SECOND EDITION

Applied Multivariate
Research

SECOND EDITION

Applied Multivariate Research

Design and Interpretation

Lawrence S. Meyers

California State University, Sacramento

Glenn Gamst

University of La Verne

A.J. Guarino

MGH Institute of Health Professions

Los Angeles | London | New Delhi
Singapore | Washington DC

Los Angeles | London | New Delhi
Singapore | Washington DC

FOR INFORMATION:

SAGE Publications, Inc.
2455 Teller Road
Thousand Oaks, California 91320
E-mail: order@sagepub.com

SAGE Publications Ltd.
1 Oliver's Yard
55 City Road
London EC1Y 1SP
United Kingdom

SAGE Publications India Pvt. Ltd.
B 1/I 1 Mohan Cooperative Industrial Area
Mathura Road, New Delhi 110 044
India

SAGE Publications Asia-Pacific Pte. Ltd.
3 Church Street
#10-04 Samsung Hub
Singapore 049483

Printed in the United States of America

A catalog record of this book is available from the Library of Congress.

9781412988117

This book is printed on acid-free paper.

Publisher: Vicki Knight
Associate Editor: Lauren Habib
Editorial Assistant: Kalie Koscielak
Production Editor: Brittany Bauhaus
Copy Editor: QuADS Prepress (P) Ltd.
Typesetter: C&M Digitals (P) Ltd.
Proofreader: Jeff Bryant
Cover Designer: Candice Harman
Marketing Manager: Nicole Elliott
Permissions Editor: Adele Hutchinson

SFI Certified Sourcing
www.sfiprogram.org
SFI-00453

12 13 14 15 16 10 9 8 7 6 5 4 3 2 1

Brief Contents

Detailed Contents

Preface to the Second Edition

This second edition of *Applied Multivariate Research: Design and Interpretation* reflects our (LSM, GG, and AJG's) continued long-distance collaboration, in concert with the valuable feedback we have received since the initial publication from our students, colleagues, and readers from around the globe. We have attempted, whenever possible, to incorporate this beneficial input into the appropriate context of this edition.

In preparing the second edition, we have reaffirmed our goals in originally writing this book:

- We hope to communicate in a relatively readable, understandable, and nonmathematical manner the conceptual bases of a range of multivariate research designs and analyses. At the same time, we have attempted to not unduly dilute or oversimplify the material.
- We want to demonstrate how to perform, interpret, and report the results of multivariate analyses in a direct and understandable manner.

In working to achieve these goals, we retained the general structure formulated in the previous edition by preparing two companion (paired) chapters for each topic. The first member of the pair is the "A" chapter; it provides the introductory and conceptual material for the topic. The second member of the pair is the "B" chapter; it presents a step-by-step description of how to perform the analysis in IBM SPSS or, where appropriate, IBM SPSS Amos. This step-by-step description includes displaying the dialog windows and syntax structures to perform the analysis, descriptions and interpretations of the output, and sample reports of the analysis results.

We have used Version 19 of IBM SPSS for the second edition, although we recognize that Version 20 is already available. Nonetheless, the dialog windows, syntax, and output we show based on Version 19 should serve as a very good guide for later versions of the software.

One overall change that readers familiar with the previous edition will notice concerns the examples we use throughout the book. In the first edition, we used data sets from GG that we were unable to share with readers due to an agreement he had with the agency from which the data were collected. In this second edition, all of the data sets used as examples are different from those older ones and are available on the Sage website (www.sagepub.com/meyers), so that interested users can replicate our analyses on the example data sets.

Despite retaining the general structure of providing pairs of chapters for each topic, this second edition represents a considerable revision of the first edition. Every chapter was extensively reviewed and, in most places, substantially rewritten to make the narrative more readable, complete, and/or current. We have also added a good deal of new material to cover topics not included in the earlier edition. The changes we have made include the following:

- We have revised somewhat the ordering and organizational schema of the chapters in an effort to more smoothly build from conceptually simpler to conceptually more complex procedures. In very global terms, we begin with basics, then cover comparisons of means, followed by prediction, analyses of structure, and finally model fitting.
- Our treatment of missing values with the IBM SPSS Missing Value Analysis module has been updated and expanded.
- We have collapsed the three pairs of MANOVA chapters down to a single pair.
- To supplement the basic statistical regression procedures, we added a pair of multiple regression chapters covering some advanced topics such as polynomial regression, mediation, interaction effects, and dummy and effect coding.
- We added a pair of chapters on multilevel modeling.
- Both the logistic regression and the discriminant analysis chapters now include three-group designs as well as the two-group designs we presented in the first edition.
- We have now included within binary logistic regression the topic of ROC curves and ROC analysis applied to the classification decision criterion.
- We have expanded on the strategy to perform exploratory principal components/factor analysis, displaying the results from several extraction techniques. We have also added to that material the procedure for performing a reliability analysis based on the factor analysis results, how to compute subscales based on the reliability analysis, and how to use the computed scales in a subsequent (albeit simple demonstration) analysis.
- We have added a new pair of chapters on multidimensional scaling.
- We have added a new pair of chapters on cluster analysis, including both hierarchical clustering and k-means clustering.
- We separated the full-information structural modeling material dealing with path analysis and structural equation modeling into separate pairs of chapters.
- We have updated the chapters on model invariance.
- We have included an Appendix covering many of the frequently used IBM SPSS Amos commands.
- Our sample reports of results now include exact probability values and confidence intervals consistent with the new APA publication guidelines.

Acknowledgments

There are many people who deserve thanks for helping us generate this second edition. Among them are the following.

Students in Glenn Gamst's graduate Advanced Statistics I and II courses provided energetic and useful feedback on versions of some of our early chapters and on near-final versions as well. Viewing the chapters through the eyes of these students was a very enlightening experience.

Eleven reviewers carefully read and provided edits on our chapters. Two of them in particular made extensive comments and suggestions, all of which we took to heart and almost all of which caused us to make modifications that we believe enhanced the quality of the book. We are most grateful to them for their efforts:

Alain d'Astous, *HEC Montreal*
Patricia L. Busk, *University of San Francisco*
Richard Feinn, *Southern Connecticut State University*
Edward D. Gailey, *Fairmont State University*
Grady L. Garner Jr., *The Chicago School of Professional Psychology*
Glenn J. Hansen, *University of Oklahoma*
Andrew Jorgenson, *University of Utah*
Xiaofen Deng Keating, *The University of Texas at Austin*
Thomas J. Keil, *Arizona State University*
E. Kevin Kelloway, *Saint Mary's University*
Marie Kraska, *Auburn University*

Most of the data sets we used as examples in this second edition were either fictitious or were modified versions of our own data sets. However, we gratefully acknowledge that two of our terrific students, Victoria Keyser of the University of La Verne and Leanne Williamson of California State University, Sacramento, each provided us with a substantial data set to use for one or more of our analyses.

We would like to express our appreciation, as well, to Angie Castillo at the University of La Verne for her invaluable skill in working with the galley proofing process. She also generously provided us with a good deal of technical support throughout the time we were writing the manuscript.

The staff at Sage was led by our publisher Vicki Knight who shared our vision for this book and provided support to us when it was needed. Kalie Koscielak was our editorial assistant. She made manuscript exchange with Sage easy and efficient and generally walked us through the publication process, for which we are very grateful. In addition we wish to thank our copyeditor Rajasree Ghosh and her team at QuADS Prepress, who did a superlative job, and Brittany Bauhaus and the rest of the production staff at Sage.

Perhaps the most significant person to acknowledge and thank is Elita Burmas, who functioned as research and technical analyst, graphic designer, and archivist in the preparation of our chapters. Elita has a psychology master's degree from California State University, Sacramento, emphasizing quantitative methods, and she was invaluable during the preparation of the first edition of the book as well as this second edition. Elita generated Windows-version screenshots of the dialog windows (transforming the Mac screenshots of LSM), ran through each of the analyses to confirm the accuracy of the output, and was instrumental in helping construct and format the Appendix with the IBM SPSS Amos commands. As before, Elita accomplished all of this with high levels of skill, grace, enthusiasm, and warmth throughout this entire process, and we will be forever grateful for her participation in this project.

We hope you find this second edition to be both readable and informative.

—Lawrence S. Meyers, *California State University, Sacramento*
—Glenn Gamst, *University of La Verne*
—A. J. Guarino, *MGH Institute of Health Professions*
June, 2012

About the Authors

Lawrence S. Meyers earned his doctorate in experimental psychology and has been a professor in the Psychology Department at California State University, Sacramento, for a number of years. He supervises research students and teaches research design courses as well as history of psychology at both the undergraduate and graduate levels. His areas of expertise include test development and validation.

Glenn Gamst is Professor and Chair of the Psychology Department at the University of La Verne, where he teaches the doctoral advanced statistics sequence. His research interests include the effects of multicultural variables on clinical outcome. Additional research interests focus on conversation memory and discourse processing. He received his PhD in experimental psychology from the University of Arkansas.

A. J. Guarino is a professor of biostatistics at Massachusetts General Hospital, Institute of Health Professions. He is the statistician on numerous National Institutes of Health grants and a reviewer on several research journals. He received his BA from the University of California, Berkeley, and a PhD in statistics and research methodologies from the Department of Educational Psychology, the University of Southern California.

PART I

THE BASICS OF MULTIVARIATE DESIGN

CHAPTER 1

An Introduction to Multivariate Design

1.1 The Use of Multivariate Designs

The use of multivariate research designs has grown very rapidly in the behavioral and social sciences throughout the past quarter century. This has been made possible in no small part by increased availability of sophisticated statistical software packages, such as IBM SPSS, SAS, and Stata, that can be installed on personal computers. But even with such increased availability of such software, behavioral and social science researchers have been using some multivariate techniques (e.g., factor analysis, multiple regression) for a very long time.

Multivariate designs can be distinguished from the univariate and bivariate designs with which readers are likely already familiar. Experimental designs that are analyzed with *t* tests or analysis of variance (ANOVA) are univariate designs, so named because there is only a single dependent variable in the design and analysis of the data (Gamst, Meyers, & Guarino, 2008). A *t* ratio or an *F* ratio is generated to test whether the group means are significantly different.

A bivariate design derives its name from the fact that there are only two variables that are analyzed together; it is exemplified by a simple correlation design. The variables in such a design are often signified as *X* and *Y* and, unless we are predicting one (the *Y* variable) from the other (the *X* variable), which variable is assigned which letter is arbitrary. The degree to which the measures are correlated is assessed with a correlation statistic, the most commonly cited one being the Pearson correlation coefficient (Pearson *r*).

1.2 The Definition of the Multivariate Domain

To be considered a multivariate research design, the study must have more variables than are contained in either a univariate or bivariate design. Furthermore, some subset of these variables must be analyzed together, that is, they must be combined in some manner to form a composite variable or *variate*. The most common way to combine variables is by forming a *weighted linear composite* where each variable is weighted in a manner determined by the analysis. This resulting weighted linear composite is known as a variate. There are several contexts where we form such variates, three examples of which are as follows:

- In an experimental design in which we wished to compare the performance of three types of memory training, we could measure two or more variables as indicators of performance. These variables could then be combined into a single weighted composite measure. For example, we could assess both number of correct responses and speed of responding in a memory task that taken together might be interpreted as reflecting performance efficiency.
- In a prediction (regression) design, we might use self-esteem, extraversion, and product knowledge to predict dollars of sales for a set of salespeople. The variate in this instance might be thought of as sales effectiveness.
- To determine which items on a personality inventory might comprise separate subscales that measure aspects of a more global construct, we might perform a factor analysis on the responses to those items. Each factor would be a weighted linear combination of the inventory items.

1.3 The Importance of Multivariate Designs

The importance of multivariate designs is becoming increasingly well recognized. It also appears that the judged utility of these designs seems to be growing as well. Here are two of the advantages of multivariate research designs over univariate research designs based on those offered by Stevens (2009):

- Many experimental treatments are likely to affect the study participants in more than one way.
- Using multiple criterion measures can paint a more complete and detailed description of the phenomenon under investigation.

A similar argument is made by Harris (2001):

However, for very excellent reasons, researchers in all of the sciences—behavioral, biological, or physical—have long since abandoned sole reliance on the classic univariate design. It has become abundantly clear that a given experimental manipulation . . . will affect many somewhat different but partially correlated aspects of the organism's behavior. Similarly, many different pieces of information about an applicant . . . may be of value in predicting his or her . . . [behavior], and it is necessary to consider how to combine all of these pieces of information into a single "best" prediction. (p. 11)

In summary, there is general consensus about the value of multivariate designs for two very general reasons. First, we all seem to agree that individuals generate many behaviors and respond in many different although related ways to the situations they encounter in their lives. Univariate analyses by definition, are, able to address this level of complexity in only a piecemeal fashion because they can examine only one aspect at a time. Multivariate analysis allows us to do this as well, but it also affords us the opportunity to examine the phenomenon under study by determining how the multiple variables interface.

The second reason why the field appears to have reached consensus on the importance of multivariate design is that we hold the causes of behavior to be complex and multivariate. Thus, predicting behavior is best done with more rather than less information. Most of us believe that several reasons explain why we feel or act as we do. For example, the degree to which we strive to achieve a particular goal, the amount of empathy we exhibit in our relationships, and the likelihood of following a medical regime may depend on a host of factors rather than just a single predictor variable. Only when we take into account a set of relevant variables—that is, when we take a multivariate approach—have we any realistic hope of reasonably accurately predicting the level—or understanding the nature—of a given construct. This, again, is the realm of multivariate design.

1.4 The General Form of a Variate

The general form of a variate—a weighted composite—is an equation or function. In the weighted linear composite shown below, each variable in the variate is symbolized by the letter X with subscripts used to differentiate one variable from another. A weight is assigned to each variable by multiplying the variable by this value; this weight is referred to as a *coefficient* in many multivariate applications. Thus, in the expression w_2X_2, the term w_2 is the weight that X_2 is assigned (multiplied by) in the weighted composite, that is, w_2 is the coefficient associated with X_2. A weighted composite of three variables would take this general form:

$$\text{weighted composite} = w_1X_1 + w_2X_2 + w_3X_3$$

These weighted composites are given a variety of names, including *variates*, *composite variables*, and *synthetic variables* (Grimm & Yarnold, 2000). Variates are therefore not directly measured by the researchers in the process of data collection but are created or computed as part of or as the result of the multivariate data analysis. Because they are not directly measured, what they assess is often referred to as a *latent construct*, and the variate is often referred to as a *latent variable*. We will have quite a bit to say about variates (weighted linear composites or latent variables) throughout this book.

1.5 The Type of Variables Combined to Form a Variate

Variates may be weighted composites of either independent variables (i.e., manipulated or predictor variables; see Section 2.3.1) or dependent variables (variables representing the outcome of the research; see Section 2.3.2), or they may be weighted composites of variables playing neither role in the analysis. Examples where the analysis creates a variate composed of independent variables are multiple regression and logistic regression designs. In these designs, two or more independent variables are combined together to predict the value of a dependent variable. For example, the number of delinquent acts performed by teenagers might be found to be predictable from the number of hours per week they play violent video games, the number of hours per week they spend doing homework (this would be negatively weighted because more homework time would presumably predict fewer delinquent acts), and the number of hours per week they spend with other teens who have committed at least one delinquent act in the past year.

Multivariate analyses can also create composites of dependent variables. The classic example of this is multivariate analysis of variance (MANOVA). This general type of design can contain one or more independent variables, but there must be at least two dependent variables in the analysis. These dependent variables are combined together into a composite, and an ANOVA is performed on this computed variate as in the case of combining number of correct responses and speed of responding mentioned above. The statistical significance of group differences on this variate is then tested by a multi-variate *F* statistic (in contrast to the univariate *F* ratio that readers have presumably studied in prior coursework).

Sometimes variables do not need to play the explicit role of either independent or dependent variable and yet will be absorbed into a weighted linear composite in the statistical analysis. This occurs in principal components and factor analysis, where we attempt to identify which variables (e.g., items on an inventory) are associated with a particular underlying dimension, component, or factor. These components or factors are weighted linear composites of the variables in the analysis.

It is possible that the prior experience of readers is such that great emphasis has been placed on the differences between dependent and independent variables. If so, it might be somewhat disconcerting to learn that variates can be composed of either class of variables. But it turns out that, in the analysis of data, dependent and independent are roles that are assigned to variables by the researchers rather than absolute attributes of the variables themselves. And just as actresses in the theater can play different roles in different productions, so too can variables play different roles in different analyses. We will discuss this matter in more detail in Section 2.3.

1.6 The General Organization of the Book

The domain of multivariate research design is quite large, and selecting which topics to include and which to omit is a difficult task for authors. Most of the multivariate procedures we cover in this book are very much related to each other in that they are different surface ways of expressing the same underlying model: the general linear model (see Section 7A.5.1). For example, ANOVA, MANOVA, multiple regression, discriminant function analysis, principal components and factor analysis, and canonical correlation analysis are all members of the general linear model family. Some of the procedures just represent different ways to conceptualize the same analysis. For example, MANOVA focuses on the differences between the groups in the analysis based on a set of quantitative variables whereas discriminant function analysis focuses on (a) the dimensions along which the groups differ on the quantitative variables and (b) the prediction of group membership based on those quantitative variables.

Separating the chapters into groupings is therefore done as a convenience for the readers. The groupings that we use, and even the ordering of the chapters within the groupings, is more of a matter of personal expression than a true classification system. Other authors would likely choose a somewhat different structuring of the topics.

1.6.1 The Chapters Are in Pairs

Beginning with the third chapter, each topic is presented by a pair of chapters labeled "A" and "B." The "A" chapter of the pair treats the topic at a relatively broad, conceptual level, focusing on the uses to which the design is often put, the rationale underlying the procedure, a description of how the procedure works, some of the decisions that are likely to be encountered in performing the analysis, and some issues of controversy when they are germane to the discussion. The "B" chapter of the pair describes in a step-by-step way how to perform the analysis in IBM SPSS (or, in the Part V chapters, IBM SPSS Amos), how to interpret the output of the analysis, and how researchers might report the results of the analysis. Most of the data sets that we use for our examples are modified versions (sometimes very substantially) of ones our students have collected in their research, and we use them with the permission of those students.

We often refer to the examples as being based on fictional studies just to reinforce the idea that the conclusions we draw from them may have little to do with the empirical world in which we live. For each procedure that we perform in our "B" chapters, we present an example of how the results might be reported. It should be emphasized that there is no one best way to report results—we just wanted to illustrate one (hopefully) acceptable way to accomplish this. Readers are encouraged to consult Cooper (2010) for his suggestions on preparing results sections for dissemination.

Sage has established a place for our materials on their website (www.sagepub.com/meyers). The following materials can be found there:

- Exercises with data files for each of the "B" chapters.
- Data files for the analyses demonstrated in each of the "B" chapters.

1.6.2 Part I: The Basics of Multivariate Design

The chapters in this part of the book introduce readers to the foundations or corner-stones of designing research and analyzing data. Our first chapter—the one that you are reading—discusses the idea of multivariate design and addresses the structure of this book.

The second chapter on fundamental research concepts covers both some basics that readers have learned about in prior courses and possibly some new concepts and terms that will be explicated in much greater detail throughout this book.

Chapters 3A and 3B cover data screening. The issues covered here are applicable to all the procedures we cover later, and so we cover them once in this pair of early chapters. We discuss ways to correct data entry mistakes, how to evaluate statistical assumptions underlying the data analysis, and how to handle missing data and outliers.

1.6.3 Part II: Comparison of Means

Part II addresses comparison of means. We begin with a description of some commonly used univariate ANOVA designs in Chapters 4A and 4B and then transition to multivariate ANOVA (MANOVA) designs in Chapters 5A and 5B. The intent of researchers using these designs is to determine which groups or conditions in a study are significantly different on the one or more dependent variables that were measured. Univariate designs assess a single dependent variable in each analysis; multivariate designs assess two or more dependent variables simultaneously in each analysis.

1.6.4 Part III: Prediction of the Value of a Single Variable

Regression procedures are used to predict the value of a single variable. Pearson correlation and simple linear regression, the soul mate of Pearson correlation, are covered in Chapters 6A and 6B. Pearson correlation is used to describe the degree of linear relationship that is observed between two measures (e.g., X and Y). In simple linear regression, one variable (e.g., X) is used as a predictor of the other (e.g., Y). Multiple regression, frequently referred to as ordinary least squares regression, is an extension of simple linear regression when we use multiple measures to predict the Y variable. The basics of this procedure are covered in Chapters 7A and 7B, and some variations of it are discussed in Chapters 8A and 8B.

When the limitations of ordinary least squares regression are exceeded, alternative regression techniques need to be called into play. Two such alternatives are presented in the next two pairs of chapters. Ordinary least squares regression assumes that the cases in the analysis are independent of each other, an assumption that is violated where cases are nested, that is, hierarchically organized. Examples of such organization are students within separate classrooms and clients of particular mental health clinics in a larger health system. In predicting an outcome variable, such as standardized test scores of the students, the children within a given classroom may be more related to each other on the outcome variable than they are to other students selected at random from the entire school or school district. To the extent that the children within a classroom are more alike than students selected at random, that is, to the extent that nesting is important, the assumption of independence is violated and we must use multilevel modeling in predicting the outcome variable. This topic is presented in Chapters 9A and 9B.

Ordinary least squares regression also assumes that the variable being predicted is measured on a quantitative scale of measurement. Yet it is often the case that we wish to predict to which group cases in the data file belong; here, group assignment is represented as a categorical variable. For example, we might want to predict whether an individual is likely to succeed or not succeed in a given program based on a set of variables. This type of prediction can be performed using binary or multinomial logistic regression, topics discussed in Chapters 10A and 10B. Prediction of a binary variable entails setting a decision point so that cases are classified or predicted as belonging to either one group or the other. One powerful and commonly used procedure used to facilitate that decision making is receiver operating characteristic (ROC) curve analysis, and this topic is included within the logistic regression chapters.

1.6.5 Part IV: Analysis of Structure

We very generally mean by structure some underlying relationships among the variables that can be brought to the surface by the statistical analysis. Often, but not always, these underlying relationships are organized into themes or dimensions. The chapters in this portion of the book meet that general criterion, but they comprise a relatively diverse set of procedures.

Discriminant function analysis, covered in Chapters 11A and 11B, is the flip side of MANOVA. It can be used to predict membership in a categorical variable, and so might easily fit in Part III; in fact, there are applications where logistic regression and discriminant function analysis are both considered possible procedures to use to analyze a given data set. But we placed discriminant function analysis here because one of its uses is to describe the dimensions along which groups differ, and with this focus, the interpretations of the obtained discriminant functions take on a decidedly structural orientation.

Principal components analysis and exploratory factor analysis, discussed in Chapters 12A and 12B, both describe the dimensions underlying a set of variables. For example, although a paper-and-pencil inventory may contain two or three dozen items, these items may tap into only three or four latent main themes or dimensions. Principal components analysis and exploratory factor analysis can be used to identify which items relate to each dimension.

Canonical correlation analysis, presented in Chapters 13A and 13B, is an extension of ordinary least squares regression in which a set of quantitative independent variables is used to predict the values of a set of quantitative dependent variables. Yet we conceive of it as structural in that the two sets of variables can be related to each other along several dimensions represented by canonical functions, and so in many ways the process of interpreting the results strongly resembles what we do in principal components and factor analysis.

Chapters 14A and 14B are devoted to multidimensional scaling. Objects or stimuli (e.g., brands of cars, retail stores) are assessed in a pairwise manner to determine the degree to which they are dissimilar. These dissimilarities are analyzed in terms of the distance between the objects. In turn, the distances between the objects are arrayed or represented in a space defined by the number of dimensions specified by the researchers who then attempt to interpret these dimensions along which the objects appear to differ.

Cluster analysis is described in Chapters 15A and 15B. Rather than using common demographic variables to define groups (e.g., females and males), we group the cases (e.g., participants in a research study, presidents of the United States, brands of beer) on the basis of how they relate based on a set of quantitative variables. These groupings are called clusters. Two different approaches to such an analysis are described in the chapter.

1.6.6 Part V: Fitting Models to Data

The chapters in this section deal with fitting (causal or predictive) models to data and determining the quality of the fit. Again, our classification schema is not perfect, as multidimensional scaling does involve fitting a dimensional solution to the data set. Nonetheless, the models referred to in the Part V chapters represent more explicit hypotheses that are tested by researchers based on their best understanding of the phenomenon under study. Most of the statistical work must be accomplished by a specialized piece of software called IBM SPSS Amos which is only available at this time with the Windows (but not the Mac) version of IBM SPSS.

Principal components analysis and, to a large extent, exploratory factor analysis (both are discussed in Chapters 12A and 12B) are analogous to an inductive approach in that researchers employ a bottom-up strategy by developing a conclusion from specific observations. That is, the researchers determine the interpretation of the factor by examining the variate that emerged from the analysis. Confirmatory factor analysis, presented in Chapters 16A and 16B, represents a deductive approach in that researchers are predicting an outcome from a theoretical framework; this strategy can be thought of as a top-down approach. Confirmatory factor analysis seeks to determine if the number of factors and their respective measured variables as specified in the model hypothesized by the researchers is supported by the data set—that is, they determine the extent to which the proposed model fits the data.

Path (sometimes called causal) structures are presented in the next two sets of chapters. When the variables in the hypothesized structure are all measured variables, we speak of path analysis, which can be analyzed through either ordinary least squares regression or IBM SPSS

Amos; this topic is treated in Chapters 17A and 17B in the context of multiple regression and Chapters 18A and 18B in the context of IBM SPSS Amos. We also discuss procedures to trim some unneeded paths from models. When we have included "factors" in the path structure—unobserved or latent variables or constructs—the analysis becomes one of structural equation modeling (SEM) and must be done in IBM SPSS Amos (or comparable specialized software); this topic is treated in Chapters 19A and 19B.

Chapters 20A and 20B deal with the issue of a given model being applicable to two or more groups. When this is the case, the model is said to be invariant with respect to those groups. For example, a specific model may fit the data obtained from both males and females or from Asian American, White American, and Latino/Latina American students. A couple of different applications are covered in the chapter.

1.7 Recommended Readings

Aiken, L. S., West, S. G., Sechrest, L., & Reno, R. R. (1990). Graduate training in statistics, methodology, and measurement in psychology: A survey of PhD programs in North America. *American Psychologist, 45,* 721–734.

Grimm, L. G., & Yarnold, P. R. (2000). Introduction to multivariate statistics. In L. G. Grimm & P. R. Yarnold (Eds.), *Reading and understanding more multivariate statistics* (pp. 3–21). Washington, DC: American Psychological Association.

Harlow, L. L. (2005). *The essence of multivariate thinking.* Mahwah, NJ: Lawrence Erlbaum.

CHAPTER 2

Some Fundamental Research Design Concepts

We start our treatment of multivariate research design with a discussion of some fundamental concepts that will serve as building blocks for the design issues contained in this book. We also introduce in this chapter some advanced concepts because they are intimately related to their more basic cousins. These advanced concepts will be revisited in greater depth in later chapters.

2.1 Populations and Samples

A *population* is composed of all entities fitting the boundary conditions of whom or what we are intending to subsume in our research. Populations are typically made up of people or other entities meeting certain criteria. In basic behavioral science research, the population of interest is often "all humans." Some applied research may target smaller and more specific populations, such as "all breast cancer survivors" or "all senior citizens in community outreach programs." Some disciplines may focus on different types of "cases" such as schools in a given school district, hospitals meeting certain criteria, stores or offices of a given corporation, and so on.

In most situations, it is not possible to include all the population members in a research study. Instead, we select a workable number of individuals or entities (*cases* is the most general label) to represent the population. That set of cases in the study is the *sample*. Very often, the intention of the researchers is to study some process or phenomenon in the sample, so that they can generalize to the population from which the sample was drawn. Generalization is one arena where research design gets interesting.

Generalizing from the sample to the population is a delicate matter, so much so that most research methods textbooks cover this topic in detail; indeed, there is enough complexity in the arena of sampling that entire books have been written on it (e.g., Fuller, 2009; Levy & Lemeshow, 2008; Lohr, 2010; S. K. Thompson, 2002). Although we do not broach the issue of selecting a sample from the population, there are a couple of issues related to samples and populations that are at least indirectly touched on in our discussions throughout this book: statistical significance and sample attrition.

One issue affecting generalization concerns tests of statistical significance. Most tests of statistical significance are based on the data obtained from our sample, but they are really testing a certain hypothesis concerning the population. That hypothesis is the null hypothesis stating (a) that the sample means we are comparing were drawn from the same population or (b) that there is no relationship between the variables that we are studying. The null hypothesis is almost always different from the research hypothesis, which typically asserts that there will be a significant difference between the treatment conditions or that there will be a significant correlation between the variables. Statistical significance is part of a larger and more complex picture that is described in Sections 2.7 and 2.8.

The second issue that affects the generalization from the sample results to the population is attrition within the sample. Attrition is usually thought of as a loss of cases over time in a longitudinal design, but multivariate analyses are subject to this concern as well. Most of the multivariate statistical procedures require participants to have valid values on all the measures. With multiple measures taken on each case, it is more likely that some of the cases will have missing data on at least one of them. When a particular case has a missing value on just one measure, that case will in many instances be removed from the entire analysis. If many participants are dropped in this manner, the possibility exists that those cases remaining in the analysis will comprise a subsample quite different from the sample as a whole. Under such a circumstance, conclusions based on the results of those analyses may not be properly generalized back to the original population. Much of Chapters 3A and 3B are devoted to dealing with the issue of missing values.

2.2 Scales of Measurement

2.2.1 Variables

It is difficult to read a textbook in research design or statistics without immediately encountering the notion of a variable. It is truly one of our fundamental concepts, and it tends to take on increasingly enriched meaning to students as they progress into more advanced coursework.

As a rather conceptual but important characterization, *a variable is an abstraction or construct that can take on different values.* These values can be, and very often are, numbers that have *quantitative* meaning. Examples of quantitatively based variables include grade point average, which can take on numerical values between 0 and 4; the number of dollars in weekly vehicle sales, which can take on values in hundreds of thousands of dollars; and a score on a standardized test such as the Graduate Record Examination (GRE) revised General Test, which can range from 130 to 170. In data files, these values will be reproduced in the same form (e.g., a case would have 3.68 recorded for grade point average, 527,000 dollars recorded for weekly vehicle sales, and 161 recorded for test score).

Alternatively, the different values that entities can take may be numbers with no quantitative meaning, such as the numbers basketball players wear on their uniforms. Values may also be names or labels for entities. Examples of these include names of people (e.g., Erin, Paul); types of animals (e.g., squirrels, skunks); and computer platforms (e.g., Mac, PC). These values are used to make *qualitative* or *categorical* distinctions between the cases. In data files, these values will often be represented by arbitrary numerical codes (e.g., we might code Mac users as 1 and PC users as 2).

All the values for variables, whether quantitatively based or categorically based, have been assigned through a set of rules defining a measurement operation. These measurement operations represent different scales of measurement.

2.2.2 Five Scales of Measurement

Although the essentials of measurement scales were known for some time before he formalized our treatment of them, it was S. S. Stevens who impressed this topic on the consciousness of behavioral scientists. As Stevens (1951) tells us, he initially broached this issue in a 1941 presentation to the International Congress for the Unity of Science. Stevens published a brief article addressing scales of measurement a few years later in *Science* (Stevens, 1946), but it was the prominent treatment of this topic in his lead chapter in the *Handbook of Experimental Psychology*, which he edited (Stevens, 1951), that most writers cite as the primary historical source.

Measurement comprises sets of rules governing the meaning of values assigned to entities. Each such set of rules defines a scale of measurement. Stevens (1951) identified four scales: nominal, ordinal, interval, and ratio in that order. Each scale includes an extra feature or rule over those in the one before it. We will add a fifth scale to Stevens's treatment—the summative response scale—placing it between the ordinal and the interval scale. Very briefly, here is the essence of each.

2.2.2.1 Nominal Scales

A *nominal* scale of measurement, sometimes called a *categorical* scale, a *qualitative* scale, or a *classification system*, has only one rule underlying its use: Cases will be identified as being different by assigning them to different categories. There is no quantitative dimension implied here at all, no implication that one entity is in any way "more" or "less" than another. Examples of nominal scales include sex and race/ethnicity categories, types of computer platforms, and arbitrary numerical codes for the categories of a variable.

Differences between the cases are defined by the nominal or classification system. For example, individuals may be classified as female or male based on biological features. Within this classification system, the set of individuals identified as, say, female, still may represent a very diverse group who may differ substantially on a host of other characteristics. Although they are all classified as the same sex, it does not mean that they are identical in any other respect.

Numerical coding of categorical variables is regularly done when we are entering data into an IBM SPSS data file. Thus, in a study comparing students who enjoy reading different kinds of books for leisure, we might use a 1 to denote a preference for science fiction, a 2 to indicate a preference for mystery novels, and a 3 to signify a preference for humor. In this situation, the numeric codes do not imply anything quantitative; they are used exclusively to represent different categories of preference.

2.2.2.2 Ordinal Scales

An *ordinal* scale of measurement uses numbers exclusively. As was true for nominal scales, different numbers represent different information. But ordinal scales add this additional rule: The numbers convey "less than" and "more than" information. This translates most easily to rank ordering of cases, and it is possible to rank order cases on any quantitative dimension.

Cases may be ranked in the order in which they align themselves on some quantitative dimension, but it is not possible from the ranking information to determine how far apart they are on the underlying dimension. For example, if we were ranking the height of three people, the one 7 feet tall would be ranked 1, the one 5 feet and 2 inches tall would be ranked 2, and the one 5 feet and 1 inch tall would be ranked 3. From the ranked data, we could not determine that two of the individuals were quite close in height.

2.2.2.3 Summative Response Scales

A *summative response* scale requires respondents to assign values to entities based on an underlying continuum defined by the anchors on the scale. The numbers are ordered, typically in an ascending way, to reflect more of the property being rated. Most common are 5-point and 7-point scales. These scales originated in the classic work of Louis Thurstone in the late 1920s (1927a, 1927b, 1928, 1929; Thurstone & Chave, 1929) in his pioneering work to develop interval-level measurement scales to assess attitudes. Based on Thurstone's time-consuming and resource-intensive scale development techniques, summative response scales were developed by Rensis Likert (pronounced "lick-ert" by the man himself) in the early 1930s to make the process more efficient (Likert, 1932), and he and his colleagues widely disseminated this scaling process later that decade (Likert, Roslow, & Murphy, 1934; Murphy & Likert, 1937). Derivatives of Likert's scale have become increasingly popular ever since.

It is called a summative scale because it is possible to add (sum) the ratings of a set of items together and divide by a constant (usually in the process of taking a mean) to obtain an individual's score on the set of items (an inventory). We will address this in a little more detail after introducing all the scales, but we wish to briefly illustrate here that the average derived from a summative response scale is meaningful, thus rendering this type of scale closer to interval-level than ordinal-level measurement. The values may not represent equal distance between adjacent numbers (as required by interval scales), but the spacing is close enough to equal to meaningfully interpret averages of the values.

To illustrate that interpreting a mean of the scale values is meaningful, let's say that we administered a short self-esteem inventory to a class of medical students. Let's further say that one item on the inventory read, "I feel that I am a worthwhile person." Assume that items were rated on a 5-point scale with higher values indicating more endorsement of the statement. Let's further say that the mean for this item based on all the students in the class was 4.75. Is that value interpretable? Yes, it indicates that the individuals in the sample on average believed pretty strongly that the content of the item was quite true for them— namely, that they were worthwhile people.

2.2.2.4 Interval Scales

An *interval* scale of measurement has all the properties of nominal, ordinal, and summative response scales but includes one more important feature. Fixed intervals between the numbers represent equal intervals. It is also worthwhile noting that interval scales may have zero points, but the zero value is an arbitrary point on the scale (this contrasts with ratio scales as noted in Section 2.2.2.5).

The most common illustration of an equal interval scale is the Fahrenheit or Celsius temperature scale. These are interval scales in the sense that a 20° difference in one region of the scale represents the same amount of difference than a 20° difference in another region of the scale. According to Stevens (1951), "Equal intervals of temperature are scaled off by noting equal volumes of expansion" (p. 27). As an example of the arbitrariness of a zero value on an interval scale of measurement, consider that 0° does not mean the absence of temperature but is the value on the Celsius scale at which water freezes and is a value on the Fahrenheit scale colder than the freezing point of water.

As was true for summative response scales, it is meaningful to average data collected on an interval scale of measurement. We may therefore say that the average high temperature in our home town this past week was 51.4 °F.

2.2.2.5 Ratio Scales

A *ratio* scale of measurement has all the properties of nominal, ordinal, summative response, and interval scales but includes one more important feature. Common examples of ratio scales are time (e.g., minutes, years) and distance (e.g., centimeters, miles). Ratio scales have an absolute zero point, where zero means absence of the property (e.g., zero distance between two objects indicates that there is no distance between them). Because of this, it is possible to interpret in a meaningful way ratios of the numbers. We can thus say that 4 hours is twice as long as 2 hours or that 3 miles is half the distance of 6 miles.

2.2.3 Algebraic Properties of the Scales

As we suggested above, the sorts of algebraic operations or manipulations that we can legitimately perform on data obtained from each of the scales of measurement is different and will thus limit the kind of data analysis we are able to appropriately use. For example, it would be inappropriate to use the three nominal codes for reading preference noted in Section 2.2.2.1 (1 for science fiction, 2 for mystery novels, and 3 for humor) as a dependent variable in, say, an analysis of variance (ANOVA) that requires a quantitatively based dependent variable to yield meaningful results.

We will discuss Stevens's classic set of four scales first. Nominal measurement is not quantitatively based. Because of that, the only operations that can legitimately be performed on the data would be that of determining equality or inequality. For example, if we were going to classify entities in our world as either "animals" and "trees," then skunks and chipmunks would be classified as animals (and thus defined as being equal or comparable in this measurement or classification system) whereas redwood trees and birch trees would be classified as trees (and thus also defined as being equal). However, diamonds and phosphorus would not be classified in this system. Based on our classifying entities, it is legitimate to count the number of occurrences we observed in each category and to compare the counts to determine which is greater. We could thus say that in a given area, there were 25 animals and 41 trees.

Ordinal measurement allows us to compare cases in a quantitative manner but only to the extent of making greater-than or less-than determinations. If students are ranked in terms of their height, we may say that one student is taller than another. But it would not make much sense to identify two students whose ranks were 1 and 7 and to add those ranks together (to say that their total rank was 8 makes no sense) or take an average of the two ranks (to say that their average rank was 4 likewise makes no sense).

Interval measurement, where the quantitative scale is marked in terms of equal intervals, allows us to perform adding (subtracting) and averaging to the operations of equality/inequality and greater-than/less-than judgments. Thus, we can legitimately add the daily temperatures for the past 7 days and divide by 7 to arrive at a meaningful value: the average temperature for the week.

Ratio measurement, with its absolute zero point, allows us to divide and multiply values to arrive at meaningful results in addition to doing all the above-mentioned operations. This allows us to say, for example, that 4 is twice as much as 2. We cannot meaningfully interpret ratios on any of the other scales. To use Fahrenheit temperature (interval measurement) as an example, we would be incorrect in asserting that 40° is twice as warm as 20°. Why? Because there is no absolute zero point to ground us. If you are not sure about this, just remember that a Celsius temperature scale is a transformation of the Fahrenheit scale. These Fahrenheit temperatures would have different values on the Celsius scale but would represent the same temperatures. And the Celsius ratio would yield a different value. This can be contrasted to the Kelvin scale of temperature where zero really does mean the absence of any heat. Using this latter scale with its absolute or true zero point, one can make ratio assertions about temperatures.

Now consider the scale we added to Stevens's list—summative response scales. It allows more operations than an ordinal scale because we can add (and subtract) its values and obtain a meaningful average. Despite this feature, however, some authors (e.g., Allen & Yen, 1979) have unequivocally placed these ratings scales within the province of ordinal measures. Historically, however, the scales have been treated more liberally. Likert (1932) himself argued that his scaling technique correlated close to 1 with the results of Thurstone's (1928; Thurstone & Chave, 1929) much more elaborate method that appeared to generate an equal interval scale that was able to assess attitudes toward a particular issue. Guilford (1954), in his book *Psychometric Methods*, allowed summative response scales to at least have more interval-like properties than rank order scales. He states that what he called rating methods "achieve the status of ordinal measurements and only approach that of interval measurements" (p. 297). Edwards (1957) goes a bit further, stating that "if our interest is in comparing the mean attitude scores of two or more groups, this can be done with summated-rating scales as well as with equal-appearing interval scales" (p. 157). Summarizing a study by Spector (1976), Ghiselli, Campbell, and Zedeck (1981) tell us, "Of particular interest with regard to Spector's research results is the finding that a majority of existing attitude scales *do* use categories of approximately equal intervals" (p. 414). Given Ghiselli et al.'s summary, it is thus possible that people might treat summative response scales psychologically (cognitively) as approximating interval measurement.

Although it may be the case that some researchers will question the degree to which the points on a summative response scale are precisely evenly spaced, the vast majority of research published in the behavioral and social sciences over the past half century or more has used summative response scales as though they met interval properties. Researchers have added the scale points, have taken means, and have used these measurements in statistical analyses that ordinarily require interval or ratio measurement to properly interpret the results. In our view, this treatment of summative response scales is acceptable, appropriate, and quite useful.

2.2.4 Qualitative Versus Quantitative Measurement

It is possible to identify two categories into which we can classify subsets of these measurement scales: qualitative (categorical) and quantitative measurements. Qualitative measurement characterizes what we obtain from the nominal scale of measurement. There is no implied underlying quantitative dimension here even if the nominal values are numerical codes. Researchers sometimes call qualitative variables by other names, such as the following:

- Categorical variables
- Nonmetric variables
- Dichotomous variables (when there are only two values or categories)
- Grouped variables
- Classification variables

It is useful for our purposes to think of quantitative measurement in a somewhat restrictive manner. Although the ordinal scale certainly presumes an underlying quantitative dimension, we would generally propose thinking in terms of those scales for which it is meaningful and informative to compute a mean. With the ability to compute a mean and all that this ability implies, the gateway is open to performing a whole range of parametric statistical procedures, such as Pearson correlation and ANOVA, as well as the host of multivariate procedures we discuss in this book. As we have seen, summative response, interval, and ratio scales meet this standard. Researchers sometimes call quantitative variables by other names, such as the following:

- Continuous variables (although technically, many quantitative variables can be assessed only in discrete steps even if the steps are very close together)
- Metric variables
- Ungrouped variables

2.3 Independent Variables, Dependent Variables, and Covariates

The concept of variable is so central to research design, measurement, and statistical analysis that we find it applied in several different contexts. Especially in multivariate analyses, variables can play different roles in different analyses. Sometimes, variables can even switch roles within a single analysis. We therefore encourage you to think of the variables in an analysis in this way—as entities specified by researchers to play their roles in a particular analysis, one role in this analysis, perhaps a second role in another analysis. The following sections present some of these different roles.

2.3.1 Independent Variables

In the prototypical experimental study, the independent variable represents the manipulation of the researchers. In a simple sense, it represents the treatment effect (what the researchers manipulate, vary, administer, etc.). Some of its features are as follows:

- It could have only two levels (e.g., control and experimental), but it could easily have three (e.g., control, placebo, and experimental) or more.
- It is only a single entity or continuum no matter how many levels represent it.
- It is often, but not always, based on qualitative measurement.

Variables are also specifically identified as independent variables in the analysis of data. In an ANOVA, for example, the independent variable is the "breakdown" variable or "factor"—a mean of the dependent variable is computed for each level of the independent variable.

In a multiple regression design, the independent variables are the predictors (of dependent or outcome variables). These predictors are most often based on quantitatively measured variables. We will discuss the idea in Section 8A.5 that this is a more general way of conceiving of independent variables whether from the standpoint of ANOVA or linear regression.

2.3.2 Dependent Variables

In the prototypical experiment, the dependent variable represents the outcome measure (response or performance) of the participants that is measured by the researchers. In a correlation design, all the measures can be thought of as dependent variables because researchers do not actively intervene by manipulating any variables (although we can also just think of them as measured variables). In general, dependent variables may be assessed on any scale of measurement. For the types of designs that we cover in this book, the dependent variables are almost always measured on one of the quantitative measurement scales.

Variables are also specifically identified as dependent variables in the analysis of data. In an ANOVA, for example, it is the variance of the dependent variable that is to be explained by the independent variables in the study. It is the variable representing the behavior of the participants. That is, when we say, "The mean for girls was 3.52," what we are really saying is, "The mean value on the dependent variable for girls was 3.52." As another example, in multiple regression analysis, the criterion variable—the variable being predicted by the independent variables—is known as the dependent variable. When we say, "The mean of the criterion variable was 816," what we are saying is, "The mean of the dependent variable in the analysis was 816."

2.3.3 Covariates

A covariate is a variable that either actually or potentially correlates (covaries) with a dependent variable. It is important to recognize the possible influence of a covariate for at least two reasons.

The first reason it is important to know about covariates is that the relationship we observe between two dependent variables or between a dependent variable and an independent variable may lead us to an incorrect conclusion. That is, we would ordinarily infer from the existence of a relationship between two variables that they are directly associated. But that association may be mediated or caused by a third heretofore anonymous variable—the covariate.

A classic but simplified example is the relatively strong correlation between ice cream sales and crime. Higher crime rates are associated with greater quantities of ice cream being sold. Yes, the two variables are correlated; conceptually, however, they are not directly but only coincidentally associated. What mediates this relationship is the weather or the season of the year. For a variety of reasons, certain types of crimes are more likely to occur—or are facilitated by—the warmer weather during the summer months. Presumably, these crimes would take place whether or not ice cream was selling well that season (assuming that ice cream sales did not index the general economic times and complicate our simplified example).

Temperature, then, appears to mediate the relationship between ice cream sales and crime rate. It is thus a *confound* in the research design in the sense that it, too, correlates with both ice cream sales and with crime rate. If we were to include it in the design and assign it the role of a covariate or mediator in the data analysis, we would find that the correlation between ice cream sales and crime rate would be weak at best once we statistically accounted for the influence of temperature.

The effects of a covariate can also be assessed in the context of ANOVA, where the analysis becomes known as an analysis of covariance (ANCOVA). To provide you with a brief hypothetical example, consider an achievement test battery that we administer to a sample of seventh-grade girls and boys. We perform an ANOVA with gender of student as the independent variable and the score in mathematical problem solving as the dependent variable. Assume that the outcome of that analysis shows us that the girls outperform the boys.

Now we note that this test in mathematical problem solving involves verbally presented problems that the students need to reason their way through. Assume that we also know that the girls have higher scores on the verbal component of the test battery. Could their greater verbal proficiency explain the girls' superior performance on the math test? To address this question, we could perform an ANCOVA. The independent variable would be gender and the dependent variable would be mathematical problem solving, the same as in the original analysis. For the ANCOVA, we would add a third variable, verbal skill, to the analysis. Verbal skill would be assigned the role of the covariate in the analysis. We could then examine the relationship between gender and mathematical problem solving when we have statistically removed from that relationship the effects of verbal ability. Thus, it is possible for researchers to statistically control for a variable that was not controlled for in the actual research procedure.

2.3.4 Fluidity of the Roles

Variables can play one role in one context and another role in another context. The discussion on ANCOVA actually contained an example of this. We indicated that we already knew that the girls scored higher on verbal ability than the boys. This suggests that an ANOVA was run with gender as the independent variable and verbal ability as the dependent variable. Furthermore, gender information was collected in a correlation methodology—a test battery was administered to a sample of children, and as is typical, some demographic and biodata information was asked of them as well. Technically, gender could be conceived of as a dependent variable under the method used for data collection, yet it was assigned the role of an independent variable in both the ANOVA and the ANCOVA.

2.4 Between-Subjects and Within-Subjects Independent Variables

Independent variables in experimental research can represent one of two types of operations corresponding to between- or within-subjects manipulations. You need to know the nature of each of your independent variables in the process of developing your research procedures as well as in structuring the ANOVA of your data.

2.4.1 Between-Subjects Variables

If the levels of the independent variables contain different participants (e.g., girls and boys; clients with schizophrenia, depression, and no pathology), then it is a between-subjects variable. The levels of the variable thus comprise separate groups of cases. Essentially, the scores in the groups are independent of each other.

2.4.2 Within-Subjects Variables

If the levels of the independent variables contain the same participants, then it is a within-subjects variable. The levels of the variable thus comprise separate conditions under which the individuals are measured. The most obvious example of a within-subjects variable is time-related measurement such as a pretest and a posttest. Here, participants are measured once before the treatment is administered and again afterward. Because individuals are measured more than once, a within-subjects variable is also known as a repeated measures variable. Essentially, the scores in the conditions are related to each other.

2.5 Latent Variables or Variates and Measured Variables

2.5.1 Latent Variables

Latent variables are constructs that we identify in the context of various theories (Raykov & Marcoulides, 2006). They are not directly measured or observed and can therefore be assessed only indirectly (Schumacker & Lomax, 2010). The idea that important determiners of human behavior remain hidden from direct view is not at all new. In his analysis of dreams first published in 1900, Sigmund Freud (1938) spoke of the difference between the manifest or conscious dream content and its latent or unconscious meaning. And Edward Chase Tolman (1932), citing his classic research on latent learning done in collaboration with Honzig, distinguished between the latent or unobservable construct of learning and the manifest or observable maze performance of his laboratory rats.

Examples of latent variables abound. Learning, motivation, job satisfaction, mental health, attitude toward life, and ethnic identification are all constructs that play important roles in existent theories. One can frame the argument that understanding and attempting to assess variables such as these are the primary reasons that we try to measure human performance in the first place.

2.5.2 Measured Variables

Measured variables are those for which we have obtained actual data. Responses to individual inventory items, choosing this object over that one in a study of choice behavior, the number of seconds children remain in physical contact with their mothers before exploring a new environment, and an indication of whether the participants are female or male are all examples of measured variables. They are in some sense tangible in that each measured variable is directly tied to data entries in the data file. Measured variables are also known by other names. These names include the following:

- *Manifest variables:* With the use of the term *latent variables*, it is historically appropriate (e.g., Freud, 1938; Tolman, 1932) to use the term *manifest variables* as a label for those variables that we measure in a study.
- *Indicator variables:* Latent variables cannot be directly assessed, but they can be indexed or indicated. Using the term *indicator variables* thus suggests that our

measured variables are serving, at least in some sense, as proxies for (partial representations of) the latent variables of interest.

- *Observed variables:* If they are measured, these variables must by definition be observed by the researchers.

2.5.3 Linking Latent Variables to Measured Variables

In many forms of multivariate research design, it is either useful or mandatory to posit the existence of latent variables. That is, discussing latent variables in general would be an exercise in pure theory unless some effort was made to study them in an empirical setting. In this empirical effort, we then identify some variables that can be directly measured to serve as indicators for the constructs.

As an example, consider the broad construct of achievement applied to the outcome of the years one spends in college obtaining a bachelor's degree. One commonly used indicator variable to represent this student effort is grade point average. This is a quantitative achievement index, and it is safe to say that, over the span of thousands of students, those whose grade point averages are in the 3.7 (A−) range have probably learned more than students whose grade point average is in the 2.0 (C) range.

Many students, however, are quick to suggest that grade point average is far from a perfect indicator of performance. Students could have learned quite a bit during their college years but, for a variety of reasons, were not able to do especially well on the exams that were the bases for assigning grades. This argument is reasonable and implies that, at least up to some point, it may be important to measure more than one indicator of a latent variable. If we had two or three valid indicators of a construct, it might be possible for us to examine what the indicators had in common in order to estimate the amount of measurement that was contained in our data.

2.5.4 Variates as Latent Variables

Latent variables can also be based on a weighted combination or composite of multiple measured variables. Such composites, as discussed in Section 1.4, are called *variates.* Combining a set of manifest variables in this way yields a variable that, although it may be extremely useful, is not itself directly measured. Hence, variates are by their very nature examples of latent variables.

Even if the terminology used here is new to you, the idea that latent constructs can be conceived as combinations of measured variables is likely to be familiar. Here is an example. We administer the 25-item Coopersmith Self-Esteem Inventory (Coopersmith, 1981) to a given sample. Items are scored 1 for every answer that affirmatively endorses an element of self-esteem (e.g., saying positive things about oneself) and 0 for every answer in the other direction. To generate an individual's self-esteem score, we add the item scores (and multiply by 4).

The self-esteem score that we obtain from the Coopersmith inventory is a linear composite of the scores on the 25 measured variables—the actual (measured, indicator) items—making up the inventory. But the composite known as self-esteem is really a latent variable or a variate. In an empirical sense, we have not measured self-esteem directly; rather, we have measured 25 separate aspects (components, facets, portions) of self-esteem and then pieced them together statistically to obtain a single value representing that construct.

Variates can also be composed of quite different measures rather than a set of related items on an inventory. For example, we could be interested in how likely students are to seek counseling from their university health center. This variate, which we might call "willingness to seek counseling," might be a function of both measured variables (e.g., family history variables, psychopathological symptoms, prior semester's grade point average) and other latent variables (e.g., personality factors, cultural values).

Much of the work accomplished by the multivariate procedures we present in this book is done to determine how the measured variables included in a composite should be weighted (combined). Factor analysis, for example, attempts to identify subsets of variables that share a common theme. The factor is a weighted composite of the variables in the analysis—some receiving more weight than others; thus, the factor can be thought of as a variate or latent variable. As another example, multiple regression analysis attempts to build a model—a composite of independent variables—to best predict a dependent variable. In multiple regression, we try to determine the most effective weights to assign to the independent variables to maximize their combined predictive power. That weighted composite of independent variables is a variate as well.

2.6 Endogenous and Exogenous Variables

In the context of path analysis and SEM, it is necessary to develop a specific model of how the variables in the study are related to or are explained by one another. In such a model, some variables are hypothesized to be explained or predicted by others. The variables being explained are the *endogenous* variables. Other variables are not presumed to be explained by the model. These are the *exogenous* variables and are present only because they are used to explain the endogenous ones. For example, if we hypothesized that both gender and ethnic identification could at least partially account for how closely patients would follow medication regimens, the exogenous variables would be gender and ethnic identification, and the endogenous variable would be compliance with the regime.

2.7 Statistical Significance

Statistical significance is a topic that is covered in most introductory textbooks and many journal articles, and for a refresher, readers might wish to consult Agresti and Finlay

(2009), Cohen (1994), Cowles and Davis (1982), Howell (1997), Jaccard and Becker (1990), Schmidt (1996), and Thompson (1996). At a very general level, we use statistical significance testing to judge how likely it is that an obtained outcome of a statistical procedure based on data from a sample (e.g., a correlation between two variables) would occur by chance given a presumed particular state of affairs in the population (e.g., that the two variables are not correlated).

Testing statistical significance is based on the probability of obtaining a particular statistical outcome (e.g., a Pearson *r* or an *F* ratio of a given value) by chance given that there is no true relationship in the population (i.e., that the null hypothesis is true). Let's use the Pearson *r* to conceptually illustrate this point. We collect data to compute a Pearson correlation by acquiring two measures (*X* and *Y*) for each person in the sample. Although the researchers may hypothesize that the two measures are related, the statistical test assumes that they are not (this is the null hypothesis). Perhaps in a prior statistics course after computing the value of the correlation, it was necessary for students to look that value up on a table in the back of the statistics text to determine if it was statistically significant (these days most statistical software packages provide the exact probabilities). The appropriate value in that table is located by entering the table with the degrees of freedom associated with the statistic.

2.7.1 Degrees of Freedom

Degrees of freedom represent a count of how many values in a set are free to vary given that certain restrictions are in place. The most common example to illustrate this is a small set of numbers whose mean value we identify in advance. If the set contains five numbers and a predetermined mean value, then we are free to select any four of them at our whim or fancy. However, with four numbers in place (any four numbers, by the way) by our free choice, the fifth number must be the one and only value that will give us our predetermined mean. Thus, we have 4 degrees of freedom in this set of five numbers.

Pagano (1986) defines degrees of freedom as well as anyone when he says that degrees of freedom "for any statistic is the number of scores that are free to vary in calculating that statistic" (p. 263). In many cases, we calculate degrees of freedom by subtracting one from the total count. To use an example with which readers are probably familiar, the total degrees of freedom in ANOVA equals the number of observations minus one, between-subjects degrees of freedom equals the number of participants minus one, and the degrees of freedom associated with an independent variable equals its number of levels minus one. In other situations, we subtract more than one from some base number. For example, we test the significance of the Pearson correlation by setting the degrees of freedom equal to the number of pairs minus two. This is because the Pearson *r* is the standardized regression coefficient (this is explained fully in Chapter 6A) in the straight-line regression equation, and any linear function must be defined by two points; that is, two points must be fixed—they are not free to vary—to define any straight-line function (Ferguson & Takane, 1989, p. 207).

2.7.2 Sampling Distributions

Sampling distributions can be produced for virtually any statistic in the context of any population parameter, but let us focus on the Pearson r for our discussion partly because the statistic itself is relatively familiar but also because some of the details of its sampling distribution may be less familiar. Consider the situation where the "true" correlation in the population (the population parameter) is equal to zero. To establish a sampling distribution for the Pearson correlation if we were to do this by hand, we would select sets of X and Y scores that are generated randomly and then correlate these sets. Because the values are generated randomly, there is, by definition, no relationship between these scores in the population. We therefore know that the value of the correlation coefficient in the population is zero; that is, we know that the null hypothesis is true. So when we randomly generate the X and Y scores, will the computed correlation for these samples always compute to zero? No—and therein lies the dilemma.

The reason the randomly generated X and Y scores will not regularly compute to zero is that they are only a sample, a subset, of the population. Because we are drawing the numbers randomly, common sense says that the numbers will not always "balance" each other exactly as they would when we drew all the values in the population. And any "imbalance" will result in a nonzero outcome.

Although any one random sampling could yield a value far removed from zero, we repeat this sampling over and over again. We do this enough number of times so that we can determine how often we obtain each value of the correlation. Granted, that's a lot of repetitions, but the result is worth the effort. What we get is a frequency distribution of correlations obtained from these random samples—a *sampling distribution*. This distribution will peak at the population value and will be "spread out" around it. The shape of this "spread" is a function of the value of the population parameter. If the population correlation value is zero, as is the case with numbers drawn randomly and then correlated, the distribution will be symmetric around the value of zero. The bulk of the computed correlations will be relatively close to zero on either side of that value, but values quite different from zero will occur with decreasing frequency as a function of their distance from zero.

The same reasoning applies to the sampling distribution for other population parameters. For example, if the population correlation is .90, then the distribution will peak at that value and will be spread out around it. But because the Pearson r cannot exceed 1.00, the spread will be very asymmetric (skewed). The sample correlations of values lower than .90 can and will range between .90 and −1.00 (decreasing frequency as a function of their distance from .90), but the sample correlations of values higher than .90 can range only between .90 and 1.00 (and will therefore "bunch up" in that small range).

2.7.3 The Role of Sample Size

Although the general shape of the sampling distribution of a statistic can be identified, its precise shape is a function of the sample size on which the statistic is based. We can use the Pearson correlation to illustrate this. Given a true population correlation of zero, hypothetically, if we were to sample an infinite number of X and Y pairs and calculate the correlation, it would compute to zero. We will obviously not be able to sample an infinite number of scores, but we could sample a gigantic number of them. Doing this many, many times will give us a sampling distribution based on this sample size. As this sample size approached infinity, the odds of obtaining a large correlation would shrink dramatically because we would be coming increasingly closer to sampling the entire population, whose true correlation value is zero.

The situation is quite different for small sample sizes. If we sampled only 10 pairs of X and Y scores (8 degrees of freedom), for example, and we randomly chose our numbers and correlated them repeatedly, we would eventually wind up with some fairly large correlation values. It is because this sample size is so far from that of the entire population that we very often would not obtain a "balancing off" in our samples, and the correlation in those samples would veer off from the true value of zero.

2.7.4 Determination of Significance

The impact of the shape of the sampling distribution and the sample size play themselves out when we look at the area under the curve of the sampling distribution. If the sampling distribution matched that of the normal curve, 95% of its area would be contained within ±1.96 standard deviation units and that any score farther away from the mean would lie in the 5% region (2.5% on either side of the distribution). By convention, scores in this 5% region are said to be relatively rare occurrences, rare enough for us to use this .05 criterion, or *alpha level*, as our default indicator of statistical significance. Other distributions will be associated with different locations corresponding to the 5% region. Two examples of sampling distributions that are not normal are as follows:

- Student's t distribution is leptokurtic for relatively small sample sizes.
- The F distribution is positively skewed.

We apply this alpha level rationale to the sampling distributions of most of the statistics we compute. Consider again the Pearson correlation. We can test the hypothesis that the one correlation value we have obtained based on data from our research sample is likely to have been drawn from a population whose true correlation value is zero (i.e., we can test the null hypothesis, explained more fully in Section 2.7.7, that our obtained correlation value is not statistically significant from zero). It turns out that for the case where the population correlation is equal to zero, a particular function of the Pearson r $[t = r * \text{SQRT}((N-2)/(1-r^2))]$

is distributed as Student's t (see Section 4A.1.2) with $N - 2$ for the degrees of freedom (Altman, 1991; Spatz, 2011; Warner, 2008), where SQRT is square root and N is the number of cases in the sample. The sampling distribution for t is *leptokurtic* (somewhat more scores fall in the tails of the distribution and somewhat fewer fall toward its center), but with relatively large sample sizes (well more than 100), the distribution becomes approximately normal.

Happily, the sampling distributions for all of the statistics we ordinarily calculate were worked out for us years ago. These days, all we need to do is access the proper table (e.g., the one for the Pearson correlation), find the entries for the appropriate sample size (or degrees of freedom in some tables), and determine the "critical value" for our alpha level. With an alpha level of .05, that critical value is the correlation value falling at the 5% demarcation for a sampling distribution with that sample size. A correlation of that value or higher is thus likely to occur by chance only 5% or less of the time in a population whose true correlation value is zero. Similar tables have been constructed for a wide range of statistics whose sampling distributions may or may not be normal.

But most of the statistical software packages such as IBM SPSS take this process one step further. Rather than just recording the .05 and .01 alpha-level critical values, these software packages are able to provide the exact probability of a particular statistical value occurring, on the assumption that the numbers generating that statistic are drawn by chance. Thus, for each statistic we calculate, we see a corresponding probability value that has already taken into account the shape of the sampling distribution and the sample size on which it was based. If our alpha level is .05, then any probability of that value or lower (e.g., .049, .002) meets our criterion for statistical significance.

It may be worthwhile to note that testing the hypothesis that an obtained correlation value was drawn from a population whose true Pearson r is some nonzero value (e.g., that an obtained Pearson r value of .42 based on a sample size of 30 does not differ significantly from a population value of .50) is a somewhat more involved process. Because of the asymmetry of its sampling distribution for population parameters that are not equal to zero, we must engage in the three following successive steps (Kirk, 2008; Warner, 2008):

1. Transform both the population and sample correlations to standard scores. Sir R. A. Fisher worked out how to do this about a century ago (Fisher, 1915) by generating a statistic known as z'. This standard score is calculated by dividing the expression $1 + r$ by the expression $1 - r$, taking the natural logarithm of that value, and dividing that log value by 2.0. Many introductory statistics texts conveniently provide such a conversion table so that users do not need to work out the hand calculations.

2. Calculate the standard error of the standardized form of our obtained correlation. The statistic z' has a standard error of one divided by the square root of the expression $N - 3$, where N is number of cases used in computing the correlation.

3. Compute the ordinary z score as the difference between the two Fisher-transformed z' scores divided by the standard error. Evaluated at an alpha level of .05, the computed z is statistically significant if it is equal to or greater than 1.96.

To establish a 95% confidence interval around a Pearson r value, multiply the standard error by 1.96. Then subtract and add that value to the Fisher-transformed z' value of the obtained correlation to generate the standardized upper and lower limits of the 95% confidence interval. Finally, convert the upper and lower limits back to Pearson r values.

2.7.5 Levels of Significance

It is not uncommon for students to think in terms of levels of significance and to verbalize this thinking when reporting the results of their statistical analysis. We have heard students say and write statements such as "highly significant," "very significant," or even "extremely significant." We would like to discourage these expressions.

Within the traditional framework of null hypothesis testing (see Section 2.7.9 for the more modern approach), one establishes an alpha level in advance of performing the statistical analysis because one needs to assert the confidence level for claiming a significant finding in advance of looking at the results. The traditional alpha level of .05 specifies that only statistics occurring less than 5% of the time are considered sufficiently unlikely to occur by chance alone. We thus attribute something else (something nonrandom or statistically significant and therefore worthy of our interpretation) to a statistic that should appear only 5% or less of the time. If we set our alpha level at .01, we would consider an outcome to be significant only if it would ordinarily occur 1% or less of the time.

Within this framework, a statistic either reaches or does not reach our established alpha level. We do not necessarily attribute any more "potency" to the effect because it reached the .001 level than if it reached the .05 level. Thus, an effect is either statistically significant or nonsignificant (not *insignificant*, by the way, but *nonsignificant*). What students hope to tap into when they speak of a result as highly significant is, in some sense of the term, the potency, strength, or magnitude of the effect that they have observed. As we will see in subsequent chapters, the instincts of students are right on target: The strength of the observed effect is very important to assess. However, it is assessed not by the level of significance but, rather, by a squared correlation coefficient; as examples, this squared correlation coefficient can be the Pearson r^2 in the case of bivariate correlation of two quantitative variables (see Section 6A.4.3), eta square in context of ANOVA (see Section 4A.4.2), the squared multiple correlation in the case of ordinary least squares multiple regression (see Section 7A.9), and phi square (for a 2×2 table) or Cramer's V (for any $R \times C$ table) in the context of chi-square.

2.7.6 Statistical Significance Versus Confidence Interval Estimation

The traditional framework of statistical significance testing has not been universally endorsed. An alternative conceptualization emphasizing confidence interval estimation has attracted both supporters and critics. The idea behind using confidence intervals can be illustrated in connection with group means: It is possible to assert something positive and tangible about the means of the groups in an experimental study. Borenstein (1994) provides the following example with respect to a controlled clinical trial by suggesting that it may be more useful to state that "the one-year survival rate was increased by 20 percentage points with a 95% confidence interval of 15 to 24 percentage points" (p. 411) than by simply stating that the difference between the experimental and control groups was statistically significant at the .05 level. Giving the range of values that is likely to be observed at a given level of confidence thus allows readers to appreciate the magnitude of measurement error associated with a particular research result. Armed with that information, readers can determine directly the extent to which the results are potentially useful to their applications of relevance.

One of the reasons for the increased interest in using confidence interval estimation over statistical significance testing is that the former permits researchers to attenuate their conclusions rather than forcing a dichotomous decision of the results being either statistically significant or not. In the case of medical research examining the effects of a particular treatment, for example, if the boundaries of a 95% confidence interval subsume an important potential benefit (perhaps possibly preventing a stroke in 1 of 30 patients) even if the experimental and control groups are not significantly different, then the possibility that the treatment may still be worthwhile may not have been ruled out (Guyatt et al., 1995).

The controversy surrounding this issue (the challenge to the traditional approach) is mounting, and we do not have the space here to provide a detailed account of it. The interested reader can consult Cohen (1994), Cumming (2012), Gliner, Leech, and Morgan (2002), Kirk (1996), Schmidt (1996), Thompson (1996), Vacha-Hasse (2001), and Wilkinson et al. (1999) for further details. Suffice it to say that significance testing, if accepted blindly without understanding its base, can be abused about as badly as any other statistical approach. Furthermore, constructing confidence intervals based on a given level of confidence is not incompatible with the underlying concept of statistical significance. In our view, the two are more akin to two sides of the same coin than they are to two competing, mutually exclusive alternatives.

2.7.7 Null Hypothesis

It may now be clear to you why such an emphasis has been placed on the null hypothesis within the tradition of testing for statistical significance. When we evaluate the value of our computed statistic against the critical values or just read from the IBM SPSS printout the exact probability of obtaining that value by chance, those critical values or probabilities make sense (can be interpreted in the way we intend) only if the true value of the statistic in the population is in fact "null" (e.g., zero for the Pearson correlation and *t*). That is, the whole premise underlying the probability tables is that no true relationship exists in the population. This premise is essentially the null hypothesis.

When we reject the null hypothesis, we are asserting that the value for the statistic we obtained occurs so infrequently by chance alone in a population where the true value is "null" that we are willing to say that something more than chance was at work. The rub is, of course, that large values of these statistics actually do occur by chance, and if our study is one of those rare occurrences, we will be in error when we reject the null hypothesis. This error is known as a Type I error, and the chance of making it is exactly equal to the value of our alpha level. That's because our alpha level indicates how often such large values do occur by chance.

We should also very briefly mention an issue in connection with testing the null hypothesis that has been raised over the years and that continues to be raised even now concerning the assumption that there is no difference at all between the population means. As Thompson (1994) states,

> There is a very important implication of the realization that the null is not literally true in the population. The most likely sample statistics from samples drawn from populations in which the null is not literally true are sample statistics that do not correspond to the null hypothesis—for example, there are some differences in sample means or *r* in the sample is not exactly 0. And whenever the null is not exactly true in the sample(s), the null hypothesis will always be rejected at some sample size. (p. 843)

In short, if the population mean difference is almost but not quite zero, which Thompson suggests has been argued many times by a variety of writers, then we need to be very careful about what we are doing in our statistical significance testing.

Even if we take the rejection of the null hypothesis at face value and say that the odds are pretty slim that the results could have occurred by chance assuming a zero difference between the means in the population, we should still ask how useful the result is to researchers. This has to do with the topic of strength of effect, and we discuss it in Chapter 4A.

2.7.8 Type I and Type II Errors

A Type I error occurs when we incorrectly reject the null hypothesis, claiming incorrectly that we have a significant group difference or a significant correlation. That is, we have obtained a large enough value of *t* or *r* with a given number of degrees of freedom to be confident that it probably did not occur by chance alone. But we make a Type I error when we are wrong in drawing such a conclusion.

A Type II error is the other side of the coin. This error occurs when we fail to find an effect that truly exists. Here, our t or r value is not large enough, given our degrees of freedom, to reach the critical value for our alpha level. We conclude that the group means do not differ significantly or that the correlation is not significantly different from zero, but we are incorrect.

Type I and Type II errors are tied to the alpha level used by researchers to decide whether or not they have obtained an effect (e.g., a group difference in an ANOVA). As we will see in more detail in Section 2.8.1, alpha level is one of the factors affecting statistical power, and so these errors are intimately tied to the issue of statistical power.

2.7.9 The Current Status of Statistical Significance Testing

As Cumming (2012) and Gliner et al. (2002) have noted, there has been increased concerns over our reliance on what is termed null hypothesis significance testing, often abbreviated NHST (e.g., Cohen, 1990, 1994; Schmidt, 1996; Thompson, 1996). Many feel that it is time to focus more attention on effect size or strength of effect, the margin of error expressed as a confidence interval, and practical significance. The American Psychological Association (APA) has (some might say finally) institutionalized a demotion of NHST in the sixth edition of the APA *Publication Manual* (APA, 2009); with the widespread use of APA style in many disciplines, this change will have noticeable effects in the scientific community. The APA *Publication Manual*, the standard for journal reporting style in the social and behavioral sciences, now requires that probabilities associated with tests of the null hypothesis be reported as exact probabilities rather than evaluations against an alpha level (e.g., we now report $p = .032$ rather than $p < .05$, and $p = .129$ rather than $p > .05$); where the statistical output yields a probability value of .000 (IBM SPSS typically reports probability values to only three decimal places), we are asked to report it as $p < .001$. APA reporting style also now maintains that effect sizes and/or confidence interval information should also be presented to readers. This change does not remove statistical significance testing from the scene, but it does widen the perspective researchers must take when presenting and evaluating their results.

2.8 Statistical Power

When we compare the means of two groups using a t test or we evaluate the correlation of two variables with a Pearson r, the null hypothesis is that the two group means do not differ (that they are drawn from the same population) or that the Pearson r does not differ from zero. Sometimes, the null hypothesis is wrong and should be rejected: The means of the groups may truly differ, or the correlation is truly greater than zero. Being able to detect such a group difference or such a nonzero correlation is thought of as statistical power. More power corresponds with greater ability to detect a true effect. An analogy can be made to the process of magnification. Think of holding a magnifying glass (using a statistical test) to the fine detail of a painting (to examine the data). As you use more powerful magnifiers—going from 2× to 5× to 10×, for example—you can see successively greater detail, distinguishing differences that were not readily apparent to the naked eye or to what was seen under the lower-power magnifier.

The individual who may be most associated with promoting the concept of statistical power is Jacob Cohen (1969, 1977, 1988). The issue is important enough, however, to have been incorporated into a range of textbooks, including those covering research methodology (e.g., Rosenthal & Rosnow, 2008), introductory statistics (e.g., Runyon, Coleman, & Pittenger, 2000), and multivariate statistics (e.g., Stevens, 2009). We will briefly discuss a few of the more important issues concerning power.

2.8.1 Definition of Power

If the null hypothesis is wrong and there is truly a difference between the means of two groups or the Pearson correlation does differ from zero, then it follows that an alternative hypothesis is true. Once such an alternative hypothesis is articulated, it is possible to compute the chances of accepting it. That probability is called beta. Power is defined as 1 − beta. Three basic factors contribute to the level of statistical power:

- Alpha level
- Effect size
- Sample size

2.8.2 Alpha Level

The alpha level we select for our research specifies the risk we are willing to run when we reject the null hypothesis. At our traditional alpha level of .05, we are willing to be wrong in rejecting the null hypothesis 5% of the time. Thus, although relatively "large" values of our statistic (e.g., *t*, *F*, *r*) can occur by chance, we consider such values occurring 5% or less of the time to be sufficiently rare that we are willing to say that something beyond chance is working. If our alpha level is set at .01, our risk is that much less of being wrong when we reject the null hypothesis; if our alpha level is set at .15, our risk is that much greater. As we have discussed in Sections 2.7.7 and 2.7.8, alpha is the probability of rejecting the null hypothesis when it is true—that is, of committing a Type I error. More stringent alpha levels (.01 is more stringent than .05) represent lower chances of committing a Type I error.

The irony is, of course, that as we make greater and greater efforts to protect ourselves from making a Type I error, we increasingly expose ourselves to committing a Type II error because the two types of errors are inexorably linked—we cannot be cautious and risky simultaneously. If researchers want to be extremely sure that there is, say, a significant difference between two groups before they commit to the assertion in print, then they are going to miss more true group differences because those differences do not meet their very strict standards. Thus, the very act of making a Type I error less likely to occur results in a greater likelihood of committing a Type II error.

The reverse is also true. To reduce the chances of committing a Type II error, researchers could make their alpha level less stringent. Say that the alpha level is shifted to .20 from the traditional .05 level. Practically, one needs a smaller value of *t* or *r* at a given number of degrees of freedom to meet this revised criterion of statistical significance. Such a change would identify more group differences to be significant and, in doing so, would reduce the chances of committing a Type II error (overlooking a true effect). But by doing so, we have increased the probability of committing a Type I error from .05 to .20.

Stevens (2009) nicely summarizes one scenario involving the trade-off between committing a Type I error and a Type II error:

> The [alpha] level set by the experimenter is a subjective decision . . . For example, if making a type I error will not have serious substantive consequences, or if sample size is small, setting [alpha] = .10 or .15 is quite reasonable . . . On the other hand, suppose we are in a medical situation where the null hypothesis is equivalent to saying a drug is unsafe, and the alternative is that the drug is safe. Here making a type I error could be quite serious, for we would be declaring the drug safe when it is not safe. This could cause some people to be permanently damaged or perhaps even killed. In this case it would make sense to make [alpha] very small, perhaps .001. (p. 4)

One can imagine an alternative scenario in which the consequences of making a Type I error are not severe but where it would be useful to increase statistical power. For example, researchers might be exploring whether a particular variation of psychotherapy can positively affect levels of depression. Assume that the treatment is otherwise benign and is not resource intensive. It may then be worthwhile in the early stages of the research to moderate one's alpha level so that a smaller difference between a control and treatment group would permit researchers to reject the null hypothesis. Although the risk of making a Type I error under these circumstances is increased, no great harm would be accrued. But the benefit of using a treatment that might be effective could outweigh the minor risks of falsely rejecting the null hypothesis.

2.8.3 Effect Size

A second factor that influences power is effect size. Larger effect sizes are associated with greater levels of statistical power. The notion of effect size relates to the magnitude of the group differences in the population (Stevens, 2009). Although there are more complex ways to index effect size (e.g., Mahalanobis distance as discussed in Section 5A.4.3), effect size in the present context can be conceived of as the difference between the two means divided by the assumed common population standard deviation (Stevens,

2009). The result of such a computation is often labeled as *d* (Cohen, 1977). In this sense, it is simply a way of standardizing raw scores and is conceptually the same structure underlying *z* scores or the *t* test.

Some writers have provided guidelines for evaluating the magnitude of effect sizes in certain applications. For example, for single sample *t* ratios, effect sizes of .20, .50, and .80 are considered to be small, medium, and large, respectively (Cohen, 1988, pp. 24–27). For Pearson *r*, effect sizes of .10, .30, and .50 are considered to be small, medium, and large, respectively (Cohen, 1988, pp. 77–81). For the eta-square statistic (indexing the amount of variance accounted for by an effect in an analysis of variance), effect sizes of .01, .06, and .14 are considered to be small, medium, and large, respectively (Cohen, 1988, pp. 285–288).

If statistical power is the ability to detect true effects, then it might not surprise anyone to learn that larger effect sizes are associated with greater levels of power. Think back to our magnifying glass analogy. A small effect size (e.g., two means differing by a fraction of a standard deviation) may require researchers to use a very strong magnifier (considerable statistical power) to find it. A very large effect size (e.g., two means differing by 10 standard deviations) may require relatively little statistical power for researchers to identify it. Effect sizes are, of course, part of the natural world that we study and, therefore, cannot be adjusted by researchers. The best we can do is to estimate the magnitude of the effect sizes we are studying so that we may accommodate them as best as possible. Relatively recent discussions concerning the reporting of effect sizes (see Wilkinson et al., 1999) encourages the practice of reporting and interpreting effect sizes in their actual research context.

2.8.4 Sample Size

Generally, we can say that researchers achieve greater power with increases in their sample size. This is the case because larger sample sizes are associated with lower standard errors and, therefore, narrower confidence intervals (these factors drive the outcome of our statistical tests of significance). Thus, larger sample sizes result in increasingly more stable and precise estimates of population parameters. From a hands-on perspective, degrees of freedom are a direct function of sample size and, all else equal, smaller values of *t*, *F*, and *r* are needed to reject the null hypothesis with greater degrees of freedom. Incorporating the size of the sample using statistical power as the context has been addressed by many researchers; a comprehensive review of this topic is provided by Maxwell, Kelley, and Rausch (2008).

We should also sound a small note of caution here. Very large sample sizes can enable us to find a statistically significant effect even when that effect is not especially strong. It is actually possible to have so much power in certain situations that small or trivial effect sizes can be distinguished. As we approach these power regions, we increasingly rely on strength-of-effect indexes to help us keep some perspective on our statistical results.

2.9 Recommended Readings

Aiken, L. S., West, S. G., Sechrest, L., & Reno, R. R. (1990). Graduate training in statistics, methodology, and measurement in psychology: A survey of PhD programs in North America. *American Psychologist, 45,* 721–734.

Cohen, J. (1994). The earth is round ($p < .05$). *American Psychologist, 49,* 997–1003.

Cowles, M., & Davis, C. (1982). On the origins of the .05 level of statistical significance. *American Psychologist, 37,* 553–558.

Gliner, J. A., Leech, N. L., & Morgan, G. A. (2002). Problems with null hypothesis significance testing (NHST): What do the textbooks say? *Journal of Experimental Education, 71,* 83–92.

Kirk, R. E. (1996). Practical significance: A concept whose time has come. *Educational and Psychological Measurement, 56,* 746–759.

Kline, R. B. (2004). *Beyond significance testing.* Washington, DC: American Psychological Association.

Mittag, K. C., & Thompson, B. (2000). A national survey of AERA members' perceptions of statistical significance tests and other statistical issues. *Educational Researcher, 29,* 14–20.

Thompson, B. (2002). "Statistical," "practical," and "clinical": How many kinds of significance do counselors need to consider? *Journal of Counseling and Development, 80,* 64–71.

Trusty, J., Thompson, B., & Petrocelli, J. V. (2004). Practical guide for reporting effect size in quantitative research in the *Journal of Counseling & Development. Journal of Counseling & Development, 82,* 107–110.

Data Screening

3A.1 Overview

Once the data from a research study—whether derived from survey, experimental, or archival methods—are in hand and have been entered into IBM SPSS, the first step that researchers should take is to examine certain properties of their data to ensure that the results of their analyses will be able to be validly interpreted. Valid interpretation rests on the two following features of the data:

- That the data are an accurate representation of what was measured
- That the data meet the underlying assumptions of the analysis procedure

The accuracy of the data involves researchers carrying out a process of *data cleaning*. Although this process is very important, there are only a few actions that researchers can carry out at this stage to detect and correct any accuracy problems. These actions are relatively simple, and we briefly discuss them in the following section.

The extent to which the data have met the important assumptions (normality, linearity, homoscedasticity, and independence of errors) underlying most of the multivariate statistical analyses we cover in this book is a complex issue involving *data screening*. There are several properties of the data that need to be examined and several possible actions to correct problems that can be carried out by researchers. We first discuss the very complicated topic of missing values, partly because it seems to follow from a discussion of the accuracy of the data and partly because most of the multivariate statistical assumptions are at risk in this arena. This is followed by a discussion of outliers, extreme values that can distort the results of a statistical analysis. We next talk about using descriptive statistics and pictorial representations in data screening. We then finish this chapter with separate discussions of each of the assumptions and what corrective measures, if any, are available to researchers.

3A.2 Value Cleaning

3A.2.1 Overview

Values in a data file are the transcribed data, which could have been hand-entered directly into IBM SPSS, imported to IBM SPSS from a spreadsheet, or downloaded from some organizational source. Most of the data on which we focus in this book is in numerical form. Thus, sales figures might be in dollars, degree of pathology or health could be represented on some quantitative scale, and so on. *Value cleaning* refers to the process of making sure, to the extent that it is possible and within the bounds of feasibility, that the values are within the limits of reasonable expectation (e.g., the age of a presumed adult is not 9 years old; a response to an item rated on a response scale of 1 through 5 is not a 6 or an otherwise out-of-bounds value).

Verification or correction of these apparently unreasonable data values can then be accomplished by examining the raw (original) sources of the data. To be able to engage in such a process suggests that these data sources are and remain available to researchers well after the data collection phase of the research has been completed. Thus, raw data (e.g., the responses to inventory items, records of dollars in sales from particular departments within a large retail store) supplied by the originating sources (e.g., respondents, original records of sales) in the context of research studies and the electronic representations of such data should be retained by researchers for an extended period of time; in this way, the original or other researchers can verify the accuracy of the entries in the data file within the limitations of the original data (e.g., handwritten values provided by respondents may not be entirely legible) and/or replicate the original or perform additional statistical analyses on the data. Most professional organizations treat this issue quite seriously (for good reason) and have published guidelines on their data retention policies that they expect members of their disciplines to follow. For example, APA in its *Publication Manual* (2009, sec. 1.08) maintains that research data should be retained for at least 5 years after publication.

3A.2.2 Qualitative Numerical Codes

Qualitative numerical coding is represented in the data file by (arbitrary) number (value) codes for the categories of a qualitative variable. An example of a variable with only two categories is gender. We might code females as 1 and males as 2 in our data file, but someone else might code males as 0 and females as 1 in their data file. Because these codes are arbitrarily assigned, both coding systems are acceptable as long as they are used consistently within any given data file. An example of a variable with more than two categories is race/ethnicity, where we might need half a dozen or more codes to represent the variable. In all situations, however, we strongly advise using adjacent (sequential) values because not doing so can affect the interpretation of certain analyses (see Section 8A.5.1.3, for an example). Participants receive one of these codes for each variable that is so coded (assuming that they responded to the questions during data collection); if they failed to respond, they would either be assigned an out-of-range value (e.g., 9) that must be defined as a missing value in the data file (this might be done to ensure that a number code was entered for every participant) or the field would be left blank for that participant.

3A.2.3 Quantitative Numerical Codes

Quantitative numerical codes represent values on the summative response, interval, or ratio scale underlying the measurement of the variable. They are not arbitrary but rather reflect the amount of the quality being assessed. As examples, we would infer that (a) a value of 4 on a 5-point summative response scale ranging from *agree very little* to *agree very much* would indicate considerable agreement, (b) 100 °C represents the particular level of temperature at which water boils, and (c) the number of hours of individual psychotherapy provided to all clients on site in a given month represents a certain amount of services that were delivered.

3A.2.4 Multiple Response Coding

Some nonmetric or qualitative variables are structured so that they might logically have *multiple responses* to a particular issue. Two examples of this are as follows:

- We might be interested in the types of music that are liked by respondents to a survey. Some of these choices might include rock, classical, jazz, blues, and country.
- We might be interested in determining which topics were included in multivariate research design textbooks. Some of these topics might be discriminant function analysis, logistic regression, cluster analysis, and path analysis.

Unlike an item requesting individuals to indicate their ethnicity, where there is only one response permitted (even with many options), people can like many different types of music and multivariate textbooks would include many topics on an extended list. To capture multiple response data, each element of interest (e.g., each type of music, each multivariate topic) should constitute its own variable. Thus, each element needs to be responded to and each will therefore be represented by a column in the IBM SPSS data file.

Sometimes the response to each element will be a binary choice (e.g., *yes/no, present/not present*). For the multivariate topics as an example, each is either included or not included in a given textbook. Other times, researchers may have more flexibility in data collection. For each music type, for example, we can ask for a binary response of *like/do not like* or we can ask for quantitative judgments by (a) using a 5-point degree-of-liking scale ranging from *very little* to *very much* or (b) asking respondents to rank order the music types, the most preferred assigned a value (rank) of 1, the next most preferred a value (rank) of 2, and so on.

Assuming for simplicity that each element is addressed in a binary manner and is coded systematically in the data file (e.g., *yes* is coded as 1 and *no* is coded as 0), we can deal with the data set in several different ways. Three of them are as follows:

- Treat each element as a separate variable. At the very least, we can tabulate frequencies of the response categories provided to each variable.
- Combine the information contained in each of the individual variables together using the **Compute** procedure of IBM SPSS (see Section 3A.13) in a manner that made sense in the research context. For example, we could code each unique response pattern (*yes* only to rock music as 1, *yes* only to classical as 2, *yes* to classical and jazz as another code, etc.). But even with just five types of music, the number of possible response patterns would likely be unmanageably large, even if we had such an enormous sample to have many respondents represented in each pattern.
- Use the **Multiple Response** procedure of IBM SPSS to summarize at one time the set of variables representing the elements. This procedure allows us to count the number of cases who have responded in a specified way (e.g., responded *yes*) to each of the variables, and it will allow us to generate frequencies of such responses as well as to perform a cross-tabulation with another variable (e.g., cross each of the music types for which respondents have indicated a liking with sex of respondent to acquire frequencies of music preference separately for female and male respondents). We do not cover the **Multiple Response** procedure in this text, but readers can consult SPSS (2006) and Wagner (2010) for instructions on its use.

3A.2.5 The Process of Value Cleaning

The value cleaning process ensures that once a given data set is in hand, a verification procedure is followed that checks for the appropriateness of numerical values for the values of each variable under study. The cleaning process begins with a consideration of the research project's unit of analysis. Often in behavioral science research, the "units of analysis"—that is, the entities to which the data are specifically related—are human respondents (in survey or archival research) and human participants (in experimental research). In such situations, the score for each variable that we have recorded in the data file (e.g., the response to a particular item on an inventory) represents something about an individual sampled by our research methodology. Generically, these units can be referred to as *cases*. Examples of other kinds of cases that can be the source of research data, as we indicated in Section 2.1, include individual mental health service providers, school districts, census tracts, and cities. Here, the value recorded for a variable in the data file represents one of these larger entities (e.g., the number of hours of individual psychotherapy provided to all clients on site in the month of April for a particular mental health facility, the average reading comprehension score on the statewide achievement test of all students in a particular district).

The challenge in value cleaning is to determine, for every case, whether each variable contains only legitimate numerical codes or values and, secondarily, whether these legitimate codes seem reasonable. For example, respondent gender (a nominal-level variable) can be arbitrarily coded as 0 for males and 1 for females. To the extent that all cases on the gender variable are coded as either 0 or 1, we can say that this variable is "clean." Notice that code cleaning does not address the correctness of an appropriately coded value—it can deal with only whether or not the variable's code is within the specified range.

It is possible that the variable is not "clean." For example, we may find a value of 2 under a gender variable that was coded 0 and 1. This is clearly an error as no such code was assigned to that variable. If it was feasible, we could attempt to determine through whatever administrative records were available to us what the proper code should be. If that strategy failed, then we should delete that value or define the value of 2 as a missing value.

We take the same approach with quantitative variables. Suppose we had collected data from a sample of 100 community mental health consumers on their global assessment of functioning (GAF) Axis V rating of the *Diagnostic and Statistical Manual of Mental Disorders*, fourth edition, text revision (*DSM-IV-TR*; American Psychiatric Association, 2000). GAF scale values can range from 1 (severe impairment) to 100 (good general functioning). Now, further suppose that our experience with these consumers has shown us that the modal (most frequent) GAF score was about 55 with minimum and maximum scores of approximately 35 and 65, respectively. If during the cleaning process, we discover a respondent with a GAF score of 2, a logically legitimate but certainly an unusual score, we would probably want to verify its authenticity through other sources if possible. For example, we might want to take a look at the original questionnaire or the actual computer-based archival record for that individual if we had access to those materials.

Such a cleaning process leads us to several options for future action. Consider the situation in which we find a very low GAF score of 2 for an individual. If our investigation shows the recorded value to be incorrect, we would substitute the correct value (e.g., 42) in its stead. Alternatively, we may confirm that the value of 2 is correct and leave it alone for the time being. Or, after confirming that it is correct, we might consider that data point to be a candidate for elimination on the proposition that it is an outlier (an extreme score) because we view the case as not being representative of the target population under study. Finally, if we deem the value to be wrong but do not have an appropriate replacement, we can treat it as a missing value (by coding directly in IBM SPSS the value of 2 as missing, by replacing it with a value that we have already specified in IBM SPSS to stand for a missing value, or by simply deleting the value and leaving the entry blank).

3A.2.6 Using Frequency Tables for Data Cleaning

A frequency table is a convenient way to summarize the obtained values for variables that contain a small to moderate number of different values or attributes. Demographic variables such as gender (with two codes), race/ethnicity (with between half a dozen and a dozen codes), and marital status (usually with no more than about six categories), along with other nominal-level variables, including questions that require simple, dichotomous "yes"–"no" options, all have a limited number of possible values that are easily summarized in a frequency table. Quantitative variables with many dozens of values are also amenable to this summarizing procedure if we are searching for the possibility of out-of-range values or even logically possible but unusual values.

An example of a demographic variable with five codes is "highest academic degree achieved." For this variable, 1 was assigned for high school (HS), 2 for a bachelor's degree (BA), 3 for a master's degree (MA), 4 for a doctoral degree (DOC), and 5 was assigned for any other degree status (Other). Table 3a.1 depicts the raw and unorganized data of 51 community mental health center providers described in a study by Gamst, Dana, Der-Karabetian, and Kramer (2001). Each respondent was assigned an arbitrary number at the time of data entry. To make it fit within a relatively small space, we have structured this table to display the data in two sets of columns. A cursory inspection of the information contained in Table 3a.1 suggests a jumble of degree statuses scattered among the 51 mental health practitioners. A coherent pattern is hard to discriminate.

A better and more readable way to display these data appears as the frequency distribution or frequency table that can be seen in Table 3a.2. Each row of the table is reserved for a particular value of the variable called "terminal degree." It aggregates the number of cases with a given value and the percentage of representation of that category in the data array. This aggregation of the data enables researchers to quickly decipher the important information contained within a distribution of values. For example, we can see in Table 3a.2 that 49% of the mental health providers had master's degrees and 20% had doctorates. Thus, a simple summary statement of this table might note that "69% of the mental health providers had graduate-level degrees."

Table 3a.2 also shows how useful a frequency table can be in the data cleaning process. Because the researchers were using only code values 1 through 5, the value of 6 represents an anomalous code in that it should not exist at all. It is for that reason that the value of 6 has no label in the table. In all likelihood, this represents a data entry error. To discover which case has this anomalous value if the data file was very large, one could have IBM SPSS list the case number and the terminal degree variable for everyone (or, to make the output easier to read, we could first select for codes on this variable that were greater than 5 and then do

Table 3a.1 Terminal Degree Status of Fifty-One Community Mental Health Center Providers

Respondent	Degree		Respondent	Degree
1	3 MA		27	1 HS
2	3 MA		28	3 MA
3	1 HS		29	3 MA
4	3 MA		30	1 HS
5	1 HS		31	3 MA
6	4 DOC		32	2 BA
7	3 MA		33	3 MA
8	4 DOC		34	2 BA
9	3 MA		35	3 MA
10	3 MA		36	2 BA
11	3 MA		37	3 MA
12	1 HS		38	3 MA
13	4 DOC		39	4 DOC
14	3 MA		40	3 MA
15	4 DOC		41	2 BA
16	6		42	3 MA
17	3 MA		43	3 MA
18	1 HS		44	4 DOC
19	4 DOC		45	5 OTHER
20	3 MA		46	3 MA
21	1 HS		47	5 OTHER
22	1 HS		48	3 MA
23	4 DOC		49	4 DOC
24	4 DOC		50	1 HS
25	3 MA		51	3 MA
26	3 MA			

Table 3a.2 Frequency Table for Fifty-One Community Mental Health Center Providers

Code	Terminal Degree	Frequency	Percentage
1	High school	9	18
2	Bachelor	4	8
3	Master's	25	49
4	Doctorate	10	20
5	Other	2	4
6		1	1
	Total	51	100

the listing). We would then discover that it was the entry for Respondent 16 that contained this out-of-range code.

3A.3 Patterns of Missing Values

During the data screening process, we encounter missing data for a variety of reasons. Respondents may refuse to answer personal questions pertaining to their income, sexual orientation, or current illegal drug use. Some respondents may not be competent to respond because of a lack of knowledge regarding a particular topic. Participants in an experiment may suffer from fatigue or lack of motivation and simply stop responding. Archival data may be missing because of data entry errors, the unavailability of certain information, or mechanical or electronic malfunctions. The key question is whether these missing values are a function of a random or a systematic process. Once this is known, a researcher can choose among a variety of methods to remove cases with missing data or to replace missing data values through an imputation process.

3A.3.1 Patterns and Mechanisms of Missing Data

Methodologists and statisticians (Enders, 2010; Little & Rubin, 2002; Rubin, 1976) often refer to two interrelated concepts regarding missing data:

- *Patterns* of missing data address typical configurations of missing values.
- *Mechanisms* of missingness (*missingness* is a term that is becoming increasingly used in this field) address relationships between the variables in the study and the missing values.

Enders (2010) has identified six typical patterns of missing data. A *univariate pattern* contains missing values on a single variable, as sometimes occurs in experimental research. A *unit nonresponse pattern* produces missing data among certain variables during survey research. *Monotone missing data patterns* typically occur in longitudinal research. They reflect participant attrition and usually resemble a "staircase" since cases who have dropped out at a study's midpoint will not have data on a subsequent measurement occasion. *General missing data patterns* have missing values scattered haphazardly throughout a data set but still can be systematically missing. A *planned missing data pattern* is a function of a survey research design that intentionally allocates missing data to certain variables across cases to reduce respondent fatigue with large questionnaires. Last, *latent variable patterns* can occur in structural equation modeling (SEM) or confirmatory factor analysis that cause the values of the latent variable to be missing for the entire sample.

These various patterns of missing data can be conceptualized as representing one of three "mechanisms of missingness" (Graham, 2009, p. 552):

- *Missing completely at random* (MCAR).
- *Missing at random* (MAR).
- *Not missing at random* (NMAR).

As the name implies, the MCAR missingness mechanism depicts the cases that have missing values to be an accidental or random sampling of all the cases. More formally, MCAR requires that missing data on a given variable *Y* are unrelated to other variables in the data set and are unrelated to the other values of variable *Y* (Enders, 2010). Hence, MCAR suggests that the data observed on average in cases with complete data are comparable to the data observed in cases with missing values. Although often claimed or implied, the MCAR assumption is seldom achieved (Allison, 2002).

The concept of MAR is a bit of a misnomer in that "random" as used in MAR has a different connotation than the "random" of MCAR. In practice, MAR implies that cases with missing values on a particular variable *Y* are systematically related to (i.e., conditional upon) one or more other variables in the data set. For example, if participants in a mental health study are given 6-month pre- and postassessments of their ability to function in the community effectively (i.e., GAF-Time-1 and GAF-Time-2), then GAF-Time-2 is dependent on GAF-Time-1. Hence, missing GAF-Time-2 values are considered MAR due to dependency on GAF-Time-1. As another example, suppose that respondents with missing data on GAF scores at termination of a treatment program were likely to be classified in the severe as opposed to the moderate diagnostic categories. These missing GAF scores would then be related to (conditional to a certain extent upon) diagnostic category, and we would conclude that the GAF score data are MAR.

Data that are MNAR are so designated because cases with a missing value on *Y* are a function of variable *Y*. For example, low-income respondents are observed to have missing data on the income question. Such a situation is not indicative of a random process, but it rather suggests that missingness depends on unobserved data (Graham, 2009).

Keeping these missing data mechanisms in mind helps guide the process of determining the seriousness of the missing data situation. If the data conform to the MCAR or MAR mechanism criteria, then perhaps we have what is termed by methodologists an *ignorable missingness* situation (we probably do not have a problem with the distribution of the missing data pattern but we may still have a problem if there are a great deal of missing data). If the missing data distributions do not meet these criteria (i.e., they are MNAR), then we are faced with a *nonignorable missingness mechanism* (Graham, 2009). Let's look at several ways of assessing this latter possibility.

3A.3.2 Statistical Tests of MCAR

Historically, two statistical methods have been used to assess the MCAR mechanism (Enders, 2010). One approach is to conduct a series of independent (separate variance) *t* tests that use an indicator variable that specifies whether the value of a variable is present or missing for a particular case as the independent variable and other continuous variables serve as dependent variables. If values of a variable are MCAR, then other continuous variables should have comparable distributions for cases separated into missing and not missing groups (i.e., the null hypothesis is accepted). Conversely, a statistically significant *t* test may suggest that the missing data mechanism is MAR or MNAR. The **Missing Value Analysis** module of IBM SPSS provides a very convenient means of conducting these tests for variables that have missing values on at least 5% of the cases. Analyses on fewer than 5% of the cases make *t* test statistics more problematic. Enders (2010) cautions against the use of univariate *t*-test comparisons, because these tests fail to incorporate the correlations among the variables, which can produce misleading results.

A second common approach to test the MCAR mechanism is to compute *Little's MCAR test* (Little, 1988), which simultaneously evaluates, with a chi-square statistic, group (missing, not missing) differences for every variable in the data set. This omnibus test of MCAR yields a null hypothesis that the missing data mechanism is MCAR if the alpha level is equal to .05 or greater. Conversely, if the test statistic is statistically significant at an alpha level less than .05, then the missing data mechanism may be MAR or MNAR. The IBM SPSS **Missing Value Analysis** module provides Little's MCAR test results as a footnote to its expectation maximization (EM) matrices. Enders (2010) cautions against reliance on this test due to its global nature and inability to pinpoint specific variables that violate MCAR.

3A.3.3 Looking for Patterns

Consider the hypothetical clinical outcome study for 15 cases represented in Table 3a.3. The left portion of the table shows the data collected by a community mental health agency for four variables. A GAF score is obtained at intake (shown as GAF-T1 for "Time 1") and again 6 months later (GAF-T2 for "Time 2"). Also recorded is the age of the client at intake and the number of counseling sessions for which the client was present. The right portion of Table 3a.3 is a tabulation of the missing data situation; it shows the absolute number of missing data points and their percentage with respect to a complete set of four data points. For example, the third case was missing a second GAF score and a record of the number of therapy sessions he or she attended. Thus, these two missing values made up 50% of the total of four data points that should have been there.

A quick inspection of Table 3a.3 indicates that missing data are scattered across all four of the variables under study. We can also note that 9 of the 15 cases (60%) have no missing

Table 3a.3 Example of a Data Set With Missing Values

Case	Variables GAF-T1	GAF-T2	Age	Sessions	Pattern # Missing	% Missing
1	51	51	30	8	0	0
2	55	—	63	4	1	25
3	40	—	57	—	2	50
4	38	50	31	10	0	0
5	80	80	19	11	0	0
6	40	—	50	2	1	25
7	55	55	19	8	0	0
8	50	70	20	8	0	0
9	62	70	20	10	0	0
10	65	75	19	7	0	0
11	—	—	38	—	3	75
12	50	61	65	9	0	0
13	40	55	—	8	1	25
14	40	50	46	9	0	0
15	32	—	44	3	1	25
# Missing in column	1	5	1	2	9	
% Missing in column	6.7	33.3	6.7	13.3	15.0	

Note. GAF-T1 = GAF at intake; GAF-T2 = GAF at Time 2; Sessions = number of treatment sessions.

data. Because almost all the multivariate procedures we talk about in this book need to be run on a complete data set, the defaults set by the statistical program (*listwise deletion* of cases) would select only these 9 cases with full data, excluding all cases with a missing value on one or more variables. This issue of sample size reduction as a function of missing data, especially when this reduction appears to be nonrandom (as in the present case), can threaten the external validity of the research and can substantially lower the power of the statistical analysis.

Further inspection of Table 3a.3 shows that one third of the sample (five respondents) had missing data on the GAF-T2 (the 6-month postintake measurement) variable. Normally, such a relatively large proportion of nonresponse for one variable would nominate it as a possible candidate for deletion (by not including that variable in the analysis, more cases would have a complete data set and thus contribute to the analysis). Nonresponse to a postmeasure on a longitudinal (multiply measured) variable is a fairly common occurrence. If this variable is crucial to our analyses, then some form of item imputation procedure (i.e., estimation of what the missing value might have been and replacement of the missing value with that estimate) may be in order.

We should also be attentive to how many missing data are associated with each measure as shown in the last two rows of Table 3a.3. As a general rule, variables containing missing data (MCAR or MAR) on 5% or fewer of the cases can be ignored (Tabachnick & Fidell, 2007). The second GAF variable, showing a third of its values as missing, has a missing value rate substantially greater than this general rule of thumb; this variable therefore needs a closer look. In the present example, although the remaining three variables exceed this 5% mark as well, the relative frequency of cases with missing data is small enough to ignore.

An important consideration at this juncture, then, is the randomness of the missing data pattern for the GAF-Time-2 variable. A closer inspection of the missing values for GAF-Time-2 indicates that they tend to occur among the older respondents. This is probably an indication of a systematic pattern of nonresponse, and thus is probably not ignorable.

Finally, we can see from Table 3a.3 that Case 11 is missing data on three of the four variables. Missing such a large proportion of data points would make a strong argument for that case to be deleted from the data analysis.

3A.4 Overview of Methods of Handling Missing Data

There are a number of established or traditional procedures for dealing with item non-response as well as more "modern" approaches. Traditional methods focus on *deleting missing cases* or using *single imputation methods* to fill in the missing values. Modern methods emphasize *maximum likelihood estimation* procedures such as EM algorithms that use all of the available data to estimate parameters of the variables with missing values (Enders, 2010) or *multiple imputation* procedures. Statisticians, methodologists, and textbook writers sometimes differ on their personal recommendations for which techniques to use under varying degrees of randomness of the missing data process. However, a consensus in favor of the more modern missing data handling approaches is now being reached.

We will examine both the traditional and modern approaches since readers will often encounter them in the research literature, and also because of their easy accessibility with statistical software like IBM SPSS. For excellent introductory overviews of the missing data topic, see Graham (2009), Graham, Cumsille, and Elek-Fisk (2003), McKnight, McKnight, Sidani, and Figueredo (2007), and Tabachnick and Fidell (2007). More advanced coverage of missing data topics can be found in Allison (2002), Enders (2010), Little and Rubin (2002), and Schafer (1997).

3A.5 Deletion Methods of Handling Missing Data

3A.5.1 Deletion Methods: Listwise

This method involves excluding from participation all cases that have missing data on the variables included in the particular analysis we are performing. We call this method *listwise* because we are deleting cases with missing data on any variable in our variable list. In this method, a single missing value on just a single variable in the analysis is cause for a case to be excluded from the statistical analysis. As we mentioned previously, this is a standard (default) practice for most computer statistical packages, including IBM SPSS.

A practical advantage of listwise deletion is that this method can be used in a variety of multivariate techniques (e.g., multiple regression, discriminant analysis), and it ordinarily requires no additional commands or computations. But the choice to invoke listwise deletion of cases has associated drawbacks or concerns, some of which are as follows:

- Listwise deletion involves the loss of cases that could have been very difficult and expensive (in time or other resources) to obtain.
- The reduction of sample size as a result of listwise deletion of cases may increase the estimate of measurement error (standard errors increase with lower sample sizes).
- Lowering the sample size may drop it below the relatively large *N* needed for most multivariate procedures.
- The loss of sample size lowers the statistical power of the analysis.
- If the cases deleted in the listwise process are not representative of the sample-as-a-whole (e.g., younger participants, patients with more severe symptoms, individuals residing in rural areas, etc. might fail to answer more questions), then the results of any statistical analysis could very well be less generalizable than researchers might ordinarily presume.

Allison (2002) gives the listwise deletion method a very strong endorsement when he notes thus:

> Listwise deletion is not a bad method for handling missing data. Although it does not use all of the available information, at least it gives valid inferences when the data are MCAR. . . . [W]henever the probability of missing data on a particular independent variable depends on the value of that variable (and not the dependent variable), listwise deletion may do better than maximum likelihood or multiple imputation. (p. 7)

While listwise deletion may be acceptable when missing data are MCAR, caution should always be exercised when using this method, as Enders (2010) notes,

> The disadvantages of listwise deletion far outweigh its advantages. The primary problem with listwise deletion is that it requires MCAR data and can produce distorted parameter estimates when this assumption does not hold. (p. 39)

3A.5.2 Deletion Methods: Pairwise

This approach computes summary statistics (e.g., means, standard deviations, correlations) from all available cases that have valid values (it is the IBM SPSS default method of handling missing values for these computations in most of the procedures designed to produce descriptive statistics). Thus, no cases are necessarily completely excluded from the data analysis. Cases with missing values on certain variables would still be included when other variables (on which they had valid values) were involved in the analysis. If we wanted to compute the mean for variables X, Y, and Z using, for example, the **Frequencies** procedure in IBM SPSS, all cases with valid values on X would be brought into the calculation of X's mean, all cases with valid values on Y would be used for the calculation of Y's mean, and all cases with valid values of Z would be used for the calculation of Z's mean. It is therefore possible that the three means could very well be based on somewhat different cases and somewhat different Ns.

Correlation presents another instance where pairwise deletion is the default. To be included in computing the correlation of X and Y, cases must have valid values on both variables. Assume that Case 73 is missing a value on the Y variable. That case is therefore excluded in the calculation of the correlations between X and Y and between Y and Z. But that case will be included in computing the correlation between X and Z if that case has valid values for those variables. It is therefore not unusual for correlations produced by the **Bivariate Correlations** procedure in IBM SPSS to be based on somewhat different cases. Note that when correlations are computed in one of the multivariate procedures where listwise deletion is in effect, that method rather than pairwise deletion is used so that the correlations in the resulting correlation matrix are based on exactly the same cases.

Although pairwise deletion can be successfully used with linear regression, factor analysis, and SEM (see Allison, 2002), this method is clearly most reliable when the data are MCAR. Furthermore, statistical software algorithms for computing standard errors with pairwise deletion show a considerable degree of variability and even bias (Allison, 2002).

Again, caution is advocated by Enders (2010),

> The primary problem with pairwise deletion is that it requires MCAR data and can produce distorted parameter estimates when this assumption does not hold. (p. 41)

Our recommendation is not to use pairwise deletion when conducting any of the multivariate data analysis procedures such as multiple regression, factor analysis, or SEM.

3A.6 Single Imputation Methods of Handling Missing Data

The next approaches to missing data that we describe are collectively referred to as single imputation procedures. To "impute" is to "ascribe" or "assign" an attribute to something. In the situation involving missing data, we "assign" a value to the piece of data that is missing. Obviously, if the piece of data is missing, then we do not know its true value, and placing in a value by the researcher may strike readers as an odd thing to do. However, these values are not assigned arbitrarily or to increase the chances of the results coming out closer to the research hypotheses but are "guesses" or "estimates" based on statistical reasoning. Single imputation methods use a single basis to replace missing values. Once the missing values are replaced with the imputed values, the statistical analysis is then conducted on the data set. The results need to be interpreted in light of the fact that the analysis used imputed values in place of the missing values.

Although single (as well as the more complex) imputation methods do preserve sample size, we urge caution in the use of these somewhat intoxicating remedies for missing data situations; all these single imputation schemes are associated with biased parameter estimates (e.g., means, standard deviations) even when the missingness mechanism is MCAR. Furthermore, permanently altering the raw data in a data set can have potentially catastrophic consequences for the beginning and experienced multivariate researcher alike. For good overviews of these procedures, see Allison (2002), Enders (2010), and Graham (2009).

3A.6.1 Single Imputation: Mean Substitution

Mean substitution calls for replacing all missing values of a variable with the mean of that variable. In its simplest form, it is probably the oldest of the imputation methods and, because this field of statistics has seen so much development over recent years, the one that is least in favor. We present this method here because readers should be aware of it, but we would urge exercising great caution if there is no alternative to use.

To illustrate a mean substitution procedure, assume that Case 24 has a missing value on variable *R*. We then compute a mean for variable *R* based on cases with valid values and then record that mean value for Case 24 as though he or she had provided that value during the original data collection. If Case 31 also had a missing value on variable *R*, we would assign the same mean value to that case as well.

In the simplest form of the procedure, the mean to be used as the replacement value is based on all the valid cases in the data file. This is both the most common and most conservative of the imputation practices. IBM SPSS conveniently provides mean imputation capabilities within many of its statistical procedures (e.g., multiple regression, factor analysis, etc.). IBM SPSS also offers as one choice in its main menu **Transform ➜ Replace Missing Values** for replacement of missing values. The choices, together with what they will accomplish, are as follows:

- *Series mean:* Replaces missing values with the mean for the entire series.
- *Mean of nearby points:* Replaces missing values with the median of valid surrounding values. The span of nearby points is the number of valid values above and below the missing value used to compute the mean.
- *Median of nearby points:* Replaces missing values with the mean of valid surrounding values. The span of nearby points is the number of valid values above and below the missing value used to compute the median.
- *Linear interpolation:* Replaces missing values using a linear interpolation (insert the average of two data points). The last valid value before the missing value and first valid value after the missing value are used for the interpolation. If the first or last case in the series has a missing value, the missing value is not replaced.
- *Linear trend at point:* Replaces missing values with the linear trend for that point. The existing series is regressed on an index variable scaled 1 to *n*. Missing values are replaced with their predicted values.

From our first statistics course on, we have been taught the rubric that the sample mean is the best estimate of the population mean. An analogous argument is offered to support using the mean substitution procedure. The best estimate of what a missing value might be is the mean of the values that we have. Now, we know that not every missing value would fall on this mean—some values would be lower and some values would be higher. But in the absence of contradictory information, we estimate that the average of these missing values would be equal to the average of the valid values. Based on that reasoning, we then substitute the mean that we have for the values that are missing.

At the same time, it is important to recognize that the true values for these missing cases would almost certainly vary over at least a modest range of scores. By substituting the same single value (the mean of our observed values) for a missing value, even granting that it is a reasonable estimate, we must accept the consequence that this procedure artificially reduces the variability of that variable.

As might be expected from what we have just said, there are at least three drawbacks to the mean substitution strategy. First, the assumption that the missing values are randomly distributed among the cases is an assumption that is not always fully tested. Second, although the mean of a distribution is the best estimate we have of the population parameter, it is still likely to occur within a certain margin of error (e.g., ±1.96 standard error units). Thus, the sample mean, although being our best estimate, may not fall at the true value of the parameter.

Third, the variance of the variable having its missing values replaced is necessarily reduced when we remove the missing value and substitute it with the mean of the valid cases. That narrowing of the variance, in turn, can distort the variable's distribution of values (Allison, 2002; Enders, 2010) and can therefore bias the statistical analysis, even when the missingness mechanism is MCAR.

A variation of this simplest mean substitution approach is to use a subgroup mean rather than a full sample mean in the substitution process. For example, if we know the ethnicity, diagnostic category, or some other information about the cases that is determined to be useful in facilitating prediction, we could calculate the mean of that subgroup and substitute that for the missing value for those individuals in that subgroup. For example, if we had reason to believe that sex was the most relevant variable with respect to variable *R*, then we would obtain separate means on *R* for women and men and substitute the former for any missing *R* values associated with women and the latter for any missing *R* values associated with men. This approach may be more attractive than sample-wise mean substitution because it narrows the configuration of cases on which the imputation is based but does require that the researchers articulate their reasoning for selecting the subgroup that they did.

This reasoning can be extended by considering not just one variable but two variables in narrowing the configuration. For example, if we had reason to believe that not only sex but age (or age category) were very relevant variables in determining the value of variable *R*, then we could use the mean of such a combination (e.g., the mean of women aged between 25 and 29) as the basis for the substitution. But as we narrow the configuration, we are using fewer cases to generate the mean that will be used as our substitute value. There are two increasingly serious drawbacks that we then face in this narrowing process: (a) The mean is based on fewer cases and thus becomes a less powerful measure of the population mean, and (b) the substituted mean will have a greater impact on statistics describing the distribution as there are fewer cases in the particular combination of categories.

3A.6.2 Single Imputation: Multiple Regression

Multiple regression will be discussed in Chapters 7A and 7B. With multiple regression, we use several independent variables to build a model (i.e., generate a regression equation) that allows us to predict a dependent variable value. When we wish to replace missing values on a particular variable, we use that variable as the dependent variable in a multiple regression procedure. A prediction equation is thus produced based on the cases with complete data. With this equation, we predict (i.e., impute, figure out the particular values to substitute for) the missing values on that variable.

This regression method is a better, more sophisticated approach than mean substitution. However, problems can arise when missing values occur on multiple independent variables or on the dependent variable (Allison, 2002). There is also a tendency to "overfit" the missing values because they are predicted from other independent variables (Tabachnick & Fidell, 2007). Such overfitting produces data that may not reflect or generalize to the population from which the original samples were drawn. This same theme is echoed by Allison (2002) who notes, "Analyzing imputed data as though it were complete data produces standard errors that are underestimated and test statistics that are overestimated" (p. 12). These concerns are also echoed by Enders (2010) who notes, "Regression imputation is superior to mean imputation, but it too has predictable biases . . . regression imputation overestimates correlations and R^2 statistics, even when the data are MCAR" (pp. 44–45).

3A.7 Modern Imputation Methods of Handling Missing Data

Most missing data authorities (e.g., Allison, 2002; Enders, 2010; Graham, 2009; Schafer & Graham, 2002) agree that modern missing data procedures provide the best options for data analysts. These procedures include (a) maximum likelihood procedures, which are typically embodied in expectation maximization (EM) algorithms, (b) full-information maximum likelihood (FIML) methods, and (c) multiple imputation (MI) analysis. IBM SPSS offers an optional module called **Missing Value Analysis**, which provides an EM algorithm and a separate MI procedure for diagnosing and imputing missing data. An additional FIML procedure is embedded in the IBM SPSS Amos software (Arbuckle, 2010). We will briefly examine each of these modern imputation approaches in turn.

3A.7.1 EM Imputation

The IBM SPSS **Missing Value Analysis** module uses a maximum likelihood method that is realized through a special EM algorithm (Enders, 2010; Graham, 2009; Little & Rubin, 2002). Maximum likelihood (see Chapter 16A) results can be similar to those obtained through least squares linear regression (Allison, 2002).

The EM algorithm is a two-step iterative process that generates maximum likelihood estimates. During the E step, regression analyses are used to estimate the missing values. Using maximum likelihood procedures, the M step makes estimates of parameters (e.g., means, variances, covariances) using the missing data replacements. The **Missing Value Analysis** EM module iterates through E and M steps until convergence or no change occurs between the steps (Allison, 2002; Graham, 2009).

When comparing EM with regression imputation procedures, Allison (2002) notes some important advantages:

The EM algorithm avoids one of the difficulties with conventional regression imputations—deciding which variables to use as predictors and coping with the fact that different missing data patterns have different sets of available predictors. Because EM always starts with the full covariance matrix, it is possible to get regression estimates for any set of predictors, no matter how few cases there may be in a particular missing data pattern. Hence, EM always uses all the available variables as predictors for imputing the missing data. (p. 20)

Although the EM algorithm, as it currently exists in the IBM SPSS software package (Version 19), is an important step forward over many of the traditional missing data methods, it does not automatically provide standard errors during this iterative process (Graham, 2009). Because of this and other limitations, some methodologists urge judicious use of the IBM SPSS EM algorithm:

> A word of caution is warranted concerning software programs that implement the EM algorithm. Some popular packages (e.g., LISREL and SPSS) offer the option of imputing the raw data after the final EM cycle. This is somewhat unfortunate because it gives the impression that a maximum likelihood approach has properly handled the missing values. In reality, this imputation scheme is nothing more than regression imputation. The only difference between EM imputation and regression imputation is that the EM approach uses a maximum likelihood estimate of the mean vector and the covariance matrix to generate the regression equations, whereas standard regression imputation schemes tend to use listwise deletion estimates of μ and Σ to build regressions ... doing so leads to ... biased parameter estimates and attenuated standard errors. (Enders, 2010, p. 113)

3A.7.2 FIML Imputation

State-of-the-art imputation procedures are reflected in FIML methodology. FIML procedures effectively handle missing data, and estimate parameters and standard errors all in one step (Graham, 2009). This efficiency comes at a price. Computer software programs must be modified to accommodate FIML-resource-intensive processes. Hence, most FIML missing data applications are currently found in SEM programs such as IBM SPSS Amos (Arbuckle, 1996, 2010). We discuss the Amos software in the context of confirmatory factor analysis and SEM in Chapters 15 through 20.

3A.7.3 MI Analysis

MI is an alternative to maximum likelihood procedures that is considered by methodologists to also be state of the art, and it is now part of the IBM SPSS **Missing Value Analysis** module (Enders, 2010). One important feature of MI analysis is that this method restores error variance typically lost in more traditional and certain EM approaches (Graham, 2009).

MI is realized in three phases as shown in Figure 3a.1: (1) imputation, (2) analysis, and (3) pooling (Enders, 2010). The imputation phase creates multiple copies (historically three to five) of the original data set, each with different estimated missing values, and this is what is shown

Figure 3a.1 Summary of Multiple Imputation Missing Values Analysis

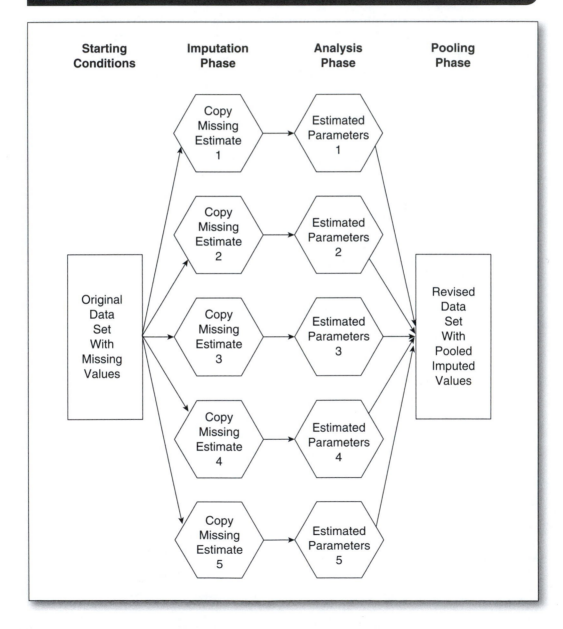

in Figure 3a.1. However, recent evidence (e.g., Enders, 2010; Graham, Olchowski, & Gilreath, 2007) indicates that creating as many as 20 separate imputed data sets may be needed to achieve sufficient statistical power for a valid statistical analysis. These missing values in each set drive the estimation of model parameters in the analysis phase. Finally, in the pooling phase the parameter estimates and standard errors are combined to produce a final set of imputed missing values (Enders, 2010).

3A.8 Recommendations for Handling Missing Data

We agree with both the sage and tongue-in-cheek advice of Allison (2002) that "the only really good solution to the missing data problem is not to have any" (p. 2). Because the likelihood of working with a data file void of missing values is low, especially in research conducted outside a controlled laboratory environment, we encourage exploration of the missing values situation. A first step could be comparing cases with and without missing values on variables of interest using independent samples *t* tests. For example, cases with missing gender data could be coded as 1 and cases with complete gender data could be coded as 0. Then a check could be made to see if any statistically significant differences emerge for this "dummy" coded independent variable on a dependent variable of choice such as a respondent's GAF score. Such an analysis may strengthen the confidence that the missing values are or are not related to a given variable under study.

When using some form of missing value imputation process, it is worthwhile to compare the statistical analysis with cases using only complete data (Tabachnick & Fidell, 2007). If no differences emerge between "complete" versus "imputed" data sets, then it becomes more likely that the missing value interventions reflect statistical reality. If they are different, then further exploration is in order.

We recommend the use of listwise case deletion with small numbers of missing values that are MCAR or MAR. Deleting variables that contain high proportions of missing data can also be an option if those variables are not crucial to a study. Mean substitution and regression imputation procedures can also be profitably employed when missing values are proportionately small (Tabachnick & Fidell, 2007), but we recommend careful pre– and post–data set appraisal as outlined above as well as consultation with a statistician as necessary. We strongly encourage the use of the new and improved IBM SPSS **Missing Value Analysis** module. As shown in Chapter 3B, this module allows users to conveniently describe or profile their missing data mechanism and impute missing data with a variety of methods.

3A.9 Outliers

Values that are extreme or unusual values on a single variable (univariate) or on a combination of variables (multivariate) are called outliers. Their presence can adversely affect the results of an analysis. This is true for a variety of reasons, but here are two. First, and most simply, the mean of a variable may no longer be a good value to capture the central tendency of the distribution of values. For example, the mean of 4, 5, 7, 8, and 86 is 22. Second, many procedures call for squaring the difference between two values, such as a least squares solution to determine the line of best fit in regression. Outliers will often yield differences that, when squared, will produce very large values that will unduly weight them in the computation.

Outliers can provide researchers with a mixed opportunity in that their existence may signal a serendipitous presence of new and exciting patterns within a data set, yet they often also signal anomalies within the data that may need to be addressed before proceeding with the statistical analyses. We should note, however, that extreme splits on dichotomous variables are more the norm than the exception in clinical and applied research. Accordingly, if the sample size is sufficiently large, these extreme differences should not pose a great problem.

3A.9.1 Causes of Outliers

Hair, Black, Babin, and Anderson (2010) identify four reasons for outliers being present in a data set.

- Outliers can be caused by data entry errors or improper attribute coding. These errors are normally caught in the data cleaning stage.
- Some outliers may be a function of extraordinary events or unusual circumstances. For example, in a human memory experiment, a participant may recall all 80 of the stimulus items correctly. As another example, some traumatic event may be experienced by a participant after completing a part of a clinical interview thereby changing the nature of participant's responses when he or she returns the following week to finish the interview. Most of the time, the safest course is to eliminate outliers produced by these circumstances—but not always. The fundamental question that should be asked is "Does this outlier represent my sample?" If "yes," then it should be included.
- There are some outliers for which we have no explanation. These unexplainable outliers are good candidates for deletion.
- There are multivariate outliers whose uniqueness occurs in their pattern of combination of values on several variables. For example, a particular combination of age, gender, and number of arrests may be quite different from other combinations (young males in certain populations will have proportionally more arrests than the other combinations of gender and age).

3A.9.2 Statistical Detection of Univariate Outliers: z Scores

Univariate outliers can be identified by an inspection of the frequency distribution or box plot for each variable. Dichotomous variables (e.g., "yes," "no") with extreme splits (e.g., 90–10%) between response options should be deleted (Tabachnick & Fidell, 2007).

For continuous variables, several options exist for determining a threshold for outlier designation. Hair et al. (2010) recommend converting the values of each variable to standard (i.e., z) scores with a mean of 0 and a standard deviation of 1. This can be accomplished easily with the **Descriptives** procedure of IBM SPSS, where z scores can be computed and saved in the data file for later profiling. As a general heuristic, Hair et al. (2010) recommend considering cases with z scores exceeding ±2.5 to be outliers. These should be carefully considered for possible deletion. Conversely, Cohen, Cohen, West, and Aiken (2003) provide this tip on outliers, stating that "if outliers are few (less than 1% or 2% of n) and not very extreme, they are probably best left alone" (p. 128).

An alternative approach to univariate detection of outliers involves inspecting histograms, box plots, and normal probability plots (Tabachnick & Fidell, 2007). Univariate outliers reveal themselves through their visible separation from the bulk of the cases on a particular variable when profiled with these graphical techniques.

3A.9.3 Graphical Detection of Univariate Outliers: Box Plots

Box plots, often called box and whiskers plots, were introduced by the statistician John Tukey (1977) in *Exploratory Data Analysis* to help researchers identify outliers. Box plots convey a considerable amount of information about the distribution in one fairly condensed display, and it is well worth mastering the terminology associated with box plots so that they become a part of your data screening arsenal. An excellent description of this topic is provided by Cohen (1996), and what we present here is heavily drawn from his treatment.

3A.9.3.1 The General Form of the Box Plot

The general form of a box and whiskers plot is shown in Figure 3a.2. According to Cohen (1996), the box plot is based on the median rather than the mean because this former measure is unaffected by extreme scores in the distribution. The "box" part of the box and whiskers plot is drawn in the middle of Figure 3a.2. The median (which is the 50th percentile or second quartile) is shown by the heavy dark line inside the box. In our drawing, the median is not at the center of the box but a bit toward its lower portion. This indicates that the distribution is somewhat positively skewed (more scores are toward the low end of the scoring continuum).

The borders of the box are set at the 25th percentile (first quartile) and the 75th percentile (third quartile) for the upper and lower border, respectively, because in our box plot, lower scores are toward the top and higher scores are toward the bottom. These quartiles are a little less than ±1 standard deviation unit but nonetheless capture the majority of the cases. As shown in Figure 3a.2, these borders are called Tukey's hinges, and the span of scores

Figure 3a.2 The General Form of a Box and Whiskers Plot Based on Cohen's (1996) Description

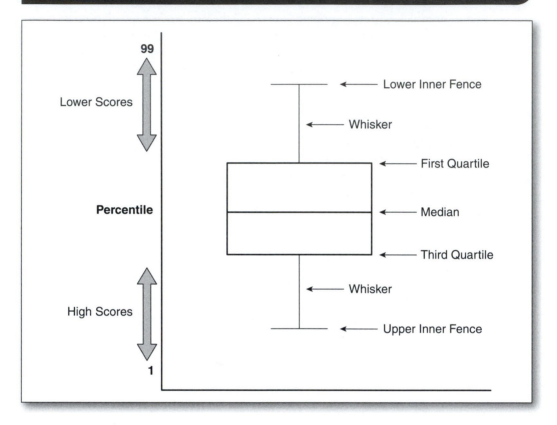

between the hinges (the distance between the first and third quartiles) is the interquartile range (IQR).

The two boundary lines appearing above and below it in Figure 3a.2 are called *inner fences*. The one toward the top is the lower inner fence and the one toward the bottom is the upper inner fence. These fences are drawn at the positions corresponding to ±1.5 IQR. That is, once we know the value for the IQR, we just multiply it by 1.5. Scores inside these fences are considered to be within the bounds of the distribution and are therefore not considered extreme.

The "whiskers" portion of the box and whiskers plot are the vertical lines perpendicular to the orientation of the box. The one at the top of the box is the lower whisker, and the one at the bottom of the box is the upper whisker. These whiskers extend only as far as the smallest and largest values that fall within the lower and upper inner fences. The upper whisker ends at the upper adjacent value and the lower whisker ends at the lower adjacent value. Because the whiskers can end before they reach the inner fences, we can tell the "compactness" of the distribution.

The regions beyond the inner fences are considered to be extreme scores by this plotting method. IBM SPSS divides this area into two regions. A data point that is farther than ±1.5 IQR but less than ±3.0 IQR is labeled by IBM SPSS as an outlier and is shown in its output as "O." A data point that exceeds this ±3.0 IQR distance is considered to be an extreme score and is given the symbol "E" in its output.

3A.9.3.2 An Example of a Box Plot

Figure 3a.3 provides an IBM SPSS box and whiskers plot of hypothetical GAF score data. As was true in our above example of the general plot, the median seems to be a little off center and toward the lower end of the box. This suggests a somewhat negative skew to the distribution. In our example, the whiskers here extend all the way to the inner fences. No scores were found in the extreme range (beyond ±3.0 IQR), but some scores in the lower portion of the distribution occupied the region between −1.5 IQR and −3.0 IQR and were marked as "O" in Figure 3a.3.

Figure 3a.3 Box Plot of Hypothetical Global Assessment of Functioning (GAF) Scores at Intake

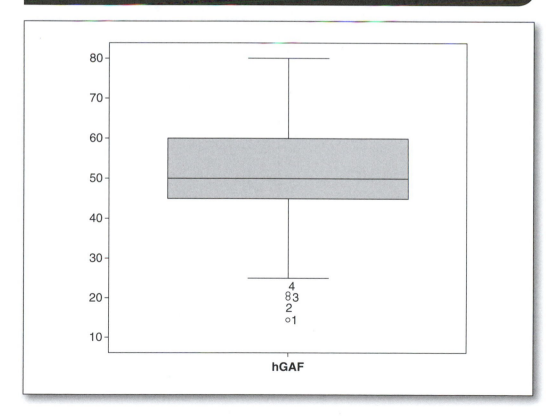

3A.9.4 Detection of Multivariate Outliers

3A.9.4.1 Detection of Multivariate Outliers: Scatterplot Matrices

After inspecting the data set for univariate outliers, an assessment for multivariate outliers is in order. As a first step in looking for outliers on a combination of variables, we recommend running bivariate (i.e., two-variable) scatterplots for combinations of key variables. In these plots, each case is represented as a point on the X and Y axes. Most cases fall within the elliptical (oval-shaped) swarm or pattern mass. Outliers are those cases that tend to lie outside the oval.

We show an example of a scatterplot matrix in Figure 3a.4. In this case, we used four variables and obtained scatterplots for each combination. For ease of viewing, we present only the upper half of the matrix. Each entry represents the scatterplot of two variables. For example, the left-most plot on the first row shows the relationship of variables A and B. It would appear, from the plot, that they might be related in a curvilinear rather than a linear

Figure 3a.4　Scatterplot Matrix of Four Quantitative Variables

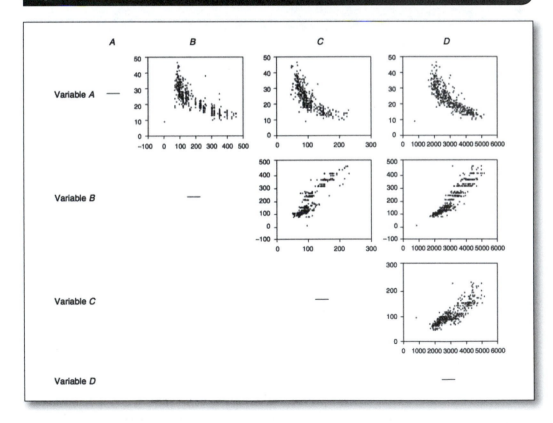

manner. On the other hand, B and C seem to be related linearly. As we will see later in this chapter, these plots are often used to look for multivariate assumption violations of normality and linearity. An alternative approach to addressing linearity with IBM SPSS, which we will not cover here, is to use the regression curve estimation procedure.

3A.9.4.2 Detection of Multivariate Outliers: Mahalanobis Distance

A more objective way of assessing for the presence of multivariate outliers is to compute the Mahalanobis distance of each case. The Mahalanobis distance statistic D^2 measures the multivariate "distance" between each case and the group multivariate mean (known as a centroid). Each case is evaluated using the chi-square distribution with a stringent alpha level of .001. Cases that reach this significance threshold can be considered multivariate outliers and possible candidates for elimination.

3A.10 Using Descriptive Statistics in Data Screening

Descriptive statistics are relatively simple but very convenient summaries of distributions of values. One descriptive statistic conveys a representation of one feature of the distribution. Most readers are quite familiar with the common measures of central tendency and variability. By examining the mean and standard deviation, for example, researchers can have a summary of the average value and the spread of scores around it. An unusual mean value (e.g., a very low score when a moderate score is expected), or exceptionally low or exceptionally high variability, would suggest careful examination of the data set.

Two descriptive statistics of great value to the process of data screening are skewness and kurtosis.

- Skewness describes the symmetry of the distribution. A symmetric distribution has a skewness value of 0. Positive values of skewness indicate that the bulk of scores are at the lower end of the continuum (the "tail" of the distribution "points" toward the positive or right side). Negative values of skewness indicate that the bulk of scores are at the higher end of continuum (the "tail" of the distribution "points" toward the negative or left side).

- Kurtosis describes the clustering of scores toward the center of the distribution. A normal distribution has a kurtosis value of 0 (mesokurtic). Positive values of kurtosis (leptokurtic) indicate that the bulk of scores are drawn in toward the middle. Negative values of kurtosis (platykurtic) indicate that the scores are more equally distributed across the entire continuum (a more rectangular distribution).

A variety of opinions can be found concerning what is an unacceptable level of skewness and kurtosis for a particular variable—that is, how far from zero the value needs to be before it is considered a substantial enough departure from normality to be mentioned. Some statisticians are more comfortable with a conservative threshold of ±0.5 as indicative of departures from normality (e.g., Hair et al., 2010; Runyon et al., 2000), whereas others prefer a more liberal interpretation of ±1.00 for skewness, kurtosis, or both (e.g., George & Mallery, 2003; Morgan, Griego, & Gloeckner, 2001). Tabachnick and Fidell (2007) suggest a more definitive assessment strategy for detecting normality violations by dividing a skewness or kurtosis value by its respective standard error and evaluating this coefficient with a standard normal table of values (z scores). But such an approach has its own pitfalls, as Tabachnick and Fidell (2007) note:

> If the sample is large, it is better to inspect the shape of the distribution instead of using formal inference because the equations for standard error of both skewness and kurtosis contain N, and normality is likely to be rejected with large samples even when the deviation is slight. (p. 44)

Another helpful heuristic, at least regarding skewness, comes from the IBM SPSS help menu, which suggests that any skewness value more than twice its standard error is taken to indicate a departure from symmetry. Unfortunately, no such heuristics are provided for determining normality violations due to extreme kurtosis. The shape of the distribution becomes of interest when researchers are evaluating their data against the assumptions of the statistical procedures they are considering using, a topic we will discuss in Section 10A.12.

3A.11 Using Pictorial Representations in Data Screening

With small data sets containing a few cases, data cleaning can be accomplished by a simple visual inspection process. However, with the typically large data sets required for most multivariate analyses, it is necessary to use computerized computational software packages such as IBM SPSS, which provides a more efficient means for screening data. We will discuss four types of output commonly used to create pictorial representations of distribution information: (1) histograms and bar graphs, (2) stem-and-leaf displays, (3) box plots, and (4) scatterplot matrices.

3A.11.1 Histograms and Bar Graphs

Some variables have a large number of possible values (e.g., GAF scores, monthly income in dollars and cents, etc.). Typically, these are variables that are measured on one of the quantitative scales of measurement. Such variables can be screened by using histograms. A histogram visually represents a frequency distribution. Values of the variable, sometimes grouped for convenience, occupy the X axis; frequency of occurrence occupies the Y axis. Commonly, bars associated with the values rise to heights dictated by how often the value occurs in the distribution of sample scores.

We discussed frequency tables in Section 3A.2.3 in the context of data cleaning. Such tables are the basis for generating histograms. When the distribution is based on a frequency count of a categorical variable, we should request a bar graph because there are typically a very small number of values or codes and because these codes just distinguish among the categories. The key factor here is that the order of the codes (numerical values) is arbitrary, and thus the "shape" of the configuration of bars carries no inherent meaning.

When the distribution is based on a frequency count of a continuous variable, we should request a histogram because there are typically a relatively large number of values and because higher values indicate more of the property (e.g., higher GAF scores indicate better functioning). The key factor here is that the order of the codes (numerical values) is meaningful, and thus the "shape" of the configuration of histogram carries inherent meaning.

An example of a histogram is shown in Figure 3a.5. These data were drawn from a portion of an Asian American community mental health consumers' sample. We can see that the distribution, although not perfect, is certainly "normal-like." Also, the first

Figure 3a.5 Histogram Showing a Frequency Count of Global Assessment of Functioning (GAF) Scores With a Normal Curve Superimposed

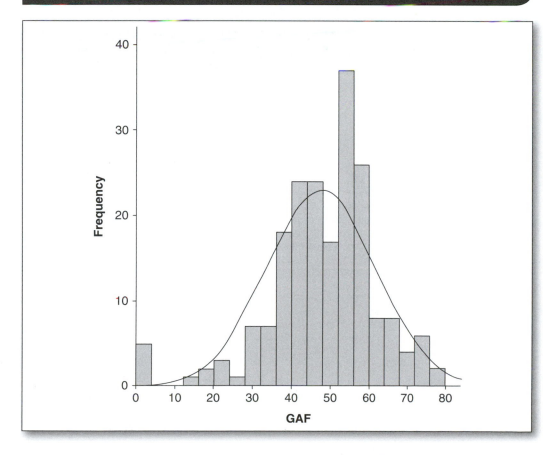

histogram bar at the far left of the figure in the range of zero on the GAF scale suggests that we might want to verify those very low values. Note also that descriptive statistics that can be generated by IBM SPSS, such as skewness and kurtosis, would provide a more precise description of the distribution's shape; normality can be directly assessed in ways that are described in Section 3A.12.1.

3A.11.2 Stem-and-Leaf Plots

Figure 3a.6 provides the "next of kin" to a histogram display called a stem-and-leaf plot. This display, also introduced by the statistician John Tukey (1977), represents hypothetical GAF scores that might have been found for a sample of individuals arriving for their first session for mental health counseling. Stem-and-leaf plots provide information about the frequency of a quantitative variable's values by incorporating the actual values of the distribution. These plots are composed of three main components.

On the far left side of Figure 3a.6 is the frequency with which a particular value (the one shown for that row) occurred. In the center of the figure is the "stem" and the far right

Figure 3a.6 Hypothetical Stem-and-Leaf Plot of Global Assessment of Functioning Scores at Intake

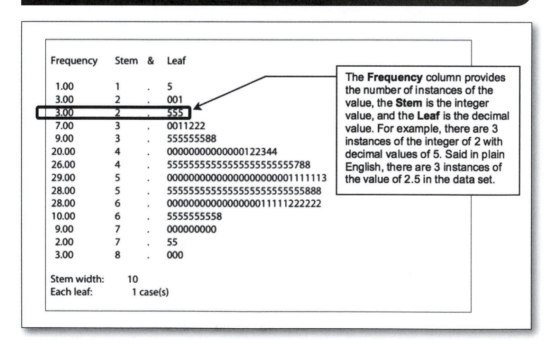

Frequency	Stem &	Leaf
1.00	1 .	5
3.00	2 .	001
3.00	2 .	555
7.00	3 .	0011222
9.00	3 .	555555588
20.00	4 .	00000000000000122344
26.00	4 .	55555555555555555555555788
29.00	5 .	00000000000000000000001111113
28.00	5 .	5555555555555555555555555888
28.00	6 .	0000000000000000011111222222
10.00	6 .	5555555558
9.00	7 .	000000000
2.00	7 .	55
3.00	8 .	000

Stem width: 10
Each leaf: 1 case(s)

The **Frequency** column provides the number of instances of the value, the **Stem** is the integer value, and the **Leaf** is the decimal value. For example, there are 3 instances of the integer of 2 with decimal values of 5. Said in plain English, there are 3 instances of the value of 2.5 in the data set.

portion is the "leaf." The stem is the base value that we combine with the leaf portion to derive the full value. For example, for the first row of Figure 3a.6, we note that the lowest GAF score value has a frequency of 1.00. With a stem of 1 and a leaf of 5, we recognize a GAF score value of 15. The next row represents scores in the low 20s. The three scores depicted here are 20, 20, and 21.

Stem-and-leaf plots ordinarily combine a range of individual values under a single stem. In Figure 3a.6, intervals of 5 values are tied to a single stem. Depending on how tightly the scores are grouped, one can have either a finer or more global picture of the distribution.

By observing the distribution of "leaves," researchers can quickly assess the general shape of the distribution; that is, they can form an impression as to whether it is normal, positively skewed (scores are more concentrated toward the low end of the distribution), or negatively skewed (scores are more concentrated toward the high end of the distribution). It is also possible to see, at least very generally without the aid of the statistical computation, whether its kurtosis is more positive (a peaked distribution among the middle values) or more negative (a relatively flat distribution) than a normal curve.

3A.12 Multivariate Statistical Assumptions Underlying the General Linear Model

Most of the statistical procedures covered in this book fall within the domain of the *general linear model* (see Sections 4A.9 and 7A.5.1). These procedures include ANOVA/ MANOVA and their covariance counterparts, ordinary least squares linear regression, discriminant function analysis, canonical correlation analysis, principal components and exploratory factor analysis, and confirmatory factor analysis and path analysis either in isolation or when combined together within the context of SEM. Underlying the proper interpretation of the results obtained through these procedures is a set of statistical assumptions, particularly those addressing normality, linearity, homoscedasticity, and independence of errors (e.g., Keppel, 1991). To the extent that one or more of these assumptions are violated, the statistical results may become biased or distorted (Gamst, Meyers, & Guarino, 2008; Hair et al., 2010; Tabachnick & Fidell, 2007) and any conclusions drawn from the results may become increasingly tenuous. We describe these assumptions here on a one-time basis rather than repeating this discussion in each of the chapters devoted to one of the general linear model procedures.

3A.12.1 Normality

The shape of a distribution of quantitative variables in a multivariate analysis should correspond to a (univariate) normal distribution. That is, the variable's frequency distribution of values should roughly approximate a bell-shaped curve. Both Stevens (2009) and Tabachnick and Fidell (2007) indicate that univariate normality violations can be assessed with statistical or graphical approaches.

3A.12.1.1 Statistical Approaches to Assessing Normality

Statistical approaches that assess univariate normality often begin with measures of skewness and kurtosis. A normally distributed variable (one exhibiting mesokurtosis) will generate skewness and kurtosis values that hover around zero. These values can be obtained with IBM SPSS through its **Frequencies, Descriptives**, and **Explore** procedures; the latter two procedures also produce significance tests, which are typically evaluated at a stringent alpha level of .01 or .001 (Tabachnick & Fidell, 2007).

Additional statistical tests include the Kolmogorov–Smirnov test and the Shapiro–Wilk test. Although both tests can be effectively employed, Stevens (2009) notes an early Monte Carlo study by Shapiro, Wilk, and Chen (1968) "that the combination of skewness and kurtosis coefficients and the Shapiro–Wilk test were the most powerful in detecting departures from normality" (p. 223). Both tests can be obtained through the IBM SPSS **Explore** procedure. Statistical significance with these measures, ideally with a stringent alpha level ($p < .001$), indicates a possible univariate normality violation.

3A.12.1.2 Graphical Approaches to Assessing Normality

Graphical approaches that assess univariate normality typically begin with an inspection of histograms or stem-and-leaf plots for each variable. However, such cursory depictions do not provide a definitive indication of a normality violation. A more precise graphical method is to use a normal probability plot, where the values of a variable are rank ordered and plotted against expected normal distribution values (Stevens, 2009). In these plots, a normal distribution produces a straight diagonal line, and the plotted data values are compared with this diagonal. Normality is assumed if the data values follow the diagonal line.

3A.12.1.3 Multivariate Approaches to Assessing Normality

The assumption of multivariate normality, although somewhat more complicated, is intimately related to its univariate counterpart. Stevens (2009) cautions researchers that just because one has demonstrated univariate normality on each variable in a data set, the issue of multivariate normality—the observations among all combinations of variables are normally distributed—may not always be satisfied. As Stevens (2009) notes, "Although it is difficult to completely characterize multivariate normality, *normality on each of the variables separately is a necessary, but not sufficient, condition for multivariate normality to hold*" (p. 222). Thus, although univariate normality is an essential ingredient to achieve multivariate normality, Stevens argues that two other conditions must also be met: (a) that linear combinations of the variables (e.g., variates) should be normally distributed and (b) that all pairwise combinations of variables should also be normally distributed (i.e., the pairwise scatterplots will be essentially elliptical).

As we noted previously, IBM SPSS offers a procedure to easily examine whether or not univariate normality is present among the variables with various statistical tests and graphical options. But it does not offer a statistical test for multivariate normality. We therefore recommend a thorough univariate normality examination coupled with a bivariate scatterplot examination of key pairs of variables. If the normality assumption appears to be violated, it may be possible to "repair" this problem through a data transformation process.

3A.12.2 Linearity

Many of the multivariate techniques we cover in this text (e.g., multiple regression, MANOVA, factor analysis) assume that the variables in the analysis are related to each other in a linear manner; that is, they assume that the best fitting function representing the scatterplot is a straight line. Based on this assumption, these procedures often compute the Pearson correlation coefficient (or a variant of it) as part of the calculations needed for the multivariate statistical analysis. As we will discuss in Chapter 6A the Pearson *r* assesses the degree of linear relationship observed between two variables. Nonlinear relationships between two variables cannot be assessed by the Pearson correlation coefficient. To the extent that such nonlinearity is present, the observed Pearson *r* would be a less representative index of the strength of the association between the two variables—it would identify less relationship strength than existed because it could capture only the linear component of the relationship.

The use of bivariate scatterplots is the most typical way of assessing linearity between two variables. Variables that are both normally distributed and linearly related to each other will produce scatterplots that are oval shaped or elliptical. If one of the variables is not normally distributed, linearity will not be achieved. We can recognize this situation because the resulting scatterplot will not take on an elliptical shape (Tabachnick & Fidell, 2007). However, there is a downside to running large numbers of bivariate scatterplots, as Tabachnick and Fidell (2007) aptly note: "Assessing linearity through bivariate scatterplots is reminiscent of reading tea leaves, especially with small samples. And there are many cups of tea if there are several variables and all possible pairs are examined" (p. 84).

Another approach (often used in the context of multiple regression) is to run a regression analysis and examine the residuals plot. Residuals depict the portion (or "left over") of the dependent variable's variance that was not explained by the regression analysis (i.e., the error component). The "cure" for nonlinearity lies in data transformation.

3A.12.3 Homoscedasticity

The assumption of homoscedasticity means that quantitative dependent variables have equal levels of variability across a range of (either continuous or categorical) independent variables (Hair et al., 2010). Violation of this assumption results in heteroscedasticity. Heteroscedasticity typically occurs when a variable is not distributed in a normal manner or when a data transformation procedure has produced an unanticipated distribution for a variable (Tabachnick & Fidell, 2007).

In the univariate ANOVA context (with one quantitative dependent variable and one or more categorical independent variables), this homoscedasticity assumption is referred to as *homogeneity of variance*, in which it is assumed that equal variances of the dependent measure are observed across the levels of the independent variables (Gamst et al., 2008).

Several statistical tests can be used to detect homogeneity of variance violations, including F max and Levene's test. The F max test is computed by working with the variance of each group and dividing the largest variance by the smallest variance. Keppel, Saufley, and Tokunaga (1992) note that any F-max value of 3.0 or greater is indicative of an assumption violation, and they recommend the use of the more stringent alpha level of $p < .025$ when evaluating an F ratio. Alternatively, Levene's test assesses the statistical hypothesis of equal variances across the levels of the independent variable. Rejection of the null hypothesis (at $p < .05$) indicates an assumption violation or unequal variability. Stevens (2009) cautions about the use of the F max test and other homogeneity variance tests because of their extreme sensitivity to violations of normality.

When more than one quantitative dependent variable is being assessed (as in the case of MANOVA), then Box's M test for equality of variance–covariance matrices is used to test for homoscedasticity. Akin to its univariate counterpart, Levene's test, Box's M tests the statistical hypothesis that the variance–covariance matrices are equal. A statistically significant ($p < .05$) Box's M test indicates a homoscedasticity assumption violation, but it too is very sensitive to any departures of normality among the variables under scrutiny (Stevens, 2009).

Typically, problems related to homoscedasticity violations can be attributed to issues of normality violations for one or more of the variables under scrutiny. Hence, it is probably best to first assess and possibly remediate normality violations before addressing the issue of equal variances or variance–covariance matrices (Hair et al., 2010; Tabachnick & Fidell, 2007). If heteroscedasticity is present, this too can be remedied by means of data transformations. However, most of the univariate and multivariate techniques that we cover in this text are fairly "robust" with respect to distributions deviating markedly from normality. In practice, this means that nominal alpha levels are minimal distorted even when normality is breached; this is particularly true when sample sizes are large.

3A.12.4 Independence of Errors

The statistical assumption of independence or independence of errors implies that the residual or error component of the dependent variable scores (i.e., the score minus the group mean) is random and independent across individual cases (Gamst et al., 2008). In practice, this means that each case is independent of other cases in the sample.

Dependence of errors, a systematic violation of the independence assumption, occurs when one dependent variable score contains information about another score. There are several ways that this can happen:

- Dependence or correlated observations may occur when intact groups of participants enter a treatment condition with previous affiliations that influence their performance on the dependent measure. This dependency (or "grouping" effect) can produce differential error components among the scores on the dependent measure.
- Dependence can also be a function of "contamination" if participants in different treatment conditions are allowed to communicate about experimental task demands.
- Dependency may also occur if the error component for each case falls into a cyclical pattern, for example, confounding the time of data collection with the ordinal position of a case within a data file. Such *autocorrelation* may produce residual error components that are not independent.
- Dependence occurs in a repeated measures design—a design in which cases are measured several times on the same dependent measure. Because the scores for any single case are more strongly related to each other than are the scores between different cases in the research, residual errors will not be independent.

Determining if the data violate the assumption of independence of error requires fairly complex statistical diagnostics. Cohen et al. (2003), in the context of multiple regression analysis, recommend plotting residuals against an ordered numeric variable (such as a case or participant number) and also computing the *Durbin–Watson* statistic (Durbin & Watson, 1971). Other independence assessment violation approaches include the computing of the *intraclass correlation coefficient* (ICC) through the IBM SPSS **Mixed Models** procedure (see Sections 9A.5 and 9B.2). Hox (2000, 2010) described the ICC as the amount of variance shared between two randomly selected individuals from the same level. Kreft and deLeeuw (2007) recommend that if the ICC accounts for 5% or less of the variance, then multilevel modeling is not required.

We agree with Stevens's (2009, p. 218) conclusion that violations of the independence of errors assumption is "*very* serious." The consequence of violating the independence assumption is the potential inflation of the specified alpha level. To avoid this unfortunate consequence, investigators are encouraged to use scrupulous research methods that include randomly sampling cases from a population, randomly assigning cases to different treatments, and ensuring that each treatment condition is independent of each other (Gamst et al., 2008).

3A.13 Data Transformations

Data transformations are mathematical procedures that can be used to modify variables that violate the statistical assumptions of normality, linearity, and homoscedasticity, or that have unusual outlier patterns (Hair et al., 2010; Tabachnick & Fidell, 2007). First, we determine the extent to which one or more of these assumptions are violated. Then, we decide whether or not the situation calls for a data transformation to correct this matter. If so, then we actually instruct IBM SPSS to change every value of the variable or variables needed to be transformed. Once the numbers have been changed in this manner, we would then perform the statistical analysis on these changed or transformed data values.

Much of our current understanding of data transformations has been informed by the earlier seminal work of Box and Cox (1964) and Mosteller and Tukey (1977). These data transformations can be easily achieved with IBM SPSS through its **Compute** procedure.

A note of caution should be expressed here. Data transformations are somewhat of a "double-edged sword." On the one hand, their use can significantly improve the precision of a multivariate analysis. At the same time, using a transformation can pose a formidable data interpretation problem. For example, a logarithmic transformation of a mental health consumer's GAF score or number of mental health service sessions will produce numbers quite different from the ordinary raw values we are used to seeing and may therefore pose quite a challenge to the average journal reader to properly interpret (Tabachnick & Fidell, 2007). Because of this apparent conflict, we recommend judicious use of data transformations.

A variety of data transformations are available. In many fields of study, certain data transformations (e.g., log transformations) are well accepted because of the distribution of the dependent variables (e.g., reaction time studies in psychology or personal income studies in economics). Using variable X as an example, some of the more popular transformations, generally, are the square root of X, (base 10 or natural) logarithm of X, inverse (1 divided by X), square of X, reflect (multiply X by -1) and square root, reflect and logarithm, and reflect and inverse. These transformations are discussed by Meyers, Gamst, and Guarino (2009).

Table 3a.4 provides some illustrations of these various transformations for some hypothetical data. The main purpose of Table 3a.4 is to remind the reader that although all these transformations were based on the same original set of five scores, the resulting data values can appear quite strange at first glance. For example, a score of 50 has a square root of 7.07, a log of 3.91, an inverse root of .02, and so on. Journal readers familiar with the original measure may be quite uncertain about the meaning of group or variable means reported in terms of these transformations.

Table 3a.4 Comparison of Common Data Transformations With Hypothetical Scores

Case	Original Value	Square Root	Log	Inverse	Square	Reflect & Square Root	Reflect & Log	Reflect & Inverse
1	1.00	1.00	0.00	1.00	1.00	10.00	2.00	0.01
2	5.00	2.24	1.61	0.20	25.00	9.80	1.98	0.01
3	25.00	5.00	3.22	0.04	625.00	8.72	1.88	0.01
4	50.00	7.07	3.91	0.02	2500.00	7.14	1.71	0.02
5	100.00	10.00	4.61	0.01	10000.00	1.00	0.00	1.00

Table 3a.4 underscores concretely the potential interpretation difficulties with which researchers are faced when they attempt to discuss even simple descriptive statistics (e.g., means and standard deviations) that are based on transformed data. One way to avoid the possibility of making confusing or misleading statements pertaining to transformed data is to provide the reader with the original variable's statistical context (e.g., minimum and maximum values or means and standard deviations reported in raw score values). Methodologists appear to be divided on their recommendations as to which transformation to use for a particular circumstance (e.g., compare Hair et al., 2010, with Tabachnick & Fidell, 2007). Nevertheless, a basic strategy in using transformations can be outlined in which a progression (escalation) of transformation strategies is employed depending on the perceived severity of the statistical assumption violation (Meyers et al., 2009). For example, Tabachnick and Fidell (2007) lobby for a data transformation progression from square root (to correct a moderate violation), to logarithm (for a more substantial violation), and then to inverse square root (to handle a severe violation). In addition, arc sine transformations can be profitably employed with proportional data, and squaring one variable in a nonlinear bivariate relationship can effectively alleviate a nonlinearity problem (Hair et al., 2010).

3A.14 Recommended Readings

Allison, P. D. (2002). *Missing data.* Thousand Oaks, CA: Sage.

Barnett, V., & Lewis, T. (1978). *Outliers in statistical data.* New York, NY: Wiley.

Berry, W. D. (1993). *Understanding regression assumptions.* Newbury Park, CA: Sage.

Box, G. E. P., & Cox, D. R. (1964). An analysis of transformations. *Journal of the Royal Statistical Society, Series B, 26,* 211–243.

Enders, C. K. (2001). A primer on maximum likelihood algorithms available for use with missing data. *Structural Equation Modeling, 8,* 128–141.

Enders, C. K. (2010). *Applied missing data analysis.* New York, NY: Guilford Press.

Enders, C. K., & Gottschall, A. C. (2011). The impact of missing data on the ethical quality of a research study. In A. T. Panter & S. K. Sterba (Eds.), *Handbook of ethics in quantitative methodology* (pp. 357–381). New York, NY: Routledge, Taylor & Francis

Fox, J. (1991). *Regression diagnostics.* Newbury Park, CA: Sage.

Gold, M. S., & Bentler, P. M. (2000). Treatments of missing data: A Monte Carlo comparison of RBHDI, iterative stochastic regression imputation, and expectation-maximization. *Structural Equation Modeling, 7,* 319–355.

Graham, J. W. (2009). Missing data analysis: Making it work in the real world. *Annual Review of Psychology, 60,* 549-576.

Molenberghs, G., & Kenward, M. G. (2007). *Missing data in clinical studies.* Chichester, England: Wiley.

Roth, P. L. (1994). Missing data: A conceptual review from applied psychologists. *Personnel Psychology, 47,* 537–560.

Rousseeuw, P. J., & van Zomeren, B. C. (1990). Unmasking multivariate outliers and leverage points. *Journal of the American Statistical Association, 85,* 633–639.

Rubin, D. (1996). Multiple imputation after 18 years. *Journal of the American Statistical Association, 91,* 473–489.

Schafer, J. L., & Graham, J. W. (2002). Missing data: Our view of the state of the art. *Psychological Methods, 7,* 147–177.

Stevens, J. P. (1984). Outliers and influential data points in regression analysis. *Psychological Bulletin, 95,* 334–344.

Tukey, J. W. (1977). *Exploratory data analysis.* Reading, MA: Addison-Wesley.

Data Screening Using IBM SPSS

I n this chapter, we cover IBM SPSS applications pertaining to data cleaning, handling of missing values and outliers, and statistical assumption violations of normality, linearity, and homoscedasticity for categorical and quantitative variables. The techniques covered here are meant to be illustrative and not necessarily exhaustive of all possible data screening techniques available.

3B.1 The Look of IBM SPSS

In this and the other "B" chapters of this book, we show in our figures both dialog windows and output tables and figures displayed on the screen by IBM SPSS. Several points about these figures should be noted. First, although we have used Version 19 for our analyses, those readers with different versions should be able to generalize what we say to other versions. Second, even with a single version of the software, different operating systems (e.g., Windows 2000, Windows XP, OS X for Mac) will generate different "looks" for the dialog screens.

As a numerical example, consider the following variables taken from a study by Keyser (2010). This study examined the relationship of cultural factors (e.g., perceived racism, individualistic vs. collectivistic orientation, ethnic identity, acculturation) on the four subscales of the California Brief Multicultural Competence Scale (CBMCS; Gamst et al., 2004), with a sample of child mental health practitioners. The data set, named **Victoria Data Screening**, is based on a subsample of five modified variables from the original data file and one additional variable. The variables are as follows:

- The gender of each mental health provider was recorded and based on self-report. This variable is labeled and named **gender**.

- Provider cultural values were examined by means of the Individualism/Collectivism Scale (INDCOL; Triandis & Gelfand, 1998). Two eight-item composite subscales were created and given the variable names **INDCOLI** and **INDCOLC** for Individualism and Collectivism, respectively. All 16 items were scored on a 9-point summative response scale (1 = *strongly disagree* to 9 = *strongly agree*).
- Provider ethnic identity was assessed with the six-item Multigroup Ethnic Identity Measure–Revised (MEIM-R; Phinney & Ong, 2007). Two three-item composite subscales were created and given the variable names **MEIMEIC** and **MIEMEIE** for ethnic identity commitment and ethnic identity exploration, respectively. All six items were scored on a 5-point summative response scale (1 = *strongly disagree* to 5 = *strongly agree*).
- At a later point in this chapter, we work with the fictitious quantitative variable labeled **depression**. Respondents endorsed a variety of symptoms representing the construct, and scores could range from 0 to 45 with higher scores indicating more depression.

3B.2 Data Cleaning: All Variables

From the main menu select **Analyze ➔ Descriptive Statistics ➔ Frequencies**, which produces the dialog window shown in Figure 3b.1. Click over the quantitative variables **INDCOLI, INDCOLC, MEIMEIC,** and **MEIMEIE**. The **Display frequency tables** checkbox

Figure 3b.1 Frequencies Main Dialogue Screen

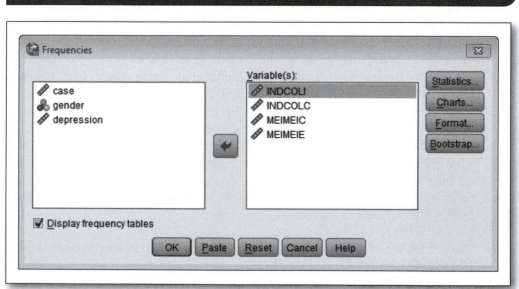

that produces frequency tables is already checked as the default, and we will retain that as part of our diagnostics. We can also use the Frequencies procedure for the categorical variable **gender** to determine if there were any more than the two codes we used for female and male (there were no problems found here); however, we will limit our present analysis to the quantitative variables for illustrative purposes.

By selecting the **Statistics** pushbutton, the dialog screen shown in Figure 3b.2 is produced. It is composed of four sections: **Percentile Values, Dispersion, Central Tendency**, and **Distribution**. In the present example, we ask for the **Mean**, **Median, Mode, Std. deviation** (standard deviation), **Minimum, Maximum, Skewness**, and **Kurtosis** values for each variable. Some of this information will be used in diagnostic decisions beyond data cleaning. Click on the **Continue** pushbutton to return to the main **Frequencies** screen.

Selecting the **Charts** pushbutton produces the screen shown in Figure 3b.3. Here, we request a **Histogram** for each variable. Checking the box for **Show normal curve on histogram** will superimpose the

Figure 3b.2 Statistics Screen

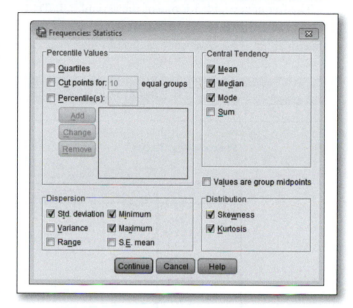

Figure 3b.3 Charts Screen

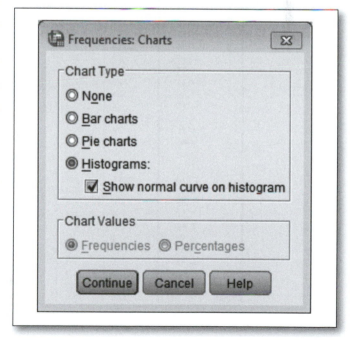

normal curve on the histogram. Click **Continue** to return to the main dialog screen and click on **OK** to obtain the output file with the results.

The frequency table for one of the variables, **INDCOLI**, is shown in Figure 3b.4. We are looking for unusual values. If this variable was in "raw" score form, perhaps responses to items on an inventory, we would expect to see values corresponding to the scale points (e.g.,

Figure 3b.4   The Frequency Table for **INDCOLI**

Frequency Table

INDCOLI Individualism

		Frequency	Percent	Valid Percent	Cumulative Percent
Valid	2.13	1	.3	.3	.3
	2.25	1	.3	.3	.6
	2.33	1	.3	.3	.8
	2.50	2	.5	.6	1.4
	2.88	4	1.1	1.1	2.5
	3.00	4	1.1	1.1	3.6
	3.13	9	2.4	2.5	6.1
	3.25	10	2.7	2.8	8.9
	3.38	8	2.2	2.2	11.1
	3.50	19	5.1	5.3	16.4
	3.57	2	.5	.6	17.0
	3.63	15	4.0	4.2	21.2
	3.71	1	.3	.3	21.4
	3.75	15	4.0	4.2	25.6
	3.86	1	.3	.3	25.9
	3.88	15	4.0	4.2	30.1
	4.00	13	3.5	3.6	33.7
	4.13	22	5.9	6.1	39.8
	4.25	24	6.5	6.7	46.5
	4.38	29	7.8	8.1	54.6
	4.50	12	3.2	3.3	57.9
	4.57	1	.3	.3	58.2
	4.63	24	6.5	6.7	64.9
	4.75	20	5.4	5.6	70.5
	4.86	2	.5	.6	71.0
	4.88	24	6.5	6.7	77.7
	5.00	24	6.5	6.7	84.4
	5.13	13	3.5	3.6	88.0
	5.25	14	3.8	3.9	91.9
	5.38	6	1.6	1.7	93.6
	5.50	5	1.3	1.4	95.0
	5.63	6	1.6	1.7	96.7
	5.75	8	2.2	2.2	98.9
	6.00	3	.8	.8	99.7
	6.38	1	.3	.3	100.0
	Total	359	96.8	100.0	
Missing	System	12	3.2		
Total		371	100.0		

1 through 9), and an unusual value would be any other number (e.g., 0, 13, 44). Here, the variable is a computed variable (an average of eight items), and so the values must fall between 1 and 9. There appear to be no unusual values here. We also note that there are 12 missing values (**Missing System** in the table). These are "system missing" because the fields are blank; had we defined a particular value as **Missing**, that would have been identified in our table.

The descriptive statistics for all four variables are shown in Figure 3b.5. Skewness and kurtosis appear to be well within the normal range, a judgment reinforced from a visual inspection of the histogram (only **INDCOLI** is presented to save space) shown in Figure 3b.6.

Figure 3b.5 Descriptive Statistics for the Variables

Statistics

		INDCOLI Individualism	INDCOLC Collectivism	MEIMEIC Ethnic Identity Commitment	MEIMEIE Ethnic Identity Exploration
N	Valid	359	359	361	360
	Missing	12	12	10	11
Mean		4.3446	5.5540	3.5896	3.6370
Median		4.3750	5.6250	3.6667	4.0000
Mode		4.38	6.00	4.00	4.00
Std. Deviation		.74191	.57689	.90607	.87984
Skewness		-.163	-.475	-.352	-.407
Std. Error of Skewness		.129	.129	.128	.129
Kurtosis		-.236	.392	-.355	-.329
Std. Error of Kurtosis		.257	.257	.256	.256
Minimum		2.13	3.38	1.00	1.00
Maximum		6.38	6.88	5.00	5.00

Here is a brief summary of what we found. There were no extreme values observed for **INDCOLI, INDCOLC, MEIMEIC**, and **MEIMEIE**. Means and standard deviations on these latter variables are all within published ranges and seem reasonable. From this initial assessment, we conclude that these variables are "clean."

Figure 3b.6   The Histogram for **INDCOLI**

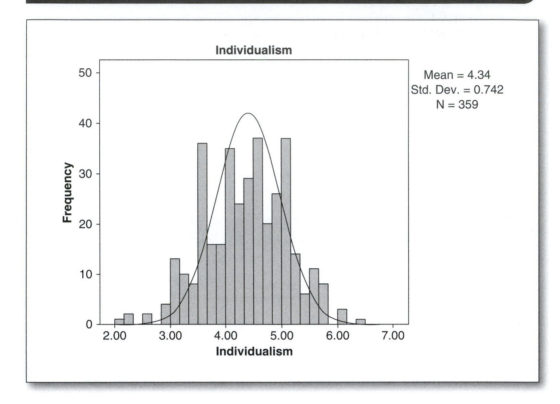

3B.3 Screening Quantitative Variables

Once the plausibility or appropriateness of each continuous variable's range of values has been established (i.e., each variable has been cleaned), we can begin to consider issues of missing values, normality, and univariate outliers with the following IBM SPSS procedures: **Frequencies, Descriptives, Explore**, and **Missing Value Analysis**. Pairwise linearity can be examined with IBM SPSS **Plot**, and assessment for multivariate outliers can be achieved through the IBM SPSS **Regression** procedure (as described in Chapter 7A). The order in which we discuss these, and the order in which we recommend these procedures be done, is as follows:

- Addressing missing values
- Dealing with univariate outliers
- Assessing assumptions
- Checking for multivariate outliers

3B.4 Missing Values: Overview

The descriptive statistics output presented in Figure 3b.5 shows that the four quantitative variables have from 10 to 12 cases each with a missing value; **gender**, not shown in the table, has 11 missing values. Because the cases with missing values on these variables represent less than 5% of the total cases (actually 3%), which is well below our threshold for possible missing value intervention, we would normally handle this situation with the IBM SPSS default of listwise deletion. However, we will use these missing value situations to demonstrate the item imputation process using the more "modern" **Missing Value Analysis** module (for those of you who have access to this module) with both the EM algorithm and the MI procedures and the more "traditional" mean substitution facility in IBM SPSS (for those of you who do not have the **Missing Value Analysis** module).

The **Missing Value Analysis** module provides a sophisticated method of addressing various missing data situations. The **Missing Value Analysis** is composed of two separate routines. One routine allows us to examine missing data by means of descriptive and inferential statistics and pattern analysis; it also provides four imputation procedures (listwise, pairwise, EM, regression). A second routine contains a MI procedure that provides further missing value pattern analysis along with multiple imputed missing value data sets.

3B.5 Missing Value Analysis

3B.5.1 Missing Value Analysis: Main Dialog Screen

For those of you who have access to this module on your IBM SPSS software, select **Analyze ➜ Missing Value Analysis** from the main menu, which produces the **Missing Value Analysis** dialog window shown in Figure 3b.7. The left panel of this window provides a list of all the variables available for analysis. We are interested in all four of our continuous variables (**INDCOLI, INDCOLC, MEIMEIC**, and **MEIMEIE**), and we have moved them over to the **Quantitative Variables** panel. We have also moved our one categorical variable **gender** over to the **Categorical Variables** panel.

On the far right side of the dialog window are the **Patterns** and **Descriptives** pushbuttons. The **Patterns** screen specifies various missing data patterns and tabulations available to us. The **Descriptives** screen allows us to generate univariate descriptive statistics for each variable and creates a temporary missing indicator variable (missing/nonmissing) that can be assessed with t tests and frequency tables.

Beneath the **Patterns** and **Descriptives** pushbuttons lies the **Estimation** panel that houses four missing value estimation checkboxes: **Listwise, Pairwise, EM**, and **Regression**. **Listwise** will display parameters (e.g., means) by omitting cases that have missing values

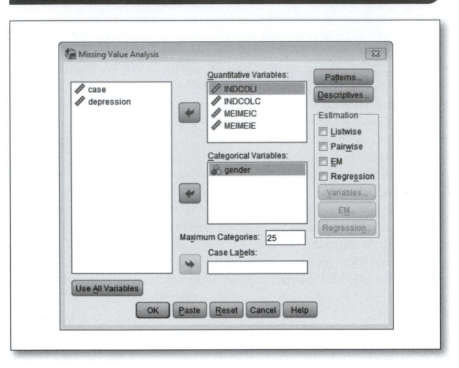

Figure 3b.7 Missing Value Analysis Main Dialog Screen

on any single variable (listwise deletion). **Pairwise** produces statistics from all available cases that have valid values on the two specified variables (pairwise deletion). **EM** estimates missing values by an iterative (two-step) process. The "E" step calculates expected values of parameters, and the "M" step calculates maximum likelihood estimates. **Regression** estimates missing values from a regression algorithm. Three additional pushbuttons are available (**Variables, EM**, and **Regression**) that provide special options, including the ability to save the newly imputed missing values in the data file, once either the **EM** or **Regression** procedure has been selected.

3B.5.2 Missing Value Analysis: Descriptives

Clicking the **Descriptives** pushbutton in the main **Missing Value Analysis** window produces the dialog screen shown in Figure 3b.8. One of the options from this dialog window is the **Univariate statistics**; this is the default, and we will keep the box checked. In the **Indicator Variable Statistics** panel we have selected **t tests with groups formed by indicator variables** (IBM SPSS instructs us not to deal with the probabilities of the *t* value being significant if we are calculating more than one, so we do not check that option) and

Crosstabulations of categorical and indicator variables. At the bottom of the window, we have modified the default of 5% to 1% in the **Omit variables missing less than [specify] % of cases** to meet the conditions of our data set where we have relatively few missing values. Click **Continue** to return to the main **Missing Value Analysis** window and click **OK** to perform the analysis.

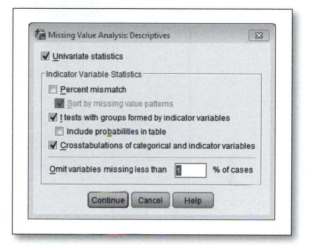

Figure 3b.8 Descriptives Screen for Missing Value Analysis

The **Univariate Statistics** output table shown in Figure 3b.9 provides an overview of the extent of missing data for the five variables. The **Missing** (**Count** and **Percent**) columns display the number and percentage of cases with missing values and provide a way of comparing the extent of missing data across variables. Inspection of Figure 3b.9 indicates that a relatively small number of cases (2.7%–3.2%) have missing values across all five variables. The means and standard deviations for the four quantitative variables are also displayed along with the number of cases with extreme values.

Figure 3b.10 presents the **Separate Variance t Tests** output. These *t* tests identify continuous (metric) variables that have unusual missing values patterns. The *t* test procedure automatically creates an indicator variable that specifies whether a value of a variable is present or missing for an individual case. Subgroup means for the indicator variable are to be compared and evaluated.

Figure 3b.9 Univariate Statistics Output

Univariate Statistics

	N	Mean	Std. Deviation	Missing Count	Missing Percent	No. of Extremes[a] Low	No. of Extremes[a] High
INDCOLI	359	4.3446	.74191	12	3.2	0	0
INDCOLC	359	5.5540	.57689	12	3.2	7	0
MEIMEIC	361	3.5896	.90607	10	2.7	4	0
MEIMEIE	360	3.6370	.87984	11	3.0	1	0
gender	360			11	3.0		

a. Number of cases outside the range (Q1 − 1.5*IQR, Q3 + 1.5*IQR).

Figure 3b.10   *t*-Test Output

Separate Variance t Tests[a]

		INDCOLI	INDCOLC	MEIMEIC	MEIMEIE
INDCOLI	t	.	−1.8	−2.6	−2.8
	df	.	11.9	11.8	10.5
	# Present	359	347	349	349
	# Missing	0	12	12	11
	Mean(Present)	4.3446	5.5444	3.5669	3.6122
	Mean(Missing)	.	5.8333	4.2500	4.4242
INDCOLC	t	−.2	.	.1	.1
	df	12.0	.	11.5	11.7
	# Present	347	359	349	348
	# Missing	12	0	12	12
	Mean(Present)	4.3432	5.5540	3.5907	3.6379
	Mean(Missing)	4.3854	.	3.5556	3.6111
MEIMEIC	t	.2	.1	.	.
	df	9.6	10.0	.	.
	# Present	349	349	361	360
	# Missing	10	10	0	0
	Mean(Present)	4.3459	5.5543	3.5896	3.6370
	Mean(Missing)	4.3000	5.5464	.	.
MEIMEIE	t	.2	−.4	.	.
	df	9.6	11.1	.	.
	# Present	349	348	360	360
	# Missing	10	11	1	0
	Mean(Present)	4.3459	5.5523	3.5856	3.6370
	Mean(Missing)	4.3000	5.6104	5.0000	.
gender	t	−.9	2.3	−1.6	−.6
	df	9.5	11.6	10.8	10.7
	# Present	349	348	350	349
	# Missing	10	11	11	11
	Mean(Present)	4.3383	5.5622	3.5776	3.6323
	Mean(Missing)	4.5625	5.2955	3.9697	3.7879

For each quantitative variable, pairs of groups are formed by indicator variables (present, missing).

a. Indicator variables with less than 2% missing are not displayed.

This output is best read across the major rows, with the information for each variable (the reference variable) presented in six rows within each major row. The **Mean (Missing)** entries are the means on the remaining variables for those cases with missing values on the reference variable, and the **# Missing** supplies the count of such cases. For example, we know from the univariate statistics that there are 12 cases with missing values on **INDICOLI**. The means of these cases on **INDICOLC, MEIMEIC**, and **MEIMEIE** are 5.8333, 4.2500, and 4.4242, respectively. Note that we see 11 missing cases for these cases on **MEIMEIE**; that is because one of these 12 cases also had a missing value on this latter variable.

The **Mean** (**Present**) entries are the means on the remaining variables for those cases with valid values on the reference variable, and the **# Present** supplies the count of such cases. For example, we know from the univariate statistics that there are 359 cases with valid values on **INDICOLI**. The means of these cases on **INDICOLC, MEIMEIC**, and **MEIMEIE** are 5.5444, 3.5669, and 3.6122, respectively.

From Figure 3b.10 we see that the missingness of **INDICOLI** significantly affects the means of **MEIMEIC** and **MEIMEIE**. For example, the mean of **MEIMEIC** is 4.25 for those cases having missing values on **INDICOLI**, as opposed to a **MEIMEIC** mean of almost 3.57 for those cases having valid values on **INDICOLI**. The same pattern is found with **MEIMEIE**. These missingness patterns may be indicative of data that are not missing at random (NMAR).

Figure 3b.11 displays an output table labeled **Crosstabulations of Categorical Versus Indicator Variables**. This table shows a cross-tabulation of all categorical variables (only **gender**

Figure 3b.11 Cross-Tabulations of the Categorical Variable

Crosstabulations of Categorical Versus Indicator Variables

gender

			Total	1 Male	2 Female	Missing SysMis
INDCOLI	Present	Count	359	57	292	10
		Percent	96.8	98.3	96.7	90.9
	Missing	% SysMis	3.2	1.7	3.3	9.1
INDCOLC	Present	Count	359	55	293	11
		Percent	96.8	94.8	97.0	100.0
	Missing	% SysMis	3.2	5.2	3.0	.0
MEIMEIC	Present	Count	361	57	293	11
		Percent	97.3	98.3	97.0	100.0
	Missing	% SysMis	2.7	1.7	3.0	.0
MEIMEIE	Present	Count	360	57	292	11
		Percent	97.0	98.3	96.7	100.0
	Missing	% SysMis	3.0	1.7	3.3	.0

Indicator variables with less than 2% missing are not displayed.

in our current example) by an automatically created indicator variable that calculates frequencies and percentage of missing and nonmissing values across levels of the categorical variable for each quantitative variable.

From the output in Figure 3b.11, we can note that for **gender**, the number of missing values for the indicator variable remains fairly constant for both males and females. For example, **INDICOLI** had only 1.7% and 3.3% missing values for males and females, respectively. Such minimal differences can probably be attributed to chance.

3B.5.3 Missing Value Analysis: Patterns

Select **Analyze** ➜ **Missing Value Analysis** from the main menu and click the **Patterns** pushbutton to produce the screen that can be seen in Figure 3b.12. Note that we have checked **Tabulated cases, grouped by missing value patterns** and the **Sort variables by missing value pattern** to produce several missing value patterns tables. In the lower half of the dialog window, we have moved all five variables in the **Missing Patterns** for panel over to the **Additional Information for** panel. This provides additional missing values pattern information. Click

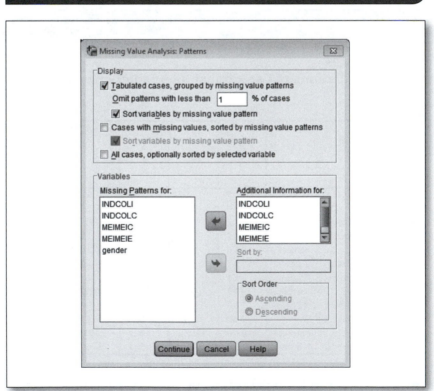

Figure 3b.12 Patterns Screen for Missing Value Analysis

Continue to return to the main **Missing Value Analysis** window and click **OK** to perform the analysis.

The output for the **Tabulated Patterns** table can be seen in Figure 3b.13. This table allows researchers to determine if the data are jointly missing or if individual cases are missing multiple variables. The first column lists subsets of cases, each of which is profiled by showing an **x** for missing values in its own row in the **Missing Patterns** columns. This part of the table shows the following:

- The first subset is the set of 327 cases having no missing values on any of the variables in the analysis.
- The second subset contains the 10 cases having missing values on the **gender** variable.
- The third subset contains the 10 cases having missing values on the **INDCOLI** variable.
- The fourth subset contains the 10 cases having missing values on two variables, **MEIMEIC** and **MEIMEIE**; such a situation is probably not indicative of a nonrandom missingness pattern due to the paucity of pairs of **MEIM** values.
- The fifth subset contains the 12 cases having missing values on the **INDCOLC** variable.

Means for the four continuous (metric) variables and frequency counts for the categorical (nonmetric) variable are also provided at each unique missing or nonmissing pattern. These means can also be used to determine if the missing data patterns are random or not.

Figure 3b.13 Tabulated Patterns Table From Missing Value Analysis Procedure

Tabulated Patterns

Number of Cases	Missing Patterns[a]					Complete if ...[b]	INDCOLI[c]	INDCOLC[c]	MEIMEIC[c]	MEIMEIE[c]	gender[d]	
	MEIMEIC	MEIMEIE	INDCOLI	gender	INDCOLC						1 Male	2 Female
327						327	4.3378	5.5518	3.5581	3.6106	53	274
10				X		337	4.5625	5.3000	3.8667	3.6667	0	0
10			X			337	.	5.8500	4.1000	4.3667	1	9
10	X	X				337	4.3000	5.5464	.	.	1	9
12					X	339	4.3854	.	3.5556	3.6111	3	9

Patterns with less than 1% cases (4 or fewer) are not displayed.

a. Variables are sorted on missing patterns.

b. Number of complete cases if variables missing in that pattern (marked with X) are not used.

c. Means at each unique pattern

d. Frequency distribution at each unique pattern

3B.5.4 Missing Value Analysis: A Test of MCAR

One additional way to address whether the data are MCAR is to compute *Little's MCAR test*. In the **Missing Value Analysis** main dialog window, select the **EM** checkbox in the **Estimation** panel as can be seen in Figure 3b.14 and click **OK**.

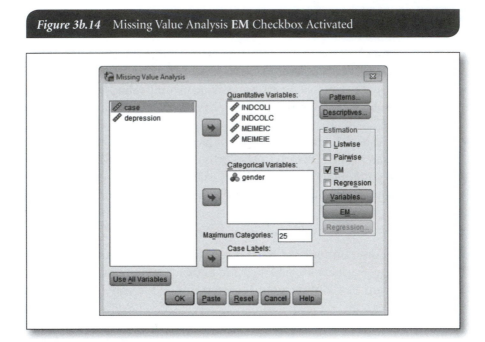

Figure 3b.14 Missing Value Analysis **EM** Checkbox Activated

The results of *Little's MCAR test* are depicted in IBM SPSS as a footnote to each **EM** parameter estimate; we display the results of the **EM Means** estimates in Figure 3b.15. *Little's MCAR test* is evaluated with a *chi-square* statistic at an alpha level set at .05. The null hypothesis for *Little's MCAR test* is that the data are MCAR. Since the present results were not statistically significant ($p > .05$), we may conclude from this omnibus missing value assessment test that the missing data are probably MCAR. Had this omnibus test been statistically significant, then this result may indicate that our data are not MCAR and may be missing at random (MAR) or NMAR. Either of these eventualities (MAR or NMAR) would probably necessitate *not* using

Figure 3b.15 Estimated Means Through EM Algorithm With Little's MCAR Test

EM Means[a]

INDCOLI	INDCOLC	MEIMEIC	MEIMEIE
4.3371	5.5612	3.5816	3.6392

a. Little's MCAR test: Chi-Square = 13.390, DF = 10, Sig. = .203

listwise deletion or the single (traditional) imputation procedures discussed in Chapter 3A. A better approach to such nonrandom missing value situations is to use a *multiple imputation* procedure.

3B.6 Multiple Imputation

3B.6.1 Multiple Imputation: Pattern Analysis

The **Multiple Imputation** procedure allows us to examine missing data patterns and to perform MIs. To begin the imputation process, go to the IBM SPSS Main Menu and click **Analyze ➜ Multiple Imputation ➜ Analyze Patterns.** This opens the Analyze Patterns dialog screen (see Figure 3b.16), where we have moved over our five variables to the **Analyze Across Variables** panel. At the bottom of the window is the **Output** panel. We will leave all three of the default IBM SPSS checkboxes activated (**Summary of missing values, Patterns of missing values, and Variables with the highest frequency of missing values**) and all other defaults in place. Click **OK.**

Figure 3b.17 depicts the output for the **Overall Summary of Missing Values.** This figure displays three pie charts that provide missing value information within the context of

Figure 3b.16 Analyze Patterns Dialog Screen

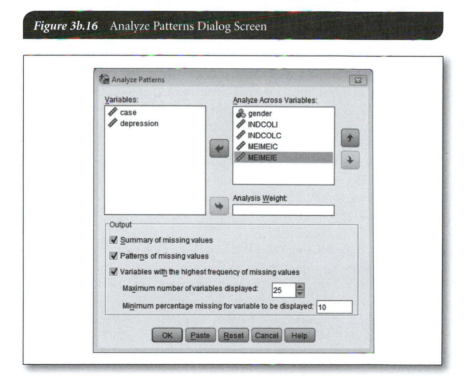

Figure 3b.17 Summary of Missing Values

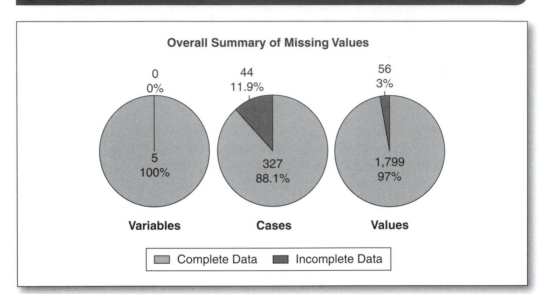

Variables, Cases, and **Values**. The Variables pie chart indicates that each one of the five variables had at least one missing value on a case. The Cases pie chart indicates that 44 (11.9%) cases had at least one missing value on a variable and that 327 (88.1%) had complete data. The Values pie chart indicates that 56 (3%) of the 1,855 values (cases *x* variables) are missing and that 1,799 (97%) are valid.

One way to interpret this summary is to calculate the ratio of the number of missing values to the number of cases. In the present data set, the ratio is 56/44 or about 1.3. This may be a warning sign to an investigator that single (traditional) imputation methods or deletion methods may not be appropriate due to the potential loss of information.

IBM SPSS provides a **Variable Summary** output table for variables with at least 10% missing values. This table was not displayed because no variable in the present analysis had more than 10% missing values. This table normally displays the number and percent of missing values for each variable in the analysis, along with their valid *N*, mean, and standard deviation.

Figure 3b.18 depicts the **Missing Value Patterns** chart. Each pattern is represented as a row in the grid and represents *a group of cases* with the same pattern of missing and nonmissing data. In the present data set, there are seven such groups of cases. Darkened squares indicate missing values. For example, **Pattern 1** indicates cases with no missing values, **Pattern 2** depicts cases with missing values on **Gender**, and **Pattern 3** represents cases that have missing values on both **MEIMEIC** and **MEIMEIE**. Note that a data set can potentially have a number of patterns equal to 2 raised to a power of the number of variables in the analysis. With five variables

Figure 3b.18 Missing Value Patterns Chart

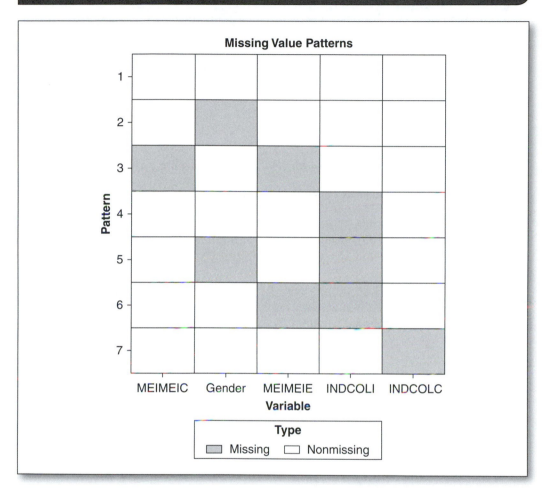

in the present example, we have 2^5 or 32 potential patterns. Only 7 of those 32 potential missing value patterns emerged in this analysis.

The **Missing Value Patterns** chart orders variables and patterns to indicate whether patterns of monotonicity exist. IBM SPSS produces this grid by ordering variables from left to right in increasing order of missingness (the least to the highest number of missing values). IBM SPSS then sorts the patterns starting with the last variable (nonmissing values then missing values), then the second to the last variable, and so on, going from right to left. These computations produce a grid that indicates whether the missing data approximate a *monotone* pattern. A monotone missing data pattern is indicated if all the missing cells and nonmissing cells are contiguous. A useful heuristic to follow is that the data are monotone if there are no "pockets" of nonmissing cells in the lower right portion of the chart and no pockets of missing cells in the upper left quadrant of the chart. The present data appear to be nonmonotone. Had the data approximated a monotone pattern, a special **Custom Monotone** MI method can be used.

Last, Figure 3b.19 is a bar graph of pattern frequencies that is automatically produced with the **Missing Value Patterns** chart. This bar graph depicts the percentage of cases for each pattern. In the present example, more than 80% of the cases have **Pattern 1**, or no missing values. **Patterns 7, 4, 3**, and **2** have the next largest amount of cases, although, in absolute terms, they represent a very small proportion.

3B.6.2 Multiple Imputation: Automatic Multiple Imputation

3B.6.2.1 The Recommended Preliminary: Setting a Random Seed

SPSS (2009) recommends setting a random seed prior to performing our MI, a procedure which will allow us to replicate this analysis should the need arise by using the same

---

Figure 3b.19   Missing Values Frequencies

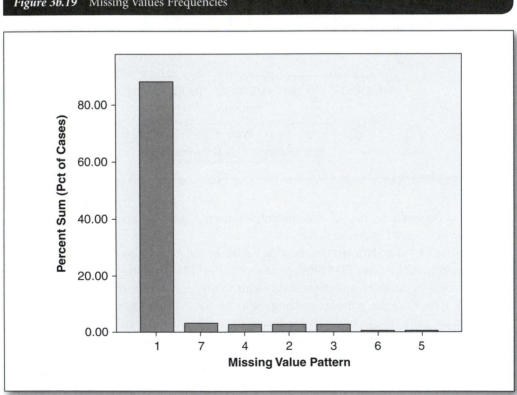

starting point as we will specify in a moment. From the main menu select **Transform ➔ Random Number Generators**, which produces the **Random Number Generators** dialog window shown in Figure 3b.20. In the **Active Generator** panel, click the **Set Active Generator** checkbox and click the **Mersenne Twister** option (this is the updated random number generator). In the **Active Generator Initialization** panel, click the **Set Starting Point** checkbox, and click the **Fixed Value** option. In the **Value** window, type **3004200** (an arbitrary starting point). Then click **OK**.

Figure 3b.20 Random Number Generators Dialog Window

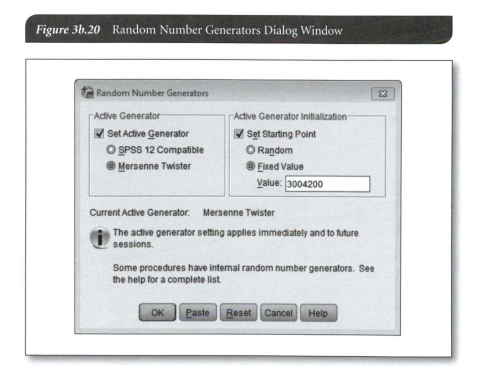

3B.6.2.2 Performing the Multiple Imputation Procedure

From the main menu select **Analyze ➔ Multiple Imputation ➔ Impute Missing Data Values**. This produces the **Impute Missing Data Values** dialog window shown in Figure 3b.21. Notice that we have moved our five variables from the **Variables** panel to the **Variables in Model** panel. We have also left the **Imputations** panel at its default setting of 5. In the **Location of Imputed Data** panel, we kept the default **Create a new dataset** option, and in the **Dataset name** panel, we have typed in **Vicmultimpute** as the name to which our multiple imputed file will be saved.

Now click the **Output** tab at the top of the dialog window. This produces the **Impute Missing Data Values Output** screen shown in Figure 3b.22, where we have retained the

Figure 3b.21 Impute Missing Data Values Dialog Window

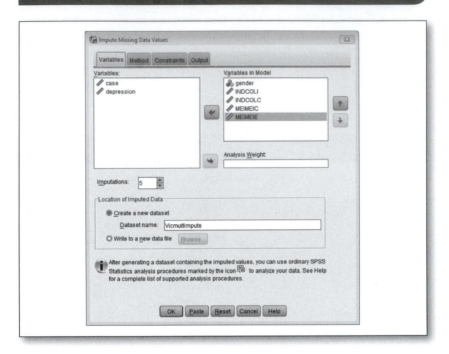

default for the **Imputation model** and selected **Descriptive statistics for variables with imputed values** in the **Display** panel. Click **OK** to perform the automatic MI.

Figure 3b.23 displays the **Imputation Specifications** table. This table confirms the specifications that we requested: **Automatic** imputation method, with **5** default imputations. We chose to create five imputed data sets to demonstrate the technique. As noted in Section 3A.7.3, Enders (2010) and Graham et al. (2007) recommend using up to 20 imputed data sets.

Figure 3b.24 displays the **Imputation Results** output table. This table provides an overview of the actual MI process that was specified. Specifically, the automatic imputation method used by IBM SPSS is called a **Fully Conditional Specification**. All five requested variables were imputed, and the imputation sequence follows the order of the variables on the *x*-axis of the **Missing Value Patterns** chart in Figure 3b.18.

The **Imputation Models** table shown in Figure 3b.25 provides additional details as to how each variable was imputed. Specifically, the variables are listed in their imputation sequence order. Quantitative variables (e.g., **MEIMEIE**) are modeled by means of linear regression as shown in the column labeled **Type**, whereas categorical variables (**gender** in this data set) are modeled with logistic regression. Each model uses all other variables as predictors as shown in the column labeled **Effects**. Last, for each variable, the number of **Missing**

Figure 3b.22 The Output Tab

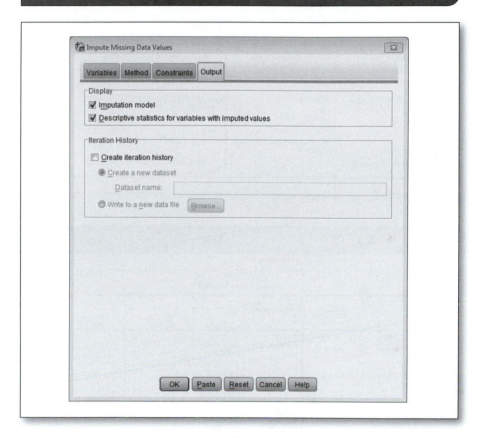

Figure 3b.23 Multiple Imputation Specifications Table

Imputation Specifications	
Imputation Method	Automatic
Number of Imputations	5
Model for Scale Variables	Linear Regression
Interactions Included in Models	(none)
Maximum Percentage of Missing Values	100.0%
Maximum Number of Parameters in Imputation Model	100

Figure 3b.24 Multiple Imputation Results

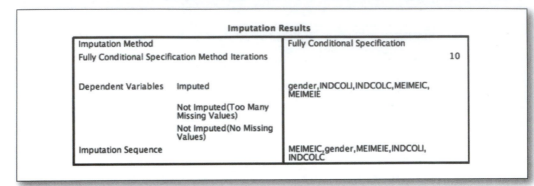

Imputation Results

Imputation Method	Fully Conditional Specification
Fully Conditional Specification Method Iterations	10
Dependent Variables Imputed	gender,INDCOLI,INDCOLC,MEIMEIC, MEIMEIE
Not Imputed(Too Many Missing Values)	
Not Imputed(No Missing Values)	
Imputation Sequence	MEIMEIC,gender,MEIMEIE,INDCOLI, INDCOLC

Figure 3b.25 Multiple Imputation Models

Imputation Models

	Model		Missing Values	Imputed Values
	Type	Effects		
MEIMEIC Ethnic Identity Commitment	Linear Regression	gender, MEIMEIE, INDCOLI, INDCOLC	10	50
gender Gender	Logistic Regression	MEIMEIC, MEIMEIE, INDCOLI, INDCOLC	11	55
MEIMEIE Ethic Identity Exploration	Linear Regression	gender, MEIMEIC, INDCOLI, INDCOLC	11	55
INDCOLI Individualism	Linear Regression	gender, MEIMEIC, MEIMEIE, INDCOLC	12	60
INDCOLC Collectivism	Linear Regression	gender, MEIMEIC, MEIMEIE, INDCOLI	12	60

Values and the number of **Imputed Values** (the number of missing values multiplied by the number of imputations) are provided.

Figure 3b.26 displays the **Descriptive Statistics** tables. Separate tables for each variable provide summary information on each of the imputed variables. For each continuous variable, the **N, Mean, Std. Deviation, Minimum**, and **Maximum** are provided for the **Original Data, Imputed Values** (all sets), and the **Complete Data After Imputation** (which

Figure 3b.26 Multiple Imputation Descriptive Statistics

gender

Data	Imputation	Category	N	Percent
Original Data		1	58	16.1
		2	302	83.9
Imputed Values	1	1	1	9.1
		2	10	90.9
	2	1	1	9.1
		2	10	90.9
	3	2	11	100.0
	4	1	1	9.1
		2	10	90.9
	5	1	2	18.2
		2	9	81.8
Complete Data After Imputation	1	1	59	15.9
		2	312	84.1
	2	1	59	15.9
		2	312	84.1
	3	1	58	15.6
		2	313	84.4
	4	1	59	15.9
		2	312	84.1
	5	1	60	16.2
		2	311	83.8

INDCOLI

Data	Imputation	N	Mean	Std. Deviation	Minimum	Maximum
Original Data		359	4.3446	.74191	2.1250	6.3750
Imputed Values	1	12	3.9832	.85017	3.2118	5.8902
	2	12	4.5344	.80309	3.7619	6.4760
	3	12	4.3665	.99168	3.1408	5.8991
	4	12	4.4340	.73513	2.6897	5.3011
	5	12	4.3301	.52500	3.4697	4.9595
Complete Data After Imputation	1	371	4.3329	.74711	2.1250	6.3750
	2	371	4.3507	.74356	2.1250	6.4760
	3	371	4.3453	.74956	2.1250	6.3750
	4	371	4.3475	.74088	2.1250	6.3750
	5	371	4.3441	.73538	2.1250	6.3750

INDCOLC

Data	Imputation	N	Mean	Std. Deviation	Minimum	Maximum
Original Data		359	5.5540	.57689	3.3750	6.8750
Imputed Values	1	12	5.4214	.34792	4.8050	5.9714
	2	12	5.8224	.83008	4.6780	7.3624
	3	12	5.5192	.55915	4.7193	6.8337
	4	12	5.5843	.42694	4.7813	6.1040
	5	12	5.4637	.43912	5.0035	6.2473
Complete Data After Imputation	1	371	5.5498	.57111	3.3750	6.8750
	2	371	5.5627	.58716	3.3750	7.3624
	3	371	5.5529	.57563	3.3750	6.8750
	4	371	5.5550	.57224	3.3750	6.8750
	5	371	5.5511	.57271	3.3750	6.8750

MEIMEIC

Data	Imputation	N	Mean	Std. Deviation	Minimum	Maximum
Original Data		361	3.5896	.90607	1.0000	5.0000
Imputed Values	1	10	3.4183	.48918	2.5195	3.9247
	2	10	4.2275	.92085	2.8602	5.5895
	3	10	3.9977	1.04872	2.7169	5.4958
	4	10	3.5433	1.06174	1.9241	5.3245
	5	10	3.5839	1.32148	1.7717	4.9149
Complete Data After Imputation	1	371	3.5850	.89742	1.0000	5.0000
	2	371	3.6068	.91110	1.0000	5.5895
	3	371	3.6006	.91099	1.0000	5.4958
	4	371	3.5883	.90899	1.0000	5.3245
	5	371	3.5894	.91720	1.0000	5.0000

MEIMEIE

Data	Imputation	N	Mean	Std. Deviation	Minimum	Maximum
Original Data		360	3.6370	.87984	1.0000	5.0000
Imputed Values	1	11	3.7041	.75422	2.2736	4.9491
	2	11	4.2870	.70132	3.1478	5.3218
	3	11	3.9690	.83542	2.7361	5.2298
	4	11	3.6189	.93774	2.3080	5.1524
	5	11	3.8408	1.31278	1.4144	5.2864
Complete Data After Imputation	1	371	3.6390	.87556	1.0000	5.0000
	2	371	3.6563	.88124	1.0000	5.3218
	3	371	3.6469	.87928	1.0000	5.2298
	4	371	3.6365	.88027	1.0000	5.1524
	5	371	3.6431	.89380	1.0000	5.2864

combines the original data and imputed values). Descriptive statistics for categorical variables include **N** and **Percent** (by category) for the **Original Data, Imputed Values**, and **Complete Data After Imputation** (combining original and imputed values).

We note from a cursory inspection of the categorical proportions (of **gender**) and the means and standard deviations of the four continuous variables that all are fairly close to the original data and are within range and appear reasonable. Had we discovered that some of the imputed values or parameter estimates were unusual (e.g., negative values or extreme minimum or maximum values), then we would need to consider running a **Custom Model** within this module. Due to space limitations, we will not be covering custom model building with multiple imputed data. The interested reader is encouraged to consult IBM SPSS documentation or seek expert advice.

3B.6.3 Structure of the Multiple Imputed Data Set

Our multiple imputed data set contains six sets of data, the original data set and (in the present example) five imputed sets. In the process of building this new data file, IBM SPSS created a new variable named **Imputation** with the label **Imputation Number** as shown in the **Variable View** in Figure 3b.27. The value of 0 is assigned to the original data set and the imputed sets are numbered 1 through M, where M is the number of imputations requested; here, M is equal to 5. Figure 3b.28 shows, in the Data View, the transition from the original data set (ending in row 371) to the first imputed data set (starting in row 372). In the present example, we had 371 original cases and used the IBM SPSS default of 5 MIs, which produced $371 + (371 * 5)$ or 2,226 cases in the new data set.

Figure 3b.27 Variable View Showing the New Imputation Variable

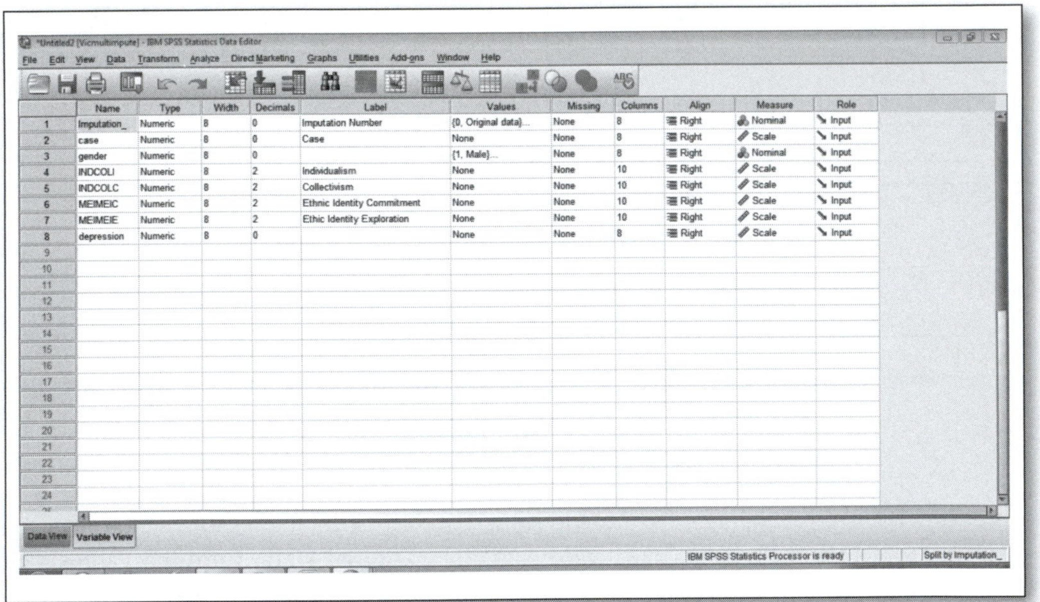

3B.6.4 Splitting the Multiple Imputed Data Set

To analyze a multiple imputed data set, IBM SPSS must be directed to recognize the imputed nature of the data file; if it does not recognize this, it will treat the data file as a single sample of cases (e.g., 2,226 unique cases in our example) rather than multiple sets of cases (e.g., multiple sets of 371 cases). The way in which we cause IBM SPSS to treat the data set as imputed is to activate the **Split File** procedure. We split the data file on the **Imputation** variable;

Figure 3b.28 Data View Showing the Transition From the Original Data to the First Imputation

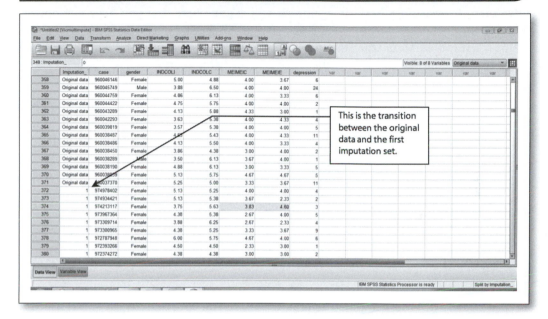

by doing so, any statistical procedure we invoke will be done separately for each value of the split variable (**Imputation** in this example).

There are two ways to accomplish this splitting. One way is to be used when you wish to work with a multiple imputed data file but do not have the **Missing Value Analysis** module. In such a situation, it is necessary to select **Data ➔ Split File** from the main menu, check the **Compare groups** and **Sort the file by grouping variables** choices, click over the **Imputation** variable to the panel labeled **Groups Based on**, and click **OK**. This is shown in Figure 3b.29.

Another way the file may be split, and the one we strongly recommend if you do have the

Figure 3b.29 Split File Dialog Screen

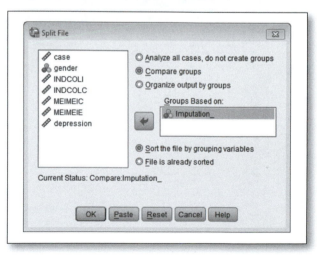

Missing Value Analysis module is to **Mark Imputed Data**. This is what is in effect when you have just built a multiple imputed data file in your current work session. However, when you open the saved data set at a later time in a different session, you must "manually" turn the markings back on again. We will assume here that you have just opened **Vicmultimpute** at the start of a new work session. All that we need to do is to select View ➔ **Mark Imputed Data** from the main menu. Marking the imputed data accomplishes three functions simultaneously and very conveniently for users:

- The data file is split on the **Imputation** variable. Performing a MI–supported procedure under this splitting strategy will not only automatically produce output for the original data and each imputation (this is what the **Data ➔ Split File** procedure will do), it will also produce output for the final pooled results. Pooled multiple imputed data in IBM SPSS typically are used to produce coefficients, means and mean differences, and counts.
- Imputed data in the data file are highlighted (see Figure 3b.30).
- A special icon (it looks like a blue ram's horn) is added to the menu options for procedures that are supported for MI pooling.

The main advantage of marking imputed data is to obtain the pooled results of a statistical procedure. With **Mark Imputed Data** turned on, as can be seen in Figure 3b.31, selecting

Figure 3b.30 With Mark Imputed Values Turned on, the Imputed Values Are Highlighted

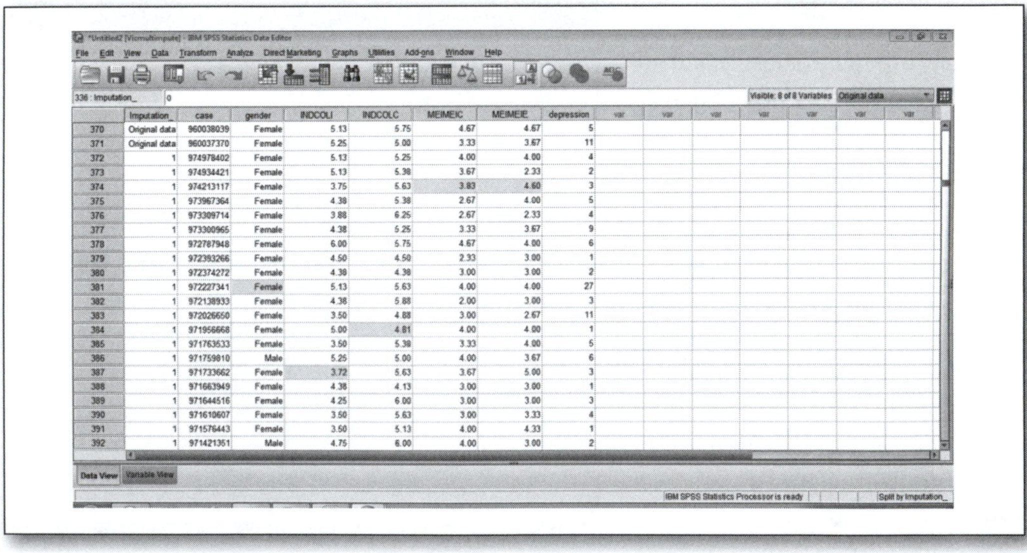

Analyze ➜ Correlate (as an example) reveals a submenu of three procedures. From this submenu, we can see that MI is supported in the **Bivariate** and **Partial** correlation procedures but not in the **Distances** procedure. IBM SPSS currently supports two levels of MI pooling. The first type of pooling is called **Naïve combination** where only the pooled parameter estimate is available. The second level of pooling is called **Univariate combination** and provides a pooled parameter estimate, its standard error, test statistic, degrees of freedom, *p* value, confidence interval, and various pooling diagnostics. The procedures that IBM SPSS currently supports for either **Naïve** or **Univariate pooling** are listed in Figure 3b.32; this list will probably change over time.

Figure 3b.31 The Path to Bivariate Correlation With Marked Icons

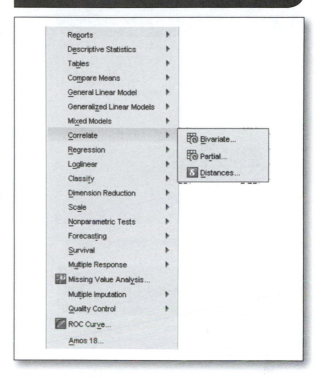

Figure 3b.32 Procedures Currently Supporting Multiple Imputation Pooling

Binary Logistic Regression	Linear Mixed Models
Binomial Test	Linear Regression
Bivariate Correlations	Means
Chi-Square Test	Multinomial Logistic Regression
Cox Regression	One-Sample Kolmogorov-Smirnov Test
Crosstabs	One-Way ANOVA
Crosstabs	Ordinal Regression
Descriptives	Paired-Samples T Test
Discriminant Analysis	Partial Correlations
Frequencies	Runs Test
Generalized Estimating Equations	T Test Independent and One-Sample
Generalized Linear Models	Test for Several Independent Samples
Generalized Linear Models Univariate	Tests for Several Related Samples
Generalized Linear Models Multivariate	Two-Independent Samples Tests
Generalized Linear Models Repeated	Two-Related Samples Tests

3B.6.5 Conducting a Statistical Analysis With Multiple Imputed Data

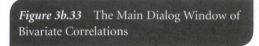

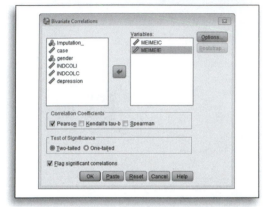

Figure 3b.33 The Main Dialog Window of Bivariate Correlations

With our marked imputed data file of **Vicmultimpute** active, we are now ready to perform an example of statistical analysis. From the main menu, select **Analyze ➔ Correlate ➔ Bivariate**, which produces the **Bivariate Correlations** dialog window shown in Figure 3b.33. Move **MEIMEIC** and **MEIMEIE** to the **Variables** panel, select Options (see Figure 3b.34) and click **Means and standard deviations**, click **Continue** to return to the main dialog window, and click **OK** to perform the analysis.

The multiple imputed **Descriptive Statistics** are shown in Figure 3b.35. The first major row shows the means and standard deviations for each variable based on the original data file (**Imputation 0**) and the next five rows provide these statistics for each of the five imputations. The final row labeled **Pooled** represents the averages of the five imputations.

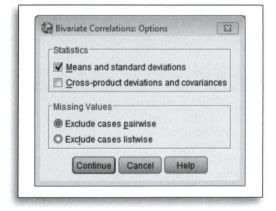

Figure 3b.34 The Options Screen of Bivariate Correlations

Figure 3b.36 presents the multiple imputed Pearson correlation results, structured analogously to the previous output. The Pearson correlation (r) between **MEIMEIE** and **MEIMEIC** in the original data was .709. The five separate imputations generated Pearson rs ranging from .705 to .724; the final pooled correlation was .712.

3B.7 Mean Substitution as a Single Imputation Approach

For those IBM SPSS users without access to the **Missing Value Analysis** module, we will briefly show how to accomplish mean substitution of missing values. We remind readers that this is not a recommended procedure because of the following:

- It makes tenuous assumptions about the pattern of missing values.
- It artificially reduces the variance and the standard error of the mean, statistics that are crucial to describing data and testing for statistical significance.

Figure 3b.35 Descriptive Statistics on the Imputed Data Set

Descriptive Statistics

Imputation Number		Mean	Std. Deviation	N
0 Original data	MEIMEIC MEIM Ethnic Identity Commitment Subscale	3.5896	.90607	361
	MEIMEIE MEIM Ethic Identity Exploration Subscale	3.6370	.87984	360
1	MEIMEIC MEIM Ethnic Identity Commitment Subscale	3.5850	.89742	371
	MEIMEIE MEIM Ethic Identity Exploration Subscale	3.6390	.87556	371
2	MEIMEIC MEIM Ethnic Identity Commitment Subscale	3.6068	.91110	371
	MEIMEIE MEIM Ethic Identity Exploration Subscale	3.6563	.88124	371
3	MEIMEIC MEIM Ethnic Identity Commitment Subscale	3.6006	.91099	371
	MEIMEIE MEIM Ethic Identity Exploration Subscale	3.6469	.87928	371
4	MEIMEIC MEIM Ethnic Identity Commitment Subscale	3.5883	.90899	371
	MEIMEIE MEIM Ethic Identity Exploration Subscale	3.6365	.88027	371
5	MEIMEIC MEIM Ethnic Identity Commitment Subscale	3.5894	.91720	371
	MEIMEIE MEIM Ethic Identity Exploration Subscale	3.6431	.89380	371
Pooled	MEIMEIC MEIM Ethnic Identity Commitment Subscale	3.5940		371
	MEIMEIE MEIM Ethic Identity Exploration Subscale	3.6444		371

From the main menu, select **Transform ➔ Replace Missing Values**, which produces the **Replace Missing Values** dialog window shown in Figure 3b.37. From the variables list panel, we moved over one of our variables for illustration purposes (**INDICOLI** whose missing values we want to replace) to the **New Variables** panel. IBM SPSS will automatically designate a new variable and variable name within the **Name** and **Method** panel (in the present case, **INDICOLI_1**) that contains the imputed replacement values for those cases having a missing value on **INDICOLI**. We have selected Series mean (in this case $M = 4.34$, the mean of the valid values). When we click **OK, INDICOLI_1** will be placed as a new variable at the

Figure 3b.36 Correlations on the Imputed Data Set

			MEIMEIC MEIM Ethnic Identity Commitment Subscale	MEIMEIE MEIM Ethic Identity Exploration Subscale
Imputation **Imputation Number**				
0 Original data	MEIMEIC MEIM Ethnic Identity Commitment Subscale	Pearson Correlation	1	.709..
		Sig. (2–tailed)		.000
		N	361	360
	MEIMEIE MEIM Ethic Identity Exploration Subscale	Pearson Correlation	.709..	1
		Sig. (2–tailed)	.000	
		N	360	360
1	MEIMEIC MEIM Ethnic Identity Commitment Subscale	Pearson Correlation	1	.705..
		Sig. (2–tailed)		.000
		N	371	371
	MEIMEIE MEIM Ethic Identity Exploration Subscale	Pearson Correlation	.705..	1
		Sig. (2–tailed)	.000	
		N	371	371
2	MEIMEIC MEIM Ethnic Identity Commitment Subscale	Pearson Correlation	1	.711..
		Sig. (2–tailed)		.000
		N	371	371
	MEIMEIE MEIM Ethic Identity Exploration Subscale	Pearson Correlation	.711..	1
		Sig. (2–tailed)	.000	
		N	371	371
3	MEIMEIC MEIM Ethnic Identity Commitment Subscale	Pearson Correlation	1	.709..
		Sig. (2–tailed)		.000
		N	371	371
	MEIMEIE MEIM Ethic Identity Exploration Subscale	Pearson Correlation	.709..	1
		Sig. (2–tailed)	.000	
		N	371	371
4	MEIMEIC MEIM Ethnic Identity Commitment Subscale	Pearson Correlation	1	.709..
		Sig. (2–tailed)		.000
		N	371	371
	MEIMEIE MEIM Ethic Identity Exploration Subscale	Pearson Correlation	.709..	1
		Sig. (2–tailed)	.000	
		N	371	371
5	MEIMEIC MEIM Ethnic Identity Commitment Subscale	Pearson Correlation	1	.724..
		Sig. (2–tailed)		.000
		N	371	371
	MEIMEIE MEIM Ethic Identity Exploration Subscale	Pearson Correlation	.724..	1
		Sig. (2–tailed)	.000	
		N	371	371
Pooled	MEIMEIC MEIM Ethnic Identity Commitment Subscale	Pearson Correlation	1	.712..
		Sig. (2–tailed)		.000
		N		371
	MEIMEIE MEIM Ethic Identity Exploration Subscale	Pearson Correlation	.712..	1
		Sig. (2–tailed)	.000	
		N	371	371

**. Correlation is significant at the 0.01 level (2–tailed).

end of our data file (see Figure 3b.38). If we wanted to use this new variable for later analyses, we would have to save the data file at this point (perhaps under a different name) so that we would have access to **INDICOLI_1** in subsequent work sessions. Note that this new variable, **INDICOLI_1**, was created for demonstration purposes only; instead, we will continue using **INDICOLI** with listwise deletion to handle its missing values.

Figure 3b.37 The Replace Missing Values Window

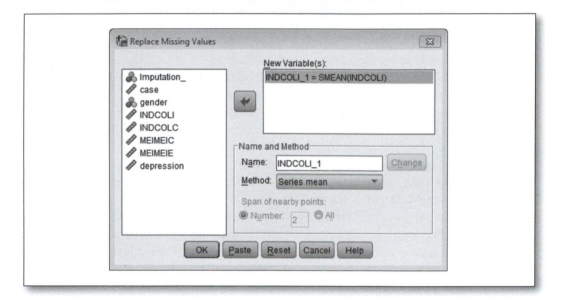

Figure 3b.38 INDICOLI_1 Has Been Placed at the End of the Data File

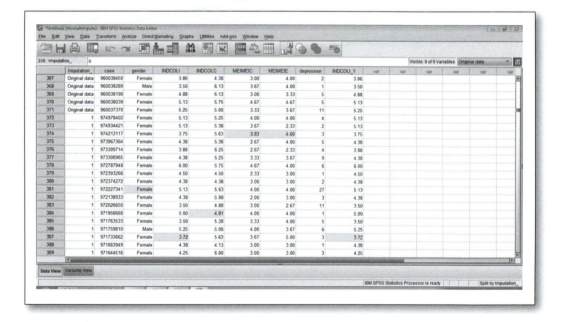

3B.8 Univariate Outliers

As we noted in Chapter 3A, univariate outliers refer to cases with extreme values on a particular variable. To assess for outliers on our quantitative variables, open **Victoria_Data_Screening** and from the main menu select **Analyze ➔ Descriptive Statistics ➔ Explore**, which opens the dialog window shown in Figure 3b.39.

Click over the four quantitative variables (**INDCOLI, INDCOLC, MEIMEIC, MEIMEIE**) to the **Dependent List** panel. The **Factor List** panel allows you to click over categorical independent variables that will "break" or profile univariate outliers by each group (or level) of the independent variable. In the present example, we will leave the **Factor List** panel blank, because our focus is on the continuous (ungrouped) variables.

Below the variable list panel (on the left side) is the **Display** panel, which allows you to toggle between a request for **Statistics** (basic descriptive statistics) or **Plots** (box plots and stem-and-leaf plots) for each variable. The IBM SPSS default is to produce both. Underneath the **Factor List** panel is the **Label Cases by** panel, which allows you to label individual cases by means of a case ID variable instead of the default IBM SPSS-generated case number. The three pushbuttons, **Statistics, Plots**, and **Options**, allow you to request additional descriptive **statistics, plots**, and ways of overriding the default (listwise) missing values option.

Selecting the **Statistics** pushbutton produces the dialog screen shown in Figure 3b.40. **Descriptives** (the default) displays basic descriptive statistics. **M-estimators** applies special maximum likelihood weights that can be applied to cases to estimate central tendency.

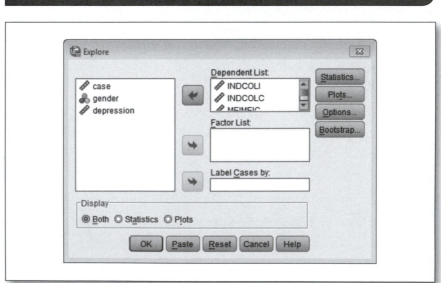

Figure 3b.39 Explore Main Dialog Window

Outliers displays cases with the five largest and smallest **Extreme Values** for each dependent variable. **Percentiles** indicates the percentage of cases falling within the 5th, 10th, 25th, 50th, 75th, 90th, and 95th percentiles. For this example, we have selected **Descriptives** and **Outliers**. Click **Continue** to return to the main dialog screen.

Click the **Plots** pushbutton to reach the dialog screen shown in Figure 3b.41. The **Boxplots** panel produces box plots for each dependent variable for each group or level of the independent variable. If no factor variable (independent variable) is selected (as in the present case), then the box plot represents the total sample. The **Descriptive** panel can produce **Stem-and-leaf** and **Histogram** plots of continuous variables, and we have selected both. The **Normality plots with tests** option will be discussed in Section 3B.9. Click **Continue** to return to the main dialog screen and click **OK** to perform the analysis.

Figure 3b.42 shows a portion of the descriptive statistics output for our variables. These results are the same as those we obtained from our **Frequencies** procedure (see Figure 3b.5) but with a few more statistics included.

Figure 3b.43 shows the **Extreme Values** table, which lists the five largest and smallest cases with **Extreme Values** on each continuous variable. For example, the five highest values of **INDICOLI** are 6.38, 6.00, 6.00, 6.00, and 5.75. Each is associated with a **Case Number**, a variable used by IBM SPSS to represent the row number in the data file. If we refer to the bottom of the **Frequency Table** in Figure 3b.4, we note that there is one value of 6.38, three values of 6.00, and eight values of 5.75. The **Extreme Values** table in Figure 3b.43 tells us in which row numbers these values can be found. The table note a by the value of 5.75 informs us that there are more values

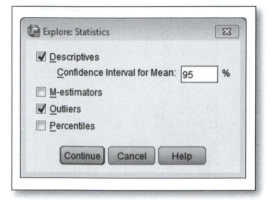

Figure 3b.40 The Statistics Window of Explore

Figure 3b.41 The Plots Window of Explore

Figure 3b.42 A Portion of the Descriptive Statistics Output

Descriptives

			Statistic	Std. Error
INDCOLI Individualism	Mean		4.3445	.04072
	95% Confidence Interval for Mean	Lower Bound	4.2644	
		Upper Bound	4.4246	
	5% Trimmed Mean		4.3499	
	Median		4.3750	
	Variance		.559	
	Std. Deviation		.74757	
	Minimum		2.13	
	Maximum		6.38	
	Range		4.25	
	Interquartile Range		1.13	
	Skewness		−.187	.133
	Kurtosis		−.232	.265
INDCOLC Collectivism	Mean		5.5443	.03164
	95% Confidence Interval for Mean	Lower Bound	5.4821	
		Upper Bound	5.6065	
	5% Trimmed Mean		5.5607	
	Median		5.6250	
	Variance		.337	
	Std. Deviation		.58077	
	Minimum		3.38	
	Maximum		6.88	
	Range		3.50	
	Interquartile Range		.75	
	Skewness		−.475	.133
	Kurtosis		.371	.265
MEIMEIC Ethnic Identity Commitment	Mean		3.5673	.04871
	95% Confidence Interval for Mean	Lower Bound	3.4714	
		Upper Bound	3.6631	
	5% Trimmed Mean		3.5890	
	Median		3.6667	
	Variance		.800	
	Std. Deviation		.89426	
	Minimum		1.00	
	Maximum		5.00	
	Range		4.00	
	Interquartile Range		1.00	
	Skewness		−.335	.133
	Kurtosis		−.347	.265
MEIMEIE Ethic Identity Exploration	Mean		3.6123	.04722
	95% Confidence Interval for Mean	Lower Bound	3.5194	
		Upper Bound	3.7051	

than the one on row 105, information we knew because we had performed the **Frequencies** procedure earlier.

The histogram for **INDICOLI** is identical to the one we produced in our Frequencies analysis (see Figure 3b.6), except for the superimposition of the normal curve, and we will not show it here. The **Stem-and-leaf plot** for the four variables can be seen in Figure 3b.44. These stem-and-leaf plots indicate that **INDCOLI** has a reasonably normal-looking distribution and that it has no univariate outliers, and that **INDCOLC, MEIMEIC**, and **MEIMEIE** had only a few extreme cases.

The stem-and-leaf findings are confirmed with the box plots of the total sample for each continuous variable shown in Figures 3b.45 and 3b.46. With regard to univariate outliers, however, the box plots provide us with an additional ingredient over the stem-and-leaf plots—the actual case number for the outliers on each variable as also shown in the **Extreme Values** table. Here we can see that **Case Numbers** 140, 243, 222, and 177 on the INDCOLC variable, Case Numbers 312 and 106 on the **MEIMEIC** variable (the box plot did not capture all of the potential outliers as the **Extreme Values** table also identified **Case Number** 215 with the same value as these other two), and **Case Numbers** 209, 106, and 164 (it did not report **Case Number** 235) on the **MEIMEIE** variable are possible candidates for deletion. In particular, because Case 106 appears to be an outlier on both **INDCOLC** and **MEIMEIE**, we would recommend its elimination from future analyses. Note that the **Extreme Values** table, with more complete information, allows us to identify other cases having missing values on multiple variables.

3B.9 Normality

3B.9.1 Assessing Normality

To address the issue of univariate normality for the quantitative (metric) variables **INDCOLI, INDCOLC, MEIMEIC, MEIMEIE**, and a new variable, depression, we begin by examining the skewness and kurtosis values for these variables. We know from the results of our previous **Frequencies** (see Figure 3b.5) and **Explore** (see Figure 3b.42) procedures that there were very modest levels of negative and positive skewness and

Figure 3b.43 Extreme Values

Extreme Values

			Case Number	Value
INDCOLI Individualism	Highest	1	323	6.38
		2	7	6.00
		3	273	6.00
		4	300	6.00
		5	105	5.75 [a]
	Lowest	1	132	2.13
		2	166	2.25
		3	253	2.33
		4	61	2.50
		5	52	2.50
INDCOLC Collectivism	Highest	1	186	6.88
		2	80	6.75
		3	173	6.75
		4	308	6.75
		5	65	6.63 [b]
	Lowest	1	177	3.38
		2	243	3.88
		3	222	3.88
		4	140	4.00
		5	214	4.13 [c]
MEIMEIC Ethnic Identity Commitment	Highest	1	38	5.00
		2	94	5.00
		3	104	5.00
		4	109	5.00
		5	112	5.00 [d]
	Lowest	1	312	1.00
		2	255	1.00
		3	106	1.00
		4	259	1.67
		5	235	1.67 [e]
MEIMEIE Ethic Identity Exploration	Highest	1	62	5.00
		2	94	5.00
		3	97	5.00
		4	104	5.00
		5	109	5.00 [d]
	Lowest	1	164	1.00
		2	235	1.33
		3	209	1.33
		4	106	1.33
		5	312	1.67 [e]

a. Only a partial list of cases with the value 5.75 are shown in the table of upper extremes.

b. Only a partial list of cases with the value 6.63 are shown in the table of upper extremes.

c. Only a partial list of cases with the value 4.13 are shown in the table of lower extremes.

d. Only a partial list of cases with the value 5.00 are shown in the table of upper extremes.

e. Only a partial list of cases with the value 1.67 are shown in the table of lower extremes.

Figure 3b.44 Stem-and-Leaf Plot for **INDCOLI** and **INDCOLC**

INDCOLI Individualism

Individualism Stem-and-Leaf Plot

```
Frequency    Stem & Leaf

     3.00     2 .  123
     6.00     2 .  558888
    29.00     3 .  00001111111112222222222333333
    64.00     3 .  5555555555555555555566666666666666677777777777777778888888888888888
    79.00     4 .  00000000000011111111111111111111112222222222222222223333333333333333333333333
    82.00     4 .  5555555555555666666666666666666666666677777777777777777777778888888888888888888888
    53.00     5 .  0000000000000000000011111111111112222222222222222333333
    17.00     5 .  55556666667777777
     4.00     6 .  0003

Stem width:     1.00
Each leaf:      1 case(s)
```

INDCOLC Collectivism

Collectivism Stem-and-Leaf Plot

```
Frequency    Stem & Leaf

     4.00 Extremes   (=<4.0)
     3.00     4 .  111
     7.00     4 .  2233333
     7.00     4 .  4455555
    17.00     4 .  66666667777777777
     9.00     4 .  888888888
    33.00     5 .  000000000000000011111111111111111
    53.00     5 .  22222222222222222222333333333333333333333333333333333
    34.00     5 .  4455555555555555555555555555555555
    57.00     5 .  666666666666666666666666677777777777777777777777777777777
    23.00     5 .  88888888888888888888888
    52.00     6 .  0000000000000000000000000000011111111111111111111111
    21.00     6 .  222222222233333333333
     7.00     6 .  4555555
     9.00     6 .  666666777
     1.00     6 .  8

Stem width:     1.00
Each leaf:      1 case(s)
```

MEIMEIC Ethnic Identity Commitment

Ethnic Identity Commitment Stem-and-Leaf Plot

```
Frequency    Stem & Leaf

     3.00 Extremes   (=<1.0)
     4.00     1 .  66
    40.00     2 .  00000000000033333333
    22.00     2 .  66666666666
    77.00     3 .  0000000000000000000333333333333333333
    32.00     3 .  666666666666666&
   109.00     4 .  000000000000000000000000000000000000000000000033333333
    12.00     4 .  666666
    38.00     5 .  0000000000000000000

Stem width:     1.00
Each leaf:      2 case(s)
```

& denotes fractional leaves.

MEIMEIE Ethic Identity Exploration

Ethic Identity Exploration Stem-and-Leaf Plot

```
Frequency    Stem & Leaf

     4.00 Extremes   (=<1.3)
     4.00     1 .  66
    33.00     2 .  0000000000033333333
    21.00     2 .  6666666666
    79.00     3 .  0000000000000000000033333333333333333333
    29.00     3 .  6666666666666666
   123.00     4 .  000000000000000000000000000000000000000000000033333333333333333
     9.00     4 .  6666
    35.00     5 .  00000000000000000

Stem width:     1.00
Each leaf:      2 case(s)
```

Figure 3b.45 Box Plots for **INDCOLI** and **INDCOLC**

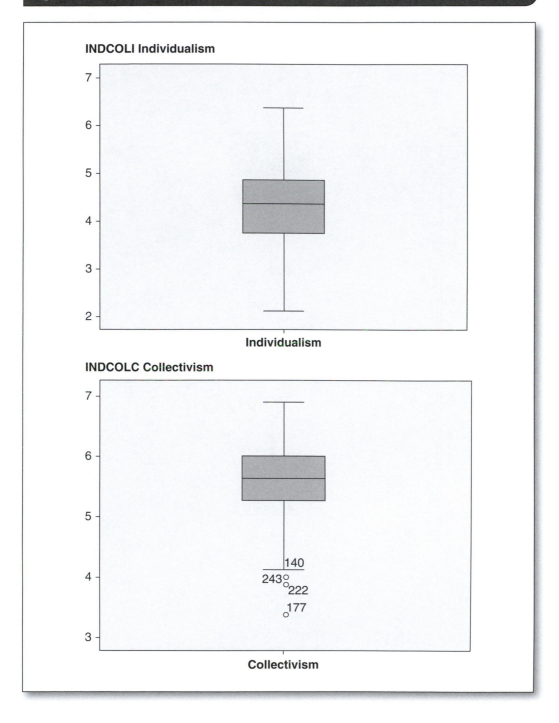

Figure 3b.46 Box Plots for **MEIMEIC** and **MEIMEIE**

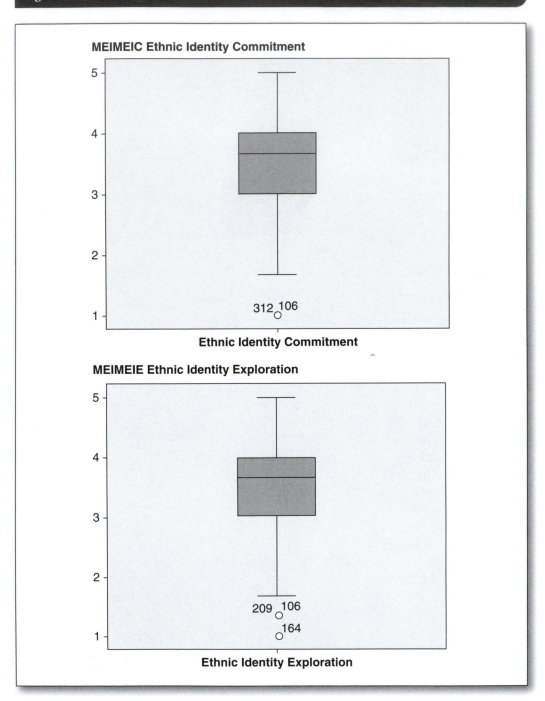

kurtosis (values range from −.187 to .371) for the **INDCOLI, INDCOLC, MEIMEIC,** and **MEIMEIE** distributions. Because these skewness and kurtosis values are within the ±1.0 range, they are likely to be normally distributed, and we deem them tentatively acceptable for our current purposes.

We have introduced the **depression** variable to illustrate a more substantial departure from normality. As described in Section 3B.2, performing a **Frequencies** procedure on **depression** (we will not repeat showing the dialog windows here) yields the descriptive statistics shown in Figure 3b.47. Of interest here is the skewness value of 2.611 and kurtosis value of 9.144. These values are brought to life by examining the histogram shown in Figure 3b.48.

Figure 3b.47 Descriptive Statistics for Depression

Statistics

depression

N	Valid	371
	Missing	0
Mean		5.85
Median		5.00
Std. Deviation		5.334
Skewness		2.611
Std. Error of Skewness		.127
Kurtosis		9.144
Std. Error of Kurtosis		.253
Minimum		1
Maximum		38

The positive skewness can be seen by the bulk of the scores toward the left and a tail pointed toward the right; the positive kurtosis (leptokurtosis) represents the scores being compressed in the lower region of the scoring continuum. It is safe to say based on this information that this distribution is far from normal.

A more complete assessment of normality can be accomplished through the **Explore** procedure. For comparison purposes, we will also analyze **INDCOLI**, although we could have selected any of the four quantitative variables we have focused on throughout this chapter. From the main menu, select **Analyze ➤ Descriptive Statistics ➤ Explore**. We have moved **INDCOLI** and **depression** into the **Dependent List** panel as shown in Figure 3b.49.

We have generated the descriptive statistics for these variables already and can therefore proceed directly to the **Plots** screen shown in Figure 3b.50. Again, because we have produced histograms for these variables earlier, there is no need to do so again. Instead, we check **Normality plots with tests**, click **Continue** to return to the main dialog window, and click **OK** to perform the analysis.

The two tests of normality for our variables computed by IBM SPSS, the Kolmogorov–Smirnov test and Shapiro–Wilk test, are shown in Figure 3b.51. The null hypothesis that is tested is that the obtained distribution of the variable is normal. As can be seen, the Kolmogorov–Smirnov test returned a statistically significant result for both variables, suggesting that both distributions are significantly different from what would be expected on the basis of a normal distribution; the Shapiro–Wilk test was almost as powerful, returning

Figure 3b.48 Histogram of Depression

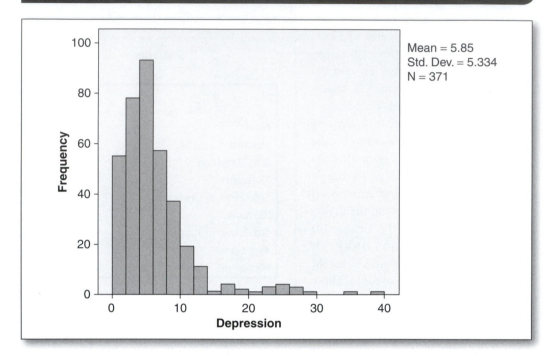

Figure 3b.49 The Main Dialog Screen for Explore

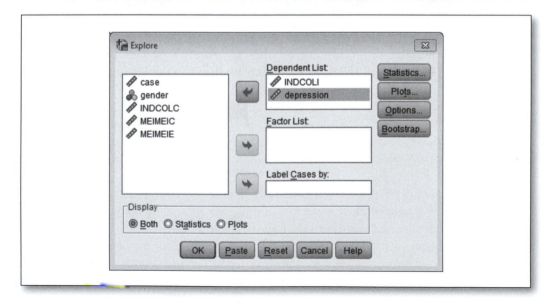

a statistically significant result for **depression** and a not-quite-significant result ($p = .051$) for **INDCOLI**. Both of these tests are very sensitive to minor (trivial) departures from normality especially with the sample size we have here—Shapiro and Wilk (1965) limited their test to sample sizes of 50 (D'Agostino, 1971)—so we need to take these results more as mildly suggestive than as definitive.

IBM SPSS also produces two normal Q–Q plots, a standard one and a detrended one; our focus is on the standard plot (the detrended plot has removed the linear trend in the data). A Q–Q plot graphs each observed value against a value that would be expected if the distribution were normal. This plot gets its name from the term *quantiles*, which are points taken at regular intervals in a cumulative distribution. A diagonal line angled from the lower left to upper right is drawn on the Q–Q plot such that, if an observed distribution were completely normal, all of the plotted points would fall directly on the line.

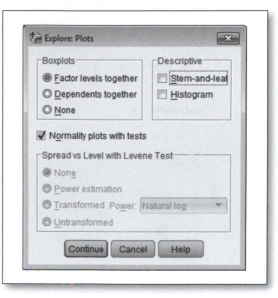

Figure 3b.50 The Plots Screen for Explore

The standard Q–Q plots for **INDCOLI** and **depression** are shown in the upper and lower graphs, respectively, in Figure 3b.52. The data points for **INDCOLI** are extremely close to the main diagonal line in the Q–Q plot. In conjunction with its skewness and kurtosis values and an inspection of its histogram, we can conclude that **INDCOLI** is distributed in an approximately normal manner. In contrast, many of the coordinate data points for **depression** depart quite far from the main diagonal line in the Q–Q plot. In conjunction with its skewness and

Figure 3b.51 Tests of Normality

Tests of Normality

	Kolmogorov–Smirnov[a]			Shapiro–Wilk		
	Statistic	df	Sig.	Statistic	df	Sig.
INDCOLI Individualism	.065	359	.001	.992	359	.051
depression	.182	359	.000	.734	359	.000

a. Lilliefors Significance Correction

Figure 3b.52   Normal Q–Q plots

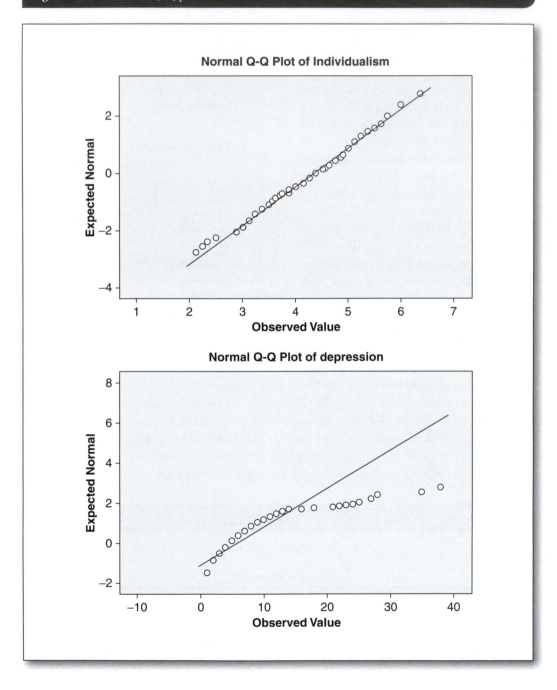

kurtosis values and an inspection of its histogram, we can conclude that **depression** is distributed in a manner quite different from normal and, thus, fails to meet the normality assumption for most of our multivariate procedures.

3B.9.2 Transforming Variables to Achieve Normality

From the output shown in Figure 3b.47, we note that the distribution of scores for the **depression** variable shows considerable positive skewness (2.611) and positive kurtosis (9.144) and is therefore a good candidate for transformation. Following our discussion of variable transformations in Section 3A.13, we choose to transform **depression** with a base-10 logarithm.

To accomplish this transformation, select from the main menu **Transform ➔ Compute Variable**, which produces the dialog screen shown in Figure 3b.53. In the top left corner is the **Target Variable** panel, where we enter a name for the new variable we are creating. We will call this new variable **log10depression**. The top right section of the window contains the **Numeric Expression** panel. Below this panel is the **Function group list**. Click **Arithmetic,**

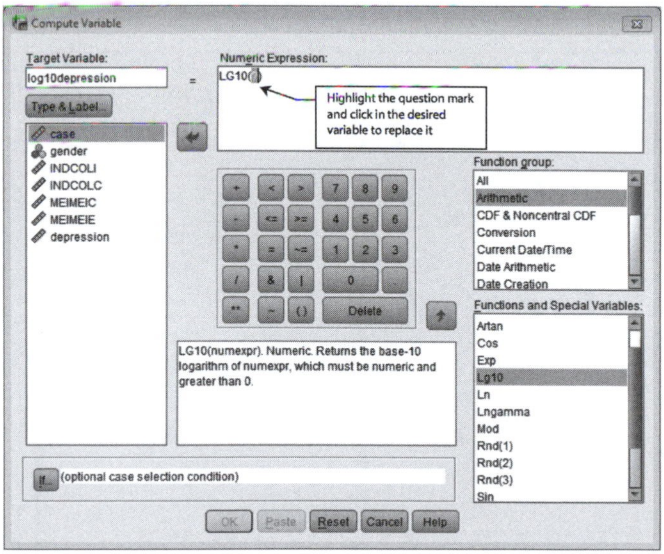

Figure 3b.53   The Compute Variable Screen With the Log 10 Function Selected

which activates a list of arithmetic functions in the companion panel **Functions and Special Variables** directly below the **Function group** panel. Scroll down on the **Function and Special Variables** list to the **Lg10** (log base-10) numeric expression, highlight it, and then click the up-arrow button to move **Lg10** into the **Numeric Expression** panel. When completed, the **Lg10** function appears in the **Numeric Expression** panel followed by a question mark enclosed in parentheses. This is shown in Figure 3b.53.

The question mark is a placeholder for a variable. To swap it out for the variable that is to be transformed, do the following in this order:

1. Highlight the question mark.

2. Highlight the variable in the variable list to be transformed (**depression** in this example).

3. Click the arrow button just to the lower left of the **Numeric Expression** panel (the arrow will be pointing toward the **Numeric Expression** panel).

When these steps have been completed, **depression** will have replaced the question mark in the parentheses, and the screen should look like the one shown in Figure 3b.54. Click **OK** and the new variable **L10dep** is saved to the end of the data file as shown in Figure 3b.55.

Figure 3b.54   The Compute Variable Screen With **Depression** Ready to Be Transformed

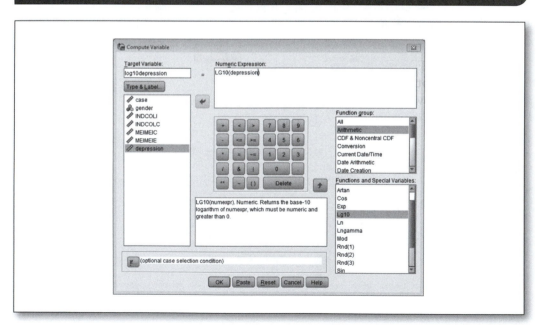

Figure 3b.55   The New Variable **log10Depression** Is Placed at the End of the Data File

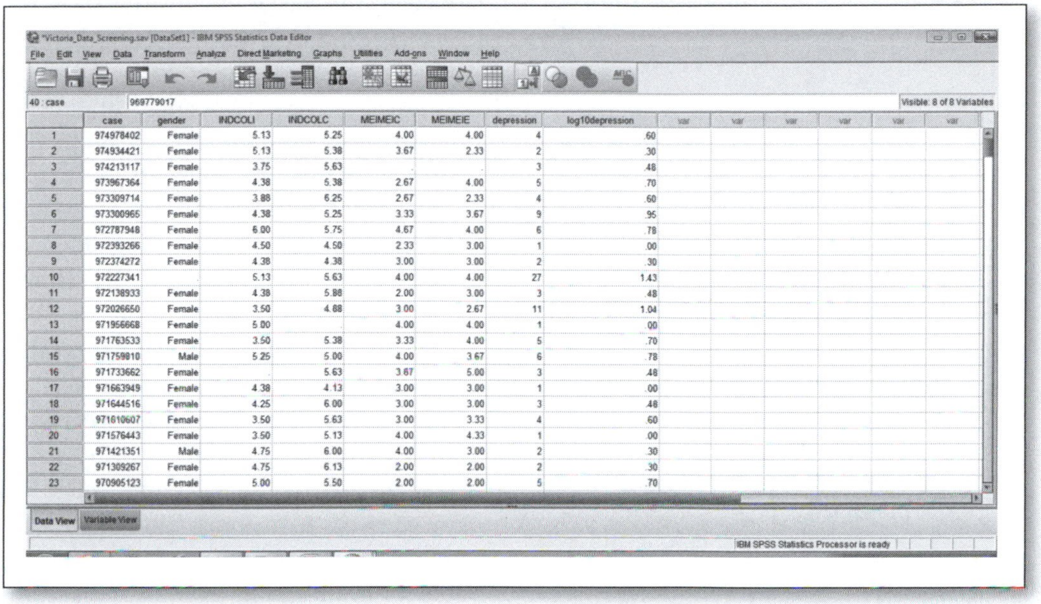

To assess our "handiwork" on our newly transformed variable, we navigate through **Analyze** ➜ **Descriptive Statistics** ➜ **Explore**. This produces the **Explore** main dialog window, and we have selected both depression and **log10depression** (see Figure 3b.56), chosen **Descriptives** in the **Statistics** window (see Figure 3b.57), and checked **Histogram** and **Normality plots with tests** in the **Plots** window (see Figure 3b.58). Click **Continue** to return to the main dialog screen, and click **OK** to perform the analysis.

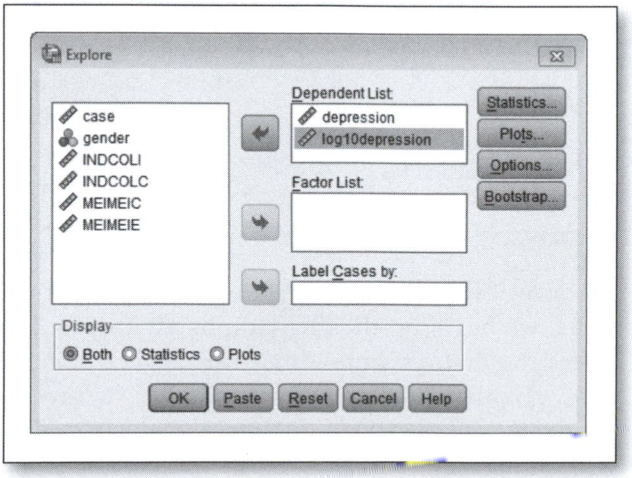

Figure 3b.59 displays descriptive statistics on the newly computed variable **log10depression** as well as the original **depression** variable (so we can compare the two). The transformation of

Figure 3b.56   The Main Dialog Screen for Explore

Figure 3b.57 The Statistics Screen for Explore

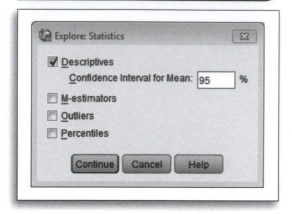

Figure 3b.58 The Plots Screen for Explore

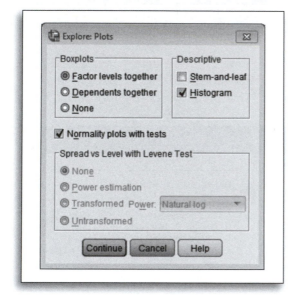

the **depression** variable into **log10depression** was successful and has reduced considerably this variable's positive skewness (e.g., from 2.611 to −.137) and kurtosis (e.g., from 9.144 to −.362). Although skewness and kurtosis are still present, they are now within acceptable limits (i.e., between ±1.0). Nonetheless, both the Kolmogorov–Smirnov and Shapiro–Wilk tests inform us that even the **log10depression** variable significantly departs from a completely normal distribution.

The histogram of **log10depression** shown in Figure 3b.60 is quite revealing. Compared with **depression** (see Figure 3b.48), **log10depression** appears to be substantially less skewed and much less compressed. It may not look like a normal distribution, but it should be acceptable for multivariate analysis. This seems to be confirmed by the normal Q–Q plot (see Figure 3b.61). Unlike **depression** (see Figure 3b.52), **log10depression** appears to be hovering relatively close to the main diagonal.

3B.10 Linearity

To determine if our quantitative variables are linearly related to each other, we will run IBM SPSS **Graphs** to examine the shape of the bivariate scatterplots for each combination of variables. Scatterplots that are elliptical or oval shaped are indicative of linearity between two variables. To produce these plots, we begin by clicking **Graphs ➔ Legacy Dialogs ➔ Scatter/Dot**, which produces the dialog window shown in Figure 3b.62. Five scatterplot options are available. Highlight **Matrix Scatter**, and click the **Define** pushbutton, which in turn produces the **Scatterplot Matrix** dialog window (see Figure 3b.63). Move over

Figure 3b.59 Descriptive Statistics and Tests of Normality

Descriptives

			Statistic	Std. Error
depression	Mean		5.85	.277
	95% Confidence Interval for Mean	Lower Bound	5.31	
		Upper Bound	6.40	
	5% Trimmed Mean		5.11	
	Median		5.00	
	Variance		28.449	
	Std. Deviation		5.334	
	Minimum		1	
	Maximum		38	
	Range		37	
	Interquartile Range		5	
	Skewness		2.611	.127
	Kurtosis		9.144	.253
log10depression	Mean		.6234	.01884
	95% Confidence Interval for Mean	Lower Bound	.5863	
		Upper Bound	.6604	
	5% Trimmed Mean		.6165	
	Median		.6990	
	Variance		.132	
	Std. Deviation		.36283	
	Minimum		.00	
	Maximum		1.58	
	Range		1.58	
	Interquartile Range		.54	
	Skewness		-.137	.127
	Kurtosis		-.362	.253

Tests of Normality

	Kolmogorov–Smirnov[a]			Shapiro–Wilk		
	Statistic	df	Sig.	Statistic	df	Sig.
depression	.181	371	.000	.744	371	.000
log10depression	.118	371	.000	.953	371	.000

a. Lilliefors Significance Correction

INDCOLI, INDCOLC, MEIMEIE, MEIMEIC, and **log10depression** into the **Matrix Variables** panel, and then click **OK.**

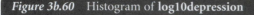

Figure 3b.60 Histogram of **log10depression**

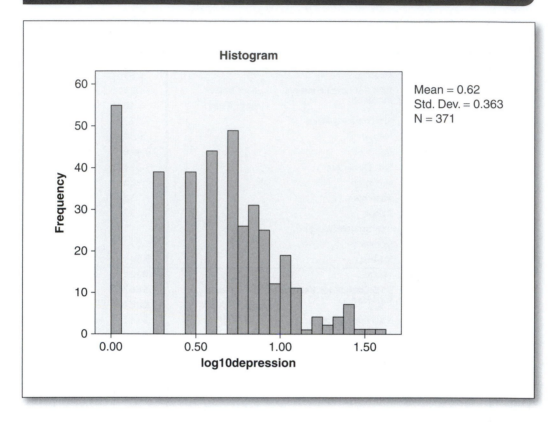

The scatterplot matrix output of the five continuous variables is presented in Figure 3b.64. This output is a matrix of the pairwise scatterplots in miniature form. Although certainly not perfect ovals, for present illustrative purposes, these scatterplots appear to depict enough linearity in the relationships of the variables to proceed with the analysis.

3B.11 Multivariate Outliers

To check for multivariate outliers among the quantitative variables, we need to calculate Mahalanobis distance for each case. This statistic is a measure of how much a case's values on the designated variables differ from the average of all cases. A large Mahalanobis distance identifies a case as having extreme values on one or more of those variables.

Figure 3b.61 Normal Q–Q plot of **log10depression**

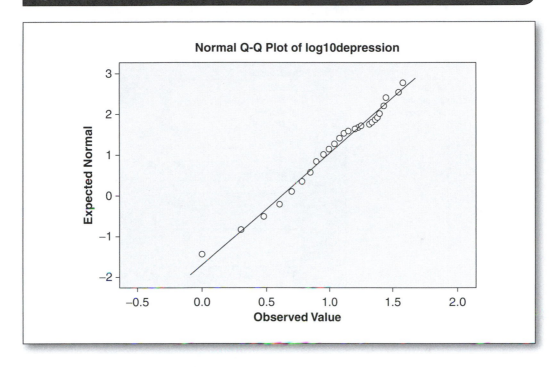

Figure 3b.62 Scatter/Dot Selection Screen

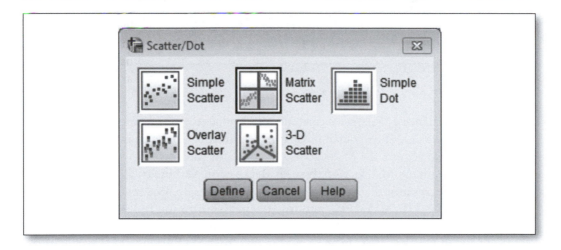

Figure 3b.63 Scatterplot Matrix Dialog Screen

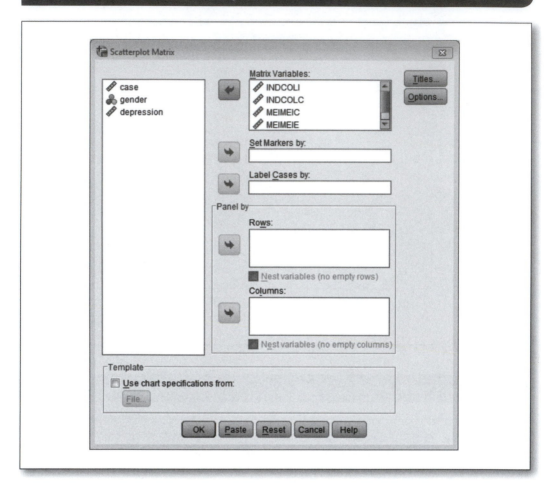

Mahalanobis distance is relatively conveniently available within **Linear Regression**, a procedure that we describe in detail in Chapter 7A; for our present purposes, we use this procedure only to acquire the Mahalanobis distance for each case.

From the main menu, select **Analyze ➜ Regression ➜ Linear**, which produces the main **Linear Regression** dialog window shown in Figure 3b.65. Move over **INDCOLI**, **INDCOLC, MEIMEIE, MEIMEIC**, and **log10depression** to the **Independent**(s) panel. When we request Mahalanobis distance, it is these variables that have been identified as the **Independent** variables in the analysis on which the distance measure is based. The **Linear Regression** procedure requires us to specify **a Dependent** variable, and so we arbitrarily designate Case to be moved into the **Dependent** panel. The results of the

Mahalanobis distance calculation are based entirely on the variables listed in the **Independent**(s) panel, and so the dependent variable in the analysis is irrelevant for our current purpose—although we have chosen to "predict" the **Case** variable to make it obvious that the results of the "prediction" are meaningless (and not of any interest here), users can select any variable they wish to serve the purely heuristic function of dependent variable.

Click the Save pushbutton. Select the **Mahalanobis** checkbox in the **Distances** panel (see Figure 3b.66), click **Continue** to return to the main dialog window, and click **OK** to perform the analysis.

Ignore the output, which is meaningless because we were predicting **Case** number. What we wished to obtain was the Mahalanobis distances for each case. Our **Save** command resulted in a new variable called **MAH_1**, which is the Mahalanobis distance values for each case on the five continuous variables, to be placed at the end of the data file as shown in Figure 3b.67.

The Mahalanobis distance values are evaluated with a chi-square (χ^2) distribution, with degrees of freedom equal to the number of variables clicked into the **Independent**(s) area (five in this case). We can assess the magnitude of the Mahalanobis distance values by consulting a *Table of Critical Values* for chi-square at a stringent alpha level of $p < .001$ (see Table A2 in Appendix A). In the present

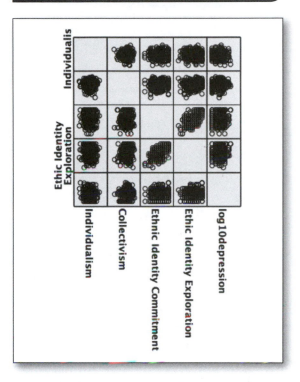

Figure 3b.64 Scatterplot Matrix Output

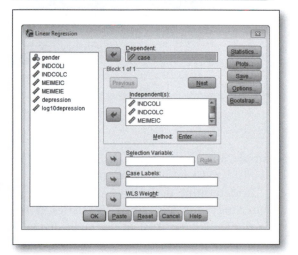

Figure 3b.65 The Main Dialog Window of Linear Regression

Figure 3b.66   The Save Dialog Window of Linear Regression

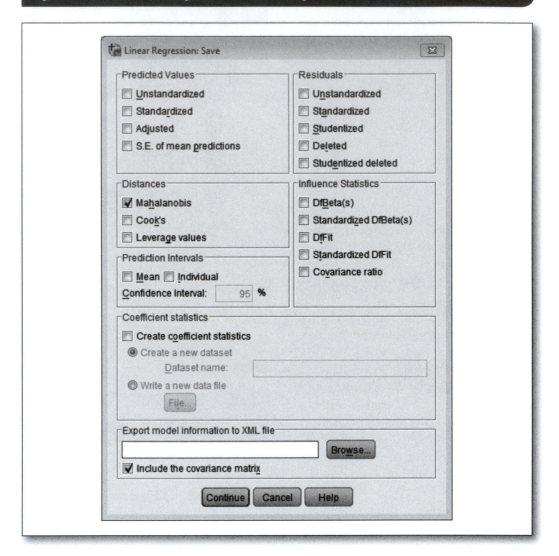

example, any case with a Mahalanobis distance value equal to or greater than 20.515 can be considered a multivariate outlier.

To determine if we have any potential multivariate outliers, select from the main menu **Analyze ➔ Descriptive Statistics ➔ Explore**, move over the new variable **MAH_1** into the **Dependent List** in the main dialog window (see Figure 3b.68), check **Outliers** in the **Statistics** screen and deselect **Descriptives** as we already have that information

Figure 3b.67 The Mahalanobis Distance for Each Case Appears as a New Variable, **MAH_1** at the End of the Data File

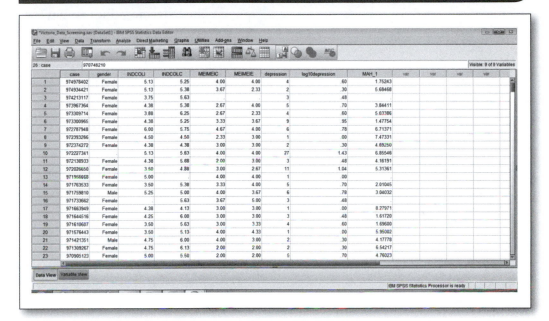

Figure 3b.68 The Main Dialog Window of Explore

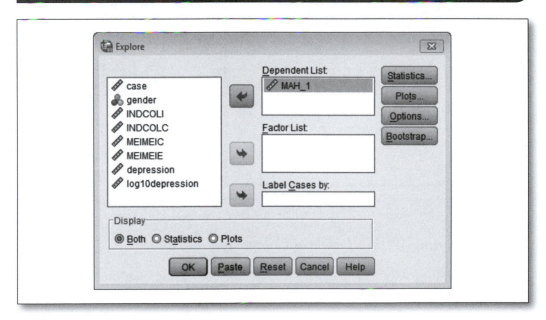

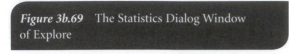

Figure 3b.69 The Statistics Dialog Window of Explore

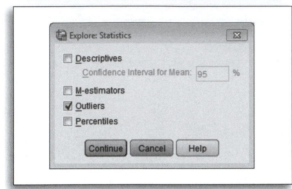

(see Figure 3b.69), click **Continue** to return to the main dialog window, and click **OK** to perform the analysis.

The **Extreme Values** output (i.e., the five highest and lowest cases) for the **MAH_1** variable are shown in Figure 3b.70. From this output, we note that the critical value associated with **Case Number 164** exceeds 20.515 (the actual value is 20.82989) and indicates that this particular case is a multivariate outlier and is a good candidate for elimination from the analysis.

Figure 3b.70 Extreme Values for Mahalanobis Distances

Extreme Values

			Case Number	Value
MAH_1 Mahalanobis Distance	Highest	1	164	20.82989
		2	222	19.03974
		3	177	18.98555
		4	253	16.63359
		5	80	15.24770
	Lowest	1	338	.29705
		2	119	.67628
		3	175	.72193
		4	348	.75399
		5	90	.79111

3B.12 Screening Within Levels of Categorical Variables

When our multivariate data analysis plan calls for comparing distributional statistics (e.g., means) for quantitative variables across two or more groups (levels of a categorical variable), it is important to consider the data for each group or level of the variable in question. To keep our example simple, assume that we are interested in the differences between females and males (the two levels of **gender**) on the variable **INDCOLI**. Because we will use here many of the procedures we have already covered, we will not show many of the dialog windows that have been already discussed—sometimes several times—in this chapter.

3B.12.1 The Distribution of Gender

We begin by inspecting the frequency output for **gender** by selecting **Analyze ➔ Descriptive Statistics ➔ Frequencies**, identifying **gender** as the variable to be analyzed, and checking the **Display frequency table** in the main dialog window. The output can be seen in Figure 3b.71. The categorical **gender** variable is disproportionately split: 16.1% of the cases who gave us this information (**Valid Percent**) were male and 83.9% of them were female; ideally we would prefer to have a fairly even split on this dichotomous variable. Because this is not an extreme or unusual bifurcation (e.g., 90% for one and 10% for the other), we will leave this variable as is and proceed with our screening. We also note that the **gender** variable contains no apparent code violations (i.e., all the values were **1**s and **2**s) and that there were 11 missing values.

Figure 3b.71 The Distribution of Gender

gender

		Frequency	Percent	Valid Percent	Cumulative Percent
Valid	1 Male	58	15.6	16.1	16.1
	2 Female	302	81.4	83.9	100.0
	Total	360	97.0	100.0	
Missing	System	11	3.0		
Total		371	100.0		

3B.12.2 Univariate Outliers

Our goal here will be to check for outliers (cases with extreme values) on **INDCOLI** within each level (or group) of **gender**. We accomplish this by selecting **Analyze ➔ Descriptive**

Figure 3b.72 The Main Dialog Window of Explore

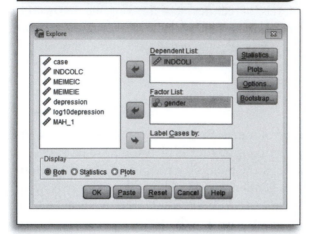

Statistics ➜ **Explore**, where we click over **INDCOLI** into the **Dependent List** and **gender** into the **Factor List** (see Figure 3b.72), select the **Outliers** checkbox in the **Statistics** window, and **Boxplots Dependent together** and **Stem-and-leaf** in the **Plots** window.

The two stem-and-leaf plots shown in Figure 3b.73 indicate that neither the male nor the female groups contain extremely high or low values on **INDCOLI**. This result is also confirmed in the **Extreme Values** (see Figure 3b.74) and box plot outputs (see Figure 3b.75).

Figure 3b.73 Stem-and-Leaf Plots for Males and Females on **INDCOLI**

INDCOLI Individualism

Stem-and-Leaf Plots

Individualism Stem-and-Leaf Plot for
gender= Male

```
Frequency    Stem &  Leaf

      1.00     2 .  8
      6.00     3 .  223333
     14.00     3 .  55555566688888
     13.00     4 .  0112222222233
     13.00     4 .  5666667778888
      7.00     5 .  0122233
      3.00     5 .  577

Stem width:      1.00
Each leaf:       1 case(s)
```

Individualism Stem-and-Leaf Plot for
gender= Female

```
Frequency    Stem &  Leaf

      3.00     2 .  123
      5.00     2 .  55888
     24.00     3 .  000011111111122222223333
     52.00     3 .  5555555555555566666666666677777777777777777778888888888
     75.00     4 .  000000000001111111111111111111122222222222222222333333333333333333333333333
     66.00     4 .  555555555566666666666666666677777777777777777788888888888888888888
     48.00     5 .  000000000000000000000001111111111222222222223333
     15.00     5 .  555666666777777
      4.00     6 .  0003

Stem width:      1.00
Each leaf:       1 case(s)
```

Figure 3b.74 Extreme Values for Males and Females on **INDCOLI**

Extreme Values

	gender				Case Number	Value
INDCOLI Individualism	1 Male	Highest	1		212	5.75
			2		288	5.75
			3		177	5.50
			4		197	5.38
			5		326	5.38
		Lowest	1		196	2.88
			2		355	3.25
			3		283	3.25
			4		217	3.38
			5		211	3.38a
	2 Female	Highest	1		323	6.38
			2		7	6.00
			3		273	6.00
			4		300	6.00
			5		105	5.75b
		Lowest	1		132	2.13
			2		166	2.25
			3		253	2.33
			4		61	2.50
			5		52	2.50

a. Only a partial list of cases with the value 3.38 are shown in the table of lower extremes.

b. Only a partial list of cases with the value 5.75 are shown in the table of upper extremes.

Figure 3b.75 Box Plots for Males and Females on **INDCOLI**

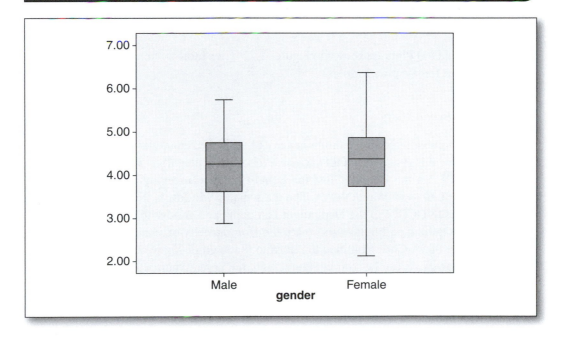

3B.12.3 Normality

After missing values and outliers have been addressed, we can check to see if **INDCOLI** is normally distributed across levels of **gender**. Select **Analyze ➜ Descriptive Statistics ➜ Explore**, place **INDCOLI** into the **Dependent List** and **gender** into the **Factor List**, and select the **Normality plots with tests** in the **Plots** window.

The Kolmogorov–Smirnov and the Shapiro–Wilk tests (see Figure 3b.76) were not significant at the .01 alpha level, with the exception of the Kolmogorov–Smirnov test for females ($p < .009$). We recommend the .01 level as a suitably stringent alpha level with these tests because of their sensitivity to any normality departures and particularly with small sample sizes. Had these normality tests been consistently statistically significant ($p < .01$), then transformation of the continuous variable, in the present example, **INDCOLI**, would potentially have been in order.

Figure 3b.76 Tests of Normality for Males and Females on **INDCOLI**

Tests of Normality

	gender	Kolmogorov-Smirnov_a			Shapiro–Wilk		
		Statistic	df	Sig.	Statistic	df	Sig.
INDCOLI Individualism	1 Male	.104	57	.195	.968	57	.141
	2 Female	.062	292	.009	.992	292	.103

a. Lilliefors Significance Correction

The normal **Q-Q Plots** are shown in Figure 3b.77. They indicate normality for **INDCOLI** across **male** and **female** practitioners.

3B.12.4 Homoscedasticity

To assess homoscedasticity or homogeneity of variance (equal variance) of the dependent variable (in this case, **INDCOLI**) across levels of the categorical variable (in this case, gender), we will run the **Levene's Test for Equality of Variances** by clicking **Analyze ➜ Compare Means ➜ One-Way ANOVA**. The main dialog window is shown in Figure 3b.78. We have moved **INDCOLI** to the **Dependent List** panel and **gender** to the **Factor** panel.

Select the **Options** pushbutton and mark the **Homogeneity of variance test** checkbox as shown in Figure 3b.79. Click Continue to return to the main dialog window, and click **OK** to perform the analysis. As can be seen in Figure 3b.80, the Levene statistic is not statistically significant ($p > .05$), telling us that there are equal variances across levels of **gender** on **INDCOLI**.

Figure 3b.77 Q–Q Plots for Males and Females on **INDCOLI**

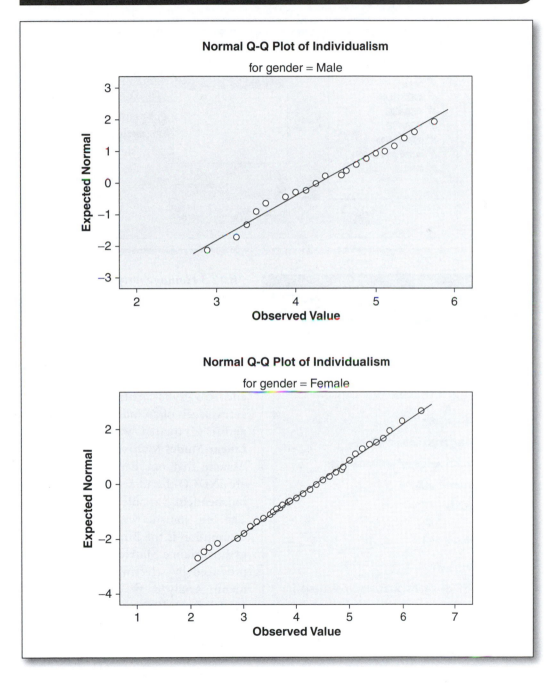

Figure 3b.78 The Main Dialog Window of One-Way ANOVA

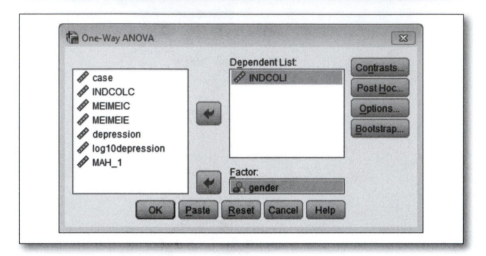

Figure 3b.79 The Options Dialog Window of One-Way ANOVA

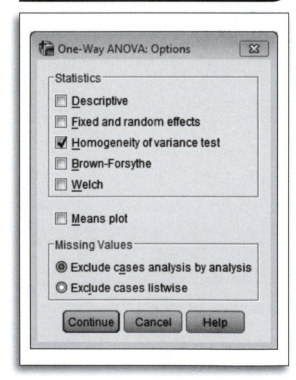

3B.12.5 Homogeneity of Variance–Covariance Matrices

The "next of kin" of the homoscedasticity assumption is the multivariate homogeneity of variance–covariance assumption, where the equality of variance–covariance matrices is examined across levels of an independent variable and is evaluated with the **General Linear Model Multivariate** procedure. Assume that our dependent variables are **INDCOLI** and **INDCOLC** and the independent variable remains gender. The test statistic we use to test this assumption is the **Box Test of Equality of Covariance Matrices**, which can be produced by selecting from the main menu **Analyze ➜ General Linear Model ➜ Multivariate**.

The main **Multivariate** dialog window is shown in Figure 3b.81. We move **INDCOLI** and **INDCOLC** to the **Dependent Variables** panel and move **gender** to the **Fixed Factor**(s) panel.

Click the **Options** pushbutton where we mark the **Homogeneity tests** checkbox in the **Options** window (see Figure 3b.82). Click **Continue** to return to the main dialog window, and click **OK** to perform the analysis.

The output table we want to examine is shown in Figure 3b.83. From that output, we can see that Box's test is

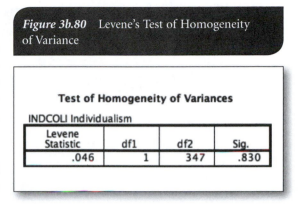

Figure 3b.80 Levene's Test of Homogeneity of Variance

Test of Homogeneity of Variances

INDCOLI Individualism

Levene Statistic	df1	df2	Sig.
.046	1	347	.830

Figure 3b.81 The Main Dialog Window of Multivariate

statistically significant ($p < .01$), suggesting that we do not have equality of variance–covariance matrices in this example. This heterogeneity of our variance–covariance matrices is probably due to the unequal numbers of males and females in the analysis.

Figure 3b.82 The Options Dialog Window of Multivariate

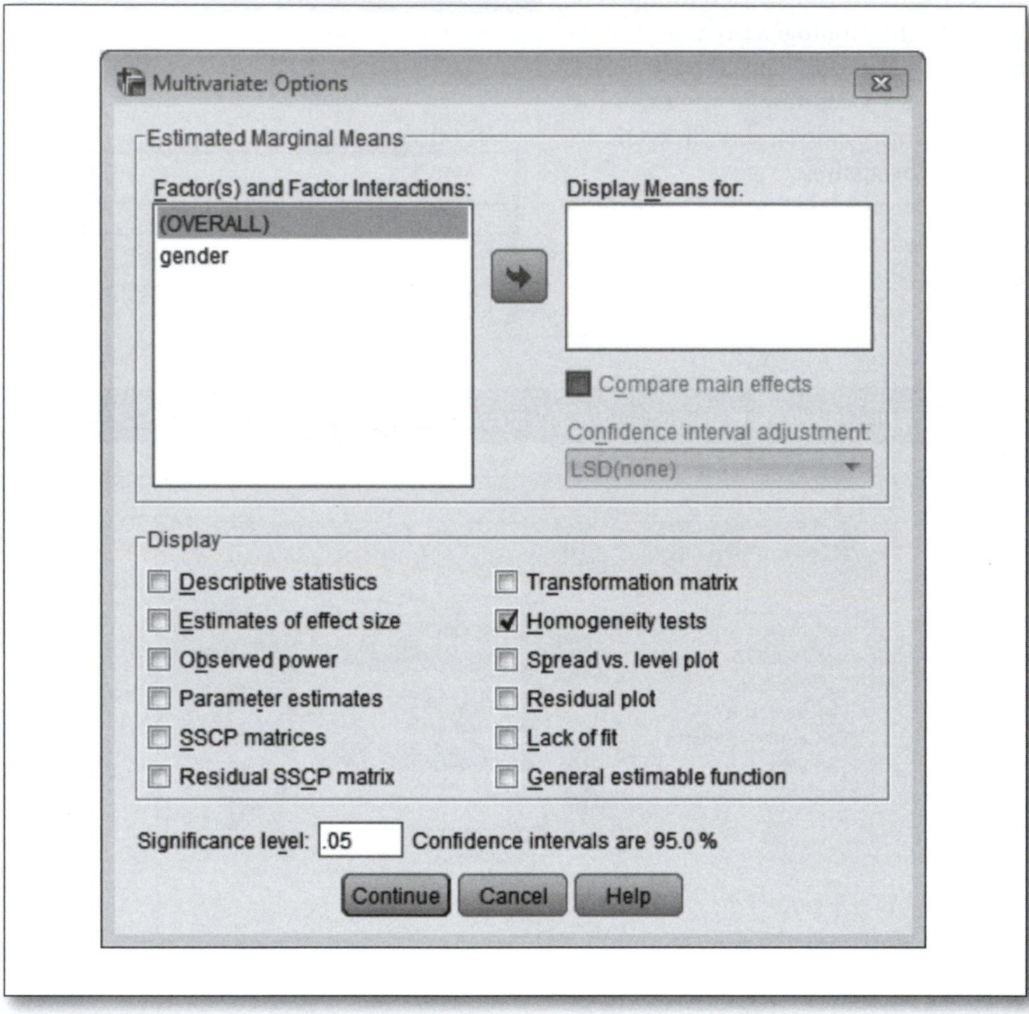

3B.13 Reporting the Results

Before proceeding with the data analysis, all variables were screened for possible code and statistical assumption violations, as well as for missing values and outliers, with IBM SPSS Frequencies, Explore, Plot, Missing Value Analysis, and Regression procedures. The 371 child mental health practitioners were screened for missing values on four initial continuous variables (INDCOLI, INDCOLC, MEIMEIE, and MEIMEIC). Using a variety of techniques, the 10 to 12 missing values per variable that were discovered were replaced (for demonstration purposes) with imputed values using the EM algorithm, the MI method, and the mean substitution procedure. No univariate outliers were detected. Because of extreme positive skewness and kurtosis of an additional variable (depression) this variable was transformed with a base-10 logarithm. Pairwise linearity was deemed satisfactory. Multivariate outliers were screened by computing Mahalanobis distance for each case on the five continuous variables; one case was identified as a potential outlier.

Figure 3b.83 Box's Test of Equality of Covariance Matrices

Box's Test of Equality of Covariance Matrices[a]

Box's M	15.467
F	5.083
df1	3
df2	116611.012
Sig.	.002

Tests the null hypothesis that the observed covariance matrices of the dependent variables are equal across groups.

a. Design: Intercept + gender

PART II

COMPARISONS OF MEANS

Univariate Comparison of Means

4A.1 Overview

4A.1.1 The Need to Compare Means

In most experimental or quasi-experimental (Shadish, Cook, & Campbell, 2002) studies, and even in many archival research programs, researchers will be faced with data collected under two or more different conditions. In such situations, we are typically interested in whether the average performance under one condition differs significantly from that of another condition in the study. Unfortunately, simply looking at the means for each condition will not be particularly informative because in almost all instances, these means will be numerically different.

The issue facing researchers is whether the mean differences they observe are *statistically significant*—that is, whether the differences are likely to recur or be reliable if the study was to be repeatedly done. Statistically, we are asking if it is likely that the two or more conditions represent different populations. To answer this question of statistical significance, it is necessary to subject the data to some statistical treatment, the simplest treatment being the *t* test and the ANOVA. These procedures in their simplest form involve analyzing only a single dependent variable and so qualify as *univariate* (one dependent variable) analyses.

4A.1.2 Brief Summary of the Origins of the t *Test and ANOVA*

The origins of the *t* distribution and the *t* test can be traced to William Sealy Gosset. According to Salsburg (2001), Gosset was hired by the Guinness Brewing Company in 1899 as a mathematician and chemist to bring statistical rigor to the beer brewing business. In the process of monitoring the beer brewing, for example, trying to estimate the yeast content based on samples drawn by the workers, Gosset, with the help and guidance of Karl Pearson (Box, 1987; Fisher, 1939), developed several innovative statistical techniques to deal with the small samples typically encountered in that industry (e.g., four farms each growing one plot of barley) and thus the error implicit in estimating the population standard deviation. He wanted to publish his discoveries but was prohibited by an agreement he had signed with Guinness, as the company was fearful of revealing trade secrets to its competitors. To abide by the letter of the agreement, Gosset consulted with Pearson, who invented the pseudonym of Student for Gosset to use, and with that, in 1908, Gosset was given the lead article in Pearson's *Biometrika* journal (Student, 1908) to introduce the *t* distribution and *t* test.

ANOVA was introduced by Sir Ronald Aylmer Fisher. Fisher worked at the Rothamsted Agricultural Station from 1919 to 1933 studying nutrition and soil types on plant growth (Salsburg, 2001). Up to the time of Fisher, the station's researchers had been using a single different fertilizer on the entire field each year while noting environmental factors such as rainfall and temperature. These researchers entertained the false hope that over a period of many years, they could eventually compare the fertilizers. Fisher revolutionized the research technique by using all of the fertilizers during the same year by dividing the field into separate plots and using different fertilizers in adjacent plots so that he could control for temperature, rainfall, drainage, and so forth. Different areas of the field would be treated in the same fashion, essentially allowing the experiment to be replicated several times. The data naturally showed variability of the yields as a function of the fertilizers in the different plots, and so he devised statistical techniques, the ANOVA and the ANCOVA (see Section 4A.8), to evaluate the overall yield results of each fertilizer against the background of such variability (e.g., Fisher, 1921, 1925, 1935; Fisher & Eden, 1927; Fisher & Mackenzie, 1923).

4A.2 Means Are Compared With Respect to Their Associated Variability

The fundamental principle involved in comparing means is as follows: Any observed mean differences must be evaluated in the context of how much variability is present in the scores of the cases in each of the groups. This mean difference may represent true differences between the conditions or may not, but the way to evaluate such a difference is against a background of score variability within each group. For example, suppose that all the individuals of one group had the same attitude score of 10, that all the individuals in another group had the same attitude score of 12, and that higher scores represented more positive attitudes toward whatever we were assessing. We could then assert without any statistical treatment of the data that the second group was significantly more positive in its attitude than the first. This assertion would be justified because there was no variability in the scores within each group. Translated into statistical language, we would say that our estimate of the population mean for each group is theoretically exact. That is, the group mean is the best estimate of the population mean and, with all cases in each group presenting us with the same score, the estimate of each population mean based on the obtained mean for the group has no associated "margin or error" (a concept we will discuss shortly).

In reality, such a situation as described above could rarely occur because measurement in the empirical world virtually always captures some variability among individuals within the same group. As a result of this variability, the estimate of the population mean based on the sample scores is somewhat less precise. That is, individuals within a single group present us with a range of scores, and so the mean of the group is now associated with some variability. Our best (and only) estimate of the population mean is still the mean of the group, but now, that mean is associated with a nonzero margin or error. To the extent that the scores of the individuals in the sample were very different, our estimate of the population mean would be increasingly less precise and the margin or error would be that much greater.

In comparing the means of two groups, where the scores in each vary, it becomes more challenging to estimate the population mean of each and determine if the two estimated population means are close enough in value to probably represent a single population (i.e., there is no significant difference between the groups) or if the two means are sufficiently different to suggest that each might represent a different population (i.e., there is a statistically significant difference between the groups).

This imprecision in estimation of population means is one way to conceptualize measurement error and is the reason why measurement error is so important to take into account in testing for the significant differences between groups. By measurement error, of course, we do not mean that researchers are constantly making mistakes (although they can err from time to time). The error to which we are referring emanates from imprecision in elements causing cases within a group to present us with different scores. Such differences can result from the instruments we use to make the measurements, the fallacy of humans as respondents and as observers, the presence of other cognitive and motor activities in the life of the respondents, and the biological, social, environmental, and cultural processes in the respondents that we do not ordinarily measure and of which we may not even be aware. This measurement error is always present in any research study. One of the primary goals in teaching students about methodology and design is the hope that they can recognize such error in the research of others and minimize this measurement error in their own research.

Assume for the sake of an example that we have two groups of respondents to an attitude-toward-life survey. Higher numbers on the 5-point response scale indicate a more positive attitude. Group A averaged 3.5 and Group B averaged 4.0. Both groups are on the positive side of the scale, but Group B has responded with a higher mean rating. The difference is 0.5 scale points.

Is Group B's attitude significantly more positive than Group A's? If there is absolutely no measurement error, then the answer is "yes." If there is measurement error, then the answer depends on the degree to which error is present. Let's quantify such error as plus or minus some amount, the so-called margin of error, much the same as the media report sampling error for political polls.

If the mean of each of the groups could have been ±0.1 different from what we observed, then the mean of Group A could have been between 3.4 and 3.6 and the mean of Group B could have been between 3.9 and 4.1. Even with this degree of measurement error, we can see that the possible ranges of the two means do not overlap. We can therefore be reasonably confident that the two groups are reliably or significantly different (that the two samples represent different populations).

Now, suppose that the mean of each of the groups could have been ±0.8 different from what we observed. The mean of Group A could now be between 2.7 and 4.3 and the mean of Group B could now be between 3.2 and 4.8. Now the potential ranges of the two means overlap quite a bit, and it is unlikely that they differ significantly. Here, the two samples more likely represent the very same population.

4A.3 The t and F Tests

The way in which we apply the margin of error to judge the relative size of the mean difference is as follows: We determine how many margin of error units are spanned by the mean difference. We thus compute the ratio of mean difference to margin of error. For a *t* test, the mean difference is literally the difference between the means, and the margin of error is the *standard error of the difference between means*; for the *F* ratio in ANOVA, the mean difference is called the *between-groups mean square* (between-groups variance) and the margin of error is the *within-groups mean square* (within-groups variance).

A *t* test can be used only in situations where there is one independent variable (the variable on which the conditions are distinguished, e.g., experimental and control) with just two levels—for example, when we are comparing the means of two groups of participants in a study. ANOVA can be used in precisely the same situation (in fact, $t^2 = F$), but it can also be used when we have more than two conditions and when we have more than one independent variable.

ANOVA is the more general form of the two-group or two-condition *t* test, and so it tends not to be widely used because we almost always have more than two independent groups or more than two conditions under which participants are measured. On the other hand, probably the most common and straightforward method of performing simple effects tests to determine the precise nature of an interaction effect (see Section 4A.5.5) is to perform pairwise *t* tests on the means of the conditions represented in the interaction. Furthermore, some post hoc tests used to determine which means are significantly different with respect to a single independent variable will also use pairwise *t* tests (Gamst et al., 2008). From this perspective, many researchers using ANOVA to perform the overall (omnibus) analysis on multiple groups or conditions will also commonly invoke *t* tests as part of their post-ANOVA follow-up analyses.

The ANOVA family of techniques is a popular and convenient way to evaluate mean differences, and we briefly treat a sample of the ANOVA designs in this chapter presuming that readers are already familiar with this topic. A comprehensive but readable presentation of a wide range of ANOVA designs can be found in Gamst et al. (2008) for those who are seeking a more complete treatment.

4A.4 One-Way Between-Subjects Designs

In the experimental scenario where we would use a between-subjects design, different individuals are assigned to different groups (levels of the independent variable)—that is, the participants or cases under each level (in each group) of the independent variable are different. This design is also appropriate for non-experimental data. For example, respondents to a survey assessing satisfaction with medical services will also almost always be asked to provide some demographic information, and some of these demographic variables can be used to designate groups (e.g., sex or ethnicity of respondents). Such groups can be used as independent variables to assess differential satisfaction with some of the services. The statistical analysis of the data would be the same regardless of the methodology under which the data were collected.

A one-way between-subjects design derives its name from the fact that there is only one between-subjects independent variable in the analysis. This variable can have as many levels as is needed to address the question under study or the hypothesis being tested. The purpose of the one-way design is to test for differences between two or three or more levels of the independent variable.

4A.4.1 Omnibus Analysis

ANOVA can be interpreted literally to mean that we analyze the variance—that is, we divide or partition the total variance of the dependent variable into its components. There are two types of components that can be identified in ANOVA designs:

- Some effects are associated with the independent variables. In the case of a one-way between-subjects design, there is only one independent variable, and hence, there is only one effect. It is generically called the *Between-Groups* or *Treatment* effect, but it can be labeled in a way that names the independent variable directly (e.g., drug effect, program type effect, etc.). It reflects mean differences between the groups.

- Some effects are associated with the variability of the cases within each group. It is subsumed under the auspice of *measurement error* in that differences in scores are observed despite the fact that they are in the same group (e.g., they have all been exposed to the same treatment level or they have all been classified into a single ethnicity group regardless of the fact that there may be substantial differences among them). In the case of a one-way between-subjects design, there is only one error component. It is generically called *Within-Groups* or *Error variance*.

The results of an ANOVA are typically consolidated into a summary table. For a one-way between-subjects design, the summary table is structured as shown in Table 4a.1. The total degrees of freedom are equal to the total number of observations minus 1 (in this design, the total number of observations is equal to the total number of cases). The between-groups degrees of freedom are equal to the number of groups or levels of the independent variable minus 1 (symbolized as $a - 1$, where a is the number of levels of independent variable A). The error degrees of freedom are equal to the difference between total and between-groups variance, which is equal to the sum of $n - 1$ of each group, where n is the number of cases in a group; when n is the same for all groups, the error degrees of freedom can be computed as $(a)(n - 1)$.

Sum of squares is the sum of the squared deviations of the appropriate scores around the appropriate mean value: For Total variance, we subtract the grand mean from each individual score; for Between-Groups variance, we subtract the group mean from the grand mean; and for Error variance, we subtract the individual score from the group mean. Mean squares are computed by dividing the sum of squares for each source of variance by its

Table 4a.1 Generic Summary Table for a One-Way Between-Subjects ANOVA

Source	Degrees of Freedom	Sum of Squares	Mean Square	F Ratio
Between-Groups	$a-1$			
Error	$(a)(n-1)$			
Total	$N-1$			

Note. N = total number of observations; a = number of groups; n = number of observations in each equal-sized group.

corresponding degrees of freedom. The F ratio for Between-Groups is computed by dividing its mean square by the mean square associated with Error. Based on the sampling distribution of the F ratio for the combination of degrees of freedom of the Between-Groups and Error, we determine if it is statistically significant. As is discussed in Section 4A.4.2, if the F ratio is statistically significant, eta square for the Between-Groups effect is computed by dividing the Between-Groups sum of squares by the total sum of squares.

4A.4.2 Strength of Effect

Statistical significance relates to the likelihood of obtaining a particular statistical outcome (e.g., an F ratio of a given value) by chance alone, given the truth of the null hypothesis (that there is no true group difference in the population). If we have a statistically significant effect of the independent variable, then we next evaluate its strength. It is very important to differentiate statistical significance and strength of effect.

There are many ways to quantify the strength of a particular effect (see Judd, McClelland, & Culhane, 1995; Kirk, 1996; Olejnik & Algina, 2000; Rosenthal, 1994; Snyder & Lawson, 1993). One very useful approach devised by Jacob Cohen (1969, 1977, 1988) is to calculate the ratio of mean difference to standard deviation, which assesses by how many standard deviation units the group means differ. This index is known as *effect size*. In the two-group case, the statistic is symbolized as d; in the multiple group case, the statistic is symbolized as f.

Another approach is to determine the percentage of variance of the dependent variable that is accounted for by the effect. One index that is sometimes used is *omega square* (Keppel, 1991; Kirk, 1995; Maxwell & Delaney, 2000), with its variation of *partial omega square* (Keppel & Wickens, 2004); omega square is used as an estimate of the population parameter.

IBM SPSS provides still an index known as a *partial eta square*, which is the ratio of the sum of squares of the effect to the sum of the sum of squares of the effect and the error sum of squares. Because it sometimes can be confused with the classical *eta square* statistic and because its interpretation is quite different from the classical eta square (Levine & Hullett, 2002), we will not request it in any of our IBM SPSS analysis setups.

Probably the most widely used index of strength of effect, and the one we use in this book, is a descriptive statistic capturing the proportion of dependent variable variance explained by (associated with) the effect of interest. In multiple regression, the statistic is called the *squared multiple correlation* and is symbolized as R^2 (Cohen et al., 2003; Darlington, 1960), and we will discuss this further in our chapters on regression.

In ANOVA, this popular index of strength of effect is called *eta square* and is symbolized as η^2 (Cohen, 1996). Eta is actually a correlation coefficient and one of its other names is the *correlation ratio* (Guilford & Fruchter, 1978; Keppel & Zedeck, 1989). Because it is based on a correlation, eta square can take on values between 0 and 1 and is interpreted as the percentage of total variance explained by a given effect. It is computed by dividing the sum of squares of the effect by the total sum of squares. This proportion can be translated directly into a percentage. For example, if the sum of squares for an effect was 50 and the total sum of squares was 300, then the proportion is 50/300 = .1667, and we could thus say that the effect accounted for 16.67% of the variance of the dependent variable. In the absence of any context, eta square values of approximately .09, .14, and .22 would be considered to be relatively weak, moderate, and strong, respectively (Gamst et al., 2008).

4A.4.3 Post-ANOVA Multiple Comparisons Tests

Having obtained a statistically significant effect of an independent variable informs us that the means of the groups are significantly different. If there are only two groups, and thus only two means, the difference is self-evident and can be directly communicated to the readers. However, it is very often the case that more than two means are subsumed within an effect. Under these circumstances, it is not self-evident which means are significantly different from which others. That is, a statistically significant effect of an independent variable informs us that there is at least one comparison of means that results in a statistical difference; however, it does not inform us of between which pairs of means the significant differences lie.

In the face of ambiguity as to which means are statistically significant when there are more than two involved, we must engage in a post-ANOVA statistical procedure, generically known as *multiple comparisons tests*, to determine this. Such procedures can involve planned or unplanned comparisons, pairwise or composite comparisons, and orthogonal or nonorthogonal comparisons. Extensive treatments of the different approaches and nuances of these procedures are available elsewhere (e.g., Gamst et al., 2008; Klockars & Sax, 1986; Toothaker, 1993). For our purposes, we will adopt the following simplified strategy:

- For between-subjects effects of stand-alone independent variables (what we will call between-subjects main effects in more complex designs), we will use one or another of the more popular post hoc tests that control for alpha level inflation (making more than one pairwise comparison increases the chances of a Type I error beyond the .05 alpha level unless the procedure can specifically compensate for that) that are available in the **Post Hoc** dialog window of IBM SPSS. These tests perform pairwise comparisons on the observed means; if two or more means are combined as they are in factorial designs, the resulting mean is a weighted average of its constituents.
- For within-subjects effects of stand-alone independent variables and for simple effects testing of interactions (see Section 4A.6), we will use Bonferroni-corrected

(for alpha-level inflation) pairwise t tests that are built into the IBM SPSS syntax structure. These tests perform pairwise comparisons on the least squares means or estimated marginal means (unweighted means that are adjusted for any covariates in the analysis); if two or more least squares means are combined as they are in factorial designs, the resulting mean is an unweighted average of its constituents. Technical information concerning least squares means may be found in the statistical literature (e.g., Hartley & Searle, 1969; Milliken & Johnson, 1984).

4A.4.4 Trend Analysis

In addition to these multiple comparisons tests, there is another analysis that we could perform if the levels of the independent variable approximated at least an interval level of measurement. This is a trend analysis. Such an analysis would be able to assess, at least indirectly, the general shape of the function (of groups represented on the X axis with the dependent variable represented on the Y axis). It assumes that the codes used for the independent variable are spaced along the X axis according to interval scale rules. The group means are then plotted to yield a function of a particular shape. A trend analysis analyzes the shape of the function.

In a one-way analysis that does not include a trend analysis, you obtain one sum of squares and one F ratio for the effect. A trend analysis partitions this overall effect of the independent variable into linear, quadratic, cubic, and other higher-order trends. The number of partitions you can request is tied to the number of groups. With only two groups, you have only two data points (the two means) and so have only one possible function: a straight-line or linear function. No partition is possible. With three groups (three means), you have the possibility of both a linear and a quadratic function and can therefore partition the effect into these two trends. With four groups, you can partition the effect into a linear, a quadratic, and a cubic trend. In general, you have one fewer trend in the partition than you have means—that is, the number of trends is equal to the degrees of freedom associated with the effect. Most researchers, if they test for trends at all, do not push beyond a cubic trend.

4A.5 Two-Way (Factorial) Between-Subjects Design

A two-way between-subjects design derives its name from the fact that there are two between-subjects independent variables in the analysis. Each of these two variables can have as many levels as is needed to address the question under study or the hypothesis being tested. When all combinations of their levels are represented in the study, we can label the design as a factorial design. The simplest factorial design is one with each variable represented by only two levels (it takes at least two levels to have any variance of an independent variable). This is called a 2 × 2 (two-by-two) design in which the two levels of one variable are factorially combined with the two levels of the other. Such a combination results in the four conditions shown in the cells of Figure 4a.1. Specifically, the four cells are a_1b_1, a_1b_2, a_2b_1, and a_2b_2. Just as was true for the one-way design, this 2 × 2 structure could have been designed either within an experimental context or superimposed on data collected through a survey methodology.

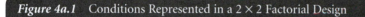

Figure 4a.1 Conditions Represented in a 2 × 2 Factorial Design

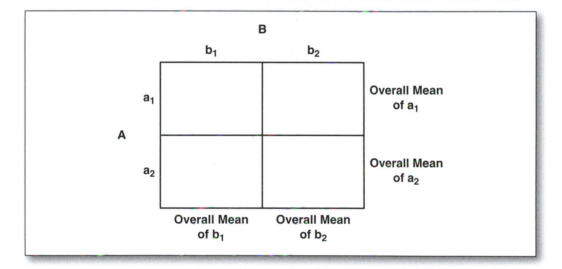

4A.5.1 Main Effects

A *main effect* involves comparing the means of the various levels of an independent variable. Each independent variable in a factorial design is associated with its own main effect. The ANOVA that we perform allows us to evaluate the statistical significance of each of them. Because there are two independent variables in a two-way design, two main effects are evaluated.

We can show the comparisons associated with the main effects by reference to Figure 4a.1. The main effect of A involves a comparison of the overall mean of a_1 and the overall mean of a_2. This comparison is based on the combined scores across the B variable (b_1 and b_2 are combined for each level of A). We see these means in the right margin of each row. The statistical question addressed by the ANOVA regarding the main effect of A is whether performance on a_1 (overall) differs on average from performance on a_2 (overall). The focus is entirely on A. An analogous situation concerns the main effect of B. Here, we focus on the column composites, comparing b_1 overall with b_2 overall. This comparison takes place across all levels of A.

4A.5.2 Interaction Effect

In addition to the two main effects, a two-way design allows us to evaluate the *interaction* of the two independent variables. The $A \times B$ (A "by" B) interaction reflects the effects associated with the various combinations of the independent variables. It is possible, for example, that the combination a_2b_2 produces quite different effects from any of the other three combinations. Such an outcome would be indicated by a significant interaction effect.

One way to conceive of what an interaction means is to imagine possible mean values plugged into the cells of Figure 4a.1. Now look at the pattern across the top row (how much higher or lower is the right one from the left one) and compare the pattern with what we see in the bottom row. If the two patterns are the same (i.e., they are parallel), there is no statistically significant interaction between the variables; if the two patterns are different (i.e., they are not parallel), there is likely to be a statistically significant interaction between the variables. When testing for the presence of an interaction, the null hypothesis is that the two patterns are parallel; a statistically significant F ratio associated with the interaction effect informs us that the patterns are not parallel.

Figure 4a.2 shows two examples of interaction patterns. Example 1 is a crossed interaction, whereas Example 2 is uncrossed. The key is that in both examples, the function for a_1 is not parallel to the function for a_2. Both examples communicate the general message of an

Figure 4a.2 Two Examples of Interaction Patterns

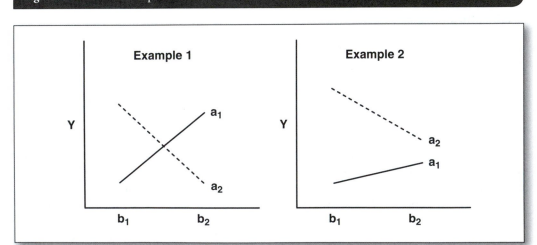

interaction: The effect of one variable (e.g., variable B) depends on (is not the same for) the level of another variable (e.g., variable A). In both examples, the mean of b_2 is higher than b_1 but only for a_1; under the a_2 condition, the means of the levels of B show the opposite pattern.

4A.5.3 Interactions Supersede Main Effects

If a significant interaction is obtained, it means that a different relationship is seen for different levels of an independent variable. For example, we see one relationship for a_1 and a different relationship for a_2. One implication of obtaining a significant interaction is that a statement of each main effect will not fully capture the results of the study. Take Example 1 in Figure 4a.2. The mean of b_1 is halfway between a_1 and a_2, and the mean of b_2 is halfway between a_1 and a_2. Those two means are just about at the same height on the Y axis and are not likely to be statistically different; thus, there is not going to be a statistically significant main effect of B. Does that mean that the level of B does not matter? No, it matters very much depending on the level of A. And such a dependency occurs because A and B interact. If it is statistically significant, the $A \times B$ interaction is the appropriate level of analysis to fully understand the results. The general strategy to follow is that if the two-way interaction is statistically significant, it deserves most or all of our attention.

4A.5.4 Omnibus Analysis

A generic summary table for a two-way between-subjects design is shown in Table 4a.2. There are three effects of interest in such a design: the main effect of A, the main effect of B, and the $A \times B$ interaction. Mean squares for each effect are computed by dividing its sum of

Table 4a.2 Generic Summary Table for a Two-Way Between-Subjects ANOVA

Source	Degrees of Freedom	Sum of Squares	Mean Square	F Ratio
A	$a-1$			
B	$b-1$			
A x B	$(a-1)(b-1)$			
Error	Residual			
Total	$N-1$			

Note. N = total number of observations; a = number of levels of A; b = number of levels of B.

squares by its degrees of freedom. The F ratios for the effects are computed by dividing each mean square value by the mean square value for the Error term. Eta square for each statistically significant effect is computed by dividing its sum of squares by the total sum of squares. In examining the results, we ordinarily assess the interaction first and then assess the main effects if warranted.

4A.5.5 Post-ANOVA Tests

If any main effect is found to be statistically significant and there were more than two levels, then it would be necessary to perform a post hoc test to determine which pairs of means were statistically different. If the interaction is found to be statistically significant, then it is necessary to perform *simple effects tests* to determine which means differ from which. In Example 2 of Figure 4a.2, for example, we can compare the two data points (means) for a_1 to determine if there is a significant rise in the function between b_1 and b_2, and we can compare the two data points for a_2 to determine if there is a significant drop in the function between b_1 and b_2. Furthermore, we can also compare the two data points at b_1 to determine if there is a significant mean difference between a_1 and a_2, and we can compare the two data points at b_2 to determine if there is a significant mean difference between a_1 and a_2. These two sets of comparisons would be accomplished through the tests of simple effects.

4A.6 One-Way Within-Subjects Design

In a within-subjects design, the same individuals are assigned to different conditions (levels of the independent variable). A one-way within-subjects design derives its name from the fact that there is only one within-subjects independent variable in the analysis, known generically as the *treatment* effect. This variable can have as many levels as is needed to address the question under study or the hypothesis being tested. The purpose of the one-way design is to test for differences between two or three or more levels of the independent variable.

For a one-way within-subjects design, we obtain two summary tables, and they are structured as shown in Table 4a.3. The two summary tables reflect the successive stages of partitioning the total variance of the dependent variable. The first partition divides the total variance into a *between-subjects* and a *within-subjects* source of variance, each receiving its own summary table in IBM SPSS. The between-subjects is not further dividable (and ordinarily of no research interest because it simply represents the individual differences among the participants with respect to their scores on the dependent variable); its degrees of freedom are equal to the number of participants or cases in the study minus 1.

The within-subjects variance can be furthered partitioned into variance attributable to the Treatment effect and variance attributable to error; this latter variance is conceptualized

Table 4a.3   Generic Summary Tables for a One-Way Within-Subjects ANOVA

Between-Subjects Variance

Source	Degrees of Freedom	Sum of Squares	Mean Square	F Ratio
Subjects	S–1			

Note. S = total number of subjects.

Within-Subjects Variance

Source	Degrees of Freedom	Sum of Squares	Mean Square	F Ratio
Treatment	a–1			
Error (Treatment × Subjects)	(a–1) (S–1)			

Note. S = total number of subjects; *a* = number of conditions.

as the different patterns of performance exhibited by the cases across the levels of the treatment variable. The Treatment degrees of freedom are equal to the number of levels of the Treatment variable minus 1, and the Error degrees of freedom are equal to the product of Treatment degrees of freedom and Subject degrees of freedom. Mean squares are computed in the standard way (sum of squares divided by degrees of freedom).

The only *F* ratio that is of relevance in this design is the one associated with the Treatment effect; it is computed as Mean Square Treatment divided by Mean Square Error. We do not compute an *F* ratio for Subjects in that we fully expect the cases to differ among themselves and, therefore, do not statistically test for individual differences. Eta square for the Treatment effect (if it is statistically significant) is computed by dividing its sum of squares by the total sum of squares associated with the within-subjects variance. With a statistically significant treatment effect, we perform pairwise *t*-test comparisons on the least squares means using a Bonferroni correction.

4A.7 Two-Way Simple Mixed Design

A mixed design contains at least one between-subjects independent variable and one within-subjects independent variable. A simple mixed design contains one of each. The simplest way to conceive of such a design is that it combines the one-way between-subjects design and the one-way within-subjects design.

4A.7.1 Omnibus Analysis

The way in which the variance is partitioned follows the same strategy as a within-subjects design, with the most global partition of between-subjects variance and within-subjects variance as shown in Table 4a.4. Each receives its own summary table in IBM SPSS.

Table 4a.4 Generic Summary Tables for a Simple Mixed Design

Between-Subjects Variance

Source	Degrees of Freedom	Sum of Squares	Mean Square	F Ratio
A	$a-1$			
Error A	$(a)(n-1)$			
Total	$S-1$			

Note. S = total number of subjects; a = number of conditions; n = number of observations in each equal sized group.

Within-Subjects Variance

Source	Degrees of Freedom	Sum of Squares	Mean Square	F Ratio
B	$b-1$			
A x B	$(a-1)(b-1)$			
Error B	$(a)(n-1)(b-1)$			
Total	$(a)(n)(b-1)$			

Note. N = total number of observations; a = number of levels of A; b = number of levels of B; n = number of observations in each equal-sized group.

The between-subjects variance is partitioned into the main effect of A and Error A. The total between-subjects degrees of freedom are equal to the number of subjects minus 1, and the main effect of A has $a - 1$ degrees of freedom. Error degrees of freedom are equal to the sum of $n - 1$ of each group, where n is the number of cases in a group; when n is the same for all groups, the Error degrees of freedom can be computed as $(a)(n - 1)$. The F ratio for the main effect of A is computed as Mean Square A divided by Mean Square Error A.

The within-subjects variance is partitioned into the main effect of B, the interaction of A and B, and Error A. The total within-subjects degrees of freedom are equal to $a \times n \times b - 1$.

Degrees of freedom for B are equal to $b - 1$, and the degrees of freedom for the A × B inter-action is the product of the degrees of freedom for each. The Error B degrees of freedom is whatever makes up the remainder of the total within-subjects degrees of freedom but can be directly calculated as shown in Table 4a.4. The *F* ratios for the main effect of B and the A × B interaction are computed as Mean Square B and Mean Square A × B each divided by Mean Square Error B. As was true for the two-way between-subjects design, we would assess the interaction first and then proceed on to the main effects.

4A.7.2 Post-ANOVA Tests

If the main effect of A is found to be statistically significant and there were more than two levels, then it would be necessary to perform a post hoc test to determine which pairs of means were statistically different. If either the main effect of B or the interaction is found to be statistically significant, then it is necessary to perform simple effects tests to determine which means differ from which.

4A.7.3 Profile Analysis

The two-way simple mixed design is also often used in *profile analysis*, an approach that compares groups on the pattern of their means from multiple measurements. Fitzmaurice and Molengerghs (2009) inform us that profile analysis originated in the work of Box (1950), Geisser and Greenhouse (1958), and Greenhouse and Geisser (1959) in evaluating longitudinal data, but the analysis has been applied to both longitudinal designs (Fitzmaurice, Laird, & Ware, 2011) as well as to general repeated measures designs not necessarily involving a time dimension (Davis, 2002; Kim & Neil, 2007).

In its most general form, two or more groups are measured under one of two circumstances:

- The groups are measured on the same dependent variable at various points in time.
- The groups are assessed on different measures (e.g., inventories assessing different personal characteristics) during the course of a research project.

The data are analyzed by using a two-way mixed ANOVA design, and the group means are plotted. In such plots—the usual way that the profile analysis results are summarized—the measures are represented on the *X* axis, and the groups are depicted by lines across the graph. When different inventories based on different scales are used in the research, it is appropriate to transform the data to *z* scores so that the profiles on the inventories can be meaningfully plotted and compared. Even a quick inspection of these plots can reveal any pattern differences of the groups over the repeated measures.

There are ordinarily three aspects of the pattern (group comparisons) on which researchers focus (Davis, 2002). These are as follows:

- *The extent to which the profiles are parallel:* A statistically significant interaction effect indicates that the functions are not parallel and that tests of simple effects are to be conducted. A nonsignificant interaction effect is our cue to examine the main effects.
- *The extent to which there are differences between the groups:* This is evaluated if there is no significant interaction by examining the main effect of the groups (the between-subjects) variable.
- *The extent to which there are differences along the time points that are measured when the measurements are across time:* This is evaluated if there is no significant interaction by examining the main effect of the within-subjects variable.

We illustrate these three patterns in Figure 4a.3 using just two groups to keep matters simple. Plot A displays the results of a profile analysis in which a statistically significant interaction is obtained. Visual inspection suggests that the two groups show virtually the opposite pattern across the measures.

Plot B shows a main effect of the grouping variable in which Group 1 is producing consistently higher scores by about 20 scale points than Group 2. If the measures represented a single dependent variable assessed at four successive times, then we would judge that there was a general increase in the magnitude of measures across time (but with a dip at the time of Measure 3). This would be represented by a statistically significant main effect of the within-subjects variable of Time.

Plot C also presents a main effect of the grouping variable in which Group 1 is yielding consistently higher scores than Group 2, although here the magnitude of the group difference varies somewhat across measures. If the measures represented a single dependent variable assessed at four successive times, then we would judge that there was a general consistency in the magnitude of the measures across time for both groups. That is, there is no main effect associated with the within-subjects variable of Time in this illustration—at each measurement, the groups are averaging a value of 40 (highlighted for the convenience of readers by the horizontal dotted line) on the dependent variable.

4A.8 One-Way Between-Subjects ANCOVA

ANCOVA provides us with a way to statistically control for one or more variables that we believe affect the dependent variable but which we cannot or choose not to experimentally control for. These variables that are statistically controlled are called *covariates*, and they are typically quantitatively measured variables.

Figure 4a.3   Three Examples of a Profile Plot

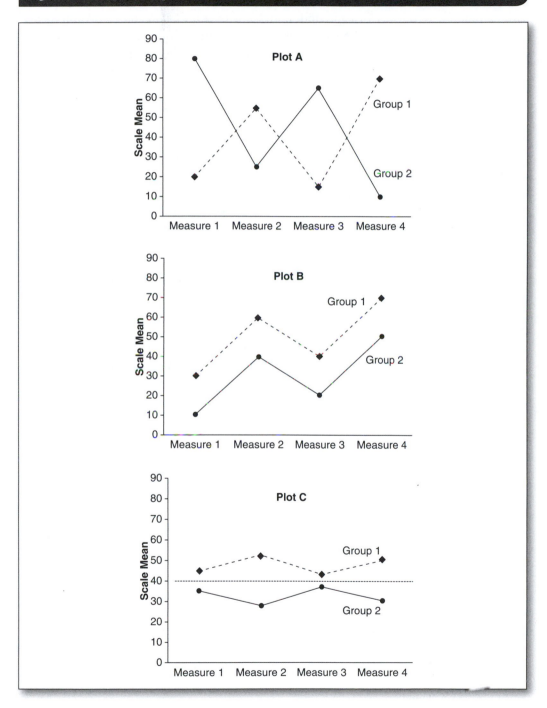

As an example of ANCOVA, assume that we intended to assess the performance of three branch offices (e.g., Boston, Dallas, and Seattle) of a particular consulting firm. Further assume that one of our performance indexes was the time it took to complete projects over a 1-year time period. An ANOVA showed that the three branch offices each completed their projects in approximately the same amount of time—that is, there were no significant differences between the offices, leading to the conclusion that the offices are comparable in performance.

But the in-house researcher in charge of performance appraisals recognizes that some projects can be more complex than others and that project complexity can be reliably measured. She therefore has her staff rate the complexity of each project completed by the offices. Thus, each value of the dependent variable (time to project completion) now also has an accompanying rating of project complexity. Scores on the complexity measure can then be used as a covariate to "adjust" the completion time of projects as part of the statistical analysis of group differences. One way to think of this, as suggested by Maxwell and Delaney (2000, p. 356), is that in an ANCOVA we evaluate group differences on the dependent variable (e.g., time to completion in our example) as if the groups were equivalent on the covariate (e.g., project complexity in our example).

Assume that the ANCOVA shows that the adjusted means of the groups are now significantly different—when statistically controlling for project complexity, the Dallas and Denver offices are taking less time than the Boston office. The ANCOVA can therefore provide a more complete picture—and many would say a more valid representation—of the performance of the three offices on the measure of the number of completed projects. More complete discussions of ANCOVA can be found in Gamst et al. (2008), Kirk (1995), Meyers et al. (2009), and Stevens (2007).

4A.8.1 The General Structure of ANCOVA

The general structure of an ANCOVA involves two major stages: (a) adjusting the scores on the dependent measure based on the covariate and (b) performing an ANOVA on the adjusted scores. We briefly discuss these in turn.

4A.8.1.1 Adjusting the Scores on the Dependent Variable Using the Covariate

In the first stage of an ANCOVA, we use a covariate (or multiple covariates) in an ANOVA design because we believe or want to consider the possibility that scores on the covariate are correlated to scores on the dependent variable. To statistically nullify or remove the effects of the covariate from the dependent variable—in a sense, to "cleanse" the dependent variable of the covariate—the first step in an ANCOVA is to predict the dependent variable from the covariate for the full sample, so that each case will have a predicted dependent variable score based on a linear regression model with the covariate as the predictor.

These predicted scores are a result of using all the linear information in the covariate and can be thought of as values of the dependent variable that are adjusted for the covariate. These adjusted scores can be quite different from the observed scores with which we started the analysis.

4A.8.1.2 Performing an ANOVA on the Adjusted Scores

Theoretically, any differences between groups that are observed on the adjusted dependent variable scores cannot be attributed to the covariate. Based on this reasoning, in the second stage of an ANCOVA, we perform an ordinary ANOVA on the adjusted scores. A significant effect in the analysis indicates that we have group differences on the adjusted scores.

4A.8.2 Additional Assumptions of ANCOVA

In addition to the assumptions underlying ANOVA—a normal distribution of the residuals (differences of the group mean from the scores), independence of errors, and equal variances—we must satisfy two other assumptions when we intend to perform an ANCOVA: (a) linearity of regression and (b) homogeneity of regression. We briefly discuss these in turn.

4A.8.2.1 Linearity of Regression

The linearity of regression assumption holds that the relationship between the covariate and the dependent variable is linear. This is in place because the adjustment process used to "remove" the effects of the covariate from the dependent variable is based on a linear regression procedure. If the relationship between the covariate and the dependent variable was not linear, then the adjustment process would be flawed, and any inferences made from the results would not be valid.

The most common and most direct way to assess this assumption is to generate a scatterplot based on the sample as a whole (ignoring the group membership of the cases), where the dependent variable is placed on the *Y* axis and the covariate is placed on the *X* axis. We illustrate in Figure 4a.4 one example of a linear relationship between the two variables. Based on a visual inspection of these data, we would conclude that the two are related linearly.

4A.8.2.2 Homogeneity of Regression

Whereas the assumption of linearity of regression is tested on the sample as a whole, the assumption of homogeneity of regression examines the regression model (covariate predicting dependent variable) separately for each group. Homogeneity of regression holds

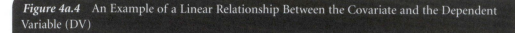

Figure 4a.4 An Example of a Linear Relationship Between the Covariate and the Dependent Variable (DV)

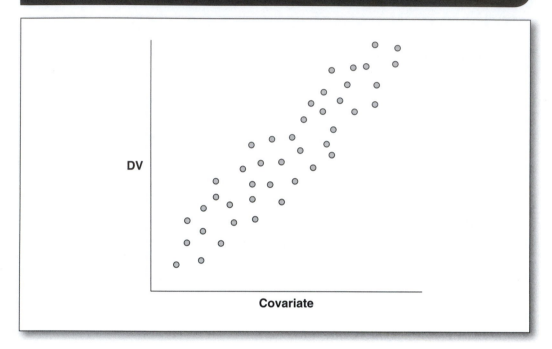

that the slope of the regression line is the same for each group. When the slopes of the regression models for the individual groups are significantly different—that is, when the slope for one group differs significantly from the slope of at least one other group—then the assumption of homogeneity of regression has been violated.

The assumption of homogeneity of regression is evaluated statistically. To test the assumption, we structure an analysis to determine if the Groups × Covariate interaction is statistically significant (where Groups represents the independent variable). Homogeneity of variance is specified by the null hypothesis that the regression lines are parallel, and so we are hoping that we obtain a nonsignificant F ratio for the interaction effect.

Testing the homogeneity of regression assumption can be illustrated in Figure 4a.5. In the graphs, a_1 and a_2 represent two groups of cases. The data points in the scatterplot are depicted by solid circles for group a_1 and open circles for group a_2, and a regression line is drawn through each set of data points. In Example 1, the slopes of the regression lines for a_1 and a_2 are not parallel, and thus, the homogeneity of regression assumption appears to be violated—that is, we would obtain a statistically significant Groups × Covariate interaction in the

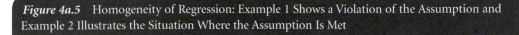

Figure 4a.5 Homogeneity of Regression: Example 1 Shows a Violation of the Assumption and Example 2 Illustrates the Situation Where the Assumption Is Met

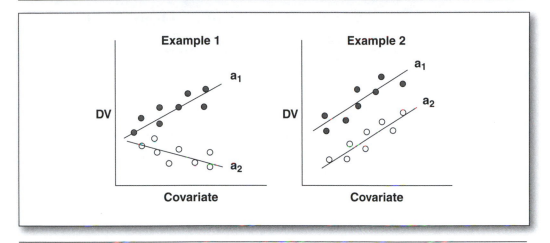

Note. DV = dependent variable.

statistical analysis. In Example 2, the slopes of the regression lines for a_1 and a_2 are approximately parallel, and thus, the homogeneity of regression assumption appears to be met—that is, the Groups × Covariate interaction would not be statistically significant.

4A.8.3 Omnibus ANCOVA Analysis

The variance in a one-way between-subjects ANCOVA is partitioned in the manner shown in the summary table in Table 4a.5. The covariate is itself an effect because we are attempting to explain the variance of the dependent variable with it. Each covariate accounts for one degree of freedom, and the effect of the independent variable *A* has *a* − 1 degrees of freedom. The *F* ratios for the covariate and the independent variable are computed by dividing the respective Mean Square values by the Mean Square associated with the Error.

4A.8.4 Post-ANCOVA Tests

The least squares means represent the adjusted means in the ANCOVA. Therefore, if a statistically significant effect of the independent variable is obtained, we are obliged to perform pairwise *t*-test comparisons on the least squares means using a Bonferroni correction.

Table 4a.5 Generic Summary Table for a One-Way Between-Subjects ANCOVA

Source	Degrees of Freedom	Sum of Squares	Mean Square	F Ratio
Covariate	1 df for each			
A	$a-1$			
Error	$[n(a-1)] - cov$			
Total	$N - 1$			

Note. N = total number of observations; n = number of observations in each equal-sized group; a = number of levels of A; cov = number of covariates.

4A.9 The General Linear Model

The approach to ANOVA that we have presented here is embedded in the general linear model, popularized in the social and behavioral sciences by Jacob Cohen (1968). The general linear model subsumes the t test, ANOVA, ANCOVA, and linear and polynomial multiple regression. This model is presented in more detail in Section 7A.5.1 in the context of multiple regression; for now, think of it as a prediction model in which the independent variables in the analysis are used to predict (explain the variance of) the dependent variable. The output can be framed, as we have done in this chapter, in terms of the partitioning of the variance and comparing means or in terms of a multiple regression model (see Chapter 7A). How we can translate between the two is shown in Sections 8A.5 and 8B.3.

It took only 10 or so years from Jacob Cohen's seminal article for others, such as Knapp (1978) and Fornell (1978), as well as Jacob Cohen (1982) himself, to realize that linear regression is a special case of an even more general linear model represented by canonical correlation analysis (see Chapters 13A and 13B). In canonical correlation analysis, a set of independent variables is used to predict a set of dependent variables. Canonical correlation analysis subsumes linear regression (canonical correlation analysis reduces to linear regression when only a single dependent variable is predicted) as well as discriminant function analysis (Knapp, 1978; see Chapters 11A and 11B). Fornell (1978) specifically brought

MANOVA (see Chapters 5A and 5B), discriminant analysis, and principal components analysis (see Chapters 12A and 12B) in addition to ANOVA under the more general tent of canonical correlation analysis.

Most of the analyses we demonstrate in Chapter 4B are performed in the procedure named **General Linear Model**. This procedure is the same fundamental technique underlying linear (ordinary least squares) regression and has been available in IBM SPSS since Version 7. In its ANOVA form, it handles both between-subjects and within-subjects factors and as part of its output presents the standard summary tables that we have described in this chapter. ANOVA is focused on the partitioning of the effects (each is a predictor of the dependent variable in an overall general linear model) into main effects associated with each independent variable and interaction effects when independent variables are considered together; thus, in examining the outcome of the analysis, we examine the individual effects.

In applying the general linear model in the context of its regression form, the focus is on the overall model and how well the set of independent variables as a whole predict the dependent variable; thus, in examining the outcome of this sort of analysis, we primarily examine how well the overall model performs and secondarily narrow our focus to the individual independent variables.

IBM SPSS has recently seen the addition of a newer procedure, the **Generalized Linear Model**, that extends the **General Linear Model** to other types of distributions. The **Generalized Linear Model** was introduced by Nelder and Wedderburn (1972). More current resources discussing this model are Dobson and Barnett (2008), Gill (2001), Hardin and Hilbe (2008), and McCullagh and Nelder (1999). An interesting interview with John Nelder that covers the development of the **Generalized Linear Model** is provided in Senn's (2003) article.

The **Generalized Linear Model** uses a maximum likelihood procedure rather than an ordinary least squares solution (see Section 6A.6.2) and appears to offer more precise parameter estimates than the **General Linear Model**. It is also orientated toward model fit techniques and covers a broader range of applications than the **General Linear Model** (e.g., it can accommodate categorical variables as dependent measures). One drawback to using the **Generalized Linear Model** is that its output does not provide standard summary tables and so researchers are unable to compute a strength-of-effect index (e.g., eta square) from the results. Because there is increased emphasis on reporting strength of effect in published research, we have chosen to focus on the **General Linear Model** in Chapter 4B, but we have performed two of the analyses (the one-way between-subjects and the simple mixed designs) in the **Generalized Linear Model** modules at the end of Chapter 4B for those who might be interested in learning the analysis setup and viewing portions of the output.

4A.10 Recommended Readings

Box, J. F. (1978). *R. A. Fisher, the life of a scientist.* New York, NY: Wiley.

Cohen, J. (1968). Multiple regression as a general data analytic system. *Psychological Bulletin, 70,* 426–443.

Ellis, M. V. (1999). Repeated measures designs. *Counseling Psychologist, 27,* 552–578.

Fisher, R. A. (1925a). Applications of Student's distribution. *Metron, 5,* 90–104.

Fisher, R. A. (1925b). *Statistical methods for research workers.* London, England: Oliver & Boyd.

Gamst, G., Meyers, L. S., & Guarino, A. J. (2008). *Analysis of variance designs: A conceptual and computational approach with SPSS and SAS.* New York, NY: Cambridge University Press.

Keppel, G., & Wickens, T. D. (2004). *Design and analysis: A researcher's handbook* (4th ed.). Upper Saddle River, NJ: Pearson Prentice Hall.

Meyers, L. S., Gamst, G., & Guarino, A. J. (2009). *Data analysis using SAS enterprise guide.* New York, NY: Cambridge University Press.

O'Brien, R. G., & Kaiser, M. K. (1985). MANOVA method for analyzing repeated measures designs: An extensive primer. *Psychological Bulletin, 97,* 316–333.

Senn, S. (2003). A conversation with John Nelder. *Statistical Science, 18,* 118–131.

Univariate Comparison of Means Using IBM SPSS

4B.1 One-Way Between-Subjects Design

A one-way between-subjects design focuses on a single between-subjects independent variable. It contains *a* number of groups where *a* is the number of levels of independent variable *A*; different cases are randomly assigned to the different groups if it is possible to do so.

4B.1.1 Numerical Example

In this hypothetical example, three different types of fertilizer (A, B, and C)—used to nourish crops of yellow sweet corn—are the levels of the independent variable. The amount of vertical growth of the plants in millimeters is the dependent variable. Seven plants are assigned to each type of fertilizer. Data are contained in the file named **Fertilizer**.

4B.1.2 Omnibus One-Way Between-Subjects Analysis Setup

Selecting **Analyze → Compare Means → One-Way ANOVA** brings us to the main dialog screen shown in Figure 4b.1. From the variables list panel on the left side, we click over **plant_growth** to the **Dependent List** and **fertilizer** to the **Factor** panel. Select the **Options** pushbutton, check **Descriptive** and **Homogeneity of variance test** in the **Options** window (see Figure 4b.2), and click **Continue** to return to the main dialog window.

Figure 4b.1   Main Dialog Window for One-Way ANOVA

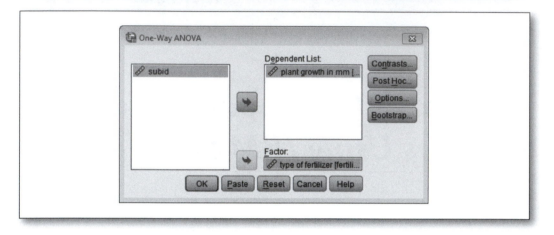

Figure 4b.2   The One-Way ANOVA Options Window

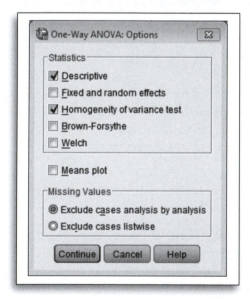

4B.1.3 Multiple Comparisons Tests

Although we could wait to see the results of the omnibus analysis, it is convenient to produce the post hoc test results while we are setting up the analysis. Selecting the **Post Ho**c pushbutton presents a wide selection of tests as shown in Figure 4b.3, and this topic of multiple comparisons (of the means of the groups in the analysis) is worthy of a brief discussion.

4B.1.3.1 Multiple Comparisons: Strategies

Some authors (e.g., Gamst et al., 2008; Keppel & Wickens, 2004) argue persuasively for the use in many experimental contexts of specified-in-advance planned comparisons (which can be produced by clicking the **Contrasts** pushbutton in the main dialog window). Alternatively, many nonexperimental situations (e.g., archival data analysis) lend themselves to a post hoc testing of all possible pairwise comparisons of between-group means. Metaphorically, planned comparisons are usually driven by specific research hypotheses. It is analogous to visiting a bookstore to purchase *Walden* by Henry David Thoreau and

Figure 4b.3 The One-Way ANOVA Post Hoc Window

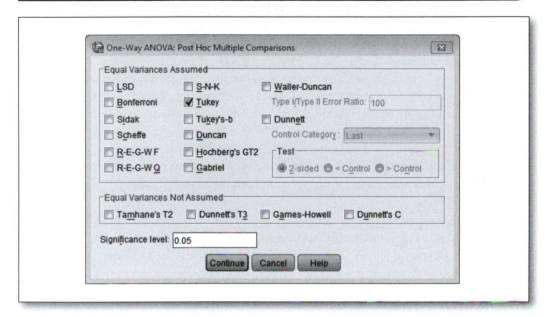

the *Lord of the Rings* trilogy by J. R. R. Tolkien. The researchers are asking the question, "Do you have these specific books in stock?" Conversely, post hoc analyses typically are only loosely driven by theoretical aims. These are analogous to visiting a bookstore hoping to find something of interest and purchasing whatever seems to interest you at the moment. The researchers are asking the question "Do you have anything interesting in stock today?"

4B.1.3.2 Multiple Comparisons: Alpha Inflation

Because the post hoc approach involves testing every possible pair of treatment means, the possibility of making a Type I error or of obtaining a false-positive result increases as we increase the number of comparisons. For example, if our independent variable has five treatment (levels) groups, then we would need to evaluate $(a(a - 1))/2 = (5 * 4)/2 = 10$ pairwise comparisons (where a is the number of treatment groups). If we multiply our alpha level by the number of comparisons—$(.05 * 10) = .5$—and round this value upward to a whole number (1), we can expect to generate 1 false positive among our 10 pairwise comparisons. To compensate for this potential exponential increase in Type I error rate, statisticians have developed a large number of multiple comparison tests that attempt to minimize Type I error and stabilize or increase statistical power in the face of statistical violations (particularly homogeneity of variance).

4B.1.3.3 Multiple Comparisons: Post Hoc Options

These multiple comparison tests compare individual pairs of means—that is, they compare each group with every other group (this is called *family-wise* comparison) with special algebraically derived formulas that are assessed with a variety of statistical distributions such as t, F, Studentized Range, and so on (Gamst et al., 2008; Keppel & Wickens, 2004; Seaman, Levin, & Serlin, 1991; Toothaker, 1993). The actual statistical algorithms that make up these post hoc tests vary in complexity and will not concern us here because IBM SPSS makes these computations for us and seamlessly evaluates each pairwise comparison for statistical significance.

We have listed below a brief summary of these multiple comparison post hoc tests as they appear in the **Post Hoc** dialog window. We first summarize the tests appropriate when the assumption of homogeneity of variance has been met:

- The **LSD** or least significant difference test uses a t test to make all possible pairwise comparisons of group means following a statistically significant omnibus F test. This test is the most liberal (i.e., it has relatively high statistical power and a greater likelihood of committing a Type I error). Most authors caution against its use (e.g., Keppel & Wickens, 2004), but there are still advocates who recommend its use (Carmer & Swanson, 1973).
- The **Bonferroni** procedure (also called the Dunn's test) uses t tests to assess all pairs of group means but controls the overall (family-wise) error rate by adjusting the operational alpha level by the number of comparisons being made. This procedure is considered a moderately conservative approach. Although often employed in the literature, this procedure tends to overcorrect with a large number of comparisons (Keppel & Wickens, 2004).
- The **Sidak** (also called Sidak–Bonferroni; the "S" is pronounced "Sh") also makes all pairwise comparisons based on a t test but uses more stringent alpha-level adjustment procedures than the Bonferroni test. This too is considered a moderate (neither too liberal nor too conservative) post hoc test.
- The **Scheffé** test conducts simultaneous pairwise comparisons of all means using the F distribution. This procedure is the most conservative (i.e., less statistical power and fewer chances of making a Type I error) of the post hoc tests. The Scheffé test may be most useful when moving into "uncharted" theoretical waters where a carefully articulated conservative stance may be most appropriate.
- **R-E-G-W-F** is the Ryan–Enoit–Gabriel–Welsch procedure based on the F test, and **R-E-G-W-Q** is the Ryan–Enoit–Gabriel–Welsch step-down procedure based on the Studentized Range. Both of these moderate procedures are modifications of the Newman–Keuls procedure. These two procedures are recommended by some authors over the use of the Newman–Keuls procedure (Keppel & Wickens,

2004); Gamst et al. (2008) recommend using the Studentized Range version of the procedure.

- The **S-N-K** (Student–Newman–Keuls) compares all pairwise combinations of means using the Studentized Range distribution. Using a stepwise procedure, means are ranked in ascending order, and extreme differences are successively tested. This moderate procedure has a tendency to inflate Type I error rate and is not recommended by some observers (Keppel & Wickens, 2004).
- The **Tukey** procedure (also called the honestly significant difference, or HSD, test) considers all pairwise comparisons by using the standard error of the mean and the Studentized Range distribution. This procedure controls the family-wise (overall) error rate at the rate for the entire set of all pairwise comparisons. This moderately conservative procedure is recommended by many commentators (e.g., Gamst et al., 2008; Keppel & Wickens, 2004).
- The **Tukey's-b** test also uses the Studentized Range distribution to make pairwise comparisons. This procedure uses an average of the Tukey HSD test and the SNK to evaluate each comparison. This test is not highly recommended (Keppel & Wickens, 2004).
- The **Duncan** test (like the SNK, REGWF, and REGWQ) is based on stepwise testing. This moderately liberal procedure rank orders the means similar to the SNK test, but it uses a family-wise control for Type I error rather than individual comparison adjustments.
- **Hochberg's GT2** test is similar to the Tukey HSD, but it was specifically designed to address unequal sample sizes.
- The **Gabriel** test is a more liberal version of the Hochberg's GT2.
- The **Waller-Duncan** test employs a Bayesian algorithm that adjusts the assessment criterion on the size of the overall *F* statistic. This approach also allows researchers to specify the ratio of Type I error to Type II error within the test comparison.
- The **Dunnett** test is useful when a control group is being compared with a set of experimental groups. The test statistic is the *t* test.

We next summarize the tests appropriate when the assumption of homogeneity of variance has not been met:

- **Tamhane's T2** test produces pairwise comparisons based on the *t* test and adjusts for unequal variances. This is considered a conservative test.
- **Dunnett's T3** provides pairwise comparisons based on the Studentized maximum modulus and can be used with unequal variances.
- The **Games-Howell** is a liberal pairwise comparison test that can be used with unequal variances.
- **Dunnett's C** is a pairwise comparison test based on the Studentized Range and can be used with unequal variances.

As far as specific recommendations go, we agree with Gamst et al. (2008), Howell (1997), and Keppel and Wickens (2004) that both the Tukey HSD and the REGWQ procedures are sound ways to control for Type I error rate. If control of Type I error rate is not a major concern but gaining statistical power is a primary goal, then the LSD test is certainly worth considering. If unequal variances are observed among the treatment groups, then the more conservative Tamhane's T2 test may be in order.

4B.1.3.4 Multiple Comparisons: Setup

On the assumption that we will meet the assumption of equal variances, we have checked **Tukey** to obtain his HSD test as shown in Figure 4b.3. Click **Continue** to return to the main dialog window, and click **OK** to perform the analysis.

4B.1.4 Omnibus One-Way Between-Subjects Analysis Output

The results of the omnibus analysis are shown in Figure 4b.4. In the top table, we see that the results of Levene's test is not statistically significant, informing us that we have not violated the assumption of equal variances. Our ANOVA yielded a statistically significant F ratio based on 2 and 18 degrees of freedom. Eta square, not provided in the output, is computed as Between Groups Sum of Squares divided by Total Sum of Squares; here, that is 798.000/1228.571 or .650. Thus, differences in fertilizer accounted for 65% of the variance in the amount of plant growth.

Figure 4b.4 Results of the Omnibus Analysis

Test of Homogeneity of Variances

plant_growth plant growth in mm

Levene Statistic	df1	df2	Sig.
1.778	2	18	.197

ANOVA

plant_growth plant growth in mm

	Sum of Squares	df	Mean Square	F	Sig.
Between Groups	798.000	2	399.000	16.680	.000
Within Groups	430.571	18	23.921		
Total	1228.571	20			

4B.1.5 Multiple Comparisons Tests Output

The results of the Tukey post hoc tests are shown in Figure 4b.5. The middle table represents a common structure that IBM SPSS uses in its output for paired comparisons. The first major numerical row labeled **1 Fertilizer A** compares Fertilizers B and C to Fertilizer A; the top line of the row is the comparison of A to B, and the second line of the row is the comparison of A to C. The column labeled **Mean Difference** is the result of the subtraction of B and C, respectively, from A. With the observed plant growth means from the top table in Figure 4b.5, we see that Fertilizer A (29.86) minus Fertilizer B (26.00) is 3.857 and that Fertilizer A (29.86) minus Fertilizer C (40.57) is −10.714.

Figure 4b.5 Results of the Post Hoc Tukey Tests

Descriptives

plant_growth plant growth in mm

	N	Mean	Std. Deviation	Std. Error	95% Confidence Interval for Mean — Lower Bound	95% Confidence Interval for Mean — Upper Bound	Minimum	Maximum
1 Fertilizer A	7	29.86	4.670	1.765	25.54	34.18	24	36
2 Fertilizer B	7	26.00	5.916	2.236	20.53	31.47	19	34
3 Fertilizer C	7	40.57	3.867	1.462	37.00	44.15	35	45
Total	21	32.14	7.838	1.710	28.58	35.71	19	45

Multiple Comparisons

plant_growth plant growth in mm
Tukey HSD

(I) fertilizer type of fertilizer	(J) fertilizer type of fertilizer	Mean Difference (I–J)	Std. Error	Sig.	95% Confidence Interval — Lower Bound	95% Confidence Interval — Upper Bound
1 Fertilizer A	2 Fertilizer B	3.857	2.614	.326	−2.81	10.53
	3 Fertilizer C	−10.714.	2.614	.002	−17.39	−4.04
2 Fertilizer B	1 Fertilizer A	−3.857	2.614	.326	−10.53	2.81
	3 Fertilizer C	−14.571.	2.614	.000	−21.24	−7.90
3 Fertilizer C	1 Fertilizer A	10.714.	2.614	.002	4.04	17.39
	2 Fertilizer B	14.571.	2.614	.000	7.90	21.24

*. The mean difference is significant at the 0.05 level.

Homogeneous Subsets

plant_growth plant growth in mm

Tukey HSD_a

fertilizer type of ...	N	Subset for alpha = 0.05 — 1	Subset for alpha = 0.05 — 2
2 Fertilizer B	7	26.00	
1 Fertilizer A	7	29.86	
3 Fertilizer C	7		40.57
Sig.		.326	1.000

Means for groups in homogeneous subsets are displayed.

a. Uses Harmonic Mean Sample Size = 7.000.

The second major row focuses on Fertilizer B and the differences of A and C, respectively, from it, and the third major row focuses on Fertilizer C and the differences of A and B, respectively, from it. Mean differences are computed in an analogous fashion to the first major row.

Looking across the row at the **Sig.** column informs us about the "level" of significance achieved by the mean difference. For example, the first line of the first row comparing Fertilizer A to Fertilizer B shows a significance level of .326. This does not meet our alpha level of .05, and thus we conclude that the mean difference of 3.857 between the two fertilizers is not statistically significant. Using this reasoning, we see that Fertilizer C, however, differs significantly from the other two. Note that there is redundancy built into the structure of the table in that each combination of fertilizers is represented twice. In reality, there are only three comparisons (A with B, A with C, and B with C).

The bottom table is provided as a way to summarize the Tukey results that we have just described. Means are placed into the same **subset** column when they are not significantly different. Here, Fertilizers A and B are in one subset, and Fertilizer C is in its own subset.

4B.1.6 Reporting One-Way Between-Subjects Results

Three different fertilizers (A, B, and C) were assessed over a 2-month period on the growth in millimeters of yellow sweet corn. The three fertilizers produced significantly different rates of growth during this time frame, $F(2, 18) = 16.680$, $p < .001$, $\eta^2 = .650$. Results of a Tukey post hoc test indicated that Fertilizer C produced significantly more growth ($M = 40.57$, $SD = 3.867$) than either Fertilizer A ($M = 29.86$, $SD = 4.670$) or Fertilizer B ($M = 26.00$, $SD = 5.916$).

4B.2 Two-Way Between-Subjects Design

A two-way between-subjects design contains two between-subjects independent variables (A and B) combined factorially such that all the combinations of the levels of A and B are represented. It contains $a \times b$ number of groups where a and b are the number of levels of independent variables A and B, respectively. Different cases are randomly assigned to the different groups if it is possible to do so.

4B.2.1 Numerical Example

In this hypothetical example, the focus is on the use of a social network website as measured by the average number of hours per week that users interact with the site (this is the dependent variable named **amount_use** in the data file). There are two independent variables, each with two levels: (a) size of the metropolitan area in which the social network user resides (1 = *large city*, 2 = *small town*) named **metropolitan_size** in the data file and (b) sex of the social network user (1 = *female*, 2 = *male*) named **sex** in the data file. Data are contained in the file named **Social_Network_Use**.

4B.2.2 Omnibus Two-Way Between-Subjects Analysis Setup

Selecting **Analyze ➜ General Linear Model ➜ Univariate** brings us to the main dialog screen shown in Figure 4b.6. From the variables list panel on the left side, we click over **amount_use** to the **Dependent Variable** panel and **metropolitan_size** and **sex** to the **Fixed Factor(s)** panel. Select the **Options** pushbutton and check **Descriptive statistics** and **Homogeneity tests** in the **Options** window (see Figure 4b.7). The checkbox for **Estimates of effect size** will produce a partial eta-square value rather than the classical eta-square value. As mentioned in Section 4A.4.2, we will not request the partial eta square but will instead compute it by hand when necessary.

Figure 4b.6 Main Dialog Window for General Linear Model

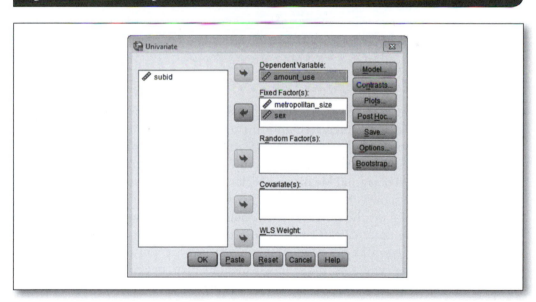

4B.2.3 Multiple Comparisons Tests Setup

As we did for the one-way between-subjects analysis setup, it is convenient to specify the post-ANOVA tests at this point. With only two levels for each independent

Figure 4b.7 The Options Window for General Linear Model

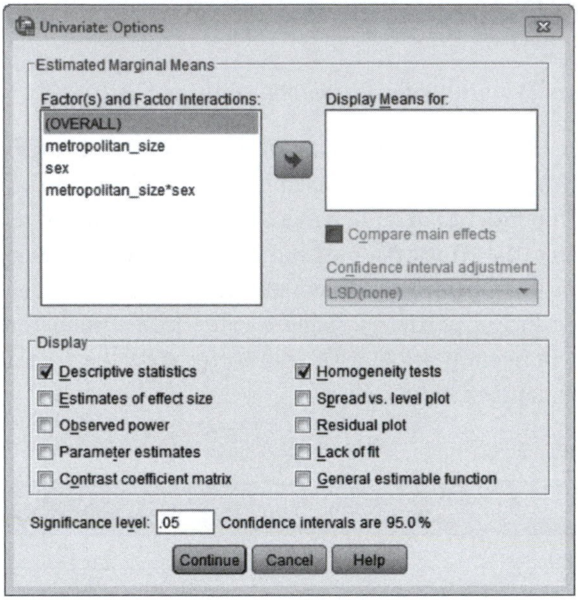

variable, we do not need to be concerned with post hoc tests as a statistically significant *F* ratio, for a main effect immediately informs us that its two means are statistically different. Thus, we focus on the interaction effect. While in the **Options** window, highlight **metropolitan_size*sex** in the **Factor(s) and Factor Interactions** panel under the heading of **Estimated Marginal Means** and click on the arrow to send it to the **Display Means for** panel as shown in Figure 4b.8. This will result in a syntax **EMMEANS =** **TABLES** subcommand for the interaction-estimated marginal (least squares) means to be displayed in the output. Click **Continue** to return to the main dialog window, and click **Paste** to open a syntax window containing the syntax you have generated. Our pointing and clicking generates this syntax, which, in turn, is what IBM SPSS uses to structure the analysis—even if this syntax is not displayed, it is what drives the analysis for IBM SPSS.

The syntax that we have generated in our pointing-and-clicking mode is displayed in Figure 4b.9. Note that the subcommand /**EMMEANS = TABLES (metropolitan_** **size*sex)** appears toward the middle of the syntax. To perform our tests of simple effects, we are going to (a) make a copy of that line and place it directly under the original and (b) add a few words of syntax to each line. The two lines should look just

Figure 4b.8 The Options Window for General Linear Model in Preparation to Set Up the Simple Effects Tests

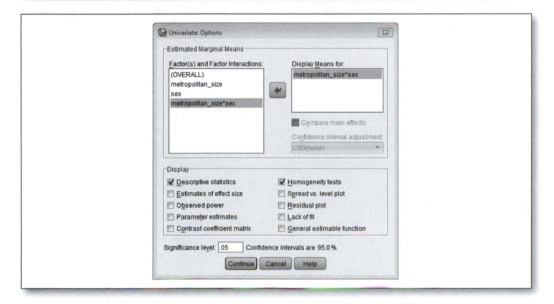

Figure 4b.9 The Syntax We Have Generated Appears in Response to Selecting the Paste Pushbutton in the Main Dialog Window

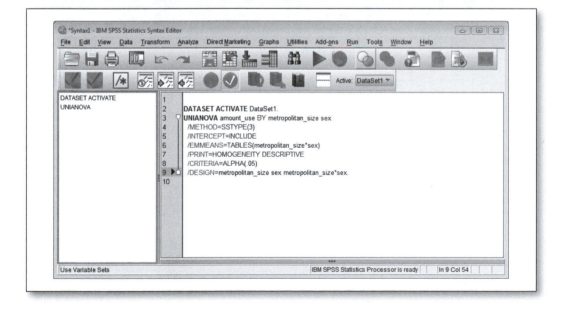

like this (as you type in the syntax window, IBM SPSS may anticipate your intentions and supply a drop-down set of choices for you—you can either select from the IBM SPSS choices, which may give the syntax a slightly different look, or you can type the syntax exactly as shown below):

/EMMEANS = TABLES (metropolitan_size*sex) compare (metropolitan_size) adj (Bonferroni)

/EMMEANS = TABLES (metropolitan_size*sex) compare (sex) adj (Bonferroni)

The top line can be translated as follows. Display a table of estimated marginal means for the combinations of **metropolitan_size** and **sex.** Then compare the means for **metropolitan_size** (large city with small town) separately for each level of the other variable (do this comparison for females and do it for males). This comparison is to be done pairwise using *t* tests with a Bonferroni adjustment or correction to avoid alpha-level inflation.

The bottom line can be translated as follows. Display a table of estimated marginal means for the combinations of **metropolitan_size** and **sex**. Then compare the means for **sex** (females with males) separately for each level of the other variable (do this comparison for large city and do it for small town). This comparison is to be done pairwise using *t* tests with a Bonferroni adjustment or correction to avoid alpha-level inflation.

Figure 4b.10   The Syntax Modified to Perform Tests of Simple Effects

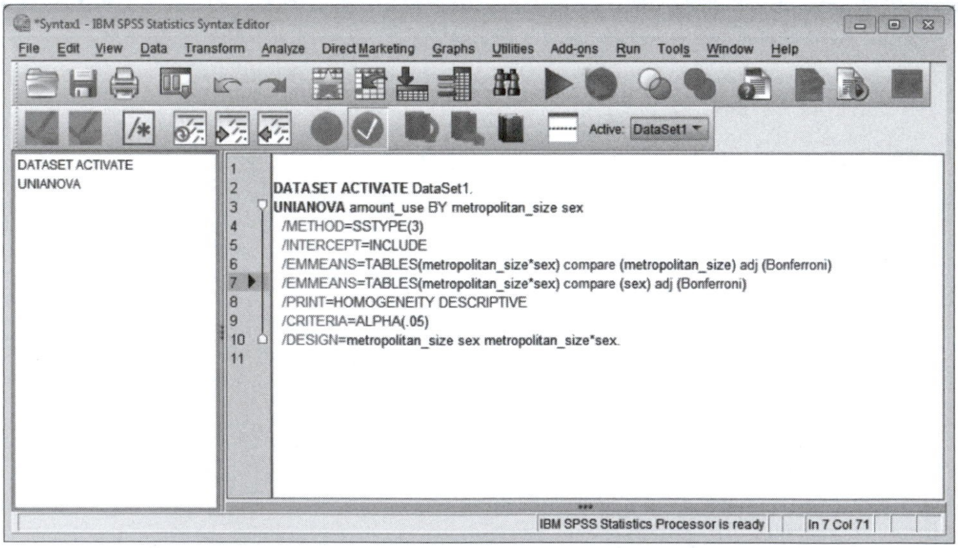

The modifications to the syntax window are shown in Figure 4b.10. Once they are made, we select **Run** ➔ **All** from the main menu to perform the analysis.

4B.2.4 Omnibus Two-Way
Between-Subjects Analysis Output

The results of the omnibus analysis are shown in Figure 4b.11. In the top table, we see that the results of Levene's test is not statistically significant, informing us that we have not violated the assumption of equal variances.

The summary table for the analysis is shown in the bottom table. ANOVA is a special case of the general linear model, which is, at a simple level, a linear regression procedure. We

---

Figure 4b.11   Results of the Omnibus Analysis

Levene's Test of Equality of Error Variances[a]

Dependent Variable:use of social network site

F	df1	df2	Sig.
1.434	3	24	.257

Tests the null hypothesis that the error variance of the dependent variable is equal across groups.

a. Design: Intercept + metropolitan_size + sex + metropolitan_size * sex

Tests of Between-Subjects Effects

Dependent Variable:use of social network site

Source	Type III Sum of Squares	df	Mean Square	F	Sig.
Corrected Model	1111.250[a]	3	370.417	90.980	.000
Intercept	11160.036	1	11160.036	2741.061	.000
metropolitan_size	378.893	1	378.893	93.061	.000
sex	22.321	1	22.321	5.482	.028
metropolitan_size * sex	710.036	1	710.036	174.395	.000
Error	97.714	24	4.071		
Total	12369.000	28			
Corrected Total	1208.964	27			

a. R Squared = .919 (Adjusted R Squared = .909)

discuss linear regression in Chapters 6, 7, and 8. In that model, the dependent variable is predicted based on the primary effects (the two main effects and the interaction for a two-way between-subjects design).

For now, those primary effects that you are used to seeing in the summary table, which are the primary effects (the effects of interest to us) and the ones we presented in Chapter 4A, represent only a part of the model (the relevant part when performing an ANOVA). That part of the model is called the *partial model* or, as IBM SPSS calls it, the *corrected model*. The *full model* contains the *Y* intercept of the regression function. Because we performed the analysis using the **General Linear Model** procedure, we obtained a more complete output than we did in the **One-Way ANOVA** procedure shown earlier.

In the summary table shown in Figure 4b.11, the rows for **Intercept** and **Total** refer to the full model and can be ignored. The row for **Corrected Model** is a composite of all three effects of interest (e.g., its sum of squares is the sum of the sum of squares for the three primary effects) and can also be ignored because the whole point of ANOVA is to partition the total variance into its components.

When examining the summary table produced by the **General Linear Model** procedure, we need examine only the three primary effects, the **Error**, and the **Corrected Total** rows. Our ANOVA yielded a statistically significant *F* ratio for all three effects. Eta square, not provided in the output, is computed as Effect Sum of Squares divided by Corrected Total Sum of Squares. For **metropolitan_size**, that is 378.893/1208.964 or .313. For **sex**, that is 22.321/1208.964 or .018. For **metropolitan_size*sex**, that is 710.036/1208.964 or .587.

4B.2.5 Simple Effects Tests Output

As was discussed in Section 4A.6.3. interaction effect supersedes main effects. Thus, we move directly to our tests of simple effects. We performed two sets of simple effects tests, the first comparing **metropolitan_size** and the second comparing **sex**. We treat each in turn.

4B.2.5.1 Simple Effects Tests Comparing *metropolitan_size*

The first set of simple effects tests called for comparing the **metropolitan_size** variable, and the results of this analysis are shown in Figure 4b.12. We see the estimated marginal means in the top table; these are identical to the observed means because we have equal sample sizes in each cell. Estimated marginal means are associated with standard errors rather than standard deviations.

Pairwise comparisons are shown in the lower table and are structured as we described in Section 4B.1.5. The two metropolitan areas (large city and small town) are compared separately for females and males. As can be seen in the first major row, female residents in a large city differ significantly in their use of social networking from those in a small town. We also see that the same can be said of males (the last major row in the table).

Figure 4b.12 Results of the Simple Effects Tests Comparing Metropolitan Areas

1. metropolitan_size * sex

Estimates

Dependent Variable:use of social network site

metropolitan_size	sex	Mean	Std. Error	95% Confidence Interval	
				Lower Bound	Upper Bound
large city	female	17.714	.763	16.140	19.288
	male	29.571	.763	27.997	31.145
small town	female	20.429	.763	18.855	22.003
	male	12.143	.763	10.569	13.717

Pairwise Comparisons

Dependent Variable:use of social network site

sex	(I) metropolitan_size	(J) metropolitan_size	Mean Difference (I-J)	Std. Error	Sig.a	95% Confidence Interval for Differencea	
						Lower Bound	Upper Bound
female	large city	small town	-2.714*	1.079	.019	-4.940	-.488
	small town	large city	2.714*	1.079	.019	.488	4.940
male	large city	small town	17.429*	1.079	.000	15.203	19.655
	small town	large city	-17.429*	1.079	.000	-19.655	-15.203

Based on estimated marginal means

*. The mean difference is significant at the .05 level.
a. Adjustment for multiple comparisons: Bonferroni.

4B.2.5.2 Simple Effects Tests Comparing **sex**

The second set of simple effects tests called for comparing the **sex** variable, and the results of this analysis are shown in Figure 4b.13. The two sexes are compared separately for a large city and a small town. As can be seen in the first major row, females and males in a large city differ significantly in their use of social networking. We also see that the same can be said of residents in a small town (the last major row in the table).

Figure 4b.13 Results of the Simple Effects Tests Comparing Female and Male Participants

2. metropolitan_size * sex

Estimates

Dependent Variable:use of social network site

metropolitan_size	sex	Mean	Std. Error	95% Confidence Interval	
				Lower Bound	Upper Bound
large city	female	17.714	.763	16.140	19.288
	male	29.571	.763	27.997	31.145
small town	female	20.429	.763	18.855	22.003
	male	12.143	.763	10.569	13.717

Pairwise Comparisons

Dependent Variable:use of social network site

metropolitan_size	(I) sex	(J) sex	Mean Difference (I-J)	Std. Error	Sig.[a]	95% Confidence Interval for Difference[a]	
						Lower Bound	Upper Bound
large city	female	male	-11.857[*]	1.079	.000	-14.083	-9.631
	male	female	11.857[*]	1.079	.000	9.631	14.083
small town	female	male	8.286[*]	1.079	.000	6.060	10.512
	male	female	-8.286[*]	1.079	.000	-10.512	-6.060

Based on estimated marginal means

*. The mean difference is significant at the .05 level.
a. Adjustment for multiple comparisons: Bonferroni.

4B.2.6 Reporting Two-Way Between-Subjects Results

The present study focused on the differences in use of a social network website (measured by the average number of hours per week that users interact with the site) as a function of type of metropolitan residence (large city or small town) and sex of user. The statistically significant main effects of metropolitan area, $F(1, 24) = 93.061$, $p < .001$, $\eta^2 = .313$, and user sex, $F(1, 24) = 5.482$, $p = .028$, $\eta^2 = .018$, can best be understood by examining the statistically significant two-way interaction, $F(1, 24) = 174.395$, $p < .001$, $\eta^2 = .587$.

The interaction is presented in Figure 4b.14. Tests of simple effects using Bonferroni-corrected t tests revealed that all pairwise comparisons were statistically significant. In both residential areas, females tended to use the social network in moderation, although somewhat more in the small town than in the large city. Males in the large city used the social network website extensively but males in small towns used the website much less compared with the other groups.

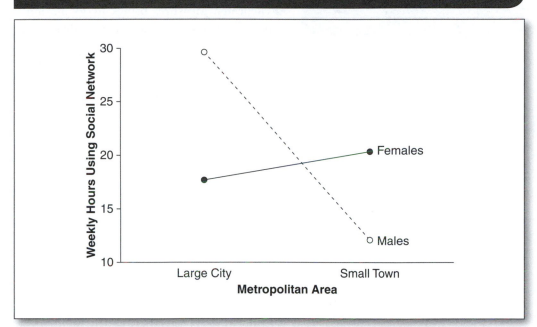

Figure 4b.14 Weekly Hours of Using a Social Network as a Function of Metropolitan Residence Area for Females and Males

4B.3 One-Way Within-Subjects Design

A one-way within-subjects design, often called a *repeated measures design*, contains one within-subjects independent variable generically labeled as the *treatment* effect. Participants are measured on the same dependent variable multiple times, and these measurements are each represented in the data file. In such a design, the subjects are conceived as their own controls.

4B.3.1 Numerical Example

In this hypothetical example, we are focusing on a medical (Drug *D*) treatment (reduction) of symptoms of Disease *X*. Seven patients are measured for the intensity of symptoms they experience prior to the treatment (named **baseline** in the data file). They are then administered the medical treatment, and their symptom intensity is measured each week for the next 3 weeks (named **week_1**, **week_2**, and **week_3** in the data file). Thus, we have four measurements (levels of the treatment variable) for each patient. Data are contained in the file named **Symptom_Reduction**.

4B.3.2 One-Way Within-Subjects Analysis Setup

Figure 4b.15 The Initial Repeated Measures Define Factor(s) Dialog Window

Figure 4b.16 The Configured Repeated Measures Define Factor(s) Dialog Window

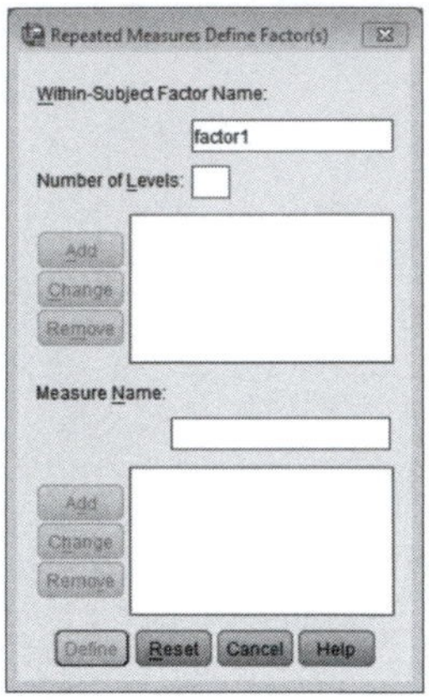

Selecting **Analyze ➔ General Linear Model ➔ Repeated Measures** brings us to the initial Repeated Measures Define Factor(s) dialog window shown in Figure 4b.15. To define a within-subjects variable, we must name it and indicate how many levels it contains. We will name the variable **med_treatment;** highlight the generic **factor1** name and replace it with our chosen name. In the **Number of Levels** panel, type in **4.** This is illustrated in Figure 4b.16. Click the **Add** pushbutton (which activates the **Define** pushbutton), and then select **Define** to reach the main dialog window.

The main dialog screen is shown in Figure 4b.17. The four vertical placeholders in the **Within-Subjects Variables** panel need to be filled with variables in the data file. From the variables list panel on the left side, we click over **baseline**, **week_1**, **week_2**, and **week_3** to the **Within-Subjects Variables** panel (highlighting the set and clicking the arrow makes this easy). As there is no between-subjects independent variable in this design, this main dialog window is now fully specified. The result of this is shown in Figure 4b.18.

Select the **Options** pushbutton and check **Descriptive statistics** under **Display** in the lower portion of the **Options** window. In the upper portion of the **Options** window labeled **Estimated Marginal Means**, highlight **med_treatment** and click the arrow to place it in the panel labeled **Display Means for.** Then check **Compare main effects** directly under that panel, and select **Bonferroni** from the drop-down menu. All this is shown in Figure 4b.19. By checking **Compare main effects** and selecting **Bonferroni**, we are requesting pairwise t tests with a Bonferroni-corrected alpha level to be applied to the means of the four conditions.

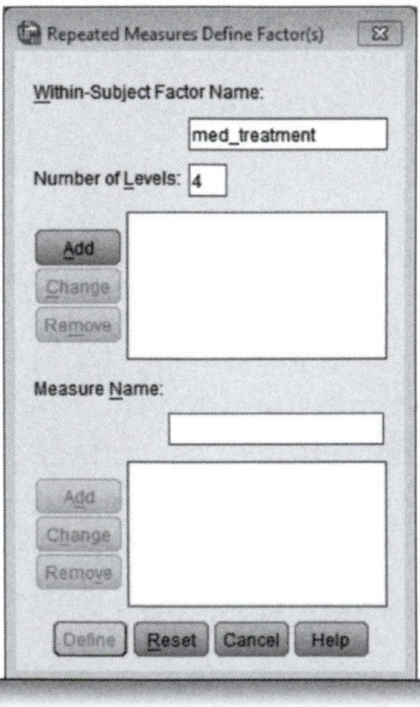

Figure 4b.17 Main Dialog Window for General Linear Model

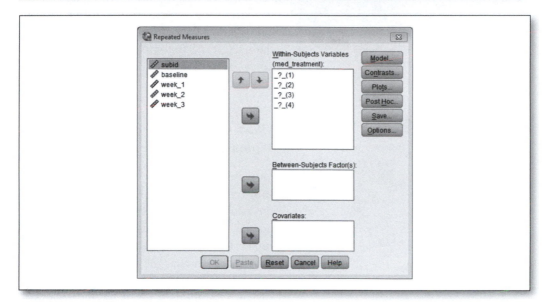

Figure 4b.18 The Configured Main Dialog Window for General Linear Model

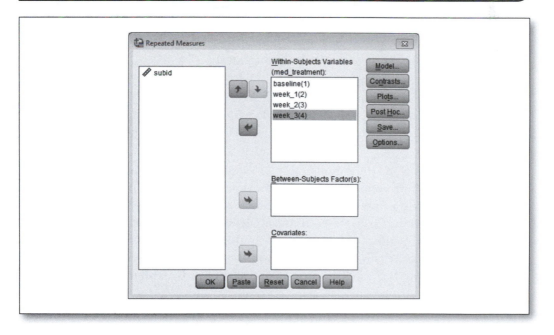

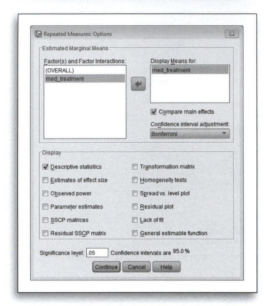

Figure 4b.19 The Options Window for General Linear Model in Preparation to Set Up the Simple Effects Tests

If our omnibus F ratio is statistically significant, we will examine these t test results to determine which means differ significantly. Click **Continue** to return to the main dialog screen, and click **OK** to perform the analysis.

4B.3.3 Omnibus One-Way Within-Subjects Analysis Output

The results of the omnibus analysis are shown in Figure 4b.20. In the top table, we see the summary table for the between-subjects portion of the variance. In a one-way within-subjects design, the only source of between-subjects variance is the individual differences between participants. IBM SPSS names this variance component **Error** in the table. Also shown is the intercept in the full model, which can be ignored for our purposes.

The middle table shown in Figure 4b.20, automatically produced by IBM SPSS in the repeated measures module, presents the results of the Mauchly test of sphericity (Mauchly, 1940). This test is applied to each within-subjects variable and is analogous to the Levene test (see Gamst et al., 2008); Mauchly's test assesses two assumptions simultaneously:

- The levels of the within-subjects variable have equal variances.
- Pairwise correlations of the levels of the within-subjects variable are equal (if the within-subjects variable has only two levels, Mauchly's test cannot be performed).

As can be seen from the middle table of Figure 4b.20, Mauchly's test returned a statistically significant result, indicating that the data have violated the sphericity assumption. Because this is not uncommon, IBM SPSS automatically generates sphericity-corrected F ratios in the form of **Greenhouse-Giesser**, **Huynh-Feldt**, and **Lower-bound** estimates. These corrections are computed by multiplying the observed degrees of freedom by the respective epsilon values shown in the table; the F ratio is then evaluated against the corrected degrees of freedom. We will use the **Greenhouse-Giesser** correction in evaluating our outcome.

The bottom table shown in Figure 4b.20 displays the summary table for the within-subjects component of the variance. Regardless of which sphericity correction is used, the

Figure 4b.20 Results of the Omnibus Analysis

Tests of Between–Subjects Effects

Measure:MEASURE_1
Transformed Variable:Average

Source	Type III Sum of Squares	df	Mean Square	F	Sig.
Intercept	24642.000	1	24642.000	380.362	.000
Error	453.500	7	64.786		

Mauchly's Test of Sphericity_b

Measure:MEASURE_1

Within Subjects Effect	Mauchly's W	Approx. Chi–Square	df	Sig.	Epsilon_a		
					Greenhouse–Geisser	Huynh–Feldt	Lower–bound
med_treatment	.021	22.053	5	.001	.376	.399	.333

Tests the null hypothesis that the error covariance matrix of the orthonormalized transformed dependent variables is proportional to an identity matrix.

a. May be used to adjust the degrees of freedom for the averaged tests of significance. Corrected tests are displayed in the Tests of Within–Subjects Effects table.

b. Design: Intercept
Within Subjects Design: med_treatment

Tests of Within–Subjects Effects

Measure:MEASURE_1

Source		Type III Sum of Squares	df	Mean Square	F	Sig.
med_treatment	Sphericity Assumed	1428.750	3	476.250	60.339	.000
	Greenhouse–Geisser	1428.750	1.128	1266.064	60.339	.000
	Huynh–Feldt	1428.750	1.197	1193.644	60.339	.000
	Lower–bound	1428.750	1.000	1428.750	60.339	.000
Error(med_treatment)	Sphericity Assumed	165.750	21	7.893		
	Greenhouse–Geisser	165.750	7.899	20.982		
	Huynh–Feldt	165.750	8.379	19.782		
	Lower–bound	165.750	7.000	23.679		

effect of **med_treatment** is statistically significant. As indicated in Section 4A.6.1, eta square is computed as the sum of squares for the effect (1428.750) divided by the total within-subjects sum of squares (1428.750 + 165.750 = 1594.500). In the present example, the eta-square value is .896.

4B.3.4 Pairwise Comparison of Means Output

Means for the within-subjects variable are shown in Figure 4b.21. Observed means are shown in the top table and estimated margin means are shown in the middle panel; with equal sample sizes, these two sets of means are the same. Note that in reporting the estimated marginal

Figure 4b.21 Results of the Simple Effects Tests Comparing Treatment

Descriptive Statistics

	Mean	Std. Deviation	N
baseline	38.00	4.811	8
week_1	29.38	5.125	8
week_2	22.25	5.175	8
week_3	21.38	3.503	8

Estimated Marginal Means

med_treatment

Estimates

Measure:MEASURE_1

med tr...	Mean	Std. Error	95% Confidence Interval	
			Lower Bound	Upper Bound
1	38.000	1.701	33.978	42.022
2	29.375	1.812	25.090	33.660
3	22.250	1.830	17.923	26.577
4	21.375	1.238	18.447	24.303

Pairwise Comparisons

Measure:MEASURE_1

(I) med _trea tmen t	(J) med _trea tmen t	Mean Difference (I–J)	Std. Error	Sig.,	95% Confidence Interval for Difference,	
					Lower Bound	Upper Bound
1	2	8.625.	1.782	.011	2.145	15.105
	3	15.750.	2.210	.001	7.715	23.785
	4	16.625.	1.068	.000	12.742	20.508
2	1	−8.625.	1.782	.011	−15.105	−2.145
	3	7.125.	.639	.000	4.801	9.449
	4	8.000.	.845	.000	4.927	11.073
3	1	−15.750.	2.210	.001	−23.785	−7.715
	2	−7.125.	.639	.000	−9.449	−4.801
	4	.875	1.231	1.000	−3.601	5.351
4	1	−16.625.	1.068	.000	−20.508	−12.742
	2	−8.000.	.845	.000	−11.073	−4.927
	3	−.875	1.231	1.000	−5.351	3.601

Based on estimated marginal means

*. The mean difference is significant at the .05 level.

a. Adjustment for multiple comparisons: Bonferroni.

means, IBM SPSS has replaced the variable names with a number corresponding to the particular level; for example, in the middle table, **baseline** is now called **med_treatment 1**, **week_1** is called **med_treatment 2**, and so on.

Pairwise comparisons are shown in the lower table and are structured as we described in Section 4B.1.5. As they are based on the estimated marginal means, the labeling of the levels corresponds to that used in the estimated marginal means table. The first major row shows the comparisons of each condition to Level 1 (**baseline**), the second major row shows the comparisons of each condition to Level 1 (**week_1**), and so on. As can be seen, all pairwise comparisons are statistically significant except for levels 3 (**week_2**) and 4 (**week_3**).

4B.3.5 Reporting One-Way Within-Subjects Results

The present study examined the effectiveness of Drug *D* in reducing symptoms associated with Disease *X* Patients were measured on symptom severity prior to the drug being administered to establish a baseline and again 1, 2, and 3 weeks after Drug *D* was administered. Using a Greenhouse–Giesser correction for the sphericity that was observed [Mauchly $W(5) = .021$, approximate $\chi^2 = 22.053$, $p = .001$], a statistically significant effect of the drug was found, $F(1.128, 7.899) = 60.339$, $p < .001$, $\eta^2 = .896$ with respect to the within-subjects variance.

Bonferroni-corrected pairwise *t* tests indicated that symptom severity at baseline ($M = 38.000$, $SE = 1.701$) significantly lessened by 1 week after treatment ($M = 29.375$, $SE = 1.812$), further lessened through the second week after treatment ($M = 22.250$, $SE = 1.830$), and then stabilized at about that same level after the third week ($M = 21.375$, $SE = 1.238$).

4B.4 Simple Mixed Design

A simple mixed design contains one between-subjects independent variable (*A*) combined factorially with one within-subjects independent variable (*B*) such that all of the combinations of the levels of A and B are represented. It contains $a \times b$ number of groups where *a* and *b* are the number of levels of independent variables *A* and *B*, respectively.

4B.4.1 Numerical Example

In this hypothetical example, we examine the effects of web-based learning (coded as **1**) versus the use of in-class exercises (coded as **2**) under the variable of **teaching_program** on learning intermediate statistics. Students were exposed to one of the two teaching programs (a between-subjects variable) and were assessed prior to the onset of the program (**start_ score**) and again when the program ended (**finish_score**). Data are contained in the file named **Teaching_Programs**.

4B.4.2 Simple Mixed Analysis Setup

Selecting **Analyze** ➔ **General Linear Model** ➔ **Repeated Measures** brings us to the initial **Repeated Measures Define Factor(s)** dialog window shown in Figure 4b.22. To

Figure 4b.22 The Initial Repeated Measures Define Factor(s) Dialog Window

Figure 4b.23 The Configured Repeated Measures Define Factor(s) Dialog Window

define a within-subjects variable, we must name it and indicate how many levels it contains. We will name the variable **pretest_posttest**; highlight the generic **factor1** name and replace it with our chosen name. In the **Number of Levels** panel, type in **2**. This is illustrated in Figure 4b.23. Click the **Add** pushbutton (which activates the **Define** pushbutton), and then select **Define** to reach the main dialog window.

The main dialog screen is shown in Figure 4b.24. The two vertical placeholders in the **Within-Subjects Variables** panel need to be filled with variables in the data file. From the variables list panel on the left side, we click over **start_score** and **finish_score** to the **Within-Subjects Variables** panel (highlighting the set and clicking the arrow makes this easy). The click over **teaching_program** leads to the **Between-Subjects Factor(s)** panel. The result of this is shown in Figure 4b.25.

Select the **Options** pushbutton, and check **Descriptive statistics** under **Display** in the lower portion of the **Options** window. In the upper portion of the **Options** window labeled **Estimated Marginal Means**, highlight the interaction effect **teaching_program*pretest_posttest**, and click the arrow to place it in the panel labeled **Display Means for** (see Figure 4b.26). This will result in a syntax **EMMEANS = TABLES** subcommand for the interaction estimated marginal (least squares) means to be displayed in the output. Click **Continue** to return to the main dialog screen, and click **Paste** to display the syntax underlying the analysis (shown in Figure 4b.27).

Figure 4b.24 Main Dialog Window for General Linear Model

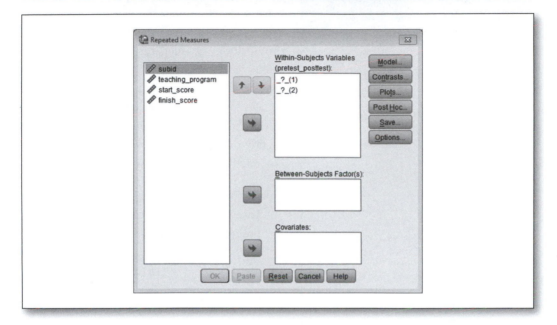

Figure 4b.25 The Configured Main Dialog Window for General Linear Model

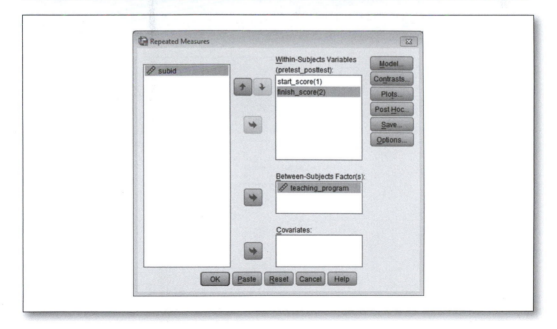

Figure 4b.26 The Options Window for General Linear Model in Preparation to Set Up the Simple Effects Tests

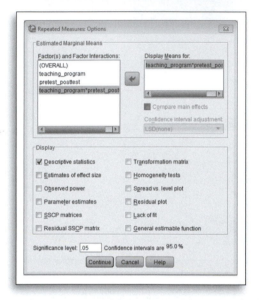

To perform our tests of simple effects, we are going to (a) make a copy of that line and place it directly under the original and (b) add a few words of syntax to each line. The two lines should look just like this (as you type in the syntax window, IBM SPSS may anticipate your intentions and supply a drop-down set of choices for you—you can either select from the IBM SPSS choices, which may give the syntax a slightly different look, or you can type the syntax exactly as shown below):

/EMMEANS = TABLES (teaching_program *pretest_posttest) compare (teaching_program) adj (Bonferroni)

/EMMEANS = TABLES (teaching_program *pretest_posttest) compare (pretest_posttest) adj (Bonferroni)

Figure 4b.27 The Syntax We Have Generated Appears in Response to Selecting the Paste Pushbutton in the Main Dialog Window

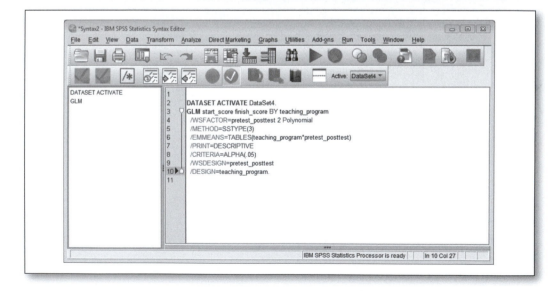

The top line can be translated as follows. Display a table of estimated marginal means for the combinations of **teaching_program** and **pretest_posttest.** Then compare the means for **teaching_program** (web-based program with in-class exercise program) separately for each level of the other variable [do this comparison for the pretest (**start_score**) and do it for the posttest (**finish_score**)]. This comparison is to be done pairwise using *t* tests with a Bonferroni adjustment or correction to avoid alpha-level inflation.

The bottom line can be translated as follows. Display a table of estimated marginal means for the combinations of **teaching_program** and **pretest_posttest**. Then compare the means for **pretest_posttest** (**start_score** with **finish_score**) separately for each level of the other variable (do this comparison for the web-based program and do it for the in-class exercise program). This comparison is to be done pairwise using *t* tests with a Bonferroni adjustment or correction to avoid alpha-level inflation.

The modifications to the syntax window are shown in Figure 4b.28. Once they are made, we select **Run ➜ All** from the main menu to perform the analysis.

Figure 4b.28 The Syntax Modified to Perform Tests of Simple Effects

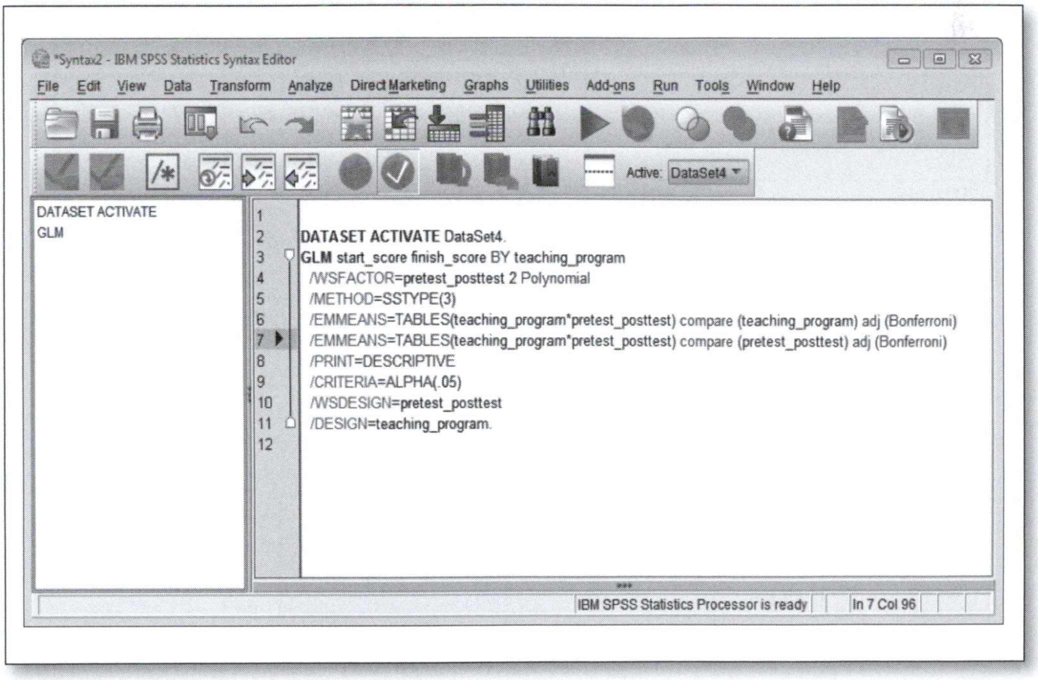

4B.4.3 Omnibus Simple Mixed Analysis Output

The results of the omnibus analysis are shown in Figure 4b.29. The bottom table shows the evaluation of the between-subjects variable, **teaching_program** in the present example. It is statistically significant. Eta square is computed as the sum of squares of the effect divided by the total between-subjects sum of squares based on the partial model. We therefore divide 612.500 by the sum of 1251.375 and 612.500 or 1863.875 to obtain 612.500/1863.875 = .329 with respect to the between-subjects variance.

Figure 4b.29   Results of the Omnibus Analysis

Mauchly's Test of Sphericity$_b$

Measure:MEASURE_1

Within Subjects Effect	Mauchly's W	Approx. Chi-Square	df	Sig.	Epsilon$_a$		
					Greenhouse-Geisser	Huynh–Feldt	Lower–bound
pretest_posttest	1.000	.000	0	.	1.000	1.000	1.000

Tests the null hypothesis that the error covariance matrix of the orthonormalized transformed dependent variables is proportional to an identity matrix.

a. May be used to adjust the degrees of freedom for the averaged tests of significance. Corrected tests are displayed in the Tests of Within–Subjects Effects table.

b. Design: Intercept + teaching_program
Within Subjects Design: pretest_posttest

Tests of Within–Subjects Effects

Measure:MEASURE_1

Source		Type III Sum of Squares	df	Mean Square	F	Sig.
pretest_posttest	Sphericity Assumed	4950.125	1	4950.125	214.972	.000
	Greenhouse-Geisser	4950.125	1.000	4950.125	214.972	.000
	Huynh–Feldt	4950.125	1.000	4950.125	214.972	.000
	Lower–bound	4950.125	1.000	4950.125	214.972	.000
pretest_posttest * teaching_program	Sphericity Assumed	684.500	1	684.500	29.726	.000
	Greenhouse-Geisser	684.500	1.000	684.500	29.726	.000
	Huynh–Feldt	684.500	1.000	684.500	29.726	.000
	Lower–bound	684.500	1.000	684.500	29.726	.000
Error(pretest_posttest)	Sphericity Assumed	322.375	14	23.027		
	Greenhouse-Geisser	322.375	14.000	23.027		
	Huynh–Feldt	322.375	14.000	23.027		
	Lower–bound	322.375	14.000	23.027		

Tests of Between–Subjects Effects

Measure:MEASURE_1
Transformed Variable:Average

Source	Type III Sum of Squares	df	Mean Square	F	Sig.
Intercept	128271.125	1	128271.125	1435.058	.000
teaching_program	612.500	1	612.500	6.852	.020
Error	1251.375	14	89.384		

In the top table, we see that Mauchly's test was not performed (because there are only two levels of the repeated measure). We therefore proceed as though we can assume sphericity.

The middle table shown in Figure 4b.29 displays the summary table for the within-subjects component of the variance. The effect of **pretest_posttest** is statistically significant, but, because the two-way interaction effect is statistically significant as well, we note that it will occupy the bulk of our attention. Eta square is computed as the sum of squares for the within-subjects effect of interest divided by the total within-subjects sum of squares (4950.125 + 684.500 + 322.375 = 5957.000). In the present example, the eta-square value for **pretest_posttest** is 4950.125/5957.000 or .831 with respect to the within-subjects variance, and the eta-square value for the interaction is 684.500/5957.000 or .115 with respect to the within-subjects variance.

4B.4.4 Simple Effects Tests Output

As was discussed in Section 4A.6.3, interaction effects supersede main effects. Thus, we move directly to our tests of simple effects performed on the interaction effect. We performed two sets of simple effects tests, the first comparing **teaching_program** and the second comparing **pretest_posttest**. We treat each in turn.

4B.4.4.1 Simple Effects Tests
Comparing *teaching_program*

The first set of simple effects tests compared the **teaching_program** variable, and the results of this analysis are shown in Figure 4b.30. We see the estimated marginal means in the top table, and the pairwise comparisons are shown in the lower table. The two teaching methods (web and class exercises) are compared separately for the **pretest_posttest 1** (pretest) and **pretest_posttest 2** (posttest). As can be seen in the first major row in the table, students in the two teaching programs performed comparably prior to initiation of the instruction (51.125 for the web-based group to 50.625 for the class exercise group). However, at the end of the specialized instruction (the second major row in the table), the two groups were significantly different. The estimated marginal means inform us that the class exercise group is outperforming the web-based group 84.750 to 66.625.

4B.4.4.2 Simple Effects Tests
Comparing *pretest_posttest*

The second set of simple effects tests compared the **pretest_posttest** variable, and the results of this analysis are shown in Figure 4b.31. We learn from the table that there was statistically significant improvement from pretest to posttest for both groups.

Figure 4b.30 Results of the Simple Effects Tests Comparing Teaching Programs

1. teaching_program * pretest_posttest

Estimates

Measure:MEASURE_1

teaching_program	pretest...	Mean	Std. Error	95% Confidence Interval	
				Lower Bound	Upper Bound
1 web based	1	51.125	2.373	46.035	56.215
	2	66.750	2.902	60.527	72.973
2 class exercises	1	50.625	2.373	45.535	55.715
	2	84.750	2.902	78.527	90.973

Pairwise Comparisons

Measure:MEASURE_1

pretest_posttest	(I) teaching_program	(J) teaching_program	Mean Difference (I–J)	Std. Error	Sig.ₐ	95% Confidence Interval for Difference_a	
						Lower Bound	Upper Bound
1	1 web based	2 class exercises	.500	3.356	.884	-6.698	7.698
	2 class exercises	1 web based	-.500	3.356	.884	-7.698	6.698
2	1 web based	2 class exercises	-18.000*	4.104	.001	-26.801	-9.199
	2 class exercises	1 web based	18.000*	4.104	.001	9.199	26.801

Based on estimated marginal means
a. Adjustment for multiple comparisons: Bonferroni.
*. The mean difference is significant at the .05 level.

Figure 4b.31 Results of the Simple Effects Tests Comparing Pretest and Posttest

2. teaching_program * pretest_posttest

Estimates

Measure:MEASURE_1

teaching_program	pretest...	Mean	Std. Error	95% Confidence Interval	
				Lower Bound	Upper Bound
1 web based	1	51.125	2.373	46.035	56.215
	2	66.750	2.902	60.527	72.973
2 class exercises	1	50.625	2.373	45.535	55.715
	2	84.750	2.902	78.527	90.973

Pairwise Comparisons

Measure:MEASURE_1

teaching_program	(I) pretest_posttest	(J) pretest_posttest	Mean Difference (I–J)	Std. Error	Sig.ₐ	95% Confidence Interval for Difference_a	
						Lower Bound	Upper Bound
1 web based	1	2	-15.625*	2.399	.000	-20.771	-10.479
	2	1	15.625*	2.399	.000	10.479	20.771
2 class exercises	1	2	-34.125*	2.399	.000	-39.271	-28.979
	2	1	34.125*	2.399	.000	28.979	39.271

Based on estimated marginal means
*. The mean difference is significant at the .05 level.
a. Adjustment for multiple comparisons: Bonferroni.

4B.4.5 Reporting Mixed Design Results

The present study compared the effects of web-based learning and the use of in-class exercises on learning intermediate statistics. Students were exposed to one of the two teaching programs and were assessed prior to the onset of the program (**start_score**) and again when the program ended. The main effects of teaching program, $F(1, 14) = 6.500$, $p = .020$, $\eta^2 = .329$ with respect to the between-subjects variance, and test scores from the pretest to the posttest, $F(1, 14) = 214.972$, $p < .001$, $\eta^2 = .831$ with respect to the within-subjects variance, were both statistically significant. These effects can be seen in the statistically significant Teaching Program × Time interaction, $F(1, 14) = 29.726$, $p < .001$, $\eta^2 = .115$ with respect to the within-subjects variance.

The interaction is presented in Figure 4b.32. Tests of simple effects using Bonferroni-corrected t tests revealed that students in the two programs performed comparably on the pretest and that both programs of instruction significantly increased test scores from the pre- to the posttest. However, at the completion of training, students in the in-class exercises program performed significantly better than those exposed to web-based instruction.

Figure 4b.32   Test Score in the Pretest and the Posttest as a Function of Instruction Using Web-Based Instruction and In-Class Exercises

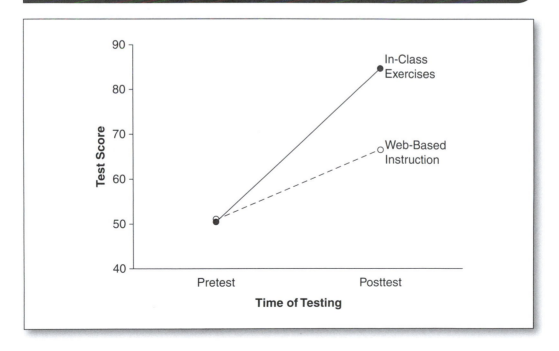

4B.5 Trend Analysis

A one-way between-subjects trend analysis partitions the total between-subjects variance of variable *A* into components representing linear and various polynomial (e.g., quadratic, cubic, quartic) functions. There are *a* − 1 such components, where *a* is the number of levels of independent variable *A*. To be meaningfully interpreted, the level of *A* should represent an equal interval scale of measurement.

4B.5.1 Numerical Example

In this hypothetical example, researchers are interested in studying marriages of teenagers between 16 and 17 years of age in which the female was pregnant at the time of getting married. Recognizing that many such marriages are likely to end in divorce, the researchers measured the degree of happiness on a 0 to 25 scale expressed by the female in the first, second, third, and fourth years of the marriage (**happiness** in the data file). They hypothesized that, on average, she would not be particularly happy during the first year while she was pregnant and gave birth, would become happier the second year as her life stabilized, would reverse that trend in the third year as she had time to evaluate her life, and then, if the marriage was to survive, she would show an increase in happiness during the fourth year. Because the research could not follow couples over a 4-year-period due to funding issues (a repeated measures design), the design was structured in a between-subjects manner with a different set of five young wives representing each of the marital years (**yr_of_marriage** in the data file). Given that the researchers believed that happiness would show two minima/maxima (reversals)—which corresponds to a cubic pattern in the data—they opted to perform a trend analysis to test their hypothesis. Data are contained in the file named **Marital_Happiness.**

4B.5.2 Trend Analysis Setup

Selecting **Analyze ➔ Compare Means ➔ One-Way ANOVA** brings us to the main dialog screen shown in Figure 4b.33. From the variables list panel on the left side, we click over **happiness** to the **Dependent List** and **yr_of_marriage** to the **Factor** panel.

Select the **Options** pushbutton, check **Descriptive** and **Homogeneity of variance test** in the **Options** window (see Figure 4b.34), and click **Continue** to return to the main dialog window.

Select the **Post Hoc** pushbutton. On the assumption that we will meet the assumption of equal variances, we have checked **Tukey** to obtain his HSD test as shown in Figure 4b.35. Click **Continue** to return to the main dialog window

Select the **Contrasts** pushbutton. Check **Polynomial**, and select **Cubic** from the drop-down menu to its right as shown in Figure 4b.36. Click **Continue** to return to the main dialog window, and click **OK** to perform the analysis.

Figure 4b.33 Main Dialog Window for One-Way ANOVA

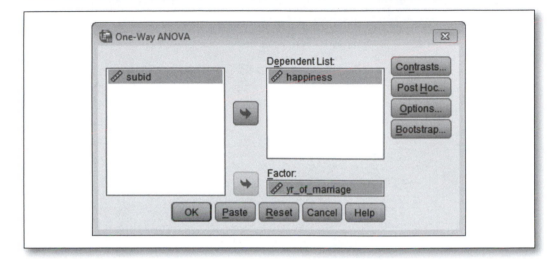

4B.5.3 Trend Analysis Output

The results of the omnibus analysis are shown in Figure 4b.37. In the top table, we see that the results of Levene's test are not statistically significant, informing us that we have not violated the assumption of equal variances.

The bottom table presents the summary table for the analysis. A one-way between-subjects ANOVA ordinarily yields a single F ratio corresponding to the main effect of the independent variable (see Figure 4b.4). That effect is shown here in the first row labeled (**Combined**) and is the overall effect; it is statistically significant and its eta-square value is 811.600/881.200 or a huge .921 in our hypothetical example. But this overall effect, with four groups, can be further partitioned into its polynomial components of linear, quadratic, and cubic trends. Each is represented in the summary table.

The trends are presented sequentially from the top-down in the summary table. The linear

Figure 4b.34 The One-Way ANOVA Options Window

Figure 4b.35   The One-Way ANOVA Post Hoc Window

One-Way ANOVA: Post Hoc Multiple Comparisons

Equal Variances Assumed

☐ LSD	☐ S-N-K	☐ Waller-Duncan
☐ Bonferroni	☑ Tukey	Type I/Type II Error Ratio: 100
☐ Sidak	☐ Tukey's-b	☐ Dunnett
☐ Scheffe	☐ Duncan	Control Category: Last
☐ R-E-G-W F	☐ Hochberg's GT2	Test
☐ R-E-G-W Q	☐ Gabriel	◉ 2-sided ◎ < Control ◎ > Control

Equal Variances Not Assumed

☐ Tamhane's T2   ☐ Dunnett's T3   ☐ Games-Howell   ☐ Dunnett's C

Significance level: 0.05

[Continue] [Cancel] [Help]

Figure 4b.36   The One-Way ANOVA Contrasts Window Configured for Our Trend Analysis

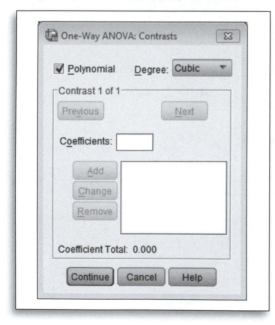

One-Way ANOVA: Contrasts

☑ Polynomial   Degree: Cubic

Contrast 1 of 1

[Previous]   [Next]

Coefficients: [____]

[Add]
[Change]
[Remove]

Coefficient Total: 0.000

[Continue] [Cancel] [Help]

contrast (evaluation) shown in the second row labeled **Linear Term** is associated with an F ratio of 119.503 and is statistically significant. Its eta-square value is 519.840/ 881.200 or .590.

Just below the linear trend is a row labeled **Deviation**, which should read in full "Polynomial trends in excess of linear" with a sum of squares of 291.760. That is what is left from the **Combined** effect when the linear partition is subtracted (811.600 − 519.84 = 291.760). This leftover sum of squares encompasses all the higher-order polynomial functions and is statistically significant; this informs us that one or more of the higher-order polynomial functions will be significant.

Next is the row labeled **Quadratic Term,** which refers to the quadratic component of the **Combined** effect. It is not statistically significant but the deviation from (one or more functions of a higher

Figure 4b.37   Results of the Omnibus Analysis

Test of Homogeneity of Variances

happiness

Levene Statistic	df1	df2	Sig.
.104	3	16	.956

ANOVA

happiness

			Sum of Squares	df	Mean Square	F	Sig.
Between Groups	(Combined)		811.600	3	270.533	62.192	.000
	Linear Term	Contrast	519.840	1	519.840	119.503	.000
		Deviation	291.760	2	145.880	33.536	.000
	Quadratic Term	Contrast	16.200	1	16.200	3.724	.072
		Deviation	275.560	1	275.560	63.347	.000
	Cubic Term	Contrast	275.560	1	275.560	63.347	.000
Within Groups			69.600	16	4.350		
Total			881.200	19			

order than) a quadratic trend is significant. Here, there is only one more higher-order function: the cubic function.

The final partition of the **Combined** effect is the cubic contrast. It is associated with an F ratio of 63.347 and is statistically significant. Its eta-square value is 275.560/881.200 or .313.

The observed means and the pairwise comparisons are shown in Figure 4b.38. As can be seen in the middle and bottom tables, all pairs of means are significantly different. We illustrate how to interpret these results in Section 4B.5.4.

Figure 4b.38   Results of the Post Hoc Tukey Tests

Descriptives

happiness

	N	Mean	Std. Deviation	Std. Error	95% Confidence Interval for Mean		Minimum	Maximum
					Lower Bound	Upper Bound		
1	5	4.60	2.074	.927	2.03	7.17	2	7
2	5	14.00	2.236	1.000	11.22	16.78	11	17
3	5	8.60	1.817	.812	6.34	10.86	6	11
4	5	21.60	2.191	.980	18.88	24.32	19	25
Total	20	12.20	6.810	1.523	9.01	15.39	2	25

(Continued)

Figure 4b.38 (Continued)

Post Hoc Tests

Multiple Comparisons

happiness
Tukey HSD

(I) yr of m...	(J) yr of m...	Mean Difference (I–J)	Std. Error	Sig.	95% Confidence Interval Lower Bound	95% Confidence Interval Upper Bound
1	2	−9.400.	1.319	.000	−13.17	−5.63
	3	−4.000.	1.319	.036	−7.77	−.23
	4	−17.000.	1.319	.000	−20.77	−13.23
2	1	9.400.	1.319	.000	5.63	13.17
	3	5.400.	1.319	.004	1.63	9.17
	4	−7.600.	1.319	.000	−11.37	−3.83
3	1	4.000.	1.319	.036	.23	7.77
	2	−5.400.	1.319	.004	−9.17	−1.63
	4	−13.000.	1.319	.000	−16.77	−9.23
4	1	17.000.	1.319	.000	13.23	20.77
	2	7.600.	1.319	.000	3.83	11.37
	3	13.000.	1.319	.000	9.23	16.77

*. The mean difference is significant at the 0.05 level.

Homogeneous Subsets

happiness

Tukey HSD$_a$

yr of ...	N	Subset for alpha = 0.05 1	2	3	4
1	5	4.60			
3	5		8.60		
2	5			14.00	
4	5				21.60
Sig.		1.000	1.000	1.000	1.000

Means for groups in homogeneous subsets are displayed.

a. Uses Harmonic Mean Sample Size = 5.000.

4B.5.4 Reporting Trend Analysis Results

A trend analysis was performed on the happiness ratings of 16- and 17-year-old females who were pregnant at the time they entered into marriage. Participants were in their first, second, third, or fourth year of marriage. The overall effect of year in marriage was statistically significant, $F(3, 16) = 62.192$, $p < .001$, $\eta^2 = .921$, and a Tukey post hoc test indicated that all group means were significantly different. The means are plotted in Figure 4b.39, and the polynomial analysis yielded two statistically significant contrasts. First, the linear trend was significant, $F(1, 16) = 119.503$, $p < .001$, $\eta^2 = .590$. That this trend was obtained was the result of happiness starting out in the first year just short of 5 and ending in the fourth year with a value in excess of 20. Of greater interest is the significant cubic component, $F(1, 16) = 63.347$, $p < .001$, $\eta^2 = .313$ indicating two significant minima/maxima in the function (at Year 2 and Year 3). As can be seen in Figure 4b.39, happiness increased from Year 1 to Year 2, decreased from Year 2 to Year 3, and then rose sharply from Year 3 to Year 4.

Figure 4b.39   Mean Happiness as a Function of Year in Marriage

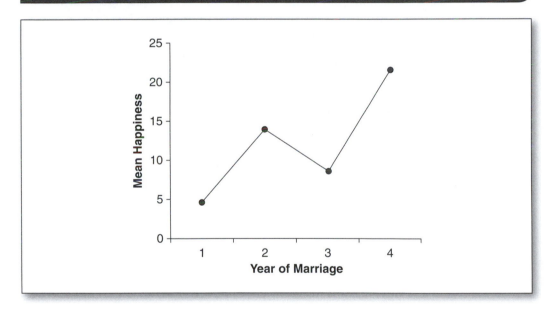

4B.6 Analysis of Covariance

ANCOVA provides us with a way to statistically control for one or more variables that may affect the dependent variable. These variables that are statistically controlled are called *covariates*, and they are usually quantitatively measured variables. Comparison of groups is accomplished by performing alpha-corrected *t* tests on the adjusted (estimated marginal) means (means that are adjusted for the effects of the covariates).

4B.6.1 Numerical Example

We will base our example here on the one discussed in Section 4A.8. As you may recall, we intended to assess the performance of three branch offices (Boston, Dallas, and Seattle) of a particular consulting firm on the average number of projects completed per month over a 1-year time period. The independent variable of branch office is named **branch_office** in the data file with codes of **1**, **2**, and **3** standing for Boston, Dallas, and Seattle, respectively; the dependent variable is named **projects_done_dv** in the data file to help you remember that it is the dependent variable in the analysis. An ANOVA showed that the three branch offices each completed approximately 35 projects each month with no significant differences between the offices, but the in-house researcher in charge of performance appraisals recognized that some projects can be more complex than others. Recognizing that project complexity can be reliably measured, she had her staff rate the complexity of each project completed by the offices and used project complexity as a covariate in the analysis. We have named this variable **complexity_cov** in the data file to help you remember that it is the covariate. Data are contained in the file named **Projects_Completed**.

4B.6.2 Evaluating the Additional ANCOVA Assumptions

The two additional assumptions we encounter with ANCOVA are linearity of regression and homogeneity of regression. We evaluate each in turn.

4B.6.2.1 Linearity of Regression

Linearity of regression is ordinarily evaluated by visually examining a scatterplot of the covariate and the dependent variable. If we determine that the relationship between these two variables is linear, then the assumption of linearity of regression will have been satisfied.

Figure 4b.40 The Scatter/Dot Window

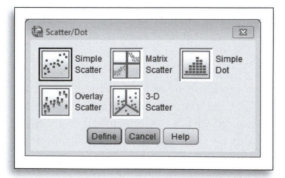

From the main IBM SPSS menu, select **Graphs ➔ Legacy Dialogs ➔ Scatter/Dot**. Selecting this path will open the window shown in Figure 4b.40. The window opens on set of possible scatterplot diagrams. Select **Simple Scatter**, and click **Define**. This will open the **Simple Scatterplot** dialog window as shown in Figure 4b.41. Drag **projects_done_dv** to the **Y Axis** panel (always place the dependent variable on the *Y* axis). Then drag **complexity_cov** to the **X Axis** panel. Click **OK**.

The result of this setup is shown in Figure 4b.42. This is a scatterplot of the two variables. Visual inspection of the plot strongly suggests that the two variables are linearly related.

We can also ask IBM SPSS to display the line of best fit (this is the least squares regression line as explained in Section 6A.6.2). To accomplish this, double click inside of the scatterplot in the IBM SPSS output. This gives us access to the **Chart Editor**. Select **Elements ➔ Fit Line at Total.** As soon as this is selected, the line of best fit will appear superimposed on the scatterplot. This is shown in Figure 4b.43. Also shown in Figure 4b.43 is the **Properties** window that automatically opened. It is set at the linear fit line, which is what we were looking to invoke;

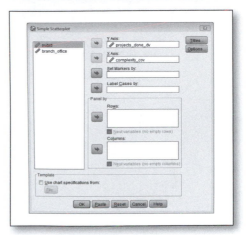

Figure 4b.41 The Dialog Window for Scatterplot

Figure 4b.42 The Scatterplot Assessing Linearity of Regression

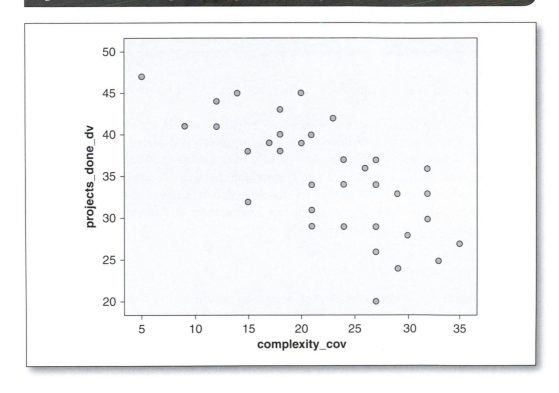

Figure 4b.43 Screen Shot of Scatterplot With Line of Best Fit and Properties Window With Linear Fit Selected

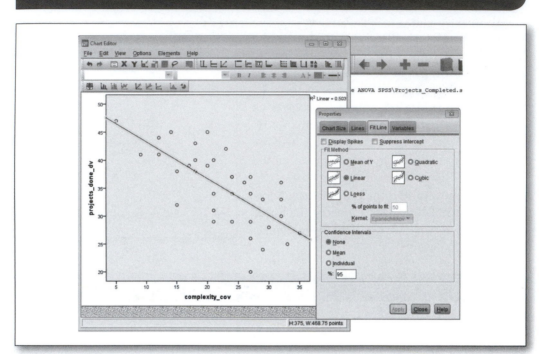

note that other fit lines (e.g., quadratic, cubic) are also available but not of interest for our purposes.

The line of best fit is shown in Figure 4b.43. As can be seen in the figure, the relationship between the dependent variable of number of projects completed and the covariate of project complexity seems to be linear. The note of **R^2 Linear = .503** informs us that the amount of total variance explained (R^2, comparable here to eta square) by the simple linear regression model (see Chapter 6A) is .503; that is, project complexity explains 50.30% of the variance of projects completed. In summary, the assumption of linearity of regression appears to have been met.

4B.6.2.2 Homogeneity of Regression

The assumption of homogeneity of regression assumes that the individual group regression functions predicting the dependent variable from the covariate are the same (they have comparable slopes to the total sample regression line shown in the scatterplot of Figure 4b.43). This assumption is tested by obtaining a nonsignificant Independent variable × Covariate interaction effect.

From the main IBM SPSS menu, select **Analyze ➜ General Linear Model ➜ Univariate.**
Selecting this path will open the dialog window shown in Figure 4b.44. We have configured
it with **branch_office** as the **Fixed Factor**, **projects_done_dv** as the **Dependent Variable**,
and **complexity_cov** as the **Covariate**.

Figure 4b.44 The Main Dialog Window of Univariate General Linear Model

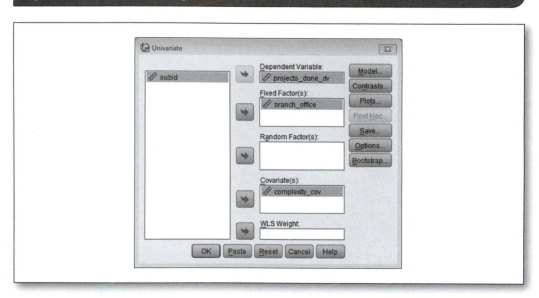

Select the **Model** pushbutton to reach the dialog screen shown in Figure 4b.45.
Select **Custom** in the area where you **Specify Model**, and select **Main effects** from the
pull-down menu under **Build Terms**. Now select **branch_office** and **complexity_cov** in
the **Factors & Covariates** panel, and click them over to the **Model** panel. This is shown
in Figure 4b.45.

Now select **Interaction** from the pull-down menu (replacing the **Main effects**
choice). Select both **branch_office** and **complexity_cov** (by holding down the **control**
button while clicking them one at a time) and use the arrow button to click them over
to the **Model** panel. The result of this is shown in Figure 4b.46. Click **Continue** to return
to the main **General Linear Model** window, and click **OK** to run the analysis.

The only output in which we are interested is the test of significance of the **branch_
office*complexity_cov** interaction shown in the summary table in Figure 4b.47. As can be
seen in the summary table, the effect is not statistically significant. We can thus presume that
the assumption of homogeneity of regression has not been violated and can proceed with
the ANCOVA.

Figure 4b.45   The Model Window of Univariate General Linear Model With the Main Effects Included

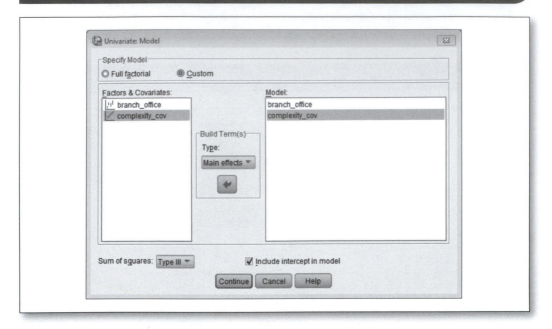

Figure 4b.46   The Model Window of Univariate General Linear Model With the Main Effects and Interaction Included

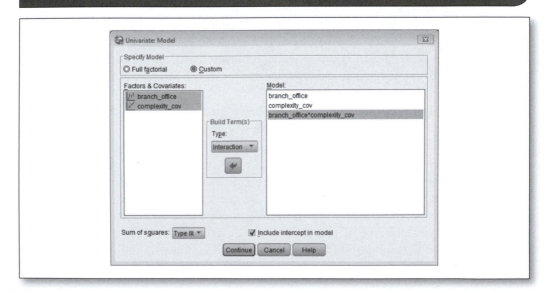

Figure 4b.47 The Results of the Custom Model Evaluating the Interaction of the Independent Variable and the Covariate

Tests of Between-Subjects Effects

Dependent Variable:projects_done_dv

Source	Type III Sum of Squares	df	Mean Square	F	Sig.
Corrected Model	1139.341[a]	5	227.868	17.376	.000
Intercept	6009.879	1	6009.879	458.293	.000
branch_office	11.001	2	5.500	.419	.661
complexity_cov	915.317	1	915.317	69.799	.000
branch_office * complexity_cov	12.147	2	6.073	.463	.634
Error	393.409	30	13.114		
Total	45843.000	36			
Corrected Total	1532.750	35			

a. R Squared = .743 (Adjusted R Squared = .701)

4B.6.3 ANCOVA Analysis Setup

From the main IBM SPSS menu, select **Analyze ➔ General Linear Model ➔ Univariate.** Selecting this path will open the main **Univariate** dialog window. Configure it as we did in examining the homogeneity of regression assumption (see Figure 4b.44), by having **branch_office** as the **Fixed Factor**, **projects_done_dv** as the **Dependent Variable**, and **complexity_cov** as the **Covariate**.

Select the **Model** pushbutton to reach the dialog window shown in Figure 4b.48. Click **Full factorial** in the area where you **Specify Model**, and click **Continue** to return to the main dialog window.

Select the **Options** pushbutton to reach the **Options** dialog window shown in Figure 4b.49. We are going to do several things in this window. In the top portion of the window devoted to **Estimated Marginal Means**, click over **branch_office** to the panel named **Display Means for** because this will cause IBM SPSS to output the adjusted group means. Then, as we did in our one-way within-subjects analysis, click the checkbox for **Compare main effects**, and select **Bonferroni** from the drop-down menu for **Confidence interval adjustment** to perform our pairwise comparisons of means, also shown in Figure 4b.49. Finally, in the lower portion of the **Options** dialog window, select **Descriptive statistics** and **Homogeneity tests** as shown in Figure 4b.50. Click **Continue** to reach the main dialog window, and click **OK** to run the analysis.

Figure 4b.48 The Model Window of Univariate General Linear Model Specifying a Full Factorial Model

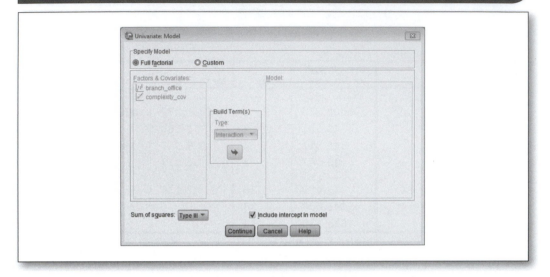

Figure 4b.49 The Options Window of Univariate General Linear Model

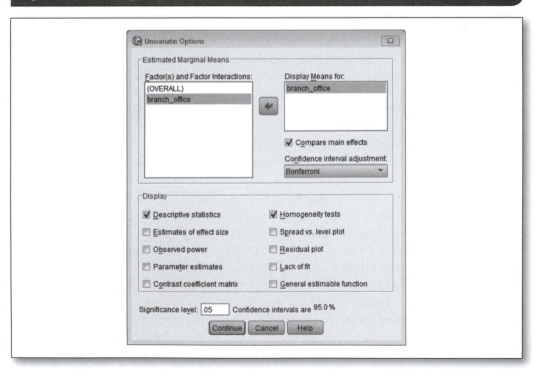

Figure 4b.50   The Results of the Levene Homogeneity of Variance Test and the Summary Table

Levene's Test of Equality of Error Variances$_a$

Dependent Variable:projects_done_dv

F	df1	df2	Sig.
.116	2	33	.891

Tests the null hypothesis that the error variance of the dependent variable is equal across groups.

a. Design: Intercept + complexity_cov + branch_office

Tests of Between–Subjects Effects

Dependent Variable:projects_done_dv

Source	Type III Sum of Squares	df	Mean Square	F	Sig.
Corrected Model	1127.195$_a$	3	375.732	29.647	.000
Intercept	7746.733	1	7746.733	611.249	.000
complexity_cov	1117.695	1	1117.695	88.191	.000
branch_office	356.080	2	178.040	14.048	.000
Error	405.555	32	12.674		
Total	45843.000	36			
Corrected Total	1532.750	35			

a. R Squared = .735 (Adjusted R Squared = .711)

4B.6.4 ANCOVA Analysis Output

The top table in Figure 4b.50 shows the results of Levene's test of the equality of error variances. The outcome is not significant, and so we appear to have met the assumption that the group variances are equal.

The bottom table in Figure 4b.50 contains the summary table for the ANCOVA. Both the covariate of project complexity and the effect of the independent variable (branch office) are statistically significant. The full eta-square value for the effects are computed by dividing the sum of squares for **Corrected Model** (1127.195, which equals the **Corrected Total** sum of squares minus the **Error** sum of squares) by the **Corrected Total** sum of squares (1532.750) presented in the summary table yielding a value of .735 (as shown in the footnote to the summary table). IBM SPSS also provides an **Adjusted R Squared** value of take-into-account error variance contributing toward successful prediction of the values of the dependent variable (this is more fully explained in Chapter 7A).

Of more immediate concern for us is the eta-square value for the branch office independent variable. It is computed by dividing its sum of squares (356.080) by the **Corrected Total** sum of squares (1532.750) to yield a value of .232.

The top portion of Figure 4b.51 presents the adjusted (estimated marginal) means for the three groups together with their standard errors. The *F* ratio for the **branch_office** effect evaluated the differences of these adjusted means. The bottom portion of Figure 4b.51 provides the results of the pairwise comparisons of the adjusted means. Based on these results, it appears that the Boston office completed significantly fewer projects when corrected for project complexity than either the Denver or Seattle offices; these latter two branch offices completed a comparable number of projects when project complexity was taken into account.

Figure 4b.51 The Results of the Multiple Comparisons Tests

Estimated Marginal Means

branch_office

Estimates

Dependent Variable:projects_done_dv

branch_office	Mean	Std. Error	95% Confidence Interval	
			Lower Bound	Upper Bound
1 Boston	30.164$_a$	1.127	27.869	32.459
2 Denver	38.707$_a$	1.075	36.518	40.897
3 Seattle	36.378$_a$	1.038	34.264	38.493

a. Covariates appearing in the model are evaluated at the following values: complexity_cov = 22.47.

Pairwise Comparisons

Dependent Variable:projects_done_dv

(I) branch_office	(J) branch_office	Mean Difference (I–J)	Std. Error	Sig.$_a$	95% Confidence Interval for Difference$_a$	
					Lower Bound	Upper Bound
1 Boston	2 Denver	−8.543.	1.648	.000	−12.707	−4.380
	3 Seattle	−6.214.	1.576	.001	−10.195	−2.234
2 Denver	1 Boston	8.543.	1.648	.000	4.380	12.707
	3 Seattle	2.329	1.463	.364	−1.367	6.025
3 Seattle	1 Boston	6.214.	1.576	.001	2.234	10.195
	2 Denver	−2.329	1.463	.364	−6.025	1.367

Based on estimated marginal means

*. The mean difference is significant at the .05 level.

a. Adjustment for multiple comparisons: Bonferroni.

4B.6.5 Reporting ANCOVA Results

A one-way between-subjects ANCOVA was performed to assess the difference in the average number of projects completed per month over a 1-year time period by the Boston, Denver, and Seattle branch offices of X Consulting Firm. Because projects involved different levels of complexity, project complexity was used as a covariate in the analysis. Data conformed to the assumptions of linearity of regression (a linear relationship was observed between the project complexity covariate and the number of projects completed dependent variable) and homogeneity of regression [the Branch Office × Project Complexity effect was not statistically significant, $F(1, 30) = 0.463$, $p = .634$].

The covariate effect was statistically significant, $F(1, 32) = 88.191$, $p < .001$. In addition, a statistically significant effect of Branch Office was obtained, $F(1, 32) = 14.048$, $p < .001$, $\eta^2 = .232$. Pairwise t tests with a Bonferroni correction indicated that the Boston office completed significantly fewer projects when corrected for project complexity (adjusted $M = 30.164$, $SE = 1.127$, 95% CI = 27.869 - 32.459) than either the Denver (adjusted $M = 38.707$, $SE = 1.075$, 95% CI = 36.518 - 40.897) or the Seattle (adjusted $M = 36.378$, $SE = 1.038$, 95% CI = 34.264 - 38.493) offices; these latter two branch offices completed a comparable number of projects when project complexity was taken into account.

4B.7 One-Way Between-Subjects Design Using Generalized Linear Models

We repeat here the one-way between-subjects design presented in Section 4B.1. As you may recall, there were three different types of fertilizer (A, B, and C) used to nourish crops of yellow sweet corn and the amount of growth of the plants was the dependent variable. Seven plants were assigned to each type of fertilizer, and the data are contained in the file named **Fertilizer.**

4B.7.1 One-Way Between-Subjects Generalized Linear Models Analysis Setup

Selecting **Analyze** ➔ **Generalized Linear Models** ➔ **Generalized Linear Models** (the module within **Generalized Linear Models** applicable to between-subjects designs) brings us to the **Type of Model** screen shown in Figure 4b.52. The default window with a **Scale Response of Linear** already checked is appropriate for our purposes. Select **Response** from the set of tabs.

In the **Response** window shown in Figure 4b.53, highlight **plant_growth** and click the arrow button to move it to the **Dependent Variable** panel.

Select the **Predictors** tab. As shown in Figure 4b.54, click **fertilizer** over to the **Factors** panel.

Figure 4b.52 The Type of Model Window of Generalized Linear Models

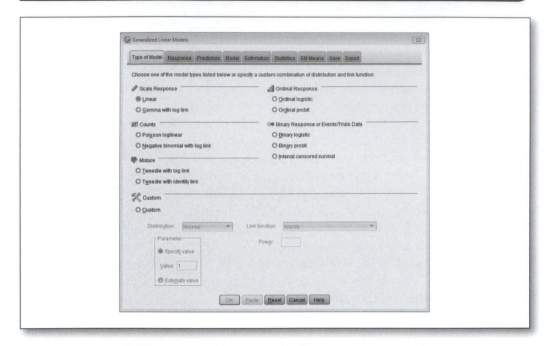

Figure 4b.53 The Response Window of Generalized Linear Models

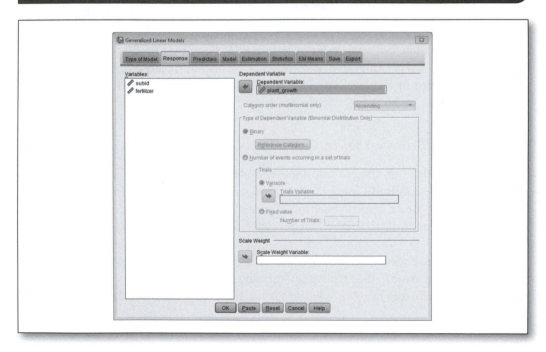

Figure 4b.54 The Predictors Window of Generalized Linear Models

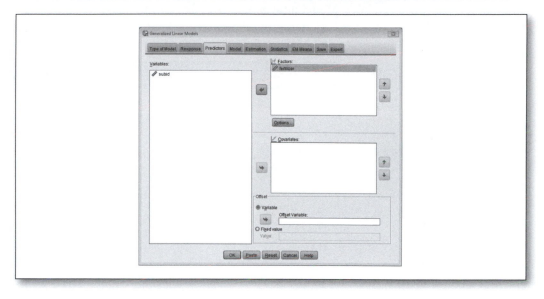

Select the **Model** pushbutton. In the **Model** window (see Figure 4b.55), make sure that **Main effects** shows in the drop-down menu for **Build Term(s) Type**. Highlight **fertilizer**, and click it into the **Model** panel.

Figure 4b.55 The Model Window of Generalized Linear Models

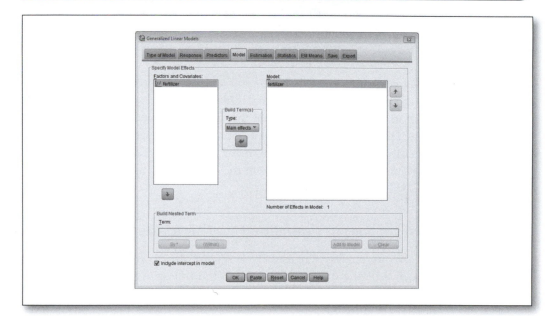

Select the **Statistics** pushbutton. In the **Statistics** window (see Figure 4b.56), retain **Wald** as the default under **Chi-square Statistics**. Under **Print**, keep the defaults of **Case processing summary**, **Descriptive statistics**, **Model information**, **Goodness of fit statistics**, and **Model summary statistics**. Remove the checkmark from **Parameter estimates.**

Figure 4b.56 The Statistics Window of Generalized Linear Models

Select the **EM Means** pushbutton. The **EM Means** window shown in Figure 4b.57 deals with the estimated marginal means. In **Generalized Linear Models**, multiple comparisons are always carried out on these means rather than the observed means. Highlight **fertilizer**, and click it over to the **Display Means for** panel. Click the cell under the **Contrast** column that is next to **fertilizer** to display the drop-down menu. Select **Pairwise**. Under **Adjustment for Multiple Comparisons,** select **Bonferroni** from the drop-down menu. Click **OK** to perform the analysis.

4B.7.2 One-Way Between-Subjects Generalized Linear Models Output

Selected results of our analysis are shown in Figure 4b.58. Although the output contains a likelihood test of the overall model (with the intercept included), the **Wald**

Figure 4b.57   The EM Means Window of Generalized Linear Models

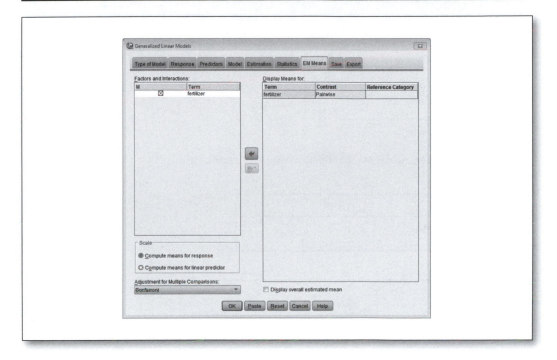

Chi-Square is used to specifically test the statistical significance of our independent variable of **fertilizer**. Wald's z^2 statistic has a chi-square distribution and, despite the concerns of some writers (e.g., Agresti, 1996; Menard, 2002), is what is used by IBM SPSS. We see from the top table of Figure 4b.58 that the effect of **fertilizer** is statistically significant with a Wald value of 38.92 based on 2 degrees of freedom. We may therefore examine the paired comparisons.

Paired comparisons of group means are based on the estimated marginal means. These means are identical to the observed means in this illustration, and the outcomes of the paired comparison tests shown in the lower table of Figure 4b.58 are extremely similar to those performed through the **One-Way ANOVA** and **Tukey** procedures (see Figure 4b.5).

4B.8 Simple Mixed Design Using Generalized Linear Models

We use here the example from Section 4B.4 where we examined the effects of web-based learning (coded as **1**) versus the use of in-class exercises (coded as **2**) under the variable of **teaching_program** on learning intermediate statistics. Students were exposed to one of the

Figure 4b.58 The Test of Significance for Our Independent Variable and the Paired Comparisons of Group Means

Tests of Model Effects

Source	Type III Wald Chi-Square	df	Sig.
(Intercept)	1058.187	1	.000
fertilizer	38.920	2	.000

Dependent Variable: plant growth in mm
Model: (Intercept), fertilizer

Estimated Marginal Means: fertilizer type of fertilizer

Estimates

fertilizer type of ...	Mean	Std. Error	95% Wald Confidence Interval Lower	Upper
1 Fertilizer A	29.86	1.711	26.50	33.21
2 Fertilizer B	26.00	1.711	22.65	29.35
3 Fertilizer C	40.57	1.711	37.22	43.93

Pairwise Comparisons

(I) fertilizer type of fertilizer	(J) fertilizer type of fertilizer	Mean Difference (I–J)	Std. Error	df	Bonferroni Sig.	95% Wald Confidence Interval for Difference Lower	Upper
1 Fertilizer A	2 Fertilizer B	3.86	2.420	1	.333	−1.94	9.65
	3 Fertilizer C	−10.71a	2.420	1	.000	−16.51	−4.92
2 Fertilizer B	1 Fertilizer A	−3.86	2.420	1	.333	−9.65	1.94
	3 Fertilizer C	−14.57a	2.420	1	.000	−20.37	−8.78
3 Fertilizer C	1 Fertilizer A	10.71a	2.420	1	.000	4.92	16.51
	2 Fertilizer B	14.57a	2.420	1	.000	8.78	20.37

Pairwise comparisons of estimated marginal means based on the original scale of dependent variable plant_growth plant growth in mm

a. The mean difference is significant at the .05 level.

two teaching programs (a between-subjects variable) and were assessed prior to the onset of the program and again when the program ended. Data for this example are contained in the file named **Teaching_Programs_Stacked**.

4B.8.1 Use of a Stacked Data Structure

The **Generalized Estimating Equations** module within **Generalized Linear Models** is where we perform analyses on designs having a within-subjects variable (within-subjects and mixed designs). This module requires a data structure known as *stacked*, *stacked column*, *univariate*, or *narrow*. Unlike the data structure (known as *multivariate*) we have used thus far and will use throughout this book, in a stacked format, each row is allowed to contain only a single value on a given dependent variable. When we have a repeated measure either in a within-subjects or a mixed design, we have by definition more than one value on the dependent variable, and so, we must place these values on different rows. In the process of accomplishing that goal, we need to create a within-subjects factor in the data file analogous to the within-subjects factor we created at the beginning of the analysis setup in the **Repeated** module of the **General Linear Model** (e.g., see Section 4B.3.2 and Figures 4b.15 and 4b.16).

Our stacked data file is shown in Figure 4b.59. The variable **subid** is an identification code for each case and will be needed in our analysis setup. Note that each case is assigned two rows in the data file because there are two values (a starting value and a finishing value) as the repeated measure. The **teaching_program** variable is the same from Section 4B.4, but we now have a variable named **start1_finish2** to represent the within-subjects factor. Note that the two rows for each case are used to accommodate these two levels of the within-subjects factor. Finally, we have the dependent variable, named **test_score** here. To make sense of the data file, consider the first two rows devoted to **subid 1**. The two rows repeat the **teaching_program** variable because the person can be in only one of the teaching methods groups. Row 1 for that case shows the value of **1 for start1_finish2**, indicating that this is the starting condition with a starting **test_score** of **50.** Row 2 for that case shows the value of **2** for **start1_finish2**, indicating that this is the finishing condition with a finishing **test_score** of **62.**

Figure 4b.59 The Data File in a Stacked (Univariate) Structure

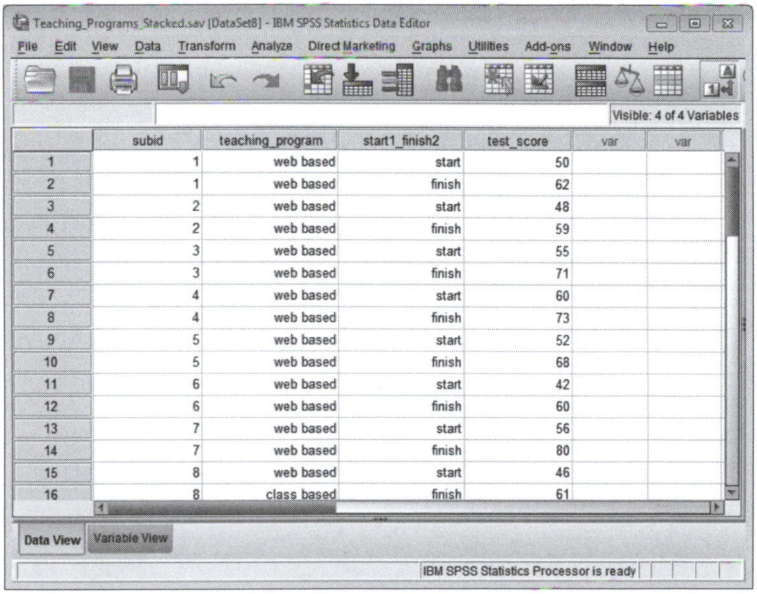

	subid	teaching_program	start1_finish2	test_score	var	var
1	1	web based	start	50		
2	1	web based	finish	62		
3	2	web based	start	48		
4	2	web based	finish	59		
5	3	web based	start	55		
6	3	web based	finish	71		
7	4	web based	start	60		
8	4	web based	finish	73		
9	5	web based	start	52		
10	5	web based	finish	68		
11	6	web based	start	42		
12	6	web based	finish	60		
13	7	web based	start	56		
14	7	web based	finish	80		
15	8	web based	start	46		
16	8	class based	finish	61		

4B.8.2 Mixed Design Generalized Linear Models Analysis Setup

Selecting **Analyze** ➜ **Generalized Linear Models** ➜ **Generalized Estimating Equations** (the module within **Generalized Linear Models** applicable to within-subjects and mixed designs) brings us to the **Repeated** screen shown in Figure 4b.60. Move **subid** from the **Variables** panel to the **Subject variables** panel to identify **subid** as our case identification variable. Move **start1_finish2** to the **Within-Subject variables** panel to identify it as the repeated measure.

Select the **Type of Model tab.** The default window (see Figure 4b.61) with a **Scale Response** of **Linear** already checked is appropriate for our purposes.

Select **Response** from the set of pushbuttons. In the **Response** window shown in Figure 4b.62, highlight **test_score** and click the arrow button to move it to the **Dependent Variable** panel.

Select the **Predictors** pushbutton. As shown in Figure 4b.63, click **teaching_program** and **start1_finish2** over to the **Factors** panel.

Select the **Model** pushbutton. In the **Model** window, make sure that **Main effects** shows in the drop-down menu for **Build Term(s) Type**. Highlight **teaching_program**, and click it into the **Model** panel. Then, do the same for **start1_finish2**. This is shown in Figure 4b.64. Then, set the **Build Term(s) Type** drop-down menu for **Interaction** (see Figure 4b.65), highlight both **teaching_program** and **start1_finish2** by holding down the shift key and move them over to the **Model** panel where they will appear as an interaction term.

Figure 4b.60   The Repeated Window of Generalized Estimating Equations

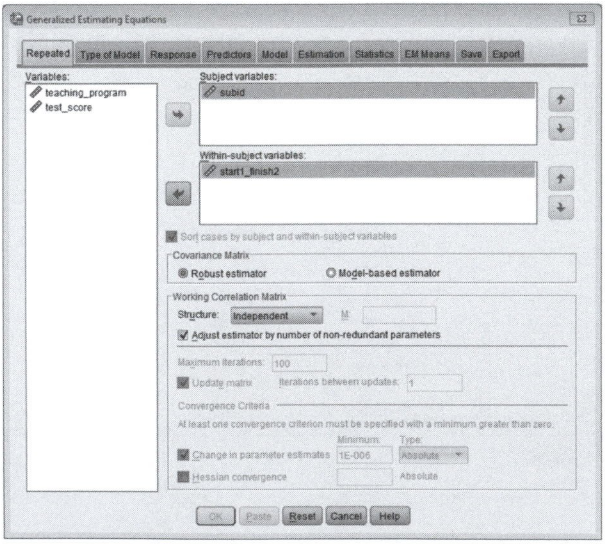

Figure 4b.61 The Type of Model Window of Generalized Estimating Equations

Figure 4b.62 The Response Window of Generalized Estimating Equations

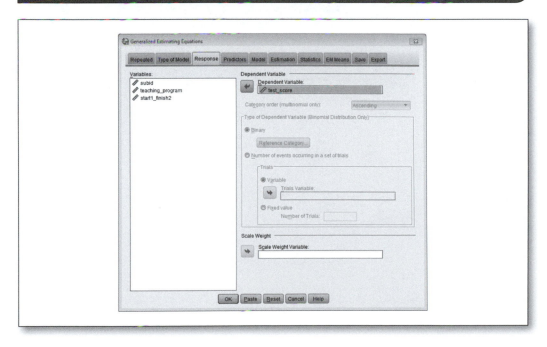

Figure 4b.63 The Predictors Window of Generalized Estimating Equations

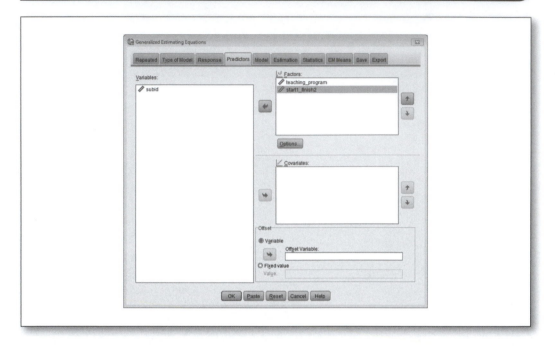

Figure 4b.64 The Model Window of Generalized Estimating Equations Placing the Main Effects in the Model

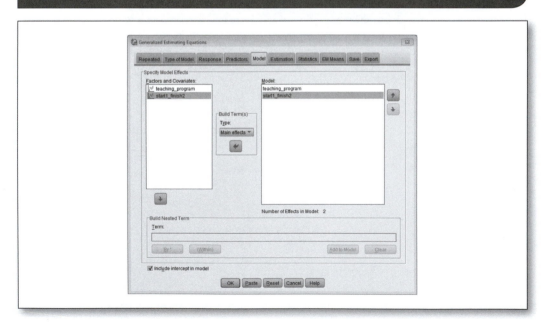

Figure 4b.65 The Model Window of Generalized Estimating Equations Placing the Interaction in the Model

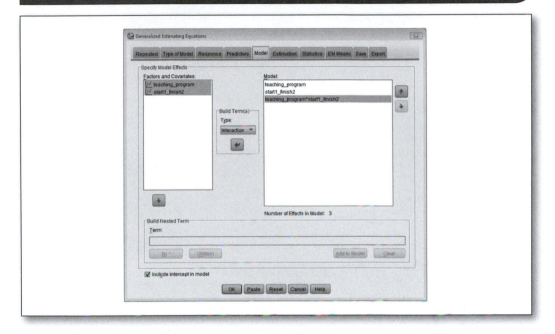

Select the **Statistics** pushbutton. In the **Statistics** window (see Figure 4b.66), retain **Wald** as the default under **Chi-square Statistics**. Under **Print**, check **Case processing summary**, **Descriptive statistics**, **Model information**, **Goodness of fit statistics**, and **Model summary statistics**.

Select the **EM Means** pushbutton. The **EM Means** window shown in Figure 4b.67 deals with the estimated marginal means. Successively highlight each of the three effects, and click them over to the **Display Means for** panel. Because each of the main effects has only two levels, there is no need to perform pairwise comparisons. But we need to perform multiple comparison tests (simple effect analysis) for the interaction. Click the cell under the **Contrast** column that is next to the interaction effect to display the drop-down menu. Select **Pairwise**. Under **Adjustment for Multiple Comparison**s, select **Bonferroni** from the drop-down menu. Click **OK** to perform the analysis.

4B.8.3 Mixed Design Generalized Estimating Equations Output

Selected results of our analysis are shown in Figure 4b.68. We see from the top table of Figure 4b.58 that all three effects are statistically significant. The probability levels shown in this analysis for **teaching_program** and **teaching_program*start1_finish2** (.028 and .001) are slightly different from those we obtained in the earlier analysis of .020 and .000 (see Figure 4b.29) but do not affect the conclusions we would draw.

Figure 4b.66 The Statistics Window of Generalized Estimating Equations

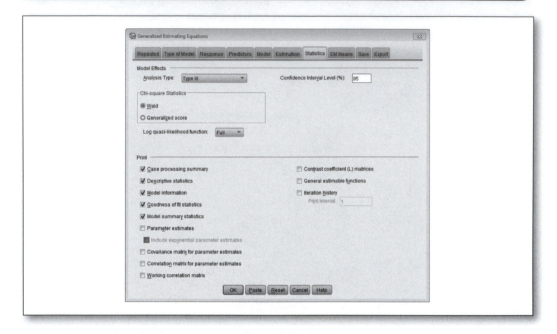

Figure 4a.67 The EM Means Window of Generalized Estimating Equations

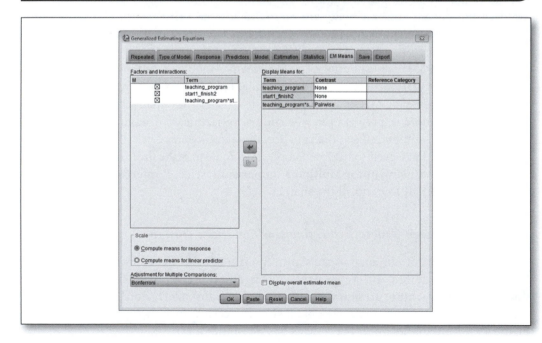

Figure 4b.68   The Tests of Significance for Our Effects and the Paired Comparisons of Group Means

Tests of Model Effects

	Type III		
Source	Wald Chi-Square	df	Sig.
(Intercept)	1349.090	1	.000
teaching_program	4.825	1	.028
start1_finish2	172.099	1	.000
teaching_program * start1_finish2	11.683	1	.001

Dependent Variable: test_score
Model: (Intercept), teaching_program, start1_finish2, teaching_program * start1_finish2

Estimated Marginal Means 3: teaching_program* start1_finish2

Estimates

teaching program	start1 finish2	Mean	Std. Error	95% Wald Confidence Interval	
				Lower	Upper
1 web based	1 start	51.13	1.932	47.34	54.91
	2 finish	67.57	2.702	62.28	72.87
2 class based	1 start	50.63	2.474	45.78	55.47
	2 finish	82.11	3.599	75.06	89.16

Pairwise Comparisons

(I) teaching program*start1_finish2	(J) teaching program*start1_finish2	Mean Difference (I-J)	Std. Error	df	Bonferroni Sig.	95% Wald Confidence Interval for Difference	
						Lower	Upper
[teaching_program=1]* [start1_finish2=1]	[teaching_program=1]* [start1_finish2=2]	−16.45ₐ	1.736	1	.000	−21.03	−11.87
	[teaching_program=2]* [start1_finish2=1]	.50	3.139	1	1.000	−7.78	8.78
	[teaching_program=2]* [start1_finish2=2]	−30.99ₐ	3.698	1	.000	−40.74	−21.23
[teaching_program=1]* [start1_finish2=2]	[teaching_program=1]* [start1_finish2=1]	16.45ₐ	1.736	1	.000	11.87	21.03
	[teaching_program=2]* [start1_finish2=1]	16.95ₐ	3.664	1	.000	7.28	26.61
	[teaching_program=2]* [start1_finish2=2]	−14.54ₐ	4.500	1	.007	−26.41	−2.67
[teaching_program=2]* [start1_finish2=1]	[teaching_program=1]* [start1_finish2=1]	−.50	3.139	1	1.000	−8.78	7.78
	[teaching_program=1]* [start1_finish2=2]	−16.95ₐ	3.664	1	.000	−26.61	−7.28
	[teaching_program=2]* [start1_finish2=2]	−31.49ₐ	3.653	1	.000	−41.12	−21.85
[teaching_program=2]* [start1_finish2=2]	[teaching_program=1]* [start1_finish2=1]	30.99ₐ	3.698	1	.000	21.23	40.74
	[teaching_program=1]* [start1_finish2=2]	14.54ₐ	4.500	1	.007	2.67	26.41
	[teaching_program=2]* [start1_finish2=1]	31.49ₐ	3.653	1	.000	21.85	41.12

Pairwise comparisons of estimated marginal means based on the original scale of dependent variable test_score
a. The mean difference is significant at the .05 level.

The estimated marginal means shown in the middle table of Figure 4b.68 are just a bit different from those of the earlier analysis (see Figure 4b.30) due to the different estimation algorithm used in **Generalized Estimating Equations**. For example, the means and standard errors obtained in the earlier analysis for the posttest for the web-based and class exercise groups were as follows. Web-Based: EMMean = 66.750, Std. Error = 2.902; Class Exercise: EMMean = 84.750, Std. Error = 2.902. In the present analysis, we found the following. Web-Based: EMMean = 67.57, Std. Error = 2.702; Class Exercise: EMMean = 82.11, Std. Error = 3.599. That difference in turn produces somewhat different mean differences as shown in the lower table in Figure 4b.68 (which displays more mean differences in a single table than we were able to generate in the earlier analysis). Nonetheless, the conclusions we would draw from the present analysis match completely those we drew earlier (see Figure 4b.30).

Multivariate Analysis of Variance

5A.1 Overview

As we saw in Chapters 4A and 4B, ANOVA is applied to designs with single quantitatively measured dependent variables and is thus conceived as a univariate procedure. Even if researchers measured more than one dependent variable, as is often the case, they can analyze only one at a time using (univariate) ANOVA. We are now ready to cross into the domain of multivariate ANOVA in which several quantitative dependent variables are simultaneously analyzed within a single ANOVA design. When we make this transition from analyzing each dependent variable separately in the univariate design domain to analyzing two or more dependent variables simultaneously, we find ourselves in the domain of *multivariate analysis of variance*, abbreviated as MANOVA.

5A.2 Working With Multiple Dependent Variables

5A.2.1 The Relationship Among the Variables

The strategy of taking more than one index or quantitative measure of the behavior of participants in a research study has much to be said in its favor. Rarely is one aspect of behavior so isolated from other aspects of the overall response that it can paint a comprehensive picture of how someone responded to a situation. If we were studying the differences between women and men in workplace behavior, for example, we would certainly expect that employees who were more satisfied with their job would in general exhibit less absenteeism than those who were less satisfied; if we were studying the differences in corporate culture between businesses, we would want to consider several features of those cultures (e.g., whether decision making can be more hierarchical or democratic, whether tasks tend to be performed sequentially or simultaneously, whether the organization can be more innovative and willing to take risks or more conservative with a higher value placed on stability). It is useful and important to take into consideration the relationship between the variables that are measured in describing differences between groups. Focusing on only one aspect of employee engagement, such as job satisfaction, or one element of corporate culture, such as willingness to take risks, provides only part of the story in which we as researchers are really interested.

5A.2.2 Combining Dependent Variables Into Variates

In measuring indexes of workplace behavior in the above example, both satisfaction and absenteeism are likely to be indicators of some more general or latent variable concerning the feelings of employees toward their job. This variate or latent variable might represent "employee engagement" and would be computed as a composite subsuming satisfaction, absenteeism, and other related variables; it would be formed in the analysis by combining the two measures into a weighted linear composite that best separates the groups (see Section 5A.2.4).

Although research questions such as those concerning workplace behavior can certainly be addressed with separate univariate statistical procedures that examine each dependent variable in isolation, such as *t* tests or one-way ANOVAs, these procedures do not permit us to examine the relationships between or among the dependent variables that we have measured. There are two intimately related and certainly not mutually exclusive perspectives through which we can examine these relationships: examining group mean differences and interpreting the latent variable or variables.

5A.2.3 Examining Group Differences

We can focus on the differences between the means of the groups. When we do this, we first examine the mean differences in the multivariate realm by examining the quantitative dependent measures collectively and simultaneously and refer to such differences as *multivariate mean differences*. Having achieved a statistically significant multivariate effect, we then examine the individual measures to determine if the group differences are obtained for each of the dependent variables in the analysis. This perspective is taken in a MANOVA procedure (and in a multivariate generalization of the *t* test called Hotelling's T^2 for the two-group independent variable context) and is what we cover in this chapter.

5A.2.4 Interpreting the Latent Variable

We can also focus on interpreting the latent variable or variables. In producing the multivariate effect in the context of examining mean differences, the dependent variables in a MANOVA design are combined into weighted linear composites (variates or latent variables). The number of such variates that are formed is a function of the number of quantitative variables on which the groups were assessed and/or the number of groups in the analysis (see Section 11A.7). The weights of the quantitative variables are determined to be those that allow each variate to maximally distinguish (differentiate, discriminate) the groups (the levels of the independent variable) in the study. Examining certain statistical elements associated with these weighted composites can inform us of the relative contribution of each dependent variable in achieving this differentiation goal, which in turn can be used by researchers to interpret the variate. This perspective is taken in a discriminant function analysis, a technique that is presented in Chapters 11A and 11B.

5A.2.5 Variates and Vectors

Single measures are often referred to as scalar measures. We use them as dependent variables in experimental designs because that single measure is considered adequate in assessing a variable of interest to the researchers. Multiple measures are often referred to as *vectors*. Vectors are a set (combination) of numbers that describe a phenomenon and is very useful in those all-too-frequent situations where no single number is sufficient to quantify the phenomenon. The variate can be thought of as an example of a vector where the variate value is computed as a weighted sum of its components.

Vectors are fairly commonly used by us in everyday living. An example of a vector from our general experience would be speed. We understand speed in a rather direct sense of how fast we are traveling. But speed is really composed of two separate physical variables: distance and time. Thus, if it takes us half an hour to travel 30 miles, we know that we are traveling at 60 miles per hour. In this case, we have divided distance by time to calculate speed. In the MANOVA designs that we will be discussing, it is appropriate to speak of vectors to represent the dependent variate. Here, the vectors are computed as a weighted sum of the dependent variables. In practice, the variables in the vectors are combined to form a variate that maximally discriminates between/among the independent variable groups.

5A.2.6 Sample Size Requirements

Because of the additional burden of analyzing simultaneously multiple dependent measures, Hotelling's T^2 or MANOVA requires larger sample sizes than its univariate t test and ANOVA counterparts. A minimal sample size requirement for the analysis to be performed is that the number of cases per group must exceed the number of dependent variables, but taking that minimum literally can lead to the absurd situation where we would theoretically allow a design with two dependent variables to be carried out with three cases per group. A more realistic minimum sample size has been suggested by some authors (e.g., Hair et al., 2010) to be at least 20 cases per group to achieve minimal levels of statistical power.

5A.3 Benefits of and Drawbacks to Using MANOVA

Using MANOVA offers several benefits to researchers and should be seriously considered when there are two or more dependent variables in an experimental design. However, there are situations in which it is either not productive or inappropriate to use the procedure. We discuss below the benefits and drawbacks of using MANOVA.

5A.3.1 Benefits of Using MANOVA

There are certain benefits associated with using a MANOVA rather than a univariate ANOVA approach in data analysis. We identify seven such benefits based on the suggestions of Bray and Maxwell (1985) and Stevens (2009).

First, single dependent measures seldom capture completely a phenomenon being studied. Multiple related measures provide researchers with a certain amount of useful redundancy (through the correlation of the multiple measures), allowing them to broaden or enhance the conceptual domain under study. For example, job satisfaction could be tapped with a single item: "How satisfied are you with your current job?" Although such a global measure will provide useful information, a better approach would be to explore separate and unique job satisfaction facets (e.g., satisfaction with pay, benefits, coworkers, location, etc.) that can initially be combined into one global job satisfaction vector. Should this variate indicate that the groups can be distinguished, then it can subsequently be decomposed into its separate job satisfaction constituents.

As we will see, the ideal situation for using MANOVA is when the dependent variables are moderately correlated. Weinfurt (1995), for example, uses an example in which the correlations between three dependent variables ranged between .21 and .36 to illustrate the appropriateness of a MANOVA design, and Tabachnick and Fidell (2007) suggest that Hotelling's T^2 or MANOVA is most efficient with moderate correlations (.6) among the dependent variables.

Second, MANOVA provides some control over the overall alpha level or Type I error rate (i.e., the chance of making a false rejection of the null hypothesis). If we were to examine gender differences (the independent variable), for example, with four job satisfaction dependent variables (pay, benefits, coworkers, and location) using four separate univariate t tests or one-way ANOVAs each evaluated at the .05 alpha level, we would expect a statistically significant effect 5% of the time for each dependent measure. In practice, the alpha level we wind up with across these four analyses actually lies someplace between 5% and 18.5% (i.e., $1 - (.95)(.95)(.95)(.95)$). Performing multiple univariate t tests or ANOVAs on variables that are related can inflate the operational alpha level (Type I error), a state of affairs often called *alpha-level inflation* or *probability pyramiding*; using MANOVA avoids this problem (see Hummel & Sligo, 1971).

Third, univariate statistical tests ignore the intercorrelation found between dependent variables as they focus on only a single dependent variable at a time. As we will see, MANOVA considers dependent variable intercorrelation by examining the variance–covariance matrices.

Fourth, MANOVA enables researchers to examine relationships between dependent variables at each level of the independent variable.

Fifth, MANOVA provides researchers with statistical guidance to reduce a large set of dependent measures to a smaller set.

Sixth, MANOVA helps identify dependent variables that produce the most group (independent variable) separation or distinction.

And seventh, MANOVA can "tease out" group differences that may become masked with univariate statistical analyses but are discovered under conditions of increased power in the multivariate situation.

5A.3.2 Drawbacks to Using MANOVA

We can identify three circumstances under which we would either not want to use MANOVA or approach MANOVA with considerable caution (see Bray & Maxwell, 1985).

5A.3.2.1 Drawbacks to Using MANOVA: Variables Relatively Uncorrelated

MANOVA should not be used if the dependent variables are relatively uncorrelated. The value of combining the variables into a weighted linear composite is so that we can take into account the relationships between them, allowing them to join forces so to speak because some of the work they are doing in explaining group differences is redundant, while another part of that work is unique to each. A significant *Bartlett's test of sphericity* ($p < .001$) is indicative of sufficient correlation between the dependent variables to proceed with the multivariate analysis or to analyze the dependent variables separately in individual ANOVAs with an adjustment to the alpha level (e.g., a Bonferroni correction) to avoid alpha-level inflation.

5A.3.2.2 Drawbacks to Using MANOVA: Variables Highly Correlated

MANOVA should not be used with a set of dependent variables that are very highly correlated (probably in the .60s but certainly in the .70s and higher). Statistically, having variables that are highly correlated can produce *multicollinearity*. Multicollinearity occurs when some dependent variables in combination perfectly or almost perfectly predict another dependent variable in the analysis. The presence of multicollinearity could cause the multivariate analysis to yield misleading results if IBM SPSS allowed the analysis to proceed in the first place. Conceptually, to the extent that variables are highly correlated, they can be said to be measuring the same construct and are therefore too redundant to be treated as individual indicators of the latent construct.

There are two common situations that we have found where students encounter this variables-are-too-highly-correlated problem. One situation occurs when students use the subscales of an inventory together with the total inventory scores as dependent variables. The subscales here are portions of the total score and thus in combination correlate very highly (sometimes almost perfectly) with the total score. The solution to this situation is to run two analyses, one using only the subscales and another using the total score.

Another situation in which we may find that the dependent variables are too highly correlated occurs when one of the dependent variables is computed from one or more of the others. For example, if researchers use the time it takes for a response to be made as well as the speed of the response as dependent variables, they will have created multicollinearity because speed is the reciprocal of time and the two are therefore perfectly correlated. As another example, we may have recorded in the data file the number of correct answers on some task (e.g., How many items were correctly recalled?). If we also calculate the percentage correct and include it as another dependent variable, the combination of the two would create perfect linear dependence that would produce multicollinearity.

Dependent variables that are highly correlated are redundant, and using them as multiple dependent variables is somewhat wasteful and counterproductive. Two possible solutions to this situation would be as follows:

- First make sure that they are positively correlated—recode one of them if necessary to accomplish this goal. Then create (using the IBM SPSS **Compute** function) a new composite dependent variable. Although there is no particular limit on the number of dependent variables you can use to build the new composite variable, we encourage judicious restraint and recommend no more than 10 dependent conceptually related variables (Bray & Maxwell, 1985).
- Delete one (or more) of the highly correlated dependent variables prior to the analysis.

5A.4 Hotelling's T^2

5A.4.1 The Derivation of Hotelling's T^2

Harold Hotelling (1931) extended the univariate t test to the multivariate arena. His statistic, known as Hotelling's T^2, is the limiting case of MANOVA. That is, the Hotelling's T^2 procedure can be applied only to a one-way design with exactly two groups, whereas a

---

Figure 5a.1 Formula for Transforming Hotelling's T^2 to a Multivariate F Ratio

$$F = \frac{(n_1 + n_2 - p - 1)}{(n_1 + n_2 - 2)p} T^2$$

MANOVA procedure can be applied to a one-way design with two or more groups. Stevens (2009) notes that Hotelling (1931) was the first to demonstrate that T^2 can be transformed into the F distribution using the conversion formula shown in Figure 5a.1. In that formula, p is the number of dependent variables and n_1 and n_2 represent the sample sizes of Groups 1 and 2, respectively. That F ratio is associated with p and $(N - p - 1)$ degrees of freedom, where N is the total sample size.

As we noted in Section 4A.3, the univariate t is a ratio of between-group variability over within-group variability or error. This ratio produces a coefficient (the t value) that can be subsequently evaluated for statistical significance. Stevens (2009) shows that Hotelling's T^2 can be computed by (a) substituting the dependent variable means with a vector of means for each group and (b) replacing the univariate error term (or denominator) by its matrix analogue S (the estimated population covariance matrix).

Using matrix algebra (see Stevens, 2009), it is possible to mathematically generalize the univariate t to its multivariate counterpart. Similar to its univariate counterpart (t), Hotelling's T^2 creates a ratio of between-group variability (based on the mean vectors) to within-group variability (as represented by the inverse of the covariance matrix). Through matrix algebra, these matrices of numbers are reduced to a single value called a *determinant* that expresses the generalized variance of a matrix. Based on this, we can make the multivariate assessment of between- to within-group variance (Harris, 2001).

5A.4.2 The Nature of Hotelling's T^2

Hotelling's T^2 creates a vector (variate or weighted linear composite) that best separates the levels or categories of the independent variable. Hotelling's T^2 tests a multivariate null hypothesis that the population mean vectors for the two groups for each of the dependent variables are equal across the two groups. For example, in a study of satisfaction with health care services where we wished to compare two different health maintenance organizations (HMO) providers, we would likely have several dependent variables assessing factors such as ease of making an appointment, quality of interaction with the treating physician, and so on. The multivariate null hypothesis is that the means of the two HMO providers are equal on ease of making an appointment, quality of interaction with the treating physician, and so on.

As is true for the univariate t, this multivariate version produces a test statistic that can be compared with a critical value to determine statistical significance (Hair et al., 2010). The main difference between the two is that the univariate t test compares two population means, whereas Hotelling's T^2 multivariate analogue compares two vectors of means (Weinfurt, 1995).

5A.4.3 Statistical Power and Hotelling's T^2

As discussed in Section 2.8, *statistical power* concerns the adequacy of the statistical test to detect an actual treatment effect. We indicated that the power of a statistical test is a function of three parameters: the alpha level, the sample size, and the effect size (i.e., the extent to which treatment groups differ on the dependent variable). Power decreases when alpha levels become more stringent and increases with increases in effect size and sample size.

We can now speak of a fourth factor affecting power: the number of dependent variables subsumed in the multivariate analysis. All else equal, greater numbers of dependent variables are associated with lower levels of power. This is shown for Hotelling's T^2 in Table 5a.1, which is adapted from Stevens (1980), but the principles apply more generally to MANOVA.

The main entries in the table (the numbers in the last four columns) are the values for power. These are probabilities for the likelihood of detecting an effect (a statistically significant mean difference), assuming that such an effect exists, and can vary between .00 and 1.00. In the absence of a good reason to modify it, the general consensus based on the recommendation of Jacob Cohen (1965, 1988) is that researchers would prefer to reach a power level of .80.

Table 5a.1 informs us how statistical power varies as a function of the number of dependent variables (ranging from two to seven) in the analysis and sample size as indexed by group size (where the two groups have equal numbers of cases). Four scenarios of different effect sizes as indexed by Mahalanobis distance, ranging from small to very large, are played out.

Consider sample size first for two dependent variables (we find the same pattern for any number of dependent variables) shown in the first four rows of the table. Increases in sample size are associated with greater power. For a small effect size, power grows from .26 for a group size of 15 to .90 for a group size of 100.

Now consider the number of dependent variables for a sample size of 100 and focus on the small effect size (we find the same pattern throughout the table). For two dependent variables, the small effect size is associated with a power of .90; for three, it is .86; for five it is .78; and for seven, it is .72. That is why it is not unusual to see recommendations in the range of 20 cases per cell to achieve minimal levels of statistical power.

Table 5a.1 Power of Hotelling's T^2 at an Alpha Level of .05 for Small Through Very Large Overall Effect Size and Group n

Number of Dependent Variables	n_a	Effect Size as Indexed by D^2			
		Small	Medium	Large	Very Large
2	15	.26	.44	.65	.95
2	25	.33	.66	.86	.97
2	50	.60	.95	1.00	1.00
2	100	.90	1.00	1.00	1.00
3	15	.23	.37	.58	.91
3	25	.28	.58	.80	.95
3	50	.54	.93	1.00	1.00
3	100	.86	1.00	1.00	1.00
5	15	.21	.32	.42	.83
5	25	.26	.42	.72	.96
5	50	.44	.88	1.00	1.00
5	100	.78	1.00	1.00	1.00
7	15	.18	.27	.37	.77
7	25	.22	.38	.64	.94
7	50	.40	.82	.97	1.00
7	100	.72	1.00	1.00	1.00

Note. D^2 is Mahalanobis distance: Group sample size assumes equal group sizes; adapted from Stevens (1980).

Source: Adapted from Stevens, J.P. (1980). Power of the multivariate analysis of variance tests. Psychological Bulletin, 88, 728–737.

5A.5 Multivariate Significance Testing With More Than Two Groups

5A.5.1 The General Null Hypothesis

The conceptual basis for Hotelling's T^2 can be extended to the more general multivariate (MANOVA) case where we have three or more (k) groups in the analysis. Here, the null hypothesis is that the means of the k groups on each of the dependent measures are equal. This multivariate null hypothesis expresses the idea that all the population mean vectors or sets are equal.

In MANOVA, the univariate sums of squares are replaced with sum of squares and cross-product (SSCP) matrices. These SSCP matrices consist of dependent variable sum of squares or variances along the diagonal of the matrix and covariances (cross-products) on the off-diagonal elements that represent the common variance shared between two variables (Weinfurt, 1995). Similar to its univariate cousin ANOVA, which partitions the total variability into sum of squares between and within components, so too, MANOVA produces an analogous matrix division. MANOVA (through its IBM SPSS **General Linear Model** procedure) produces a total SSCP matrix (**T**) that can be separated into a between-group SSCP matrix (**B**) and a within-group SSCP matrix (**W**). Symbolically, these matrix components form the following multivariate analogue to the univariate sum of squares partitioning:

$$T = B + W$$

Total SSCP Matrix = Between SSCP Matrix + Within SSCP Matrix

As we noted earlier in Section 5A.4.1 in connection with Hotelling's T^2, these matrices of coefficients are converted into single values called *determinants* through matrix algebraic manipulations conducted within the IBM SPSS **General Linear Model** procedure. Determinants reflect the generalized variance of each matrix. Thus, **T** (the determinant for the SSCP) reflects the multivariate generalization of how the cases in each independent variable level or group deviate from the grand mean of each dependent variable. Similarly, **B** (the between-group SSCP matrix) reflects the differential treatment effects on the set of dependent variables and is the multivariate generalization of the univariate between-group sum of squares. Finally, **W** (the within-group SSCPs matrix) is the multivariate generalization of the univariate within-group sum of squares and represents how the cases in each level or group of the independent variable deviate from the dependent variable means (Stevens, 2009).

5A.5.2 Multivariate Tests of Statistical Significance

Because it is the two-group special case of the more general MANOVA procedure, most statistical software packages do not routinely display a Hotelling's T^2 value and its corresponding degrees of freedom and level of significance. Instead, the null hypothesis is commonly evaluated with four multivariate test statistics: Pillai's trace, Wilks' lambda, Hotelling's trace (the Hotelling–Lawley trace), and Roy's largest characteristic root. These tests assess the multivariate between- and within-group variability, and the output of most statistical software are converted to an approximate multivariate (Rao's) *F* value, which is evaluated much as any other *F* statistic. All four of these multivariate tests will produce the same approximate *F* value when the independent variable has only two levels (Tabachnick & Fidell, 2007) but will differ to a certain extent when there are three or more groups in the analysis. With three or more levels (groups) of the independent variable, these approximate multivariate *F* values tend to differ slightly, but all tend to yield the same statistically significant or not significant decision. Although researchers tend to focus on the approximate *F* values in assessing statistical significance, the values of the statistics themselves and how they are computed are interesting. We quickly mention what the values mean here and discuss their computation, and thus, a more complete characterization of them has been made in Sections 13A.5 and 13A.6.

The most prominent of these tests in the research literature is Wilks' lambda, which is basically a ratio of **W** to (**B** + **W**). The value of Wilks' lambda represents the proportion of the total variance that is not explained by the effect. In practice, if the independent variable has a statistically significant effect on the dependent variables—that is, if treatment effects are present—then **B** (the treatment variance–covariance) will be relatively large and **W** (the residual or error variance–covariance) will be small. Because Wilks' lambda is an inverse criterion, smaller values provide more evidence of treatment effects (Stevens, 2009).

Although Wilks' lambda is most typically reported in the literature, Pillai's trace is the other side of the variance–unexplained/explained coin. The Wilks statistic informs us of the amount of unexplained variance associated with an effect, whereas the Pillai statistic informs us of the amount of explained variance associated with an effect (think of it as a multivariate version of eta square). If we added the values of the Wilks and Pillai statistics in the two-group situation, the total would be 1.00. With more than two groups in the multivariate analysis, the amount of explained variance (eta square) can be computed by subtracting the value of Wilks' lambda from 1.00 (Huberty & Olejnik, 2006).

Pillai's trace should be reported if the dependent variables are plagued by significant heterogeneity of variance–covariance matrices. Some researchers believe it to be the most robust to assumption violations of the four statistics and will use it generally instead of Wilks' lambda (e.g., Norman & Streiner, 2008). It is the multivariate test to be used when this assumption of homogeneity (assessed by Box's M test) is found to be statistically significant.

Hotelling's trace, also known as the Hotelling–Lawley trace, is different from Hotelling's T^2, although the one can be converted to the other (Warner, 2008). Hotelling's trace, in simplified form until we reach Sections 13A.5 and 13A.6, is the ratio of variance attributable to the effect (e.g., an independent variable) to the error variance.

Roy's largest characteristic root provides an estimate of the upper boundary of the F statistic and may return a statistically significant result when the other three statistics do not. Under most circumstances, we would abide by the outcome of the other three multivariate tests if the conclusion drawn from Roy's largest characteristic root differs from them but, with one group having considerably different mean values on one or more dependent variables from the other groups, Roy's largest characteristic root may be a better index of an effect (e.g., Johnson & Wichern, 1999).

A statistically significant effect, as evidenced by the above tests (at the .05 level or less) indicates that group differences on the dependent variate exist. Concretely, if we obtained a significant Wilks' lambda or Pillai's trace for the effect of the independent variable (e.g., three types of HMOs), we would conclude that group differences existed on the weighted composites (dependent variates) of the measures.

5A.6 What to Do After a Significant Multivariate Effect

Once a statistically significant multivariate effect has been established (i.e., we reject the null hypothesis that our independent variable groupings are equal on the weighted composite dependent variates), researchers need to examine the nature of the variates. There are a number of established procedures available to do this, which we will now briefly review. It should be noted at this juncture that if the multivariate test is *not* significant, we would normally not proceed with any further analysis. Instead, we would conclude that the levels of the independent variable are not differentially distributed on the dependent measures.

5A.6.1 Multiple Univariate t or F Tests

Perhaps the most popular procedure to follow up multivariate significance is to conduct separate *t* tests or ANOVAs on each dependent variable with an adjusted alpha level (e.g., Hair et al., 2010; Stevens, 2009; Weinfurt, 1995). The adjustment to the alpha level we suggest is a *Bonferroni correction*, which adjusts the alpha level to reduce the possibility of operating with an inflated Type I error rate due to the use of multiple univariate tests. A Bonferroni adjustment is made by dividing the omnibus alpha level (typically .05) by the number of dependent variables. With three groups in the study, for example, we would divide .05 by 3 yielding a Bonferroni-corrected alpha level of .017.

If a statistically significant effect of the independent variable is obtained for any of the dependent variables using the corrected alpha level, then multiple comparisons tests (see Section 5B.4.2) would be performed for those particular effects. If post hoc tests (as opposed to planned comparisons, see Section 4A.4.3) are performed, then traditionally a test is selected that protects against alpha-level inflation. This is the strategy we use in the present chapter.

5A.6.2 Roy–Bargmann Step-Down Analysis

Step-down analysis is an alternative procedure for assessing each dependent variable separately following a statistically significant multivariate effect (Bray & Maxwell, 1985; Tabachnick & Fidell, 2007; Weinfurt, 1995). Here, a univariate *F* value is computed for each dependent variable after controlling for the effects of the remaining dependent measures in the analysis. This procedure is analogous to hierarchical regression (see Section 8A.2) in that we require that the dependent measures have a logical, theoretically based, a priori causal ordering. The dependent variables would then be evaluated in that order.

Consider an example with the three dependent variables dealing with client functioning. These three variables consist of GAF posttest, satisfaction with the mental health services that were provided, and the number of visits clients made to the facility to illustrate this step-down process. Assume that our literature review or clinical experience led us to the understanding that GAF posttest scores, which reflect the general state of client functioning after treatment, are a major determinant of their assessment of service satisfaction. In turn, satisfaction with the services they receive is a major reason or cause for how often clients actually come to the mental health facility. Under these conditions, we would have a reasonable foundation on which to base a step-down analysis.

The first step-down F would examine GAF posttest scores and would be the same as a standard univariate F test. The second step-down F would examine service satisfaction while holding GAF posttest scores constant. Here, GAF posttest scores would essentially be treated as a covariate, and thus, all remaining step-down "steps" are really separate ANCOVAs. The third step-down F would test mental health visits while holding both GAF posttest scores and service satisfaction constant. From this procedure, the investigator can determine the relative contribution of the dependent measures producing the multivariate effect.

We certainly recommend this approach if you are working with correlated multiple dependent measures *and* if these measures contain some logical hierarchical ordering. However, we will not emphasize this procedure because of issues of pragmatics and continuity. In IBM SPSS, Roy–Bargmann step-down analyses can be produced only through the syntax-based **MANOVA** procedure and not through the menu-driven **General Linear Model—Multivariate** procedure. The interested reader should consult Tabachnick and Fidell (2007) regarding IBM SPSS programming details for step-down analysis. We note in passing that step-down analyses can also be achieved through a series of ANCOVAs. For example, we can perform one ANCOVA using GAF posttest scores as the dependent variable and satisfaction as a covariate and then perform a second ANCOVA using GAF posttest scores as the dependent variable and both satisfaction and number of visits as covariates.

5A.6.3 Discriminant Function Analysis

As we will note in Chapter 11A, MANOVA is the other side of the discriminant function analysis coin. In these two analyses, the same variables take on different roles: The quantitative dependent variables in the MANOVA procedure are assigned the role of predictors or independent variables in discriminant analysis. In both analyses, these variables are combined into a linear composite that best differentiates the levels of the categorical variable. The categorical variable that plays the role of an independent variable in MANOVA takes on the role of dependent variable in discriminant analysis in that we are predicting membership in one of the groups.

Conducting a discriminant analysis following a statistically significant T^2 or MANOVA allows us to better understand the nature of the variates. These variates describe the potentially complex—and therefore potentially interesting—ways in which the groups can be said to differ. We strongly recommend that evaluating group differences in the traditional MANOVA procedure be accompanied by a discriminant function analysis; in Chapter 11B, we illustrate how the two work together.

5A.7 Advantages of Multivariate Factorial Designs

Thus far, we have addressed the multivariate analysis of a single independent variable. In the univariate statistical domain, where we examine one dependent variable at a time, these single-factor analyses can provide very useful information. This is also true in the multivariate domain as well, where two or more dependent measures are profitably assessed by means of a single categorical independent variable.

Challenges arise when researchers work with multiple independent variables (in the univariate or multivariate context) in a study. If they opt to analyze one independent variable at a time, they will drive up Type I (false-positive) error rates. Furthermore, single-factor independent variable designs (either univariate or multivariate) do not allow researchers to determine how independent variables jointly affect the dependent measure(s). The solution to this is to make use of factorial designs. Gamst et al. (2008) and Keppel and Wickens (2004) note several distinct advantages that univariate factorial designs have over single-factor approaches, although these advantages are also recognized by most researchers in the field. Our discussion is based on their thoughts, but we have extended the arguments to subsume the multivariate domain as well.

5A.7.1 Simultaneous Manipulation of Independent Variables

A univariate factorial design is defined as the joint or simultaneous manipulation of two or more independent variables to determine their unique and joint effect on a single dependent variable. Likewise, a multivariate factorial design examines the unique and joint effects of two or more independent variables on two or more dependent variables—both collectively (the dependent variate) and separately (as in the univariate case). Accordingly, factorial designs provide researchers with a richer context within which they may explore the phenomenon under study.

Adding an additional independent variable to the use of a single one can potentially increase the *ecological validity* or real-world meaningfulness of the study. This is true for at least two general reasons: First, most phenomena we wish to study in the social and behavioral sciences are observed in the presence of a host of conditions. Up to a point, the more of these conditions we can treat or manipulate as independent variables in a study or assess in the context of a correlation design, the more we are able to reproduce the real-world conditions and thus explain the operations of these variables. Second, as we will note in our discussion of multiple regression in Chapter 7A, we tend to believe that most of the phenomena we study are multiply determined. For the same reason that we would include multiple potential predictors in a regression study, we would want to include more than one independent variable in an experimental design.

5A.7.2 Main Effect and Interactions

A second advantage of univariate and multivariate factorial designs is found by examining the concepts of main effects and interaction effects. In the univariate situation, main effects reflect the separate treatment effects of one independent variable averaged (or collapsed) over the levels of the other independent variable(s) on a single dependent measure. Similarly, main effects in the multivariate context refer to the separate effects of one independent variable collapsed over the levels of the other independent variable(s) on a set or vector of dependent variable means. Each independent variable is considered to be a single main effect. For example, Factor A might be type of treatment and Factor B could be gender of client. Assessing the main effects of each independent variable (Factor A and Factor B) is analogous to conducting single-factor analyses in the univariate and multivariate contexts.

But factorial designs also provide us with a new ingredient that is not present in the single-factor case. This new component is the interaction effect, which assesses the joint influence of two or more independent variables. In the univariate two-factor case, an interaction depicts how the variables combine to influence the dependent measure. This combinatory effect occurs when one independent variable changes at the different levels of the second independent variable. Similarly, an interaction effect in the multivariate context depicts how two (or more) independent variables combine to influence the composite dependent variate. Thus, a second advantage of factorial designs lies in their ability to show how independent variables combine or interact to influence the dependent measure(s).

5A.8 A Strategy for Examining Two-Way Between-Subjects MANOVA Results

Performing a factorial multivariate analysis is, from the standpoint of researchers using IBM SPSS, not all that more complicated than what is entailed in performing an analogous univariate analysis. Users identify the set of dependent variables and a set of independent variables, specify the elements of the analysis, and click **OK**. Examining the multivariate statistical output is a little more complex than what we did for the ANOVA output. We outline in this section the strategy (the logic) to follow once the data are prepared for the analysis. Although we do not explicitly cover it, the strategy we outline could also generally be applied to a multivariate analysis of covariance design (a MANCOVA design).

5A.8.1 Step 1: Perform the Omnibus Multivariate Analysis

The first step is to perform the overall or omnibus multivariate analysis. For a two-way between-subjects design, there are three multivariate effects of interest: the main effect of independent variable A, the main effect of independent variable B, and the $A \times B$ interaction. The dependent variable in an omnibus multivariate analysis is the variate. This variate is computed as a weighted linear composite of the individual dependent variables, and its value for each case is known as a discriminant score (see Section 11A.6.1). This first step in the analysis is completed when we note which, if any, of the three multivariate effects are statistically significant.

5A.8.2 Step 2: Examine the Interaction Effects

The rule of interactions superseding the main effects that was described for the univariate analysis in Section 4A.5.3 applies in the multivariate setting as well. As may be recalled, explicating a statistically significant two-way interaction will incorporate any statistically significant main effects. Thus, we first examine the multivariate two-way interaction of A and B.

The multivariate effects are based on the variate—the weighted linear composite of the set of dependent variables—as the dependent variable in the analysis. These effects are composed of the univariate effects (in combination). The IBM SPSS output will provide the univariate ANOVAs for each dependent variable for each of the three effects in addition to the tests of significance for the multivariate effects. If the interaction effect is statistically significant, we are then interested in examining the univariate interaction effects that compose it.

The decision strategy that we use to interpret the results of the multivariate two-way interaction effect is shown schematically in the top portion of Figure 5a.2. Here is a summary of that strategy:

- If the multivariate interaction is statistically significant, we examine the univariate interaction effects; there will be one for each dependent variable in the analysis.
- For each univariate interaction that is statistically significant based on a Bonferroni correction for alpha inflation, we perform the simple effects analyses and interpret the results for that dependent variable. We are very likely (but are not absolutely guaranteed) to obtain at least one statistically significant effect.

Figure 5a.2 Decision Strategy for Interpreting Multivariate and Univariate Effects From a Two-Way Between-Subjects Design

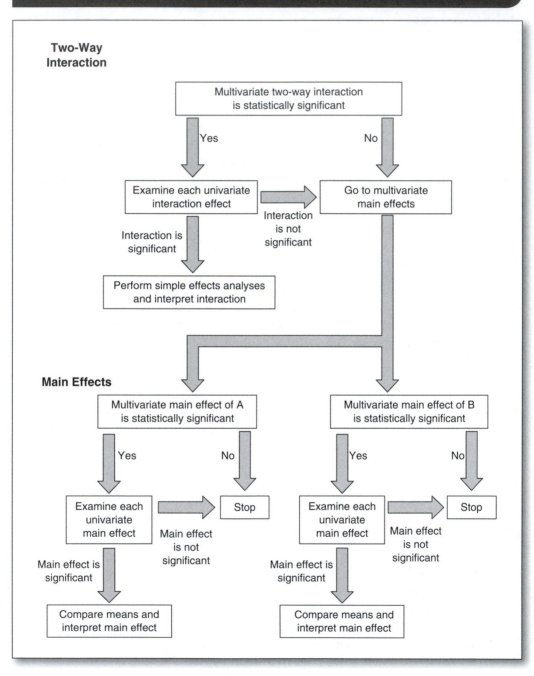

- For each univariate interaction that is not statistically significant, we enter the decision strategy for the main effects.
- If the multivariate interaction is not statistically significant, we enter the decision strategy for the main effects.

5A.8.3 Step 3: Examine the Relevant Main Effects

With a statistically significant multivariate interaction effect obtained in the omnibus analysis, some dependent variables may have yielded statistically significant univariate $A \times B$ interaction effects and others may not. For those that did yield significant effects, we would generally stop with the simple effects analysis and not examine any main effects of either A or B (as the story we would learn from such an examination would be incomplete—an interaction informs us that the effect of one independent variable depends on the level of the other). But for those dependent variables not yielding a statistically significant univariate $A \times B$ interaction effect, we would examine the multivariate main effects of A and B. The general strategy that we use to interpret the results of the main effects is shown schematically in the bottom portion of Figure 5a.2. Here is a summary of that strategy:

- If a multivariate main effect is statistically significant, we examine the univariate main effects for those dependent variables that were not involved in a statistically significant interaction.
- For each such univariate main effect that is statistically significant based on a Bonferroni correction for alpha inflation, we perform any multiple comparisons tests that are needed and interpret the results.
- If a multivariate main effect is not statistically significant, we do not report statistical significance for any univariate effect.

5A.8.4 An Application of the Strategy to Examine the MANOVA Results

Consider a somewhat more concrete example of how we go about examining the multivariate and univariate results. Assume that we have independent variables A and B, each with three levels. Further assume that all three multivariate effects (the two main effects and the interaction) were statistically significant. Finally, assume that we have five dependent variables in the analysis. The Bonferroni-corrected alpha level (used to evaluate the univariate effects) is .05 divided by the number of dependent variables; with five dependent variables in the analysis, we compute it as .05/5, yielding a value of .01. Our strategy to examine the results is as follows:

- With a statistically significant multivariate interaction effect, we first examine the five univariate interaction effects separately. Assume that only the $A \times B$ interaction effects for DV_1 (dependent variable 1) and DV_2 have achieved the Bonferroni-corrected alpha level of .01.

- We would then conduct simple effects tests on the $A \times B$ interaction effect for DV_1 and then again separately for DV_2 as discussed in Section 4A.5.5 and as shown in Section 4B.2.

- We would next evaluate the univariate main effects of A and B but only for DV_3, DV_4, and DV_5 (unless we have good reasons to examine the main effects for DV_1 and DV_2) because DV_3, DV_4, and DV_5 were not involved in a statistically significant univariate interaction effect. Unlike the $A \times B$ interaction that supersedes (conceptually encompasses) the main effects of A and B, the main effect of one independent variable does not influence the interpretation of the other main effect. Thus, we are permitted to examine the univariate main effects for both independent variable A and independent variable B for DV_3, DV_4, and DV_5.

- Let us now assume that in examining the main effect of independent variable A, DV_3 and DV_4 each achieved an alpha level equal to or better than our Bonferroni-corrected alpha level of .01. Because there are three levels of independent variable A, we would perform multiple comparisons tests for DV_3 and then again for DV_4 as discussed in Section 4A.4.3 and as shown in Section 4B.1.

- Finally, let us assume that in examining the main effect of independent variable B, DV_4 and DV_5 achieved an alpha level equal to or better than our Bonferroni-corrected alpha level of .01. Because there are three levels of independent variable B, we would perform multiple comparisons tests for DV_4 and then again for DV_5.

5A.9 The Time Dimension in Multivariate Data Analysis

Most of the statistical designs covered in this book are cross-sectional in nature. That is, the statistical analysis is employed on a set of observations (cases) that represents a single point in time. Cross-sectional data sets are represented by self-report questionnaires completed by a random sample of college freshmen on their first day of class, averages of standardized test scores reported by school districts, and exit interview data gleaned from interviews of a sample of voters exiting their precinct polling station. Such designs capture behavior, attitudes, opinions, and feelings at one moment in time, much like a photographic snapshot.

The construct of time has historically been studied by means of univariate and multivariate analysis of variance procedures. In the univariate situation, participants or cases are measured more than once on a dependent variable. For example, clients could be given a mental health evaluation at initial intake, at 6 months into their treatment, and again at the end of their first treatment year. These three longitudinal snapshots of client functioning (sometimes referred to as trend analysis) can be used to track treatment progress over time. To evaluate change, we would use a within-subjects design in which the three periodic assessments would constitute the repeated measure. Alternatively, we could incorporate a second dependent variable (e.g., client satisfaction) into this same experimental design scenario and use MANOVA to analyze the effects of these multiple dependent measures over time (e.g., Keppel & Wickens, 2004; Tabachnick & Fidell, 2007).

A variety of longitudinal data analysis designs are gaining considerable momentum in the multivariate literature (Diggle, Heagerty, Liang, & Zeger, 2002; Hand & Crowder, 1996) that represent more complex and sophisticated approaches to the study of time-related effects. These methods include panel data analysis, cohort analysis, multilevel linear modeling, and survival analysis. Although each technique is unique, they also share some fundamental commonalities, such as focusing on responses or behavior over time and using methods related to multiple regression analysis (see Allison, 1990). We will briefly note each in passing.

5A.9.1 Panel Data Analysis

Panel studies (or linear panel analyses) are based on repeatedly measuring the same set of participants over time. For example, a metropolitan newspaper might locate a small group of undecided registered Republican and Democrat voters ($N = 20$) via a telephone interview 1 year prior to a presidential election. These individuals become the panel, and their political attitudes and preferences can be assessed on a monthly basis, right up to the November election. For overviews of this method, see Cronbach and Furby (1970), Finkel (1995), Hsiao (2003), Kessler and Greenberg (1981), and Menard (1991).

5A.9.2 Cohort Data Analysis

Cohort analysis compares one or more groups of individuals at different points in time. Different participants are selected from the same cohort at each test point. Cohorts are assumed to consist of individuals who have experienced similar significant life events and personal contexts; in some sense, they have entered some sort of system at the same time. Here are two examples:

- Individuals in a large corporation are selected to start a 6-month management training program. Although they may differ on many characteristics (age, geographic region of origin), they make up a cohort based on training. We could study their success in the training program and follow up every year to determine their effectiveness as managers.
- Individuals born between 1946 and 1964 are known as the "baby boomer" generation and make up a cohort based on age. A sample of these persons could be surveyed at 5- or 10-year intervals to examine their attitudes about world political events or domestic social policy or to track changes in their personal values and spiritual orientation.

A number of methodological issues affect the proper assessment of cohort data, including participant age effects, cohort status effects, and the time period, all of which influence the variability within the study and must be accounted for. These issues can be addressed in part by means of dummy coding and interaction analysis (Glenn, 2005; Mason & Fineberg, 1985; Mason & Wolfinger, 2001; Rodgers, 1982).

5A.9.3 Multilevel Linear Modeling

Multilevel linear modeling was originally developed to study nested data (levels of variables are specific to one level of another variable)—for example, mental health clients nested within specific therapeutic programs, who are in turn nested within mental health agencies (see Chapters 9A and 9B for overviews). One assumption underlying the analysis of this sort of structure is that clients within a cluster will share certain commonalities because of their shared context. The multilevel modeling approach is also referred to as hierarchal linear models, linear mixed models, random coefficient models, or random effects models. The dependent variables in multilevel linear modeling can be either continuous or categorical (see Kenny, Bolger, & Kashy, 2002; Raudenbush & Bryk, 2002, for useful overviews).

Multilevel linear modeling has also been extended to the analysis of longitudinal data where the research goal is to examine change and the factors that affect both intra- and interindividual change (e.g., Hox, 2000, 2010; MacCallum, Kim, Malarkey, & Kiecolt-Glaser, 1997; Raudenbush, 2001; Singer & Willett, 2003; Weinfurt, 2000). At least three major approaches to multilevel linear modeling can be identified (see Diggle et al., 2002; Singer & Willett, 2003). One approach is called *marginal analysis*, where the investigator builds a model that focuses on the dependent variable average and how this mean changes over time. A second approach is to develop transition models that focus on how the dependent variable is a function of or depends on previous values of the dependent measure and other variables. A third multilevel linear modeling longitudinal approach is to construct a random effects model where the focus becomes how regression coefficients vary among participants. Several recent and readable applications of multilevel linear modeling to longitudinal data can be found in Lane and Zelinski (2003) and O'Connell and McCoach (2004).

5A.9.4 Survival Analysis

Survival analysis, also called event history analysis, encompasses a number of methods (e.g., life table analysis, Kaplan–Meier method, Cox regression model) that predict the survival time between two events for one or more groups of participants or cases (e.g., Hosmer & Lemeshow, 2002; Klein & Moeschberger, 2003; Kleinbaum & Klein, 2005; Lee & Wang, 2003; Singer & Willett, 1991; Wright, 2000). These methods were first developed in the medical, epidemiological, and biological fields to examine the survival times of patients undergoing various types of medical treatment and hence the suggested name of the procedure.

Survival analysis has been successfully extended to other fields, including the social and behavioral sciences, as well as business and marketing. For example, Gamst (1985) used this approach to determine the length of time individuals would continue to subscribe to a newspaper under different financial incentive scenarios. Survival analysis can be applied to a host of interesting and very important topics (e.g., how long adolescents will remain in high school before dropping out, how long patients are likely to follow a medication regime before putting their medicine aside). Generally, we are interested in the length of time that cases in a target group remain "active" or "alive" (in either a literal or figurative sense).

The challenge in survival analysis is that the original number of participants can be quite variable between two points in time. Participants may continue to survive, or they may quit, drop out, or become lost to follow-up. These latter situations are called *censored* events and must be taken into account to produce accurate survival curve estimates. Several descriptive methods (e.g., life tables and Kaplan–Meier survival functions) are available for estimating survival times for a sample or comparing the survival of two or more groups. Regression models (e.g., Cox, 1972) are also available to examine the contribution of continuous (metric) independent variables to survival time.

5A.10 Recommended Readings

Bird, K. D., & Hadzi-Pavlovic, D. (1983). Simultaneous test procedures and the choice of a test statistic in MANOVA. *Psychological Bulletin, 93,* 167–178.

Bochner, A. P., & Fitzpatrick, M. A. (1980). Multivariate analysis of variance: Techniques, models, and applications in communication research. In P. R. Monge & J. N. Cappella (Eds.), *Multivariate techniques in human communication research* (pp. 143–174). New York, NY: Academic Press.

Bock, R. D., & Haggard, E. A. (1968). The use of multivariate analysis of variance in behavioral research. In D. K. Whitla (Ed.), *Handbook of measurement and assessment in behavioral sciences* (pp. 100–142). Reading, MA: Addison-Wesley.

Box, G. E. P., Hunter, W. P., & Hunter, J. S. (1978). *Statistics for experimenters.* New York, NY: Wiley.

Cole, D. A., Maxwell, S. E., Avery, R., & Salas, E. (1994). How the power of MANOVA can both increase and decrease as a function of the intercorrelations among dependent variables. *Psychological Bulletin, 115,* 465–474.

Everitt, B. S. (1979). A Monte Carlo investigation of the robustness of Hotelling's one and two sample T^2 tests. *Journal of the American Statistical Association, 74,* 48–51.

Gabriel, K. R. (1969). A comparison of some methods of simultaneous inference in Manova. In P. R. Krishnaiah (Ed.), *Multivariate analysis–II* (pp. 67–86). New York, NY: Academic Press.

Hakstian, A. R., Roed, J. C., & Lind, J. C. (1979). Two-sample T^2 procedure and the assumption of homogeneous covariance matrices. *Psychological Bulletin, 56,* 1255–1263.

Hand, D. J., & Taylor, C. C. (1987). *Multivariate analysis of variance and repeated measures.* London, England: Chapman & Hall.

Harris, R. J. (1993). Multivariate analysis of variance. In L. K. Edwards (Ed.), *Applied analysis of variance in behavioral science* (pp. 255–296). New York, NY: Marcel Dekker.

Holloway, L. N., & Dunn, O. J. (1967). The robustness of Hotelling's T^2. *Journal of the American Statistical Association, 62,* 124–136.

Hotelling, H. (1931). The generalization of Student's ratio. *Annals of Mathematical Statistics, 2,* 360–378.

Huberty, C. J. (1989). Multivariate analysis versus multiple univariate analyses. *Psychological Bulletin, 105,* 302–308.

Huberty, C. J., & Morris, J. D. (1989). Multivariate analysis versus multiple univariate analyses. *Psychological Bulletin, 105,* 302–308.

Hummel, T. J., & Sligo, J. (1971). Empirical comparison of univariate and multivariate analysis of variance procedures. *Psychological Bulletin, 76,* 49–57.

Lauter, J. (1978). Sample size requirements for the T^2 test of MANOVA (tables for one-way classification). *Biometrical Journal, 20,* 389–406.

Lix, L. M., & Keselman, H. J. (2004). Multivariate tests of means in independent groups designs: Effects of covariance heterogeneity and nonnormality. *Evaluation & the Health Professions, 27,* 45–69.

McDonald, R. A., Seifert, C. F., Lorenzet, S. J., Givens, S., & Jaccard, J. (2002). The effectiveness of methods for analyzing multivariate factorial data. *Organizational Research Methods, 5,* 255–274.

Mudholkar, G. S., & Subbaiah, P. (1980). MANOVA multiple comparisons associated with finite intersection tests. In P. R. Krishnaiah (Ed.), *Multivariate analysis V* (pp. 467–482). Amsterdam, Netherlands: North-Holland.

O'Brien, R. G., & Kaiser, M. K. (1985). MANOVA method for analyzing repeated measures designs: An extensive primer. *Psychological Bulletin, 97,* 316–333.

Olson, C. L. (1974). Comparative robustness of six tests in multivariate analysis of variance. *Journal of the American Statistical Association, 69,* 894–908.

Olson, C. L. (1976). On choosing a test statistic in MANOVA. *Psychological Bulletin, 83,* 579–586.

Olson, C. L. (1979). Practical considerations in choosing a MANOVA test statistic: A rejoinder to Stevens. *Psychological Bulletin, 86,* 1350–1352.

Rulon, P. J., & Brooks, W. D. (1968). On statistical tests of group differences. In D. K. Whitla (Ed.), *Handbook of measurement and assessment in behavioral sciences* (pp. 60–99). Reading, MA: Addison-Wesley.

Shaffer, J. P., & Gillo, M. W. (1974). A multivariate extension of the correlation ratio. *Educational and Psychological Measurement, 34,* 521–524.

Spector, P. E. (1977). What to do with significant multivariate effects in multivariate analyses of variance. *Journal of Applied Psychology, 62,* 158–163.

Stevens, J. P. (1972). Four methods of analyzing between variation for the k group MANOVA problem. *Multivariate Behavioral Research, 7,* 499–522.

Stevens, J. P. (1980). Power of the multivariate analysis of variance tests. *Psychological Bulletin, 88,* 728–737.

Thomas, D. (1992). Interpreting discriminant functions: A data analytic approach. *Multivariate Behavioral Research, 27,* 335–362.

Weinfurt, K. P. (1995). Multivariate analysis of variance. In L. G. Grimm & P. R. Yarnold (Eds.), *Reading and understanding multivariate statistics* (pp. 245–276). Washington, DC: American Psychological Association.

Wilkinson, L. (1975). Response variable hypotheses in the multivariate analysis of variance. *Psychological Bulletin, 82,* 408–412.

Zwick, R. (1986). Rank and normal scores alternatives to Hotelling's T^2. *Multivariate Behavioral Research, 21,* 169–186.

Multivariate Analysis of Variance Using IBM SPSS

5B.1 Numerical Example

The data set that we will be using throughout Chapter 5B is called **Victoria MANOVA**. It has 348 mental health practitioners as the cases. These practitioners were assessed on their perceived degree of multicultural counseling skills as well as on some demographic measures.

The following are categorical demographic variables:

- **Gender** (1 = *male*, 2 = *female*)
- **Ethnicity** (1 = *White American*, 2 = *Latino/a American*, 3 = *African American*, 4 = *Asian American/Pacific Islander*, 5 = *missing*)
- **Original_Ethnicity** (1 = *White American*, 2 = *Latino/a American*, 3 = *African American*, 4 = *Asian American/Pacific Islander*, 5 = *Other*). This was the original ethnicity variable with the category of Other.
- **DIMEIMEIE** (Dichotomous MEIM Ethnic Identity Exploration: 1 = *low*, 2 = *high*)
- **DISMASDSI** (Dichotomous Stephenson Multigroup Acculturation Scale [SMAS] Dominant Society Immersion: 1 = *low*, 2 = *high*)
- **DIINDCOLC** (Dichotomous INDCOL Collectivism Scale: 1 = *low*, 2 = *high*)

Four additional quantitative variables are also in the data file. These are the subscales of the CBMCS (Gamst et al., 2004):

- **CBMCSSD** (CBMCS Sociocultural Diversities)
- **CBMCSACB** (CBMCS Awareness of Cultural Barriers)
- **CBMCSMK** (CBMCS Multicultural Knowledge)
- **CBMCSSC** (CBMCS Sensitivity and Responsiveness to Consumers)

5B.2 Alternatives to Performing a MANOVA Analysis

IBM SPSS provides two separate procedures for conducting a MANOVA. The **General Linear Model** procedure is menu driven and is therefore similar in function to all the other IBM SPSS statistical procedures reviewed in this book. It is the one we will use in this chapter.

An alternative way to conduct a MANOVA with IBM SPSS is through the use of the older, syntax-based **MANOVA** procedure. The **MANOVA** procedure generates much of the same output that the **General Linear Model** procedure produces, but it can also compute Roy–Bargmann step-down analyses (recall that these analyses test for group mean differences on a single dependent measure while controlling for the other dependent variables). We use the **MANOVA** procedure to generate our canonical correlation analysis in Chapters 13A and 13B.

5B.3 Two-Group MANOVA

For the present example of a two-group MANOVA, we will designate **Gender** as the single (binary) independent variable and the four CBMCS subscales (**CBMCSSD**, **CBMCSACB**, **CBMCSMK**, **CBMCSSC**) as the four quantitative dependent variables.

5B.3.1 Two-Group MANOVA Setup

The two-group MANOVA is the equivalent of Hotelling's T^2. From the main menu, select **Analyze ➜ General Linear Model ➜ Multivariate**, which produces the **Multivariate** main dialog window shown in Figure 5b.1. Move the four dependent variables (**CBMCSSD**, **CBMCSACB**, **CBMCSMK**, and **CBMCSSC**) from the variables list panel to the **Dependent Variables** panel and move **Gender** to the **Fixed Factor(s)** panel.

Selecting the **Options** pushbutton brings us to the window shown in Figure 5b.2. In the **Display** area, check **Descriptive statistics**, **Estimates of effect size** (see first bullet below), **Residual SSCP matrix** (this is the only way we can obtain Bartlett's test of sphericity to evaluate whether or not there is statistically significant correlation between the dependent variables), and **Homogeneity tests** (to acquire Levene's test for equality of variances for each dependent variable across the levels of the independent variable).

The other checkboxes provide the following information:

- **Estimates of effect size** produces *partial eta-square* values rather than full eta-square values. Each is computed as the ratio of the sum of squares for the effect divided by the sum of sum of squares for the effect and the sum of squares for the error term appropriate to that effect. In the case of a one-way between-subjects design, the partial eta-square value and the

Figure 5b.1 The Main Multivariate Dialog Window

Figure 5b.2 The Options Window of Multivariate

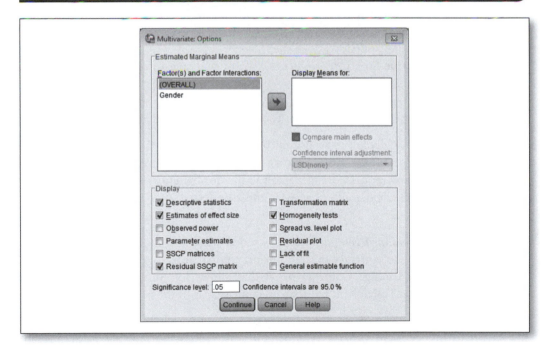

full eta-square value that we have talked about in our previous chapters are equal, and so we can generate them here. In the case of other designs, these values will be different, and we recommend not requesting the partial eta square unless you are very familiar with how to interpret this statistic. The full eta square is simple enough to calculate (sum of squares for the effect divided by the corrected total sum of squares) from the information in the summary table.

- **Observed power** evaluates whether an F test will detect differences between groups (see Section 2.8 for a discussion of statistical power). Note that such "after-the-fact" calculations have come under criticism for providing meaningless post hoc diagnostics (Keppel & Wickens, 2004).

- **Parameter estimates** provides parameter estimates, t tests, confidence intervals, and power for each test.

- **SSCP matrices** produces sum of squares and cross-products matrices.

- **Transformation matrix** generates a transformation of the dependent variables.

- **Spread vs. level plots** displays group variability and is useful in detecting the source of heterogeneity of variance.

- **Residual plots** produces plots of observed, standardized, and predicted residuals to help identify outliers.

- **Lack of fit** tests the adequacy of the multivariate model. If this test is statistically significant, it suggests that the current multivariate model is inadequate.

- **General estimable function** produces a table of general estimable functions that can be used to test custom hypotheses.

Each of the remaining pushbuttons produces its own dialog window that we briefly review:

- The **Model** is usually left in its default setting, **Full factorial**, which requests that all main effects, interaction effects, and covariates be tested. In the present example, the full model is appropriate and requested. The default setting for the **Sum of squares** is set at **Type III** sum of squares, which requests that each effect be tested after adjusting for all other model effects.

- **Contrasts** or *planned comparisons* are needed when the independent variable has three or more groups and you have specific a priori comparisons to test. A pull-down menu can be found in the **Change Contrast** panel that allows for **Simple** or more complex (**Special**) comparisons. The default requests no contrasts, as in the present example.

- **Plots** generates line graphs that display dependent variable means at each level of the **Factor** or independent variable. The default is to request no plots, as in the present example.

- The **Post Hoc** window allows researchers to perform *post hoc* or *multiple comparisons tests* after a statistically significant omnibus univariate *F* test indicates differences between the (three or more) levels of the independent variable. We will talk more about these tests in Section 5B.3.2. The default, no post hoc tests, is in place with the current example because our independent variable (Gender) has only two levels.

- **Save** allows researchers to save various predicted values, case diagnostics, and residuals; it also provides the opportunity to save certain statistics to the data file.

After completing the dialog window specifications, click **Continue** to return to the main dialog window, and click **OK** to perform the analysis.

5B.3.2 Two-Group MANOVA Output

5B.3.2.1 Descriptive Output

Figure 5b.3 presents the descriptive information for the analysis. The **Between-Subjects Factors** table indicates one factor (independent variable) with two levels containing relatively large but unequal sample size. The **Descriptive Statistics** table provides each dependent measure's observed means, standard deviations, and sample sizes for each level of the independent variable.

Figure 5b.3 Descriptive Information

Between–Subjects Factors

			Value Label	N
Gender Gender	1		Male	133
	2		Female	215

Descriptive Statistics

	Gender Gender	Mean	Std. Deviation	N
CBMCSSD CBMSC Sociocultural Diversities Subscale	1 Male	2.7658	.45340	133
	2 Female	2.7855	.43604	215
	Total	2.7780	.44221	348
CBMCSACB CBMCS Awareness of Cultural Barriers Subscale	1 Male	3.3010	.38634	133
	2 Female	3.2995	.39653	215
	Total	3.3001	.39211	348
CBMCSMK CBMCS Multicultural Knowledge Subscale	1 Male	2.5350	.59949	133
	2 Female	2.4609	.64826	215
	Total	2.4892	.63022	348
CBMCSSC CBMCS Sensitivity to Consumers Subscale	1 Male	3.3284	.36005	133
	2 Female	2.9092	.62228	215
	Total	3.0694	.57422	348

5B.3.2.2 The Box and Bartlett Tests

The outcome of **Box's Test of Equality of Covariance Matrices** presented in the upper portion of Figure 5b.4 is statistically significant (Box's $M = 62.407$, $p < .001$), indicating that the dependent variable covariance matrices are not equal across the levels of the independent variable (**Gender**). **Bartlett's Test of Sphericity** (in the lower portion of Figure 5b.4) is statistically significant (approximate chi-square = 272.783, $p < .001$), indicating sufficient correlation between the dependent measures to proceed with the analysis.

Figure 5b.4 Box's and Bartlett's Tests

Box's Test of Equality of Covariance Matrices[a]

Box's M	62.407
F	6.157
df1	10
df2	367037.006
Sig.	.000

Tests the null hypothesis that the observed covariance matrices of the dependent variables are equal across groups.

a. Design: Intercept + Gender

Bartlett's Test of Sphericity[a]

Likelihood Ratio	.000
Approx. Chi-Square	272.783
df	9
Sig.	.000

Tests the null hypothesis that the residual covariance matrix is proportional to an identity matrix.

a. Design: Intercept + Gender

5B.3.2.3 The Multivariate Test

The "heart" of the MANOVA output lies in the **Multivariate Tests** output shown in Figure 5b.5. This table is composed of two parts. The top portion of the table (**Intercept**) evaluates whether the overall CBMCS mean differs from zero. Because of its statistical significance, we conclude that it does differ from zero, indicating that the CBMCS variate varies in the population.

Of more importance is the evaluation of the effect of the independent variable (**Gender**) in the bottom half of the table. Recall that when we evaluate a univariate t or F statistic, we are assessing a ratio of between-group variability (i.e., treatment effects plus error) to within-group variability (i.e., error or nuisance variation, measurement error). In the multivariate situation, we are no longer dividing a single number that represents between-group variability by a single number that represents within-group variability. Rather, we are dividing (actually inverting) two

Figure 5b.5 The Multivariate Tests

Multivariate Tests[b]

Effect		Value	F	Hypothesis df	Error df	Sig.	Partial Eta Squared
Intercept	Pillai's Trace	.989	7519.060[a]	4.000	343.000	.000	.989
	Wilks' Lambda	.011	7519.060[a]	4.000	343.000	.000	.989
	Hotelling's Trace	87.686	7519.060[a]	4.000	343.000	.000	.989
	Roy's Largest Root	87.686	7519.060[a]	4.000	343.000	.000	.989
Gender	Pillai's Trace	.149	15.042[a]	4.000	343.000	.000	.149
	Wilks' Lambda	.851	15.042[a]	4.000	343.000	.000	.149
	Hotelling's Trace	.175	15.042[a]	4.000	343.000	.000	.149
	Roy's Largest Root	.175	15.042[a]	4.000	343.000	.000	.149

a. Exact statistic

b. Design: Intercept + Gender

matrices or vectors (between and within) of numbers. Because the end result of this matrix manipulation is not a single number, as in the univariate situation, multivariate tests have been developed that translate these matrix-based ratios into a single value that can be evaluated as an *F* statistic.

Four multivariate tests are commonly employed in computerized statistical programs: Pillai's trace, Wilks' lambda, Hotelling's trace, and Roy's largest characteristic root. As we noted in Chapter 5A, Wilks' lambda is most typically reported in the literature, followed by Pillai's trace if the Box's *M* test is statistically significant (as we have discovered in the present example), indicating heterogeneity of variance–covariance matrices. All these tests evaluate the null hypothesis of no independent variable (group) differences in the population on the dependent variate.

An actual value for each multivariate test statistic is displayed in the **Value** column of the table (e.g., Pillai's trace = .149) and is translated by IBM SPSS into an *F* value that is evaluated with specific hypothesis (between groups) and error (within groups) degrees of freedom. Remember that the *F* values will always be the same in a two-group Hotelling's T^2 analysis. This statistically significant multivariate test tells us there are reliable multivariate differences between gender groups on the composite dependent CBMCS variate. We should also note in passing, however, that we are accounting for a moderate proportion of the total variance (.149, or about 15%) with this independent variable (the partial eta square is equal to the full eta square in this design).

Note that the value of Wilks' lambda is .851, which is the total amount of unexplained variance of the dependent variate in the multivariate analysis. If we subtract this value from 1.00, we obtain .149, the total amount of explained variance. Note also that .149 is the value of Pillai's trace, which gives us a direct estimate of the amount of explained variance. We will provide more description on how these multivariate test statistics are generated in Chapter 13A in the context of canonical correlation analysis.

5B.3.2.4 The Levene Test

Because the multivariate test is statistically significant, we can proceed with an assessment of each dependent measure. Shown in Figure 5b.6 are the results of the **Levene Test of Equality of Error Variances**. These are tests for homogeneity of variance violations for each dependent variable. The evaluations of the first three dependent measures are not statistically significant ($p > .05$), indicating equal error variance across levels of **Gender**. The one exception is the **CBMCSSC** variable, whose Levene test was statistically significant ($p < .001$), indicating unequal error variance across the levels of **Gender**. For the purposes of this example, we will use a stringent alpha level of .001 for evaluation of any effects related to the **CBMCSSC** dependent variable (see Gamst et al., 2008, for more details).

Figure 5b.6 The Levene Test

Levene's Test of Equality of Error Variances[a]

	F	df1	df2	Sig.
CBMCSSD CBMSC Sociocultural Diversities Subscale	.236	1	346	.627
CBMCSACB CBMCS Awareness of Cultural Barriers Subscale	.549	1	346	.459
CBMCSMK CBMCS Multicultural Knowledge Subscale	1.636	1	346	.202
CBMCSSC CBMCS Sensitivity to Consumers Subscale	44.565	1	346	.000

Tests the null hypothesis that the error variance of the dependent variable is equal across groups.

a. Design: Intercept + Gender

5B.3.2.5 Tests of the Univariate Effects

Each dependent variable is evaluated separately in the **Tests of Between-Subjects Effects** presented in Figure 5b.7. The F values obtained from these analyses are identical to running separate univariate ANOVAs for each dependent measure. This output

Figure 5b.7 Tests of the Univariate Effects

Tests of Between-Subjects Effects

Source	Dependent Variable	Type III Sum of Squares	df	Mean Square	F	Sig.	Partial Eta Squared
Corrected Model	CBMCSSD CBMSC Sociocultural Diversities Subscale	.032[a]	1	.032	.162	.688	.000
	CBMCSACB CBMCS Awareness of Cultural Barriers Subscale	.000[b]	1	.000	.001	.973	.000
	CBMCSMK CBMCS Multicultural Knowledge Subscale	.450[c]	1	.450	1.134	.288	.003
	CBMCSSC CBMCS Sensitivity to Consumers Subscale	14.435[d]	1	14.435	49.954	.000	.126
Intercept	CBMCSSD CBMSC Sociocultural Diversities Subscale	2532.246	1	2532.246	12918.227	.000	.974
	CBMCSACB CBMCS Awareness of Cultural Barriers Subscale	3579.888	1	3579.888	23217.347	.000	.985
	CBMCSMK CBMCS Multicultural Knowledge Subscale	2050.865	1	2050.865	5165.540	.000	.937
	CBMCSSC CBMCS Sensitivity to Consumers Subscale	3197.036	1	3197.036	11063.883	.000	.970
Gender	CBMCSSD CBMSC Sociocultural Diversities Subscale	.032	1	.032	.162	.688	.000
	CBMCSACB CBMCS Awareness of Cultural Barriers Subscale	.000	1	.000	.001	.973	.000
	CBMCSMK CBMCS Multicultural Knowledge Subscale	.450	1	.450	1.134	.288	.003
	CBMCSSC CBMCS Sensitivity to Consumers Subscale	14.435	1	14.435	49.954	.000	.126
Error	CBMCSSD CBMSC Sociocultural Diversities Subscale	67.823	346	.196			
	CBMCSACB CBMCS Awareness of Cultural Barriers Subscale	53.350	346	.154			
	CBMCSMK CBMCS Multicultural Knowledge Subscale	137.372	346	.397			
	CBMCSSC CBMCS Sensitivity to Consumers Subscale	99.981	346	.289			
Total	CBMCSSD CBMSC Sociocultural Diversities Subscale	2753.437	348				
	CBMCSACB CBMCS Awareness of Cultural Barriers Subscale	3843.290	348				
	CBMCSMK CBMCS Multicultural Knowledge Subscale	2294.113	348				
	CBMCSSC CBMCS Sensitivity to Consumers Subscale	3393.053	348				
Corrected Total	CBMCSSD CBMSC Sociocultural Diversities Subscale	67.855	347				
	CBMCSACB CBMCS Awareness of Cultural Barriers Subscale	53.350	347				
	CBMCSMK CBMCS Multicultural Knowledge Subscale	137.822	347				
	CBMCSSC CBMCS Sensitivity to Consumers Subscale	114.415	347				

a. R Squared = .000 (Adjusted R Squared = −.002)
b. R Squared = .000 (Adjusted R Squared = −.003)
c. R Squared = .003 (Adjusted R Squared = .000)
d. R Squared = .126 (Adjusted R Squared = .124)

summarizes standard ANOVA output (i.e., sum of squares, degrees of freedom, mean squares, *F* values, significance level, and partial eta-square values) for each dependent variable.

The left side of the table specifies the **Source**. The **Corrected Model** source is identical to the **Gender** source because, with the exception of the intercept, it consolidates all model effects and there is only the one **Gender** effect. The **Intercept** (as we noted previously) tests whether each mean differs significantly from zero and is not of much interest to us.

Gender is where we focus our attention, because this evaluates the effect of the **Gender** independent variable for each dependent variable. To evaluate these effects, we use a Bonferroni-corrected alpha level to avoid alpha inflation. We therefore divide .05 by the number of ANOVAs and obtain .05/4 or a Bonferroni-corrected alpha level of .0125. However, in evaluating the **CBMCSSC** variable, which has violated the homogeneity of variance, we invoke an alpha level of .001. As we can see, a statistically significant effect of **Gender** was evidenced for the **CBMCSSC** subscale but not for the other three CBMCS subscales. Thus, we can conclude that the statistically significant multivariate effect we found was "driven" in part by the impact of **Gender** on the **CBMCSSC** self-appraisals of these mental health practitioners.

To see the specific manner in which provider gender affected their judgments regarding the **CBMCSSC** subscale, we examine the observed group means shown in Figure 5b.3. We may now say that males had statistically significant higher **CBMCSSC** scores ($M = 3.33$, $SD = 0.36$) than did females ($M = 2.91$, $SD = 0.62$). No statistically significant differences were observed for the other dependent measures.

5B.3.3 Reporting the Results of a Two-Group MANOVA

A Hotelling's T^2 or two-group between-subjects multivariate analysis of variance was conducted on four dependent variables: CBMCS Sociocultural Diversities, CBMCS Awareness of Cultural Barriers, CBMCS Multicultural Knowledge, and CBMCS Sensitivity and Responsiveness to Consumers subscales. The independent variable was gender of mental health practitioner.

The sample consisted of 348 child mental health practitioners (215 females, 133 males). Due to a statistically significant ($p < .001$) Box's test of equality of the variance–covariance matrices, indicating that the observed covariance matrices of the dependent variables were unequal across independent variable groups, a Pillai's trace was employed to evaluate all multivariate effects.

Using Pillai's trace as the criterion, the composite dependent variate was significantly affected by gender, Pillai's trace = .149, $F(4, 343) = 15.04$, $p < .001$. Univariate ANOVAs were conducted on each dependent measure separately to determine the locus of the statistically significant multivariate effect. The only statistically significant univariate effect was associated with the CBMCS Sensitivity and Responsiveness to Consumers subscale, $F(1, 346) = 49.95$, $p < .001$, $\eta^2 = .126$; male mental health providers achieved higher sensitivity and responsiveness [$M = 3.33$, $SD = 0.36$, 95% CI (3.27, 3.39)] than females [$M = 2.91$, $SD = 0.62$, 95% CI (2.83, 2.99)].

5B.4 k-Group MANOVA

The ingredients for a *k*-group MANOVA require a categorical independent variable with three or more levels or groups and at least two quantitative conceptually related dependent measures. The two-group MANOVA is the limiting case of a *k*-group MANOVA and was discussed in Section 5B.2 to introduce the analysis. The present numerical example is an extension of the previous numerical example of community mental health child practitioners. The dependent variables will remain the same as in the previous analysis: **CBMCSSD, CBMCSACB, CBMCSMK,** and **CBMCSSC.** The independent variable is practitioner **Ethnicity.**

5B.4.1 Recoding to Create Our Independent Variable

As indicated in Section 5B.1, the **Original_Ethnicity** variable had five categories, and it was likely that one or more of those categories does not have sufficient sample size to be included in our analysis. To investigate this, we select **Analyze ➔ Descriptive Statistics ➔ Frequencies**, the dialog window for which is shown in Figure 5b.8. We move **Original_ Ethnicity** into the **Variable(s)** panel and click **OK**.

The output in Figure 5b.9 shows disproportionate numbers of practitioners by ethnic/racial group. Specifically, **White American, Latino/a American, Asian American Pac**

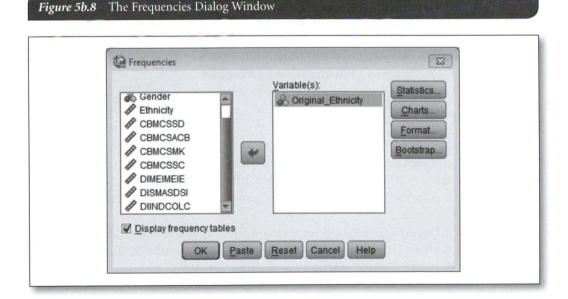

Figure 5b.9 Output From the Frequencies Procedure

Original_Ethnicity Original Practitioner Ethnicity

		Frequency	Percent	Valid Percent	Cumulative Percent
Valid	1 White American	154	44.3	44.3	44.3
	2 Latino/a American	69	19.8	19.8	64.1
	3 African American	48	13.8	13.8	77.9
	4 Asian American Pac Islander	60	17.2	17.2	95.1
	5 Other	17	4.9	4.9	100.0
	Total	348	100.0	100.0	

Islander, and **African American** practitioners combined represent 95.1% of the total ($N = 348$) practitioners, but those in the **Other** category total to just 17. To reduce somewhat the disproportionate subsample sizes, we suggest the following:

- Copy the **Original_Ethnicity** variable (click on the top of the column in the data file) to a new column (it will be given the default name of **VAR000001**).
- At the bottom of the data file, click **Variable View**.
- Name **VAR000001** as **Ethnicity**.
- Click in the **Missing** cell for **Ethnicity** (see Figure 5b.10) to display the dialog window shown in Figure 5b.11.
- Select the **Discrete missing values** button, and type **5** in the first panel.
- Click **OK** to define **5** as a **missing value** on **Ethnicity**.

5B.4.2 k-Group MANOVA Setup

From the main menu, select **Analyze ➔ General Linear Model ➔ Multivariate**, which produces the **Multivariate** main dialog window shown in Figure 5b.12. Move the four dependent variables (**CBMCSSD, CBMCSACB, CBMCSMK,** and **CBMCSSC**) from the variables list panel to the **Dependent Variables** panel, and move **Ethnicity** to the **Fixed Factor(s)** panel.

Selecting the **Options** pushbutton brings us to the window shown in Figure 5b.13. In the **Display** area, check **Descriptive statistics, Residual SSCP Matrix** (this is the only way we can obtain **Bartlett's Test of Sphericity** to evaluate whether or not there is statistically significant correlation between the dependent variables), and **Homogeneity tests** (to acquire Levene's test for equality of variances for each dependent variable across the levels of the

Figure 5b.10 Setting the Other Category in Ethnicity to Missing: The Variable View Screen

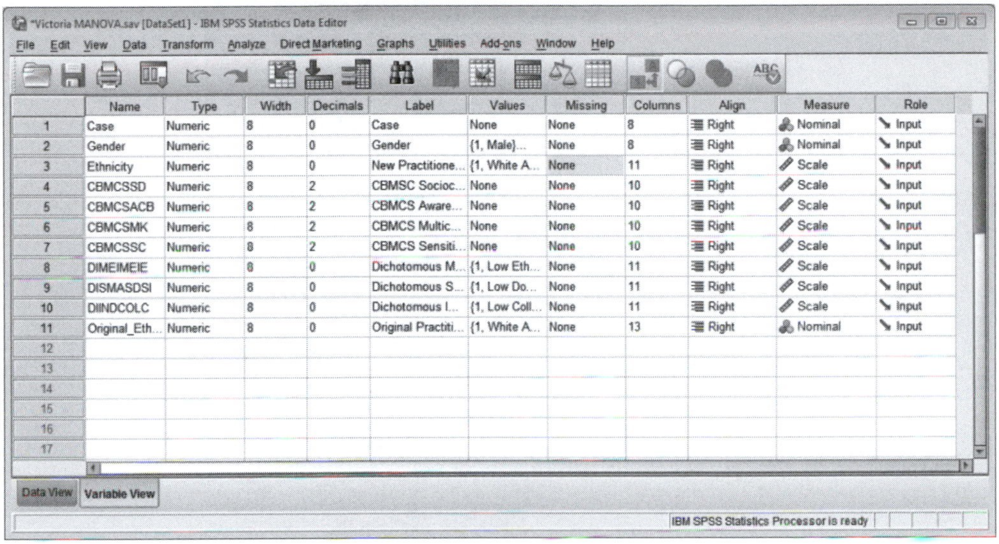

independent variable). We will not request (by selecting the **Estimates of effect size** checkbox) the partial eta square here as mentioned in Section 4A.4.2 but instead calculate it when needed (for a statistically significant effect).

Selecting the **Post Hoc** pushbutton accesses the **Multivariate: Post Hoc Multiple Comparisons for Observed Means** dialog window (see Figure 5b.14). Highlighting the independent variable (**Ethnicity**) in the **Factor(s)** panel and clicking the arrow button to its right moves this variable into the **Post Hoc Tests for** panel and activates the **Equal Variances Assumed** and **Equal Variances Not Assumed** panels (at the bottom of

Figure 5b.11 Setting the Other Category in Ethnicity to Missing: The Missing Values Screen

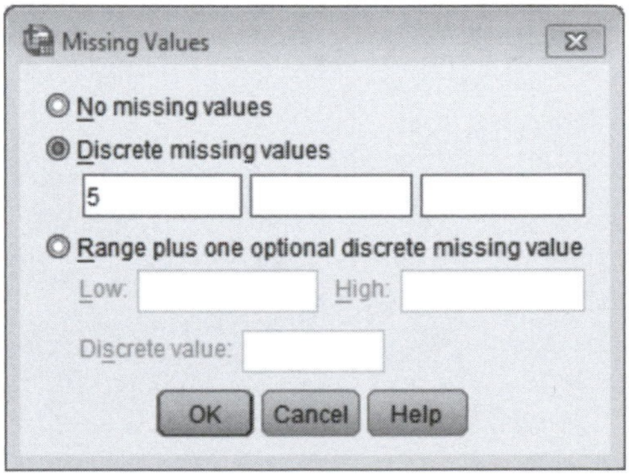

Figure 5b.12   The Main Multivariate Dialog Window

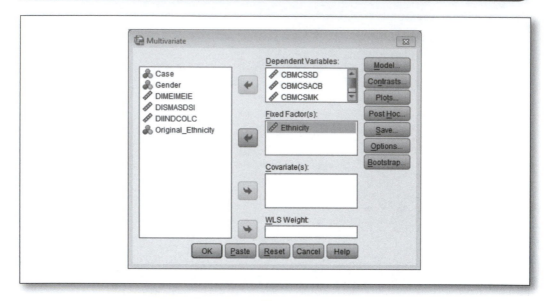

Figure 5b.13   The Options Window of Multivariate

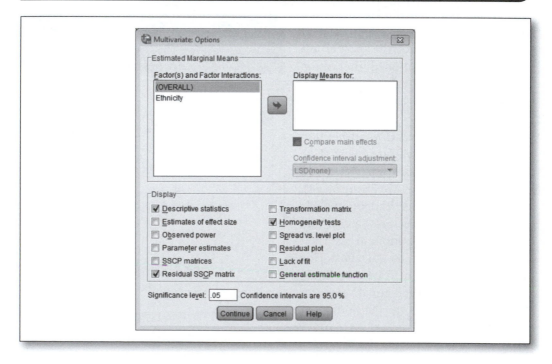

the dialog window). In the present example, we have selected two of the post hoc tests as can be seen in Figure 5b.14. If a dependent variable does not violate the equal variances assumption, we will use the REGWQ procedure as recommended by Gamst et al. (2008). However, the different ethnic/racial groups, especially with different sample sizes, are also likely to exhibit sufficiently different variances on some of the dependent variables to violate the equal variances assumption. In anticipation of such a violation, we have also requested the **Tamhane's T2** post hoc test.

Figure 5b.14   The Post Hoc Window

Once we have completed the **Post Hoc** dialog window, we are ready to perform the analysis. Clicking **Continue** brings us back to the main dialog window, and clicking **OK** runs the analysis.

5B.4.3 k-*Group MANOVA Output*

5B.4.3.1 Descriptive Output

Figure 5b.15 displays the **Between-Subjects Factors** table. We note disproportionate or unequal cell sample sizes among the four groups. The **Descriptive Statistics** table shown next in Figure 5b.15 depicts each dependent measure's observed (unadjusted) means, standard deviations, and sample sizes at each level of the independent variable.

Figure 5b.15 Descriptive Information

Between–Subjects Factors

		Value Label	N
Ethnicity Ethnicity	1	White American	154
	2	Latino/a American	69
	3	African American	48
	4	Asian American Pac Islander	60

Descriptive Statistics

	Ethnicity Ethnicity	Mean	Std. Deviation	N
CBMCSSD CBMSC Sociocultural Diversities Subscale	1 White American	2.7786	.44680	154
	2 Latino/a American	2.8271	.41749	69
	3 African American	2.7351	.44984	48
	4 Asian American Pac Islander	2.7210	.44403	60
	Total	2.7720	.44031	331
CBMCSACB CBMCS Awareness of Cultural Barriers Subscale	1 White American	3.3186	.37655	154
	2 Latino/a American	3.2696	.36406	69
	3 African American	3.2708	.47229	48
	4 Asian American Pac Islander	3.2906	.39273	60
	Total	3.2964	.39099	331
CBMCSMK CBMCS Multicultural Knowledge Subscale	1 White American	2.1240	.62036	154
	2 Latino/a American	2.7558	.43365	69
	3 African American	2.7583	.47393	48
	4 Asian American Pac Islander	2.8000	.45844	60
	Total	2.4702	.62576	331
CBMCSSC CBMCS Sensitivity to Consumers Subscale	1 White American	3.0204	.53149	154
	2 Latino/a American	2.8988	.61101	69
	3 African American	3.4793	.53261	48
	4 Asian American Pac Islander	3.0720	.53924	60
	Total	3.0710	.57613	331

5B.4.3.2 The Box and Bartlett Tests

The outcome of **Box's Test of Equality of Covariance Matrices** presented in the upper portion of Figure 5b.16 is statistically significant (Box's $M = 60.421$, $p < .001$), indicating that the dependent variable covariance matrices are not equal across the levels of the independent variable. The unequal variances may be a function of the unequal group sample sizes. In the present example, we elect to proceed with the analysis rather than transform the dependent measures, but we will use Pillai's trace to assess the multivariate effect. **Bartlett's Test of Sphericity** (in the lower portion of Figure 5b.16) is statistically significant (approximate chi-square = 247.403, $p < .001$), indicating sufficient correlation between the dependent measures to proceed with the analysis.

5B.4.3.3 The Multivariate Tests

The **Multivariate Tests** output table appears next in Figure 5b.17. Our primary interest is in the bottom half of this table. The section of the table labeled **Ethnicity** followed by four multivariate tests evaluates the multivariate null hypothesis of no independent variable differences in the population on the dependent (CBMCS) variate.

When **Box's M** test is statistically significant (as in the present case), heterogeneity of variance–covariance matrices is present, necessitating the use of the **Pillai's Trace** multivariate test because of its robustness in the presence of unequal dependent variate variance. We note a **Pillai's Trace** value of .463, which is subsequently translated into an F statistic of 14.858. This F statistic is evaluated at degrees of freedom of 12 and 978. At these degrees of freedom, the F value is statistically significant ($p < .001$). We can determine from **Pillai's Trace** that it would appear that **Ethnicity** accounts for nearly 46% of the total variance,

Figure 5b.16 Box's and Bartlett's Tests

Box's Test of Equality of Covariance Matrices[a]

Box's M	60.421
F	1.959
df1	30
df2	121566.660
Sig.	.001

Tests the null hypothesis that the observed covariance matrices of the dependent variables are equal across groups.

a. Design: Intercept + Ethnicity

Bartlett's Test of Sphericity[a]

Likelihood Ratio	.000
Approx. Chi-Square	247.403
df	9
Sig.	.000

Tests the null hypothesis that the residual covariance matrix is proportional to an identity matrix.

a. Design: Intercept + Ethnicity

but subtracting the **Wilks' lambda** value of .579 (the amount of unexplained variance) from 1.00 yields a value of .421 as a more conservative estimate. If we wished to express these results in the more conservative manner, we would say that we obtained a statistically significant effect of ethnicity, $F(12, 978) = 14.858$, $p < .001$, 1 − Wilks' lambda = .421; if we wished to express these results in a less conservative manner, we would say

---

Figure 5b.17 The Multivariate Tests

Multivariate Tests[c]

Effect		Value	F	Hypothesis df	Error df	Sig.
Intercept	Pillai's Trace	.987	6220.814[a]	4.000	324.000	.000
	Wilks' Lambda	.013	6220.814[a]	4.000	324.000	.000
	Hotelling's Trace	76.800	6220.814[a]	4.000	324.000	.000
	Roy's Largest Root	76.800	6220.814[a]	4.000	324.000	.000
Ethnicity	Pillai's Trace	.463	14.858	12.000	978.000	.000
	Wilks' Lambda	.579	16.381	12.000	857.515	.000
	Hotelling's Trace	.655	17.603	12.000	968.000	.000
	Roy's Largest Root	.518	42.227[b]	4.000	326.000	.000

a. Exact statistic

b. The statistic is an upper bound on F that yields a lower bound on the significance level.

c. Design: Intercept + Ethnicity

---

that we obtained a statistically significant effect of ethnicity, $F(12, 978) = 14.858$, $p < .001$, Pillai's trace = .463.

5B.4.3.4 The Levene Test

Because our multivariate test is statistically significant, we can proceed with a separate assessment of each dependent measure. Figure 5b.18 displays the results of the **Levene's Test of Equality of Error Variances**, which tests for homogeneity of variance violations for each dependent measure. In the present example, one of the four dependent variables (**CBMCSMK**) has a statistically significant **Levene's test**, indicating heterogeneity (unequal) variances among the groups on that dependent measure. This is not entirely surprising because the **Box's M** test also indicated heterogeneity (of the variance–covariance matrices) among the combined dependent variate. Thus, in evaluating the effect of the **CBMCSMK** subscale, we will exercise interpretive caution because of the unequal variability among the treatment groups and increase the stringency of the alpha level we use to evaluate statistical significance.

5B.4.3.5 Tests of the Univariate Effects

The **Tests of Between-Subjects Effects** shown in Figure 5b.19 evaluates each dependent variable separately. Of particular interest is the middle portion of the table labeled **Ethnicity** that depicts the separate univariate ANOVAs for each dependent variable. We

Figure 5b.18 The Levene Tests

Levene's Test of Equality of Error Variances[a]

	F	df1	df2	Sig.
CBMCSSD CBMSC Sociocultural Diversities Subscale	.201	3	327	.895
CBMCSACB CBMCS Awareness of Cultural Barriers Subscale	2.157	3	327	.093
CBMCSMK CBMCS Multicultural Knowledge Subscale	6.918	3	327	.000
CBMCSSC CBMCS Sensitivity to Consumers Subscale	1.637	3	327	.181

Tests the null hypothesis that the error variance of the dependent variable is equal across groups.

a. Design: Intercept + Ethnicity

apply a Bonferroni adjustment in considering the statistical significance of these univariate effects. With four dependent variables, we divide our alpha level of .05 by four, the number of dependent variables, to obtain an adjusted alpha level of .0125. We use that for the three dependent variables that did not violate the equal variances assumption. For the **CBMCSMK** subscale, we will use a criterion of .001 in evaluating this latter dependent variable.

Two of the four CBMCS subscale dependent measures (**CBMCSMK** and **CBMCSSC**) were statistically significant, with the output displaying a probability of .000 because of the limited number of printed decimal places; this translates for us as a probability less than .001 and meets both the Bonferroni-adjusted alpha level of .0125 for the **CBMCSSC** subscale (which met the homogeneity assumption) and the again-adjusted Bonferroni-adjusted alpha level of .001 for the **CBMCSMK** subscale (which violated the homogeneity assumption).

To determine the eta-square values, we divide the sum of squares for the measure by the sum of squares for its **Corrected Total**. Thus, for **CBMCSMK**, we divide 34.594 by 129.219 to obtain .26; for **CBMCSSC**, we divide 10.442 by 109.537 to obtain .10.

The other two CBMCS subscales (**CBMCSSD** and **CBMCSACB**) were not statistically significant. Apparently, differences among the four ethnic/racial groups on **CBMCSMK** and **CBMSCSC** contributed to the multivariate effect.

Figure 5b.19 Tests of the Univariate Effects

Tests of Between-Subjects Effects

Source	Dependent Variable	Type III Sum of Squares	df	Mean Square	F	Sig.
Corrected Model	CBMCSSD CBMSC Sociocultural Diversities Subscale	.438[a]	3	.146	.751	.523
	CBMCSACB CBMCS Awareness of Cultural Barriers Subscale	.159[b]	3	.053	.345	.793
	CBMCSMK CBMCS Multicultural Knowledge Subscale	34.594[c]	3	11.531	39.849	.000
	CBMCSSC CBMCS Sensitivity to Consumers Subscale	10.442[d]	3	3.481	11.486	.000
Intercept	CBMCSSD CBMSC Sociocultural Diversities Subscale	2092.202	1	2092.202	10767.385	.000
	CBMCSACB CBMCS Awareness of Cultural Barriers Subscale	2956.441	1	2956.441	19223.674	.000
	CBMCSMK CBMCS Multicultural Knowledge Subscale	1862.918	1	1862.918	6437.742	.000
	CBMCSSC CBMCS Sensitivity to Consumers Subscale	2658.986	1	2658.986	8774.337	.000
Ethnicity	CBMCSSD CBMSC Sociocultural Diversities Subscale	.438	3	.146	.751	.523
	CBMCSACB CBMCS Awareness of Cultural Barriers Subscale	.159	3	.053	.345	.793
	CBMCSMK CBMCS Multicultural Knowledge Subscale	34.594	3	11.531	39.849	.000
	CBMCSSC CBMCS Sensitivity to Consumers Subscale	10.442	3	3.481	11.486	.000
Error	CBMCSSD CBMSC Sociocultural Diversities Subscale	63.539	327	.194		
	CBMCSACB CBMCS Awareness of Cultural Barriers Subscale	50.290	327	.154		
	CBMCSMK CBMCS Multicultural Knowledge Subscale	94.625	327	.289		
	CBMCSSC CBMCS Sensitivity to Consumers Subscale	99.094	327	.303		
Total	CBMCSSD CBMSC Sociocultural Diversities Subscale	2607.330	331			
	CBMCSACB CBMCS Awareness of Cultural Barriers Subscale	3647.123	331			
	CBMCSMK CBMCS Multicultural Knowledge Subscale	2149.012	331			
	CBMCSSC CBMCS Sensitivity to Consumers Subscale	3231.144	331			
Corrected Total	CBMCSSD CBMSC Sociocultural Diversities Subscale	63.977	330			
	CBMCSACB CBMCS Awareness of Cultural Barriers Subscale	50.449	330			
	CBMCSMK CBMCS Multicultural Knowledge Subscale	129.219	330			
	CBMCSSC CBMCS Sensitivity to Consumers Subscale	109.537	330			

a. R Squared = .007 (Adjusted R Squared = −.002)
b. R Squared = .003 (Adjusted R Squared = −.006)
c. R Squared = .268 (Adjusted R Squared = .261)
d. R Squared = .095 (Adjusted R Squared = .087)

5B.4.3.6 Post Hoc Paired Comparisons

To determine specifically which groups differ significantly on the **CBMCSMK** and **CBMCSSC** dependent measures, pairwise comparisons were performed using the IBM SPSS default of alpha = .05. The results of the post hoc tests are presented in Figure 5b.20.

Figure 5b.20 A Portion of the Post Hoc Tests Showing the Multiple Comparisons for Two Dependent Variables That Were Statistically Significant in the Omnibus Analysis

Post Hoc Tests

New Practitioner Ethnicity

Multiple Comparisons

Dependent Variable		(I) New Practitioner Ethnicity	(J) New Practitioner Ethnicity	Mean Difference (I–J)	Std. Error	Sig.	95% Confidence Interval	
							Lower Bound	Upper Bound
CBMCSMK CBMCS Multicultural Knowledge Subscale	Tamhane	1 White American	2 Latino/a American	−.6318*	.07228	.000	−.8240	−.4395
			3 African American	−.6343*	.08473	.000	−.8616	−.4070
			4 Asian American/Pacific Islander	−.6760*	.07747	.000	−.8826	−.4693
		2 Latino/a American	1 White American	.6318*	.07228	.000	.4395	.8240
			3 African American	−.0025	.08605	1.000	−.2337	.2287
			4 Asian American/Pacific Islander	−.0442	.07892	.994	−.2553	.1669
		3 African American	1 White American	.6343*	.08473	.000	.4070	.8616
			2 Latino/a American	.0025	.08605	1.000	−.2287	.2337
			4 Asian American/Pacific Islander	−.0417	.09046	.998	−.2845	.2012
		4 Asian American/Pacific Islander	1 White American	.6760*	.07747	.000	.4693	.8826
			2 Latino/a American	.0442	.07892	.994	−.1669	.2553
			3 African American	.0417	.09046	.998	−.2012	.2845

Based on observed means.
The error term is Mean Square(Error) = .303.
*. The mean difference is significant at the

Homogeneous Subsets

CBMCSSC CBMCS Sensitivity to Consumers Subscale

	New Practitioner Ethnicity	N	Subset	
			1	2
Ryan–Einot–Gabriel–Welsch Range[a]	2 Latino/a American	69	2.8988	
	1 White American	154	3.0204	
	4 Asian American/Pacific Islander	60	3.0720	
	3 African American	48		3.4793
	Sig.		.198	1.000

Means for groups in homogeneous subsets are displayed.
Based on observed means.
The error term is Mean Square(Error) = .303.

Note. The Tamhane test is shown in the top panel for the multicultural knowledge subscale (where homogeneity of variance was violated), and the homogeneous subsets for the Ryan–Einot–Gabriel–Welsch Studentized Range tests are shown in the bottom panel for the sensitivity to consumers subscale.

The results of the two post hoc tests for all four dependent variables are shown in the full output. It is the responsibility of the researchers to apply these tests only to the dependent variables that achieved statistical significance based on their evaluation. We therefore focus on (and therefore show in Figure 5b.20) only the **Ethnicity** effect for the **CBMCSMK** and **CBMCSSC** dependent measures.

The top panel of Figure 5b.20 displays the **CBMCSMK** pairwise comparisons based on the Tamhane test because homogeneity of variance was violated. This table is structured as we described in Section 4B.1.5. For example, we can see that the **Mean Difference** between **White American** and **Latino/a American** practitioners was $-.6318$ and was statistically significant at the $p < .05$ level. Additionally, **White American** practitioners also achieved a statistically significant ($p < .05$) **Mean Difference** of $-.6343$ compared with **African American** practitioners. Finally, **White American** practitioners garnered a statistically significant ($p < .05$) **Mean Difference** of $-.6760$ compared with **Asian American Pacific Islanders**. Examining the comparisons in the remaining portion of the top panel indicates that none of the non-White groups differed significantly from each other.

By referring back to the earlier **Descriptive Statistics** table (Figure 5b.15), we can see more clearly what these pairwise comparison results are telling us. Specifically, **White American** practitioners had significantly lower **CBMCSMK** scores ($M = 2.12$, $SD = 0.62$) than did **Latino/a American** practitioners ($M = 2.76$, $SD = 0.43$). Similarly, **White American** practitioners also had lower **CBMCSMK** scores than did **African American** practitioners ($M = 2.76$, $SD = 0.47$) and **Asian American/Pacific Islander** practitioners ($M = 2.80$, $SD = 0.46$). It is also clear that the means of the non-White groups are extremely similar to each other. Thus, it appears that the **White American** practitioners view themselves as less knowledgeable in multicultural matters than the other three groups of practitioners.

The **CBMCSSC** pairwise comparisons are based on the REGWQ test because this dependent variable exhibited homogeneity of variance. The output is in the form of **Homogenous Subsets** and is shown in the lower panel of Figure 5b.20. This format displays the means for the groups sorted into "subsets." Groups whose mean is contained in the same subset do not differ significantly; means in different subsets are statistically different. As can be seen in Figure 5b.20, **Subset 1** contains the **Latino/a American**, **White American**, and **Asian American Pacific Islander** groups with means ranging between approximately 2.90 and 3.07; these means do not differ significantly. **Subset 2** contains the **African American** group with a mean of approximately 3.48, and, because it is in its own subset, we know that this group is significantly different from the other groups. Thus, it appears that the **African American** practitioners view themselves as more sensitive to consumers than the other three groups of practitioners.

5B.4.3.7 Reporting the Results of a k-Group MANOVA

A four-group one-way between-subjects multivariate analysis of variance was performed on four CBMCS subscale dependent variables: CBMCSSD, CBMCSACB, CBMCSMK, and CBMCSSC. The independent variable was practitioner race/ethnicity (White American, Latino/a American, African American, Asian American/Pacific Islander).

A total of 331 child mental health practitioners participated in this study. Practitioner race/ethnicity was distributed as follows: Latino/a American (20.8%), White American (46.5%), African American (14.5%), and Asian American/Pacific Islander (18.2%). A statistically significant Box's *M* test ($p < .001$) indicated unequal variance–covariance matrices of the dependent variables across levels of practitioner race/ethnicity and thus necessitated the use of Pillai's trace in assessing the multivariate effect.

Using Pillai's trace as the criterion, the dependent variate was significantly affected by practitioner race/ethnicity, Pillai's trace = .463, $F(12, 978) = 14.86$, $p < .001$, 1 − Wilks' lambda = .421. Univariate ANOVAs were conducted on each dependent measure separately to determine the locus of the statistically significant multivariate effect. Those dependent variables not violating the homogeneity of variance assumption were evaluated against a Bonferroni-adjusted alpha level of .0125 (.05 divided by 4). Neither the Sociocultural Diversity nor the Awareness of Cultural Barriers subscales were statistically significant, *F*s < 1. Practitioner race/ethnicity significantly affected only the CBMCS Sensitivity and Responsiveness to Consumers subscale scores $F(3, 327) = 11.49$, $p < .001$, $\eta^2 = .095$.

The CBMCS Multicultural Knowledge subscale violated the homogeneity assumption as assessed by the Levene test, $F(3, 327) = 6.92$, $p < .05$. To evaluate this univariate effect, a more stringent alpha level of .001 was used. Against this alpha level, the practitioner race/ethnicity effect was statistically significant, $F(3, 327) = 39.85$, $p < .001$, $\eta^2 = .268$.

The Ryan, Einot, Gabriel, and Welsch Studentized Range test, used for CBMCS Sensitivity and Responsiveness to Consumers subscale as the assumption of equal variances was not violated, indicated that African American practitioners viewed themselves as more sensitive to consumers [*M* = 3.48, *SD* = 0.53, 95% CI (3.32, 3.63)] than their White American [*M* = 3.02, *SD* = 0.53, 95% CI (2.94, 3.11)], Latino/a American [*M* = 2.90, *SD* = 0.61, 95% CI (2.75, 3.05)], and Asian American/ Pacific Islander [*M* = 3.07, *SD* = 0.54, 95% CI (2.93, 3.21)] counterparts. Tamhane post hoc tests, used because heterogeneity of variance was obtained, suggested that White American practitioners had lower CBMCS Multicultural Knowledge subscale scores [*M* = 2.12, *SD* = 0.62, 95% CI (2.03, 2.22)] than the African American practitioners [*M* = 2.76, *SD* = 0.47, 95% CI (2.62, 2.90)] and Asian American/Pacific Islander practitioners [*M* = 2.80, *SD* = 0.46, 95% CI (2.68, 2.92)].

5B.5 Two-Way Between-Subjects Factorial MANOVA

The design we use here is a 2 × 2 between-subjects MANOVA. The independent variables are dichotomized variables based on a median split: Ethnic Identity Exploration (**DIMEIMEIE**) and Dominant Society Immersion (**DIMASDSI**), which provide measures of provider ethnic identity and acculturation, respectively. It should be noted that these variables are simply used to present an example analysis. Because they are quantitative variables, dichotomizing the variables loses a good deal of the information they contain and is therefore not a recommended procedure; an alternative and technically better (preferred) procedure is to use them in a regression analysis (see Sections 8A.6 and 8B.4). The dependent variables are the four CBMCS subscales: **CBMCSSD**, **CBMCSACB**, **CBMCSMK**, and **CBMCSSC**. Again, to avoid redundancy, assume that pertinent issues relating to missing values, outliers, linearity, normality, and homogeneity of variance–covariance matrices were addressed.

5B.5.1 Two-Way MANOVA Setup

From the main menu, select **Analyze ➔ General Linear Model ➔ Multivariate**, which produces the **Multivariate** main dialog window shown in Figure 5b.21. Move the four dependent variables (**CBMCSSD**, **CBMCSACB**, **CBMCSMK**, and **CBMCSSC**)

Figure 5b.21   The Main Multivariate Dialog Window

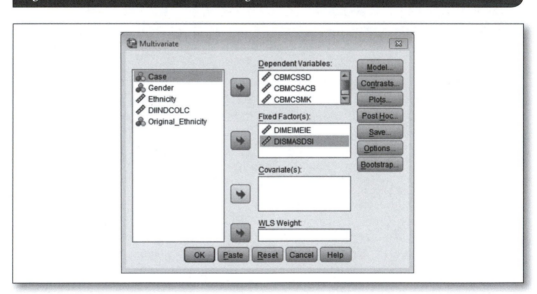

from the variables list panel to the **Dependent Variables** panel and move **DIMEIMEIE** and **DIMASDSI** to the **Fixed Factor(s)** panel. The **Options** window is configured in the same way as the prior analysis (see Section 5B.4.2) as shown in Figure 5b.22. Click **Continue** to return to the main dialog window, and click **OK** to perform the analysis.

Figure 5b.22   The Options Window of Multivariate

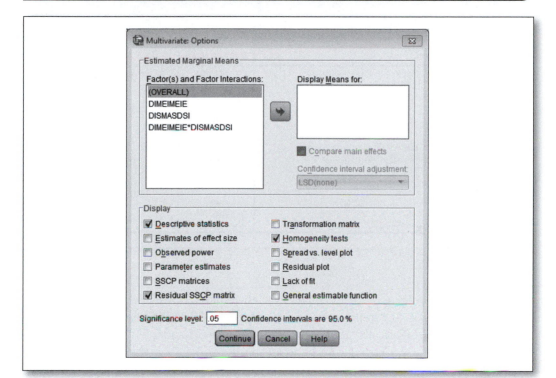

5B.5.2 Two-Way MANOVA Output

5B.5.2.1 Descriptive Output

Figure 5b.23 displays the **Between-Subjects Factors** table output, which provides counts or sample size for each independent variable broken by treatment or level. We note large and unequal sample sizes among the various treatment conditions.

The **Descriptive Statistics** table shown next in Figure 5b.24 presents each dependent variable's observed mean, standard deviation, and sample size for each treatment combination.

5B.5.2.2 The Box and Bartlett Tests

Box's Test of Equality of Covariance Matrices, shown in Figure 5b.25, is statistically significant (Box's $M = 51.126$, $p < .014$), which indicates that the dependent variable covariance matrices are not equal across the levels of the independent variables.

Figure 5b.23 Sample Size Information

Between–Subjects Factors

		Value Label	N
DIMEIMEIE Dichotomous MEIM Ethnic Identity Exploration	1	Low Ethnic Identity Exploration	264
	2	High Ethnic Identity Exploration	83
DISMASDSI Dichotomous SMAS Dominant Society Immersion	1	Low Dominant Society Immersion	181
	2	High Dominant Society Immersion	166

This observed heterogeneity or unequal covariance matrices will necessitate the use of Pillai's trace to assess our multivariate effects. **Bartlett's Test of Sphericity**, also shown in Figure 5b.25, is statistically significant (approximate chi-square = 232.684, $p < .001$). This indicates sufficient correlation between the dependent variables to proceed with the analysis.

5B.5.2.3 The Multivariate Tests

The **Multivariate Tests** output table appears in Figure 5b.26. We will focus on the bottom three fourths of the table, which includes the **DIMEIMEIE**, **DISMASDSI**, and **DIMEIMEIE*DISMASDSI**. These correspond to the two multivariate main effects and the one interaction effect.

Because the Box's M test was statistically significant, indicating inequality of the variance–covariance matrices of the dependent variables across levels of our independent variables, we will use Pillai's trace to evaluate our multivariate main effects and interaction. Typically, if statistical significance is or is not found with one of the four multivariate tests, the other three tests will also reflect a similar result.

We begin by examining the multivariate interaction effect (**DIMEIMEIE*DISMASDSI**) that yielded a Pillai's trace value of .007; the associated F value of .560, evaluated with degrees of freedom of 4 and 340, is not statistically significant ($p < .692$), indicating that the multivariate interaction effect of Ethnic Identity Exploration × Dominant Society Immersion does not account for a significant proportion of the variance.

Figure 5b.24 Descriptive Statistics

Descriptive Statistics

	DIMEIMEIE Dichotomous MEIM Ethnic Identity ...	DISMASDSI Dichotomous SMAS Dominant Societ...	Mean	Std. Deviation	N
CBMCSSD CBMSC Sociocultural Diversities Subscale	1 Low Ethnic Identity Exploration	1 Low Dominant Society Immersion	2.6600	.41600	139
		2 High Dominant Society Immersion	2.7882	.43160	125
		Total	2.7207	.42749	264
	2 High Ethnic Identity Exploration	1 Low Dominant Society Immersion	2.8787	.47283	42
		2 High Dominant Society Immersion	3.0418	.40230	41
		Total	2.9593	.44437	83
	Total	1 Low Dominant Society Immersion	2.7107	.43838	181
		2 High Dominant Society Immersion	2.8508	.43733	166
		Total	2.7778	.44283	347
CBMCSACB CBMCS Awareness of Cultural Barriers Subscale	1 Low Ethnic Identity Exploration	1 Low Dominant Society Immersion	3.1971	.35083	139
		2 High Dominant Society Immersion	3.2835	.41918	125
		Total	3.2380	.38639	264
	2 High Ethnic Identity Exploration	1 Low Dominant Society Immersion	3.5119	.30442	42
		2 High Dominant Society Immersion	3.4740	.38762	41
		Total	3.4932	.34640	83
	Total	1 Low Dominant Society Immersion	3.2702	.36500	181
		2 High Dominant Society Immersion	3.3305	.41865	166
		Total	3.2990	.39218	347
CBMCSMK CBMCS Multicultural Knowledge Subscale	1 Low Ethnic Identity Exploration	1 Low Dominant Society Immersion	2.3838	.58077	139
		2 High Dominant Society Immersion	2.3672	.62421	125
		Total	2.3759	.60063	264
	2 High Ethnic Identity Exploration	1 Low Dominant Society Immersion	2.8762	.54092	42
		2 High Dominant Society Immersion	2.7951	.63638	41
		Total	2.8361	.58780	83
	Total	1 Low Dominant Society Immersion	2.4981	.60719	181
		2 High Dominant Society Immersion	2.4729	.65212	166
		Total	2.4860	.62829	347
CBMCSSC CBMCS Sensitivity to Consumers Subscale	1 Low Ethnic Identity Exploration	1 Low Dominant Society Immersion	2.9784	.58331	139
		2 High Dominant Society Immersion	3.0494	.54516	125
		Total	3.0120	.56562	264
	2 High Ethnic Identity Exploration	1 Low Dominant Society Immersion	3.2617	.54902	42
		2 High Dominant Society Immersion	3.2439	.59668	41
		Total	3.2529	.56961	83
	Total	1 Low Dominant Society Immersion	3.0441	.58644	181
		2 High Dominant Society Immersion	3.0974	.56279	166
		Total	3.0696	.57504	347

Figure 5b.25 Box's and Bartlett's Tests

Box's Test of Equality of Covariance Matrices[a]

Box's M	51.126
F	1.653
df1	30
df2	69943.775
Sig.	.014

Tests the null hypothesis that the observed covariance matrices of the dependent variables are equal across groups.

a. Design: Intercept + DIMEIMEIE + DISMASDSI + DIMEIMEIE * DISMASDSI

Bartlett's Test of Sphericity[a]

Likelihood Ratio	.000
Approx. Chi–Square	232.684
df	9
Sig.	.000

Tests the null hypothesis that the residual covariance matrix is proportional to an identity matrix.

a. Design: Intercept + DIMEIMEIE + DISMASDSI + DIMEIMEIE * DISMASDSI

Next, we examine the multivariate main effect of Ethnic Identity Exploration (**DIMEIMEIE**). The Pillai's trace value of .142 is subsequently translated into an F value of 14.063 and evaluated at hypothesis (between groups) and error (within groups) degrees of freedom of 4 and 340. This F value is statistically significant ($p < .001$). This indicates that the differences between the two practitioner exploration groups on the dependent variate are significant and account for approximately 14% of the total multivariate variance.

Last, we look at the multivariate main effect of practitioner Dominant Society Immersion (**DISMASDSI**). The Pillai's trace value of .028 is translated into an F value of 2.431 and evaluated at 4 and 340 (between- and within-groups degrees of freedom, respectively). This F is also statistically significant ($p < .047$) and indicates immersion differences on the dependent variate. This multivariate main effect is accounting for about 3% of the variance.

5B.5.2.4 The Levene Test

Because both multivariate main effects were found to be statistically significant, we can proceed with a separate assessment of each dependent variable for each main effect. This process is begun with an inspection of the **Levene's Test of Equality of Error Variances** output in Figure 5b.27. For three dependent measures, the test is not statistically significant ($p > .05$), indicating homogeneity or equality of variances among the groups on each dependent measure. However, one dependent measure (**CBMCSACB**) was statistically significant, indicating that the error variance of this dependent variable is unequal across groups. Extra caution will need to be exercised when interpreting this dependent measure, and we will evaluate effects associated with this subscale at a more stringent alpha level of .001. We can now proceed with univariate ANOVAs for both main effects on each dependent variable.

Figure 5b.26 The Multivariate Tests

Multivariate Tests[b]

Effect		Value	F	Hypothesis df	Error df	Sig.
Intercept	Pillai's Trace	.988	6725.669[a]	4.000	340.000	.000
	Wilks' Lambda	.012	6725.669[a]	4.000	340.000	.000
	Hotelling's Trace	79.126	6725.669[a]	4.000	340.000	.000
	Roy's Largest Root	79.126	6725.669[a]	4.000	340.000	.000
DIMEIMEIE	Pillai's Trace	.142	14.063[a]	4.000	340.000	.000
	Wilks' Lambda	.858	14.063[a]	4.000	340.000	.000
	Hotelling's Trace	.165	14.063[a]	4.000	340.000	.000
	Roy's Largest Root	.165	14.063[a]	4.000	340.000	.000
DISMASDSI	Pillai's Trace	.028	2.431[a]	4.000	340.000	.047
	Wilks' Lambda	.972	2.431[a]	4.000	340.000	.047
	Hotelling's Trace	.029	2.431[a]	4.000	340.000	.047
	Roy's Largest Root	.029	2.431[a]	4.000	340.000	.047
DIMEIMEIE * DISMASDSI	Pillai's Trace	.007	.560[a]	4.000	340.000	.692
	Wilks' Lambda	.993	.560[a]	4.000	340.000	.692
	Hotelling's Trace	.007	.560[a]	4.000	340.000	.692
	Roy's Largest Root	.007	.560[a]	4.000	340.000	.692

a. Exact statistic

b. Design: Intercept + DIMEIMEIE + DISMASDSI + DIMEIMEIE * DISMASDSI

Figure 5b.27 The Levene Tests

Levene's Test of Equality of Error Variances[a]

	F	df1	df2	Sig.
CBMCSSD CBMSC Sociocultural Diversities Subscale	.346	3	343	.792
CBMCSACB CBMCS Awareness of Cultural Barriers Subscale	4.382	3	343	.005
CBMCSMK CBMCS Multicultural Knowledge Subscale	1.109	3	343	.345
CBMCSSC CBMCS Sensitivity to Consumers Subscale	.745	3	343	.526

Tests the null hypothesis that the error variance of the dependent variable is equal across groups.

a. Design: Intercept + DIMEIMEIE + DISMASDSI + DIMEIMEIE * DISMASDSI

5B.5.2.5 Tests of the Univariate Effects

These univariate F tests can be found in the **Tests of Between-Subjects Effects** in Figure 5b.28. Of particular interest is the upper-middle portion of the table labeled **DIMEIMEIE**

Figure 5b.28 Tests of the Univariate Effects

Tests of Between-Subjects Effects

Source	Dependent Variable	Type III Sum of Squares	df	Mean Square	F	Sig.
Corrected Model	CBMCSSD CBMSC Sociocultural Diversities Subscale	5.228[a]	3	1.743	9.545	.000
	CBMCSACB CBMCS Awareness of Cultural Barriers Subscale	4.632[b]	3	1.544	10.901	.000
	CBMCSMK CBMCS Multicultural Knowledge Subscale	13.528[c]	3	4.509	12.569	.000
	CBMCSSC CBMCS Sensitivity to Consumers Subscale	4.004[d]	3	1.335	4.146	.007
Intercept	CBMCSSD CBMSC Sociocultural Diversities Subscale	2038.785	1	2038.785	11167.267	.000
	CBMCSACB CBMCS Awareness of Cultural Barriers Subscale	2860.617	1	2860.617	20196.113	.000
	CBMCSMK CBMCS Multicultural Knowledge Subscale	1713.488	1	1713.488	4776.057	.000
	CBMCSSC CBMCS Sensitivity to Consumers Subscale	2477.934	1	2477.934	7698.178	.000
DIMEIMEIE	CBMCSSD CBMSC Sociocultural Diversities Subscale	3.519	1	3.519	19.275	.000
	CBMCSACB CBMCS Awareness of Cultural Barriers Subscale	4.028	1	4.028	28.435	.000
	CBMCSMK CBMCS Multicultural Knowledge Subscale	13.360	1	13.360	37.239	.000
	CBMCSSC CBMCS Sensitivity to Consumers Subscale	3.603	1	3.603	11.192	.001
DISMASDSI	CBMCSSD CBMSC Sociocultural Diversities Subscale	1.339	1	1.339	7.333	.007
	CBMCSACB CBMCS Awareness of Cultural Barriers Subscale	.037	1	.037	.261	.610
	CBMCSMK CBMCS Multicultural Knowledge Subscale	.151	1	.151	.420	.518
	CBMCSSC CBMCS Sensitivity to Consumers Subscale	.045	1	.045	.138	.710
DIMEIMEIE * DISMASDSI	CBMCSSD CBMSC Sociocultural Diversities Subscale	.019	1	.019	.105	.746
	CBMCSACB CBMCS Awareness of Cultural Barriers Subscale	.244	1	.244	1.720	.191
	CBMCSMK CBMCS Multicultural Knowledge Subscale	.066	1	.066	.183	.669
	CBMCSSC CBMCS Sensitivity to Consumers Subscale	.124	1	.124	.387	.535
Error	CBMCSSD CBMSC Sociocultural Diversities Subscale	62.621	343	.183		
	CBMCSACB CBMCS Awareness of Cultural Barriers Subscale	48.583	343	.142		
	CBMCSMK CBMCS Multicultural Knowledge Subscale	123.057	343	.359		
	CBMCSSC CBMCS Sensitivity to Consumers Subscale	110.407	343	.322		
Total	CBMCSSD CBMSC Sociocultural Diversities Subscale	2745.274	347			
	CBMCSACB CBMCS Awareness of Cultural Barriers Subscale	3829.846	347			
	CBMCSMK CBMCS Multicultural Knowledge Subscale	2281.153	347			
	CBMCSSC CBMCS Sensitivity to Consumers Subscale	3384.053	347			
Corrected Total	CBMCSSD CBMSC Sociocultural Diversities Subscale	67.849	346			
	CBMCSACB CBMCS Awareness of Cultural Barriers Subscale	53.215	346			
	CBMCSMK CBMCS Multicultural Knowledge Subscale	136.585	346			
	CBMCSSC CBMCS Sensitivity to Consumers Subscale	114.411	346			

a. R Squared = .077 (Adjusted R Squared = .069)

b. R Squared = .087 (Adjusted R Squared = .079)

c. R Squared = .099 (Adjusted R Squared = .091)

d. R Squared = .035 (Adjusted R Squared = .027)

and **DISMASDSI** that present the separate univariate ANOVAs for each dependent variable on each main effect. With four dependent variables, we use a Bonferroni-corrected alpha level of .0125 (.05/4 = .0125); however, because the **CBMCSACD** subscale violated the homogeneity of variance assumption, we will increase the stringency of the alpha level for that measure to .001.

For the ethnic identity exploration (**DIMEIMEIE**) main effect, we find that all four dependent variable (CBMCS subscales) are statistically significant. Specifically, **CBMCSSD** $F(1, 343) = 19.275$, $p < .0125$, $\eta^2 = .052$ (3.519 divided by 67.849); **CBMCSACD** $F(1, 343) = 28.435$, $p < .001$, $\eta^2 = .076$ (4.028 divided by 53.215); **CBMCSMK** $F(1, 343) = 37.239$, $p < .0125$, $\eta^2 = .098$ (13.360 divided by 136.585); and **CBMCSSC** $F(1, 343) = 11.192$, $p < .0125$, $\eta^2 = .031$ (3.603 divided by 114.411). Hence, differences between the two ethnic identity groups (high and low) on each of the four CBMCS subscales produced the multivariate main effect of ethnic identity exploration.

An inspection of the means and standard deviations (see Figure 5b.24) reveals a consistent pattern among the practitioners for the ethnic identity exploration independent variable across the four CBMCS subscales: High ethnic identity exploration was associated with greater CBMCS subscale scores than low ethnic identity exploration. Specifically, on Sociocultural Diversities, practitioners with high ethnic identity scored higher ($M = 2.959$, $SD = 0.444$) than did practitioners with low ethnic identity ($M = 2.721$, $SD = 0.427$); on Awareness of Cultural Barriers, practitioners with high ethnic identity scored higher ($M = 3.493$, $SD = 0.346$) than did practitioners with low ethnic identity ($M = 3.238$, $SD = 0.386$); on Multicultural Knowledge, practitioners with high ethnic identity scored higher ($M = 2.836$, $SD = 0.588$) than did practitioners with low ethnic identity ($M = 2.376$, $SD = 0.601$); and last, on Sensitivity to Consumers, practitioners with high ethnic identity ($M = 3.253$, $SD = 0.570$) scored higher than did practitioners with low ethnic identity ($M = 3.012$, $SD = 0.566$). These mean differences produced the statistically significant multivariate effect of ethnic identity exploration.

For the statistically significant multivariate effect of dominant society immersion (**DISMASDSI**), only one of the four CBMCS subscale dependent measures (**CBMCSSD**) reached statistical significance, $F(1, 343) = 7.333$, $p < .0125$, $\eta^2 = .020$ (1.339 divided by 67.849). The other three CBMCS dependent measures were not statistically significant, $Fs < 1$.

We do not have the means and standard deviations of these two groups directly in the table and could either compute weighted averages by using a calculator or quickly perform the analysis again by switching the order of the two independent variables. We opt for the latter. The main dialog window is shown in Figure 5b.29, this time with **DISMASDSI** moved over first, performing the analysis again and presenting only the top portion of the **Descriptive Statistics** table as can be seen in Figure 5b.30

An inspection of relevant means in Figure 5b.30 indicates that on Sociocultural Diversities, practitioners with high dominant society immersion scored higher ($M = 2.851$, $SD = 0.437$) than did practitioners with low dominant society immersion ($M = 2.711$, $SD = 0.438$). This mean difference produced the statistically significant multivariate main effect of dominant

Figure 5b.29   The Main Dialog Window With a Different Order of the Independent Variables

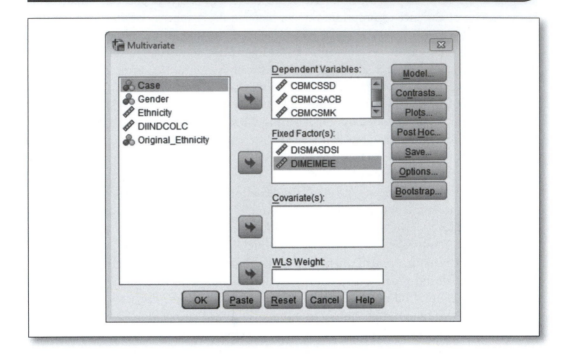

society immersion. We should note that, had one or both of the present independent variables contained three or more groups (levels), we would have conducted some form of multiple comparison tests to determine the locus of the effect. With two-group independent variables (as in the present example), we can simply inspect the respective means to determine the locus of the multivariate main effect.

5B.5.3 Reporting the Results of a Two-Way MANOVA

A two-way between-subjects multivariate analysis of variance was performed on four dependent variables: CBMCS Sociocultural Diversities, Awareness of Cultural Barriers, Multicultural Knowledge, and Sensitivity and Responsiveness to Consumers. The independent variables were child mental health practitioner, Ethnic Identity Exploration (high, low), and Dominant Society Immersion (high, low).

A statistically significant Box's *M* test ($p = .014$) indicated inequality of variance–covariance matrices of the dependent variables across levels of the independent variables. Hence, Pillai's trace was used to evaluate all multivariate effects.

Using Pillai's trace as the criterion, the multivariate interaction effect of Ethnic Identity Exploration × Dominant Society Immersion was not statistically significant ($F < 1$), indicating that the unique joint effect of these two variables did not account for a significant portion of the variance. Both, multivariate main effects of ethnic identity exploration and dominant society immersion, were statistically significant, Pillai's trace = .142, $F(4, 340) = 14.06$, $p < .001$ and Pillai's trace = .028, $F(4, 340) = 2.43$, $p = .047$, respectively.

Univariate ANOVAs were conducted on each dependent measure separately to determine the locus of the statistically significant multivariate main effects of ethnic identity exploration and dominant society immersion. With four dependent variables in the analysis, these effects are evaluated against a Bonferroni-adjusted alpha level of .0125 (.05/4). However, based on the results of the Levene test, the subscale of Awareness of Cultural Barriers violated homogeneity of variance, $F(3, 343) = 4.38$, $p = .005$; thus, statistical significance is evaluated for that measure against a more stringent alpha level of .001.

Practitioner ethnic identity exploration significantly affected all four CBMCS dependent measures: Sociocultural Diversities, $F(1, 343) = 19.28$, $p < .001$, $\eta^2 = .05$; Awareness of Cultural Barriers, $F(1, 343) = 28.44$, $p < .001$, $\eta^2 = .08$; Multicultural Knowledge, $F(1, 343) = 37.24$, $p < .001$, $\eta^2 = .10$; Sensitivity and Responsiveness to Consumers, $F(1, 343) = 11.19$, $p = .001$, $\eta^2 = .03$. An examination of the four CBMCS subscale means (see Table 5b.1) indicates a consistent pattern of higher CBMCS subscale scores for practitioners with high Ethnic Identity Exploration compared with their low Ethnic Identity Exploration counterparts.

The locus of the statistically significant multivariate main effect of Dominant Society Immersion was a function of one CBMCS subscale: Sociocultural Diversities, $F(1, 343) = 7.333$, $p = .007$, $\eta^2 = .020$. Examination of the relevant means in Table 5b.1 indicates that practitioners with high Ethnic Identity Exploration scored significantly higher than their low Ethnic Identity Exploration counterparts. Caution should be exercised in interpreting these results because of the small amount of variance accounted for with the present independent variables.

Figure 5b.30 A Portion of the Descriptive Statistics Output

Descriptive Statistics

	DISMASDSI Dichotomous SMAS Dominant Societ...	DIMEIMEIE Dichotomous MEIM Ethnic Identity ...	Mean	Std. Deviation	N
CBMCSSD CBMSC Sociocultural Diversities Subscale	1 Low Dominant Society Immersion	1 Low Ethnic Identity Exploration	2.6600	.41600	139
		2 High Ethnic Identity Exploration	2.8787	.47283	42
		Total	2.7107	.43838	181
	2 High Dominant Society Immersion	1 Low Ethnic Identity Exploration	2.7882	.43160	125
		2 High Ethnic Identity Exploration	3.0418	.40230	41
		Total	2.8508	.43733	166
	Total	1 Low Ethnic Identity Exploration	2.7207	.42749	264
		2 High Ethnic Identity Exploration	2.9593	.44437	83
		Total	2.7778	.44283	347
CBMCSACB CBMCS Awareness of Cultural Barriers Subscale	1 Low Dominant Society Immersion	1 Low Ethnic Identity Exploration	3.1971	.35083	139
		2 High Ethnic Identity Exploration	3.5119	.30442	42
		Total	3.2702	.36500	181
	2 High Dominant Society Immersion	1 Low Ethnic Identity Exploration	3.2835	.41918	125
		2 High Ethnic Identity Exploration	3.4740	.38762	41
		Total	3.3305	.41865	166
	Total	1 Low Ethnic Identity Exploration	3.2380	.38639	264
		2 High Ethnic Identity Exploration	3.4932	.34640	83
		Total	3.2990	.39218	347
CBMCSMK CBMCS Multicultural Knowledge Subscale	1 Low Dominant Society Immersion	1 Low Ethnic Identity Exploration	2.3838	.58077	139
		2 High Ethnic Identity Exploration	2.8762	.54092	42
		Total	2.4981	.60719	181
	2 High Dominant Society Immersion	1 Low Ethnic Identity Exploration	2.3672	.62421	125
		2 High Ethnic Identity Exploration	2.7951	.63638	41
		Total	2.4729	.65212	166

Table 5b.1 Means and Standard Deviations of Low and High Groups on the Four Dependent Variables for Ethnic Identity Exploration and Dominant Society Immersion

Ethnic Identity Exploration

	Sociocultural Diversity		Barrier Awareness		Multicultural Knowledge		Sensitivity	
	Low	High	Low	High	Low	High	Low	High
M	2.72	2.96	3.24	3.49	2.39	2.84	3.01	3.25
SD	0.43	0.44	0.39	0.35	0.60	0.59	0.57	0.57

Dominant Society Immersion

	Sociocultural Diversity		Barrier Awareness		Multicultural Knowledge		Sensitivity	
	Low	High	Low	High	Low	High	Low	High
M	2.71	2.85	3.27	3.33	2.50	2.47	3.04	3.10
SD	0.44	0.44	0.37	0.42	0.61	0.65	0.59	0.56

PART III

PREDICTING THE VALUE OF A SINGLE VARIABLE

Bivariate Correlation and Simple Linear Regression

6A.1 The Concept of Relationship

Determining whether the groups in an analysis differed on one or more dependent variables, a topic discussed in Chapters 4A through 5B, addressed a specific aspect of a more general question. This more general question, perhaps the most basic question that research is designed to answer, is whether two variables are related to each other. Chapters 4A through 5B approached this question by considering only the relationship between an independent variable (or a combination of independent variables) and one or more dependent variables. Although the computational strategy was that of ANOVA/MANOVA, we indexed the strength of the relationship by the squared eta correlation.

As a general rule, a correlation coefficient is an index of the degree to which two or more variables are associated with or related to each other, and a squared correlation coefficient is an index of the strength of that relationship (see Section 4A.4.2). The procedure used to determine if two variables are related falls into the domain of bivariate correlation. It is *bivariate* because we are addressing the relationship between two ("bi") variables. Although our focus in this chapter will be on bivariate correlation, we will see in Chapters 7A and 7B that it is possible to deal with relationships involving more than two variables.

Probably the most widely used bivariate correlation statistic is the Pearson product–moment correlation coefficient, commonly called the Pearson correlation. It is abbreviated as *r*. The Pearson *r* indexes the extent to which a linear relationship exists between two quantitatively measured variables. A good way to think about a relationship or an association between two variables is in terms of *covariation*. In its most basic form, covariation deals with the patterns exhibited by the two variables being evaluated. For this evaluation to be meaningful, the data must be arranged pairwise—that is, the data must be arranged so that the two pieces of information (one for each variable) derived from the same person or case are linked to each other. This is shown schematically below. We then wind up with two lists or distributions of scores that are paired with each other.

Person	Variable X	Variable Y
A	A's score on X	A's score on Y
B	B's score on X	B's score on Y
C	C's score on X	C's score on Y

With the data in the form shown above, the amount of covariation that exists between the two variables summarizes how the differences in one variable correspond with the differences in the other. That we have differences is a crucial point. It is difference that creates pattern—it is difference that provides information. Just as a canvas of a single, uniform color would not ordinarily be considered a work of art, a list of identical numbers could have no pattern or no variation, and with no variation, they could not covary with some other set of numbers. With no covariation, there can be no correlation.

6A.2 Different Types of Relationships

Just as it is possible for two people to have different types of relationships with each other (e.g., positive or negative), the same is also possible for two variables. We can demonstrate with the use of a series of small data sets how to generally read these covariation patterns that signify different types of relationships between the variables. Bear in mind at the outset that what we are looking for is a pattern based on the linked distributions.

6A.2.1 Perfect Positive Relationships

Consider the data in Table 6a.1. We have made the pattern more apparent in the table by ordering the list from the lowest to the highest based on the X score. These data are plotted in the accompanying Figure 6a.1. In a correlation analysis, each participant contributes two scores: an X score and a Y score. Because a standard graph also has X and

Table 6a.1 Covariation Pattern Example 1: Perfect Positive Correlation

Person	Variable X	Variable Y
A	10	20
B	25	35
C	30	40
D	50	60
E	60	70

Figure 6a.1 A Perfect Positive Correlation

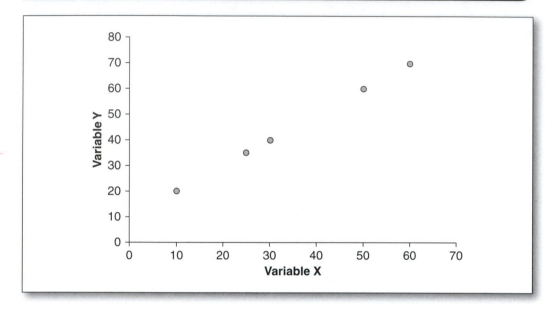

Y axes, participants can be depicted by data points. Such a plot is known as a *scatterplot*. In Figure 6a.1, individuals' scores on the two variables are shown by a dot indicating where they coincide on the axes. For example, the data point in Figure 6a.1 representing Person A is at the coordinate, where $X = 10$ and $Y = 20$.

The covariation pattern shown in Table 6a.1 and Figure 6a.1 is as follows: Every *Y* score is 10 points greater than its corresponding *X* score. Given this lockstep correspondence, the relationship is as strong as it can be. We can see this in Figure 6a.1 in that each data point is precisely in line with all the others. If we fit a straight line through this lockstep array of data points, that line would intersect all the data points.

When we calculate the Pearson *r* for this set of data points, we would find it to be +1.00. The positive sign simply means that higher values on *X* are associated with higher values on *Y*. A positive correlation thus indicates what is known as a *direct* relationship.

The presence of such a clear covariation pattern makes very accurate prediction possible. Given that these two variables are perfectly correlated, we could precisely predict someone's *Y* score if we knew how that person had scored on *X*. For example, someone with an *X* score of 15 should have a *Y* score of 25. Prediction is thus founded on correlation; statistically, it is handled through a procedure called *regression*. Perfect prediction (where there is no margin of error) as illustrated in Figure 6a.1 is obtained when the correlation between the two variables is +1.00.

6A.2.2 Perfect Negative Relationships

To reinforce the idea of a perfect relationship, consider the data in Table 6a.2, which have been plotted in Figure 6a.2. Again in this table, we have ordered the data on the *X* variable to make the pattern easier to observe, although the pattern becomes quite clear when one examines the figure. As can be seen, higher scores on *X* are associated with lower scores on *Y*. This signifies an *inverse* relationship and results in a negative correlation.

Table 6a.2 Covariation Pattern Example 2: Perfect Negative Correlation

Person	Variable X	Variable Y
F	22	68
G	24	67
H	26	66
I	28	65
J	30	64

The covariation shown in Table 6a.2 and depicted in Figure 6a.2 is also in lockstep: Every gain of 2 points in *X* is associated with a decrement of 1 point in *Y*. In the figure, the data points all fall on a straight line. Thus, we have a perfect relationship. If we calculated the Pearson *r*, it would turn out to be −1.00. With this perfect correlation, we could again perfectly predict the value of *Y* from a knowledge of how the person scored on *X*.

Figure 6a.2 A Perfect Negative Correlation

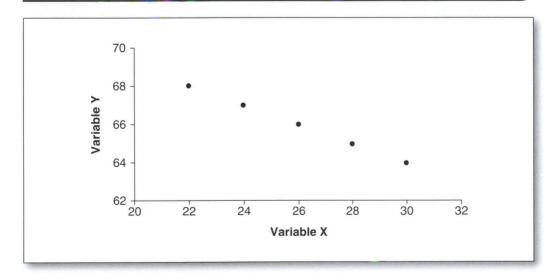

6A.2.3 Nonperfect Positive Relationships

Table 6a.3 shows a positive correlation (a direct relationship) between the two variables, although the relationship is not absolutely perfect. This is perhaps more clearly seen in the plot of these data points as shown in Figure 6a.3. As we can see (a) higher scores on X are generally, but not absolutely, associated with higher scores on Y, and (b) even when higher scores on one variable are associated with higher scores on the other variable, there is still some variability in the amount of such differences. Thus, prediction cannot be perfect; that is, our prediction of a Y value given a particular value of X is going to be accurate to a certain extent, but there will still be some margin of error associated with that prediction.

Table 6a.3 Covariation Pattern Example 3: Positive Correlation

Person	Variable X	Variable Y
K	100	55
L	110	47
M	115	67
N	125	71
O	140	70

It is possible to draw a straight line that "best fits" the array of points, and this has been approximated in Figure 6a.3. Because the data points are not in lockstep—that is, because the covariation is not perfect—they do not fall exactly on this line of best fit. But even without perfection, it is possible to see that there is still quite a bit of covariation present. For these data, the r value is .731. In predicting Y from a knowledge of X,

Figure 6a.3 A Positive Correlation

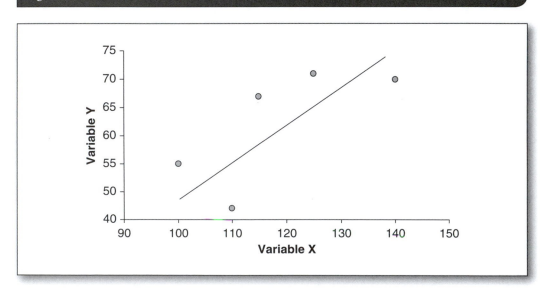

we would do much better than chance, but our prediction could not be perfect because the relationship between the two variables is not perfect.

6A.2.4 Absence of Relationship With Variance on Both Variables

Table 6a.4 and the accompanying Figure 6a.4 illustrate the situation where there is no relationship at all between the two variables. Lower scores on *X* are not systematically associated with either lower or higher scores on *Y*. That is, *X* scores of 15 and 16 (i.e., lower *X* scores) are linked to *Y* scores of 87 and 48 (i.e., they are linked to both lower and higher *Y* scores). Likewise, higher scores on *X* are not systematically associated with either lower or higher scores on *Y*. That is, *X* scores of 33 and 34 are linked to *Y* scores of 52 and 90.

Table 6a.4 Covariation Pattern Example 4: Zero Correlation With Variance on both Variables

Person	Variable X	Variable Y
P	15	87
Q	16	48
R	33	52
S	34	90
T	40	64

The lack of any systematic covariation between the two variables can also be seen in Figure 6a.4. The data points appear to be found all over the set of axes, and the line of best fit actually turns out to lie in a position that is parallel to the *X* axis. The slope of this line is

Figure 6a.4 A Zero Correlation With Variance on Both Variables

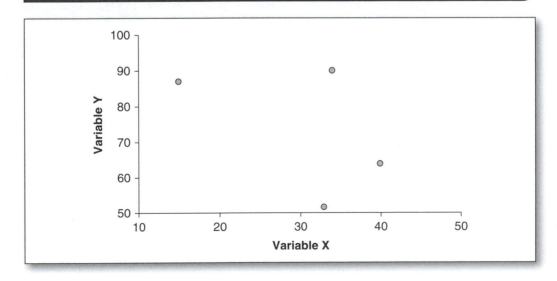

virtually zero (we will discuss slope in Section 6A.6.5), a mathematical indication that the Pearson r would yield a value very close to zero (it's actually −.033).

Notice that with a correlation of zero, there is no predictability. Given such a situation, we could predict the Y value corresponding to a given X value at a rate no better than chance. Another way to think about this lack of predictability is to realize that knowing a person's X score does not improve our ability to predict how he or she would score on Y. Here, our best prediction of Y based on knowing that someone scored a particular X value is the mean of the Y variable itself (which is not terribly helpful).

6A.2.5 Absence of Relationship With No Variance on One Variable

Table 6a.5 Covariation Pattern Example 5: Zero Correlation With No Variance on One Variables

Person	Variable X	Variable Y
U	50	75
V	50	80
W	50	85
X	50	90
Y	50	95

We stated earlier that there needed to be variation for there to be the possibility of a pattern. Table 6a.5 depicts a situation in which there is no variation in the X variable. These data are plotted in Figure 6a.5, which shows that the data points are vertically stacked over the X value of 50. Every value of Y is associated with an X value of 50. Without variation on both variables, there can be no possibility of covariation, so the correlation (the covariation) in Figure 6a.5 is zero.

Figure 6a.5 A Zero Correlation With No Variance on One Variable

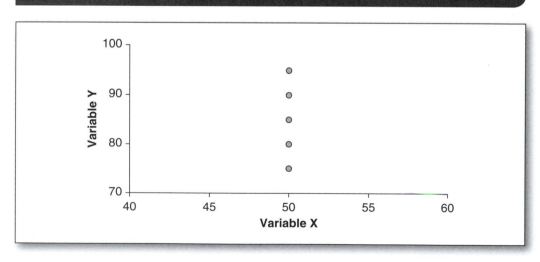

6A.2.6 Covariation Is Not the Same Thing as Mean Difference

Before leaving the topic of the different types of relationships that can exist between two variables, it is important to briefly reinforce an important point that was probably made in the first statistics course that readers have taken. The point is this: To say that two variables are significantly positively or negatively correlated does not provide information concerning whether or not the means of the variables are significantly different, that is, *covariation and mean difference are separate statistical matters.* We illustrate this idea using the data presented in Table 6a.6.

Table 6a.6   Scores of Five Persons on Variables *X*, *Y*, *Z1*, and *Z2*

Person	Variable X	Variable Y	Variable Z1	Variable Z2
K	100	55	10,000	140
L	110	47	11,000	125
M	115	67	11,500	115
N	125	71	12,500	110
O	140	70	14,000	100
Mean	118	62	11,800	118

In Table 6a.6, the data for variables *X* and *Y* are reproduced from Table 6a.3, where we indicated that the correlation between them was .731. If the relationship we see in the table was obtained for a larger sample of persons, say a sample size of even a dozen cases, this correlation would be statistically significant.

Variables *X* and *Y* also have quite different means as may be seen in Table 6a.6; the mean of variable *X* is 118, and the mean of variable *Y* is 62. Even with this very small sample size of 5, a one-way within-subjects ANOVA yields a statistically significant mean difference, $F(1, 4) = 144.516$, $p < .001$. That the Pearson correlation is only addressing covariation and is not addressing mean differences may be difficult for some to distinguish, given that both the correlation and the mean difference are substantial.

To drive the point home that correlation (covariation) and mean difference are separate statistical issues, we have included variables *Z1* and *Z2* in Table 6a.6. Consider variable *Z1*. To obtain these values, we multiplied the values for variable *X* by 100, and the variable *Z1* mean of 11,800 is considerably larger than the means for variables *X* and *Y*. But if we were to correlate variable *Z1* with variables *X* and *Y*, we would obtain the following outcomes:

- The Pearson r for variable $Z1$ with variable X is 1.00 (not surprising as $Z1$ is a linear transformation of X).
- The Pearson r for variable $Z1$ with variable Y is .731 (the same correlation that holds between variables X and Y despite the substantially higher mean of $Z1$ relative to X).

Now consider variable $Z2$. To obtain these values, we have simply inverted the values of variable X (e.g., Person K has the lowest value of 100 on X but now has the highest value of 140 on $Z2$). Thus, the mean of variable $Z2$ is identical to the mean of variable X—both are 118. Examining the relationship between variables X and $Z2$ quickly reveals the observation that higher scores on the one are associated with lower scores on the other. This pattern is extremely consistent, and the Pearson correlation coefficient of $-.962$ statistically confirms our visual inspection of the data. Thus, despite the means being identical, the variables are quite strongly related to each other.

The lessons to be learned from these oversimplified examples are as follows:

- Two variables can be highly correlated whether their means are of equal magnitudes or are quite different in magnitude.
- Correlation indexes the degree to which two variables covary or are in synchrony with each other but does not speak to absolute differences in magnitude of the values taken on by the variables.
- Positive and negative correlations signify direct and inverse relationships, respectively. The strength of the relationship is indexed by r^2, and so direct and inverse relationships can indicate relatively weaker or relatively stronger relationships depending on the absolute value of r (this is more fully addressed in Section 6A.4).

6A.3 Statistical Significance of the Correlation Coefficient

Researchers are concerned about two aspects of the calculated value of a correlation: whether or not it is statistically significant and the strength of the relationship it is indexing. We briefly treat statistical significance here and discuss strength of relationship in Section 6A.4.

6A.3.1 Interpretation of Statistical Significance

Most popular statistics texts (e.g., Agresti & Finlay, 2009; Runyon et al., 2000) cover the calculation of a Pearson correlation coefficient, and we will not repeat those details here. After obtaining the value of the correlation coefficient from a computation or a printout, the first thing that most researchers wish to determine (assuming that their sample size is not extremely large as discussed in Section 6A.3.2) is whether or not the correlation significantly differs from zero. Note that such reasoning applies equally to positive and negative correlation coefficients, in that a correlation of, say, .72 is as "far" away from a correlation of zero as a correlation of −.72.

The null hypothesis is that the correlation between the two variables is zero in the population, implying that there is no observed relationship between them. For us to achieve statistical significance at the given alpha level (typically .05), the coefficient must be "large enough" ("far enough" away from a zero value), given the sample size (technically, given the degrees of freedom). IBM SPSS actually provides us in the output with the exact probability of the correlation value occurring by chance, permitting us to apply to our results whatever alpha level is appropriate for our research. When we say that our correlation coefficient is statistically significant at the .05 level, we are saying that the chances of that value of a correlation occurring by chance, given this many degrees of freedom, is less than 5 times out of 100, assuming that the null hypothesis is true. Because the correlation is so unlikely to occur by chance, we assert that a relationship between the two variables does really exist.

Statistical significance tells us how confident we can be that an obtained correlation is different from zero. If a computed correlation coefficient reaches the .05 alpha level, for example, then we know that correlations of that magnitude or greater occur by chance only 5% or less of the time if the null hypothesis is true. We therefore permit ourselves to assert that in this particular instance, our obtained Pearson r differs "significantly" from a value of zero. In that sense, we maintain that a correlation "is significant at the .05 alpha level." Obtaining a statistically significant correlation using an alpha level of .01 would permit us to say that correlations of that magnitude or greater occur by chance only 1% or less of the time if the null hypothesis is true.

6A.3.2 Statistical Significance and Sample Size

The key element in determining whether the correlation is statistically significant is the sample size on which the correlation is based. This is because the sampling distribution of r changes with the size of the sample contributing data to the analysis.

With a sample size as small as 9 (i.e., 7 degrees of freedom, which is determined by subtracting 2 from the number of cases because we lose 1 degree of freedom for each variable in this analysis), we need a Pearson r of about .67 or better to achieve statistical significance at the .05 level (two-tailed, where the direction of the effect is not specified in advance). With an N of 27 (degrees of freedom of 25), a Pearson r of about .38 is the threshold value for significance. By the time we reach a sample size around 100, an r value of about .20 is significant at an alpha level of .05, and we need an r value of only about .10 to be significant if we had about 400 cases. With approximately 1,000 cases, a correlation coefficient (r) of about .062 would be statistically significant at the .05 alpha level. We invite readers to examine for themselves a table of critical values for the Pearson correlation to see a more complete picture of this relationship. Such a table is provided by virtually all introductory statistics texts (e.g., Runyon et al., 2000).

It is important to test the statistical significance of any Pearson r we have computed in our research, especially when we have used small- or moderate-sized samples. This is the case because we can obtain what appears to be a relatively high value of the correlation coefficient that turns out to be statistically no different from a correlation of zero. A correlation of .61 might be thought of as reasonably high but if our sample size was nine cases, then such a value would not be statistically significant at the .05 level.

As we work with larger and larger samples, however, we do not need a particularly high value of the correlation to reach significance, so statistical significance testing becomes increasingly less important an issue. With larger sample sizes, the issue of the practical worth of the correlation becomes increasingly relevant. For example, if we have found a correlation between two variables to be .07 based on 4,000 participants, it may be statistically different from zero, but in very many of the circumstances that we might study, the magnitude of the relationship may be thought of as quite small. The important point here is that the concept of *statistical significance* is not the same thing as *strong relationship*. We learn from the correlation being significant that the relationship exists (it is statistically different from zero) but nothing more.

6A.4 Strength of Relationship

Statistical significance is only a portion of the information we wish to glean from a correlation analysis. If a correlation is statistically significant, we maintain that there is more than a null relationship between the variables. But relationships can vary considerably in strength, and knowledge of the strength of a relationship is often the ultimate goal of our research in the first place. Strength of relationship can be thought of in terms of predictive ability. In attempting to predict the value of the Y variable given a certain value of the X variable, prediction becomes increasingly precise with increasingly stronger relationships between the two variables.

6A.4.1 Guidelines for Assessing Relationship Strength

A conventional frame of reference within which we can evaluate the magnitude of a correlation coefficient has been provided by Jacob Cohen (1988). He suggested that in the absence of context, one might regard correlations of .5, .3, and .1 as large, moderate, and small, respectively. But Cohen and many other authors (e.g., Chen & Popovich, 2002) are quick to point out that we almost always have some sort of context within which we can more appropriately judge the size of a correlation. For example, sometimes, in a large correlation table of personality variables, we may not wish to focus on correlations much below the middle .20s. In other contexts, some researchers will initially select variables to place on subscales of an inventory only if they are correlated with a factor at .40 or better.

But there are times when even a very small correlation is worth its weight in gold. Chen and Popovich (2002) provide a telling example, stating that "a small correlation can be very impressive, as well as extremely important for various reasons. Recall that Dr. Jonas Salk's experiment only showed a correlation of [−.01] between polio vaccine and paralytic polio" (pp. 42–43).

This very same theme has been emphasized by several authors (e.g., Cohen, 1990, 1994; Kirk, 1996; B. Thompson, 2002). B. Thompson (2002), for example, distinguishes between statistical significance, practical significance, and clinical significance. The idea is to capture the utility or practical worth of the relationship for specific applications. As a general strategy, we would want to evaluate the magnitude of the correlation twice—once regarding whether it is statistically different from zero and, if it is, then whether the strength of the relationship is large enough to matter for the application in question.

6A.4.2 Relationship Strength Is Shared Variance

To say that two variables are correlated or related is to say that they covary. To say that two variables covary is also to say that they share variance. We have pictured the amount of variance shared by two variables in Figure 6a.6. The variables are depicted by rectangles

Figure 6a.6 Diagrams Showing No Relationship, a Weak Relationship, and a Strong Relationship

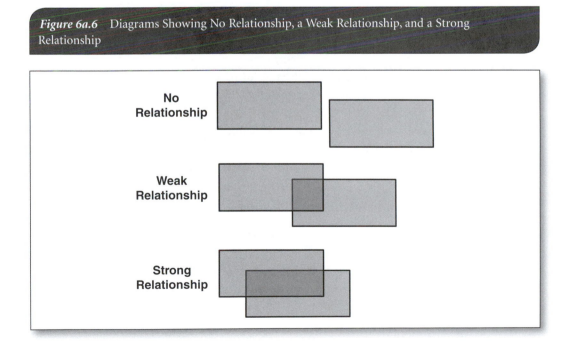

(although it is very common to use circles as well) and are shown in pairs to represent different degrees or strengths of relationship. Using a geometric figure that has an area reminds us that the variable represented has a certain amount of variance; if a variable had zero variance (all participants had the same value as shown for variable X in Table 6a.5 above), we would draw it as a vertical line.

Variables can bear different strengths of relationship to each other. We show a range of these possibilities in Figure 6a.6. The variables in the pair at the top are next to each other but do not overlap. This represents the fact that they are independent of—not correlated with or related to—each other. The Pearson r is zero. The variable pair in the middle overlap, but to a very limited extent. This represents the fact that they are correlated with or related to each other, but that the relationship is not particularly strong. The Pearson r may be in the neighborhood of .25. The variable pair at the bottom overlap considerably. This represents the fact that they are correlated with or related relatively strongly to each other. The Pearson r here may be in the neighborhood of .80.

6A.4.3 Indexing Relationship Strength by r^2

It is possible to quantify the strength of the relationship in a very convenient way: It is the square of the correlation. For the Pearson r, the strength of the relationship is indexed by r^2, which is often called the *coefficient of determination*. The squared correlation value can be translated to a percentage. For example, if we calculated a Pearson correlation of .60, the r^2 would be .36. Note that if the correlation was −.60, the r^2 would still be .36 (remember that positive and negative correlations just indicate whether the observed relationship is direct or inverse, respectively, but in no way address the strength of the relationship). Given an r^2 of .36, we could then say that

- the two variables shared 36% of each other's variance and
- the X variable accounted for or explained 36% of the variance of the Y variable.

If r^2 is the percentage of variance in Y that is explained by X, 36% in this case, then the remaining portion of Y's variance $(1 - r^2)$ is $1 - .36$ or .64 and is unexplained. This residual variance, indexed by the expression $1 - r^2$, is called the *coefficient of nondetermination*.

6A.4.4 Alternative Measures of Strength of Relationship

Although we will use r^2 as our index of relationship strength for the Pearson correlation, other indexes have been suggested (Chen & Popovich, 2002). Cohen (1988) has suggested using r itself as the gauge, and Rosenthal (1991) has proposed the ratio of $r^2/(1 - r^2)$. This latter ratio evaluates the amount of explained variance with respect to the amount of unexplained variance.

Table 6a.7 Values of r, r^2, and Percentage of Shared Variance

Pearson r	Pearson r^2	% Shared Variance
.10	.01	01%
.20	.04	04%
.30	.09	09%
.40	.16	16%
.50	.25	25%
.60	.36	36%
.70	.49	49%
.80	.64	64%
.90	.81	81%

6A.4.5 Relation of r and r²

Table 6a.7 presents the Pearson r value in increments of .10 together with the r^2 values and the percentage of variance shared by the two variables. As can be seen from Table 6a.7, a difference of .10 in terms of r represents rather different jumps in strength of relationship depending on the magnitude of the correlation. For example, when we compare a correlation of .20 with one of .30, we see an increase in explained variance from 4% to 9%, but when we compare a correlation of .80 with a correlation of .90, we see a jump in explained variance from 64% to 81%.

The squared correlation is assessed on a ratio scale of measurement. We are therefore able to say that an r^2 of .40 represents twice as strong a relationship as does an r^2 of .20. Examples of r values, their associated r^2 values, and the corresponding percentage of shared or explained variance are shown in Table 6a.7. Looked at from the other direction, we would also say, for example, that a correlation of .70 (49% shared variance) represents a relationship almost twice as strong as one with a Pearson r of .50 (25% shared variance). These r^2 values help us to gain a bit of perspective on their corresponding r values, and researchers will ordinarily bear these in mind in the process of interpreting their results. In this book, time after time we will emphasize the squared correlation rather than the correlation itself.

6A.4.6 Calculating the Mean Correlation

There are a couple of methods available to compute the mean correlation of a set of correlation values. *Neither of these methods involves computing an ordinary average.* The Pearson *r* is far from interval measurement, and averaging numbers whose intervals are not close to being equal can lead to a distorted and improper result (for a more complex analysis of this issue, see Silver & Dunlap, 1987).

The most commonly used way of determining the mean correlation is to convert the *r* values to Fisher *z'* values (see Section 2.7.4). These *z'* scores (which are measured on an interval scale of measurement) can be averaged. Once the mean of these *z'* values is obtained, we use the conversion table to determine the *r* value that corresponds to the mean *z'* score just computed. We can illustrate this by assuming that we have three Pearson correlations of .10, .20, and .80. The Fisher *z'* scores obtained from a conversion table for these correlations are .100, .203, and 1.099, respectively. Averaging these *z'* scores yields .4673. Converting this *z'* value back to a Pearson *r* value yields an *r* of approximately .44.

We can also compute a quick approximation to the average correlation. Given that the squared correlation is assessed on a ratio scale of measurement, we can calculate a mean r^2 value for a set of such values and take the square root to convert back to *r*. We can illustrate this as follows. If we have three Pearson correlations of .10, .20, and .80, the r^2 values associated with them are .01, .04, and .64. The mean r^2 value is .230, which corresponds to an *r* value of approximately .4796. We can thus say that the average correlation of the set was very approximately .48, a value somewhat higher than what we would regard as the more precise representation obtained when using the Fisher *z'* transformation.

The above example may have served an instructional purpose to illustrate the two different procedures to compute an average correlation, but with such discrepant values, we would be surprised if any researchers would wish to average those particular correlations. If a measure of central tendency is desired, an alternative to computing a mean is to determine the median. With correlation values of .10, .20, and .80, the median is .20 but does not really capture the central tendency of our small set; with many more values, however, the median would become an increasingly better index.

6A.5 Pearson Correlation Using a Quantitative Variable and a Dichotomous Nominal Variable

A general assumption underlying the interpretation of a Pearson *r* is that the two variables are each measured on a quantitative scale. This is so because the interpretation of the correlation rests on the proposition that larger values on a variable represent more of the assessed quantity than do smaller values. With this assumption in place, the ordering of the numbers is tied to some underlying property of the things that are measured (e.g., five symptoms are more than three symptoms).

6A.5.1 Why a Dichotomous (Two-Category) Predictor Variable Works

The interpretation of a Pearson correlation also can make sense if one of the variables has only two categories, and it is useful here to imagine that the variable with two categories can logically or reasonably be used to predict the other variable (that is quantitative). Thus, we specify here that the predictor or *X* variable is *dichotomous* (it contains only two levels) and that the dependent or *Y* variable has been assessed on a *quantitative* scale of measurement.

A convenient way to explain the logic of how a dichotomous *X* variable can appropriately be analyzed with the Pearson *r* is to use the following hypothetical example. Assume that we have measured the verbal ability of entry-level middle school students; assume that this verbal ability variable would be our *Y* variable in a regression approach. The set of children was composed of both girls and boys; assume that this sex variable would be our *X* variable in a regression approach. Thus, we wish to predict verbal ability based on the sex of the child.

A portion of the data set is shown in Table 6a.8. Furthermore, assume that the pattern shown in this small portion of the data is representative of the larger sample. We have organized the rows of Table 6a.8 to make it easier to see what we admit are rather exaggerated results. Looking only at the **Sex** and **Verbal Score** columns, our results are clear. For this sample and for this measure, the girls appear to have greater verbal ability than the boys. Now the only thing we need to do is achieve the statistical outcome that tells us this very same thing.

To calculate a Pearson correlation, both variables have to be numeric. We therefore need to arbitrarily code sex. Common choices are 0 and 1 or 1 and 2 to represent the different

Table 6a.8　Relationship of a Dichotomous Variable and a Quantitative Variable

Child	Sex	Verbal Score	Sex Coding	
			Alternative A Coding of Sex	**Alternative B** Coding of Sex
A	Girl	545	1	2
B	Girl	612	1	2
C	Girl	627	1	2
D	Boy	497	2	1
E	Boy	534	2	1
F	Boy	559	2	1

sexes of the children; we will use the codes of 1 and 2 here by way of illustration. So far, so good. Now we come to a decision point: Who gets coded as 1 and who gets coded as 2? As the choice is arbitrary, assume that we decided to code the girls as 1 and the boys as 2. This is shown as coding Alternative A in Table 6a.8.

We now perform the Pearson procedure. What are we going to find? Well, the data in Table 6a.8 inform us that higher verbal scores are associated with 1s (these are the girls) and lower verbal scores are associated with 2s (these are the boys). Under this specific coding scheme, the value of the Pearson r for the entire sample must show an inverse relationship (a negative correlation). This is so because higher verbal scores are tied to "lower" sex codes (1s) and lower verbal scores are tied to "higher" sex codes (2s). When we perform the calculation on the data shown in Table 6a.8 and round to two decimal places, we obtain a Pearson r of approximately −.72. The strength of this relationship is indexed by r^2, giving us a value of approximately .52.

Let's return to our decision point regarding what group was given what code and institute the opposite coding strategy. This is shown in Table 6a.8 as coding Alternative B in which girls are coded as 2 and boys are coded as 1. With only the coding scheme altered, we see that the same higher verbal scores are now associated with 2s and that the same lower verbal scores are now associated with 1s. The reality, however, is still the same—the girls are scoring higher than the boys and, of course, by the same degree, because the underlying reality has not been altered by the arbitrary coding schema.

If the reality is unchanged, then the statistical outcome should tell us the same story. And, of course, it does. The Pearson correlation must turn out to be +.72 because now the higher verbal scores are linked with "higher" sex codes (2s) and lower verbal scores are linked with "lower" sex codes (1s). And r^2 is the same at .52.

The lesson learned from this example is as follows. When a dichotomous variable is used as one of the variables in computing a Pearson r, the same numeric value will be obtained regardless of which category was coded as 1 and which was coded as 2. The only consequence of using the alternative coding scheme is that the valence of the correlation will be different.

6A.5.2 Why an X Variable With Three or More Categories Will Not Work

A dichotomous variable can be accommodated by the Pearson correlation procedure in that there are only two possible coding schemas. Because the groups will be coded either 1 and 2 or 2 and 1, the numerical value of the Pearson r will be identical under both coding schemas, differing only in whether it is positive or negative. Once we have three or more categories, the situation is not as clean.

We provide an illustration of some hypothetical data in Table 6a.9 to demonstrate the point. Our quantitative variable is math score and our categorical variable is eye color. We have specified three different eye colors. In coding this categorical variable, there are many more options, and we show three such alternative coding schemas in Table 6a.9. And the problem is now that different numerical values of the Pearson r

Table 6a.9 Relationship of a Dichotomous Variable and a Quantitative Variable

| | | | | Eye Color Coding | |
| | Eye | Math | Alternative A Coding of | Alternative B Coding of | Alternative C Coding of |
Child	Color	Score	Eye Color	Eye Color	Eye Color
A	Green	627	1	3	2
B	Green	642	1	3	2
C	Blue	545	2	1	1
D	Blue	559	2	1	1
E	Brown	434	3	2	3
F	Brown	497	3	2	3

would be obtained between math score and eye color depending on which coding schema for eye color was used.

The key to remembering why the situation of a variable with three or more categories will not work (why we would obtain different numerical values of the Pearson r for each coding alternative) is that we can no longer simply swap the codes and obtain the same numerical result, that is, if the swapping strategy fails under at least one coding schema, then we cannot properly use the Pearson correlation procedure. Inspection of the data in Table 6a.9 reveals that correlating math score with each of the alternative eye color coding schemas will produce different results. These are specifically the following:

- The Pearson correlation between math score and eye color using Alternative A is −.964. Higher math scores are consistently associated with lower eye color codes (e.g., math scores in the 600s are associated with the code of 1 for eye color, math scores in the 400s are associated with the code of 3 for eye color).
- The Pearson correlation between math score and eye color using Alternative B is .470. Higher math scores are associated to a certain extent but not exceptionally consistently with higher eye color codes (e.g., math scores in the 600s are associated with the code of 3 for eye color, but math scores in the 500s are associated with the code of 1 for eye color).
- The Pearson correlation between math score and eye color using Alternative C is −.493. Higher math scores are associated to a certain extent but not exceptionally consistently with lower eye color codes (e.g., math scores in the 400s are associated with the code of 3 for eye color, but math scores in the 500s are associated with the code of 1 for eye color).

One can ask the following question: "If we obtain different results with different coding schemas, which result is correct?" The answer to this question is an emphatic "None of them because the Pearson correlation procedure is the wrong statistical technique to apply to the issue."

Will IBM SPSS compute a Pearson correlation between eye color in our example (or ethnicity, or occupation, or geographic region or any other categorical variable if it has more than two categories) and math score for this data set? Yes, of course, because the software will do pretty much anything that we tell it to do. Should we so instruct the software? No, because we have more than two codes for the categorical variable. Should we interpret the outcome of the correlation procedure if someone less knowledgeable actually performed the computation? No, because the numerical value is dependent on the particular coding schema used, and so the result is not appropriately interpretable.

So what is the proper analysis for these data? The simplest answer to this question is that we should perform a one-way between-subjects ANOVA here with eye color as the independent variable and math score as the dependent variable. We have discussed this procedure in Chapters 4A and 4B. An alternative and more complex way of performing the ANOVA is to dummy code or effect code the eye color variable in a multiple regression analysis to predict math score (see Section 8A.5).

6A.6 Simple Linear Regression

When we focus on two variables in a research study, computing their correlation gives us most of the information that we ordinarily want. However, as we mentioned several times already, the Pearson correlation between two variables can be used as a basis for the prediction of the values for one variable given a knowledge of the values on the other. When our attention turns to prediction, we are in the realm of regression analysis.

In the situation where we use a single variable to predict another single variable, the particular procedure is called *simple linear regression.*

- It is *simple* because only one predictor (independent variable) is involved.
- It is *linear* because we apply a straight-line function to the data and are computing a Pearson correlation.
- It is *regression* because we are predicting something.

The concept of regression and the initial procedure to calculate it leads back to Sir Francis Galton (Stanton, 2001), "the late 19th-century geographer, meteorologist, and statistician . . . perhaps best known for his study of the inheritance of both physical and intellectual characteristics" (Meyers et al., 2009, p. 155). Based on his observations that (a) relatively heavy and relatively light sweet pea plants each tended to produce seeds of less extreme weight and (b) relatively tall and relatively short men tended to have offspring who were closer to average height, Galton (1886) introduced the concept of regression. It was this framework that enabled him 2 years later (Galton, 1888) to introduce the notion of *co-relation*. His index of co-relation was symbolized as *r* to stand for regression. In the following decade, Galton's collaborator and eventual biographer, Karl Pearson, formalized a product–moment correlation coefficient in 1896 known today as the Pearson *r* (he retained Galton's choice of symbol). The earlier portion of this chapter was devoted to this index of co-relation; we now turn to the somewhat earlier published concept of regression, showing where Galton's original conception has led us over the past century or so.

6A.6.1 An Overview of the Regression Process

The easiest way to conceive of simple linear regression is to imagine a straight line, the regression line, fitted to a scatterplot, something we have talked about briefly earlier in the chapter. This straight regression line would be oriented in the same direction as the oval characterizing the relationship of the variables and would run through the middle of it. The regression line is used as the basis for predicting the variable on the *Y* axis from a knowledge of the variable on the *X* axis.

If we wished to do so at a slight sacrifice of precision, this prediction process could be done pictorially as in Figure 6a.7. In this figure, a simplified scatterplot is outlined in an oval

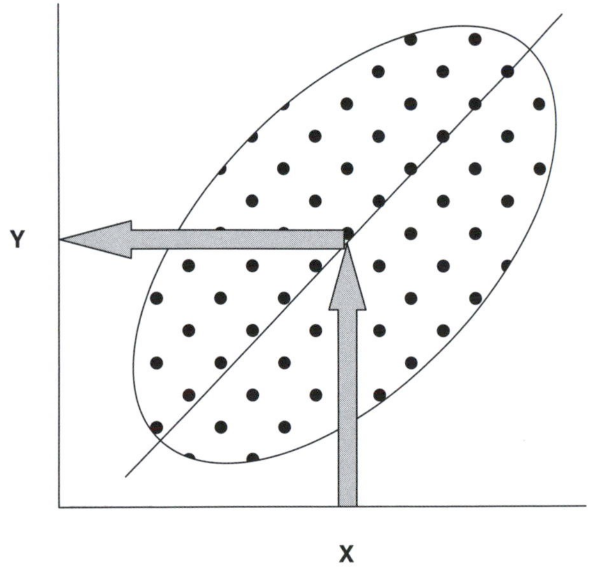

Figure 6a.7 Predicting *Y* From a *X* Based on the Regression Line

with a least squares regression line drawn through it. To predict a Y value based on some X value, we would start with that X value, locate it on the X axis, draw a line straight up to the regression line, hang a sharp 90° turn toward the Y axis, and continue in a horizontal direction until we reached the Y axis. The value at the place where we encountered the Y axis would be our predicted Y value. Of course, the more precise way of predicting Y from a knowledge of X is to do it algebraically based on the equation for that straight regression line.

6A.6.2 The Least Squares Solution

The goal of simple linear regression is to find the proper location (i.e., the particular linear equation) for the regression line. It is found by applying the *least squares algorithm.* The least squares solution is a way of fitting a straight line—the regression line in this case—to an array of data. There is only one place in the array where this solution may be satisfied. The least squares algorithm underlying the solution deals with the distances of the data points from the line.

- It is a *squares* rule because the distance between each data point and the line is required to be squared. All these squared distances are then added together. This sum is then used to satisfy the second portion of the procedure.
- It is a *least* squares rule because the regression line is placed at the position where the sum of the squared distances between the data points and the straight line is minimal.

This least squares solution is often referred to as *ordinary least squares* to distinguish it from the other, more specialized calculations of least squares (e.g., generalized, weighted), which we do not cover in this text. We will use "least squares" and "ordinary least squares" interchangeably.

6A.6.3 Raw Scores and Standard Scores

We enter raw data into data files. Raw data are literally the data values derived from the measurement operations we were using in our research study. Sometimes, the metrics used to measure the two variables differ considerably. In the example shown earlier in Table 6a.2, the scales have rather different magnitudes. The X scores range from the teens to the 20s whereas the Y scores range in the 60s.

As the metrics used to assess the two variables become increasingly more discrepant, it is more difficult to keep track of and deal with the raw values (e.g., how much above or below the sample mean is a participant with a given score). Although we never want to lose or give up raw data, it is often desirable to also convert (transform) the raw scores to standardized scores so that their relative magnitudes can be assessed instantly; in the context of regression, the basic standardized score—the *z* score—is used.

A *z* score, as you may recall from previous coursework, indicates how many standard deviation units a particular score lies from the mean of the distribution. For example, a distribution may have a mean of 80 and a standard deviation of 5. Thus, for that set of scores, a raw score of 80 has a *z* score of zero because it is exactly at the mean, a raw score of 85 has a *z* score of 1.00 because it lies exactly 1 standard deviation above the mean, and a raw score of 70 has a *z* score of −2.00 because it lies exactly 2 standard deviation units below the mean.

This transformation from raw scores to *z* scores is accomplished, as can be seen above, by examining the distance between the score and the mean (by subtracting the mean from the score) and determining how many standard deviations that distance represents (dividing that distance by the standard deviation). The formula for this transformation is therefore as follows:

$$Z = \frac{X - \text{Mean}}{\text{Standard deviation}}$$

In this formula, we subtract the sample mean from the score of interest (designated as X) and divide that difference by the standard deviation of the sample.

The usefulness of *z* scores is found in the fact that we can immediately interpret these scores based on the fact that the *z* scale has a mean of 0 and a standard deviation of 1 in the normal distribution. For example, 95% of the area of the normal curve is subsumed between ±1.96 *z* scores. We automatically know that a *z* score of 1.50 is 1.5 standard deviations above the mean, that a *z* score of −.75 is .75 standard deviations below the mean, and so on.

One nice thing about using such a standardized scale is that if both variables are transformed to their respective *z* scales, we can immediately grasp the magnitude of every score in the analysis without trying to remember the details of the raw score measurement. We are also in a much better position to immediately compare variables with each other. Partly because of these benefits of the *z* scale, most computerized statistical programs, such as IBM SPSS, work in both raw score as well as standardized score mode when they perform a regression analysis. The output of these programs presents us with the regression solution—that is, the equation for the regression line—in both raw score and standard score form.

6A.6.4 The Regression Equations

We talk about the regression line in terms of an equation or model. Although it is really just one function, IBM SPSS displays the components of the model in two forms—one for the raw scores and another for the standardized scores. This equation serves as the regression *model*, the representation of the predictive relationship between the two variables.

6A.6.4.1 The Raw Score Model

The raw score model or equation for predicting *Y* based on a knowledge of *X* is that of a straight line. It is as follows:

$$Y_{pred} = a + bX$$

The symbols in this model represent the following:

- Y_{pred} is the predicted value of the variable that is being predicted. It is often called the *criterion variable*, the *dependent variable*, or the *outcome variable*.
- *X* is the value of the variable used as the basis of the prediction. It is often called the *predictor variable* or the *independent variable*.
- *b* is the coefficient of the *X* variable. It is the amount by which the *X* variable is weighted or multiplied and so is often called the *raw score coefficient, raw score weight, b weight,* or *b coefficient*. Mathematically, it is the slope of the line. It indicates how much change in Y_{pred} is associated with a change in one unit of *X*.
- *a* is the *Y* intercept of the line. It is the place where the line crosses the *Y* axis and can be thought of as the value of Y_{pred} when *X* = 0. The *Y* intercept is a *constant* and is often called that.

A straight line can be drawn on a set of axes once the *Y* intercept and the slope are computed. The object of the work done on the raw scores in simple linear regression is to figure out these two values.

You will note that the term *bX* in the equation is preceded by a plus sign. This is the generic way to represent the additive nature of this term, but it does not require that the term is always positive. It is possible that *bX* could take on a negative value. This will happen when the predictor variable is negatively correlated with the criterion variable. In such a case, we would obtain a negative *b* value and, therefore, would need to subtract *bX* from the constant in order to acquire the predicted *Y* value.

We can now also express the ordinary least squares solution in different words. Remember that the dots in the scatterplot (see Figure 6a.7) mark the actual data points and the regression line represents the prediction model. The distance between the line and any one of the data points therefore is the distance between the predicted *Y* value and the actual *Y* value. In wording the least squares solution in this alternative way, we can say that we find this difference between every person's predicted and actual *Y* value, square each difference, and then add these squared values together. The regression line may thus be said to occupy the place where the sum of the squared differences between the predicted and actual *Y* scores is at a minimum.

6A.6.4.2 The Standardized Model

The standardized score model for predicting *Y* based on a knowledge of *X* is also a straight-line function. It is as follows:

$$Y_{z\,pred} = \beta X_z$$

The symbols in this model represent the following:

- $Y_{z\,pred}$ is the *z* score value that is being predicted. As we have seen, it can be called the *criterion, dependent,* or *outcome variable* in this context.
- X_z is the *z* score value of the variable used as the basis of the prediction. As we have also seen, it is called the *predictor* or *independent variable.*
- β is the coefficient of the X_z variable. It is the Greek letter beta. Beta is the amount by which the standardized *X* variable is weighted or multiplied and so is often called the *standardized coefficient, standardized weight, beta weight,* or *beta coefficient.* In simple linear regression, this beta weight is the Pearson *r*. Mathematically, it is the slope of the line based on the standardized *X* and *Y* scores.
- Note that the constant drops out of the standardized equation. This is because the standardized regression line always passes through the point of origin of the axis set. The origin is the place where both *X* and *Y* are equal to zero. In effect, the constant is still in the equation, but its value is zero; thus, there is no sense in writing it in.

Also, as was true for the raw score model, the expression βX_z could be negative; that is, the Pearson *r* (or beta coefficient in the equation) could be negative, indicating an inverse relationship between the predictor and criterion variables.

6A.6.5 Interpreting a Regression Model

In simple linear regression, the raw score and beta coefficients represent the slope of the respective regression lines. Larger absolute values indicate greater slopes than smaller values. The constant in the raw score model indicates the *Y* intercept.

How we may interpret these features of the model can be illustrated by the regression line and accompanying information shown in Figure 6a.8. The small data set used to generate

Figure 6a.8 Interpreting the Values of a Regression Equation

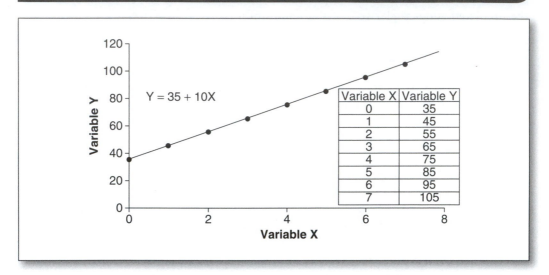

the model is shown inside the axes of the graph. There are eight cases. The first case has an X value of 0 and a Y value of 35, the second case has an X value of 1 and a Y value of 45, and so on. The correlation between the two variables is 1.00, and thus the prediction of Y from X is perfect; this would not occur in empirical research, but it is very convenient for us to illustrate how to interpret the regression model.

The raw score regression model predicting Y from a knowledge of X based on the data set is as follows:

$$Y_{pred} = 35 + 10X$$

The constant—the Y intercept—in the model takes on the value of 35. It can be seen from Figure 6a.8 that (by our design to make this clear) the first case has an X value of 0. The Y value for that individual is 35. This may also be seen in the regression line—it crosses the Y axis at a value (height) of 35.

The b coefficient of 10 is the slope of the line; this means that a 1-unit change in X corresponds to an increment of 10 units in Y_{pred}. This can be seen in the plotted line and the small table of data shown in Figure 6a.8. For example, the change or difference between values of 2 and 3 on variable X is a difference of 1 unit, and that 1-unit change corresponds to a change of 10 units on variable Y (it has a value of 55 at X = 2 and a value of 65 at X = 3). Based on the model, we can predict the Y value of any other case to which these sample results can be generalized. For example, if one person had an X value of 8, we would predict that her Y value would be equal to 115, that is, 35 + 10(8) = 35 + 80 = 115.

6A.7 Statistical Error in Prediction: Why Bother With Regression?

There is an interesting question that some students ask at this point: Using the regression model to predict Y scores of the participants must lead to errors because most of the scores in an actual research study are not really on the regression line. But we know the actual scores of these participants—their data were used to generate the statistical analysis. So why use the regression model to predict the Y value when we can do better (in fact, we would make no errors) by just looking up everyone's score?

The answer is that the regression equation is treated as a model (or "theory") for how one variable in general can be used to predict the other. We collected data on a particular sample only as a way to build this model. We are not necessarily interested in these particular participants per se. Rather, we hope that they are sufficiently representative of the population we wish to characterize so that they can provide us with a solid base on which to build a model. Thus, with the regression function, (a) we can predict how some future individuals who did not participate in the study might perform on Y if we knew how they did on X and/or (b) we can better understand the general relationship between X and Y.

Because the regression model is a summary of the data and because the correlation in a real-world data set virtually never reaches the value of 1.00, researchers recognize that some amount of prediction error comes with the territory. This is shown in pictorial form in Figure 6a.9. We have drawn three scatterplots depicting differing strengths of relationship based on a large number of data points.

The top scatterplot of Figure 6a.9 shows a nonperfect but relatively strong relationship. The Y value we predict given a particular value of X is based on the regression model. But note that even for a relatively strong relationship, scores on the Y variable from the highest Y value to the lowest Y value are also associated with that given X value. When we identify the Y value corresponding to regression model as our predicted Y value, we must recognize that there is a certain amount of prediction error associated with such a prediction. How much prediction error is, schematically speaking, a function to the degree of compression of the oval, or more precisely, it is a function of the spread of scores around the regression line. And the spread of scores around the regression line can be indexed by the strength of the relationship between X and Y, namely, r^2. In short, a stronger relationship between X and Y results in less prediction error. And, perhaps obviously, as we just discussed in Section 6A.6.5, a perfect relationship between X and Y results in no prediction error at all.

The middle scatterplot of Figure 6a.9 shows a relatively weak relationship. Again, there is a range of Y scores associated with the X value that we are using as our predictor. And once again our best prediction is based on the regression model. Here, however, the spread of scores in the scatter is wider—indicative of a relatively weak relationship between X and

Figure 6a.9 Predicting *Y* From *X* for a Range of Relationship Strengths

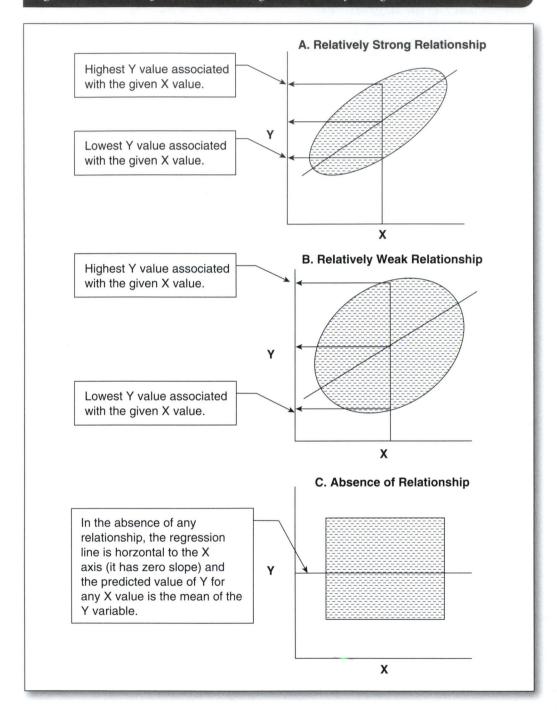

Y—and so our prediction is that much less precise. In short, a weaker relationship between *X* and *Y* results in more prediction error.

The lower scatterplot of Figure 6a.9 pictures a situation where there is no correlation between the two variables. The shape of the scatterplot resembles a square (some would draw it as a circle, but no one would call it an oval). Because there is no relationship between *X* and *Y*, knowing the *X* value does not help us in predicting the corresponding *Y* value. Our best guess about the *Y* value—that is, Y_{pred}—in the absence of useful information is therefore the mean of the *Y* variable. This is reinforced by looking at the regression line: Its slope is zero (the line is horizontal), and its *Y* intercept is the mean of the *Y* variable.

6A.8 How Simple Linear Regression Is Used

Whereas correlation—especially Pearson correlation—is used extensively, simple linear regression is infrequently used. The reason simple linear regression is used so little is that it is just too simple. Most of us would agree that human behavior is multiply determined. We act the way we act, believe the way we believe, and are the way we are based on many considerations rather than just one: our upbringing, our adult histories, our stimulus environment, our current motivational state, and so on. To use just one variable to predict another is neither adequate nor reasonable for most purposes.

So why have we devoted these pages to a topic that is not widely used? Because our treatment of simple linear regression lays a solid foundation for *multiple* linear regression (and its more complex variations); the attempt to predict *Y* is based on a set of theoretically relevant variables. Multiple regression has a great deal of intuitive appeal for those researchers who believe that much of human behavior is determined by the combination of many factors. We cover the topic of multiple regression in Chapters 7A and 7B.

6A.9 Factors Affecting the Computed Pearson r and Regression Coefficients

For both the Pearson correlation and simple linear regression, several factors can adversely affect either the computations or our interpretation of the result. We quickly mention three of them here.

6A.9.1 Outliers

We indicated in Chapter 3A that it was important to identify and deal with outliers during data screening. They can be particularly troublesome in computing the Pearson *r* as well as the regression statistics. The easiest way to conceptualize this is by recalling that the regression model is fit by the ordinary least squares algorithm in which the sum of squared deviations from the line of best fit is minimal. Outliers by definition will lie quite a distance away from the middle range of scores. Under ordinary least squares, large distances become disproportionately influential when they are squared. The effect of this disproportionate influence is that an outlier will tend to attract the line of best fit toward itself as the algorithm works hard to minimize the squared distances; as a result, it will move away from the bulk of scores in the middle of the distribution and become less representative of these latter values. All else equal, researchers attempt to intervene in such situations by removing outliers, allowing a maximum value for outliers, or transforming the data to reduce or eliminate the presence of outliers.

6A.9.2 Range (Variance) Restriction

We gave an example in Section 6A.2.5 in which the correlation was zero because we had no variance on the X variable. Generally, low variability on one of the variables will produce a low value of the Pearson correlation, which will result in very little prediction power using a regression model. This situation is often called *range restriction*, but it is probably more appropriately thought of as *variance restriction* because variance is a useful framework within which to understand correlation.

Although range or variance restriction applies to the numbers in the data analysis, sometimes the reason we see such restriction in the data can be traced to a weakness in the research design. The key issue on which to focus is that, to the extent that range restriction is present in the research sample, it will reduce the value of the obtained correlation coefficient. As a result, an obtained statistical result from a certain piece of research may or may not have all that much external validity depending on the variability in the population. We illustrate this with the following example.

A team of researchers intends to study the relationship between age and self-esteem. They have hypothesized that older individuals will generally have higher self-esteem than younger people. Statistically, they are expecting to obtain a reasonably strong positive correlation. They run their study, however, in a small liberal arts college where the entire freshman class takes the introductory psychology course that makes up their sample. Based on data from 75 participants, the researchers find that their obtained Pearson r is not significantly different from zero.

What happened? If we assume that their hypothesis was reasonable and that age and self-esteem are really positively correlated in the general population, then why did they not obtain that result in their study? The answer is likely to be range restriction. Small liberal arts colleges generally attract students directly out of high school who are probably very similar in age. If the youngest participant in their study was 18 years old and their oldest participant was 19 years old, how much of a relationship between age and anything would we expect to find? The answer is, not much. Age simply does not vary enough in the sample to covary with anything. To appropriately test for a relationship involving an age variable, the researchers should have sampled from a much more age-diverse population.

6A.9.3 Nonlinearity

We have seen that linearity has played a prominent role in our discussions during this chapter. We have repeatedly said that the Pearson correlation assesses the degree of *linear relationship* observed between two variables, and we have seen that the regression line is a linear function. If two variables are strongly related but not in a linear manner, then the value of the Pearson r may be close to zero and the simple linear regression model may fail to show any significant prediction.

Two examples of nonlinear relationships are illustrated in Figure 6a.10. The upper scatterplot pictures a pure quadratic relationship between the two variables; here, Y is relatively strongly related to the square of X. But because there is no linear relationship between the two variables, the Pearson r would be zero and the least squares regression line would be horizontal to the X axis. Note that a zero value for the Pearson r indicates merely that there is no observed *linear* relationship between the variables, *but it should not be interpreted to indicate that the variables are unrelated.*

The lower scatterplot of Figure 6a.10 suggests that X and Y are related in a roughly linear manner from the low through midrange of X.

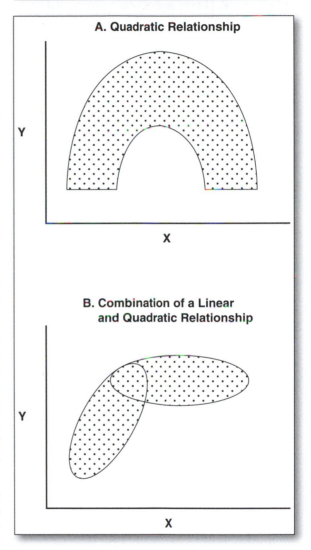

Figure 6a.10 Examples of Nonlinear Relationships

A. Quadratic Relationship

Y

X

B. Combination of a Linear and Quadratic Relationship

Y

X

From the mid-range to upper range of X, the scatterplot levels out suggesting that the different X values are associated with approximately the same Y value. Because it is possible to fit a straight nonhorizontal ordinary least squares line through this entire scatterplot, the Pearson r would yield a nonzero value. But because the relationship is more complex, the Pearson correlation will underestimate the degree of relationship between X and Y.

6A.10 Recommended Readings

Baggaley, A. R. (1964). *Intermediate correlational methods.* New York, NY: Wiley.

Chambers, W. V. (2000). Causation and corresponding correlations. *Journal of Mind and Behavior, 21,* 437–460.

Cohen, B. H. (1996). *Explaining psychological statistics.* Pacific Grove, CA: Brooks/Cole.

Cowles, M. (1989). *Statistics in psychology: An historical perspective.* Hillsdale, NJ: Lawrence Erlbaum.

Diamond, S. (1959). *Information and error: An introduction to statistical analysis.* New York, NY: Basic Books.

Galton, F. A. (1886). Regression towards mediocrity in hereditary stature. *Journal of the Anthropological Institute, 15,* 246–263.

Galton, F. A. (1888). Co-relations and their measurement, chiefly from anthropometric data. *Proceedings of the Royal Society of London, 40,* 42–73.

Lorenz, F. O. (1987). Teaching about influence in simple regression. *Teaching Sociology, 15,* 173–177.

Salsburg. D. (2001). *The lady tasting tea.* New York, NY: W. H. Freeman.

Stigler, S. M. (1989). Francis Galton's account of the invention of correlation. *Statistical Science, 4,* 73–86.

Stigler, S. M. (1999). *Statistics on the table: The history of statistical concepts and methods.* Cambridge, MA: Harvard University Press.

Bivariate Correlation and Simple Linear Regression Using IBM SPSS

T his chapter will briefly demonstrate how to perform Pearson product–moment correlations and simple (bivariate) linear regressions with IBM SPSS. We will use the data file **Personality** in these demonstrations.

6B.1 Bivariate Correlation: Analysis Setup

6B.1.1 Main Dialog Window

To produce a bivariate correlation matrix, we begin by selecting **Analyze ➔ Correlate ➔ Bivariate**. This brings us to the **Bivariate Correlations** dialog window shown in Figure 6b.1. From the variables list panel on the left side, we click over the variables for which we wish to obtain bivariate correlations. The two variables we intend to correlate are negative affect named **negafect** in the data file and self-esteem named **esteem** in the data file. Click over these variables into the **Variables** panel as shown.

In the lower half of the **Bivariate Correlations** dialog window is the **Correlation Coefficients** area with three checkboxes for **Pearson** (the default), **Kendall's tau-b**, and **Spearman**. The Pearson *r* correlation, as we noted in Chapter 4A, is the most common measure of linear association between two variables and is what we have selected to compute. Kendall's tau-b is a nonparametric measure of association for ordinal or ranked variables that also takes ties into account. The Spearman *rho*, also based on rank, is a nonparametric version of the Pearson correlation.

Underneath this area lies the **Test of Significance** panel, where researchers can specify either a **Two-tailed** (default) significance level, which tests a null hypothesis for which the

Figure 6b.1 Bivariate Correlations Main Dialog Window

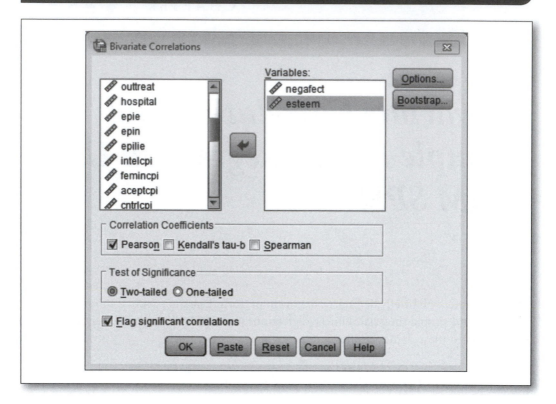

direction of an effect is not specified in advance, or a **One-tailed** significance level, for which the direction of an effect is specified in advance. We have chosen a two-tailed significance test. At the bottom is the **Flag significant correlations** checkbox, which is checked (default) and identifies significant coefficients at the .05 level with a single asterisk and those significant at the .01 level with two asterisks. This provides an extra visual cue when examining the output and is very often a helpful choice.

6B.1.2 Options Window

By selecting the **Options** pushbutton, the **Bivariate Correlations: Options** dialog window is produced, shown as in Figure 6b.2.

The **Statistics** panel at the top of the **Options** dialog window has two checkboxes for **Means and standard deviations** for each case and **Cross-product deviations and covariances** for each pair of variables. To keep the output simpler, we have chosen to obtain only the means and standard deviations.

Figure 6b.2 Bivariate Correlations: Options Window

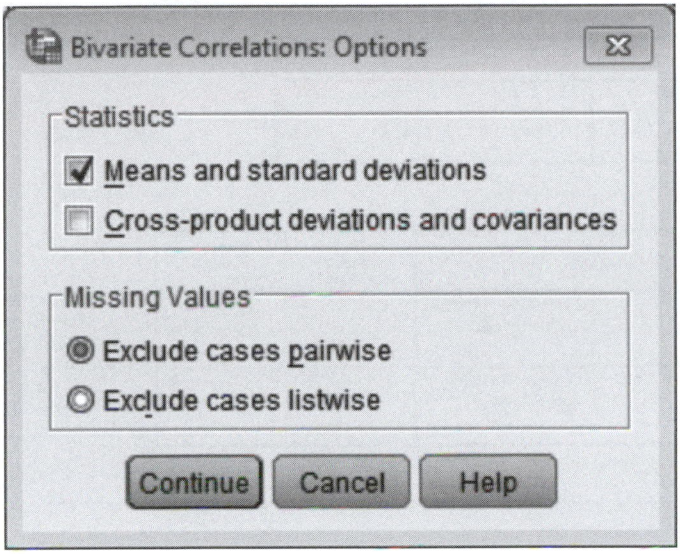

The **Missing Values** panel also has two checkboxes, the **Exclude cases pairwise** (default) checkbox allows you to exclude cases with missing values for either or both of the pair of variables involved in the correlation and the **Exclude cases listwise** checkbox eliminates cases that have missing values on any of the variables being correlated. With only one pair of variables, the choice is irrelevant. With more than two variables, the choice can make a difference depending on the extent to which there are missing data. If the analysis is restricted to only correlation, then **Exclude cases pairwise** will produce the most descriptive results. If the analysis is a prelude to another procedure, such as multiple regression, then **Exclude cases listwise** will be more relevant to that later analysis. Clicking the **Continue** pushbutton returns us to the original main dialog window, where selecting the **OK** pushbutton instructs IBM SPSS to perform the analysis.

6B.1.3 Output From the Correlation Analysis

Figure 6b.3 shows the output from the correlation analysis. The upper table provides the means and standard deviations of the variables as well as the number of cases in the analysis. The lower case presents a "square" correlation matrix. It is square because of this:

Figure 6b.3 Results of the Correlation Analysis

Descriptive Statistics

	Mean	Std. Deviation	N
esteem self-esteem: coopersmith	71.2417	20.94656	422
negafect negative affect: mpq	5.7962	3.73418	422

Correlations

		esteem self-esteem: coopersmith	negafect negative affect: mpq
esteem self-esteem: coopersmith	Pearson Correlation	1	-.569..
	Sig. (2-tailed)		.000
	N	422	422
negafect negative affect: mpq	Pearson Correlation	-.569..	1
	Sig. (2-tailed)	.000	
	N	422	422

The three entries in order are the Pearson *r*, the probability of the *r* value occurring by chance if the null hypothesis is true, and the sample size used for the computation.

**. Correlation is significant at the 0.01 level (2-tailed).

Focusing on the numerical part of the table, if you drew a diagonal from the upper left to the lower right, the outputs above the diagonal and below the diagonal are the same, that is, there is redundant information in a square correlation matrix.

IBM SPSS outputs a value of 1.00 for the correlation of the variable with itself, and this is a quick way to locate the diagonal of the correlation matrix in larger matrixes. Each other entry provides three pieces of information that may be obvious, but we will identify them anyway:

- The top entry is the Pearson *r* value. Here it is −.569. This is not surprising in that we would expect individuals with higher levels of self-esteem to exhibit lower negative affect (they experience lower levels of negative emotions).
- The second entry is the probability of obtaining that correlation if the null hypothesis was true given the sample size. Evaluated against a .05 alpha level, the correlation is statistically significant. Given that it is statistically significant, we should recognize that the strength of the relationship as indexed by r^2 is approximately .32. Thus, we may say that the two variables share approximately 32% of their variances.
- The third entry is the sample size, which in this analysis was 422. Thus, there were 420 degrees of freedom ($N - 2$) against which the null hypothesis of a correlation of zero was tested.

6B.2 Simple Linear Regression

6B.2.1 Main Regression Dialog Window

For purposes of illustrating simple linear regression, assume we are interested in predicting our self-esteem variable based on negative affect. Selecting **Analyze ➔ Regression ➔ Linear** brings us to the **Linear Regression** main dialog window displayed in Figure 6b.4. From the variables list panel, we click over **esteem** to the **Dependent** panel and **negafect** to the **Independent(s)** panel. The **Method** drop-down menu will be left at its default setting of **Enter**, which requests a standard regression analysis.

Figure 6b.4 Linear Regression Main Dialog Window

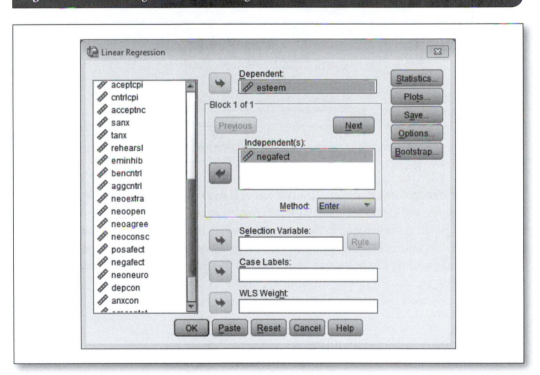

6B.2.2 Statistics Tab

Selecting the **Statistics** pushbutton brings us to the **Linear Regression: Statistics** dialog window shown in Figure 6b.5. By default, **Estimates** in the **Regression Coefficients** panel is checked. This instructs IBM SPSS to print the value of the regression coefficient and related measures. We also checked the following: **Model fit**, which provides *R*-square, adjusted

Figure 6b.5 Linear Regression Statistics Window

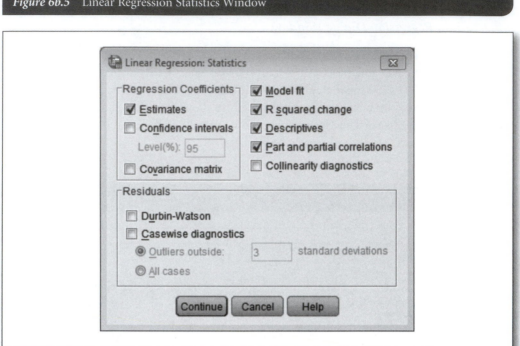

R-square, the standard error, and an ANOVA table; **R squared change**, which is useful when there are multiple predictors that are being entered in stages so you can see where this information is placed in the output; **Descriptives**, which provides the means and standard deviations of the variables as well as the correlation table; and **Part and partial correlations**, which produces the partial and semipartial correlations and convey important information when multiple predictors are used. Clicking **Continue** returns us to the main dialog window, and selecting **OK** produces the analysis.

6B.2.3 Simple Linear Regression Output

We will examine the output of the analysis in the order we suggest that you proceed. Figure 6b.6 contains descriptive information and is identical to the output from the bivariate correlation analysis we described earlier. The upper table contains the means and standard deviations of the variables, and the lower table shows the square correlation matrix.

Figure 6b.7 displays the test of significance of the model using an ANOVA. There are 421 ($N - 1$) total degrees of freedom. With only a single predictor, the **Regression**

Figure 6b.6 Descriptive Statistics Results of the Regression Analysis

Descriptive Statistics

	Mean	Std. Deviation	N
esteem self–esteem: coopersmith	71.2417	20.94656	422
negafect negative affect: mpq	5.7962	3.73418	422

Correlations

		esteem self–esteem: coopersmith	negafect negative affect: mpq
Pearson Correlation	esteem self–esteem: coopersmith	1.000	–.569
	negafect negative affect: mpq	–.569	1.000
Sig. (1–tailed)	esteem self–esteem: coopersmith	.	.000
	negafect negative affect: mpq	.000	.
N	esteem self–esteem: coopersmith	422	422
	negafect negative affect: mpq	422	422

effect has one degree of freedom. If the **Regression** effect is statistically significant (which it is here), it means that prediction of the dependent variable is accomplished better than can be done by chance. If the **Regression** effect is not statistically significant, then there is little point (other than satisfying one's curiosity) in looking at the rest of the results.

Figure 6b.7 Statistical Significance of the Regression Model

ANOVA$_b$

Model		Sum of Squares	df	Mean Square	F	Sig.
1	Regression	59702.816	1	59702.816	200.578	.000$_a$
	Residual	125014.530	420	297.654		
	Total	184717.346	421			

a. Predictors: (Constant), negafect negative affect: mpq

b. Dependent Variable: esteem self–esteem: coopersmith

Figure 6b.8 Model Summary and Coefficients

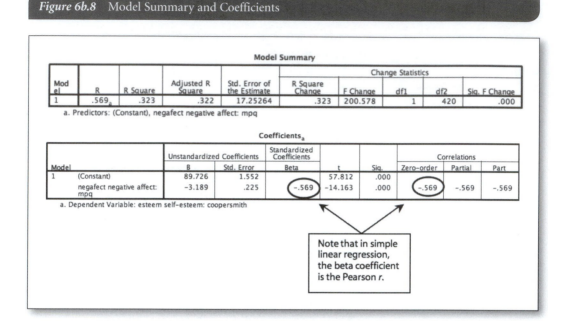

Note that in simple linear regression, the beta coefficient is the Pearson *r*.

Figure 6b.8 presents the results of the analysis. The upper table in Figure 6b.8 labeled **Model Summary** provides an overview of the results. Of primary interest are the **R Square** and **Adjusted R Square** values, which here are .323 and .322, respectively. We learn from these that negative affect explained approximately one third of the variance of self-esteem. The loss of so little strength in computing the **Adjusted R Square** value is primarily due to our relatively large sample size. With only one predictor entered into the model, **R Square Change** went from zero before the model was fitted to the data to .323 when the variable was entered.

The lower table in Figure 6b.8 labeled **Coefficients** provides the details of the results. The *Y* intercept of the raw score model is labeled as the **Constant**, and it has a value here of 89.726. Of primary interest here are the raw (**B**) and standardized (**Beta**) coefficients, which are −3.189 and −.569, respectively. In simple linear regression, the beta value is the Pearson *r*, and so this latter value can be anticipated from the correlation analysis. The *t* statistic tests whether or not the regression coefficient is statistically significant. In the present case, it is statistically significant (not surprising in that we know that the correlation between the two variables is statistically significant), and we conclude that negative affect is a significant predictor of self-esteem.

The raw score regression *b* coefficient indicates the change we predict in the dependent variable for every unit change in the predictor. Thus, for every one-point increase in the inventory score assessing negative affect, we predict 3.189 *fewer* points on the inventory measuring self-esteem. Note that we predict *fewer* points because there is an inverse relationship between negative affect and self-esteem—had the relationship been a direct one, we would have predicted an increase in the criterion variable for a unit increase in the predictor.

In the three **Correlations** columns in the right portion of the table, the **zero-order** correlation is the Pearson correlation; the other two correlations, which take on the same value as the Pearson *r* here, will be discussed in Chapter 7A in the context of multiple linear regression.

Based on the information contained in the lower table of Figure 6b.8, we can write the simple linear regression model fit to this data set:

$$\text{Self-esteem} = 89.726 - 3.189 \,(\text{negative affect})$$

6B.3 Reporting Results

Simple linear regression is not a type of analysis that is found in the research literature because of its simplicity. Nonetheless, we include a sample report of the results for the sake of completeness.

> Negative affect was used to predict self-esteem using ordinary least squares regression. A statistically significant degree of prediction was obtained, $F(1, 421) = 200.578$, $p < .001$, $R^2 = .323$, Adjusted $R^2 = .322$. The standardized regression coefficient was $-.569$, the raw regression coefficient was -3.189 ($SE = 0.225$), and the intercept was 89.726. Negative affect explained approximately one third of the variance of self-esteem.

Multiple Regression: Statistical Methods

7A.1 General Considerations

Multiple regression is a very useful extension of simple linear regression in that we use several quantitative (metric) or dichotomous variables rather than just one such variable to predict a value of a quantitatively measured criterion variable. It has become a very popular technique to employ in the social and behavioral sciences. Most researchers believe that using more than one predictor or potentially explanatory variable can paint a more complete picture of how the world works than is permitted by simple linear regression because constructs in the behavioral sciences are believed to be multiply determined. Using only a single variable as a predictor or explanatory variable will at best capture only one of those sources. In the words of one author (Thompson, 1991), multivariate methods such as multiple regression have accrued greater support in part because they "best honor the reality to which the researcher is purportedly trying to generalize" (p. 80).

Based on what we have already discussed regarding simple linear regression, it may be clear that multiple regression can be used for predictive purposes, such as estimating from a series of entrance tests how successful various job applicants might perform on the job, and this is what is covered in this chapter and in Chapter 7B. These regression procedures are known as statistical regression methods in the very general sense that once the researchers identify the variables to be used as predictors, they relinquish all control of the analysis to the software and the mathematical algorithms programmed in it to carry out the analysis. This is not necessarily a bad thing in that we are trying to maximize the predictive work of our variables.

But the regression technique can also guide researchers toward explicating or explaining the dynamics underlying a particular construct by indicating which variables in combination might be more strongly associated with it. In this sense, the model that emerges from the analysis can serve an explanatory purpose as well as a predictive purpose. In most analyses where researchers have an interest in explanation in addition to prediction, it is common for them to play a more active role in the structuring of the statistical analysis. Regression topics that are often used for this purpose are discussed in Chapters 8A and 8B.

7A.2 A Range of Regression Methods

As was true for simple linear regression, multiple regression generates two variations of the prediction equation, one in raw score form and the other in standardized form. These equations are extensions of the simple linear regression models and thus still represent linear regression, that is, they are still linear equations but use multiple variables as predictors. Because the variables are weighted in the equation (so that they maximize prediction), the set of variables in that weighted combination can be labeled as a *variate*. The main work done in multiple regression is to build the prediction equation. This involves generating the weighting coefficients—the *b* coefficients and the *Y* intercept for the raw score equation and the beta coefficients for the standardized equation.

Several different methods are available to researchers to build the variate or linear function; these can be organized into two subsets or classes. One subset of methods relies exclusively on statistical decision-making criteria built into the software procedures to decide at which point in the process which predictors are to be entered into the equation. These are ordinarily called, as a class, *statistical* methods. The most popular of these statistical methods include the standard, forward, backward, and stepwise methods, although others (not covered here), such as the Mallows Cp method (e.g., Mallows, 1973) and the maxi *R*-squared and mini *R*-squared (see Freund & Littell, 2000), have been developed as well. In using the statistical methods, researchers permit the computer software to autonomously carry out the analyses. The present chapter discusses these statistical methods.

The other subset of methods calls for the researchers to determine which predictors are to be entered into the regression equation at each stage of the analysis or even how the predictors are configured or arranged as a set. Thus, the researchers rather than the software program assume a certain amount of control over the regression procedure. These researcher-based decisions regarding order of entry or configuration of the variables are often derived from the theoretical model of the empirical research literature with which the researchers are working, although it is possible to use these procedures in a more exploratory fashion. Some of these methods are addressed in Chapter 8A.

7A.3 The Variables in a Multiple Regression Analysis

The variables in a multiple regression analysis fall into one of two categories: One is the variable being predicted and the others are the variables used as the basis of prediction. We briefly discuss each in turn.

7A.3.1 The Variable Being Predicted

The variable that is the focus of a multiple regression design is the one being predicted. In the regression equation, as we have already seen for simple linear regression, it is designated as an upper case Y_{pred}. This variable is known as the *criterion variable* or *outcome variable* but is often referred to as the *dependent variable* in the analysis. It needs to have been assessed on one of the quantitative scales of measurement.

7A.3.2 The Variables Used as Predictors

The variables used as predictors comprise a set of measures designated in the regression equation with upper case Xs and are known as the *predictor variables* or the *independent variables* in the analysis. In many research design courses, the term *independent variable* is reserved for a variable in the context of an experimental study, but the term is much more generally applied because ANOVA (used for the purpose of comparing the means of two or more groups or conditions) and multiple regression are just different expressions of the same general linear model (see Section 8A.5). In the underlying statistical analysis, whether regression or ANOVA, the goal is to predict (explain) the variance of the dependent variables based on the independent variables in the study.

Talking about independent and dependent variables can get a bit confusing when the context is not made clear. In one context, predicting the variance of the dependent variable is what the statistical analysis is designed to accomplish, and it does so on the basis of a data set that already exists; such a context is the statistical analysis of the data.

Another context is the research methodology and data collection process itself. In this context, experimental studies are distinguished from regression or correlation studies by the procedures used to acquire the data. Some of the differences in the typical nature of independent variables in experimental and regression studies within this methodology and data collection context are listed in Table 7a.1. For example, in experimental studies, independent variables are often manipulated by the researchers and many times can be called treatment effects, and dependent variables can be some sort of behaviors measured under one or more of the treatment conditions. However, independent variables may also be configured after-the-fact in correlation designs (e.g., we may define different groups of respondents to a survey medical treatment satisfaction based on the class of medication patients were prescribed) rather than be exclusively based on manipulated conditions. In regression designs, it is usual for all of the variables (the variable to be predicted as well as the set of predictor variables) to be measured in a given "state of the system" (e.g., we administer a battery of personality inventories, we ask employees about their attitudes on a range of work satisfaction issues, we extract a set of variables from an existing archival database).

These two contexts map to each other but not necessarily completely, and that is where confusion can arise. For example, when we speak of an experimental design, such as a 2 × 3 between-subjects design, our experimental conditions are configured within the

Table 7a.1 Some Differences in How Independent Variables Are Treated in Experimental and Regression Studies

Independent Variables in Experimental Study	Independent Variables in Regression Study
Often actively manipulated but can also be an enduring (e.g., personality) characteristic of research participants.	Usually an enduring (e.g., personality) characteristic of research participants but could be changeable over time (e.g., attitudes).
Uncorrelated so long as cells in the design have equal sample sizes; as cells contain increasingly unequal sample sizes, the independent variables become more correlated.	All else equal, we would like them to be uncorrelated, but they should be correlated to some extent if that more appropriately reflects the relationships in the population.
Usually nominal (qualitatively measured) variables.	Usually quantitatively measured variables.
Usually coded into a relatively few levels or categories.	Fully continuous if possible but more likely to be discrete with wide range and small steps.

methodological infrastructure to ensure that each group will be exposed to a different combination of the independent variables via some appropriate strategy (e.g., randomized blocks) that is usually not contained in the name of the design. It is also the case that the ANOVA (statistical) procedure that is used to analyze the data is also named a 2×3 between-subjects design. But such isomorphism between contexts is not always the case. In a regression design, all variables are measured over the course of the study without methodologically distinguishing between the variable that is to be the dependent variable and those that are to be the predictors. To minimize the potential for confusion, our discussion will remain in the context of the statistical analysis; should we refer to the methodological context, we will make that explicit.

7A.4 Multiple Regression Research

7A.4.1 Research Problems Suggesting a Regression Approach

If the research problem is expressed in a form that either specifies or implies prediction, multiple regression becomes a viable candidate for the design. Here are some examples of research objectives that imply a regression design:

- We want to predict one variable from a combined knowledge of several others.
- We want to determine which variables of a larger set are better predictors of some criterion variable than others.
- We want to know how much better we can predict a variable if we add one or more predictor variables to the mix.
- We want to examine the relationship of one variable with a set of other variables.
- We want to statistically explain or account for the variance of one variable using a set of other variables.

7A.4.2 The Statistical Goal in a Regression Analysis

The statistical goal of multiple regression is to produce a model in the form of a linear equation that identifies the best weighted linear combination of independent variables in the study to optimally predict the criterion variable. That is, in the regression model—the statistical outcome of the regression analysis—each predictor is assigned a weight. Each predictor for each case is multiplied by that weight to achieve a product, and those products are summed together with the constant in the raw score model. The final sum for a given case is the predicted score on the criterion variable for that case.

The weights for the predictor variables are generated in such a way that, across all of the cases in the analysis, the predicted scores of the cases are as close to their actual scores as is possible. Closeness of prediction is defined in terms of the ordinary least squares solution. This strategy underlying the solution or model describes a line for which *the sum of the squared differences between the predicted and actual values of the criterion variable is minimal.* These differences between the predictions we make with the model and the actual observed values are the prediction errors. The model thus can be thought of as representing the function that minimizes the sum of the squared errors. When we say that the model is fitted to the data to "best" predict the dependent variable, what we technically mean is that the sum of squared errors has been minimized.

Because the model configures the predictors together to maximize prediction accuracy, the specific weight (contribution) assigned to each independent variable in the model is relative to the other independent variables in the analysis. Thus, we can say only that when considering this particular set of variables, this one variable is able to predict the criterion to such and such an extent. In conjunction with a different set of independent variables, the predictive prowess of that variable may turn out to be quite different.

It is possible that variables not included in the research design could have made a substantial difference in the results. Some variables that could potentially be good predictors may have been overlooked in the literature review, measuring others may have demanded too many resources, and still others may not have been amenable to the measurement instrumentation available to researchers at the time of the study. Our working assumption is that the model is *fully specified*, that is, that we have captured all of the important variables that are predictive of our outcome variable; with this assumption in place, we can draw inferences about the phenomenon we are studying from the results of our analysis. To the extent that potentially important variables were omitted from the research, the model is said to be *incompletely specified* and may therefore have less external validity than is desirable.

Because of these concerns, we want to select the variables for inclusion in the analysis based on as much theoretical and empirical rationale as we can bring to bear on the task. It is often a waste of research effort to realize after the fact that a couple of very important candidate predictors were omitted from the study. Their inclusion would have potentially produced a very different dynamic and would likely have resulted in a very different model than we have just obtained.

7A.5 The Regression Equations

Just as was the case for simple linear regression, the multiple regression equation is produced in both raw score and standardized score form. We discuss each in turn.

7A.5.1 The Raw Score Equation

The multiple regression raw score equation or model is an expansion of the raw score equation for simple linear regression and is the embodiment of the *general linear model* that was introduced more than two centuries ago by Adrien Marie Legendre in 1805 (Stigler, 1990). It is as follows:

$$Y_{pred} = a + b_1X_1 + b_2X_2 + \cdots + b_nX_n$$

In this equation, Y_{pred} is the predicted score on the criterion variable, the Xs are the predictor variables in the equation, and the bs are the weights or coefficients associated with the predictors. These b weights are also referred to as *partial regression coefficients* (Kachigan, 1986) because each reflects the relative contribution of its independent variable when we are statistically controlling for the effects of all the other predictors. Each b weight informs us of how many units (and in what direction) the predicted Y value will increment for a one-unit change in the corresponding X variable (we will show this by example in a moment), statistically controlling for the other predictors in the model. Because this is a raw score equation, it also contains a constant, shown as a in the equation (representing the Y intercept).

All the variables are in raw score form in the model even though the metrics on which they are measured could vary widely. If we were predicting early success in a graduate program, for example, one predictor may very well be average GRE-Revised test performance (the mean of the verbal and quantitative subscores), and the scores on this variable are probably going to be in the 150 to 165 range. Another variable may be grade point average, and this variable will have values someplace in the middle to high 3s on a 4-point grading scale. We will say that success is evaluated at the end of the first year of the program and is measured on a scale ranging from the low 50 to 75 (just to give us three rather different metrics for our illustration here).

The b weights computed for the regression model are going to reflect the raw score values we have for each variable (the criterion and the predictor variables). Assume that the results of this hypothetical study show the b coefficient for grade point average to be 7.00 and for GRE to be about .50 with a Y intercept value of −40.50. Thus, controlling for the effects of GRE, a one-unit change in grade point average (e.g., the difference between 3.0 and 4.0) is associated with a 7-point increase (because of the positive sign in the model) in the predicted success criterion variable. Likewise, controlling for the effects of grade point average, a one-unit change in GRE score is associated with a 0.50-point increase in the predicted success criterion variable. Putting these values into the equation would give us the following prediction model:

$$Y_{pred} = -40.50 + (7)(gpa) + (.5)(GRE)$$

Suppose that we wished to predict the success score of one participant, Erin, based on her grade point average of 3.80 and her GRE score of 160. To arrive at her predicted score, we place her values into the variable slots in the raw score form of the regression equation. Here is the prediction:

$$Y_{pred} = -40.50 + (7)(gpa) + (.5)(GRE)$$

$$Y_{pred\ Erin} = -40.50 + (7)(gpa_{Erin}) + (.5)(GRE_{Erin})$$

$$Y_{pred\ Erin} = -40.5 + (7)(3.80) + (.5)(160)$$

$$Y_{pred\ Erin} = -40.50 + (26.6) + (80)$$

$$Y_{pred\ Erin} = 66.10$$

We therefore predict that Erin, based on her grade point average and GRE score, will score a little more than 66 on the success measure. Given that the range on the success measure is from 50 to 75, it would appear, at least on the surface, that Erin would be predicted to have performed moderately successfully. We would hope that this level of predicted performance would be viewed in a favorable light by the program to which she was applying.

This computation allows you to see, to some extent, how the *b* weights and the constant came to achieve their respective magnitudes. We expect a success score between 50 and 75. One predictor is grade point average, and we might expect it to be someplace in the middle 3s. We are therefore likely to have a partial regression weight much larger than 1.00 to get near the range of success scores. But the GRE scores are probably going to be in the neighborhood of 150 plus or minus, and these may need to be lowered to get near the success score range by generating a partial regression weight likely to be less than 1.00. When the dust settles, the weights overshoot the range of success scores, requiring the constant to be subtracted from their combination.

Because the variables are assessed on different metrics, it follows that you cannot see from the *b* weights which independent variable is the stronger predictor in this model. Some of the ways by which you can evaluate the relative contribution of the predictors to the model will be discussed shortly.

7A.5.2 The Standardized Equation

The multiple regression standardized score equation or model is an expansion of the standardized score equation for simple linear regression. It is as follows:

$$Y_{z\,pred} = \beta_1 X_{z1} + \beta_2 X_{z2} + \cdots + \beta_n X_{zn}$$

Everything in this model is in standardized (*z*) score form. Unlike the situation for the raw score equation, all the variables are now measured on the same metric—the mean and standard deviation for all the variables (the criterion and the predictor variables) are 0 and 1, respectively.

In the standardized equation, $Y_{z\,pred}$ is the predicted *z* score of the criterion variable. Each predictor variable (each *X* in the equation) is associated with its own weighting coefficient symbolized by the lowercase Greek letter β and called a *beta weight*, *standardized regression coefficient*, or *beta coefficient*, and just as was true for the *b* weights in the raw score equation, they are also referred to as *partial regression coefficients*. These coefficients usually compute to a decimal value between 0 and 1, but they can exceed the range of ±1 if the predictors are correlated enough between themselves (an undesirable state of affairs that should be avoided either by removing all but one of the highly intercorrelated predictors or by combining them into a single composite variable).

Each term in the equation represents the *z* score of a predictor and its associated beta coefficient. With the equation in standardized form, the *Y* intercept is zero and is therefore not shown.

We can now revisit the example used above where we predicted success in graduate school based on grade point average and GRE score. Here is that final model, but this time in standard score form:

$$Y_{z\,pred} = b_1 X_{z1} + b_2 X_{z2} \cdots + \beta_n X_{zn}$$

$$Y_{z\,pred} = (.31)(gpa_z) + (.62)(GRE_z)$$

We can also apply this standardized regression model to individuals in the sample—for example, Erin. Within the sample used for this study, assume that Erin's grade point average of 3.80 represents a z score of 1.80 and that her GRE score of 160 represents a z score of 1.25 (at the time we are writing, the standard deviation of the GRE-scaled scores was yet to be determined). We can thus solve the equation as follows:

$$Y_{z\,pred} = b_1 X_{z1} + b_2 X_{z2} + \ldots + b_n X_{zn}$$

$$Y_{z\,pred} = (.31)(gpa_z) + (.62)(GRE_z)$$

$$Y_{z\,pred\,Erin} = (.31)(gpa_{z\,Erin}) + (.62)(GRE_{z\,Erin})$$

$$Y_{z\,pred\,Erin} = (.31)(1.80) + (.62)(1.25)$$

$$Y_{z\,pred\,Erin} = (.558) + (.775)$$

$$Y_{z\,pred\,Erin} = 1.33$$

We therefore predict that Erin, based on her grade point average and GRE score, will score about 1.33 SD units above the mean on the success measure. Given that the range on the success measure is from 50 to 75, it would appear, at least on the surface, that Erin would be predicted to have performed moderately successfully and would hopefully be positively evaluated at this stage in her application process.

7A.6 The Variate in Multiple Regression

Multivariate procedures typically involve building, developing, or solving for a weighted linear combination of variables. This weighted linear combination is called a *variate*. The variate in this instance is the entity on the right side of the multiple regression equation composed of the weighted independent (predictor) variables.

Although the variate is a weighted linear composite of the measured variables in the model, it is often possible to view this variate holistically as representing some underlying dimension or construct—that is, to conceive of it as a *latent variable*. In the preceding example where we were predicting success in graduate school, the variate might be interpreted as "academic aptitude" indexed by the weighted linear combination of grade point average and GRE score. From this perspective, the indicators of academic aptitude—grade point average and GRE score—were selected by the researchers to be used in the study. They then used the regression technique to shape the most effective academic aptitude variate to predict success in graduate school.

Based on the previous example, the academic aptitude variate is built to do the best job possible to predict a value on a variable. That variable is the predicted success score. Note that the result of applying the multiple regression model—the result of invoking the linear weighted composite of the predictor variables (the variate)—is the predicted success score and not the actual success score. For most of the cases in the data file, the predicted and the actual success scores of the students will be different. The model minimizes these differences, but it cannot eliminate them. Thus, the variable "predicted success score" and the variable "actual success score" are different variables, although we certainly hope that they are reasonably related to each other. The variate that we have called academic aptitude generates the predicted rather than the actual value of the success score (we will see in Section 18A.4 that the structural equation used in structural equation modeling predicts the actual *Y* value because the prediction error is included as a term in the model).

7A.7 The Standard (Simultaneous) Regression Method

The *standard regression method*, also called the *simultaneous* or the *direct method*, is what most authors refer to if they leave the regression method unspecified. It is currently the most widely used of the statistical methods. Under this method, all the predictors are entered into the equation in a single "step" (stage in the analysis). The standard method provides a full model solution in that all the predictors are part of it.

The idea that these variables are entered into the equation simultaneously is true only in the sense that the variables are entered in a single statistical step or block. But that single step is not at all simple and unitary; when we look inside this step, we find that the process of determining the weights for independent variables is governed by a coherent but complex strategy.

7A.7.1 The Example to Be Used

Rather than referring to abstract predictors and some amorphous dependent variable to broach this topic, we will present the standard regression method by using an example with variables that have names and meaning. To keep our drawings and explication manageable, we will work with a smaller set of variables than would ordinarily be used in a study conceived from the beginning as a regression design. Whereas an actual regression design might typically have from half a dozen to as many a dozen or more variables as potential predictors, we will use a simplified example of just three predictors for our presentation purposes.

The dependent variable we use for this illustration is self-esteem as assessed by Coopersmith's (1981) Self-Esteem Inventory. Two of the predictors we use for this illustration are Tellegen's (1982) measures of the number of positive and negative affective behaviors a person ordinarily exhibits. The third independent variable represents scores on the Openness scale of the NEO (Neuroticism–Extroversion–Openness) Five-Factor Personality Inventory (Costa & McCrae, 1992). Openness generally assesses the degree to which respondents appear to have greater aesthetic sensitivity, seek out new experiences, and are aware of their internal states.

7A.7.2 Correlations of the Variables

It is always desirable to initially examine the correlation matrix of the variables participating in a regression analysis. This gives researchers an opportunity to examine the interrelationships of the variables, not only between the dependent variable and the independent variables but also between the independent variables themselves.

In examining the correlation matrix, we are looking for two features primarily. First, we want to make sure that no predictor is so highly correlated with the dependent variable as to be relatively interchangeable with it; correlations of about .70 and higher would suggest that such a predictor might best be entered in the first block of a hierarchical analysis (see Section 8A.2) rather than proceed with the standard regression analysis that we cover here. Second, we want to make sure that no two predictors are so highly correlated that they are assessing the same underlying construct; again, correlations of about .70 and higher would suggest that we might want to either remove one of the two or combine them into a single composite variable before performing a standard regression analysis.

Table 7a.2 displays the correlation matrix of the variables in our example. We have presented it in "square" form where the diagonal from upper left to lower right (containing the value 1.000 for each entry) separates the matrix into two redundant halves. As can be seen, the dependent variable of self-esteem is moderately correlated with both Positive Affect and Negative Affect but is only modestly correlated with Openness. It can also be seen that Positive Affect and Negative Affect correlate more strongly with each other than either does with Openness.

7A.7.3 Building the Regression Equation

The goal of any regression procedure is to predict or account for the variance of the criterion variable. In this example, that variable is Self-Esteem. At the beginning of the

Table 7a.2 Correlation Matrix of the Variables in the Regression Analysis

	Self-Esteem	**Positive Affect**	**Negative Affect**	**Openness**
Self-Esteem	1.000	.555	−.572	.221
Positive Affect	.555	1.000	−.324	.221
Negative Affect	−.572	−.324	1.000	−.168
Openness	.221	.221	−.168	1.000

process, before the predictors are entered into the equation, 100% of the variance of Self-Esteem is unaccounted for. This is shown in Figure 7a.1. The dependent variable of self-esteem is in place, and the predictors are ready to be evaluated by the regression procedure.

On the first and only step of the standard regression procedure, all the predictors are entered as a set into the equation. But to compute the weighting coefficients (*b* coefficients for the raw score equation and beta coefficients for the standardized equation), the predictors must be individually evaluated. To determine the weights, which represent the contribution of each predictor given all of the other predictors in the set, and this is the essence of standard regression, *each predictor's weight is computed as though it had entered the equation last.*

The purpose of treating each predictor as if it was the last to enter the model is to determine what predictive work it can do over and above the prediction attributable to the rest of

Figure 7a.1 Predictors Assembled Prior to the Regression Analysis

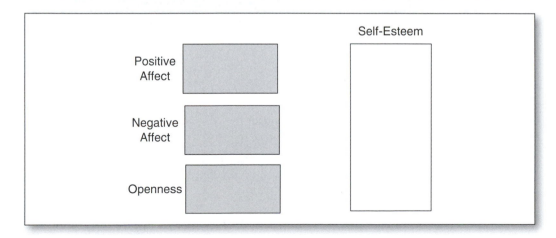

the predictors. In this manner, standard regression focuses on the unique contribution that each independent variable makes to the prediction when *statistically controlling* for all the other predictors. These other predictors thus behave as a set of *covariates* in the analysis in that the predictive work that they do as a set is allowed to account for the variance of the dependent variable before the predictive work of a given predictor is evaluated. Because these other predictors are afforded the opportunity to perform their predictive work before the given predictor, we say that we have statistically controlled for these other predictors. Each predictor is evaluated in turn in this manner, so that the regression coefficient obtained for any predictor represents the situation in which all of the other predictors have been statistically controlled.

This process is illustrated in Figure 7a.2. To evaluate the effectiveness of Positive Affect, the variables of Negative Affect and Openness are inserted as a set into the model. These two variables act as covariates (we are statistically controlling for them) in determining the weight that Positive Affect will receive in the regression model. Together, Negative Affect and Openness have accounted for some of the variance of Self-Esteem (shown as diagonal lines in Figure 7a.2).

With these two other variables in the equation for the moment, we are ready to evaluate the contribution of Positive Affect. The criterion variable or dependent variable (Self-Esteem here) is the focus of the multiple regression design. It is therefore the variance of Self-Esteem that we want to account for or predict, and our goal is to explain as much of it as possible with our set of independent variables. We face an interesting but subtle feature of multiple regression in its efforts to maximize the amount of dependent variable variance that we can explain. In the context of multiple regression, our predictors must account for separate portions—rather than the same portion—of the dependent variable's variance. This is the key to understanding the regression process. With

Figure 7a.2   Evaluating the Predictive Power of Positive Affect

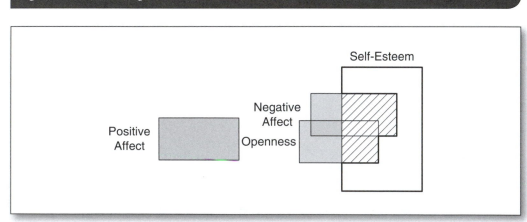

Negative Affect and Openness already in the model, and thus already accounting for some of the variance of Self-Esteem, Positive Affect, as the last variable to enter, must target the variance in Self-Esteem that remains—the *residual* variance of Self-Esteem. The unaccounted for (residual) portion of the variance of Self-Esteem is shown by the blank portion of its rectangle in Figure 7a.2.

After the computations of the *b* and beta coefficients for Positive Affect have been made, it is necessary to evaluate another one of the predictors. Thus, Positive Affect and another predictor (e.g., Negative Affect) are entered into the equation, and the strategy we have just outlined is repeated for the remaining predictor (e.g., Openness). Each independent variable is put through this same process until the weights for all have been determined. At the end of this complex process, the final weights are locked in and the results of the analysis are printed.

7A.8 Partial Correlation

Most statistical software packages, such as IBM SPSS, routinely compute and have available for output other statistical information in addition to the regression weights and the constant. One such statistic is the *partial correlation*. In the context of our present discussion, this is a good place to broach that subject.

As the term implies, a partial correlation is a correlation coefficient. Everything that we have described about correlation coefficients (e.g., the Pearson *r*) applies equally to the particular coefficient known as a partial correlation. But as the term also implies, a partial correlation is special. When you think of the Pearson *r*, you envision an index that captures the extent to which a linear relationship is observed between one variable and another variable. A partial correlation describes the linear relationship between one variable and a part of another variable. Specifically, *a partial correlation is the relationship between a given predictor and the residual variance of the dependent variable* when the rest of the predictors have been entered into the model. We discuss this in somewhat more detail in Section 7A.10.2.

Consider the situation depicted in Figure 7a.2. Negative Affect and Openness have been entered into the model (for the moment) so that we can evaluate the effectiveness of Positive Affect. The variance of Self-Esteem accounted for by Negative Affect and Openness is shown by diagonal lines, and the residual variance of Self-Esteem is shown by the remaining blank area. The partial correlation is the correlation between Positive Affect and the residual variance of Self-Esteem when the effects of Negative Affect and Openness have been statistically removed, controlled, or "partialled out." Such a correlation is called a *partial correlation*. A partial correlation describes the linear relationship between two variables when the effects of other variables have been statistically removed from one of them. In this sense, the variables already in the model are conceived of as *covariates* in that their effects are statistically accounted for prior to evaluating the relationship of Positive Affect and Self-Esteem. Once the regression procedure has determined how much Positive Affect can contribute to the set of predictors already in the model (how much of the residual variance of Self-Esteem it can explain), the software starts the process of computing the weight that Positive Affect will receive in the model.

7A.9 The Squared Multiple Correlation

Assume that each of the three predictors has been evaluated in a single but obviously complex step or block, so that we know their weights and can construct the model. We will discuss the specific numerical results shortly, but first we need to cover three additional and important concepts and their associated statistical indexes: the squared multiple correlation, the squared semipartial correlations, and the structure coefficients.

The first of these is the squared multiple correlation, symbolized by R^2 and illustrated in Figure 7a.3. All three predictors are now in the model, and based on our discussion in the last two sections, it likely makes sense to you that all three variables in combination are accounting for the amount of Self-Esteem variance depicted by the entire filled area in Figure 7a.3.

You are already familiar with the idea that the degree of correlation between two variables can be pictured as overlapping figures (we have used squares to conform to pictorial style of path analysis and structural equation modeling that we cover in the later chapters, but introductory statistics and research methods texts tend to use circles). For the case of the Pearson r (or any bivariate correlation), the shaded or overlapping area would show the strength of the correlation, and its magnitude would be indexed by r^2.

Figure 7a.3 All Three Predictors Are Now in the Model

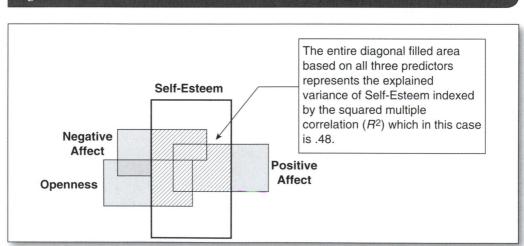

The entire diagonal filled area based on all three predictors represents the explained variance of Self-Esteem indexed by the squared multiple correlation (R^2) which in this case is .48.

The relationship shown in Figure 7a.3 is more complex than what is represented by r^2, but it is conceptually similar. Three variables are drawn as overlapping with Self-Esteem. Nonetheless, this still represents a correlation, albeit one more complex than a bivariate correlation. Specifically, we are looking at the relationship between the criterion (Self-Esteem) on the one hand and the three predictors (Positive Affect, Negative Affect, and Openness) on the other hand. When we have three or more variables involved in the relationship (there are four here), we can no longer use the Pearson correlation coefficient to quantify the magnitude of that linear relationship—the Pearson r can index the degree of relationship only when two variables are being considered. The correlation coefficient we need to call on to quantify the degree of a more complex relationship is known as the *multiple correlation*. It is symbolized as an uppercase italic R. That said, the Pearson r is really the limiting case of R, and thus the bulk of what we have said about r applies to R.

A multiple correlation coefficient indexes the degree of linear association of one variable with a set of other variables, and the *squared multiple correlation* (R^2), sometimes called the *coefficient of multiple determination,* tells us the strength of this complex relationship. In Figure 7a.3, the diagonally shaded area—the overlap of Positive Affect, Negative Affect, and Openness with Self-Esteem—represents the R^2 for that relationship. This R^2 value can be thought of in a way analogous to r^2; that is, it can be thought of in terms of explained or accounted-for variance of the dependent variable. In this case, we are explaining the variance of Self-Esteem. The R^2 value represents one way to evaluate the model. Larger values mean that the model has accounted for greater amounts of the variance of the dependent variable.

The second feature important to note in Figure 7a.3 is that the three predictors overlap with each other, indicating that they correlate with one another (as we documented in Table 7a.2). The degree to which they correlate affects the beta weights these variables are assigned in the regression equation, so the correlations of the predictors become a matter of some interest to researchers using a regression design.

7A.10 The Squared Semipartial Correlation

7A.10.1 The Squared Semipartial Correlation Itself

We have redrawn with a bit of a variation in Figure 7a.4 the relationship between the three predictors and the dependent variable previously shown in Figure 7a.3. In Figure 7a.4, we have distinguished the variance of Self-Esteem that is uniquely associated with only a single predictor by using a solid fill and have retained the diagonal area to represent variance that overlaps between two or all of the predictors. The amount of variance explained uniquely by a predictor is indexed by another correlation statistic known as the *squared semipartial correlation*, often symbolized as sr^2. It represents the extent to which variables do independent predictive work when combined with the other predictors in

Figure 7a.4 A Depiction of the Squared Semipartial Correlations

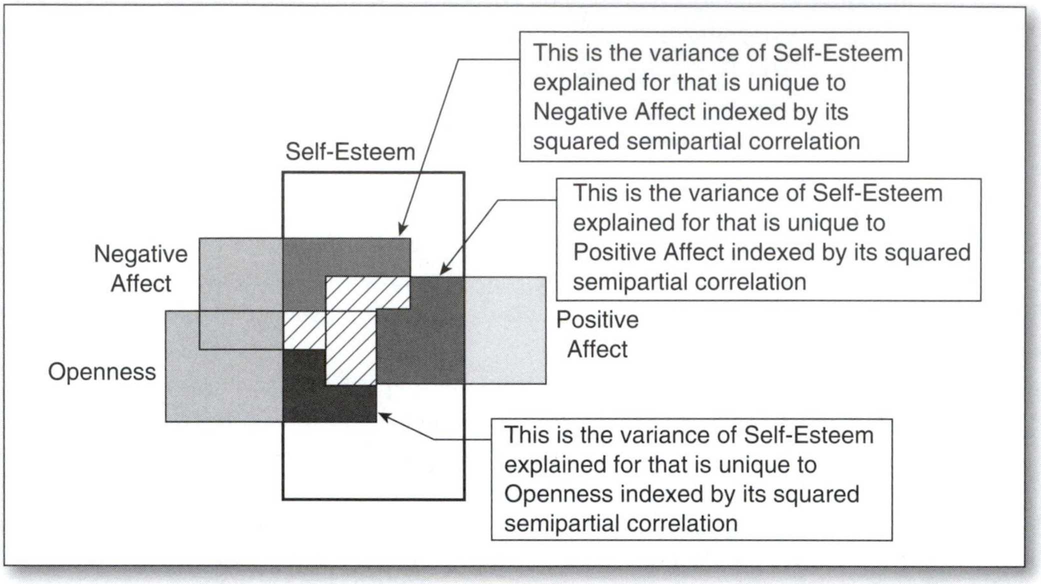

Note. The solid fill represents self-esteem variance accounted for that is unique to each predictor; the diagonal fill represents self-esteem variance accounted for common to two or more predictors.

the model. Each predictor is associated with its own squared semipartial correlation. The semipartial correlation describes the linear relationship between a given predictor and the variance of the dependent variable.

7A.10.2 The Difference Between the Squared Semipartial Correlation and the Squared Partial Correlation

Distinguishing between the squared semipartial and squared partial correlations is subtle but very important because these represent descriptions of two similar but different relationships between each predictor and the dependent variable. To simplify our discussion, we have drawn in Figure 7a.5 only two generic predictor (independent) variables (IV_1 and IV_2) for a given generic dependent variable.

In Figure 7a.5, the labels of lowercase letters identify different areas of the variance of the predictor and dependent variables so that we may contrast the squared semipartial correlation coefficient with the squared partial correlation coefficient. These different variance areas are as follows:

- Area **a** is the variance of the dependent variable that is explained but cannot be attributed uniquely to either predictor.
- Area **b** is the variance of the dependent variable that is explained uniquely by IV_1.
- Area **d** is the variance of the dependent variable that is explained uniquely by IV_2.
- Area **c** is the variance of IV_1 that is not related to the dependent variable.
- Area **e** is the variance of IV_2 that is not related to the dependent variable.
- Area **f** (the blank area of the dependent variable labeled twice in the figure) is the variance of the dependent variable that is not explained by either predictor (it is the residual variance of the dependent variable once the model with two predictors has been finalized).

Consider Area **b** in Figure 7a.5, although an analogous analysis can be made for Area **d**. This is the variance of the dependent variable that is explained only by IV_1. Because we are dealing with squared correlations that are interpreted as a percent of variance explained, we must compute a proportion or percent, that is, we must compute the value

Figure 7a.5 Contrasting the Squared Semipartial and Squared Semipartial Correlations for IV_1

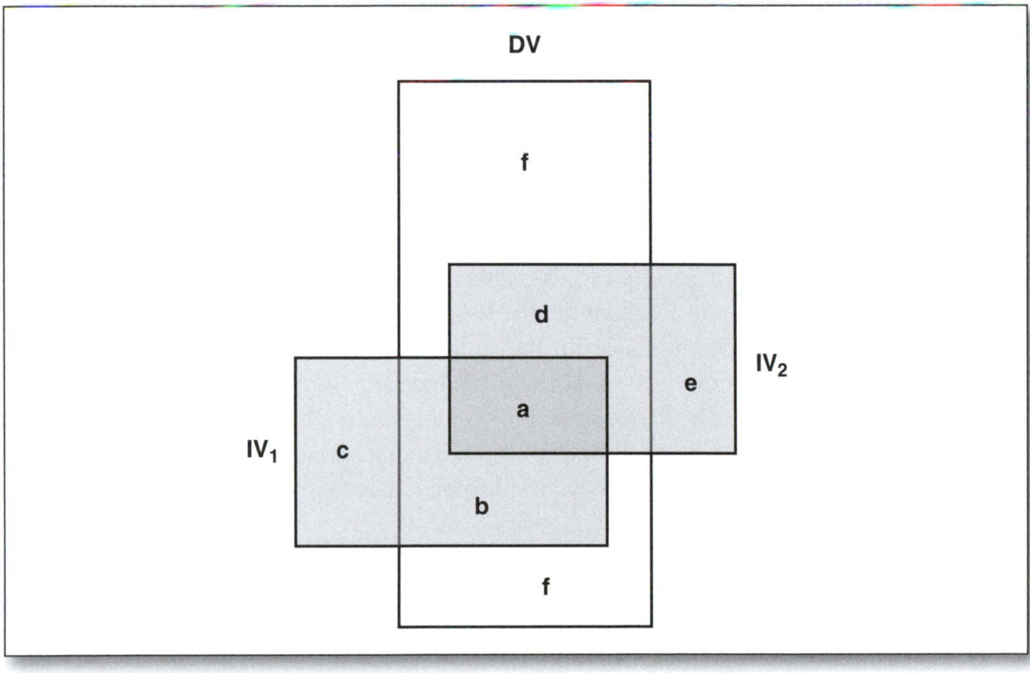

Note. The squared semipartial correlation is computed as **b**/(**a** + **b** + **d** + **f**) and the squared partial correlation is computed as **b**/(**b** + **f**). IV = independent variable; DV = dependent variable.

of a ratio between two variances. Area **b** is the conceptual focus of both the squared semipartial correlation as well as the squared partial correlation for IV_1; because it is the focus of the proportion we calculate, it must be placed in the numerator in the computation for both the squared semipartial correlation and the squared partial correlation. Stated in words, both the squared semipartial correlation and the squared partial correlation associated with IV_1 each describe the percentage of variance attributable to the unique contribution of IV_1.

The difference between the two indexes is what representation of the variance is placed in the denominator of the ratio. The denominator of a ratio provides the frame of reference. In the present situation, we wish to know the percentage of variance attributable to the unique contribution of IV_1 with respect to one of two frames of reference:

- The frame of reference used in computing the squared semipartial correlation is the total variance of the dependent variable. In Figure 7a.5, the denominator would be **a + b + d + f**. Thus, the computation of the squared semipartial correlation for IV_1 is **b/(a + b + d + f)**. What we obtain is the percent of variance of the dependent variable that is associated with the unique contribution of IV_1.
- The frame of reference used in computing the squared partial correlation between the predictor and the dependent variable is only that portion of the variance of the dependent variable remaining when the effects of the other predictors have been removed (statistically removed, nullified). In Figure 7a.5, the denominator would be **b + f**. Thus, the computation of the squared partial correlation for IV_1 is **b/(b + f)**. What we obtain is the percent of variance of the dependent variable not predicted by the other predictor(s) that is associated with the unique contribution of IV_1.

Given that the frame of reference for the squared partial correlation contains only Areas **b** and **f** whereas the frame of reference for the squared semipartial correlation contains Areas **b**, **f**, **a**, and **d**, it follows that the denominator for the squared semipartial correlation will always be larger than the denominator for the squared partial correlation (unless the other areas have a zero value). Because (in pictorial terms) we are asking about the relative size of Area **b** in for both squared correlations, the upshot of this straightforward arithmetic is that the squared partial correlation will almost always have a larger value than the squared semipartial correlation. This explanation may be summarized as follows:

- The squared semipartial correlation represents the proportion of variance of the dependent variable uniquely explained by an independent variable when the other predictors are taken into consideration.
- The squared partial correlation is the amount of explained variance of the dependent variable that is incremented by including an independent variable in the model that already contains the other predictors.

When the regression model is finally in place, as it is in Figure 7a.5, our interest in the squared partial correlation fades because it was more useful in constructing the model, and our interest shifts to the squared semipartial correlation. Thus, when examining Figure 7a.5 or the numerical results of the regression analysis, what interests us is the variance of the dependent variable that is uniquely explained by each predictor, that is, we are interested in the squared semipartial correlation associated with each predictor (in Figure 7a.5, that would be Areas **b** and **d** with respect to the total variance of the dependent variable).

7A.10.3 The Squared Semipartial Correlation and the Squared Multiple Correlation

In Figure 7a.5, the squared multiple correlation (R^2) can be visualized as the proportion of the total variance of the dependent variable covered by Areas **a**, **b**, and **d**. That is, the squared multiple correlation takes into account not only the unique contributions of the predictors (Areas **b** and **d**) but also the overlap between them (Area **a**). The squared semipartial correlations focus only on the unique contributions of the predictors (Areas **b** and **d**).

Note that the sum of Area **b** (the variance of the dependent variable uniquely explained by IV$_1$) and Area **d** (the variance of the dependent variable uniquely explained by IV$_2$) does not cover all of the shaded area (it does not take into account Area **a**). Translated into statistical terms, the sum of the squared semipartial correlations—the total amount of variance uniquely associated with individual predictors—does not equal the squared multiple correlation. The reason for this is that the predictor variables are themselves correlated and to that extent will overlap with each other in the prediction of the dependent variable that they are attempting to predict.

Generally, we can tell how well the model fits the data by considering the value of the squared multiple correlation. But we can also evaluate how well the model works on an individual predictor level by examining the squared semipartial correlations (Tabachnick & Fidell, 2007). With the squared semipartial correlations, we are looking directly at the unique contribution of each predictor within the context of the model, and, clearly, independent variables with larger squared semipartial correlations are making a larger unique contribution.

There are some limitations in using squared semipartial correlations to compare the contributions of the predictors. The unique contribution of each variable in multiple regression is very much a function of the correlations of the variables used in the analysis. It is quite likely that within the context of a different set of predictors, the unique contributions of these variables would change, perhaps substantially. Of course, this argument is true for the beta coefficients as well.

Based on this line of reasoning, one could put forward the argument that it would therefore be extremely desirable to select predictors in a multiple regression design that are not at all correlated between themselves but are highly correlated with the criterion variable. In such a fantasy scenario, the predictors would account for different portions of the dependent variable's variance, the squared semipartial correlations would themselves be substantial, the overlap of the predictors would be minimal, and the sum of the squared semipartial correlations would approximate the value of the squared multiple correlation.

This argument may have a certain appeal at first glance, but it is not a viable strategy for both practical and theoretical reasons. On the practical side, it would be difficult or perhaps even impossible to find predictors in most research arenas that are related to the criterion variable but at the same time are not themselves at least moderately correlated. On the theoretical side, it is desirable that the correlations between the predictors in a research study are representative of those relationships in the population. All else equal, to the extent that variables are related in the study as they are in the outside world, the research results may be said to have a certain degree of external validity.

The consequence of moderate or greater correlation between the predictors is that the unique contribution of each independent variable may be relatively small in comparison with the total amount of explained variance of the prediction model because the predictors in such cases may overlap considerably with each other. Comparing one very small semipartial value with another even smaller semipartial value is often not a productive use of a researcher's time and runs the risk of yielding distorted or inaccurate conclusions.

7A.11 Structure Coefficients

In our discussion of the variate, we emphasized that there was a difference between the predicted value and the actual score that individuals obtained on the dependent variable. Our focus here is on the predicted score, which is the value of the variate for the particular values of the independent variables substituted in the model. The *structure coefficient* is the bivariate correlation between a particular independent variable and the predicted (not the actual) score (Dunlap & Landis, 1998). Each predictor is associated with its own structure coefficient.

A structure coefficient represents the correlation between one of the variables that is a part of the variate and the weighted linear combination itself. Stronger correlations indicate that the predictor is a stronger reflection (indicator, gauge, marker) of the construct underlying the variate. Because the variate is a latent variable, a structure coefficient can index how well the variable can serve as an indicator or marker of the construct represented by the variate. This feature of structure coefficients makes them extremely useful in multivariate analyses, and we will make considerable use of them in the context of discriminant function analysis (Chapters 11A and 11B), principal components and factor analysis (Chapters 12A and 12B), and canonical correlation analysis (Chapters 13A and 13B).

The numerical value of the structure coefficient is not contained in the output of IBM SPSS but is easy to compute with a hand calculator using the following information available in the output:

$$\text{Structure coefficient} = \frac{r_{xi\,y}}{R}$$

where $r_{xi\,y}$ is the Pearson correlation between the given predictor (x_i) and the actual (measured) dependent variable, and R is the multiple correlation.

7A.12 Statistical Summary of the Regression Solution

There are two levels of the statistical summary of the regression solution, a characterization of the effectiveness of the overall model and an assessment of the performance of the individual predictors. Examining the results for the overall model takes precedence over dealing with the individual predictors—if the overall model cannot predict better than chance, then there is little point in evaluating how each of the predictors fared.

We have performed the analysis for the regression design that we have been discussing, and the results of that analysis are summarized in Table 7a.3. For each predictor, we show its raw (b) and standardized (beta) regression weighting coefficients, the t value associated with each regression weight, the Pearson correlation (r) of each predictor with the dependent variable, the amount of Self-Esteem variance each predictor has uniquely explained (squared semipartial correlation), and the structure coefficient associated with each predictor. We will discuss each statistic in Section 7A.14. The constant is the Y intercept of the raw score model and is shown in the last line of the table, and the R^2 and the adjusted R^2 values are shown in the table note.

Table 7a.3 Summary of the Example for Multiple Regression

Variables in Model	b	Beta	t	r	Squared Semipartial Correlation	Structure Coefficient
Positive Affect	2.89	.40	10.61*	.55	.14	.80
Negative Affect	−2.42	−.43	−11.50*	−.57	.16	−.82
Openness	0.11	.06	1.64	.22	.00	.32
Constant (Y intercept)	56.66					

Note. Dependent variable is Self-Esteem. $R^2 = .48$, Adjusted $R^2 = .48$.
*$p < .05$.

7A.13 Evaluating the Overall Model

The overall model is represented by the regression equation. The partial regression coefficients are the weights associated with the predictors and are used (in combination with the constant in the raw score variant of the equation) to predict the value of the dependent variable. There are two questions that we address in evaluating the overall model, one involving a somewhat more complex answer than the other:

- Is the model statistically significant?
- How much variance is explained by the model?

7A.13.1 Is the Model Statistically Significant?

The simpler of the two questions to answer concerns the statistical significance of the model. The issue is whether the predictors as a set can account for a statistically significant amount of the variance of the dependent variable. This question is evaluated by using an ANOVA akin to a one-way between-subjects design, with the single "effect" in the ANOVA procedure as the regression model itself. The degrees of freedom associated with the total variance and its partitions are as follows:

- The degrees of freedom for the total variance are equal to $N-1$ where N is the sample size.
- The degrees of freedom for the regression model (the effect) is equal to v (standing for predictor *variables*), the number of predictor variables in the model.
- The degrees of freedom for the error term is equal to $(N-1) - v$; that is, it is equal to the total degrees of freedom minus the number of predictors in the model.

The null hypothesis tested by the F ratio resulting from the ANOVA is that prediction is no better than chance, that is, that the predictor set cannot account for any of the variance of the dependent variable (i.e., $R^2 = 0$). If the F ratio from the ANOVA is statistically significant, then it can be concluded that the model as a whole accounts for a statistically significant percentage of the variance of the dependent variable (i.e., $R^2 > 0$). In our example analysis, the effect of the regression model was statistically significant, $F(3, 416) = 129.32$, $p < .05$, $R^2 = .48$, adjusted $R^2 = .48$. We would therefore conclude that the three independent variables of Positive Affect, Negative Affect, and Openness in combination significantly predicted Self-Esteem.

7A.13.2 How Much Variance Is Explained by the Model?

7A.13.2.1 Variance Explained: The Straightforward Portion of the Answer

The more complex of the two questions to answer (because the straightforward answer is only a part of the story) concerns how much variance of the dependent variable is explained by the model. We can answer this question at one level in a straightforward manner for the moment by examining the value of R^2. In our example, the value for R^2, shown in the table note below Table 7a.3, was .48 when rounded to two decimal places. The straightforward answer to the question, then, is that the three predictors in this particular weighted linear combination were able to explain about 48% of the variance of Self-Esteem.

We should also consider the magnitude of the obtained R^2. One would ordinarily think of .48 as reasonably substantial, and most researchers should not be terribly disappointed with R^2s considerably less than this. In the early stages of a research project or when studying a variable that may be complexly determined (e.g., rate of spread of an epidemic, recovery from a certain disease, multicultural sensitivity), very small but statistically significant R^2s may be cause for celebration by a research team. Just as we suggested in Sections 2.8.2 and 4A.4.2, for eta square, in the absence of any context R^2 values, .10, .25, and .40 might be considered to be small, medium, and large, respectively (Cohen, 1988); however, we conduct our research within a context, and so the magnitude of the effect must be considered with respect to the theoretical and empirical milieu within which the research was originally framed.

7A.13.2.2 Variance Explained: R^2 Is Somewhat Inflated

At another level, the answer to question of how much variance is explained by the regression model has a more complex aspect to it. The reason it is more complex is that the obtained R^2 value is actually somewhat inflated. Two major factors drive this inflation:

- The inevitable presence of error variance
- The number of predictors in the model relative to the sample size

We can identify two very general and not mutually incompatible strategies that can be implemented (Darlington, 1960; Yin & Fan, 2001) to estimate the amount of R^2 inflation (as we will see in a moment, the ordinary terminology focuses on R^2 *shrinkage*, the other side of the R^2 inflation coin); one set of strategies is empirical and is focused on error variance; another set of strategies is analytic and is focused on the number of predictors with respect to sample size.

7A.13.2.3 Variance Explained: Empirical Strategies for Estimating the Amount of R^2 Shrinkage

Because it is a human endeavor, there is always some error of measurement associated with anything we assess. If this error is random, as we assume it to be, then some of that measurement error will actually be working in the direction of enhanced prediction.

The multiple regression algorithm, however, is unable to distinguish between this chance enhancement (i.e., blind luck from the standpoint of trying to achieve the best possible R^2) and the real predictive power of the variables, so it uses everything it can to maximize prediction—it generates the raw and standardized regression weights from both true and error sources combined. By drawing information from both true score variance and error variance because it cannot distinguish between the two sources in fitting the model to the data, multiple regression procedures will overestimate the amount of variance that the model explains (Cohen et al., 2003; Yin & Fan, 2001).

The dynamics of this problem can be understood in this way: In another sample, the random dictates of error will operate differently, and if the weighting coefficients obtained from our original regression analysis are applied to the new sample, the model will be less effective than it appeared to be for the original sample, that is, the model will likely yield a somewhat lower R^2 than was originally obtained. This phenomenon is known by the term *R^2 shrinkage*. R^2 shrinkage is more of a problem when we have relatively smaller sample sizes and relatively more variables in the analysis. As sample size and the number of predictors reach more acceptable proportions (see Section 7A.13.2.4), the inflation of R^2 becomes that much less of an issue.

Empirical strategies estimating the amount of R^2 shrinkage call for performing a regression analysis on selected portions of the sample, an approach generally known as a *resampling* strategy. In the present context, resampling can be addressed through procedures such as *cross-validation*, *double cross-validation*, and the use of a *jackknife* procedure.

To perform a cross-validation procedure, we ordinarily divide a large sample in half (into two equal-sized subsamples, although we can also permit one sample to be larger than the other) by randomly selecting the cases to be assigned to each. We then compute our regression analysis on one subsample (the larger one if unequal sample sizes were used) and use those regression weights to predict the criterion variable of the second "hold-back" sample (the smaller one if unequal sample sizes were used). The R^2 difference tells us the degree of predictive loss we have observed. We can also correlate the predicted scores of the hold-back sample with their actual scores; this is known as the *cross-validation coefficient*.

Double cross-validation can be done by performing the cross-validation process in both directions—that is, performing the regression analysis on each subsample and applying the results to the other. In a sense, we obtain two estimates of shrinkage rather than one, that is, we can obtain two cross-validation coefficients. If the shrinkage is not excessive, and there are few guidelines as to how to judge this, we can then perform an analysis on the combined sample and report the double cross-validation results to let readers know the estimated generalizability of the model.

The jackknife procedure was introduced by Quenouille (1949) and is currently treated (e.g., Beasley & Rodgers, 2009; Chernick, 2008; Efron, 1979; Fuller, 2009; Wu, 1986) in the context of *bootstrapping* (where we draw with replacement repeated subsamples from our sample to estimate the sampling distribution of a given parameter). The jackknife procedure is also called, for what will be obvious reasons, a *leave-one-out* procedure.

Ordinarily, we include all of the cases with valid values on the dependent and independent variables in an ordinary regression analysis. To apply a jackknife procedure, we would temporarily remove one of those cases (i.e., leave one of those cases out of the analysis), say Case A, perform the analysis without Case A, and then apply the regression coefficients obtained in that analysis to predict the value of the dependent variable for Case A. We then "replace" Case A back into the data set, select another case to remove, say Case B, repeat the process for Case B, and so on, until all cases have had their *Y* score predicted.

The comparison of these jackknifed results with those obtained in the ordinary (full-sample) analysis gives us an estimate of how much shrinkage in explained variance we might encounter down the road. IBM SPSS does not have a jackknife procedure available for multiple regression, but that procedure is available for discriminant function analysis (see Section 11A.10.3.4).

7A.13.2.4 Variance Explained: Analytic Strategies for Estimating the Amount of R^2 Shrinkage

In addition to capitalizing on chance, R^2 can also be mathematically inflated by having a relatively larger number of predictors relative to the size of the sample, that is, R^2 can be increased simply by increasing the number of predictors we opt to include in the model for a given sample size (e.g., Stuewig, 2010; Wooldridge, 2009; Yin & Fan, 2001). The good news here is that statisticians have been able to propose ways to "correct" or "adjust" the obtained R^2 that takes into account both the sample size and the number of predictors in the model. When applied to the obtained R^2, the result is known as an *adjusted* R^2. This adjusted R^2 provides an estimate of what the R^2 might have been had it not been inflated by the number of predictors we have included in the model relative to our sample size. All of the major statistical software packages report in their output an adjusted R^2 value in addition to the observed R^2.

To further complicate this scenario, there are two different types of adjusted R^2 values that are described in the literature, and there is no single way to compute either of them. Some of these formulas (e.g., Olkin & Pratt, 1958; Wherry, 1931) are intended to estimate the population value of R^2, whereas others (e.g., Browne, 1975; Darlington, 1960; Rozeboom, 1978) are intended to estimate the cross-validation coefficient (Yin & Fan, 2001). Yin and Fan (2001) made a comparison of the performance of 15 such formulas (some estimating the population value of R^2 and others estimating the cross-validation coefficient), and Walker (2007) compared four estimates of the cross-validation coefficient in addition to a bootstrap procedure.

Our interest here is with the adjusted R^2 as an estimate of the population value of R^2. The algorithm that is used by IBM SPSS Version 19 to compute its adjusted R^2 value

Figure 7a.6 The IBM SPSS Formula, the Wherry Formulas 1 and 2, and the Okin–Pratt Formula for Computing the Adjusted R^2 as an Estimate of the Population R^2

IBM SPSS 19: $\quad$ Adjusted $R^2 = R^2 - \dfrac{(1 - R^2)\,(v)}{N - (v + 1)}$

Wherry – 1: $\quad$ Adjusted $R^2 = 1 - \dfrac{N}{N - v}\,(1 - R^2)$

Wherry – 2: $\quad$ Adjusted $R^2 = 1 - \dfrac{N - 1}{N - v}\,(1 - R^2)$

Olkin – Pratt: $\quad$ Adjusted $R^2 = 1 - \left[\dfrac{(N - 3)\,(1 - R^2)}{N - v - 1}\right]\left[1 + \dfrac{(2)\,(1 - R^2)}{N - v + 1}\right]$

Note. In the formulas to complete the adjusted R^2 value, R^2 is the obtained value from the analysis, N is the sample size, and v is the number of predictor variables in the model.

(SPSS, 2010) and three other well-known formulas, the Wherry formulas 1 and 2, and the Olkin–Pratt formula, are presented in Figure 7a.6. They all contain the following three elements:

- The obtained value of R^2 from the multiple regression analysis
- The sample size, designated as N
- The number of predictor variables in the model, which we are designating as v

Although these formulas are somewhat different and when solved will lead to somewhat different adjusted values of R^2, the estimates appear to be relatively close to each other from the standpoint of researchers. For example, we assumed that a hypothetical research study used a sample size of 100 (what we would regard as too small an N), eight predictor variables (an excessive number of predictors for that sample size), and obtained an R^2 of .25. The resulting adjusted R^2 values from each of the formulas were as follows:

- IBM SPSS Version 19 algorithm: .184066
- Wherry Formula 1: .1847827
- Wherry Formula 2: .1929349
- Olkin–Pratt formula: .1876552

Considering that these values hover around .18 or .19, the adjusted R^2 values appear to be approximately three quarters the magnitude of the observed R^2 value. In our view, this is a considerable amount of estimated shrinkage.

We can contrast this hypothetical result with our worked example presented in Table 7a.3. In our worked example, the adjusted R^2 value rounded to .48, giving us virtually the same value as the unadjusted R^2 (the actual R^2 was .48257 and the IBM SPSS adjusted R^2 was .47883). That such little adjustment was made to R^2 is most likely a function of the sample size to number of variables ratio we used (the analysis was based on a sample size of 420 cases; with just three predictors, our ratio was 140:1).

Yin and Fan (2001) suggested that good quality estimates of adjusted R^2 values were obtained with most of the R^2 estimation formulas they evaluated when the ratio of sample size to number of predictors was 100. In research environments where there is a limited number of potential cases who may be recruited for a study (e.g., a university, hospital, or organizational setting), such a ratio may be difficult to achieve. In more restrictive settings where we must accept pragmatic compromises to get the research done, our recommendations are that the sample size should generally be no less than about 200 or so cases and that researchers use at least 20 but preferably 30 or more cases per predictor.

7A.14 Evaluating the Individual Predictor Results

7A.14.1 Variables in the Model

The predictor variables are shown in the first column of Table 7a.3. This represents a complete solution in the sense that all the independent variables are included in the final equation regardless of how much (or how little) they contribute to the prediction model.

7A.14.2 The Regression Equations

Using the raw and standardized regression weights, and the Y intercept shown in Table 7a.3, we have the elements of the two regression equations. These are produced below.

The raw score equation is as follows:

$$\text{Self-esteempred} = 56.66 + (2.89)(\text{pos affect}) - (2.42)(\text{neg affect}) + (.11)(\text{open})$$

The standardized equation is as follows:

$$\text{Self-esteem}z \text{ pred} = (.40)(\text{pos affect}z) - (.43)(\text{neg affect}z) + (.06)(\text{open}z)$$

7A.14.3 t Tests

IBM SPSS tests the significance of each predictor in the model using t tests. The null hypothesis is that a predictor's weight is effectively equal to zero when the effects of the other predictors are taken into account. This means that when the other predictors act as covariates and this predictor is targeting the residual variance, according to the null hypothesis the predictor is unable to account for a statistically significant portion of it; that is, the partial correlation between the predictor and the criterion variable is not significantly different from zero. And it is a rare occurrence when every single independent variable turns out to be a significant predictor. The t-test output shown in Table 7a.3 informs us that only Positive Affect and Negative Affect are statistically significant predictors in the model; even with our large sample size, Openness does not receive a strong enough weight to reach that touchstone.

7A.14.4 b Coefficients

The b and beta coefficients in Table 7a.3 show us the weights that the variables have been assigned at the end of the equation-building process. The b weights are tied to the metrics on which the variables are measured and are therefore difficult to compare with one another. But with respect to their own metric, they are quite interpretable. The b weight for Positive Affect, for example, is 2.89. We may take that to mean that when the other variables are controlled for, an increase of 1 point on the Positive Affect measure is, on average, associated with a 2.89-point gain in Self-Esteem. Likewise, the b weight of -2.42 for Negative Affect would mean that, with all of the other variables statistically controlled, every point of increase on the Negative Affect measure (i.e., greater levels of Negative Affect) corresponds to a lower score on the Self-Esteem measure of 2.42 points.

Table 7a.3 also shows the Y intercept for the linear function. This value of 56.66 would need to be added to the weighted combination of variables in the raw score equation to obtain the predicted value of Self-Esteem for any given research participant.

7A.14.5 Beta Coefficients

7A.14.5.1 General Interpretation

The beta weights for the independent variables are also shown in Table 7a.3. Here, all the variables are in z score form and thus their beta weights, within limits, can be compared with each other. We can see from Table 7a.3 that Positive Affect and Negative Affect have beta weights of similar magnitudes and that Openness has a very low beta value. Thus, in achieving the goal of predicting Self-Esteem to the greatest possible extent (to minimize the sum of the squared prediction errors), Positive Affect and Negative Affect are given much more weight than Openness.

7A.14.5.2 The Case for Using Beta Coefficients to Evaluate Predictors

Some authors (e.g., Cohen et al., 2003; Pedhazur, 1982, 1997; Pedhazur & Schmelkin, 1991) have cautiously argued that, at least under some circumstances, we may be able to compare the beta coefficients of the predictors with each other. That is, on the basis of visual examination of the equation, it may be possible to say that predictors with larger beta weights contribute more to the prediction of the dependent variable than those with smaller weights.

It is possible to quantify the relative contribution of predictors using beta weights as the basis of the comparison. Although Kachigan (1986) has proposed examining the ratio of the squared beta weights to make this comparison, that procedure may be acceptable only in the rare situation when those predictors whose beta weights are being compared are uncorrelated (Pedhazur & Schmelkin, 1991). In the everyday research context, where the independent variables are almost always significantly correlated, we may simply compute the ratio of the actual beta weights (Pedhazur, 1982, 1997; Pedhazur & Schmelkin, 1991), placing the larger beta weight in the numerator of the ratio. This ratio reveals how much more one independent variable contributes to prediction than another within the context of the model.

This comparison could work as follows. If we wanted to compare the efficacy of Negative Affect (the most strongly weighted variable in the model) with the other (less strongly weighted) predictors, we would ordinarily limit our comparison to only the statistically significant ones. In this case, we would compare Negative Affect only with Positive Affect. We would therefore compute the ratio of the beta weights (Negative Affect/Positive Affect) without carrying the sign of the beta through the computation (.43/.40 = 1.075). Based on this ratio (although we could certainly see this just by looking at the beta weights themselves), we would say that Negative Affect was 1.075 times a more potent predictor in this model. Translated to ordinary language, we would say that Negative Affect and Positive Affect make approximately the same degree of contribution to the prediction of Self-Esteem in the context of this research study with the present set of variables.

7A.14.5.3 Concerns With Using the Beta Coefficients to Evaluate Predictors

We indicated above that even when authors such as Pedhazur (1982, 1997; Pedhazur & Schmelkin, 1991) endorse the use of beta coefficient ratios to evaluate the relative contribution of the independent variables within the model, they usually do so with certain caveats. Take Pedhazur (1997) as a good illustration:

> Broadly speaking, such an interpretation [stating that the effect of one predictor is twice as great as the effect of a second predictor] is legitimate, but it is not free of problems because the Beta[s] are affected, among other things, by the variability of the variable with which they are associated. (p. 110)

Thus, beta weights may not be generalizable across different samples.

Another concern regarding the use of beta coefficients to evaluate predictors is that beta weight values are partly a function of the correlations between the predictors themselves. That is, a certain independent variable may predict the dependent variable to a great extent in isolation, and one would therefore expect to see a relatively high beta coefficient associated with that predictor. Now place another predictor that is highly correlated with the first predictor into the analysis, and all of a sudden, the beta coefficients of both predictors can plummet (because each is evaluated with the other treated as a covariate). The first predictor's relationship with the dependent variable has not changed in this scenario, but the presence of the second correlated predictor could seriously affect the magnitude of the beta weight of the first. This "sensitivity" of the beta weights to the correlations between the predictors places additional limitations on the generality of the betas and thus their use in evaluating or comparing predictive effectiveness of the independent variables.

The sensitivity of a beta coefficient associated with a given predictor to the correlation of that predictor with other predictors in the model can also be manifested in the following manner: If two or three very highly correlated predictors were included in the model, their beta coefficients could exceed a value of 1.00, sometimes by a considerable margin. Ordinarily, researchers would not include very highly correlated variables in a regression analysis (they would either retain only one or create a single composite variable of the set), but there are special analyses where researchers cannot condense such a set of variables (see Section 8B.2, for an example); in such analyses, researchers focus on R^2 or (depending on the analysis) the change in R^2 and ignore these aberrant beta coefficient values.

Recognizing that the value of a beta coefficient associated with a variable is affected by, among other factors, the variability of the variable, the correlation of the variable with other predictors in the model, and the measurement error in assessing the variable, Jacob Cohen (1990) in one of his classic articles titled "Things I Have Learned (So Far)" went so far as to suggest that in many or most situations, simply assigning unit or unitary weights (values of 1.00) to all significant predictors can result in at least as good a prediction model as using partial regression coefficients to two decimal values as the weights for the variables. Cohen's strategy simplifies the prediction model to a yes/no decision for each potential predictor, and although it is not widely used in regression studies, it is a strategy that is commonly used in connection with factor analysis where a variable is either included with a unitary weight or not included when we construct the subscales that are used to represent a factor (see Section 12B.14).

7A.14.5.4 Recommendations for Using Betas

We do not want to leave you completely hanging at this point in our treatment, so we will answer the obvious questions. Should you use the beta weights to assess the relative strengths of the predictors in your own research? Yes, although we have considerable sympathy with the wisdom expressed by Cohen (1990) of using unit weights. Should beta coefficients be the only index you check out? No. The structure coefficients and the squared semipartial correlations should be examined as well. And, ultimately, using the raw regression weights to inform us of how much of a change in the dependent variable is associated with a unit difference in the predictor, given that all of the other predictors are acting as covariates, will prove to be a very worthwhile interpretation strategy.

7A.14.6 Pearson Correlations of the Predictors With the Criterion Variable

The fourth numerical column in Table 7a.3 shows the simple Pearson correlations between Self-Esteem and each of the predictors. We have briefly described the correlations earlier. For present purposes, we can see that the correlations between Self-Esteem and Positive Affect and Openness are positive. This was the case because each of these variables is scored in the positive direction—higher scores mean that respondents exhibit greater levels of self-esteem and more positive affective behaviors and that they are more open to new or interesting experiences. Because higher scores on the Self-Esteem scale indicate greater positive feelings about oneself, it is not surprising that these two predictors are positively correlated with it. On the other hand, Negative Affect is negatively correlated with Self-Esteem. This is also not surprising in that individuals who exhibit more negative affective behaviors are typically those who have lower levels of self-esteem.

7A.14.7 Squared Semipartial Correlations

The next to last column of Table 7a.3 displays the squared semipartial correlations for each predictor. These correlations are shown in the IBM SPSS printout as "part correlations" and appear in the printout in their nonsquared form. This statistic indexes the variance accounted for uniquely by each predictor in the full model. What is interesting here, and this is pretty typical of multiple regression research, is that the sum of these squared semipartial correlations is less than the R^2. That is, .14, .16, and .00 add up to .30 and not to the R^2 of .48.

The reason these squared semipartial correlations do not add to the value of R^2 is that the independent variables overlap (are correlated) with each other. Here, 30% of the variance is accounted for uniquely by the predictors, whereas (by subtraction) 18% of the accounted-for variance is handled by more than one of them. We therefore have some but not a huge amount of redundancy built into our set of predictors.

Using the squared semipartial correlations as a gauge of the relative strength of the predictors results in an evaluation similar to the one we made based on comparing the beta weights. From this perspective, Positive Affect and Negative Affect are approximately tied in their unique contribution to the prediction model under the present research circumstances.

7A.14.8 The Structure Coefficients

The last column in Table 7a.3 shows the structure coefficients, which index the correlation of each variable with the weighted linear combination (the variate). These coefficients needed to be hand calculated because IBM SPSS does not provide them. For each independent variable in the table, we divided the Pearson r representing the correlation of the independent variable and the dependent variable (shown in the fourth numerical column) by the multiple correlation. To illustrate, the square root of .48 (the R^2) is approximately .69. For Positive Affect's structure coefficient, we divided .55 by .69 to obtain .80.

The structure coefficients indicate that Positive Affect and Negative Affect correlate reasonably highly with the variate. In this example, using the structure coefficients as a basis to compare the contribution of the predictors presents the same picture as those painted by the beta weights and the squared semipartial correlations. Such consistency, however, is not always obtained.

Beta coefficients and structure coefficients differ in at least two important ways.

- A beta coefficient associated with its predictor reflects the correlations of that predictor with the other predictors in the analysis. A structure coefficient does not take into account the degree to which that predictor correlates with the other predictors.
- Beta weights can exceed the range of ±1 when the predictors are relatively highly correlated with each other. Many researchers are not keen on interpreting beta weights greater than unity. Structure coefficients are bounded by the range ±1 because they are correlation coefficients, thus making them pretty clearly interpretable.

Our recommendations are consistent with what we offered above for beta weights. We concur with Thompson and Borrello (1985) that the structure coefficients are a useful companion index of relative predictor contribution. Unlike the beta coefficients and the squared semipartial correlations, structure coefficients are not affected by the correlations between the predictors although, as is true for all of the regression statistics, the structure coefficients could change substantially if a different set of predictors happened to be used.

Pedhazur (1982) notes that structure coefficients will show the same pattern of relationships as the Pearson correlations of the predictors and the criterion. Because of this, Pedhazur is not convinced of the utility of structure coefficients. Nonetheless, in our view, by focusing on the correlation between the predictor and the variate, we believe that structure coefficients may add a nuance to the interpretation of the regression analysis that we think is worthwhile. Furthermore, we make extensive use of structure coefficients in other analyses (e.g., factor analysis, discriminant function analysis, canonical correlation analysis) for reasons that are also applicable to the regression context.

7A.15 Step Methods of Building the Model

The step methods of building the regression equation that we briefly cover here are part of the class of statistical regression methods, and it will be clear from our descriptions just how the software programs are in charge of the decision process for selecting the ordering of the predictors as the model is built. We cover here the forward method, the backward method, and the stepwise method. These methods construct the model one step at a time rather than all at once as the standard method does.

The primary goal of these step methods is to build a model with only the "important" predictors in it, although importance is still relative to the set of predictors that are participating in the analysis. The methods differ primarily in how they structure to steps in entering or removing variables from the model.

7A.16 The Forward Method

In the forward method, rather than placing all the variables in the model at once, IBM SPSS adds independent variables to the model, one variable or step at a time. At each step, we enter the particular variable that adds the most predictive power at that time. If we were working with the set of variables we used to illustrate the standard regression method, Negative Affect would be entered first. We know this because, with no variables in the model at the start and building the model one variable at a time, the variable correlating most strongly with Self-Esteem would be entered first.

In the forward method, once a variable is entered into the model, it remains in the model. For the next step, the variable with the highest partial correlation (the correlation between the residual variance of Self-Esteem and each remaining predictor with Negative Affect acting as a covariate because it is already in the model) is entered if that partial correlation is statistically significant. In this case, Positive Affect would be entered.

This process is repeated for each remaining predictor with the variables in the model all acting as covariates. We would find, with Negative Affect and Positive Affect in the model, that Openness would not be entered; that is, it would not account for a significant amount of the residual variance accounted for by Negative Affect and Positive Affect. Because that is the entire set of predictors, the forward procedure would stop at the end of the second step.

7A.17 The Backward Method

The backward method works, not by adding significant variables to the model but, rather, by removing nonsignificant predictors from it one step at a time. The very first action performed by the backward method is the same one used by the standard method; it enters all the predictors into the equation regardless of their worth. But whereas the standard method stops here, the backward method is just getting started.

The model with all the variables in it is now examined, and the significant predictors are marked for retention. Nonsignificant predictors are then evaluated, and the most expendable of them—the one whose loss would least significantly decrease the R^2—is removed from the equation. A new model is built in the absence of that one independent variable, and the evaluation process is repeated. Once again, the most expendable independent variable is removed. This removal process and model reconstruction process continues until there are only significant predictors remaining in the equation. In our example, Openness would have been removed at the first opportunity. The method would have stopped at that point because both remaining predictors would have been significant predictors.

7A.18 Backward Versus Forward Solutions

Backward regression does not always produce the same model as forward regression even though it would have in our simplified example. Here is why: Being entered into the equation in the forward method requires predictors to meet a more stringent criterion than variables being retained in the equation in the backward method. This creates a situation in which it is more difficult to get into the equation than to remain in it. Stringency or difficulty is defined statistically by the alpha or probability level associated with entry and removal.

Predictors earn their way into the equation in the forward method by significantly predicting variance of the dependent variable. The alpha level governing this entry decision is usually the traditional .05 level. By most standards, this is a fairly stringent criterion. When we look for predictors to remove under the backward method, the alpha level usually drops to .10 as the default in most programs. This means that a predictor needs to be significant at only .10 (not at .05) to retain its place in the equation. Thus, an independent variable is eligible to be removed from the equation at a particular step in the backward method if its probability level is greater than .10 (e.g., $p = .11$), but it will be retained in the equation if its probability level is equal to or less than .10 (e.g., $p = .09$).

The consequences of using these different criteria for entry and removal affect only those variables whose probabilities are between the entry and removal criteria. To see why this is true, first consider variables that are not within this zone.

- If a variable does not meet the standard of $p = .10$, it is removed from the equation. This variable would also by definition not meet the .05 alpha-level criterion for entry either, so there is no difference in the outcome for this predictor under either criterion—it is not going to wind up in the equation in either the forward or backward methods.
- If a variable does meet the .05 criterion, it will always be allowed entry to the equation and will certainly not be removed by the backward method; again, there is no difference in outcome for such a predictor under either method.

Variables with probability levels between these two criteria are in a more interesting position. Assume that we are well into the backward process, and at this juncture, the weakest predictor is one whose probability is .08. This variable would not have been allowed into the equation by the forward method if it were considered for entry at this point because to get in, it would have to meet a .05 alpha level to achieve statistical significance. However, under the backward method, this variable was freely added to the equation at the beginning, and the only issue here is whether it is to be removed. When we examine its current probability level and find it to be .08, we determine that this predictor is "significant" at the .10 alpha level. It therefore remains in the equation. In this case, the model built under the backward method would incorporate this predictor, but the model built under the forward method would have excluded it.

7A.19 The Stepwise Method

The stepwise method of building the multiple regression equation is a fusion of the forward and backward methods. The stepwise and forward methods act in the same fashion until we reach the point where a third predictor is added to the equation. The stepwise method therefore begins with an empty model and builds it one step at a time. Once a third independent variable is in the model, the stepwise method invokes the right to remove an independent variable if that predictor is not earning its keep.

Predictors are allowed to be included in the model if they significantly ($p \le .05$) add to the predicted variance of the dependent variable. With correlated independent variables, as

Figure 7a.7 The Unique Contribution of Variable *K* Is Reduced by Addition of Variable *L*

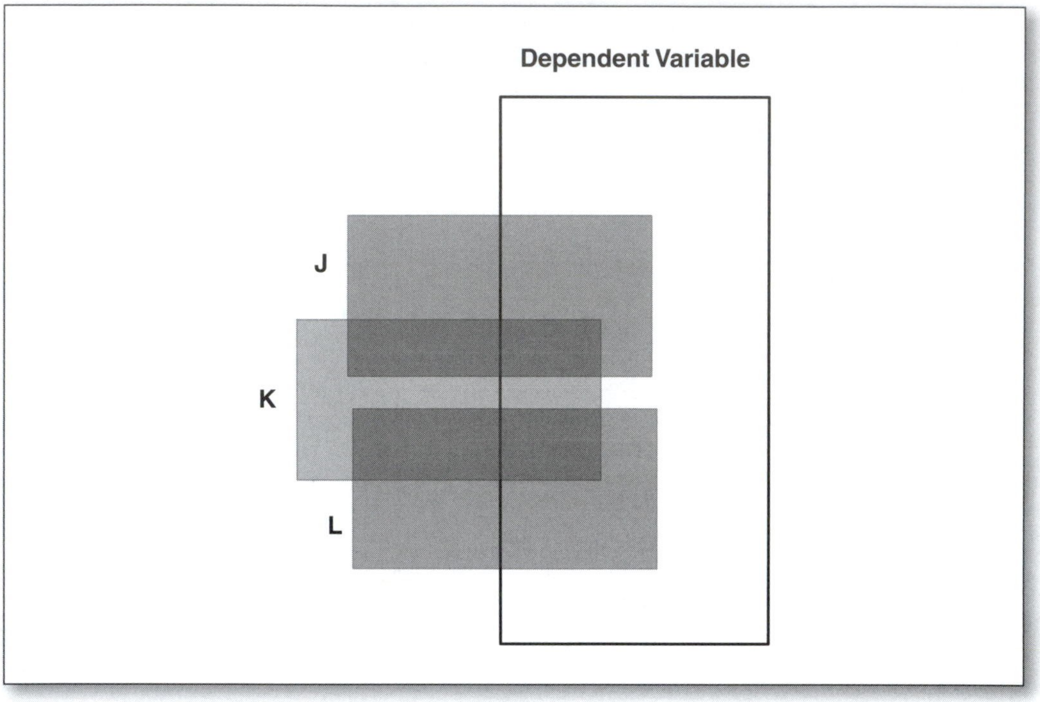

we have seen, the predictors in the equation admitted under a probability level of .05 can still overlap with each other. This is shown in Figure 7a.7.

In Figure 7a.7, predictor *J* was entered first, *K* was entered second, and *L* was just entered as the third predictor. We are poised at the moment when *L* joined the equation. Note that between predictors *J* and *L*, there is very little work that can be attributed uniquely to *K*. At this moment, the squared semipartial correlation associated with *K* (showing its unique contribution to the prediction model) is quite small.

In the forward method, the fact that *K*'s unique contribution has been substantially reduced by *L*'s presence would leave the procedure unfazed because it does not have a removal option available to it. But this is the stepwise method, and it is prepared to remove a predictor if necessary. When the amount of unique variance that *K* now accounts for is examined with variables *J* and *L* acting as covariates, let's presume that it is not significant at the removal criterion of .10 (say its *p* value is .126). *K* is thus judged to no longer be contributing effectively to the prediction model, and it is removed from the equation. Of course, as more predictors are entered into the equation, the gestalt could change dramatically, and *K* might very well be called on to perform predictive duties later in the analysis.

We have just described the reason that the entry criterion is more severe than the removal criterion. It can be summarized as follows. If getting into the equation was easier than getting out, then variables removed at one step might get entered again at the next step because they might still be able to achieve that less stringent level of probability needed for entry. There is then a chance that the stepwise procedure could be caught in an endless loop where the same variable kept being removed on one step and entered again on the next. By making entry more exacting than removal, this conundrum is avoided.

7A.20 Evaluation of the Statistical Methods

7A.20.1 Benefits of the Standard Method

The primary advantage of using the standard model is that it presents a complete picture of the regression outcome to researchers. If the variables were important enough to earn a place in the design of the study, then they are given room in the model even if they are not adding very much to the R^2. That is, on the assumption that the variables were selected on the basis of their relevance to theory or at least on the basis of hypotheses based on a comprehensive review of the existing literature on the topic, the standard model provides an opportunity to see how they fare as a set in predicting the dependent variable.

7A.20.2 Benefits of the Step Methods

The argument for using the stepwise method is that we end up with a model that is "lean and mean." Each independent variable in it has earned the right to remain in the equation through a hard, competitive struggle. The argument for using the forward and backward methods is similar to the one used by those advocating the stepwise method. The forward and backward methods give what their users consider the essence of the solution by excluding variables that add nothing of merit to the prediction.

7A.20.3 Criticisms of the Statistical Methods as a Set

One criticism of all the statistical methods is that independent variables with good predictive qualities on their own may be awarded very low weight in the model. This can happen because their contribution is being evaluated when the contributions of the other predictors have been partialled out. Such "masking" of potentially good predictors can lead researchers to draw incomplete or improper conclusions from the results of the analysis. One way around this problem is for the researchers to exercise some judgment in which variables are entered at certain points in the analysis, and this is discussed in Chapter 8. This issue is also related to multicollinearity, a topic that we discuss later in Section 7A.21.

The step methods have become increasingly less popular over the years as their weaknesses have become better understood and as hierarchal methods and path approaches have gained in popularity. Tabachnick and Fidell (2007), for example, have expressed serious concerns about this group of methods, especially the stepwise method, and they are not alone. Here is a brief summary of the interrelated drawbacks of using this set of methods.

- These methods, particularly the stepwise method, may need better than the 20 to 1 ratio of cases to independent variables because there are serious threats to external validity (Tabachnick & Fidell, 2007). That is, the model that is built may overfit the sample because a different sample may yield somewhat different relationships (correlations) between the variables in the analysis and that could completely change which variables were entered into the model.
- The statistical criteria for building the equation identify variables for inclusion if they are better predictors than the other candidates. But "better" could mean "just a tiny bit better" or "a whole lot better." One variable may win the nomination to enter the equation, but the magnitude by which the variable achieved that victory may be too small to matter to researchers.
- If the victory of getting into the model by one variable is within the margin of error in the measurement of another variable, identifying the one variable as a predictor at the expense of the other may obscure viable alternative prediction models.
- Variables that can substantially predict the dependent variable may be excluded from the equations built by the step methods because some other variable or combination of variables does the job a little bit better. It is conceivable that several independent variables taken together may predict the criterion variable fairly well, but step procedures consider only one variable at a time.

7A.20.4 Balancing the Value of All the Statistical Methods of Building the Model

The standard method works well if we have selected the independent variables based on theory or empirical research findings and wish to examine the combined predictive power of that set of predictors. But because they are functioning in combination, the weights of the predictors in the model are a function of their interrelationships; thus, we are not evaluating them in isolation or in subsets. The standard method will allow us to test hypotheses about the model as a whole; if that is the goal, then that is what should be used.

The stepwise methods are intended to identify which variables should be in the model on purely statistical grounds. Such an atheoretical approach is discouraged by many researchers. On the other hand, there may be certain applications where all we want is to obtain the largest R^2 with the fewest number of predictors, recognizing that the resulting model may have less external validity than desired. Under these conditions, some researchers may consider using a step method.

Before one decides that one of the statistical procedures is to be used, it is very important to consider alternative methods of performing the regression analysis. Although they do require more thoughtful decision making rather than just entering the variables and selecting a statistical method, the flexibility and potential explanatory power they afford more than compensate for the effort it takes to run such analyses. Some of these procedures are discussed in Chapter 8A.

7A.21 Collinearity and Multicollinearity

Collinearity is a condition that exists when two predictors correlate very strongly; *multicollinearity* is a condition that exists when more than two predictors correlate very strongly. Note that we are talking about the relationships between the predictor variables only and not about correlations between each of the predictors and the dependent variable.

Regardless of whether we are talking about two predictors or a set of three or more predictors, multicollinearity can distort the interpretation of multiple regression results. For example, if two variables are highly correlated, then they are largely confounded with one another; that is, they are essentially measuring the same characteristic, and it would be impossible to say which of the two was the more relevant. Statistically, because the standard regression procedure controls for all the other predictors when it is evaluating a given independent variable, it is likely that neither predictor variable would receive any substantial weight in the model. This is true because at the time the procedure evaluates one of these two predictors, the other is (momentarily) already in the equation accounting for almost all the variance that would be explained by the first. The irony is that each on its own might very well be a good predictor of the criterion variable. On the positive side, with both variables in the model, the R^2 value will be appropriately high, and if the goal of the research is to maximize R^2, then multicollinearity might not be an immediate problem.

When the research goal is to understand the interplay of the predictors and not simply to maximize R^2, multicollinearity can cause several problems in the analysis. One problem caused by the presence of multicollinearity is that the values of the standardized regression coefficients of the highly correlated independent variables are distorted, sometimes exceeding the ordinarily expected range of ±1. A second problem is that the standard errors of the regression weights of those multicollinear predictors can be inflated, thereby enlarging their confidence intervals, sometimes to the point where they contain the zero value. If that is the case, you could not reliably determine if increases in the predictor are associated with increases or decreases in the criterion variable. A third problem is that if multicollinearity is sufficiently great, certain internal mathematical operations (e.g., matrix inversion) are disrupted, and the statistical program comes to a screeching halt.

Identifying collinearity or multicollinearity requires researchers to examine the data in certain ways. A high correlation is easy to spot when considering only two variables. Just examine the Pearson correlations between the variables in the analysis as a prelude to multiple regression. Two variables that are very strongly related should raise a "red flag." As a general rule of thumb, we recommend that two variables correlated in the middle .7s or higher should probably not be used together in a regression or any other multivariate analysis. Allison (1999a) suggests that you "almost certainly have a problem if the correlation is above .8, but there may be difficulties that appear well before that value" (p. 64).

One common cause of multicollinearity is that researchers may use subscales of an inventory as well as the full inventory score as predictors. Depending on how the subscales have been computed, it is possible for them in combination to correlate almost perfectly with the full inventory score. We strongly advise users to employ either the subscales or the full inventory score, but not all of them in the analysis.

Another common cause of multicollinearity is including in the analysis variables that assess the same construct. Researchers should either drop all but one of them from the analysis or consider the possibility of combining them in some fashion if it makes sense. For example, we might combine height and weight to form a measure of body mass. As another example, we might average three highly correlated survey items; principal components analysis and exploratory factor analysis, discussed in Chapters 12A and 12B, can be used to help determine which variables might productively be averaged together without losing too much information.

A less common cause of an analysis failing because of multicollinearity is placing into the analysis two measures that are mathematical transformations of each other (e.g., number of correct and incorrect responses; time and speed of response). Researchers should use only one of the measures rather than both of them.

Multicollinearity is much more difficult to detect when it is some (linear) combination of variables that produces a high multiple correlation in some subset of the predictor variables. We would worry if that correlation reached the mid .8s, but Allison (1999a, p. 141) gets concerned if those multiple correlations reached into the high .7s (R^2 of about .60). Many statistical software programs will allow us to compute multiple correlations for different combinations of variables so that you can examine them. Thus, we can scan these correlations for such high values and take the necessary steps to attempt to fix the problem.

Most regression software packages have what is called a *tolerance* parameter that tries to protect the procedure from multicollinearity by rejecting predictor variables that are too highly correlated with other independent variables. Conceptually, tolerance is the amount of a predictor's variance not accounted for by the other predictors ($1 - R^2$ between predictors). Lower tolerance values indicate that there are stronger relationships (increasing the chances of obtaining multicollinearity) between the predictor variables. Allison (1999a) cautions that tolerances in the range of .40 are worthy of concern; other authors have suggested that tolerance values in the range of .1 are problematic (Myers, 1990; Stevens, 2009).

A related statistic is the *variance inflation factor* (VIF), which is computed as 1 divided by tolerance. A VIF value of 2.50 is associated with a tolerance of .40 and is considered problematic by Allison (1999a); a VIF value of 10 is associated with a tolerance of .1 and is considered problematic by Cohen et al. (2003), Myers (1990), and Stevens (2009).

7A.22 Recommended Readings

Berk, R. A. (2003). *Regression analysis: A constructive critique.* Thousand Oaks, CA: Sage.

Berry, W. D. (1993). *Understanding regression assumptions* (Sage University Papers Series on Quantitative Applications in the Social Sciences, series no. 07-92). Newbury Park, CA: Sage.

Cohen, J. (1968). Multiple regression as a general data analytic system. *Psychological Bulletin, 70,* 426–443.

Darlington, R. B. (1960). *Regression and linear models.* New York, NY: McGraw-Hill.

Darlington, R. B. (1968). Multiple regression in psychological research and practice. *Psychological Bulletin, 69,* 161–182.

Draper, N. R., Guttman, I., & Lapczak, L. (1979). Actual rejection levels in a certain stepwise test. *Communications in Statistics, A8,* 99–105.

Fox, J. (1991). *Regression diagnostics.* Newbury Park, CA: Sage.

Green, S. A. (1991). How many subjects does it take to do a multiple regression analysis. *Multivariate Behavioral Research, 26,* 499–510.

Kahane, L. H. (2001). *Regression basics.* Thousand Oaks, CA: Sage.

Lopez, R. P., & Guarino, A. J. (2011). Uncertainty and decision making for residents with dementia. *Clinical Nursing Research, 20,* 228–240.

Lorenz, F. O. (1987). Teaching about influence in simple regression. *Teaching Sociology, 15,* 173–177.

Park, C., & Dudycha, A. (1974). A cross-validation approach to sample size determination. *Journal of the American Statistical Association, 69,* 214–218.

Schafer, W. D. (1991). Reporting nonhierarchical regression results. *Measurement and Evaluation in Counseling and Development, 24,* 146–149.

Schroeder, L. D., Sjoquist, D. L., & Stephan, P. E. (1986). *Understanding regression analysis: An introductory guide.* Beverly Hills, CA: Sage.

Sherry, A., & Henson, R. K. (2005). Conducting and interpreting canonical correlation analysis in personality research: A user-friendly primer. *Journal of Personality Assessment, 84*(1), 37–48.

Stevens, J. P. (2009). *Applied multivariate statistics for the social sciences* (5th ed.). New York, NY: Routledge Taylor & Francis.

Thompson, B. (1989). Why won't stepwise methods die? *Measurement and Evaluation in Counseling and Development, 21,* 146–148.

Trusty, J., Thompson, B., & Petrocelli, J. V. (2004). Practical guide for reporting effect size in quantitative research in the *Journal of Counseling & Development. Journal of Counseling & Development, 82,* 107–110.

Weiss, D. J. (1972). Canonical correlation analysis in counseling psychology research. *Journal of Counseling Psychology, 19,* 241–252.

Multiple Regression: Statistical Methods Using IBM SPSS

This chapter will demonstrate how to perform multiple linear regression with IBM SPSS first using the standard method and then using the stepwise method. We will use the data file **Personality** in these demonstrations.

7B.1 Standard Multiple Regression

7B.1.1 Main Regression Dialog Window

For purposes of illustrating standard linear regression, assume that we are interested in predicting self-esteem based on the combination of negative affect (experiencing negative emotions), positive affect (experiencing positive emotions), openness to experience (e.g., trying new foods, exploring new places), extraversion, neuroticism, and trait anxiety. Selecting the path **Analyze ➔ Regression ➔ Linear** opens the **Linear Regression** main dialog window displayed in Figure 7b.1. From the variables list panel, we move over **esteem** to the **Dependent** panel and **negafect**, **posafect**, **neoopen**, **neoextra**, **neoneuro**, and **tanx** to the **Independent(s)** panel. The **Method** drop-down menu will be left at its default setting of **Enter**, which requests a standard regression analysis.

7B.1.2 Statistics Window

Selecting the **Statistics** pushbutton opens the **Linear Regression: Statistics** dialog window shown in Figure 7b.2. By default, **Estimates** in the **Regression Coefficients** panel is checked. This instructs IBM SPSS to print the value of the regression coefficient and

Figure 7b.1 Main Dialog Window for Linear Regression

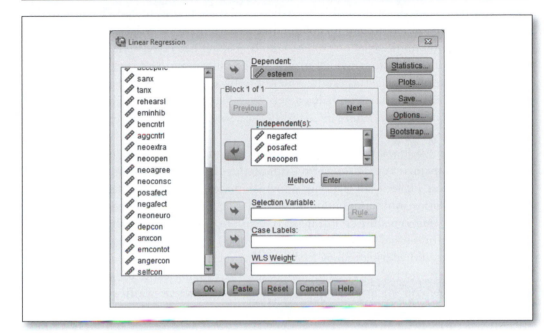

Figure 7b.2 The Linear Regression Statistics Window

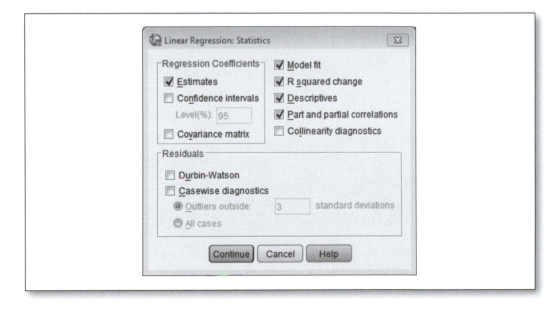

related measures. We also retained the following defaults: **Model fit**, which provides *R*-square, adjusted *R*-square, the standard error, and an ANOVA table; **R squared change**, which is useful when there are multiple predictors that are being entered in stages so that we can see where this information is placed in the output; **Descriptives**, which provides the means and standard deviations of the variables as well as the correlations table; and **Part and partial correlations**, which produces the partial and semipartial correlations and conveys important information when multiple predictors are used. Clicking **Continue** returns us to the main dialog screen.

7B.1.3 Options Window

Select the **Options** pushbutton; this displays the **Linear Regression: Options** dialog window shown in Figure 7b.3. The top panel is applicable if we were using one of the step methods, and we will discuss this in Section 7B.2. We have retained the defaults of including the *Y* intercept (the constant) in the equation and of excluding cases listwise. The choice **Exclude cases listwise** (sometimes called listwise deletion) means that all cases must have valid values on all of the variables in the analysis in order to be included; a missing value on even one of the variables is sufficient to exclude that case. Selecting this choice ensures that the set of variables, and thus the regression model, is based on the same set of cases. So long as there is relatively little missing data, this choice is best. Clicking **Continue** returns us to the main dialog box, and selecting **OK** produces the analysis.

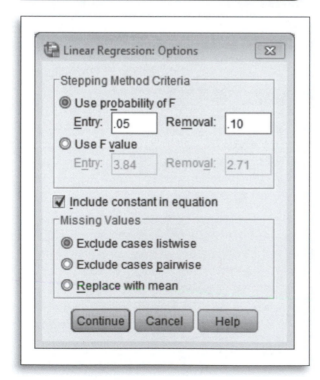

Figure 7b.3 The Linear Regression Options Window

7B.1.4 Multiple Regression Output

We will examine the output of the analysis in the order we suggest that you proceed. Figure 7b.4 contains descriptive information. The upper table contains the means and standard deviations of the variables, and the lower table shows the square correlation matrix. The correlation results are divided into

Figure 7b.4 Descriptive Statistics and Correlations Output for Standard Regression

Descriptive Statistics

	Mean	Std. Deviation	N
esteem self–esteem: coopersmith	71.2952	20.95292	420
negafect negative affect: mpq	5.7786	3.73029	420
posafect positive affect: mpq	7.7048	2.90970	420
neoopen openness: neo	55.4607	10.90952	420
neoextra extraversion: neo	55.8324	11.28265	420
neoneuro neuroticism: neo	50.5394	11.14793	420
tanx trait anxiety: spielberger	38.3262	10.59431	420

Correlations

		esteem self–esteem: coopersmith	negafect negative affect: mpq	posafect positive affect: mpq	neoopen openness: neo	neoextra extraversion: neo	neoneuro neuroticism: neo	tanx trait anxiety: spielberger
Pearson Correlation	esteem self–esteem: coopersmith	1.000	−.572	.555	.221	.425	−.693	−.724
	negafect negative affect: mpq	−.572	1.000	−.324	−.168	−.218	.712	.713
	posafect positive affect: mpq	.555	−.324	1.000	.221	.528	−.441	−.528
	neoopen openness: neo	.221	−.168	.221	1.000	.051	−.227	−.183
	neoextra extraversion: neo	.425	−.218	.528	.051	1.000	−.347	−.375
	neoneuro neuroticism: neo	−.693	.712	−.441	−.227	−.347	1.000	.809
	tanx trait anxiety: spielberger	−.724	.713	−.528	−.183	−.375	.809	1.000
Sig. (1–tailed)	esteem self–esteem: coopersmith		.000	.000	.000	.000	.000	.000
	negafect negative affect: mpq	.000		.000	.000	.000	.000	.000
	posafect positive affect: mpq	.000	.000		.000	.000	.000	.000
	neoopen openness: neo	.000	.000	.000		.148	.000	.000
	neoextra extraversion: neo	.000	.000	.000	.148		.000	.000
	neoneuro neuroticism: neo	.000	.000	.000	.000	.000		.000
	tanx trait anxiety: spielberger	.000	.000	.000	.000	.000	.000	
N	esteem self–esteem: coopersmith	420	420	420	420	420	420	420
	negafect negative affect: mpq	420	420	420	420	420	420	420
	posafect positive affect: mpq	420	420	420	420	420	420	420
	neoopen openness: neo	420	420	420	420	420	420	420
	neoextra extraversion: neo	420	420	420	420	420	420	420
	neoneuro neuroticism: neo	420	420	420	420	420	420	420
	tanx trait anxiety: spielberger	420	420	420	420	420	420	420

three major rows: the first contains the Pearson *r* values, the second contains the probabilities of obtaining those values if the null hypothesis was true, and the third provides sample size.

The dependent variable **esteem** is placed by IBM SPSS on the first row and column, and the other variables appear in the order we entered them into the analysis. The study represented by our data set was designed for a somewhat different purpose, so our choice of variables was a bit limited. Thus, the correlations of self-esteem with the predictor variables in the analysis are higher than we would ordinarily prefer, and many of the other variables are themselves likewise intercorrelated more than we would prefer. Nonetheless, the example is still useful for our purposes.

Figure 7b.5 displays the results of the analysis. The middle table shows the test of significance of the model using an ANOVA. There are 419 ($N - 1$) total degrees of freedom. With six predictors, the **Regression** effect has 6 degrees of freedom. The **Regression** effect is statistically significant indicating that prediction of the dependent variable is accomplished better than can be done by chance.

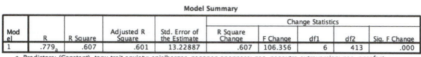

Figure 7b.5 The Results of the Standard Regression Analysis

Model Summary

Mod el	R	R Square	Adjusted R Square	Std. Error of the Estimate	Change Statistics				
					R Square Change	F Change	df1	df2	Sig. F Change
1	.779ₐ	.607	.601	13.22887	.607	106.356	6	413	.000

a. Predictors: (Constant), tanx trait anxiety: spielberger, neoopen openness: neo, neoextra extraversion: neo, posafect positive affect: mpq, negafect negative affect: mpq, neoneuro neuroticism: neo

ANOVA_b

Model		Sum of Squares	df	Mean Square	F	Sig.
1	Regression	111675.183	6	18612.531	106.356	.000ₐ
	Residual	72276.207	413	175.003		
	Total	183951.390	419			

a. Predictors: (Constant), tanx trait anxiety: spielberger, neoopen openness: neo, neoextra extraversion: neo, posafect positive affect: mpq, negafect negative affect: mpq, neoneuro neuroticism: neo

b. Dependent Variable: esteem self-esteem: coopersmith

Coefficients_a

Model		Unstandardized Coefficients		Standardized Coefficients	t	Sig.	Correlations		
		B	Std. Error	Beta			Zero-order	Partial	Part
1	(Constant)	96.885	7.294		13.283	.000			
	negafect negative affect: mpq	-.386	.264	-.069	-1.462	.144	-.572	-.072	-.045
	posafect positive affect: mpq	1.338	.293	.186	4.564	.000	.555	.219	.141
	neoopen openness: neo	.088	.062	.046	1.420	.156	.221	.070	.044
	neoextra extraversion: neo	.185	.069	.099	2.684	.008	.425	.131	.083
	neoneuro neuroticism: neo	-.477	.106	-.254	-4.505	.000	-.693	-.216	-.139
	tanx trait anxiety: spielberger	-.646	.117	-.326	-5.511	.000	-.724	-.262	-.170

a. Dependent Variable: esteem self-esteem: coopersmith

The upper table in Figure 7b.5 labeled **Model Summary** provides an overview of the results. Of primary interest are the **R Square** and **Adjusted R Square** values, which are .607 and .601, respectively. We learn from these that the weighted combination of the predictor variables explained approximately 60% of the variance of self-esteem. The loss of so little strength in computing the **Adjusted R Square** value is primarily due to our relatively large sample size combined with a relatively small set of predictors. Using the standard regression procedure where all of the predictors were entered simultaneously into the model, **R Square Change** went from zero before the model was fitted to the data to .607 when the variable was entered.

The bottom table in Figure 7b.5 labeled **Coefficients** provides the details of the results. The **Zero-order** column under **Correlations** lists the Pearson *r* values of the dependent variable (self-esteem in this case) with each of the predictors. These values are the same as those shown in the correlation matrix of Figure 7b.4. The **Partial** column under **Correlations** lists the partial correlations for each predictor as it was evaluated for its weighting in the model (the correlation between the predictor and the dependent variable when the other predictors are treated as covariates). The **Part** column under **Correlations** lists the semipartial correlations for each predictor once the model is finalized; squaring these values informs us of the percentage of variance each predictor uniquely explains. For example, trait anxiety accounts uniquely for about 3% of the variance of self-esteem ($-.170 * -.170 = .0289$ or approximately .03) given the other variables in the model.

The *Y* intercept of the raw score model is labeled as the **Constant** and has a value here of 98.885. Of primary interest here are the raw (**B**) and standardized (**Beta**) coefficients, and their significance levels determined by *t* tests. With the exception of negative affect and openness, all of the predictors are statistically significant. As can be seen by examining the beta weights, trait anxiety followed by neuroticism followed by positive affect were making relatively larger contributions to the prediction model.

The raw regression coefficients are *partial regression coefficients* because their values take into account the other predictor variables in the model; they inform us of the predicted change in the dependent variable for every unit increase in that predictor. For example, positive affect is associated with a partial regression coefficient of 1.338 and signifies that for every additional point on the positive affect measure, we would predict a gain of 1.338 points on the self-esteem measure. As another example, neuroticism is associated with a partial regression coefficient of $-.477$ and signifies that for every additional point on the neuroticism measure, we would predict a decrement of .477 points on the self-esteem measure.

This example serves to illustrate two important related points about multiple regression analysis. First, it is the model as a whole that is the focus of the analysis. Variables are treated akin to team players weighted in such a way that the sum of the squared residuals of the model is minimized. Thus, it is the set of variables in this particular (weighted) configuration that maximizes prediction—swap out one of these predictors for a new variable and the whole configuration that represents the best prediction can be quite different.

The second important point about regression analysis that this example illustrates, which is related to the first, is that a highly predictive variable can be "left out in the cold," being "sacrificed" for the "good of the model." Note that negative affect correlates rather substantially with self-esteem ($r = -.572$), and if it was the only predictor it would have a beta weight of $-.572$ (recall that in simple linear regression the Pearson *r* is the beta weight of the predictor), yet in combination with the other predictors is not a significant predictor in the multiple regression model. The reason is that its predictive work is being accomplished by one or more of the other variables in the analysis. But the point is that just because a variable receives a modest weight in the model or just because a variable is not contributing a statistically significant degree of prediction in the model is not a reason to presume that it is itself a poor predictor.

It is also important to note that the IBM SPSS output does not contain the structure coefficients. These are the correlations of the predictors in the model with the overall predictor variate, and these structure coefficients help researchers interpret the dimension underlying the predictor model (see Section 7A.11). They are easy enough to calculate by hand (the Pearson correlation between the predictor and the criterion variable divided by the multiple correlation), and we incorporate these structure coefficients into our report of the results in Section 7B.1.5.

7B.1.5 Reporting Standard Multiple Regression Results

Negative affect, positive affect, openness to experience, extraversion, neuroticism, and trait anxiety were used in a standard regression analysis to predict self-esteem. The correlations of the variables are shown in Table 7b.1. As can be seen, all correlations, except for the one between openness and extraversion, were statistically significant.

The prediction model was statistically significant, $F(6, 413) = 106.356$, $p < .001$, and accounted for approximately 60% of the variance of self-esteem ($R^2 = .607$, Adjusted $R^2 = .601$). Self-esteem was primarily predicted by lower levels of trait anxiety and neuroticism, and to a lesser extent by higher levels of positive affect and extraversion. The raw and standardized regression coefficients of the predictors together with their correlations with self-esteem, their squared semipartial correlations and their structure coefficients, are shown in Table 7b.2. Trait anxiety received the strongest weight in the model followed by neuroticism and positive affect. With the sizeable correlations between the predictors, the unique variance explained by each of the variables indexed by the squared semipartial correlations was quite low. Inspection of the structure coefficients suggests that, with the possible exception of extraversion whose correlation is still relatively substantial, the other significant predictors were strong indicators of the underlying (latent) variable described by the model, which can be interpreted as well-being.

7B.2 Stepwise Multiple Regression

We discussed the forward, backward, and stepwise methods of performing a regression analysis in Chapter 5A. To illustrate how to work with these methods, we will perform a

Table 7b.1 Correlations of the Variables in the Analysis ($N = 420$)

Variable	2	3	4	5	6	7
1. Self-Esteem	−.572	.555	.221	.425	−.693	−.724
2. Negative Affect	--	−.324	−.168	−.218	.712	.713
3. Positive Affect		--	.221	.528	−.441	−.528
4. Openness			--	.051	−.227	−.183
5. Extraversion				--	−.347	−.375
6. Neuroticism					--	.809
7. Trait Anxiety						--

Note. All correlations except that between Openness and Extraversion were statistically significant ($p < .001$).

Table 7b.2 Standard Regression Results

Model	b	SE-b	Beta	Pearson r	sr²	Structure Coefficient
Constant	96.885	7.294				
Negative Affect	−.386	.264	−.069	−.572	.002	−.734
Positive Affect*	1.338	.293	.186	.555	.020	.712
Openness	.088	.062	.046	.221	.002	.284
Extraversion*	.185	.069	.099	.425	.007	.546
Neuroticism*	−.477	.106	−.254	−.693	.019	−.890
Trait Anxiety*	−.646	.117	−.326	−.724	.029	−.929

Note. The dependent variable was Self-Esteem. $R^2 = .607$, Adjusted $R^2 = .601$. sr^2 is the squared semi-partial correlation.
* $p < .05$.

stepwise analysis on the same set of variables that we used in our standard regression analysis in Section 7B.1. We will use the data file **Personality** in these demonstrations. In the process of our description, we will point out areas of similarity and difference between the standard and step methods.

7B.2.1 Main Regression Dialog Window

Select the path **Analyze ➔ Regression ➔ Linear**. This brings us to the **Linear Regression** main dialog window displayed in Figure 7b.6. From the variables list panel, we click over **esteem** to the **Dependent** panel and **negafect, posafect, neoopen, neoextra, neoneuro**, and **tanx** to the **Independent(s)** panel. The **Method** drop-down menu contains the set of step methods that IBM SPSS can run. The only one you may not recognize is **Remove**, which allows a set of variables to be removed from the model together. Choose **Stepwise** as the **Method** from the drop-down menu as shown in Figure 7b.6.

Figure 7b.6 Main Dialog Window for Linear Regression

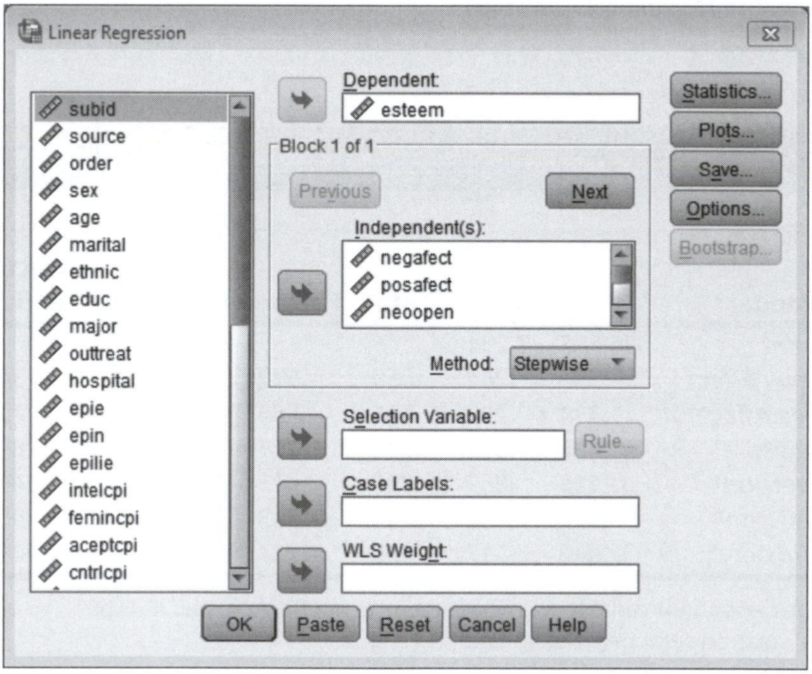

7B.2.2 Statistics Window

Selecting the **Statistics** pushbutton brings us to the **Linear Regression: Statistics** dialog window shown in Figure 7b.7. This was already discussed in Section 7B.1.2. Clicking **Continue** returns us to the main dialog box.

Figure 7b.7 The Linear Regression Statistics Window

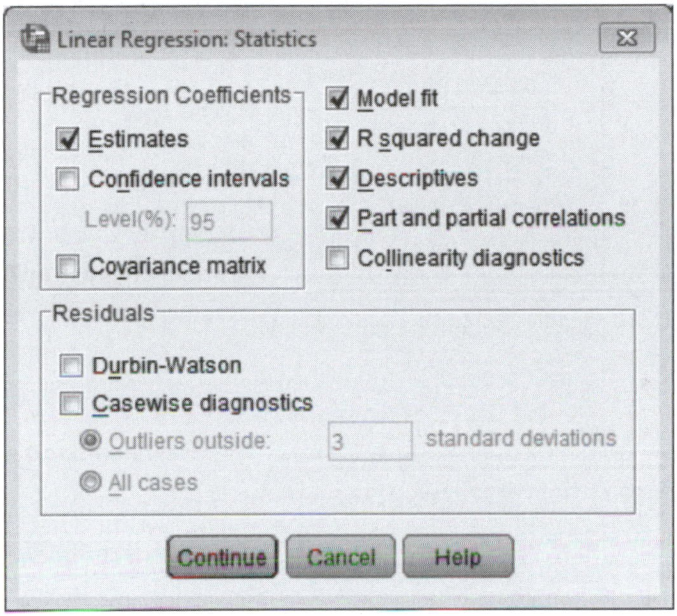

7B.2.3 Options Window

Selecting the **Options** pushbutton brings us to the **Linear Regression: Options** dialog window shown in Figure 7b.8. The top panel is now applicable as we are using the stepwise method. To avoid looping variables continually in and out of the model, it is appropriate to set different "significance" levels for entry and exit. The defaults used by IBM SPSS are common settings, and we recommend them. Remember that in the stepwise procedure, variables already entered into the model can be removed at a later step if they are no longer contributing a statistically significant amount of prediction.

Earning entry to the model is set at an alpha level of .05 (e.g., a variable with a probability of .07 will not be entered) and is the more stringent of the two settings. But to be removed, a variable must have an associated probability of greater than .10 (e.g., a variable with an associated probability of .12 will be removed but one with an associated probability of .07 will remain in the model). In essence, it is more difficult to get in than be removed. This is a good thing and allows the stepwise procedure to function. Click **Continue** to return to the main dialog window, and click **OK** to perform the analysis.

Figure 7b.8 The Linear Regression Options Window

7B.2.4 Stepwise Multiple Regression Output

The descriptive statistics are identical to those presented in Section 7B.1.4, and we will skip those here. Figure 7b.9 displays the test of significance of the model using an ANOVA. The four ANOVAs that are reported correspond to four models, but don't let the terminology confuse you. The stepwise procedure adds only one variable at a time to the model as the model is "slowly" built. At the third step and beyond, it is also possible to remove a variable from the model (although that did not happen in our example). In the terminology used by IBM SPSS, each step results in a model, and each successive step modifies the older model and replaces it with a newer one. Each model is tested for statistical significance.

Examining the last two columns of the output shown in Figure 7b.9 informs us that the final model was built in four steps; each step resulted in a statistically significant model. Examining the **df** column shows us that one variable was added during each step (the degrees of freedom for the **Regression** effect track this for us as they are counts of the

Figure 7b.9 Tests of Significance for Each Step in the Regression Analysis

ANOVA$_e$

Model		Sum of Squares	df	Mean Square	F	Sig.
1	Regression	96502.996	1	96502.996	461.281	.000$_a$
	Residual	87448.394	418	209.207		
	Total	183951.390	419			
2	Regression	104086.724	2	52043.362	271.736	.000$_b$
	Residual	79864.666	417	191.522		
	Total	183951.390	419			
3	Regression	109881.931	3	36627.310	205.712	.000$_c$
	Residual	74069.460	416	178.052		
	Total	183951.390	419			
4	Regression	110934.239	4	27733.560	157.626	.000$_d$
	Residual	73017.152	415	175.945		
	Total	183951.390	419			

a. Predictors: (Constant), tanx trait anxiety: spielberger

b. Predictors: (Constant), tanx trait anxiety: spielberger, posafect positive affect: mpq

c. Predictors: (Constant), tanx trait anxiety: spielberger, posafect positive affect: mpq, neoneuro neuroticism: neo

d. Predictors: (Constant), tanx trait anxiety: spielberger, posafect positive affect: mpq, neoneuro neuroticism: neo, neoextra extraversion: neo

e. Dependent Variable: esteem self-esteem: coopersmith

number of predictors in the model). We can also deduce that no variables were removed from the model since the count of predictors in the model steadily increases from 1 to 4.

This latter deduction is verified by the display shown in Figure 7b.10, which tracks variables that have been entered and removed at each step. As can be seen, trait anxiety, positive affect, neuroticism, and extraversion have been entered on Steps 1 through 4, respectively, without any variables having been removed on any step.

Figure 7b.11, the **Model Summary**, presents the **R Square** and **Adjusted R Square** values for each step along with the amount of **R Square Change**. In the first step, as can be seen from the footnote beneath the **Model Summary** table, trait anxiety was entered into the model. The **R Square** with that predictor in the model was .525. Not coincidentally, that is the square of the correlation between trait anxiety and self-esteem ($.724^2 = .525$), and is the value of **R Square Change**.

On the second step, positive affect was added to the model. The **R Square** with both predictors in the model was .566; thus, we gained .041 in the value of **R Square** (.566 − .525 = .041), and this is reflected in the **R Square Change** for that step. By the time we arrive at the end of the fourth step, our **R Square** value has reached .603. Note that this

Figure 7b.10 Variables That Were Entered and Removed

Variables Entered/Removeda

Model	Variables Entered	Variables Removed	Method
1	tanx trait anxiety: spielberger	.	Stepwise (Criteria: Probability-of-F-to-enter <= .050, Probability-of-F-to-remove >= .100).
2	posafect positive affect: mpq	.	Stepwise (Criteria: Probability-of-F-to-enter <= .050, Probability-of-F-to-remove >= .100).
3	neoneuro neuroticism: neo	.	Stepwise (Criteria: Probability-of-F-to-enter <= .050, Probability-of-F-to-remove >= .100).
4	neoextra extraversion: neo	.	Stepwise (Criteria: Probability-of-F-to-enter <= .050, Probability-of-F-to-remove >= .100).

a. Dependent Variable: esteem self-esteem: coopersmith

value is very close to but not identical to the R^2 value we obtained under the standard method.

The **Coefficients** table in Figure 7b.12 provides the details of the results. Note that both the raw and standardized regression coefficients are readjusted at each step to reflect the additional variables in the model. Ordinarily, although it is interesting to observe the dynamic changes taking place, we are usually interested in the final model. Note also that the values of the regression coefficients are different from those associated with the same variables in the standard regression analysis. That the differences are not huge is due to the fact that these four variables did almost the same amount of predictive work in much the same configuration as did the six predictors accomplished using the standard method. If economy of model were relevant, we would probably be very happy with the trimmed model of four variables replacing the full model containing six variables.

Figure 7b.13 addresses the fate of the remaining variables. For each step, IBM SPSS tells us which variables were not entered. In addition to tests of the statistical significance of each variable, we also see displayed the partial correlations. This information together tells us what will happen in the following step. For example, consider Step 1, which contains the five excluded variables. Positive affect has the highest partial correlation (.294), and it is statistically significant; thus, it will be the variable next entered on Step 2. On the second step, with four variables (of the six) excluded, we see that neuroticism with a statistically significant partial correlation of

Figure 7b.11 Model Summary

Model Summary

Model	R	R Square	Adjusted R Square	Std. Error of the Estimate	Change Statistics R Square Change	F Change	df1	df2	Sig. F Change
1	.724a	.525	.523	14.46398	.525	461.281	1	418	.000
2	.752b	.566	.564	13.83915	.041	39.597	1	417	.000
3	.773c	.597	.594	13.34360	.032	32.548	1	416	.000
4	.777d	.603	.599	13.26442	.006	5.981	1	415	.015

a. Predictors: (Constant), tanx trait anxiety: spielberger

b. Predictors: (Constant), tanx trait anxiety: spielberger, posafect positive affect: mpq

c. Predictors: (Constant), tanx trait anxiety: spielberger, posafect positive affect: mpq, neoneuro neuroticism: neo

d. Predictors: (Constant), tanx trait anxiety: spielberger, posafect positive affect: mpq, neoneuro neuroticism: neo, neoextra extraversion: neo

Figure 7b.12 The Results of the Stepwise Regression Analysis

Coefficients_a

Model		Unstandardized Coefficients B	Std. Error	Standardized Coefficients Beta	t	Sig.	Correlations Zero-order	Partial	Part
1	(Constant)	126.197	2.652		47.588	.000			
	tanx trait anxiety: spielberger	−1.432	.067	−.724	−21.477	.000	−.724	−.724	−.724
2	(Constant)	103.366	4.427		23.347	.000			
	tanx trait anxiety: spielberger	−1.183	.075	−.598	−15.742	.000	−.724	−.611	−.508
	posafect positive affect: mpq	1.722	.274	.239	6.293	.000	.555	.294	.203
3	(Constant)	114.095	4.665		24.459	.000			
	tanx trait anxiety: spielberger	−.706	.111	−.357	−6.386	.000	−.724	−.299	−.199
	posafect positive affect: mpq	1.679	.264	.233	6.364	.000	.555	.298	.198
	neoneuro neuroticism: neo	−.567	.099	−.302	−5.705	.000	−.693	−.269	−.177
4	(Constant)	105.775	5.751		18.392	.000			
	tanx trait anxiety: spielberger	−.698	.110	−.353	−6.345	.000	−.724	−.297	−.196
	posafect positive affect: mpq	1.384	.289	.192	4.793	.000	.555	.229	.148
	neoneuro neuroticism: neo	−.549	.099	−.292	−5.537	.000	−.693	−.262	−.171
	neoextra extraversion: neo	.167	.068	.090	2.446	.015	.425	.119	.076

a. Dependent Variable: esteem self-esteem: coopersmith

−.269 wins the struggle for entry next. By the time we reach the fourth step, there is no variable of the excluded set that has a statistically significant partial correlation for entry at Step 5; thus, the stepwise procedure ends after completing the fourth step.

Figure 7b.13 The Results of the Stepwise Regression Analysis

Excluded Variables$_e$

Model		Beta In	t	Sig.	Partial Correlation	Collinearity Statistics Tolerance
1	negafect negative affect: mpq	−.112$_a$	−2.350	.019	−.114	.492
	posafect positive affect: mpq	.239$_a$	6.293	.000	.294	.721
	neoopen openness: neo	.091$_a$	2.680	.008	.130	.967
	neoextra extraversion: neo	.179$_a$	5.058	.000	.240	.859
	neoneuro neuroticism: neo	−.311$_a$	−5.625	.000	−.266	.346
2	negafect negative affect: mpq	−.139$_b$	−3.034	.003	−.147	.488
	neoopen openness: neo	.062$_b$	1.872	.062	.091	.945
	neoextra extraversion: neo	.106$_b$	2.777	.006	.135	.709
	neoneuro neuroticism: neo	−.302$_b$	−5.705	.000	−.269	.346
3	negafect negative affect: mpq	−.061$_c$	−1.296	.196	−.063	.434
	neoopen openness: neo	.038$_c$	1.180	.239	.058	.928
	neoextra extraversion: neo	.090$_c$	2.446	.015	.119	.704
4	negafect negative affect: mpq	−.070$_d$	−1.487	.138	−.073	.432
	neoopen openness: neo	.047$_d$	1.446	.149	.071	.918

a. Predictors in the Model: (Constant), tanx trait anxiety: spielberger

b. Predictors in the Model: (Constant), tanx trait anxiety: spielberger, posafect positive affect: mpq

c. Predictors in the Model: (Constant), tanx trait anxiety: spielberger, posafect positive affect: mpq, neoneuro neuroticism: neo

d. Predictors in the Model: (Constant), tanx trait anxiety: spielberger, posafect positive affect: mpq, neoneuro neuroticism: neo, neoextra extraversion: neo

e. Dependent Variable: esteem self-esteem: coopersmith

7B.2.5 Reporting Stepwise Multiple Regression Results

Negative affect, positive affect, openness to experience, extraversion, neuroticism, and trait anxiety were used in a stepwise multiple regression analysis to predict self-esteem. The correlations of the variables are shown in Table 7b.1. As can be seen, all correlations except for the one between openness and extraversion were statistically significant.

The prediction model contained four of the six predictors and was reached in four steps with no variables removed. The model was statistically significant, $F(4, 415) = 157.626$, $p < .001$, and accounted for approximately 60% of the variance of self-esteem ($R^2 = .603$, Adjusted $R^2 = .599$). Self-esteem was primarily predicted by lower levels of trait anxiety and neuroticism, and to a lesser extent by higher levels of positive affect and extraversion. The raw and standardized regression coefficients of the predictors together with their correlations with self-esteem, their squared semi-partial correlations, and their structure coefficients are shown in Table 7b.3. Trait anxiety received the strongest weight in the model followed by neuroticism and positive affect; extraversion received the lowest of the four weights. With the sizeable correlations between the predictors, the unique variance explained by each of the variables indexed by the squared semipartial correlations, was relatively low: trait anxiety, positive affect, neuroticism, and extraversion uniquely accounted for approximately 4%, 2%, 3%, and less than 1% of the variance of self-esteem. The latent factor represented by the model appears to be interpretable as well-being. Inspection of the structure coefficients suggests that trait anxiety and neuroticism were very strong indicators of well being, positive affect was a relatively strong indicator of well-being, and extraversion was a moderate indicator of well-being.

Table 7b.3 Stepwise Regression Results

Model	b	SE-b	Beta	Pearson r	sr^2	Structure Coefficient
Constant	105.775	5.751				
Trait Anxiety	−.698	.110	−.353	−.724	.038	−.932
Positive Affect*	1.384	.289	.192	.555	.022	.714
Neuroticism*	−.549	.099	−.292	−.693	.029	−.892
Extraversion*	.167	.068	.090	.425	.006	.547

Note. The dependent variable was Self-Esteem. $R^2 = .603$, Adjusted $R^2 = .599$.
sr^2 is the squared semi-partial correlation.
* $p < .05$.

Multiple Regression: Beyond Statistical Regression

8A.1 A Larger World of Regression

Statistical regression, in the form of either the standard method or one of the step methods, has proven to be a very useful tool for researchers. But perhaps it is partly because the current software packages such as IBM SPSS have made this technique so easy to use—place some measures in a data file, identify the dependent and independent variables, select some checkboxes for particular output, and click **OK** to perform the analysis—that we have tended to yield control of regression analyses to the software a little too frequently. That is, simply placing a set of variables in a regression analysis and seeing how they work together to predict the outcome variable may be appropriate under some research circumstances but there are many occasions under which it is more appropriate—and sometimes necessary—for researchers to take a more active role in the data analysis.

With some extra work on our part—not necessarily a lot of work in many instances—it is possible to perform variations of statistical regression, and that is what this chapter is all about. Our sense is that times are changing and that researchers are now being much more proactive in using a regression approach to analyze their data, looking to incorporate a more explicit aspect of explanation to supplement the prediction aspect of the analysis. This chapter discusses some variations that allow us to move past statistical regression.

8A.2 Hierarchical Linear Regression

8A.2.1 Overview

Hierarchical regression, at least in its simplest incarnation, is perhaps the procedure most similar to standard regression that we cover in this chapter in that all of the independent variables are still placed into the model—the difference here is that the variables are entered into the model in steps (called *blocks* or *models* in the context of hierarchical regression) rather than all at once. What makes a hierarchical approach different is that the researchers rationally determine which variables they would like to use as covariates at each step of their choosing in the analysis. Particular attention is paid to the amount of predictability (explanation) that is gained—assessed by the change in R^2—with each new block of variables added to the previous model in forming a new (expanded) model.

Selection of covariates should be based on a particular theory or should rest on a solid empirical basis in which the research literature has shown the need to take into account the relationship(s) between the criterion variable and one or more of the predictors. Several labels are applied to this sort of variation of researcher control: *sequential analysis*, *covariance analysis*, *hierarchical analysis*, and *block-entry analysis* are among the most common. We will use the term *hierarchical analysis* in our presentation.

8A.2.2 An Example

We use a simplified example to illustrate hierarchical regression in the context of delivering community mental health services to a diverse population in which 368 mental health providers completed a set of inventories. Suppose we are interested in predicting one particular aspect of the self-perceived level of cultural competence acknowledged by professional mental health providers: awareness of cultural barriers faced by their clientele. Assume that the potential predictor variables we have in the data file include measures of racial attitudes (specifically, a subscale assessing institutional discrimination), ethnic identity (specifically, a subscale assessing ethnic identity exploration), a collectivism orientation measure, a social desirability measure, a variable dealing with the length of time spent as a provider in mental health, and a variable indicating whether or not the provider received specialized training in multicultural counseling. Further assume that the research question of interest concerns the prediction of awareness of cultural barriers based on the strengths of their racial attitudes, ethnic identity, and collective orientation.

Under the standard regression method, all of the variables would be entered into the model in a single step, and the regression weights would then be examined if the model was statistically significant. We would also examine the R^2 and the adjusted R^2 to determine how effectively the model fared. Under a step method, the stepwise method for example, the best predictor would be entered into the model first, the next best would be entered second, and so forth. Variables could be removed as needed after the third variable was entered. And, as would be true for the standard method, we would also examine the R^2 and the adjusted R^2.

The structure of the hierarchical analysis and the results are shown in Figure 8a.1. Let us assume that both the research literature as well as theoretical issues guide the researchers through the following reasoning. The goal of the research is to predict the reported level of

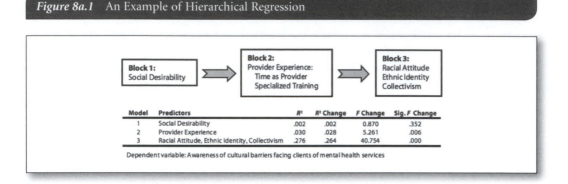

Figure 8a.1 An Example of Hierarchical Regression

Model	Predictors	R^2	R^2 Change	F Change	Sig. F Change
1	Social Desirability	.002	.002	0.870	.352
2	Provider Experience	.030	.028	5.261	.006
3	Racial Attitude, Ethnic Identity, Collectivism	.276	.264	40.754	.000

Dependent variable: Awareness of cultural barriers facing clients of mental health services

provider awareness of cultural barriers faced by clients receiving mental health services based on the levels of racial attitudes, ethnic identity, and collective orientation of practitioners. But we will assume that there is good reason to believe that responses to the survey items for the dependent variable might be affected by clinicians trying to respond in a manner that they felt was more socially desirable or appropriate. In anticipation of this possibility, the researchers administered an inventory designed to measure that characteristic. To statistically control for social desirability effects, the researchers entered this variable in the first step, called a "Block" by IBM SPSS.

The result of that step is shown in the table below the flow chart. The row labeled **Model 1 Social Desirability** summarizes some of the results for entering the **Social Desirability** variable into the model. The R^2 value reached .002, representing a quite small change from an R^2 value of zero (since this was the first variable placed into the model). The F value associated with the ANOVA evaluating the statistical significance of the model had a p value of .352. Using an alpha level of .05, we would conclude that **Social Desirability** did not account for a statistically significant amount of the variance of **Awareness of Cultural Barriers**. Such a finding would help assure the researchers that responses by providers indicating their awareness of barriers facing their clientele were not likely to be influenced by a need to present themselves in a more socially acceptable light.

The researchers might also have been concerned that the experience of the practitioners as indexed here by their time in practice and having received specialized multicultural training could make a difference in the prediction of awareness of barriers. Thus, while controlling for the effects of **Social Desirability**, the researchers enter in a second step or "Block" the time-in-practice and having-received-specialized-multicultural-training variables next into the model. The variables are entered together (although they could be themselves entered sequentially) as the researchers wish to treat them together as predictors in a single step.

The result of that step is shown in the second row of the table labeled **Model 2 Provider Experience**. Remember that **Social Desirability** is already in the model and thus is acting as a covariate. When the variables Time as Provider and Specialized Training (comprising **Provider Experience**) are entered in Block 2, the regression weights for **Social Desirability** (not shown) are recomputed to accommodate the additional variables in the model (as described in Chapter 7A). Entering the **Provider Experience** variables with **Social Desirability** being used as a covariate raised the R^2 by .028 (from an R^2 for Model 1) to an R^2 of .030 for Model 2. This change in R^2 was statistically significant ($p = .006$). Thus, **Provider Experience** added about 3% explained **Awareness of Cultural Barriers** variance when controlling for the effects of **Social Desirability**.

Finally, in the third and final block, the researchers have entered their three focal variables of **Institutional Discrimination**, **Ethnic Identity Exploration**, and **Collectivism**. And the weights of the other three variables already in the model are once again recomputed now that three more variables have been added. The last row of the table shows that the increase of R^2 by .264 to a final value of .276 was statistically significant. Thus, statistically controlling for **Provider Experience** and **Social Desirability**, **Institutional Discrimination**, **Ethnic Identity Exploration**, and **Collectivism** added predictive power to the model—that is, these latter three variables contributed prediction (about 26% of accounted for variance) over and above what the other three variables could offer.

Note that at the very end of the hierarchical regression analysis, the final model is identical to what would be obtained when using the standard method. That is, all of the variables are in the model, and the weighting of each has been determined by using all of the other variables as covariates. The difference, however, is that by using a hierarchical method of entry, it is possible to see the dynamic interplay among the variables that was not available when using the standard method.

8A.2.3 Other Issues in the Context of Hierarchical Regression

In addition to exploring the theoretical consequences of varying the order of entry of the predictors and in addition to determining the result of using certain variables as covariates, other issues can be broached by using a sequential form of regression analyses. Here are two examples:

- A very "expensive" variable achieved substantial weight in the model. To collect data on this predictor might take a great deal of time, trouble, and/or funding. It may be worthwhile to ask if any combination of variables in the model could do almost as good a job but "work for cheaper research wages."
- A set of variables received negligible weights in the model, but these are easy to measure (e.g., they may be subscales of a single inventory). Similar measures might have been weighted substantially but could be more difficult to work with. It may make sense to investigate the R^2 consequences of replacing the latter with the former.

8A.3 Suppressor Variables

8A.3.1 Overview

Suppressor variables, when included in regression models, increase R^2, but they accomplish this feat in a somewhat different way from what we have already discussed. Suppressor variables often are not correlated particularly strongly with the criterion variable itself. Rather, they are correlated in a special way with one or more of the other predictor variables, and that is where they do their job.

A suppressor variable works by correlating with what is usually thought of as a source of error in another predictor (Darlington, 1960). Pedhazur (1982) describes it well in saying that by correlating with the error in another predictor, the suppressor variable helps "purify" that predictor and thereby enhances its predictive power. Often, under these conditions, this suppressor variable will then be given a negative weight in the equation (assuming that the predictor it is partially suppressing is positively correlated with the dependent variable). Tabachnick and Fidell (2007) have provided the following rubric to help identify a suppressor variable:

- The correlation between it and the criterion variable is substantially smaller than its beta weight.

Or

- Its Pearson correlation with the criterion and its beta weight have different signs. (p. 149)

Other signs that we may have a suppressor variable in the equation are offered by Pedhazur (1982):

- It may have a near-zero correlation with the criterion variable but yet it is a significant predictor in the regression model.
- It may have little or no correlation with the criterion variable but is correlated with one or more of the predictors. (pp. 104–105)

8A.3.2 An Example

Conceptualizing how a suppressor variable does its work is not an easy matter. Guilford's example (Guilford & Fruchter, 1978) is better than most, and we will present it to you as a way to exemplify this somewhat elusive concept.

J. P. Guilford, one of the great pioneers in measurement and psychometrics, did research for the Air Force during World War II to develop selection procedures for pilots. He speaks of a vocabulary test that slightly negatively correlated with success in pilot training. His research team had also used a reading test in the study (the trainees read passages and answered questions about them), which turned out to correlate positively with success in pilot training.

At first, it must have seemed odd that a vocabulary test slightly negatively correlated with pilot success but that a reading test correlated positively with pilot training success. But Guilford soon realized that the reading test correlated positively with pilot success not because it measured some verbal skill but rather because of the content it presented to the trainees. This content tapped into their experience with mechanical devices and their ability to visualize information contained in the passages.

According to Guilford's appraisal of the situation, the score these trainees received on the reading test was a function of three factors—mechanical experience, visualization, and, of course, verbal comprehension—only two of which (mechanical experience and visualization) were viable predictors of pilot success. The third factor measured by the reading test, verbal comprehension, did not predict success, something he already knew from the results of his vocabulary test. This third factor in the reading test actually represented, from the standpoint of predicting training success, error variance.

Now consider the relationship between the vocabulary test and the reading test. Roughly speaking, the vocabulary test was a measure of verbal comprehension or something that correlated highly with it. From this perspective, the reading test and the vocabulary test share common variance. But not just any variance, mind you. The variance they share is common to what they both measure—verbal comprehension or its kin.

How a suppressor variable works lies, in this example, with what happens when you make use of the correlation between the vocabulary and the reading tests. If the vocabulary test was placed in the regression model together with the reading test, even though it could not directly predict pilot success, it would have the opportunity to correlate with that portion of the reading test assessing verbal comprehension. By virtue of that correlation, it would account for (statistically control for or negate) that portion of the reading test's variance attributable to verbal comprehension and thus make the reading test a better predictor than it would be in the absence of the vocabulary test. All that we would need to do is subtract that error variance out.

Based on this reasoning, Guilford tells us that the

> combination of a vocabulary test with the reading test, with a negative weight for the vocabulary test [to subtract out this variance accounted for by the vocabulary test], would have improved predictions [of pilot success] over those possible with the reading test alone. (Guilford & Fruchter, 1978, p. 182)

That is, including the vocabulary test would have accounted for and subtracted out the variance due to verbal comprehension in the reading test (which was not contributing to the prediction of success anyhow), freeing up the other components of the reading test (the parts assessing mechanical experience and visualization) to more purely predict success in pilot training. In this context, the vocabulary test would have operated as a suppressor variable.

8A.4 Linear and Nonlinear Regression

For the purposes of this book, we can distinguish between three types of regression models (Cohen et al., 2003): a form we will call *completely linear*, another form of linear model called *intrinsically linear* (Pedhazur, 1982), and a form of nonlinear model called *intrinsically nonlinear* (Pedhazur, 1982) or *general curve fitting* (Darlington, 1960). We briefly discuss each in turn.

8A.4.1 Completely Linear Models

In the completely linear model, both the variables specified by the model (the dependent and the independent variables) as well as the parameters (the coefficients and the intercept) are in their "regular" form. We then multiply each variable by its weight and add the results of that multiplication together (adding the constant in the raw score equation) to obtain the predicted value of the criterion variable. We have seen this type of model throughout Chapter 7A and thus far in the present chapter.

If there is only one predictor in the model, as is the case in simple linear regression, the equation can be represented geometrically as a straight line in two-dimensional space (in a space defined with X and Y axes). With two predictors in the model, the equation may be represented geometrically as a tilted plane in three-dimensional space (illustrated well by Darlington, 1960). If you think of a room in a house, the two predictor variables cover the floor (the width and the length) of the room and the criterion variable is mapped to the walls (height). Imagine a pitched and tilted ceiling to this room that can be dropped down inside the walls of the room. This ceiling represents the plane described by a regression model with two predictors. Although it has one more dimension to it than the straight line, it is still a completely linear model composed of flat, straight surfaces. Models with more than two predictors, even though we cannot easily picture them, are also linear in this sense.

8A.4.2 Intrinsically Linear Models

8A.4.2.1 Overview

Another class of linear models has the same basic structure of completely linear models in that (a) each variable has an associated coefficient, (b) we multiply each variable by its coefficient to obtain its weighted value, and (c) we add the results of that multiplication together (adding the constant in the raw score equation) to obtain the predicted value of the criterion variable. Furthermore, the function of best fit is still based on the least squares rule.

The difference between completely linear models and intrinsically linear models is that in the latter, the variables themselves are not in their "regular" or raw form; rather, they have been "altered" in some manner. In this sense, we can say that the model is *linear with respect to its parameters*—in that the regression weights are still in "regular" form and we add the weighted variables together to obtain the predicted score—but that the model is *nonlinear in its variables*. We can think of an intrinsically linear model as one that combines variables that are themselves not linear in the best weighted linear combination to maximally predict the dependent variable.

Variables in an intrinsically linear model can be altered in several different nonlinear ways. Two such ways are special coding strategies, such as dummy and effect coding, and evaluating interaction effects. These topics are given their own treatment in Sections 8A.5 and 8A.6, respectively. Transformations of dependent and independent variables is another such alteration, and we deal with that here.

A transformation is used either to bring the data more closely in line with the underlying assumptions of regression or because it makes more sense to frame the relationships between the predictor and criterion variables in terms of a transformed variable. We have already discussed a transformation to a standardized scale (a *z*-score transformation) that is routinely performed by virtually every statistical software program in computing a regression solution, although this type of transformation still keeps the variables in linear form. Other transformations are generally applied to the dependent or criterion variable, and still other transformations are generally applied to the independent or predictor variables that convert them to a nonlinear form.

8A.4.2.2 Log Transformation

One common transformation of the criterion variable (other than standardizing it) is to use its natural logarithm as the value to be predicted (Allison, 1999a). Such a transformation, which we described in Chapter 3A, may help reduce the degree of heteroscedasticity in the measure. Another transformation, often applied to predictor variables, is to subject them to a log (usually base 10) transformation. We would tend to use this type of transformation where we expect the criterion and predictor variables to increase together up to some point but then expect the dependent variable to level off with further increases in the predictor. For example, in predicting income from education, we might expect that higher income levels are associated with increasingly more education up to some point but that more education would not alter income level beyond some point (Allison, 1999).

8A.4.2.3 Logit Transformation

Another transformation of the dependent variable is a logit transformation, provided the criterion variable is a proportion (Allison, 1999a). If the criterion variable is symbolized by Y, then this transformation takes the following form:

$$\text{log of the expression} \left[\frac{Y}{1-Y} \right]$$

8A.4.2.4 Polynomial Transformations

A common transformation of the predictor variables is to use a polynomial function in which the value of one or more of the independent variables is raised to a power (e.g., X^2). This is called *polynomial* or *curvilinear* regression. A second-order polynomial function, known as a quadratic function, has the predictor raised to the second power. We might use this transformation when we expect the criterion variable to first increase together with the predictor and then to decrease with further increases in values of the predictor variable. For example, using age as a predictor of physical agility, we would expect agility to increase up to some age level but to then show a decrease with further increases in age. A quadratic function has one "bend" in the curve. In contrast, a cubic function (a third-order polynomial in which a predictor X is raised to the power of 3) has two "bends" in the functions and is substantially more complex to interpret. Most researchers would not use a polynomial function in excess of a third order. In the case of a single predictor with just a few values, an alternative strategy is to use a trend analysis (see Chapter 4A).

8A.4.3 Intrinsically Nonlinear Models

There is a whole set of models that do not take a linear form. That is, even if the variables are altered in some manner as described in Section 8A.4.2, there are models that are not linear with respect to their parameters. These models cannot be transformed to produce a linear function and are called as a set of *intrinsically nonlinear models*. Intrinsically nonlinear models cannot be analyzed through a procedure that uses ordinary least squares and are best handled by other curve-fitting techniques. They are represented by equations of different forms. Darlington (1960) gives the following example of an intrinsically nonlinear model:

$$Y_{\text{pred}} = (b_1 X_1 + b_2 X_2)(b_3 X_3 + b_4 X_4)$$

Allison (1999) gives an example as well:

$$Y_{\text{pred}} = 1 + A_X^B$$

We do not treat intrinsically nonlinear models in this book, but interested readers can consult Cohen et al. (2003), Freund, Wilson, and Ping (2006), and Vittinghoff, McCulloch, Glidden, and Shiboski (2011) for more information on this topic.

8A.5 Dummy and Effect Coding

In his classic *Psychological Bulletin* article, Jacob Cohen (1968) explicitly told us that the *t* test, ANOVA, ANCOVA, and linear and polynomial regression analysis were the same fundamental procedure, something that mathematical statisticians knew long before behavioral scientists came to this understanding. It is therefore possible to evaluate main effects as well as interactions of independent variables in either an ANOVA procedure or an ordinary least squares regression procedure. Perhaps the clearest demonstration of the truth of Cohen's message can be seen in working with dummy and effect coding. In Chapter 8B, we will directly show the correspondence between these two approaches. Here, we present the more conceptual discussion of this topic.

8A.5.1 The Elements of Dummy and Effect Coding

As we demonstrated in Section 6A.5, it is appropriate to perform a Pearson correlation analysis with a dichotomously coded qualitative (categorical) variable (e.g., sex) and a quantitatively measured variable (e.g., verbal ability). In the example that we used, the sex of the children was coded as 1 and 2, with the correlation yielding the same value regardless of which sex was assigned which code (just the sign of the correlation was different). And because Pearson correlation and ordinary least squares regression are so intimately connected, we could use that dichotomously coded sex variable as an independent variable to predict the quantitative criterion variable of verbal ability.

Without repeating the explanation of why it is so, we also indicated in Section 6A.5 that if a qualitative variable had three or more categories, then performing a Pearson correlation procedure would be inappropriate. However, such categorical variables can conditionally be properly used in ordinary least squares regression as predictors of a quantitatively measured variable. The condition we must meet is that the categorical variable needs to be specially coded before it can be so used. Although there are several coding strategies available, we will limit our discussion to two of the more commonly used strategies: dummy coding and effect coding.

The processes of dummy coding and effect coding involve making decisions about four major elements:

- The number of codes or code sets that are required
- The categories that are to be coded

- The values that are to be used as the codes
- How the categorical variable is represented in the regression analysis

We treat each in turn, illustrating these elements in the context of the following hypothetical example. The categorical independent or predictor variable in the regression analysis is to be the cover of a new textbook on statistics. In our scenario, there has been some uncertainty over what the color of the cover should be. The publisher has therefore asked the graphic designer to mock up three covers in different colors: red, blue, and green. Eight students were shown the book with the red cover, 8 were shown the book with the blue cover, and 8 were shown the book with the green color. The dependent variable is an evaluation rating of the book. The 24 students were asked to look over the book and rate on a 10-point scale the extent to which they viewed it in a positive light; higher values indicate more positive reactions. The book publisher intends to place the text into production with the cover that draws the most favorable ratings.

8A.5.1.1 The Number of Code Sets Required

The required number of code sets (new variables to be created in the data file) representing a categorical variable is equal to the degrees of freedom of the categorical variable, which is the number of categories minus one ($k - 1$). Thus, with the three categories (three colors) we have in our example, we need two code sets (two new variables need to be created). If we had four categories we would need three code sets, if we had five categories we would need four code sets, and so on. This is true for both dummy and effect coding.

8A.5.1.2 The Categories to Be Coded

Each code set that we create represents one of the k number of categories comprising the variable. But given that the number of code sets required is $k - 1$, one of the categories will not have its own code set. That may strike you a little odd, but it is not a problem; however, it does mean that the researchers must make a conscious decision regarding which categories are assigned their own code set and which one category is not. Dummy and effect coding handle this element somewhat differently.

8A.5.1.3 The Values Used as Codes

True dummy coding uses the values of 0 and 1 in the coding scheme, and that is what we will presume in the rest of our discussion of dummy coding. Other coding values may be used but we would not recommend them to users of this book. Specifically,

- It is possible to use any set of adjacent numbers as codes (e.g., 1 and 2, 2 and 3, and so on). We would label such coding as quasi-dummy coding. Under these alternative code values, the *b* coefficient will be the same as when 0 and 1 are used, but the *Y* intercept will be different depending on the code values and will be less immediately interpretable.
- It is possible to use any set of nonadjacent numbers as codes (e.g., 1 and 4, 37 and 90, and so on). Under this condition, both the *b* coefficient and the *Y* intercept will reflect the relationship between the coded values and will make interpretation extremely less direct.

Effect coding uses the values of 1, 0, and −1. As is true for dummy coding, using different numeric codes will affect the values of the *b* coefficients, the *Y* intercept, or both and make interpretation potentially quite difficult.

8A.5.1.4 Representing the Categorical Variable in the Regression Analysis

A code set is created by generating a new column in the data file. This code set therefore becomes, by definition, a variable. The number of code sets required to capture a qualitative (categorical) variable (as we indicated previously) is equal to $k - 1$. We therefore need two code sets—two new variables—for our three book color covers. A categorical variable is represented in the regression analysis by *all* of its code sets as predictors in the same analysis. In the example, to represent the color of the book cover where we have three colors, we would need two variables in the regression analysis; specifically, we would need the two code set variables created for the variable of color cover.

8A.5.2 Dummy Coding

The key decision to be made in dummy coding is determining which category or group will serve as the *reference* category. It is the performance of each of the other categories with respect to the reference category that forms the basis of the analysis. A statistically significant model is obtained when one or more of the other categories (the nonreference or comparison categories) differ(s) significantly from the reference group on the dependent variable. Put in prediction terms, a statistically significant model is obtained when the predicted score on the dependent variable for one or more of the other categories (the nonreference or comparison categories) differ(s) from that of the reference category.

If the overall model is statistically significant, then the regression coefficients of the individual predictor variables should be examined. For each predictor variable, the null hypothesis is that the mean of that predictor (one of the colors in the present example) does not differ significantly from the mean of the reference group. With a statistically significant model, at least one of the category groups (predictors) should achieve statistical significance.

The way to decide on which group best serves as the reference category is to bear in mind that each of the other groups will be compared with it. Sometimes, the choice is relatively easy to make:

- If we have two or more new teaching curricula as well as the current one in the study, we probably would like to compare (at least at first) the new ones with the old one. Thus, the old curriculum would be a strong candidate for the reference group.
- If we were evaluating two or more experimental drugs to treat Disease X and also had the currently used drug in the study, we probably would like to compare (at least at first) the new drugs with the old one. Thus, the old drug condition would be a strong candidate for the reference group.

Sometimes, as is the case in our book cover example, there is no compelling reason to choose one category over another as the reference group; researchers can then exercise their professional (or even personal) judgment or, if all else fails, frame an arbitrary judgment. Thus, believing that the red or blue covers would produce better sales, we thus arbitrarily choose the green cover to serve as the reference category. This choice means that we code for the red and the blue covers.

The dummy coding schema is shown in Table 8a.1. The first column represents the color of the book cover that participants were shown: They judged the red, the blue, or the green cover. The second column is the dummy coding for the red cover: We code as 1 those students who evaluated the red cover, and we code as 0 those students who did not evaluate the red cover (those who evaluated either the blue or the green cover). This will be one of the two predictor variables in the regression analysis. The third column is the dummy coding for the blue cover: We code as 1 those students who evaluated the blue cover, and we code as 0 those students who did not evaluate the blue cover (those who evaluated either the red or green covers). This will be the second of the two predictor variables in the regression analysis. These two predictors together represent the categorical variable of book cover color.

Looking at the rows in Table 8a.1 gives a sense of what it means to be a reference category. Because we have coded for red and blue, each has a code of 1 someplace on its row. But the coding for green seen on the last row shows only

Table 8a.1 Dummy Coding Strategy for the Covers of the Three Book Colors

Book Cover Color	Code for Red Cover	Code for Blue Cover
Red	1	0
Blue	0	1
Green	0	0

a 0 code. That information immediately identifies green as the reference group in the to-be-performed regression analysis.

8A.5.3 Effect Coding

The key decision to be made in effect coding is determining which category or group will be excluded from the coding schema and therefore will not be directly addressed in the regression analysis. The performance of each of the other categories will be compared with the grand mean—the mean on the dependent variable of the entire sample. A statistically significant model is obtained when one or more of the coded-for categories differs significantly from the grand mean of the dependent variable. Put in prediction terms, a statistically significant model is obtained when the predicted score on the dependent variable for one or more of the coded-for categories differs from that of the grand mean.

If the overall model is statistically significant, then, as we do for dummy coding, the regression coefficients of the individual predictor variables should be examined. For each individual predictor, the null hypothesis is that the mean of that predictor (one of the colors in the present example) does not differ significantly from the grand mean of the sample. With a statistically significant model, at least one of the category groups should achieve statistical significance.

The group that is excluded from the analysis under effect coding is analogous to the reference group in dummy coding. Let us assume that we select the green category as the one we will not code. The effect coding schema is shown in Table 8a.2, which is structured in the same manner as Table 8a.1. The second column is the effect coding for the red cover: We code as 1 those students who evaluated the red cover, we code as 0 those students who evaluated the blue cover, and we code as −1 those students who evaluated the green cover. This will be one of the two predictor variables in the regression analysis. The third column is the effect coding for the blue cover: We code as 1 those students who evaluated the blue cover, we code as 0 those students who evaluated the red cover, and we code as −1 those students who evaluated the green cover. This will be the second of the two predictor variables in the regression analysis. These two predictors together represent the categorical variable of book cover color.

Looking at the rows in Table 8a.2 gives a sense of what it means to be an excluded category. Because we have coded for red and blue, each has a code of 1 someplace on its row just as we saw for dummy coding. The effect coding for green seen on the last row shows all codes of −1. Seeing that green is

Table 8a.2   Effect Coding Strategy for the Covers of the Three Book Colors

Book Cover Color	Code for Red Cover	Code for Blue Cover
Red	1	0
Blue	0	1
Green	−1	−1

coded as −1 across the board immediately identifies it as the excluded group in the to-be-performed regression analysis.

8A.6 Moderator Variables and Interactions

Consider the case where we have two predictors, X_1 and X_2. At the end of the regression analysis, each predictor is associated with a regression weight. For example, b_1 is the coefficient of X_1. This coefficient is an estimate of the slope of the function for X_1 controlling for X_2. An assumption underlying such an interpretation is that the value of b_1 is the same across the range of X_2; that is, whether or not X_1 and X_2 are correlated, the regression function for X_1 is independent of X_2 (Aiken & West, 1991). This same reasoning can be applied to X_2.

Now suppose that this independence assumption is not true. Instead, the relationship between X_1 and the criterion variable differs for different levels of X_2. With the relationship between X_1 and the criterion depending on the level of X_2, the variable X_2 is thought of as a *moderator variable* when evaluating the prediction of the criterion variable from X_1—in that we need to take into account the level of X_2 in describing the relationship between X_1 and the criterion. When this is the case, we say that X_1 and X_2 *interact* (see Section 4A.5.2).

Here are two examples of interactions that illustrate how different relationships between one predictor and a criterion variable might be expected at different levels of another predictor:

- As predictors of the degree of liberal attitudes held by people, we measure socioeconomic status and age. Let's look at socioeconomic status predicting liberal attitudes at two levels of age. Among younger people, we might find that higher levels of socioeconomic status predict more liberalism; among older people, we might find that higher levels of socioeconomic status predict less liberalism. If such a result was obtained, we would say that age and socioeconomic status interact in affecting (predicting) liberalism (Darlington, 1960).
- In predicting the self-assurance of managers, we use as independent variables how long participants have been managers as well as their actual managerial ability. Let's focus here on predicting self-assurance from the number of years the managers have held such a position but develop that prediction model separately for high and low ability levels. We might find that high-ability managers become more self-assured with increased time as a manager but that managers with low ability become less self-assured the longer they have been in the position. Thus, time as manager and managerial ability would interact in predicting self-assurance (Aiken & West, 1991).

In the regression examples we discussed thus far, the independent variables have always "stood alone" with their regression weights. That is, we have always dealt with situations where the regression coefficient was the weight assigned to the predictor to represent one element of the regression model. Interactions involve estimating the coefficient (weight) of the product of two predictors. Usually, these two predictors are also included separately in the model. Thus, at minimum, we would have X_1, X_2, and X_1X_2 as three predictors in the models. In this structure, each would be associated with its own regression weight. Our minimal model would then be as follows:

$$Y_{pred} = a + b_1X_1 + b_2X_2 + b_3X_1X_2$$

In the above equation, the term X_1X_2 represents the interaction and $b_3X_1X_2$ represents the weighted interaction effect in the prediction model. The two terms preceding it in the equation contain the stand-alone weighted predictors and are known as the *simple main effects* (Pedhazur, 1982) of the variables. As we will discuss in a moment, these regression simple main effects differ from the full main effects we see in ANOVA and so must be interpreted with great caution (if at all).

In ANOVA and MANOVA, interaction terms are automatically inserted into the model and are treated as so standard a source of variance that experimental researchers tend to take the presences of interaction terms for granted. In configuring a regression analysis, researchers must explicitly create the interaction terms and then include these interaction terms as predictor variables in the model over and above the stand-alone variables. The decision of which if any interaction terms to include in the model is a judgment of the researchers based on what to them are reasonable grounds (e.g., theoretical, heuristic).

In the regression solution, if the coefficient associated with the interaction was statistically significant, we must be careful about interpreting the results of the stand-alone variables (the simple main effects). In the first example above, it would be inappropriate to speak of the slope of socioeconomic status in general (interpret the *b* coefficient associated with socioeconomic status) because the nature of the relationship would depend on age; in the second example, it would be inappropriate to speak of the overall slope of time as a manager (interpret the *b* coefficient associated with time in position) because the nature of the relationship depends on ability level.

When there is a significant interaction between predictors, it is necessary to explore its nature in more detail. In ANOVA and MANOVA, such exploration takes the form of performing simple effect analysis on the categorical independent variables. An analogous procedure is employed in regression. Because the variables in regression are almost always quantitatively measured, we examine the *simple slopes*, the slope of a predictor under different levels of the other predictor. To illustrate this for the first example, we would want to predict liberalism with socioeconomic status at different values of age. In some situations, we might have a theoretical or practical reason for selecting certain ages on which to focus. Under such circumstances, we should use those particular ages in the regression model to determine the slope (the regression coefficient) specific to those age levels. If there was no theoretical basis to select particular ages, Aiken and West (1991) appear to offer the same recommendation of Cohen et al. (2003) to use values corresponding to +1 *SD*, the mean, and −1 *SD*; we would thus estimate the *b* coefficient at each of these three values in the distribution. In our example, if the mean age was 36 and the standard deviation was 10, then the ages corresponding to these three locations would be 26, 36, and 46. We would then estimate the *b* coefficient for socioeconomic status at each of these three age levels. You should note that this means generating separate regression models to represent the relationship between the predictor (e.g., socioeconomic status) and criterion (e.g., liberalism) variables at each level (+1, 0, and −1 *SD* units) of the moderator variable (e.g., age).

With an interaction effect included in the model, we should interpret the simple main effects with great care. Allison (1999a), using an example of years of schooling and age predicting income, makes this clear:

> What you must always remember is that in models with interactions, the main-effect coefficients have a special (and often not very useful) meaning. The coefficient . . . for age . . . can be interpreted as the effect of age when schooling is 0. Similarly, the coefficient . . . for schooling can be interpreted as the effect of schooling when age is 0. . . . In general, whenever you have a product term in a regression model, you should not be concerned about the statistical significance (or lack thereof) of the main effects of the two variables in the product. That doesn't mean that you can delete the main effects from the model. Like the intercept in any regression equation, those terms play an essential role in generating correct predictions for the dependent variable. (p. 168)

If the interaction term is significant, then we must focus our attention on simplifying the interaction effect. This means examining the simple slopes. If the interaction is not significant, then we should perform another regression analysis without the interaction term being included. That model will include only the main effects and can be interpreted in the ways described in the context of ANOVA (see Chapter 4A).

We described the shape of the function in a two-predictor model to be a plane—the roof of a room serves as a suitable image. In a model that includes the interaction term of these two predictors, the surface can be thought of as "warped" (Darlington, 1960). Imagine a room with walls of different heights; represented geometrically, the roof that would be fitted to such a room would represent the surface of an interaction.

It has been argued (e.g., Aiken & West, 1991; Darlington, 1960) that when interaction terms are included in the model, the predictor and the moderator variables should be *centered*; that is, the grand mean of the variable (the mean of the entire sample) should be subtracted from each score on the variable to create a new (transformed) variable representing a deviation score.

The regression model that we ordinarily produce showing us a significant interaction represents the situation for the case where the predictor and moderator variables take on a value of zero. Yet it is very often the case that zero is not a possible value for these variables, and it is almost always the case that zero is not a representative value for these variables. For example, scores on a summative response scale may have values of 1 through 5, and scores on many national administered standardized exams (e.g., GRE revised General Test) have scores ranging from 130 to 170. For these measures, no one has achieved a valid score of zero.

Assume that we wanted to center scores on the GRE for a sample of graduate student applicants. If the mean GRE verbal score of the sample was 160, then a person whose original score was 164 would have a deviation score of +4. The mean of the predictor will thus have a transformed value of zero. When the predictor and moderator variables are centered in this manner, the ordinary regression solution will still show the prediction model appropriate for zero values of the predictor and moderator variables, but now, this centered zero value is the mean of each distribution. The result of centering is that the regression model now represents the case for the typical score in the study.

In generating the regression lines for ±1 *SD* from the mean, the predictor and moderator variables should be recentered twice—once at the value corresponding to +1 *SD* and again at the value corresponding to −1 *SD*. For each recentering operation, a regression analysis should be conducted so that each of these two functions can be obtained and the data points plotted.

Although centering is common practice, some authors have argued that it may not be worthwhile (Kromrey & Foster-Johnson, 1998) for linear regression. Our recommendation is to always center your predictor and moderator variables as Aiken and West (1991) have suggested. The idea here is that centering does not adversely affect the statistical analysis and, in our view, has the added advantage of facilitating the interpretation of the results in many circumstances.

8A.7 Simple Mediation

In statistical regression, when we have used the original variables and/or some polynomial variation of them, when we have used dummy and effect codes, or when we have incorporated interaction effects as a part of the model, all of the predictors are treated as having equal status in the sense that they are all entered into the model simultaneously or, in the case of the step procedures, the predictors equally vie for inclusion in the model. An exception to the equality of status was seen in hierarchal regression, where some predictors are given precedence by the researchers in entering the model so that they can serve as covariates for other predictors to be entered subsequently. But even in hierarchal regression, at the end of the analysis, we have the full solution without regard to the order that the variables were previously entered—that is, at the end of the analysis, all predictors have been afforded equal status.

Analysis of mediation effects presents us with the opportunity to structure the predictors in a different and potentially more interesting and useful manner. Rather than each independent variable simply doing its best to predict the outcome variable, we arrange the predictors into a *path structure*. We treat in some depth the topic of path analysis and its more general approach—structural equation modeling—in several chapters at the end of this book. We could therefore place our discussion of mediation in that context. But, historically, mediation, at least in its simplest form known as *simple mediation*, has been traditionally treated as a topic in the context of regression. We will therefore follow this tradition by discussing simple mediation in the present regression chapter. Here, we consider only models containing just three variables: an independent variable, a mediating variable, and an outcome variable; we will revisit this topic when we discuss the more general case of path analysis in Chapters 17A and 17B.

8A.7.1 The Concept of Mediation

Mediation analysis was brought front and center as a powerful analysis strategy through the seminal article by Baron and Kenny (1986), whose definition still captures what is meant by mediation today:

> In general, a given variable may be said to function as a mediator to the extent that it accounts for the relation between the predictor and the criterion. (p. 1176)

The classic illustration of simple mediation is shown in Figure 8a.2. The top diagram in Figure 8a.2 labeled **Scenario A: Unmediated Model** represents the direct prediction of dependent variable Y based on independent variable X and is the situation we have dealt with in simple linear regression. If there is a statistically significant correlation between X and Y, then X will significantly predict Y. But there are times when we either recognize or hypothesize that the observed predictive power of X can be explained either fully or in part by another predictor variable that has not been specified in the model (and thus represents a specification error).

This idea of a specification error is captured in the "third variable problem" that is addressed in many introductory statistics texts (e.g., Ferguson & Takane, 1989). A common (and exaggerated) example of the third variable problem is the positive correlation between ice cream sales and number of crimes: We can predict to a certain extent the crime rate on a given day by knowing how much ice cream was sold that day. But that relationship would lead to a spurious causal conclusion. Rather, ice cream sales are related to the daily

Figure 8a.2 Scenario A: An Unmediated Model With the Independent Variable (*X*) Directly Affecting the Dependent or Outcome Variable (*Y*) and Scenario B: A Mediated Model Where a Mediator Variable (*M*) Is Presumed to Intervene Between *X* and *Y*

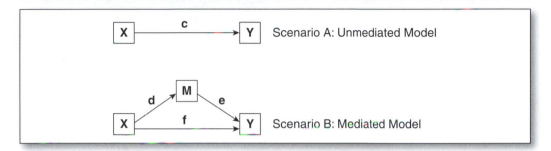

temperature, and warmer days are more conducive to many types of crimes. This third variable problem is the vehicle that leads textbook writers to introduce the topic of partial correlation, which provides a nice bridge to multiple regression analysis. Using daily temperature as a covariate—that is, partialling out the variance of crime rate due to temperature—should substantially reduce or reduce to zero the correlation between ice cream sales and crime rate.

The third variable problem leads us to a more complex but more complete conceptualization in terms of mediation, and this is illustrated in the bottom diagram of Figure 8a.2 labeled **Scenario B: Mediated Model**. Here, that "third variable" is placed in a path structure as mediator variable *M*. In this model, the predictive power of *X* is evaluated with the effects of *M* taken into account.

8A.7.2 The Conditions for Using Mediation

For researchers to invoke the notion of mediation, it makes sense that three conditions are true. These conditions are as follows:

- *X* must significantly predict *Y* in isolation (Scenario A in Figure 8a.2). That is, it makes no sense to speak of a mediated effect of *X* on *Y* if *X* and *Y* are not correlated in the first place (i.e., we cannot mediate a relationship that does not exist).
- If *X* is going to "act through" *M* to influence *Y*, then *X* must significantly predict *M* in the mediation model. If there is no significant prediction of *X* to *M*, *X* cannot "act through" a variable that supposedly mediates it.
- If *X* is going to "act through" *M* to influence *Y*, then *M* must significantly predict *Y* in the mediation model. Again, the idea of "act through" implies that the effect of *X* is being "carried to" *Y* through *M*. If no effect is being "carried to" *Y*, then *X* cannot "act through" *M* to affect *Y*.

8A.7.3 Conceptualizing Mediation

Perhaps the most straightforward way to think about simple mediation analysis is that it compares the "strengths" or power of X to predict Y under the two scenarios. These strengths are labeled in Figure 8a.2 as **c** and **f** for the unmediated and mediated models, respectively. In a mediation analysis, these strengths are represented by the regression coefficients generated via regression analyses, and we ordinarily assume that **c**, the *direct path* from X to Y or the *direct effect* of X on Y, is significantly greater than zero for us to bother with the analysis (this is Rule 1 in Section 8A.7.2). When we compare **c** and **f**, one of four possible results will ordinarily occur:

- The regression coefficient of X (**f**) will not be statistically significant with M in the model. Thus, the presence of mediator M has eradicated the direct predictive power of X. Such a result is labeled as *perfect mediation* (Preacher & Hayes, 2004) or *complete mediation* (James & Brett, 1984).
- The regression coefficient of X (**f**) will still be statistically significant with M in the model; however, the mediated regression coefficient of X (**f**) will be reliably lower than what it was (**c**) in the unmediated model. Thus, the presence of mediator M has diminished but not eliminated the direct predictive power of X. Such a result is labeled as *partial mediation* (Preacher & Hayes, 2004).
- The regression coefficient of X (**f**) will be the same with M in the model as regression coefficient **c** in the unmediated model. Thus, the presence of mediator M has not affected the direct predictive power of X. Such a result is labeled as the absence of mediation.
- The regression coefficient of X (**f**) will be stronger with M in the model compared with the regression coefficient **c** in the unmediated model. Thus, the presence of mediator M appears to have enhanced the predictive power of X. Such a result is labeled as a suppression effect (as described in Section 8A.3) in that the mediator M has accounted for some of the variance of X that is not contributing to the prediction of Y.

8A.7.4 An Example of a Mediation Analysis

Mediation analysis has enjoyed considerable application in a variety of behavioral and social science fields. For example, it has been applied to health-related physical activity (e.g., Spink & Nickel, 2010), family communication patterns (e.g., Letbetter, 2009), prevention research (e.g., MacKinnon & Dwyer, 1993), evaluation research (e.g., Judd & Kenny, 1981), age-related cognitive decline (e.g., Salthouse, Atkinson, & Berish, 2003), age of first sexual experience (e.g., Kahn, Rosenthal, Succop, Ho, & Burk, 2002), and counseling psychology (e.g., Frazier, Tix, & Barron, 2004).

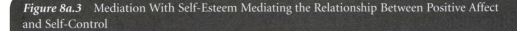

Figure 8a.3 Mediation With Self-Esteem Mediating the Relationship Between Positive Affect and Self-Control

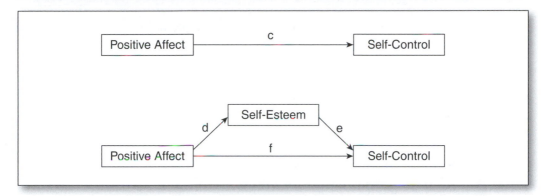

The path structures for the example that we use are drawn in Figure 8a.3. Assume for the sake of our present example that we wished to predict the level of self-control exhibited by individuals; this characteristic is often used as an index of learned resourcefulness (Rosenbaum, 1990). We initially use an individual's level of positive affect as a predictor based on the presumption for this example that positively oriented individuals will be better able to solve problems (will be more resourceful) than those who are less positive. This is shown in the upper portion of Figure 8a.3.

Furthermore, assume that we do indeed find that positive affect significantly predicts self-control. The issue may then arise about self-esteem potentially acting as a mediator of the relationship between positive affect and self-control, shown in the lower portion of Figure 8a.3, with the idea in mind that individuals with higher self-esteem may be more positive but may also be more reliant on their own abilities to solve problems. We will use this contrived example as a way to make concrete some of the ideas we cover in our discussion of mediation.

8A.7.5 The Individual Constituents of a Mediation Analysis

A mediation analysis can be performed using standard ordinary least squares regression. The necessary information is generated by three separate regression analyses (Judd & Kenny, 1981; MacKinnon, 2008; MacKinnon & Dwyer, 1993; Preacher & Hayes, 2004). These analyses can be recognized in the context of Figures 8a.2 and 8a.3. Although we will make this point in more detail in the context of path analysis in Chapters 17A and 17B, any variable that is pointed to by one or more arrows in the path structure serves as a dependent variable in a separate regression analysis. As may be seen in Figures 8a.2 and 8a.3, three such regression analyses are called for in the path structure we have drawn because there are three variables in the combined two scenarios that are pointed to by arrows. These analyses based on the generic labels in Figure 8a.2 are as follows:

- In the regression analysis for Scenario A, we use X to predict Y.
- In the first regression analyses for Scenario B, we use X to predict M.
- In the second regression analyses for Scenario B, we use X and M together to predict Y.

We can apply this strategy to our example shown in Figure 8a.3. The three regression analyses we will perform are as follows:

- We use Positive Affect to predict Self-Control.
- We use Positive Affect to predict Self-Esteem.
- We use Positive Affect and Self-Esteem together to predict Self-Control.

Table 8a.3 shows the results of our regression analyses that are specifically applicable to the mediation analysis. To help readers visualize which analysis relates to what elements in the mediation structure, we have keyed in Table 8a.3 to Figure 8a.3 by specifying the path pertaining to each analysis. Let's examine the results of the analyses one at a time.

The first analysis addressed the direct effect of Positive Affect on Self-Control designated as path **c** in Figure 8a.3. As shown in Table 8a.3, the b coefficient was 0.071 and the beta coefficient was .402. A t test indicated that the coefficients were greater than zero—that is, we had a statistically significant amount of prediction.

The second analysis addressed the relationship of Positive Affect and the hypothesized mediator Self-Esteem, and this is shown in the second row of Table 8a.3. In this analysis, the b coefficient was 4.000 and the beta coefficient was .554. A t test indicated that the

Table 8a.3 Results of the Three Regression Analyses

Path From Figure 8a.3		b	SE of b	Beta	r	t	p	R^2
c	(Positive Affect to Self Control)	0.071	0.008	.402	.402	9.002	.000	.162
d	(Positive Affect to Self-Esteem)	4.000	0.293	.554	.554	13.655	.000	n/a
e	(Self-Esteem to Self-Control)	0.009	0.001	.343	.461	6.717	.000	.243
f	(Positive Affect to Self-Control)	0.037	0.009	.212	.402	4.151	.000	

Note. r is the correlation of the predictor and outcome variable.

coefficients were greater than zero—that is, we had a statistically significant amount of prediction of Self-Esteem from Positive Affect.

The third analysis addressed the combined effects of Self-Esteem and Positive Affect in predicting Self-Control. Both predictors were statistically significant.

At this early stage of the mediation analysis, it is useful to compare the predictive strengths associated with path **c** and path **f**. These are indexed by the coefficients in each analysis. For the beta coefficients, for example, the direct path **c** has a beta weight of .402, whereas in the mediated analysis, path **f** has a beta weight of .212. This same pattern holds for the *b* coefficients. Thus, at least on visual inspection, we can tentatively say that there appears to be a mediation effect; specifically, visual inspection suggests that there is an indirect effect of Positive Affect on Self-Control that acts through Self-Esteem. This would appear to be a partial mediation effect as the path from Positive Affect to Self-Control is statistically significant in the mediated model.

8A.7.6 Testing the Statistical Significance of the Mediated Effect

8A.7.6.1 Overview

Our above conclusion that (partial) mediation occurred was tentative in that it was based only on visual inspection of the regression coefficients. As you might guess, the proposition that variable *M* mediated the effect of variable *X* on variable *Y* can be evaluated statistically. In fact, there are several ways to perform this statistical evaluation.

Probably the most widely known and most frequently used approach to test the statistical significance of a mediation effect is the Sobel test (Sobel, 1982, 1986) and its variants, the Aroian test (Aroian, 1944/1947), and the Goodman test (Goodman, 1960). These tests evaluate the null hypothesis that the indirect effect of the independent variable on the outcome variable through the mediator is zero. Because they were designed to be used on larger samples of a couple of hundred or more and because they assume that the sampling distribution of the indirect effect is normal (it really tends to be somewhat skewed), this family of tests has relatively low statistical power (MacKinnon, Lockwood, Hoffman, West, & Sheets, 2002) and has come under criticism of late (e.g., Hayes, 2009; Preacher & Hayes, 2004). In fact, there are more sophisticated and statistically powerful procedures that have been developed to address this issue (see Hayes, 2009), such as bootstrapping (e.g., Bollen & Stine, 1990; Cheong, MacKinnon, & Khoo, 2003; Mallinckrodt, Abraham, Wei, & Russell, 2006; Preacher & Hayes, 2004, 2008; Shrout & Bolger, 2002).

Despite their weaknesses, the Sobel test and its variations are still commonly used and are relatively simple to apply. Given the popularity of this family of tests, we present them here as one way to illustrate the testing of statistical significance of the mediation effect.

MacKinnon et al. (2002), in their comparison of mediation methods, gave relatively high (though not perfect marks) to another test of mediation, the Freedman–Schatzkin test

(Freedman & Schatzkin, 1992). This test assesses the relative strengths of the paths from the X variable to the Y variable in the unmediated model versus the mediated model. Using the path letters shown in Figure 8a.2, the Freedman–Schatzkin test compares the values of paths **c** and **f** based on a Student's t test. This test addresses the intuitive issue for most of us as described in Section 8A.7.3: If X appears to predict Y and if M is a viable mediator in that relationship, then the power of X to predict Y should be lessened or negated with M in the model. The Freedman–Schatzkin test, in addition to being relatively highly regarded, is also very appealing because it is a direct test of what most of us conceptually mean by mediation. The test is just as easy to apply as the Sobel family of tests, and we illustrate how to perform this test as well.

8A.7.6.2 The Values to Use in the Sobel Family of Equations

The Sobel family of tests produce z scores whose values can be directly applied to the normal distribution. Thus, a z score of 1.96 corresponds to an alpha level of .05, a z score of 2.58 corresponds to an alpha level of .01, and so on. Computation can proceed directly by taking certain values from the output of the regression analyses and inserting them into one of the equations in the family. The four values from the IBM SPSS output that are used in the computation, keyed to Figure 8a.3, are as follows:

- The b coefficient for path **d** from the independent variable (Positive Affect) to the mediator (Self-Esteem).
- The standard error of the b coefficient for path **d** from the independent variable (Positive Affect) to the mediator (Self-Esteem).
- The b coefficient for path **e** from the mediator (Self-Esteem) to the outcome variable (Self-Control).
- The standard error of the b coefficient for path **e** from the mediator (Self-Esteem) to the outcome variable (Self-Control).

8A.7.6.3 The Sobel Family Equations and the Solution

The Sobel test and its variants use the same basic equation to compute the value of z. The differences are that Aroian's test adds an extra value to and Goodman's test subtracts that value from the Sobel test. The equations are shown in Figure 8a.4. The terms **d** and **e** refer to the b (raw score) coefficients specified in Section 8A.7.6.2, and the **SE** terms are the standard errors associated with these coefficients. The expression **SQRT** represents the square root function.

Of the three variations, Baron and Kenny (1986) popularized Aroian's equation, and it is the one we recommend if you are using a member of this equation family (an interactive calculation tool for the Sobel family of tests can be found on the website http://quantpsy.org/sobel/sobel.htm put together by Kristopher J. Preacher and Geoffrey J. Leonardelli). Given

Figure 8a.4 The Equations for the Sobel, Aroian, and Goodman Tests Evaluating the Null Hypothesis (Assessed Through a *z* Test) That the Indirect Effect of the Independent Variable on the Outcome Variable Through the Mediator Is Zero

$$\text{The Sobel test: } z = \frac{(d*e)}{\sqrt{(e^2 * SE_d^2 + d^2 * SE_e^2)}}$$

$$\text{The Aroian test: } z = \frac{(d*e)}{\sqrt{(e^2 * SE_d^2 + d^2 * SE_e^2 + (SE_d^2 * SE_e^2))}}$$

$$\text{The Goodman test: } z = \frac{(d*e)}{\sqrt{(e^2 * SE_d^2 + d^2 * SE_e^2 - (SE_d^2 * SE_e^2))}}$$

Note. The raw regression (*b*) coefficients for the paths are shown by lowercase letters and refer to the paths labeled in Figure 8a.2. Each **SE** value refers to the standard error associated with the raw regression coefficient for the specified subscripted path.

the values shown in Table 8a.3, the computation using an inexpensive hand calculator is as follows:

$$Z = 4 * .009/\text{SQRT} (.009^2 * .293^2 + 4^2 * .001^2 + .293^2 * .001^2)$$

$$Z = .036/\text{SQRT} (.000081 * .085849 + 16 * .00001 + 085849 * .00001)$$

$$Z = .036/\text{SQRT} (.0000069 + .000016 + .0000008)$$

$$Z = .036/\text{SQRT} (.0000237)$$

$$Z = .036/.0048682$$

$$Z = 7.3949303$$

This value of approximately 7.3949 is close to what would be obtained using more sophisticated computational machinery. For example, the calculation for the Aroian test performed by entering our values in the calculator on Preacher and Leonardelli's website (which no doubt carries many more decimal points than our $5.00 solar calculator) yielded a value of 7.500006218. Our result (intended to show you the process step by step) is quite close to that of the computer and, in this case, leads to the same conclusion.

We should note that the sampling distribution of the indirect effect is more likely to be skewed than normal, and so the Aroian procedure, which assumes normality, is relatively conservative (it is less likely to find statistical significance than a more powerful test). Despite a bit of deficiency in power, however, we did find that our z value of approximately 7.40 (or 7.50) is clearly statistically significant (it exceeds a z value of 1.96 considerably). We may therefore conclude that there was a statistically significant amount of mediation observed in our path structure—that is, Self-Esteem significantly mediated the effect of Positive Affect on Self-Control.

8A.7.6.4 The Freedman–Schatzkin Equation and the Solution

The Freedman–Schatzkin test produces a Student t whose value must be evaluated on a table of critical Student t values. The five values contained in the IBM SPSS output that are used in the computation, the first four of which are keyed to Figure 8a.3, are as follows:

- The b coefficient for path **c** from the independent variable (Positive Affect) to the outcome variable (Self-Control) in the unmediated model.
- The standard error of the b coefficient for path **c** from the independent variable (Positive Affect) to the outcome variable (Self-Control) in the unmediated model.
- The b coefficient for path **f** from the independent variable (Positive Affect) to the outcome variable (Self-Control) in the mediated model.
- The standard error of the b coefficient for path **f** from the independent variable (Positive Affect) to the outcome variable (Self-Control) in the mediated model.
- The Pearson correlation coefficient of the independent variable (Positive Affect) and the mediator variable (Self-Control).

The equation for computing the Freedman–Schatzkin test is displayed in Figure 8a.5. Given the values shown in Table 8a.3, the computation using an inexpensive hand calculator is as follows:

$$t = 0.071 - 0.037/\mathrm{SQRT}\,((0.008^2 + 0.009^2) - (2 * 0.008 * 0.009 * \mathrm{SQRT}\,(1 - .402))$$

$$t = 0.034/\mathrm{SQRT}\,((0.000145) - (2 * 0.000072 * .838396))$$

$$t = 0.034/\mathrm{SQRT}\,((0.000145) - (0.0001206))$$

$t = 0.034/0.0049396$

$t = 6.8831484$

$$\text{The Freedman-Schatzkin test: } t = \frac{c - f}{\sqrt{(SE_c^2 + SE_f^2) - (2 * SE_c * SE_f * \sqrt{(1 - r_{XM}^2)})}}$$

Note. The raw regression (*b*) coefficients for the paths are shown by lowercase letters and refer to the paths labeled in Figure 8A.2. Each **SE** value refers to the standard error associated with the raw regression coefficient for the specified subscripted path. The expression r_{XM} refers to the Pearson correlation coefficient specifying the relationship between the independent variable (X) and the mediator variable (M).

The Student t value obtained from the Freedman–Schatzkin test is evaluated with $N - 2$ degrees of freedom. For this analysis, assume that our sample size was 422, and thus, we need to evaluate our obtained t value against a sampling distribution based on 420 degrees of freedom. Appendix A Table A1 displays critical t values for selected degrees of freedom. It may be seen from this table that the ordinarily leptokurtic sampling distribution of t for smaller sample sizes has given way to a virtually normal distribution for large sample sizes such as we have here. Thus, the critical t value applicable to our worked example for an alpha of .05 is closer to 1.96 (associated with infinite degrees of freedom) than to the highest tabled value of 1.98 associated with 120 degrees of freedom. Our obtained value of approximately 6.88 exceeds these tabled values. We may therefore conclude that the path between Positive Affect and Self-Control was significantly lower in the mediated model compared with the unmediated model. Given that the path is statistically significant in the mediated model, we would conclude that partial mediation was observed.

8A.7.7 The Strength of the Mediated Effect

It is also possible to calculate the relative strength of the mediation effect using the beta coefficients that are associated with the paths in our mediation model. Figure 8a.6 shows the computational steps in determining the relative strength of the mediation effect, and Figure 8a.7 presents our model with the path (beta) coefficients shown (transcribed from

Table 8a.3). Assuming that the analyses are based on the same cases and that the model is reasonably fully specified, it is meaningful to compare these beta coefficients with each other using the following steps:

- The strength of the *indirect effect* as shown in Figure 8a.6 is taken as the product of the **d** and **e** path coefficients in the mediated model (see Figure 8a.3). In the present example, we would multiply .554 and .343 to achieve a value of approximately .190. This value of .190 is the value (or strength) of the indirect effect.
- The *total direct effect* as shown in Figure 8a.6 is represented in both the unmediated and the mediated model. Its value or strength is .402. This value is the beta coefficient in the unmediated model. It is also the sum of the indirect effect (.190) and the beta path coefficient **f** (.212) in the mediated model—that is, .190 + .212 = .402.
- The *relative strength of the mediated effect* as shown in Figure 8a.6 is indexed by the ratio of the indirect effect to the total direct effect. In our example, we would compute the proportion .190/.402 to obtain approximately .4726. Thus, with the constraints indicated above, we would mildly assert that in our example approximately 47.26% of the effect of Positive Affect on Self-Control is mediated through Self-Esteem.

Figure 8a.6   The Relative Strength of the Mediated Effect

The Relative Strength of the Mediated Effect:

indirect effect = Beta$_d$ * Beta$_e$

direct effect = Beta$_c$

or

direct effect = indirect effect + Beta$_f$

relative strength of mediated effect = $\dfrac{\text{indirect effect}}{\text{direct effect}}$

Note. The beta coefficients for the paths are shown by subscripted lowercase letters and refer to the paths labeled in Figure 8a.2.

Figure 8a.7 The Path (beta) Coefficients From the Mediation Analysis

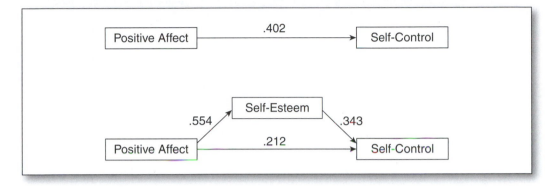

8A.8 Recommended Readings

Alvarez, A. N., & Juang, L. P. (2010). Filipino Americans and racism: A multiple mediation model of coping. *Journal of Counseling Psychology, 57*, 167–178.

Baron, R. M., & Kenny, D. A. (1986). The moderator-mediator variable distinction in social psychological research: Conceptual, strategic, and statistical considerations. *Journal of Personality and Social Psychology, 51*, 1173–1182.

Bauer, D. J., Preacher, K. J., & Gil, K. M. (2006). Conceptualizing and testing random indirect effects and moderated mediation in multilevel models: New procedures and recommendations. *Psychological Methods, 11*, 142–163.

Berk, R. A. (2003). *Regression analysis: A constructive critique.* Thousand Oaks, CA: Sage.

Berry, W. D. (1993). *Quantitative applications in the social sciences: Vol. 92. Understanding regression assumptions.* Newbury Park, CA: Sage.

Conger, A. J., & Jackson, D. N. (1972). Suppressor variables, prediction, and the interpretation of psychological relationships. *Educational and Psychological Measurement, 32*, 579–599.

Fairchild, A. J., MacKinnon, D. P., Taborga, M. P., & Taylor, A. B. (2009). *R2* effect-size measures for mediation analysis. *Behavior Research Methods, 41*, 486–498.

Hardy, M. A. (1993). *Regression with dummy variables.* Newbury Park, CA: Sage.

Hayes, A. F. (2009). Beyond Baron and Kenny: Statistical mediation analysis in the new millennium. *Communication Monographs, 76*, 408–420.

Jaccard, J., & Wan, C. K. (1995). Measurement error in the analysis of interaction effects between continuous predictors using multiple regression: Multiple indicator and structural equation approaches. *Psychological Bulletin, 117*, 348–357.

Maassen, G. H., & Bakker, A. B. (2001). Suppressor variables in path models: Definitions and interpretations. *Sociological Methods & Research, 30*, 241–270.

MacKinnon, D. P. (2008). *Introduction to statistical mediation analysis.* New York, NY: Lawrence Erlbaum.

MacKinnon, D. P., Fairchild, A. J., & Fritz, M. S. (2007). Mediation analysis. *Annual Review of Psychology, 58*, 593–614.

MacKinnon, D. P., Krull, J. L, & Lockwood, C. M. (2000). Equivalence of the mediation, confounding and suppression effect. *Prevention Science, 1*, 173–181.

McClelland, G. H. (1993). Statistical difficulties of detecting interactions and moderator effects. *Psychological Bulletin, 114,* 376–390.

Preacher, K. J., Hayes, A. F. (2004). SPSS and SAS procedures for estimating indirect effects in simple mediation models. *Behavior Research Methods, Instruments, & Computers, 36,* 717–731.

Preacher, K. J., Rucker, D. D., & Hayes, A. F. (2007). Assessing moderated mediation hypotheses: Theory, method, and prescriptions. *Multivariate Behavioral Research, 42,* 185–227.

Schafer, W. D. (1991). Reporting hierarchical regression results. *Measurement and Evaluation in Counseling and Development, 24,* 98–100.

Tzelgov, J., & Henik, A. (1991). Suppression situations in psychological research: Definitions, implications, and applications. *Psychological Bulletin, 109,* 524–536.

West, S. G., Aiken, L. S., & Krull, J. L. (1996). Experimental personality designs: Analyzing categorical by continuous variable interactions. *Journal of Personality, 64,* 1–48.

Multiple Regression: Beyond Statistical Regression Using IBM SPSS

8B.1 Hierarchical Linear Regression

We use the example of hierarchical linear regression that was described in Section 8A.2.2. In that example, we were interested in predicting the level of awareness of cultural barriers believed to be faced by their clientele as reported by mental health practitioners. The key predictors we used were a subscale assessing institutional discrimination, a subscale assessing ethnic identity exploration, and collectivism orientation. Control variables were social desirability and two sample characteristics variables dealing with the length of time spent as a provider in mental health and whether or not the practitioners had received specialized training in multicultural counseling. The data set we use here is **Victoria**.

8B.1.1 Hierarchical Regression Analysis Setup

Selecting the path **Analyze ➜ Regression ➜ Linear** from the main menu brings us to the **Linear Regression** main dialog window displayed in Figure 8b.1. From the variables list panel, we click over **CBMCSACB** (California Brief Multicultural Competence Scale Awareness of Cultural Barriers subscale) to the **Dependent** panel and **MCSDS** (Marlowe–Crowne Social Desirability scale) to the **Independent(s)** panel. This will be the first "block" or "set" of variables in the hierarchical analysis. The **Method** drop-down menu will be left at its default setting of **Enter**, which specifies that the variables we have in the panel will be entered simultaneously in that block (with only one variable, it does not matter anyway).

Figure 8b.1 The First Block of the Hierarchical Analysis Will Enter Social Desirability Into the Model

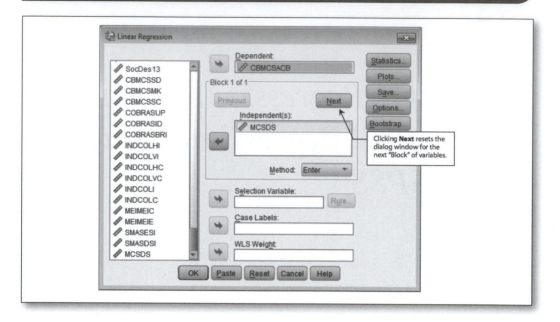

Click the **Next** pushbutton to reset the window so that the second block of variables can be specified.

With the main dialog window reset and the **Independent(s)** panel now empty, place **YearMenHlth** (years of mental health experience) and **MCWorkshp** (*yes* coded as 1 and *no* coded as 0 for having participated in a multicultural workshop for mental health practitioners) into the **Independent(s)** panel (see Figure 8b.2). This will be the second block or set of variables in the hierarchical analysis. The **Method** drop-down menu will be left at its default setting of **Enter**, which specifies that the variables we have in the panel will be entered simultaneously in that block (although we have not done so, we could have specified one of the step methods). Click the **Next** pushbutton to reset the window so that the third and final block of variables can be specified.

Once again we are presented with an empty **Independent(s)** panel into which we now place **COBRASID** (Color-Blind Racial Attitudes Scale Institutional Discrimination subscale)**, MEIMEIE** (Multigroup Ethnic Identity Measure Ethnic Identity Exploration subscale), and **INDCOLC** (Individual/Collectivism scale Collectivism subscale) as shown in Figure 8b.3. The **Method** drop-down menu will be left at its default setting of **Enter**, which specifies that these variables will be entered simultaneously. Set up the **Statistics** window as we have done in the previous chapters (see Figure 8b.4), click **Continue** to return to the main dialog window, and select **OK** to perform the analysis.

Figure 8b.2 The Second Block of the Hierarchical Analysis Will Enter the Two Experience Variables Into the Model

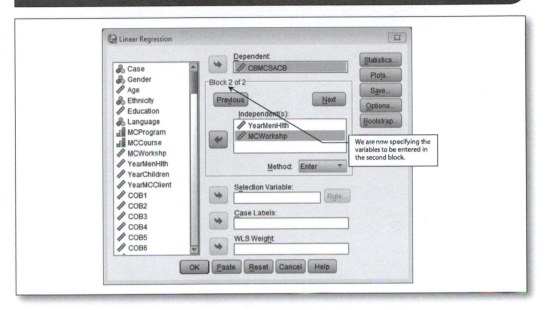

Figure 8b.3 The Third and Final Block of the Hierarchical Analysis Will Enter Institutional Discrimination, Ethnic Identity Exploration, and Collectivism Into the Model

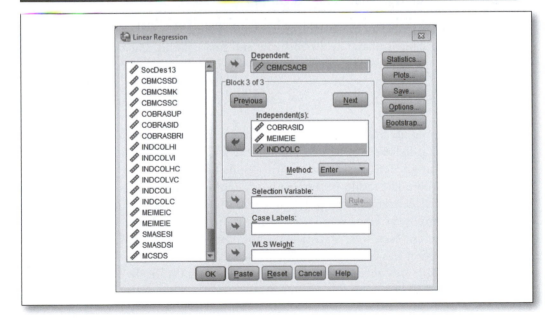

Figure 8b.4 The Statistics Window

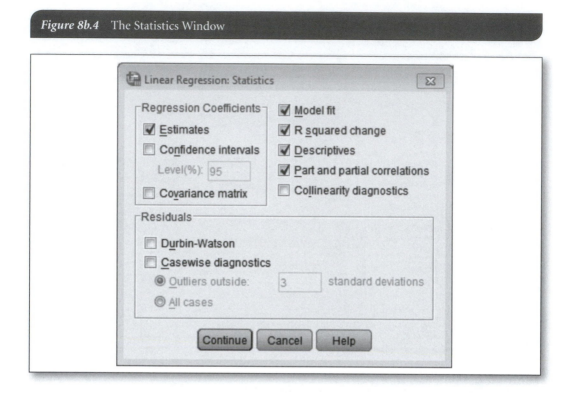

8B.1.2 Hierarchical Regression Analysis Output

The correlation matrix of the variables is shown in Figure 8b.5. As we have already seen, the dependent variable is placed in the first row and first column. The correlations of the other predictors are quite modest, with the highest being associated with institutional discrimination. As can be seen, awareness of cultural barriers is not significantly ($p = .176$) correlated with social desirability ($r = -.049$), and thus, its effect as a covariate is likely to be minimal.

Figure 8b.6 presents the results of the significance testing of the models. This output and the output that follows is structured akin to the way in which the output from a step analysis is structured. Here, each model corresponds to each block of variables that we entered in succession. The results of the first block confirm what we saw from the correlation matrix: Social desirability did not significantly increase our predictive ability. The second block, composed of the experience variables, and the third block, composed of our predictors of interest, each were statistically significant, that is, a statistically significant amount of prediction was obtained for each of these blocks.

The main results are contained in the two tables shown in Figure 8b.7. We can see in the **Model Summary** that the R^2 value went from .002 to .030 to .276 over the three hierarchical

Figure 8b.5 Correlations of the Variables

Correlations

		CBMCSACB CBMCS Awareness of Cultural Barriers Subscale	MCSDS Marlowe–Crowne Social Desirability Scale	YearMenHlth Exp Mental Health	MCWorkshp Train MC Workshop	COBRASID CoBRAS Institutional Discriminatio n	MEIMEIE MEIM Ethic Identity Exploration Subscale	INDCOLC INDCOL Collectivism Subscale
Pearson Correlation	CBMCSACB CBMCS Awareness of Cultural Barriers Subscale	1.000	-.049	-.029	-.147	-.436	.288	.168
	MCSDS Marlowe–Crowne Social Desirability Scale	-.049	1.000	.029	-.092	.032	.106	.154
	YearMenHlth Exp Mental Health	-.029	.029	1.000	-.260	.075	.046	.092
	MCWorkshp Train MC Workshop	-.147	-.092	-.260	1.000	.041	-.220	-.144
	COBRASID CoBRAS Institutional Discrimination	-.436	.032	.075	.041	1.000	-.155	.053
	MEIMEIE MEIM Ethic Identity Exploration Subscale	.288	.106	.046	-.220	-.155	1.000	.184
	INDCOLC INDCOL Collectivism Subscale	.168	.154	.092	-.144	.053	.184	1.000
Sig. (1–tailed)	CBMCSACB CBMCS Awareness of Cultural Barriers Subscale	.	.176	.287	.002	.000	.000	.001
	MCSDS Marlowe–Crowne Social Desirability Scale	.176	.	.290	.040	.268	.021	.002
	YearMenHlth Exp Mental Health	.287	.290	.	.000	.077	.189	.039
	MCWorkshp Train MC Workshop	.002	.040	.000	.	.216	.000	.003
	COBRASID CoBRAS Institutional Discrimination	.000	.268	.077	.216	.	.001	.155
	MEIMEIE MEIM Ethic Identity Exploration Subscale	.000	.021	.189	.000	.001	.	.000
	INDCOLC INDCOL Collectivism Subscale	.001	.002	.039	.003	.155	.000	.
N	CBMCSACB CBMCS Awareness of Cultural Barriers Subscale	368	368	368	368	368	368	368
	MCSDS Marlowe–Crowne Social Desirability Scale	368	368	368	368	368	368	368
	YearMenHlth Exp Mental Health	368	368	368	368	368	368	368
	MCWorkshp Train MC Workshop	368	368	368	368	368	368	368
	COBRASID CoBRAS Institutional Discrimination	368	368	368	368	368	368	368
	MEIMEIE MEIM Ethic Identity Exploration Subscale	368	368	368	368	368	368	368
	INDCOLC INDCOL Collectivism Subscale	368	368	368	368	368	368	368

Figure 8b.6 Statistical Significance of the Models

ANOVA$_d$

Model		Sum of Squares	df	Mean Square	F	Sig.
1	Regression	.140	1	.140	.870	.352$_a$
	Residual	59.088	366	.161		
	Total	59.228	367			
2	Regression	1.800	3	.600	3.804	.010$_b$
	Residual	57.428	364	.158		
	Total	59.228	367			
3	Regression	16.329	6	2.722	22.902	.000$_c$
	Residual	42.899	361	.119		
	Total	59.228	367			

In hierarchical regression output, the model is reconfigured based on the new variables added and evaluated after each block.

a. Predictors: (Constant), MCSDS Marlowe–Crowne Social Desirability Scale

b. Predictors: (Constant), MCSDS Marlowe–Crowne Social Desirability Scale, YearMenHlth Exp Mental Health, MCWorkshp Train MC Workshop

c. Predictors: (Constant), MCSDS Marlowe–Crowne Social Desirability Scale, YearMenHlth Exp Mental Health, MCWorkshp Train MC Workshop, COBRASID CoBRAS Institutional Discrimination, INDCOLC INDCOL Collectivism Subscale, MEIMEIE MEIM Ethic Identity Exploration Subscale

d. Dependent Variable: CBMCSACB CBMCS Awareness of Cultural Barriers Subscale

Figure 8b.7 The Main Regression Results

Model Summary

Mod el	R	R Square	Adjusted R Square	Std. Error of the Estimate	Change Statistics				
					R Square Change	F Change	df1	df2	Sig. F Change
1	.049ₐ	.002	.000	.40180	.002	.870	1	366	.352
2	.174ᵦ	.030	.022	.39720	.028	5.261	2	364	.006
3	.525ᵧ	.276	.264	.34472	.245	40.754	3	361	.000

a. Predictors: (Constant), MCSDS Marlowe–Crowne Social Desirability Scale

b. Predictors: (Constant), MCSDS Marlowe–Crowne Social Desirability Scale, YearMenHlth Exp Mental Health, MCWorkshp Train MC Workshop

c. Predictors: (Constant), MCSDS Marlowe–Crowne Social Desirability Scale, YearMenHlth Exp Mental Health, MCWorkshp Train MC Workshop, COBRASID CoBRAS Institutional Discrimination, INDCOLC INDCOL Collectivism Subscale, MEIMEIE MEIM Ethic Identity Exploration Subscale

Coefficients_a

Model		Unstandardized Coefficients		Standardized Coefficients	t	Sig.	Correlations		
		B	Std. Error	Beta			Zero-order	Partial	Part
1	(Constant)	3.434	.126		27.264	.000			
	MCSDS Marlowe–Crowne Social Desirability Scale	−.006	.007	−.049	−.933	.352	−.049	−.049	−.049
2	(Constant)	3.711	.152		24.392	.000			
	MCSDS Marlowe–Crowne Social Desirability Scale	−.008	.007	−.062	−1.202	.230	−.049	−.063	−.062
	YearMenHlth Exp Mental Health	−.020	.015	−.072	−1.349	.178	−.029	−.071	−.070
	MCWorkshp Train MC Workshop	−.146	.046	−.172	−3.198	.002	−.147	−.165	−.165
3	(Constant)	3.273	.226		14.500	.000			
	MCSDS Marlowe–Crowne Social Desirability Scale	−.011	.006	−.087	−1.900	.058	−.049	−.100	−.085
	YearMenHlth Exp Mental Health	−.012	.013	−.042	−.903	.367	−.029	−.047	−.040
	MCWorkshp Train MC Workshop	−.072	.041	−.085	−1.776	.077	−.147	−.093	−.080
	COBRASID CoBRAS Institutional Discrimination	−.029	.003	−.405	−8.871	.000	−.436	−.423	−.397
	MEIMEIE MEIM Ethic Identity Exploration Subscale	.086	.022	.188	3.982	.000	.288	.205	.178
	INDCOLC INDCOL Collectivism Subscale	.112	.032	.160	3.449	.001	.168	.179	.154

a. Dependent Variable: CBMCSACB CBMCS Awareness of Cultural Barriers Subscale

blocks of variables, with the R^2 change being statistically significant for the second and third blocks.

The **Coefficients** table tracks the changes in the model as variables were entered. After the second block, not having participated in a multicultural workshop predicts greater awareness when social desirability and years of experience are statistically controlled, which may be of some theoretical and practical interest to the researchers. But the dynamics evolve. After the third and final block where only the primary three variables—institutional discrimination, ethnic identity exploration, and collectivism—emerge as the statistically significant predictors in the model controlling for the other variables. The workshop variable is no longer statistically significant at the .05 level and social desirability is very close to statistical significance, and these trends might provide the impetus to further research.

8B.1.3 Reporting Hierarchical Multiple Regression Results

A three-stage hierarchical linear regression analysis was used to predict the level of awareness of cultural barriers believed to be faced by their clientele as reported by mental health practitioners. In the first block, social desirability was entered as a covariate; in the second block, the number of years spent as a provider in mental health and whether or not the practitioners had received specialized training in multicultural counseling were simultaneously entered; in the third block, institutional discrimination, ethnic identity exploration, and collectivism orientation were entered simultaneously as the primary variables of interest.

The correlations of the variables are shown in Table 8b.1. As can be seen, the awareness of barriers variable correlated most strongly with institutional discrimination and ethnic identity exploration.

Results of the hierarchical regression analysis are shown in Table 8b.2. Social desirability, entered on the first block, was not a significant covariate, $F(1, 366) = 0.870$, $p = .352$. When the two experience variables were added on the second block, the prediction model was statistically significant, $F(3, 364) = 3.804$, $p = .010$, $R^2 = .030$, Adjusted $R^2 = .022$. In the second block, not having participated in a multicultural workshop modestly predicted greater awareness of cultural barriers.

For the final block, the model increased substantially in its predictive power, $F(6, 361) = 22.902$, $p < .001$, $R^2 = .276$, Adjusted $R^2 = .264$. The strongest predictor of the set was institutional discrimination followed by ethnic identity exploration and a collectivism orientation. Generally, with all other variables in the analysis statistically controlled, those whose views on discrimination have been negatively driven by the culture, who are more inclined to explore their ethnic identity, and who have more of a collectivist orientation reported greater awareness of their clientele's cultural barriers. Based on the structure coefficients, it appears that the latent variable described by the model is best indicated by institutional discrimination.

8B.2 Polynomial Regression

8B.2.1 The Example for Polynomial Regression

Our example for polynomial regression is based on a set of real test data that have been substantially modified and simplified for the present purposes. It has been known since the middle of the past century (Lord, 1953; Mollenkopf, 1949; Thorndike, 1951) that the value of the standard error of measurement (a statistic that estimates measurement error and

Table 8b.1 Correlations of the Variables in the Analysis ($N = 368$)

Variable	2	3	4	5	6	7
1. Aware Barriers	−.049	−.029	−.147*	−.436*	.288*	.168*
2. Social Desire	--	.029	−.092*	.032	.106*	.154*
3. Years Exp		--	−.260	.075	.046	.092
4. Workshop			--	.041	−.220	−.144
5. Inst Discriminate				--	−.155	.053
6. Ethnic Identity					--	.184
7. Collectivism						--

Note. Aware Barriers = California Brief Multicultural Competence Scale Awareness of Cultural Barriers subscale; Social Desire = Marlowe-Crowne Social Desirability scale; Years Exp = years of mental health experience; Workshop = Yes coded as 1 and no coded as 0 indicating having participated in a multicultural workshop for mental health practitioners; Inst Discriminate = Color-Blind Racial Attitudes Scale Institutional Discrimination subscale; Ethnic Identity = Multigroup Ethnic Identity Measure Ethnic Identity Exploratory subscale.
* $p < .05$.

which serves as a basis to establish confidence intervals—margins of error—around scores) varies across the range of test scores; when focusing on any single test score, it is known as the conditional standard error of measurement.

Based on the analysis of some test data collected from an entry-level state selection exam that one of the authors and a team of his graduate students developed for a large job classification, it was possible to estimate the standard error of measurement over a range of test scores. The pattern of the data is shown in the scatterplot of Figure 8b.8. The data are contained in the file named **Polynomial**. In this modified and simplified version of the data set, a standard error of measurement was estimated for test scores ranging from 15 to 45 items correct.

As can be seen from Figure 8b.8, there appear to be two minimum/maximum locations in the function, a maximum between the test scores of 20 and 30 and a minimum just over a test score of 40. The presence of two such minimum/maximum locations suggests that a cubic (X^3) function would represent the relationship between test score and the standard error.

For the purposes of this example, assume that we wished to generate the model that best represented the relationship between the estimated standard error of measurement

Table 8b.2 Hierarchical Regression Results ($N = 368$)

Block	R^2	Model	b	SE-b	Beta	Pearson r	sr^2	Structure Coefficient
1	.002	Constant	3.273	.226				
		Social Desire	−.006	.007	−.049	−.049	.002	
2	.030	Constant	3.273	.226				
		Social Desire	−.008	.007	−.062	−.049	.004	
		Years Exp	−.012	.013	−.042	−.029	.002	
		Workshop*	−.072	.041	−.085	−.147	.006	
3	.276	Constant	3.273	.226				
		Social Desire	−.011	.006	−.087	−.049	.007	−.093
		Years Exp	−.012	.013	−.042	−.029	.002	−.055
		Workshop	−.072	.041	−.085	−.147	.006	−.280
		Inst Discriminate*	−.029	.003	−.405	−.436	.158	−.830
		Ethnic Identity*	.086	.022	.188	.288	.032	.549
		Collectivism*	.112	.032	.160	.169	.024	.322

Note. Aware Barriers = California Brief Multicultural Competence Scale Awareness of Cultural Barriers subscale; Social Desire = Marlowe-Crowne Social Desirability scale; Years Exp = years of mental health experience; Workshop = Yes coded as 1 and no coded as 0 indicating having participated in a multicultural workshop for mental health practitioners; Inst Discrim = Color-Blind Racial Attitudes Scale Institutional Discrimination subscale; Ethnic Identity = Multigroup Ethnic Identity Measure Ethnic Identity Exploratory subscale. sr^2 is the squared semi-partial correlation.
* $p < .05$.

and test score. Given the observed pattern of the scatterplot, we might hypothesize that an important aspect of the function (assessed by R^2) was cubic but that a significant quadratic aspect of the function might materialize [because that portion of the function to the left of a test score of 40 appears to give a strong impression of a quadratic (X^2) relationship]. Furthermore, because the data generally "angle downward" from left to right (a negatively sloped straight line), some of the variance would likely be explained by a linear component.

8B.2.2 Polynomial Regression Setup

To examine the polynomial relationship between the estimated standard error of measurement and test score, the first step is to build the quadratic and cubic variables to use as additional predictors. We thus computed the squared (quadratic) and cubic values of **test_score**, the syntax for which is shown in Figure 8b.9. In the syntax, the double asterisks indicate "exponent." These variables are already contained in the data file.

Figure 8b.8 A Scatterplot of Standard Error of Measurement Across Test Scores

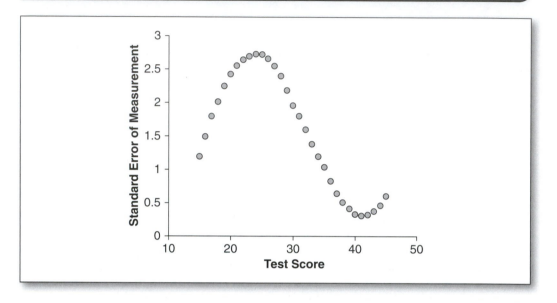

Figure 8b.9 Syntax to Compute the Quadratic and Cubic Predictor Variables

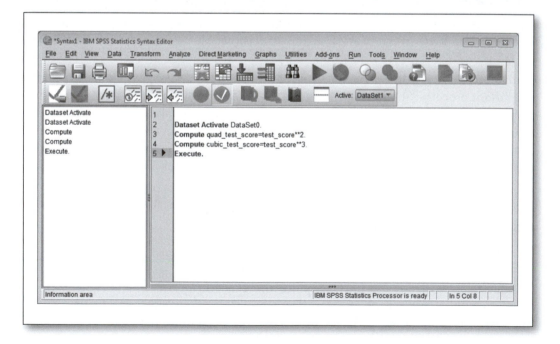

Figure 8b.10 The First Block of the Hierarchical Analysis Will Enter the Original Test Score Variable Into the Model

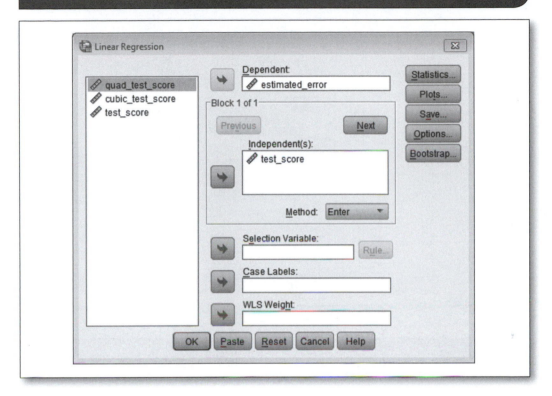

Although we could enter the linear (original) test score variable together with the two polynomial variables into a standard regression analysis, by entering them hierarchically, we can see the cubic model as it is "being built." Thus, from the main menu select the path **Analyze ➔ Regression ➔ Linear**. From the variables list panel, we click over **estimated_error** to the **Dependent** panel and **test_score** to the **Independent(s)** panel (see Figure 8b.10). Click **Next** to reach Block 2, and enter **quad_test_score** in the **Independent(s)** panel (see Figure 8b.11). Click **Next** again to reach Block 3, and enter **cubic_test_score** in the **Independent(s)** panel (see Figure 8b.12). Set up the **Statistics** window as we have done previously (see Figure 8b.13), click **Continue** to return to the main dialog window, and select **OK** to perform the analysis.

8B.2.3 Polynomial Regression Output

The descriptive statistics and the correlations are shown in Figure 8b.14. The correlations are Pearson *r*s, which are assessing the linear relationship between the

Figure 8b.11 The Second Block of the Hierarchical Analysis Will Enter the Quadratic Test Score Variable Into the Model

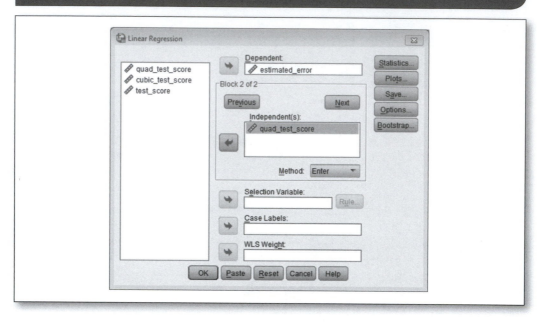

Figure 8b.12 The Third Block of the Hierarchical Analysis Will Enter the Cubic Test Score Variable Into the Model

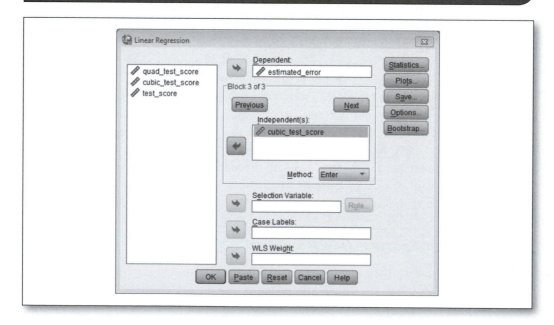

Figure 8b.13 The Linear Regression: Statistics Window

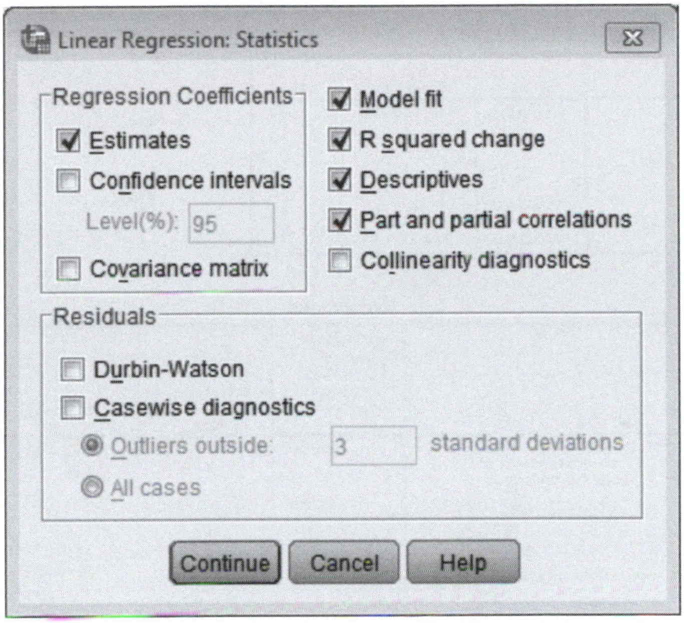

variables. The relationships between the dependent variable (estimated standard error of measurement) and the three predictors (the first row of the **Correlations** table) are negative because for much of the test score range, higher test scores are associated with lower error estimates.

Figure 8b.15 presents the results of the significance testing of the models. All three models are statistically significant, which can be understood in the context of the model summary information shown in Figure 8b.16. Model 1 contains only the linear (original) test score variable, and the R^2 value is .578. That a statistically significant linear component was obtained is not surprising. A best-fitting straight line would angle from the upper left to the lower right of the scatterplot shown in Figure 8b.8. In very general terms, estimated error is relatively high at low test scores and is relatively lower at higher test score levels. But while that is true, this is far too general a summary of the relationship to sufficiently capture the observed pattern of the data.

Model 2 contains both the linear and quadratic components. Entering the quadratic term raised the R^2 by .182 to a total R^2 value of .774. Finally, the third model contains the linear, quadratic, and cubic terms. Adding the cubic variable raised the R^2 by .221 to

Figure 8b.14   Descriptive Statistics and the Correlations of the Variables

Descriptive Statistics

	Mean	Std. Deviation	N
estimated_error standard error of measurement	1.5523	.88688	31
test_score raw score on test	30.00	9.092	31
quad_test_score	980.00	550.340	31
cubic_test_score	34200.00	26675.551	31

Correlations

		estimated_error standard error of measurement	test_score raw score on test	quad_test_score	cubic_test_score
Pearson Correlation	estimated_error standard error of measurement	1.000	-.770	-.819	-.840
	test_score raw score on test	-.770	1.000	.991	.969
	quad_test_score	-.819	.991	1.000	.993
	cubic_test_score	-.840	.969	.993	1.000
Sig. (1-tailed)	estimated_error standard error of measurement	.	.000	.000	.000
	test_score raw score on test	.000	.	.000	.000
	quad_test_score	.000	.000	.	.000
	cubic_test_score	.000	.000	.000	.
N	estimated_error standard error of measurement	31	31	31	31
	test_score raw score on test	31	31	31	31
	quad_test_score	31	31	31	31
	cubic_test_score	31	31	31	31

a total R^2 value of .995 and pretty much completes the picture of the relationship. By considering all three terms in the model, we have accounted for almost 100% of the variance of the dependent variable. Thus, the full model provides a very good fit to the data.

The main regression results are shown in Figure 8b.17. Note that the beta coefficients are substantially in excess of 1.00, an outcome obtained when the predictors are highly correlated (see Section 7A.14.5.3). This is to be expected in that the linear variable and its squared and cubic counterparts are (must be) extremely correlated with each other.

Figure 8b.15 Statistical Significance of the Models

ANOVA_d

Model		Sum of Squares	df	Mean Square	F	Sig.
1	Regression	13.979	1	13.979	42.153	.000_a
	Residual	9.617	29	.332		
	Total	23.597	30			
2	Regression	18.267	2	9.134	47.988	.000_b
	Residual	5.329	28	.190		
	Total	23.597	30			
3	Regression	23.472	3	7.824	1700.055	.000_c
	Residual	.124	27	.005		
	Total	23.597	30			

a. Predictors: (Constant), test_score raw score on test

b. Predictors: (Constant), test_score raw score on test, quad_test_score

c. Predictors: (Constant), test_score raw score on test, quad_test_score, cubic_test_score

d. Dependent Variable: estimated_error standard error of measurement

Figure 8b.16 The Model Summary Results

Model Summary

Model	R	R Square	Adjusted R Square	Std. Error of the Estimate	Change Statistics				
					R Square Change	F Change	df1	df2	Sig. F Change
1	.770_a	.592	.578	.57587	.592	42.153	1	29	.000
2	.880_b	.774	.758	.43627	.182	22.529	1	28	.000
3	.997_c	.995	.994	.06784	.221	1130.966	1	27	.000

a. Predictors: (Constant), test_score raw score on test

b. Predictors: (Constant), test_score raw score on test, quad_test_score

c. Predictors: (Constant), test_score raw score on test, quad_test_score, cubic_test_score

Figure 8b.17 The Main Regression Results

Coefficients_a

Model		Unstandardized Coefficients		Standardized Coefficients	t	Sig.	Correlations		
		B	Std. Error	Beta			Zero-order	Partial	Part
1	(Constant)	3.805	.362		10.510	.000			
	test_score raw score on test	-.075	.012	-.770	-6.493	.000	-.770	-.770	-.770
2	(Constant)	-.464	.940		-.494	.625			
	test_score raw score on test	.237	.066	2.432	3.574	.001	-.770	.560	.321
	quad_test_score	-.005	.001	-3.230	-4.747	.000	-.819	-.668	-.426
3	(Constant)	-17.097	.516		-33.150	.000			
	test_score raw score on test	2.111	.057	21.645	37.254	.000	-.770	.990	.520
	quad_test_score	-.071	.002	-44.176	-36.147	.000	-.819	-.990	-.505
	cubic_test_score	.001	.000	22.052	33.630	.000	-.840	.988	.470

a. Dependent Variable: estimated_error standard error of measurement

8B.2.4 Reporting Polynomial Regression Results

A three-stage hierarchical polynomial linear regression analysis (entering the linear, quadratic, and cubic terms successively) was used to predict the estimated value of the standard error of measurement as a function of test score. The scatterplot of estimated standard error of measurement as a function of test score shown in Figure 8b.8 strongly suggests a curvilinear relationship, which was confirmed by the results of the analysis. All three models were statistically significant: the linear component, $F(1, 29) = 13.979$, $p < .001$, $R^2 = .592$, Adjusted $R^2 = .578$, the combined linear and quadratic components, $F(2, 28) = 9.134$, $p < .001$, $R^2 = .774$, Adjusted $R^2 = .758$, and the combined linear, quadratic, and cubic components, $F(3, 27) = 7.824$, $p < .001$, $R^2 = .995$, Adjusted $R^2 = .994$. It appears that a cubic function containing both the linear and quadratic terms almost fully accounts for the shape of the function. The details of the models are shown in Table 8b.3.

Table 8b.3 Polynomial Regression Results ($N = 31$)

Block	R^2	Model	b	SE-b	Beta	Pearson r	sr^2
1	.592	Constant	3.805	.362			
		Linear Test Score*	−.075	.012	−.770	−.770	.593
2	.774	Constant	−.464	.940			
		Linear Test Score*	.237	.066	2.432	−.770	.103
		Quadratic Test Score*	−.005	.001	−3.230	−.819	.182
3	.995	Constant	−17.097	.516			
		Linear Test Score*	2.111	.057	21.645	−.770	.270
		Quadratic Test Score*	−.071	.002	−44.176	−.819	.255
		Cubic Test Score*	.001	.000	22.052	−.840	.221

Note. sr^2 is the squared semi-partial correlation.
* $p < .05$.

8B.3 Dummy and Effect Coding

8B.3.1 The Example for Dummy and Effect Coding

We will use the example of dummy and effect coding that was described in Section 8A.5, which involved the evaluation of books whose only difference was the color of the

Figure 8b.18 Data File With the Dummy and Effects Coding

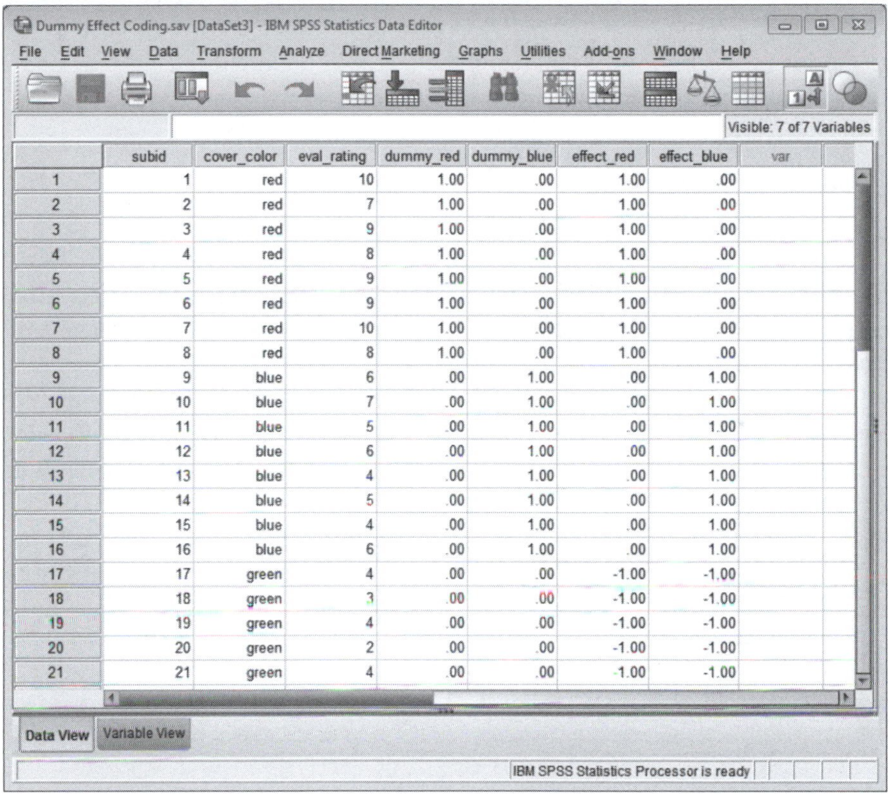

	subid	cover_color	eval_rating	dummy_red	dummy_blue	effect_red	effect_blue	var
1	1	red	10	1.00	.00	1.00	.00	
2	2	red	7	1.00	.00	1.00	.00	
3	3	red	9	1.00	.00	1.00	.00	
4	4	red	8	1.00	.00	1.00	.00	
5	5	red	9	1.00	.00	1.00	.00	
6	6	red	9	1.00	.00	1.00	.00	
7	7	red	10	1.00	.00	1.00	.00	
8	8	red	8	1.00	.00	1.00	.00	
9	9	blue	6	.00	1.00	.00	1.00	
10	10	blue	7	.00	1.00	.00	1.00	
11	11	blue	5	.00	1.00	.00	1.00	
12	12	blue	6	.00	1.00	.00	1.00	
13	13	blue	4	.00	1.00	.00	1.00	
14	14	blue	5	.00	1.00	.00	1.00	
15	15	blue	4	.00	1.00	.00	1.00	
16	16	blue	6	.00	1.00	.00	1.00	
17	17	green	4	.00	.00	-1.00	-1.00	
18	18	green	3	.00	.00	-1.00	-1.00	
19	19	green	4	.00	.00	-1.00	-1.00	
20	20	green	2	.00	.00	-1.00	-1.00	
21	21	green	4	.00	.00	-1.00	-1.00	

book cover. The data file is shown in Figure 8b.18 and is contained in **Dummy Effect Coding**. The variable **cover_color** is the original coding for the book cover: Red is coded as 1, blue is coded as 2, and green is coded as 3 (the variable labels for this variable are shown in the data file). The variable **eval_rating** is the quantitative rating provided by the students in evaluating how positively they view the book (based on a 10-point response scale with higher values indicating more positive ratings). The variables **dummy_red** and **dummy_blue** dummy code for the red and blue colors, respectively, and together would comprise the representation of book color in a regression analysis; in this analysis, the green book cover is treated as the reference category. In an analogous manner, the variables **effect_red** and **effect_blue** effect code for the red and blue colors, respectively, and together would comprise the representation of book color in a regression analysis; in this analysis, the green book cover is not directly coded.

8B.3.2 The Analysis Strategy to Illustrate the Coding

We will illustrate how to perform and interpret dummy and effect coding by quickly performing three relatively simple analyses: an ANOVA, a regression analysis using dummy coding, and a regression analysis using effect coding. In doing so, we will display the setup and the output for each in turn. Following that, we will highlight related portions of each output describing how they interface with each other.

8B.3.3 Analysis of Variance

8B.3.3.1 ANOVA Setup

The ANOVA is very straightforward. From the main IBM SPSS menu, select **Analyze ➔ Compare Means ➔ One-Way ANOVA**. Click **cover_color** to the **Factor** panel, and click **eval_rating** to the **Dependent List** (see Figure 8b.19).

In the **Options** screen, check the box for **Descriptive** as shown in Figure 8b.20. We do not need to deal with homogeneity of variance because the data set was developed to meet the assumption of equal group variances. Click **Continue** to return to the main **One-Way ANOVA** screen.

We will perform the REGWQ post hoc test to perform all pairwise comparisons. In the **Post Hoc** window, select the **R-E-G-W Q** test as shown in Figure 8b.21. Click **Continue** to

---

Figure 8b.19   The Main One-Way ANOVA Window

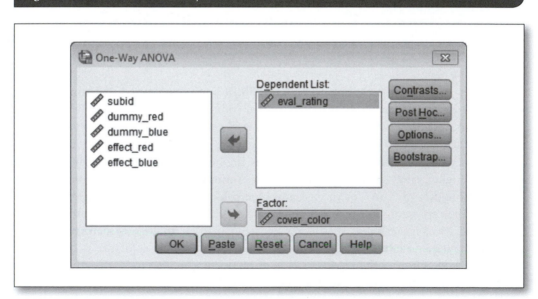

return to the main **One-Way ANOVA** screen and click **OK** to perform the analysis.

8B.3.3.2 ANOVA Output

The output of the ANOVA is shown in Figure 8b.22, and we will return to the ANOVA summary table (the middle table in the figure) and the means and standard deviations. There is a statistically significant effect of the color of the book cover; with 2 and 21 degrees of freedom, the F ratio of 37.848 exceeds our alpha level of .05 ($p < .001$). The value of eta square is approximately .783 (104.083/132.958). We learn from the post hoc test that all three means differ significantly from each other:

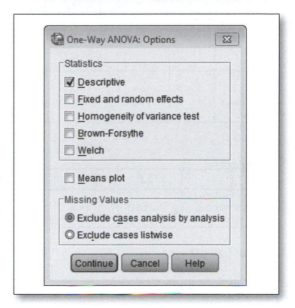

Figure 8b.20 The Main One-Way ANOVA Options Window

Figure 8b.21 The Main One-Way ANOVA Post Hoc Multiple Comparisons Window

Figure 8b.22 The Output of the ANOVA

Descriptives

eval_rating

	N	Mean	Std. Deviation	Std. Error	95% Confidence Interval for Mean		Minimum	Maximum
					Lower Bound	Upper Bound		
1 red	8	8.75	1.035	.366	7.88	9.62	7	10
2 blue	8	5.38	1.061	.375	4.49	6.26	4	7
3 green	8	3.75	1.389	.491	2.59	4.91	2	6
Total	24	5.96	2.404	.491	4.94	6.97	2	10

ANOVA

eval_rating

	Sum of Squares	df	Mean Square	F	Sig.
Between Groups	104.083	2	52.042	37.848	.000
Within Groups	28.875	21	1.375		
Total	132.958	23			

Post Hoc Tests

Homogeneous Subsets

eval_rating

Ryan–Einot–Gabriel–Welsch Range

cover_color	N	Subset for alpha = 0.05		
		1	2	3
3 green	8	3.75		
2 blue	8		5.38	
1 red	8			8.75
Sig.		1.000	1.000	1.000

Means for groups in homogeneous subsets are displayed.

Students preferred the red over the blue book cover, and they preferred the blue over the green book cover.

8B.3.4 Dummy Coded Regression

8B.3.4.1 Dummy Coded Regression Setup

From the main IBM SPSS menu, select **Analyze ➔ Regression ➔ Linear**. Click **dummy_red** and **dummy_blue** to the **Independent(s)** panel, and click **eval_rating** to the **Dependent** panel (see Figure 8b.23). Note that these two dummy variables together (in combination) represent the independent variable of book cover color in this analysis.

Figure 8b.23 The Main Linear Regression Window

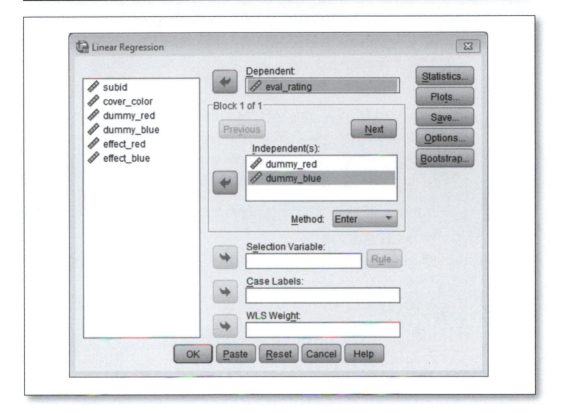

In the **Statistics** window, check the boxes corresponding to **Estimates, Model fit, R squared change, Descriptives**, and **Part and partial correlations** (see Figure 8b.24). Click **Continue** to return to the main window, and click **OK** to perform the analysis.

8B.3.4.2 Dummy Coded Regression Output

The output of the dummy coded regression analysis is shown in Figure 8b.25. In the top table we see the means of the variables, with the means for the two dummy coded variables reflecting the coding schema and the mean for the evaluation ratings corresponding with the grand mean shown in the ANOVA table (see Figure 8b.22).

The model is statistically significant; with 2 and 21 degrees of freedom, the *F* ratio of 37.848 exceeds our alpha level of .05 ($p < .001$). The value of R^2 is .783. Both regression coefficients are statistically significant. The null hypothesis that is tested by the *t* test is that each color (red and blue here) is not statistically different from the reference category. Based on our results, we reject the null hypothesis, an outcome that is not

Figure 8b.24   The Linear Regression: Statistics Window

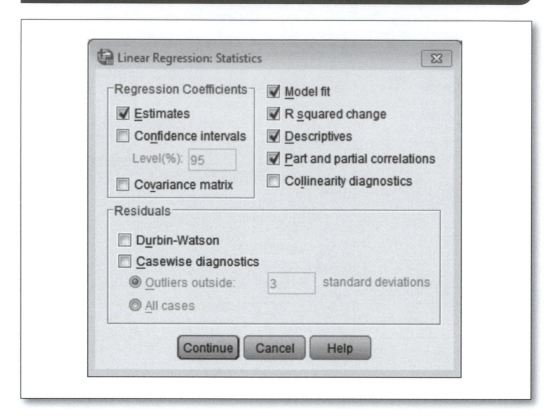

surprising as we know the results of the REGWQ post hoc test performed as part of the One-Way ANOVA.

8B.3.5 Effects Coded Regression

8B.3.5.1 Effects Coded Regression Setup

From the main IBM SPSS menu, select **Analyze ➜ Regression ➜ Linear**. Click **effect_red** and **effect_blue** to the **Independent(s)** panel, and click **eval_rating** to the **Dependent** panel (see Figure 8b.26). Analogous to the dummy coded regression analysis, the two effect coded variables together represent the independent variable of book cover color in this analysis. In the **Statistics** window (not shown), check the boxes corresponding to **Estimates, Model fit, R squared change, Descriptives**, and **Part and partial correlations**. Click **Continue** to return to the main window, and click **OK** to perform the analysis.

Figure 8b.25   Output From the Dummy Coded Regression Analysis

Descriptive Statistics

	Mean	Std. Deviation	N
eval_rating	5.96	2.404	24
dummy_red	.3333	.48154	24
dummy_blue	.3333	.48154	24

Model Summary

Model	R	R Square	Adjusted R Square	Std. Error of the Estimate	R Square Change	F Change	df1	df2	Sig. F Change
					Change Statistics				
1	.885ₐ	.783	.762	1.173	.783	37.848	2	21	.000

a. Predictors: (Constant), dummy_blue, dummy_red

ANOVA_b

Model		Sum of Squares	df	Mean Square	F	Sig.
1	Regression	104.083	2	52.042	37.848	.000ₐ
	Residual	28.875	21	1.375		
	Total	132.958	23			

a. Predictors: (Constant), dummy_blue, dummy_red
b. Dependent Variable: eval_rating

Coefficients_a

Model		Unstandardized Coefficients		Standardized Coefficients	t	Sig.	Correlations		
		B	Std. Error	Beta			Zero-order	Partial	Part
1	(Constant)	3.750	.415		9.045	.000			
	dummy_red	5.000	.586	1.001	8.528	.000	.839	.881	.867
	dummy_blue	1.625	.586	.325	2.772	.011	–.175	.518	.282

a. Dependent Variable: eval_rating

8B.3.5.2 Effects Coded Regression Output

The output of the effect coded regression analysis is shown in Figure 8b.27. In the top table, we see the means of the variables. The only mean that is useful is the one for the evaluation ratings with a value of 5.96. This is the grand mean for the dependent variable (as also shown in Figures 8b.22 and 8b.25).

The model is statistically significant; with 2 and 21 degrees of freedom, the *F* ratio of 37.848 exceeds our alpha level of .05 ($p < .001$). The value of R^2 is .783. Note that only one regression coefficient is statistically significant. The null hypothesis that is tested by this *t* test is that each color (red and blue here) is not statistically different from the grand mean. Based on our results, we reject the null hypothesis for the red cover—it is significantly different from the grand mean. However, we cannot reject the null

Figure 8b.26 The Main Linear Regression Window

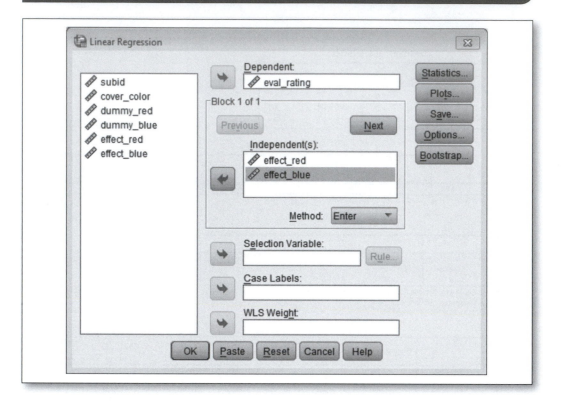

hypothesis concerning the blue cover—its evaluation rating is not significantly different from the overall sample mean.

8B.3.6 Interface of the Three Analyses

8B.3.6.1 Summary and Model Summary Tables

Each analysis produced an ANOVA summary table containing the same numerical output. The eta-square value computed from the ANOVA summary table output was .783. Note that this same value is identified in both the dummy coding and effect coding **Model Summary** tables as **R square** (see Figures 8b.25 and 8b.27, respectively). Thus, the variable of book cover color accounts for 78.3% of the variance of the evaluation ratings.

8B.3.6.2 Group Means and Regression Coefficients

We have taken screenshots of portions of the output of the three analyses we have performed and have placed them in Figure 8b.28. In the top panel we have the group means

Figure 8b.27 Output From the Effect Coded Regression Analysis

Descriptive Statistics

	Mean	Std. Deviation	N
eval_rating	5.96	2.404	24
effect_red	.0000	.83406	24
effect_blue	.0000	.83406	24

Model Summary

Model	R	R Square	Adjusted R Square	Std. Error of the Estimate	Change Statistics				
					R Square Change	F Change	df1	df2	Sig. F Change
1	.885a	.783	.762	1.173	.783	37.848	2	21	.000

a. Predictors: (Constant), effect_blue, effect_red

ANOVAb

Model		Sum of Squares	df	Mean Square	F	Sig.
1	Regression	104.083	2	52.042	37.848	.000a
	Residual	28.875	21	1.375		
	Total	132.958	23			

a. Predictors: (Constant), effect_blue, effect_red
b. Dependent Variable: eval_rating

Coefficientsa

Model		Unstandardized Coefficients		Standardized Coefficients	t	Sig.	Correlations		
		B	Std. Error	Beta			Zero-order	Partial	Part
1	(Constant)	5.958	.239		24.893	.000			
	effect_red	2.792	.339	.968	8.247	.000	.867	.874	.839
	effect_blue	-.583	.339	-.202	-1.723	.100	.282	-.352	-.175

a. Dependent Variable: eval_rating

from the one-way ANOVA, in the middle panel we have the *b* coefficients for the dummy coding regression analysis, and in the bottom panel we have the *b* coefficients for the effect coding regression analysis. These means and coefficients represent different viewpoints depicting precisely the same information. Let's use the regression analyses as our base and focus on each component of the models separately.

For the dummy coded analysis, the constant (the *Y* intercept) was 3.750. This value is the mean of the reference category (the mean rating of the book with the green cover), which can be seen in the top panel of Figure 8b.28. For the effect coded analysis, the constant (the *Y* intercept) is 5.958. This is the value of the grand mean of the dependent variable (mean evaluation rating for all 24 students). We note that if there were unequal sample sizes across the groups, the *Y* intercept in an effect coded regression will equal the unweighted (estimated marginal, least squares) mean of the cell means.

Figure 8b.28 Means From the ANOVA Output and Regression Coefficients From the Dummy Coding and Effect Coding Analyses

eval_rating

	N	Mean	Std. Deviation
1 red	8	8.75	1.035
2 blue	8	5.38	1.061
3 green	8	3.75	1.389
Total	24	5.96	2.404

		Unstandardized Coefficients	
Model		B	Std. Error
1	(Constant)	3.750	.415
	dummy_red	5.000	.586
	dummy_blue	1.625	.586

		Unstandardized Coefficients	
Model		B	Std. Error
1	(Constant)	5.958	.239
	effect_red	2.792	.339
	effect_blue	-.583	.339

The regression coefficient for **dummy_red** was 5.000. This represents the difference between the mean red rating and the mean rating for the reference category (green), that is, red mean − green mean or 8.75 − 3.75 = 5.000. The regression coefficient for **effect_red** is 2.792. This represents the difference between the mean red rating and the grand mean, that is, red mean − grand mean or 8.75 − 5.96 = 2.79 (actually, 2.792 to be more precise).

The regression coefficient for **dummy_blue** was 1.625. This represents the difference between the mean blue rating and the mean rating for the reference category (green), that is, 5.38 − 3.75 = 1.63. The regression analysis was actually providing more precision here in displaying a value of 1.625 rather than rounding it to 1.63. The regression coefficient for **effect_blue** is −0.583. This represents the difference between the mean blue rating and the grand mean, that is, blue mean − grand mean or 5.38 − 5.96 = −0.58 (actually, −0.583 to be more precise).

8B.4 Interaction Effects of Quantitative Variables in Regression

Interaction effects of quantitative variables can be assessed using ordinary least squares regression. We will use an example from the **Personality Interaction** data set for the simplest case where we have two variables as predictors (self-esteem and depression). We wish to examine the prediction of neuroticism by each variable and their interaction. The stages of the analysis will be as follows:

1. Specifying the variables and their roles in the analysis.

2. Centering the predictor variables.

3. Constructing the interaction variable.

4. Performing the primary regression analysis.

5. Performing additional regression analyses at ± 1 *SD* unit of the moderator variable.

6. Plotting the simple slopes on one set of axes to view the functions.

8B.4.1 The Variables and Their Roles

We will use **neoneuro** (a measure of neuroticism) as the dependent variable. When working with two-way interaction effects (the interaction of two independent variables), it is useful to think of one of the independent variables as taking on the role of the predictor variable and the other taking on the role of the moderator variable. The difference between these roles is that we conceive of the predictor relating to the dependent variable differently (i.e., there is a separate prediction model) at different levels of the moderator variable if the interaction is statistically significant. In this sense, the moderator variable is said to moderate or regulate the relationship between the predictor and the dependent variables. For example, if sex was the moderator variable in an interaction effect, then there would be different regression models relating the predictor and criterion variables for females and males.

When using continuous independent variables, the choice of which variable assumes which role is often somewhat arbitrary. For the sake of this present example, we will designate self-esteem as the predictor variable and depression as the moderator variable.

8B.4.2 Centering the Predictor and Moderator Variables

The importance of centering, as spelled out by Aiken and West (1991), becomes clear when you appreciate this fact: The regression equation that we obtain from a multiple regression analysis shows the model when the predictor and moderator each has a value of zero. When there is no statistically significant interaction, that's perfectly okay because the model can then be applied as it stands to any values of the predictor variables.

However, when there is a statistically significant interaction, the parameters of the model—the intercept and the regression weight of the predictor variable—differ with the level of the moderator variable. Thus, the zero level for the predictor and moderator variables (the place described by the model) is just one of an infinite number of different values each of which will have somewhat different prediction parameters given that the interaction is statistically significant. In a sense, there is not just one model but an infinite number of them. And with the predictor and moderator values set to zero, the model produced by the analysis can present a distorted picture of the results either because one or both of these variables may not actually have a measured zero value or the measured value of zero exists but is an extreme rather than a typical value. It is the rare case that a value of zero for the predictor and moderator variables represents a typical value in those distributions.

Centering the predictor and moderator variables solves this typicality problem. Remember that the regression model will always be applicable to zero values of the predictor and moderator variables—this cannot be changed. But centering "moves" the zero value to the mean (the center) of the distribution for both the predictor and the moderator variables. When we view the regression results after centering, we see the model applied to the typical case rather than to an extreme or impossible case.

8B.4.3 Constructing the Variables

To center a variable is to subtract the mean from each of the values on the variable (Variable – Mean of the Variable) to obtain a deviation score. Creating an interaction term involves multiplying the two centered variables whose interaction we are targeting. Setting up the analysis therefore involves these initial three steps: (a) computing a centered predictor variable, (b) computing a centered moderator variable, (c) computing an interaction term representing the product of the two centered variables.

Accomplishing these steps first requires us to obtain the means of the predictor and moderator variables. Because these means must be based only on the cases that will be in our regression analysis once we have centered the variables, we need to obtain our means from a preliminary, "throw-away" regression analysis. Select **Analyze ➜ Regression ➜ Linear** from the main menu, and place **esteem** and **beckdep** in the **Independent(s)** panel and **neo-neuro** in the **Dependent** panel as shown in Figure 8b.29. Select the **Statistics** pushbutton, check **Descriptives** as shown in Figure 8b.30 (which will give us the *listwise* means and standard deviations), click **Continue** to return to the main dialog window, and click **OK** to perform the analysis.

The means and standard deviations for the variables are shown in Figure 8b.31. We also show the square correlation matrix. These variables are correlated much stronger than we would ordinarily prefer but will serve to illustrate what is needed in our example.

Figure 8b.29   The Main Linear Regression Window

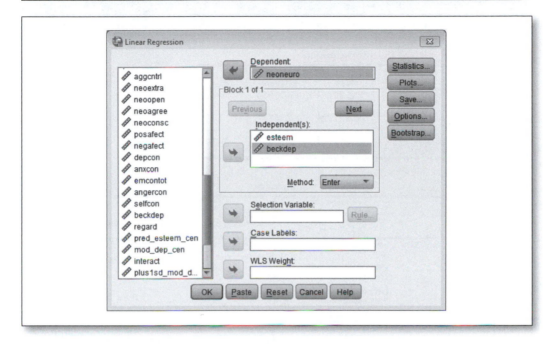

Figure 8b.30   The Linear Regression: Statistics Window

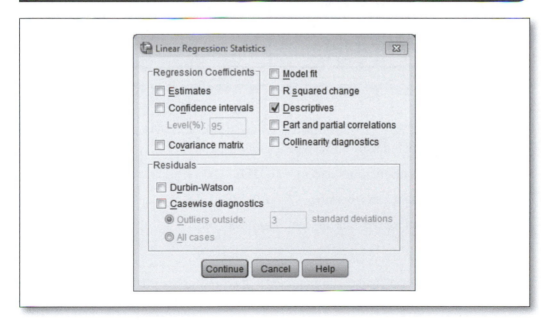

Figure 8b.31 The Descriptive Statistics and Correlations Based on the Noncentered Variables

Descriptive Statistics

	Mean	Std. Deviation	N
neoneuro neuroticism: neo	50.5298	11.15953	419
esteem self–esteem: coopersmith	71.3317	20.96459	419
beckdep Beck depression: bdi	7.4177	6.92542	419

Correlations

		neoneuro neuroticism: neo	esteem self– esteem: coopersmith	beckdep Beck depression: bdi
Pearson Correlation	neoneuro neuroticism: neo	1.000	-.693	.608
	esteem self–esteem: coopersmith	-.693	1.000	-.654
	beckdep Beck depression: bdi	.608	-.654	1.000
Sig. (1-tailed)	neoneuro neuroticism: neo	.	.000	.000
	esteem self–esteem: coopersmith	.000	.	.000
	beckdep Beck depression: bdi	.000	.000	.
N	neoneuro neuroticism: neo	419	419	419
	esteem self–esteem: coopersmith	419	419	419
	beckdep Beck depression: bdi	419	419	419

To compute the new variables, open a syntax window by selecting **File ➔ New ➔ Syntax** and, as shown in Figure 8b.32, type the following:

compute pred_esteem_cen = esteem – 71.3317.

compute mod_dep_cen = beckdep – 7.4177.

compute interact = pred_esteem_cen * mod_dep_cen.

execute.

The first two lines of syntax compute centered scores for the predictor and moderator variables. We have gone out of our way to name the new variables in such a way that you can

Figure 8b.32 The Syntax to Generate the Variables in the Analysis

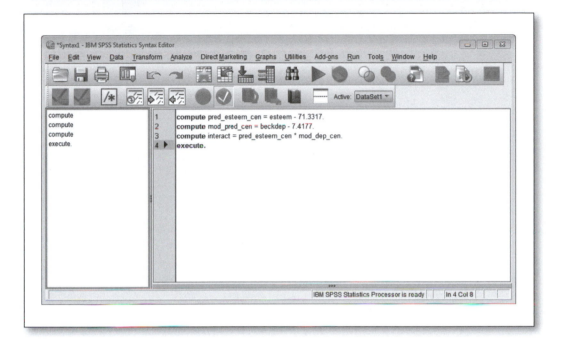

recognize their roles in the analysis and the fact that they are centered. Each case in the data file will have as their values for each centered variable the difference between their original score and the mean. Once you have typed this syntax, select **Run ➜ All** from the main menu. These new variables will be placed at the end of the data file (see Figure 8b.33). It is a good idea to save the data file with these new variables in it.

8B.4.4 Performing the Centered Regression Analysis

With our three new variables now computed and in the data file, we are ready to perform the main analysis on the centered variables. Select **Analyze ➜ Regression ➜ Linear** from the main menu and place **neoneuro** in the **Dependent** panel. In the **Independent(s)** panel, place **pred_esteem_cen**, **mod_dep_cen**, and **interact** as shown in Figure 8b.34. Select the **Statistics** pushbutton, and check all of the usual choices (see Figure 8b.35). Click **Continue** to return to the main dialog window, and click **OK** to perform the analysis.

Figure 8b.36 contains the **Descriptive Statistics** and **Correlations** tables for this centered analysis. Note that the means of the predictor and moderator variables are now zero,

Figure 8b.33 The New Variables Are Placed at the End of the Data File

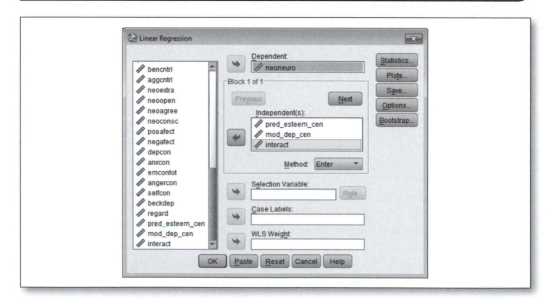

Figure 8b.34 The Main Linear Regression Window With the Centered Variables Specified

Figure 8b.35 The Linear Regression: Statistics Window

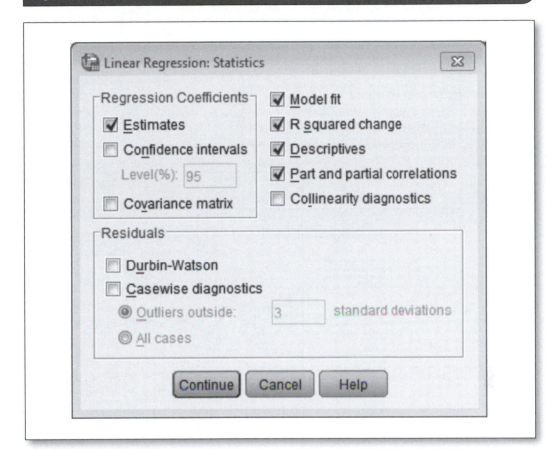

but their standard deviations are exactly what they were before we centered the variables. Note also that the correlations involving the centered variables are exactly what they were before we centered them—centering does not change the relationships between variables but simply shifts the zero point.

The main regression results are presented in Figure 8b.37. The model is statistically significant, and the R^2 is a substantial .531. The **Coefficients** table informs us that the interaction is statistically significant. With that effect in play, the two variables composing the interaction and which are also statistically significant here are exerting what are called *simple main effects* (Pedhazur, 1982); that is, the effect of one in isolation (e.g., the predictor of self-esteem) depends on the particular value of the other (e.g., the moderator of depression). Because these simple main effects cannot be interpreted in the same way as the effects for

Figure 8b.36 The Descriptive Statistics and Correlations Based on the Centered Variables

Descriptive Statistics

	Mean	Std. Deviation	N
neoneuro neuroticism: neo	50.5298	11.15953	419
pred_esteem_cen centered predictor self-esteem	.0000	20.96459	419
mod_dep_cen centered moderator depression	.0000	6.92542	419
interact interaction of centered esteem and depression	-94.6899	203.84405	419

Correlations

		neoneuro neuroticism: neo	pred_esteem_cen centered predictor self-esteem	mod_dep_cen centered moderator depression	interact interaction of centered esteem and depression
Pearson Correlation	neoneuro neuroticism: neo	1.000	-.693	.608	-.336
	pred_esteem_cen centered predictor self-esteem	-.693	1.000	-.654	.467
	mod_dep_cen centered moderator depression	.608	-.654	1.000	-.608
	interact interaction of centered esteem and depression	-.336	.467	-.608	1.000
Sig. (1-tailed)	neoneuro neuroticism: neo	.	.000	.000	.000
	pred_esteem_cen centered predictor self-esteem	.000	.	.000	.000
	mod_dep_cen centered moderator depression	.000	.000	.	.000
	interact interaction of centered esteem and depression	.000	.000	.000	.
N	neoneuro neuroticism: neo	419	419	419	419
	pred_esteem_cen centered predictor self-esteem	419	419	419	419
	mod_dep_cen centered moderator depression	419	419	419	419
	interact interaction of centered esteem and depression	419	419	419	419

these variables if there were no interaction involved, our focus in this analysis shifts to the interaction effect. The model at the centered values of zero for the predictor and the moderator variables is as follows:

$$\text{Neuroticism} = 51.113 - (.282)\,(\text{self-esteem}) + (.532)\,(\text{depression}) + (.006)\,(\text{esteem} * \text{depression})$$

8B.4.5 Additional Analyses at ±1 SD for the Moderator Variable

The statistically significant interaction informs us that the prediction model for self-esteem (our arbitrarily identified predictor) differs across the range of values of depression

Figure 8b.37 The Regression Results Based on the Centered Variables

Model Summary

Model	R	R Square	Adjusted R Square	Std. Error of the Estimate	Change Statistics				
					R Square Change	F Change	df1	df2	Sig. F Change
1	.728a	.531	.527	7.67386	.531	156.325	3	415	.000

a. Predictors: (Constant), interact interaction of centered esteem and depression, pred_esteem_cen centered predictor self–esteem, mod_dep_cen centered moderator depression

ANOVAb

Model		Sum of Squares	df	Mean Square	F	Sig.
1	Regression	27617.071	3	9205.690	156.325	.000a
	Residual	24438.584	415	58.888		
	Total	52055.655	418			

a. Predictors: (Constant), interact interaction of centered esteem and depression, pred_esteem_cen centered predictor self–esteem, mod_dep_cen centered moderator depression

b. Dependent Variable: neoneuro neuroticism: neo

Coefficientsa

Model		Unstandardized Coefficients		Standardized Coefficients	t	Sig.	Correlations		
		B	Std. Error	Beta			Zero–order	Partial	Part
1	(Constant)	51.113	.435		117.446	.000			
	pred_esteem_cen centered predictor self–esteem	-.282	.024	-.530	-11.847	.000	-.693	-.503	-.398
	mod_dep_cen centered moderator depression	.532	.080	.330	6.622	.000	.608	.309	.223
	interact interaction of centered esteem and depression	.006	.002	.112	2.636	.009	-.336	.128	.089

a. Dependent Variable: neoneuro neuroticism: neo

(our arbitrarily identified moderator). We are thus in a bad-news/good-news situation. The bad news is that the model we have just obtained is only one of an infinite number of the set of models that characterize the relationship between self-esteem and neuroticism. The good news is that we do not have to generate an infinite number of models in order to understand the nature of the moderation or to communicate the results in professional circles—examining just two more models will provide us with a sufficient amount of information to accomplish these two goals in almost all situations.

The model we presently have describes prediction at the centered value of zero for the moderator variable of depression. Our goals are (a) to re-center the moderator variable at *1 SD unit above* where it is now and build a second prediction model and (b) to re-center the moderator variable at *1 SD unit below* where it is now and build a third prediction model. The key piece of information we need for these computations, which appears in the upper table of Figure 8b.36, is the standard deviation of the depression variable; that value is 6.92542.

8B.4.5.1 An Additional Analysis at +1 SD
for the Moderator Variable

In centering the moderator variable depression 1 *SD* above where it is now (it is currently centered on the mean), a score of +6.92542 needs to be our new zero point. The way we get that value to be zero is to subtract 6.92542 from it, which tells us that the deviations (centering) in general must be computed by *subtracting* this value from each previously centered score. Once we do that, we need to compute a new interaction term because we will have a new moderator variable. Here is the command structure that will make this happen:

compute plus1sd_mod_dep_cen = mod_dep_cen - 6.92542.

compute interact_plus1sd = pred_esteem_cen * plus1sd_mod_dep_cen.

execute.

Type this syntax in a syntax window as shown in Figure 8b.38 (or run each compute command separately using a **Compute** window by selecting **Transform ➔ Compute Variable**) and select **Run ➔ All** from the main menu. These new variables will be placed at the end of the data file. We advise you to save the data file with these new variables in it.

Figure 8b.38 The Syntax to Generate the Variables in the Analysis

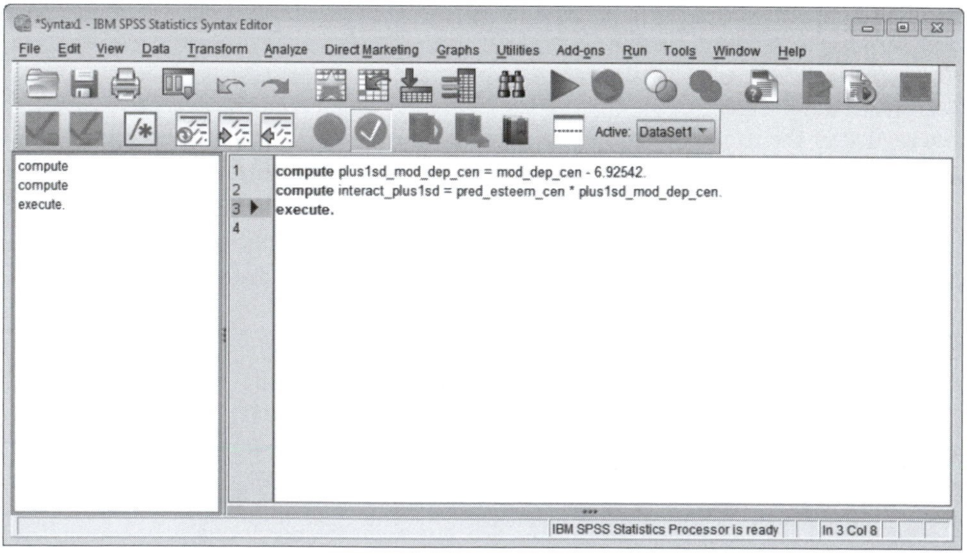

Then, perform a standard regression analysis using **pred_esteem_cen**, **plus1sd_mod_dep_cen**, and **interact_plus1sd**, as the independent variables and **neoneuro** as the dependent variable (see Figure 8b.39).

Figure 8b.40 presents the **Descriptive Statistics** and **Correlations** tables for the analysis. Note that the mean of **plus1sd_mod_dep_cen** is −6.9255. This is as it should be. We have centered the scores at a value of +1 *SD* but the mean is still in the same place it always was, in this instance, 6.9255 units (1 *SD* unit) below our centered value. Note that the correlations between the two centered variables and their correlation with the dependent variable are unchanged—only the correlations involving the interaction term have changed (because we multiplied different values here to compute it).

The ANOVA results and the **Model Summary** are identical to what we have shown before, and we will not present them again. The **Coefficients** table is presented in Figure 8b.41. Note that the *b* weight for the interaction term (.006) is the same as it has always been. That's because the interaction is an omnibus effect descriptive of the data as a whole. Note also that the *b* weight of the moderator variable (.532) has not changed either. That's because our focus is on the predictor whose equation changes with different

Figure 8b.39 The Main Linear Regression Window With the Variables Specified for the Analysis at + 1 *SD* for the Moderator Variable of Depression

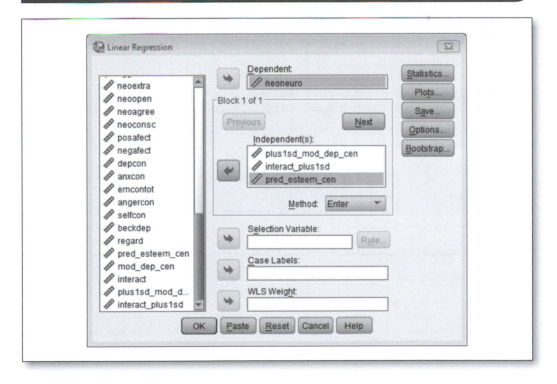

Figure 8b.40 The Descriptive Statistics and Correlations Based on the Variables Specified for the Analysis at + 1 *SD* for the Moderator Variable of Depression

Descriptive Statistics

	Mean	Std. Deviation	N
neoneuro neuroticism: neo	50.5298	11.15953	419
pred_esteem_cen centered predictor self-esteem	.0000	20.96459	419
plus1sd_mod_dep_cen	-6.9255	6.92542	419
interact_plus1sd	-94.6902	187.06885	419

Correlations

		neoneuro neuroticism: neo	pred_esteem_cen centered predictor self-esteem	plus1sd_mod_dep_cen	interact_plus1sd
Pearson Correlation	neoneuro neuroticism: neo	1.000	-.693	.608	.172
	pred_esteem_cen centered predictor self-esteem	-.693	1.000	-.654	-.267
	plus1sd_mod_dep_cen	.608	-.654	1.000	-.155
	interact_plus1sd	.172	-.267	-.155	1.000
Sig. (1-tailed)	neoneuro neuroticism: neo	.	.000	.000	.000
	pred_esteem_cen centered predictor self-esteem	.000	.	.000	.000
	plus1sd_mod_dep_cen	.000	.000	.	.001
	interact_plus1sd	.000	.000	.001	.
N	neoneuro neuroticism: neo	419	419	419	419
	pred_esteem_cen centered predictor self-esteem	419	419	419	419
	plus1sd_mod_dep_cen	419	419	419	419
	interact_plus1sd	419	419	419	419

Figure 8b.41 The Regression Results Based on the Variables Specified for the Analysis at + 1 *SD* for the Moderator Variable of Depression

Coefficients_a

Model		Unstandardized Coefficients		Standardized Coefficients	t	Sig.	Correlations		
		B	Std. Error	Beta			Zero-order	Partial	Part
1	(Constant)	54.795	.781		70.175	.000			
	pred_esteem_cen centered predictor self-esteem	-.240	.027	-.450	-8.810	.000	-.693	-.397	-.296
	plus1sd_mod_dep_cen	.532	.080	.330	6.622	.000	.608	.309	.223
	interact_plus1sd	.006	.002	.103	2.636	.009	.172	.128	.089

a. Dependent Variable: neoneuro neuroticism: neo

levels of the moderator. Compared with the model where the moderator is centered at its mean, this function is somewhat less steep. That is, the *b* coefficient—the slope of the function controlling for the other predictors—for the "base" centered model was −.282 (see Figure 8b.37), but here it is −.240. The value of the intercept has also changed a bit since we are now looking at the model from the perspective of relatively high depression (remember that the depression variable is centered at 1 *SD* unit above the mean for depression). The model at the centered values of zero for the predictor and +1 *SD* for the moderator is as follows:

$$\text{Neuroticism} = 54.795 - (.240) \text{ (self-esteem)} + (.532) \text{ (depression)} + (.006) \text{ (esteem}^* \text{depression)}$$

8B.4.5.2 An Additional Analysis at −1 SD for the Moderator Variable

In centering the moderator variable depression 1 *SD* below where it was originally centered (which is at the mean), a score of −6.92542 needs to be our new zero point. The way we get that value to be zero is to add 6.92542 to it, which tells us that the deviations (centering) in general must be computed by *adding* this value from each previously centered score. Once we do that, we need to again compute a new interaction term because we will have a new moderator variable. Here is the command structure that will make this happen:

compute minus1sd_mod_dep_cen = mod_dep_cen + 6.92542.

compute interact_minus1sd = pred_esteem_cen * minus1sd_mod_dep_cen.

execute.

We will assume here that you have computed the new variables and have performed a standard regression analysis using **minus1sd_mod_dep_cen**, **interact_minus1sd**, and **pred_esteem_cen** as the independent variables and **neoneuro** as the dependent variable.

Figure 8b.42 presents the **Descriptive Statistics** and **Correlations** tables for that analysis. Note that the mean of **minus 1sd_mod_dep_cen** is 6.9254. This is as it should be. We have centered the scores at a value of −1 *SD*, but the mean is still in the same place it always was, in this instance, 6.9255 units (1 *SD* unit) above our centered value. Note that the correlations between the two centered variables and their correlation with the dependent variable are unchanged—only the correlations involving the interaction term have changed.

Figure 8b.42   The Descriptive Statistics and Correlations Based on the Variables Specified for the Analysis at – 1 *SD* for the Moderator Variable of Depression

Descriptive Statistics

	Mean	Std. Deviation	N
neoneuro neuroticism: neo	50.5298	11.15953	419
pred_esteem_cen centered predictor self-esteem	.0000	20.96459	419
minus1sd_mod_dep_ cen	6.9254	6.92542	419
interact_minus1sd	-94.6896	300.44883	419

Correlations

		neoneuro neuroticism: neo	pred_esteem_cen centered predictor self-esteem	minus1sd_mod_dep_ cen	interact_minus1sd
Pearson Correlation	neoneuro neuroticism: neo	1.000	-.693	.608	-.563
	pred_esteem_cen centered predictor self-esteem	-.693	1.000	-.654	.800
	minus1sd_mod_dep_ cen	.608	-.654	1.000	-.728
	interact_minus1sd	-.563	.800	-.728	1.000
Sig. (1-tailed)	neoneuro neuroticism: neo	.	.000	.000	.000
	pred_esteem_cen centered predictor self-esteem	.000	.	.000	.000
	minus1sd_mod_dep_ cen	.000	.000	.	.000
	interact_minus1sd	.000	.000	.000	.
N	neoneuro neuroticism: neo	419	419	419	419
	pred_esteem_cen centered predictor self-esteem	419	419	419	419
	minus1sd_mod_dep_ cen	419	419	419	419
	interact_minus1sd	419	419	419	419

The ANOVA results and the **Model Summary** are identical to what we have shown before, and we will not present them here. The **Coefficients** table is presented in Figure 8b.43. Note that the *b* weight for the interaction term (.006) is the same as it has always been because the interaction is an omnibus effect descriptive of the data as a whole. Note also that the *b* weight of the moderator variable (.532) has not changed either. That's because our focus is on the predictor whose equation changes with different levels of the moderator. Compared with the model where the moderator is centered at its mean, this function is somewhat steeper. That is, the *b* coefficient—the slope of the function controlling for the other predictors—for the "base" centered model is −.282 (see Figure 8b.9), but here it is

Figure 8b.43 The Regression Results Based on the Variables Specified for the Analysis at − 1 *SD* for the Moderator Variable of Depression

Coefficients

Model		Unstandardized Coefficients		Standardized Coefficients	t	Sig.	Correlations		
		B	Std. Error	Beta			Zero-order	Partial	Part
1	(Constant)	47.430	.622		76.195	.000			
	pred_esteem_cen centered predictor self-esteem	−.325	.030	−.610	−10.721	.000	−.693	−.466	−.361
	minus1sd_mod_dep_cen	.532	.080	.330	6.622	.000	.608	.309	.223
	interact_minus1sd	.006	.002	.166	2.636	.009	−.563	.128	.089

a. Dependent Variable: neoneuro neuroticism: neo

−.325. The value of the intercept has also changed a bit since we are now looking at the model from the perspective of relatively low depression (the depression variable is centered at 1 *SD* unit below the mean for depression). The model at the centered values of zero for the predictor and −1 *SD* for the moderator is as follows:

$$\text{Neuroticism} = 47.430 - (.325)\,(\text{self-esteem}) + (.532)\,(\text{depression}) + (.006)\,(\text{esteem}^* \text{depression})$$

8B.4.6 Plotting the Simple Slopes

8B.4.6.1 Plotting the Simple Slopes in IBM SPSS

We have now generated the equations of self-esteem predicting neuroticism for three reference points of the moderator variable of depression: (a) the model at the mean of depression, (b) the model at a relatively high level of depression (+1 *SD*), and (c) the model at a relatively low level of depression (−1 *SD*). These models can be plotted. The resulting plots are called *plots of simple slopes*, in the sense that we are simplifying the interaction by taking snapshots of the function at three different levels of the moderator variable.

In plotting the simple slopes for the interaction, the dependent variable is placed on the *Y* axis, the predictor variable is placed on the *X* axis, and the levels of the moderator variable are depicted by separate lines. Since these are straight-line functions, all we need are two data points for each function to be plotted. Aiken (2005) recommended using values of the predictor variable at ±1.5 *SD* units as the points to be generated for the plot (because they subsume the bulk of the distribution). For continuous predictor and moderator variables such as we have here, it is useful to plot the three functions that we have generated.

The mean of **pred_esteem_cen** is 0 with a standard deviation (see one of the previously shown **Descriptive Statistics** tables) of 20.96469. Thus, +1.5 *SD* units corresponds to a **pred_esteem_cen** value of 31.447 (20.96469 * 1.5 = 31.447) and −1.5 *SD* corresponds to a **pred_esteem_cen** value of −31.447.

Although it is not pretty, it is possible to obtain a graph of these functions through IBM SPSS. The syntax to do this (based on Aiken, 2005) is provided in the top portion of Figure 8b.44. Briefly, we compute the three simple slope functions and then graph the pairs in "overlay" fashion on the same set of axes. The resulting graphic display is shown in the bottom portion of Figure 8b.44.

Figure 8b.44   Self-Esteem as a Predictor of Neuroticism at Depression Values of − 1 *SD*, Its Mean (0 *SD*), and + 1 *SD*

Syntax to graph functions as −1 SD, 0 SD, and +1 SD

```
COMPUTE function_neg1sd_dep = 47.430 - .325 * pred_esteem_cen.
COMPUTE function_zerosd_dep = 51.113 - .282 * pred_esteem_cen.
COMPUTE function_plus1sd_dep = 54.795 - .240 * pred_esteem_cen.
TEMPORARY .
select if ((pred_esteem_cen ge -31.447) and (pred_esteem_cen le 31.447)).
GRAPH
    /SCATTERPLOT (OVERLAY) = pred_esteem_cen pred_esteem_cen red_esteem_cen
    with function_neg1sd_dep function_zerosd_dep function_plus1sd_dep (PAIR)
    /TITLE = "Regression of neuroticsm on centered self-esteem" .
EXECUTE .
```

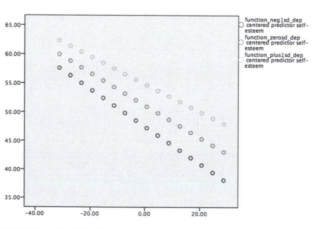

Regression of neuroticsm on centered self−esteem

8B.4.6.2 Plotting the Simple Slopes by Hand

There are three linear functions to be graphed: (a) the function for depression at +1 SD, (b) the function for depression at its mean, and (c) the function for depression at −1 SD. For each, all we need are two data points to plot the straight line. We will take these two data points to be ±31.447. For each of the three models, we solve the equation once for a self-esteem value of +31.447 and again for a self-esteem value of −31.447.

The computations for the function at the mean of the moderator variable of depression are as follows:

$$\text{Predicted neuroticism} = 51.113 + (-.282)(\text{self-esteem}) = 51.113 + (-.282)$$
$$(31.447) = 42.245$$

$$\text{Predicted neuroticism} = 51.113 + (-.282)(\text{self-esteem}) = 51.113 + (-.282)$$
$$(-31.447) = 59.981$$

The computations for the function at +1 SD for the moderator variable of depression are as follows:

$$\text{Neuroticism} = 54.795 - (.240)(\text{self-esteem}) = 54.795 + (-.240)(31.447) = 47.248$$

$$\text{Neuroticism} = 54.795 - (.240)(\text{self-esteem}) = 54.795 + (+.240)(31.447) = 62.342$$

The computations for the function at −1 SD for the moderator variable of depression are as follows:

$$\text{Neuroticism} = 47.430 - (.325)(\text{self-esteem}) = 47.430 +$$
$$(-.325)(31.447) = 37.210$$

$$\text{Neuroticism} = 47.430 - (.325)(\text{self-esteem}) = 47.430 +$$
$$(+.325)(31.447) = 57.650$$

We have placed the results of these computations in Table 8b.4. One way to graph these is to place such a table in Excel or some comparable software. If you work in Excel, you can highlight the table and select the **Chart Wizard** to construct the basic graph. Once the graph is built, you can customize it by right-clicking on each separate feature (that is how we constructed Figure 8b.45).

Table 8b.4 The Data Points in Preparation for Graphing the Interaction

Function	Self-Esteem at −1 SD	Self-Esteem at +1 SD
Depression at +1 *SD*	62.342	47.248
Depression at its Mean	59.981	42.245
Depression at −1 *SD*	57.650	37.210

Figure 8b.45 Self-Esteem Predicting Neuroticism at Depression Values of − 1 *SD*, its mean, and + 1 *SD*

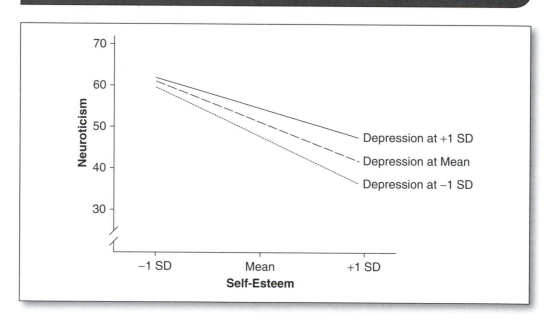

8B.4.7 Reporting Multiple Regression Interaction Results

Self-esteem and depression, as well as their interaction, were used as predictors of neuroticism. In preparation for the analysis and in accord with the recommendations of Aiken and West (1991) and Cohen et al. (2003), the two predictors were centered.

The correlations of the variables are shown in Table 8b.5. As can be seen, the variables were quite highly correlated with one another.

Self-esteem, depression, and the Self-esteem × Depression interaction significantly predicted neuroticism, $F(3, 415) = 156.325$, $p < .001$, $R^2 = .531$, Adjusted $R^2 = .527$. Results of the standard regression analysis are shown in Table 8b.6. Because the interaction was a statistically significant predictor, two additional analyses were performed treating depression as a moderator variable. The first analysis was carried out at a depression level of +1 *SD* unit by recentering the depression variable at that value; the intercept and raw regression coefficient for self-esteem were 54.795 and −.240 (*SE* = 0.027), respectively. The second analysis was carried out at a depression level of −1 *SD* unit by recentering the depression variable at that value; the intercept and raw regression coefficient for self-esteem were 47.430 and −.325 (*SE* = 0.030), respectively.

Based on this set of three regression analyses, a graphic representation of the interaction effect is presented in Figure 8b.45. Neuroticism decreases with increasing levels of self-esteem across the range of depression, but the rate of decrease is more pronounced at lower levels of depression. Generally, it appears that the presence of a higher level of depression can act as a resisting force for lowering neuroticism with increases in self-esteem.

8B.5 Mediation

8B.5.1 The Mediation Model Example

We will use the example of simple mediation that was described in Section 8A.7, the model for which is shown in Figure 8b.46. As you may recall, we are examining the possibility that the effect of positive affect on self-control might be mediated by considering the level of self-esteem. The data are contained in the data file **Personality**. Three regression analyses are called for in the path structure: We will use positive affect to predict self-control, we will use positive affect to predict self-esteem, and we will use positive affect and self-esteem together to predict self-control.

Table 8b.5 Correlations of the Variables in the Analysis (*N* = 419)

Variable	Self-Esteem	Depression
Neuroticism	−.693*	.608*
Self-Esteem	--	−.654*
Depression		--

* p < .05.

Table 8b.6 Regression Results for the Interaction Based on the Centered Variables ($N = 419$)

Model	b	SE-b	Beta	Pearson r	sr²
Constant	51.113	.435			
Self-Esteem*	−.282	.024	−.530	−.693	.158
Depression*	.532	.080	−.330	.608	.050
Interaction*	.006	.002	.112	−.336	.008

Note. sr² is the squared semi-partial correlation.
* p < .05.

Figure 8b.46 Mediation Model to Be Evaluated

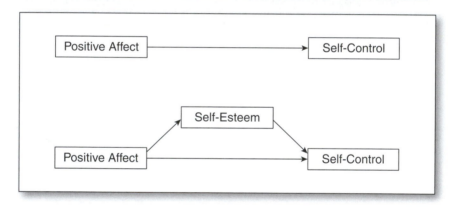

8B.5.2 Evaluating the Direct Effect of Positive Affect on the Dependent Variable of Self-Control

Select **Analyze ➔ Regression ➔ Linear** from the main menu. Place **selfcon** in the **Dependent** panel and **posafect** in the **Independent(s)** panel as shown in Figure 8b.47. Select the **Statistics** pushbutton, and check all of the usual choices (see Figure 8b.48). Click **Continue** to return to the main dialog window, and click **OK** to perform the analysis. The results of the analysis are shown in Figure 8b.49. Positive affect significantly predicts self-control; its *b* coefficient was 0.071 and its beta coefficient was .402.

Figure 8b.47 The Main Linear Regression Window

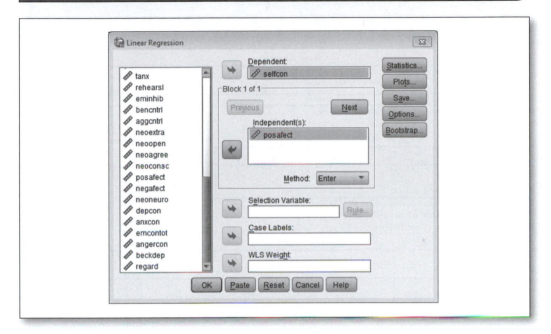

Figure 8b.48 The Linear Regression: Statistics Window

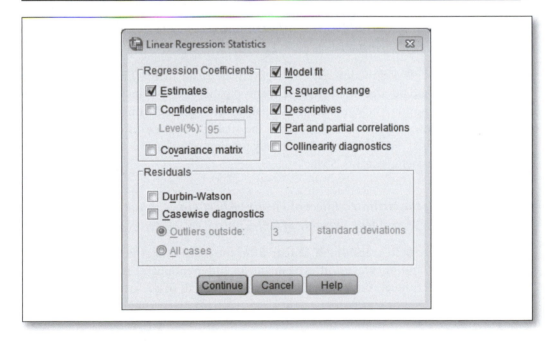

Figure 8b.49 The Regression Results Evaluating the Direct Effect of Positive Affect on the Dependent Variable of Self-Control

Model Summary

Model	R	R Square	Adjusted R Square	Std. Error of the Estimate	Change Statistics				
					R Square Change	F Change	df1	df2	Sig. F Change
1	.402a	.162	.160	.46672	.162	81.045	1	420	.000

a. Predictors: (Constant), posafect positive affect: mpq

ANOVA_b

Model		Sum of Squares	df	Mean Square	F	Sig.
1	Regression	17.654	1	17.654	81.045	.000a
	Residual	91.488	420	.218		
	Total	109.141	421			

a. Predictors: (Constant), posafect positive affect: mpq
b. Dependent Variable: selfcon self-control: Rosenbaum sched: rscs

Coefficients_a

Model		Unstandardized Coefficients		Standardized Coefficients	t	Sig.	Correlations		
		B	Std. Error	Beta			Zero-order	Partial	Part
1	(Constant)	3.524	.065		54.633	.000			
	posafect positive affect: mpq	.071	.008	.402	9.002	.000	.402	.402	.402

a. Dependent Variable: selfcon self-control: Rosenbaum sched: rscs

8B.5.3 Evaluating the Effect of Positive Affect on the Mediator Variable of Self-Esteem

Select **Analyze ➤ Regression ➤ Linear** from the main menu. Place **esteem** in the **Dependent** panel and **posafect** in the **Independent(s)** panel as shown in Figure 8b.50. Select the **Statistics** pushbutton, and check all of the usual choices. Click **Continue** to return to the main dialog window, and click **OK** to perform the analysis. The results of the analysis are shown in Figure 8b.51. Positive affect significantly predicts self-control; its *b* coefficient was 4.000 and the beta coefficient was .554.

8B.5.4 Evaluating the Mediated Effect of Positive Affect via Self-Esteem on the Dependent Variable of Self-Control

Select **Analyze ➤ Regression ➤ Linear** from the main menu. Place **selfcon** in the **Dependent** panel and **posafect and esteem** in the **Independent(s)** panel as shown in Figure 8b.52. Select the **Statistics** pushbutton, and check all of the usual choices. Click

Figure 8b.50 The Main Linear Regression Window

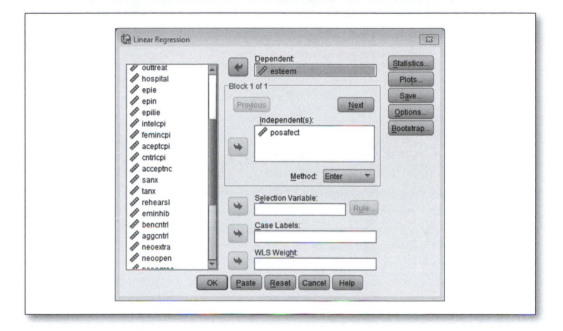

Figure 8b.51 The Regression Results Evaluating the Direct Effect of Positive Affect on the Mediator of Self-Esteem

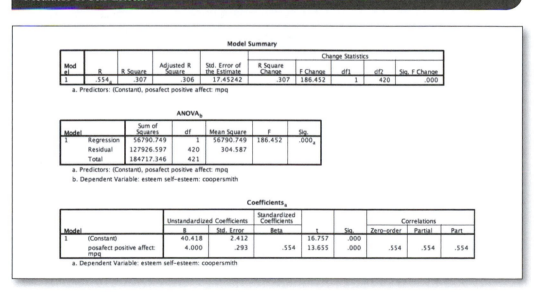

Model Summary

Mod el	R	R Square	Adjusted R Square	Std. Error of the Estimate	R Square Change	F Change	df1	df2	Sig. F Change
1	.554[a]	.307	.306	17.45242	.307	186.452	1	420	.000

a. Predictors: (Constant), posafect positive affect: mpq

ANOVA[b]

Model		Sum of Squares	df	Mean Square	F	Sig.
1	Regression	56790.749	1	56790.749	186.452	.000[a]
	Residual	127926.597	420	304.587		
	Total	184717.346	421			

a. Predictors: (Constant), posafect positive affect: mpq
b. Dependent Variable: esteem self-esteem: coopersmith

Coefficients[a]

Model		Unstandardized Coefficients		Standardized Coefficients	t	Sig.	Correlations		
		B	Std. Error	Beta			Zero-order	Partial	Part
1	(Constant)	40.418	2.412		16.757	.000			
	posafect positive affect: mpq	4.000	.293	.554	13.655	.000	.554	.554	.554

a. Dependent Variable: esteem self-esteem: coopersmith

Figure 8b.52 The Main Linear Regression Window

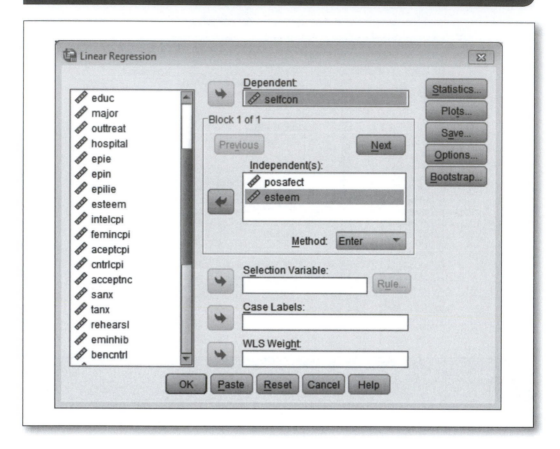

Continue to return to the main dialog window, and click **OK** to perform the analysis. The results of the analysis are shown in Figure 8b.53. Both predictors were statistically significant. The *b* and beta coefficients for positive affect here controlling for self-esteem are .037 and .212, down from the values of .071 and .402, respectively, that we saw in analyzing its direct effect. Self-esteem was associated with a *b* coefficient of .008 and a beta coefficient of .343 when controlling for positive affect.

The results of the Aroian test (the formula for which was shown in Figure 8a.4), which was discussed and computed in Section 8A.7.6.3, demonstrated a statistically significant mediation effect ($z = 7.3949303$), with a relative strength of effect of approximately .47 (see Section 8A.7.5). We have also seen that the Freedman–Schatzkin test (see Section 8A.7.6.4) yielded a statistically significant result as well, $t(419) = 6.8831484$, $p < .05$.

Figure 8b.53 The Regression Results Evaluating the Mediated Effect of Positive Affect Via Self-Esteem on the Dependent Variable of Self-Control

Model Summary

Model	R	R Square	Adjusted R Square	Std. Error of the Estimate	Change Statistics				
					R Square Change	F Change	df1	df2	Sig. F Change
1	.493$_a$	.243	.240	.44398	.243	67.338	2	419	.000

a. Predictors: (Constant), esteem self-esteem: coopersmith, posafect positive affect: mpq

ANOVA$_b$

Model		Sum of Squares	df	Mean Square	F	Sig.
1	Regression	26.548	2	13.274	67.338	.000$_a$
	Residual	82.594	419	.197		
	Total	109.141	421			

a. Predictors: (Constant), esteem self-esteem: coopersmith, posafect positive affect: mpq

b. Dependent Variable: selfcon self-control: Rosenbaum sched: rscs

Coefficients$_a$

Model		Unstandardized Coefficients		Standardized Coefficients	t	Sig.	Correlations		
		B	Std. Error	Beta			Zero-order	Partial	Part
1	(Constant)	3.187	.079		40.208	.000			
	posafect positive affect: mpq	.037	.009	.212	4.151	.000	.402	.199	.176
	esteem self-esteem: coopersmith	.008	.001	.343	6.717	.000	.461	.312	.285

a. Dependent Variable: selfcon self-control: Rosenbaum sched: rscs

8B.5.5 Reporting the Results of the Mediation Analysis

The hypothesis that some of the predictive effect of positive affect on self-control is mediated by self-esteem was tested by performing three regression analyses, the results of which are shown in Table 8b.7. In the first model shown in Table 8b.7, positive affect significantly predicted the outcome variable of self-control, $F(1, 420) = 81.045$, $p < .001$, $R^2 = .162$, Adjusted $R^2 = .160$; its b coefficient was .071 ($SE = 0.008$) and its beta coefficient was .402. In the second model shown in Table 8b.7, positive affect also significantly predicted the mediator variable of self-esteem, $F(1, 420) = 186.452$, $p < .001$, $R^2 = .307$, Adjusted $R^2 = .306$; its b coefficient was 4.000 ($SE = 0.293$) and the beta coefficient was .554.

In the mediated analysis (shown as the third model in Figure 8b.7), both positive affect and self-esteem significantly predicted the outcome variable of self-control, $F(2, 419) = 67.338$, $p < .001$, $R^2 = .243$, Adjusted $R^2 = .240$. The b and beta coefficients for positive affect controlling for self-esteem were .037 ($SE = 0.009$) and .212, down from the values of .071 and .402, respectively, when analyzing its direct effect. Self-esteem was associated with a b coefficient of .008 ($SE = 0.001$) and a beta coefficient of .343 when controlling for positive affect. The entire path structure with the coefficients is shown in Figure 8b.54.

To test the statistical significance of the mediation effect, both the Aroian test (1944/1947), a variation of the Sobel test suggested by Baron and Kenny (1986), and the Freedman–Schatzkin (Freedman & Schatzkin, 1992) test were performed. The results of both the Aroian test indicated that the mediation effect was statistically significant, $z = 7.39$, $p < .05$, and the Freedman–Schatzkin test, $t(420) = 6.88$, $p < .05$, indicated that the effect of positive affect on self-control was significantly reduced when self-esteem was included as a mediator.

The ratio of the indirect to the total direct effect was used as an index of relative strength of the mediated effect. The indirect effect, computed as the product of the mediated path coefficients of .554 and .343, was .190, the total direct effect was .402, and the ratio of the two is approximately .4726. It thus appears that approximately 47.26% of the effect of positive affect on self-control is mediated through self-esteem.

Table 8b.7 Mediation Analysis Results ($N = 422$)

Model	R^2	Variables	b	SE-b	Beta	Pearson r	sr^2
1	.162	Constant	3.524	.065			
		Positive Affect*	.071	.008	.402	.402	.162
2	.307	Constant	40.418	2.412			
		Positive Affect*	4.000	.293	.554	.554	.307
3	.243	Constant	3.187	.079			
		Positive Affect*	.037	.009	.212	.402	.031
		Self-Esteem*	.008	.001	.343	.461	.081

Note. Model 1: Positive affect predicting self-control; Model 2: Positive affect predicting self-esteem; Model 3: Positive affect and self-esteem predicting self-control. sr^2 is the squared semi-partial correlation.
* $p < .05$.

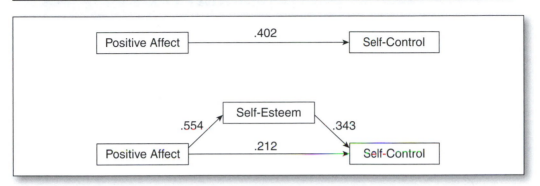

Multilevel Modeling

9A.1 The Name of the Procedure

In this chapter, we present an extension of the ordinary least squares multiple regression analyses described in Chapters 7A and 8A. We are calling this type of design *multilevel modeling*, but it is also known by other names including the following:

- Multilevel linear modeling
- Hierarchical linear modeling
- Contextual modeling
- Mixed models

9A.2 The Rise of Multilevel Modeling

Behavioral and social researchers are rapidly incorporating multilevel modeling into their mainstream data analysis techniques, and it is clear that this trend will continue into the foreseeable future. In fact, Goldstein (2011a, p. 342) has suggested that "this general methodology has now reached a stage of maturity, as witnessed by its routine use and its incorporation into major statistical packages." Multilevel modeling is a complex topic and the mathematical underpinnings are not easily simplified for less quantitatively oriented readers (although we will make such an attempt here). Chapters in Cohen et al. (2003) and Tabachnick and Fidell (2007) summarize the important aspects of the topic. Other sources that treat the topic in more depth include Bickel (2007), Goldstein (2011b), Heck and Thomas (2008), Heck, Thomas, and Tabata (2010), Hox (2010), Hox and Roberts (2010), Kim (2009), Kreft and de Leeuw (2007), Luke (2004), Raudenbush and Bryk (2002), Singer (1998), Snijders and Bosker (2012), Stevens (2009), and Van de Vijver, van Hemert, and Poortinga (2008).

9A.3 The Defining Feature of Multilevel Modeling: Hierarchically Structured Data

Because multilevel modeling is a statistical regression technique, our focus is on predicting the value of a quantitative dependent variable. The way to recognize that we may need to apply multilevel modeling to the research problem is when we have a data set that is *hierarchically structured*.

The idea that data are hierarchically structured means that the cases in the research do not comprise a single relatively homogeneous set of individuals or other entities but are themselves organized or structured into sets of cases. Examples of such a scenario abound. As one example, assume that we have an interest in predicting the success or productivity of automobile salespeople in a large metropolitan area such as Washington, D.C. We use as a measure of success the number of dollars of car sales during the past calendar year. Each salesperson has some value on this variable, and we can invoke certain predictors (e.g., years of experience, whether the salespeople are female or male) to attempt to explain the variance of the dependent variable. If it were as simple as this, we could apply an ordinary least squares regression procedure in this instance. But it is not that simple.

The salespeople work in car dealerships, and different dealerships may, for various reasons (e.g., location, reputation, business practice), sell different numbers of vehicles. The sales figure of any one salesperson is likely to be a function not only of his or her individual characteristics (e.g., years of experience, sex) but also of the dealership where he or she is employed. If we think of the individual characteristics of the salespeople as first-level (often referred to as the *micro-level*) or Level 1 explanatory variables, then dealership can be thought of as a second-level (*macro-level*) or Level 2 variable. If this study were expanded to other metropolitan areas (e.g., Dallas–Fort Worth, Chicago, New York, Miami), then metro area could be incorporated as a third-level (a higher-order macro-level) or Level 3 variable. The different units within macro-level variables are often called *groups*; thus, in our example, salespeople would be said to belong to different groups (i.e., dealerships). Multilevel modeling is appropriate (needed) here insofar as the macro-level variables contribute to the prediction of the dependent variable, for example, sales success.

A convenient way to describe or conceive of a hierarchical structure is to say that the micro-level "units" (cases or participants) to which the individual characteristics are attached are *nested* within the Level 2 units or groups, that the Level 2 groups are nested within the Level 3 groups, and so on. In our car sales example, the salespeople are nested within dealerships, and dealerships are nested within metropolitan areas. In this sense, the Level 3 variable provides a *context* for the Level 2 groups, and the Level 2 variable provides a *context* for the Level 1 cases.

Hierarchically structured research data sets are not at all uncommon. Other examples include the following:

- Researchers wish to assess achievement of elementary school students. These students are nested within classroom or by teachers who are in turn nested within schools in a district (which can be nested within regions of a state, and so on).
- Researchers wish to assess the effectiveness of a leadership workshop using a pretest–posttest design (pretest scores and posttest scores are nested within cases).

9A.4 Nesting and the Independence Assumption

In Section 3A.12.4, we discussed the assumption of independence, sometimes called the assumption of independence of errors, as one of the four assumptions underlying much of multivariate statistical analysis. The ANOVA/MANOVA and regression procedures treated in the intervening chapters, and the techniques to be treated in subsequent chapters that are manifestations of the general linear model, all require those assumptions to be met. An exception to this rule is multilevel modeling.

In hierarchical (contextual) data structures where Level 1 units are nested within Level 2 groups, it is typically true that the independence assumption is violated. We can illustrate this by referring back to our car sales example. Let's say that we have drawn a sample of 44 dealerships in the metropolitan Washington, D.C., area, and that each dealership has on average 10 salespeople, giving us 440 Level 1 units. If the assumption of independence was holding, then the sales figures predicted from the individual characteristics of the salespeople (e.g., years of experience, sex) would maximize our predictive power. But the data would clearly show that some dealerships were selling more product than others, and thus the sales figures for salespeople within a dealership are going to be correlated even though we will see individual differences between those salespeople.

The observation that salespeople within dealerships are on average more alike on the dependent measure than salespeople between dealerships—more generally, that there are correlations between the Level 1 units within Level 2 groups—is known as *clustering* (not to be confused with formal cluster analysis procedures discussed in Chapters 15A and 15B). To the extent that we see correlations or clustering within the Level 2 groups, we have violated the assumption of independence. That is, the first-level units—the salespeople in our example—are not simply randomly selected members of a larger population; rather, the sales figures of staff within a given dealership are likely to be more related to each other than they are to the sales figures of salespeople randomly selected from the other dealerships.

This independence violation is pervasive in multilevel modeling designs. Some examples include the following:

- Certain aspects of the medical records of patients who see the same primary care physician will likely be more similar than those aspects from randomly selected patients elsewhere in the same clinic or from other clinics.

- The performance of elementary school students in the same classroom or with the same teacher will be more similar than the performance of a randomly selected set of students.

Once we recognize that the data from our Level 1 units (salespeople in our example) are likely to exhibit a clustering effect that will violate our assumption of independence, it is necessary to engage in a statistical analysis that takes such clustering into account. Goldstein (2011a) has gone so far as to suggest that failing to acknowledge and deal with clustering in a data set is ethically questionable, in that the results of a statistical analysis that does not take clustering into account when clustering matters (an analysis that erroneously assumes all of the observations are independent of each other) is likely to return results that are at best incomplete but are quite likely to be either misleading or incorrect.

9A.5 The Intraclass Correlation as an Index of Clustering

The degree to which clustering is observed—the correlation of the Level 1 units within the Level 2 groups—can be assessed by the *intraclass correlation* (ICC). The ICC gained recognition some time ago in the context of being used to assess the reliability of rater judgments (Shrout & Fleiss, 1979), particularly because it was able to be conceptualized within the generalizability theory that was originally proposed by Cronbach, Nageswari, and Gleser (1963) and Cronbach, Gleser, Nanda, and Rajaratnam (1972). As we briefly suggested in Section 3A.12.4, it turns out that the ICC is also applicable in the context of multilevel modeling.

Using a two-level hierarchy to simplify our discussion, the ICC can be conceived in the context of a one-way between-subjects ANOVA in which the independent variable is the Level 2 variable and the dependent variable is the variable that is being predicted. In our car sales example, the independent variable would be the car dealerships and the dependent variable would be numbers of dollars of sales. The ICC indexes the extent to which cases within a Level 2 group (a dealership) are more similar to each other than to a random sample of cases drawn across all of the Level 2 groups. More formally, the ICC is the percentage of variance of the dependent variable that is attributable to the Level 2 variable. Other ways that the ICC can be thought of are as follows:

- The ICC represents the similarity of cases within the same Level 2 group.
- The ICC informs us of the homogeneity (or lack thereof) of cases within the Level 2 groups.
- The ICC characterizes how much the cases in the Level 2 resemble each other (on the dependent variable).
- The ICC indexes the dependence between cases in the Level 2 groups.

The ICC functions more as though it was a squared correlation coefficient such as eta square and less like a Pearson correlation. It is often symbolized by the lower case Greek letter rho (ρ) and can take on values between 0 and 1. To the extent that the ICC is closer to zero, the amount of variance associated with the Level 2 variable is relatively small. ANOVA/MANOVA and ordinary least squares regression assume that the ICC is zero; in fact, this is one way to operationally define the independence assumption. To the extent that the ICC is greater than zero, membership in a Level 2 unit contributes to prediction and thus indicates that the independence assumption is violated.

9A.6 Consequences of Violating the Independence Assumption

Violating the independence assumption can result in a substantial increase in making a Type I error (incorrectly rejecting the null hypothesis). This happens because of the following chain of events:

- Sample size is conceptually distorted, which leads to
- underestimating the standard errors, which leads to
- an inflated alpha level.

9A.6.1 Sample Size Distortion

In ordinary least squares regression, we assume that our sample is composed of N independent cases, that is, we assume that the ICC is equal to zero. Were we to mistakenly apply this procedure to our car sales example, we would perform a standard regression analysis with a sample of 440 salespeople. But the more likely scenario is that the ICC is greater than zero, and so rather than having 440 independent observations *we have fewer than 440 independent observations*. How many fewer depends on the value of the ICC. In the hypothetical situation where the ICC was equal to 1—all of the variance of the dependent variable was explained by dealership—there would be no variation of sales figures within a dealership. In such an instance, we would effectively have 44 independent observations, one for each dealership, rather than 440 independent observations.

9A.6.2 Underestimating Standard Errors

If we performed an ordinary least squares regression on the 440 cases using some individual characteristics of the salespeople (e.g., years of experience, sex) to predict sales figures, the statistical significance tests for the regression coefficients would be based on an N of 440. These significance tests use an estimate of the standard errors in the computation, and the estimated standard errors, in turn, are a function of sample size. Larger sample sizes are associated with greater precision and narrower confidence intervals, factors that increase the chances of obtaining a statistically significant effect. To illustrate this, consider that a Pearson *r* of approximately .09 is needed to achieve statistical significance at an alpha level of .05 with an *N* of 440 but that a Pearson *r* of approximately .29 is needed to achieve statistical significance at an alpha level of .05 with an *N* of 44. Thus, to the extent that the ICC takes on values greater than zero, the standard errors in ordinary least squares regression are going to be increasingly underestimated. This underestimation generates confidence intervals that are far too narrow. Unduly narrow confidence bands will result in regression coefficients improperly reaching statistical significance at a rate much greater than 5 times in 100 (the presumed alpha level), a situation known as alpha inflation.

9A.6.3 Alpha-Level Inflation

As demonstrated by Barcikowski (1981) using a procedure described by Walsh (1947), the extent to which alpha inflation intrudes into a statistical analysis is a function of the value of the ICC. Barcikowski reported his results in tabular form, and his table, which we show in Table 9a.1, is widely reproduced in many textbooks.

The information in Table 9a.1 presents what we regard as one of the most sobering set of results in the arena of multivariate research design. The entries in the table are the alpha levels for an ANOVA under the specified conditions, since that was Barcikowski's (1981) focus, but his analysis applies equally to regression or to any other procedure that is part of the general linear model. Barcikowski played out the effective alpha levels under two specified sets of conditions: four different cell sample sizes and six different values of the ICC.

Table 9a.1 Effective Alpha Levels for Determining Statistical Significance in ANOVA as a Function of Cell Size and Value of ICC (Based on Barcikowski, 1981)

n per cell	Value of the Intraclass Correlation					
	.00	.01	.05	.20	.40	.80
10	.05	.06	.11	.28	.46	.75
25	.05	.08	.19	.46	.63	.84
50	.05	.11	.30	.59	.74	.89
100	.05	.17	.43	.70	.81	.92

Source: Based on Barcikowski, R. S. (1981). Statistical power with group mean as the unit of analysis. *Journal of Educational Statistics, 6,* 267–285.

In Table 9a.1, each row represents a different cell size for ANOVA, and covers a span from 10 to 100 (these values would be multiplied by the number of groups of the Level 2 variable to determine a sample size N for ordinary least squares regression). The columns represent some example values of the ICC.

Each coordinate (entry) in the table depicts the effective alpha level for the analysis with a certain number of cases in each cell and a certain value of the ICC. For an ICC whose value is zero (the first column under **Value of the Intraclass Correlation**), the effective alpha level is constant at .05 for all Ns. This is so because, with an ICC of zero, there is no effect of the Level 2 variable (there is no clustering effect), and so the number of cases in the analysis is also the number of independent observations. This condition satisfies the independence assumption and thus results in no alpha-level inflation.

That situation changes even for the situation where the ICC is .01, a value just barely above zero. For a cell size of 100, the effective alpha level is no longer .05 but rather .17. With increasingly higher ICCs for a cell size of 100, the effective alpha level (alpha-level inflation) increases dramatically, reaching .70 with an ICC of .20 and .81 with an ICC of less than.40.

Barcikowski's (1981) results teach us two very important and related lessons:

- Alpha inflation is a serious threat to the valid interpretation of results when we assume independence but when there is a clustering effect in the data. To remove this threat to validity, we need to analyze our data using a procedure such as multilevel modeling that takes this clustering into account.
- What may be judged as substantial values of the ICC must be made in the context of Barcikowski's table. Even an ICC of .01 can wreak havoc on the alpha level with the sample sizes in triple figures, a common sample size used in regression analyses. That is, the likelihood of committing a Type I error when we assume independence but when there is a clustering effect in the data can be substantial. It is very likely, then, that once a hierarchical structure is included in the research design, an analysis that takes into account that multilevel structure needs to be applied.

9A.7 Some Ways in Which Level 2 Groups Can Differ

With several Level 2 groups in the research study, it is likely that the groups will differ in some ways, and we have illustrated this point in the left column of Figure 9a.1 (which is modeled on figures presented by Kreft & de Leeuw, 2007). We will use our car sales example to make this illustration concrete. Assume that we are predicting sales productivity in number of dollars of sales (represented on the Y axis) based on the number of years of experience of the sales staff (represented on the X axis). Each graph shows only four regression models (one for each of four dealerships) for the sake of readability, but

Figure 9a.1 Ordinary Least Squares Regression Contrasted With the Random Coefficient Model for Parallel Slopes/Different Intercepts, Different Slopes/Common Intercept, and Different Slopes/Different Intercepts for the Level 2 Units

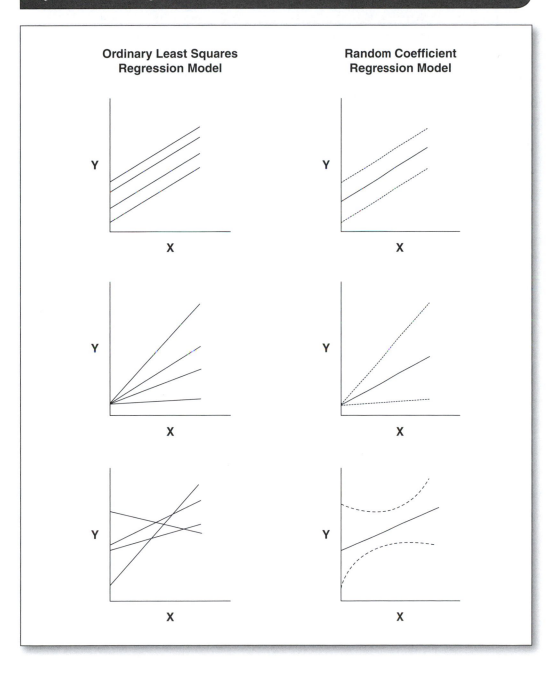

remember that we have data for 44 dealerships in our example and so the situation would be far more complicated.

The top graph in the left column of Figure 9a.1 illustrates a situation in which the slopes for the dealerships are very similar but the models differ in their Y intercept. The similarity in slopes suggests that sales figures increase to the same degree with more sales staff experience, but the difference in intercepts indicates that the dealerships differ in the amount of sales dollars that they produce.

The middle graph in the left column of Figure 9a.1 illustrates a situation in which the slopes for the dealerships are quite different but the Y intercepts are the same. Such a pattern would suggest that, although there are still dealership differences, years of experience of the sales staff is of little importance in some dealerships (ones whose slope is almost parallel to the X axis) but is of considerable importance in others.

The lower graph in the left column of Figure 9a.1 illustrates a situation in which both the slopes and intercepts differ by dealerships. This represents the most complex scenario.

9A.8 The Random Coefficient Regression Model

9A.8.1 Generality of Approach

If we were limited to ordinary least squares regression, we might be tempted to generate 44 separate regression models for our example, one for each dealership. Such an outcome would be less than satisfying, however. Our purpose in framing this hypothetical study was to predict the success of car salespeople in a large metropolitan area such as Washington, D.C, not to separately predict the success of car salespeople in Silver Spring, Arlington, Bethesda, Alexandria, and all of the other areas in Washington, D.C., containing dealerships. And so we should hope to produce a single general model that subsumes all of the dealerships rather than a set of individual dealership models.

Multilevel modeling is the technique that will provide us with a more general model. It is able to accomplish this goal, at least in part, by using the *random coefficient model* rather than ordinary least squares. In the random coefficient model, the individual slopes and intercepts of each Level 2 group are not separately estimated as stand-alone parameters, but are taken into account in producing the more general multilevel model. As Cohen et al. (2003) say,

> [The random coefficient] model provides accurate estimates of relationships of individual level [Level 1] predictors to a dependent variable while at the same time taking into account clustering and providing accurate estimates of the standard errors of regression coefficients so that alpha inflation is avoided. (p. 544)

In the random coefficient model, the coefficients have two components, an average part and a variable part (analogous to the mean and standard deviation). This idea is illustrated in the right column of Figure 9a.1 (again modeled on figures presented by Kreft & de Leeuw, 2007). Each of the three scenarios already described is handled in the random coefficient model to its right. The dashed lines depict the variability around the overall or general solution, what Kreft and de Leeuw (2007) call the macro variance, giving a sense of the differences attributable to the Level 2 groups.

9A.8.2 Fixed and Random Coefficients

In ordinary least squares regression, where we are analyzing data from independent observations, we assume that there are population (fixed) parameters for the *Y* intercept and the slopes of the predictors. The regression procedure is designed to estimate those fixed values, and so are themselves regarded as fixed coefficients.

In multilevel modeling, the cases in the Level 2 groups, and often the Level 2 groups themselves, are most often samples from a larger and possibly ever-changing population. For example, some salespeople at the dealerships may stop working there and others may take their place, a new dealership may open somewhere in the metropolitan area, another dealership may change ownership and adopt different business practices, and so on. We may therefore consider the data to be a random sample from some probability distribution. Treating the coefficients as fixed would allow us to speak only of the particular data set. If we wish to generalize to the population, we must treat the variables as random variables (de Leeuw & Kreft, 1986). Multilevel modeling treats the slopes and intercepts of the Level 1 model as random variables in the Level 2 analysis. These random variables take on values that are a sample of the more general population. Taken together, we can derive estimates of what the typical values of those variables may be and obtain as well a sense of how variable those values may be. This is dealt with in the statistical treatment of the data, rendering the data processing more complex than ordinary least squares regression but at the same time providing for more generalizable results.

9A.8.3 Guidelines for Sample Sizes

As a general rule, greater sample sizes generate greater amounts of statistical power because they are associated with smaller standard errors, thus driving the estimates toward greater precision. The issue, of course, is that we ordinarily do not have the resources (or inclination) to measure millions of cases to ensure a microscopic-sized standard error term (and even if we did, there is a point of diminishing returns where we gain very little with greater sample sizes). Hox (2010) suggests a 30–30 rule of thumb for appropriate sample sizes in multilevel modeling designs; that is, researchers should strive for 30 groups with at least

30 cases within each group. If we were interested in evaluating interaction effects between Level 1 and Level 2 variables (see Section 9A.8.3.4), then Hox recommends a 50–20 rule of thumb in which we would look to capture 50 groups with about 20 cases per group. If we were interested in evaluating the random components in the model, then a 100–10 rule of thumb is proposed.

9A.9 Centering the Variables

Although centering is not typically done in ordinary least squares regression procedures, we indicated in Section 8A.6 that it is most useful to do when we are examining interaction effects. As you may recall, centering a variable involves subtracting the mean from each score. The scores that are therefore analyzed by the regression procedure are deviation scores rather than raw scores. Using simple linear regression to illustrate this, the slope (the regression coefficient) is unaffected by centering, and the *Y* intercept still reflects the value of the dependent variable when the predictor is zero. Without centering, the zero point of the predictor is a raw score value that is often not meaningful (e.g., 0 on a 1–5 scale, 0 intelligence); with centering, the zero point of the predictor is its mean.

In multilevel modeling, unlike ordinary least squares regression, centering the predictors is virtually standard operating procedure for most researchers. Centering is desirable because it reduces the degree of multicollinearity between (a) predictors in the model and (b) the random slopes and intercepts (Cohen et al., 2003). The process of centering always involves subtracting the mean from the raw score. But in multilevel modeling, the question that must be answered is which mean to use, and the answer is complicated.

9A.9.1 The Centering Options

The two types of centering that are commonly discussed in the context of multi-level modeling (Cohen et al., 2003; Kreft & de Leeuw, 2007) are *grand mean centering* and *group mean centering*. The differences between these two strategies are discussed below.

9A.9.1.1 Grand Mean Centering

Grand mean centering involves using the overall mean of the entire sample. To obtain this mean, distinctions between the Level 2 groups are ignored. The result of this grand mean centering strategy is that the standing of individual cases in their own group is lost; the deviation score informs us only of the standing of the cases with respect to every other case in the entire sample. Despite the loss of relative standing in the group, we do not lose a sense of group differences. For example, for those groups whose mean score is relatively high, many or most of the cases associated with it will have positive deviation scores.

9A.9.1.2 Group Mean Centering

Group mean centering involves subtracting each individual group mean from the score on the variable for those cases within that particular group. To obtain this mean, each group is treated separately. The mean of the predictor for only those cases in a particular group is computed, and that mean is subtracted from the scores of those cases. The result of group mean centering is that the standing of an individual case with respect to the entire sample is lost; the deviation score informs us only of the standing of that case with respect to the other cases in the particular group. Here, it does not matter if a particular group has a high average score or a low average score; the deviation score will only reflect a case's standing relative to that group mean. As a result of group mean centering, information with respect to group differences is lost as each group will have a mean of zero.

9A.9.2 Centering the Level 2 Predictor

Assuming for the sake of simplicity that we have just one predictor at Level 2, the Level 2 counterpart of the Level 1 predictor. Using our car sales example, we would have a variable representing years of experience for the dealership, that is, we would average the years of experience for salespeople within a given dealership. In the data file, we might have a variable called **dealership_experience**. All salespeople in Dealership A would have the mean value for Dealership A as their data points for this variable, all salespeople in Dealership B would have the mean value for Dealership B as their data points for this variable, and so on. Because salespeople within a dealership would have the same value on the Level 2 predictor, group mean centering makes no sense (everyone in each group would have a deviation score of zero).

The centering choices are thus limited to two options: using the noncentered raw scores or centering the scores based on the grand mean of that variable. Common practice is to adopt grand mean centering for the Level 2 predictor (Enders & Tofighi, 2007).

9A.9.3 Centering the Level 1 Predictor

We will assume for the sake of simplicity that we have just one predictor at Level 1, the years of experience of the salespeople from our car sales example. In the data file, we might have a variable called **salesperson_experience**. Each case would have a value representing his or her particular number of years of experience. We want to center this variable, but the choice between grand mean centering and group mean centering needs to be considered carefully. The consensus view (e.g., Cohen et al., 2003; Enders & Tofighi, 2007; Kreft & de Leeuw, 2007; Kreft, de Leeuw, & Aiken, 1995) is that there is no single answer to the question; rather, the centering strategy that is selected should be consonant with the focus of the research.

Mostly everyone supports the idea that researchers should carefully consider the centering strategy in light of the purpose of the research, but exactly what should be considered and what should be decided on the basis of that consideration is still an evolving story. To address this issue, we adopt the general perspective outlined by Enders and Tofighi (2007). These authors identified four broadly framed research questions and discussed the logic underlying the two different types of centering for each, ultimately providing their recommended centering strategies. We present here some of their conclusions together with our own recommendations. In creating this synopsis, we have broken apart their last research question concerning interaction effects so that we discuss five broad research questions; interested readers are advised to access the original article for a more complete discussion of the underlying logic. Remember, as we address these research questions, we wish to determine what centering strategy to use for the Level 1 variable in the analysis.

9A.9.3.1 The Research Is Focused on the Level 1 Predictor

If the primary purpose of the research is to assess the ability of the Level 1 variable to predict the dependent variable, then removing the variance attributable to the Level 2 groups will result in a purer picture of that relationship (Enders & Tofighi, 2007). In our example, we might be interested in the degree to which years of experience of the individual salespeople predicts sales figures, but we would not be interested in the degree to which the average years of sales experience of the salespeople in a dealership predicts sales figures. A convenient way to negate the Level 2 grouping factor is to use group mean centering. The mean of each group on the centered scores is always zero, and so the variance contributed by group membership is zero.

9A.9.3.2 The Research Is Focused on the Level 2 Predictor

If the primary purpose of the research is to assess the ability of the Level 2 variable to predict the dependent variable, then we recommend using Level 2 grand mean centering. Grand mean centering retains the integrity of the differences in the Level 2 groups. This strategy calls for subtracting the grand mean (this is the same value that would be obtained from the weighted average of the group means) from each group mean. For example, a group with cases whose values on the dependent variable are relatively high will have relatively large positive deviation scores.

9A.9.3.3 The Research Is Focused on Both Levels

If researchers have an interest in examining both levels of the hierarchy, then Enders and Tofighi (2007) argue that both the individual scores and the differences between the groups at Level 2 need to be considered. Assuming an ICC greater than zero and triple figures for sample size (i.e., assuming there are contextual effects), we recommend that Level 1 and Level 2 group mean centering is done.

9A.9.3.4 The Research Is Focused on Cross-Level or Level 1 Interactions

We have discussed interactions between Level 1 predictors in Section 8A.6, and those are possible to evaluate in multilevel models as well. What is new here are *cross-level interactions*. A cross-level interaction includes a Level 1 variable and a Level 2 variable in the effect. In our car sales example, we used years of experience of the salespeople as the Level 1 variable. Suppose we introduced a Level 2 variable capturing at least one element of the convenience of accessing the dealership. This convenience factor might be indicated by miles to the nearest freeway exit. If we named that variable **dealership_convenience**, we could then construct an interaction term named **salesperson_experience*dealership_convenience** to represent the interaction term. When the research issue focuses on either Level 1 interactions or cross-level interactions, Enders and Tofighi (2007) recommend using group mean centering.

9A.9.3.5 The Research Is Focused on Level 2 Interactions

It is also possible for the focus of the research to be on interactions between Level 2 variables. In our car sales example, we discussed in Section 9A.8.2 a Level 2 variable of **dealership_experience**, and in Section 9A.8.3.4, we introduced another Level 2 variable of **dealership_convenience**. It is possible that the interaction of these two Level 2 variables, **dealership_experience*dealership_convenience**, was the primary focus. In this scenario, we recommend using Level 2 grand mean centering.

9A.10 The Process of Building the Multilevel Model

9A.10.1 Assembling the Measured Variables

The process of building the multilevel model proceeds in a systematic manner. The first task we must accomplish is to assemble the measured variables that we will use in the analysis, that is, to identify those variables in the data that have been collected for the research that we anticipate incorporating in the model. Using our car dealership example to illustrate this, the following list of variables in the original data file (together with their status in the hierarchy) will be involved in our analysis:

- Dealership is a Level 2 variable.
- Years of experience of the salesperson is a Level 1 variable.
- The sex of the sales person is a categorical Level 1 variable.
- The average years of experience representing the dealership (the average experience of its sales staff) is a Level 2 variable.
- The outcome variable is sales success as measured by the number of dollars of car sales in a given time period (e.g., monthly) is a Level 1 variable.

9A.10.2 Assess the Unconditional Model to Compute the ICC

Our design of the car sales study presumed that we were going to apply a multilevel model to predict successful sales performance. Inherent in this presumption is that the data exhibit a hierarchical structure, that is, that the ICC is sufficiently greater than zero to justify conceiving of the data as being hierarchically organized. We test this presumption by generating what is called the *unconditional model* and sometimes referred to as the *null model* or the *empty model*; it is referred to as unconditional because the only factor in the model is the Level 2 dealership variable that defines the hierarchy. The ICC may be computed from the results of evaluating this model. Let us assume that we determine from this analysis that Dealership accounts for a practical enough portion of the variance to justify a multilevel modeling approach, say approximately 20% of the variance in this case.

9A.10.3 Computing Centered Variables for the Analysis

We will be using for this example two centered variables in our multilevel model. Centered variables need to be computed through IBM SPSS. The variables that we need to generate are as follows:

- A Level 1 dealership experience group-centered variable. This represents the deviation of each sales person's years of experience from the average years of experience for his or her dealership.
- A Level 2 dealership experience variable centered on the grand mean. This represents the deviation of each dealership's average years of experience from the average years of experience for the entire sample of sales people.

9A.10.4 Classifying the Predictors as Factors or Covariates

In setting up the multilevel analysis, it will be necessary to identify which predictors are factors and which are covariates. The rule governing this distinction is straightforward:

- Factors are categorical variables. If a variable has multiple values (e.g., race/ethnicity might have five different categories), IBM SPSS will automatically dummy code the variable.
- Quantitative variables are called covariates, by definition, in this context.

9A.10.5 Determining the Fixed and Random Effects

In setting up the multilevel analysis, it will also be necessary to determine which of the predictors are to be used as fixed effects, random effects, or (in some analyses) as both. Distinctions between fixed and random effects are complex. Very generally, an effect is said to be fixed if the values of a variable in the study represent the full set of possible values in the population, and an effect is said to be random if the values of a variable in the study represent a sample of the possible values in the population that we want to generalize.

We can suggest additional guidelines to help make this distinction:

For fixed effects:

- A factor should be considered as fixed if the researchers are interested in the mean differences on the outcome variable between or among its levels.
- A covariate should be considered as fixed if the researchers are interested in predicting the amount of change in the outcome variable that is associated with a one-unit change of the covariate; that is, if researchers wish to obtain the slope of the covariate.

For random effects:

- A factor should be considered as random if the researchers are interested in the amount of variance of the dependent variable explained by the factor.
- A covariate should be considered as random if the researchers are interested in the amount of variance of the dependent variable explained by the covariate.

It is not uncommon in multilevel models to include interaction effects. The following guidelines apply to these:

- Interactions with only fixed effects are considered fixed interaction effects.
- Interactions with only random effects are considered random interaction effects.
- Interactions with both fixed effects and random effects are considered random interaction effects.

9A.10.6 Building the Multilevel Models

The process of developing a multilevel model is ordinarily done in a multistep manner. That is, researchers generate a series of hypothesized models in succession and evaluate them. We have already begun that process in assessing the unconditional model. The general strategy is to add (and at times remove) predictors (individual variables and interactions) from the successively built models; these latter models are referred to as *conditional models* because they contain predictors in addition to the Level 2 grouping variable. Decisions of which predictors to add or remove are based on theoretical, empirical, and rational grounds as well as on the specific interests of the researchers.

With respect to our example, several options are open to us. With approximately 80% of the variance not accounted for by the Level 2 dealership variable, there is quite a bit of sales volume variance remaining to be explained. Some researchers might opt to first examine the Level 2 predictor of each dealership's years of experience. Other researchers might be more interested in first evaluating the effect of the Level 1 predictor representing the deviation of each sales person's years of experience from the average years of experience for his or her dealership. Still other researchers might be primarily interested in evaluating the interaction of the sex of the salesperson with either the Level 1 or Level 2 dealership variables. Once the researchers have decided on this first step, this decision process is repeated for each subsequent addition or removal decision until the researchers achieve a satisfactory understanding of the interrelationships among the predictors.

9A.10.7 The Analysis Procedure for Multilevel Models

ANOVA and multiple regression, as examples of the general linear model, use ordinary least squares to calculate the prediction equation and to determine the amount of explained variance. The computational technique underlying multilevel modeling is a maximum likelihood method. Maximum likelihood is used to estimate the values of the parameters that would result in the highest likelihood of the actual data matching the proposed model. This method always requires iterative solutions.

In the IBM SPSS procedure for computing multilevel models, two variations of the maximum likelihood procedure are available: Full-information maximum likelihood (often abbreviated as FIML) and restricted maximum likelihood (often abbreviated as REML). In the process of estimating the fixed effects in the model, degrees of freedom are lost. The FIML method does not account for this loss of degrees of freedom and could therefore result in biased estimates. In contrast, the REML method does take into account the loss of degrees of freedom used in estimating the fixed effects, resulting in smaller standard errors than produced by the FIML method (Kim, 2009). We suggest using the restricted technique, which is the IBM SPSS default.

9A.11 Recommended Readings

Enders, C. K., & Tofighi, D. (2007). Centering predictor variables in cross-sectional multilevel models: A new look at an old issue. *Psychological Methods, 12,* 121–138.

Hox, J. (2010). *Multilevel analysis: Techniques and applications* (2nd ed.). New York, NY: Psychology Press.

Kreft, I., & de Leeuw, J. (2007). *Introducing multilevel modeling.* London, England: Sage.

Peugh, J. L., & Enders, C. K. (2005). Using the SPSS mixed procedure to fit cross-sectional and longitudinal multilevel models. *Educational and Psychological Measurement, 65,* 717–741.

Raudenbush, S. W., & Bryk, A. S. (2002). *Hierarchical linear models: Applications and data analysis methods* (2nd ed.). Thousand Oaks, CA: Sage.

Multilevel Modeling Using IBM SPSS

9B.1 Numerical Example

We will use the fictitious car sales example of multilevel modeling we have described in Section 9A.3, where we were interested in focusing on car sales of sales people in automobile dealerships located in the Washington D.C. metropolitan area. The outcome variable is **sales**, measured as thousands of dollars in sales in a given time period. Our Level 2 variable is **dealership**; in our example data set, we have 20 dealerships represented. A total of 813 salespersons (named **salesperson** in the data file) across the 20 dealerships are represented. For each sales person, we have recorded their **sex** (with *females* coded as 0 and *males* coded as 1) and their years of experience (**experience** in the data file). The data set we use is **Dealership**. A portion of the data file is pictured in Figure 9b.1.

9B.2 Assessing the Unconditional Model

Before we launch into multilevel modeling, it is necessary to determine if the data have a hierarchical structure. We therefore want to assess the extent to which there are sufficient differences among the levels of the Level 2 variable (**dealership** in this case) to violate the assumption of independence. This is accomplished by placing **dealership** in the model as the only predictor of **sales** and determining if it is statistically significant. If it is significant, we then want to calculate the value of the ICC.

   Select the path **Analyze ➔ Mixed Models ➔ Linear** from the main menu. This brings us to the preliminary **Linear Mixed Models** dialog window named **Specify Subjects and Repeated** displayed in Figure 9b.2. From the variables list panel, we click over **dealership** to the **Subjects** panel. This identifies **dealership** as the clustered variable. Click **Continue** to reach the main dialog window shown in Figure 9b.3.

Figure 9b.1 A Portion of the Data File

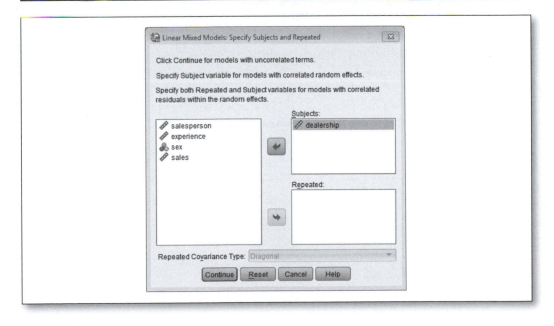

Figure 9b.2 Preliminary Dialog Window of Linear Mixed Models

Figure 9b.3 Main Dialog Window of Linear Mixed Models

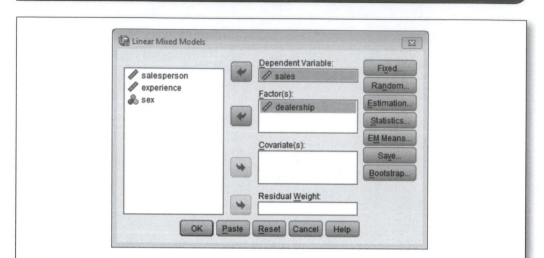

In the main dialog window, place **sales** into the **Dependent Variable** panel and place **dealership** into the **Factor(s)** panel. Because **dealership** represents a sample of the possible values in the population that we want to generalize, we define **dealership** as a random effect. We therefore select the **Random** pushbutton.

Selecting **Random** brings us to the dialog screen presented in Figure 9b.4. Move **dealership** from the **Factors and Covariates** panel to the **Model** panel by highlighting the variable and clicking the **Add** pushbutton. Then move **dealership** from the **Subject Groupings** panel to the **Combinations** panel by highlighting the variable and clicking the arrow button. Click **Continue** to reach the main dialog window.

Select the **Statistics** pushbutton. In the **Statistics** window (see Figure 9b.5), check **Parameter estimates** and **Tests for covariance parameters**, click **Continue** to reach the main dialog window, and click **OK** to perform the analysis.

Figure 9b.6 shows the **Model Dimension** and **Information Criteria** tables. The **Model Dimension** table displays the number of parameters that were estimated. In this model, there were three estimated parameters:

- The value of the intercept of the fixed effects, which represents the grand mean for **sales**
- The **dealership** parameter, which is the amount of variance in **sales** attributable to the **dealership** variable
- The value of the residual variance (variance of sales not accounted for by **dealership**)

Figure 9b.4 Random Effects Window of Linear Mixed Models

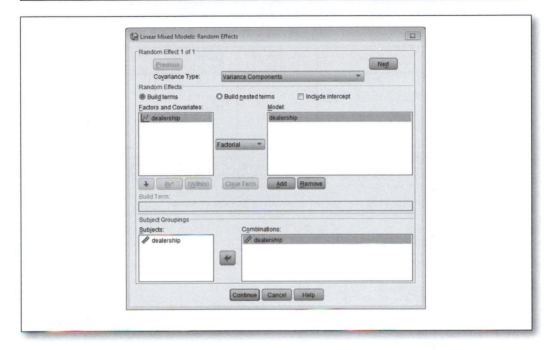

Figure 9b.5 Statistics Window of Linear Mixed Models

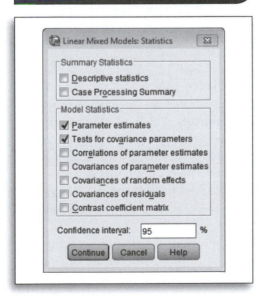

The **Information Criteria** table displays the goodness-of-fit measures. We are most interested in the fit assessed via the **−2 Restricted Log Likelihood** technique. This value is 7397.059 and is not directly interpretable; rather, it serves as a baseline against which other models can be compared. Values smaller than what we have obtained here indicate a better fit than this unconditional model. As **−2 Restricted Log Likelihood** is distributed as chi-square, we can test whether a subsequently generated model shows a statistically significant improvement in model fit through a chi-square difference evaluation using the difference in number of estimated parameters as the degrees of freedom for that statistical significance test.

Figure 9b.6 Parameter Estimates and Model Fit Output for the Unconditional Model

Model Dimension[b]

		Number of Levels	Covariance Structure	Number of Parameters
Fixed Effects	Intercept	1		1
Random Effects	dealership[a]	20	Variance Components	1
Residual				1
Total		21		3

a. As of version 11.5, the syntax rules for the RANDOM subcommand have changed. Your command syntax may yield results that differ from those produced by prior versions. If you are using version 11 syntax, please consult the current syntax reference guide for more information.

b. Dependent Variable: sales Thousands of Dollars in Sales.

Information Criteria[a]

−2 Restricted Log Likelihood	7397.059
Akaike's Information Criterion (AIC)	7401.059
Hurvich and Tsai's Criterion (AICC)	7401.074
Bozdogan's Criterion (CAIC)	7412.458
Schwarz's Bayesian Criterion (BIC)	7410.458

The information criteria are displayed in smaller–is–better forms.

a. Dependent Variable: sales Thousands of Dollars in Sales.

Figure 9b.7 displays the estimates of the covariance parameters for the random effects. The column labeled **Estimate** contains the estimated variance between dealerships (shown on the row named **dealership Variance**), which in this example is 133.858957. The row labeled **Residual**, which in this example is 495.742630, represents the remaining (unexplained or within-dealership) variance. The statistical significance of **dealership** variance, that is, whether it accounts for a statistically significant percentage of the total variance, is evaluated by a Wald statistic (a chi-square). In our example, the proportion of variance accounted for by **dealership** is statistically significant.

We next compute by hand the value of the proportion of variance accounted for by **dealership**, which is the ICC. The total variance is equal to the sum of the variances of

Figure 9b.7 Amount of Variance Explained by the Dealership Variable for the Unconditional Model

Covariance Parameters

Estimates of Covariance Parameters[a]

Parameter		Estimate	Std. Error	Wald Z	Sig.	95% Confidence Interval	
						Lower Bound	Upper Bound
Residual		495.742630	24.894836	19.913	.000	449.273971	547.017569
dealership	Variance	133.858957	47.491676	2.819	.005	66.780636	268.314611

a. Dependent Variable: sales Thousands of Dollars in Sales.

dealership and **Residual** or 133.858957 + 495.742630 = 629.60158. The ICC is computed as the ratio of **dealership** variance to total variance: In this example, the ICC is equal to 133.858957/629.60158 or .2126089, which rounds to .21. Therefore, we can say that **dealership** accounts for approximately 21% of the total variance of **sales**. This value is sufficiently large for us to determine that there is a clustering effect and that we may proceed with developing our multilevel models.

Three points are worth making about this 21% value. First, although we can assert that 21% of the variance of sales is attributable to the differences among the 20 dealerships, we have not determined anything about the nature of these differences. That is, we do not know from this analysis what is "causing" or "driving" the differences among the dealerships. To address this issue, we would need to introduce one or more Level 2 variables that we believe could be accounting for these differences. For example, we might hypothesize that some dealerships have on average more experienced staff who are presumably better able to build better customer relationships or who can close sales deals better than those in other dealerships. The point is that all we know at this juncture is that the dealerships differ.

The second point that is important to be made about the result is that if **dealership** is accounting for 21% of the variance, there remains 79% of the variance that is unaccounted for. This 79% unaccounted for portion of the total variance is, at the most general level, attributable to differences *within* the dealerships, that is, it is attributable to differences among the individual 813 salespeople working within the dealerships. Such individual differences are represented by Level 1 predictors. Some candidate variables that may be associated with these individual differences could be differences in the amount of sales experience these salespeople have and whether they are female or male.

The third point that is important to make is that some of the total variance may be associated with interactions between the variables. Interactions between Level 1 variables may be hypothesized to be important. For example, we may wish to explore the interaction between sex of salesperson and their level of experience. Interactions between Level 1 and Level 2 variables can also be hypothesized to be important. For example, we may wish to explore the interaction between sex of salesperson (a Level 1 variable) and the average experience of the salespeople with each dealership (a Level 2 variable).

9B.3 Centering the Variables

To begin our model building, we need to center the covariates (the quantitative variables used as predictors). In our example, the only covariate we have is **experience**. We will center this variable in two different ways:

- We will group-mean center the 813 individual **experience** scores. This is Level 1 centering in that one of the 20 group means is being subtracted from scores *tied directly to the* (*Level 1*) *individual cases* in that particular group. In this process, we will compute the mean of each of the 20 groups and subtract it from the respective scores of those salespeople in that particular group.
- We will grand-mean center the 20 **dealership** experience values. This is Level 2 centering in that the grand mean is being subtracted from scores *tied to the* (*Level 2*) **dealership** variable. In this process, we will compute the grand mean of all the **experience** scores (or the weighted mean of the group means) and subtract it from each of the 20 group means. This computation results in all cases within a single group having the same numerical value for their deviation score.

9B.3.1 Level 1 Centering of the Individual Experience Scores

As a preliminary step to group centering the individual **experience** scores, we need to obtain the means for each of the 20 groups on the **experience** variable. Select the path **Data ➔ Aggregate** from the main menu as shown in Figure 9b.8. From the variables list panel, click over **experience** to the **Summaries of Variable(s)** panel. The experience variable is automatically represented in this latter panel by the expression **experience_mean = Mean(experience)**, which indicates that IBM SPSS will compute a mean of the variable (this is the default function and is what we want to do) and assign that mean value to each case under the newly created variable of **experience_mean**. Now move **dealership** to the **Break Variable(s)** panel. This instructs the software to compute the mean just described separately for each level of **dealership**. Click **OK** to perform the aggregation.

The results of this aggregation are shown in Figure 9b.9, where the boundary between **dealership 1** and **dealership 2** is visible. Note that the mean **experience** for **dealership 1** is

Figure 9b.8 The Aggregate Data Window

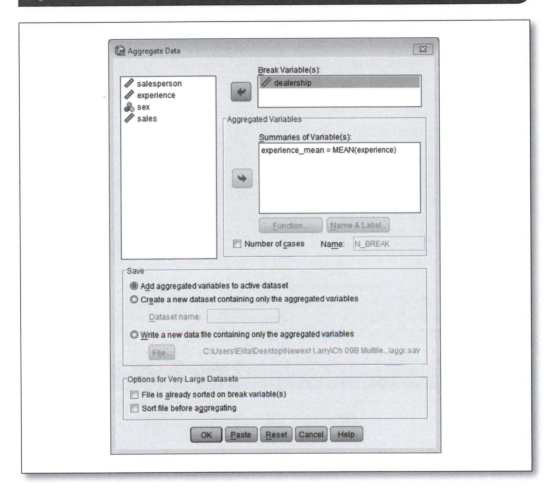

14.30 and the mean **experience** for **dealership 2** is 16.72. Each case within a given group is assigned the same value on this variable.

Now that we have the 20 mean **experience** values (one for each group), we can now center the individual salespeople's **experience** scores on their respective group means. Select **Transform ➔ Compute Variable** from the main menu as shown in Figure 9b.10. We type the name of our new variable in the panel labeled **Target Variable**; here, we will choose the very long but descriptive name **grp_cent_experience_Level1** to indicate that this variable is

Figure 9b.9 A Portion of the Data File With the Group Means Computed

Figure 9b.10 The Compute Variable Window

experience of the individual salespeople centered on their own group and that it is a Level 1 centered variable.

Move **experience** into the **Numeric Expression** panel by highlighting it and clicking the arrow pointing toward the right between the list of variables and the **Numeric Expression** panels. Click the minus sign from the keypad just below the **Numeric Expression** panel and then move **experience_mean** into the **Numeric Expression** panel directly following the minus sign. Click **OK** to perform the computation. The results of this computation are shown in Figure 9b.11. Each case has a value that represents the deviation of his or her **experience** score from his or her group mean.

9B.3.2 Level 2 Centering of the Dealership Experience Scores

To perform the centering operation for the dealership variable at Level 2 (subtracting the grand mean from each of the 20 group means), we must obtain the value of the grand mean of **experience**. Select **Analyze ➔ Descriptive Statistics ➔ Descriptives** from the main menu as shown in Figure 9b.12. Move **experience** into the **Variable(s)** panel. Click **OK** to perform the computation. The default output is shown in Figure 9b.13. From the table, we confirm that our sample size is 813 and we determine that the grand mean for **experience** is 16.53.

We are now in a position to compute the Level 2 grand mean centered dealership experience variable. Select **Transform ➔ Compute Variable** from the main menu as shown in Figure 9b.14. We type the name of our new variable in the panel labeled **Target Variable**; here, we will choose the name **grand_dealer_experience_Level2** to indicate that this variable is the mean experience of each of the 20 dealerships centered on the grand mean of the entire sample and that it is a Level 2 centered variable.

Move **experience_mean** into the **Numeric Expression** panel by highlighting it and clicking the arrow pointing toward the right between the list of variable and the **Numeric Expression** panels. Click the minus sign from the keypad just below the **Numeric Expression** panel and then type in the grand mean of 16.53. Click **OK** to perform the computation. The results of this computation are shown in Figure 9b.15, where the boundary between **dealership 1** and **dealership 2** is visible. Note that the deviation value for **dealership 1** is −2.23 and that the deviation value for **dealership 2** is 0.19. Each case within a given group is assigned the same value on this variable.

9B.4 Building the Multilevel Models: Overview

Once the centered variables are computed, we are ready to evaluate our models. The general strategy is to begin with simpler models and move toward more complex ones in a manageable

Figure 9b.11   A Portion of the Data File With the Group-Centered Level 1 Experience Values Computed

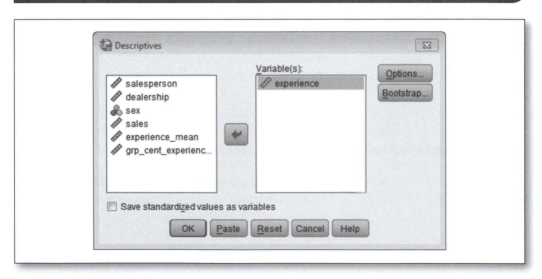

Figure 9b.12   Main Dialog Window of Descriptives

Figure 9b.13 Descriptives Default Output

Descriptive Statistics

	N	Minimum	Maximum	Mean	Std. Deviation
experience Years of Experience	813	2	24	16.53	3.673
Valid N (listwise)	813				

Figure 9b.14 The Compute Variable Window

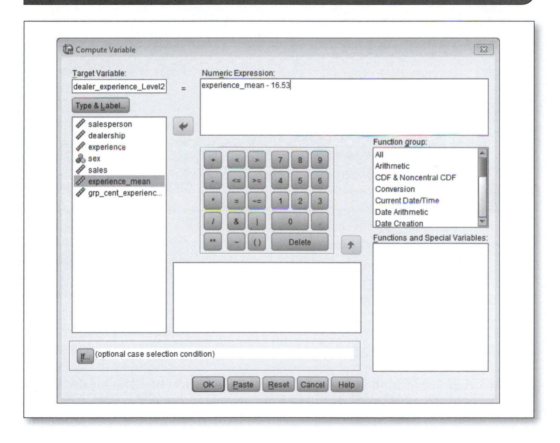

number of steps. But how many steps are taken and in which order the effects are evaluated are individual but educated decisions made by the researchers based on theoretical, practical, and intuitive considerations. The key is that there is no necessarily correct or lockstep ordering of these analyses; the only provision is that the researchers have a reasonable basis for the strategy that they have used. For our present example, different researchers might adopt

Figure 9b.15 A Portion of the Data File With the Grand Mean Centered Level 2 Dealership Experience Values Computed

	dealership	experience	sex	sales	experience_mean	grp_cent_experience_Level1	grand_dealer_experience_Level2
38	1	16	0	22	14.30	1.70	-2.23
39	1	16	0	59	14.30	1.70	-2.23
40	1	16	1	12	14.30	1.70	-2.23
41	1	18	0	52	14.30	3.70	-2.23
42	1	18	0	83	14.30	3.70	-2.23
43	1	18	0	35	14.30	3.70	-2.23
44	1	18	0	45	14.30	3.70	-2.23
45	1	20	0	94	14.30	5.70	-2.23
46	1	20	0	30	14.30	5.70	-2.23
47	1	20	0	19	14.30	5.70	-2.23
48	2	10	1	49	16.72	-6.72	.19
49	2	12	0	39	16.72	-4.72	.19
50	2	12	0	21	16.72	-4.72	.19
51	2	14	0	82	16.72	-2.72	.19
52	2	14	0	75	16.72	-2.72	.19
53	2	14	0	28	16.72	-2.72	.19
54	2	14	1	47	16.72	-2.72	.19
55	2	16	1	31	16.72	-.72	.19
56	2	16	0	76	16.72	-.72	.19
57	2	16	0	38	16.72	-.72	.19
58	2	16	0	38	16.72	-.72	.19

somewhat different strategies in formulating the model-building steps; the one we demonstrate here is to be treated as illustrative rather than as prescriptive.

9B.5 Building the First Model

We have determined that there is a substantial clustering effect based on the **dealership** variable (the ICC informed us that **dealership** accounted for about 21% of the variance). We therefore choose to evaluate the Level 2 dealership experience variable in our first hierarchical model to determine if the average experience of the dealership (the average years of experience of the sales staff in each particular dealership) can explain (account for) any of the 21% of the variance in **sales** with which **dealership** is associated.

9B.5.1 The First Model: Setup

Select **Analyze** ➔ **Mixed Models** ➔ **Linear** from the main menu. This brings us to the preliminary **Linear Mixed Models** dialog window displayed in Figure 9b.16. From the variables list panel, we click over **dealership** to the **Subjects** panel. This identifies **dealership** as the clustered variable. Click **Continue** to reach the main dialog window shown in Figure 9b.17.

Figure 9b.16 Preliminary Dialog Window of Linear Mixed Models

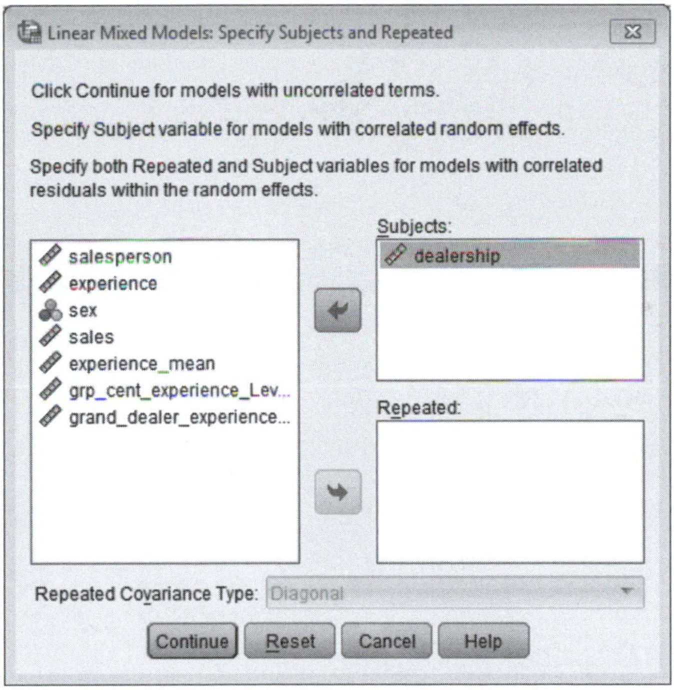

In the main dialog window place **sales** into the **Dependent Variable** panel and place **grand_dealer_experience_Level2** into the **Covariate(s)** panel. Selecting **Fixed** brings us to the dialog screen presented in Figure 9b.18. Move the Level 2 variable **grand_dealer_experience_Level2** from the **Factors and Covariates** panel to the **Model** panel by

Figure 9b.17 Main dialog Window of Linear Mixed Models

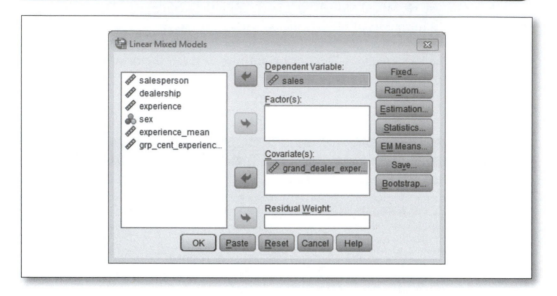

Figure 9b.18 Fixed Effects Window of Linear Mixed Models

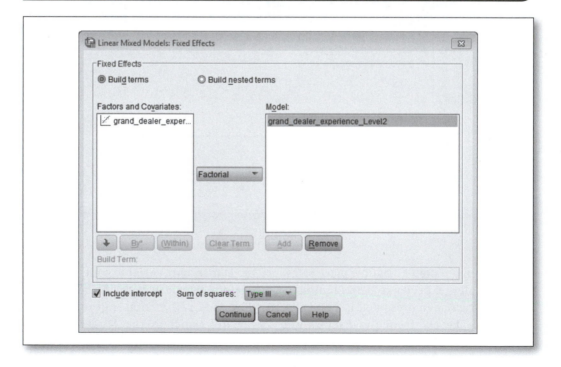

highlighting the variable and clicking the **Add** pushbutton. Click **Continue** to reach the main dialog window.

Select **Random** from the main dialog window, which brings us to the dialog screen presented in Figure 9b.19. Check the box for **Include intercept** toward the top of the screen. Move **dealership** from the **Subject Groupings** panel to the **Combinations** panel by highlighting the variable and clicking the arrow button. Click **Continue** to reach the main dialog window.

Select the **Statistics** pushbutton. In the **Statistics** window (see Figure 9b.20), check **Parameter estimates** and **Tests for covariance parameters**, click **Continue** to reach the main dialog window, and click **OK** to perform the analysis.

9B.5.2 The First Model: Output

Figure 9b.21 shows the **Model Dimension** and **Information Criteria** tables. The **Model Dimension** table displays the number of parameters that were estimated.

Figure 9b.19   Random Effects Window of Linear Mixed Models

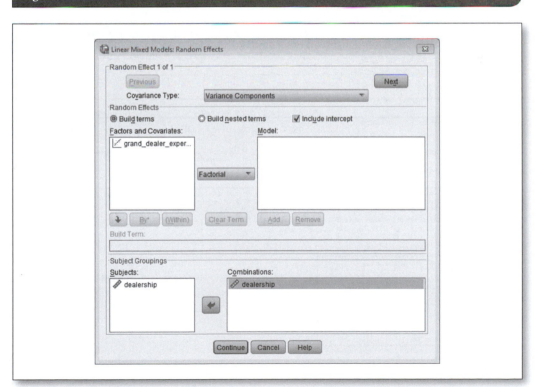

Figure 9b.20 The Statistics Window of Linear Mixed Models

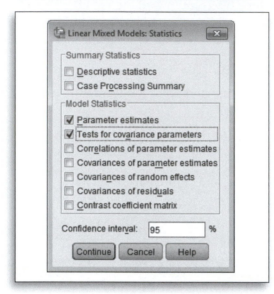

In this model, there were four estimated parameters:

- The value of the intercept of the fixed effects
- The slope for the **grand_dealer_experience_Level2** variable. This indicates how much of a change would be expected in **sales** (in thousands of dollars) for each year increase in **grand_dealer_experience_Level2**
- The value of the intercept of the random effects
- The value of the **Residual** variance (variance of sales not accounted for by **grand_dealer_experience_Level2**

Figure 9b.21 Parameter Estimates and Model Fit Output for Model 1

Model Dimension[b]

		Number of Levels	Covariance Structure	Number of Parameters	Subject Variables
Fixed Effects	Intercept	1		1	
	grand_dealer_experience_Level2	1		1	
Random Effects	Intercept[a]	1	Variance Components	1	dealership
Residual				1	
Total		3		4	

a. As of version 11.5, the syntax rules for the RANDOM subcommand have changed. Your command syntax may yield results that differ from those produced by prior versions. If you are using version 11 syntax, please consult the current syntax reference guide for more information.

b. Dependent Variable: sales Thousands of Dollars in Sales.

Information Criteria[a]

-2 Restricted Log Likelihood	7367.343
Akaike's Information Criterion (AIC)	7371.343
Hurvich and Tsai's Criterion (AICC)	7371.358
Bozdogan's Criterion (CAIC)	7382.739
Schwarz's Bayesian Criterion (BIC)	7380.739

The information criteria are displayed in smaller-is-better forms.

a. Dependent Variable: sales Thousands of Dollars in Sales.

The **Information Criteria** table displays the goodness of fit measures. The **−2 Restricted Log Likelihood** value is 7367.343. Recall that the unconditional model showed us a **−2 Restricted Log Likelihood** value of 7397.059. We have lost 29.716 units, suggesting that there has been an improvement in the fit of the present model over that of the unconditional model.

Whether this gain in fit is statistically significant can be quickly evaluated. From the main menu, select **Transform ➔ Compute Variable**. We have assigned the name **model_improvement** to our to-be-computed **Target Variable**. Activate **Significance** in the **Function group** panel, and choose **Sig.Chisq** (short for "testing the significance of a change in chi-square") from the **Functions and Special Variables** panel by clicking the upward arrow to the upper left of the **Functions and Special Variables** panel so that it will appear in the **Numeric Expression** panel. Once **Sig.Chisq** is in the **Numeric Expression** panel, a highlighted question mark inside parentheses will be seen (see Figure 9b.22).

Figure 9b.22 The Compute Variable Screen With SIG.CHISQ Function Placed in the Numeric Expressions Panel

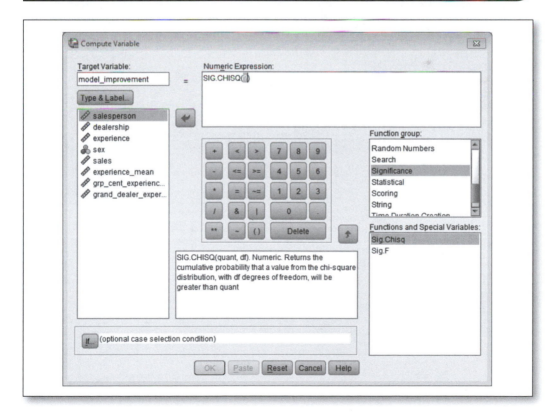

Replace the question mark by typing in the value of the difference in the **−2 Restricted Log Likelihood** fit measure, followed by a comma and the difference in the total number of parameters (IBM SPSS calls these degrees of freedom in the window) that were estimated in the two models. In the present example, our difference in **−2 Restricted Log Likelihood** was 29.716 (**−2 Restricted Log Likelihood** has a chi-square distribution and, in such a distribution, a value of 29.716 for 1 degree of freedom is quite large), and we went from 3 parameters in unconditional model to 4 parameters in the present model for a difference of 1 parameter. We have typed this information in the **Sig.Chisq** function Figure 9b.23. Click **OK** to perform the computation.

The result of this computation is placed in the data file for each case (many users whom we have informally spoken with have wondered why this output information

Figure 9b.23 The Compute Variable Screen With SIG.CHISQ Function Now Specified in the Numeric Expressions Panel

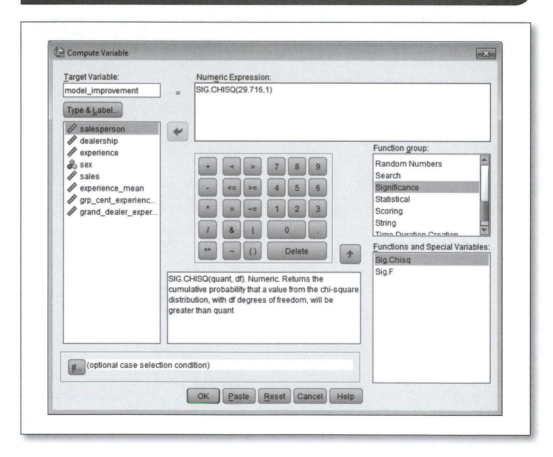

could not be more simply designed to just print out the single outcome as a small output table). We show this result in Figure 9b.24. The entry is .00 ($p < .01$), which is the probability of obtaining the observed improvement by chance if the null hypothesis was true. As can be seen (831 times), the improvement is statistically significant. We may therefore conclude that the model fit significantly improved by adding **grand_dealer_experience_Level2** to the model.

The fixed and random components of the model are presented in Figure 9b.25. The upper table describes the fixed effects. The value of the intercept appears in the column labeled **Estimate**. This is the grand mean of **sales** controlling for (removing the effects of) the Level 2 variable of **grand_dealer_experience_Level2**. The value of 5.353932 is the slope of the linear function using the Level 2 variable to predict **sales**. As we can see in the column labeled **Sig.**, the slope is significantly different ($p < .01$) from a value of zero. We can therefore say that for every year of experience of dealerships, we would predict an increase (on the average) of approximately 5.35 thousand dollars in sales for the dealership.

Figure 9b.24 The Result of the Computation Is Placed in the Data File for Each Case

	xperience_mean	grp_cent_experience_Level1	grand_dealer_experience_Level2	model_improvement	var	var	var
38	14.30	1.70	-2.23	.00			
39	14.30	1.70	-2.23	.00			
40	14.30	1.70	-2.23	.00			
41	14.30	3.70	-2.23	.00			
42	14.30	3.70	-2.23	.00			
43	14.30	3.70	-2.23	.00			
44	14.30	3.70	-2.23	.00			
45	14.30	5.70	-2.23	.00			
46	14.30	5.70	-2.23	.00			
47	14.30	5.70	-2.23	.00			
48	16.72	-6.72	.19	.00			
49	16.72	-4.72	.19	.00			
50	16.72	-4.72	.19	.00			
51	16.72	-2.72	.19	.00			
52	16.72	-2.72	.19	.00			
53	16.72	-2.72	.19	.00			
54	16.72	-2.72	.19	.00			
55	16.72	-.72	.19	.00			
56	16.72	-.72	.19	.00			
57	16.72	-.72	.19	.00			
58	16.72	-.72	.19	.00			

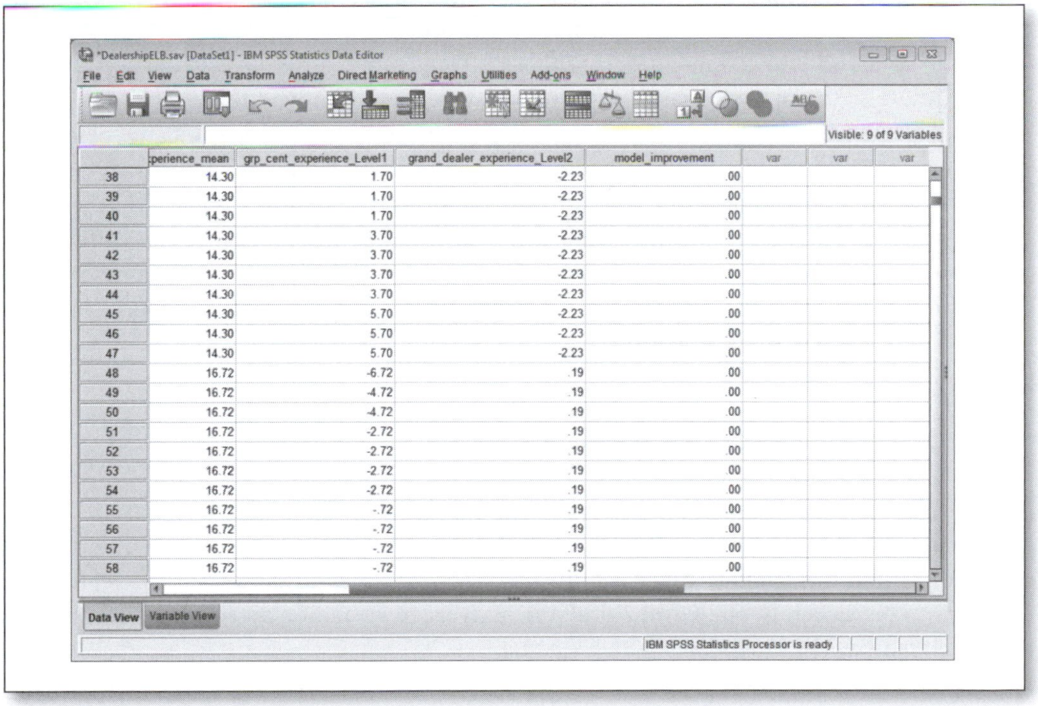

Figure 9b.25   Slope and Amount of Variance Explained by the Level 2 Variable for Model 1

Estimates of Fixed Effects[a]

Parameter	Estimate	Std. Error	df	t	Sig.	95% Confidence Interval	
						Lower Bound	Upper Bound
Intercept	57.285405	1.329611	18.760	43.084	.000	54.500082	60.070728
grand_dealer_ experience_Level2	5.353932	.679302	17.836	7.882	.000	3.925832	6.782032

a. Dependent Variable: sales Thousands of Dollars in Sales.

Estimates of Covariance Parameters[a]

Parameter		Estimate	Std. Error	Wald Z	Sig.	95% Confidence Interval	
						Lower Bound	Upper Bound
Residual		495.383670	24.858222	19.928	.000	448.981677	546.581282
Intercept [subject = dealership]	Variance	22.500463	11.333710	1.985	.047	8.383640	60.387946

a. Dependent Variable: sales Thousands of Dollars in Sales.

The lower table in Figure 9b.25 shows the estimates of the covariance parameters for the random effects. The column labeled **Estimate** contains (on the row labeled **Intercept (subject = dealership)**) the estimated variance of sales dollars between dealerships controlling for the effects of the Level 2 variable of **grand_dealer_experience_Level2**. This value is 22.500463, and the total variance controlling for the effects of the Level 2 variable is 22.500463 + 495.383670 or 517.88413. Dealership differences thus account for approximately .04 of the variance of sales when we have removed the effects of average dealer experience. This percentage of variance is statistically significant at the 5% alpha level ($p = .047$), but it is substantially down from the approximately 21% of the variance accounted for by **dealership** in the unconditional model. It thus appears that average dealership years of experience is a very important factor in explaining the differences (heterogeneity) among the 20 dealerships. It is still worthy of note that there are still dealership differences remaining after we have statistically removed the effects of average dealership years of experience.

9B.6 Building the Second Model

We have determined from our unconditional model that there is a substantial Level 2 clustering effect on **sales** based on the **dealership** variable, and we have determined from our first model that much of the variance of **sales** attributable to **dealership** appears to be driven by the Level 2 variable of average years of experience of the staff in the dealerships.

We now wish to shift the focus to Level 1 and ask about the degree of prediction of **sales** we might obtain when considering the 813 individual salespeople. Given that the average dealership experience affects **sales**, we opt to consider the individual experience variable with the effects of dealership experience removed from our analysis. Because our Level 1 group-centered experience variable does in fact remove or negate this dealership effect (the mean of each group in that centering strategy is zero), we can use this Level 1 variable in place of the Level 2 variable we used in the prior model.

9B.6.1 The Second Model: Setup

Select **Analyze ➔ Mixed Models ➔ Linear** from the main menu. In the preliminary **Linear Mixed Models** dialog window, click over **dealership** to the **Subjects** panel, and click **Continue** to reach the main dialog window shown in Figure 9b.26. In the main dialog window, place **sales** into the **Dependent Variable** panel and place **grp_cent_experience_Level1** into the **Covariate(s)** panel.

Select **Fixed**, which brings us to the dialog screen presented in Figure 9b.27. Move the Level 1 variable **grp_cent_experience_Level1** from the **Factors and Covariates** panel to the **Model** panel (to obtain an estimated slope) by highlighting the variable and clicking the **Add** pushbutton. Click **Continue** to reach the main dialog window.

Select **Random** from the main dialog window to reach the dialog screen presented in Figure 9b.28. From the drop-down menu for **Covariance Type**, select **Unstructured**, so that

Figure 9b.26 Main Dialog Window of Linear Mixed Models

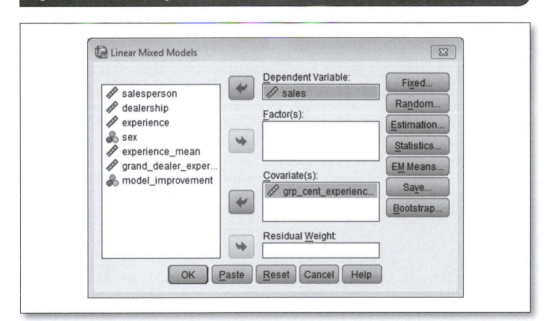

Figure 9b.27 Fixed Effects Dialog Window of Linear Mixed Models

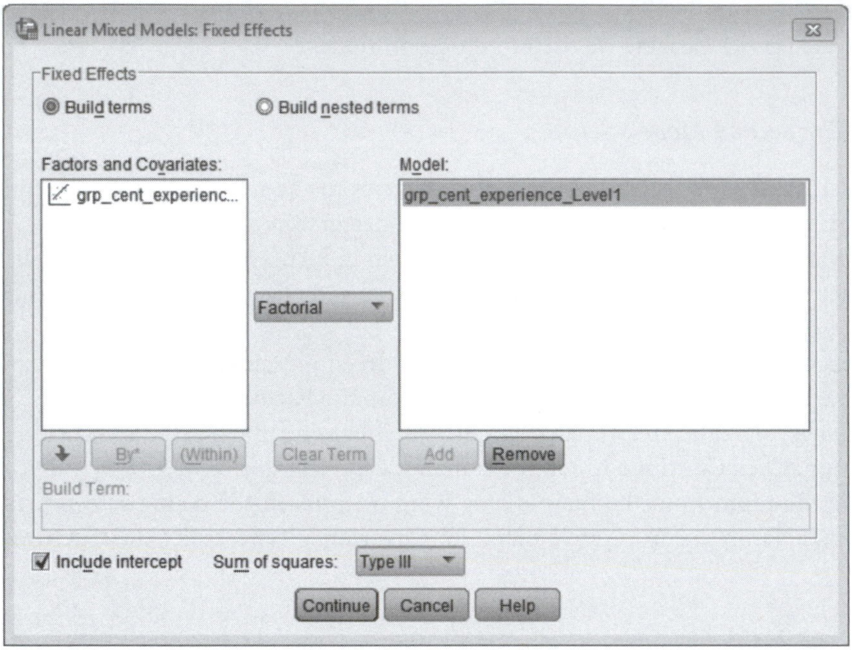

we can obtain information to compare the intercepts and slopes of the 20 dealerships. Check the box for **Include intercept** under the **Covariance Type** drop-down menu. Move **grp_cent_experience_Level1** from the **Factors and Covariates** panel to the **Model** panel (to obtain an estimated variance of the intercepts and slopes for this variable) by highlighting the variable and clicking the **Add** pushbutton. Move **dealership** from the **Subject Groupings** panel by highlighting it and clicking the arrow button. Click **Continue** to reach the main dialog window.

Select the **Statistics** pushbutton. Check **Parameter estimates** and **Tests for covariance parameters** in the **Statistics** window, click **Continue** to reach the main dialog window, and click **OK** to perform the analysis.

9B.6.2 The Second Model: Output

Figure 9b.29 shows the **Model Dimension** and **Information Criteria** tables. The **Model Dimension** table informs us that there were six estimated parameters in the current model. The **Information Criteria** table displays the goodness-of-fit measures. The **−2 Restricted**

Figure 9b.28   Random Effects Dialog Window of Linear Mixed Models

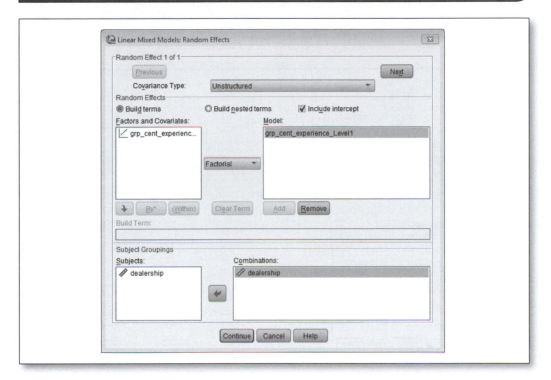

Log Likelihood value is 7338.059. Recall that the unconditional model showed us a -2 **Restricted Log Likelihood** value of 7397.059. We have lost 59.000 units with a difference of 3 parameters (degrees of freedom). When placed into our evaluation of the chi-square difference (not shown), this gain in model fit over the unconditional model was statistically significant.

The fixed and random components of the model are presented in Figure 9b.30. The upper table describes the fixed effects. The value of the intercept (58.345440) appears in the column labeled **Estimate**. This is the expected (predicted) **sales** in thousands of dollars for the 813 salespeople (controlling for **dealership**), given that they have the average years of experience in their particular dealership.

The value of 1.924102 is the slope of the linear function using the Level 1 variable of 813 individual salesperson experience to predict **sales**, which is significantly different ($p < .01$) from a value of zero. We can therefore say that for every year of experience of the salesperson, we would predict an increase (on the average) of approximately 1.92 thousand dollars in sales.

Figure 9b.29 Parameter Estimates and Model Fit Output for Model 2

Model Dimension_b

		Number of Levels	Covariance Structure	Number of Parameters	Subject Variables
Fixed Effects	Intercept	1		1	
	grp_cent_experience_Level1	1		1	
Random Effects	Intercept + grp_cent_experience_Level1_a	2	Unstructured	3	dealership
Residual				1	
Total		4		6	

a. As of version 11.5, the syntax rules for the RANDOM subcommand have changed. Your command syntax may yield results that differ from those produced by prior versions. If you are using version 11 syntax, please consult the current syntax reference guide for more information.

b. Dependent Variable: sales Thousands of Dollars in Sales.

Information Criteria_a

−2 Restricted Log Likelihood	7338.059
Akaike's Information Criterion (AIC)	7346.059
Hurvich and Tsai's Criterion (AICC)	7346.109
Bozdogan's Criterion (CAIC)	7368.852
Schwarz's Bayesian Criterion (BIC)	7364.852

The information criteria are displayed in smaller-is-better forms.

a. Dependent Variable: sales Thousands of Dollars in Sales.

Figure 9b.30 Fixed and Random Effects Output for Model 2

Estimates of Fixed Effects_a

Parameter	Estimate	Std. Error	df	t	Sig.	95% Confidence Interval	
						Lower Bound	Upper Bound
Intercept	58.345440	2.707576	19.069	21.549	.000	52.679807	64.011074
grp_cent_experience_Level1	1.924102	.301676	20.312	6.378	.000	1.295435	2.552770

a. Dependent Variable: sales Thousands of Dollars in Sales.

Covariance Parameters

Estimates of Covariance Parameters_a

Parameter		Estimate	Std. Error	Wald Z	Sig.	95% Confidence Interval	
						Lower Bound	Upper Bound
Residual		456.273822	23.136854	19.721	.000	413.107044	503.951226
Intercept + grp_cent_experience_Level1 [subject = dealership]	UN (1,1)	134.775556	47.468526	2.839	.005	67.579398	268.786807
	UN (2,1)	.731354	3.796098	.193	.847	−6.708861	8.171569
	UN (2,2)	.541638	.514850	1.052	.293	.084063	3.489900

a. Dependent Variable: sales Thousands of Dollars in Sales.

The lower table in Figure 9b.30 shows the estimates of the covariance parameters for the random effects. The columns labeled **Estimate** and **Sig.** are what we focus on here. The top row labeled **Residual** represents the unexplained variance of **sales**. In this example, the value of the unexplained variance is 456.273822 and, as can be seen in the **Sig.** column, is statistically significant. We learn from this that there is a significant amount of variance that is not accounted for by this model.

The next three rows are labeled as **UN (1,1)**, **UN (2,1)**, and **UN (2,2)**. The abbreviation **UN** stands for the type of covariance matrix known as "unstructured" (in which covariances parameters are not related); this is what we requested from the drop-down menu in the **Random Effects** dialog window. The numbers in parentheses after **UN** refer to coordinates in a particular output table that we did not request and so can be ignored for our purposes. The three specific parameters of the variance in the order that we suggest examining these results are as follows:

- **UN (1,1)**: *The variance of the intercepts.* Intercepts are the mean **sales** for each of the 20 dealerships controlling for the experience of the individuals within the groups. The value of 134.775556 in the **Estimate** column is the variance of those means controlling for (in this model) the differences in dealership experience. As we can see from the **Sig.** column, the variance of the intercepts is statistically significant and indicates that the means of the 20 dealerships differ significantly.
- **UN (2,2)**: *The variance of the slopes.* Slopes are the amount of increase in **sales** dollars for each year of experience for each of the 20 dealerships, controlling for the experience of the individuals within the groups. The value of 0.541638 in the **Estimate** column is the variance of those slopes, controlling for (in this model) the differences in dealership experience. As we can see from the **Sig.** column, the variance of the slopes is not statistically significant and indicates that the slopes of the 20 dealerships are comparable.
- **UN (2,1)**: *The covariance between the slopes and the intercepts.* This parameter addresses the issue of the relationship between the slope (how steep the function is for a given **dealership**) and intercept (the mean of the dealership) for the prediction equation for each **dealership**, controlling for the experience of the individuals within the groups. This relationship is quantified and compared across dealerships. For Dealership 1, the relationship is this, for Dealership 2 the relationship is that, and so on for 20 relationships. The value of 0.731354 is the composite value, which is then tested for significance. In this case, this value is not statistically significant, and indicates that the slope–intercept relationships are consistent across all 20 dealerships.

9B.7 Building the Third Model

From our second model, we have determined that the Level 1 of variable years of experience of the 813 individual salespeople is predictive of their **sales** volume controlling for **dealership**. We now choose to add to the second model the Level 1 variable of **sex** of salesperson.

9B.7.1 The Third Model: Setup

Select **Analyze** ➔ **Mixed Models** ➔ **Linear** from the main menu. In the preliminary **Linear Mixed Models** dialog window, click over **dealership** to the **Subjects** panel, and click **Continue** to reach the main dialog window shown in Figure 9b.31. In the main dialog window, place **sales** into the **Dependent Variable** panel, place **grp_cent_experience_Level1** into the **Covariate(s)** panel, and place **sex** into the **Factor(s)** panel.

Select **Fixed**, which brings us to the dialog screen presented in Figure 9b.32. Move both **grp_cent_experience_Level1** and **sex** from the **Factors and Covariates** panel to the **Model** panel (to obtain an estimated mean of **sales** for salespeople with respect to their **dealership** as well as their **sex**) by highlighting the variables and clicking the **Add** pushbutton. Click **Continue** to reach the main dialog window.

Select **Random** from the main dialog window to reach the dialog screen presented in Figure 9b.33. From the drop-down menu for **Covariance Type**, select **Unstructured**, so that we can obtain information to compare the intercepts and slopes of the 20 dealerships. Check the box for **Include intercept** under the **Covariance Type** drop-down menu. Move **grp_cent_experience_Level1** from the **Factors and Covariates** panel to the **Model** panel (to

Figure 9b.31　Main Dialog Window of Linear Mixed Models

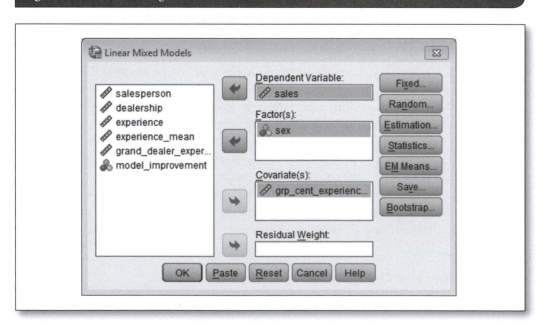

Figure 9b.32   Fixed Effects Dialog Window of Linear Mixed Models

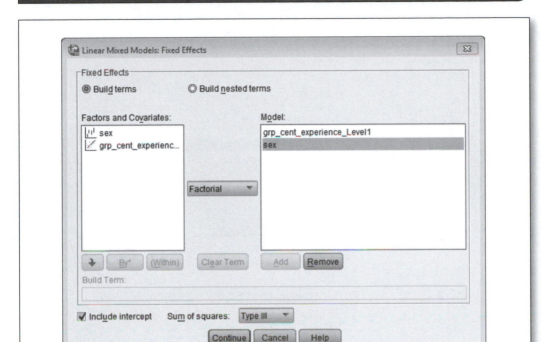

obtain an estimated variance of the intercepts and slopes for **sales** with respect to their **dealership**) by highlighting the variable and clicking the **Add** pushbutton. Move **dealership** from the **Subject Groupings** panel by highlighting it and clicking the arrow button. Click **Continue** to reach the main dialog window.

Select the **Statistics** pushbutton. Check **Parameter estimates** and **Tests for covariance parameters** in the **Statistics** window, click **Continue** to reach the main dialog window, and click **OK** to perform the analysis.

9B.7.2 The Third Model: Output

Figure 9b.34 shows the **Model Dimension** and **Information Criteria** tables. The **Model Dimension** table informs us that there were 7 estimated parameters in this third model. The **Information Criteria** table displays the goodness-of-fit measures. The **−2 Restricted Log Likelihood** value is 7300.958. Recall that the second model showed us a **−2 Restricted Log Likelihood** value of 7338.059 with 6 parameters. We have lost 37.101 units with a difference

Figure 9b.33 Random Effects Dialog Window of Linear Mixed Models

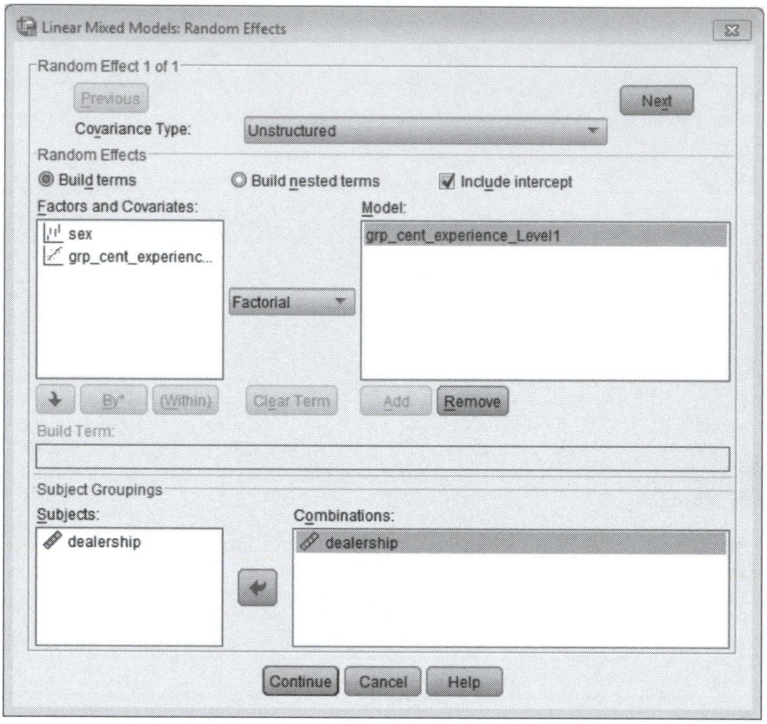

of 1 parameter (degree of freedom). When placed into our evaluation of the chi-square difference (not shown), this gain in model fit over the second model was statistically significant.

The fixed and random components of the model are presented in Figure 9b.35. The upper table describes the fixed effects. The value of the intercept (47.330915) appears in the column labeled **Estimate**. This is the expected (predicted) **sales** in thousands of dollars for the 813 salespeople (controlling for **dealership** and **sex**), given that they have the average years of experience in their particular dealership.

The value of 1.547253 is the slope of the linear function using the Level 1 variable of 813 individual salespersons' experience to predict **sales** when we are controlling for **sex**; this slope is significantly different ($p < .01$) from a value of zero. We can therefore say that, controlling for **sex**, for every year of experience of the salesperson we would predict an increase (on the average) of approximately 1.55 thousand dollars in sales.

The value of 14.812901 is the slope of the linear function using the Level 1 **sex = 0** variable to predict **sales** when we are controlling for individual experience within each

Figure 9b.34 Parameter Estimates and Model Fit Output for Model 3

Model Dimension_b

		Number of Levels	Covariance Structure	Number of Parameters	Subject Variables
Fixed Effects	Intercept	1		1	
	grp_cent_experience_Level1	1		1	
	sex	2		1	
Random Effects	Intercept + grp_cent_experience_Level1_a	2	Unstructured	3	dealership
Residual				1	
Total		6		7	

a. As of version 11.5, the syntax rules for the RANDOM subcommand have changed. Your command syntax may yield results that differ from those produced by prior versions. If you are using version 11 syntax, please consult the current syntax reference guide for more information.

b. Dependent Variable: sales Thousands of Dollars in Sales.

Information Criteria_a

–2 Restricted Log Likelihood	7300.958
Akaike's Information Criterion (AIC)	7308.958
Hurvich and Tsai's Criterion (AICC)	7309.008
Bozdogan's Criterion (CAIC)	7331.747
Schwarz's Bayesian Criterion (BIC)	7327.747

The information criteria are displayed in smaller-is-better forms.

a. Dependent Variable: sales Thousands of Dollars in Sales.

dealership; this slope is significantly different ($p < .01$) from a value of zero. To interpret this value, we must recall three pieces of information:

- The dependent variable of **sales** was measured in thousands of dollars in a given time period.
- *Females* were coded as 0 and *males* were coded as 1 in the data file.
- The value of the slope uses the group with the lowest code as the reference group; here, females are that group.

We can therefore say that, controlling for individual experience within each dealership, females produced approximately 14.81 thousand dollars (i.e., $14,810) more than males for their sales figures.

The slope of 0 for the entry **sex = 1** simply indicates that males cannot be compared with themselves. IBM SPSS describes this in the first footnote to the table and

Figure 9b.35 Fixed and Random Effects Output for Model 3

Estimates of Fixed Effects[b]

Parameter	Estimate	Std. Error	df	t	Sig.	95% Confidence Interval	
						Lower Bound	Upper Bound
Intercept	47.330915	2.895036	43.170	16.349	.000	41.493181	53.168648
grp_cent_experience_Level1	1.547253	.294335	18.648	5.257	.000	.930414	2.164091
[sex=0]	14.812901	2.460635	532.529	6.020	.000	9.979158	19.646644
[sex=1]	0[a]	0	.	.	.	.	.

a. This parameter is set to zero because it is redundant.
b. Dependent Variable: sales Thousands of Dollars in Sales.

Covariance Parameters

Estimates of Covariance Parameters[a]

Parameter		Estimate	Std. Error	Wald Z	Sig.	95% Confidence Interval	
						Lower Bound	Upper Bound
Residual		442.484229	22.472577	19.690	.000	400.559994	488.796424
Intercept + grp_cent_experience_Level1 [subject = dealership]	UN (1,1)	89.815797	33.142802	2.710	.007	43.576468	185.120035
	UN (2,1)	−1.724007	3.190174	−.540	.589	−7.976632	4.528618
	UN (2,2)	.449149	.511724	.878	.380	.048150	4.189681

a. Dependent Variable: sales Thousands of Dollars in Sales.

arbitrarily shows a 0 number (any symbol could have been used); this entry is not to be interpreted.

The lower table in Figure 9b.35 shows the estimates of the covariance parameters for the random effects. The columns labeled **Estimate** and **Sig.** are what we focus on here. The top row labeled **Residual** represents the unexplained variance of **sales**. In this example, the value of the unexplained variance is 442.484229 and is statistically significant. Thus, there is a significant amount of variance that is not accounted for by this model.

The next three rows are labeled as **UN (1,1)**, **UN (2,1)**, and **UN (2,2)**. The three specific parameters of the variance in the order that we suggest examining these results are as follows:

- **UN (1,1)**: *The variance of the intercepts*. Intercepts are the mean **sales** for each of the 20 dealerships, controlling for the experience of the individuals within the groups and **sex**. The value of 89.815797 in the **Estimate** column is the variance of those means, controlling for (in this model) the differences in dealership experience and **sex**. As we can see from the **Sig.** column, the variance of the intercepts is statistically significant and indicates that the means of the 20 dealerships differ significantly.
- **UN (2,2)**: *The variance of the slopes*. Slopes are the amount of increase in **sales** dollars for each year of experience for each of the 20 dealerships, controlling for the experience of the individuals within the groups and **sex**. The value of 0.449149 in the

Estimate column is the variance of those slopes, controlling for (in this model) the differences in dealership experience and **sex**. As we can see from the **Sig.** column, the variance of the slopes is not statistically significant and indicates that the slopes of the 20 dealerships are comparable.

- **UN (2,1)**: *The covariance between the slopes and the intercepts.* This parameter addresses the issue of the relationship between the slope (how steep the function is for a given **dealership**) and intercept (the mean of the dealership) for the prediction equation for each **dealership**, controlling for the experience of the individuals within the groups and **sex**. The value of -1.724007 is not statistically significant, indicating that the slope–intercept relationships are consistent across all 20 dealerships.

9B.8 Building the Fourth Model

From our third model, we have determined that the Level 1 of variables of years of experience as well as the sex of the 813 individual salespeople is predictive of their **sales** volume controlling for **dealership**. We now choose to add to the third model, as the final step in our model-building process, the interaction of these two Level 1 variables (**sex*grp_cent_experience_Level1**). In Section 9B.8.1 below, we will not show the dialog windows that are configured as we described for the third model.

9B.8.1 The Fourth Model: Setup

Select **Analyze** ➜ **Mixed Models** ➜ **Linear** from the main menu. In the preliminary **Linear Mixed Models** dialog window, click over **dealership** to the **Subjects** panel, and click **Continue** to reach the main dialog window. Just as we did for the previous model, in the main dialog window, place **sales** into the **Dependent Variable** panel, place **grp_cent_experience_Level1** into the **Covariate(s)** panel, and place **sex** into the **Factor(s)** panel.

Select **Fixed**, which brings us to the dialog screen presented in Figure 9b.36. Move both **sex** and **grp_cent_experience_Level1** from the **Factors and Covariates** panel to the **Model** panel (to obtain an estimated mean of **sales** for salespeople with respect to their **dealership** as well as their **sex**) by highlighting the variables and clicking the **Add** pushbutton. Then choose **Interaction** in the drop-down menu, and select both **sex** and **grp_cent_experience_Level1** (by pressing the shift key while selecting them). Click the **Add** pushbutton to place the interaction term in the **Model** panel, and click **Continue** to reach the main dialog window.

Select **Random** from the main dialog window. From the drop-down menu for **Covariance Type**, select **Unstructured**, so that we can obtain information to compare the intercepts and slopes of the 20 dealerships. Check the box for **Include intercept** under the **Covariance Type** drop-down menu. Move **grp_cent_experience_Level1** from the **Factors and Covariates** panel to the **Model** panel (to obtain an estimated variance of the

Figure 9b.36 Fixed Effects Dialog Window of Linear Mixed Models

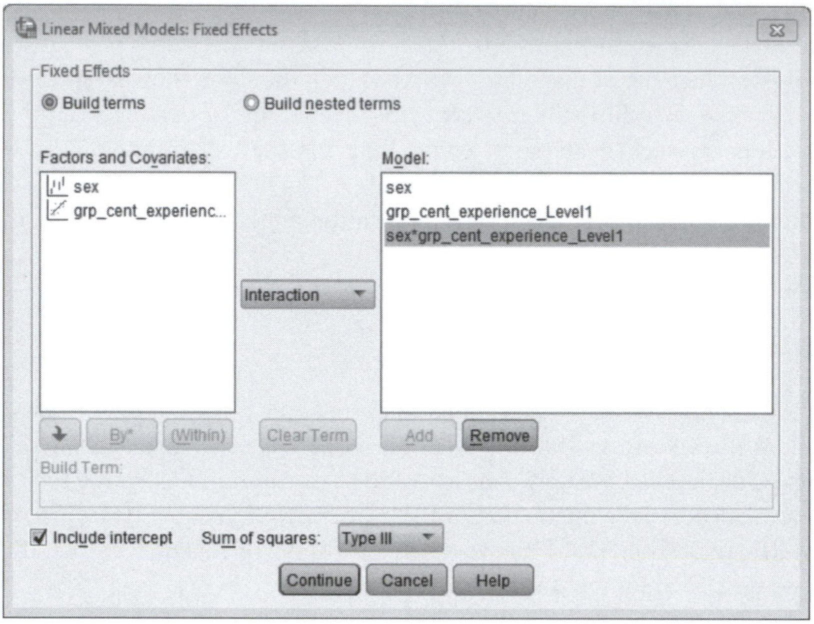

intercepts and slopes for **sales** with respect to their **dealership**) by highlighting the variable and clicking the **Add** pushbutton. Move **dealership** from the **Subject Groupings** panel by highlighting it and clicking the arrow button. Click **Continue** to reach the main dialog window.

Select the **Statistics** pushbutton. Check **Parameter estimates** and **Tests for covariance parameters** in the **Statistics** window, click **Continue** to reach the main dialog window, and click **OK** to perform the analysis.

9B.8.2 The Fourth Model: Output

Figure 9b.37 shows the **Model Dimension** and **Information Criteria** tables. The **Model Dimension** table informs us that there were 8 estimated parameters in this fourth model. The **Information Criteria** table displays the goodness-of-fit measures. The **−2 Restricted Log Likelihood** value is 7281.487. Recall that the third model showed us a **−2 Restricted Log Likelihood** value of 7300.958 with 7 parameters. We have lost 19.471 units with a difference of 1 parameter (degree of freedom). When placed into our evaluation of the chi-square difference (not shown), this gain in model fit over the third model was statistically significant.

Figure 9b.37 Parameter Estimates and Model Fit Output for Model 4

Model Dimension_b

		Number of Levels	Covariance Structure	Number of Parameters	Subject Variables
Fixed Effects	Intercept	1		1	
	sex	2		1	
	grp_cent_experience_Level1	1		1	
	sex * grp_cent_experience_Level1	2		1	
Random Effects	Intercept + grp_cent_experience_Level1_a	2	Unstructured	3	dealership
Residual				1	
Total		8		8	

a. As of version 11.5, the syntax rules for the RANDOM subcommand have changed. Your command syntax may yield results that differ from those produced by prior versions. If you are using version 11 syntax, please consult the current syntax reference guide for more information.

b. Dependent Variable: sales Thousands of Dollars in Sales.

Information Criteria_a

−2 Restricted Log Likelihood	7281.487
Akaike's Information Criterion (AIC)	7289.487
Hurvich and Tsai's Criterion (AICC)	7289.537
Bozdogan's Criterion (CAIC)	7312.270
Schwarz's Bayesian Criterion (BIC)	7308.270

The information criteria are displayed in smaller-is-better forms.

a. Dependent Variable: sales Thousands of Dollars in Sales.

The fixed and random components of the model are presented in Figure 9b.38. The upper table describes the fixed effects. The value of the intercept (46.321371) appears in the column labeled **Estimate**. This is the expected (predicted) **sales** in thousands of dollars for the 813 salespeople (controlling for group-level experience, **sex**, and the interaction of group and **sex**).

The value of 15.422006 is the slope of the linear function using the Level 1 **sex = 0** variable to predict **sales** when we are controlling for both individual experience within each dealership and the interaction effect; this slope is significantly different ($p < .01$) from a value of zero. This indicates that, controlling for individual experience within each dealership and the interaction, females produced approximately 15.42 thousand dollars (i.e., $15,420) more than males for their sales figures.

Figure 9b.38 Fixed and Random Effects Output for Model 4

Estimates of Fixed Effects[b]

Parameter	Estimate	Std. Error	df	t	Sig.	95% Confidence Interval	
						Lower Bound	Upper Bound
Intercept	46.321371	2.913691	41.445	15.898	.000	40.438970	52.203772
[sex=0]	15.422006	2.399803	437.304	6.426	.000	10.705425	20.138587
[sex=1]	0[a]	0	.	.	.	.	.
grp_cent_experience_Level1	-.116165	.422583	19.428	-.275	.786	-.999326	.766996
[sex=0] * grp_cent_experience_Level1	2.436586	.518765	44.811	4.697	.000	1.391617	3.481554
[sex=1] * grp_cent_experience_Level1	0[a]	0	.	.	.	.	.

a. This parameter is set to zero because it is redundant.
b. Dependent Variable: sales Thousands of Dollars in Sales.

Covariance Parameters

Estimates of Covariance Parameters[a]

Parameter		Estimate	Std. Error	Wald Z	Sig.	95% Confidence Interval	
						Lower Bound	Upper Bound
Residual		434.691827	22.031760	19.730	.000	393.585862	480.090885
Intercept + grp_cent_experience_Level1 [subject = dealership]	UN (1,1)	95.341299	34.754865	2.743	.006	46.665042	194.791709
	UN (2,1)	-5.341548	3.377652	-1.581	.114	-11.961625	1.278528
	UN (2,2)	.299887	.474726	.632	.528	.013474	6.674606

a. Dependent Variable: sales Thousands of Dollars in Sales.

The value of −0.116165 is the slope of the linear function using the Level 1 variable of 813 individual salesperson experience to predict **sales** when we are controlling for **sex** and the interaction of sex and group experience; this slope is not significantly different ($p = .786$) from a value of zero and indicates that there is no relationship within dealership experience (group) and sales, controlling for both sex and the interaction of sex and group experience. This group experience outcome is different from what we obtained in the third model and has occurred because we now have the interaction term in our fourth model.

The value of 2.436586 is the slope for the interaction using females as the reference category (again, the males are arbitrarily assigned an estimated slope of zero). We interpret this as follows: For each additional year of experience, women earned 2.43 thousand dollars more than men. This interaction effect supplies us with a nuance that was not able to be recognized by the third model. That is, in the third model, we learned that women produced more sales dollars than males and that more experience generated more sales dollars. By introducing the interaction term, the main effect of experience was no longer a viable predictor of sales; rather, the interaction "fine-tuned" our appreciation of the role that experience played. We now have learned that, at least in our simulated data set, women capitalize more effectively on their experience than men to the tune of 2.43 thousand dollars per year of experience.

The lower table in Figure 9b.38 shows the estimates of the covariance parameters for the random effects. The top row labeled **Residual** represents the unexplained variance of **sales**. In this example, the value of the unexplained variance is 434.691827 and is statistically significant. Thus, there is a significant amount of variance that is not accounted for by this model.

The next three rows are labeled as **UN (1,1)**, **UN (2,1)**, and **UN (2,2)**. The three specific parameters of the variance in the order that we suggest examining these results are as follows:

- **UN (1,1)**: *The variance of the intercepts.* Intercepts are the mean **sales** for each of the 20 dealerships, controlling for the experience of the individuals within the groups, **sex**, and the interaction. The value of 95.341299 in the **Estimate** column is the variance of those means, controlling for (in this model) the differences in dealership experience, **sex**, and the interaction. This variance of the intercepts is statistically significant and indicates that the means of the 20 dealerships differ significantly.
- **UN (2,2)**: *The variance of the slopes.* Slopes are the amount of increase in **sales** dollars for each year of experience for each of the 20 dealerships, controlling for the experience of the individuals within the groups and **sex**. The value of −5.341548 in the **Estimate** column is the variance of those slopes, controlling for (in this model) the differences in dealership experience, **sex**, and the interaction. This variance of the slopes is not statistically significant and indicates that the slopes of the 20 dealerships are comparable.
- **UN (2,1)**: *The covariance between the slopes and the intercepts.* This parameter addresses the issue of the relationship between the slope (how steep the function is for a given **dealership**) and intercept (the mean of the dealership) for the prediction equation for each **dealership**, controlling for the experience of the individuals within the groups, **sex**, and the interaction. The value of 0.299887 is not statistically significant, indicating that the slope–intercept relationships are consistent across all 20 dealerships.

9B.9 Reporting Multilevel Modeling Results

A sample of 20 automobile dealerships in the Washington D.C. metropolitan area participated in a two-level multilevel modeling study of sales productivity as measured by the dollar amount of sales produced by their sales staff during a typical month. Data for two Level 1 predictors, the number of years of sales experience and whether the salesperson was female or male, were collected for each of the 813 salespeople. In addition, a Level 2 variable was generated to reflect the average years of experience of sales staff representing each of the 20 dealerships.

The unconditional model yielded a statistically significant estimated dealership variance of 133.859 (Wald $Z = 2.819$, $p = .005$) as well as a statistically significant estimated residual variance of 495.743 (Wald $Z = 19.913$, $p < .001$). The intraclass correlation coefficient was calculated to be .2126, indicating that approximately 21% of the total variance of sales dollars was associated with the dealership groupings and that the assumption of independence was violated.

To address a possible basis for this clustering effect, we computed the Level 2 variable of dealership experience—the average years of experience of the sales staff in each dealership. This variable was centered on the grand mean and added to the model. This model (−2 log likelihood = 7367.343, $df = 4$) offered a significantly better fit to the data than did the unconditional model (−2 log likelihood = 7397.059, $df = 3$) as determined by a chi-square difference test. The variance of dealership controlling for average dealership experience was 22.500; this was statistically significant (Wald $Z = 1.985$, $p = .047$), now accounting for approximately 4% of the total variance (down from 21% when average years of dealership experience was not included in the model). The slope of dealership experience was statistically significant, $t(17.836) = 7.882$, $p < .001$, indicating that for every year of dealership experience, an increase (on the average) of approximately 5.35 thousand dollars in sales for the dealership ($SE = 0.679$) would be predicted.

In the second model, average dealership experience was replaced with the Level 1 variable of years of experience for the 813 salespeople. This variable was centered with respect to the particular dealership at which the individual was employed and entered into the model. The fit of this model (−2 log likelihood = 7338.059, $df = 6$) was significantly better than that of the unconditional model. Although the intercepts (means) for the 20 dealerships differed significantly, their slopes did not. Overall, the slope for years of individual sales experience was statistically significant, $t(20.312) = 6.278$, $p < .001$; for every year of experience of the salesperson an increase (on the average) of approximately 1.92 thousand dollars ($SE = 0.302$) in sales would be predicted.

In the third model, sex of the salesperson was added to the number of years of experience for each of the 813 salespeople as a second Level 1 predictor. Model fit (−2 log likelihood = 7300.958, $df = 7$) significantly improved over the second model. The slopes of both predictors were statistically significant, $t(18.648) = 5.257$, $p < .001$ for group-centered individual experience and $t(532.529) = 6.020$, $p < .001$ for sex. Controlling for sex, for every year of experience of the salesperson, we would predict an increase (on the average) of approximately 1.55 thousand dollars in sales ($SE = 0.294$); controlling for individual experience within each dealership, females produced approximately 14.81 thousand dollars more than males ($SE = 2.460$).

In the fourth and final model, the interaction of the Level 1 variables of years of experience and sex was added to the third model. Model fit (-2 log likelihood = 7281.487, $df = 8$) was significantly better than the third model. Years of experience no longer yielded a statistically significant slope, $t(19.428) = -0.275$, $p > .05$, but both the slope of sex, $t(437.304) = 6.426$, $p < .001$, and the slope of the Experience × Sex interaction, $t(44.811) = 4.697$, $p < .001$, were statistically significant. For the effect of sex, it was found that, controlling for individual experience within each dealership and the interaction, females produced approximately 15.42 thousand dollars more than males overall ($SE = 2.400$). The interaction fine-tunes this effect by indicating that women earned 2.43 thousand dollars more than men ($SE = 0.519$) for every year of experience when controlling for both individual experience within each dealership and sex.

Binary and Multinomial Logistic Regression and ROC Analysis

10A.1 Overview

10A.1.1 Regression as Discussed in Prior Chapters

The regression analyses we discussed in Chapters 6A, 7A, and 8A were based on the general linear model in which a quantitatively measured dependent variable is predicted by a set of independent variables that are preferably quantitatively measured but that can be dichotomous. A linear function was fit to the data using the ordinary least squares algorithm where the squared deviations from the function was minimized and thus defined the line of best fit. These ordinary least squares regression designs are extremely useful research tools and have very widespread application.

In Chapter 9A, we expanded beyond the general linear modeling approach to analyze data that were hierarchically organized. Maximum likelihood rather than ordinary least squares was used to estimate the parameter values in the process of fitting a model to the data. Furthermore, the model contained predictors at each level of the research methodology hierarchy. Despite these substantial changes to the model-building strategy, the dependent (outcome) variable was still assessed on a quantitative scale of measurement.

10A.1.2 Types of Logistic Regression

This chapter addresses a regression approach where the dependent variable is categorical; the independent variables here may still be quantitative or dichotomous, or some of each. The categorical dependent variable could be a dichotomous (binary) dependent variable, and designs using such outcome variables are generally known as binary logistic regression designs. On the other hand, the dependent grouping variable could have more than two categories, and designs using such outcome variables are generally known as polytomous or multinomial logistic regression designs. As we will see in Chapter 10B, the IBM SPSS multinomial logistic regression analysis procedure uses one of the categories as the reference group, akin to the reference category in dummy coding (see Section 8A.5.2) and dummy codes the other categories so that we perform multiple binary logistic analyses even when we have more than two categories of the dependent variable. Thus, any single logistic regression analysis specifies a binary outcome as its dependent variable.

10A.1.3 The Prevalence of Logistic Regression

Many research studies in the social and behavioral sciences (e.g., psychology, education, criminal justice, marketing, medical research) investigate dependent (outcome) variables of a categorical nature. Pedhazur (1997) illustrates some of these designs with binary outcome variables:

> The ubiquity of such variables in social and behavioral research is exemplified by a yes or no response to diverse questions about behavior (e.g., voted in a given election), ownership (e.g., of a personal computer), educational attainment (e.g., graduated from college), status (e.g., employed), to name but some. Among other binary response modes are agree-disagree, success-failure, presence-absence, and pro-con. (p. 714)

The use of logistic regression is increasing because of the wide availability of statistical software packages that include the procedure. Hosmer and Lemeshow (2000) report that the use of logistic regression has "exploded during the past decade" (p. ix), having expanded from its origins in biomedical research to fields such as business and finance, criminology, ecology, engineering, health policy, linguistics, and wildlife biology. Logistic regression has become so popular that Huck (2004) predicts, "It may soon overtake multiple regression and become the most frequently used regression tool of all!" (p. 438). More complete treatments of logistic regression may be found in Agresti (2007), Hosmer and Lemeshow (2000), Kleinbaum, Klein, and Pryor (2002), Menard (2002, 2010), Pampel (2000), and Wright (1995).

10A.2 The Variables in Logistic Regression Analysis

In a typical logistic regression analysis, there will always be one binary dependent variable in a single analysis (although it could be a dummy coded variable in the case of multinomial logistic regression) and a set of independent variables that may be either dichotomous or quantitative or some combination thereof. Furthermore, the dichotomous predictor variables need not be truly binary; for example, researchers may transform a highly skewed quantitative dependent variable into a dichotomous variable with approximately equal numbers of cases in each category. And akin to what we have seen in multiple regression, some of the independent variables in logistic regression analysis may serve as covariates to allow researchers to hold constant or statistically control for these variable(s) to better assess the unique effects of the other independent variables.

10A.3 Assumptions of Logistic Regression

Although logistic regression makes fewer assumptions than linear regression (e.g., homogeneity of variance and normality of errors are not assumed), logistic regression does require the following:

- There must be an absence of perfect multicollinearity.
- There must be no specification errors (i.e., all relevant predictors are included and irrelevant predictors are excluded).
- The independent variables must be measured at the summative response scale, interval, or ratio level (although dichotomous or dummy coded categorical variables are also allowed).
- There must be independence of errors—each observation is independent of the other observations.
- The independent variables must be linearly related to the log odds (this will make more sense to readers when we discuss log odds in Section 10A.7).
- The dependent variable must be binary.

Logistic regression also requires larger samples than does ordinary least squares regression for valid interpretation of the results. Although statisticians disagree on the precise sample requirements, Pedhazur (1997) suggests using at least 30 times as many cases as parameters being estimated.

10A.4 Coding of the Binary Variables in Logistic Regression

As we discussed in Section 8A5.1.3, a binary variable can be coded using any set of adjacent numbers as codes or, although we strongly advise against it, any set of nonadjacent numbers. However, the coding schema that is traditionally recommended (e.g., Hosmer & Lemeshow, 2000), and the one that IBM SPSS employs, calls for using the values of 0 and 1. This coding schema should be used for both the binary predictor (independent) variables as well as for the binary outcome (dependent) variable using the strategies described in the following two sections.

10A.4.1 Coding of the Binary Predictor Variables

10A.4.1.1 Coding of the Binary Predictor Variables in Binary Logistic Regression

It is not uncommon in logistic regression designs for researchers to use categorical (binary) predictors. Two such examples are as follows:

- Gender (female vs. male) may be predictive of (related to) an event occurring or not (e.g., pass or fail, select one program over another).
- Having a family history of a certain medical condition (yes vs. no) may be predictive of whether or not individuals are diagnosed with that condition themselves.

In the **Binary Logistic Regression** procedure of IBM SPSS, such predictors should be coded as 1 and 0 based on the following consideration: Those cases who comprise the focus category for the researchers or who possess some attribute of research interest should be coded as 1 and the others coded as 0. In the former example, females (if they were the focus of the study) would be coded as 1 and males would be coded as 0; in the latter example, those having a family history of the medical condition would be coded as 1 and those with no such history would be coded as 0.

Identifying the focus category for a particular research study often appears to be somewhat unclear to students who will point out, for example, that gender is composed of both females and males or that having a family history of a certain condition has meaning only if others do not have such a family history. And they are correct—both groups together comprise the variable and thus both groups are equally relevant. Nonetheless, one of the two categories must be the focus, that is, one of the two categories must be coded as 1 in the data file.

The way to deal with the dilemma of determining the focus category is to follow this rubric: Verbalize a hypothetical result in both ways and select the one that represents the preferred verbalization—that verbalization will capture the focus group. For example, assume we are predicting program success (fail or succeed) based on gender and we must decide how to code the gender variable. The analysis results in logistic regression are stated in terms of an odds ratio. Assume that females are more likely to succeed (males are more likely to fail). The two alternative verbalizations are as follows:

- Females are twice as likely as males to succeed in the program.
- Males are half as likely as females to succeed in the program.

If the researchers prefer females to be the focus of the sentence (to be verbalized first in the former sentence example), then **female** is the focus category and should be coded as 1 in the data file (with **male** coded as 0). If the researchers prefer males to be the focus of the sentence (to be verbalized first in the latter sentence example), then **male** is the focus category and should be coded as 1 in the data file (with **female** coded as 0). That is, the odds statement will be output in IBM SPSS in terms of the focus category. Thus, if **female** is the focus category, the odds ratio for success in the above example would be 2.00; if **male** was the focus category, the odds ratio for success in the above example would be 0.50. Both values describe the same empirical reality, so the choice is usually a matter of preference on the part of the researchers.

10A.4.1.2 Coding of the Binary Predictor Variables in Multinomial Logistic Regression

In the **Multinomial Logistic Regression** procedure of IBM SPSS, at least in Versions 18 and 19 of the software, the treatment of binary predictors is switched from some earlier versions. In Version 19, the focus category of a binary predictor is associated with the code of 0 (or the lower code), and the other category to which the focus category is compared in the odds ratio is associated with the code of 1 (or the higher code).

Because this coding treatment does not appear to be consistent across versions, users of the IBM SPSS software should examine the two-way frequency tabulation of the binary predictor with the multinomial outcome variable. As a general rule, the odds ratio should reflect the relative proportion of cases in this array. For example, if in the response group compared with the reference group (see Section 10A.4.2 for the definitions of these groups) the percentage of females was much greater than the percentage of males, and if female was the focus category, then the odds ratio should be greater than 1.00. By anticipating whether the odds ratio should be greater or less than 1.00, it is possible to make a rapid assessment of whether or not the coding is what is expected. If it is not, just reverse the coding on the binary predictor and perform the analysis again.

10A.4.2 Coding of the Categorical Outcome Variable

10A.4.2.1 Coding of the Outcome Variable in Binary Logistic Regression

In binary logistic regression, the dependent (outcome) variable is always dichotomous. In a very general sense, cases or outcomes coded as 1 are referred to (or are thought of) as the *response group, comparison group,* or *target group*; these outcomes usually represent the expected, hoped-for, or desired result. Cases or outcomes coded as 0 are sometimes called the *referent group, reference group, base group,* or *control group*; these outcomes usually represent the alternative result. The ultimate objective of logistic regression is to predict a case's group membership on the dependent variable by calculating the probability that a case will belong to the category coded as 1 (e.g., desired outcome). For example, if the outcome variable was successful completion of a program (e.g., a training program or a rehabilitation program), we would code successful completion of the program as 1 and unsuccessful program completion as 0.

There are certain advantages to using this 1 and 0 coding scheme. One advantage is that the mean of the dependent variable is equal to the proportion of 1s in the distribution, thus allowing researchers to immediately know this second piece of information from the first. Consider the situation where there are 100 people in the sample. If 30 of them are coded 1, then the mean of the distribution is .30, which is the proportion of 1s in the data set. The mean of the distribution is also the probability of drawing a person coded as 1 at random from the sample. Therefore, the indexes of proportion and probability with respect to the value or code of 1 are the same.

The mean of a binary distribution coded as 1 and 0 is denoted as P, the proportion of 1s. The proportion of 0s is $1 - P$, which is sometimes denoted as Q. The variance of such a distribution is PQ. In the above example where there are thirty 1s in a set of 100 cases, the variance of the distribution is .21 (computed as $.3 * .7 = .21$) and the standard deviation is the square root of PQ or .458.

10A.4.2.2 Coding of the Outcome Variable in Multinomial Logistic Regression

In multinomial logistic regression, the outcome variable has three or more categories. IBM SPSS allows for maximum flexibility here. Users can use any numerical coding schema, although we recommend using 1, 2, 3, and so on. For example, if we have three groups—art majors, business majors, and psychology majors—we could code these groups (arbitrarily) as 1 for art majors, 2 for business majors, and 3 for psychology majors.

When we identify the multinomial outcome variable in the main dialog window of IBM SPSS, we are also asked to specify which category we wish to identify as the reference group in the analysis. Each of the remaining groups is then used separately as a target group in separate analyses, thus keeping the outcome variable in each analysis as binary. For example, if we wished to have psychology students as the reference group given the example coding schema above, we would specify **Last Category** in the IBM SPSS dialog window (because the code of **3** is highest or "last" category)—one analysis would contrast art students to psychology students and the other would contrast business students to psychology students. If we wished to have business students as the reference group given the example coding schema above, we would specify **Custom** and type the code value of **2** in the IBM SPSS dialog window—here, one analysis would contrast art students to business students and the other analysis would contrast psychology students to business students.

10A.5 The Logistic Regression Model

Conceptually, logistic regression and ordinary least squares linear regression are analogous. Both methods produce prediction equations. Recall from Chapter 7A that in multiple regression analysis, the ordinary least squares strategy is used to calculate the prediction of a quantitative dependent variable. The regression function is a straight line; that is, the prediction model is a linear combination of the independent variables. Things are a bit different in logistic regression.

10A.5.1 Least Squares Is Not Appropriate in Logistic Regression

Because the dependent variable in logistic regression is dichotomous, using the least squares technique to calculate the prediction of a categorical dependent variable is inappropriate for two reasons. The first reason why the least squares technique is not appropriate is as follows: Because the dependent variable is dichotomous, the equal variance assumption underlying linear multiple regression is almost always violated. Recall that in multiple regression, there is the assumption that the variance of Y is constant across values of X (this is an assumption of homoscedasticity). Requiring equal variances is an unreasonable condition to meet in logistic regression for at least two reasons:

- The variance is calculated by multiplying the proportion of 1s by the proportion of 0s. Thus, the notion of "equal variances" of the 1s and 0s does not make sense because we have to work with both proportions to compute the variances in the first place.
- If we take "equal variances" to mean an equal proportion of 1s and 0s (which must be .5 and .5), then we place an unnecessary restriction on the variables that can be used in the analysis. Most variables are probably going to show different numbers of 1s and 0s in the set, and we would certainly be interested in using some of these as dependent variables in a logistic regression analysis.

The second reason the least squares technique is not appropriate is as follows: The least squares method can produce predicted values greater than 1 and less than 0, and such values are inadmissible (and nonsensical) for a 0 and 1 coded variable. This means that the linear function that we use in multiple regression is inappropriate here. Instead, the shape of the best-fit line in logistic regression is *sigmoidal* or S shaped.

10A.5.2 The Logistic Function

An ordinary least squares regression function is represented by a straight line. For the situation in which we are using a single quantitative predictor to predict a quantitative outcome variable, we are predicting that given amount of change of the X variable is predicted to result in a certain amount of change in the Y variable. This function is continuous and constant throughout the ranges of X and Y. Based on this continuous function, we can predict a given value on the outcome variable from the value of the predictor variable. But in the case of a binary outcome variable, there are only two values for the outcome. As indicated above, the linear prediction function is not applicable under these circumstances.

Superimposing an imaginary linear prediction function in a binary outcome design is illustrated in Figure 10a.1. Variable X is the predictor here, and for the sake of exposition, assume that it is a quantitative variable. The outcome variable is Y. Notice that if researchers were to use least squares for a dichotomous outcome, the equation would suggest that a change in the predictor variable has a constant effect on the outcome variable, a relationship that does not apply here.

If a straight-line function is not workable, what sort of function is better? The answer provided by logistic regression is, perhaps not surprisingly, a logistic (S-shaped or sigmoidal) function as shown in Figure 10a.1. This function allows us to predict the probability that the outcome is a 1 based on the value of the predictor variable. This function is interesting in that it is relatively flat at both the low and high levels of X. Notice in Figure 10a.1 that the

Figure 10a.1 Comparing the Ordinary Least Squares (Linear Probability) Model and the Logistic Regression Model

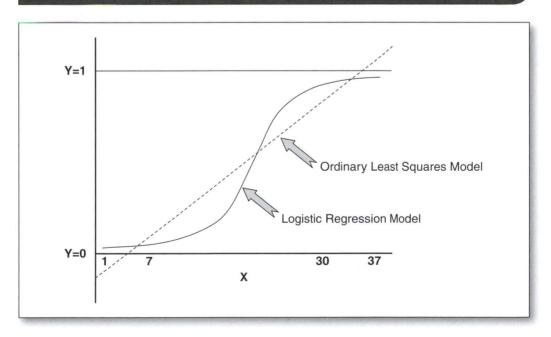

corresponding Y values for Xs in the range of 1 through 7 are all around 0. This suggests that differences in this range of X do not make much of a difference in outcome. Let X be the amount of distress individuals are experiencing at a given time in their lives, with lower values indicating less distress, and let Y be the probability of seeking therapy. Then the logistic function indicates that people experiencing little stress, whether at levels of 1 or 6 or anyplace in between, are not likely to enter therapy.

An analogous situation is seen at the upper end of the X range where again the function is quite flat. Individuals experiencing lots of distress, whether as low as 30 or as high as 37, are all very likely to seek therapy. Again, distress level within this range does not make much of a difference in prediction.

So where is the "real action" in prediction? It is in the midrange of X where different distress levels are associated with different probabilities of seeking therapy. In fact, the steeper the slope in this range, the more differentiating would be the different distress levels. And it makes sense that prediction of who will seek therapy is more uncertain in this range of distress.

In essence, what we have said is that distress level (X) does not have a constant effect on the probability of seeking therapy (Y). And that may make it apparent why least squares multiple regression is not applicable here.

The point is that a linear function defines a situation in which the predictor and the criterion bear a constant relationship to each other; that is, this much difference in the predictor results in that much difference in the criterion over the entire range of the predictor. When a constant relationship is not descriptive of the relationship, least squares, with its fit of a linear function, is not an acceptable strategy to use. This is where the logistic regression model, with its S-shaped function that relates predictors to probabilities of events occurring, takes on a considerable amount of predictive power.

10A.6 Logistic Regression and Odds

10A.6.1 Probability

Probability is the likelihood that an event will occur and is constrained to lie between 0 and 1. The constraints at 0 and 1 make it unrealistic to construct a linear equation for predicting probabilities (ordinary least squares will cause these bounds to be exceeded).

Probability is often expressed as a decimal value. To compute it, take the number of occurrences and divide it by the total number of possibilities. For example, the probability of rolling a 4 on a six-sided die is 1 divided by 6 or .167. One would therefore say that the probability of that event occurring is about .17. Thus, out of 100 attempts, we would expect in the long run that about 17 of them would result in rolls of 4.

We can apply this idea to a simple logistic regression design, where we wish to predict successfully completing a rehabilitation program as the outcome variable (it is either successful

Table 10a.1 Fictional Data Illustrating Gender Differences in Program Success

	Program Successful	Program Not Successful	Total Count
Females	200	100	300
Males	50	150	200
Total	250	250	500

or not successful) based on the individuals being either female or male (as the predictor variable). The fictional data for this example are shown in Table 10a.1.

Notice that an equal proportion (50%) of the participants in our example experienced success and failure in the program, that is, 250 were classified under **Program Successful** and 250 were classified under **Program Not Successful**. Thus, the probability of a study participant being successful is .50. The key issue, however, is whether this proportion is the same for males and females. The first step would be for the researcher to calculate the odds of success separately for females and males.

10A.6.2 Odds

Odds in this example represent the probability of belonging to one group (success) divided by the probability of not belonging to that group (not being successful). Odds are computed by the formula $(P/1 - P)$, where P is the probability of an event occurring (of the outcome being a 1) and $1 - P$ is the probability of an event not occurring (of the outcome being a 0).

Unlike probability, which is bounded by 0 and 1, odds can range from 0 to an extremely high value. If the chances of an event occurring are greater than not occurring, then the odds will be greater than 1. If the chances of an event failing to occur are greater, then the odds will be less than 1. If there is an equal chance of the event occurring or not occurring, then the odds equal 1. Odds of 1 are considered the equivalent of the null hypothesis in logistic regression.

In this study, the odds of a male being successful are .33 (50 males were successful divided by 150 who were not). This means that for every male who was successful, three males were not successful. The odds for females being successful are 200/100 or 2. This means that a female is twice as likely to be successful in the program than not.

10A.6.3 Odds Ratio

In logistic regression, one of the important results is to obtain the *odds ratio*. It is what researchers need to calculate to answer the research question in most logistic regression studies. In this study, the question of whether there is a gender difference in program success is answered by calculating an odds ratio.

The odds ratio is, as may be obvious from its name, a ratio of the odds for each group. It is a way of comparing whether the probability of a certain event is the same for two groups. The numerator represents the odds of the event occurring (program success) for the target group (the group coded as 1—let's say it is the females in this example), and the denominator represents the odds of the event occurring (program success) for the referent group (the group coded as 0—let's say it is the males in this example).

Analogous to odds, an odds ratio of 1 implies that the event is equally likely for the two groups. An odds ratio greater than 1 indicates that the likelihood of an event occurring is more likely in the group coded 1 than in the group coded 0. An odds ratio less than 1 suggests that the event is less likely to occur in the group coded 1 than in the group coded 0. In our hypothetical example, the odds ratio is computed by dividing the odds of females being successful in the program by the odds of males being successful in the program.

Given that the female odds were calculated as 2 and the male odds were calculated as .33, we divide 2 by .33 to obtain 6. We interpret this outcome as follows: Women in this sample were six times more likely than males to be successful in the program.

Women were coded as 1 because they were the focus of our study. Had men been our focus, we would have coded the males as 1 and the females as 0. The odds ratio would then have been .33/2 = .167, and we would then say that males were one sixth as likely to be successful in the program.

10A.6.4 Adjusted Odds Ratio

The odds ratio just discussed would be considered "simple" or "unadjusted" because no other predictor variables were included in the analysis. Frequently, logistic regression would employ a set of independent variables to predict or explain the dichotomous dependent variable. When multiple variables are used as predictors in a logistic analysis, the odds ratio for any one predictor variable is referred to as an *adjusted odds ratio* to indicate the contribution of a particular variable when other variables are statistically controlled or held constant.

10A.7 The Logistic Regression Model

10A.7.1 The Logistic Regression Model: The Predictor Side

Just as in linear regression, logistic analysis will produce a single constant (*a*) and a regression coefficient (*b*) or weight for each predictor in the model. Recall that the *b* coefficients in linear regression are derived through the use of ordinary least squares estimation. In logistic regression, the *b* coefficients are calculated through maximum likelihood estimation after transforming the dependent variable into a logit variable (described in Section 10A.7.2). Unlike what we saw for ordinary least squares regression, a standardized model is not ordinarily produced in parallel to the raw score model; thus, we work only with the raw regression coefficients and the constant in logistic regression.

10A.7.2 The Logistic Regression Model: The Outcome Variable

The fundamental entity that is predicted in logistic regression is the probability of the occurrence of an event (the code of 1 on the outcome variable). But for calculation purposes the probability of an event is transformed to odds. It is possible to create a linear relationship between the predictors and odds. Although a number of functions work, one of the most useful is the logit function. It is the *natural log* (abbreviated ln) transformation of the odds that a case belongs to the target group (the group coded as 1); it is known as the *natural log odds* but is often simply called the *log odds* (assuming readers know that it is the natural log). This transformation "bends" the data to fit the sigmoidal curve. The ultimate objective of logistic regression is to predict a case's group membership. This translates to the probability or likelihood of an event occurring for a given value of a predictor variable—more specifically, the probability or likelihood of a case's membership in the target group.

10A.7.3 The Logistic Regression Model: The Full Equation

The general form of the logistic regression equation with *v* number of independent variables is as follows:

$$\ln[\text{odds}] = a + b_1 X_1 + b_2 X_2 + \cdots + b_v X_v$$

The left side of the equation represents the log odds for the predicted dependent variable in a linear model. The *b* coefficients indicate the change in log odds of membership for any 1-unit change in the independent variables controlling for the other predictors in the model. In this sense, logistic regression is in reality linear regression using the logit as the outcome variable.

The values for the constant (*a*) and the *b* weights are calculated through maximum likelihood estimation after transforming the dependent variable into a logit variable. Maximum likelihood estimation seeks to maximize the log likelihood, which reflects how likely it is (the odds) that the observed values of the dependent variable may be predicted from the observed values of the independent variable(s). An iterative process is used in conjunction with maximum likelihood estimation that starts with an initial arbitrary "guesstimate" and then determines the direction and magnitude of the logit coefficients. Thus, the b coefficients in logistic regression indicate the change in log odds of membership in the dependent variable code of 1 for any 1-unit change in the independent variable controlling for the other predictors. This increase in log odds is not easily interpreted. The b coefficients will eventually allow the researcher to predict the probability of membership of the target group. But remember that the logistic regression equation does not directly predict the probability of an event occurring; rather, it predicts the log odds that an observation will have an outcome (a code) of 1. We therefore need to engage in a two-step process to calculate the probability for a case belonging to the target group.

10A.8 Calculating the Chances of Cases Belonging to the Target Group

To make the general logistic regression equation more interpretable, it can be expanded in such a manner that ln, the natural log odds, is the predicted group membership. We can symbolize predicted group membership as $\text{group}_{\text{pred}}$. Thus,

$$\text{group}_{\text{pred}} = \ln\ [\text{odds}] = a + b_1 X_1 + b_2 X_2 + \cdots + b_v X_v$$

Because the logit (i.e., the natural logarithm of an odds ratio) is difficult to interpret, the log odds are transformed into probabilities by taking the antilog (the number corresponding to a logarithm) of the above equation. This is accomplished as follows:

$$\frac{e^{group_{pred}}}{1 + e^{group_{pred}}} = \text{predicted probability}$$

That is, the log odds (represented as $\text{group}_{\text{pred}}$) are now inserted into the antilog function where e (the exponential function) takes on the value of 2.7182. This is the antilog equation that transforms the log odds to probabilities.

10A.9 Binary Logistic Regression With a Single Binary Predictor

10A.9.1 Obtaining the Predicted Probability

We will briefly walk through the example contained in Table 10a.1 of program success being predicted by the gender of the participant. Determining a case's group membership requires calculating the log odds and then transforming the log odds to predicted probability. The first step in calculating the logistic equation for our hypothetical example is based on the linear equation, $\text{group}_{pred} = a + b_1 X_1$. Note that there is only one predictor (X_1) in the equation because there is only one predictor (gender) in our example study. With more predictors, there would be more terms.

In this example, the values of X_1 will be 1 for females and 0 for males, and group_{pred} is the ln of the odds of a case in the target group. Assume that the logistic regression, through maximum likelihood estimation analysis that was performed by IBM SPSS, yielded values of -1.099 for the constant and 1.792 for the b weight. The resulting formula demonstrates the relationship between the regression equations.

$$\text{group}_{pred} = \ln\,[\text{odds}] = a + b_1 X_1 + b_2 X_2 + \cdots + b_n X_n$$

$$\text{group}_{pred} = -1.099 + 1.792\,(\text{gender})$$

This is a linear formula. The logistic regression equation to be addressed in the second step is nonlinear. Thus, for a female,

$$\text{group}_{pred} = -1.099 + 1.792(1)$$

$$\text{group}_{pred} = 0.693$$

For the second step, the value of .693 is now inserted into the following formula, known as the antilog, to transform the log odds to probabilities:

$$\frac{e^{\text{group}_{pred}}}{1 + e^{\text{group}_{pred}}} = \text{Predicted probability}$$

Recall that e is the exponential function and has a value of approximately 2.718. Thus, for a female, the logit equation would be $2.718^{693}/(1 + 2.718^{693}) = .667$.

The analogous computations for a male would be as follows:

$$\text{group}_{pred} = -1.099 + 1.792(0)$$

$$\text{group}_{pred} = -1.099$$

$$\text{predicted probability} = \frac{2.718^{1.009}}{1 + 2.718^{1.009}} = .250.$$

10A.9.2 Obtaining the Odds Ratio

The calculated probabilities from the logistic analysis can now be used to predict group membership. For this, we need to apply a decision rule for this prediction, a rule based on the predicted probability. The rule used is as follows: If the predicted probability is .5 or greater, then the outcome is program success (coded as 1); if the probability is less than .5, the case is classified as not having achieved program success (coded as 0).

In this example, females would be classified as successful in the program because the calculated probability (.667) exceeds .5. Males, however, would be classified as not being successful because their calculated probability (.250) is less than .5.

The odds ratio can be calculated directly from e (which has a value of 2.718) and the b coefficient. We simply raise e to the b power. In the present example,

$$e^b = \text{odds ratio}$$

$$e^{1.792} = \text{odds ratio}$$

$$2.718^{1.792} = 6.0$$

As indicated, we interpret the odds ratio here (with females coded as 1) as signifying that women in this sample demonstrated success in the program six times more than males.

10A.10 Binary Logistic Regression With a Single Quantitative Predictor

Assume that we were examining success in a managerial training program and that we had administered a conscientiousness inventory to participants just as they started the program. Scores on the inventory could range from 10 through 90 with higher scores indicative of greater conscientiousness. The raw data for a small number of cases drawn in this fictional study from a larger data set are shown in Table 10a.2. Those who were successful in the program are shown as 1s, and those not successful are shown as 0s. Conscientiousness scores for the cases shown in the table range from a low of 35 to a high of 80.

Recall that odds are the probability of belonging to one group (successful completion of the program) divided by the probability of not belonging to that group (not successfully completing the program). Visual inspection of the data contained in Table 10a.2, even though there we show only 46 of the 500 cases in the data file, reveals a relatively clear pattern. In the low regions of conscientiousness scores shown in the table, 0s predominate under program outcome, indicating that most of these cases are not successful. In the high regions of conscientiousness scores shown in the table, 1s predominate under program success, indicating that most of these cases are successful. In the midrange region of conscientiousness, we find a mixture of 0s and 1s. Although even this limited set of cases would resemble an S-shaped curve if plotted on a set of axes, the entire set of 500 would yield a very clear sigmoidal function.

Table 10a.2 Fictional Data Illustrating Conscientiousness and Program Success

Success	Conscientiousness	Success	Conscientiousness
0	35	1	60
0	35	1	60
0	40	1	60
0	40	1	60
1	40	0	65
1	40	0	65
0	45	1	65
0	45	1	65
0	45	1	65
0	45	1	70
0	50	1	70
0	50	1	70
0	50	1	70
0	50	1	70
0	50	1	75
0	50	1	75
1	50	1	75
1	50	1	75
0	55	1	80
0	55	1	80
0	60	1	80
0	60	1	80
1	60	1	80

Note. Success is coded as 0 for not successful and 1 for successful.

We can now talk about the data in terms of odds. Assume that in the larger data set, 10 cases had conscientiousness scores of 15. Of these 10 individuals, 1 of them (10% or .10) was successful in the program and 9 of them (90% or .90) were not. Thus, the odds of program success for individuals with a low score of 15 are .11 (.10/.90 = .11). This indicates that for every 1 person with a conscientiousness score of 15 who succeeds in the program, there are 9 who do not.

We can examine the odds of program success for cases whose conscientiousness scores are more in the midrange of the distribution. At a conscientiousness score of 55, for example, we find that an equal number of cases did and did not achieve program success. Therefore, the odds of program success with a conscientiousness score of 55 are 1 (.50/.50 = 1), indicating that there is an equal chance of succeeding and not succeeding. Using the same reasoning process, we find that the odds of success with a conscientiousness score of 85 are 9 (.90/.10 = 9). At this very high level of conscientiousness, for every 9 individuals who succeed in the program, there is 1 who does not.

Applying a logistic function makes intuitive sense here. There is little change in the probability of success at low or high conscientiousness levels. That is, there is little difference between those who are not very conscientious and those who are just a little conscientious; these individuals, as a general rule, simply do not succeed in the program. At the same time, there is also little difference between those who are very conscientious and those who are extremely conscientious; these individuals in our database will generally achieve success. The uncertainty in predicting success is in the midrange of the conscientiousness continuum; increasingly higher conscientiousness in this more narrow range of scores is associated with an increasing likelihood that individuals will succeed in the program.

Given such a pattern across the conscientiousness range means that the relationship between the predictor and the predicted values is nonlinear. Note also that in our larger hypothetical data set, the odds of success with a low conscientiousness score was .11 (.10/.90 = .11), whereas the odds of success with a high conscientiousness score was 9 (.90/.10 = 9). These odds reveal an asymmetry (odds of .11 and 9) that may be reconciled through the logit transformation.

The logit transformation resolves both the asymmetrical issue concerning the odds as well as the calculations of different probabilities at different predictor values. Recall that once we calculate the constant (a) and the b coefficient through maximum likelihood estimation, a probability can be eventually derived by using the two-step procedure previously described. The formula is this: $\text{group}_{\text{pred}} = \text{logit} = a + b_1 X_1$, where X_1 is now the conscientiousness score. This logistic regression analysis yielded a constant value of -7.734 and a b weight of .139. Thus, for a conscientiousness score of, say, 35, the probability of an individual being in the target (successful program completion) group is as follows:

$$\text{group}_{\text{pred}} = -7.734 + .139(35)$$

$$\text{group}_{\text{pred}} = -2.869$$

This value of -2.869 can now be inserted into the antilog equation to transform the log odds to probabilities, where $e = 2.718$.

$$\text{predicted probability} = \frac{2.718^{-2.869}}{1 + 2.718 - 2.869} = .053$$

For a conscientiousness score of 80, the results would be

$$group_{pred} = -7.734 + .139(80)$$

$$group_{pred} = 3.386$$

$$predicted\ probability = \frac{2.718^{3.386}}{1+2.718^{3.386}} = .966$$

In this example, a conscientiousness score of 35 would result in an individual being classified as someone who is likely to be unsuccessful because the calculated probability (.053) is less than .5. However, a conscientiousness score of 80 would result in an individual being classified as someone who is likely to be successful because that person's calculated probability (.966) exceeds .5.

To calculate the odds ratio in this example, we raise e to the power of b. For this example,

$$e^{139} = 1.149$$

This tells us that the odds of successful program completion are 1.149 times greater for a person who had a conscientiousness score of, say, 35, than for a person with a conscientiousness score of 34. For a quantitative variable in general, the odds ratio indicates the odds of the target outcome occurring (the outcome coded as 1) when comparing one level of a predictor with another. For example, when comparing the likelihood of success of individuals with a conscientiousness score of 35 to those of 37, one multiplies the regression coefficient by the size of the difference in quantitative scores before raising e to the power of the coefficient. Thus, the difference between a conscientiousness score of 35 and 37 (a 2-unit increase) would be calculated as follows:

$$e^{(2\ *\ .139)} = e^{278} = 1.320$$

We would therefore say that those scoring a 37 on conscientiousness are 1.32 times more likely to succeed in the program than those scoring 35. If there is a 10-point difference on scores, the equation would be

$$e^{(10\ *\ .139)} = e^{1.39} = 4.01$$

and our interpretation would be that those who scored 70 are 4.01 times more likely to succeed in the program than those scoring 60.

The key thing to remember in interpreting an odds ratio is that, by definition, we are comparing one set of cases with another on the outcome coded as 1 in the data file. The odds ratio changes as a function of the "distance" between the two sets. How much of a change is predicted is a function of b, the regression weight, which is the power to which we raise e. The only issue is how many bs we need, which is told to us by the distance between the sets. If the difference is 2 (conscientiousness scores of 35 and 37, conscientiousness scores of 63 and 65, and so on), then we multiply b by that difference in the power function (e raised to the power of twice b when comparing those who scored 37 with those who scored 35 or when comparing those who scored 65 with those who scored 63).

10A.11 Binary Logistic Regression With a Categorical and a Quantitative Predictor

As is true for ordinary least squares regression, using multiple predictors to develop a logistic regression model is the norm. To provide a sense of the interplay of predictors, we briefly discuss the situation where we have both a categorical and a quantitative predictor by combining the above two examples. Assume that we are predicting program success where successful completion is coded as 1 and unsuccessful completion is coded as 0. Both gender (females coded as 1 and males coded as 0) and conscientiousness are used as predictors. When more than one predictor variable is used in a logistic analysis, researchers must examine the contribution of one variable when other variables are controlled or held constant.

The maximum likelihood estimation method for this data set yielded a constant (a) of -8.35, ab_{gender} of 2.129, and $ab_{conscientiousness}$ score of .131. Thus, for a male (coded as 0) with a conscientiousness score of 40, the probability of program success (target group coded as 1) is as follows:

$$group_{pred} = -8.35 + 2.129(0) + .131(40) = -3.11$$

$$predicted\ probability = \frac{2.718^{3.11}}{1 + 2.718^{-3.11}} = -.042$$

Because the predicted probability of group membership is below .5, this respondent would be predicted to be unsuccessful in the program. However, for a female with a conscientiousness score of 75, the equation would be as follows:

$$group_{pred} = -8.35 + 2.129(1) + .131(75) = 3.604$$

$$predicted\ probability = \frac{2.718^{3.604}}{1 + 2.718^{3.604}} = .973$$

Because the predicted probability of group membership is greater than .5, this respondent would be predicted to be successful in the program.

With multiple variables (two in this simple situation) used as predictors in the logistic analysis, the odds ratio is now referred to as an *adjusted odds ratio* to indicate the contribution of a particular variable when other variables are controlled or held constant. The odds ratio for gender is now $e^{2.129} = 8.404$. This indicates that females (coded as 1) are 8.40 times more likely to be successful in the program when we have statistically controlled for conscientiousness level. Another way to interpret this result would be to imagine that for the condition in which males and females had identical conscientiousness scores, females are about 8.4 times more likely than males to achieve program success.

10A.12 Evaluating the Logistic Model

Logistic regression produces a number of tests to assess the viability of the model (i.e., the regression equation). These tests are as follows:

- −2 log likelihood ratio
- Omnibus chi-square
- Pseudo R^2
- Hosmer and Lemeshow test
- Wald test of significant coefficients

10A.12.1 The −2 Log Likelihood Ratio

If researchers have no information other than the outcome, known as the *constant-only model,* then our best guess is the most prevalent outcome of the study (assuming that the two outcomes are not identical). Assume that in our program completion example, based on the entire data set, that program success was the more common outcome (56.5% in this sample). Thus, without considering any other information (gender or conscientiousness level), the likelihood or probability is that an individual will be successful in the program.

The likelihood ratio can be used to evaluate whether or not the set of the independent variables improves prediction of the dependent variable better than chance. Because each case is independent of the others, the probability of program success can be computed as the percentage of the sample succeeding in the program (the percentage of 1s in the sample) raised to the power equal to the number of cases in the sample. For our small example data set of 46 cases shown in Table 10a.2, 26 were successful. That represents 56.5% of the sample. We thus raise .565 to the 46th power. The result is approximately .00000000000392. This is not an unusual magnitude to obtain because we are raising some decimal value to a power equal to the sample size.

Given that these likelihood values are ordinarily very small, the natural log of the likelihood is usually reported instead in the output. We calculate this value by multiplying the natural log of the above value (the percentage of 1s raised to the power of the sample size) by −2. This outcome (i.e., −2 times the log likelihood) is referred to as the −2 log likelihood or −2LL. Taking the natural log of the likelihood transforms a typically very small number into a "reasonably large" value that is more familiar to most of us. For example, the natural log of .0000000000039 is −26.262. Multiplying this natural log by −2 yields a value of 52.52.

Why not just leave the natural log of the likelihood alone (it's certainly a large enough value for most of us) instead of multiplying it by −2? The answer is that the distribution of −2LL is distributed as chi-square, whereas log likelihood by itself is not. Thus, we can use the −2LL to evaluate the statistical significance of the logistic regression model. Specifically, this test assesses whether or not the contribution of at least one predictor (independent) variable is significantly different from zero.

10A.12.2 Omnibus Chi-Square Test

The omnibus test of model coefficients is another absolute measure of the validity of the model. The model chi-square is a statistical test of the null hypothesis that all the coefficients are zero. It is equivalent to the overall *F* test in linear regression. The model chi-square value is the difference between the constant-only model (containing no predictors) and the full model (i.e., with constant and predictors). If the chi-square reached statistical significance, we would conclude that the set of independent variables improves prediction of the outcome over the situation where they are not used.

10A.12.3 Pseudo R^2

The Cox and Snell and the Nagelkerke tests are two alternative ways to compute a pseudo R^2 estimate. They are used to estimate the percentage of variance in the dependent variable explained by the independent variables and are thus analogous to but are not the same as the R^2 generated in multiple regression analysis. Technically, a true R^2 cannot be computed in logistic regression, and that is why the term *pseudo* is used. Nonetheless, the values can very roughly be interpreted in similar ways to the way we interpret R^2 in ordinary least squares regression.

The pseudo R^2 in logistic regression is defined as $(1 - L_{full})/L_{reduced}$, where $L_{reduced}$ represents the log likelihood for the "constant-only" model and L_{full} is the log likelihood for the full model with constant and predictors. Usually, the Nagelkerke pseudo R^2 is preferred because it can achieve a maximum value of 1, unlike the Cox and Snell pseudo R^2.

10A.12.4 Hosmer and Lemeshow Test

The Hosmer and Lemeshow test of model fit is another absolute measure to assess whether the predicted probabilities match the observed probabilities. Researchers are ordinarily seeking a nonsignificant *p* value for this test because the goal of the research is to derive a set of independent variables that will accurately predict the actual probabilities. Thus, the researcher does not want to reject the null hypothesis.

This test is performed on the entire sample as an overall test of model fit and is what most researchers will examine first. In addition, IBM SPSS also provides a "fine-tuned" or detailed level of analysis as well, dividing the sample into multiple groups ordered from highest to lowest in being expected to be the target group (those who are coded as 1). For each group, the output contains the observed frequencies and the expected values of the two outcomes. There are no significance tests for these separate groups.

10A.12.5 Wald Test of Significant Coefficients

The Wald test is used to test the statistical significance of the unique contribution of each coefficient (*b*) in the model. These coefficients indicate the amount of change expected in the log odds when there is a 1-unit change in the predictor variable with all the other variables in the model held constant. A coefficient close to 0 suggests that there is no change due to the predictor variable. The Wald test is analogous to the *t* test in multiple regression.

Several authors have identified problems with the use of the Wald statistic. Menard (2002) warns that for large coefficients, standard error is inflated, lowering the Wald statistic (chi-square) value, and Agresti (2007) and Enders (2010) state that the likelihood ratio test is more reliable for small sample sizes than the Wald test. Gould, Pitblado, and Sribney (2006) suggest using the likelihood ratio test because they believe that the Wald test uses an inappropriate variance estimate in its calculation. All that said, the decision between the two tests is still complicated, and the issue remains a point of discussion (see Millar, 2011).

10A.12.6 Classification Results

One of the results available from a logistic regression analysis is a **Classification Table** showing the percentage of the cases whose group membership was correctly classified. We would consult such a table if the model yielded statistically significant prediction of the outcome variable. Recall that we are predicting the probability of a case being a member of the target group (the group coded as 1 in the data file). Given a statistically significant logistic model, common sense (as well as painful experience) tells us that our predictions will not be perfect. It is informative to determine just how well we did by consulting the **Classification Table**. Such a determination is especially useful because it is very possible that the model (applied under a certain "setting") does a better job predicting one of the groups (e.g., the target group) than the other, and it is important for researchers to be aware of such differential successful prediction. The details and nuances of dealing with such information and potentially changing the "setting" to modify the rate of successful classification are discussed more completely starting in Section 10A.14.5.

10A.13 Strategies for Building the Logistic Regression Model

As was the case for ordinary least squares regression, there are several strategies available to generate the logistic regression model. These are analogous to those we have seen for multiple regression. There are somewhat different choices available in binomial and multinomial logistic regression.

10A.13.1 Strategies Available in a Binary Logistic Regression Model

The following strategies for building the model are available in binomial logistic regression. These are available within a hierarchical entry procedure such that any of these methods can be selected to apply to all of the variables entered at any hierarchical step (block of variables).

- *Standard selection method:* In this procedure, we enter all of the predictors simultaneously. Each is evaluated statistically controlling for the effects of the others (i.e., with the others used as covariates). We recommend this strategy unless there is an explicit reason for choosing one of the others in this list.
- *Forward selection (conditional):* This is a stepwise procedure. Entry is based on a statistically significant regression coefficient and removal is based on the conditional parameter estimates associated with the likelihood ratio.
- *Forward selection (likelihood ratio):* This is a stepwise procedure. Entry is based on a statistically significant regression coefficient, and removal is based on the maximum partial likelihood estimates associated with the likelihood ratio.
- *Forward selection (Wald):* This is a stepwise procedure. Entry is based on a statistically significant regression coefficient and removal is based on the probability of the Wald statistic.
- *Backward elimination (conditional):*. All variables are entered and then one variable is removed if warranted at each step. Removal is based on the conditional parameter estimates associated with the likelihood ratio.
- *Backward elimination (likelihood ratio):* All variables are entered and then one variable is removed if warranted at each step. Entry is based on a statistically significant regression coefficient, and removal is based on the maximum partial likelihood estimates associated with the likelihood ratio.
- *Backward elimination (Wald):* All variables are entered and then one variable is removed if warranted at each step. Removal is based on the probability of the Wald statistic.

10A.13.2 Strategies Available in Multinomial Logistic Regression Model

The following strategies for building the model are available in multinomial logistic regression:

- *Standard selection method:* In this procedure, we enter all of the predictors simultaneously. Each is evaluated statistically controlling for the effects of the others (i.e., with the others used as covariates). As with binary logistic regression, this is our suggested strategy.
- *Forward entry:* The variable that is associated with the "most significant" is added to the model at each step. Once entered, variables are not removed. The process ends when none of the remaining variables would significantly contribute to prediction.
- *Backward elimination:* All variables are entered into the model and then one variable is removed if warranted at each step. Variables are removed if their elimination does not substantially change the statistical significance of the model. The "least significant" variable is removed if more than one are not statistically significant.
- *Forward stepwise:* This is a combination of the forward and backward methods starting with an empty model and placing predictors in it.
- *Backward stepwise:* All variables are entered into the model and then the forward and backward methods are combined until all variables remaining in the model contribute significantly to prediction.

10A.14 ROC Analysis

10A.14.1 ROC Analysis: Overview

A receiver operating characteristic (ROC pronounced "R-O-C" rather than "rock") analysis can be applied to a judgment situation in which a decision between two possible events must be made based on a quantitative measure. The ROC analysis provides a statistical assessment of the accuracy of the decision strategy that is used for prediction, but its strong appeal to researchers using binary logistic regression is that its results are also able to document how modifications to the decision strategy would affect classification accuracy. Binary logistic regression aligns exceptionally well with an ROC analysis under the given conditions:

- In binary logistic regression, we have a quantitative measure—the predicted probability of a case being a member of the target group—on which a binary decision is made.
- In binary logistic regression, we decide between two possible events—we classify each case into either the target or reference group based on the predicted probability of a case being a member of the target group.

An ROC analysis is well suited to integrate with binary logistic regression, where there are exactly two groups or outcomes, but it is not applicable to multinomial logistic regression because there are three or more groups or outcomes. To predict group membership in multinomial logistic regression, separate prediction functions are generated for each of the groups, and each case is classified into the group with the highest predicted probability value.

During the Second World War, ROC analysis was used by the U.S. military (Green & Swets, 1966) where radar operators needed to determine if the blips on the screen represented enemy warplanes or something more benign such as a flock of birds. ROC analysis was later applied to signal detection and decision theory in the 1950s (e.g., Barlow, 1957; Macmillan & Creelman, 2005; Swets, 1973; Swets, Tanner, & Birdsall, 1961). In this latter application, research subjects attempt to detect the presence of some stimulus signal against some level of interfering background or noise (e.g., a tone against white noise); it has been suggested that signal detection theory had its origins in the psychophysics research of Gustav Fechner (Link, 1994). Signal detection theory's general thrust was to deal with decisions under circumstances where there was uncertainty of the outcome. Currently, ROC analysis in concert with decision theory is applied extensively in medical research (e.g., Soreide, 2009; Soreide, Korner, & Soreide, 2011).

10A.14.2 ROC Analysis: The Classification Table

Because it is perfectly suited for it, it is not surprising that one of the contexts in which ROC analysis has been applied is binary logistic analysis. Figure 10a.2 provides a binary logistic classification table organized in the manner provided by IBM SPSS (it is more common in the decision arena for the groups to be listed in the reverse order), the outcomes for which are labeled in terms of a decision context and ROC.

Figure 10a.2 Decision Outcome of Binary Choice

		Predicted Group	
		Reference Group	Target Group
Actual Group	**Reference Group**	True Negatives (specificity)	False Positives
	Target Group	False Negatives	True Positives (Sensitivity)

In most research situations, the target group has the condition that we wish to iden-tify (predict) and is thought of as the *positive* outcome; this condition could be newly hired personnel who are successful in completing a required training program, patients who might have a particular immunity or those who are afflicted by a certain disease, convicted offenders who will not re-offend on release from prison, and so on. These cases are distinguished from the corresponding alternative outcome of the respective reference groups, and their status (e.g., those unsuccessful in the training program, those offenders who will commit another crime on release) is labeled as the *negative* outcome.

The cells in the array shown in Figure 10a.2 are labeled with respect to those outcomes and (reading across the rows) are as follows:

- *True negatives:* These are the cases who have been correctly predicted as having the negative outcome. The proportion of all reference group members that is represented by these cases is known as *specificity.*
- *False positives:* These are the cases with the negative outcome (reference group members) who have incorrectly been predicted to have the positive outcome.
- *False negatives:* Members of the target group who have been predicted to have a negative outcome.
- *True positives:* These are the cases who have been correctly predicted as having the positive outcome. The proportion of all reference group members that is represented by these cases is known as *sensitivity.*

10A.14.3 ROC Analysis: The ROC Curve

Perhaps one of the classic visual depictions of human performance in the social and behavioral sciences is the ROC curve, which is usually placed in a graph together with a diagonal line representing a random model that has no predictive power. This curve is a representation of how well group membership can be predicted for combinations of true- and false-positive rates. We show a stylized ROC curve in Figure 10a.3. The axes of the graph are as follows:

- The *X* axis represents the false-positive rate with values between 0 (no false positives) and 1 (100% false positives). It is very often designated as 1 – specificity.
- The *Y* axis represents the true-positive rate with values between 0 (no true positives) and 1 (100% true positives). It is very often designated as sensitivity.

The ROC curves rise from the region of the origin toward the upper-right portion of the graphing area. The flat diagonal line is our visual baseline for random success at predicting group membership, and researchers want the decision marker (one coordinate on the ROC curve) for predicting case membership to lie as far from the diagonal line as is possible or

Figure 10a.3 A Generic ROC Curve

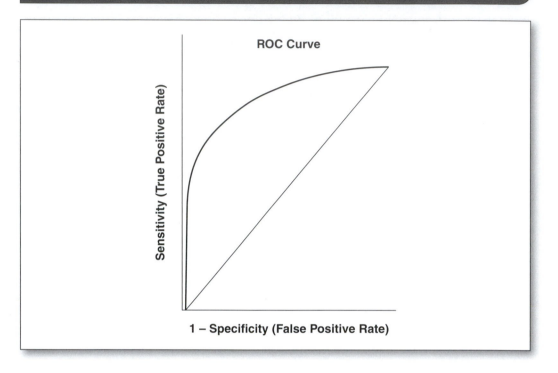

reasonable. Generally speaking, the further the marker (the decision criterion) is from baseline, the more accurate will be the decisions that are made.

The bow of the ROC curve meets the diagonal line depicting the random model at its endpoints. When the false-positive rate (1 − specificity) and the true-positive rate (sensitivity) are both near a value of 0, then we are very close to classification prediction that is essentially random; with both of these near the value of 1, we are also hovering around the diagonal line as well. Using a decision criterion in either of these regions would not be a satisfactory research outcome.

10A.14.4 ROC Analysis: The Area Under the ROC Curve

The degree to which the ROC curve bows away from the random model projection is an indication of how well the model generating the quantitative prediction index, the logistic function in our present circumstance, can discriminate between the two possible outcomes in the study. This degree of bow can be indexed by the area under the curve, often abbreviated in the research literature as AUC. The AUC is also known as the *c statistic* or *c index*.

Table 10a.3 Guidelines for Evaluating Discriminating Ability of the Logistic Model Based on the Area Under the ROC Curve (AUC)

AUC Range	Guideline
.50–.60	No discrimination
.60–.70	Poor
.70–.80	Acceptable/fair/good
.80–.90	Very good
.90 and higher	Excellent

The diagonal line is a good marker for us. Consider the entire area within the axes to represent 100%; we may then say that half of the area (.50 of the area) lies under the diagonal line. An ROC curve that fell very close to the diagonal line would likewise have an AUC value in the range of .50. The area under the ROC curve thus provides an index of how much better than the random model a given logistic function was able to differentiate the groups.

Rubrics for evaluating how well the logistic function can differentiate the groups based on AUC values are available. Mandrekar (2010), for example, provides a set of guidelines of the discriminating ability of the function, but there is no general consensus in the field about this. We present in Table 10a.3 our own guidelines based partly on Mandrekar (2010) but with our own take on this matter as well. Researchers typically hope that their model will exceed an AUC value of .80, celebrate when their AUC hits .90, and stoically accept values in the low to middle .70s.

10A.14.5 ROC Analysis: The Decision Threshold

The ROC curve pictures the overall accuracy of the model, but the success of correctly predicting group membership depends on the location of the particular decision criterion coordinate on the curve. That location would be the *decision threshold* or *cut value* that the researchers have adopted for their study.

We need to establish a decision threshold because the basis of classification—the result obtained from the binary logistic analysis—is a quantitative measure, namely, the predicted probability of a case being a member of the target group (the group coded as 1 in the data file). These probability values range relatively continuously from close to zero to close to 1.00. It is therefore necessary to draw a line in the sand—to identify a probability value (the "setting" as we called it in Section 10A.12.6) that marks out a decision threshold. Cases whose probability value falls below that threshold would be classified as (predicted to be) members of the reference group, and cases whose probability value falls at or above that threshold would be classified as (predicted to be) members of the target group.

Selection of that decision threshold is, to say the least, a delicate matter because it always involves a trade-off in predictive effectiveness. We present a visual schematic in Figure 10a.4 to illustrate this trade-off. Recall that the binary logistic regression model is predicting the probability of a case being a member of the target group. The horizontal axis in Figure 10a.4 is exactly that: the probability of a case belonging to the target group. The reference group and the target group are depicted by overlapping distributions on that horizontal axis. Note that if the distributions did not overlap at all we would have little need to perform a statistical analysis in the first place and if they overlapped completely there would be nothing to gain by performing such an analysis; thus, overlap is the norm in this sort of study.

The goal in a prediction/classification binary logistic regression study is to predict group membership, and the basis for that prediction is what the logistic function

Figure 10a.4 Predicting Group Membership With Two Different Cut Thresholds as Shown by the Tinted Arrows

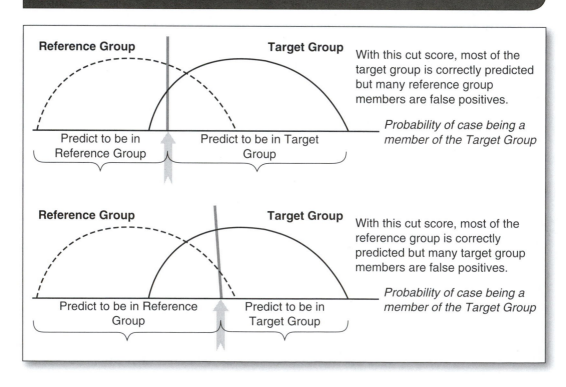

generates—the predicted probability of belonging to the target group, that is, the chances that a case is coded as 1 in the data file. Any case whose predicted probability value falls below the cut score is predicted to belong to the reference group; any case whose predicted probability value falls at or above the cut score is predicted to belong to the target group.

Here is the trade-off: Because the groups overlap, we cannot identify a cut value that will provide us with perfect prediction. We illustrate the situation for two different classification thresholds in Figure 10a.4.

In the upper graph, the cut value, shown by the tinted arrow and vertical line, is situated toward the far left portion of the target group's distribution—cases whose probability was equal to or greater than that value would result in them being classified as a target group member, and cases whose probability was less than that value would result in them being classified as a reference group member. Under this threshold, we would do very well in correctly predicting membership of cases in the target group, misclassifying only a relatively small percentage of them; that is, we would have a high rate of true positives (high sensitivity). At the same time, a relatively large proportion of reference group members would be misclassified as belonging in (predicted as belonging to) the target group because their scores fall at or to the right of (the scores are equal to or greater than) the decision threshold; thus, we would have a relatively high rate of false positives (the value of 1 − specificity would be relatively high).

In the lower graph in Figure 10a.4, the cut value is situated toward the far right portion of the reference group's distribution. Under this decision threshold, we would do very well in correctly predicting membership of cases in the reference group, misclassifying only a relatively small percentage of them; that is, we would have a high rate of true negatives (we would have high specificity). At the same time, our rate of correctly classifying target group members (true-positive predictions or sensitivity) would be relatively low and our false-negative rate would therefore rise.

We learn from this illustration that more accurately predicting one group's membership will, at least to a certain extent, reduce the accuracy of predicting the other. How well we are able to achieve high levels of either sensitivity or specificity depends on the value we use for our threshold criterion, and the effect of using any given threshold value depends on the shape of the ROC curve.

10A.14.6 ROC Analysis: Coordinates of the ROC Curve

An informed decision about where to set the threshold value can be made based on the results of an ROC analysis. In addition to obtaining the AUC value and the ROC curve, IBM SPSS allows us to obtain a range of coordinates (combinations of true positives or sensitivity values and false positives or 1 − specificity values) that define the ROC curve. Associated with each set is the predicted probability of a case being classified as belonging to the target group. It is the cutoff based on these probabilities that we

Table 10a.4 Coordinates of an ROC Curve

Predicted Probability of a Case Being in Target Group	True Positive Rate (Sensitivity)	False Positive Rate (1 – Specificity)	Positive Likelihood Ratio (True Positive Rate/ False Positive Rate)	Positive Predictive Value (# True Positives/ # True Positives + # False Positives)
.150	.99	.98	1.01	.62
.450	.89	.60	1.48	.70
.475	.87	.48	1.81	.74
.500	.80	.40	2.00	.76
.525	.77	.28	2.75	.81
.550	.74	.22	3.36	.84
.900	.10	.02	5.00	.90

Note. The positive predictive value is based on a total of 400 target group cases and 250 reference group cases in this fictional example.

use as our decision threshold. We show a simplified version of some fictitious output similar to that provided by IBM SPSS in Table 10a.4. The first three columns mimic the IBM SPSS output. To that output, we added two additional columns and will describe them after explaining the IBM SPSS output.

10A.14.6.1 Coordinates of the ROC Curve: The Plotted Values

The first column in Table 10a.4 is the predicted probability of a case being a member of the target group. These probabilities are generated from the binary logistic regression model. We have presented "adjacent" probabilities between .450 and .550 and then a more extreme probability in either direction across a gap that we have left empty to visually simplify the displayed information. These probabilities correspond to classification decision rules. Note that the "adjacent" probabilities are not continuous. This lack of continuity occurs because the point is to classify cases, and cases are counted only in whole number increments; thus, the probabilities corresponding to fractions of cases drop out of the compilation. Associated with each probability are the true-positive and false-positive rates. These are summary statistics of the frequencies in the classification table.

To illustrate how to read the information in Table 10a.4, consider the middle row where we see the probability of a case being predicted to be in the target group as .500. Using this value as the classification criterion means that if a case has a predicted probability as computed from the logistic function between .000 and .499, that case will be classified (predicted) as a reference group member; if a case has a probability as computed from the logistic function between .500 and .999, that case will be classified (predicted) as a target group member.

The true-positive rate (sensitivity) and false-positive rate (1 – specificity) are shown in the second and third columns, respectively, of Table 10a.4. These are the values that are plotted as the data points for the ROC curve: sensitivity on the Y axis and (1 – specificity) on the X axis. To illustrate, consider the probability of .500 as the threshold criterion. Under this setting, the true-positive rate (shown in the second column of Table 10a.4) would be .80; that is, we would correctly classify 80% of the target group members as being in the target group (and therefore we would wrongly classify 20% of the target group members). Furthermore, the false-positive rate (shown in the third column of Table 10a.4) would be .40; that is, we would incorrectly classify 40% of the reference group members as being in the target group (and therefore we would correctly classify 60% of the reference group members). The coordinate ($X = .40$, $Y = .80$) is one of the data points on the ROC curve. Generally, the ROC curve is what we see when we connect all the data point coordinates shown in Table 10a.4.

10A.14.6.2 Coordinates of the ROC Curve: The Positive Likelihood Ratio

The fourth column of Table 10a.4 displays the *positive likelihood ratio*, something that is not supplied in the IBM SPSS output (there is also a negative likelihood ratio, but we will focus here on true-positive and false-positive classifications). The positive likelihood ratio is the ratio of the true-positive rate to the false-positive rate. For example, the decision criterion of .500 is associated with a true-positive rate of .80 and a false-positive rate of .40, yielding a positive likelihood ratio of .80/.40 or 2.00; thus, we learn that by using a .500 decision threshold, we would achieve twice as many true positives as false positives. The likelihood ratio is commonly used by researchers to help assess the consequences of using a given classification cut value (e.g., Chatburn, 2011; Gorunescu, 2011). It provides an efficient way to compare the classification effects of various decision cut values.

10A.14.6.3 Coordinates of the ROC Curve: The Positive Predictive Value

The last column of Table 10a.4 displays the *positive predictive value*, another ratio not supplied in the IBM SPSS output (similar to the likelihood ratio, there is also a negative predictive value, but our focus here is on true-positive and false-positive classifications). The positive predictive value is used extensively in evaluating classification results in a variety of research fields (e.g., Flicker et al., 1997; Jewell, 2011; Klee et al., 2000; Mandel et al., 2000). It is computed as the ratio of the number of true-positive cases in the classification results to the combined total of the number of true-positive cases and the number of false-positive cases in the classification results. We interpret it as the chances that cases classified in (predicted as being members of) the target group truly belong to that group; higher values of the positive predictive value are therefore associated with greater confidence in a positive classification.

We can illustrate how to compute this value by using the decision threshold of .500 as an example. The true-positive rate is .80 in this fictional example. Thus, of a target group containing 400 cases, 80% of them would be correctly classified under a decision threshold of .500; we therefore would have .80 * 400 or 320 of them as true positives. The false-positive rate in our example is .40. Thus, if the reference group contained 250 cases, 40% of them would be falsely classified as target group members under a decision threshold of .500; we therefore would have .40 * 250 or 100 of them as false positives. The positive predictive value is therefore 320/(320 + 100), which computes to .76.

10A.14.6.4 Coordinates of the ROC Curve: Using All of the Information

As can be seen from Table 10a.4, the positive likelihood ratio and the positive predictive value are very much in tune with each other: Higher values represent, from the positive perspective, better outcomes (we have proportionally more true than false positives). The general strategy, then, is to select a classification threshold with a relatively large positive likelihood ratio and a reasonably high positive predictive value so that we have proportionally fewer false-positive decisions. That strategy, however, comes with a caveat.

The likelihood ratio and predictive value are quite useful but should not be used alone, as the absolute rates of true and false positives themselves are often as important as the ratio. Examining the classification cut value of .900 can illustrate why. The positive likelihood ratio informs us that we have 5.00 times more true than false positives and the positive predictive value is a very impressive .90, what appears on the surface to be a very desirable outcome. At the same time, our sensitivity is only .10—we can correctly predict the proper group membership of 10% of the target group. That is not a very high true-positive rate. But at that rate, our false-positive rate is extremely low at .02—we will predict only 2% of the reference group incorrectly as target group members.

Contrast the decision criteria of .500 and .900 to that of .550 in Table 10a.4. The threshold of .550 is associated with a positive likelihood ratio of 3.36 (much higher than the 2.00 value associated with the decision threshold of .500 although much lower than the likelihood ratio of 5.00 associated with the decision threshold of .900), and its positive predictive value is .84 (higher than the .76 value associated with the decision threshold of .500 although lower than the .90 value associated with the decision threshold of .900). At a threshold of .550, our sensitivity (true-positive rate) is .74 and our false-positive rate is .22.

10A.14.7 ROC Analysis: Decision Making
Using the Coordinates of the ROC Curve

So how do researchers decide on the decision threshold they wish to use to classify cases? The answer is "It depends." The table of coordinates of the ROC curve, by displaying the consequences of using a range of decision criteria, can serve as the basis for researchers to decide on the criterion they wish to adopt in their study, but researchers will ultimately need to evaluate the potential alternative decision criteria by considering the application arena in which they are working. The following two scenarios suggest some of the dynamics that might enter into the decision of what criterion one might wish to adopt.

In the first scenario, a medical research team hypothesizes that a new diagnostic procedure can potentially identify early symptoms of a life-threatening disorder. Detection of the symptoms would then lead physicians to perform additional diagnostic tests. Under these circumstances, a very high premium might be placed on a true-positive outcome, whereas the consequences of false positives (increased medical laboratory time, patient concern, and medical costs for what may be unnecessary tests) are not as dire. Thus, it might be appropriate to establish a threshold of .450 based on Table 10a.4 to obtain a true-positive rate of 89% and accept an associate false-positive rate of 60%; even decision criteria lower than .450 (not shown in Table 10a.4) might be worth considering as well.

In the second scenario, job candidates are put through an extensive battery of tests to become an air traffic controller. A binary logistic regression analyses is used to predict success. Because selecting someone who will fail at the job could cost the lives of most passengers on the plane that crashed due to an error committed by an air traffic controller, it would seem that every effort should be made to keep the false-positive rate low. Given the high level of potential risk involved in a false-positive classification, an argument could be made for establishing a .900 classification criterion. The advantage of using this criterion is that the goal of maximizing the safety of the flying public would be achieved (we would have only a 2% false-positive rate). Its disadvantage, however, is that a large proportion of qualified job applicants would be rejected (we would have only a 10% true-positive rate). If the acceptance rate of truly qualified job candidates was sufficiently low to discourage enough qualified individuals from applying—thus creating unfilled vacancies and cancelled flights as a result—perhaps the .900 cut would be judged as too drastic. We cannot resolve these issues here, but we bring them up because they enter into the cost–benefit or risk analysis in which researchers and administrators would need to engage once the ROC analysis was performed.

10A.14.8 ROC Analysis: The Decision Threshold in Binary Logistic Regression

In performing a binary logistic analysis, the default threshold criterion in IBM SPSS is a probability level of .500. That threshold might be appropriate for many research studies, especially those that have no immediate practical application and so it may be less necessary for a risk analysis such as we have just described to be conducted. But there is a dialog window in the analysis setup where we can specify our cut score, and we suggest that in many circumstances the selection of a decision criterion should be informed by the results of the ROC analysis.

10A.15 Recommended Readings

Allison, P. D. (1999b). Comparing logit and probit coefficients across groups. *Sociological Methods and Research, 28,* 186–208.

Cox, D. R., & Snell, E. J. (1989). *Analysis of binary data* (2nd ed.). London, England: Chapman & Hall.

DeMaris, A. (1992). *Logit modeling: Practical applications.* Newbury Park, CA: Sage.

Estrella, A. (1998). A new measure of fit for equations with dichotomous dependent variables. *Journal of Business and Economic Statistics, 16,* 198–205.

Fox, J. (2000). *Multiple and generalized nonparametric regression.* Thousand Oaks, CA: Sage.

Hosmer, D. W., Jr., & Lemeshow, S. (2000). *Applied logistic regression* (2nd ed.). New York, NY: Wiley.

Menard, S. (2002). *Applied logistic regression analysis* (2nd ed.). Thousand Oaks, CA: Sage.

Pampel, F. C. (2000). *Logistic regression: A primer.* Thousand Oaks, CA: Sage.

Rice, J. C. (1994). Logistic regression: An introduction. In B. Thompson (Ed.), *Advances in social science methodology* (Vol. 3, pp. 191–245). Greenwich, CT: JAI Press.

Wright, R. E. (1995). Logistic regression. In L. G. Grimm & P. R. Yarnold (Eds.), *Reading and understanding multivariate statistics* (pp. 217–244). Washington, DC: American Psychological Association.

Binary and Multinomial Logistic Regression and ROC Analysis Using IBM SPSS

10B.1 Binary Logistic Regression

10B.1.1 Numerical Example

In binary logistic regression, the outcome variable is represented by only two categories. Here, we will use **Program Success** as our outcome variable. The target or response outcome category is **program_success**, coded as 1 in the data file; it will be compared with the reference category of **no success**, coded as 0 in the data file. One predictor variable is **gender_F1**. The focus predictor category is **female**, coded as 1 in the data file (hence the name of the variable to remind us of the coding); it will be compared with **male**, which is coded as 0. Our second predictor is the quantitative variable named **conscientious**, which was assessed on a 10-point scale with higher values indicating greater conscientiousness. The data are contained in the file named **Program Success**.

10B.1.2 Binary Logistic Regression Analysis Setup

From the main menu, select **Analyze ➔ Regression ➔ Binary Logistic**, which opens up the **Logistic Regression** main dialog box as shown in Figure 10b.1. We place **program_success** in the **Dependent** panel. The two predictors, **gender_F1** and **conscientious**, are placed in the **Covariates** panel. We will enter these two predictors simultaneously, so we leave the default **Method** at **Enter**.

Figure 10b.1 The Main Binary Logistic Dialog Window

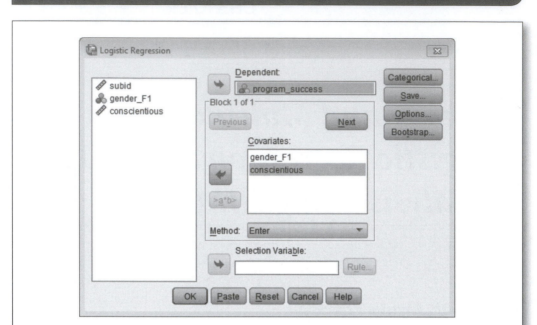

Select the **Options** pushbutton. As shown in Figure 10b.2, under **Statistics and Plots** we have marked the **Hosmer-Lemeshow goodness-of-fit** and the **CI for exp (B) at 95%**; this latter selection will give us the 95% confidence interval for our odds ratios. For **Display**, we have kept the default showing the results **At each step** even though under the **Enter Method** there is only one step (choosing **At last step** gives us the same output here). Keep the default on the checkbox to **Include constant in the model**. For this analysis, we will keep the default **Classification cutoff** at 0.5; in Section 10B.2, we will see how to use an ROC analysis to evaluate and possibly change the value of this decision threshold. Click **Continue** to return to the main dialog window, and click **OK** to perform the analysis.

10B.1.3 Binary Logistic Regression Analysis Output

10B.1.3.1 Administrative Output

Figure 10b.3 shows what we are calling administrative output. The upper table labeled **Case Processing Summary** provides information on the number of cases in the analysis and is useful as a check of our expected number of cases. The **Dependent Variable Encoding**

Figure 10b.2   The Options Dialog Window of Binary Logistic Regression

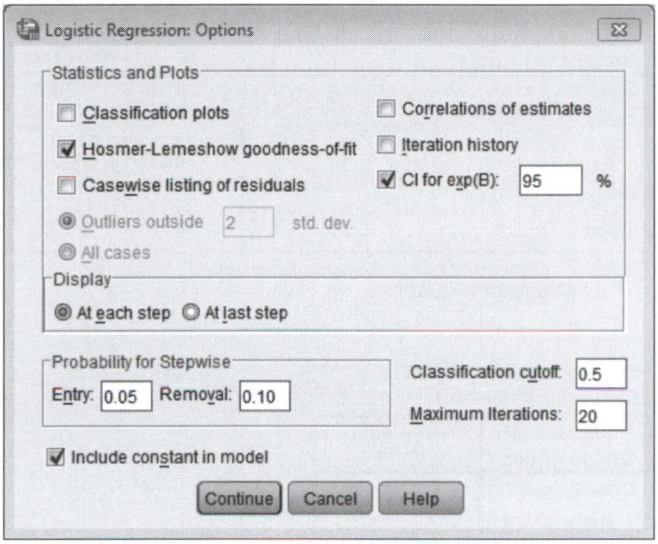

table documents what IBM SPSS has done with our coding schema: It "internally recodes" for the duration of the analysis our binary outcome variable as follows:

- The lower value is assigned a code of 0 and becomes the reference category.
- The higher code is assigned a value of 1 and becomes the target category.

Not wishing to give up any control to a software application, we have coded our variable originally in the proper way. Note that our coding schema is preserved in the "internal recode" that was made.

10B.1.3.2 Block 0 Output

Figure 10b.4 presents the results of what IBM SPSS calls **Block 0**. This is the intercept-only model, computed with only the constant in the equation but without any of the predictor variables included. The **Classification Table** is the top table and simply counts the number of cases in each binary outcome. With only the intercept in the model, our prediction is based only on the frequencies in that table: 141 cases were not successful and 278 cases were. Thus, if we had no additional information, our best guess is that a program participant would be successful, and our classification would be 66.3% correct.

Figure 10b.3 Administrative Output

Case Processing Summary

Unweighted Cases[a]		N	Percent
Selected Cases	Included in Analysis	419	98.6
	Missing Cases	6	1.4
	Total	425	100.0
Unselected Cases		0	.0
Total		425	100.0

a. If weight is in effect, see classification table for the total number of cases.

Dependent Variable Encoding

Original Value	Internal Value
0 no success	0
1 success	1

Figure 10b.4 Block 0: The Intercept-Only Model

Block 0: Beginning Block

Classification Table[a,b]

			Predicted		
			program_success		
Observed			0 no success	1 success	Percentage Correct
Step 0	program_success	0 no success	0	141	.0
		1 success	0	278	100.0
	Overall Percentage				66.3

a. Constant is included in the model.
b. The cut value is .500

Variables in the Equation

		B	S.E.	Wald	df	Sig.	Exp(B)
Step 0	Constant	.679	.103	43.113	1	.000	1.972

Variables not in the Equation

			Score	df	Sig.
Step 0	Variables	gender_F1	100.750	1	.000
		conscientious	28.605	1	.000
	Overall Statistics		114.126	2	.000

Note that 278 is approximately twice as large as 141 (two thirds of the sample are successful and one third are not successful). It should therefore be no surprise that the odds ratio shown in the middle **Variables in the Equation** table under the column labeled **Exp (B)** is 1.972; this informs us that, with no information about the participants, a random program participant is 1.972 (almost twice) as likely to be successful as opposed to being unsuccessful in the program. Just to complete our understanding, the bottom table called **Variables not in the Equation** reminds us that we have yet to use our independent variables to predict program success.

10B.1.3.3 Model Evaluation Output

Figure 10b.5 shows the tables evaluating the model with the predictors included. This is **Block 1** or **Step 1** and is our only step because we entered both of our predictors together.

Figure 10b.5 Evaluation of the Model That Includes the Predictors

Omnibus Tests of Model Coefficients

		Chi–square	df	Sig.
Step 1	Step	121.109	2	.000
	Block	121.109	2	.000
	Model	121.109	2	.000

Model Summary

Step	−2 Log likelihood	Cox & Snell R Square	Nagelkerke R Square
1	414.119[a]	.251	.348

a. Estimation terminated at iteration number 5 because parameter estimates changed by less than .001.

Hosmer and Lemeshow Test

Step	Chi–square	df	Sig.
1	7.375	7	.391

Contingency Table for Hosmer and Lemeshow Test

		program_success = 0 no success		program_success = 1 success		
		Observed	Expected	Observed	Expected	Total
Step 1	1	28	30.583	12	9.417	40
	2	27	29.131	18	15.869	45
	3	29	24.721	15	19.279	44
	4	25	24.565	27	27.435	52
	5	13	11.858	36	37.142	49
	6	10	7.087	40	42.913	50
	7	4	3.616	28	28.384	32
	8	2	5.522	56	52.478	58
	9	3	3.917	46	45.083	49

Had we chosen to use a hierarchical strategy with more predictors, we would have had multiple blocks to view.

The top table is the **Omnibus Tests of Model Coefficients** containing the model chi-square, a statistical test of the null hypothesis that all the coefficients are zero. It is equivalent to the overall F test in linear regression. The **Model** chi-square value (in the last row) is 121.109. In this example, the null hypothesis is rejected because the significance is less than .05 (shown by the .000 under the **Sig.** heading). We would thus conclude that the set of independent variables significantly predicts the outcome. The other two tests, **Block** and **Step**, have the same value as the **Model** statistic because all the variables were entered together.

The **Model Summary** table, also shown in Figure 10b.5, presents three measures of how well the logistic regression model fits the data. With all the variables in the model, the goodness-of-fit **−2 Log likelihood** (−2LL) statistic is 414.119. This fit statistic is usually not interpreted directly but is useful when comparing different logistic models. The **Cox & Snell** pseudo R^2 is .251 and the **Nagelkerke** pseudo R^2, which is always the higher of the two, is .348. Based on the **Nagelkerke** pseudo R^2, we would thus conclude that about a third of the variance of program success is explained by the variables in our model.

The **Hosmer and Lemeshow Test** provides a formal test assessing whether the predicted probabilities match the observed probabilities. Researchers are seeking a nonsignificant p value for this test because the goal of the research is to derive predictors that will accurately predict the actual probabilities. If the predictions are consonant with the observed values, then there should be little discrepancy between them; that is, there should not be a significant difference between them. Thus, researchers do not want to reject the null hypothesis (the null hypothesis is that the predictions and observed values do not differ). In this example, the goodness-of-fit statistic is 7.375, distributed (and tested) as a chi-square value, and is associated with a p value of .391, indicating an acceptable (close enough) match between predicted and observed probabilities.

The **Contingency Table for Hosmer and Lemeshow Test**, shown in the bottom table of Figure 10b.5, demonstrates more details of the **Hosmer and Lemeshow** test. This output divides the data into approximately 10 equal groups (9 groups for this example) based on the outcome variable. These groups are defined by increasing order of success in the program and (unfortunately for a student just learning to read logistic regression output) are called "steps" in the table. The first group (**Step 1**) represents those participants least likely to succeed. The observed frequencies were that 28 cases did not succeed and 12 cases did succeed. Notice for all the groups how closely the observed and the expected frequencies (based on the prediction model) match. This is why the **Hosmer and Lemeshow** test was not statistically significant; this is a desirable result.

10B.1.3.4 Classification Table and Odds Ratio

The results of using the model to predict program success are shown in Figure 10b.6. The **Variables in the Equation** table presents the b coefficient (written as an uppercase "B" by

Figure 10b.6   The Coefficients Tables and Classification

Variables in the Equation

		B	S.E.	Wald	df	Sig.	Exp(B)	95% C.I.for EXP(B)	
								Lower	Upper
Step 1[a]	gender_F1	2.218	.249	79.411	1	.000	9.191	5.643	14.971
	conscientious	.191	.047	16.620	1	.000	1.211	1.104	1.328
	Constant	−1.689	.356	22.495	1	.000	.185		

a. Variable(s) entered on step 1: gender_F1, conscientious.

Classification Table[a]

			Predicted		
			program_success		Percentage Correct
Observed			0 no success	1 success	
Step 1	program_success	0 no success	84	57	59.6
		1 success	45	233	83.8
Overall Percentage					75.7

a. The cut value is .500

IBM SPSS) and the standard error (S.E.) of b for each predictor. These coefficients indicate the amount of change expected in the log odds when there is a 1-unit change in the predictor variable with all the other variables in the model held constant. A coefficient close to 0 suggests that there is no change due to the predictor variable.

The **Sig.** column represents the p value for testing whether a predictor is significantly associated with seeking psychotherapy exclusive of any of the other predictors. The logistic coefficients can be used in a manner similar to linear regression coefficients to generate predicted values. In this example,

$$\text{program success} = -1.689 + 2.218\ (\textbf{gender\_F1}) + 0.191\ (\textbf{conscientious}).$$

Conscientiousness is a quantitative variable that can take on a wide range of values, and thus, the expression 0.191 (**conscientious**) can likewise take on a wide range of values. But because gender is dichotomously coded, there are only two values possible for the expression 2.218 (**gender_F1**): For females (who are coded as 1), the value of the expression will be 2.218 * 1 or 2.218; for males (who are coded as 0), the value of the expression will be 2.218 * 0 or 0.

The **Exp (B)** column provides the odds ratios associated with each predictor (adjusting for the other predictor) with the 95% confidence interval associated with each provided in the final two columns. The adjusted odds ratio for gender is 9.191, although there is a relatively wide confidence interval surrounding this estimate. Taken at its face value, however, this odds ratio indicates that females (because they were coded as 1 to make them the research focus) are 9.191 times more likely than males in this sample to be successful in the program, controlling for conscientiousness.

The adjusted odds ratio for conscientiousness is 1.211 with a somewhat narrow confidence interval. Because conscientiousness is a quantitatively assessed variable, we can interpret this odds ratio of 1.211 to mean that an increase of 1 on the conscientiousness measure increases the odds of program success by 1.211 times, controlling for gender. Using a conscientiousness score of 1 as a comparison base (it's one of the lowest scores in the data file, and we need to compare something with something else when talking about an odds ratio), we can say that the odds of program success are 1.211 times greater for a person who had a conscientiousness score of 2 than for a person with a conscientiousness score of 1. Any score can serve as a base. To compute the odds ratio for a different conscientiousness value, one multiplies the regression coefficient by the size of the increase over a base score before raising e to the power of the coefficient.

The **Classification Table** is presented in Figure 10b.6 and indicates how well the model classifies cases into the two categories of the outcome variable. The overall predictive accuracy is 75.7%, although the model predicted better for success (83.8%) than for no success (59.6%) due in large part to the nearly 2:1 ratio of success to no success. Recall from Block 0 that without considering any of our predictors, the likelihood or probability of a correct prediction was 66.3%. We can now see that, with our predictors included in the model, the overall predictive accuracy of 75.7% appears to be a noticeable, if not breathtaking, improvement.

10B.1.4 Reporting the Results of Binary Logistic Regression

A standard binary logistic regression was used to model the binary variable of success in the Compulsive Researchers Rehabilitation Program (using unsuccessful completion of the program as the reference category). The predictor variables in this study were the binary variable of gender with females as the focus category and the quantitative variable of conscientiousness, with higher scores indicating greater levels of conscientiousness. Based on a classification threshold predicted probability of target group membership as .5, results of the logistic analysis indicated that the two-predictor model provided a statistically significant prediction of success, $\chi^2(2, N = 419) = 121.109$, $p < .001$. The Nagelkerke pseudo R^2 indicated that the model accounted for approximately 35% of the total variance. Classification success for the cases based on a classification cutoff value of .500 for predicting membership in the successful group was moderately high, with an overall prediction success rate of 75.7% and correct prediction rates of 83.8% for successful program participants and 59.6% for those not successful in the program.

Table 10b.1 presents the partial regression coefficients, the Wald test, odds ratio [Exp(B)], and the 95% confidence intervals (CI) for odds ratios for each predictor. The Wald test indicated that both gender and conscientiousness were statistically significant predictors of success. The influence of gender was strong; females were approximately nine times (CI = 5.643, 14.971) more likely than males to succeed in the program, adjusting for conscientiousness. For each single-point increase in the conscientiousness score, there was a 1.211 times greater likelihood of program success, controlling for gender.

Table 10b.1 Binary Logistic Regression Results

Model	b	SE-b	Wald	df	Exp (B)	95% CI Exp (B)
Intercept*	−1.689	0.356	22.495	1	0.185	
Gender*	2.218	0.249	79.411	1	9.191	5.643–14.971
Conscientiousness*	0.191	0.047	16.620	1	1.211	1.104–1.328

Note. The dependent variable was program success with success as the target category and no success as the reference category; females were the focus group of the Gender variable; Nagelkerke $R^2 = .348$.
* $p < .05$.

10B.2 ROC Analysis

10B.2.1 Save Predicted Probabilities From the Logistic Regression

We will perform an ROC analysis on the binary logistic regression example we described in Section 10B.1. As the initial step in this ROC analysis, it is necessary to repeat the binary regression analysis with the exception that we now wish to save the predicted probability values of belonging to the target group (the group coded as 1) for each case. From the main menu, select **Analyze** ➔ **Regression** ➔ **Binary Logistic**. Place **program_success** in the **Dependent** panel and place **gender_F1** and **conscientious** in the **Covariates** panel.

Select the **Save** pushbutton, and check **Probabilities** in the **Predicted Values** area of the **Save** window as shown in Figure 10b.7. Click **Continue** to return to the main dialog window, and click **OK** to perform the analysis.

The results of this analysis are exactly the same as we have discussed in Section 10B.1; the only difference is that the predicted values are now added as a variable named **PRE_1**

Figure 10b.7 The Save Dialog Window of Binary Logistic Regression

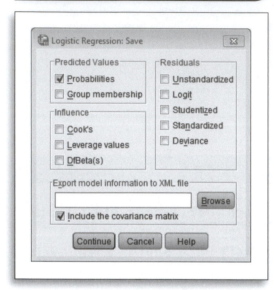

(this stands for "predicted values, first analysis") to the data file. We show a portion of the data file in Figure 10b.8. The **PRE_1** values are the predicted probabilities of a case belonging to the target group. Any probability lower than the threshold criterion is classified by the software as a reference group member, and any probability equal to or higher than the threshold criterion is classified by the software as a target group member.

The prediction of group membership is easy once we know the threshold value. As this was what we did in the analysis described in Section 10B.1, we kept it simple by not specifying such a value. Our silence was taken by IBM SPSS as an acceptance of its default value of .500; this cut value is provided in a footnote to the

Figure 10b.8 A portion of the Data File With the Predicted Probabilities Saved as PRE_1

	subid	program_success	gender_F1	conscientious	PRE_1
1	1	1	1	10	.92005
2	2	0	0	6	.36803
3	3	1	1	8	.88699
4	4	1	0	6	.36803
5	5	0	0	4	.28426
6	6	1	1	10	.92005
7	7	1	1	9	.90480
8	8	0	0	6	.36803
9	9	0	0	6	.36803
10	10	0	0	3	.24698
11	11	1	1	8	.88699
12	12	1	1	0	.62932
13	13	1	1	9	.90480
14	14	1	1	4	.78496
15	15	1	1	4	.78496
16	16	1	1	4	.78496
17	17	1	1	5	.81551
18	18	1	0	9	.50837
19	19	0	1	4	.78496
20	20	0	0	3	.24698
21	21	1	1	8	.88699
22	22	1	1	9	.90480
23	23	1	1	7	.86634

classification table shown in Figure 10b.6. To illustrate how the decision threshold works, consider the first two cases shown in the data file in Figure 10b.8. **Subid 1** has a probability of .92005 of belonging to the target group and, with a cut value of .500, would be classified (predicted) as belonging to that group (a true-positive classification). **Subid 2** has a probability of .36803 of belonging to the reference group and, with a cut value of .500, would be classified (predicted) as belonging to that group (a true-negative classification).

10B.2.2 An ROC Analysis Is Worth Considering

As we discussed in Section 10B.1, the binary logistic regression analysis resulted in an overall correct percentage classification rate of 75.7% (see Figure 10b.6). But a more detailed examination of the classification results from the standpoint of ROC is informative. Our true-positive rate (sensitivity) was 83.3%, suggesting a very effective prediction outcome. However, our true-negative rate (specificity) was a rather less impressive 59.6%; that is, with only two possible outcomes, flipping an unbiased coin would probably yield a true-negative rate of about 50%, a value not all that far below what we were able to achieve here.

We can approach the issue of potentially revising our decision criterion from at least two possible directions. First, we can ask what the risk is of false-positive classifications. Given that our rate here is equal to 40.4% (1 – specificity), classifying an unsuccessful case as someone who is successful might be quite costly depending on the program under study. Under these circumstances, we might want to explore alternative decision thresholds that would provide proportionally fewer false-positive classifications. Second, we can ask if our prediction model can be made more effective by reducing the false-positive rate while preserving a decent sensitivity level. To explore this option, we would want to determine if an alternative decision threshold might be invoked. From either direction, we would be led to an ROC analysis where we can determine the effects of a range of decision criteria.

10B.2.3 Performing the ROC Analysis

From the main menu, select **Analyze ➜ ROC Curve**. This opens the main dialog window as shown in Figure 10b.9. Move the variable **PRE_1** (predicted probabilities that we saved from the logistic regression analysis) into the **Test Variable** panel. The **State Variable** is our outcome variable **program_success**, and for the **Value of State Variable** type 1 (the target group that the **PRE_1** values are predicting) in the panel.

As also shown in Figure 10b.9, select the following under **Display**:

- **ROC Curve:** This causes the ROC curve to be provided in the output.
- **With diagonal reference line:** This causes the diagonal reference line to be included with the ROC curve.

- **Standard error and confidence interval**: The primary piece of output for us here is the area under the ROC curve.
- **Coordinate points of the ROC Curve**: This provides a set of possible decision criteria and the effects of applying them.

Click **OK** to perform the analysis.

10B.2.4 The Output From the ROC Analysis

The ROC curve is shown in Figure 10b.10. The false-positive rate (1 − specificity) is represented on the X axis, and the true-positive rate (sensitivity) is represented on the Y axis. The curve has the expected bow shape, although it could be more pronounced. This visual impression is reinforced by the proportion of the total AUC (or c statistic). In the table below the ROC curve in Figure 10b.10, we see under **Area** the value of **.812**. Based on our guidelines in Table 10a.3, we have just crossed into the very good discriminating ability of the logistic model, and most researchers would not complain about that result. However, its standard error is .022, and a 95% confidence interval would subsume 1.96 * .022 or .043 standard error units on either side. Placing this interval around our obtained AUC gives

Figure 10b.9 The Main Receiver Operating Characteristic Curve Dialog Window

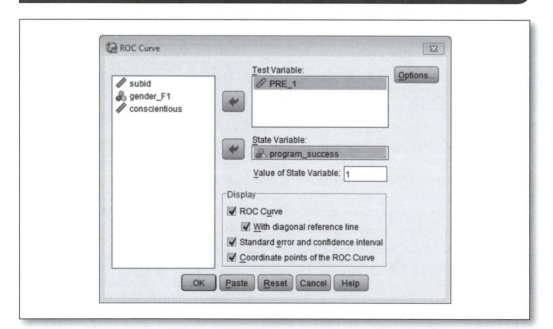

Figure 10b.10   The Receiver Operating Characteristic Curve and the Area Under It

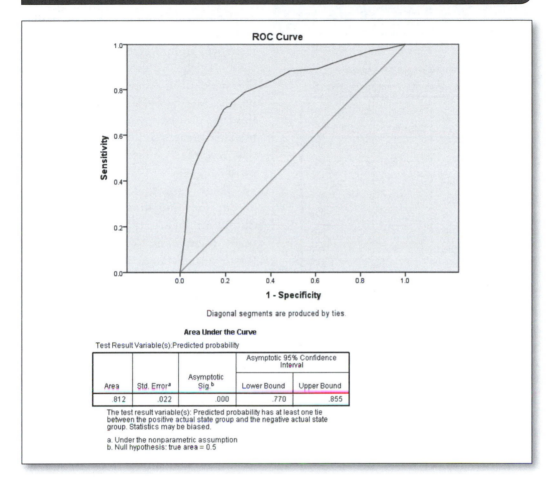

Diagonal segments are produced by ties.

Area Under the Curve

Test Result Variable(s):Predicted probability

Area	Std. Error[a]	Asymptotic Sig.[b]	Asymptotic 95% Confidence Interval	
			Lower Bound	Upper Bound
.812	.022	.000	.770	.855

The test result variable(s): Predicted probability has at least one tie between the positive actual state group and the negative actual state group. Statistics may be biased.

a. Under the nonparametric assumption
b. Null hypothesis: true area = 0.5

us an interval of .769 to .855; thus, we are probably someplace in the good to very good range (see Table 10a.3) for the discriminating ability of the model.

The coordinates of selected points along the ROC curve are shown in Figure 10b.11 in the right two columns of the **Coordinates of the Curve** output. We can find the classification criterion represented by our default logistic regression model by computing the sensitivity and 1 – specificity rates. The computation is as follows:

- **Sensitivity** is the true-positive rate. From the classification results in Figure 10b.6, we can see that the **Percentage Correct** value for the **success** (the target) groups was 83.8% or a sensitivity value of .838. By most standards, this represents a very good true-positive proportion.

Figure 10b.11 The Coordinate Values of the Receiver Operating Characteristic Curve

Coordinates of the Curve

Test Result Variable(s):Predicted probability

Positive if Greater Than or Equal To[a]	Sensitivity	1 - Specificity
.0000000	1.000	1.000
.1693545	.996	.986
.1979602	.993	.965
.2300538	.982	.922
.2656209	.971	.844
.3045057	.957	.801
.3463915	.935	.730
.3907960	.892	.610
.4370819	.881	.482
.4844874	.838	.404
.5321732	.788	.284
.5926505	.741	.227
.6510411	.727	.220
.6930913	.723	.206
.7321644	.712	.191
.7679341	.687	.177
.8002352	.651	.163
.8290458	.612	.135
.8544608	.565	.106
.8766628	.468	.064
.8958931	.367	.035
.9124266	.165	.021
1.0000000	.000	.000

The test result variable(s): Predicted probability has at least one tie between the positive actual state group and the negative actual state group.

a. The smallest cutoff value is the minimum observed test value minus 1, and the largest cutoff value is the maximum observed test value plus 1. All the other cutoff values are the averages of two consecutive ordered observed test values.

• **Specificity** is the true-negative rate. From the classification results in Figure 10b.6, we can see that the **Percentage Correct** value for the **no success** (the reference) group was 59.6% or a sensitivity value of .596. We can therefore compute the value of 1 − specificity (our false-positive rate) as .404. By many standards, this false-positive rate is relatively high and in many research contexts would be a value that researchers might wish to lower if possible.

These coordinates (.838 and .404) are in the **Coordinates of the Curve** output in Figure 10b.11, and we have made them easy to find by enclosing them in a rectangle. These coordinates correspond to a decision threshold of .4844874 as shown in the leftmost column under the heading **Positive if Greater Than or Equal To**. This value is not exactly equal to the default cut value of .500 because the process of classification presumes whole numbers (even IBM SPSS cannot classify a third of a case). That is, if the designated cut value does not result in classifying whole numbers of cases, the decision threshold is moved to the nearest decimal value that permits us to keep the cases intact. Here, the threshold had to be decreased from .500 to .4844874.

The output does not provide us with the likelihood ratios or predictive values, but we present the positive likelihood ratios and the positive predictive values in Table 10b.2. Table 10b.2 duplicates the values in the **Coordinates of the Curve** output but adds the positive likelihood ratios and positive predictive values. In Table 10b.2, we can see that for the classification criterion of .4844874, the positive likelihood ratio is 2.07 and the positive predictive value is .80.

We are now able to explore our options, and it is easier to work with Table 10b.2 than with the IBM SPSS output in Figure 10b.11 due to the presence of the likelihood ratios and predictive values. The next highest threshold in the output is .5321732 with a positive likelihood ratio of 2.77 and a positive predictive value of .85. The jump from 2.07 to 2.77 in likelihood ratio and from .80 to .85 in predictive value does result in a noticeable relative reduction of false positives. The sensitivity (true-positive rate) is only lowered a little to .788,

Table 10b.2 Coordinates of the Receiver Operating Characteristic (ROC) Curve and the Positive Likelihood Ratios of Sensitivity (True Positives) to False Positives

Classification Cutoff Value	Sensitivity (True Positive Rate)	False Positive Rate	Positive Likelihood Ratio	Positive Predictive Value
.0000000	1.000	1.000		
.1693545	.996	.986	1.01	.67
.1979602	.993	.965	1.03	.67
.2300538	.982	.922	1.07	.68
.2656209	.971	.844	1.15	.69
.3045057	.957	.801	1.19	.70
.3463915	.935	.730	1.28	.72
.3907960	.892	.610	1.46	.74
.4370819	.881	.482	1.83	.78
.4844874	.838	.404	2.07	.80
.5321732	.788	.284	2.77	.85
.5926505	.741	.227	3.26	.87
.6510411	.727	.220	3.30	.87
.6930913	.723	.206	3.51	.87
.7321644	.712	.191	3.73	.88
.7679341	.687	.177	3.88	.88
.8002352	.651	.163	3.99	.89
.8290458	.612	.135	4.53	.90
.8544608	.565	.106	5.33	.91
.8766628	.468	.064	7.31	.94
.8958931	.367	.035	10.49	.95
.9124266	.165	.021	7.86	.93
1.0000000	.000	.000		

Note. The False Negative Rate = 1 – Specificity; the Positive Likelihood Ratio = Sensitivity/False Positive Rate. The Positive Predictive Value = number of True Positive classifications/(number of True Positive classifications + number of False Positive classifications) based on Target Group (Success in program) *n* of 278 and a Reference Group (No Success in program) *n* of 141.

but the value of 1 − specificity (our false-positive rate) drops quite a bit to .284 (and thereby gives us a true-negative rate of .716). As we move down the rows of Table 10b.2, the positive likelihood and positive predictive values steadily increase (until the last viable entry with a decision threshold of .9124266), thus providing generally increasingly smaller proportions of false positives; the trade-off is that our sensitivity decreases as well.

How low a false-positive rate and how high a sensitivity rate are appropriate in the research context is an educated judgment that must be made by the researchers. Ours is a fictional example, and so for the sake of this example, we will illustrate the effect of changing the decision threshold in our binary logistic regression analysis from the default of .500 to .6930913. Thus, we will perform a new logistic regression analysis with this new cut value, projecting that our revised sensitivity (true-positive rate) will be .723 and that our revised false-positive rate will be .206.

10B.2.5 Performing a Logistic Regression Analysis With Revised Cut Value

From the main menu, select **Analyze** ➜ **Regression** ➜ **Binary Logistic**. Place **program_success** in the **Dependent** panel and place **gender_F1** and **conscientious** in the **Covariates** panel.

Select the **Options** pushbutton. As shown in Figure 10b.12, mark the **Hosmer-Lemeshow goodness-of-fit**, the **CI for exp (B)** at 95%, and the box for **Include constant in the model**. In the panel for **Classification cutoff**, type in the value of .6930913. Click **Continue** to return to the main dialog window, and click **OK** to perform the analysis.

10B.2.6 Output of Logistic Regression Analysis With Revised Cut Value

The output of the binary logistic regression analysis is exactly the same as what we described in Section 10A.1.3 (e.g., the Nagelkerke R^2 is .348; the odds ratio for our gender variable is 9.191) with one exception. The **Classification Table**, shown in Figure 10b.13, is now based on a decision criterion of .6930913 (shown to three decimal places in the footnote of the table) rather than the default of .500. As we know from our ROC curve, the degree to which we can correctly predict group membership based on the logistic function is different from our default analysis. The overall percentage of correct classifications has dropped very slightly from 75.7% in the original analysis to 74.7% in the revised cut value analysis, but our attention is focused more specifically on predicting membership separately in each of the two groups.

One projection we made from the ROC analysis was that our sensitivity (true-positive rate) would drop from .838 to .723. As seen in the **Percentage Correct** column of the **Classification Table**, the row for **success** shows a value of **72.3**, a percentage projection right on the money. A second projection we made from the ROC analysis was that our false-positive

Figure 10b.12 The Options Dialog Window of Binary Logistic Regression With the Revised Decision Threshold Entered

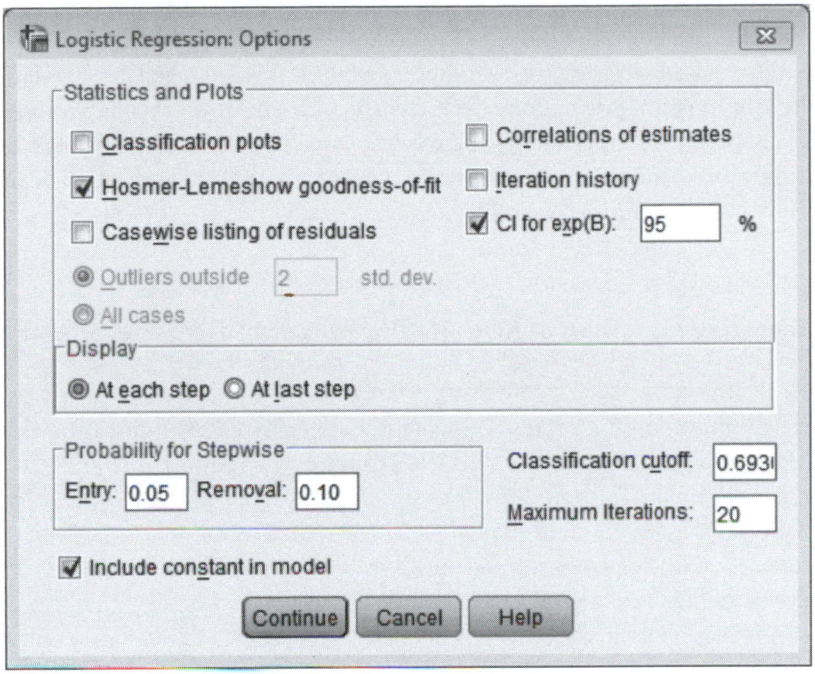

Figure 10b.13 The Revised Classification Table

Classification Table[a]

			Predicted		
			program_success		
Observed			no success	success	Percentage Correct
Step 1	program_success	no success	112	29	79.4
		success	77	201	72.3
	Overall Percentage				74.7

a. The cut value is .693

rate (1 − specificity) would drop substantially from .404 to .206. As seen in the **Percentage Correct** column of the **Classification Table**, the row for **no success** shows that there were 29 unsuccessful cases who were predicted to be successful (these are the false-positive classifications). Given that there were 141 unsuccessful cases (112 + 29 = 141), 29 cases represents 20.56% of them.; rounding this value to one decimal place gives us 20.6% and another percentage projection right on the money.

Using the revised decision threshold of .6930913 has reduced by a relatively small amount the true-positive rate and the overall correct classification rate; however, it has done a substantially better job of reducing the false-positive rate. Overall, considering the losses and the gains in prediction accuracy, the revised decision criterion appears to be distinguishably superior to the default original solution.

10B.2.7 Reporting the Results of ROC-Modified Binary Logistic Regression

A standard binary logistic regression was used to model the binary variable of success in the Compulsive Researchers Rehabilitation Program (using unsuccessful completion of the program as the reference category). The predictor variables in this study were the binary variable of gender with females as the focus category and the quantitative variable of conscientiousness, with higher scores indicating greater levels of conscientiousness. Results of the logistic analysis indicated that the two-predictor model provided a statistically significant prediction of success, $\chi^2(2, N = 419) = 121.109$, $p < .001$. The Nagelkerke pseudo R^2 indicated that the model accounted for approximately 35% of the total variance.

Table 10b.1 presents the partial regression coefficients, the Wald test, odds ratio [Exp(B)], and the 95% confidence intervals (CI) for odds ratios for each predictor. The Wald test indicated that both gender and conscientiousness were statistically significant predictors of success. The influence of gender was strong; females were approximately nine times (CI = 5.643, 14.971) more likely than males to succeed in the program, adjusting for conscientiousness. For each single-point increase in the conscientiousness score, there was a 1.211 times greater likelihood of program success, controlling for gender.

Classification success for the cases based on a classification cutoff value of .500 for predicting membership in the successful group was moderately high, with an overall prediction success rate of 75.7%. The true-positive rate indexing the sensitivity of the model was .838, and the false-positive rate (1 − specificity) was .404 (i.e., the true-negative rate indexing the specificity of the model was .596). This classification cutoff corresponded to a positive likelihood ratio of 2.07 and a positive predictive value of .80.

In an effort to determine if the performance of the model could be improved by using an alternative decision threshold, the predicted probabilities of membership in the successful group were subjected to an ROC analysis. The ROC curve is presented in Figure 10b.14, and the area under the curve (AUC) was .812 (*SE* = .022); both visual inspection and the AUC value suggest that the fit of the logistic regression model is in the acceptable to very good range.

Coordinates of the ROC curve corresponding to whole number predictions of group membership are shown in Table 10b.2. The original classifications under a nominal probability of .500 corresponded to the actual decision criterion of .4844847. Inspection of Table 10b.2 suggests that by moving to a revised classification threshold of .6930913, the sensitivity of the model would drop only to .723, but the false-positive rate (1 – specificity) would drop substantially to .206. Translated to frequency counts, a revised classification threshold of .6930913 would permit 201 of the 278 successful cases to be correctly classified (true-positive frequency) with 29 of the 141 unsuccessful cases incorrectly classified (false-positive frequency). This alternative decision threshold was associated with a positive likelihood ratio of 3.51 and a positive predictive value of .87.

Using the revised decision threshold of .6930913 reduced by a relatively small amount the true-positive rate and the overall correct classification rate; however, it has done a substantially better job of reducing the false-positive rate. Overall, considering the losses and gains in prediction accuracy, the revised decision criterion appears to be distinguishably superior to the default original solution.

10B.3 Multinomial Logistic Regression

10B.3.1 Numerical Example

In multinomial logistic regression, the outcome variable is represented by three or more categories. Here, we will use **Political Party** as our outcome variable. The target or response outcome categories are **Republican** and **Democrat**, coded as 1 and 2, respectively, in the data file; each will be compared with the reference category of **Independent**, coded as 3 in the data file. One predictor variable is **gender_F0_focus**. The focus predictor category is **female**, coded as 0 in the data file because we are using IBM SPSS Version 19 that (unlike binary logistic where the focus category is coded as 1) treats the category with the 0 code as the focus category (hence the name of the variable to remind us of the coding); it will be compared with **male**, which is coded as 1.

Our other three predictors are quantitative variables named **pro_capital_punishment**, **pro_welfare_reform**, and **pro_fed_support_ed** (short for federal support of education). Each of these latter variables was assessed on a 10-point scale with higher

Figure 10b.14 The Receiver Operating Characteristic Curve for the Predicted Probabilities of Membership in the Successful Group

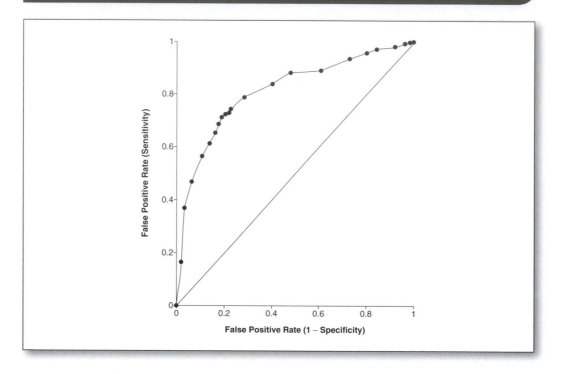

values indicating greater support for the position. The data are contained in the file named **Political Party**.

10B.3.2 Multinomial Logistic Regression Analysis Setup

From the main menu, select **Analyze ➔ Regression ➔ Multinomial Logistic**, which opens up the **Multinomial Logistic Regression** main dialog box as shown in Figure 10b.15. We move **political_party** to the **Dependent** panel. The default in IBM SPSS is to designate the last category (ascending, that is, from lower to higher values) in the coding schema as the **Reference Category**, and so we leave it. However, we show in Figure 10b.16 what the window looks like when the **Reference Category** pushbutton is selected; in the **Dependent** panel, the **Reference Category** is indicated by adding (**Last**) to the end of the variable name so that it now reads **political_party(Last)**. The predictor **gender_F0_focus** is a categorical variable and so is moved to the **Factor(s)** panel. The three quantitative predictor variables are moved to the **Covariate(s)** panel.

Figure 10b.15 The Main Multinomial Logistic Regression Dialog Window

Select the **Statistics** pushbutton. As shown in Figure 10b.17, we have checked the **Case processing summary**; under **Model,** we have marked the **Pseudo R-square**, **Step summary**, **Model fitting information**, and **Classification table**. Under **Parameters**, we have checked **Estimates** and **Likelihood ratio tests**. Click **Continue** to return to the main dialog window, and click **OK** to perform the analysis.

10B.3.3 Multinomial Logistic Regression Analysis Output

10B.3.3.1 Model Fit Output

The upper table in Figure 10b.18 shows the model fit information. The

Figure 10b.16 The Reference Category Screen of Multinomial Logistic Regression

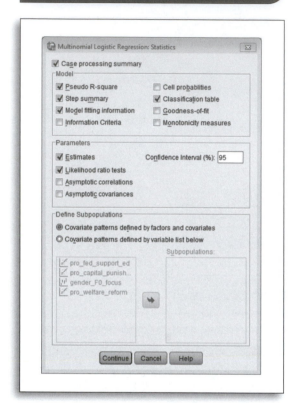

Figure 10b.17 The Statistics Dialog Window of Multinomial Logistic Regression

Final model has a −2 log likelihood value of 361.378, which is statistically significant. We may therefore conclude that we can predict at a better than chance level using our set of predictors. The Nagelkerke Pseudo R^2 value, as seen in the lower table of Figure 10b.18, is .379. We are therefore able to account for approximately 38% of the variance associated with choice of political party made by participants in this sample.

10B.3.3.2 Likelihood Ratio Tests

Figure 10b.19 shows the **Likelihood Ratio Tests**. The column labeled **−2 Log Likelihood of Reduced Model** provides the values for each component of the model so that it can be separately evaluated. The column immediately to its right labeled **Chi-Square** is the difference between the intercept-only model with a −2 log likelihood of 361.378 and the consequences of including each of the other predictors in the model. The difference between the two is listed in the **Chi-Square** column and tested for significance. As can be seen, only two predictors were statistically significant: **pro_capital_punishment** and **gender_F0_focus**, controlling for **pro_welfare_reform** and **pro_fed_support_ed**.

10B.3.3.3 Classification Table and Parameter Estimates

The results of using the model to predict political party are shown in Figure 10b.20. The **Parameter Estimates** table (the top table in Figure 10b.20) is divided into two major rows, one for **Republican** and another for **Democrat**. This is done because there are three categories of **political_party**. We used **Independent** as our reference categories, and so each of the other two categories are contrasted to it in separate logistic regression analyses so that the outcome variable is always binary. The first analysis used **Republican** as the target group and **Independent** as the reference group; the second analysis used **Democrat** as the target group and **Independent** as the reference group.

Figure 10b.18   Model Fit Information

Model Fitting Information

Model	Model Fitting Criteria	Likelihood Ratio Tests		
	–2 Log Likelihood	Chi–Square	df	Sig.
Intercept Only	477.653			
Final	361.378	116.275	8	.000

Pseudo R–Square

Cox and Snell	.337
Nagelkerke	.379
McFadden	.187

Figure 10b.19   Likelihood Tests of the Predictors

Likelihood Ratio Tests

Effect	Model Fitting Criteria	Likelihood Ratio Tests		
	–2 Log Likelihood of Reduced Model	Chi–Square	df	Sig.
Intercept	361.378[a]	.000	0	.
pro_capital_punishment	406.045	44.667	2	.000
pro_welfare_reform	364.471	3.093	2	.213
pro_fed_support_ed	363.587	2.209	2	.331
gender_F0_focus	463.283	101.905	2	.000

The chi–square statistic is the difference in –2 log–likelihoods between the final model and a reduced model. The reduced model is formed by omitting an effect from the final model. The null hypothesis is that all parameters of that effect are 0.

a. This reduced model is equivalent to the final model because omitting the effect does not increase the degrees of freedom.

Figure 10b.20 The Parameter Estimates and Classification Tables

Parameter Estimates

political_party[a]		B	Std. Error	Wald	df	Sig.	Exp(B)	95% Confidence Interval for Exp(B) Lower Bound	95% Confidence Interval for Exp(B) Upper Bound
1 Republican	Intercept	−3.587	1.235	8.441	1	.004			
	pro_capital_punishment	.523	.137	14.453	1	.000	1.686	1.288	2.208
	pro_welfare_reform	−.004	.110	.001	1	.974	.996	.803	1.236
	pro_fed_support_ed	−.025	.121	.043	1	.835	.975	.769	1.237
	[gender_F0_focus=0]	2.427	.436	30.944	1	.000	11.329	4.817	26.647
	[gender_F0_focus=1]	0[b]	.	.	0	.	.	.	.
2 Democrat	Intercept	4.468	1.099	16.541	1	.000			
	pro_capital_punishment	−.464	.145	10.214	1	.001	.629	.473	.836
	pro_welfare_reform	−.172	.105	2.672	1	.102	.842	.685	1.035
	pro_fed_support_ed	−.164	.114	2.071	1	.150	.848	.678	1.061
	[gender_F0_focus=0]	−1.808	.427	17.953	1	.000	.164	.071	.379
	[gender_F0_focus=1]	0[b]	.	.	0	.	.	.	.

a. The reference category is: 3 Independent.

b. This parameter is set to zero because it is redundant.

Classification

Observed	Predicted 1 Republican	Predicted 2 Democrat	Predicted 3 Independent	Percent Correct
1 Republican	67	6	22	70.5%
2 Democrat	13	58	21	63.0%
3 Independent	33	28	35	36.5%
Overall Percentage	39.9%	32.5%	27.6%	56.5%

The left side of the table presents the *b* coefficient and the standard error (S.E.) for each predictor. These coefficients indicate the amount of change expected in the log odds when there is a 1-unit change in the predictor variable with all the other variables in the model held constant. As we saw in the **Likelihood Ratio Tests** table, only **pro_capital_punishment** and **gender_F0_focus** were statistically significant. The logistic coefficients can be used in a manner similar to linear regression coefficients to generate predicted values.

The **Exp (B)** column provides the odds ratios associated with each predictor (adjusting for the other predictor), with the 95% confidence interval associated with each provided in the final two columns. For **Republican**, the adjusted odds ratio for gender is 11.329, although there is a relatively wide confidence interval surrounding this estimate. Taken at its face value, however, this odds ratio indicates that females (because they were coded as 0 to make them the research focus) are 11.329 times more likely than males in this sample to be **Republican** rather than **Independent**, controlling for their attitudes toward capital punishment, welfare reform, and educational funding.

For **Republican**, the adjusted odds ratio for **pro_capital_punishment** is 1.686 with a somewhat narrow confidence interval. Because **pro_capital_punishment** is a quantitatively assessed variable, we can interpret this odds ratio of 1.686 to mean that an increase of 1 on the **pro_capital_punishment** measure increases the odds of being **Republican** rather than being **Independent** by 1.686 times, controlling for gender and the other variables. Using a **pro_capital_punishment** score of 1 as a comparison base (it's one of the lowest scores in the data file, and we need to compare something with something else when talking about an odds ratio), we can say that the odds of being **Republican** rather than being **Independent** are 1.686 times greater for a person who had a **pro_capital_punishment** score of 2 than for a person with a **pro_capital_punishment** score of 1, controlling for their attitudes toward capital punishment, welfare reform, and educational funding.

For **Democrat**, the adjusted odds ratio for gender is 0.164. This odds ratio indicates that females are one sixth as likely as males in this sample (1/6 = .167) to be **Democrat** rather than **Independent**, controlling for their attitudes toward capital punishment, welfare reform, and educational funding. Note that if males had been the focus category, we would have obtained a greater-than-one odds ratio of 1/0.167 or 6.097 (it might be easier for some to characterize an odds ratio that is greater than 1.00) and would have interpreted that to indicate that males were approximately six times more likely than women to be **Democrat**.

For **Democrat**, the adjusted odds ratio for **pro_capital_punishment** is 0.629, indicating that an increase of 1 on the **pro_capital_punishment** measure increases the odds of being **Democrat** rather than **Independent** by 0.629 times, controlling for gender and the other variables. Using a **pro_capital_punishment** score of 1 as a comparison base, we can say that the odds of being **Democrat** rather than **Independent** are about two thirds for a person who had a **pro_capital_punishment** score of 2 than for a person with a **pro_capital_punishment** score of 1, controlling for gender and the attitudes toward welfare reform and educational funding. Again, the other side of the coin is also true. Given that 1/0.629 is 1.589, we could also say that **Independents** were 1.589 times more likely than **Democrats** to be **pro_capital_punishment**.

The **Classification Table** is also shown in Figure 10b.20. It indicates how well the model classifies cases into the three categories of the outcome variable. The overall predictive accuracy is 56.5%, but that differed across the three parties. Republicans (70.5%) and Democrats (63.0%) were much more accurately predicted than Independents (36.5%).

10B.3.4 Reporting the Results of Multinomial Logistic Regression

A standard multinomial logistic regression was used to predict the political party of the respondents in the sample. Three political parties, Republican, Democrat, and Independent, were represented; Independent was used as the reference category. One binary predictor variable, gender, was used in this study, with females as the focus category. Three quantitative predictor variables assessing support of capital punishment, welfare reform, and federal funding of education were also used, with higher scores indicating more positive attitudes toward the issue.

Results of the multinomial logistic analysis indicated that the four-predictor model provides a statistically significant prediction of success, −2 Log Likelihood = 361.275, $\chi^2(8, N = 283) = 116.275$, $p < .001$. The Nagelkerke pseudo R^2 indicated that the model accounted for approximately 38% of the total variance. Prediction success for the cases used in the development of the model was modest, with an overall prediction success rate of 56.5% and correct prediction rates of 70.5%, 63.0%, and 36.5% for Republican, Democrat, and Independent, respectively.

The upper portion of Table 10b.3 presents the regression coefficients, the Wald test, adjusted odds ratio [Exp(B)], and the 95% confidence intervals (CI) for odds ratios for each predictor contrasting Republican to Independent. The Wald test indicated that both gender and attitude toward capital punishment were statistically significant predictors of political party. The influence of gender was strong; females were approximately 11 times (CI = 4.817, 26.647) more likely than males to be Republican rather than Independent, adjusting for the measured political attitudes. For each single-point increase in support of capital punishment, respondents were 1.686 times more likely to be Republican than Independent, controlling for gender and attitudes toward welfare reform and federal support of education.

The lower portion of Table 10b.3 presents the regression coefficients, the Wald test, adjusted odds ratio [Exp(B)], and the 95% confidence intervals for odds ratios for each predictor contrasting Democrat to Independent. The Wald test again indicated that both gender and attitude toward capital punishment were statistically significant predictors of political party. The influence of gender was once again strong; females were approximately one sixth as likely as males (CI = 0.071, 0.379) to be Democrat rather than Independent, adjusting for the measured political attitudes. For each single-point increase in support of capital punishment, there was slightly less than a two-thirds chance (0.629) that respondents were Democrat rather than Independents, controlling for gender and attitudes toward welfare reform and federal support of education.

Table 10b.3   Multinomial Logistic Regression Results

Model	b	SE-b	Wald	df	Exp (B)	95% CI Exp (B)
Republican						
Intercept*	−3.587	1.235	8.441	1		
Gender*	2.427	0.436	30.944	1	11.329	4.817–26.647
Pro Capital Punish*	0.523	0.137	14.453	1	1.686	1.288–2.208
Pro Welfare Reform	−0.004	0.110	0.001	1	0.996	0.803–1.236
Pro Fed Ed Support	−0.025	0.121	0.043	1	0.835	0.769–1.237
Democrat						
Intercept*	4.468	1.099	16.541	1		
Gender*	−1.808	0.427	17.963	1	0.164	0.071–0.379
Pro Capital Punish*	−0.464	0.145	10.214	1	0.629	0.473–0.836
Pro Welfare Reform	−0.172	0.105	2.672	1	0.842	0.685–1.035
Pro Fed Ed Support	−0.164	0.114	2.071	1	0.848	0.678–1.061

Note. The dependent variable was political party with Independent as the reference category; females were the focus group of the Gender variable; Multinomial Nagelkerke R^2 = .379.
* $p < .05$.

PART IV

ANALYSIS OF STRUCTURE

Discriminant Function Analysis

11A.1 Overview

11A.1.1 Purposes of Discriminant Function Analysis

We use discriminant function analysis in a situation where we have several quantitative measures of participants from two or more groups. Discriminant function analysis can serve two distinct but compatible purposes:

- *Classification:* We can classify cases into the groups that are used in the analysis, based on a weighted linear composite of the quantitative variables used in the data analysis. This approach is sometimes referred to as *predictive* or *classificatory* discriminant function analysis. For example, if we have youths who have been convicted of a criminal offense, we may want to predict which of them might be amenable to a rehabilitative counseling treatment program and which are not likely to be successful in such a program.

- *Explanation:* We generate a set of weighted linear combinations (variates) of the quantitative variables that best differentiates our groups. These variates together serve as our model of group differences. This approach is sometimes referred to as *descriptive* (Huberty, 1994; Stevens, 2009) or *explanatory* discriminant function analysis. For example, we may wish to determine the ways in which academically successful middle school children differ on personality and temperament factors from those who are not academically successful.

From a classification perspective, we ordinarily apply the model to the current sample. Even though the model was developed based on this sample, it will not function perfectly, that is, it will not correctly classify all of the cases into their proper groups. How far the prediction is from perfection is one way to evaluate the quality of the solution. We can also apply the model to cases that were not in the original sample, either to a "holdout" sample from our original source allowing us to cross-validate our findings or to a sample that will be drawn sometime in the future.

If the primary purpose of researchers is to gain understanding of the nature of the variates, then a descriptive discriminant function analysis would be performed. In descriptive discriminant function analysis, we interpret the latent construct (the underlying dimension) represented by the variate. In most research studies, both the classification and the explanatory aspects of the analysis are of interest and the results pertaining to both aspects are reported.

11A.1.2 The Dependent and Independent Variables in Discriminant Function Analysis

The groups in discriminant function analysis are represented on a nonmetric (e.g., categorical) scale of measurement. Our goals are to predict group membership of the cases and to describe or characterize how the groups differ. The groups are the focus of our prediction and description interests, and the analysis is designed to maximally account for group differences. Thus, in discriminant function analysis, using oversimplified language for the moment, we would say that the categorical variable representing the groups plays the role of a *dependent variable* in the statistical analysis of the data (analogous to a certain extent to the outcome variable in ordinary least squares regression). Using more precise language, as we will see in Section 11A.6.1, the dependent variable is a quantitative value called a discriminant score that is used to index group differences.

The quantitative variables in the analysis are used as the predictors of group membership. They are configured into a weighted linear combination to characterize how the groups differ. Thus, in discriminant function analysis, these quantitative variables play the roles of *independent variables* in the data analysis (analogous to the predictor or independent variables in ordinary least squares regression).

We recognize that the terminology can appear confusing and even contradictory at times to those unfamiliar with these analytic procedures. For example, in a MANOVA—an alternative way to view discriminant function analysis (see Section 11A.3)—the categorical grouping variable is the independent variable and the quantitative variables are the dependent variables, whereas these roles are reversed in discriminant function analysis. The key to avoiding confusion is to recall our discussion in Section 2.3, where we indicated that variables may be called on to take on different roles in different analyses. We will remind readers from time to time during this chapter about the roles these variables are assigned in the data analysis in an effort to minimize confusion.

11A.1.3 Additional Resources

Most multivariate textbooks have chapters describing discriminant function analysis. Readers wishing to obtain more information may wish to consult Duarte Silva and Stam (1995), Lattin, Carroll, and Green (2003), Stevens (2009), and Warner (2008). Books by Huberty (1994), Huberty and Olejnik (2006), and Klecka (1980) may also prove helpful.

11A.2 Discriminant Function Analysis and Logistic Analysis Compared

The purpose of a discriminant function analysis is similar to that of logistic regression (discussed in Chapters 10A and 10B), and we discuss the choice of the procedure to use in Section 11A.4. We use discriminant function analysis to develop a weighted composite of variables to predict membership in two or more groups (Cooley & Lohnes, 1971). For both logistic regression and discriminant function analysis, the variable that is predicted is categorical and can be represented by two or more groups. Three of the differences between the procedures are as follows:

- In logistic regression, the predictor variables may be either continuous, dichotomous (categorical variables can be used if they are first dummy coded), or a combination of both. In discriminant function analysis, the predictors are continuous variables (Duarte Silva & Stam, 1995).
- Logistic regression fits a sigmoidal-shaped function (a function curved in two directions such as an S-shaped function) to the data (although it is linear with respect to the logit or log odds of the outcome variable—see Section 10A.7.3) and requires fewer assumptions to be met. Discriminant function analysis fits a linear function to the data and requires all of the assumptions of the general linear model to be met.
- In multinomial logistic analysis, separate functions are generated to compare each of the target groups with the common reference group. In discriminant function analysis with three or more groups, multiple functions are generated that differentiate the groups in a somewhat more complex (and, some may argue, interesting) manner.

11A.3 Discriminant Function Analysis and MANOVA

We discussed in Sections 4A.9 and 7A.5.1 the idea that the general linear model is used to predict the value of a variable from a weighted linear composite of some other variables (a variate). Exactly which variables predict which other variables and what role each of these plays in the analysis are largely the features that distinguish the various procedures in applying the general linear model.

Discriminant function analysis is the alternative way to view MANOVA (see Section 5A.2.3) and is thus a member of the general linear model family of procedures. When we perform a MANOVA, our focus is on any differences we observe between the groups on any of the quantitative variables we used in our study; the structure of MANOVA calls for the group (categorical) variable to be the independent variable and the quantitative variables to be the dependent variables. Our focus in a discriminant function analysis is on how the different weighted linear combinations of the quantitative variables in the variates predict group membership and/or explain differences between the groups; the structure of discriminant function analysis calls for the group (categorical) variable to be the dependent variable (again, we will be more precise in Section 11A.6.1) and the quantitative variables to be the independent variables. In reality, the one-way MANOVA and discriminant function analysis involve exactly the same overall tests of statistical significance, and so it is not unusual to see both MANOVA and discriminant function analysis combined together in reporting results for multiple groups with multiple quantitative measures obtained for the cases.

It is easy to find these different roles played by the variables a bit confusing:

- The categorical variable is the independent variable and the quantitative variables are dependent variables in MANOVA.
- The categorical variable is the dependent variable and the quantitative variables are the independent variables in discriminant function analysis.

One way to cope with this potential confusion is to primarily direct our attention to the sets of variables themselves and then to secondarily invoke their roles in the context of the data analysis. MANOVA and discriminant function analysis are fundamentally the same analysis even though they are treated as separate analytic procedures at the surface level. For both analyses, we are trying to explicate the differences between the groups. The emphases of the two procedures in terms of the sets of variables themselves are as follows:

- In MANOVA, we are focused on differences between the groups based on the means of quantitative variables.
- In discriminant function analysis, we address how the groups differ on the weighted linear composite of the quantitative variables and the extent to which we can predict group membership based on the composite of the quantitative variables.

11A.4 Assumptions Underlying Discriminant Function Analysis

Discriminant function analysis conforms to the general linear model and therefore makes the same rigorous assumptions as multiple regression, including linearity, multivariate normality, independence of predictors, homoscedasticity, absence of multicollinearity, and the presumption that outliers are not adversely affecting the results of the analysis; it also presumes the use of near-interval data for the quantitative variables in the analysis.

As is true for some of the other general linear model techniques, discriminant function analysis is fairly robust to violations (it can withstand some minor violations) of most of these assumptions. However, it is highly sensitive to outliers, and these should be resolved as described in Chapter 3A prior to the analysis. If one group contains extreme outliers, the mean of that group will be biased (the mean will be drawn toward an outlier and away from the bulk of the other values) and the variance will be disproportionally increased (the squared difference between the outlier and the mean will result in an exceptionally large value in the calculation of the variance). Because overall significance tests are calculated on pooled variances (i.e., the average variance across all groups), these significance tests in the presence of outliers are prone to a Type I error—that is, reporting statistical significance erroneously in the presence of outliers (McLachlan, 1992).

Because discriminant function analysis assumes that the quantitative predictor variables are normally distributed, violation of this assumption suggests that we should probably opt for logistic regression. Recall that logistic regression can accommodate both dichotomous and continuous variables, and the predictors do not have to be normally distributed, be linearly related, or demonstrate equal variance within each group (Tabachnick & Fidell, 2007). Logistic regression is sometimes preferable to discriminant analysis in studies where the variables violate multivariate normal distributions within the criterion groups (Klecka, 1980). However, if the assumption of normality is not violated, logistic regression is less powerful than discriminant analysis (Lachenbruch, 1975; Press & Wilson, 1978).

11A.5 Sample Size for Discriminant Analysis

Besides the assumptions presented above, there are issues concerning sample size that need to be taken into account. Discriminant analysis permits the groups to be of different sample sizes, but the sample size of the smallest group should exceed the number of predictor variables (by a lot). The maximum number of quantitative independent variables should be taken as $N - 2$, where N is the sample size. Although this minimum sample size may allow the analysis to be conducted, it is certainly not recommended (Huberty, 1994). The recommended sample size for the smallest group should be at least 20 times the number of predictors.

11A.6 The Discriminant Function

11A.6.1 The General Form of the Discriminant Function

Recall that the purpose of multiple regression is to develop a linear function (i.e., the best weighted linear combination of the independent variables) that predicts some quantitative measure (the criterion variable or dependent variable) from a set of other quantitative variables (predictors or independent variables). This linear equation—the prediction model—is generated to achieve the goal of maximally predicting the scores on the dependent variable.

An analogous purpose underlies discriminant function analysis. The quantitative variables (the independent variables in the analysis) are configured into a weighted linear combination to calculate or predict a value known as a *discriminant score*. The unstandardized discriminant coefficients are used in the equation for making the prediction, much as *b* coefficients are used in regression in making predictions. For each case, we multiply the score on each predictor by its discriminant coefficient or weight and add the constant. The result of this computation yields the discriminant score. The generic form for a discriminant function is as follows:

$$DS = a + w_1 X_1 + w_2 X_2 + \ldots + w_v X_v$$

In this equation, DS is the discriminant score (which is a multivariate composite of all of the quantitative variables). This discriminant function offers the best differentiation of the groups. That is, the discriminant scores of cases within each of the groups are generated such that the groups are maximally separated.

The discriminant scores are computed in such a way that they are centered (see Sections 8A.6 and 9A.8) on the sample as a whole. This allows us to quickly evaluate the differences of the group composite means (centroids), knowing (because the discriminant scores have been centered in the computation) that the overall centroid of the sample is zero. In the final solution, the discriminant means for the groups are as far apart as is possible given the data set.

The *X*s in the discriminant function are the quantitative predictor variables in the equation, and the *w*s are the discriminant weights or coefficients associated with the raw score values of the predictors. Analogous to multiple regression, these discriminant weights reflect the relative contribution of its independent variable when the effects of all the other predictors are statistically controlled. The equation also contains a constant, shown as *a* in the equation (representing the *Y* intercept). Thus, when we solve the variate (the expression to the right of the equal sign) for a particular case, we obtain the discriminant score for that case.

We indicated earlier in this chapter that the categorical variable represented by the groups was the dependent variable in a discriminant function analysis but warned that to express the idea in that way was an oversimplification. A more precise way to express this idea is to explain that the dependent variable in the analysis is the discriminant score. Each case in each group becomes associated with a particular discriminant score computed by using the discriminant function. We can thus compute an average discriminant score for the cases in each group, and the differences between these means can represent the extent to which the groups differ based on the quantitative independent variables represented in the discriminant function.

11A.6.2 Maximum Likelihood Is Used to Generate the Discriminant Function

Unlike the multiple regression equation where we use the ordinary least squares solution, the weights in the discriminant function are derived through the maximum likelihood method (the same strategy used in logistic regression). The maximum likelihood method uses an iterative process that starts with an initial arbitrary "guesstimate" of the weights and then determines the direction and magnitude of the discriminant coefficients to minimize the number of classification errors.

In the classification process, each case is predicted to be a member of one of the groups based on his or her discriminant score value. That is, the underlying algorithm compares the discriminant score value of each case with a specific discriminant cutoff value. The cutoff score that is used is the one that results in the fewest classification errors. When group sizes are equal, the cutoff score is based on the mean scores (the centroids) of the groups (i.e., a case is assigned to the group whose centroid is the closest one to the case's discriminant score). If the group sizes are unequal, the cutoff score is calculated from the weighted means.

11A.7 The Number of Discriminant Functions That Can Be Extracted

Groups, whether they are composed of people, school districts, states, businesses, or works of art, can differ along several dimensions. For example, a group of art majors may differ from a group of business majors along dimensions such as their approach to life (e.g., their degree of being creative or enterprising), their orientation toward information (e.g., their reliance on feelings or empirical data), and so on.

In discriminant analysis, there are two or more groups that we are attempting to differentiate (this categorical variable is the dependent variable in the analysis). The analysis allows researchers to describe some dimensions along which the groups in the analysis vary, where each dimension is represented by a discriminant function. The number of discriminant functions (dimensions) we are able to obtain is limited to the smaller number of the following:

- The number of predictor (quantitative independent) variables in the analysis
- The degrees of freedom for the groups ($k - 1$, where k is the number of groups)

Since we almost always have more predictors than groups, the latter criterion is the one usually governing the number of obtained functions. For example, with two groups we can assess just one dimension, with three groups we can assess two dimensions, and so on.

Each dimension is represented by a separate and independent discriminant function. For example, in the case of a three-group discriminant function analysis, the general form of the function shown in Section 11A.6.1 applies to each of the two functions we generate. Each function contains all of the predictors, but the weights or coefficients will differ from function to function. We will discuss this idea in more detail as we develop this chapter, but it is important to keep in mind that these dimensions that are represented by the discriminant functions each apply to the groups as a set. That is, just as art majors and business majors can differ in more than one way, so it is that the groups we study in discriminant function analysis can differ (on the set of predictor variables) in more than one way. Each of those coexistent dimensions is indicated by one of the discriminant functions.

11A.8 Dynamics of Extracting Discriminant Functions

We say that discriminant functions are "fit to" or "extracted from" the data because each function accounts for a portion of the total variance of the discriminant scores. We are thus explaining the between-groups variance with each discriminant function. The term *extraction* is used in the sense that we start with 100% of the total between-groups variance as unexplained and chip away at that with our functions until (hopefully) very little of that variance remains unexplained.

Discriminant functions are extracted sequentially, that is, first one function is extracted, the situation is examined, and then the next function is extracted. This process continues until all of the possible number of functions have been extracted.

Each discriminant function is independent of (orthogonal to) each of the others. Thus, the between-groups variance accounted for by the first extracted discriminant function is sacrosanct; subsequently extracted functions must target the residual variance—variance that is not yet explained. This allows us to add the variance explained by multiple functions to obtain the total amount of between-groups variance that is explained. We ordinarily report that the full set of functions explained such and such percentage of the total variance (the variance between the discriminant scores of the different groups) as well as indicate the relative contribution of each extracted function.

In the dynamics of extracting the discriminant functions, the variance explained by each function is directly related to its precedence in the order of extraction. The first discriminant function will account for more variance than any of the others, the second will account for more variance than all but the first, and so on. Not all of the discriminant functions are likely to be statistically significant if there are several of them. With each subsequent function explaining increasingly less variance than the last, at some point nonsignificant amounts of explained variance will start to be associated with the functions. And researchers may opt to not interpret even some of the later functions that are still statistically significant but substantially less compelling.

11A.9 Testing Statistical Significance

11A.9.1 Wilks' lambda

The null hypothesis in discriminant function analysis is that the groups do not differ in their discriminant scores, that is, they do not differ on the composite of the quantitative independent variables. We use Wilks' lambda to assess the null hypothesis, a multivariate statistical test that we have seen in the context of MANOVA (see Section 5A.5.2); it is in fact the same Wilks' lambda—its value will be the same whether the analysis is performed in the MANOVA or the discriminant function procedure of IBM SPSS. A statistically significant Wilks' lambda indicates that the full set of discriminant functions in combination is successful in distinguishing the groups better than we would expect on the basis of chance.

Wilks' lambda is an index of the variance that is not explained, and the difference between it and 1.00 indexes the amount of explained variance. In discriminant function analysis, Wilks' lambda is converted into a chi-square with degrees of freedom equal to the product of the number of predictors and the number of functions that are extracted; this chi-square value is then tested for statistical significance.

11A.9.2 Eigenvalues

Eigenvalues are indexes of explained variance. We will discuss this concept in considerable detail in the contexts of principal components/exploratory factor analysis (see Section 12A.9.3) and canonical correlation analysis (see Section 13A.5.2). For our present purposes, think of an eigenvalue very generally as a ratio of explained variance to error variance that resembles a signal-to-noise ratio. Larger eigenvalues indicate proportionally more explained variance than error variance. Ratios greater than 1.00 indicate more "signal" (explained variance); ratios less than 1.00 indicate more "noise." The explanatory ability of a discriminant function and, to a certain extent, the likelihood of it being clearly interpreted can be thought of as a function of the magnitude of the eigenvalue.

11A.9.3 Precedence of Testing Statistical Significance

We made the point at the end of Section 11A.7 that groups can differ in many ways—for example, art majors may be different from business majors along many dimensions. We can therefore speak of the differences between those two groups holistically or separately by dimensions. This is, at least very roughly, what is done in discriminant function analysis. We test the set of discriminant functions for statistical significance based on Wilks' lambda using chi-square.

Assume for the sake of example that we had five groups (a rather large number in this sort of design) and a dozen quantitative independent variables. We could therefore extract a total of four discriminant functions ($k-1$, where k is the number of groups). The order or precedence of the Wilks' lambda significance tests, diagrammed in Figure 11a.1, is as follows:

Figure 11a.1   Order (Precedence) of Testing Statistical Significance Using an Example With Four Discriminant Functions

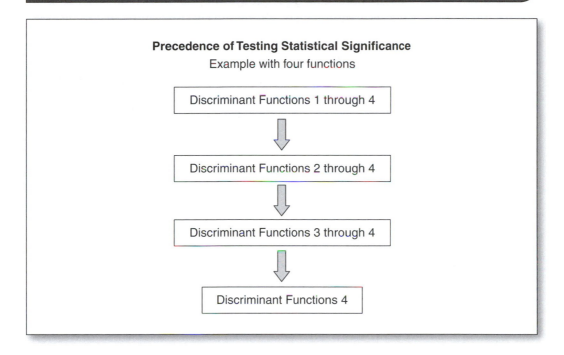

• The first test of statistical significance is performed on all of the functions combined. If four functions were extracted, for example, then Wilks' lambda would be based on Functions 1 through 4 as a set. If the associated chi-square value is statistically significant, then at least one of the included functions is significant. Specifically, at least one function can distinguish between the groups, that is, at least one function can distinguish between the mean discriminant scores of the groups (the dependent variable) better than we expect by chance. The one function that we therefore know to be statistically significant is the first one, because that function will account for more variance than any of the others. It is also possible that some or all of the other functions (Functions 2, 3, and 4) could be statistically significant as well. If the set is not statistically significant, then none of the included functions are significant.

• The second test of statistical significance is performed as a set on all functions extracted after the first. For example, if four discriminant functions were extracted, then Wilks' lambda would be based on Functions 2 through 4 as a set. If the set is statistically significant, then at least one of the included functions is significant. The one function that we therefore know to be statistically significant is the second one, because that function will account for more variance than any of the others in that set. It is also possible that one or both of the other functions (Functions 3 and 4) could be statistically significant as well. If the set is not statistically significant, then none of the included functions are significant.

• The third test of statistical significance is performed as a set on all functions extracted after the second. For example, if four discriminant functions were extracted, then Wilks' lambda would be based on Functions 3 through 4 as a set. If the set is statistically significant, then at least one of the two included functions is significant. That significant function will be the third one, since we know that it will account for more variance than the fourth function. If the set is not statistically significant, then neither of the included functions is significant.

• Tests of sets of discriminant functions are continued in this manner until the last extracted function is tested on its own.

11A.10 Evaluating the Quality of the Solution

There are three aspects of the output of discriminant function analysis that we can use to judge how well the variables were able to differentiate the groups: Wilks' lambda, the canonical correlations and the eigenvalues, and the classification results.

11A.10.1 Wilks' lambda

The full set of discriminant functions is tested for statistical significance by determining the value of the Wilks' lambda and converting that to a chi-square value. That Wilks' lambda value is directly interpreted as the amount of variance not explained by the set of functions, and subtracting that value from 1.00 informs us of how much variance the set of functions explained. For example, if a set of four functions together yielded a Wilks' lambda value of .25, then $1.00 - .25 = .75$, or 75% of the variance can be said to be explained. It is possible in some discriminant function analyses to account for more than 50% of the variance, but the success of any one analysis should be evaluated in the context of the existing research and the use to which the research will be put rather than by absolute standards.

11A.10.2 Canonical Correlations and the Eigenvalues

Each discriminant function is associated with a canonical correlation and an eigenvalue. These two statistics will paint the same picture because, as we will discuss in Section 13.5, they are intimately related to each other. Eigenvalues are best suited to compare functions within a single analysis; larger values indicate that the function accounts for more variance.

Canonical correlations are true correlations (analogous to Pearson correlations between two individually measured variables) representing the relationship between the weighted linear composite of predictor (independent) variables (the predictor variate) and the discriminant scores (the dependent variable) for that function. It is common practice to square these correlations, and the *squared canonical correlations* are indexes of the amount of variance (of the discriminant scores) explained by the variate, analogous to the R^2 we obtain in multiple regression. Squared canonical correlations are often symbolized as R_c^2.

The values of the eigenvalues and squared canonical correlations are systematically related to the precedence of the functions. Functions extracted earlier will have larger eigenvalues and higher canonical correlations. Typically, the first function is a dominant one; functions extracted toward the end of the process, even if they are statistically significant, usually have quite low canonical correlations and are often but not always ignored in the interpretation.

11A.10.3 Classification Results

11A.10.3.1 Classification Results: Hits and Misses

Unlike the binary logistic regression situation where we had target and reference groups and were thus able to use terms such as *true positive* and *false positive* classifications (see Section 10A.14.2), the classification table for discriminant function analysis entails using more lackluster terminology. Here, we say that the performance of the discriminant function model is evaluated by examining the rates of correct classifications ("hits") and misclassifications ("misses"). As was true for logistic regression, the classification table, also called the prediction matrix, is simply a table in which the rows are the observed group membership of the cases and the columns are the predicted group membership of the cases. Such a table in general form is shown in Figure 11a.2.

When prediction is perfect (which is not going to happen in empirical research), all cases will lie on the upper left to lower right diagonal of Figure 11a.2. The percentage of cases on the diagonal is the percentage of correct classifications and is called the *hit ratio*. This hit ratio is not compared with zero but with the percentage that would have been correctly classified by chance.

Figure 11a.2 General Form of a Classification Table

		Predicted Group		
		Group 1	**Group 2**	**Group 3**
Actual Group	**Group 1**	Hit	Miss	Miss
	Group 2	Miss	Hit	Miss
	Group 3	Miss	Miss	Hit

11A.10.3.2 Classification Results: Incorporating Group Sizes

In generating the predicted group membership of cases, one factor that can (optionally) be taken into account is the relative sample sizes of the groups. For example, consider a situation in which Group 1 contained 900 cases and Group 2 contained 100 cases. If we were to classify these 1,000 cases into the two groups and had no empirical (statistical) basis to use their scores on a set of quantitative variables as a guide, we can do a lot better than chance (50–50) if we took account of the group sizes. In such a situation, because 9 of every 10 cases on average were members of Group 1, we can beat the 50–50 odds by heavily biasing our guesses toward the 90–10 proportion in classifying cases (e.g., if we blindly guessed each case to be a member of Group 1, we would be incorrect just 10% of the time).

Built into the procedure used by IBM SPSS in performing a discriminant function analysis is a consideration of how to deal with the relative size of the groups in the analysis. For many research purposes, we would prefer the classification process to be focused exclusively on the potency of our predictive variables and not to take advantage of differences in group size to "help" us classify cases. To negate the influence of group size, we can instruct IBM SPSS to treat the group sizes as though they were equal and so we would receive no added cue from that information in classifying cases.

Occasionally though, there are instances where (a) our group sizes are representative of what would be found in the population to which we wish to generalize our results and (b) we want to make use of the group size information in classifying our cases. For example, medical researchers may hope to differentiate patients with a particular disease from those who do not have it. If the disease affects only 3% of their sample and if that is representative of its incidence in the population, it may make sense to use the group sizes (those with and those without the disease) as added information in using the model to predict the group membership of cases because that is the situation medical practitioners will face in a clinical setting where the classification will be made.

In summary, there are just two possible bases for the strategy used by IBM SPSS in establishing a decision criterion for predicting group membership:

- Treat the groups as though they had equal sample sizes.
- Use the relative sample sizes of the groups in shaping the decision criterion.

A third alternative may have occurred to readers who were impressed with the power and elegance of the ROC analysis as discussed in Section 10A.2. This alternative might be to apply such a strategy here. We can certainly apply the ROC analysis to a two-group discriminant function analysis by saving the probabilities of group membership and obtaining the ROC curve and the *c* statistic (the AUC) to evaluate the accuracy of the model. But alas, we cannot use the ROC **Coordinates of the Curve** output to revise our decision criterion in the discriminant function analysis. The reason why we could do so in binary logistic regression and cannot do so here is as follows:

- The IBM SPSS binary logistic regression module is specific to binary logistic regression. Thus, there will always be two outcome groups and so it is reasonable to allow users to specify their own cut value for predicting membership in the target group. In the multinomial logistic regression module, where there are three or more groups in the analysis, we cannot set our own cut value; instead, predicted probabilities are computed for all three groups and each case is classified into the group with the highest probability value for that particular case.

- The IBM SPSS discriminant function analysis module is general, accommodating two or more groups in the analysis. The algorithm for classifying cases must therefore be the most general one available, and it mirrors the strategy used in multinomial logistic regression: Predicted probabilities are computed for all groups and each case is classified into the group with the highest probability value for that particular case.

11A.10.3.3 Classification Results: Is Classification Better Than Chance?

Assuming that we have specified in our analysis setup that we wish to treat the group sizes as though they were equal to negate any influence of group size being used as additional information, there is a statistical test to determine if prediction of group membership is better than what we would expect on the basis of chance. Chance, in this application, is the expectation that we would be correct 1 of k times, where k is the number of groups. For example, with two groups, we would expect to be correct 1 of 2 times (50%), with three groups we would expect to be correct 1 of 3 times (approximately 33%), and so on.

The determination of correctly classifying cases at a significantly better than chance level can be assessed using Press' Q statistic (Press, 1972; also see Hair et al., 2010; James & Hatten,

Figure 11a.3 Formula for and Application of Press' Q Statistic

$$\text{Press'} \ Q = \frac{[N - (n*k)]^2}{N(k-1)}$$

Where: N = total number of cases in sample
n = number of cases correctly classified
k = number of groups in the analysis

Example Classification Results

		Predicted Group		
		Group 1	Group 2	Total
Actual	Group 1	70	30	100
Group	Group 2	20	80	100
	Total	90	110	200

Example Classification Results

$N = 200$
$n = 70 + 80 = 150$
$k = 2$

$$\text{Press'} \ Q = \frac{[200 - (150*2)]^2}{200(2-1)}$$

$$\text{Press'} \ Q = \frac{[200 - (300)]^2}{200}$$

$$\text{Press'} \ Q = \frac{10,000}{200}$$

$$\text{Press'} \ Q = 50$$

1995); this statistic is not available in the IBM SPSS output and must be computed by hand. The Q statistic is a function of the total number of cases, the number of cases that have been correctly classified by the model, and the number of groups in the analysis; its computational formula is shown in Figure 11a.3. Press' Q can be described by a chi-square distribution with 1 degree of freedom (the critical value for chi-square with 1 degree of freedom and thus for Q, using an alpha level of .05, is 3.841).

We illustrate the application of Press' Q in Figure 11a.3. In this two-group example, the discriminant function allows us to correctly classify 70 of the 100 cases in Group 1 and 80 of the 100 cases in Group 2. The value of Press' Q in this example is 50; evaluated against the critical value for chi-square with 1 degree of freedom of 3.841 (see Table A2 in Appendix A), our value is statistically significant ($p < .05$), and so we would conclude that we are able to correctly classify cases at a better than chance level. Given that our hit proportion is 150–200 or 75%, we would judge that under most circumstances, this successful rate of classification is practically significant as well.

We suggest two cautions in applying Press' Q test of statistical significance. First, large sample sizes increase the power of this test (because it is linked to the chi-square test, which is itself sensitive to the increased power afforded by larger sample sizes) such that, at some point, a trivial percentage of correct classification difference between the performance of the model and guessing on the basis of chance can reach statistical significance. Thus, researchers should always consider how much better than chance their model permits prediction to be rather than to just be concerned with statistical significance. Second, disproportionate sample sizes can render the outcome of the assessment of statistical significance ambiguous at best (Morrison, 1969).

11A.10.3.4 Classification Results: Two Strategies

There are two different ways in which the classification analysis can be performed in IBM SPSS. The default classification procedure uses all of the cases in deriving the discriminant model. Because all cases were used to perform the analysis and to derive the model in the first place, such a procedure will yield a better (more accurate) classification rate than if we tried to predict the group membership of brand new cases. Thus, such a procedure will provide results that are overly favorable (biased) toward the model and should not be taken at face value.

The second variation is to perform a jackknife classification procedure (see Section 7A.13.2.3), called by IBM SPSS the **Leave-one-out** method (it can be performed by simply checking a box in the **Classification** dialog window as is illustrated in Section 11B.1.3). In this procedure, one of the cases is omitted in deriving the discriminant solution. Then an assessment (prediction) is made of the group to which that case is likely to belong, based on the model that was derived from all of the other cases. The outcome is noted, and the process is repeated after replacing the first case back into the analysis and removing the second case. This continues until all cases have had their turn at being removed from the analysis and their group membership predicted based on the cases that were included in the analysis.

The jackknife or **Leave-one-out** procedure is one form of cross-validation and will always result in a poorer rate of correct classification (because the classification rubric is based on an incomplete sample) than was true for when the entire sample was used. However, because the cases whose group membership are predicted have not been involved in the analysis (and therefore were not used to derive the discriminant function), there is less bias in the results. Generally, researchers prefer a method that is less biased, and so we regard the **Leave-one-out** method to be a preferable way to evaluate the classification outcome.

11A.11 Coefficients Associated With the Interpretation of Discriminant Functions

There are four sets of coefficients that can be obtained in a discriminant function analysis: raw discriminant coefficients, standardized discriminant coefficients, structure coefficients, and classification function coefficients. Each is discussed below.

11A.11.1 Raw Discriminant Coefficients

The raw discriminant coefficients are the weights linked to the predictor variables when the predictors are in raw score form. They are analogous to b weights in ordinary least squares regression and symbolized by the letter "w" in the general discriminant model shown in Section 11A.6.1. When applying the discriminant model to a new sample, for example, we would rely on these raw discriminant coefficients because the standardized coefficients are specific to our sample and would therefore not necessarily be an exact fit to a future sample.

Each raw score of each predictor variable is multiplied by its corresponding weight, and the results, together with the constant, are summed to yield a discriminant score. As we indicated in Section 11A.6.1, the discriminant scores are centered. Thus, the (grand) mean (centroid) is zero, allowing us to quickly judge the differences between it and the group composite means (centroids).

11A.11.2 Standardized Discriminant Coefficients

The standardized discriminant coefficients are the weights linked to the predictor variables when the predictors are in standardized or *z*-score form. They are analogous to beta weights in ordinary least squares regression. They are combined together in a weighted linear composite to yield a standardized discriminant score.

Researchers may also want or need to assess the relative importance of the discriminating variables. Recall that in multiple regression, the relative importance can be assessed by comparing beta weights. In discriminant function analysis, the standardized discriminant function coefficients are used to assess relative importance. Note that the standardized discriminant coefficients will change if variables are added to or deleted from the equation. It should also be noted that the drawbacks to using beta weights in multiple regression discussed in Section 7A.12.2.6.3 apply analogously to standardized discriminant coefficients.

11A.11.3 Structure Coefficients

We have discussed structure coefficients in the context of multiple regression in Section 7A.11 and have shown how to interpret them in Section 7B.1.5; we will also have occasion to focus on them again in the context of principal components/factor analysis and canonical correlation analysis. A structure coefficient is the correlation between an individual variable and the variate as a whole. In the case of discriminant function analysis, since the value of the predictor variate is equal to the discriminant score, we can say that a structure coefficient is the correlation between a given predictor and the discriminant score. Because it is independent of the correlations among the predictors, it can be used as an indicator (as a basis for the interpretation) of the nature of the variate (the discriminant function).

The discriminant function is a weighted linear composite of the variables composing it. Because it is not a directly measured variable but rather was "put together" by statistically combining measured variables, we treat the variate as representing a *latent* construct or factor, that is, one that was not directly observed in the study. The measured variables in the composite combine to create this latent variable and form the key to its interpretation. Measured variables that are more strongly related to (correlated with) the latent factor have more in common with the construct and are therefore better indicators of what it is; measured variables that are more weakly related to (correlated with) the latent factor have less in common with the construct and are therefore less relevant indicators of what it is. The structure coefficients provide the index of how strongly the measured variables are indicators of the underlying factor.

To illustrate how structure coefficients can be used to interpret a discriminant function, a fictional set of measured predictor variables and the structure coefficient associated with each variable for a single fictional discriminant function are shown in Table 11a.1. Assume that higher scores on the variables represent the following:

Table 11a.1 Hypothetical Set of Structure Coefficients Illustrating How to Interpret a Discriminant Function

Measured Variable	Structure Coefficient
Depression	.90
Self-Esteem	−.89
Anxiety	.88
Neuroticism	.85
Extrinsic Orientation	.17
Intelligence	.10

- *Depression:* Negative feelings about oneself
- *Self-Esteem:* Positive feelings about oneself
- *Anxiety:* Feelings of apprehension and fear
- *Neuroticism:* A tendency to experience negative emotional states and instability
- *Extrinsic Orientation:* Valuing financial success, social recognition, and appearance
- *Intelligence:* An ability to learn, retain knowledge, and think abstractly and originally

We can see in Table 11a.1 that the structure coefficients for the first four listed variables are all very high, informing us that Depression, Self-Esteem, Anxiety, and Neuroticism share a great deal of variance with the variate as a whole (the latent factor). Furthermore, higher values of Depression, Anxiety, and Neuroticism and lower values of Self-Esteem are associated with higher levels of the latent construct. Neither Extrinsic Orientation nor Intelligence, however, has much to do with whatever the latent variable is.

The interpretation of the discriminant function—the interpretation of the latent factor—is the answer to this question: "What construct is indicated by higher levels of Depression, Anxiety, and Neuroticism and lower values of Self-Esteem?" Our answer to this question, and thus our interpretation of the construct, is *demoralization*. We use this label to represent the latent factor based on the work of Tellegen et al. (2003). With more than one discriminant function, we would use the same strategy to interpret each.

11A.11.4 Classification Function Coefficients

On the basis of the quantitative predictor variables, cases are predicted to belong to one group or another. This prediction is called a classification process, and because we know from the data file to which group a case truly belongs, we can determine the accuracy of the predicted classification. This in turn is one way to assess the efficacy of the model. It also allows us to project how well we would be able to predict group membership if we were to apply the model to a new sample (e.g., how well we could predict individuals with a certain disease given the results of various medical tests).

Cases are classified on the basis of classification function coefficients. Each predictor variable is associated with a classification coefficient for each group. Because we are dealing with raw scores, there is also a constant for each group.

We present a hypothetical set of classification coefficients for a three-group discriminant function analysis in the upper portion of Figure 11a.4. These are the classification weights of the quantitative independent variables for each group that have been generated by the statistical analysis. To classify each case in each group, we would multiply these values by the raw variable values. Each group has its own distinct set of classification weights, and each quantitative independent variable is weighted differently in predicting membership in each group. For example, variable *A* is weighted 0.259 for Group 1, 0.046 for Group 2, and −0.008 for Group 3.

We have also illustrated in Figure 11a.4 the process by which these weights are used to generate the predicted group membership of each case. Just below the classification coefficients in Figure 11a.4 is a portion of the data file containing variables *A* through *D* for the first three cases (called **Subid**). The variable labeled **Group** indicates the actual group to which each case belongs. Thus, the individuals who are identified as **Subid # 1**, **Subid # 2**, and **Subid # 3** are members of Groups 3, 2, and 3, respectively.

Each case is classified separately and the results eventually tallied in the classification table. Just below the raw data in Figure 11a.4 are the computations for **Subid # 1**. Her score on variable *A* is 5, and that is multiplied by the classification coefficient specific to a group. For example, for Group 1, we multiply 5 by 0.259, for Group 2 we multiply 5 by 0.046, and

Figure 11a.4 The Classification Coefficients Together With the First Few Cases in the Data File and the Process Illustrating How to Use the Classification Coefficients to Predict Group Membership: Highest Total Value Is Most Likely Group to Which the Case Belongs (Bolded in the Lower Table)

Classification Coefficients

	Group 1	Group 2	Group 3
Variable A	0.259	0.046	−0.008
Variable B	0.732	1.001	1.218
Variable C	23.766	23.997	23.967
Variable D	1.691	1.505	1.331
Constant	−116.295	−115.029	−118.414

A Portion of a Data File

Subid	Group	Variable A	Variable B	Variable C	Variable D
1	3	5	65	4.47	40.09
2	2	7	59	3.61	62.60
3	3	1	65	4.75	34.84

Classifying Subid # 1

	Group 1	Group 2	Group 3
Variable A	0.259*5	0.046*5	−0.008*5
Variable B	0.732*65	1.001*65	1.218*65
Variable C	23.766*4.47	23.997*4.47	23.967*4.47
Variable D	1.691*40.09	1.505*40.09	1.331*40.09
Constant	−116.295	−115.029	−118.414
Total	106.606	119.672	**121.208**

Classifying Subid # 2

	Group 1	Group 2	Group 3
Variable A	0.259*7	0.046*7	−0.008*7
Variable B	0.732*59	1.001*59	1.218*59
Variable C	23.766*3.61	23.997*3.61	23.967*3.61
Variable D	1.691*62.60	1.505*62.60	1.331*62.60
Constant	−116.295	−115.029	−118.414
Total	120.358	**125.194**	123.233

for Group 3 we multiply 5 by −0.008. This process is repeated for each variable. We then add all the values including the constant to arrive at a **Total** for each group for **Subid # 1**. Thus, for **Subid # 1**, the total for Group 1 is 106.606, the total for Group 2 is 119.672, and the total for Group 3 is 121.208.

The prediction of group membership is based on the highest total value of the classification coefficients applied to the scores of a given case. For **Subid # 1**, as can be seen in the bolded total in the display, the highest value is 121.208 and corresponds to Group 3. Thus, **Subid # 1** would be classified into (predicted to belong in) Group 3. By similar reasoning, **Subid # 2** would be predicted to belong to Group 2. For these two cases, the predictions represent "hits" in that the cases are correctly classified.

11A.12 Different Discriminant Function Methods

There are two different general methods by which researchers can build the variate or linear function in IBM SPSS:

- We can enter all the quantitative independent variables into the equation at once. This is the standard method and is akin to standard multiple regression.
- We can use one of the available stepwise methods. These are akin to stepwise multiple regression in that quantitative independent variables may be entered or removed based on the particular statistical criteria applicable to the particular stepwise procedure.

11A.12.1 The Standard Method

The standard discriminant function method, also known as the simultaneous or direct method, is what most authors refer to if they leave the method unspecified. Under this method, all the predictors (the quantitative independent variables) are entered into the equation in a single "step" (stage in the analysis). The standard method provides a full-model solution in that all the predictors are part of it. Just as is true for multiple regression, the weight of each variable is determined when all of the other quantitative independent variables are statistically controlled.

11A.12.2 The Stepwise Methods

The set of stepwise strategies to develop the discriminant function is the alternative to the standard method. Stepwise methods begin with an empty equation and build it one step at a time. Once a third predictor is in the model, these stepwise methods invoke the right to remove an independent variable if that predictor is not earning its keep (in a statistical sense). Predictors are allowed to be included in the equation if they significantly add to the predictive function. With correlated predictor variables, as we have seen for multiple regression, the predictors in the equation admitted under a probability level of .05 can still overlap with each other.

There are five variations of stepwise methods available in IBM SPSS. They differ in the type of criterion used to evaluate whether the quantitative independent variables are making enough of a contribution to prediction to enter them into the model or, if they are already in the model, whether they have the necessary level of statistical significance to remain. These five variations are Wilks' lambda, Unexplained Variance, Mahalanobis Distance, Smallest *F* Ratio, and Rao's *V*. We briefly present each below.

11A.12.2.1 Wilks' lambda

The criterion here is, not surprisingly, Wilks' lambda. Because it is one index of unexplained variance, the goal is to lower it. At each step, the variable that most lowers Wilks' lambda is entered into the model; the variable whose removal will not effectively raise Wilks' lambda is a target for removal.

11A.12.2.2 Unexplained Variance

The criterion here is the amount of unexplained variance. At each step, the variable that most lowers the amount of unexplained variance is entered into the model; the variable whose removal will not effectively raise the amount of unexplained variance is a target for removal. This procedure should result in very similar results to those produced by the Wilks' lambda method.

11A.12.2.3 Mahalanobis Distance

Each group can be summarized by a centroid, the multivariate mean of all of the variables in the data set or over all of the cases in that group. Mahalanobis distance is a way to measure such distances. Discriminant function analysis will build a function that maximizes the Mahalanobis distances or separation between the groups from the overall sample centroid. At each step, the variable that most increases the Mahalanobis distance between the groups and the sample centroid is entered into the model; the variable whose removal will not effectively decrease the Mahalanobis distance between the groups is a target for removal.

11A.12.2.4 Smallest F Ratio

The criterion here is the *F* ratio. At each step, the variable that maximizes the *F* ratio based on the Mahalanobis distance between the groups is entered into the model; the variable whose removal will not effectively raise the *F* ratio based on the Mahalanobis distance between the groups is a target for removal.

11A.12.2.5 Rao's V

Rao's *V* is a variation of Mahalanobis distance to assess the differences between groups. At each step, the variable that maximizes the increase in Rao's *V* is entered into the model; the variable whose removal will not effectively lower Rao's *V* is a target for removal.

11A.12.3 The Criteria for Entry and Removal

For each of the stepwise methods summarized above, it is necessary to specify a criterion for entry and removal of a variable. As discussed in Section 7A.17 in the context of stepwise multiple regression, the entry criterion is always more stringent than the removal criterion (to avoid placing the analysis in an endless loop where the same variable is entered and removed an infinite number of times). It is possible to indicate particular *F* ratios as the criteria or probabilities. The latter is conceptually simpler and is what most users opt for, and as was true for multiple regression, the most commonly used choices are .05 for entry into the model and .10 for removal from the model.

11A.13 Recommended Readings

Efron, B. (1975). The efficiency of logistic regression compared to normal discriminant analysis. *Journal of the American Statistical Association, 70*, 892–898.

Huberty, C. J. (1984). Issues in the use and interpretation of discriminant analysis. *Psychological Bulletin, 95*, 156–171.

Huberty, C. J., & Barton, R. M. (1989). An introduction to discriminant analysis. *Measurement and Evaluation in Counseling and Development, 22*, 158–168.

Huberty, C. J., Wisenbaker, J. M., & Smith, J. C. (1987). Assessing predictive accuracy in discriminant analysis. *Multivariate Behavioral Research, 22*, 307–329.

Joachimsthaler, E. A., & Stam, A. (1990). Mathematical programming approaches for the classification problem in two-group discriminant analysis. *Multivariate Behavioral Research, 25*, 427–454.

Konishi, S., & Honda, M. (1990). Comparison procedures for estimation of error rates in discriminant analysis under non-normal populations. *Journal of Statistical Computing and Simulation, 36*, 105–115.

Lopez, R. P., & Guarino, A. J. (2011). Uncertainty and decision making for residents with dementia. *Clinical Nursing Research, 20*, 228–240.

McLaughlin, M. L. (1980). Discriminant analysis. In P. Monge & J. Cappella (Eds.), *Multivariate techniques in human communication research* (pp. 175–204). New York, NY: Academic Press.

Panel on Discriminant Analysis, Classification and Clustering. (1989). Discriminant analysis and clustering. *Statistical Science, 4*, 34–69.

Press, S. J., & Wilson, S. (1978). Choosing between logistic regression and discriminant analysis. *Journal of the American Statistical Association, 73*, 699–705.

Ragsdale, C. T., & Stam, A. (1992). Introducing discriminant analysis to the business statistics curriculum. *Decision Sciences, 23*, 724–745.

Spicer, J. (2005). *Making sense of multivariate data analysis.* Thousand Oaks, CA: Sage.

Thomas, D. (1992). Interpreting discriminant functions: A data analytic approach. *Multivariate Behavioral Research, 27*, 335–362.

CHAPTER **11B**

Discriminant Function Analysis Using IBM SPSS

In this chapter, we will first perform a two-group discriminant function analysis and then perform a three-group analysis. The data set we will use for both analyses is named **Discriminant**.

11B.1 Two-Group Discriminant Function Analysis Setup

11B.1.1 The Initial Dialog Window

Selecting the path **Analyze ➔ Classify ➔ Discriminant** from the main menu brings us to the **Discriminant Analysis** main dialog window displayed in Figure 11b.1. Move the following variables into the **Independents** panel: **beckdep**, **regard**, **selfcon**, **neoextra**, **neoopen**, **neoagree**, **neoconsc**, and **negafect**. These will be the quantitative predictor variables assessing depression, self-regard, self-control, extraversion, agreeableness, conscientiousness, and negative affect, respectively.

Move **recruitment_source** into the **Grouping Variable** panel. This variable represents the source of the participants in this fictional study. Some participants ($n = 359$) were recruited from several noncounseling (e.g., university, work environment) sources (coded as 1 in the data file), whereas others ($n = 264$) were clients at various counseling clinics (coded as 2 in the data file).

Note in Figure 11b.1 that IBM SPSS has placed the expression (**??**) next to **recruitment_source** in the Grouping Variable panel. We need to specify the coding of **recruitment_source** to replace the (**??**). Click the **Define Range** pushbutton to reach the dialog window shown in Figure 11b.2. Our lowest coded value is 1 and our highest is 2, and we have specified that in the window. Clicking **Continue** to return to the main dialog window shows

▶ 609

Figure 11b.1 The Main Discriminant Analysis Dialog Window Before Defining the Range of the Grouping Variable

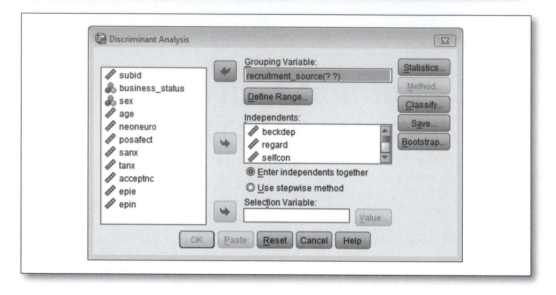

Figure 11b.2 Defining the Range of the Grouping Variable From the Main Discriminant Analysis Dialog Window

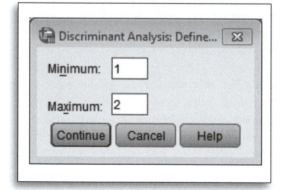

us in Figure 11b.3 that our codes have been incorporated in the **Grouping Variable** panel.

11B.1.2 The Statistics Window

Selecting the **Statistics** pushbutton brings us to the screen shown in Figure 11b.4. In the **Descriptives** section of the screen, check all three boxes. **Means** allows us to obtain the means and standard deviations of the quantitative variables, **Univariate ANOVAs** generates a between-groups ANOVA for each quantitative variable, and **Box's M** tests the equality of the group covariance matrixes. Under **Function Coefficients** we check **Fisher's** (for the classification coefficients) and **Unstandardized** (for the unstandardized discriminant function coefficients) in the section (the standardized discriminant function coefficients are part of the defaults for the output and so we do not have a checkbox for them). Click **Continue** to return to the main dialog window.

Figure 11b.3 The Main Discriminant Analysis Dialog Window After Defining the Range of the Grouping Variable

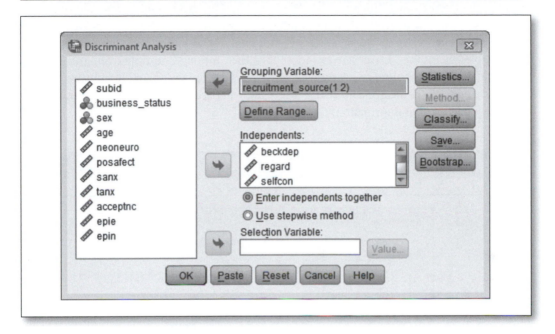

Figure 11b.4 The Statistics Window of Discriminant Analysis

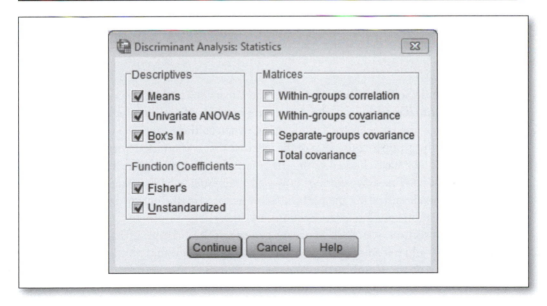

11B.1.3 The Classify Window

Select the **Classify** pushbutton. As can be seen in Figure 11b.5, we have checked **All groups equal** in the **Prior Probabilities** section of the window. Our group sample sizes are not equal, but that is a sampling issue. We do not want the analysis to use the different proportions of our group *n*s as a cue to classify cases; rather, we want *all* of the classification work to be based on the variables themselves. If we were to choose the other option (**Compute from group sizes**), we would give the procedure an advantage that we consider unfair in that the software "knows" that more cases are in the noncounseling group and will base its classification of group membership in part on that information.

Figure 11b.5   The Classification Window of Discriminant Analysis

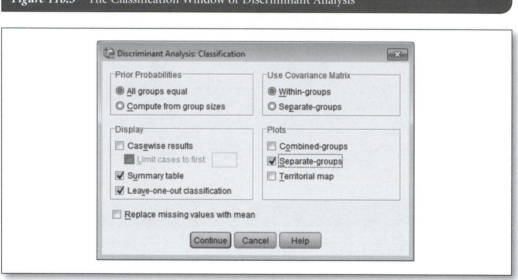

We leave the default of **Within-groups** as the **Covariance Matrix** to use and choose to **Display** the **Summary table** and the **Leave-one-out classification**. The **Summary table** method uses all of the cases in the computation, whereas the **Leave-one-out classification** method predicts the group membership of the one case that was omitted from the analysis (see Section 11A.10.3). We have checked both. The results from the **Summary table** method will provide us with a baseline assessment of how well the model is performing; the results from the **Leave-one-out classification** method will allow us to assess the performance of the model under cross-validation conditions (see Section 11A.10.3.4).

In the **Plots** section, we check **Separate-groups**. If we had more than two groups in the analysis, we would have also checked **Combined-groups**, but that plot is not available for a two-group design (the **Combined-groups** plots multiple discriminant functions on one set of axes, but we have only one function in a two-group analysis, and so there is no plot produced by IBM SPSS—if the box is checked, the IBM SPSS output will politely inform us that we should not have requested it). Click **Continue** to return to the main dialog window and **OK** to perform the analysis.

11B.2 Two-Group Discriminant Function Analysis Output

11B.2.1 Descriptive Statistics

The means and standard deviations of each of the predictor variables are shown in Figure 11b.6. These statistics are shown for each group separately as well as for the sample

Figure 11b.6 Descriptive Statistics Output

Group Statistics

recruitment_source source of subjects		Mean	Std. Deviation	Valid N (listwise) Unweighted	Weighted
1 non counseling	beckdep	6.7209	6.42774	369	369.000
	regard	56.5122	9.71694	369	369.000
	selfcon	4.1004	.50243	369	369.000
	neoextra	57.0475	10.47856	369	369.000
	neoopen	55.6344	10.63737	369	369.000
	neoagree	48.5493	11.83393	369	369.000
	neoconsc	44.6709	10.86287	369	369.000
	negafect	5.5285	3.67496	369	369.000
2 counseling	beckdep	12.5606	8.20902	264	264.000
	regard	46.6174	11.90278	264	264.000
	selfcon	3.8463	.50200	264	264.000
	neoextra	46.8974	12.91374	264	264.000
	neoopen	54.1159	12.79305	264	264.000
	neoagree	43.6872	11.79082	264	264.000
	neoconsc	42.8114	11.64671	264	264.000
	negafect	7.5038	3.67190	264	264.000
Total	beckdep	9.1564	7.77202	633	633.000
	regard	52.3855	11.73780	633	633.000
	selfcon	3.9944	.51728	633	633.000
	neoextra	52.8143	12.58643	633	633.000
	neoopen	55.0011	11.59977	633	633.000
	neoagree	46.5215	12.04794	633	633.000
	neoconsc	43.8954	11.22495	633	633.000
	negafect	6.3523	3.79799	633	633.000

as a whole. Visual inspection of the means gives the strong suggestion that the groups are quite different on many of the predictors. It would appear that cases in the counseling group may be more depressed, have lower self-regard, are less extraverted and agreeable, and report somewhat more negative affect than cases in the noncounseling group.

11B.2.2 Homogeneity of Covariance

Figure 11b.7 displays the assessment of homogeneity of covariance matrices. **Box's M** (shown in the lower table) is statistically significant, suggesting that we have violated the assumption of homogeneity of variance, but the test is an extremely powerful test, and with our large sample size, it is not surprising that it reached statistical significance. We should note that the discriminant function analysis is robust to the violation of homogeneity of variance assumption, provided the data do not contain extreme outliers (i.e., z scores greater than the absolute value of 4).

The **Log Determinants** table, also presented in Figure 11b.7 (shown in the upper table), provides an additional way to assess the homogeneity of the groups. Larger log determinants correspond to a greater difference between the covariance matrices of the groups. The **Rank**

Figure 11b.7 Homogeneity of Covariance Assessed by Log Determinants and by Box's *M*

Box's Test of Equality of Covariance Matrices

Log Determinants

recruitment_source source of subjects	Rank	Log Determinant
1 non counseling	8	27.131
2 counseling	8	28.087
Pooled within-groups	8	27.803

The ranks and natural logarithms of determinants printed are those of the group covariance matrices.

Test Results

Box's M		173.049
F	Approx.	4.740
	df1	36
	df2	1.083E6
	Sig.	.000

Tests null hypothesis of equal population covariance matrices.

column provides the number of independent variables (i.e., eight in this study). Because discriminant analysis assumes homogeneity of covariance matrices between groups, the determinants should be relatively equal. In the present example, this is the case, suggesting that the groups are exhibiting relatively homogeneous degrees of covariance.

11B.2.3 Univariate ANOVAs

The group differences on the predictor variables are evaluated by computing a **Wilks' lambda** statistic for each predictor; these are displayed in the table of **Tests of Equality of Group Means** as shown in Figure 11b.8. **Wilks' lambda** is then converted to an *F* ratio and tested for significance. As can be seen, all but one of the predictor variables (**neoopen**) were statistically significant at the .05 alpha level. If we apply a Bonferroni correction to that nominal alpha level (to protect for alpha-level inflation) by dividing .05 by the number of predictors (.05/8), we obtain approximately .006. Using that .006-corrected alpha level, we would judge that a second predictor (**neoconsc**) failed to reach statistical significance as well.

Figure 11b.8 Univariate Analyses of Variances on the Predictors

Tests of Equality of Group Means

	Wilks' Lambda	F	df1	df2	Sig.
beckdep	.863	100.574	1	631	.000
regard	.827	132.036	1	631	.000
selfcon	.941	39.388	1	631	.000
neoextra	.842	118.724	1	631	.000
neoopen	.996	2.644	1	631	.104
neoagree	.960	26.057	1	631	.000
neoconsc	.993	4.245	1	631	.040
negafect	.934	44.494	1	631	.000

11B.2.4 Eigenvalue, Canonical Correlation, and Wilks' lambda

The global discriminant function results are contained in Figure 11b.9. **Wilks' lambda** is reported in the lower table of Figure 11b.9. Its value is .745, and when tested for significance via a chi-square test, it is statistically significant. This is the same value of **Wilks'**

Figure 11b.9 Summary of the Discriminant Functions

Eigenvalues

Function	Eigenvalue	% of Variance	Cumulative %	Canonical Correlation
1	.342[a]	100.0	100.0	.505

a. First 1 canonical discriminant functions were used in the analysis.

Wilks' Lambda

Test of Function(s)	Wilks' Lambda	Chi–square	df	Sig.
1	.745	184.586	8	.000

lambda that we would have obtained had we performed a MANOVA on these same variables. We may conclude that a statistically significant proportion of the variance of the discriminant scores is accounted for by the discriminant function. The value of **Wilks' lambda** represents the percentage of variance that is not explained. Subtracting this value from 1.00 indicates the proportion of explained variance. In this instance, $1.00 - .745 = .255$. Thus, the discriminant function explains approximately 26% of the variance in the discriminant scores.

The upper table shows the **Canonical Correlation** value of .505. This is the correlation of the discriminant function with the discriminant scores. The **Eigenvalue** associated with this function has a value of 0.342. Squaring the canonical correlation of .505 gives us the squared canonical correlation value of .255, the same value we obtained by subtracting **Wilks' lambda** from 1.00. This is another way to determine the proportion of variance of the discriminant scores that were explained by the discriminant function.

11B.2.5 Discriminant Function Coefficients

Figure 11b.10 presents the **Canonical Discriminant Function Coefficients**. On the left are the raw score coefficients; on the right are the standardized coefficients. These are the weights by which the raw scores or the z-score values of the variables are multiplied and summed together to produce a discriminant score for each case, and they comprise the raw score and standardized score versions of the discriminant model. Based on the standardized coefficients, it appears that when these variables are combined together to distinguish the groups, extraversion (**neoextra**) and self-regard (**regard**) are weighted more heavily than the other predictors.

Figure 11b.10 Unstandardized and Standardized Discriminant Function Coefficients

Canonical Discriminant Function Coefficients	Function 1
beckdep	−.037
regard	.043
selfcon	.335
neoextra	.046
neoopen	−.008
neoagree	.009
neoconsc	−.023
negafect	.000
(Constant)	−4.651

Unstandardized coefficients

Standardized Canonical Discriminant Function Coefficients	Function 1
beckdep	−.264
regard	.462
selfcon	.168
neoextra	.537
neoopen	−.095
neoagree	.102
neoconsc	−.260
negafect	.000

11B.2.6 Structure Coefficients

The structure coefficients are shown in Figure 11b.11. These are the correlations between the variables and the variate (the weighted linear composite or latent variable) as a whole. We interpret the discriminant function primarily on the basis of these coefficients. The coefficients are conveniently ordered for us in a descending fashion in the **Structure Matrix** to facilitate reading the table. We note that self-regard (**regard**), extraversion (**neoextra**), and self-control (**selfcon**) are positively correlated with the variate and that depression (**beckdep**) and negative affect (**negafect**) are negatively correlated with the variate. Thus, the variate is oriented toward the positive end of the latent construct and can be interpreted as a generally positive life orientation.

11B.2.7 Classification Results

Figure 11b.12 presents the **Functions at Group Centroids** table. These centroids (multivariate means) are in Mahalanobis distance units and can be thought of as standard deviation units or as z scores. The sample as a whole has a centroid (akin to the grand mean) of zero. The noncounseling group centroid is 0.494, about half a standard deviation unit above the overall sample centroid; the counseling group centroid is −0.691, almost three quarters of a standard deviation below the overall sample centroid. Visual depictions of the distribution of discriminant scores in each group are shown in the histograms in Figure 11b.13.

Figure 11b.11 Structure Coefficients

Structure Matrix

	Function
	1
regard	.782
neoextra	.741
beckdep	−.682
negafect	−.454
selfcon	.427
neoagree	.347
neoconsc	.140
neoopen	.111

Pooled within–groups correlations between discriminating variables and standardized canonical discriminant functions
 Variables ordered by absolute size of correlation within function.

Figure 11b.12 Group Centroids

Functions at Group Centroids

recruitment_source source of subjects	Function
	1
1 non counseling	.494
2 counseling	−.691

Unstandardized canonical discriminant functions evaluated at group means

The **Classification Function Coefficients** are shown in the upper portion of Figure 11b.14. These are in raw score form and are weights by which we would multiply the variables to achieve a classification value for each group for an individual case. The group associated with the largest classification value is the group to which that case is predicted to belong.

Hits and misses in the classification effort are shown in the lower portion of Figure 11b.14. The major output row labeled **Original** has used all of the cases in performing the discriminant function analysis. When we use this solution to classify each case, we are somewhat biasing our result toward successful classification. Thus, of 369 noncounseling cases, 290 are predicted to be in the noncounseling group (these are "hits") and 79 are predicted to be in the counseling group (these are "misses"). Of the 264 noncounseling cases, 79 are predicted to be in the noncounseling group and 185 are predicted to be in the counseling group. Overall, as shown in **Footnote b** at the bottom of the table, 75.0% of the cases were correctly classified. In the procedure where the case whose group membership is to be predicted is omitted from the analysis (the leave-one-out analysis), labeled as **Cross-validated** in the table, correct classifications was almost as good at 74.9%. With smaller sample sizes and with a less clear solution, we would expect the **Cross-validated** hit rate to show a more substantial drop.

We may compute Press' Q (see Section 11A.10.3.3) to assess whether the **Cross-validated** hit rate exceeded chance expectation. We have 633 cases in the sample; of these, 289 were correctly classified as noncounseling and 185 were correctly classified as counseling for a total of 474. Using these values, Press' Q is 156.75. Evaluated against the

Figure 11b.13 Separate Group Plots

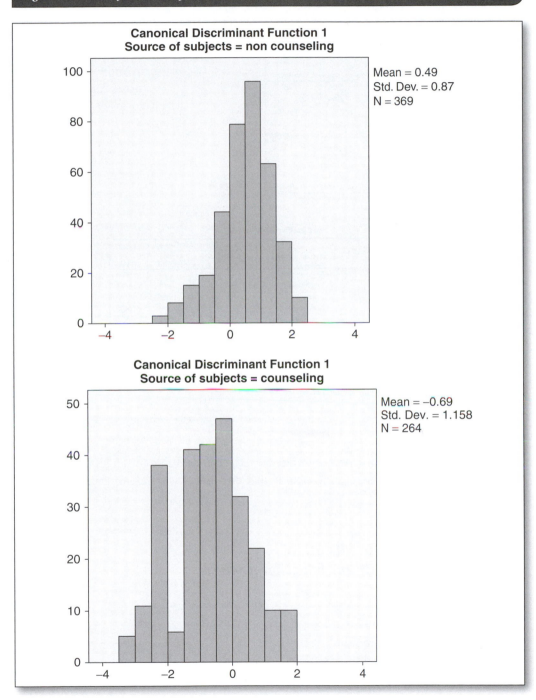

Figure 11b.14 Classification Function Coefficients and the Classification Table

Classification Function Coefficients

	recruitment_source source ...	
	1 non counseling	2 counseling
beckdep	.700	.743
regard	.596	.545
selfcon	15.683	15.286
neoextra	.211	.155
neoopen	.215	.225
neoagree	.275	.265
neoconsc	.001	.028
negafect	1.774	1.774
(Constant)	−75.639	−70.245

Fisher's linear discriminant functions

Classification Results[b,c]

			Predicted Group Membership		Total
			1 non counseling	2 counseling	
Original	Count	1 non counseling	290	79	369
		2 counseling	79	185	264
	%	1 non counseling	78.6	21.4	100.0
		2 counseling	29.9	70.1	100.0
Cross-validated[a]	Count	1 non counseling	289	80	369
		2 counseling	79	185	264
	%	1 non counseling	78.3	21.7	100.0
		2 counseling	29.9	70.1	100.0

a. Cross validation is done only for those cases in the analysis. In cross validation, each case is classified by the functions derived from all cases other than that case.

b. 75.0% of original grouped cases correctly classified.

c. 74.9% of cross-validated grouped cases correctly classified.

chi-square distribution with 1 degree of freedom, the critical value for an alpha level of .05 (3.841) was exceeded; we therefore conclude that our model was able to classify cases at a better than chance level.

11B.3 Reporting the Results of a Two-Group Discriminant Function Analysis

A two-group discriminant analysis was performed on noncounseling and counseling participants using depression, self-regard, self-control, extraversion, openness, agreeableness, conscientiousness, and negative affect as discriminating (predictor) variables. The obtained discriminant function accounted for a statistically significant percentage of the between-group differences, Wilks' $\Lambda = .745$, $\chi^2(3, N = 633) = 184.59$, $p < .001$, $R_c^2 = .255$. Using a leave-one-out cross-validation strategy, 74.9% of the cases were correctly classified, Press' $Q = 156.75$, $p < .05$.

Table 11b.1 presents the discriminant function coefficients for the raw and standardized forms of the variables. Extraversion and self-regard were most strongly weighted in the linear composite; depression and conscientiousness also were assigned moderate weights. The latent construct represented by the discriminant function can be interpreted with respect to the structure coefficients, which are shown in Table 11b.2. Higher levels of the latent variable are indicated primarily by higher levels of self-regard and extraversion and lower levels of depression. Other, but weaker, indicators are less negative affect and more self-control and agreeableness. Overall, the discriminant function appears to represent a positive and social approach to life.

The group means on the discriminant variables are shown in Table 11b.3. Separate one-way between-subjects ANOVAs using a Bonferroni-corrected alpha level of .006 indicated that all of the predictor variables but openness and conscientiousness yielded a statistically significant difference between the groups.

Table 11b.1 Raw and Standardized Discriminant Function Coefficients

Measured Variable	Raw Score Coefficients	Standardized Coefficients
Depression	−0.037	−.264
Self-Regard	0,043	.462
Self-Control	0,335	.168
Extraversion	0.046	.537
Openness	−0,008	−.095
Agreeableness	0.009	.102
Conscientiousness	−0.023	−.260
Negative Affect	0.000	.000
Constant	−4.651	

Table 11b.2 Structure Coefficients

Measured Variable	Structure Coefficients
Depression	−.682
Self-Regard	.782
Self-Control	.427
Extraversion	.741
Openness	.111
Agreeableness	.347
Conscientiousness	.140
Negative Affect	−.454

11B.4 Three-Group Discriminant Function Analysis Setup

11B.4.1 The Initial Dialog Window

Selecting the path **Analyze ➔ Classify ➔ Discriminant** from the main menu brings us to the **Discriminant Analysis** main dialog window displayed in Figure 11b.15. Move the following variables into the **Independents** panel: **beckdep**, **regard**, **selfcon**, **neoneuro**, **neoextra**, **neoopen**, **neoagree**, and **neoconsc**. These will be the quantitative predictor variables assessing depression, self-regard, self-control, neuroticism, extraversion, openness, agreeableness, and conscientiousness, respectively.

Table 11b.3 Means and Standard Deviations of the Variables for Each Group

Measured Variable	Non-Counseling Group		Counseling Group	
	M	SD	M	SD
Depression	6.72	6.43	12.56	8.21
Self-Regard	56.51	9.72	46.62	11.91
Self-Control	4.10	0.50	3.84	0.50
Extraversion	57.05	10.48	46.90	12.91
Openness	55.63	10.64	54.12	12.79
Agreeableness	48.55	11.83	43.69	11.79
Conscientiousness	44.67	10.86	42.81	11.65
Negative Affect	5.53	3.67	7.50	3.67

Figure 11b.15 The Main Discriminant Analysis Dialog Window After Defining the Range of the Grouping Variable

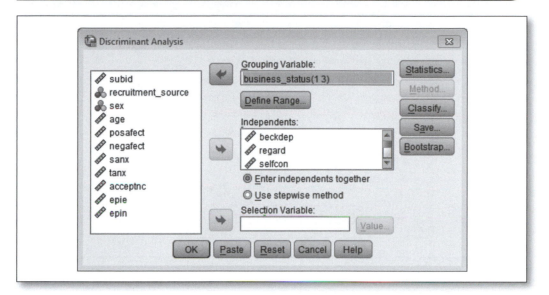

Move **business_status** into the **Grouping Variable** panel. This grouping variable represents the three groups of the participants in this fictional study. Some employees ($n = 145$) were recruited from businesses that had filed for bankruptcy but were still open; these were coded as 1 in the data file). Other employees ($n = 229$) were recruited from businesses that were stable and were not in financial stress but were not expanding; we labeled these "steady state" and coded them as 2 in the data file. The third group was composed of employees from businesses that were in a state of rapid expansion, coded as 3 in the data file. All the participants completed the inventories assessing their personal characteristics at the time. Click **Define Range** to establish these codes as described in Section 11B 1.1. Figure 11b.15 shows the window after already defining the range of the **business_status** variable by showing the variable as **business_status(1 3)**.

11B.4.2 The Statistics Window

Select the **Statistics** pushbutton. As shown in Figure 11b.16, check **Means, Univariate ANOVAs,** and **Box's M** in the **Descriptives** section of the screen and check **Fisher's** (for the classification coefficients) and **Unstandardized** in the **Function Coefficients** section. Click **Continue** to return to the main dialog window.

Figure 11b.16 The Statistics Window of Discriminant Analysis

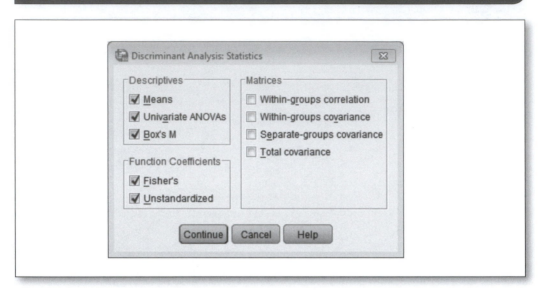

11B.4.3 The Classify Window

Select the **Classify** pushbutton. As can be seen in Figure 11b.17, we have checked **All groups equal** in the **Prior Probabilities** section of the window. We choose to **Display** the

Figure 11b.17 The Classification Window of Discriminant Analysis

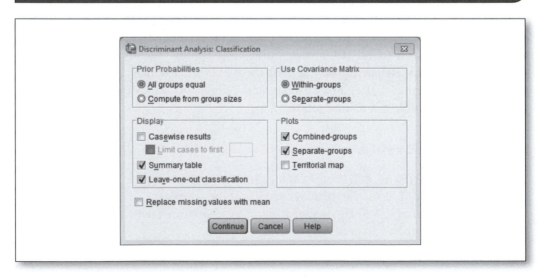

Summary table and the **Leave-one-out classification**; the former uses all of the cases in the computation, whereas the latter predicts the group membership of the one case that was omitted from the analysis. In the **Plots** section, we check **Combined-groups** and **Separate-groups**. Click **Continue** to return to the main dialog window and **OK** to perform the analysis.

11B.5 Three-Group Discriminant Function Analysis Output

11B.5.1 Descriptive Statistics

The means and standard deviations of each of the predictor variables are shown in Figure 11b.18. These statistics are shown for each group separately (from which we may look at indications of group differences) as well as for the sample as a whole. Visual inspection of the means gives the strong suggestion that the groups are quite different on many of the predictors; generally speaking, employees from businesses in bankruptcy appear to be in more dire straits than those in the other two types of companies.

11B.5.2 Homogeneity of Covariance

Figure 11b.19 displays the assessment of homogeneity of covariance matrices. **Box's M** (shown in the lower table) is statistically significant but it is an extremely powerful test, and with our large sample size, it is not surprising that it reached statistical significance. Recall, however, that the discriminant function analysis is robust to the violation of homogeneity of variance assumption.

The **Log Determinants** table, presented also in Figure 11b.19 (shown in the upper table), provides an additional way to assess the homogeneity of the groups. Larger log determinants correspond to a greater difference between the covariance matrices of the groups. The **Rank** column provides the number of independent variables (i.e., eight in this study). Because discriminant analysis assumes homogeneity of covariance matrices between groups, the determinants should be relatively equal. In the present example, the log determinants are relatively similar, suggesting that the groups are exhibiting relatively homogeneous degrees of covariance.

11B.5.3 Univariate ANOVAs

The group differences on the predictor variables are evaluated by computing a Wilks' lambda statistic in the table of **Tests of Equality of Group Means** as shown in Figure 11b.20. **Wilks' lambda** is then converted to an F ratio and tested for significance. As can be seen, all of the predictor variables were statistically significant at the .05 alpha level. If we apply a Bonferroni correction to that nominal alpha level (to protect for alpha-level

Figure 11b.18 Descriptive Statistics Output

Group Statistics

business_status financial status of business		Mean	Std. Deviation	Valid N (listwise)	
				Unweighted	Weighted
1 bankruptcy	beckdep	18.4621	8.37574	145	145.000
	regard	37.2517	7.22773	145	145.000
	selfcon	3.6255	.50544	145	145.000
	neoneuro	66.3253	7.65660	145	145.000
	neoextra	44.0397	12.24871	145	145.000
	neoopen	52.7634	12.54515	145	145.000
	neoagree	40.5809	13.50701	145	145.000
	neoconsc	38.7657	10.18847	145	145.000
2 steady state	beckdep	8.6769	5.17843	229	229.000
	regard	51.4170	7.02156	229	229.000
	selfcon	3.9753	.42116	229	229.000
	neoneuro	53.5585	6.81634	229	229.000
	neoextra	53.3882	11.96425	229	229.000
	neoopen	53.9871	11.05835	229	229.000
	neoagree	45.6679	10.10016	229	229.000
	neoconsc	44.3662	12.21000	229	229.000
3 rapid expansion	beckdep	4.2008	3.46568	254	254.000
	regard	62.1220	6.33680	254	254.000
	selfcon	4.2298	.47570	254	254.000
	neoneuro	43.3233	7.51283	254	254.000
	neoextra	57.2991	10.80371	254	254.000
	neoopen	57.3912	11.17124	254	254.000
	neoagree	50.6869	11.33657	254	254.000
	neoconsc	46.2805	9.98008	254	254.000
Total	beckdep	9.1258	7.79533	628	628.000
	regard	52.4761	11.74022	628	628.000
	selfcon	3.9975	.51819	628	628.000
	neoneuro	52.3665	11.48228	628	628.000
	neoextra	52.8115	12.63648	628	628.000
	neoopen	55.0814	11.61080	628	628.000
	neoagree	46.5234	12.09587	628	628.000
	neoconsc	43.8473	11.25663	628	628.000

Figure 11b.19 Homogeneity of Covariance Assessed by Log Determinants and by Box's *M*

Box's Test of Equality of Covariance Matrices

Log Determinants

business_status financial status of business	Rank	Log Determinant
1 bankruptcy	8	29.609
2 steady state	8	27.872
3 rapid expansion	8	26.548
Pooled within–groups	8	28.454

The ranks and natural logarithms of determinants printed are those of the group covariance matrices.

Test Results

Box's M		448.534
F	Approx.	6.110
	df1	72
	df2	713326.570
	Sig.	.000

Tests null hypothesis of equal population covariance matrices.

Figure 11b.20 Univariate Analyses of Variances on the Predictors

Tests of Equality of Group Means

	Wilks' Lambda	F	df1	df2	Sig.
beckdep	.505	305.867	2	625	.000
regard	.335	621.251	2	625	.000
selfcon	.799	78.738	2	625	.000
neoneuro	.403	462.909	2	625	.000
neoextra	.837	60.986	2	625	.000
neoopen	.972	9.165	2	625	.000
neoagree	.894	36.912	2	625	.000
neoconsc	.933	22.381	2	625	.000

inflation), by dividing .05 by the number of predictors (.05/8), we obtain approximately .006. Using that .006-corrected alpha level, we would still judge that all of them reached statistical significance.

If researchers were interested in which groups differed on each of the quantitative independent variables, they could perform a MANOVA followed by multiple comparisons tests to obtain that information (see Chapter 5A). We have done so by clicking over the quantitative variables to the **Dependent Variables** panel and **business_status** to the **Fixed Factor(s)** panel and selecting the **R-E-G-W-Q** test in the **Post Hoc** window (see Section 5B.4.2). The multivariate and univariate tests of significance yielded the same results shown in Figure 11b.20 (of course the same results were obtained, since our discriminant function analysis is the same analysis that is performed in the MANOVA procedure but just taken from a somewhat different perspective). In Figure 11b.21, we present the results of the REGWQ tests for each of the quantitative variables.

11B.5.4 Eigenvalues, Canonical Correlations, and Wilks' lambda

The global discriminant function results are contained in Figure 11b.22. **Wilks' lambda** is reported in the lower table of Figure 11b.22. Recall that with three groups in the analysis, we extract two discriminant functions. As described in Section 11A.9.3, the functions are evaluated in a reductionistic manner, and that can be seen in the lower table. The first assessment is made of all the functions taken together (**1 through 2**) shown in the first row.

Wilks' lambda is .206 for that full set; it is converted into a chi-square with degrees of freedom equal to the product of the number of predictors (8) and the number of functions that are extracted (2). Here the chi-square value is 981.330 and, with 16 degrees of freedom, is statistically significant. This **Wilks' lambda** value is the same that we obtained when we performed the MANOVA on these same variables as described in Section 11B.5.3. The value of **Wilks' lambda** represents the percentage of variance that is not explained. Subtracting this value from 1.00 indicates the proportion of explained variance. In this instance, $1.00 - .206 = .794$. Thus, the full set of two discriminant functions explains approximately 79% of the variance in the discriminant scores.

In the reduction process, after testing the statistical significance of the first two functions together, the second discriminant function is tested on its own (if there were d discriminant functions, the second through d functions would have been tested). Here, **Wilks' lambda** has a value of .966. It is statistically significant but, on its own, accounts for a very small percentage of the variance in the discriminant scores.

The upper table in Figure 11b.22 shows the **Canonical Correlation** value for each individual discriminant function. The first function is associated with a canonical correlation value of .887, and thus its squared canonical correlation is approximately .787;

Figure 11b.21 Results of the Ryan, Einot, Gabriel, and Welsch Studentized Range Tests for Each of the Quantitative Variables Performed in the Multivariate Analysis of Variance Procedure

beckdep

Ryan–Einot–Gabriel–Welsch Range[a]

financial status of business	N	Subset		
		1	2	3
3 rapid expansion	254	4.20		
2 steady state	229		8.68	
1 bankruptcy	145			18.46
Sig.		1.000	1.000	1.000

Means for groups in homogeneous subsets are displayed.
Based on observed means.
The error term is Mean Square(Error) = 30.808.

a. Alpha =

neoextra

Ryan–Einot–Gabriel–Welsch Range[a]

financial status of business	N	Subset		
		1	2	3
1 bankruptcy	145	44.0397		
2 steady state	229		53.3882	
3 rapid expansion	254			57.2991
Sig.		1.000	1.000	1.000

Means for groups in homogeneous subsets are displayed.
Based on observed means.
The error term is Mean Square(Error) = 134.034.

a. Alpha =

regard

Ryan–Einot–Gabriel–Welsch Range[a]

financial status of business	N	Subset		
		1	2	3
1 bankruptcy	145	37.25		
2 steady state	229		51.42	
3 rapid expansion	254			62.12
Sig.		1.000	1.000	1.000

Means for groups in homogeneous subsets are displayed.
Based on observed means.
The error term is Mean Square(Error) = 46.276.

a. Alpha =

neoopen

Ryan–Einot–Gabriel–Welsch Range[a]

financial status of business	N	Subset	
		1	2
1 bankruptcy	145	52.7634	
2 steady state	229	53.9871	
3 rapid expansion	254		57.3912
Sig.		.364	1.000

Means for groups in homogeneous subsets are displayed.
Based on observed means.
The error term is Mean Square(Error) = 131.389.

a. Alpha =

selfcon

Ryan–Einot–Gabriel–Welsch Range[a]

financial status of business	N	Subset		
		1	2	3
1 bankruptcy	145	3.6255		
2 steady state	229		3.9753	
3 rapid expansion	254			4.2298
Sig.		1.000	1.000	1.000

Means for groups in homogeneous subsets are displayed.
Based on observed means.
The error term is Mean Square(Error) = .215.

a. Alpha =

neoagree

Ryan–Einot–Gabriel–Welsch Range[a]

financial status of business	N	Subset		
		1	2	3
1 bankruptcy	145	40.5809		
2 steady state	229		45.6679	
3 rapid expansion	254			50.6869
Sig.		1.000	1.000	1.000

Means for groups in homogeneous subsets are displayed.
Based on observed means.
The error term is Mean Square(Error) = 131.272.

a. Alpha =

neoneuro

Ryan–Einot–Gabriel–Welsch Range[a]

financial status of business	N	Subset		
		1	2	3
3 rapid expansion	254	43.3233		
2 steady state	229		53.5585	
1 bankruptcy	145			66.3253
Sig.		1.000	1.000	1.000

Means for groups in homogeneous subsets are displayed.
Based on observed means.
The error term is Mean Square(Error) = 53.304.

a. Alpha =

neoconsc

Ryan–Einot–Gabriel–Welsch Range[a]

financial status of business	N	Subset	
		1	2
1 bankruptcy	145	38.7657	
2 steady state	229		44.3662
3 rapid expansion	254		46.2805
Sig.		1.000	.060

Means for groups in homogeneous subsets are displayed.
Based on observed means.
The error term is Mean Square(Error) = 118.621.

a. Alpha =

Figure 11b.22 Summary of the Discriminant Functions

Eigenvalues

Function	Eigenvalue	% of Variance	Cumulative %	Canonical Correlation
1	3.687[a]	99.1	99.1	.887
2	.035[a]	.9	100.0	.183

a. First 2 canonical discriminant functions were used in the analysis.

Wilks' Lambda

Test of Function(s)	Wilks' Lambda	Chi-square	df	Sig.
1 through 2	.206	981.330	16	.000
2	.966	21.214	7	.003

therefore, in this first function, approximately 79% of the variance of the dependent variate is explained or predicted by the predictor variate. Its eigenvalue is 3.687, and of the total amount of explained variance of the set of functions, the first function is responsible for 99.1%.

The second function is associated with a canonical correlation value of .183, and its squared canonical correlation is approximately .033; thus, in this second function, approximately 3% of the variance of the dependent variate is explained or predicted by the predictor variate. This second discriminant function also lags well behind the first with an eigenvalue of 0.035, and of the total amount of explained variance of the set of functions, the second function is responsible for 0.9%.

Here is how we know how much of the explained variance can be attributed to each discriminant function. Because the functions are orthogonal (independent of each other), the eigenvalues are additive. Adding the two eigenvalues yields a total of 3.722. Of that total, the eigenvalue for the first function represents 3.687 of the 3.722 and 3.687/3.722 = .9906 or 99.1% of the explained variance, and the eigenvalue for the second function represents .035 of the 3.722, and .035/3.722 = .0094 or 0.9% of the explained variance.

Remember, though, that we have explained only 79% of the total variance; these percentages described above (99.1% for the second function and just less than 1% for the second function) are partitioning this 79% of the variance explained by the set of discriminant functions—there is still 21% of the total variance that remains unexplained by the set of discriminant functions.

11B.5.5 Discriminant Function Coefficients

Figure 11b.23 presents the **Canonical Discriminant Function Coefficients**. On the left are the raw score coefficients; on the right are the standardized coefficients. These are the weights for each function by which the raw scores or the *z*-score values of the variables are multiplied and summed together to produce a discriminant score for each case, and they comprise the raw score and standardized score versions of the discriminant model. Based on the standardized coefficients, it appears that when these variables are combined together to distinguish the groups, self-regard (**regard**) and neuroticism (**neoneuro**) are weighted more heavily than the other predictors in the first function and that depression (**beckdep**) is weighted more heavily than the other predictors in the second function.

Figure 11b.23   Unstandardized and Standardized Discriminant Function Coefficients

Canonical Discriminant Function Coefficients

	Function 1	Function 2
beckdep	.052	.142
regard	-.099	.031
selfcon	-.183	.082
neoneuro	.076	-.065
neoextra	.000	-.027
neoopen	.005	.020
neoagree	-.004	.018
neoconsc	.015	-.033
(Constant)	.713	1.077

Unstandardized coefficients

Standardized Canonical Discriminant Function Coefficients

	Function 1	Function 2
beckdep	.290	.787
regard	-.674	.212
selfcon	-.085	.038
neoneuro	.558	-.474
neoextra	.002	-.309
neoopen	.056	.225
neoagree	-.046	.203
neoconsc	.160	-.355

11B.5.6 Structure Coefficients

The structure coefficients for each function are shown in Figure 11b.24. These are the correlations between the variables and the variate (the weighted linear composite) as a whole. We interpret the discriminant functions primarily on the basis of these coefficients. The coefficients are conveniently ordered for us in a descending fashion for each function in the **Structure Matrix** to facilitate reading the table.

Figure 11b.24   Structure Coefficients

Structure Matrix

	Function 1	Function 2
regard	−.734*	.089
neoneuro	.634*	−.195
selfcon	−.261*	.001
neoagree	−.178*	.172
beckdep	.511	.711*
neoextra	−.227	−.373*
neoopen	−.083	.328*
neoconsc	−.136	−.296*

Pooled within–groups correlations between discriminating variables and standardized canonical discriminant functions
Variables ordered by absolute size of correlation within function.

*. Largest absolute correlation between each variable and any discriminant function

We interpret each discriminant function separately, remembering that the first is overwhelmingly more potent than the second. For the first function, we note that self-regard (**regard**) and neuroticism (**neoneuro**) are relatively strong indicators of the latent construct. Higher levels of the construct are thus associated with more self-regard and less neuroticism; we opt to label the latent construct as an unhealthy adaptation toward life. The latent construct for the second function is indicated primarily by more depression (**beckdep**) and, to a limited degree, by lower levels of extraversion (**neoextra**) and conscientiousness (**neoconsc**) and higher levels of openness (**neoopen**); we opt to label the latent construct as representing a lack of caring about self and others.

11B.5.7 Classification Results

Figure 11b.25 presents the **Functions at Group Centroids** table. These centroids (multivariate means) are in Mahalanobis distance units and can be thought of as standard deviation units or as z scores. Because there are two functions, there are two sets of centroids: one for each function. As we discussed in Section 11B.5.4, canonical correlations, eigenvalues, and Wilks' lambda informed us that the first discriminant function accounted for 99% of the explained variance and that the second function accounted for just less than 1% of the explained variance.

Figure 11b.25   Group Centroids

Functions at Group Centroids

business_status financial status of business	Function 1	Function 2
1 bankruptcy	3.068	.163
2 steady state	.182	−.245
3 rapid expansion	−1.916	.128

Unstandardized canonical discriminant functions evaluated at group means

The centroids shown in Figure 11b.25 illustrate this information as well. Note that the centroids corresponding to the first function are very far apart (remembering that these Mahalanobis distances can be thought of in z-score terms). The Bankruptcy and Rapid Expansion groups are separated considerably from about a distance of 3 units from the center for the Bankruptcy group to a distance of almost −2 units from the center for the Rapid Expansion group. Our Steady State group is almost at the center of the space (the midpoint of 0). All three groups are relatively quite far from each other with respect to the first function.

The situation is different for the second function. There are two features of note. First, the centroids hover near the center of the space. Specifically, all are within a distance of about .25 from the center. Second, the Steady State group seems to be relatively separated from the other two groups to the extent that such a spread can be interpreted as any sort of separation.

Figure 11b.26 shows the separate group plots. Unlike what was seen in the two-group analysis, these plots are more complex. Function 1 distances are represented on the X axis

Figure 11b.26 Separate Group Plots

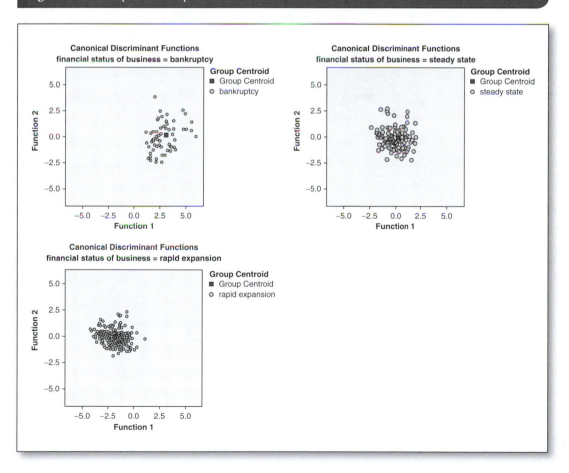

and Function 2 distances are represented on the *Y* axis for each group. The data points depict the cases in each group, and the darkened data point is the centroid of the two-function space.

A somewhat easier-to-interpret plot is shown in the combined groups plot in Figure 11b.27. The axes are the same as for the separate group plots, but all three groups are placed

Figure 11b.27 Combined Group Plot

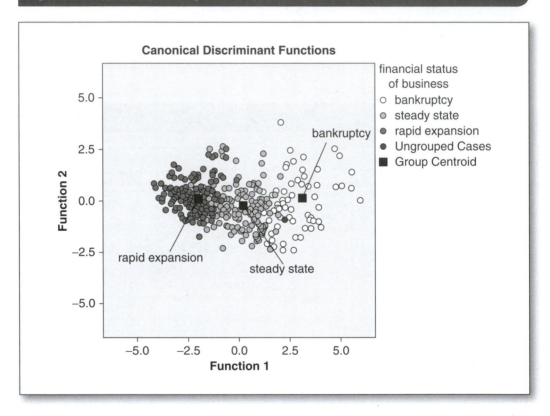

into the same space using different colors (that may not be easily discerned in the grey-tone version of the output shown in the figure) to represent the group data points. The darkened data points are the overall centroids of the three groups. Horizontal separation visually depicts the relatively even and substantial spacing among the groups with respect to the first function. Vertical separation, such as it is, corresponds to the separation of the groups on the second function.

Although the combined groups plot in Figure 11b.27 has the advantage of allowing us to see the information for all three groups on a single set of axes, IBM SPSS has not scaled the axes to match the actual values of the centroids. To compensate for this, we have plotted the group centroids ourselves in Figure 11b.28 using the coordinates shown in Figure 11b.25. With the understanding that each axis is scaled to the approximate range of the centroid values, and with the understanding that the relatively small Function 2 differences may be pictorially exaggerated, we can see from the display in Figure 11b.28 (as well as from the table in Figure 11b.25) that the three groups are quite differentiated along Function 1 and that the Bankruptcy and Rapid Expansion groups appear to be somewhat differentiated from the Steady State group along Function 2.

Figure 11b.28 Simplified and Properly Scaled Combined Group Plot

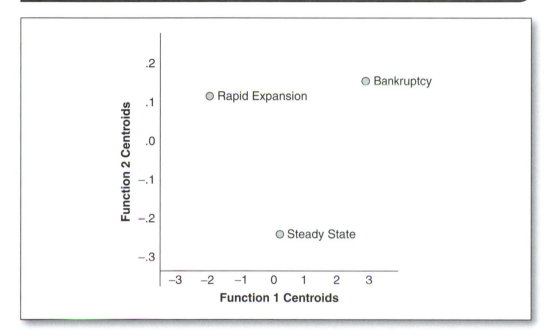

The **Classification Function Coefficients** are shown in the upper portion of Figure 11b.29. These are in raw score form and are weights by which we would multiply the variables to achieve a classification value for each group for an individual case. The group associated with the largest classification value is the group to which that case is predicted to belong.

Hits and misses in the classification effort are shown in the lower portion of Figure 11b.29. The major output row labeled **Original** has used all of the cases in performing the discriminant function analysis. When we use this solution to classify each case, we are somewhat biasing our result toward successful classification. Thus, of 145 Bankruptcy

Figure 11b.29 Classification Function Coefficients and the Classification Table

Classification Function Coefficients

	business_status financial status of business		
	1 bankruptcy	2 steady state	3 rapid expansion
beckdep	.350	.141	.084
regard	.569	.842	1.062
selfcon	19.751	20.244	20.658
neoneuro	1.782	1.588	1.403
neoextra	.205	.216	.205
neoopen	.291	.269	.266
neoagree	.229	.234	.249
neoconsc	.238	.209	.166
(Constant)	-131.283	-129.108	-132.001

Fisher's linear discriminant functions

Classification Results[b,c]

		business_status financial status of business	Predicted Group Membership			Total
			1 bankruptcy	2 steady state	3 rapid expansion	
Original	Count	1 bankruptcy	133	12	0	145
		2 steady state	13	176	40	229
		3 rapid expansion	0	26	228	254
		Ungrouped cases	5	0	0	5
	%	1 bankruptcy	91.7	8.3	.0	100.0
		2 steady state	5.7	76.9	17.5	100.0
		3 rapid expansion	.0	10.2	89.8	100.0
		Ungrouped cases	100.0	.0	.0	100.0
Cross-validated[a]	Count	1 bankruptcy	131	14	0	145
		2 steady state	20	167	42	229
		3 rapid expansion	0	28	226	254
	%	1 bankruptcy	90.3	9.7	.0	100.0
		2 steady state	8.7	72.9	18.3	100.0
		3 rapid expansion	.0	11.0	89.0	100.0

a. Cross validation is done only for those cases in the analysis. In cross validation, each case is classified by the functions derived from all cases other than that case.

b. 85.5% of original grouped cases correctly classified.

c. 83.4% of cross-validated grouped cases correctly classified.

cases, 133 are predicted to be in the Bankruptcy group (these are "hits"), 12 are predicted to be in the Steady State group, and none are predicted to be in the Rapid Expansion group. Of the 229 Steady State cases, 176 are predicted to be in that group, 13 are predicted to be in the Bankruptcy group, and 40 are predicted to be in the Rapid Expansion group. Finally, of the 254 Rapid Expansion cases, 228 are predicted correctly, 26 are predicted to be in the Steady State group, and none are predicted to be in the Bankruptcy group.

Overall, as shown in **Footnote b** at the bottom of the table, 85.5% of the cases were correctly classified. In the procedure where the case whose group membership is to be predicted is omitted from the analysis, labeled as **Cross-validated** in the table, correct classifications was almost as good at 83.4%.

We may compute Press' Q (see Section 11A.10.3.3) to assess whether the **Cross-validated** hit rate exceeded chance expectation. We have 628 cases in the analysis; of these, 131 were correctly classified to be in the Bankruptcy group, 167 were correctly classified to be in the Steady State group, and 226 were correctly classified to be in the Rapid Expansion group for a total of 524. Using these values, Press' Q is 709.50. Evaluated against the chi-square distribution with 1 degree of freedom, the critical value for an alpha level of .05 (3.841) was exceeded; we therefore conclude that our model was able to classify cases at a better than chance level.

11B.6 Reporting the Results of a Three-Group Discriminant Function Analysis

A three-group discriminant analysis was performed on employees from businesses that were in bankruptcy, in steady state, or in a state of rapid expansion. Measures of depression, self-regard, self-control, neuroticism, extraversion, openness, agreeableness, and conscientiousness were used as discriminating (predictor) variables. The obtained discriminant functions in combination accounted for a statistically significant percentage of the between-group differences, Wilks' $\Lambda = .206$, $\chi^2(16, N = 625) = 981.33$, $p < .001$, overall $R_c^2 = .794$. Using a leave-one-out cross-validation strategy, 83.4% of the cases were correctly classified, Press' $Q = 709.50$, $p < .001$. The first function was dominant, accounting for approximately 99% of the explained variance; the second function, however, was also statistically significant, step-down second function Wilks' $\Lambda = .966$, $\chi^2(7, N = 625) = 21.21$, $p = .003$, $R_c^2 = .033$.

Table 11b.4 presents the discriminant function coefficients for the raw and standardized forms of the variables for each function. For the first discriminant function, self-regard and neuroticism were most strongly weighted in the linear composite; for the second discriminant function, depression was most strongly weighted, with neuroticism, conscientiousness, and extraversion also receiving moderate weights.

The latent constructs represented by the discriminant functions can be interpreted with respect to the structure coefficients, which are shown in Table 11b.5. For the first function, higher levels of the latent variable are indicated primarily by lower levels of self-regard and higher levels of neuroticism and depression; this construct appears to represent an unhealthy adaptation toward life. The latent construct for the second function is indicated primarily by more depression and, to a limited degree, by lower

(Continued)

(Continued)

levels of extraversion and conscientiousness and higher levels of openness; this construct appears to represent a lack of caring about self and others.

The group centroids are shown in Figure 11b.28. The differences in centroid values are relatively substantial along Function 1 (a healthy adaptation toward life) with all three groups strongly differentiated from each other; those undergoing bankruptcy reported a healthy adaptation toward life, whereas those in businesses undergoing rapid expansion reported a relatively unhealthy adaptation toward life, and those in steady state businesses reported a midrange adaptation toward life. The differences in centroid values are much more modest along Function 2 (lack of caring), with those in the bankruptcy and rapid expansion groups appearing to be somewhat more caring and those in the steady state group appearing to be somewhat less caring.

The group means on the discriminant variables are shown in Table 11b.6. Separate one-way between-subjects ANOVAs using a Bonferroni-corrected alpha level of .006 yielded a statistically significant difference between the groups for all of the predictor variables. Ryan, Einot, Gabriel, and Welsch Studentized Range tests indicated that (a) those in the bankruptcy group reported higher levels of depression, self-regard, self-control, neuroticism, extraversion, and agreeableness than those in the steady state group, who in turn were higher on these characteristics than employees in the rapid expansion group; (b) that employees in the steady state and rapid expansion groups were not significantly different on conscientiousness but were both more conscientious than those in the bankruptcy group; and (c) that employees in the rapid expansion group were more open than those in the bankruptcy and steady state groups, with these latter two sets of employees not differing on this characteristic.

Table 11b.4　Raw and Standardized Discriminant Function Coefficients

Measured Variable	Raw Score Coefficients		Standardized Coefficients	
	Function 1	Function 2	Function 1	Function 2
Depression	0.052	0.142	.290	.787
Self-Regard	−0.099	0.031	−.674	.212
Self-Control	−0.183	0.082	−.085	.038
Neuroticism	0.076	−0.065	.558	−.474
Extraversion	0.000	−0.027	.002	−.309
Openness	0.005	0.020	.056	.225
Agreeableness	−0.004	0.018	−.046	.203
Conscientiousness	0.015	−0.033	.160	−.355
Constant	0.713	1.077		

Table 11b.5 Structure Coefficients

Measured Variable	Structure Coefficients	
	Function 1	**Function 2**
Depression	.511	.711
Self-Regard	−.734	.089
Self-Control	−.261	.001
Neuroticism	.634	−.195
Extraversion	−.227	−.373
Openness	−.083	.328
Agreeableness	−.178	.172
Conscientiousness	−.136	−.296

Table 11b.6 Means and Standard Deviations of the Variables for Each Group

Measured Variables	Bankruptcy Business		Steady State Business		Rapidly Expanding Business	
	M	*SD*	*M*	*SD*	*M*	*SD*
Depression	18.46	8.38	8.68	5.18	4.20	3.47
Self-Regard	37.25	7.23	51.42	7.02	62.12	6.34
Self-Control	3.63	0.51	3.98	0.42	4.23	0,48
Neuroticism	66.33	7.66	53.56	6.82	43.32	7.51
Extraversion	44.04	12.25	53.39	11.96	57.30	10.80
Openness	52.76	12.55	53.99	11.06	57.39	11.17
Agreeableness	40.58	13.51	45.67	10.10	50.69	11.34
Conscientiousness	38.77	10.19	44.37	12.21	46.28	9.98

Principal Components Analysis and Exploratory Factor Analysis

12A.1 Orientation and Terminology

The informal term *data crunching* generally refers to a process in which a considerable quantity of data is reduced down to a more manageable or consolidated whole. Principal components analysis and exploratory factor analysis are the quintessential data-crunching procedures. Their general purpose is to identify a relatively small number of themes, dimensions, components, or factors underlying a relatively large set of variables. They do this by distinguishing sets of variables that have more in common with each other than with the other variables in the analysis. What the subsets of variables have in common are the underlying components or factors.

Both principal components analysis and factor analysis are *exploratory* procedures. In this context, that means we are not testing a null hypothesis about the population value of a particular statistic nor are we distinguishing between dependent and independent variables; rather, we are describing relationships among variables existent in the data set. This does not prohibit researchers from having hopes or expectations regarding the factor structure that emerges from the analysis, but it does mean that there is no statistical hypothesis that is being tested. Exploratory factor analysis can be contrasted with *confirmatory factor analysis* (see Chapters 16A and 16B), where a certain factor structure is specified and the procedure then tests how well the data fit that structure. We adopt the common convention here of dropping the term *exploratory* when referring to the factor analysis techniques we cover in this chapter and using the term *confirmatory* when referring to the factor analysis techniques we cover in Chapters 16A and 16B.

Principal components analysis and factor analysis are very closely related exploratory data reduction techniques that are generally quite similar but differ in important ways both statistically and conceptually. Many researchers use the term *factor analysis* in a generic way to refer to both principal components analysis and factor analysis (Gorsuch, 1983). To ease readers into the topic, we will use this generic term in the beginning of our discussion, but we will soon need to distinguish between principal components analysis and factor analysis.

12A.2 How Factor Analysis Is Used in Psychological Research

One of the most common applications of factor analysis is in test development and test scoring, and the examples we present here are drawn from this domain. Using factor analysis in this context, researchers analyze the correlations between responses of participants to a relatively large number of test items. Their goals are to choose the items that will appear on the final version of the instrument and to determine if the construct assessed by the inventory can best be measured by reasonable and viable subscales (Gamst, Liang, & Der-Karabetian, 2011). The factors will indicate which items should be assigned to which subscale. This process can also be used in validating the structure of a test or inventory. Researchers will have reported the factor structure of their measure, but it is useful to determine the extent to which that structure is replicable and the extent to which it will generalize to somewhat different populations.

Another potential application of factor analysis might be to help researchers organize or conceptualize a set of measures that they have obtained in the context of a research program. For example, researchers may have administered a large battery of cognitive tests to a sample of participants to determine which ones might be assessing a similar mental process. Here, each factor will represent a subset of measures that are relatively strongly related to each other. Further analyses can then be conducted based on the factors rather than on the individual measures themselves; for example, we can examine group differences in a MANOVA using the factors as dependent variables, we can predict group membership through logistic regression or discriminant analysis using the factors as predictors, or we can predict the value of a quantitative variable in multiple regression with the factors as the predictor variables.

12A.3 Origins of Factor Analysis

A very readable and informative history of the development of factor analysis is provided in the beginning of Harry Harmon's (1960, 1967) classic text. Harmon tells us that the origins of this statistical technique can be traced to Charles Spearman (1904), who is considered to be the father of factor analysis, although Anastasi and Urbana (1997) suggest that an earlier article by Karl Pearson (1901) might have established a beginning on which Spearman (1904) could build. In any case, Spearman proposed a two-factor theory of intelligence by identifying a general intelligence factor (which came to be symbolized as *g*) underlying all cognitive abilities as well as factors specific to particular abilities (e.g., memory for number sequences, ability to perceive spatial relations). Harmon (1960) goes on to say that Spearman's (1904) two-factor approach gave way to the extraction of several factors and credits Garnett (1919) as the driving force behind that. Finally, factor analysis was transformed into the modern form that we now use through the seminal work of Louis Leon Thurstone (1931, 1935). Principal components analysis also has its start in the article by Pearson (1901) but was developed in large part by Harold Hotelling (1933, 1936b) at about the same time that Thurstone (1931, 1935) was revamping factor analysis.

12A.4 The General Organization of This Chapter

In describing factor analysis, we start with a simplified and conceptual example. Once this foundation is established, we discuss the extraction phase of the procedure and follow it with a discussion of the rotation phase. We close with guidelines for determining an acceptable solution and provide some rubrics for selecting a sample size appropriate for the analysis.

12A.5 Where the Analysis Begins: The Correlation Matrix

Factor analysis attempts to summarize and synthesize the relationships between the variables contained in the analysis. It starts at the same place that many of the other multivariate procedures begin—with the correlation matrix showing the Pearson correlations between pairs of variables. Bivariate correlations assess the degree to which the variables are associated or related. A correlation matrix contains these pairwise correlations for all the variables. To make the relationships of the variables that much easier to see, in the following discussion, we will talk about correlations that are either extremely high or extremely low.

12A.5.1 A Three-Variable Example

In very simplified form, factor analysis is a statistical procedure designed to determine which variables are more intimately related to each other than to other variables. Intimacy in this context is quantifiable in terms of Pearson correlation values. Consider the very small correlation matrix shown in Table 12a.1. These are correlations of the responses to Questions A, B, and C on a hypothetical survey or inventory. With only three variables in the matrix, it is relatively easy to see, without any elaborate statistical procedure such as factor analysis, that Items A and B are very strongly correlated but that neither is related much to Item C.

The obtained Pearson r value of .87 describes the association between A and B. From this value, we know that responses to Item B are very predictable from a knowledge of the responses to Item A. For Pearson r values of .12 and .07 obtained between C and A and C and B, respectively, we know that responses to Item C are not at all predictable from the responses participants gave to either Item A or Item B.

Table 12a.1 Correlation Matrix for Variables A Through C

Variable	B	C
A	.87	.12
B	--	.07

12A.5.2 A Four-Variable Example

Now consider a slightly larger set of variables in an expansion of the preceding example, which we will use to broach the topic of factor analysis. In this somewhat larger set of variables, we have added Item D to the original three survey questions. The correlation matrix that includes this newly added variable is displayed in Table 12a.2. Here, we see that D is strongly related to C but is not related to A and B. At this juncture, we can then draw the inference that A and B have much in common, that C and D have much in common, and that A and B have little in common with C and D.

Another way to verbalize what we can infer from the relationships between the survey questions is to say that the set of four variables shown in Table 12a.2 really represents two sets of two variables each. Because factors distinguish sets of variables that have more in common with each other than with the other variables in the analysis, we may then also say that the four variables represent two underlying factors. From the correlations of these variables, Items A and B appear to be the primary indicators of one factor, and Items C and D appear to be the primary indicators of the other factor. In essence, what we have just done from our examination of the correlation matrix is to perform a conceptually based factor analysis.

The factors that we have identified are not themselves directly measured variables. Instead, they are latent variables (*variates* or *weighted linear composites*). When we perform the factor analysis, each factor would be composed of the four variables in the analysis, but the variables would have different weights in the two factors.

Table 12a.2 Correlation Matrix for Variables A Through D

Variable	B	C	D
A	.87	.12	.11
B	--	.07	.17
C			.86

In one variate or factor, A and B would each weighted quite highly, whereas C and D would have negligible weights. We therefore say that A and B are strong indicators of that factor (and that C and D are weak indicators of that factor). The situation is reversed in the other variate. There, C and D would each be weighted quite highly, whereas A and B would have negligible weights. In this case, C and D would be the strong indicators of that factor (and A and B would be weak indicators).

As we have seen in other multivariate designs (e.g., regression analysis, discriminant analysis), it is also useful to examine the relationship (correlation) between each of the variables contained in the linear composite and the variate as a whole. Such correlations are called *structure coefficients*. The weights assigned to the variables in the linear composite and the structure coefficients both provide us with a perspective for interpreting the variate or factor.

The weights of the variables as well as the structure coefficients associated with the variables are each ordinarily shown in a table called a *factor matrix*. Such tables are a standard feature in the output of a factor analysis procedure. We show such a factor matrix in Table 12a.3 for variables A through D. In this table, the variables in the analysis occupy the rows and the factors occupy the columns. These factors were obtained from the results of the rotation phase of the analysis (we will talk about rotation in Section 12A.13); we therefore refer to this factor matrix as a *rotated factor matrix*.

We used an orthogonal strategy for the rotation on which the factor matrix in Table 12a.3 is based (we will explain this in our discussion of rotation); because of this, the numerical entries in the table represent at the same time (a) the weights of the variables in the linear composite as well as (b) the structure coefficients. Either way of viewing these values is acceptable in the process of interpreting the results of the factor analysis. The rotated factor matrix is one of the main ingredients involved in a statistical solution to the factor analysis procedure. A convenient way to examine the rotated factor matrix is to first focus on the rows of the table to understand how the variables are behaving across the factors. Once we have digested this information, we can concentrate on the columns in an effort to interpret the factors.

Using this strategy, we first examine the rows of Table 12a.3. Remember that we can view the table entries as structure coefficients. From this perspective, the top two rows of this rotated factor matrix show the correlations of variables A and B with each of the two factors. Variable B is (slightly) more strongly correlated with Factor 1 than is variable A. Reading across these first two rows reveals a consistent

Table 12a.3   Two-Factor Rotated Matrix for Variables A Through D

Variable	Factor 1	Factor 2
A	.96439	.05828
B	.96563	.06356
C	.03566	.96422
D	.08635	.96065

story: A and B are both strongly correlated with Factor 1 and are not correlated with Factor 2. The last two rows of Table 12a.3 show the correlations of C and D with each of the two factors. Reading across these rows, we can see that variables C and D are not correlated with Factor 1 but are strongly correlated with Factor 2.

We can now focus on the columns (the factors) of this rotated factor matrix. In this matrix, each factor is composed of a weighted combination of the four variables, and we can view the numbers in the table as representing those weights. The key to dealing with the information contained in the rotated factor matrix is to notice the difference in the pattern of the weights in the two factors. Looking first at Factor 1, we find that it is strongly exemplified by variables A and B and weakly represented by C and D. That is, A and B have been weighted quite strongly, and C and D have been weighted quite weakly in the establishment of Factor 1. An analogous finding is obtained for Factor 2 in which C and D have received the very substantial weights, whereas the weights assigned to A and B are negligible.

The process of examining the columns or factors of the rotated factor matrix is the way that the factors are "interpreted" by researchers—knowing that the content of Items A and B in effect unveils the essence of Factor 1 because these variables are the primary indicators of this factor and knowing that the content of Items C and D discloses the essence of Factor 2 because they are the primary indicators of that factor. We will talk about this later in the chapter.

12A.5.3 A Six-Variable Example

Let's expand the example further by adding two additional variables, E and F, to the correlation matrix. This is shown in Table 12a.4. There are many more relationships to deal with now given the inclusion of these two additional variables. But because we are building on what we presented in the previous table and because we are still working with correlations that are relatively near 1 and 0, it is still possible to discern the interrelationships between the six variables contained in Table 12a.4. Because we have constructed this example with an unambiguous interpretation in mind, we have made E strongly related to A and B, whereas we have made F strongly related to C and D. Given this pattern, it is not surprising that we have built this example such that E and F have no substantial relationship.

Although there is more information in Table 12a.4 than in the prior correlation matrices, we can still identify two factors based on the correlations between the pairs of

Table 12a.4 Correlation Matrix for Variables A Through F

Variable	B	C	D	E	F
A	.87	.12	.11	.92	.08
B		.07	.17	.89	.13
C			.86	.10	.88
D				.14	.91
E					.06

variables; that is, we can still identify two relatively distinct sets of survey items. One set of variables (one factor) is composed of Inventory Questions A, B, and E, and the other set of questions is composed of C, D, and F. Analogous to what we stated above, we can say here that A, B, and E have a great deal in common and that C, D, and F, likewise, have a great deal in common. That is, it appears that the variables within each set share a great deal of variance and that there is not much shared variance (not much of a relationship) between the two sets.

Just as in the prior example, what we have essentially done here for this more complex correlation matrix is to again perform a conceptually based factor analysis of the variables A, B, C, D, E, and F. We have determined that there are two factors underlying this set of variables. One of the factors was represented by A, B, and E, and the other factor was represented by C, D, and F. Each set of variables shares a great deal of variance. The factor is, at a conceptual level, that shared variance, and the factor would ordinarily be labeled as whatever it is that the items in the set have in common.

Our conceptually based factor analysis coincides very well with the results of the statistical analysis that we performed on these correlations. We show in Table 12a.5 the rotated factor matrix from that analysis. To make it easier to glean information from the table, we have sorted the values (the structure coefficients) by factor in descending order within each factor (we can specify such sorting in an IBM SPSS dialog window). The disadvantage of sorting is that the variables are in a different order from that in the data file, but the advantage, which usually far outweighs the disadvantage, is that the variables indicative of a given factor are all grouped together in the table.

In looking at the rows of this matrix, we can see a very general pattern—variables are strongly correlated with one of the factors while showing no substantial correlation with the other factor. Note that even though the pattern is quite similar, the values of these correlations are different from those shown in the prior rotated factor matrix for variables A through D. This is to be expected because the two variates (factors) represented in Table 12a.5 are linear composites of six rather than four variables and therefore depict entities that are at least somewhat different from those in Table 12a.3.

Examining the columns (the factors) in Table 12a.5 reaffirms and extends the story that emerged in the previous example. Factor 1 here is best indicated by Survey Questions A, B, and E (with C, D, and F playing little role in that composite). In contrast, Factor 2 is best signified by Questions C, D, and F (with A, B, and E playing little role in that composite).

Table 12a.5 Two-Factor Rotated Matrix for Variables A Through F

Variable	Factor 1	Factor 2
E	.97136	.04630
A	.96344	.05026
B	.95153	.07340
F	.03577	.96865
D	.09035	.95795
C	.04405	.94933

12A.5.4 Introducing a Little Fuzziness
Into the Example: Modest Relationship Strengths

We will now expand our example one final time to illustrate another point. We have added Items G and H to our set of variables, and we show the entire correlation matrix in Table 12a.6. We acknowledge that the table is beginning to get very cluttered, but stay with us for just a little longer.

Table 12a.6 Correlation Matrix for Variables A Through H

Variable	B	C	D	E	F	G	H
A	.87	.12	.11	.92	.08	.61	.08
B		.07	.17	.89	.13	.57	.15
C			.86	.10	.88	.14	.56
D				.14	.91	.09	.60
E					.06	.55	.07
F						.08	.58
G							.07

We have written in correlations for G that tie it to A, B, and E but not to the other variables. Similarly, we have written in correlations for H that tie it to C, D, and F but not to the other variables. Thus, we still have two factors represented by the variables in this matrix—A, B, E, and G on the one hand and C, D, F, and H on the other hand. And we can still say that the variables within each factor have a great deal more in common with each other than they have with those in the other factor.

But here we have much more diversity in the strengths of the relationships of the variables within each factor. Consider the factor represented by A, B, E, and G. If you look at the correlations for these variables, you will see that the first three of them are tied together quite strongly. Given that the correlation for A–B is .87, for A–E is .92, and for B–E is .89, we understand that there is a large amount of shared variance among this trio. Although G is related to these three, the ties are not nearly that strong. The correlations for G–A, G–B, and G–E are .61, .57, and .55, respectively. A similar situation exists for the second factor.

When we think in terms of factors, we would say that one factor is represented by variables A, B, E, and G and another factor is indexed by variables C, D, F, and H. But given the ties that bind them together, we hope you can see that G is less related to its factor than are A, B, and E and that H is less related to its factor than are C, D, and F.

Table 12a.7 Two-Factor Rotated Matrix for Variables A Through H

Variable	Factor 1	Factor 2
A	.95558	.04616
E	.94828	.04119
B	.93463	.08318
G	.73099	.06213
F	.03521	.95125
D	.08330	.94641
C	.05697	.92905
H	.05845	.73754

This conceptual treatment is reinforced by the statistical outcome of the analysis. We present the rotated factor matrix for this two-factor solution in Table 12a.7. Once again, the results are unambiguous in that variables correlate substantially with one factor and do not correlate with the other factor. Variables G and H, because they are less related to the other variables in their respective factors as we have described above, show a relatively lower (but still substantial) correlation with their respective factor.

Examining the columns of the rotated factor matrix in Table 12a.7, we see that the factors are clearly differentiated. Factor 1 is best represented by A, E, and B, and Factor 2 is best represented by F, D, C, and H. Yet in these two sets of variables, G and H are less potent indicators of their respective factor than the other three variables in the set. When we discuss how to interpret a factor, we will focus on the content of those variables that are more strongly related to the factor. Here, for example, we would focus more heavily on A, E, and B to interpret Factor 1 and on F, D, and C to interpret Factor 2.

In the everyday world of research, the fuzziness we introduced into this last correlation matrix will be closer to what will be obtained than the exaggerated examples we used earlier. That is, although a number of variables may be correlated with a factor to a certain extent, not all will be strongly correlated with it. Some variables will have a stronger relationship with (overlap more with, be better indicators of) the factor than other variables. Generally, we expect the variables to have different weights when we obtain the linear function that defines the factor. In the process of choosing a name for (interpreting) a factor, something that researchers almost always have to (and want to) do, we should allow ourselves to be more influenced by variables that are more strongly related to (correlated with) the factor than those that are more weakly related to it.

12A.6 Acquiring Perspective on Factor Analysis

This last example, with variables A through H, is really an oversimplified, almost-best-case illustration of the factor analysis process. We started with a set of eight variables—it would be unlikely that we would have such a small number of items if we were actually developing a test, survey, or inventory—and reduced them down to two pretty clear factors. Because this was a contrived example, it worked out to be a wonderfully clean solution. That is, we lost very little information in the process of this data crunching. Even given the simplicity of our example, however, looking at some of the issues and implications of what went on will provide a good foundation for appreciating what factor analysis is all about.

12A.6.1 The Importance of Individual Variables

The importance of the individual variables in a factor analysis (particularly when these variables are items on an inventory or survey) presents us with one of the great ironies of behavioral and social research. It can be best illustrated in the context of test development. As you have no doubt already learned, developing good-quality items that assess the proper content of a construct is an absolute requirement of proper test development. The presence of poorly written items and items that are not germane to the topic can adversely affect the assessment process by substantially lowering the validity and reliability of the instrument (due to inflation or deflation of the item correlations).

Faced with a well-understood and well-documented content domain, the number of different items that can be generated is, if not infinite, then very, very large. Yet of the zillions of items that can potentially be written to measure a construct, only four or five dozen are likely to ever be produced, and only about two or three dozen may ever be included on the preliminary versions of the inventory. These few dozen items will be used to represent a content domain that could be composed of thousands of potential items.

We do not write thousands of items for a very good reason. There would be too much redundancy in the set to justify the effort—it is just too much work for no real gain. But it is naive to believe that the two or three dozen items we did write are completely independent of each other. By virtue of the fact that the items are all related to the same global construct, we would expect that they bear some relation to each other. Now, common sense tells us that for many of the constructs we wish to assess, there are going to be sets of items that are more related to each other than to other items in the inventory, something that we have already illustrated and that occurs time and time again.

For the sake of this illustration, assume that A through H completely represent the content domain that the inventory is designed to measure. But these are eight of thousands of potential items that could have been written. Based on the content domain, Item A could just as easily have been written as AA, B as BB, and so on, where AA is a variation of A, BB is a variation of B, and so forth.

Assume that the relationships of these items are represented in Table 12a.6. If that is true, and if we had written AA instead of A, BB instead of B, and so on through HH instead of H, then it would be reasonable to expect that AA, BB, EE, and GG would form one factor and that CC, DD, FF, and HH would form a second factor.

We could carry out this example further using AAA through HHH, AAAA through HHHH, and so on for hundreds of variations. And in each case, we would expect the same sort of factor structure to emerge. As long as all these items were of good quality, it should not matter if we used A or AA or AAA or AAAA in our inventory. As long as that part of the content domain was covered, and written well, we should be happy.

So here is the irony. Although we sweat to carefully write specific test items that are clear, unambiguous, and unitary, and although test takers are responding to these specific items, in a larger sense, the items are not important in and of themselves but are important only insofar as they represent a particular part of the content domain. Whether we had used A or AA or AAA or AAAA in combination with B or BB or BBB or BBBB and C or CC . . ., we should still find that the As, Bs, Es, and Gs would emerge as one factor and that the Cs, Ds, Fs, and Hs would emerge as a second factor.

What is important at the level of interpreting what the inventory is measuring is not the individual items (most of the time) but, rather, the fewer number of factors that underlie these items. For, although we could envision writing thousands or millions or zillions of items for this content domain, they would still represent only the two general factors that describe this construct. In some sense, then, although the items are the concrete entities of the measurement enterprise, what are more "real," or certainly more useful, are the more abstract (latent) factors underlying these items.

12A.6.2 How Much Information Is Lost in the Crunch

One of the hopes of researchers using factor analysis is that not much information is lost in the process of reducing a large number of variables down to a fewer number of factors. The outcome of this hope will be reflected in the quality of the solution. To the extent that variables are strongly related to their factors and not strongly related to the other factors, we say that the factor solution is a good one where not much information is lost. To the extent that the results depart from this ideal, we say that the solution is less good. We will show you how to make this assessment after covering the basics of factor analysis.

12A.6.3 When Visual Inspection No Longer Works

We have used contrived and simplified small examples to illustrate the essence of factor analysis. If everything was always this easy, we would have very limited use for the actual statistical procedures available on IBM SPSS and other statistical software. But the real world of research often uses more than eight variables, and it is always the case that the interrelationships of the variables are more complicated than presented even in our most extended example. And so it happens that we can rarely rely exclusively on visual inspection of the correlation matrix to tell us what our factors are. Fortunately, we can direct a computerized statistical package such as IBM SPSS to process the correlations by performing mathematical routines in place of our visual inspection. We must always bear in mind, however, that at the end of this mathematical processing, we still need to interpret the results as researchers, that is, we need to interpret the results at the human level.

12A.7 Distinctions Within Factor Analysis

We have been using the term *factor analysis* as a generic label to stand for a process that allows us to identify a few components, factors, or dimensions that underlie a larger set of variables. The generic label of factor analysis subsumes a set of related statistical techniques. It is now time to briefly outline some distinctions that need to be made under the generic factor analysis label; we will cover these in greater depth as we develop this chapter.

12A.7.1 Principal Components Analysis and Factor Analysis

One primary distinction that needs to be made is between *principal components analysis* and *factor analysis*. From the standpoint of a nonstatistician, the differences are likely to appear minor, as the output and interpretation of the results of these procedures are virtually the same. However, there are statistical differences that are noteworthy for the present chapter (additional aspects of such differences are presented in Sections 12A.10 and 16A.4):

- We always start the analysis with the correlation matrix having values of 1.00 on the diagonal. In principal components analysis, these diagonal values are retained. In factor analysis, these values of 1.00 are replaced with other values (e.g., the squared multiple correlation between the variable and the other variables in the analysis) to represent the relationship of each variable with the other variables in the analysis.
- In principal components analysis, we focus on (look to explain) the *total variance* of the variables. In factor analysis, we focus on (look to explain) the *common variance* of the variables (the amount of variance the variables share, which is always less than the total variance).
- Principal components analysis is mathematically less complex a procedure than factor analysis.
- Principal components analysis refers to a single procedure. Factor analysis represents a family of procedures (e.g., principal axis, unweighted least squares [ULS], maximum likelihood) defined by the way in which the factors are extracted.

12A.7.2 An Extraction Phase and a Rotation Phase

Principal components analysis and factor analysis are ordinarily conducted in two successive phases—the extraction phase is done first, followed by the rotation phase. Each phase can be accomplished using different analytic methods. In the extraction phase, one can "extract" factors via several alternative processes, or one can extract components (a simpler kind of factor that we will actually use to illustrate the extraction process). From a technical perspective, we would call what we were doing either a factor analysis or a principal components analysis depending on the analytic technique used in the extraction phase. Once components or factors have been extracted, most researchers rotate them before interpreting the results. Not surprisingly, different rotation procedures may be applied as well.

12A.7.3 Our Approach

The most straightforward way we have found to describe the extraction process is to focus on a principal components analysis because it is a bit simpler to explicate than a factor analysis (simpler does not imply better—many researchers prefer one of the factor analysis procedures over principal components analysis). In this discussion, we will use the term *component* rather than *factor* as a label for the variate. Following that, we will conceptually distinguish between principal components analysis and factor analysis, and we will briefly characterize some of the extraction methods that fall under the category of factor analysis. We will then address the rotation process, discussing both orthogonal and oblique strategies, and cover how components and factors are interpreted.

12A.8 The First Phase: Component Extraction

12A.8.1 The Concept of Extraction

As has been true for the other multivariate procedures that we have covered, the goal of the extraction process is to account for variance. At the start of the extraction process, all the variance is unaccounted for; when it finishes, it will have accounted for all the variance. A solution will be selected by researchers someplace between these extremes but presumably with more rather than less variance explained. Akin to the process of extraction in discriminant function analysis (see Section 11A.8), what is being "extracted" is variance, that is, we are extracting or explaining variance. Components are extracted one at a time. Each successively identified component will account for (extract) a certain amount of the total original variance.

12A.8.2 What Is a Component?

A component is a weighted linear combination of the variables being analyzed—a variate. The mathematical function describing this straight line contains all the variables in the analysis. Each variable is weighted based on its contribution or relationship to the principal component in much the same way as is done in multiple regression. The value of this variate is analogous to the dependent variable in a multiple regression analysis (Pedhazur & Schmelkin, 1991) and to the discriminant score in discriminant function analysis.

12A.8.3 Does the Component Refer to a Subset of the Sample?

A component is a weighted linear combination of the variables being analyzed based on all of the cases in the data file. Components just specify particular weights computed for the variables. Each component subsumes all of the cases. They are analogous to the dimensions identified in a discriminant function analysis (see Section 11B.5.6) in that components represent the different ways along which the variables in the set may be thought of as differing.

12A.8.4 The Total Variance Is Equal to the Number of Variables

In principal components analysis, variance is being extracted from the total variance of the variables in the analysis. Each variable can be thought of as contributing one unit of variance to that total. If there are eight variables in the analysis, for example, then the total amount of variance is equal to eight.

In addition to equaling the total variance, the number of variables also equals the total number of components that it is possible to extract from the set. When all eight components are extracted from a set of eight variables, we say that the analysis has gone to completion in the sense that it has accounted for all the variance. IBM SPSS will take the analysis to completion in its first pass through the data; however, we will wish to stop far short of that in identifying a principal components solution that we wish to interpret.

12A.8.5 The Extraction Process

Although the extraction process is done at a mathematical level, we will explain what is happening with a pictorial illustration. This picture that we construct is, admittedly, oversimplified. Despite that limitation, however, it can capture the important features of the first few steps in component extraction. We will first put the picture with all its props in place, then tell you the rules of extraction, and finally describe the process itself.

12A.8.6 A Pictorial Illustration

Imagine a glass cube hovering in the air in front of you. It is punctuated by a few dark dots suspended inside of this space as drawn in Figure 12a.1. The dots in the picture are the variables in the analysis. The glass cube represents at least the visible part of the component/factor or

Figure 12a.1 Variables Located Closer Together Are More Correlated Than Those Located Farther Apart

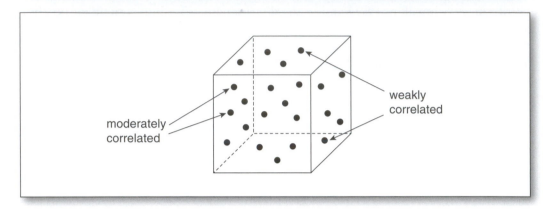

multidimensional space defined by the positions of the variables. We have asked you to imagine a three-dimensional space (a cube) because that is a shape that people can see in their mind's eye and a shape that we can draw. There are actually more than three dimensions in this space. In fact, there are as many dimensions as there are variables in the analysis. This multidimensional space (sometimes referred to as hyperspace) is the site of the component extraction process.

In this image of a cuboid factor space, the positions of the dark dots (representing the variables) relative to each other are determined by their correlations. Variables that are more strongly correlated are closer to each other. We depict this in Figure 12a.1, where two data points that are relatively close to each other are shown as being moderately correlated, and two data points far apart are shown as being very weakly related to each other. The idea that correlation is a gauge of distance is important and will be elaborated on later in our discussion.

Now include in this image a set of laser beams, each a little bit longer than our little cuboid space. We have complete control over where we aim these lasers. These laser beams are straight lines, and they will be the components once they are positioned in this multidimensional space. We have as many of these components as there are variables in this multidimensional space because the extraction process will run to completion.

12A.8.7 The Rules of Component Extraction

Extraction is the fitting of lines (components) into this multidimensional space one component at a time. The laser beams will play the role of the components. Here are the rules governing the extraction of components from this multidimensional space:

1. Every component must pass through the gravitational center of that space.

2. Once the first component has been thrust (fit) into the space, all succeeding components must intersect the one or ones already in the space at right (90°) angles.

3. When a component is fit into this multidimensional space, it must account for all the variance that it is possible for it to account for, that is, it must occupy the one orientation that meets the criterion for best fit.

4. If there are already components in the space, a newly extracted component must account for variance not already explained by the ones already there.

12A.8.8 Extracting Components

Do not let the terminology get in the way of your understanding of the extraction process. Principal components are fitted into the multidimensional space and represent the lines of best fit. Best fit is defined in terms of accounting for the most variance and, as we will see shortly, meets the least squares rule for fitting straight lines to data arrays.

The term *extraction* is used to convey the idea that these components, these fitted straight lines or variates, are accounting for or extracting variance from the system. Thus, we start with all the variance unexplained. When we fit the first component to the variables, we will account for a certain amount of variance. It is in this sense that we have extracted variance. Ultimately, when all the components have been fitted, all the variance will have been extracted, that is, explained.

Let's extract our first component. Using our pictorial illustration, we must position one of the components through the center of this factor space at any angle such that we come as close as possible to *all* the variables. The position that our beam should occupy is solvable once we identify the rule governing the choice of this position—namely, that there is only one place (i.e., only one linear function) where the sum of squared distances of the variables from the line are a minimum; all we need to do is apply the least squares rule (or permit the software to do it for you). We have illustrated this in Figure 12a.2. Thus successful, in pictorial terms we now have a factor space with a laser beam through its gravitational center.

This is the first extracted component and will have accounted for a certain amount of variance. In fact, because this is the very first component, it will have been positioned in the best place in the entire space. This is given to us in Rule 4 in Section 12A.8.7. It will thus have accounted for (extracted) more variance than any subsequently fitted line.

As we will see by the end of Section 12A.9.3, the distance between the points and the line is the gauge of explained variance. For example, in the very unlikely event that all of the points were aligned in a straight line, that is, that a straight line fitted through these points would run directly through their centers, then 100% of the variance would

Figure 12a.2 The First Component Is Placed at the Optimal Location as Defined by the Least Squares Rule

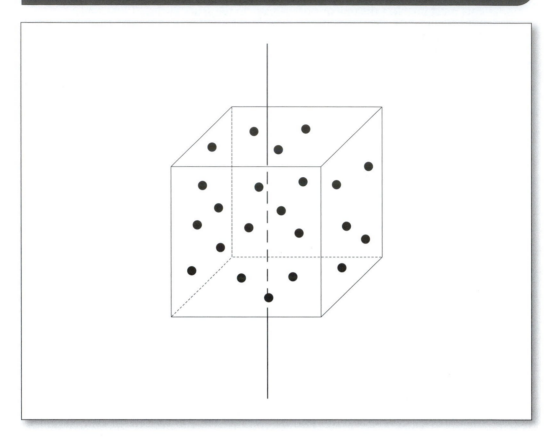

be explained. To the extent that the points were closely distributed around the line, a relatively large proportion the variance would be accounted for; to the extent that the points were distributed more distantly around the line, a relatively smaller proportion the variance would be explained.

We will next extract (fit) the second component (Rule 1 states that we must do this process one component at a time). Extracted components are to intersect each other at 90° according to Rule 3 above. This means that the components during this extraction phase are orthogonal to each other, that is, they are independent of (uncorrelated with) each other. In our imaginary factor space, we will take a second laser beam and position it perpendicular to the one already in place (Rule 3) as shown in Figure 12a.3. It, too, must intersect the factor space's center (Rule 2), and it, too, must occupy the best place left to it given that the first component has the very best absolute place (Rule 4).

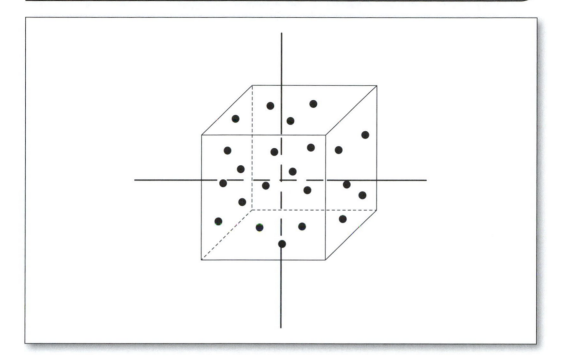

Figure 12a.3 The Second Component Is Placed in the Next Most Optimal Location Orthogonal to the First

Applying the least squares rule will yield the information necessary to place this second component appropriately.

The third component to be extracted must also intersect the factor space's center and must be perpendicular to the components (two thus far) that have been identified to this point. This component must also occupy the best place left to it, given that the first and second components have taken the very best and next best absolute places already. This is pictured in Figure 12a.4. With the third component extracted from this component space, our imaginary factor space now has three components sticking out of it.

Unfortunately, it is impossible for us to provide you with a visual representation of the imaginary factor space once we have extracted more than three components because we will have run out of tangible dimensions for the universe in which we live. Through the wonders of mathematics, however, any number of dimensions beyond three can be put in place, but if the image with three straight lines made sense to you, it is not necessary to stretch your visual imaging beyond that.

Figure 12a.4   The Third Component Is Placed in the Third Most Optimal Location Orthogonal to the First

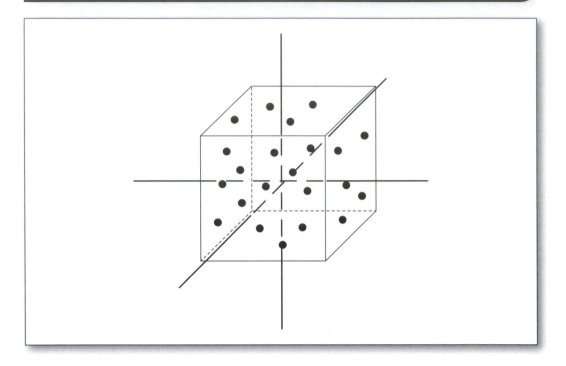

12A.8.9 Point of Diminishing Returns

One can continue on in the manner just described, extracting as many components as there are variables. But it will also be true that once the first few components have been fit, there will not be any decent places for the other components to be positioned (i.e., they will not account for very much variance), and their existence will be superfluous. Thus, a *complete solution* as it is called is not very interesting; the real issue in principal components analysis is to stop the process when "enough" components have been extracted.

12A.9 Distances of Variables From a Component

12A.9.1 Correlation as a Distance Measure

We have already indicated that correlation can be used as a measure of distance between variables. It is time to more fully discuss this idea. When we say that two variables are highly correlated, we are also saying that they are strongly related to or are associated with each other. For the Pearson r, the strength of relationship is indexed by r^2.

Picturing the correlation between two variables as overlapping rectangles as was done in Chapter 6A (Figure 6a.6), the area common to them (the overlap) is r^2. The stronger the relationship the more overlap we would draw. If we were able to take two variables and continuously make them more and more related, we would see the two rectangles start off with little overlap and gradually move toward each other as the strength of relation increased. In this diagrammatic way, it can be seen that the variables are indeed getting physically closer as they become increasingly more related. Thus, it is that correlation (actually the correlation squared) can be used as a measure of distance, although the verbalization of it may at first sound backward (it's not):

- Weaker correlations represent more distance between the variables (they are farther apart).
- Stronger correlations represent less distance between the variables (they are closer together).

12A.9.2 Distance Between a Component and the Variables

Components are weighted linear combinations of the variables in the analysis, and we could compute a component score for each participant on each component if we so wished. This would be done by taking the person's score on the first variable and multiplying by its coefficient (weight), taking the person's score on the second variable and multiplying that by its coefficient, and so on and then adding all those values together to achieve a single value for the component for that case.

Once we had the numeric value of each component for each participant, we could then correlate the component score with the score for each variable to obtain the structure coefficients. To compute a correlation, all we need are two quantitative values. In this situation, one value would be the score on the component, and the other would be the score on the variable under consideration. Listing these pairs of numbers for each participant gives us the setup to compute a Pearson r. These correlations are structure coefficients. Once we obtained these, we could generate the r^2 for each component–variable pairing.

The squared correlations—these r^2 values or squared structure coefficients—are directly translatable into distance indexes. Keeping with our pictorial illustration, we have these components passing near some variables and farther from other variables. We can use the r^2 values to let us know how close each variable is to the component. A large r^2 tells us that the two entities—here, the component and the variable—are quite close to each other, whereas a small r^2 tells us that they are relatively far apart.

This idea is schematized in Figure 12a.5. For simplicity, we show five data points at different distances from the component or variate (assume for this example that there are only five variables in the analysis and that we have pictured the situation after the rotation phase

Figure 12a.5 The Squared Variable–Component Correlation Coefficient Is an Indicator of the Distance Between the Variable and the Factor, and the Sum of the Squared Correlations Is the Eigenvalue of the Component

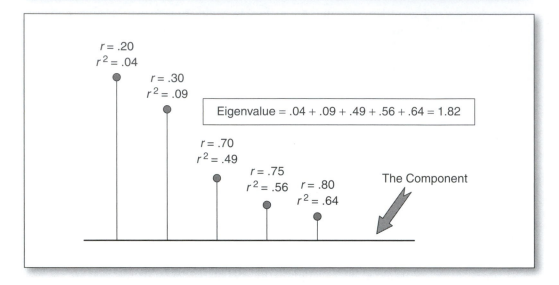

has been completed). These distances are measured in terms of the strength of association (correlation) between the variate and the variable. As can be seen, the smallest distances represent the strongest correlations between the component and the variable, the middle distances represent a relatively moderate correlation, and the largest distances represent a relatively weak correlation.

12A.9.3 Eigenvalues

Distances of the variables to the component, measured in terms of r^2, are quite important. We (well, the software) can use these correlations to apply the least squares rule and thus determine the proper location of the component. That is, the sum of squares of the distances of the variables to the line is minimal at the position of the component. If distance is measured in terms of r^2, then we can simply add all the r^2 values to obtain the sum of these squares for each component. The sum of these squared correlations for each component over the full set of variables is called an *eigenvalue*. In terms of the least squares rule, this optimal position where the squared distances are minimal represents the best or closest fit of the line to the data points. We have illustrated the computation of an eigenvalue in Figure 12a.5, where we have summed all of the r^2 values. In this situation, the eigenvalue of the component is 1.82.

Each component has an associated eigenvalue. This makes sense in that it is possible to assess the distance (again measured in terms of correlation) between any given data point and any given component. We have illustrated this in Table 12a.8, which shows the two-component rotated component matrix for the analysis pictured in Figure 12a.5. Assume that we have determined that there are two components underlying these five variables. Further assume that the distances of the variables we provided to you earlier were between the variables and Component 1 and are reproduced in the first numerical column of Table 12a.8. But because there is a second component in the solution (intersecting the first at 90°), one can examine the distances of the variables from that second component as well.

Table 12a.8 Two-Factor Rotated Matrix for Variables V Through Z

Variable	Component 1	Component 2
V	.80	.05
W	.75	.10
X	.70	.20
Y	.20	.85
Z	.30	.70

The positioning of the variables on these factors is shown in Figure 12a.6. Each variable occupies a coordinate coinciding to the distance it lies from each component. For example, variable V correlates .80 with Component 1 and thus lies relatively close to it, but it correlates only .05 with Component 2 and so lies quite far from that component. In Figure 12a.6, variable V is placed at the (Component 1, Component 2) coordinate of (.80, .05).

Figure 12a.6 Variables V Through Z Arrayed Along Two Components

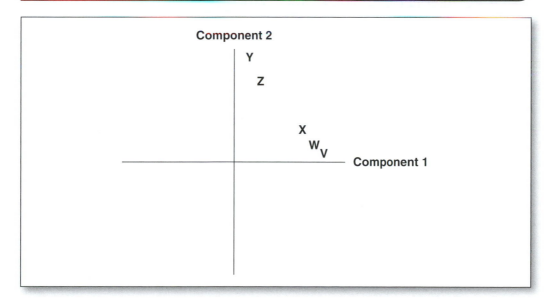

The eigenvalue for each component is the sum of the squared correlations (the squares of the structure coefficients) of the variables in the analysis. As we have seen, the eigenvalue for Component 1 is 1.82. Because we have supplied the correlations of the variables with the second component in Table 12a.8, it is now possible to also calculate the eigenvalue for this component. The r^2 values for variables V, W, X, Y, and Z are .0025, .01, .04, .72, and .49, and the sum of these values is 1.26; this is the eigenvalue of the second component.

Eigenvalues are a direct measure of the amount of explained variance. With five variables in the analysis, and with each variable contributing one unit of variance, we know that the total variance is equal to 5.00 units. This value of 5.00 is in "eigenvalue units" in the sense that this value is also equal to the sum of the eigenvalues for all of the five components if the analysis was taken to completion (all of the possible components were extracted).

In our example, the eigenvalue associated with the first component is 1.82. We can therefore say that 1.82/5.00 or .364 or 36.4% of the total variance is accounted for by the first component. By the same reasoning, the second component with an eigenvalue of 1.26 is accounting for 25.2% of the total variance. Furthermore, because the components are orthogonal to each other, their explained variance is additive; thus, we can also assert that the first two components cumulatively account for 61.6% of the total variance. If we were to extract the remaining three components, compute their eigenvalues, and add them to what we have already calculated, we would find that the five factors together (cumulatively) accounted for 100% of the total variance.

12A.10 Principal Components Analysis Versus Factor Analysis

12A.10.1 Causal Flow

We have indicated that the numerical value of the component for any single case is analogous to the dependent variable in a multiple regression analysis or the discriminant score in a discriminant function analysis predictable by the weighted linear composite of the variables in the analysis. In this sense, principal components are latent variables or composites descriptive of the information contained in the measured variables (the variables in the analysis). These components can be said to "arise from" the measured variables. From a causal modeling perspective, the causal flow is from the measured variables to the latent components.

Factor analysis shifts this conception around. The measured variables are taken as "indicators" of the factors. Here, the causal flow is from the factor (still a latent variable) to the measured indicator variables. This is one of the reasons why, at least at a conceptual level, some researchers prefer factor analysis over principal components analysis. We can illustrate this by using inventory items. Items such as "I feel worthless," "I can't concentrate," "I feel I am a failure," and "I feel extremely unhappy" do not just coincidentally wind up on an inventory and happen by sheer luck to be interpretable as relating to depression. Instead, researchers started with an understanding or model of depression and, based on that model, built items to represent that construct. The items of the inventory (the variables in a factor analysis) emanated from the latent variable or construct of depression, and this causal flow underlies factor analysis and not principal components analysis (the counterargument is that both principal components analysis and factor analysis would yield the same structure and that principal components analysis, as the simpler procedure, is therefore preferred).

12A.10.2 Variance Explained

Another difference between principal components analysis and factor analysis is how each identifies the target variance that is to be explained. Principal components analysis, as we have seen, deals with the total amount of variance in the data set. We thus measured the magnitudes of the first few components by how much of the total variance they can explain.

In factor analysis, the total variance of each variable is partitioned into two segments. One segment is common or shared (overlapping) variance—variance that is shared by the variables in the analysis. The other segment is variance unique to each variable itself. Only the common variance is used in factor analysis. This approach is adopted because it is argued that if the point of factor analysis is to describe the structure of the set of variables in the analysis, then we should really be looking only at the shared or common variance of the variables. That is, the factor structure should be descriptive of what the variables have in common rather than including what is idiosyncratic (unique) about them. Factor analysis therefore deals only with the shared variance—the covariance—of the variables in the analysis. The magnitudes of the factors are thus measured by how much of the common variance (the covariance) they can account for.

These two perspectives partly play themselves out in how the correlation matrix is prepared for the component or factor extraction process. As we have already seen, the extraction process begins with the correlation matrix, examples of which are shown in the Tables 12a.1 through 12a.4 and Table 12a.6 near the beginning of this chapter. The main issue at hand is the value that is to be used on the diagonal of the matrix, the place representing the correlation of each variable to itself. In those tables, we did not actually place values on the diagonal. This was done to enable the tables to be more easily read by having fewer numbers in them but also to avoid raising the issue of what to place on the diagonal before we were ready to discuss it more fully.

Students are taught in their early statistics course that a variable correlated with itself should yield a value of 1.00. This value of 1.00, however, represents all the variance (the total variance) of the variable. It is therefore an acceptable value to be used in principal components analysis because this procedure analyzes the total variance.

But using 1s on the diagonal of the correlation matrix is not appropriate in factor analysis. Rather, factor analysis will use some estimate of a variable's *communality* on the diagonal. Communality estimates are intended to represent how much a variable has in common with the remaining variables in the analysis. For example, if variable *J* shares 83% of its variance with the other variables (with the remaining variance being unique to that variable), then the value that would be used for the diagonal element for variable *J* in many variations of factor analyses would be .83 instead of 1.00.

Each variable in the analysis is associated with its own communality. It is the sum of the squared correlations between the variable and the other variables (we square the correlations in the factor matrix and add across the rows). Communalities thus give an indication of the degree to which a variable was represented in the factor solution.

We can briefly illustrate the idea of communality, which is symbolized in texts as h^2, by contrasting principal components analysis with principal axis factor analysis. In the full principal components solution, each variable's communality will be equal to 1 because all its variance will have been accounted for in the solution. For a less than full solution, say a three-component solution, a variable's communality will be less than that; it will be the sum of the squared correlations for that variable in the three-component factor matrix.

In the full principal axis solution (see Section 12A.11), each variable's initial communality will be less than 1 because only the common variance and not the unique variance will be considered. It is these values that are originally placed on the diagonal of the correlation matrix; it will be estimated in an iterative fashion in the extraction process until a stabilized value is reached. Finally, in a less than full solution, a variable's communality will be computed in the same manner as was done for principal components (sum the squared correlations across the row of the factor matrix), but again because only the common variance is analyzed, these communalities will be less than those corresponding communalities computed for a principal components analysis.

12A.11 Different Extraction Methods

Partitioning the variance of the variables into common and unique variance and then deciding on how to perform the extraction process have given rise to several alternative procedures developed under the aegis of factor analysis. We summarize some of the more popular ones here and mention principal components analysis as well.

- *Principal components analysis* uses 1s on the diagonal of the correlation matrix in the process of extraction and is the method described above. It is not a factor analysis procedure but represents its own procedure called, appropriately enough, *principal components.*

- *Principal axis factoring* (also called *principal factors*) differs from principal components analysis mainly by using estimates of communalities (a measure of shared variance) on the diagonal in the extraction process. IBM SPSS does this by starting with squared multiple correlations (a measure of the relationship between a particular variable and the set of remaining variables in the analysis—hence the term *communality*), but alternative methods (e.g., choosing the largest correlation in the row of the correlation matrix) can be used instead. Many software packages such as IBM SPSS then reestimate these communality values via an iterative process to achieve a "better" estimate of this shared variance. Once stable estimates have been achieved, a factor analysis is performed in the manner already described above for principal components analysis.

- *Unweighted least squares* factoring and *generalized least squares* factoring both attempt to minimize the off-diagonal differences between the observed and reproduced correlation matrices (because factors are meant to represent the relationships between the variables, one should be able to perform a "back-to-the-future" operation of "reproducing" or estimating the values in the original correlation matrix). Communalities are derived from the solution rather than estimated from it. The two procedures differ in that ULS weights all variables equally whereas generalized least squares factoring gives greater weight to variables more strongly related to other variables in the set (those with higher communality values).

- *Maximum likelihood* factor extraction is related to the generalized least squares method in that it, too, uses weights proportional to the relatedness of the variables. However, maximum likelihood calculates weights on the factors for the variables that maximize the probability of having sampled the correlation matrix from a multivariate normally distributed population. Thompson (2004) contrasts the ordinary least squares approach with maximum likelihood theory by noting that rather than trying to reproduce the sample data, the maximum likelihood procedure attempts to use the sample data to directly estimate the population covariance matrix. He goes on to say that "estimating population parameters with a statistical theory that optimizes the estimation . . . is very appealing. Better estimation of population parameters should yield more replicable results" (p. 127). Maximum likelihood, as we will see in the following chapters, is extensively used in confirmatory factor analysis, path analysis, and SEM.

- *Alpha* factoring also starts with communality estimates on the diagonal. Its extraction strategy is designed to maximize the reliability (defined by Cronbach's coefficient alpha) of the factors.

- In *image factoring*, the common (shared) factor variance is estimated via multiple regression to predict the value of the variable. This predicted value is known as the "image" of the variable. The "anti-image" of the variable is the difference between the actual and predicted values. Factor extraction is performed on the image covariance matrix containing the squared images on the diagonal.

12A.12 Recommendations Concerning Extraction

Based on the preceding discussion, it may seem that principal components analysis and the various forms of factor analysis might each yield vastly different results in this extraction phase. One of the pleasant surprises experienced by students when they actually perform these various procedures on the same data set is that the extraction results are quite often remarkably similar given a relatively large sample size, reasonable reliability of the measurements, and a stable dimensional structure. The primary difference between the outputs of these two general approaches is that principal components analysis will account for more variance than the factor analyses. This discrepancy occurs because factor analysis targets only the common variance, which is always less than the total variance dealt with by principal components analysis.

So what extraction procedure should you use in your own research? Some researchers (e.g., Kazelskis, 1978) have argued that principal components analysis, by focusing on the total variance, can provide a somewhat inflated solution (e.g., it will account for more variance and will show higher correlations between the variables and the factors) than the data really warrant, and the argument can be made to either correct the component correlations or to use one of the factor analysis methods. At the same time, a look through the research journals suggests that principal components analysis is an increasingly popular extraction technique (Bryant & Yarnold, 1995).

Traditional wisdom suggests that there is probably not going to be much difference in the interpretation based on either principal components analysis or factor analysis, especially when analyzing more than two dozen or so variables that are all reasonably related to the dimensions tapped into by the components or factors (Gorsuch, 1983; Stevens, 2009). However, we will see in Chapter 12B that there are exceptions to this traditional wisdom.

Theoretically, principal components analysis is conceptually simpler than factor analysis. Principal components analysis attempts to summarize or aggregate sets of correlated variables and in that sense is relatively empirical (inductive). From the same standpoint, factor analysis is more complex in that factors are thought of more as causes that underlie or drive the correlations between the variables. Although both procedures are considered exploratory, factor analysis is more related to theory development (Tabachnick & Fidell, 2007). We will discuss the tie between factor analysis and theory more explicitly in our treatment of confirmatory factor analysis (see Chapters 16A and 16B).

Here is our general recommendation. For many applications, principal components analysis should probably be sufficient to meet the needs of most readers, but we recommend examining the results of several different extraction procedures (as we demonstrate in Chapter 12B) to determine how stable the solution appears to be. If you opt for factor analysis, our tastes run toward ULS, generalized least squares, maximum likelihood, or principal axis solutions.

In discussing the next phase of the analysis, the rotation phase, there is little value for us to distinguish between principal components analysis and factor analysis. We will therefore talk in terms of factor analysis to keep our language simple, but please note that what we say is applicable to principal components analysis as well.

12A.13 The Rotation Process

12A.13.1 Introduction

By virtue of the mathematical procedure underlying the extraction process, the first extracted factor accounts for the most variance, the second extracted factor accounts for the next largest portion of the variance, and so on. Researchers and statisticians have argued that the mathematically based placement of these factors (in the multidimensional factor space) does not optimize the interpretability of the solution. Hence, once the number of factors to be interpreted is decided, the factors are rotated. By *rotation*, we mean the pivoting of the first *n* number of extracted factors around their point of intersection. The outcome of this rotation phase is what researchers ordinarily interpret.

Factor rotation is designed to achieve simple structure (we will discuss this in a moment). From the histories presented by Harmon (1960) and Harris (2001), we learn that Thurstone (1947) was the first person to explicate the concept of rotation to achieve his standards for simple structure. However, Thurstone's stringent criteria for realizing this state were unable to be satisfied by most data sets, prompting several statisticians in the early 1950s (Carroll, 1953; Ferguson, 1954; Neuhaus & Wrigley, 1954; Tucker, 1955) to develop an alternative rotational procedure known as *quartimax*.

Although quartimax was an improvement over Thurstone's (1947) method, it did not generally meet the needs of most researchers. Quartimax tended to identify one general factor that correlated with most of the variables in the analysis. This outcome was problematic to many investigators in that some of the variables captured by this general factor were not necessarily related to each other. Thus, the quartimax rotation strategy did not really distinguish subsets of related variables (i.e., separate factors) that would be of use to researchers. This problem was finally solved in 1958 when Kaiser published the results of his dissertation on another alternative strategy to factor rotation. Kaiser's publication introduced to the field the rotation strategy known as *varimax* that most researchers currently prefer (if they are performing an orthogonal rotation strategy as discussed in Section 12A.14 rather than an oblique rotation strategy as discussed in Section 12A.15).

12A.13.2 The Goal of Simple Structure: The Least Squares Rule in Operation

The least squares rule, as used in the factor extraction process, has an awful lot to be said in favor of its use, but at least one of its properties becomes something of a liability here. This rule really represents moderation, compromise, and a lack of commitment. It is the "one solution fits all" approach that is less than desirable in many situations. To minimize the squared distance from all the variables taken together, the line (factor) cannot afford to come too close to some variables because it would have to then be terribly far from others. In the world of squared distances, large distances become magnified in importance (because distances are squared in determining the best fit). Positioning of the factor thus becomes a very delicate matter.

The result of this least squares strategy of compromise is shown schematically in Figure 12a.7. It is a very simplified picture of the first extracted factor fitted to a set of eight variables, J through Q, before any rotation process has been accomplished. As you can see, the line of best fit is not all that far from the eight variables, but neither does it come all that near any of them.

Figure 12a.7   In Minimizing the Sum of the Squared Distances of the Data Points to the Factor, the Position of This Factor Represents a Compromise

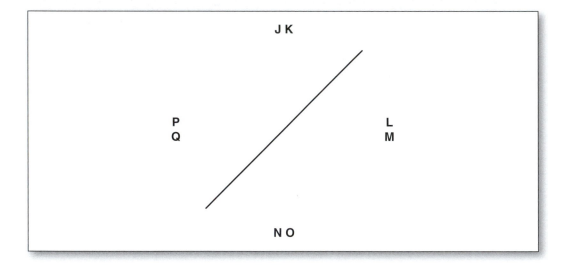

In Figure 12a.8, we have added the second extracted factor to the mix (we are still in the extraction phase here). This second factor is also subject to the least squares rule, and it is positioned as conservatively as the first. This situation is a bit at odds with the goal of simple structure.

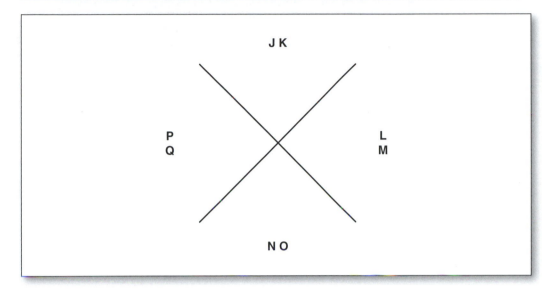

Figure 12a.8 In Minimizing the Sum of the Squared Distances of the Data Points to the Factor, the Position of all Factors (Two in This Figure) Represents a Compromise

12A.13.3 Achieving Simple Structure

Rotation of the extracted factor structure does not change the amount of variance explained but simply redistributes the variance across the factors to facilitate interpretation by trying to achieve "simple structure." Simple structure is obtained when the correlations of the variables with the factors would be either very high (values near 1) or very low (values near 0). Rotation is an iterative process of "twisting" or "pivoting" the factor structure in the multidimensional space until a satisfactory "fit" is established.

To be moved closer to some variables in this rotation process (to achieve correlations closer to 1), each factor must actually move farther away from other variables (and thus reduce those correlations closer to the target of 0). Because the factors are being rotated together, we care less about newly computed eigenvalues but more about how clear the simple structure becomes. Most researchers do not even compute the new eigenvalues of the factors once rotation has been done. In fact, we do not ordinarily keep track of which rotated factor was originally which extracted factor.

Figure 12a.8 showed the (hypothetical) outcome after extracting the second factor from the data. For this example, assume that we have made the decision to stop the extraction process at this point and to rotate these first two factors. We show the results of this rotation in Figure 12a.9.

Figure 12a.9   Rotating the Two Extracted Factors Allows Us to Come Closer to Achieving Our Goal of Obtaining Simple Structure

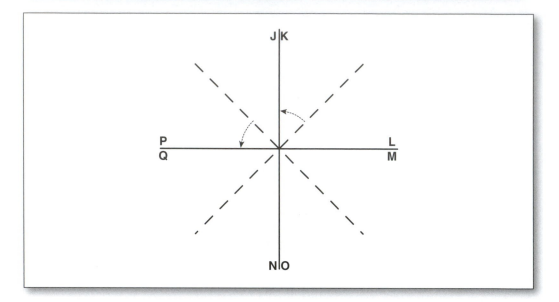

In the rotation process that we are using (a varimax rotation—we will describe this shortly), the factors are kept at a 90° angle of intersection with each other and so will remain orthogonal to each other after the rotation is completed (we will explain this in the following section of this chapter). In our mind's eye when we imagine this rotation process, we imagine putting some very powerful glue on the intersection point of the factors so that when they are rotated or pivoted they will move as a single structure.

We have used lighter dashed lines in Figure 12a.9 to show the original position of the factors and have used a solid black line to show the position of the factors following this varimax rotation process. Each factor has been repositioned closer to four of the variables at the expense of moving away from the other four. We have not changed the total amount of variance accounted for, but that total variance has been redistributed in the process of striving to achieve simple structure. If we were interpreting the two-factor solution, it is this rotated solution with which we would be working.

We can illustrate this process numerically as well by drawing on one of our previous (and simpler) examples. We presented toward the beginning of this chapter in Table 12a.3 the rotated factor matrix for the four-variable example of Items A through D, which demonstrated a two-factor structure in a numerical manner. Here, in Table 12a.9, we reproduce that information again, but this time we also show the factor matrix prior to rotation (the factor matrix resulting from the extraction process).

As we can see from the top portion of Table 12a.9, the least squares solution shown for the prerotation result (the factor matrix resulting from the extraction phase) was truly a compromise. Variable B, for example, correlated about .74 with Factor 1 and about −.63 with Factor 2. And variable C, as another example, correlated almost equally with both factors. The extraction process placed the two factors such that they were moderately close to all the variables. As a consequence, although the factors were not all that far from the variables, neither were they especially close to at least some of them. Thus, all four variables are correlated with both factors, with correlations ranging from the low .6s to the low .7s.

It is now possible to appreciate why we prefer to work with the results of the rotation process. Recall the correlation matrix, the place where the factor analysis all started. In our discussion of that matrix, it was very clear that there were two viable factors represented by the four variables—one factor composed primarily of A and B and another composed primarily of C and D. But that structure is not apparent from the factor matrix following the extraction phase. Even though variables A and B are not related to variables C and D, all four are substantially correlated to each of the factors. The extraction process, driven by the least squares rule, has succeeded in having all the variables as related as possible to all the factors but has not differentiated sets of variables for us.

The rotation phase picks up from where the extraction process leaves off. Once we identify the number of factors with which we want to work, we abandon the least squares rule. Instead, we allow the rotation process to be driven by the goal of simple structure so that the relationships between the variables can reemerge from the blandness of ordinary least squares.

In the bottom portion of Table 12a.9, we see the dramatic structural change as a result of the rotation process. The factors were given an opportunity to make a commitment—to achieve simple structure. Factor 1 was thus placed quite close to (it was allowed to correlate quite strongly with) A and B, and Factor 2 was thus placed quite close to C and D. Of course, in the process of committing to A and B, Factor 1 wound up much farther away from C and D. That turned out to be acceptable, however, because

Table 12a.9 Two-Factor Extracted and Rotated Matrix for Variables A Through D (with only the rotated factor matrix shown in Table 12a.3)

Variable	Factor 1	Factor 2
Extracted Factor Matrix		
A	.73073	−.63204
B	.73530	−.62913
C	.69914	.66497
D	.73292	.62701
Rotated Factor Matrix		
A	.96439	.05828
B	.96563	.06356
C	.03566	.96422
D	.08635	.96065

the position of Factor 2 worked out well to complement that of Factor 1. Thus, the rotation process accomplished the goal of achieving simple structure, and our effort to interpret the factor analysis results was thus facilitated.

Although the factors were repositioned in the factor space, the total amount of variance accounted for in this two-factor solution remained unchanged. This can be easily verified by simply computing the sum of all the squared prerotated correlations and comparing them with the sum of all the squared rotated correlations. If you do the math, both sets of squared correlations sum to the value of 3.73669.

12A.14 Orthogonal Factor Rotation

The term *orthogonal* is a statistical concept indicating that two or more entities are independent of (not correlated with) one another. An orthogonal rotation strategy keeps the factors independent of each other during the rotation process. Geometrically, factors are orthogonal if they cross each other at 90°. In Figure 12a.9, we retained the 90° angle between the factors when we rotated them, and in all the previous examples of rotated factor matrices involving variables A through H, the results were based on the orthogonal rotation strategy known as varimax.

Three methods of orthogonal rotation are available in most statistical packages:

• *Varimax* rotation, introduced by Kaiser (1958) as an alternative to the quartimax strategy, simplifies the correlations within each factor (the columns of the factor matrix) by striving toward 1s and 0s. It simplifies the factors (the columns of the factor matrix). Varimax rotation works toward having some factors correlate quite strongly with some variables (correlations nearer to 1) but more weakly with the other variables (correlations nearer to 0). Because it is focused on the factors (as are the researchers most of the time), this method is the most frequently used orthogonal rotation strategy.

• *Quartimax* rotation, resulting from the work done in the early 1950s, simplifies the variables (the rows of the factor matrix). It does this by having a variable correlate more strongly (nearer to 1) to one factor and more weakly (nearer to 0) to all other factors. As we have already described, this strategy tends to drive the rotated solution toward a single general factor. Quartimax rotation is infrequently used today not only because it is variable oriented rather than factor oriented but also because researchers do not often prefer one dominant factor.

• *Equimax* rotation attempts to effect a compromise between varimax and quartimax rotational strategies; it, too, has failed to electrify the interests of most researchers.

12A.15 Oblique Factor Rotation

The key difference between orthogonal and oblique rotation is that oblique rotation does not require the rotation process to keep the factors uncorrelated. In geometric terms, the mandate that the factors remain at 90° is no longer in effect. Instead of gluing the factors together as we had imagined for orthogonal rotation, here we suggest that forming an image of the factors connected by means of a hinge at their point of intersection. This would allow the factors to be pivoted if necessary to form an oblique angle (an angle that is not a right or 90° angle)—hence the term *oblique rotation*—rather than being forced to remain perpendicular to each other. A convenient way to imagine this is to picture a pair of scissors with the blades representing the factors; opening and closing the scissors allows the blades to intersect at different angles. Software packages such as IBM SPSS can determine the optimal angle needed to best fit the data points.

There are two oblique rotation methods available in IBM SPSS, Direct Oblimin and Promax, and both are widely used. In the direct oblimin rotation, the amount of correlation permitted between factors is under the control of the researcher, although most software programs such as IBM SPSS have default values that are usually fine (IBM SPSS uses the term *delta* value) for how much correlation is permitted if the researchers do not specify a value (IBM SPSS's default is a delta value of zero).

Promax involves three steps that are "invisible" to users. First, the factors are subjected to a varimax rotation. Then the resulting coefficients are raised to a power called "kappa"; in IBM SPSS, the default value of kappa is 4. Raising the coefficients to a power has the effect of driving them toward the extremes of 0 and 1, thus simplifying them. Finally, the factors based on the simplified coefficients are obliquely rotated. Promax and direct oblimin will almost always provide comparable solutions.

Oblique rotation permits the factors to be correlated up to a certain degree. But to permit a particular degree of correlation to exist between factors is not to require that the factors achieve that much correlation. Rather, the correlation value is a ceiling or maximum that is permitted should the factors exhibit that much relationship. The idea here is to permit the factors some leeway so that if they do correlate only somewhat, the factor structure would be allowed to incorporate that in the solution.

So why set a limit at all? Because the situation is similar to the hands of an analog clock where the minute hand can come closer and closer to the hour hand and at some point overlap it. If two factors are allowed to be placed extremely close to each other, perhaps intersecting each other at 5° or 10°, one can question whether the two factors are all that different from each other. It is therefore useful to set some sort of limit to prevent the factors from being located too close to each other.

We have provided an illustration of a successful oblique rotation. Figure 12a.10 shows an array of eight variables named A through H. If we select a two-factor solution to rotate using an orthogonal strategy, we must keep the factors oriented at 90°. As you

Figure 12a.10 An Array of Variables A Through H Shown in Two Dimensions With an Orthogonal Rotation of Two Factors

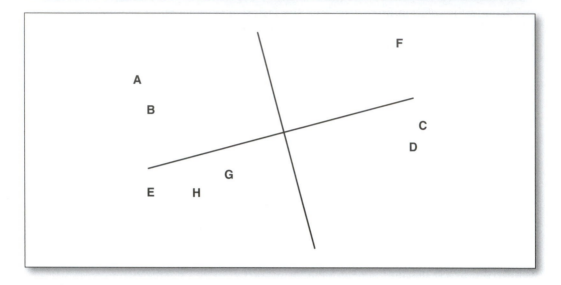

may be able to discern, the "fit" (how close we can come to achieving simple structure) will not be particularly good under these conditions (we will not draw the various ways to place two factors at 90° in the rotation process but show one fit location in Figure 12a.10).

An oblique rotation will provide a much better fit to the data points, and we illustrate that in Figure 12a.11. With the factors no longer constrained to intersect at 90°, they can be placed in a better position to achieve simple structure. Now it can be seen that variables A, B, C, and D appear to be relatively strongly related to one factor, and variables E, F, G, and H appear to be relatively strongly related to the other factor.

12A.16 Choosing Between Orthogonal and Oblique Rotation Strategies

In most studies, researchers present in their report the results of just one of the factor rotation strategies. When it is possible to do so, the decision as to which one is more appropriate can be made on the basis of the theory or model from which the study was generated. That is, ideally, the model has indicated whether the factors should be correlated or not, and that direction may well be sufficient for researchers to commit to one or the other strategy.

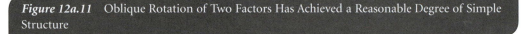

Figure 12a.11 Oblique Rotation of Two Factors Has Achieved a Reasonable Degree of Simple Structure

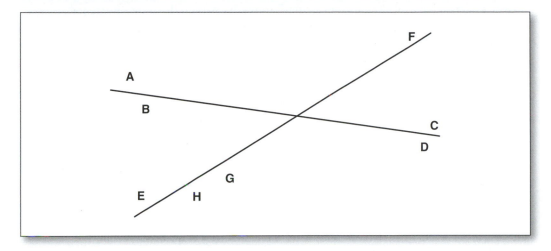

In the absence of any solid expectations, we strongly suggest that researchers initially perform an oblique rotation solution (although research reported in the professional journals tends to lean more heavily toward performing a varimax rotation without exploring the reasonableness of an oblique rotation strategy). The strategy we suggest permits researchers to examine the factor correlations that are provided as part of the oblique rotation output. Based on these computed factor correlations, researchers can determine whether an oblique or orthogonal rotation strategy is more appropriate for their analysis.

Our strategy is this: Perform an oblique rotation. Norman and Streiner (2008) suggest that a promax rotation be used. Then examine the factor correlations and apply the following very general rule of thumb to start the decision making:

- If some of the factors are correlated in the range of the high .3s or higher, most researchers would probably opt to work with an oblique rotation.
- If some of the factors are correlated in the middle teens or lower, many researchers would probably opt to work with an orthogonal (most likely varimax) solution.
- If some of the factors are correlated between these two ranges, the decision is less clear-cut and may vary substantially among researchers. In situations where the decision is less clear cut, it is our bias (as we believe it is the safest and more conservative approach) to retain the oblique rotation results rather than moving to a varimax solution (the two will not be very different from each other in any case).

12A.17 The Factor Analysis Printout

Although we will cover this in a more hands-on way in our worked example in Chapter 12B, there are certain parts of the output that have immediate use in helping researchers accept a particular solution to the factor analysis. We will briefly cover these features here by returning to the context of our simplified and hypothetical eight-variable example with variables A through H.

12A.17.1 Variance Accounted for in the Initial Solution

As we have seen, eigenvalues indicate the amount of variance each factor has accounted for. For the extraction phase, the first component or factor will have the largest eigenvalue, the second component or factor will have the next largest eigenvalue, and so on. This is one of the first portions of the output that researchers examine. There is a table in the output that looks similar to what we have presented in Table 12a.10, summarizing the first part of the extraction process when the analysis goes to completion. The example used in this table shows the solution of variables A through H from an earlier example in this chapter. The correlation matrix for these variables was presented in Table 12a.6.

Because there are eight variables in the analysis, the total amount of variance is equal to 8. After the first factor is in place, we can compute the correlation between each variable and the factor. We then square these correlations and sum them to achieve the eigenvalue of the factor. Eigenvalues are directly interpretable in terms of variance accounted for.

Table 12a.10 Eigenvalues and Variance Accounted for in an Eight-Variable Factor Analysis of Variables A Through H as part of the Initial Extraction Using Principal Components Analysis

Factor	Eigenvalue	% Variance	Cumulative % Variance
1	3.64341	45.5	45.5
2	2.81393	35.2	80.7
3	.58015	7.3	88.0
4	.53570	6.7	94.7
5	.19279	2.4	97.1
6	.10758	1.3	98.4
7	.07462	.9	99.4
8	.05181	.7	100.0

The first factor has explained approximately 3.64 units of the variance. Because there are 8 variables in the analysis, the total amount of variance is equal to 8.00. The proportion of 3.64 to 8.00 is .455, that is, 3.64 is 45.5% of 8.00.

In Table 12a.10, we see that the first component has an eigenvalue of 3.64341; that is, the first factor has accounted for about 3.64 units of variance. Because the total amount of variance is 8, dividing 3.64 by 8 tells us the proportion of the total variance extracted by the first component. That turns out to be 45.5%, and this is shown in the next column of Table 12a.10. By the same reasoning, the second component accounts for 35.2% of the total variance. Together, as shown in the last column of the table, the first two components have accounted for almost 81% of the variance.

As shown in Table 12a.10, the extraction process has gone to completion in the sense that all eight components have been extracted. Together, these eight components have cumulatively accounted for all the variance. Because the usual goal in such an analysis is to account for the most variance with the fewest number of factors, we certainly want to work with fewer than all the eight factors extracted here.

Although this solution is a bit exaggerated, it does demonstrate some valid and important points.

- The first factor always accounts for the most variance, the second factor for the next most variance, and so forth.
- Our focus is almost always on the cumulative percentage of variance explained. Here, the first two factors accounted for an incredible 80.7% of the variance.
- It is not an issue here, but factors that cannot muster enough strength to achieve an eigenvalue of 1 are ordinarily not going to be part of the solution. That is, researchers are not usually going to go that far down the list of possible factors to select.
- Researchers have the desire to work with factor solutions that appear to capture enough of the variance to provide confidence that they did not lose too much information in the data-crunching process. A very rough rule of thumb proposed by some authors (e.g., Tabachnick & Fidell, 2007) is that the solution that is accepted should account for at least 50% of the variance.
- The factor solution is cumulative, starting with the first factor. When we select a factor solution, what we are really saying is that we select the first *n* number of factors.
- In the example, we would select the two-factor solution as most viable. We saw this in the correlation matrix shown earlier in this chapter. As you can see from Table 12a.10, we gain a chunk of variance by reaching down to the second factor. The third factor is not contributing an awful lot of explained variance, and its eigenvalue is less than 1. We will say more about how to select the number of factors in a moment.

12A.17.2 Eigenvalue Plot (Scree Plot)

Another part of the printout that we would want to examine is the plot of eigenvalues, known as a *scree plot.* It is a visual depiction of the first two columns of Table 12a.10. In real-world data sets where the solution is not oversimplified by textbook writers, researchers can sometimes see the pattern more clearly than in the table. The idea behind this graphical way to determine the number of factors in a solution was introduced by Raymond B. Cattell in 1966.

In a scree plot, eigenvalues are represented on the *Y* axis and the factors are represented on the *X* axis. An idealized curve might look like a negatively decelerating curve (similar to Ebbinghaus's forgetting curve). Generally, as one part of the decision process aimed at determining the number of factors there should be in the solution, we look for where the scree plot is still reasonably dropping (factors are still contributing to variance accounted for in potentially meaningful ways) and where it starts to straighten out (the point of diminishing returns where no gain is made by choosing additional factors).

The scree plot for our eight-variable example is presented in Figure 12a.12. As can be seen in Figure 12a.12, by the time we reach the third factor the function is pretty much attenuated, visually suggesting that the two-factor solution is probably the most viable.

Figure 12a.12   A Scree Plot of the Initial Solution for Variables A Through H

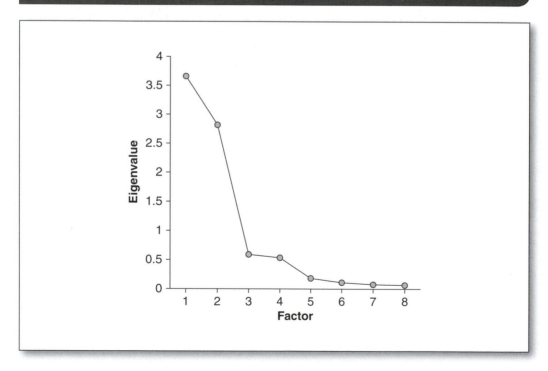

12A.17.3 The Rotated Factor Matrix

12A.17.3.1 Varimax Rotated Factor Matrix

What is finally interpreted by researchers is the rotated factor matrix. Using our simplified eight-variable example, this matrix is shown in Table 12a.7. These results represent the varimax rotated solution. Looking down the columns, we can see that varimax rotation has done a good job in achieving simple structure (of course, we constructed this example to exaggerate this point). Generally, the correlations of the variables to the factors are either relatively high or relatively low.

12A.17.3.2 Obliquely Rotated Factor Matrix

In an orthogonal rotation, the values in the rotated factor matrix represent both the correlations (structure coefficients) of the variables with the factors and the weights (akin to beta weights in multiple regression) of the variables (pattern coefficients) in the linear function defining the variate (factor). The structure coefficients are equal to the weights in an orthogonal rotation precisely because the factors are independent of each other.

In an oblique rotation strategy, the factors are permitted to be correlated (and virtually always are, at least a little). Because the factors are no longer independent of (orthogonal to) each other, the weights of the variables in the linear function (variate, factor) are no longer equal to the structure coefficients. Therefore, instead of the single rotated factor matrix produced by an orthogonal rotation strategy, an oblique rotation strategy generates two somewhat different rotated factor matrices, one presenting the weights of the variables in the linear function (pattern matrix) and one presenting the correlations of the variables with the factors (structure matrix).

- The *pattern matrix* presents what are called pattern coefficients. Pattern coefficients are the weights that have been assigned to variables in the linear functions (factors). This is analogous to what is done in regression, and pattern coefficients are essentially multiple regression beta weights. To the extent that the factors are relatively strongly correlated, these coefficients can (and occasionally do) go beyond the range of ±1.

- The *structure matrix* presents the structure coefficients, a statistic that we have discussed in the context of ordinary least squares regression and discriminant function analysis. Structure coefficients depict the correlations between the variables and the factors (variates). They are true correlations and are therefore bounded by the range of ±1. Generally, these values tend to be just a bit higher than those of the pattern coefficients (except when the factors are very highly correlated), but using these coefficients in interpreting the factor solution should often result in the same characterization of the factors as using the pattern coefficients.

12A.17.3.3 The Magnitude of the Variable Weights

In the context of a rotated factor matrix, the attention of researchers is focused on the magnitude of the structure and/or pattern coefficients. Many researchers call these values by the colloquial and generic label of *loadings*. The key question here is how large a coefficient or "loading" should be before we accept it as sufficiently relating to the factor to commit ourselves to that interpretation. Comrey and Lee (1992) have characterized coefficients of .7 as excellent, .63 as very good, .55 as good, .45 as fair, and .32 as close to minimal. Few if any authors recommend going below about .3. Tabachnick and Fidell (2007) have argued for .32 as rock bottom, Gorsuch (1983) has suggested that .3 may be too small, especially if there are many variables in the analysis, and Stevens (2009) has recommended .40 to achieve practical worth.

Our recommendation is to base your decision in part on your sample size. With less than about 200 cases, think in terms of values in the .40 to .45 range as minimal. With larger samples, we suggest using about .40 as your rough guide, but variables with coefficients or "loadings" in the high .3s might be captured as well with a clear factor structure.

These recommendations address the interpretation of a rotated factor solution but may be too lenient if you wish to build a composite subscale based only on the subset of variables that you define as "loading" on the factor. At least under certain circumstances, variables with coefficients much below .5 can actually reduce the reliability of scales, especially those built from a combination of close to a dozen variables.

12A.18 Interpreting Factors

12A.18.1 Discerning the Common Quality

For the purposes of this example, we will accept a variable as related to a factor if it has produced a structure or pattern coefficient of .4 or better. The interpretation process starts by examining the variables in Table 12a.7 row by row. For each row where we get a relatively high coefficient, we mark the result. Thus, we would say that variables A, E, B, and G all "load" on or correlate with Factor 1, and that variables F, D, C, and H all "load" on or correlate with Factor 2.

Interpretation of the solution is now possible to make by examining the columns. Recall two points:

- A factor or component is what the variables correlated with it have in common.
- Variables more highly correlated with the factor or component share more in common with it.

Thus, Factor 1 can be identified by emphasizing the content of A, E, and B, and Factor 2 can be identified by emphasizing the content of F, D, and C.

To illustrate this idea, assume that A, E, and B were the following items on an inventory:

I try to avoid being in a crowd.

I tend to stay away from parties.

I don't enjoy social events.

These three variables all correlate relatively strongly with the factor. What is the factor, that is, what underlying theme or quality do these items have in common or tap into? Given the kernels of avoiding crowds, staying away from parties, and disliking social events, we can infer that the idea that ties them together is something like social avoidance; thus, "social avoidance" is a reasonable interpretation of the factor.

12A.18.2 Negative Factor Coefficients

This illustration, by the way, is based on Scale 0, Social Introversion, of the Minnesota Multiphasic Personality Inventory–2 (MMPI-2). Although we have given the essence of the items rather than reproducing the items verbatim, it is worth noting that the second and third items are reverse worded on the inventory. The items would thus be something like the following:

I try to avoid being in a crowd.

I like parties.

I enjoy social events.

If the factor is truly social avoidance, then the last two items would be negatively correlated with the factor. The variable weights on the factor might look like what is shown in Table 12a.11. Thus, respondents who were more socially avoidant would try harder to avoid crowds (positive correlation) but would be less enthused with parties (negative correlation) and would enjoy social events to a lesser extent (negative correlation).

The negative values associated with variables E and B in Table 12a.11 simply indicate that the relationship between each of those variables and the factor is an inverse one. Remember that a correlation of .94 represents the same strength of relationship as −.94 because r^2 is always positive. Positive and negative structure or pattern coefficients simply reflect the way the variable is measured (e.g., the way an item is worded in an

Table 12a.11 Example of a Social Avoidance Factor

Variable	Content	Structure Coefficient
A	I try to avoid being in a crowd.	.95558
E	I like parties.	−.94828
B	I enjoy social events	−.93463

inventory); stronger relationships, whether direct or inverse, still reflect more association on the factor.

12A.18.3 Recommendations

It may not surprise you to learn that different authors have offered alternative viewpoints as to which obliquely rotated factor matrix researchers should use for their interpretation and hence which they should report to readers. Hair et al. (2010), Mertler and Vannatta (2001), and Tabachnick and Fidell (2007) have proposed that the pattern matrix be used. On the other hand, Thompson (1984, 1991) has stressed the importance of the structure coefficients in interpreting classical parametric analyses, and Courville and Thompson (2001) have argued that the structure coefficients are important in factor analysis as well as in regression. In addition, Diekhoff (1992), Gorsuch (1983), and Pedhazur and Schmelkin (1991) urge that both structure and pattern coefficients be considered in interpreting factors.

Although it is possible that the pattern and structure matrices would provide somewhat different impressions about the nature of the underlying factor structure, it is frequently the case that the two pictures they present are relatively consonant with one another. That is, although the pattern coefficients may be somewhat larger if the factors are highly correlated and the structure coefficients may be somewhat higher if the factors are not highly correlated, they will very often result in a very similar interpretation. Thus, variables easily meeting our criterion for being accepted as relatively strongly representing a factor (e.g., variables correlating in the range of .70 where our criterion is .40) are likely to emerge on the same factor in both the pattern and structure matrices. We do urge you to examine both matrices to determine if this sort of an outcome holds for your particular data analysis.

For the purposes of this discussion, we will assume that both the pattern and structure matrices yield similar interpretations. Because both ways of viewing the results are viable and useful, the choice as to which rotated factor matrix to present probably comes down to the language used in articulating the framework from which the research was derived. That is, if the theoretical framework conceptualized the factor coefficients in terms of weights or in terms of correlations to the variate, then that is very likely the language you would want to maintain and that, in turn, tells you which of the two matrices you would present in communicating your results.

If that framework is neutral on which viewpoint is more reasonable to take, then your choice of which matrix to present may be driven by how comfortable you are in talking about weights versus structure coefficients. It seems to us that somewhat more researchers report the pattern matrix, and that alternative is a perfectly reasonable reporting strategy to follow. But the structure matrix presenting the variable–factor correlations may sometimes turn out to be a little clearer and a little easier to discuss and might therefore be considered for reporting on those occasions. To us, viewing the correlations of the variables to the factors in interpreting the factor analysis results is more intuitive, and so our personal preference is to report the structure matrix when we have used an oblique rotation.

12A.19 Selecting the Factor Solution

12A.19.1 There Is No Easy Answer

As you can deduce from our discussions in this chapter, there is no agreement on a single factor extraction method to use. And unless the factors are substantially correlated, in which case you should use an oblique rotation, it is often a close call as to whether to report a varimax or an oblique rotation. Thus, you cannot follow a prescribed formula to achieve your factor analytic solution. In one of the editions of his classic testing textbook, Lee Cronbach (1970) said it very plainly: "There is no one 'right' way to do a factor analysis any more than there is a 'right' way to photograph Waikiki Beach" (p. 315). Cronbach's words are true even today.

The solution finally accepted by researchers is an informed but ultimately a subjective choice. Tabachnick and Fidell (2007) suggested that at least for analyses containing up to about 40 variables, the number of factors whose eigenvalue is higher than 1.00 can be estimated in advance by dividing the number of variables by 3 to 5. In the majority of analyses, however, researchers are unlikely to accept that many components or factors in their final decision.

12A.19.2 The Issue of the Number of Factors to Extract

Statistically, it is possible to extract as many factors or components as there are variables in the analysis, and in fact, the first pass through the analysis that is made using principal components does just that, that is, the analysis is taken to completion and the total amount of variance is extracted by the time we reach the last component. Examining this output in either tabular form or as a scree plot informs us that increasing amounts of variance are explained with increasing numbers of components. That information can be used to suggest, at least approximately, the number of factors we wish to include in the final (rotated) solution.

In a typical or idealized set of results, in which the scree plot drops off in an inverted J-shaped pattern, two general subpatterns can be seen. First, the first few factors or components are accounting for relatively large portions of the variance. These factors should certainly be included in the final rotated solution. Second, the last many factors are accounting for relatively small portions of the variance. These factors should certainly not be included in the final rotated solution. The key issue is where we draw the line between those factors or components that are included in the final rotated solution and those that are not included. Specifying a technique that will answer the question of how many factors or components to include has become something of a "holy grail" of the factor analysts.

12A.19.3 Suggested Statistical Solutions to the Number of Factors Question

According to Lautenschlager (1989), probably the most widely used method in the past to identify the number of factors researchers should include in their reported solution was originally proposed by Kaiser (1960). It calls for bringing into the rotation phase those factors or components whose eigenvalue exceed 1.000; in fact, this is the current default in IBM SPSS. However, this strategy will often include more factors in the final solution than is appropriate (Cliff, 1988), and so the number of factors or components with eigenvalues exceeding 1.000 is often viewed today as a rough upper boundary (usually too high) of the number of factors or components to accept in the final solution.

Another widely known solution to the question of the appropriate number of factors to extract was provided by Raymond B. Cattell (1966) in a classic article titled "The Scree Test for the Number of Factors." He suggested that we include those factors in the solution corresponding to a drop in the scree plot and not to include those factors where the scree plot has (roughly) straightened out. This suggestion is not a bad one, but such a dividing line must be identified by visual inspection of the scree plot and can be judged to be at somewhat different locations by different researchers if the scree plot does not sharply level off. As a technical answer to the question of the number of factors to extract, this suggestion has come under some criticism (e.g., Crawford & Koopman, 1979; Hayton, Allen, & Scarpello, 2004; Streiner, 1998; Zwick & Velicer, 1986).

Two increasingly popular methods have been proposed to identify the number of factors that should be brought into the rotation phase. One is Velicer's (1976) partial correlation test (minimum average partial or MAP test). Another method that has gained increased popularity is parallel analysis, first proposed by Horn (1965) but explicated and developed later by many others (e.g., Allen & Hubbard, 1986; Glorfeld, 1995; Franklin et al., 1995; Humphreys & Montanelli, 1975; Montanelli & Humphreys, 1976; Patil, Singh, Mishra, & Donavan, 2008; Watkins, 2006). The MAP method partials out each successive factor and assesses the shared and error variance that remains (O'Connor, 2000; Watkins, 2006), whereas parallel analysis compares solutions based on the actual data obtained in the research with random results.

Although various statistical methods for determining the number of factors have been compared over the years (e.g., Férre, 1995; Peres-Neto, Jackson, & Somers, 2005; Weng & Cheng, 2005; Zwick & Velicer, 1986), the MAP test and especially parallel analysis (e.g., Liu & Rijmen, 2008) have fared well in such evaluations. However, neither IBM SPSS nor SAS have these techniques built into their interface and thus remain beyond the reach of many or most researchers. As one remedy for that, O'Connor (2000) has written IBM SPSS syntax and SAS code to perform both Velicer's (1976) MAP test and parallel analysis.

12A.19.4 Our Recommendations

The choice of the factor solution is based on multiple features of the results, including the following:

- *The theoretical and empirical milieu:* Research is carried out in a context that allows researchers to speculate in advance of data collection what some of the themes underlying the data might be. Thus, although the guidelines here may appear quite data driven, they must always be taken with respect to what the researchers already know about the content domain under study.

- *The plot of the eigenvalues:* You do not want to get into the region of diminishing returns and will most likely select a solution before you reach that point.

- *The amount of variance accounted for by different solutions:* Accepting more factors will allow you to account for more of the variance, but at some point you may be identifying more factors than is reasonable for the construct. You can begin to see this when you find that the content of and the labels for a couple of the factors are difficult to tell apart. At that point, the increased amount of accounted-for variance is probably doing more harm than good.

- *The number of variables used to represent factors:* It is appropriate to have a decent number of variables taken as illustrating the factor, although how many comprise a "decent" number is a subjective decision (generally no fewer than three or four variables, and many researchers would argue for half a dozen or more). This is true for at least two reasons:

(a) You want to be clear what the factor is, and more variables correlating relatively strongly with the factor give you more information on which to base your interpretation; and (b) if you plan to create subscales based on the factor structure, you need enough variables that are highly correlated to the factor to achieve an acceptable level of reliability.

- *The magnitudes of the coefficients:* Even if you use a lenient structure or pattern coefficient criterion of .40, variables correlated with the factor near this lower limit are clearly not strongly related to the factor. Ideally, you should have enough variables in the .7 range or higher to not worry about bringing in variables that are in the .4s.

- *The reasonableness of the interpretation:* If you have to articulate a bottom line for characterizing what researchers finally select, this feature is it. As characterized by Johnson and Wichern (1999), ultimately the selection of a factor structure does not rest on any single quantitative basis but rather on what they call a "wow" criterion: "If, while scrutinizing the factor analysis, the investigator can shout 'Wow, I understand these factors,' the application is deemed successful" (p. 565). As it turns out, reasonableness emerges from the other considerations already mentioned. That is, solutions accounting for relatively small percentages of the variance (e.g., less than 40%) will tend not to have many variables with strong correlations showing up on the factors and are unlikely to be conducive to clear and forthright interpretation.

One strategy that we have found to be helpful in selecting the factor structure that is most reasonably interpreted is trying out a small range of factor solutions based on the scree plot and the amount of variance accounted for. Our intent in this process is to try to "surround" the solution that is most likely to be accepted (e.g., if we guess that either the three- or four-factor solution is going to be eventually selected, we would perform the two-, three-, four-, and five-factor solutions and attempt to interpret each of them). This process can be thought of as laying out the evolution of the factor structure, and it very often helps researchers with factor interpretation by making them aware of which variables have formed stable groupings over the multiple-solution set. The bottom line, however, always rests squarely on the sensibility of the interpretation of the factor structure as formulated by the researchers.

12A.20 Sample Size Issues

One final although very important issue to address is the sample size needed to support a principal components analysis or factor analysis. These procedures are two of the large-sample statistical procedures that we discuss in this book. Guidelines for judging the adequacy of the sample size for such analyses are available from several sources (e.g., Bryant & Yarnold, 1995; Comrey & Lee, 1992; Gorsuch, 1983; Hutcheson & Sofroniou, 1999). Comrey and Lee (1992), for example, have provided the following very general evaluations of the adequacy of various sample sizes for factor analysis: 50 is very poor, 100 is poor, 200 is fair, 300 is good, 500 is very good, and 1,000 is excellent.

It is useful to think about the sample size for the analysis not only in general as suggested by Comrey and Lee (1992) but also in terms of the ratio of participants to variables in the analysis (e.g., number of survey items). Our general recommendation is this: *Do not drop below an N of 200. Start with a target ratio of 20 participants for every variable. With a larger number of variables, you can back off in this sample size to number of variables ratio.*

Here are some examples that may help illustrate our recommendations. If you are analyzing a 10-item inventory, plan to collect data on at least 200 participants. If you are analyzing a 25-item inventory, run at least 300 participants. If you are analyzing a 90-item inventory, we suggest using close to 500 participants.

12A.21 Recommended Readings

Cattell, R. B. (1966). The scree test for the number of factors. *Multivariate Behavioral Research, 1*, 245–276.

Conway, J. M., & Huffcutt, A. I. (2004). A review and evaluation of exploratory factor analysis practices in organizational research. *Organizational Research Methods, 6*, 147–168.

Eysenck, H. J. (1952). The uses and abuses of factor analysis. *Applied Statistics, 1*, 45–49.

Fabrigar, L. R., Wegener, D. T., MacCallum, R. C., & Strahan, E. J. (1999). Evaluating the use of exploratory factor analysis in psychological research. *Psychological Methods, 4*, 272–299.

Gorsuch, R. L. (1990). Common factor analysis versus component analysis: Some well and little known facts. *Multivariate Behavioral Research, 25*, 33–39.

Gorsuch, R. L. (2003). Factor analysis. In J. A. Schinka & W. F. Velicer (Eds.), *Handbook of psychology: Vol. 2. Research methods in psychology* (pp. 143–164). Hoboken, NJ: Wiley.

Hayton, J. C., Allen, D. G., & Scarpello, V. (2004). Factor retention decisions in exploratory factor analysis: A tutorial on parallel analysis. *Organizational Research Methods, 7*, 191–205.

Kline, P. (1994). *An easy guide to factor analysis.* New York, NY: Routledge.

Mulaik, S. (1972). *The foundations of factor analysis.* New York, NY: McGraw-Hill.

Pett, M. A., Lackey, N. R., & Sullivan, J. L. (2003). *Making sense of factor analysis: The use of factor analysis for instrument development in health care research.* Thousand Oaks, CA: Sage.

Spearman, C. (1904). "General intelligence," objectively determined and measured. *American Journal of Psychology, 15*, 201–293.

Thompson, B. (2004). *Exploratory and confirmatory factor analysis: Understanding concepts and applications.* Washington, DC: American Psychological Association.

Wood, J. M., Tataryn, D. J., & Gorsuch, R. L. (1996). Effects of under- and overextraction on principal axis factor analysis with varimax rotation. *Psychological Methods, 1*, 254–365.

Zwick, W. R., & Velicer, W. F. (1986). Comparison of five rules for determining the number of components to retain. *Psychological Bulletin, 99*, 432–442.

CHAPTER **12B**

Principal Components Analysis and Exploratory Factor Analysis Using IBM SPSS

12B.1 Numerical Example

The numerical example we use in this chapter is based on responses to the Aspirations Index (Kasser & Ryan, 1993, 1996), an inventory assessing personal values or goals. The inventory assesses both extrinsic goals that are more materialistically oriented and intrinsic goals that are more closely aligned to personal development. Within each general domain, subsets of items assess more specific exemplars of these goals. The version of the inventory that was used within the context of a larger research project run in 2010 by Leanne Williamson, one of our graduate students, is shown in Table 12b.1. In this version, intrinsic orientation and extrinsic orientation are both represented by three subscales. Items said to comprise each subscale are also shown in Table 12b.1; participants used a 9-point summative response scale to indicate the extent to which the content of the item applied to them. The data file contains 310 cases and is named **Leanne**; the 30 individual items—the variables to be factor analyzed—are named **aspire01** through **aspire30**.

Although there is a hypothesized structure to this inventory (which suggests that we might wish to engage in a confirmatory factor analysis procedure as discussed in Chapters 16A and 16B), for the purposes of this chapter we will apply the exploratory procedures of principal components and factor analysis to our data set. To illustrate how to perform and interpret the results of the analyses as well as to demonstrate how

Table 12b.1   The Structure of the Aspirations Inventory Used in Data Collection

Orientation	Sub-Scale	Item Number and Exact Wording
Intrinsic Orientation	Self-Acceptance	1. I will choose what I do, instead of being pushed along by life. 7. At the end of my life, I will look back on my life as meaningful and complete. 13. I will gain increasing insight into why I do the things I do. 19. I will know and accept who I really am. 25. I will continue to grow and learn new things.
	Community Feelings	3. I will assist people who need it, asking nothing in return. 9. I will work for the betterment of society. 15. I will work to make the world a better place. 21. I will help others improve their lives. 27. I will help people in need.
	Affiliation	2. I will feel that there are people who really love me, and whom I love. 8. I will have good friends that I can count on. 14. I will share my life with someone I love. 20. I will have committed, intimate relationships. 26. I will have deep, enduring relationships.
Extrinsic Orientation	Social Recognition	4. I will be recognized by lots of different people. 10. My name will be known by many people. 16. I will be admired by many people. 22. I will be famous. 28. My name will appear frequently in the media.
	Financial Success	6. I will be financially successful. 12. I will have a job that pays very well. 18. I will have many expensive possessions. 24. I will be rich. 30. I will have enough money to buy everything I want.
	Appealing Appearance	5. I will successfully hide the signs of aging. 11. I will have people comment often about how attractive I look. 17. I will keep up with fashions in hair and clothing. 23. I will achieve the "look" I've been after. 29. My image will be one others find appealing.

researchers might work with the resulting factor structure in subsequent analyses, we do the following:

- We perform a preliminary principal components analysis (without rotation) to obtain the scree plot and determine how much variance is explained as a function of the number of components.

- We then extract and rotate two components/factors, expecting to see a separation between the global intrinsic items and the global extrinsic items.
- Following that, we extract and rotate six components/factors, hoping to see a separation between the six subscales, but being prepared to deal with whatever results we obtain.
- We then evaluate the reliability of item sets defined by the factor structure that we have accepted.
- Based on the outcome of the reliability analysis, we build the corresponding scales/subscales.
- We correlate the scales/subscales that we have computed.
- Finally, we use the scales/subscales as dependent variables in an exploratory one-way between-subjects MANOVA.

12B.2 Preliminary Principal Components Analysis

12B.2.1 Preliminary Principal Components Analysis Setup

Selecting the path **Analyze ➔ Dimension Reduction ➔ Factor** from the main menu brings us to the **Factor Analysis** main dialog window displayed in Figure 12b.1. We have highlighted and moved **aspire01** through **aspire30** into the **Variables** panel.

Figure 12b.1   The Main Factor Analysis Window

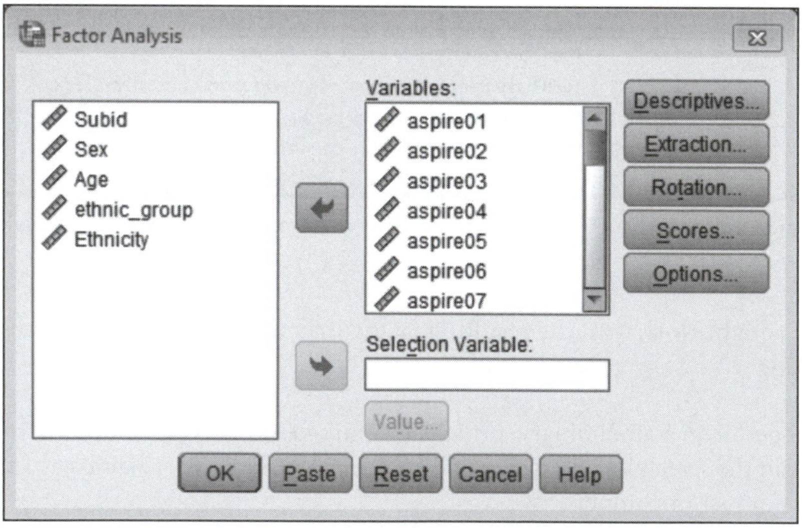

12B.2.1.1 Descriptive Statistics

Select the **Descriptives** pushbutton and check **Univariate descriptives** and **Initial solution** under **Statistics** as shown in Figure 12b.2. The **Statistics** section provides two options. The **Univariate descriptives** will provide the number of valid cases, mean, and standard deviation for each variable. The **Initial solution** checkbox will produce an initial (unrotated) solution including the complete analysis (all 30 components extracted) and a snapshot of the number of components we would wish to bring into the rotation phase if in fact we requested a rotation of the structure. It will also provide the communalities, eigenvalues, and percentage of variance explained. We have requested that both sets of statistics be included in the output.

The **Correlation Matrix** section displays eight separate options, including a Pearson correlation matrix (**Coefficients**)

Figure 12b.2 The Descriptives Window of Factor Analysis

with **significance levels** for all variables in the analysis. These Pearson coefficients should be scanned to check for consistent patterns of variability or relationships between variables. We recommend this inspection be conducted during the initial data screening and univariate/multivariate assumption violation check discussed in Chapters 3A and 3B and so will not do it here.

Choose the **KMO and Bartlett's test of sphericity** checkbox as shown in Figure 12b.2. This produces the Kaiser–Meyer–Olkin (KMO) measure of sampling adequacy, which is a rough indicator of how adequate the correlations are for factor analysis. As a general heuristic (see Kaiser, 1970, 1974), a value of .70 or above is considered adequate. Bartlett's test of sphericity provides a test of the null hypothesis that none of the variables are significantly correlated. This test should yield a statistically significant outcome before proceeding with the factor analysis. Click **Continue** to return to the main dialog window.

12B.2.1.2 Component Extraction

Selecting the **Extraction** pushbutton produces the dialog window shown in Figure 12b.3. This screen is composed of five sections: **Method**, **Analyze**, **Display**, **Extract**, and **Maximum Iterations for Convergence**.

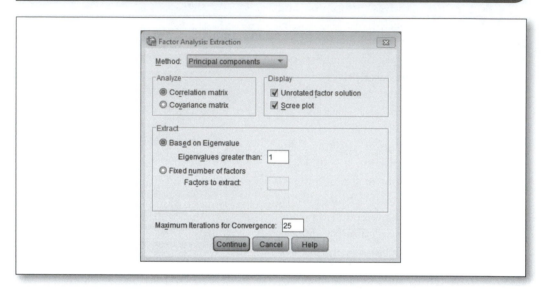

Figure 12b.3 The Extraction Window of Factor Analysis

The **Method** drop-down menu allows us to choose from one of seven methods of factor (or component) extraction. We have chosen **Principal components** (the default option) in this preliminary analysis but there are several other choices including principal factors, generalized least squares and ULS, and maximum likelihood. In the **Analyze** panel, we have chosen to analyze the **Correlation matrix**. The **Display** panel allows us to obtain an **Unrotated factor solution** and a **Scree plot**. The **Extract** panel defaults to selecting factors or components whose eigenvalues exceed 1.00; this is a reasonable choice to make given that we are performing the preliminary analysis. Finally, the **Maximum Iterations for Convergence** section defaults at 25 iterations or algorithmic passes to achieve a solution; this will work for our data set, but it is sometimes necessary to raise this value to 100 or greater for data sets that have a less well-defined structure. Click **Continue** to return to the main dialog window.

12B.2.1.3 Component Rotation

The **Rotation** dialog window, shown in Figure 12b.4, consists of three sections: **Method**, **Display**, and **Maximum Iterations for Convergence**. The **Method** section provides for a variety of factor rotation methods. For this preliminary analysis, we have chosen **None** and therefore do not need to **Display** anything. Click **Continue** to return to the main dialog window.

12B.2.1.4 Options

The **Options** window is shown in Figure 12b.5. The **Missing Values** section allows researchers to **Exclude cases listwise** (the default), which is what we have selected. This option excludes any cases missing one or more values on any of the variables in the analysis; thus, all cases included in the analysis have valid values on all of the variables.

The **Coefficient Display Format** section allows us to sort the factor weightings by size and to suppress weightings with absolute values less than a specified value. Sorting coefficients by size usually makes it easier for researchers to comprehend the results, and we will choose this form of display when we request the two-factor and later the six-factor rotated solution. Click **Continue** to return to the main dialog window and **OK** to perform the analysis.

12B.2.2 Preliminary Principal Components Analysis Output

12B.2.2.1 Descriptive Statistics

A portion of the **Descriptive Statistics** output is shown in Figure 12b.6. The mean, standard deviation, and sample size are displayed for each variable. Examining the sample size is especially important as that assures us that we have not lost too many cases; here, we analyzed data for 301 of the 310 cases in the data file.

The results of the KMO and Bartlett's test of sphericity appear in Figure 12b.7. A KMO coefficient in the middle .8s suggests that the data are suitable for principal components

Figure 12b.4   The Rotation Window of Factor Analysis

Figure 12b.5   The Options Window of Factor Analysis

Figure 12b.6 A Portion of the Descriptive Statistics Output

Descriptive Statistics

	Mean	Std. Deviation	Analysis N
aspire01 I will choose what I do, instead of being pushed along by life.	7.72	1.457	301
aspire02 I will feel that there are people who really love me, and whom I love.	8.34	1.172	301
aspire03 I will assist people who need it, asking nothing in return.	7.72	1.413	301
aspire04 I will be recognized by lots of different people.	5.33	2.284	301
aspire05 I will successfully hide the signs of aging.	4.43	2.387	301
aspire06 I will be financially successful.	7.61	1.407	301
aspire07 At the end of my life, I will look back on my life as meaningful and complete.	8.30	1.334	301
aspire08 I will have good friends that I can count on.	8.23	1.153	301
aspire09 I will work for the betterment of society.	7.31	1.635	301
aspire10 My name will be known by many people.	4.55	2.325	301
aspire11 I will have people comment often about how attractive I look.	4.15	2.310	301
aspire12 I will have a job that pays very well.	7.38	1.662	301
aspire13 I will gain increasing insight into why I do the things I do.	7.31	1.465	301
aspire14 I will share my life with someone I love.	8.46	1.184	301

analysis. Likewise, a statistically significant Bartlett's test enables us to reject the null hypothesis of lack of sufficient correlation between the variables. These two results give us confidence to proceed with the analysis.

Figure 12b.7 Kaiser–Meyer–Olkin and Bartlett Test Output

KMO and Bartlett's Test		
Kaiser–Meyer–Olkin Measure of Sampling Adequacy.		.853
Bartlett's Test of Sphericity	Approx. Chi–Square	4751.733
	df	435
	Sig.	.000

12B.2.2.2 Explained Variance

The **Total Variance Explained** output is presented in Figure 12b.8. The first major set of three columns labeled **Initial Eigenvalues** shows the analysis that has been taken to completion. Thus, by the time we reach the 30th component, we have extracted 100% of the variance (because there are 30 items in the full inventory). What draws our immediate attention is that seven components have eigenvalues of 1.00 or greater, and for most researchers most of the time, that would indicate the maximum number of components they would accept (and most often they would accept fewer for their final solution).

The first two components each make great strides in accounting for the variance—almost 25% and 16%, respectively, cumulatively accounting for about 41% of the total variance. Gains in total variance explained for the next few components still jump in somewhat good-sized chunks—almost 8%, 5.5%, better than 4%, and almost 4% for the third through sixth components, respectively. The first six components cumulatively account for better than 62% of the variance.

The second major set of three columns labeled **Extraction Sums of Squared Loadings** conveys the same information (because this was a principal components analysis) for all components whose eigenvalue was better than 1.00 (as we specified in the **Options** dialog window).

The percentages shown in the **Total Variance Explained** table are based on the eigenvalues. With 30 variables in the analysis, there are 30 units of total variance. The first component had a computed eigenvalue of 7.422, which represents 24.739% of 30, and the second component had a computed eigenvalue of 4.819, which represents 16.062% of 30, and so on.

12B.2.2.3 The Scree Plot

The **Scree Plot** output is presented in Figure 12b.9 and simply plots the eigenvalues shown in Figure 12b.8 for each component. Visual inspection of the plot suggests that the

Figure 12b.8 Total Variance Explained by the Analysis

Total Variance Explained

Component	Initial Eigenvalues			Extraction Sums of Squared Loadings		
	Total	% of Variance	Cumulative %	Total	% of Variance	Cumulative %
1	7.422	24.739	24.739	7.422	24.739	24.739
2	4.819	16.062	40.801	4.819	16.062	40.801
3	2.356	7.854	48.655	2.356	7.854	48.655
4	1.654	5.514	54.169	1.654	5.514	54.169
5	1.276	4.254	58.423	1.276	4.254	58.423
6	1.161	3.870	62.293	1.161	3.870	62.293
7	1.039	3.465	65.758	1.039	3.465	65.758
8	.937	3.125	68.883			
9	.843	2.810	71.693			
10	.808	2.693	74.386			
11	.785	2.617	77.003			
12	.694	2.313	79.316			
13	.607	2.023	81.338			
14	.568	1.895	83.233			
15	.535	1.783	85.016			
16	.511	1.702	86.718			
17	.461	1.535	88.253			
18	.421	1.405	89.658			
19	.390	1.301	90.959			
20	.367	1.224	92.183			
21	.338	1.126	93.309			
22	.293	.978	94.287			
23	.277	.924	95.211			
24	.258	.860	96.071			
25	.244	.814	96.885			
26	.228	.759	97.643			
27	.211	.703	98.347			
28	.175	.583	98.930			
29	.170	.567	99.497			
30	.151	.503	100.000			

Extraction Method: Principal Component Analysis.

function appears to level out in the general neighborhood of the fifth or sixth component. If we were examining the output with no hypothesized factor structure presented in the research literature, and if we were using this plot to help us envision how many components are likely to be included in the final rotated solution, we might be inclined to consider the four-component, five-component, and six-component solutions as potentially viable candidates.

Figure 12b.9 The Scree Plot

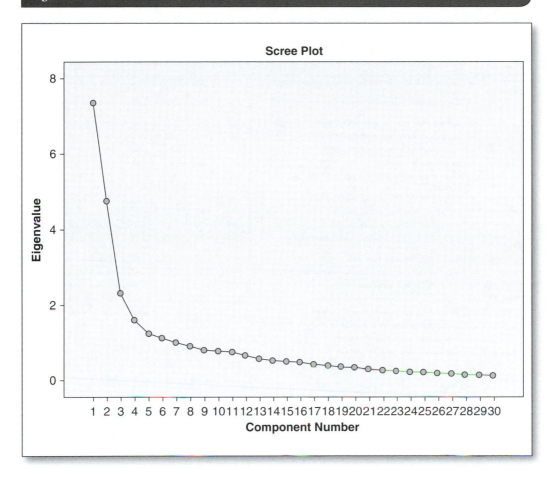

12B.2.2.4 The Component Matrix

We present the **Component Matrix** in Figure 12b.10 more for information than for interpretation purposes as this is not a rotated matrix. The entries are the correlations between the variables and the components at the end of the extraction phase (the entries are extraction structure coefficients) for all components whose eigenvalues are better than 1.00 (seven components in this analysis). Note that the first component overall has the largest correlations compared with the other components. How much larger? That is told to us by the eigenvalues. If we were to square each of the structure coefficients for the first component and add these squared values $(.143^2 + .284^2 + .226^2 + \ldots + .533^2)$, the result would be

Figure 12b.10 The Component Matrix

Component Matrix[a]

	Component						
	1	2	3	4	5	6	7
aspire01 I will choose what I do, instead of being pushed along by life.	.143	.330	.249	−.17	−.10	.418	.416
aspire02 I will feel that there are people who really love me, and whom I love.	.284	.469	.303	.298	−.03	−.11	−.03
aspire03 I will assist people who need it, asking nothing in return.	.226	.547	−.21	−.23	.029	−.04	−.04
aspire04 I will be recognized by lots of different people.	.642	.002	−.12	−.05	−.50	−.13	.209
aspire05 I will successfully hide the signs of aging.	.556	−.17	−.02	−.04	.090	−.25	.459
aspire06 I will be financially successful.	.577	−.05	.545	−.31	.019	−.21	−.07
aspire07 At the end of my life, I will look back on my life as meaningful and complete.	.300	.409	.461	−.01	−.10	.045	.241
aspire08 I will have good friends that I can count on.	.342	.417	.219	.057	.155	−.13	.132
aspire09 I will work for the betterment of society.	.359	.508	−.36	−.32	.066	−.17	−.03
aspire10 My name will be known by many people.	.731	−.17	−.15	−.00	−.42	−.04	.090
aspire11 I will have people comment often about how attractive I look.	.698	−.36	−.15	.111	.273	.046	.170
aspire12 I will have a job that pays very well.	.556	−.00	.541	−.40	−.04	−.17	−.10
aspire13 I will gain increasing insight into why I do the things I do.	.418	.338	.036	−.07	.069	.450	−.02
aspire14 I will share my life with someone I love.	.365	.476	.279	.476	−.05	−.18	−.05
aspire15 I will work to make the world a better place.	.359	.595	−.39	−.20	.031	−.16	−.03
aspire16 I will be admired by many people.	.711	−.12	−.13	−.08	−.29	−.00	.120
aspire17 I will keep up with fashions in hair and clothing.	.619	−.35	−.18	.091	.436	−.07	.140
aspire18 I will have many expensive possessions.	.630	−.47	.030	.005	.188	−.07	−.09
aspire19 I will know and accept who I really am.	.326	.498	.158	−.07	.103	.481	.101
aspire20 I will have committed, intimate relationships.	.361	.376	.146	.615	.013	−.00	−.11
aspire21 I will help others improve their lives.	.339	.634	−.37	−.09	.138	−.05	−.06
aspire22 I will be famous.	.625	−.36	−.25	.143	−.30	.124	−.17
aspire23 I will achieve the "look" I've been after.	.641	−.35	−.15	.060	.278	.107	.079
aspire24 I will be rich.	.594	−.36	.344	−.11	.010	−.02	−.36
aspire25 I will continue to grow and learn new things.	.329	.460	−.04	−.22	−.04	.296	−.36
aspire26 I will have deep, enduring relationships.	.390	.497	.131	.472	.009	−.04	−.07
aspire27 I will help people in need.	.366	.587	−.40	−.05	.142	−.16	−.13
aspire28 My name will appear frequently in the media.	.534	−.39	−.29	.168	−.29	.172	−.19
aspire29 My image will be one others find appealing.	.598	−.30	−.15	.187	.201	.269	.032
aspire30 I will have enough money to buy everything I want.	.533	−.32	.370	−.19	.185	.047	−.21

Extraction Method: Principal Component Analysis.

a. 7 components extracted.

the eigenvalue for the first component, 7.422. The analogous computation for the other components would provide their eigenvalues as well.

12B.2.2.5 Communalities

It is also possible to add the squared structure coefficients across the rows of the component matrix, obtaining a total for each variable. The result of that operation gives us the

Communalities of the variables as displayed in Figure 12b.11. Communality is a measure of how much variance of a variable has been captured in the component structure. It is computed by summing the squared structure coefficients for that variable, that is, squaring the correlations between a variable and each of the components (the values on each row of the component matrix) and then taking the sum of those squared correlations. Generally speaking, variables with communality values less than .50 are not substantially captured by the component structure and are thus possible candidates for removal from the analysis.

Figure 12b.11 The Communalities Output

Communalities

	Initial	Extraction
aspire01 I will choose what I do, instead of being pushed along by life.	1.000	.579
aspire02 I will feel that there are people who really love me, and whom I love.	1.000	.496
aspire03 I will assist people who need it, asking nothing in return.	1.000	.454
aspire04 I will be recognized by lots of different people.	1.000	.740
aspire05 I will successfully hide the signs of aging.	1.000	.626
aspire06 I will be financially successful.	1.000	.781
aspire07 At the end of my life, I will look back on my life as meaningful and complete.	1.000	.542
aspire08 I will have good friends that I can count on.	1.000	.402
aspire09 I will work for the betterment of society.	1.000	.660
aspire10 My name will be known by many people.	1.000	.781
aspire11 I will have people comment often about how attractive I look.	1.000	.762
aspire12 I will have a job that pays very well.	1.000	.807
aspire13 I will gain increasing insight into why I do the things I do.	1.000	.504
aspire14 I will share my life with someone I love.	1.000	.703
aspire15 I will work to make the world a better place.	1.000	.714
aspire16 I will be admired by many people.	1.000	.648
aspire17 I will keep up with fashions in hair and clothing.	1.000	.767
aspire18 I will have many expensive possessions.	1.000	.668
aspire19 I will know and accept who I really am.	1.000	.637
aspire20 I will have committed, intimate relationships.	1.000	.683
aspire21 I will help others improve their lives.	1.000	.690
aspire22 I will be famous.	1.000	.749
aspire23 I will achieve the "look" I've been after.	1.000	.663
aspire24 I will be rich.	1.000	.748
aspire25 I will continue to grow and learn new things.	1.000	.595
aspire26 I will have deep, enduring relationships.	1.000	.647
aspire27 I will help people in need.	1.000	.708
aspire28 My name will appear frequently in the media.	1.000	.706
aspire29 My image will be one others find appealing.	1.000	.620
aspire30 I will have enough money to buy everything I want.	1.000	.648

Extraction Method: Principal Component Analysis.

The column labeled **Initial** is based on the complete solution in which all 30 components were extracted. Because extracting all 30 components explains 100% of the total variance, each variable is "fully captured" in this complete solution; hence, each variable has a communality of 1.00.

Of greater interest is the output for the column labeled **Extraction**. These values represent the communalities based only on those components that were extracted in the analysis. In our analysis, we requested that components with eigenvalues greater than 1.00 be extracted and so seven components were extracted. These are shown in the component matrix (see Figure 12b.10). Consider the communality of the first variable, **aspire01**. We see from the **Communalities** output that it has a communality value of .579. This value is the sum of the squared correlation values for that variable as seen in the component matrix: that is—$(.143)^2 + (.330)^2 + (.249)^2 + (-.175)^2 + (-.103)^2 + (.418)^2 + (.416)^2 = .579$, when all 16 of the decimal places (only 3 of which are shown) are used.

12B.3 Principal Components Analysis
With a Promax Rotation: Two-Component Solution

Based on our preliminary analysis, it appears that more than two components/factors are needed to describe the underlying structure of the 30 items on the inventory. Nonetheless, it is useful to perform the two-component/factor analysis first in this particular example because (a) it will serve as a relatively simple illustration of the general procedure, and (b) there is good reason to believe that the items generally align along two very global dimensions. To save page space, we will display only those dialog boxes in the setup in which somewhat different specifications from those already illustrated are needed, and in presenting the output, we will display only output that is specific to the particular analysis.

12B.3.1 Principal Components Analysis With a
Promax Rotation: Two-Component Solution Setup

Select the path **Analyze ➜ Dimension Reduction ➜ Factor** from the main menu. Highlight and move **aspire01** through **aspire30** into the **Variables** panel. Select the **Descriptives** pushbutton and check **Univariate descriptives**, **Initial solution**, and **KMO and Bartlett's test of sphericity**. Click **Continue** to return to the main dialog window.

In the **Extraction** dialog window shown in Figure 12b.12 select **Principal components**, **Correlation matrix**, **Unrotated factor solution**, and **Scree plot**. Click **Fixed number of factors** and in the **Factors to extract** panel type in **2**. Click **Continue** to return to the main dialog window.

Figure 12b.12 The Extraction Window of Factor Analysis

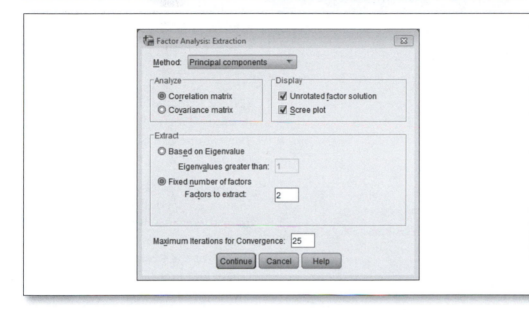

In the **Rotation** dialog window, as shown in Figure 12b.13, select **Promax** and keep the default for **Kappa** at 4 (the power to which the coefficients will be raised in the second phase of the **Promax** procedure). We invoke an oblique rotation strategy, **Promax** in this analysis, to obtain the component correlations. Based on these correlations, we will be able to determine if we can revert to a varimax rotation or if we should stay with an oblique rotation. Click **Continue** to return to the main dialog window.

In the **Options** window shown in Figure 12b.14, check **Exclude cases listwise** and, to make the output easier to read, **Sorted by size**. This latter specification will sort the variables by the value of the structure coefficients within each of the two components, allowing us at a glance to

Figure 12b.13 The Rotation Window of Factor Analysis

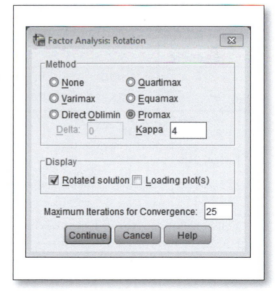

Figure 12b.14 The Options Window of Factor Analysis

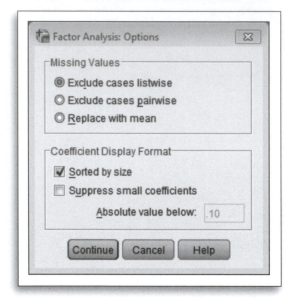

Figure 12b.15 The Correlations of the Components

Component Correlation Matrix

Component	1	2
1	1.000	.182
2	.182	1.000

Extraction Method: Principal Component Analysis.
Rotation Method: Promax with Kaiser Normalization.

determine which variables correlate most strongly with each component. Click **Continue** to return to the main dialog window and click **OK** to perform the analysis.

12B.3.2 Principal Components Analysis With a Promax Rotation: Two-Component Solution Selected Output

Because the extraction phase of this analysis is identical to that of our preliminary analysis, we already know that the two-component solution accounts for 40.80% of the total variance (see Figure 12b.8). Of immediate interest is the correlation between the two components, and we show that in Figure 12b.15. In this analysis, the two components have a correlation of .182. As indicated in Section 12A.16, this value is probably low enough to justify reverting to a varimax solution should researchers be so inclined. For us, we opt to stay with this oblique solution (the varimax rotated component matrix would be very similar to what we obtained here).

In an oblique rotation procedure, we obtain two rotated matrixes, the pattern matrix and the structure matrix. We show the structure matrix in Figure 12b.16 (the pattern matrix is very similar). The entries are sorted (as we specified in the **Options** dialog window). Variables more strongly correlated with the first component (the ordering of components is arbitrary) are listed in order of the magnitude of the correlation, followed by those most strongly correlated with the second component.

Figure 12b.16 The Two-Component Rotated Structure Matrix: Principal Components/Promax

Structure Matrix

	Component 1	Component 2
aspire11 I will have people comment often about how attractive I look.	.787	.096
aspire18 I will have many expensive possessions.	.767	-.02
aspire10 My name will be known by many people.	.740	.269
aspire23 I will achieve the "look" I've been after.	.732	.069
aspire22 I will be famous.	.720	.055
aspire17 I will keep up with fashions in hair and clothing.	.710	.062
aspire16 I will be admired by many people.	.699	.304
aspire24 I will be rich.	.691	.038
aspire29 My image will be one others find appealing.	.669	.094
aspire28 My name will appear frequently in the media.	.648	-.01
aspire30 I will have enough money to buy everything I want.	.619	.036
aspire04 I will be recognized by lots of different people.	.584	.367
aspire05 I will successfully hide the signs of aging.	.577	.176
aspire06 I will be financially successful.	.550	.280
aspire12 I will have a job that pays very well.	.509	.314
aspire21 I will help others improve their lives.	.049	.715
aspire15 I will work to make the world a better place.	.084	.693
aspire27 I will help people in need.	.093	.691
aspire26 I will have deep, enduring relationships.	.152	.630
aspire09 I will work for the betterment of society.	.120	.622
aspire14 I will share my life with someone I love.	.137	.599
aspire19 I will know and accept who I really am.	.093	.595
aspire03 I will assist people who need it, asking nothing in return.	-.01	.578
aspire25 I will continue to grow and learn new things.	.111	.565
aspire02 I will feel that there are people who really love me, and whom I love.	.067	.547
aspire08 I will have good friends that I can count on.	.141	.538
aspire13 I will gain increasing insight into why I do the things I do.	.242	.516
aspire20 I will have committed, intimate relationships.	.175	.514
aspire07 At the end of my life, I will look back on my life as meaningful and complete.	.106	.507
aspire01 I will choose what I do, instead of being pushed along by life.	-.00	.352

Extraction Method: Principal Component Analysis.
Rotation Method: Promax with Kaiser Normalization.

We see from the output that **aspire11** ("I will have people comment often about how attractive I look") correlated most strongly with Component 1 at .787, **aspire18** ("I will have many expensive possessions") correlated next most strongly at .767, and so on. The last variable that was still correlating more strongly with Component 1 than with Component 2 was **aspire12** ("I will have a job that pays very well") at .509; it is associated with Component 1 because the structure coefficient of .509 is higher than its structure coefficient for Component 2 (.314).

If the name of this component was not already known to us—a situation that is relatively commonly experienced—we would examine the content of the items most strongly correlated with the component and introduce a label that we believed was descriptive. By focusing on those items with the highest structure coefficients and identifying their commonality as the label for the component or factor, we can achieve some theoretical clarity on what is sometimes a very large amount of separate pieces of information.

In the present example, the label has already been put forward in the research literature; nonetheless, it is a worthwhile effort to examine for ourselves the content of these items and to determine what we believe the items have in common (a process that we urge readers to carry out for each component or factor that we discuss in this chapter). That said, it is apparent to us that these variables are indicative of extrinsic goal orientation.

An analogous pattern may be seen for Component 2. The variable having the highest structure coefficient for that component was **aspire21** ("I will help others improve their lives") at .715, then **aspire15** ("I will work to make the world a better place") at .693, and so on. Using our own reasoning in thinking about the content of these items (but obviously informed by the label existent in the research literature already), we determine (agree) that Component 2 can be interpreted as intrinsic goal orientation.

12B.4 ULS Analysis With a Promax Rotation: Two-Factor Solution

Different extractions can sometimes make a difference in the outcome to the extent that the component/factor structure is less distinct. In this two-component/factor analysis, the more commonly used factor analysis methods yield very similar structures to what we saw with principal components, suggesting that the two dimensions are quite robust. We will use the ULS extraction procedure to quickly show the results of a factor analysis.

We set up this analysis in the same way as we did in Section 12B.3 except that we request a ULS extraction in the extraction dialog window as shown in Figure 12b.17.

The correlation of the factors is shown in Figure 12b.18. Although certainly in the same order of magnitude as the principal components, these ULS factors correlate to a slightly greater extent at .199. Again, some researchers might consider this a sufficiently low correlation to revert to a varimax rotation, but we are quite comfortable with our decision to use an oblique rotation here.

The **Total Variance Explained** output is presented in Figure 12b.19. Note that the **Initial Eigenvalues** columns provide the same information as we have previously seen. That is the case because those columns are based on a principal components analysis (even though we specified ULS extraction). Furthermore, because the scree plot includes all components/factors, it is also based on this same information.

Figure 12b.17 The Extraction Window of Factor Analysis

The consequences of using ULS as our extraction technique are shown in the set of columns labeled **Extraction Sums of Squared Loadings**. Because we have performed a factor analysis rather than a principal components analysis, it is the common variance rather than the total variance that is to be explained. Thus, the values in these columns will differ from the corresponding values in the **Initial Eigenvalues** columns. In the ULS analysis, the eigenvalue associated with the first factor has a value of 6.843, and that represents only 22.81% of the total variance. Ultimately, because the total variance is composed of common variance and unique variance, and because factor analysis

Figure 12b.18 The Correlations of the Components

Factor Correlation Matrix

Factor	1	2
1	1.000	.199
2	.199	1.000

Extraction Method:
Unweighted Least Squares.
Rotation Method: Promax
with Kaiser Normalization.

attempts to explain only the common variance, a factor analysis will always explain less of the total variance than a principal components analysis. Here, the first two factors

Figure 12b.19 Total Variance Explained: Unweighted Least Squares/Promax

Total Variance Explained

Factor	Initial Eigenvalues			Extraction Sums of Squared Loadings			Rotation Sums of Squared Loadings[a]
	Total	% of Variance	Cumulative %	Total	% of Variance	Cumulative %	Total
1	7.422	24.739	24.739	6.843	22.810	22.810	6.450
2	4.819	16.062	40.801	4.194	13.981	36.791	5.028
3	2.356	7.854	48.655				
4	1.654	5.514	54.169				
5	1.276	4.254	58.423				
6	1.161	3.870	62.293				
7	1.039	3.465	65.758				
8	.937	3.125	68.883				
9	.843	2.810	71.693				
10	.808	2.693	74.386				
11	.785	2.617	77.003				
12	.694	2.313	79.316				
13	.607	2.023	81.338				
14	.568	1.895	83.233				
15	.535	1.783	85.016				
16	.511	1.702	86.718				
17	.461	1.535	88.253				
18	.421	1.405	89.658				
19	.390	1.301	90.959				
20	.367	1.224	92.183				
21	.338	1.126	93.309				
22	.293	.978	94.287				
23	.277	.924	95.211				
24	.258	.860	96.071				
25	.244	.814	96.885				
26	.228	.759	97.643				
27	.211	.703	98.347				
28	.175	.583	98.930				
29	.170	.567	99.497				
30	.151	.503	100.000				

Extraction Method: Unweighted Least Squares.

a. When factors are correlated, sums of squared loadings cannot be added to obtain a total variance.

accounted for 36.79% of the total variance whereas the first two principal components accounted for 40.80% of the total variance.

The last column in the **Total Variance Explained** table is labeled **Rotation Sums of Squared Loadings**. These are the eigenvalues associated with each factor. Most researchers do not attend much to them in general because in attempting to achieve simple structure they will be closer in value to each other than they were in the extraction phase. Furthermore, the factors are almost always correlated with each other under an oblique rotation strategy.

Under these circumstances, we cannot meaningfully add the eigenvalues as was done in the extraction phase where the extracted factors were orthogonal.

The structure matrix is shown in Figure 12b.20. The variables are correlating in the identical fashion to what was obtained with the principal components analysis. Were we to use any of the other factor analysis procedures (e.g., maximum likelihood, principal factors) to generate a two-factor solution, the factor structure we see in Figure 12b.20 would be seen using these other procedures as well; therefore, we will not present those analyses here.

Figure 12b.20   The Two-Component Rotated Structure Matrix: Unweighted Least Squares/Promax

Structure Matrix

	Factor 1	Factor 2
aspire11 I will have people comment often about how attractive I look.	.771	.108
aspire18 I will have many expensive possessions.	.750	-.01
aspire10 My name will be known by many people.	.720	.277
aspire23 I will achieve the "look" I've been after.	.707	.082
aspire22 I will be famous.	.693	.069
aspire17 I will keep up with fashions in hair and clothing.	.682	.075
aspire16 I will be admired by many people.	.676	.308
aspire24 I will be rich.	.659	.048
aspire29 My image will be one others find appealing.	.637	.104
aspire28 My name will appear frequently in the media.	.613	-.00
aspire30 I will have enough money to buy everything I want.	.581	.046
aspire04 I will be recognized by lots of different people.	.557	.360
aspire05 I will successfully hide the signs of aging.	.541	.179
aspire06 I will be financially successful.	.516	.270
aspire12 I will have a job that pays very well.	.476	.299
aspire21 I will help others improve their lives.	.057	.692
aspire15 I will work to make the world a better place.	.089	.668
aspire27 I will help people in need.	.099	.665
aspire26 I will have deep, enduring relationships.	.154	.591
aspire09 I will work for the betterment of society.	.122	.589
aspire14 I will share my life with someone I love.	.139	.556
aspire19 I will know and accept who I really am.	.098	.550
aspire03 I will assist people who need it, asking nothing in return.	-.00	.537
aspire25 I will continue to grow and learn new things.	.114	.524
aspire02 I will feel that there are people who really love me, and whom I love.	.072	.499
aspire08 I will have good friends that I can count on.	.141	.493
aspire13 I will gain increasing insight into why I do the things I do.	.234	.478
aspire20 I will have committed, intimate relationships.	.172	.471
aspire07 At the end of my life, I will look back on my life as meaningful and complete.	.107	.459
aspire01 I will choose what I do, instead of being pushed along by life.	.003	.309

Extraction Method: Unweighted Least Squares.
 Rotation Method: Promax with Kaiser Normalization.

12B.5 Wrap-Up of the Two-Factor Solution

There are some relatively clear inferences that we can draw from the previous analyses. Items can be clearly separated into the global dimensions of extrinsic and intrinsic goal orientation. It does not matter whether these dimensions are principal components or factors—they are sufficiently robust to emerge regardless of the extraction technique used. Furthermore, these dimensions do not appear to be strongly correlated.

12B.6 Looking for Six Dimensions

Despite the clarity of these two dimensions, there is likely to be more structure than is captured just by these global dimensions. We can explain up to about 41% of the total variance depending on our analytic technique, but it is at least an informal ambition of many researchers to break the 50% explained variance barrier and a fragile hope to exceed the 60% explained variance mark. Achieving this level of explanation requires us to extract more than two components or factors from the present data set. Given (a) the hypothesized subscale structure, (b) that six components explains a bit more than 62% of the total variance, and (c) that in our visual examination of the scree plot we did allow for the possibility of a six-component/factor solution being potentially viable, we opt here to generate a small set of solutions targeting six dimensions.

12B.7 Principal Components Analysis With a Promax Rotation: Six-Component Solution

We set up our analysis as we have done previously in this chapter, so that we will work with a **Promax** rotation. The only difference worthy of a screen shot is the **Extraction** dialog window (see Figure 12b.21) where we requested a **Principal components** analysis, have checked **Fixed number of factors**, and have set **Factors to extract** at **6**. We have also left **Scree plot** unchecked as we already have generated it in prior analyses.

The **Component Correlation Matrix** is shown in Figure 12b.22. Some pairs of components are not correlated at all (the correlations are effectively zero)—for example, the correlation between Component 1 and Component 2 is −.001 and the correlation between Component 1 and Component 6 is .019. Other components are modestly correlated—for example, the correlation between Component 2 and Component 3 is .139 and the correlation between Component 3 and Component 4 is .130. But there is considerable correlation between some of the other components—for example, the correlation between Component 1 and Component 3 is .572 and the correlation between Component 2 and Component 4 is .401. With these rather substantial correlations in the mix, it is appropriate to use an oblique rather than orthogonal rotation strategy, and so we will not explore a varimax rotation in our solution set.

Figure 12b.21 The Extraction Window of Factor Analysis

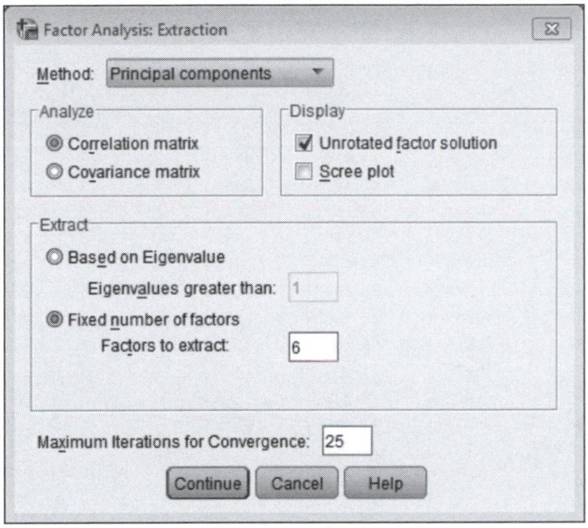

Figure 12b.22 The Correlations of the Components: Principal Components/Promax

Component Correlation Matrix

Component	1	2	3	4	5	6
1	1.000	−.001	.572	.053	.304	.019
2	−.001	1.000	.139	.401	.095	.358
3	.572	.139	1.000	.130	.324	.112
4	.053	.401	.130	1.000	.235	.400
5	.304	.095	.324	.235	1.000	.216
6	.019	.358	.112	.400	.216	1.000

Extraction Method: Principal Component Analysis.
Rotation Method: Promax with Kaiser Normalization.

The **Total Variance Explained** output, presented in Figure 12b.23, once again presents the same information as we have previously seen in the **Initial Eigenvalues** columns because those columns are based on a principal components analysis. As this is a principal components analysis, the set of columns labeled **Extraction Sums of Squared Loadings** repeats the first six sets of rows from the prior columns. Thus, the six-component solution accounts for 62.29% of the total variance.

Figure 12b.23 Total Variance Explained: Principal Components/Promax

Total Variance Explained

Component	Initial Eigenvalues			Extraction Sums of Squared Loadings			Rotation Sums of Squared Loadings[a]
	Total	% of Variance	Cumulative %	Total	% of Variance	Cumulative %	Total
1	7.422	24.739	24.739	7.422	24.739	24.739	5.662
2	4.819	16.062	40.801	4.819	16.062	40.801	4.412
3	2.356	7.854	48.655	2.356	7.854	48.655	5.252
4	1.654	5.514	54.169	1.654	5.514	54.169	4.084
5	1.276	4.254	58.423	1.276	4.254	58.423	4.139
6	1.161	3.870	62.293	1.161	3.870	62.293	3.176
7	1.039	3.465	65.758				
8	.937	3.125	68.883				
9	.843	2.810	71.693				
10	.808	2.693	74.386				
11	.785	2.617	77.003				
12	.694	2.313	79.316				
13	.607	2.023	81.338				
14	.568	1.895	83.233				
15	.535	1.783	85.016				
16	.511	1.702	86.718				
17	.461	1.535	88.253				
18	.421	1.405	89.658				
19	.390	1.301	90.959				
20	.367	1.224	92.183				
21	.338	1.126	93.309				
22	.293	.978	94.287				
23	.277	.924	95.211				
24	.258	.860	96.071				
25	.244	.814	96.885				
26	.228	.759	97.643				
27	.211	.703	98.347				
28	.175	.583	98.930				
29	.170	.567	99.497				
30	.151	.503	100.000				

Extraction Method: Principal Component Analysis.

a. When components are correlated, sums of squared loadings cannot be added to obtain a total variance.

The **Structure Matrix** is shown in Figure 12b.24. These components generally but not precisely correspond to the hypothesized subscales that presumably exist within the inventory. Even though the variables are ordered by the value of their coefficients on the components (we specified **Sorted by size** in the **Options** dialog window), the table is relatively complicated; we will therefore treat the results component by component; readers are referred to Table 12b.1 for the hypothesized structure.

Figure 12b.24 The Six-Component Rotated Structure Matrix: Principal Components/Promax

Structure Matrix

	Component					
	1	2	3	4	5	6
aspire11 I will have people comment often about how attractive I look.	.852	.061	.535	.098	.303	.044
aspire17 I will keep up with fashions in hair and clothing.	.838	.100	.390	.063	.268	-.07
aspire23 I will achieve the "look" I've been after.	.807	.046	.487	.039	.269	.076
aspire18 I will have many expensive possessions.	.761	-.07	.503	.012	.452	-.07
aspire29 My image will be one others find appealing.	.749	-.00	.486	.111	.154	.191
aspire05 I will successfully hide the signs of aging.	.512	.179	.426	.142	.416	-.07
aspire15 I will work to make the world a better place.	.022	.840	.186	.316	.064	.289
aspire27 I will help people in need.	.092	.812	.141	.398	.008	.264
aspire21 I will help others improve their lives.	.048	.809	.105	.391	-.00	.372
aspire09 I will work for the betterment of society.	.053	.796	.179	.210	.139	.257
aspire03 I will assist people who need it, asking nothing in return.	-.08	.655	.055	.252	.079	.342
aspire10 My name will be known by many people.	.507	.187	.870	.177	.382	.115
aspire22 I will be famous.	.616	-.01	.809	.044	.160	.052
aspire04 I will be recognized by lots of different people.	.304	.294	.780	.241	.375	.135
aspire16 I will be admired by many people.	.500	.238	.766	.158	.399	.181
aspire28 My name will appear frequently in the media.	.578	-.06	.751	-.01	.062	.028
aspire14 I will share my life with someone I love.	.025	.296	.129	.829	.231	.255
aspire26 I will have deep, enduring relationships.	.095	.362	.150	.791	.121	.344
aspire20 I will have committed, intimate relationships.	.154	.212	.160	.783	.051	.277
aspire02 I will feel that there are people who really love me, and whom I love.	-.05	.280	.051	.688	.249	.300
aspire08 I will have good friends that I can count on.	.069	.384	.019	.524	.337	.296
aspire07 At the end of my life, I will look back on my life as meaningful and complete.	-.09	.213	.071	.512	.447	.463
aspire12 I will have a job that pays very well.	.237	.123	.303	.200	.888	.253
aspire06 I will be financially successful.	.309	.081	.304	.235	.879	.186
aspire24 I will be rich.	.548	-.14	.464	.078	.658	.091
aspire30 I will have enough money to buy everything I want.	.536	-.12	.306	.030	.648	.157
aspire19 I will know and accept who I really am.	.046	.365	.037	.403	.188	.775
aspire13 I will gain increasing insight into why I do the things I do.	.199	.337	.196	.311	.185	.676
aspire25 I will continue to grow and learn new things.	.010	.483	.167	.257	.168	.606
aspire01 I will choose what I do, instead of being pushed along by life.	-.12	.145	.021	.194	.196	.605

Extraction Method: Principal Component Analysis.
Rotation Method: Promax with Kaiser Normalization.

12B.7.1 First Principal Components/Promax Rotated Component

The first component appears to subsume, ordered by the strength of the structure coefficients, Items 11 (" I will have people comment often about how attractive I look"), 17 ("I will keep up with fashions in hair and clothing"), 23 ("I will achieve the 'look' I've been after"), 18 ("I will have many expensive possessions"), 29 ("My image will be one others find appealing"), and 5 ("I will successfully hide the signs of aging"). These match up closely but not perfectly with those items said to represent the Extrinsic Orientation goal of Appealing Appearance. We have also captured here Item 18, "I will have many expensive possessions," which was hypothesized to be a part of the Financial Success item set. But its presence here makes a good deal of sense because it seems as though the respondents are interpreting this item from an appearance perspective—expensive possessions are a means of showing oneself to the world in a presumably appealing manner.

12B.7.2 Second Principal Components/Promax Rotated Component

The second component appears to subsume, ordered by the strength of the structure coefficients, Items 15 ("I will work to make the world a better place"), 27 ("I will help people in need"), 21 ("I will help others help others improve their lives"), 9 ("I will work for the betterment of society"), and 3 ("I will assist people who need it, asking nothing in return"). These match up perfectly with those items said to represent the Intrinsic Orientation goal of Community Feeling.

12B.7.3 Third Principal Components/Promax Rotated Component

The third component appears to subsume, ordered by the strength of the structure coefficients, Items 10 ("My name will be known by many people"), 22 ("I will be famous"), 4 ("I will be recognized by lots of different people"), 16 ("I will be admired by many people"), and 28 ("My name will appear frequently in the media"). These match up perfectly with those items said to represent the Extrinsic Orientation goal of Social Recognition.

12B.7.4 Fourth Principal Components/Promax Rotated Component

The fourth component appears to subsume, ordered by the strength of the structure coefficients, Items 14 ("I will share my life with someone I love"), 26 ("I will have deep, enduring relationships"), 20 ("I will have committed, intimate relationships"), 2 ("I will feel that there are people who really love me, and whom I love"), 8 ("I will have good friends that I can count on"), and 7 ("At the end of my life, I will look back on my life as meaningful and complete"). These match up closely but not perfectly with those items said to represent the Intrinsic Orientation goal of Affiliation. Item 7 is picked up in this set but presumably should be part of Self-Acceptance. It is clearly possible to interpret this item as an "acceptance of life" item, and so it does make sense that it correlates with this component. We note that this item correlates relatively strongly with Components 5 and 6 as well, one of which is the Self-Acceptance item group. It is possible that this item really taps into several different elements and is therefore a less pure indicator of any one of them. If we were building a subscale to represent Affiliation based only on this analysis (remember that we have other analyses as well), we would carefully evaluate the issue of whether to include Item 7.

12B.7.5 Fifth Principal Components/Promax Rotated Component

The fifth component appears to subsume, ordered by the strength of the structure coefficients, Items 12 ("I will have a job that pays very well"), 6 ("I will be financially successful"), 24 ("I will be rich"), and 30 ("I will have enough money to buy everything I want"). These match up closely but not perfectly with those items said to represent the Extrinsic Orientation goal of Financial Success. The hypothesized structure includes Item 18, but that item correlated most strongly with Component 1, Appealing Appearance. The item is "I will have many expensive possessions." Items 12, 6, 24, and 30 specifically deal with money, whereas Item 18, as indicated earlier, may have more to do with appearance. We do note, however, that the item is also moderately correlated with Component 5.

12B.7.6 Sixth Principal Components/Promax Rotated Component

The sixth component appears to subsume, ordered by the strength of the structure coefficients, Items 19 ("I will know and accept who I really am"), 13 ("I will gain increasing insight into why I do the things I do"), 25 ("I will continue to grow and learn new things"), and 1 ("I will choose what I do, instead of being pushed along by life"). These match up closely but not perfectly with those items said to represent the Intrinsic Orientation goal of Self-Acceptance. Missing here is Item 7, an item that we noted may be tapping into several different elements.

12B.8 ULS Analysis With a Promax Rotation: Six-Component Solution

We set up our analysis as we have done for the six-component analysis but this time specifying **Unweighted least squares** as the extraction method.

The **Component Correlation Matrix** is shown in Figure 12b.25. Generally, we see the same pattern of correlations as we did in the principal components analysis, although these

Figure 12b.25 The Correlations of the Components: Unweighted Least Squares/Promax

Factor Correlation Matrix

Factor	1	2	3	4	5	6
1	1.000	−.001	.070	.633	.360	.080
2	−.001	1.000	.448	.160	.066	.437
3	.070	.448	1.000	.166	.255	.509
4	.633	.160	.166	1.000	.369	.194
5	.360	.066	.255	.369	1.000	.335
6	.080	.437	.509	.194	.335	1.000

Extraction Method: Unweighted Least Squares.
Rotation Method: Promax with Kaiser Normalization.

are of somewhat greater magnitude. But a surface examination may give the impression of a major discrepancy: Principal Component 1 was correlated .572 with Component 3 and .053 with Component 4; here, ULS Factor 1 is correlated .070 with Component 3 and .633 with Component 4.

This provides us with a fortuitous opportunity to point out that the rotated component or factor numbers can get all twisted up in the process of rotation. We will see that the items in the Component 3 set are the items captured in ULS Factor 4. The lesson is this: Do not be concerned with matching different solutions based on the component or factor number—focus instead on the variables that are most strongly associated with a component or factor.

The **Total Variance Explained** output is presented in Figure 12b.26. The ULS procedure accounted for 53.642% of the total variance, about 8.65% less than the

Figure 12b.26 Total Variance Explained: Unweighted Least Squares/Promax

Total Variance Explained

Factor	Initial Eigenvalues			Extraction Sums of Squared Loadings			Rotation Sums of Squared Loadings[a]
	Total	% of Variance	Cumulative %	Total	% of Variance	Cumulative %	Total
1	7.422	24.739	24.739	7.012	23.372	23.372	5.565
2	4.819	16.062	40.801	4.351	14.503	37.876	4.051
3	2.356	7.854	48.655	1.962	6.539	44.414	3.752
4	1.654	5.514	54.169	1.237	4.125	48.539	5.108
5	1.276	4.254	58.423	.902	3.007	51.546	3.834
6	1.161	3.870	62.293	.629	2.096	53.642	3.236
7	1.039	3.465	65.758				
8	.937	3.125	68.883				
9	.843	2.810	71.693				
10	.808	2.693	74.386				
11	.785	2.617	77.003				
12	.694	2.313	79.316				
13	.607	2.023	81.338				
14	.568	1.895	83.233				
15	.535	1.783	85.016				
16	.511	1.702	86.718				
17	.461	1.535	88.253				
18	.421	1.405	89.658				
19	.390	1.301	90.959				
20	.367	1.224	92.183				
21	.338	1.126	93.309				
22	.293	.978	94.287				
23	.277	.924	95.211				
24	.258	.860	96.071				
25	.244	.814	96.885				
26	.228	.759	97.643				
27	.211	.703	98.347				
28	.175	.583	98.930				
29	.170	.567	99.497				
30	.151	.503	100.000				

Extraction Method: Unweighted Least Squares.

a. When factors are correlated, sums of squared loadings cannot be added to obtain a total variance.

principal components analysis due to its focus on only the variance common to the 30 items.

The **Structure Matrix** for the ULS/Promax analysis is shown in Figure 12b.27. We will discuss the results separately by factor.

Figure 12b.27 The Six-Component Rotated Structure Matrix: Unweighted Least Squares/Promax

Structure Matrix

	Factor 1	2	3	4	5	6
aspire11 I will have people comment often about how attractive I look.	.832	.053	.101	.555	.303	.100
aspire17 I will keep up with fashions in hair and clothing.	.817	.086	.071	.411	.264	-.02
aspire23 I will achieve the "look" I've been after.	.763	.044	.050	.506	.275	.102
aspire18 I will have many expensive possessions.	.749	-.09	.018	.516	.431	.002
aspire29 My image will be one others find appealing.	.686	.017	.109	.493	.194	.178
aspire05 I will successfully hide the signs of aging.	.496	.139	.141	.423	.358	.057
aspire15 I will work to make the world a better place.	.027	.815	.342	.194	.070	.332
aspire21 I will help others improve their lives.	.038	.779	.407	.127	.001	.417
aspire27 I will help people in need.	.085	.773	.410	.159	.014	.330
aspire09 I will work for the betterment of society.	.063	.737	.244	.192	.126	.311
aspire03 I will assist people who need it, asking nothing in return.	-.06	.573	.278	.068	.066	.364
aspire14 I will share my life with someone I love.	.041	.312	.790	.140	.241	.334
aspire26 I will have deep, enduring relationships.	.096	.377	.736	.162	.141	.402
aspire20 I will have committed, intimate relationships.	.140	.242	.710	.171	.088	.328
aspire02 I will feel that there are people who really love me, and whom I love.	-.02	.286	.596	.068	.230	.368
aspire08 I will have good friends that I can count on.	.075	.341	.459	.085	.270	.390
aspire10 My name will be known by many people.	.549	.184	.190	.858	.384	.180
aspire22 I will be famous.	.628	.003	.047	.771	.181	.076
aspire16 I will be admired by many people.	.534	.228	.176	.721	.389	.242
aspire04 I will be recognized by lots of different people.	.371	.283	.255	.705	.362	.204
aspire28 My name will appear frequently in the media.	.576	-.04	-.01	.687	.103	.030
aspire12 I will have a job that pays very well.	.287	.107	.220	.329	.889	.339
aspire06 I will be financially successful.	.357	.062	.253	.330	.863	.278
aspire24 I will be rich.	.562	-.14	.087	.476	.608	.158
aspire30 I will have enough money to buy everything I want.	.526	-.12	.046	.352	.579	.207
aspire19 I will know and accept who I really am.	.039	.377	.408	.076	.199	.723
aspire13 I will gain increasing insight into why I do the things I do.	.173	.347	.326	.219	.219	.547
aspire25 I will continue to grow and learn new things.	.027	.456	.292	.167	.176	.516
aspire07 At the end of my life, I will look back on my life as meaningful and complete.	-.03	.226	.466	.089	.381	.478
aspire01 I will choose what I do, instead of being pushed along by life.	-.07	.180	.216	.018	.175	.418

Extraction Method: Unweighted Least Squares.
Rotation Method: Promax with Kaiser Normalization.

12B.8.1 First ULS/Promax Rotated Factor

The first ULS factor appears to subsume, ordered by the strength of the structure coefficients, Items 11, 17, 23, 18, 29, and 5. These duplicate the principal components analysis and match up closely but not perfectly with those items said to represent the Extrinsic Orientation goal of Appealing Appearance. We have also captured here Item 18 ("I will have many expensive possessions"), which was hypothesized to be a part of the Financial Success item set but makes good sense to be included here.

12B.8.2 Second ULS/Promax Rotated Factor

The second ULS factor appears to subsume, ordered by the strength of the structure coefficients, Items 15, 27, 21, 9, and 3. These duplicate the principal components analysis and match up perfectly with those items said to represent the Intrinsic Orientation goal of Community Feeling.

12B.8.3 Third ULS/Promax Rotated Factor

The third ULS factor appears to subsume, ordered by the strength of the structure coefficients, Items 14, 26, 20, 2, and 8. These match up closely but not perfectly with principal components analysis (Component 4) in that Item 7 was captured by principal components in this item set. Here, the item set matches perfectly the composition of the hypothesized Intrinsic Orientation goal of Affiliation.

12B.8.4 Fourth ULS/Promax Rotated Factor

The fourth ULS factor appears to subsume, ordered by the strength of the structure coefficients, Items 10, 22, 16, 4, and 28. These match up perfectly with those items said to represent the Extrinsic Orientation goal of Social Recognition.

12B.8.5 Fifth ULS/Promax Rotated Factor

The fifth ULS factor appears to subsume, ordered by the strength of the structure coefficients, Items 12, 6, 24, and 30. These duplicate the principal components analysis and match up closely but not perfectly with those items said to represent the Extrinsic Orientation goal of Financial Success. The hypothesized structure includes Item 18, but that item correlated most strongly with Factor 1, Appealing Appearance. The item is "I will have many expensive possessions." Items 12, 6, 24, and 30 specifically deal with money, whereas Item 18, as indicated earlier, may have more to do with appearance. We do note, however, that the item is also moderately correlated with Factor 5.

12B.8.6 Sixth ULS/Promax Rotated Factor

The sixth ULS factor appears to subsume, ordered by the strength of the structure coefficients, Items 19, 13, 25, 7, and 1. These match up perfectly with those items said to represent the Intrinsic Orientation goal of Self-Acceptance. Included here is Item 7, an item that was not captured in the corresponding component of the principal component analysis.

12B.9 Principal Axis Factor Analysis With a Promax Rotation: Six-Component Solution

To quickly illustrate that the different extraction procedures do not always produce the same outcome, we set up our analysis as we have done for the six-component analysis, but this time we specified **Principal axis factoring** as the extraction method.

The **Component Correlation Matrix** is shown in Figure 12b.28. This configuration of correlations looks quite different from what we have seen for the principal components and ULS analyses and signifies that we should expect to see some noticeable differences in this solution.

Figure 12b.28 The Correlations of the Components: Principal Axis/Promax

Factor Correlation Matrix

Factor	1	2	3	4	5	6
1	1.000	.020	.048	.348	.519	.474
2	.020	1.000	.507	.135	.251	.004
3	.048	.507	1.000	.309	.166	.089
4	.348	.135	.309	1.000	.290	.330
5	.519	.251	.166	.290	1.000	.310
6	.474	.004	.089	.330	.310	1.000

Extraction Method: Principal Axis Factoring.
Rotation Method: Promax with Kaiser Normalization.

The **Total Variance Explained** output is presented in Figure 12b.29. It looks very similar to what was obtained with the ULS solution.

The **Structure Matrix** for the Principal Axis/Promax analysis is shown in Figure 12b.30. We will discuss the results separately by factor.

12B.9.1 First Principal Axis/Promax Rotated Factor

The first principal axis factor appears to subsume, ordered by the strength of the structure coefficients, Items 17, 11, 23, 18, 29, and 5. These duplicate the prior two analyses and match up closely but not perfectly with those items said to represent the Extrinsic Orientation

Figure 12b.29   Total Variance Explained: Principal Axis/Promax

Total Variance Explained

Factor	Initial Eigenvalues			Extraction Sums of Squared Loadings			Rotation Sums of Squared Loadings[a]
	Total	% of Variance	Cumulative %	Total	% of Variance	Cumulative %	Total
1	7.422	24.739	24.739	7.025	23.418	23.418	5.456
2	4.819	16.062	40.801	4.343	14.477	37.895	4.364
3	2.356	7.854	48.655	1.957	6.523	44.417	3.881
4	1.654	5.514	54.169	1.229	4.095	48.513	4.001
5	1.276	4.254	58.423	.936	3.120	51.633	3.999
6	1.161	3.870	62.293	.612	2.039	53.672	3.247
7	1.039	3.465	65.758				
8	.937	3.125	68.883				
9	.843	2.810	71.693				
10	.808	2.693	74.386				
11	.785	2.617	77.003				
12	.694	2.313	79.316				
13	.607	2.023	81.338				
14	.568	1.895	83.233				
15	.535	1.783	85.016				
16	.511	1.702	86.718				
17	.461	1.535	88.253				
18	.421	1.405	89.658				
19	.390	1.301	90.959				
20	.367	1.224	92.183				
21	.338	1.126	93.309				
22	.293	.978	94.287				
23	.277	.924	95.211				
24	.258	.860	96.071				
25	.244	.814	96.885				
26	.228	.759	97.643				
27	.211	.703	98.347				
28	.175	.583	98.930				
29	.170	.567	99.497				
30	.151	.503	100.000				

Extraction Method: Principal Axis Factoring.

a. When factors are correlated, sums of squared loadings cannot be added to obtain a total variance.

goal of Appealing Appearance. We have also captured here Item 18 ("I will have many expensive possessions"), which was hypothesized to be a part of the Financial Success item set but makes good sense to be included here.

Figure 12b.30 The Six-Component Rotated Structure Matrix: Principal Axis/Promax

Structure Matrix

	Factor					
	1	2	3	4	5	6
aspire17 I will keep up with fashions in hair and clothing.	.844	.067	.050	.233	.379	.266
aspire11 I will have people comment often about how attractive I look.	.837	.065	.100	.307	.476	.405
aspire23 I will achieve the "look" I've been after.	.749	.069	.054	.302	.364	.466
aspire18 I will have many expensive possessions.	.745	-.08	.009	.424	.406	.432
aspire29 My image will be one others find appealing.	.657	.064	.126	.248	.331	.481
aspire05 I will successfully hide the signs of aging.	.530	.118	.123	.309	.481	.156
aspire21 I will help others improve their lives.	.040	.788	.412	.015	.172	.003
aspire15 I will work to make the world a better place.	.049	.787	.333	.042	.303	-.04
aspire27 I will help people in need.	.092	.757	.398	.009	.208	.020
aspire09 I will work for the betterment of society.	.081	.717	.241	.103	.282	-.02
aspire03 I will assist people who need it, asking nothing in return.	-.06	.587	.292	.077	.128	-.04
aspire25 I will continue to grow and learn new things.	-.01	.533	.337	.255	.087	.188
aspire19 I will know and accept who I really am.	-.00	.474	.466	.293	.042	.079
aspire13 I will gain increasing insight into why I do the things I do.	.140	.423	.374	.292	.160	.181
aspire14 I will share my life with someone I love.	.048	.327	.763	.227	.197	-.00
aspire26 I will have deep, enduring relationships.	.083	.413	.733	.169	.144	.108
aspire20 I will have committed, intimate relationships.	.128	.275	.705	.117	.140	.133
aspire02 I will feel that there are people who really love me, and whom I love.	-.02	.322	.599	.244	.087	.009
aspire07 At the end of my life, I will look back on my life as meaningful and complete.	-.05	.291	.497	.414	.100	.021
aspire08 I will have good friends that I can count on.	.071	.376	.472	.284	.120	-.00
aspire01 I will choose what I do, instead of being pushed along by life.	-.10	.247	.260	.229	.004	.017
aspire12 I will have a job that pays very well.	.282	.153	.235	.859	.326	.176
aspire06 I will be financially successful.	.359	.096	.256	.819	.342	.160
aspire24 I will be rich.	.530	-.08	.099	.655	.282	.525
aspire30 I will have enough money to buy everything I want.	.497	-.06	.069	.629	.189	.400
aspire10 My name will be known by many people.	.554	.193	.187	.373	.819	.525
aspire04 I will be recognized by lots of different people.	.388	.279	.248	.330	.775	.327
aspire16 I will be admired by many people.	.539	.246	.182	.387	.701	.420
aspire22 I will be famous.	.593	.040	.051	.235	.531	.792
aspire28 My name will appear frequently in the media.	.540	-.01	-.00	.157	.446	.751

Extraction Method: Principal Axis Factoring.
Rotation Method: Promax with Kaiser Normalization.

12B.9.2 Second Principal Axis/Promax Rotated Factor

The second principal axis factor appears to subsume, ordered by the strength of the structure coefficients, Items 21, 15, 27, 9, 3, 25, 19, and 13. This item set captures those items in the Intrinsic Orientation goal of Community Feeling but adds three items from Self-Acceptance: Items 25 ("I will continue to grow and learn new things"), 19 ("I will know and accept who I really am"), and 13 ("I will gain increasing insight into [my behavior] why I do the things I do"). This result is consistent with the idea that all of these items are within the intrinsic domain but do not appear to have a clear underlying theme as a group.

12B.9.3 Third Principal Axis/Promax Rotated Factor

The third principal axis factor appears to subsume, ordered by the strength of the structure coefficients, Items 14, 26, 20, 2, 7, 8, and 1. This item set captures the items comprising the Intrinsic Orientation goal of Affiliation but adds the remaining two items from Self-Acceptance: Items 7 ("At the end of my life, I will look back on my life as meaningful and complete") and 1 ("I will choose what I do, instead of being pushed along by life"). This result is also consistent with the idea that all of these items are within the intrinsic domain but do not appear to have a clear underlying theme as a group.

12B.9.4 Fourth Principal Axis/Promax Rotated Factor

The fourth principal axis factor appears to subsume, ordered by the strength of the structure coefficients, Items 12, 6, 24, and 30. These duplicate the prior two analyses and match up closely but not perfectly with those items said to represent the Extrinsic Orientation goal of Financial Success. The hypothesized structure includes Item 18, but that item correlated most strongly with Factor 1, Appealing Appearance. The item is "I will have many expensive possessions." Items 12, 6, 24, and 30 specifically deal with money, whereas Item 18, as indicated earlier, may have more to do with appearance.

12B.9.5 Fifth Principal Axis/Promax Rotated Factor

The fifth principal axis factor appears to subsume, ordered by the strength of the structure coefficients, Items 10, 4, and 16. These represent three of the five items hypothesized to indicate the Extrinsic Orientation goal of Social Recognition.

12B.9.6 Sixth Principal Axis/Promax Rotated Factor

The sixth principal axis factor appears to subsume, ordered by the strength of the structure coefficients, Items 22 and 28, the remaining two items in the hypothesized Social Recognition indicator.

12B.10 Wrap-Up of the Six-Factor Solution

The picture of the factor structure emerging when we asked for a six-dimension solution can be characterized as fuzzier than the structure seen with just two dimensions. The different extraction procedures that we have presented yielded different outcomes, and others that we have not shown are more closely aligned with either principal axis factoring (e.g., maximum likelihood) or ULS (e.g., alpha factoring). Given that the former set of solutions do not appear to be amenable to viable or parsimonious interpretations, given the high level of regard held in the professional literature for the theoretical framework within which the Aspirations Index was developed, given that the principal components and ULS solutions were very consistent with the hypothesized inventory structure, and given that the principal components and ULS solutions were easily interpretable, we opt to utilize one of these latter two rather than the alternative solutions represented by principal axis factoring. Because the ULS solution matches almost exactly with the hypothesized inventory structure, and because the hypothesized structure appears to make intuitive sense, we chose to adopt the ULS solution as a basis for subsequent data analysis.

We do note that, although researchers attempt to honor the factor structure of an inventory as reported in the research literature, we will make an exception here: We will place Item 18 on the Appealing Appearance subscale even though the authors of the inventory scored in on the Financial Success subscale. We caution readers that such a strategy is best done with great caution and as a suggested modification to be more strongly endorsed only with replications based on substantial sample sizes.

One of the purposes of performing a factor analysis is to create subscales corresponding to the factor structure. In the present six-factor solution, we would build six subscales, each containing only the inventory items that correlated most strongly and at least in excess of .30 or .40 with the particular factor. Because we know that there are also two underlying global factors, we will also compute two additional scales representing extrinsic and intrinsic goal orientation. But before we are ready to build the scales and subscales, it is necessary to perform a reliability analysis.

12B.11 Assessing Reliability: General Principles

12B.11.1 The Concept of Reliability

Reliability is an inverse index of measurement error. More formally, a reliability coefficient theoretically expresses the proportion of true score variance to observed score variance (e.g., Lord & Novick, 1968). Reliability coefficients theoretically vary between a high of 1.00, indicating that we have only true score variance and that there is no measurement error, and a low of .00, indicating that we have no true score variance and that all of the variance we observe is due to measurement error. With a reliability value of 1.00, the test score is a completely reliable index of whatever characteristic was assessed; with a reliability value of .00, the test score relates no viable information about the characteristic that was assessed.

The most commonly used reliability coefficient in the context of classical test theory is Cronbach's coefficient alpha (Cronbach, 1951), an extension of the generalized split half reliability coefficient (the so-called KR-20 coefficient) of Kuder and Richardson (1937). Within classical test theory, coefficient alpha is an index of internal consistency, quantifying the degree to which test takers respond in a consistent manner to the items in the set. It is a function of the correlations between the pairs of items, but it can be inflated by the number of items in the set (see Embretson & Reise, 2000). Rough guidelines for interpreting the value of the coefficient are as follows: .90 or better is outstanding, high to middle .8s is very good, .80 or the low .8s is good, high to middle .7s is acceptable, .70 or the low .7s is borderline acceptable, high to middle .6s may be okay for research purposes, the low .6s are problematic, and anything below that is not acceptable. More complete coverage of reliability and coefficient alpha can be found in Allen and Yen (1979), Cortina (1993), Kaplan and Saccuzzo (2008), and Nunnally and Bernstein (1994).

12B.11.2 Using the Reliability Procedure Before Computing the Scales

Before computing any scales based on a factor analysis, it is strongly advisable to assess the reliability of the scales in advance of the time that they are computed. The **Reliability** procedure in IBM SPSS is nicely designed to accomplish this. In setting up the analysis, we specify a set of variables (the ones that we anticipate being on our scale or subscale) and request reliability output. Based on the output, we can make one of the following determinations and engage in the associated actions:

- We can determine that the results are satisfactory as they stand. If this is our judgment, then the item set for that scale is now identified and we would next compute a permanent variable to be added to the data file representing that particular item set.
- We can determine that the item set needs to be modified to achieve an acceptable level of reliability. If this is our judgment, then we would make a change in the item set (e.g., remove an item) and perform the **Reliability** analysis again. We would continue in this manner until we have reached an outcome that was either satisfactory or was one that we could live with. Having reached that point, we would next compute a permanent variable based on the revised item set to be added to the data file representing the particular item set.
- We can determine that the situation is hopeless in that any reasonable combination of items based on the factor analysis will not achieve an acceptable reliability level. We would then plan on not computing a scale based on the item set and may wish to revisit the factor analysis with the intent of reducing (or, less frequently, increasing) the number of factors extracted.

12B.11.3 Item Groups on Which We Focus

One set of scales on which we focus is that composed of the two global dimensions—intrinsic and extrinsic goal orientation. The item structure hypothesized to comprise these dimensions was supported in our analyses, and so we will use the structure shown in Tables 12b.1 and 12b2.

Table 12b.2 The Structure of the Aspirations Inventory Resulting From the Factor Analysis and Reliability Analysis

Orientation	Sub-Scale	Item Number and Exact Wording
Intrinsic Orientation	Self-Acceptance	1. I will choose what I do, instead of being pushed along by life.
		7. At the end of my life, I will look back on my life as meaningful and complete.
		13. I will gain increasing insight into why I do the things I do.
		19. I will know and accept who I really am.
		25. I will continue to grow and learn new things.
	Community Feelings	3. I will assist people who need it, asking nothing in return.
		9. I will work for the betterment of society.
		15. I will work to make the world a better place.
		21. I will help others improve their lives.
		27. I will help people in need.
	Affiliation	2. I will feel that there are people who really love me, and whom I love.
		8. I will have good friends that I can count on.
		14. I will share my life with someone I love.
		20. I will have committed, intimate relationships.
		26. I will have deep, enduring relationships.
Extrinsic Orientation	Social Recognition	4. I will be recognized by lots of different people.
		10. My name will be known by many people.
		16. I will be admired by many people.
		22. I will be famous.
		28. My name will appear frequently in the media.
	Financial Success	6. I will be financially successful.
		12. I will have a job that pays very well.
		24. I will be rich.
		30. I will have enough money to buy everything I want.
	Appealing Appearance	5. I will successfully hide the signs of aging.
		11. I will have people comment often about how attractive I look.
		17. I will keep up with fashions in hair and clothing.
		18. I will have many expensive possessions.
		23. I will achieve the "look" I've been after.
		29. My image will be one others find appealing.

The second set of scales on which we focus are the six subscales identified in the inventory. We will base our item sets on the ULS/promax six-factor solution, which supported the hypothesized structure shown in Table 12b.1 with one exception—the fate of Item 18. Although the bias of most researchers is to respect the subscale structure of published scales, we feel that the results are sufficiently compelling to make the exception regarding Item 18. Thus, we will set up the reliability analysis with that item placed in the Appealing Appearance subscale rather than in the Financial Success subscale. This revised structure is shown in Table 12b.2.

12B.12 Assessing Reliability: The Global Domains

12B.12.1 Assessing Reliability: The Intrinsic Global Domain Analysis Setup

From the main menu, select **Analyze ➔ Scale ➔ Reliability Analysis**. This opens the main dialog window. Move over to the **Items** panel in any order all of those items shown in Table 12b.2 that are associated with Intrinsic Orientation. Then, as shown in Figure 12b.31, type in the scale name **Intrinsic** in the **Scale label** panel; this will help us in reading our output.

Figure 12b.31 The Main Dialog Window of Reliability

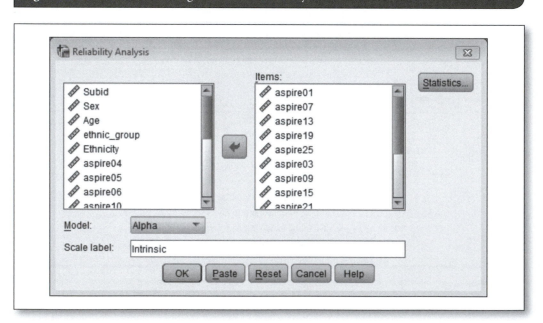

Selecting the **Statistics** pushbutton brings us to the window shown in Figure 12b.32. Under **Descriptives for** select **Item** to obtain the item descriptive statistics and **Scale if item deleted** to obtain the reliability of the item set if an item was not included. Under **Inter-Item** there is an opportunity to obtain the **Correlations** between the pairs of items, and we have checked it. With 15 items in our set, the table will be relatively large, but it is a good idea to examine the interitem relationships. Click **Continue** to return to the main window and click **OK** to perform the analysis.

Figure 12b.32   The Statistics Window of Reliability

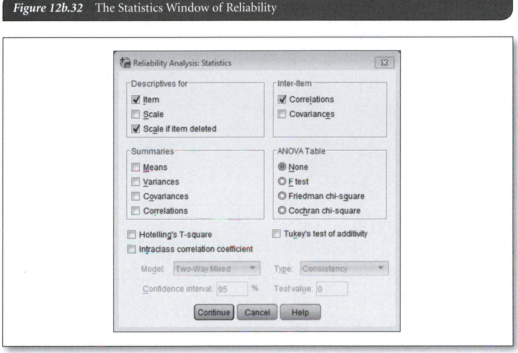

12B.12.2 Assessing Reliability:
Intrinsic Global Domain Selected Output

The interitem correlations are shown in Figure 12b.33. The items in this set are generally not very strongly correlated (this is a desired finding). The majority of the correlations are below .30 and only a handful are in the .5s. The highest correlation by a large margin is between Item 9 ("I will work for the betterment of society") and Item 15 ("I will work to make the world a better place") at .703. These two items have much common variance, and some researchers might be inclined to remove one of them; we choose to keep them both in the scale.

Figure 12b.33 The Interitem Correlations

Inter-Item Correlation Matrix

	aspire01 I will choose what I do, instead of being pushed along by life.	aspire07 At the end of my life, I will look back on my life as meaningful and complete.	aspire13 I will gain increasing insight into why I do the things I do.	aspire19 I will know and accept who I really am.	aspire25 I will continue to grow and learn new things.	aspire03 I will assist people who need it, asking nothing in return.	aspire09 I will work for the betterment of society.	aspire15 I will work to make the world a better place.	aspire21 I will help others improve their lives.	aspire27 I will help people in need.	aspire02 I will feel that there are people who really love me, and whom I love.	aspire08 I will have good friends that I can count on.	aspire14 I will share my life with someone I love.	aspire20 I will have committed, intimate relationships.	aspire26 I will have deep, enduring relationships.
aspire01 I will choose what I do, instead of being pushed along by life.	1.000	.321	.172	.319	.188	.197	.127	.116	.170	.119	.209	.175	.124	.082	.205
aspire07 At the end of my life, I will look back on my life as meaningful and complete.	.321	1.000	.208	.344	.189	.145	.184	.160	.195	.142	.325	.373	.329	.266	.327
aspire13 I will gain increasing insight into why I do the things I do.	.172	.208	1.000	.469	.329	.189	.273	.326	.318	.237	.191	.157	.250	.286	.240
aspire19 I will know and accept who I really am.	.319	.344	.469	1.000	.362	.322	.231	.269	.337	.273	.268	.332	.274	.277	.283
aspire25 I will continue to grow and learn new things.	.188	.189	.329	.362	1.000	.343	.355	.406	.333	.343	.220	.208	.181	.125	.314
aspire03 I will assist people who need it, asking nothing in return.	.197	.145	.189	.322	.343	1.000	.372	.395	.489	.502	.251	.286	.214	.140	.178
aspire09 I will work for the betterment of society.	.127	.184	.273	.231	.355	.372	1.000	.703	.524	.537	.138	.278	.158	.141	.250
aspire15 I will work to make the world a better place.	.116	.160	.326	.269	.406	.395	.703	1.000	.606	.587	.230	.257	.314	.186	.270
aspire21 I will help others improve their lives.	.170	.195	.318	.337	.333	.489	.524	.606	1.000	.708	.235	.259	.246	.261	.324
aspire27 I will help people in need.	.119	.142	.237	.273	.343	.502	.537	.587	.708	1.000	.269	.271	.234	.252	.408
aspire02 I will feel that there are people who really love me, and whom I love.	.209	.325	.191	.268	.220	.251	.138	.230	.235	.269	1.000	.358	.580	.350	.380
aspire08 I will have good friends that I can count on.	.175	.373	.157	.332	.208	.286	.278	.257	.259	.271	.358	1.000	.354	.269	.355
aspire14 I will share my life with someone I love.	.124	.329	.250	.274	.181	.214	.158	.314	.246	.234	.580	.354	1.000	.552	.551
aspire20 I will have committed, intimate relationships.	.082	.266	.286	.277	.125	.140	.141	.186	.261	.252	.350	.269	.552	1.000	.617
aspire26 I will have deep, enduring relationships.	.205	.327	.240	.283	.314	.178	.250	.270	.324	.408	.380	.355	.551	.617	1.000

The heart of the output is contained in a little table called **Reliability Statistics** that is shown in Figure 12b.34. We focus on the first column labeled **Cronbach's Alpha** and note that the value is .859; this would be judged as a very good reliability. The second column, labeled **Cronbach's Alpha Based on Standardized Items**, is applicable only if our items are standardized; if our items were standardized (they are not standardized in our data set), we would use this column rather

Figure 12b.34 The Reliability Statistics

Reliability Statistics

Cronbach's Alpha	Cronbach's Alpha Based on Standardized Items	N of Items
.859	.862	15

than the first one to asses our reliability. The last column labeled **N of Items** just gives us the number of items we included in the item set.

Item-Total Statistics are shown in Figure 12b.35. Information for each variable in the set is on its own row. The main purpose of producing this table is to enable researchers to diagnose a problem with an item (should a problem exist) and to learn the consequence of removing that item from the item set. The first two columns, **Scale Mean if Item Deleted** and **Scale Variance if Item Deleted** report the mean and variance of the items in the set if the item on that row was removed from the set.

Figure 12b.35 The Item-Total Statistics

Item-Total Statistics

	Scale Mean if Item Deleted	Scale Variance if Item Deleted	Corrected Item–Total Correlation	Squared Multiple Correlation	Cronbach's Alpha if Item Deleted
aspire01 I will choose what I do, instead of being pushed along by life.	111.11	126.869	.290	.189	.862
aspire07 At the end of my life, I will look back on my life as meaningful and complete.	110.51	124.729	.408	.286	.855
aspire13 I will gain increasing insight into why I do the things I do.	111.51	122.395	.436	.309	.854
aspire19 I will know and accept who I really am.	110.48	124.782	.528	.391	.850
aspire25 I will continue to grow and learn new things.	110.70	126.593	.480	.316	.852
aspire03 I will assist people who need it, asking nothing in return.	111.11	121.159	.496	.368	.851
aspire09 I will work for the betterment of society.	111.51	116.677	.544	.547	.848
aspire15 I will work to make the world a better place.	111.59	112.681	.611	.628	.844
aspire21 I will help others improve their lives.	111.21	116.997	.639	.590	.843
aspire27 I will help people in need.	111.05	117.047	.620	.616	.844
aspire02 I will feel that there are people who really love me, and whom I love.	110.49	124.769	.471	.401	.852
aspire08 I will have good friends that I can count on.	110.60	125.021	.469	.295	.852
aspire14 I will share my life with someone I love.	110.37	123.420	.518	.554	.850
aspire20 I will have committed, intimate relationships.	110.67	123.461	.443	.481	.853
aspire26 I will have deep, enduring relationships.	110.58	122.244	.564	.557	.848

The column labeled **Corrected Item-Total Correlation** is the correlation between the particular item on the row and the other items taken together in the set. Specifically, each case has a score on the item in question and a score representing the total of the other items. The "correction" refers to the exclusion of the particular item from the calculated total score. These two variables (the score on the item and the score on the corrected total score of the items in the set) are then correlated. Positive values indicate that higher scores on the item correspond to higher scores on the total of the other items. This is the desired result and indicates that the item in question is a good indicator of the total subscale score. Correlations in the .2s and .3s are not uncommonly obtained and would be judged as quite good. Correlations in the table are mostly between .40 and .63 and would be judged to be unusually high.

The last two columns of the **Item-Total Statistics** are relatively straightforward. The **Squared Multiple Correlation** is the value of R^2 from a multiple regression in which the variable in question is predicted from the other variables in the set. **Cronbach's Alpha if Item Deleted** is what the alpha coefficient would be if the item on the particular row was not included in the set. Deleting items that are poor indicators of the total would actually raise the value of coefficient alpha. Here, with items that are all somewhat interrelated, removing any one of them (except **aspire01**) lowers the reliability by a small margin; the slight loss in reliability is due to a reduced item count and demonstrates the sensitivity of coefficient alpha to the number of items in the set.

12B.12.3 Assessing Reliability: The Extrinsic Global Domain

We have repeated the analysis for the items in the extrinsic global dimension and will summarize but not take the space to show the very similar output. Most of the items in the Social Recognition set tended to correlate in the .6s and .7s, which would suggest that that these items are uncomfortably similar to each other. A couple of other item pairs in the other two sets correlated quite highly as well. The other correlations were in the more moderate range. Between the moderate correlations and those high correlations, however, Cronbach's alpha coefficient was driven to .912. This would ordinarily be interpreted as excellent reliability, but we should be a little less enthusiastic in embracing such a finding given the several extremely high interitem correlations that were obtained.

12B.12.4 Assessing Reliability: Interpreting the Reliability of the Two Global Domains

Despite some less than desired high correlations among some of the extrinsic items, the item sets contain no item whose inclusion reduces the reliability by any margin beyond the simple loss of an item. We can therefore take the item sets as they stand and compute intrinsic and extrinsic scales.

12B.13 Assessing Reliability:
The Six Item Sets Based on the ULS/Promax Structure

From the main menu select **Analyze** ➔ **Scale** ➔ **Reliability Analysis**. This opens the main dialog window. Move over to the **Items** panel all of those items shown in Table 12b.2 that are associated with Self-Acceptance. Then, type in the scale name **Self-Acceptance** in the **Scale label** panel. Configure the **Statistics** dialog window as described in Section 12B.12.1 and then perform the analysis. Repeat this for each item set.

The results are summarized in Table 12b.3. All of the item sets, with the exception of Self-Acceptance, demonstrated extremely good levels of reliability given the small numbers of items in each set. The Self-Acceptance items were on average correlated less strongly than those in the other sets, and the reliability of .656 with no "offending" item is still useable to a certain extent for research purposes. We therefore accept the item sets as they stand and can now compute subscales based on them.

Table 12b.3 Reliabilities for the Six Sub-Scales

Item Sets From ULS/Promax	Cronbach Alpha
Self-Acceptance	.656
Community Feelings	.856
Affiliation	.794
Social Recognition	.862
Financial Success	.823
Appealing Appearance	.871

12B.14 Computing Scales Based on the ULS Promax Structure

12B.14.1 Strategies for Computing Scales

One way to compute scores on each factor is to use the pattern coefficients to construct four linear composites, each of which would be composed of all the variables. IBM SPSS has the capability (in the **Save** dialog window) to save these values (i.e., save the factor scores). This strategy assumes that the weights are generalizable across samples; however, such an assumption is tenuous at best, and we prefer to not use factor scores.

Alternatively, and more simply, we can compute scales with each variable weighted equally (i.e., using unitary weights for the items). This strategy presumes that each item or variable we identify as an indicator of the factor is largely as good as any other and that it is not worthwhile to make fine-grained distinctions between them based on factor weights that might differ if we measured another sample of cases. We adopt this very commonly used strategy here.

12B.14.2 Computing the New Variables

We will compute the six subscales (one at a time) based on the structure shown in Table 12b.2. We have chosen to do these first just because there are fewer variables (items) involved in each computation and it will therefore be easier to show and describe. We will discuss the first computation in detail to illustrate the process.

From the main menu, select **Transform ➔ Compute Variable**, which brings us to the dialog window shown in Figure 12b.36. For the first subscale dealing with the Self-Acceptance item set, we type the name of the to-be-computed subscale, **acceptance**, in the **Target Variable** panel. Select **Statistical** from the **Function group** panel in the left portion of the dialog window and then **Mean** from the **Functions and Special Variables** panel under it. This is shown in Figure 12b.36. Then click the "up" arrow immediately left of the **Functions and Special Variables** panel. That places the **Mean** function in the **Numeric Expression** panel as shown in Figure 12b.37. When this operation is run, it will produce a mean value of these variables for every case in the data file.

Figure 12b.36   Configuring the Compute Variable Dialog Window

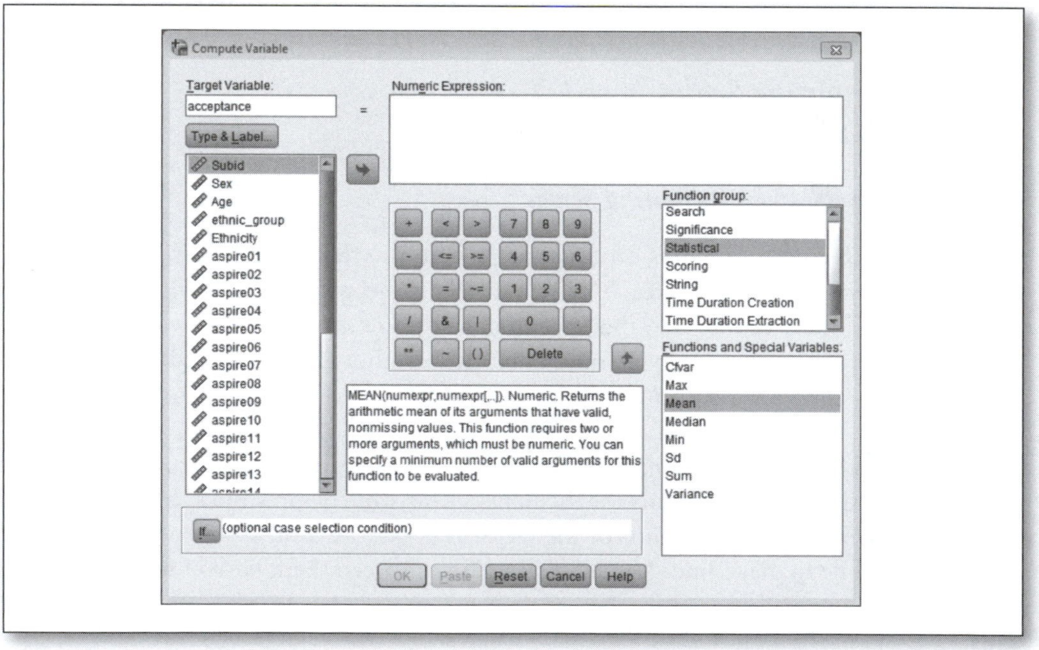

Figure 12b.37 The Compute Variable Dialog Window With the Mean Function in the Numeric Expression Panel

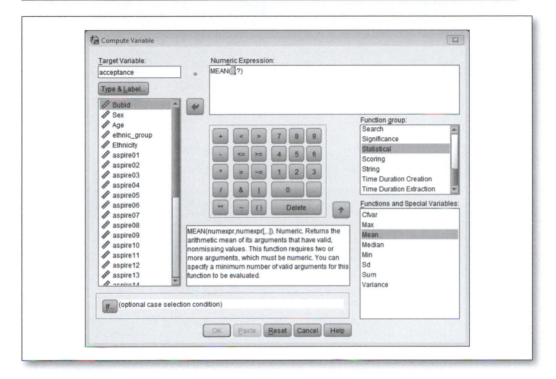

The **Mean** function in the **Numeric Expression** panel contains the word **MEAN** and two question marks in parentheses separated by a comma. The first thing we do is require that a mean is to be computed only when a case has a valid value on all of the items. To accomplish this, we note from Table 12b.2 that Self-Acceptance, the first subscale we will compute, has five items. We therefore place our cursor after the word **MEAN** and type a period followed by the number **5**. This is shown in Figure 12b.38. Generally, the **MEAN.n** specification requires that there be at least **n** valid values within the scores for a given participant before IBM SPSS will compute a mean for a case; with four or fewer valid values, the case will be assigned a missing value as the mean.

Now the question marks need to be replaced by the variables whose mean we wish to compute. Each variable must be separated from the next by a comma; although spaces are not required, we recommend them. Variables can be placed in the expression by highlighting the question mark (at least for the first two variables) and then either selecting them from the variable list and clicking them over using the arrow immediately to the right of the variable panel or double-clicking the variables directly. For

Figure 12b.38 The Compute Variable Dialog Window With the Specification Set to Require Five Valid Values for a Mean to Be Compute for a Case

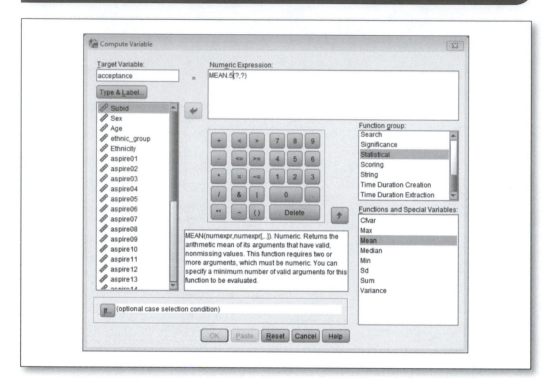

example, the first variable of the Self-Acceptance item set is **aspire01**. We therefore highlight the first question mark, select **aspire01**, and double-click it. We then type a space following the comma. The result, shown in Figure 12b.39, is that the first question mark has been replaced by **aspire01**. We then repeat the process for **aspire07**, place a comma and space after that, double-click **aspire13**, and so on. The completed panel for Self-Acceptance is shown in Figure 12b.40. Click **OK** to perform the computing operation.

Shown in Figure 12b.41 is a screen shot of a portion of the data file with the new variable **acceptance** in place at the end of the data set. Note that Case 1 has an **acceptance** value of 8.60; this is the mean for the five variables related to Self-Acceptance for Case 1. Because there is a value for Case 1 in the data file, we know that he or she had valid values on all five items. Case 18, on the other hand, has an empty cell (a missing value) for **acceptance**; therefore, that case was missing a value on one or more of the Self-Acceptance items.

Figure 12b.39 The Compute Variable Dialog Window With the Variable aspire01 Placed in the Function

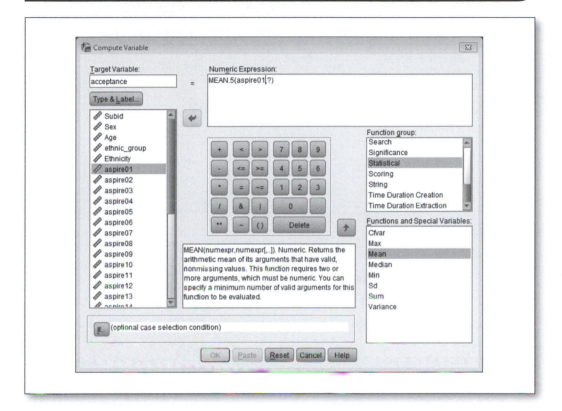

We immediately save the data file under a new name to distinguish it from the original data file that contains no computed subscales. Select **File ➔ Save As** and give it a new name. We have given it the name **Leanne Scales**. Click the **Variables** pushbutton to obtain the **Save Data As: Variables** dialog window as shown in Figure 12b.42. Variables that are checked (selected) will be included in the new data file. Leave all variables checked and click **Continue**. You may then save the file to the location you specify.

We have computed the remaining five subscales and the two global scales of intrinsic and extrinsic goal orientation, being sure to specify the correct number of items in the **.n** portion of the **MEAN** function. The product of that work is shown in Figure 12b.43 where we present a portion of the data file with all of the computed variables in it. We strongly recommend saving this data file now that the subscales have been computed.

Figure 12b.40 The Compute Variable Dialog Window With the Item Set for Self-Acceptance Specified

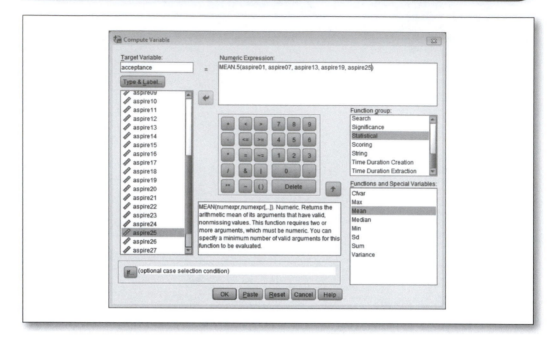

Figure 12b.41 A Portion of the Data File With the First Subscale Computed

Figure 12b.42 The IBM SPSS Save Data As: Variables Dialog Window

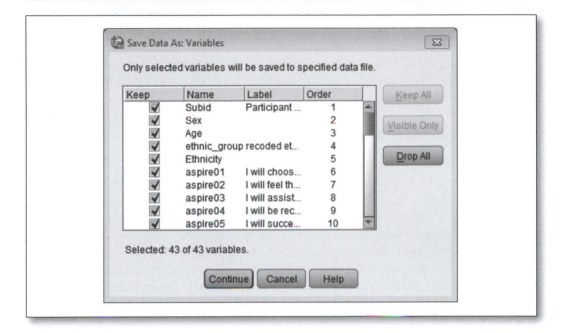

Figure 12b.43 A Portion of the Data File With All of the Scales Computed

12B.15 Using the Computed Variables in Further Analyses

In addition to the item variables, our data file contained a variable named **Sex** indicating the sex of the participants (females were coded as 1 and males were coded as 2). To illustrate the use of the computed scales in subsequent analyses, we will perform a simple one-way between-subjects MANOVA using **Sex** as the independent variable and the computed scales as the dependent variables. As a prelude to our MANOVA, we will examine the correlations between the pairs of scales.

12B.15.1 Correlations of the Computed Variables

Using subscales and full scales as dependent variables in the same MANOVA can be problematic in that we could have an issue with multicollinearity (a combination of dependent variables correlating close to 1.00 as discussed in Section 5A.3.2). To assess that possibility, we examine the correlations of the global scales and subscales.

We use the data file **Leanne Scales** for this analysis. From the main menu, select **Analyze** ➔ **Correlate** ➔ **Bivariate**, which produces the **Bivariate Correlations** main dialog window shown in Figure 12b.44. Move the eight variables representing the computed scales (**acceptance**, **community**, **affiliation**, **social_recognition**, **financial**, **appearance**, **intrinsic**, and **extrinsic**) from the variables list panel to the **Variables** panel. Click **OK** to perform the analysis.

Figure 12b.44   The Bivariate Correlations Dialog Window

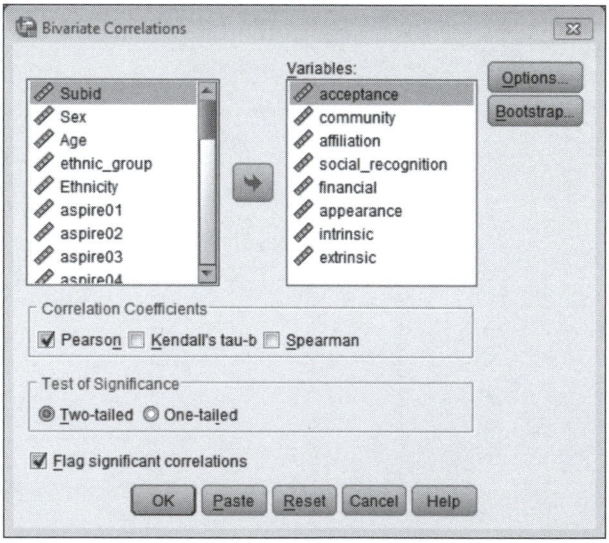

The correlations between the scales is shown in Figure 12b.45, where we note that the global scales are substantially and not surprisingly correlated with their respective subscales. That is, the Extrinsic global scale correlates .910 with Appealing Appearance, .849 with Social Recognition, and .728 with Financial Success; the Intrinsic global scale, not quite as strongly but still at an uncomfortable level, correlates .834 with Community Feelings, .774 with Self-Acceptance, and .766 with Affiliation.

Figure 12b.45 The Correlations Between the Pairs of Scales

Correlations

		acceptance	community	affiliation	social_recognition	financial	appearance	intrinsic	extrinsic
acceptance	Pearson Correlation	1	.450**	.488**	.176**	.239**	.076	.774**	.176**
	Sig. (2-tailed)		.000	.000	.002	.000	.188	.000	.002
	N	306	306	306	304	305	304	306	301
community	Pearson Correlation	.450**	1	.407**	.192**	−.025	.067	.834**	.101
	Sig. (2-tailed)	.000		.000	.001	.667	.242	.000	.080
	N	306	309	309	307	308	307	306	304
affiliation	Pearson Correlation	.488**	.407**	1	.172**	.180**	.120*	.766**	.175**
	Sig. (2-tailed)	.000	.000		.002	.002	.036	.000	.002
	N	306	309	309	307	308	307	306	304
social_recognition	Pearson Correlation	.176**	.192**	.172**	1	.436**	.653**	.238**	.849**
	Sig. (2-tailed)	.002	.001	.002		.000	.000	.000	.000
	N	304	307	307	307	306	305	304	304
financial	Pearson Correlation	.239**	−.025	.180**	.436**	1	.526**	.141*	.728**
	Sig. (2-tailed)	.000	.667	.002	.000		.000	.014	.000
	N	305	308	308	306	308	306	305	304
appearance	Pearson Correlation	.076	.067	.120*	.653**	.526**	1	.117*	.910**
	Sig. (2-tailed)	.188	.242	.036	.000	.000		.041	.000
	N	304	307	307	305	306	307	304	304
intrinsic	Pearson Correlation	.774**	.834**	.766**	.238**	.141*	.117*	1	.190**
	Sig. (2-tailed)	.000	.000	.000	.000	.014	.041		.001
	N	306	306	306	304	305	304	306	301
extrinsic	Pearson Correlation	.176**	.101	.175**	.849**	.728**	.910**	.190**	1
	Sig. (2-tailed)	.002	.080	.002	.000	.000	.000	.001	
	N	301	304	304	304	304	304	301	304

**. Correlation is significant at the 0.01 level (2-tailed).
*. Correlation is significant at the 0.05 level (2-tailed).

These correlations are unacceptably high for the global scales and the subscales to be used together as a set of dependent variables in a MANOVA. Consider the Extrinsic dimension. Not only does it correlate .91 with one of its subscales, it correlates .83 with another and .77 with a third. If all three subscales are in the model together, the multiple correlation between them as a set and the Extrinsic scale will actually be equal to 1.00 (we used the three subscales to predict the Extrinsic value in a multiple regression to determine this value, but even without having performed the analysis, we would expect a very high multiple correlation simply based on the Pearson correlation values). This illustrates exactly what is meant by multicollinearity. Such an outcome is to be expected in most situations, and the way to deal with it is to perform separate analyses if we wish to assess group differences on the global Extrinsic dimension as well as its subscales. If we were to use all four of these measures as dependent variables in a MANOVA, IBM SPSS would exclude the Extrinsic dimension in the multivariate analysis (although it would still produce univariate ANOVAs for all four).

The correlations between the six subscales present a more acceptable set of results. There is one correlation in excess of .60 (Social Recognition with Appealing Appearance at .653) and another in the .5s (Financial Success with Appealing Appearance at .526), but the remainder are under .50. The fact that the subscales within each of the global domains share a moderate amount of variance is to be expected as they are, by definition, related in a fundamental way to each other. For the purposes of performing a MANOVA, however, we should not have a multicollinearity problem. Therefore, we will perform one MANOVA using the two global scales as dependent variables (to demonstrate the use of the global dimensions) and a second MANOVA using the six subscales as dependent variables (which, because it looks at the global dimensions in a more detailed manner, is what we would report). A detailed treatment of how to perform a MANOVA is contained in Chapter 5B; here, we assume that readers are familiar with the procedure and present the analysis setup and results in a more succinct manner.

12B.15.2 A MANOVA Using
the Global Dimensions as Dependent Variables

We use the data file **Leanne Scales** for this and the next analysis. From the main menu, select **Analyze ➔ General Linear Model ➔ Multivariate** to reach the **Multivariate** main dialog window shown in Figure 12b.46. Move the two dependent variables (**intrinsic** and **extrinsic**) from the variables list panel to the **Dependent Variables** panel and move **Sex** to the **Fixed Factor(s)** panel.

Select the **Options** pushbutton. In the **Display** area, as shown in Figure 12b.47, check **Descriptive statistics, Residual SSCP matrix,** and **Homogeneity tests**. Click **Continue** to return to the main dialog window and click **OK** to perform the analysis.

The results of Box's test for multivariate and Levene's test for the individual dependent variables in terms of homogeneity of variance are shown in Figure 12b.48. **Box's Test of Equality of Covariance Matrices** is statistically significant (Box's $M = 11.099$, $p = .012$), indicating that the dependent variable covariance matrices are not equal across the levels of the independent variable. It is therefore appropriate to report Pillai's trace for the multivariate test of significance (this is a technical point only, because with only two groups in our MANOVA, all of the multivariate F ratios will be the same). Levene's test, also shown in Figure 12b.48, indicates that the global intrinsic scale but not the global extrinsic scale

Figure 12b.46   The Main General Linear Model Multivariate Window

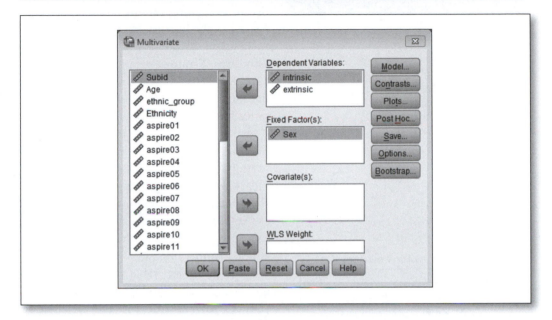

Figure 12b.47   The Options Window of General Linear Model Multivariate

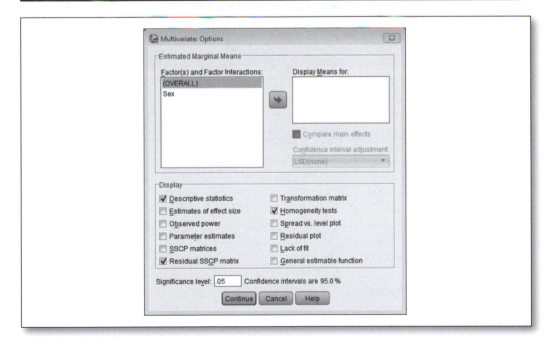

Figure 12b.48 The Results of Box's Test and Levene's Test

Box's Test of Equality of Covariance Matrices[a]

Box's M	11.099
F	3.656
df1	3
df2	203116.651
Sig.	.012

Tests the null hypothesis that the observed covariance matrices of the dependent variables are equal across groups.

a. Design: Intercept + Sex

Levene's Test of Equality of Error Variances[a]

	F	df1	df2	Sig.
intrinsic	17.665	1	297	.000
extrinsic	.160	1	297	.689

Tests the null hypothesis that the error variance of the dependent variable is equal across groups.

a. Design: Intercept + Sex

appeared to violate the assumption of equal variances; we therefore want to be conservative in evaluating the univariate effect with respect to the intrinsic dimension.

The multivariate test values and their associated F ratios are presented in Figure 12b.49. Because there are only two groups in the analysis, all tests of the multivariate F ratios for **Sex** return the same value and were statistically significant; nonetheless, we note that Pillai's trace is significant. We may thus examine the univariate ANOVA results. Pillai's trace here represents the multivariate eta square, the amount of variance explained by **Sex**: 5.5%; we can also compute eta square by subtracting the value of Wilks' lambda from 1.00 ($1.00 - .945 = .055$).

The summary table for the univariate results is presented in Figure 12b.50. Sex differences for the intrinsic goal orientation measures are statistically significant, but the sexes do not appear to differ on the amount of extrinsic goal orientation they endorsed.

Figure 12b.49 The Multivariate Results

Multivariate Tests[b]

Effect		Value	F	Hypothesis df	Error df	Sig.
Intercept	Pillai's Trace	.986	10776.678[a]	2.000	296.000	.000
	Wilks' Lambda	.014	10776.678[a]	2.000	296.000	.000
	Hotelling's Trace	72.815	10776.678[a]	2.000	296.000	.000
	Roy's Largest Root	72.815	10776.678[a]	2.000	296.000	.000
Sex	Pillai's Trace	.055	8.565[a]	2.000	296.000	.000
	Wilks' Lambda	.945	8.565[a]	2.000	296.000	.000
	Hotelling's Trace	.058	8.565[a]	2.000	296.000	.000
	Roy's Largest Root	.058	8.565[a]	2.000	296.000	.000

a. Exact statistic

b. Design: Intercept + Sex

Figure 12b.50 The Univariate Results

Tests of Between-Subjects Effects

Source	Dependent Variable	Type III Sum of Squares	df	Mean Square	F	Sig.
Corrected Model	intrinsic	9.815[a]	1	9.815	16.916	.000
	extrinsic	.209[b]	1	.209	.095	.758
Intercept	intrinsic	12367.050	1	12367.050	21314.562	.000
	extrinsic	4714.667	1	4714.667	2153.009	.000
Sex	intrinsic	9.815	1	9.815	16.916	.000
	extrinsic	.209	1	.209	.095	.758
Error	intrinsic	172.324	297	.580		
	extrinsic	650.372	297	2.190		
Total	intrinsic	18938.178	299			
	extrinsic	7630.720	299			
Corrected Total	intrinsic	182.139	298			
	extrinsic	650.580	298			

a. R Squared = .054 (Adjusted R Squared = .051)

b. R Squared = .000 (Adjusted R Squared = −.003)

At $p < .001$ for the intrinsic dimension, we have no concern about the violation of equal variances exhibited for that dependent measure. The eta-square value for **intrinsic** is computed as its sum of squares of 9.815 divided by the Corrected Total sum of squares of 182.139 or .05.

Figure 12b.51 shows the group means. It can be seen that females have somewhat stronger intrinsically oriented goals than males.

Figure 12b.51 The Descriptive Statistics

Descriptive Statistics

	Sex	Mean	Std. Deviation	N
intrinsic	1 female	8.0157	.69997	234
	2 male	7.5764	.95332	65
	Total	7.9202	.78180	299
extrinsic	1 female	4.8456	1.48944	234
	2 male	4.7815	1.44417	65
	Total	4.8317	1.47755	299

12B.15.3 A MANOVA Using the Six Subscales as Dependent Variables

We set up the analysis in the same way as described in Section 12B.15.2, except that we use the six subscales rather than the two global dimensions as dependent variables. The results of Box's test for multivariate and Levene's test for the individual dependent variables in terms of homogeneity of variance are shown in Figure 12b.52. **Box's Test of Equality of Covariance Matrices** is statistically significant (Box's $M = 80.822$, $p < .001$), indicating that the dependent variable covariance matrices are not equal across the levels of the independent variable. Levene's test indicates that the three intrinsic subscales (**acceptance**, **community**, and **affiliation**) but not the three extrinsic subscales appeared to violate the assumption of equal variances.

Figure 12b.52 The Results of Box's Test and Levene's Test

Box's Test of Equality of Covariance Matrices[a]

Box's M	80.822
F	3.712
df1	21
df2	51693.811
Sig.	.000

Tests the null hypothesis that the observed covariance matrices of the dependent variables are equal across groups.

a. Design: Intercept + Sex

Levene's Test of Equality of Error Variances[a]

	F	df1	df2	Sig.
acceptance	5.290	1	297	.022
community	15.999	1	297	.000
affiliation	22.539	1	297	.000
social_recognition	1.057	1	297	.305
financial	.003	1	297	.953
appearance	1.663	1	297	.198

Tests the null hypothesis that the error variance of the dependent variable is equal across groups.

a. Design: Intercept + Sex

The multivariate test values and their associated F ratios are presented in Figure 12b.53. Because there are only two groups in the analysis, all tests of the multivariate F ratios for **Sex**

Figure 12b.53   The Multivariate Results

Multivariate Tests[b]

Effect		Value	F	Hypothesis df	Error df	Sig.
Intercept	Pillai's Trace	.989	4227.553[a]	6.000	292.000	.000
	Wilks' Lambda	.011	4227.553[a]	6.000	292.000	.000
	Hotelling's Trace	86.868	4227.553[a]	6.000	292.000	.000
	Roy's Largest Root	86.868	4227.553[a]	6.000	292.000	.000
Sex	Pillai's Trace	.120	6.634[a]	6.000	292.000	.000
	Wilks' Lambda	.880	6.634[a]	6.000	292.000	.000
	Hotelling's Trace	.136	6.634[a]	6.000	292.000	.000
	Roy's Largest Root	.136	6.634[a]	6.000	292.000	.000

a. Exact statistic

b. Design: Intercept + Sex

return the same value and were statistically significant; nonetheless, we note that Pillai's trace is significant. We may thus examine the univariate ANOVA results. Pillai's trace here represents the multivariate eta square, the amount of variance explained by **Sex**: 12%; eta square can also be obtained by subtracting the value of Wilks' lambda from 1.00 ($1.00 - .880 = .120$).

Note that these results are very similar to what we obtained when analyzing the global dimensions. This happened because the three subscales of each global dimension and the global dimensions themselves are almost interchangeable with each other (due to multicollinearity), so whether we use the global dimensions or the subscales that represent them should make little difference in the results of the analysis.

The summary table is presented in Figure 12b.54. Applying a Bonferroni correction to the univariate ANOVAs ($.05/\#$ dependent variables $= .05/6 = .008$) indicates that the **community** and **affiliation** scales are statistically significant ($p = .002$ and $p < .001$, respectively). That the **acceptance** scale does not achieve statistical significance using the Bonferroni-corrected alpha level is an acceptable result, given that this subscale did violate the assumption of homogeneity of variance; the stringency of the corrected alpha level should be sufficient to protect us from committing a Type I error for the other two scales.

The eta-square value for **community** is computed as its sum of squares of 14.824 divided by the Corrected Total sum of squares of 447.571 or .03; the eta-square value for **affiliation** is computed as its sum of squares of 14.064 divided by the Corrected Total sum of squares of 236.016 or .06.

Figure 12b.55 shows the group means. It can be seen that females have somewhat stronger community- and affiliation-oriented goals than males.

Figure 12b.54 The Univariate Results

Tests of Between–Subjects Effects

Source	Dependent Variable	Type III Sum of Squares	df	Mean Square	F	Sig.
Corrected Model	acceptance	3.234[a]	1	3.234	4.712	.031
	community	14.824[b]	1	14.824	10.174	.002
	affiliation	14.064[c]	1	14.064	18.820	.000
	social_recognition	4.631[d]	1	4.631	1.531	.217
	financial	.014[e]	1	.014	.005	.943
	appearance	8.162[f]	1	8.162	2.399	.122
Intercept	acceptance	12634.586	1	12634.586	18407.721	.000
	community	11065.899	1	11065.899	7594.684	.000
	affiliation	13461.445	1	13461.445	18013.147	.000
	social_recognition	3568.205	1	3568.205	1180.081	.000
	financial	8885.622	1	8885.622	3358.659	.000
	appearance	3485.424	1	3485.424	1024.447	.000
Sex	acceptance	3.234	1	3.234	4.712	.031
	community	14.824	1	14.824	10.174	.002
	affiliation	14.064	1	14.064	18.820	.000
	social_recognition	4.631	1	4.631	1.531	.217
	financial	.014	1	.014	.005	.943
	appearance	8.162	1	8.162	2.399	.122
Error	acceptance	203.853	297	.686		
	community	432.746	297	1.457		
	affiliation	221.952	297	.747		
	social_recognition	898.038	297	3.024		
	financial	785.739	297	2.646		
	appearance	1010.468	297	3.402		
Total	acceptance	19110.200	299			
	community	17388.040	299			
	affiliation	20746.240	299			
	social_recognition	5934.600	299			
	financial	13861.063	299			
	appearance	6424.278	299			
Corrected Total	acceptance	207.087	298			
	community	447.571	298			
	affiliation	236.016	298			
	social_recognition	902.668	298			
	financial	785.753	298			
	appearance	1018.631	298			

a. R Squared = .016 (Adjusted R Squared = .012)

b. R Squared = .033 (Adjusted R Squared = .030)

c. R Squared = .060 (Adjusted R Squared = .056)

d. R Squared = .005 (Adjusted R Squared = .002)

e. R Squared = .000 (Adjusted R Squared = −.003)

f. R Squared = .008 (Adjusted R Squared = .005)

Figure 12b.55   The Descriptive Statistics

Descriptive Statistics

	Sex	Mean	Std. Deviation	N
acceptance	1 female	8.0060	.77369	234
	2 male	7.7538	1.00298	65
	Total	7.9512	.83362	299
community	1 female	7.6444	1.09705	234
	2 male	7.1046	1.54277	65
	Total	7.5271	1.22553	299
affiliation	1 female	8.3966	.74855	234
	2 male	7.8708	1.19501	65
	Total	8.2823	.88994	299
social_recognition	1 female	4.0368	1.68880	234
	2 male	4.3385	1.91014	65
	Total	4.1023	1.74043	299
financial	1 female	6.6165	1.63290	234
	2 male	6.6000	1.60310	65
	Total	6.6129	1.62381	299
appearance	1 female	4.3390	1.88776	234
	2 male	3.9385	1.67772	65
	Total	4.2520	1.84884	299

12B.16 Reporting the Results

An exploratory factor analysis of the 30 items of the Aspirations Index was performed on the data from 310 university students. Prior to running the analysis with IBM SPSS, the data were screened by examining descriptive statistics on each item, interitem correlations, and possible univariate and multivariate assumption violations. From this initial assessment, all variables were found to be interval-like, variable pairs appeared to be bivariate normally distributed, and all cases were independent of one another. Because of the large sample size, the variables-to-cases ratio was deemed adequate. The Kaiser–Meyer–Olkin measure of sampling adequacy was .85, indicating that the present data were suitable for principal components analysis. Similarly, Bartlett's test of sphericity was significant ($p < .001$), indicating sufficient correlation between the variables to proceed with the analysis.

(Continued)

(Continued)

A total of seven factors had eigenvalues greater than 1.00, cumulatively accounting for 65.76% of the total variance. The Aspirations Index is said to have two global dimensions, intrinsic and extrinsic goal orientation. In the first set of analyses, two factors were extracted. All extraction methods yielded the same structure, and the results for the unweighted least squares (ULS) procedure are reported here. The first two factors cumulatively accounted for 36.79% of the total variance. A promax rotation indicated that the factors were correlated .20, and the structure coefficients from the promax rotation are presented in Table 12b.4. As can be seen, the structure coefficients are of reasonable but not notably large magnitude owing to the relatively small amount of variance explained by this structure. Nonetheless, the two factors clearly distinguished between an extrinsic goal orientation (Factor 1) and an intrinsic goal orientation (Factor 2). For example, Item 11 ("I will have people comment often about how attractive I look") and Item 18 ("I will have many expensive possessions") correlated relatively strongly with the extrinsic factor and Item 21 ("I will help others improve their lives") and Item 15 ("I will work to make the world a better place") correlated relatively strongly with the intrinsic factor.

Based on the subscales that are said to comprise the Aspirations Index, six factors were extracted accounting for 53.64% of the total variance in the ULS solution. Many of the correlations between pairs of factors within each of the global domains were in excess of .40, strongly suggesting the appropriateness of an oblique rotation strategy; thus, promax rotation was used in conjunction with several extraction techniques. Some of the extraction techniques (e.g., principal factors, maximum likelihood) yielded the essence of four of the subscales but broke apart two of them, whereas others (e.g., principal components, ULS) yielded outcomes extremely similar or almost identical to the proposed inventory structure; the ULS procedure was in this latter set, and the results of that analysis are presented in Table 12.5.

The six-factor ULS promax rotated structure mirrored the existent scoring schema of the Aspirations Index with one exception. The items associated with each subscale are summarized in Table 12b.2. The one exception to the hypothesized structure was Item 18 ("I will have many expensive possessions"). This item did not correlate most strongly with the Financial Success item set as expected from the scoring system of the Aspirations Index (although a moderate correlation was obtained) but was captured in the Appealing Appearance item set instead. It would seem that from the perspective of the respondents, owning expensive possessions may be more for the purpose of displaying them to others than for the purpose of accumulating wealth.

Subscales were constructed based on the organization shown in Table 12b.2. The internal consistency of each subscale as assessed by coefficient alpha is shown in Table 12b.3. With the exception of Self-Acceptance, whose reliability is relatively low, the other subscales exhibited very good internal consistency.

A MANOVA was used to evaluate sex differences on the six subscales. Box's test of Equality of Covariance Matrices was statistically significant (Box's $M = 80.822$, $p < .001$), indicating that the dependent variable covariance matrices are not equal across the levels of the independent variable. Levene's test indicates that the three intrinsic subscales (acceptance, community, and affiliation) but not the extrinsic subscales appeared to violate the assumption of equal variances.

A statistically significant multivariate effect was obtained, Pillai's trace $= .120$, $F(6, 292) = 6.634$, $p < .001$. Using a Bonferroni-corrected alpha level of .006 to evaluate the six univariate effects indicated that the two of the intrinsic subscales showed a sex difference. Community Feelings demonstrated a significant effect, $F(1, 297) = 10.174$, $p = .002$, eta square $= .03$, with females ($M = 7.64$, $SD = 1.10$, 95% $CI = 7.50, 7.79$) reporting somewhat stronger community-oriented feelings than males ($M = 7.10$, $SD = 1.54$, 95% $CI = 6.72, 7.49$). Affiliation also demonstrated a significant effect, $F(1, 297) = 18.820$, $p < .001$, eta square $= .06$, with females ($M = 8.40$, $SD = 0.75$, 95% $CI = 8.30, 8.49$) reporting somewhat stronger affiliation-oriented goals than males ($M = 7.87$, $SD = 1.20$, 95% $CI = 7.57, 8.17$).

Table 12b.4 Structure Coefficients: 2-Factor ULS/Promax Solution

Item Number and Wording	Factor 1	Factor 2
11 I will have people comment often about how attractive I look.	.771	.108
18 I will have many expensive possessions.	.750	-.015
10 My name will be known by many people.	.720	.277
23 I will achieve the "look" I've been after.	.707	.082
22 I will be famous.	.693	.069

(Continued)

Table 12b.4 (Continued)

Item Number and Wording	Factor 1	Factor 2
17 I will keep up with fashions in hair and clothing.	**.682**	.075
16 I will be admired by many people.	**.676**	.308
24 I will be rich.	**.659**	.048
29 My image will be one others find appealing.	**.637**	.104
28 My name will appear frequently in the media.	**.613**	-.001
30 I will have enough money to buy everything I want.	**.581**	.046
04 I will be recognized by lots of different people.	**.557**	.360
05 I will successfully hide the signs of aging.	**.541**	.179
06 I will be financially successful.	**.516**	.270
12 I will have a job that pays very well.	**.476**	.299
21 I will help others improve their lives.	.057	**.692**
15 I will work to make the world a better place.	.089	**.668**
27 I will help people in need.	.099	**.665**
26 I will have deep, enduring relationships.	.154	**.591**
09 I will work for the betterment of society.	.122	**.589**
14 I will share my life with someone I love.	.139	**.556**
19 I will know and accept who I really am.	.098	**.550**
03 I will assist people who need it, asking nothing in return.	-.006	**.537**
25 I will continue to grow and learn new things.	.114	**.524**
02 I will feel that there are people who really love me, and whom I love.	.072	**.499**
08 I will have good friends that I can count on.	.141	**.493**
13 I will gain increasing insight into why I do the things I do.	.234	**.478**
20 I will have committed, intimate relationships.	.172	**.471**
07 At the end of my life, I will look back on my life as meaningful and complete.	.107	**.459**
01 I will choose what I do, instead of being pushed along by life.	.003	**.309**

Table 12b.5 Structure Coefficients: 6-Factor ULS/Promax Solution

Item Number and Wording	Factor					
	1	2	3	4	5	6
11 I will have people comment often about how attractive I look.	**.832**	.053	.101	.555	.303	.100
17 I will keep up with fashions in hair and clothing.	**.817**	.086	.071	.411	.264	-.020
23 I will achieve the "look" I've been after.	**.763**	.044	.050	.506	.275	.102
18 I will have many expensive possessions.	**.749**	-.090	.018	.516	.431	.002
29 My image will be one others find appealing.	**.686**	.017	.109	.493	.194	.178
05 I will successfully hide the signs of aging.	**.496**	.139	.141	.423	.358	.057
15 I will work to make the world a better place.	.027	**.815**	.342	.194	.070	.332
21 I will help others improve their lives.	.038	**.779**	.407	.127	.001	.417
27 I will help people in need.	.085	**.773**	.410	.159	.014	.330
09 I will work for the betterment of society.	.063	**.737**	.244	.192	.126	.311
03 I will assist people who need it, asking nothing in return.	-.060	**.573**	.278	.068	.066	.364
14 I will share my life with someone I love.	.041	.312	**.790**	.140	.241	.334
26 I will have deep, enduring relationships.	.096	.377	**.736**	.162	.141	.402
20 I will have committed, intimate relationships.	.140	.242	**.710**	.171	.088	.328
02 I will feel that there are people who really love me, and whom I love.	-.021	.286	**.596**	.068	.230	.368
08 I will have good friends that I can count on.	.075	.341	**.459**	.085	.270	.390
10 My name will be known by many people.	.549	.184	.190	**.858**	.384	.180
22 I will be famous.	.628	.003	.047	**.771**	.181	.076
16 I will be admired by many people.	.534	.228	.176	**.721**	.389	.242
04 I will be recognized by lots of different people.	.371	.283	.255	**.705**	.362	.204
28 My name will appear frequently in the media.	.576	-.045	-.012	**.687**	.103	.030
12 I will have a job that pays very well.	.287	.107	.220	.329	**.889**	.339
06 I will be financially successful.	.357	.062	.253	.330	**.863**	.278
24 I will be rich.	.562	-.143	.087	.476	**.608**	.158
30 I will have enough money to buy everything I want.	.526	-.127	.046	.352	**.579**	.207
19 I will know and accept who I really am.	.039	.377	.408	.076	.199	**.723**
13 I will gain increasing insight into why I do the things I do.	.173	.347	.326	.219	.219	**.547**
25 I will continue to grow and learn new things.	.027	.456	.292	.167	.176	**.516**
07 At the end of my life, I will look back on my life as meaningful and complete.	-.035	.226	.466	.089	.381	**.478**
01 I will choose what I do, instead of being pushed along by life.	-.077	.180	.216	.018	.175	**.418**

Canonical Correlation Analysis

13A.1 Overview

Canonical correlation analysis can be viewed as an extension of multiple regression analysis with a strong flavoring of principal components analysis and is a more general case of discriminant function analysis and MANOVA. In multiple regression, we use a set of quantitative independent variables to predict a single quantitative dependent variable; in canonical correlation analysis, we use a set of quantitative independent variables (labeled as covariates) to predict not one but rather a set of quantitative dependent variables. In multiple regression, we obtain the raw and standardized coefficients; in canonical analysis, we also obtain raw and standardized coefficients. In multiple regression, we use the structure coefficients to interpret the weighted linear composite of predictors (the predictor variate); in canonical analysis, we use the structure coefficients to interpret the weighted linear composites of both the predictors (the predictor variate) and the dependent variables (the dependent variate).

Canonical correlation analysis has much of the feel of principal components analysis (and factor analysis). The dynamics of extracting components or factors are very similar to the way in which canonical functions are extracted. In principal components analysis and factor analysis, we use structure coefficients to interpret the components or factors; in canonical analysis also, we use the structure coefficients to interpret the predictor and the dependent variates.

Canonical correlation analysis is also intimately related to MANOVA and discriminant function analysis; in fact (as we will see in Chapter 13B), to conduct a canonical correlation analysis in IBM SPSS, we must use the older syntax to perform a MANOVA and must include the discriminant function analysis command structure as part of our syntax. In MANOVA and discriminant analysis, we obtain one or more discriminant functions that represent one or more dimensions along which the groups differ; in canonical correlation analysis, we obtain multiple canonical functions that represent different dimensions along which the predictor variables are related to the dependent variables.

Canonical correlation was introduced by Harold Hotelling (1936a). It is a member of the set of procedures comprising the general linear model, but one that is far more conducive to exploratory rather than hypothesis testing research (see Cohen et al., 2003). Additional sources that may be consulted on this topic include Hair et al. (2010), Lattin et al. (1993), Levine (1977), Lutz and Eckert (1994), Stevens (2009), Takane and Hwang (2002), and Thompson (1984, 1991).

13A.2 Canonical Functions or Roots

13A.2.1 The Definition of a Canonical Function or Root

Canonical correlation analysis relates the two sets of variables by creating weighted linear composites for each of them in a set of predictive equations (dependent variables weighted linear composite = predictor or covariate variables weighted linear composite). Each weighted linear composite—the dependent variables and the covariates—thus constitutes a variate. The coefficients or weights are selected in such a way as to maximize the amount of explained variance of the set of dependent variables—that is, the weights maximize the correlation of the variates.

The equation that depicts the relationship of the dependent and predictor variates is called a *canonical function* or *canonical root*, and it can be represented in either raw score or standardized form. Unlike multiple regression and more like discriminant function analysis and principal components analysis, there are typically several functions resulting from the analysis. To illustrate this, here are the first two canonical functions in their most general form:

$$w * DV_{11} + w * DV_{12} + \ldots + w * DV_{1u} = w * IV_{11} + w * IV_{12} + \ldots + w * IV_{1v}$$

$$w * DV_{21} + w * DV_{22} + \ldots + w * DV_{2u} = w * IV_{21} + w * IV_{22} + \ldots + w * IV_{2v}$$

In the above equation, w is the weight or canonical coefficient (raw or standardized) of the dependent variable or independent variable in the respective variate. Note that there are two subscripts to each variable because there are multiple canonical functions. The subscripting is adopted from Stevens (2009), where we place the function number as the first subscript and the variable number as the second number in the subscript. Thus, DV_{12} is the second dependent variable in the first canonical function, and IV_{2v} is the vth predictor of the second function.

13A.2.2 The Maximum Number of
Canonical Functions or Roots That Can Be Extracted

Akin to discriminant function analysis, where the set of variables can be weighted differently in different discriminant functions, and principal components analysis, where the set of variables can be weighted differently in different components, the two variates in the canonical function can be related to each other in more than a single way. That is, the relationship between a set of dependent variables and a set of predictor variables is potentially rather complex, and complex relationship often needs to be represented by not one but by c number of functions, where c is the smaller of the following:

- The number of dependent variables
- The number of predictor or independent variables

For example, if there were six dependent variables and nine predictor variables, the maximum number of canonical functions that could be computed would be six.

13A.3 The Index of Shared Variance

The overall correlation between the two sets of variables is called the *overall canonical correlation* and is often symbolized as R_c, a statistic that we have already seen in discriminant function analysis (see Section 11A.10.2). Its squared value, the *overall squared canonical correlation*, is often symbolized as R_c^2. The multiple correlation that we obtain in multiple regression is a special (limiting) case of the overall canonical correlation (where there is only one dependent variable) in much the same way as the Pearson correlation is a special (limiting) case of the multiple correlation (where there is only one predictor variable).

The overall squared canonical correlation summarizes the value of the total amount of variance shared by the set of canonical functions (the full solution) and represents the strength of the complex relationship between the set of dependent and predictor variables. We usually suppress the term *overall* for this statistic (each canonical function can also have its own squared canonical correlation, and thus, we must be very specific when talking about the squared canonical correlation for a particular function—see Section 13A.5.3).

The full set of functions will account for 100% of the *explained* or *common* variance of the variables, but it is virtually always true that we will not explain all of the variance. That is, there may be variance that is more specific to one or some of the variables but is not shared across the entire set, and such variance cannot be explained by the canonical functions. This situation is analogous to what we have seen in factor analysis where it is the common rather than total variance that is the focus of the analysis.

13A.4 The Dynamics of Extracting Canonical Functions

To "extract" a function is to account for a portion of the total variance of the dependent variable set. Canonical functions (canonical roots) are extracted from the total variance in a manner analogous to the way in which principal components and discriminant functions are extracted. Thus,

- Canonical functions are extracted sequentially.
- Each canonical function is orthogonal to (independent of) the others.
- Each canonical function accounts for more variance than those extracted subsequently.

The variables in the canonical functions are weighted such that the amount of explained variance of the set of dependent variables associated with the predictor variables is maximized. The first function that is extracted, akin to what happens in principal components analysis, is the most substantial one—it accounts for more of the total variance than any of the other subsequently extracted functions.

Once the first function is extracted, the focus of the analysis shifts to the residual variance (the amount of unexplained variance remaining). Because the second canonical function targets this residual variance, it is orthogonal to (independent of) the first function, and the amount of variance it explains can be added to the amount of variance explained by the first function to yield the total amount of variance cumulatively explained by the first two canonical functions. The second function is also generated such that the variates are maximally correlated.

Once this second function is extracted, the focus of the analysis shifts to the remaining (residual) variance, and the third canonical function is extracted such that the correlation between the variates (the variance explained) is maximized. This third function is orthogonal to the first and second canonical functions. We continue in this manner until all of the canonical functions have been extracted down to the specified alpha level in the analysis setup.

Canonical functions that are extracted earlier will account for more variance than those extracted later. In canonical correlation analysis, the amount of variance accounted for usually falls off quite sharply past the first function. It is therefore not uncommon for researchers to interpret only the first one or two functions in a typical study.

13A.5 Testing Statistical Significance

13A.5.1 Overview

The null hypothesis in canonical correlation analysis is that we cannot explain any of the variance of the set of dependent variables based on the predictor variable set. That null hypothesis is tested in the same manner as is done in MANOVA. Four different multivariate significance tests are computed: Pillai's trace, Hotelling's trace, Wilks' lambda, and (although not evaluated for statistical significance—see Section 13A.6) Roy's greatest (largest) characteristic root. If these tests return a statistically significant outcome, then we can conclude that the overall squared canonical correlation is more than zero (i.e., we can use the predictor variables to explain at least some of the variance associated with the set of dependent variables). We would then go on to interpret as many of the statistically significant individual canonical functions that were warranted based on the amount of explained variance associated with each respective function.

The canonical correlation output allows us to discuss in a little more detail than we have done in previous chapters—but still in a somewhat qualitative way—how each of the multivariate tests is computed. To get to that discussion, we first need to apply the concept of eigenvalues to the present context and then introduce the notion of *theta values*.

13A.5.2 Eigenvalues

In principal components analysis, we made extensive use of eigenvalues to describe the amount of variance each component explains. In canonical correlation analysis, we find a comparable use for them. As was true for discriminant functions (see Section 11A.9.2), each canonical function is associated with an eigenvalue describing the amount of variance it explains. The eigenvalue of each successive canonical function will be smaller than the prior one since each successive root will explain less and less of the data.

In the context of canonical analysis, we can conceptualize the eigenvalue as a ratio of the variance of the canonical function to the estimated error variance. Dividing the variance explained based on the function by an estimate of the error variance provides a count of the number of error units the effect spans. This is what a univariate t test does—it counts the number of error variance units spanned by the mean difference—and what an F test does—it counts the number of error variance units spanned by the variance of the effect.

This effect-to-error variance ratio can be viewed as a signal-to-noise ratio. If the ratio is equal to 1, then the variance attributable to the root (or to the effect in general) is equal to the variance attributable to error. To the extent that the ratio is less than 1, there is more error than signal (i.e., the noise can overpower the signal), making the signal (the effect) that much more difficult to detect. To the extent that the ratio exceeds 1, the signal is stronger than the noise making the signal more apparent. An eigenvalue of 5, for example, indicates, again very roughly, that the variance attributable to the canonical function is five times greater than the error variance. Generally, researchers are hesitant to interpret canonical functions whose eigenvalues are substantially lower than 1.

13A.5.3 Theta Values (Squared Canonical Correlations)

Each eigenvalue is associated with a *theta value*—another term for the squared canonical correlation for a given canonical root. Theta, or the squared canonical correlation, is an index of the strength of the relationship between the dependent and the predictor variate for that canonical function. Thus, the theta value for root *r* is equal to the squared canonical correlation for root *r*.

The theta value for any given canonical function can be computed from the eigenvalue associated with that function. Specifically, it is computed as the eigenvalue divided by one plus the eigenvalue. In general terms,

$$\text{Theta for root } r = \frac{\text{Eigenvalue of root } r}{1 + \text{Eigenvalue of root } r}$$

Squared canonical correlations (theta values but are not so labeled in the output) for each root or function, as well as the canonical correlation values, are contained in the IBM SPSS output when eigenvalues are requested.

13A.6 The Multivariate Tests

The four multivariate tests can be computed from theta values and/or the eigenvalues. Very briefly, the following provide the computation for each:

- Pillai's trace is the sum of the theta (squared canonical correlation) values across the full set of canonical functions.
- Hotelling's trace is the sum of the eigenvalues across the full set of canonical functions.
- Wilks' lambda is equal to the product of all (1 − theta) values across the full set of canonical functions.
- Roy's largest characteristic root is the largest theta value when considering the full set of canonical functions or roots (this will be the theta value for the first canonical function because this first function will account for more variance than any subsequently extracted function).

Researchers tend to have their own favorite multivariate test. The Wilks test is widely used, and we recommend it if no assumption violations are found. If Box's *M* test is statistically significant (it is very powerful and may find small differences in the population variance–covariance matrices to be statistically significant even if these differences are not compelling) or any of the other multivariate assumptions are violated, then the Pillai test may gain researchers some robustness in their evaluation of the effect and is to be preferred. Roy's method is appropriate to use in MANOVA if one group differs quite a bit from the other groups (e.g., Johnson & Wichern, 1999); since we have no groups in canonical correlation analysis, Roy's statistic is not tested for significance.

13A.7 Redundancy Index

Although the overall squared canonical correlation is an extension of the squared multiple correlation, there is a subtle difference in how we interpret each. The squared multiple correlation indexes the amount of variance of the dependent variable that is explained by the regression model (the prediction variate); the overall squared canonical correlation represents the amount of variance that is shared between the set of dependent and predictor variates. To estimate the amount of variance in the dependent variates explained by the predictor variates, we use a redundancy index.

A redundancy index is used to indicate the amount of variance in the dependent variates explained by the predictor variates. One widely used measure is that proposed by Stewart and Love (1968) that can be used to determine how well the information in the dependent variables can be reconstructed based on the information from the predictor set (Tacq, 1997). It is also possible to use Stewart and Love's index to determine how well the information in the predictor variables can be reconstructed based on the information from the dependent variable set. It should be noted that these two uses do not yield the same numerical value because they address different issues; hence, the redundancy index is *asymmetric*.

The redundancy index has received criticisms in the research literature (e.g., Cramer & Nicewander, 1979; Huo & Budescu, 2009); for example, it is not sensitive to correlations between the variables with the dependent and predictor variable sets. At least partially as a consequence of such criticisms, it seems that the index has been used less widely recently (Raykov & Marcoulides, 2008; Stevens, 2009; Thompson, 2000a).

An alternative measure to assess the amount of explained variance was proposed by Cramer and Nicewander (1979). All we do is calculate the *average squared canonical correlation*. For example, if we extracted five functions and the squared canonical correlations were .84, .47, .14, .07, and .04 for the first through fifth functions, respectively, then the Cramer–Nicewander index would be .312. We would interpret this value as follows: The set of predictor variates accounted for approximately 31% of the variance of the dependent variates.

13A.8 Coefficients Associated With the Canonical Functions

There is a set of three coefficients produced by IBM SPSS for the predictor variables as well as for the dependent variables in each canonical function: Two sets of coefficients represent the weighting of the variables in the functions and one set represents the structure coefficients.

13A.8.1 Weighting Coefficients

One set of weighting coefficients—the raw canonical coefficients—is associated with the raw score values of the variables; these coefficients are akin to the raw score coefficients in regression. A second set of weighting coefficients—the standardized canonical coefficients—is associated with the standardized values of the variables; these coefficients are akin to the beta weights or coefficients in regression. These two types of coefficients are useful and important, but it is the third set of coefficients on which researchers tend to focus in canonical analysis—the structure coefficients.

13A.8.2 Structure Coefficients

We introduced structure coefficients in the context of regression, where they helped us interpret the meaning of the prediction variate, and relied on them in the context of discriminant analysis and principal components/factor analysis in our efforts to interpret the discriminant functions and rotated components and factors, respectively. Structure coefficients are the correlations between the individual variables and the variate. They are used to interpret canonical functions in precisely the same way as we use them in discriminant function analysis and factor analysis—as we did for a discriminant function or a factor, the interpretation of the variate is based on the strength of the structure coefficients that may be treated as "loadings" of the variables on the variates.

IBM SPSS allows us to orthogonally rotate the dependent variates (no option is available for oblique rotation or to rotate the predictor variates) to achieve simple structure just as we do in factor analysis. But many researchers (including us) tend not to opt for this strategy for at least a couple of reasons. First, the importance of the function is a useful piece of information that needs to be taken into account in the interpretation of canonical functions—rotation would tend to equalize the importance of the functions. Second, the dependent variables in the analysis are not really chosen to represent different aspects of a larger construct as they are in factor analysis; instead, they are chosen to capture potentially different effects that may result from the presence of a set of conditions represented by the predictors. It therefore may not be clear what simple structure (the goal we hope to achieve when rotating the factors or components) really means in a canonical correlation context.

13A.9 Interpreting the Canonical Functions

To interpret a given canonical function (e.g., Canonical Function c), we suggest the following steps:

1. Examine the structure coefficients associated with the dependent variables comprising Canonical Function c to determine how we would interpret or characterize the variate.

2. Examine the structure coefficients associated with the predictor variables comprising Canonical Function c to determine how we would interpret or characterize the variate.

3. Generate the interpretation of the canonical function in the form "Higher levels of [predictor variate interpretation] is associated with or predictive of [higher/lower] levels of [dependent variate interpretation]." For example, we might say that higher levels of academic and social achievement during college appears to predict greater success in an early management career as indexed by faster advancement and higher year-end bonuses.

13A.10 Recommended Readings

Guarino, A. J. (2004). A comparison of first and second generation multivariate analysis: Canonical correlation analysis and structural equation modeling. *Florida Journal of Educational Research, 42,* 22–40.

Harlow, L. L. (2005). *The essence of multivariate thinking.* Mahwah, NJ: Lawrence Erlbaum.

Muller, K. E. (1982). Understanding canonical correlation through the general linear model and principal components. *American Statistician, 36,* 342–354.

Sherry, A., & Henson, R. K. (2005). Conducting and interpreting canonical correlation analysis in personality research: A user-friendly primer. *Journal of Personality Assessment, 84,* 37–48.

Thompson, B. (1991). A primer on the logic and use of canonical correlation analysis. *Measurement and Evaluation in Counseling and Development, 24,* 80–95.

Weiss, D. J. (1972). Canonical correlation analysis in counseling psychology research. *Journal of Counseling Psychology, 19,* 241–252.

Canonical Correlation Analysis Using IBM SPSS

his chapter will demonstrate how to perform canonical correlation analysis with IBM SPSS. We will use the data file **Personality** in these demonstrations.

13B.1 Canonical Correlation: Analysis Setup

Canonical correlation analysis cannot be performed by making selections from the menu system. Instead, we must perform the analysis through syntax using the MANOVA procedure (an older way to perform a multivariate ANOVA). Select the path **File ➔ New ➔ Syntax** to open a new syntax window. The cursor is placed on the first line when the window opens, and we have typed the syntax to perform the analysis as shown in Figure 13b.1.

Here is what the syntax means. MANOVA is structured similarly to all of IBM SPSS's ANOVA procedures. After the name of the procedure (**MANOVA**) is the list of dependent variables (**eminhib, rehearsl**, and so on). The keyword **with** informs IBM SPSS that the variables following it are covariates (our predictors in this canonical correlation analysis). Here, we are predicting the set of dependent variables based on **posafect, negafect, selfcon**, and so on.

We are using only the specification **signif** on the **print** subcommand (there are other specifications available) requesting, in the order as listed, the multivariate *F* tests (**MULTIV**), the eigenvalues and canonical correlations associated with each of the canonical functions (**EIGEN**), and the dimension reduction analysis (**DIMENR**). The **DISCRIM** subcommand is asking IBM SPSS to perform a discriminant function analysis and to display from that analysis the raw (**raw**) and standardized (**stan**) canonical coefficients and the correlations (**cor**) between the variables and the variate (the structure coefficients). We are also specifying the alpha level (**alpha**) needed to justify extracting a canonical function; the default is .25,

Figure 13b.1 The Syntax to Perform a Canonical Correlation Analysis

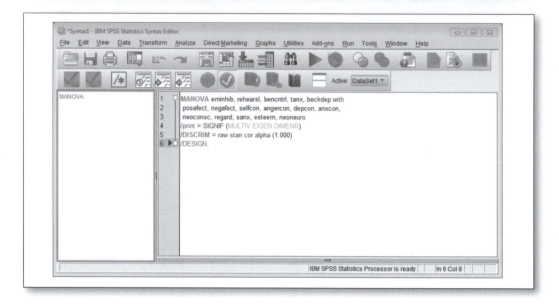

which will ordinarily limit the number of extracted functions. Since it is useful to see the full solution, especially for illustration purposes, we are specifying an alpha level of **1.000**—this makes sure that all of the functions are extracted. To perform the analysis, select **Run ➔ All** from the main menu.

13B.2 Canonical Correlation: Overview of Output

Having performed the canonical correlation analysis through an older procedure, the format of the output is tied to older technology—courier font in tables that could be printed by the dot matrix printers of that bygone era. An example of this is shown in Figure 13b.2, where

Figure 13b.2 Number of Cases in the Analysis

```
419 cases accepted.
  0 cases rejected because of out-of-range factor values.
  6 cases rejected because of missing data.
  1 non-empty cell.

  1 design will be processed.
```

we obtain a count of our cases. Here, we have 419 cases in the analysis, with 6 cases being deleted because of missing values. If you cannot see all of the output that we describe below, double-click on it to expose everything.

13B.3 Canonical Correlation: Multivariate Tests of Significance

The multivariate tests of statistical significance are shown in Figure 13b.3. As we indicated in Section 13A.6, Roy's largest characteristic root is not evaluated for significance. Each of the others is translated into a multivariate *F* test, and each was found to be statistically significant. We may therefore conclude that there is a statistically significant relationship between the set of dependent variables and the set of predictors (covariates).

Figure 13b.3 Multivariate Tests of Statistical Significance

```
EFFECT .. WITHIN CELLS Regression
Multivariate Tests of Significance (S = 5, M = 2 1/2, N = 200 1/2)

Test Name         Value        Approx. F    Hypoth. DF    Error DF       Sig. of F

Pillais           1.55567       16.71141        55.00      2035.00          .000
Hotellings        6.48783       47.34934        55.00      2007.00          .000
Wilks              .06485       27.38228        55.00      1868.98          .000
Roys               .84221
```

The total amount of shared variance between the predictors and the dependent variables can be determined by examining the value of Wilks' lambda, which is .06485 in our example. This is the amount of variance remaining once we have taken into consideration the full set of canonical functions. In this instance, approximately 6.5% of the total variance of the dependent variable set is not shared and thus R_c^2—the total amount of shared variance—is approximately 93.5% (this is perhaps somewhat more variance than might typically be explained in most research studies).

13B.4 Canonical Correlation: Eigenvalues and Canonical Correlations

We present the table of **Eigenvalues and Canonical Correlations** in Figure 13b.4. In this analysis, there were five canonical functions or roots extracted, and each is given a row in the table. Five roots were extracted in that there were 5 dependent variables and 11 predictors, and the number of functions extracted is equal to the smaller set size.

Figure 13b.4 Eigenvalues and Canonical Correlations

```
Eigenvalues and Canonical Correlations

Root No.       Eigenvalue         Pct.      Cum. Pct.    Canon Cor.     Sq. Cor

    1            5.33760       82.27103     82.27103       .91772        .84221
    2             .87366       13.46610     95.73712       .68285        .46628
    3             .16230        2.50168     98.23881       .37369        .13964
    4             .07528        1.16032     99.39912       .26459        .07001
    5             .03898         .60088    100.00000       .19370        .03752
```

Each root (canonical function) has the following information associated with it as shown in each of the remaining five columns:

- *Eigenvalue:* This is the amount of variance associated with each canonical function. For example, the first function has an eigenvalue of 5.33760.

- *Percent of variance:* This is the percentage of shared variance (not the total variance) that is attributed to each function. In this case, the sum of the eigenvalues is 6.48782. The eigenvalue for the first function is 5.33760, which is approximately 82.27% of that total.

- *Cumulative percent of variance:* This is the amount of shared variance attributable to the first c functions. With only one function extracted, the cumulative percentage of shared variance is approximately 82.27%; with two functions extracted, we have reached better than 95% of the shared variance; and so on. When all five functions have been extracted, all of the shared (not the total) variance is accounted for.

- *Canonical correlation:* This is the canonical correlation between the dependent variate and the predictor variate of each function. For example, the first function has a canonical correlation value of .91772.

- *Squared canonical correlation:* This is the squared canonical correlation, which is also the theta value as described in Section 13A.5.3, for each function. For example, the first function has a squared canonical correlation or theta value of .84221, indicating that for the first root the predictor variate explained approximately 84% of the variance of the dependent variate. Note that this is the largest theta or squared canonical correlation (eigenvalue/1 + eigenvalue = 5.33760/6.33760 = .84221), and thus, it is the value taken on by Roy's largest characteristic root (see Figure 13b.3). The average of these squared canonical correlations (the mean of .84221, .46628, .13964, .07001, and .03752) is the value of Cramer–Nicewander's index, a value in this instance of approximately .312. We would thus infer that the set of predictor variates accounted for approximately 31% of the variance of the dependent variates.

13B.5 Canonical Correlation: Dimension Reduction Analysis

The **Dimension Reduction Analysis** is shown in Figure 13b.5. This analysis assesses the statistical significance of the canonical functions using Wilks' lambda. The way in which it assesses significance may seem a bit indirect, but it works in the same way that we have seen in the case of evaluating discriminant functions (see Section 11A.9.3). Each row of the table tests the significance of a set of functions in a reductionistic manner (hence the name of the analysis). Here is what the output reveals row by row:

Figure 13b.5 Dimension Reduction Analysis

Dimension Reduction Analysis

Roots	Wilks L.	F	Hypoth. DF	Error DF	Sig. of F
1 TO 5	.06485	27.38228	55.00	1868.98	.000
2 TO 5	.41102	10.13255	40.00	1533.78	.000
3 TO 5	.77010	4.10124	27.00	1183.45	.000
4 TO 5	.89510	2.89152	16.00	812.00	.000
5 TO 5	.96248	2.26664	7.00	407.00	.028

- The first row tests the statistical significance of the entire set of functions (**Roots 1 TO 5**). The Wilks' lambda is .06485, its *F* value is 27.38228, and it is statistically significant. We thus learn that the entire set of functions is statistically significant. Thus, akin to what we have seen in dealing with discriminant functions, at least the first function (the one accounting for more variance than any of the others) is statistically significant.

- The second row tests the statistical significance of the second, third, fourth, and fifth functions taken together (**Roots 2 TO 5**). The Wilks' lambda is .41102 (there is more unexplained variance), its *F* value is 10.13255, and it is statistically significant. We thus learn that this set of functions is still statistically significant and may conclude that at least the second function was statistically significant.

- The third row tests the statistical significance of the third, fourth, and fifth functions taken together (**Roots 3 TO 5**). The Wilks' lambda is .77010 (there is still more unexplained variance), its *F* value is 4.10124, and it is statistically significant. We thus learn that this set of functions is still significant and may conclude that at least the third function was statistically significant.

- The fourth row tests the statistical significance of the fourth and fifth functions taken together (**Roots 4 TO 5**). The Wilks' lambda is .89510, its *F* value is 2.89152, and it is statistically significant. We thus learn that this set of functions is still statistically significant and may conclude that at least the fourth function in isolation was statistically significant.

- The fifth and last row tests the statistical significance of the fifth function in isolation (**Roots 5 TO 5**). The Wilks' lambda is .96248, its F value is 2.26664, and it is statistically significant using an alpha level of .05. We thus learn that this fifth function is statistically significant.

13B.6 Canonical Correlation: How Many Functions Should Be Interpreted?

We may have all five of the canonical functions reaching statistical significance, but it would be poor research judgment to interpret all of them. The picture painted by the eigenvalues, individual squared canonical correlations (see Figure 13b.4), and the values of Wilks' lambda for each of the functions (see Figure 13b.5) is relatively clear. We certainly want to interpret the first function as it accounts for the bulk of explained variance. Functions three through five are clearly adding very little explained variance and do not merit interpretation.

How to deal with the second function is less clear-cut. Some researchers would argue against interpreting it because its eigenvalue is below 1.00 and because it is not accounting for all that much of the explained variance. Our recommendation to those who are facing a similar set of results is to take a look at it and interpret it if it contributes to an understanding of the general issue under study. We take this position because it looks much more substantial than the last three functions and because canonical correlation analysis is an exploratory technique at best. As a consequence, researchers should not be drawing particularly powerful conclusions from such results but instead using them to formulate tentative models or generate some new ideas of how to better understand the phenomenon under study. Here, as a way to illustrate the process, we will interpret both the first and second canonical functions.

13B.7 Canonical Correlation: The Coefficients in the Output

Figure 13b.6 presents the coefficients for the dependent variables; the coefficients for the predictor variables are displayed in an analogous manner. The three types of coefficients are tabled in the following order: raw canonical coefficients, standardized canonical coefficients, and structure coefficients (labeled in the output as **Correlations between Dependent and canonical variables**). For our interpretation purposes, we want to focus on the structure coefficients for the dependent and the predictor variables.

Figure 13b.6 How the Coefficients Are Shown in the Output

This is the portion of the output table that pertains to the structure coefficients for the dependent variate.

Raw canonical coefficients for DEPENDENT variables
Function No.

Variable	1	2	3	4	5
eminhib	-.05137	.31811	.14378	.03675	-.01049
rehears1	-.04811	-.08336	.07231	.30633	.21231
bencntrl	.02682	.04404	-.33923	.22677	-.04481
tanx	-.06296	-.02819	-.02927	.01463	-.13073
beckdep	-.02924	.02865	-.08938	-.08947	.15519

Standardized canonical coefficients for DEPENDENT variables
Function No.

Variable	1	2	3	4	5
eminhib	-.15270	.94557	.42738	.10925	-.03119
rehears1	-.15007	-.26003	.22558	.95561	.66230
bencntrl	.07559	.12410	-.95600	.63907	-.12628
tanx	-.66759	-.29895	-.31036	.15508	-1.38619
beckdep	-.20253	.19844	-.61897	-.61964	1.07478

Correlations between DEPENDENT and canonical variables
Function No.

Variable	1	2	3	4	5
eminhib	-.38354	.88814	.19500	.15813	-.03279
rehears1	-.65178	-.26268	.23444	.55390	.38003
bencntrl	.50317	.33411	-.67295	.41043	-.11780
tanx	-.96538	-.12586	-.07720	-.01918	-.21419
beckdep	-.79546	.06457	-.31744	-.31324	.40520

13B.8 Canonical Correlation: Interpreting the Dependent Variates

Figure 13b.7 shows the structure coefficients for the five dependent canonical variates separated from the larger table of Figure 13b.6. We approach each variate (column) as we would approach the component or factor "loadings"—higher values of the structure coefficients indicate a stronger relationship between the individual variable and the variate as a whole.

Each column provides the structure coefficients for the function whose number appears at the top of the column. Researchers examine the set of coefficients for each function with an eye toward interpreting what construct is depicted by the function. In this way, researchers impose meaning on the numeric output and can exercise a certain amount of synthesis and creativity.

Figure 13b.7 Structure Coefficients for the Dependent Variates

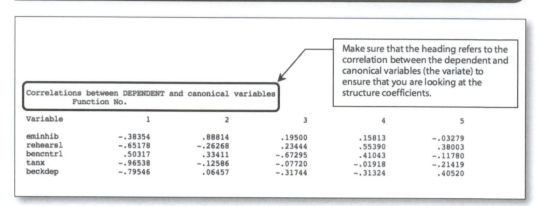

For the first dependent canonical function (for the column labeled as **1**), the variate appears to be indicated by (in order of the magnitude of the structure coefficients) the following:

- Lower levels of trait anxiety (**tanx** with a structure coefficient of −.96538)
- Lower levels of depression (**beckdep** with a structure coefficient of −.79546)
- Lower levels of rehearsal—the tendency to repeatedly play out mentally actions that will be taken in the future (**rehearsl** with a structure coefficient of −.65178)
- Higher levels of benign control—the tendency to control behavior and thoughts in a positive manner (**bencntrl** with a structure coefficient of .50317)

One interpretation of this variate might be that it represents emotional stability.

The second dependent canonical variate is indicated primarily by greater levels of emotional inhibition (**eminhib** with a structure coefficient of .88814).

13B.9 Canonical Correlation: Interpreting the Predictor Variates

Figure 13b.8 shows the structure coefficients for the five predictor canonical variates. We approach each variate (column) as we did for the dependent variates. The first predictor canonical variate appears to be indicated by (in order of the magnitude of the structure coefficients) the following:

- Lower levels of neuroticism (**neoneuro** with a structure coefficient of −.88888)
- Higher levels of self-esteem (**esteem** with a structure coefficient of .83675)

Figure 13b.8   Structure Coefficients for the Predictor Variates

```
Correlations between COVARIATES and canonical variables
         CAN. VAR.

Covariate            1             2             3             4             5

posafect          .58990       -.09613        .23934       -.17690        .17053
negafect         -.79124       -.29686        .23223        .32817        .13512
selfcon           .54155        .08532       -.53906        .10113        .07169
angercon         -.29249        .73501        .06135        .20492       -.20989
depcon           -.39252        .79639        .25847        .02062        .02788
anxcon           -.29249        .55255        .11547        .09506        .33012
neoconsc          .38275        .10460       -.50310        .48652        .25602
regard            .70462       -.02086        .04067       -.00525       -.16759
sanx             -.73941       -.05921       -.19736       -.39718       -.07172
esteem            .83675       -.10077        .08230        .08619       -.27465
neoneuro         -.88888       -.15107        .05012        .10774       -.24387
```

- Lower levels of negative affect (**negafect** with a structure coefficient of −.79124)
- Lower levels of state anxiety (**sanx** with a structure coefficient of −.73941)
- Higher levels of self-regard (**regard** with a structure coefficient of .70462)
- Higher levels of positive affect (**posafect** with a structure coefficient of .58990)
- Higher levels of self-control (**selfcon** with a structure coefficient of .54155)

One interpretation of this variate is that it might represent something akin to a positive attitude toward self.

The second predictor canonical variate appears to be indicated by the following:

- Higher levels of depression control—the tendency to actively control and suppress feelings of depression (**depcon** with a structure coefficient of .79639)
- Higher levels of anger control—the tendency to actively control and suppress feelings of anger (**angercon** with a structure coefficient of .73501)
- Higher levels of anxiety control—the tendency to actively control and suppress feelings of anxiety (**anxcon** with a structure coefficient of .55255)

This variate appears to represent control of certain negative feelings.

13B.10 Canonical Correlation: Interpreting the Canonical Functions

We are now ready to interpret the canonical functions by bringing into one sentence for each function what we have said about the dependent and predictor portions of it already. The interpretations, not earthshaking and perhaps almost trivial because of our example data set, are as follows:

- The first function appears to indicate that a positive attitude toward self is predictive of emotional stability.
- The second function appears to indicate that controlling certain negative feelings associated with depression, anger, and anxiety is predictive of general emotional inhibition.

13B.11 Reporting Canonical Correlation Analysis Results

A canonical correlation analysis was used to explore the relationships between sets of personality variables. The dependent variables were emotional inhibition, rehearsal, benign control, trait anxiety, and depression. The predictor variables were positive affect, negative affect, self-concept, anger control, depression control, anxiety control, conscientiousness, self-regard, state anxiety, self-esteem, and neuroticism.

With 419 cases in the analysis, the relationship between the sets of variables was statistically significant, Wilks' lambda = .06, R_c^2 = .94, Approximate $F(55, 1868.98)$ = 27.38, $p < .001$. All five functions were extracted. Eigenvalues, percentages of variance explained, and the squared canonical correlations for each function are shown in Table 13b.1. The first function accounted for approximately 82% of the explained variance, and the second function added somewhat more than 13% to that. The dimension reduction analysis indicated that all five functions were statistically significant, but only the first two, which cumulatively accounted for more than 95% of the explained variance, were interpreted. Based on the Cramer–Nicewander (1979) index, it appears that approximately 31% of the variance of the dependent variates was explained by the predictor variates.

The structure coefficients for the first two functions for the predictor and dependent variables are shown in Tables 13b.2 and 13b.3, respectively. The first predictor function is associated with lower levels of neuroticism, negative affect, and state anxiety and higher levels of self-esteem, self-regard, positive affect, and self-control; the first dependent function is associated with lower levels of trait anxiety, depression, and rehearsal (the tendency to repeatedly play out mentally actions that will be taken in the future). Taken together, the first function appears to indicate that a positive attitude toward self is predictive of emotional stability.

The second predictor function is associated with higher levels of depression control, anger control, and anxiety control (the tendency to actively control and suppress these feelings); the second dependent function is associated with higher levels of emotional control. This second function appears to indicate that controlling certain negative feelings associated with depression, anger, and anxiety is predictive of general emotional inhibition.

Table 13b.1 Eigenvalues, Cumulative Percentage of Explained Variance, and Squared Canonical Correlations for Each Canonical Function

Function	Eigenvalue	Percent Variance Explained	Squared Canonical Correlation
1	5.34	82.27	.84
2	0.87	13.47	.47
3	0.16	2.50	.14
4	0.08	1.16	.07
5	0.04	0.60	.04

Table 13b.2 Structure Coefficients for the First Two Predictor Canonical Variates

Predictor Variable	Function 1	Function 2
Positive Affect	.59	−.10
Negative Affect	−.79	−.30
Self-Control	.54	.09
Anger Control	−.29	.74
Depression Control	−.40	.80
Anxiety Control	−.29	.55
Conscientiousness	.38	.10
Self-Regard	.70	−.02
State Anxiety	−.74	−.06
Self-Esteem	.84	−.10
Neuroticism	−.89	−.15

Table 13b.3 Structure Coefficients for the First Two Dependent Canonical Variates

Dependent Variable	Function 1	Function 2
Emotional Inhibition	−.38	.89
Rehearsal	−.65	−.26
Benign Control	.50	.33
Trait Anxiety	−.97	−.13
Depression	−.80	.06

Multidimensional Scaling

14A.1 Overview

14A.1.1 The Nature of the Analysis

Multidimensional scaling (MDS) is a set of statistical techniques used to model (describe) the dimensional structure underlying a set of objects or stimuli. It was introduced and named by Warren S. Torgerson (1952, 1958) and advanced by Shepard (1962) and Kruskal (1964a). More complete descriptions of MDS can be found in Borg and Groenen (2005), Davison (1983), Giguère (2007), Kruskal and Wish (1978), Lattin et al. (2003), Schiffman, Reynolds, and Young (1981), Stalans (1995), Takane, Jung, and Oshima-Takane (2009), Young and Hamer (1987, 1994), and Young and Harris (2008).

The focus of MDS is on the degree to which objects or stimuli are dissimilar to each other. Dissimilarity data can take on several different forms that we will describe in Section 14A.6, but the common element is that dissimilarity is an index of the relative distance between objects (the proximity of the objects to each other)—objects more dissimilar are further apart. These objects are then arranged in multidimensional space based on their dissimilarity. The space is defined by the number of dimensions it contains, and it is up to the researchers to specify the number of dimensions they select to represent an acceptable structure or solution.

At a very global level, the dimensions in MDS resemble a factor structure as described in Chapters 12A and 12B in that researchers strive to interpret the dimensions. But because we are working with dissimilarity data in MDS, the "feel" of the analysis and interpretation of the results differs from principal components/factor analysis. One of the striking differences between principal components/factor analysis and MDS is that, in a major application of MDS, raters in the data collection process are asked to compare pairs of objects or stimuli so as to provide the researchers with dissimilarity judgments. Furthermore, none of the strong assumptions required for proper interpretation of the results from procedures based on the general model add linear are applicable to MDS.

14A.1.2 Some Constraints on
the Interpretation of the Solution

Because objects are being compared on the extent of their dissimilarity, the following features or issues apply to MDS:

- The objects should be members of the same class of entities (e.g., music types, brands of cars, department stores, cities) so that a comparison of similarity/dissimilarity (proximity) can meaningfully be made.

- If raters are involved, they must be sufficiently familiar with the objects so that they can meaningfully make the requested comparisons (typically by using a summative response scale assessing degree of perceived dissimilarity). For example, if the stimuli were a set of major personality theorists (e.g., Freud, Allport, Bandura), it would be unreasonable to ask a group of chemistry undergraduate majors to rate the dissimilarities of the theories, but it would be appropriate to have a group of clinical psychology graduate students accomplish that task.

- If objective data are used, a measure must be selected such that it is meaningful to assess proximity with it. For example, in comparing cities, it is reasonable (if not obvious) to use the number of miles between cities as a measure of distance.

- The dimensions along which the objects are arrayed in the MDS solution are interpreted in terms of the characteristics along which the objects are similar and/or different.

14A.1.3 Fitting Dimensions to the Data

MDS uses the proximity information in the data to configure the objects in the space defined by the number of dimensions specified by the researchers. By examining how the objects are arrayed in the given space, and knowing the "true" distances between the objects (information contained in the raw data), the MDS procedure is able to (a) determine how good the fit is between the array and the data and (b) rearrange the configuration to improve the fit. The goal of the MDS procedure is to settle on a configuration that maximizes the goodness of fit.

14A.2 The Paired Comparison Method

Comparing stimuli by having raters judge which member of a pair has more (or less) of a quality has a long and rich history. Gustov Fechner (1860) developed a method called *constant stimuli* in which a set of *comparison* stimuli were each separately compared with a *standard* stimulus. On one trial, observers would be presented with two stimuli, one of which was the standard stimulus and the other was one of the comparison stimuli, and were to indicate which stimulus had a greater intensity (e.g., which weight was heavier or which sound was louder). On another trial, observers would again be presented with the standard stimulus, but this time it was paired with one of the other comparison stimuli, and again, they were to indicate which had the greater intensity. Trials would continue in this manner with several measurements taken for each standard stimulus–comparison stimulus pairing. Fechner used the outcome of these measurements to estimate the difference threshold for the standard stimulus (the intensity that was just noticeably more or less intense) and to generate a quantitative relationship between the intensity of the physical stimulus and the psychological representation of it. Sixteen years later (in 1876) in his study of aesthetics, Fechner asked his subjects to evaluate their preferences for certain geometric figures (rectangles and triangles); this aesthetics research stands as a historical bridge between his original psychophysical methods and the paired comparisons method.

The *method of paired comparisons* was introduced in 1894 by a German researcher named J. Cohn (cited in Gescheider, 1977, and Woodworth & Schlosberg, 1954) in an article published in Wilhelm Wundt's *Philosophical Studies*. In Cohn's procedure, every stimulus (a colored card) in a set was paired with every other stimulus in that set. On each trial, an observer judged which of the two stimuli possessed more of a characteristic (e.g., which of the two colors was preferred). This was a more complex procedure than what Fechner had done in 1860 and 1876, but by pairing every stimulus with every other stimulus, a good deal of information could be obtained. Cohn's procedure became reasonably well-known in short order. For example, Wundt used the method in his research on feelings (Titchener, 1908), and Titchener (1901) constructed one of the experiments in his laboratory manual to study affect using this method; for both Wundt and Titchener, observers were shown pairs of squares of different colors and were asked to indicate which was more pleasant.

The method of paired comparisons achieved widespread recognition in the hands of Louis L. Thurstone when he introduced the law of comparative judgment (Thurstone, 1927a) as a way to transform paired comparison data into interval-level measurement. Thurstone applied the paired comparisons method to study attitudes by having his participants rate socially relevant features of the stimuli rather than the preferences for or the pleasantness of colors as Cohn and Titchener, respectively, proposed. For example, Thurstone (1927b) presented his raters with various criminal offenses (e.g., burglary, arson, kidnapping, homicide) and had them indicate which one of the pair was the more serious offense.

14A.3 Dissimilarity Data in MDS

The MDS procedure is performed on data representing the dissimilarities between pairs of stimuli. These dissimilarities are very often assessed in the form of subjective appraisals about the degree of likeness (similarity) or unlikeness (dissimilarity) between a pair of objects. For example, respondents might indicate how similar or different various types of music are (e.g., rock, pop, jazz, classical, and hip-hop). However, dissimilarity data can also be based on other forms of assessment. For example, we can use objectively measured dissimilarities between pairs of objects such as the flying or driving distance (in miles) between pairs of cities, and dissimilarities can also be calculated from frequencies of occurrences or choices between pairs of individuals or variables.

14A.4 Similarity/Dissimilarity Conceived as an Index of Distance

In the context of covering principal components analysis in Section 12A.9.1, we discussed the idea that correlation can be conceived as a measure of distance. By analogous reasoning, dissimilarity can also be viewed as an index of distance. If several stimuli are contained in a multidimensional space, then stimuli that are more similar to each other can be depicted by being placed closer to each other and stimuli that are more dissimilar to each other can be depicted by being placed further from each other.

MDS analyzes dissimilarities as distance-like data by mapping each object as a point in a multidimensional space (typically two or three dimensions). These data are sometimes referred to as *proximity* or *dissimilarly* data and can be arrayed in a *proximity matrix* (or *dissimilarity matrix*). A fictional illustration of a proximity matrix is shown in Table 14a.1. Assume that some college students compared five different types of music. Ratings were completed on a 9-point summative response scale, where 1 represented *very similar* and 9 represented *very dissimilar*. Thus, Pop music and Hip-Hop were judged as relatively similar, whereas Jazz and Rock were judged as relatively dissimilar.

Table 14a.1   Proximity Matrix for Dissimilarity Ratings for Five Types of Music

Variable	Hip-Hop	Pop	Jazz	Classical	Rock
Hip-Hop	–	2	5	9	4
Pop		–	8	9	3
Jazz			–	5	8
Classical				–	9
Rock					–

Note. All pairs of music types compared on summative response scale (1 = *Very Similar* to 9 = *Very Dissimilar*).

14A.5 Dimensionality in MDS

As the term implies, MDS represents the stimuli along dimensions of the multidimensional space in which the stimuli are arrayed. We usually limit ourselves to two or three dimensions so that we can more easily conceptualize the results of the analysis. To illustrate this, Figure 14a.1 presents the five types of music shown in the dissimilarity matrix arranged in a two-dimensional space. Based on the array, researchers attempt to interpret the dimensions.

Figure 14a.1 Hypothetical Multidimensional Space of Average Dissimilarity Ratings for Five Types of Music

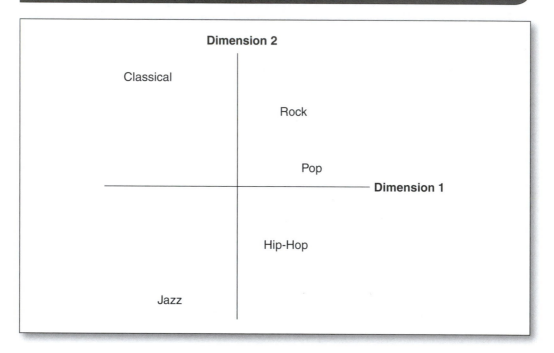

For Dimension 1, Pop, Rock, and Hip-Hop are located more toward the right pole, and Classical and Jazz are located more toward the left pole. One possible interpretation is that it might represent a sort of populist dimension, with the right pole capturing more of a popular or mass appeal and the left pole capturing more of an academic or esoteric appeal.

For Dimension 2, Classical and Rock are located more toward the top pole, and Jazz and, to a certain extent, Hip-Hop are located more toward the bottom pole. One possible interpretation is that it might represent a sort of structural dimension, with the top pole capturing music that followed certain structural rules and the bottom pole capturing music that could be of a more improvisational nature.

We can also speak about the music as being located in certain quadrants. For example, we might say that Classical music is quite structured and esoteric, whereas Jazz can be quite improvisational and somewhat esoteric.

MDS as a statistical technique is used to depict perceptions of the similarity of a set of objects. The utility of MDS is particularly helpful in identifying concepts, dimensions, and social/psychological structure in embryonic domains (Giguère, 2007). Regardless of how these dissimilarity perceptions are captured, these data are relegated to a single (aggregated) matrix of paired dissimilarities or multiple (disaggregated) matrices of individual respondent dissimilarity judgments. From these measures or judgments of dissimilarity that are assembled in the proximity matrix (or matrices), an MDS technique is employed that estimates the relative position of each object in multidimensional space given a specified number of dimensions in that space. Pairs of objects with scores that indicate greater similarity will be depicted as closer together in multidimensional space, and objects assessed as dissimilar will be located farther apart.

There are some limitations to the interpretation of the solutions generated by MDS that are worth noting, although they should not be taken as reasons not to perform the analysis. First, the dimensions that emerge from the analysis reflect the specific objects used in the data collection. In our music example, for instance, the dimensional structure might be somewhat different if we had included other music types in the ratings. Second, interpretation of a dimension might be a bit ambiguous, in that one researcher might offer one interpretation and a second researcher might offer another somewhat different interpretation. Finally, even if the solutions yield interpretable dimensions, they may not be informative to theory or even generally all that interesting.

14A.6 Data Collection Methods

Because the data collection methods are somewhat unique when an individual evaluates the perceived similarity or dissimilarity of two objects or stimuli, we will briefly consider some of the most popular methods employed by investigators. Takane et al. (2009) have dichotomized these techniques into the two broad classifications of *direct judgments* and *indirect judgments*, and we follow their dichotomy in the following discussion.

14A.6.1 Direct Judgment Methods

Most MDS studies employ some type of direct judgment of dissimilarity. We briefly note four types.

14A.6.1.1 Direct Judgment: Rating Methods

Rating methods reflect perhaps the most typical MDS data collection technique, where respondents are asked to evaluate the degree of similarity or dissimilarity between two objects (or stimuli) by means of a rating scale. This method results in a symmetric matrix of dissimilarities that will take the form of $(n(n-1))/2$, where $n=$ the number of objects being evaluated. For example, respondents could be asked to evaluate their perceptions of pairs of local department stores on a 9-point summative response scale, where 1 represents *very similar* and 9 represents *very dissimilar*. Stimuli or objects are typically presented in random orderings for each respondent to reduce the possibility of presentation order bias.

14A.6.1.2 Direct Judgment: Multiple Ratio Methods

These are variations of the method of constant stimuli devised by Fechner described in Section 14A.2. Multiple ratio (also referred to as *magnitude estimation* tasks) methods have their roots in early psychophysical investigations (e.g., Stevens, 1971; Torgerson, 1958). In these tasks, a stimulus or stimulus pair serves as a standard or reference object on each trial. Participants are asked to make dissimilarity judgments between the standard and a series of experimental stimuli (e.g., tones varying in loudness).

14A.6.1.3 Direct Judgment: Rank-Order Methods

The most typical method in the rank-order genre is the *conditional rank-ordering* task. This task also employs a standard object or stimulus. One object in a set is designated as the standard, and the participant is asked to pick the most dissimilar object among the remaining objects. Once selected, that object is given the highest rank and is excluded from the comparison set. Participants once again select from the reduced set the object that is most dissimilar to the standard. That object is then given the second highest rank and is excluded from the comparison set. This comparison process is done in an iterative fashion until a complete set of ranked dissimilarity judgments have been made.

14A.6.1.4 Direct Judgment: Sorting Methods

Sorting methods have participants sorting or dividing a set of objects into as many categories of dissimilarity as they choose. Pairs of objects in the same category or subgroup are coded as "1," and pairs of objects from different groups are coded as "0" (Giguère, 2007; Schiffman et al., 1981).

14A.6.2 Indirect Methods

As the name implies, indirect methods employ circuitous routes to obtain dissimilarity data. Often, dissimilarity is a function of a participant's performance on a discrimination judgment task.

14A.6.2.1 Indirect Methods: Confusion Data Methods

These confusion methods are sometimes referred to as *same–different* judgment tasks. In a typical study, participants are presented in very brief exposures (fractions of a second) with pairs of stimuli (e.g., two uppercase letters) and are asked to judge whether they are the same or different (on some trials, the same letter will be presented, but on other trials, the two letters will be different). One underlying assumption of these methods is that more physically similar pairs of objects will be, the more difficult it will be to discriminate them. Hence, letters that are often confused are considered relatively similar, whereas letters that are seldom confused are considered relatively dissimilar. For example, observers will relatively often confuse the letters (fail to accurately detect the differences between) O and Q, E and F, and V and U, but they will hardly ever confuse A and R, M and F, and Y and P (Townsend, 1971). Confusability can therefore be deemed to be a measure of dissimilarity (Giguère, 2007)—that is, stimuli not easily confused can be thought of as relatively dissimilar, and stimuli easily confused can be thought of as relatively similar. Alternatively, confusion matrices can be developed where the proportion of stimuli misjudged as another stimulus becomes the measure of dissimilarity.

14A.6.2.2 Indirect Methods: Frequency of Co-Occurrence Methods

Respondent frequency data can be used to provide dissimilarity data. For example, famous politicians (e.g., Obama and Clinton) can be assessed in terms of perceived personality traits. Individuals who share more traits in common can be considered more similar, and conversely, individuals who share fewer personality traits are more dissimilar. It is also possible to use the frequency of social interactions to determine intimacy dissimilarity (Takane et al., 2009).

14A.6.2.3 Indirect Methods: Reaction Time

Many of the same–different (confusion method) tasks employ reaction time (typically recorded in milliseconds) as the measure of dissimilarity. The assumption is that more "cognitive work" is involved in discriminating between two similar stimuli than is involved in discriminating between two dissimilar stimuli. A further assumption is that more cognitive processing will result in longer times before participants can reach a decision, and thus, shorter reaction times presumably indicate greater stimulus dissimilarity and longer reaction times presumably indicate greater stimulus similarity.

14A.7 Similarity Versus Dissimilarity

MDS is a set of statistical tools for the analysis of similarity or dissimilarity data, often collectively referred to as *proximity* data to underscore that the data represent the distance between stimuli or object points in a multidimensional space. Proximity data are best "captured" as dissimilarities because "similarities are not as robust as dissimilarities for the SPSS Statistics Multidimensional Scaling procedure" (Young & Harris, 2008, p. 351). Therefore, most MDS practitioners convert their similarity data into dissimilarity values so that greater perceived dissimilarities are associated with greater perceived distances (Giguère, 2007).

14A.8 Distance Models

14A.8.1 Euclidian Distance Between Objects

Objects or stimuli in an MDS analysis are represented as points in a multidimensional space. Objects that are viewed as more similar are located closer together and objects that are more dissimilar are located farther apart from each other. The multidimensional space (sometimes called the *perceptual map*) that chronicles this configuration of proximities is typically realized by means of a *Euclidean distance model* or one of its offshoots. Other models such as the *city block distance model* will not be examined in this chapter but are described by Attneave (1950) and Hubert, Arabie, and Hesson-Mcinnis (1992). We also discuss a range of distance models, including city block, in Section 15A.3.5 of our chapter on clustering.

Euclidean distance provides a familiar framework for representing the distance between objects. Consider the two points shown in Figure 14a.2. These points are in the two-dimensional space defined by Dimensions 1 and 2. The location of points is given by a coordinate in which its position is defined by its value on Dimension 1 and Dimension 2, respectively. Thus, in Figure 14a.2, one point lies at the coordinate (2, 5), and the other point lies at coordinate (4, 3).

The distance between the two points, labeled as C in Figure 14a.2, is the hypotenuse of the right triangle ABC (Giguère, 2007; Young & Harris, 2008). This distance can be computed by the Pythagorean theorem ($C^2 = A^2 + B^2$, with C being the value of the square root of $[A^2 + B^2]$). The distance B can be computed as the distance between the Dimension 1 values of the two points; in our example that would be $4 - 2$, or 2. The distance A can be computed as the distance between the Dimension 2 values of the two points; in our example that would be $5 - 3$, or 2. Now we have the following:

$$C^2 = 2^2 + 2^2$$

$$C^2 = 4 + 4$$

$$C^2 = 8$$

$$C = 2.828$$

A common variant of the Euclidian distance model is the *weighted Euclidean distance model*. As we will see in Section 14A.10.3, this type of distance model is employed when

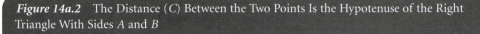

Figure 14a.2 The Distance (*C*) Between the Two Points Is the Hypotenuse of the Right Triangle With Sides *A* and *B*

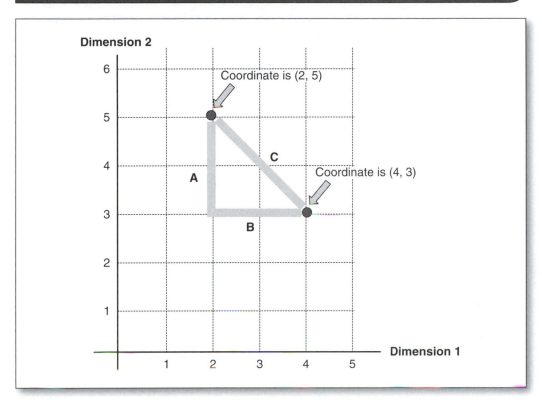

researchers collect proximity data from a group of participants but have reason to believe that there are systematic individual differences present among the data (Takane et al., 2009).

14A.8.2 Alternating Least Squares Scaling

Once the distances between the objects are determined, they are used in the MDS analysis. IBM SPSS utilizes the MDS algorithm known as *ALSCAL*. ALSCAL stands for alternating least squares scaling and was created by Takane, Young, and de Leeuw (1977). Alternating least squares is a more sophisticated variation of the ordinary least squares strategy described in Section 7A.4. According to Takane et al. (1977),

The alternating least squares (ALS) method is a general approach to parameter estimation which involves subdividing the parameters into several subsets, and then obtaining least squares estimates for one of the parameter subsets under the assumption that all remaining parameters are in fact known constants. The estimation is then alternately repeated for first one subset and then another until all subsets have been so estimated. This entire process is then iterated until convergence (which is assured) is obtained. (p. 18)

The procedure locates the coordinates for each object and configures them in the multidimensional space of a given number of dimensions such that the calculated distances between points (sometimes referred to as *disparities*) coincide with the original dissimilarity judgments respondents made between pairs of objects (Giguère, 2007; Jaworska & Chupetlovska-Anastasova, 2009; Young & Harris, 2008).

14A.9 A Classification Schema for MDS Techniques

MDS techniques can be conceptualized on the basis of three data characteristics (e.g., Arce & Garling, 1989; Giguère, 2007; Young & Hamer, 1987; Young & Harris, 2008):

- The measurement level of data
- The "shape" of the data
- The type of conditionality present in the data matrix

Each characteristic will be examined briefly.

14A.9.1 Measurement Level of Data

Proximity data used in MDS analyses, as in other multivariate statistical techniques, range between nominal and ordinal on one hand (known jointly as *nonmetric* measurement) and summative response and interval- and ratio-level data on the other (known jointly as *metric* measurement). Although any level of dissimilarity data can be examined with MDS, nominal-level analyses are fairly rare and will not be addressed in this chapter; hence, the major distinction of relevance here is between ordinal-level dissimilarity data on one hand and summative response and interval- and ratio-level data on the other.

14A.9.2 Data Shape

In MDS, *data shape* refers to the type of matrix in which the proximities or dissimilarities data are configured. Data shapes can be either *square* or *rectangular*. Square data can be further classified into *symmetric* or *asymmetric*.

Square data (both symmetric and asymmetric) utilize rows and columns that contain the same set of objects (e.g., city names, department stores, movie stars). Hence, these data reflect dissimilarity between pairs of objects (Young & Harris, 2008) because all of the objects are compared with each other. Data are said to be *symmetric* if the order of presentation of objects (or stimuli) has no appreciable effect on respondents' dissimilarity judgments. For example, the rated dissimilarity of Target versus Nordstrom department stores should be the same as Nordstrom versus Target. Conversely, if presentation order affects dissimilarity judgments, then the data are *asymmetric.*

We have *rectangular* data when the objects designated by the rows of the matrix do not coincide with the columns (Giguère, 2007). For example, the rows could represent individual respondents (e.g., community mental health clients), and the columns could represent separate subscale scores on various clinical outcome measures. These data are always asymmetric, and the resulting MDS configurations are "often not robust" (Young & Harris, 2008, p. 341). Rectangular data with MDS will not be emphasized in this chapter.

14A.9.3 Data Matrix Conditionality

The conditionality of the data matrix is primarily a function of the role of two elements (Giguère, 2007):

- The extent to which individual differences are assumed to be present
- The shape of the data

Three conditionality states can be evidenced:

- *Matrix conditional:* Data matrices are *matrix conditional* when the dissimilarities within a specific matrix can be directly compared with one another because each object is measured on the same scale but cannot be compared with other data matrices because of the assumed individual differences among participants. Most dissimilarity data are considered conditional.

- *Matrix unconditional:* Data matrices are *matrix unconditional* when the dissimilarities within a specific matrix can be directly compared with one another because each object is measured on the same scale and can be compared with other data matrices because of the negligible individual differences among participants.

- *Row conditional:* Data matrices are considered *row conditional* when meaningful comparisons for asymmetric and rectangular matrices can be made among only the rows of each matrix. For example, if the evaluations were of martial arts forms contestants, the master judge ratings would comprise the rows, and the individual forms contestants would occupy separate column locations in a rectangular matrix.

14A.10 Types of MDS Models

14A.10.1 Classical MDS

When a single matrix of dissimilarities (or a single matrix that is averaged across participants) is utilized (based on either metric or nonmetric data) to perform the analysis, it is referred to as *Classical MDS* (CMDS). Examples of CMDS would be a matrix of flying distances (in miles) among several California cities or a matrix of department store dissimilarity judgments averaged over 20 participants. The IBM SPSS ALSCAL algorithm creates a multidimensional space given the specified number of dimensions that best aligns with the original dissimilarity data. In metric CMDS, this alignment is accomplished by linearly transforming the raw dissimilarity data by means of the following equation (Young & Harris, 2008):

$$\text{Linear transformation of } \mathbf{S} = \mathbf{D}^2 + \mathbf{E}$$

In this equation, the linear transformation of the dissimilarity matrix ($\mathbf{S}$) equals the fitting of the squared Euclidean distances ($\mathbf{D}^2$) by the ALSCAL algorithm plus the sum of the squared errors ($\mathbf{E}$) or residuals between the original dissimilarity judgments and the computed disparities.

For nonmetric CMDS, the alignment of the multidimensional space with the original dissimilarly data is accomplished by a monotonic transformation of the raw dissimilarity data. A monotonic transformation is one that preserves the rank order of the values although the intervals between the values may not be preserved. Nonmetric CMDS minimization algorithms (minimizing the discrepancy between the distances in the array and those represented in the raw data—that is, maximizing goodness of fit) are more difficult to achieve due to their iterative nature and require more computer resources (Young & Harris, 2008). The equation, analogous to metric CMDS, is as follows (Young & Harris, 2008):

$$\text{Monotonic transformation of } \mathbf{S} = \mathbf{D}^2 + \mathbf{E}$$

14A.10.2 Replicated MDS

Replicated MDS (RMDS) was developed to extend the MDS analysis to multiple matrices of dissimilarity data (McGee, 1968). In RMDS, Euclidean distances are produced for each matrix of dissimilarities (e.g., for each respondent) under the assumption that the multidimensional space (perceptual map) is the *same* for each matrix (or respondent). As in CMDS, a single multidimensional configuration is produced. Because each matrix in RMDS is assumed to be a "replicate" of each other, no systematic differences are assumed other than individual response biases to the original dissimilarity scale (Young & Harris,

2008). The equations, analogous to what we described for CMDS, are as follows (Young & Harris, 2008):

For metric RMDS:

$$\text{Linear ransformation of } \mathbf{S}_k = \mathbf{D}^2 + \mathbf{E}_k$$

For nonmetric RMDS:

$$\text{Monotonic transformation of } \mathbf{S}_k = \mathbf{D}^2 + \mathbf{E}_k$$

In the above equations, *k* is the dissimilarity matrix for each respondent.

The point to remember about RMDS is that a linear or monotonic transformation of the individual dissimilarity matrices provides a method for accounting for any possible response bias on the part of each respondent (e.g., not considering all points on a 9-point Likert-type response scale) since all matrices are considered to be related (except for error) in the final establishment of a common multidimensional space (Giguère, 2007; Young & Harris, 2008).

14A.10.3 Weighted MDS

Weighted MDS (WMDS; also known as *individual differences scaling* or *INDSCAL*) extends CMDS to the multiple matrix situation (as does RMDS); however, WMDS does not assume that the multidimensional configuration is the same for each matrix (i.e., for each respondent). Hence, WMDS allows for differences (typically cognitive or perceptual) among the participants (as exhibited in the dissimilarity matrices) through the IBM SPSS ALSCAL algorithm by building the typical (unweighted) stimulus space configuration as well as a weighted stimulus space.

The *unweighted* space represents information that is shared or is common across individuals or matrices (Young & Harris, 2008). The *weighted* space (*W*), sometimes referred to as an individual's *personal stimulus space*, represents information about the stimulus structure that is *unique* to the individual. Weights can vary between 0.0 and 1.0 for each individual (*k*) on each dimension (*a*) of the stimulus, with larger W_{ka} weights indicating greater importance of the dimension to the individual and smaller-weight (W_{ka}) values indicating less importance (Young & Harris, 2008).

Carroll and Chang (1970) developed the first metric WMDS protocol. Takane et al. (1977) created the ALSCAL algorithm that incorporates both metric and nonmetric optimization solutions to proximity data used by IBM SPSS. The equations, analogous to what we described for RMDS, are as follows (Young & Harris, 2008):

For metric RMDS:

$$\text{Linear transformation of } \mathbf{S}_k = \mathbf{D}^2 + \mathbf{E}_k$$

WMDS creates M unique or individual distance matrices ($\mathbf{D}_k$) for each raw data matrix ($\mathbf{S}_k$). Thus, the equation is read as the M linear transformations of the data matrices ($\mathbf{S}_k$) is equal to the squared Euclidean distance for each matrix ($\mathbf{D}_k{}^2$) plus the sum of the squared errors for each matrix ($\mathbf{E}_k$).

For nonmetric RMDS:

$$\text{Monotonic transformation of } \mathbf{S}_k = \mathbf{D}^2 + \mathbf{E}_k$$

This is read as the M monotonic transformations of the data matrices ($\mathbf{S}_k$) is equal to the squared Euclidean distance for each matrix ($\mathbf{D}_k{}^2$) plus the error for each individual matrix ($\mathbf{E}_k$).

14A.10.4 A Decision Tree for Determining the Appropriate MDS Model

Figure 14a.3 provides a convenient heuristic for linking various data characteristics and MDS models (adapted from Giguère, 2007). The decision matrix helps researchers focus attention on important data characteristics such as shape, number of matrices, whether individual differences are salient, matrix conditionality, and the measurement level of the data in determining the appropriate MDS model. For example, if researchers working with several square matrices are assuming that there are enough individual differences to affect the proximity judgments and if their data matrices are conditional and have interval-level data, then they should use the metric WMDS procedure.

14A.11 Assessing Model Fit

One of the challenges of MDS analyses is to determine the degree of fit between the original dissimilarity data and the distance models used. Researchers need to assess the quality of fit in order to determine the confidence that they place in the interpretation of the results and how robust they judge the solution to be. IBM SPSS provides several MDS fit indexes.

14A.11.1 Stress as a Fit Index

The most common measure of fit is known as *Stress*. Kruskal (1964a, b) developed Stress as the difference between the input raw disparities and the output distances in the subsequent multidimensional map (Davison, 1983; Jawovska & Chupetlovska-Anastasova, 2009). Stress can vary between a maximum value of 1 and a minimum value of 0. As is true in everyday life, less stress is better. Although there are no hard-and-fast rules governing the interpretation of Stress values, Kruskal and Wish (1978) and Giguère (2007) have provided the heuristics that can be seen in Table 14a.2. Thus, in the absence of any other context,

Figure 14a.3 Giguère's (2007) Decision Matrix Relating Characteristics of the Data and Multidimensional Scaling Models

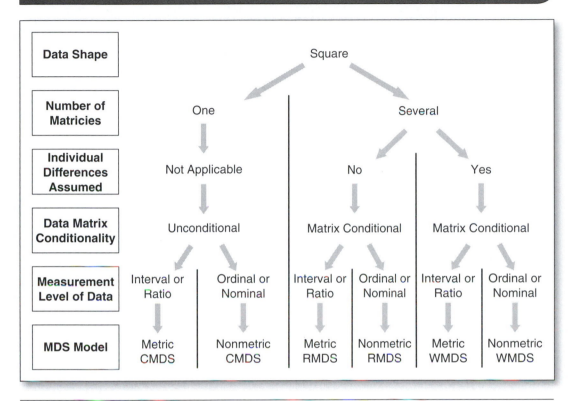

Source: Adapted from Giguère (2007).

Stress values below .10 are to be desired and Stress values above .20 should be of concern to researchers.

That said, caution should always be exercised when interpreting Stress values, as Stress values tend to increase with metric MDS models or high levels of data error and tend to decrease with nonmetric MDS models of the perceptual map (Giguère, 2007).

Stress is also a function of the number of dimensions that are used to represent the data. That is, any data set can be fit perfectly

Table 14a.2 Level of Fit for ranges of STRESS values

Fit Level	Stress Value Range
Perfect	.00
Excellent	.025 to ≤ .05
Good	.05 to ≤ .10
Fair	.10 to ≤ .20
Poor	> .20

Note. From Kruskal and Wish (1978) and Giguère (2007).

if we use $n - 1$ dimensions, where n is the number of objects being compared. But of course, we do not want to use that many dimensions as it defeats the purpose of trying to synthesize the information contained in the dissimilarities. Most of the time, we will attempt to map the data to two dimensions as it is the easiest to depict and interpret. In our desire to compress the relationships into two dimensions, we might very well raise the level of Stress observed in the fit.

14A.11.2 S-Stress as a Fit Index

A second measure of fit also produced with the IBM SPSS ALSCAL algorithm (for CMDS, RMDS, or WMDS) is called *S-stress*. It was originally developed by Takane et al. (1977) and creates an "iteration history," which includes, for each iteration, the S-stress value and its improvement over the previous iteration. S-stress is derived from the stress measure and differs only in that it is defined by means of squared distances and squared disparities (Davison, 1983). For RMDS or WMDS, the S-stress is adjusted to account for the multiple matrices (Giguère, 2007; Young & Harris, 2008). It should be noted that IBM SPSS optimizes (i.e., fits the model with) S-stress and not Stress (Young & Harris, 2008), and consequently, the Stress measure is only provided for the last iteration (which defaults in IBM SPSS at 30). Generally, the quality of the fit as indexed by S-stress is judged by the same rubric that is used for Stress.

14A.11.3 R^2 as a Fit Index

A third measure of fit that is commonly employed in MDS research is the *squared correlation index* or R^2 (note that IBM SPSS labels this as RSQ). RSQ indicates the amount of input data variance accounted for by the MDS model. A value of R^2 that is equal to or greater than .60 is typically considered an acceptable fit.

14A.11.4 The Weirdness Index as a Fit Index

As we noted previously, one important difference between weighted and unweighted Euclidean models is that WMDS produces both a group or collective multidimensional space and an individual space (derived from the group space) for each participant or matrix of data (see Giguère, 2007; Young & Harris, 2008, for details on the weighting algorithm used to produce each individual space). The *weirdness index* provides a means of evaluating individual participant weights used to create the individual multidimensional space by comparing each participant's weight or data matrix with the general configuration. Weirdness index values range from 0 to 1. A participant associated with a weirdness value of 0.00 indicates that his or her weights are proportional to the average weight of all the participants (hence they are considered typical). With larger values of the index, the participant is considered more atypical or "weird." Participants with weirdness index scores greater than .5 are considered outliers and are possible candidates for elimination from the analysis (Giguère, 2007).

14A.11.5 Goodness-of-Fit Graphs as a Fit Index

14A.11.5.1 Linear Fit Scatterplots

In CMDS, a perceptual map or multidimensional configuration is produced along with a default linear-fit scatterplot that depicts disparities (i.e., transformed data) against distances. A linear plot with little scatter reflects a good fit of the data. Sometimes increasing the number of IBM SPSS iterations can reduce the nonlinearity of this plot (Giguère, 2007).

14A.11.5.2 Transformation Scatterplots

In nonmetric MDS, a transformation scatterplot is produced that displays observations (original data) by disparities (transformed data). A smooth positive monotonic function indicates a good fit. If the function resembles a series of horizontal steps, then a *degenerate solution* is present and indicates a poor data fit. Nonmetric RMDS and WMDS provide separate transformation scatterplots for each participant or matrix. Participants with transformation scatterplots that are not monotonically positive can be considered outliers and are good candidates for elimination from the analysis (Giguère, 2007).

14A.11.5.3 Scree Plots

It is generally recommended that researchers perform multiple MDS analyses on the dataset, each time requesting a different number of dimensions as a solution (e.g., Giguère, 2007; Young & Harris, 2008). The IBM SPSS ALSCAL algorithm allows investigators to use from one to six dimensions (although two or three dimensions are most often used due to ease of interpretability). The goal of the researchers should be to capture the best fit of the data with the use of the fewest possible dimensions.

An effective way to compare solutions with different numbers of dimensions is with a *scree plot* (Cattell, 1966), directly analogous to what we discussed for eigenvalues in principal components analysis and factor analysis (see Section 12A.17.2). In the context of MDS, the scree plot is focused on S-stress values rather than eigenvalues, but its interpretation is consistent with how it is used in principal components analysis and factor analysis. We have provided an example of a scree plot in Figure 14a.4. The number of dimensions corresponding to the flattening of the plot, what some call the place where an "elbow" appears, usually indicates the maximum and perhaps appropriate number of dimensions researchers should select for their MDS solution configuration. However, a final determination of dimensionality

Figure 14a.4 An Example of a Scree Plot of S-Stress Values

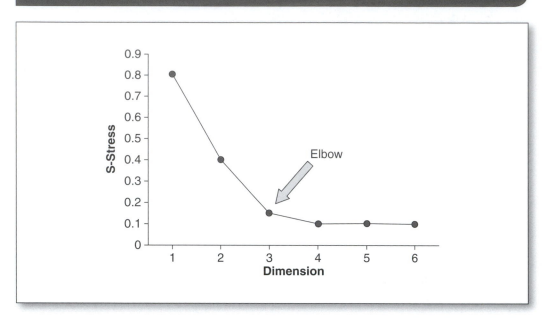

will always rest with the researchers and their ability to provide theoretically meaningful labels of each dimension captured by the data.

We note here that IBM SPSS does not produce the scree plot in Version 19 or earlier. For those users who wish to obtain this information, they can generate all the dimensional solutions and examine (or plot for themselves) the S-stress values associated with each solution.

14A.12 Recommended Readings

Arabie, P., Carroll, J. D., & DeSarbo, W. S. (1987). *Three-way scaling and clustering.* Newbury Park, CA: Sage.

Carroll, J. D., & Arabia, P. (1998). Multidimensional scaling. In M. H. Birnbaum (Ed.), *Handbook of perception and cognition: Vol. 3. Measurement, judgment and decision making* (pp. 179–250). San Diego, CA: Academic Press.

Carroll, J. D., & Wish, M. (1974). Models and methods for three-way multidimensional scaling. In D. H. Krantz, R. C. Atkinson, R. D. Luce, & P. Suppes (Eds.), *Contemporary developments in mathematical psychology: Vol. 2. Measurement, psychophysics, and neural information processing* (pp. 57–105). San Francisco, CA: W. H. Freeman.

Cox, T. F., & Cox, M. A. A. (2001). *Multidimensional scaling* (2nd ed.). Boca Raton, FL: Chapman & Hall.

Davison, M. L. (1983). *Multidimensional scaling.* New York, NY: Wiley.

Everitt, B. S., & Rabe-Hesketh, S. (1997). *The analysis of proximity data*. New York, NY: Wiley.

Giguère, G. (2007). Collecting and analyzing data in multidimensional scaling experiments: A guide for psychologists using SPSS. *Tutorials in Quantitative Methods for Psychology, 2,* 26–37.

Green, P. E., & Rao, V. R. (1972). *Applied multidimensional scaling: A comparison of approaches and algorithms*. Hinsdale, IL: Dryden Press.

Jacoby, W. G. (1991). *Data theory and dimensional analysis*. Newbury Park, CA: Sage.

Jaworska, N., & Chupetlovska-Anastasova, A. (2009). A review of multidimensional scaling (MDS) and its utility in various psychological domains. *Tutorials in Quantitative Methods for Psychology, 5,* 1–10.

Kruskal, J. B. (1964b). Nonmetric multidimensional scaling: A numerical method. *Psychometrika, 29,* 115–129.

Kruskal, J. B., & Wish, M. (1978). *Multidimensional scaling*. Beverly Hills, CA: Sage.

Lattin, J. M., Carroll, J. D., & Green, P. E. (2003). *Analyzing multivariate data*. Pacific Grove, CA: Brooks/Cole.

Norusis, M. J. (2008). *SPSS statistics 17.0: Advanced statistical procedures companion*. Upper Saddle River, NJ: Prentice Hall.

Romney, A. K., Shepard, R. N., & Nerlove, S. B. (1972). *Multidimensional scaling: Theory and applications in the behavioral sciences: Vol. 2. Applications*. New York, NY: Seminar Press.

Schiffman, S. S., Reynolds, M. L., & Young, F. W. (1981). *Introduction to multidimensional scaling theory, methods, and application*. New York, NY: Academic Press.

Shepard, R. N., Romney, A. K., & Nerlove, S. B. (1972). *Multidimensional scaling: Theory and application in the behavioral science: Vol. 1. Theory*. New York, NY: Seminar Press.

Stalans, L. J. (1995). Multidimensional scaling. In L. G. Grimm & P. R. Yarnold (Eds.), *Reading and understanding multivariate statistics*. Washington, DC: American Psychological Association.

Takane, Y., Jung, S., & Oshima-Takane, Y. (2009). Multidimensional scaling. In R. E. Millsap & A. Maydeu-Olivares (Eds.), *The Sage handbook of quantitative methods in psychology* (pp. 219–242). Thousand Oaks, CA: Sage.

Torgerson, W. S. (1958). *Theory and method of scaling*. New York, NY: Wiley.

Young, F. W., & Hamer, R. M. (1987). *Multidimensional scaling: History, theory, and applications*. Hillsdale, NJ: Lawrence Erlbaum.

Multidimensional Scaling Using IBM SPSS

14B.1 The Structure of This Chapter

We present three examples that demonstrate MDS analyses using metric CMDS, nonmetric CMDS, and metric WMDS.

14B.2 Metric CMDS

14B.2.1 Metric CMDS: Our Numeric Example

Recall that CMDS utilizes a single matrix of dissimilarity data. We will use the data set in **Metric CMDS CA City Flying Mileage**; a screenshot of those data are shown in Figure 14b.1. This data file contains the flying mileage (as opposed to driving mileage) between 10 California cities ranging from Crescent City (a coastal city in the far north of the state) to San Diego (in the far southern region). For example, the distance between Fresno and Crescent City is 422 miles (1 mile = 1.61 kilometers) and the distance from San Francisco to Los Angeles is 338 miles.

14B.2.2 Metric CMDS: The Data Structure

Note that the data file is structured quite differently from what we have seen in the previous chapters. Because the family of MDS procedures operates on proximity data between pairs of objects, the data must be entered in that form. We thus directly enter a proximity matrix into the data file. Because such data are symmetric (i.e., they reside in a symmetric matrix), mileages above the matrix diagonal do not need to be entered—the elements above the diagonal are mirror images of the lower diagonal counterparts.

Figure 14b.1 Flying Mileage for Pairs of California Cities

	City	Crescent_City	Fresno	La_Verne	Los_Angeles	Riverside	Sacramento	San_Bernardino	San_Diego	San_Francisco	San_Jose	var	var
1	Crescent	0	.	.	.	.	.	.	.	.	.		
2	Fresno	422	0	.	.	.	.	.	.	.	.		
3	La Verne	636	215	0	.	.	.	.	.	.	.		
4	Los Angeles	627	209	37	0	.	.	.	.	.	.		
5	Riverside	655	233	22	55	0	.	.	.	.	.		
6	Sacramento	254	168	382	373	400	0	.	.	.	.		
7	San Bernardino	649	228	28	64	14	396	0	.	.	.		
8	San Diego	734	313	100	109	85	480	96	0	.	.		
9	San Francisco	304	158	354	338	375	86	373	446	0	.		
10	San Jose	329	128	324	308	344	94	343	417	31	0		
11													
12													
13													
14													

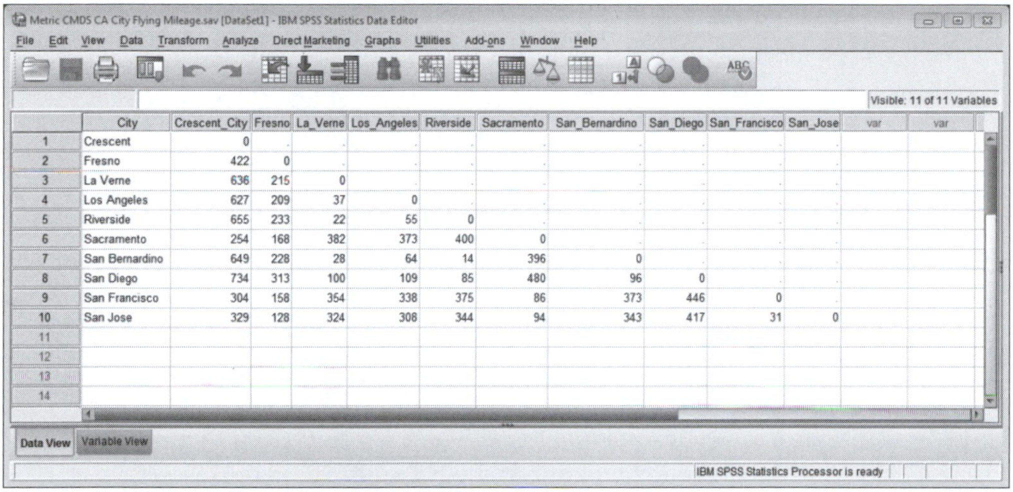

14B.2.3 Metric CMDS: Analysis Setup

Selecting the path **Analyze ➔ Scale ➔ Multidimensional Scaling** (**ALSCAL**) from the main menu brings us to the **Multidimensional Scaling** main dialog window displayed in Figure 14b.2. We have highlighted and moved our 10 California city variables to the **Variables** panel. **Individual Matrices for** is not activated in the present example. In the **Distances** panel, we have kept the default **Data are distances** with its default setting at **Square symmetric** for **Shape** because here the data that we have entered are distances and the shape of the distances matrix is square and is symmetric.

Selecting the **Model** pushbutton produces the **Model** dialog window shown in Figure 14b.3. This dialog screen consists of four separate panels. The **Level of Measurement** panel (in the upper left portion of the window) allows us to indicate the measurement level of our data: **Ordinal**, **Interval**, or **Ratio.** For the present example, we have activated the **Ratio** level as our distance measure is miles. The **Conditionality** panel provides three options: **Matrix** (for data measured on the same measurement scale), **Row** (for rectangular data matrices where the data cannot be compared with data in other matrices), and **Unconditional** (unconditional data matrices can be compared with each other). The default **Matrix** option is selected in the present example.

The **Dimensions** panels in Figure 14b.3 allow us to specify the **Minimum** and **Maximum** number of dimensions (solutions) we wish to obtain. IBM SPSS allows for one

Figure 14b.2 The Main Dialog Window for Multidimensional Scaling (ALSCAL)

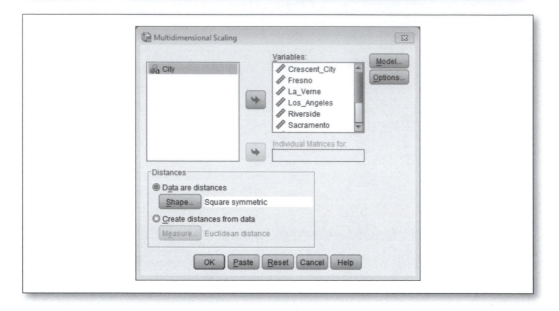

Figure 14b.3 The Model Dialog Window for Multidimensional Scaling (ALSCAL)

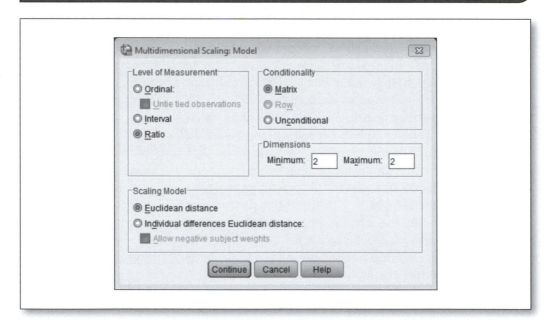

to six dimensions to be specified. In the present example we have requested the default **Minimum** and **Maximum** of **2** dimensions. Last, the **Scaling Model** panel offers either a **Euclidean distance** (appropriate for CMDS analyses) or an **Individual differences Euclidean distance** option (appropriate for RMDS or WMDS analyses). The **Euclidean** distance option is activated for the present analysis. Click **Continue** to return to the main dialog screen.

Select the **Options** pushbutton. This dialog window (see Figure 14b.4) consists of two general areas and an additional option. In the **Display** panel, we have activated two options: (a) the **Group plots**, which produces the CMDS perceptual map or **Derived Stimulus Configuration**, and **Scatterplot of Linear Fit**, and (b) **Data matrix**, which reproduces the original data matrix. The **Individual subject plots** (not activated) provides perceptual maps for each participant during an RMDS or WMDS analysis. The **Model and options summary** (not activated) documents the various IBM SPSS **Data Options**, **Model Options**, **Output Options**, and **Algorithmic Options** requested by the researchers.

The **Criteria** panel has the following three options: **S-stress convergence**, **Minimum s-stress value**, and **Maximum iterations**. We recommend for most situations leaving these values in their default state as in the present example. The **Treat distances less than**

Figure 14b.4   The Options Dialog Window for Multidimensional Scaling (ALSCAL)

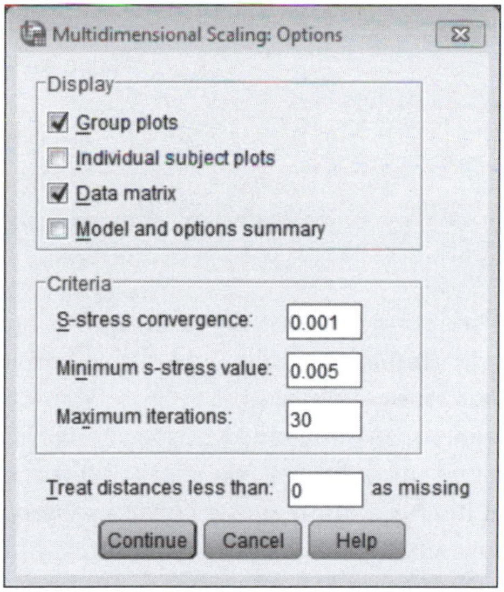

[**a to-be-filled-in value**] **as missing** option was also kept at its default value of **0**. Click **Continue** to return you to the main window, and click **OK** to perform the analysis.

14B.2.4 Metric CMDS: Selected Output

The two-dimensional Euclidean distance solution that we requested is accomplished by means of a series of iterations, which are ultimately realized in the final perceptual map. The **Iteration history** (produced by default) is shown in Figure 14b.5. The lack of table formatting and the use of the Courier font tell us that this output is a carryover from the ancient days of wide-carriage dot matrix line printers.

Figure 14b.5 Iteration History and Fit Indexes

```
Iteration history for the 2 dimensional solution (in squared distances)

            Young's S-stress formula 1 is used.

        Iteration     S-stress       Improvement

            1             .00106

                    Iterations stopped because
                    S-stress is less than    .005000


                        Stress and squared correlation (RSQ) in distances

                    RSQ values are the proportion of variance of the scaled data (disparities)
                            in the partition (row, matrix, or entire data) which
                            is accounted for by their corresponding distances.
                            Stress values are Kruskal's stress formula 1.



                For  matrix
        Stress  =   .00182     RSQ =  .99999

            Configuration derived in 2 dimensions
```

Despite such ancient script, the information conveyed is appropriate and current. It consists of two stress indexes (**Young's S-stress** and Kruskal's **Stress** Index) and the squared correlation (**RSQ**) in distances. By default, IBM SPSS MDS procedures are set at a maximum of 30 iterations, a value that we retained in specifying the analysis **Options**. Recall that S-stress and Stress values range from 1 (poor fit) to 0 (perfect fit). The software will continue to cycle through iterations until S-stress has improved (decreased) to a value of less than 0.005 (the default setting). In the present example, the software needed only a single iteration because the resulting **Young's S-stress** value of **.00106 exceeded** immediately (i.e., the value was lower than) the default minimum of 0.005. Two other measures of fit are also displayed in Figure 14b.5.

Kruskal's **Stress** (not explicitly labeled as such) can be interpreted in a manner akin to S-stress. It is labeled in the lower left portion of the output as **Stress** and has a value in our example of **.00182**. **RSQ**, the squared correlation coefficient between the Euclidean distances and the raw data, is **.99999**. All three fit indexes indicate excellent correspondence between the California city flying mileages and the two-dimensional Euclidean model.

The near-perfect linear fit between data and distances can also be represented visually in the **Scatterplot of Linear Fit Euclidean distance model**—sometimes referred to as a *Shepard diagram*—shown in Figure 14b.6. This figure displays on the horizontal axis the original raw distance data (after standardization) by the Euclidean distances between pairs of objects on the vertical axis. Note the near-perfect linear relationship, which is reflected in the **RSQ** value of **.99**. The lack of scatter reflects the high quality of the mileage data and their relative lack of error.

Figure 14b.7 displays the **Optimally scaled data (disparities) for subject 1**. Note that **subject 1** refers to the original raw data matrix of paired city mileages—from the standpoint of IBM SPSS, there is only one "subject" represented in the data file because there is only one proximity matrix. The matrix in Figure 14b.7 represents the transformed raw data based on the ALSCAL least squares algorithm employed by IBM SPSS and can be referred to collectively as disparities that are linearly related to the original dissimilarity data.

Figure 14b.6 Scatterplot of Linear Fit Euclidean Distance Model

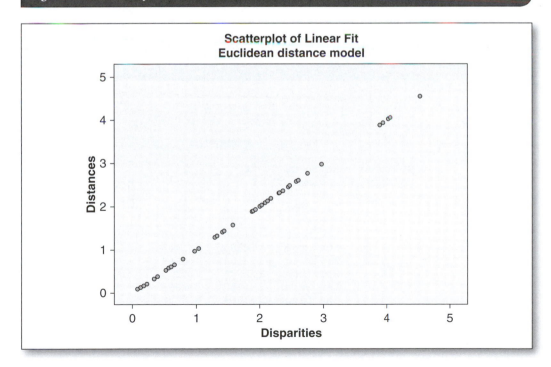

Figure 14b.7 Scaled Disparities

```
                    Optimally scaled data (disparities) for subject    1

          1         2         3         4         5         6         7         8         9        10

 1      .000
 2     2.612      .000
 3     3.937     1.331      .000
 4     3.882     1.294      .229      .000
 5     4.055     1.442      .136      .340      .000
 6     1.572     1.040     2.365     2.309     2.476      .000
 7     4.018     1.411      .173      .396      .087     2.452      .000
 8     4.544     1.938      .619      .675      .526     2.972      .594      .000
 9     1.882      .978     2.192     2.092     2.322      .532     2.309     2.761      .000
10     2.037      .792     2.006     1.907     2.130      .582     2.123     2.582      .192      .000
```

With confidence in the quality of the derived solution, we can examine the two-dimensional solution that was produced by the procedure. The Dimension 1 and Dimension 2 coordinates for each city are shown in Figure 14b.8. These coordinates are then used by the MDS procedure to locate or position each object (e.g., city) in a two-dimensional configuration or space.

The visual depiction of the two-dimensional space where these coordinates are plotted, known as a *perceptual map*, is shown in Figure 14b.9. This two-dimensional configuration depicts objects (i.e., cities) as points in a multidimensional space. A schematic map of

Figure 14b.8 Stimulus Coordinates for the Metric Classical Multidimensional Scaling Solution

Stimulus Coordinates

Dimension

Stimulus Number	Stimulus Name	1	2
1	Crescent	2.8330	.2283
2	Fresno	.2231	.1514
3	La_Verne	−1.1009	.0616
4	Los_Ange	−1.0304	−.1468
5	Riversid	−1.2189	.1240
6	Sacramen	1.2629	.1239
7	San_Bern	−1.1859	.2201
8	San_Dieg	−1.7004	−.0858
9	San_Fran	1.0481	−.3686
10	San_Jose	.8695	−.3081

Figure 14b.9 Perceptual Map of California City Flying Mileage for the Metric Classical Multidimensional Scaling Solution

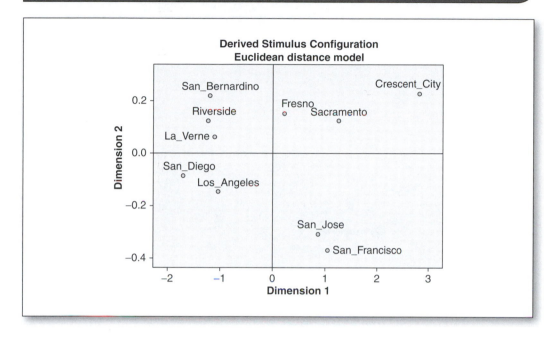

California showing the cities in our example presented in Figure 14b.10 may be used to help interpret the dimensional structure for readers not familiar with where these cities are approximately located.

Generally, objects that are closer to each other are more similar. Here, similarity is defined in terms of flying mileage between cities. Thus, the adjacent cities of San Bernardino, Riverside, and La Verne are relatively close together (they are all in the upper left quadrant of the perceptual map) because the mileage between them is rather small (one would drive from one to the other location rather than fly, although given the traffic on the Los Angeles freeways, we do not guarantee a quick trip). On the other hand, Crescent City and San Diego are located at the far northern and southern ends of the state, that is, they are more dissimilar or have greater distance in flying mileage between them.

The orientation of the two dimensions is determined by the IBM SPSS ALSCAL algorithm and is arbitrary; it is based entirely on distances, with Dimension 1 having the longest distances followed by Dimension 2 and so on if there are more dimensions in the solution. In this display, Dimension 1 (the horizontal dimension) appears to represent a North–South dimension, with North on the right and South on the left. Thus, Crescent City is the northernmost city in our set and is farthest toward the right, whereas San Diego is the southernmost city in our set and is farthest toward the left. Dimension 2 seems to be something that a software routine rather than a human thinker

Figure 14b.10 Map of California Showing the 10 Cities in Our Example

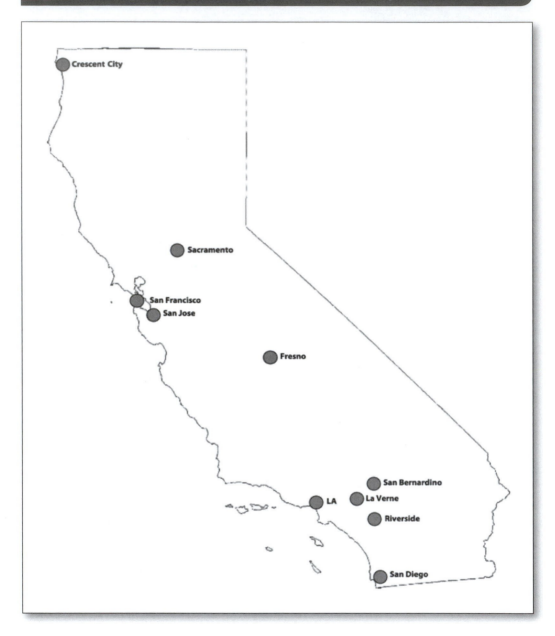

would produce; we interpret it as a binary pairing dimension. Cities below the midline have one other city quite nearby and thus are paired with another city. Because San Jose and San Francisco are physically very close, they are paired and placed lowest in the plot;

San Diego and Los Angeles are somewhat further apart but still represent a pair, and they are located closer to the midline. Cities above the midline are not paired with exactly one other city. Those in the upper left quadrant, San Bernardino, Riverside, and La Verne, are all located fairly close to each other in Southern California and represent a triad of cities. Fresno, Sacramento, and Crescent City, located in the upper right quadrant, can be thought of as loners in the set of cities used in the analysis, stretched across the wide expanse of Northern and Central California (although Sacramento is not all that far from the San Francisco–San Jose pair).

14B.2.5 Reporting Metric CMDS Results

The flying distances (in miles) of 10 California cities were examined by means of a metric CMDS analysis. The 45 paired city distances (i.e., $n(n − 1)/2 = (10 * 9)/2 = 90/2 = 45$) were entered into the IBM SPSS Multidimensional Scaling (ALSCAL) procedure for analysis. Convergence was achieved after one iteration, resulting in a Young's S-stress value of .001, Kruskal's Stress value of .002, and an R^2 value of .99, all of which indicate an excellent fit of the Euclidean model to the data. The two-dimensional Derived Stimulus Configuration (or perceptual map) can be seen in Figure 14b.9.

Dimension 1 (the horizontal dimension) appears to represent a North–South dimension, with North on the right and South on the left. Thus, Crescent City is the northernmost city in the set of cities used in the analysis and is farthest toward the right, whereas San Diego is the southernmost city in the set and is farthest toward the left. Dimension 2 seems to be something that a software routine would produce; we interpret it as a binary pairing dimension. Cities below the midline have one other city quite nearby. Because San Jose and San Francisco are physically very close, they are lowest in the plot; San Diego and Los Angeles are somewhat further apart and they are located closer to the midline. Cities above the midline are not paired with exactly one other city. Those in the upper left quadrant, San Bernardino, Riverside, and La Verne, are all located fairly close to each other in Southern California and represent a triad of cities. Fresno, Sacramento, and Crescent City, located in the upper right quadrant, are relative loners in the set of cities used in the analysis, stretched across the wide expanse of Northern and Central California.

14B.3 Nonmetric CMDS

14B.3.1 Nonmetric CMDS: Our Numeric Example

To demonstrate nonmetric CMDS we will use California city flying mileages but have presented the distances in terms of ranks. This data set can be found in **Nonmetric CMDS CA City Flying Mileage**. A screenshot of the data set can be seen in Figure 14b.11.

Figure 14b.11 Flying Mileage Rankings for Pairs of California Cities

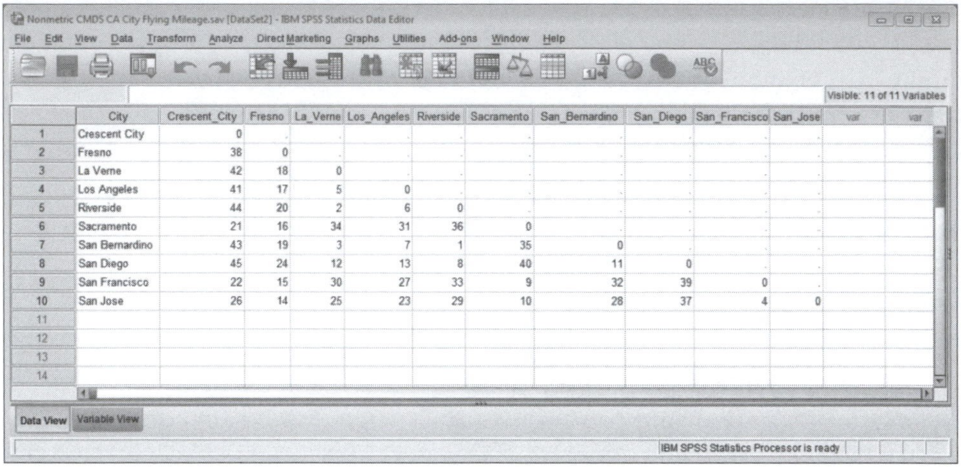

City	Crescent_City	Fresno	La_Verne	Los_Angeles	Riverside	Sacramento	San_Bernardino	San_Diego	San_Francisco	San_Jose
Crescent City	0									
Fresno	38	0								
La Verne	42	18	0							
Los Angeles	41	17	5	0						
Riverside	44	20	2	6	0					
Sacramento	21	16	34	31	36	0				
San Bernardino	43	19	3	7	1	35	0			
San Diego	45	24	12	13	8	40	11	0		
San Francisco	22	15	30	27	33	9	32	39	0	
San Jose	26	14	25	23	29	10	28	37	4	0

The data for this example were derived from the metric data shown in Figure 14b.1. Those 45 mileage differences shown in the metric data set were placed on a list and rank ordered from closest distance to furthest distance. The resulting ranks were then transcribed into the data file shown in Figure 14b.11. For example, Riverside and San Bernardino were the two closest cities, separated by only 14 miles; this difference was assigned a rank of 1. In the nonmetric (ordinal) data set, their proximity is therefore represented by a value of 1. On the other hand, San Diego and Crescent City were furthest apart at 734 miles; this difference was assigned a rank of 45. In the nonmetric (ordinal) data set, their proximity is therefore represented by a value of 45. The remaining values shown in the nonmetric data file represent the ranks assigned to all of the differences in mileage between the respective cities.

Note that a considerable amount of information is lost when we convert ratio-level data to ordinal data, and it is a practice we emphasize that you should avoid. We have performed this conversion here only for the sake of using an example that is already familiar to you in order to illustrate the nonmetric form of the analysis. The only time that such a nonmetric analysis should be performed is when the original data are themselves ordinal.

14B.3.2 Nonmetric CMDS: Analysis Setup

Select the path **Analyze ➔ Scale ➔ Multidimensional Scaling (ALSCAL)** from the main menu and configure it in the same way as we did in the metric CMDS analysis (see Figure 14b.12).

Figure 14b.12 The Main Dialog Window for Multidimensional Scaling (ALSCAL)

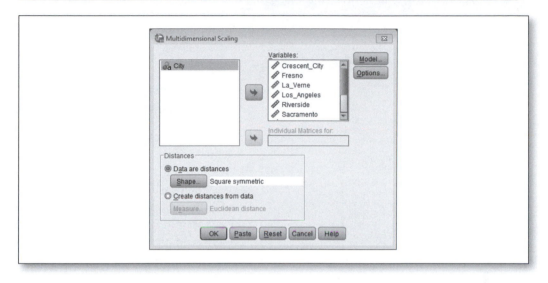

In the **Model** dialog window (see Figure 14b.13), we have accepted the default activation of **Ordinal** in the **Level of Measurement** panel because our data consist of ordinal level ranks. For the remaining panels, we accept the IBM SPSS defaults as we did in the metric analysis.

Figure 14b.13 The Model Dialog Window for Multidimensional Scaling (ALSCAL)

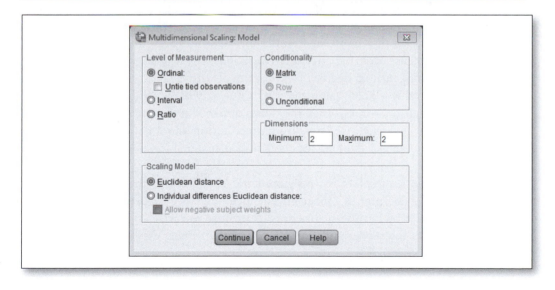

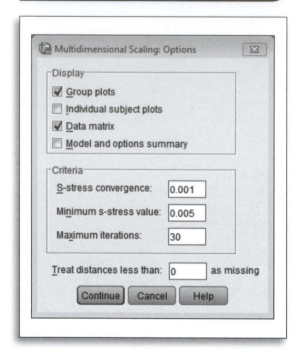

Figure 14b.14 The Options Dialog Window for Multidimensional Scaling (ALSCAL)

Clicking the **Options** pushbutton produces the **Multidimensional Scaling: Options** dialog screen (see Figure 14b.14), which we have configured akin to the metric analysis.

14B.3.3 Nonmetric CMDS: Selected Output

The **Iteration history** and fit indexes together with a warning message from IBM SPSS are shown in Figure 14b.15. Occasionally, when conducting nonmetric CMDS analyses, IBM SPSS will produce a cautionary warning (as in the present example) indicating that the total number of parameters being estimated, 20 in the present example (i.e., 10 California cities in two dimensions), is large in comparison with the number of data values in our raw data dissimilarity matrix—(i.e., $10(10 - 1))/2 = 45$). This warning will typically not appear in a metric or quantitative CMDS. We agree with Young and Harris (2008) that caution should be invoked when interpreting output under this warning.

The consequences of working with ordinal-level measurement rather than ratio data—there is a loss in precision because a difference between two adjacent ranks do not convey any information about the distance between cities (e.g., cities ranked 17 and 18 could be 30 miles or 100 apart)—can be seen in the **Iteration history** and stress indexes.

S-stress convergence occurred after seven iterations, beginning with an **S-stress** value of **.02292** and reaching its final degree of improvement with a value of **.00533** at Iteration 7. Kruskal's **Stress** value is **.02081** and the **RSQ** value is **.99839**. Although the present fit indexes suggest a slightly poorer fit than the values obtained in the previous metric CMDS example (to be expected when we compare ratio to ordinal level data), these fit indexes nevertheless indicate an excellent fit for the two-dimensional Euclidean model and the transformed data.

We obtain three scatterplots in this nonmetric analysis, and they are presented in Figure 14b.16. The **Scatterplot of Linear Fit Euclidean distance model** plots disparities or transformed raw data by Euclidean distances. A positive linear relationship confirms an excellent fit between the model and the data. Note the minor level of scatter for small

Figure 14b.15 Iteration History and Fit Indexes

```
>Warning # 14654
>The total number of parameters being estimated (the number of stimulus
>coordinates plus the number of weights, if any) is large relative to the
>number of data values in your data matrix.  The results may not be reliable
>since there may not be enough data to precisely estimate the values of the
>parameters.  You should reduce the number of parameters (e.g. request fewer
>dimensions) or increase the number of observations.
>Number of parameters is 20.  Number of data values is 45

Iteration history for the 2 dimensional solution (in squared distances)

                Young's S-stress formula 1 is used.

        Iteration      S-stress        Improvement

            1            .02292
            2            .01571          .00721
            3            .01153          .00418
            4            .00887          .00266
            5            .00714          .00173
            6            .00603          .00111
            7            .00533          .00070

                    Iterations stopped because
            S-stress improvement is less than    .001000


                            Stress and squared correlation (RSQ) in distances

                    RSQ values are the proportion of variance of the scaled data (disparities)
                        in the partition (row, matrix, or entire data) which
                        is accounted for by their corresponding distances.
                        Stress values are Kruskal's stress formula 1.



                For  matrix
        Stress  =   .02081      RSQ =   .99839

            Configuration derived in 2 dimensions
```

distances and disparities. This result is an artifact of the S-stress formula, which tends to underfit small disparities and overfit large ones (Young & Harris, 2008).

The **Scatterplot of Nonlinear Fit Euclidean distance model** plots observations or original raw data by Euclidean distances. As was true for the linear fit plot, we expect a positive function (as in the present case) indicating excellent fit.

The **Transformation Scatterplot Euclidean distance model** is shown as the bottom plot in Figure 14b.16. This diagram shows the raw data by the transformed data (or disparities). An excellent fit is represented by an increasing function from left to right. If similarities (instead of dissimilarities) are plotted, the function is reversed (i.e., from upper left to lower right). Note that transformations that depict horizontal steps may indicate a *degenerate solution* and poor model fit.

Figure 14b.16 Scatterplot of Linear Fit and Nonlinear Fit, and the Transformation Scatterplot

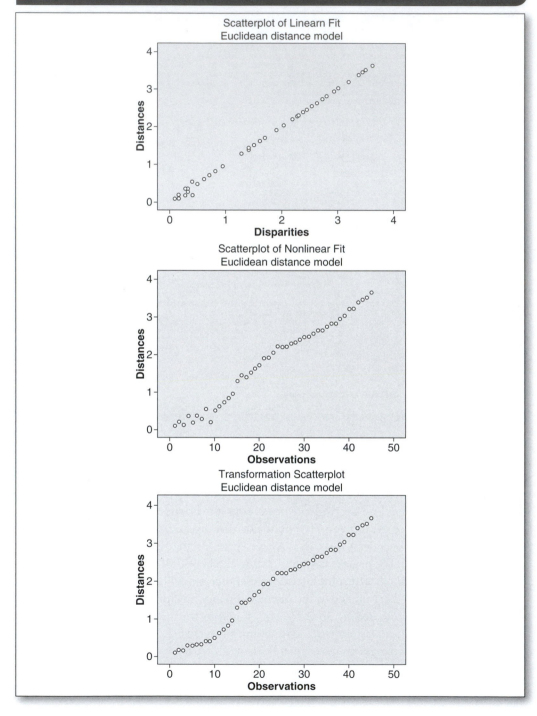

Figures 14b.17 and 14b.18 display the **Stimulus Coordinates** and the perceptual map or **Derived Stimulus Configuration Euclidean distance model**, respectively. Although similar to

Figure 14b.17 Stimulus Coordinates for the Nonmetric CMDS Solution

Stimulus Coordinates

Stimulus Number	Stimulus Name	Dimension 1	Dimension 2
1	Crescent	1.9961	-1.3918
2	Fresno	.1285	.8612
3	La_Verne	-1.0820	-.0280
4	Los_Ange	-.9067	-.0613
5	Riversid	-1.2529	-.1210
6	Sacramen	1.4920	.4327
7	San_Bern	-1.1792	-.0735
8	San_Dieg	-1.5351	-.5695
9	San_Fran	1.3173	.3844
10	San_Jose	1.0220	.5667

Figure 14b.18 Perceptual Map of California City Flying Mileage for the Nonmetric Classical Multidimensional Scaling Solution

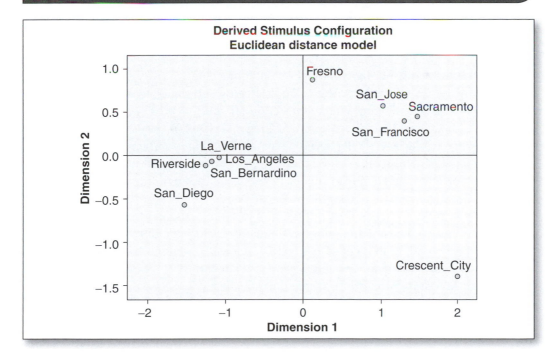

the metric CMDS configuration, the objects in the present nonmetric configuration are less dispersed. Dimension 1 (the horizontal dimension) still appears to order the cities from north (right) to south (left), and those cities on the left side of the midline are thought of as Southern California cities whereas those to the right of the midline thought of as Central California (Fresno), Central or Northern California (San Jose, San Francisco, and Sacramento), or Northern California (Crescent City).

It is unclear to us how to interpret Dimension 2, but this lack of clarity does serve to underscore the potential consequences of reducing the richness of the information contained in ratio-level data by converting the data to an ordinal scale of measurement. It does not always happen that the underlying dimensions become somewhat distorted, but the fact that it happened in our example suggests that it may happen frequently enough to be of concern.

Despite the lack of clarity for Dimension 2, the groupings in the quadrants of the perceptual map make a certain amount of sense. The clump of Riverside, La Verne, San Bernardino, and Los Angeles represents the general Los Angeles area; San Diego is near enough to still be a part of the broad Southern California region, but it is far enough away to be somewhat distinct. The other clump of San Jose, San Francisco, and Sacramento captures a very strong association between the two Bay Area cities (San Jose and San Francisco) and the relatively strong association between the Bay Area and the state capital (a steady workday commuter stream flows from Sacramento into the Bay Area in the morning and back out in the evening). Fresno and Crescent City are each relatively far from all of the other cities represented in the data set and stand alone and far from the other data points in the plot.

14B.3.4 Reporting Nonmetric CMDS Results

The ranked flying distances (in miles) of 10 California cities were examined by means of a nonmetric CMDS analysis. The ranked (1 = closest distance to 45 = farthest distance) 45 paired city distances (i.e., $n(n - 1)/2 = (10 * 9)/2 = 90/2 = 45$) were entered into the IBM SPSS Multidimensional Scaling (ALSCAL) procedure for analysis. Convergence was achieved after seven iterations, resulting in a Young's S-stress value of .005, Kruskal's Stress value of .021, and an R^2 value of .99, all of which indicate an excellent fit of the Euclidean model to the data. The two-dimensional Derived Stimulus Configuration (or perceptual map) can be seen in Figure 14b.18. Dimension 1 appears to order the cities from north (right) to south (left), and those cities on the left side of the midline are thought of as Southern California cities whereas those to the right of the midline thought of as Central California (Fresno), Central or Northern California (San Jose, San Francisco, and Sacramento), or Northern California (Crescent City). It is unclear how to interpret Dimension 2.

Despite the lack of clarity for Dimension 2, the groupings in the perceptual map make a certain amount of sense. The grouping of Riverside, La Verne, San Bernardino, and Los Angeles represents the general LA area; San Diego is nearby but somewhat distinct. The other grouping of San Jose, San Francisco, and Sacramento captures a relatively strong association between the Bay Area and the state capitol, with a steady commuter stream linking the two areas. Fresno and Crescent City are each quite far from all of the other cities represented in the data set.

14B.4 Metric WMDS

14B.4.1 Metric WMDS: Our Numeric Example

Recall that WMDS (or INDSCAL) employs the Euclidean distance model in the context of multiple dissimilarity matrices (individual respondents) that could differ from each other on the basis of cognitive or perceptual differences assumed to be involved in the dissimilarity judgments. For the present example, 20 graduate students from one of our universities were asked to make dissimilarity judgments on pairs of the following local department stores: JCPenney, Kohl's, Target, Macy's, Nordstrom's, Sears, and Walmart. Each respondent was given a separate randomized list of 21 ($n(n - 1)/2$ or $(7 * 6)/2 = 42/2 = 21$) paired department stores on which to make dissimilarity judgments. The students rated each pair of department stores on a 9-point summative response scale of 1 (*very similar*) to 9 (*very dissimilar*).

This data set can be found in a file labeled **Metric WMDS Retail Stores**. Note that this data file includes 20 individual symmetric matrices embedded in one file. It can be partially seen in Figure 14b.19. To perform a WMDS analysis, the data must be entered in IBM SPSS matrix form. Only the bottom portion of the matrix and the diagonal elements are typed in. Figure 14b.19 displays the complete data from the first three individual respondent (or subject) matrices of dissimilarity data.

We have included **Sub_ID** as the first variable in the file to provide a subject number identification code for each line of each dissimilarity matrix. For example, **Subject 1** has **1** at the beginning of the seven lines of data that comprise his or her symmetric matrix. The **Subject** variable serves no functional purpose because the IBM SPSS ALSCAL algorithm already "knows" the beginning and end points of each of the 20 symmetric matrices embedded in the data set (Giguere, 2007), but it is important to include this identification code so that we can verify the data entry on a later occasion if needed.

The remaining seven variables in the columns of the file represent the store name matching the order of the unlabeled rows. For example, consider the responses of the first

Figure 14b.19 A Portion of the Data File for Metric Weighted Multidimensional Scaling

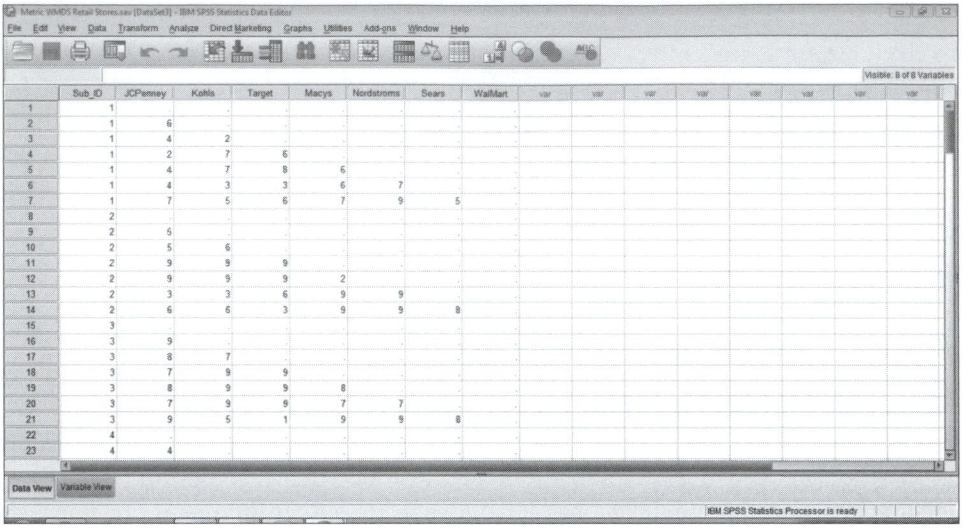

	Sub_ID	JCPenney	Kohls	Target	Macys	Nordstroms	Sears	WalMart
1	1	.	.	.	.	.	.	.
2	1	6	.	.	.	.	.	.
3	1	4	2	.	.	.	.	.
4	1	2	7	6	.	.	.	.
5	1	4	7	8	6	.	.	.
6	1	4	3	3	6	7	.	.
7	1	7	5	6	7	9	5	.
8	2	.	.	.	.	.	.	.
9	2	5	.	.	.	.	.	.
10	2	5	6	.	.	.	.	.
11	2	9	9	9	.	.	.	.
12	2	9	9	9	2	.	.	.
13	2	3	3	6	9	9	.	.
14	2	6	6	3	9	9	8	.
15	3	.	.	.	.	.	.	.
16	3	9	.	.	.	.	.	.
17	3	8	7	.	.	.	.	.
18	3	7	9	9	.	.	.	.
19	3	8	9	9	8	.	.	.
20	3	7	9	9	7	7	.	.
21	3	9	5	1	9	9	8	.
22	4	.	.	.	.	.	.	.
23	4	4	.	.	.	.	.	.

graduate student (**Subject 1**). The first row represents JCPenney; we know this because we can see that the first column, to which it is keyed, is displayed in the data file. The entry is blank because the student did not compare any store with itself, but the cell needs to be included in the data matrix for completeness.

The following row contains an entry of **6** (on the 9-point summative response scale) and represents a comparison between JCPenney and Kohl's. We know this because the second row must correspond to the second column, which is labeled as such. The third row represents Target, and **Subject 1** determined that it was somewhat different from JCPenney (with a rating of **4**) and relatively similar to Kohl's (with a rating of **2**).

It is worth noting that the graduate students did not all fully agree on the degree to which the stores were dissimilar. **Subject 2**, for example, rated Target and Kohl's relatively dissimilar (with a rating of **6** that can be seen on Line 10 of the data file).

14B.4.2 Metric WMDS: Analysis Setup

Select the path **Analyze ➔ Scale ➔ Multidimensional Scaling (ALSCAL)** from the main menu and configure it as shown in Figure 14b.20 analogously to what we have done before.

Figure 14b.20   The Main Dialog Window for Multidimensional Scaling (ALSCAL)

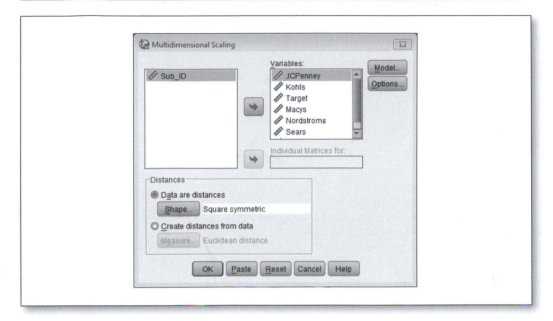

In the **Model** dialog window (see Figure 14b.21), we have selected **Interval** in the **Level of Measurement** specification because our data consist of responses to a summative scale rating system that we treat as approximating interval data. Because our data file now contains the data for individual respondents, and because individuals are almost always going to exhibit some differences, we specify that the **Scaling Model** is now **Individual differences Euclidean distance**. In the **Conditionality** area, we still specify **Matrix**, and we are still requesting that **Dimensions** are to be held at a **Minimum** and **Maximum** of **2**. We configure the **Options** dialog window as we have done before (see Figure 14b.22).

14B.4.3 Metric WMDS: Selected Output

The **Iteration history** and fit indexes are shown in Figure 14b.23. In the present example, the **Iteration history** indicates convergence after seven iterations. The analysis yielded a **Young's S-stress** value of **.34975**, indicating a relatively mediocre fit. This result is followed by separate **Stress** and **RSQ** values for each of the 20 respondents or matrices. For example, **Subject 1** (represented in the output as **Matrix 1**) had a **Stress** value of **.390** and an **RSQ** value of **.142**, **Subject 2** (represented in the output as **Matrix 2**) had a **Stress** value of **.160** and an **RSQ** value of **.879**, and so on.

Figure 14b.21 The Model Dialog Window for Multidimensional Scaling (ALSCAL)

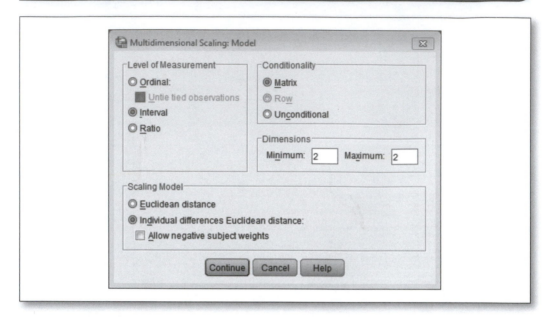

Figure 14b.22 The Options Dialog Window for Multidimensional Scaling (ALSCAL)

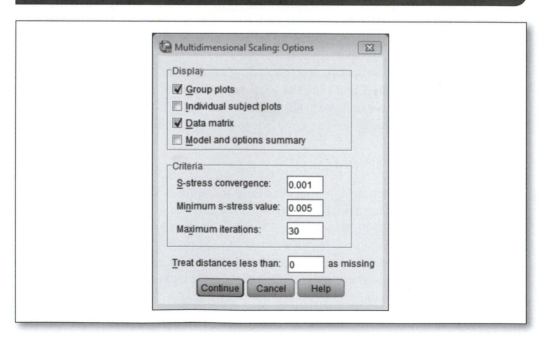

Figure 14b.23   Iteration History and Fit Indexes

```
Iteration history for the 2 dimensional solution (in squared distances)

        Young's S-stress formula 1 is used.

        Iteration    S-stress    Improvement

            0          .39281
            1          .40072
            2          .36763       .03309
            3          .35791       .00972
            4          .35405       .00386
            5          .35190       .00215
            6          .35059       .00131
            7          .34975       .00084

                Iterations stopped because
        S-stress improvement is less than    .001000


            Stress and squared correlation (RSQ) in distances

        RSQ values are the proportion of variance of the scaled data (disparities)
                in the partition (row, matrix, or entire data) which
                is accounted for by their corresponding distances.
                Stress values are Kruskal's stress formula 1.

Matrix   Stress   RSQ   Matrix   Stress   RSQ   Matrix   Stress   RSQ   Matrix   Stress   RSQ
   1      .390   .142      2      .160   .879      3      .373   .216      4      .307   .479
   5      .345   .365      6      .302   .504      7      .400   .254      8      .349   .322
   9      .332   .378     10      .219   .775     11      .368   .231     12      .337   .389
  13      .172   .890     14      .327   .429     15      .334   .383     16      .237   .721
  17      .187   .868     18      .220   .783     19      .302   .568     20      .304   .518


    Averaged (rms) over matrices
Stress =    .30678      RSQ =   .50475

    Configuration derived in 2 dimensions
```

The Stress values range from **.160** to **.400** and the **RSQ** values range from **.142** to **.890**. An average (collapsed across all 20 matrices) Kruskal's **Stress** was **.30678** and average **RSQ** was **.50475**, both of which indicate a fairly tepid model fit.

The **Subject Weights** shown in Figure 14b.24 indicate the importance of each dimension to each respondent or participant. Also displayed is the **Weirdness** index for each respondent. When the **Subject Weights** are fairly proportional to the average weights for each dimension (which are **.2545** and **.2503** for Dimensions 1 and 2, respectively, in our example) as shown below the last two columns of values, then the **Weirdness** index will be low as is the case for **Subject 1 (Weirdness = .1042)**. Conversely, **Subject 7** whose **Weirdness** index is **.5662** has a relatively high **Subject Weight** of **.4759** on **Dimension 1** and a low **Subject Weight** of .1652 on **Dimension 2**. Subjects (or respondents) with **Weirdness** indexes that are greater than .50 may be considered atypical or outliers and are possible candidates for elimination from subsequent analyses.

Euclidean distances or **Optimally scaled data (disparities)** are computed and displayed for each respondent. Recall that that these "disparities" represent the transformed raw data based on the ALSCAL least squares algorithm employed by IBM SPSS. We show a portion of this output in Figure 14b.25.

Figure 14b.24   Subject Weights

```
Subject weights measure the importance of each dimension to each subject.
Squared weights sum to RSQ.

A subject with weights proportional to the average weights has a weirdness of
zero, the minimum value.
A subject with one large weight and many low weights has a weirdness near one.
A subject with exactly one positive weight has a weirdness of one,
the maximum value for nonnegative weights.


                        Subject Weights

                                      Dimension
       Subject   Weird-      1           2
       Number     ness

          1      .1042     .2904       .2412
          2      .4388     .8512       .3930
          3      .0382     .3226       .3353
          4      .2410     .3944       .5691
          5      .2279     .5002       .3396
          6      .2857     .6045       .3718
          7      .5662     .4759       .1652
          8      .0970     .4344       .3649
          9      .0633     .4175       .4515
         10      .5439     .8266       .3029
         11      .0310     .3351       .3444
         12      .3762     .2984       .5477
         13      .5633     .3234       .8865
         14      .1388     .5152       .4048
         15      .0679     .4185       .4559
         16      .1664     .5241       .6683
         17      .3931     .4347       .8239
         18      .5051     .8212       .3292
         19      .3315     .3837       .6483
         20      .4287     .3176       .6457
Overall importance of
each dimension:            .2545       .2503
```

The plot of the **Derived Subject Weights** can be seen in the top plot of Figure 14b.26. This plot depicts how each respondent's assessments of the store pairings were weighted on the two dimensions of the Euclidean distance model. We note a small grouping of respondents (e.g., 2, 18, and 10) that weight Dimension 1 very high and Dimension 2 relatively low.

The **Scatterplot of Linear Fit Individual differences (weighted) Euclidean distance model** can be seen in the lower plot of Figure 14b.26. This plot shows some scatter and departure from linearity, indicating that the model fit is reasonable but not ideal.

For WMDS models, IBM SPSS provides a table of **Flattened Subject Weights** and a plot of **Flattened Subject Weights Individual differences (weighted) Euclidean distance model** as shown in Figure 14b.27. Young and Harris (2008) note that a common mistake made by data analysts is to regard the distances between individual subject weights instead of examining the angle between subject vectors. To help remedy this problem, IBM SPSS calculates

Figure 14b.25 A Portion of the Optimally Scaled Disparities

Optimally scaled data (disparities) for subject 1

	1	2	3	4	5	6	7
1	.000						
2	1.152	.000					
3	.938	.723	.000				
4	.723	1.260	1.152	.000			
5	.938	1.260	1.367	1.152	.000		
6	.938	.830	.830	1.152	1.260	.000	
7	1.260	1.045	1.152	1.260	1.474	1.045	.000

Optimally scaled data (disparities) for subject 2

	1	2	3	4	5	6	7
1	.000						
2	1.089	.000					
3	1.089	1.358	.000				
4	2.163	2.163	2.163	.000			
5	2.163	2.163	2.163	.284	.000		
6	.552	.552	1.358	2.163	2.163	.000	
7	1.358	1.358	.552	2.163	2.163	1.895	.000

Optimally scaled data (disparities) for subject 3

	1	2	3	4	5	6	7
1	.000						
2	1.368	.000					
3	1.248	1.128	.000				
4	1.128	1.368	1.368	.000			
5	1.248	1.368	1.368	1.248	.000		
6	1.128	1.368	1.368	1.128	1.128	.000	
7	1.368	.887	.407	1.368	1.368	1.248	.000

Optimally scaled data (disparities) for subject 4

	1	2	3	4	5	6	7
1	.000						
2	.913	.000					
3	1.688	1.688	.000				
4	.913	.913	1.688	.000			
5	1.688	1.688	1.688	1.688	.000		
6	.913	.913	1.688	.913	1.688	.000	
7	1.688	1.688	.913	1.688	2.076	1.688	.000

flattened weights. These more intuitive coefficients transform raw subject weights into distance coordinates. The flattening algorithm reduces r dimensions to $r - 1$ or in the present case $2 - 1 = 1$ dimension and labeled as **Variable 1** on the Y-axis in Figure 14b.27. From this plot, we can see that respondents with relatively low and symmetrical subject weights on the two dimensions will appear in the middle of the plot (e.g., Subjects 1, 11, 3, and 15), and subjects with relatively high weights on one or the other dimensions will appear near the top or bottom of the Y axis (e.g., Subjects 7, 10, 18, 20, 17, and 13).

Figure 14b.26 Scatterplot of Derived Subject Weights and Linear Fit

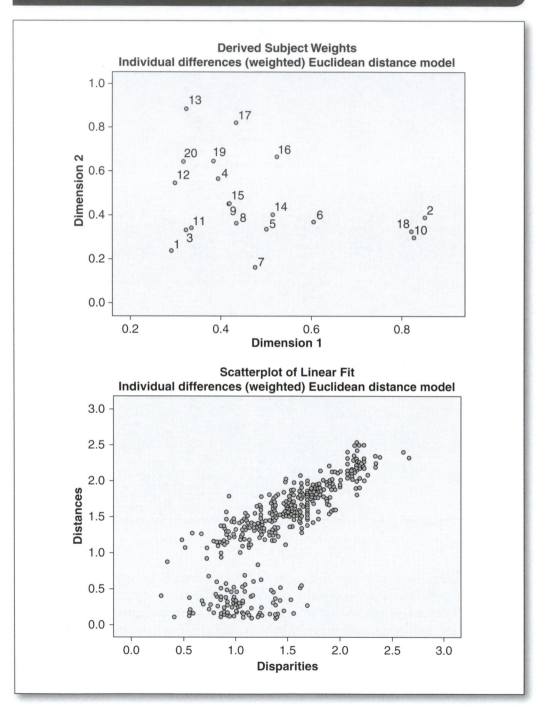

Figure 14b.27 Flattened Subject Weights Table and Plot

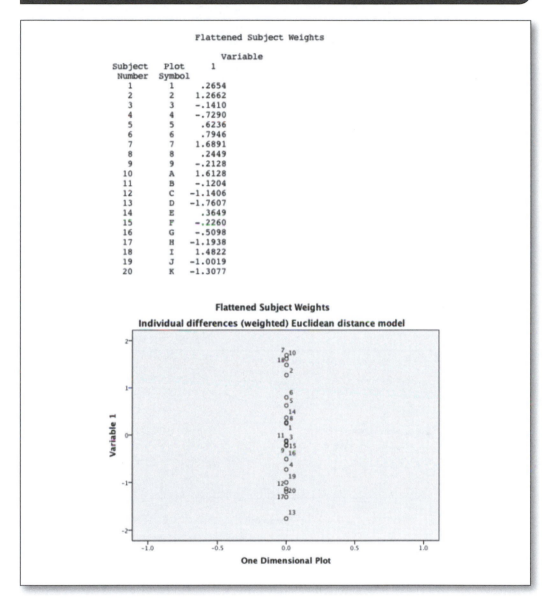

The **Stimulus Coordinates** and the perceptual map or **Derived Stimulus Configuration Individual differences (weighted) Euclidean distance model** are displayed in Figure 14b.28. Three obvious sets of store clusters can be discerned in this two-dimensional configuration. **Dimension 1** (on the horizontal axis) can be

Figure 14b.28 Stimulus Coordinates and Perceptual Map

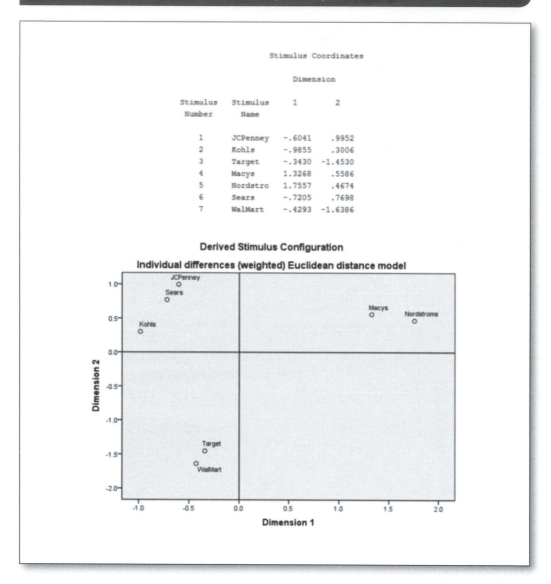

Stimulus Coordinates

Dimension

Stimulus Number	Stimulus Name	1	2
1	JCPenney	-.6041	.9952
2	Kohls	-.9855	.3006
3	Target	-.3430	-1.4530
4	Macys	1.3268	.5586
5	Nordstro	1.7557	.4674
6	Sears	-.7205	.7698
7	WalMart	-.4293	-1.6386

Derived Stimulus Configuration

Individual differences (weighted) Euclidean distance model

considered a "Cost" dimension; in the display, lower cost is toward the left and higher cost is toward the right. **Dimension 2** (vertical dimension) can be construed as a "Perceived Value" dimension; greater perceived value is toward the top and lower perceived value is toward the bottom.

With the dimensions identified, we can now interpret the three store groupings. Nordstrom's and Macy's are clustered together and appear to be perceived as higher-cost and higher–perceived value stores. Kohl's, Sears, and JCPenney also grouped together and appear to be viewed as lower-cost and higher–perceived value stores. Last, Walmart and Target grouped together and represent respondents' perceptions of lower cost and lower perceived value. The fourth quadrant of the perceptual map (high cost, low perceived value) was empty because none of the pairs of stores were seen as reflecting those attributes (we suspect that few retail stores could be viable in this quadrant).

One final caveat is in order. The sample consisted of a set of psychology graduate students. Such a sample is not likely to be representative of the population as a whole or of the subset of the population likely to extensively shop at these retail stores. What we see in Figure 14b.28 is the collective judgment of our set of stores as seen through the eyes of these students, and the image portrayed may be quite different from that built on the judgments of different sets of consumers.

14B.4.4 Reporting Metric WMDS Results

Twenty respondents were asked to judge the similarity/dissimilarity of seven major department stores. Each respondent was given a separate randomized list of 21 ($n(n - 1)/2$ or $(7 * 6)/2 = 42/2 = 21$) paired department stores on which they made dissimilarity judgments. Respondents rated each pair of department stores on a 9-point summative response scale (1 = *very similar*, 9 = *very dissimilar*). Each of the 20 respondents' data was entered as 20 contiguous symmetric data matrices in one IBM SPSS data file and analyzed with the weighted multidimensional scaling (WMDS or individual differences scaling, INDSCAL) procedure. Convergence was achieved after seven iterations, resulting in a Young's S-stress value of .350, Kruskal's Stress (averaged over all 20 respondents) value of .307, and an R^2 value of .50, indicating a moderate to good fit of the weighted Euclidean model to the data. Weirdness index values ranged from .03 to .57 with four respondents yielding index values greater than .50. Based on a comparison of two- and three-dimensional analyses, the two-dimensional model was deemed the best fit. The two-dimensional Derived Stimulus Configuration (or perceptual map) can be seen in Figure 14b.28.

Dimension 1 appears to depict a *cost* dimension, whereas Dimension 2 expresses a *perceived value* dimension. Accordingly, Nordstrom's and Macy's (in the upper right quadrant) can be viewed as higher cost and higher perceived value, whereas Kohl's, Sears, and JCPenney (clustered in the upper left quadrant) can be considered as lower cost and higher perceived value. Wal-Mart and Target (clustered in the lower left quadrant) represent lower cost and lower perceived value. The empty lower right quadrant represents higher cost and lower perceived value and indicates that respondents did not judge any of the seven pairs of stores to reflect those attributes. The scatterplot of linear fit (see Figure 14b.26) indicates some scatter and departure from linearity, which suggests the model fit is reasonable but not ideal.

Cluster Analysis

15A.1 Introduction

Cluster analysis, at least on a superficial level, bears a certain resemblance to MDS analysis that was covered in Chapters 14A and 14B. In both types of analyses, we use the proximities (distances) between cases to organize them (Davison, 1983). But we ordinarily manage the information differently in the two approaches—in MDS, we attempt to identify the dimensions along which we can understand the dissimilarities among the cases; in cluster analysis, we analyze the cases so that we can obtain groupings or clusters of them.

Cluster analysis does not involve testing any null hypothesis, but we assume that the variables included in the analysis are relevant to the task at hand (DeStefano, 2012; Everitt, Landau, Leese, & Stahl, 2011). The result of the procedure is therefore not a statistic that has a sampling distribution (e.g., the F ratio or the Pearson r) that can be tested for statistical significance. Rather, this type of analysis is exploratory, and the outcome is the best structuring of the cases that we could do given the variables that are used and the specifications that the researchers selected for performing the analysis. The strong assumptions that must be met to properly interpret the results of procedures based on the general linear model do not apply to cluster analysis.

15A.2 Two Types of Clustering

Bock (2008) provides a detailed history of cluster analysis, the beginnings of which can be traced back to the 1950s. Cluster analysis rapidly gained popularity during the 1960s and 1970s as a result of the book written by Sokal and Sneath (1963).

There are two types of cluster analyses that we cover in this chapter. The first type that we cover is known as *hierarchical clustering*. Although this technique has many other uses (e.g., it can be used in certain variations of the second type of clustering that we will cover), a common use is to sort a relatively small number of cases into subgroups or clusters on the basis of several quantitative variables. The second type of cluster analysis that we cover is one of the *iterative-agglomerative clustering* procedures—specifically, the *k-means clustering* procedure. This is a classic technique whose primary purpose is to identify from a relatively large sample a few subgroups of cases based on a relatively small set of variables. We will discuss hierarchical clustering first and then move on to a discussion of *k*-means clustering.

15A.3 Hierarchical Clustering

One of the main uses of hierarchical clustering is to cluster or group a small to moderate number of cases based on several quantitative attributes. The process is hierarchical in that once joined in a cluster, the cases are forever bound together in that analysis.

15A.3.1 Overview

The cases that are clustered or grouped can be any kind of entity. For example, they could be individuals such as prominent world leaders, members of a particular social network, workers in a particular office, or graduate students working at an internship site. They could also be other kinds of entities such as branch offices of a large corporation, countries comprising the European Union, patrol districts of a law enforcement organization, or even brands of beers—this last application was actually one of the early hierarchical clustering examples used in an SPSS manual (SPSS, 1988).

For the hierarchal clustering procedure to be properly performed, each case must be measured on a set of quantitative variables. To illustrate, members of a social network could be assessed on variables such as the number of siblings they have, the number of hours they spend on non–work related Internet sites, the number of books they read each year, the degree to which they endorse a particular political orientation (e.g., conservative), their annual income, and so on. The hierarchical clustering procedure can then be applied to determine which members of the social network are most similar, based on the variables on which the cases have been measured.

Just as was true for all of the statistical techniques that we have covered in this book, the results that we obtain from the hierarchical clustering analysis depend on the data serving as its base. For example, we can say that two members of the social network, Kasey and Leanne, are sufficiently similar to each other to be joined or linked together in a cluster very early in the analysis, but that assessment is made on the basis of the specific variables that have been used as clustering variables in the analysis; had we used a different set of variables Kasey and Leanne might well have been linked much later in the analysis.

15A.3.2 The Clustering Process

Hierarchical clustering proceeds one step at a time. During each step, one linking or clustering of cases occurs in the clustering process; this linking is known as a step, and how this linking is accomplished is discussed in Section 15A.3.6. At the start of the analysis, each case can be thought of as a cluster (yes, it is an odd way to speak of single cases but it helps conceptualize the hierarchal clustering process). Thus, at the start there are *n* clusters (where *n* is the number of cases). In the first step of the analysis, the two entities that are most similar to one another or are, in the language of clustering, *closest* to one another (i.e., have the least "distance" between them as described in Section 15A.3.5) are combined or joined into a single cluster. This cluster is a new entity in that the two cases comprising it are joined together and will remain so throughout the remaining steps of the analysis.

Let's say (to follow our social network illustration) that Kasey and Leanne are joined together in this first step. Once this first linking has been accomplished, we are now left with *n* − 1 entities remaining to be clustered. One of these remaining entities is the Kasey–Leanne cluster; the remaining entities are separate members of the social network.

In the second step, the least distant or closest two of the remaining entities are combined into a single cluster leaving (*n* − 1) − 1 or *n* − 2 entities still remaining to be clustered. Let's say that in this second step of our social network illustration, Chuck and Kamilah are linked. This process is carried out step after step. On the third step, any of the following is possible:

- A new member could be linked to the Kasey–Leanne cluster.
- A new member could be linked to the Chuck–Kamilah cluster.
- The Chuck–Kamilah cluster could be linked to the Kasey–Leanne cluster.
- Two other individual cases could be joined together into a new cluster.

At each step, a new cluster can be formed between any two entities that remain. Generally, entities that are most similar based on the set of variables in the analysis are clustered together in earlier steps. This process continues until there is only one "giant" entity remaining, that is, the analysis goes to completion. Thus, no matter how dissimilar two entities may be, they are ultimately going to be joined together by the end of the analysis. It is the researcher's task to determine which step or solution (how many clusters) prior to the analysis having reached completion is most appropriate for their particular research question.

15A.3.3 Separating Two Issues: Distance and Linking

In our description above, we quickly alluded to two different aspects of the data analysis that we now need to more explicitly discuss. Entities can be assessed on the *distance* that lies between them, and the treatment is similar to how this issue is treated in MDS (see Section 14A.8). Distance is a quantitative index defining the similarities of the clusters or entities remaining in the analysis at each step. There are several algorithms available to compute distance, and researchers need to select (from an IBM SPSS drop-down menu) the particular distance measure they wish to use for the analysis.

The two clusters or entities having the smallest distance between them as determined by the distance measure that has been used are linked together in a cluster (or a larger cluster). There are several methods available to *link* entities together, and researchers also need to select (from an IBM SPSS drop-down menu) the particular linking algorithm they wish to use for the analysis.

Assessing the distance between entities and linking them together presumes that these mathematical procedures can be applied to the data set such that we can properly interpret the outcome. To ensure proper interpretation, we must first standardize our variables.

15A.3.4 Standardizing the Variables

Because of the way the distances are computed and the strategy used to link the clusters, it is necessary that the results of the numerical computations be interpretable. Calculating distances involves subtracting, adding, and sometimes squaring scores for cases on the variables used as the basis of clustering. Thus, variables whose values are "large" relative to other variables could inappropriately "overshadow" those variables. For example, a variable such as the number of individuals with whom the cases have been in Internet contact during the past month could have values in the 100s; however, another variable assessing the degree to which they enjoy live theater might be assessed on a 5-point summative response scale.

To numerically equalize all the variables that will be used to cluster cases, we transform the values to standardized scores prior to the analysis. The **Hierarchal Clustering** procedure in IBM SPSS has a checkbox to request that a transformation to z scores be made if the data are not already in that form. Once the variables are transformed to z scores, each will have a mean value of 0 and a standard deviation value of 1. Thus, the subtracting, adding, and squaring of scores is performed on variables that are scaled along the same metric. In our descriptions of distance measures and linkage strategies, readers should assume that all references to numerical calculations are intended to be applied to the z-score form of the variables.

15A.3.5 Distance Measures

There are several distance measures that are available in IBM SPSS. Most of these distance measures are computed by subtracting corresponding values for one entity from those of another entity. Distances are computed between sets of cases or clusters. We briefly describe each of the distance measures below. Our recommendations are presented in Section 15A3.7.

15A.3.5.1 Squared Euclidian Distance

We discussed Euclidian distance in Section 14A.8.1 in the context of MDS. This distance measure (we discuss its squared value here) also can be used in cluster analysis. The first stage of computing the squared Euclidian distance between Entity A and Entity B involves matching these entities on each of the clustering variables and subtracting corresponding values. To make the computations more understandable, we will illustrate this in a concrete way. Assume that we are computing the squared Euclidian distance between Kasey and Leanne. Further assume that although there are many clustering variables in the analysis, we will focus on just two of them (the number of fiction books read each year and the degree to which they identify themselves as spiritual individuals) to simplify our discussion. Recall that these and all the other variables have already been converted to z scores.

The squared Euclidian distance between Kasey and Leanne based on these two variables is obtained in three stages:

1. In the first stage, which is the most involved stage, we subtract corresponding scores on the variables. To illustrate, we subtract Leanne's z score from Kasey's z score on each variable. Specifically, for books read we would have Kasey's value minus Leanne's value, and for spirituality we would have Kasey's value minus Leanne's value. We would continue on for all of the cluster variables.

2. In the second computation stage we square the result of each subtraction. This removes any negative values we have accrued in the subtractions.

3. In the third computation stage we add all of these squared values. The result of this is the squared Euclidian distance between Kasey and Leanne.

15A.3.5.2 Euclidian Distance

Euclidian distance is the square root of squared Euclidian distance. We simply take the result of the third-stage computation of squared Euclidian distance and compute its square root.

15A.3.5.3 City Block Distance

City block distance (also called Manhattan distance for what may be an obvious yet geocentric reason) is computed in the same way as squared Euclidian distance, with the following exceptions:

1. In the first stage, where we subtract the two values of corresponding variables, the absolute (rather than ordered) difference is computed. This results in only positive values associated with the differences. Because we have only positive values there is no reason to square the differences to remove negative values.

2. In the second computation stage, we add all of these absolute difference values. The result of this is the city block distance between Kasey and Leanne.

15A.3.5.4 Chebychev Distance

Chebychev distance is computed starting in the same way that we do for the city block distance algorithm, but it is simpler:

1. In the first stage, where we subtract the two values of corresponding variables, the absolute (rather than ordered) difference is computed. This results in only positive values associated with the differences.

2. In the second stage, only the single largest absolute difference is used. The result of this is the Chebychev distance between Kasey and Leanne.

15A.3.5.5 Minkowski Distance

Minkowski distance is one of the "power" algorithms available in IBM SPSS. It starts in a manner similar to the city block computation and then gets more complex:

1. In the first stage, where we subtract the two values of corresponding variables, the absolute (rather than ordered) difference is computed. This results in only positive values associated with the differences.

2. In the second stage, each absolute difference is raised to the power p, where p is a value selected by the researchers. To the extent that the Minkowski procedure is used, values of p of 2 and 4 may be a bit more common.

3. In the third computation stage, we add all of these values.

4. In the fourth stage, the sum of the values is raised to the power $1/p$. The result of this is the Minkowski distance between Kasey and Leanne.

15A.3.5.6 Power Metric Distance

The power metric distance algorithm is very similar to the Minkowski procedure except that the power factor in stages two and four can be of different values:

1. In the first stage, where we subtract the two values of corresponding variables, the absolute (rather than ordered) difference is computed. This results in only positive values associated with the differences.

2. In the second stage, each absolute difference is raised to the power p, where p is a value selected by the researchers. To the extent that the Minkowski procedure is used, values of p of 2 and 4 are probably a bit more common.

3. In the third computation stage, we add all of these values.

4. In the fourth stage, the sum of the values is raised to the power $1/r$, where r is a value selected by the researchers. To the extent that the power metric procedure is used, values of r of 2 and 4 may be a bit more common. The result of this is the power metric distance between Kasey and Leanne.

15A.3.6 Linkage Methods

Once the distances between cases or clusters have been computed, a decision must be made regarding which entities will be joined or linked into a cluster. Analogous to distance measures, there are several linkage methods that are available in IBM SPSS. Most of the linkage methods available in IBM SPSS involve comparing the distances between all pairs of clusters and using a particular rule to decide which pair is closest. We briefly describe each of the linkage methods below, and our recommendations are presented in Section 15A3.8.

15A.3.6.1 Unweighted Pair-Group Method With Arithmetic Averages Method

The *unweighted pair-group method with arithmetic averages* method is also called the *average linkage between groups* method. In this method, the average distance between all "cross-pairs" of entities (cases or clusters) is calculated, where a cross-pair is a pairing of variables from each different cluster. To illustrate, assume that at this particular step in the analysis, Cluster A contained Kasey and Leanne and Cluster B contained Chuck and Kamilah. The cross-pairs would be (Kasey, Chuck), (Kasey, Kamilah), (Leanne, Chuck), and (Leanne, Kamilah). Four distances (measured by one of the measures described above) would be derived, one for each cross-pair, and the average of these four distances would then be computed. This average would be the average linkage between groups for the joining of Clusters A and B. The average linkage between groups for all cluster combinations is derived, and the one combination resulting in the smallest average distance is accepted as the cluster pair that will be merged at this step of the analysis.

15A.3.6.2 Average Linkage Within Groups Method

The average linkage within groups method is a bit more complex than the method we just described. Here, all cluster combinations are also explored, but what is calculated is the average distance between all cases within each potentially new cluster. Using the above illustration, we would derive the average distance for all possible cross-pairs: (Kasey, Leanne), (Kasey, Chuck), (Kasey, Kamilah), (Leanne, Chuck), (Leanne, Kamilah), and (Chuck, Kamilah). This process would be repeated for all other cluster combinations. The pair of clusters with the smallest average distance is the one selected as the cluster pair that will be merged at this step of the analysis.

15A.3.6.3 Nearest Neighbor Method

The nearest neighbor method is also called the *single linkage* method. It focuses on only the smallest distance between two cases in different clusters. To illustrate this, assume that Cluster A contained Kasey and Leanne, Cluster B contained Chuck and Kamilah, and Cluster C contained Kelly and Pedro. The analysis would then proceed as follows.

We would first deal with the distances between the cases in Cluster A and the other clusters. We would therefore compute the distance between Kasey and Chuck, Kasey and Kamilah, Kasey and Kelly, and Kasey and Pedro. Then, we would compute the distance between Leanne and Chuck, Leanne and Kamilah, Leanne and Kelly, and Leanne and Pedro. All distances would be compared, and only the smallest distance would be retained.

We would next deal with the distances between the cases in Cluster B and the other clusters. We would therefore compute the distance between Chuck and Kasey, Chuck and Leanne, Chuck and Kelly, and Chuck and Pedro. We would then repeat this process for Kamilah. All distances would be compared, and only the smallest distance would be retained.

Finally, we would deal with the distances between the cases in Cluster C and the other clusters. We would therefore compute the distance between Kelly and each of the others followed by the same computation for Pedro. All distances would be compared, and only the smallest distance would be retained.

When the dust finally settled, we would have three distances in this illustration. Each distance represented the smallest distance in the comparison of clusters. We now would in this final moment determine the smallest distance of these three. The cluster pair corresponding to that distance is accepted as the cluster pair that will be merged at this step of the analysis.

15A.3.6.4 Furthest Neighbor Method

The furthest neighbor method is also called the *complete linkage* method. This procedure is the same as the nearest neighbor method except that what is retained in each pairwise cluster comparison is the largest distance rather than the smallest distance. When the dust raised by this complete linkage method finally settled, we would again have three distances in this illustration. Each distance is now represented by the largest distance in the comparison of clusters. We would now in this final moment determine the smallest distance of these three. The cluster pair corresponding to that distance is accepted as the cluster pair that will be merged at this step of the analysis.

15A.3.6.5 Ward's Method

Ward's (1963) method deals with the sum of the squared within-cluster distances for each potential cluster (similar to the traditional "sum of squares" as the sum of the deviations of scores around a mean in ANOVA) at this step in the analysis. The procedure is as follows:

1. We first compute the mean for each clustering variable.

2. Next, for each case the mean is subtracted from the score and the difference is squared.

3. Then, the squared deviations are summed across variables and cases.

4. This process yields a sum of the squared within-cluster distances. The cluster pair corresponding to the smallest value is accepted as the cluster pair that will be merged at this step of the analysis.

15A.3.6.6 The Centroid and Median Methods

The proper name for the centroid method is the *unweighted pair-group centroid method*; the proper name for median method is the *weighted pair-group centroid method*. These methods are extremely similar to each other, and so we cover them at one time. A centroid is an average as is a mean; the difference is that a mean is the central value of a single variable whereas a centroid is the central value when multiple variables are combined.

The same general computational procedure is applicable to both methods. According to Norusis (2011, p. 373), "For each cluster, the means for all variables are calculated. Then, for each case, the squared Euclidean distance to the cluster means is calculated. These distances are summed for all of the cases." The cluster pair with the smallest value is accepted as the cluster pair that will be merged at this step of the analysis.

The two methods differ in how the centroids are weighted:

In the centroid method, the centroid of a merged cluster is a weighted combination of the centroids of the two individual clusters, where the weights are proportional to the sizes of the clusters . . . [in the median method] the two clusters being combined are weighted equally in the computation of the centroid, regardless of the number of cases in each. This allows small groups to have an equal effect on the characterization of larger clusters into which they are merged. (Norusis, 2011, pp. 373–374)

15A.3.7 Distance and Linkage Recommendations

Given the many distance and linkage methods measures, it can be difficult to decide which to use in a particular analysis. If we were limited to a single analysis, we would probably select squared Euclidian distances and the average distance between groups linkage method. But users can perform any number of analyses that they wish, and if there is no theoretical reason for using one or another of the distance measures or linkage methods, then we suggest exploring several combinations before deciding on the one that will be most useful for their purposes. The constraint to adopting such a strategy is to always bear in mind that this is an exploratory analysis and is being used pragmatically and judiciously to help the researchers describe possible relationships among the cases in the study.

15A.3.8 The Output of Interest

Although there are several sets of results that are contained in the output of a hierarchical cluster analysis, the most well-known (and probably the most useful to most researchers) is the *icicle plot*. IBM SPSS can display this plot in different ways but the most traditional view, and the one that inspired the name, is the vertical plot. It is called an icicle plot, because in its vertical display, it resembles frozen water as it has dripped from an overhang.

We have created fictional results for our social network to illustrate hierarchical clustering and present the results in three versions of a vertical icicle plot in Figure 15a.1. The top display is close to what can be seen in previous versions of IBM SPSS output, and with a little imagination, one can make out icicles (of a sort) hanging from a roof; *X*s were used because early printers (dot matrix line printers) could not generate true graphics. We show this display because (a) readers may see it in some publications and (b) the presence of the *X*s may make the results a little easier to see. In the middle display, we have supplied a tinted version of the top plot to help readers see the pattern. The bottom plot is very similar to the current IBM SPSS display in which the *X*s are no longer provided.

Here is how to read the plot. The cases who are to be clustered are presented as column headings. They have already been ordered in terms of when they are linked together in a cluster (the software uses the statistical results to format the display) so that the display is readable. In our simplified illustration, we have only six cases, and so the cluster procedure starts with six clusters; however, the six-cluster situation is not shown in the display—we pick up the display after the first cluster has been formed.

Figure 15a.1 Vertical Icicle Plots of a Hierarchical Clustering Solution (*Top*: Older SPSS Version; *Middle*: Tinted Version of Older Output; *Bottom*: Current IBM SPSS Output)

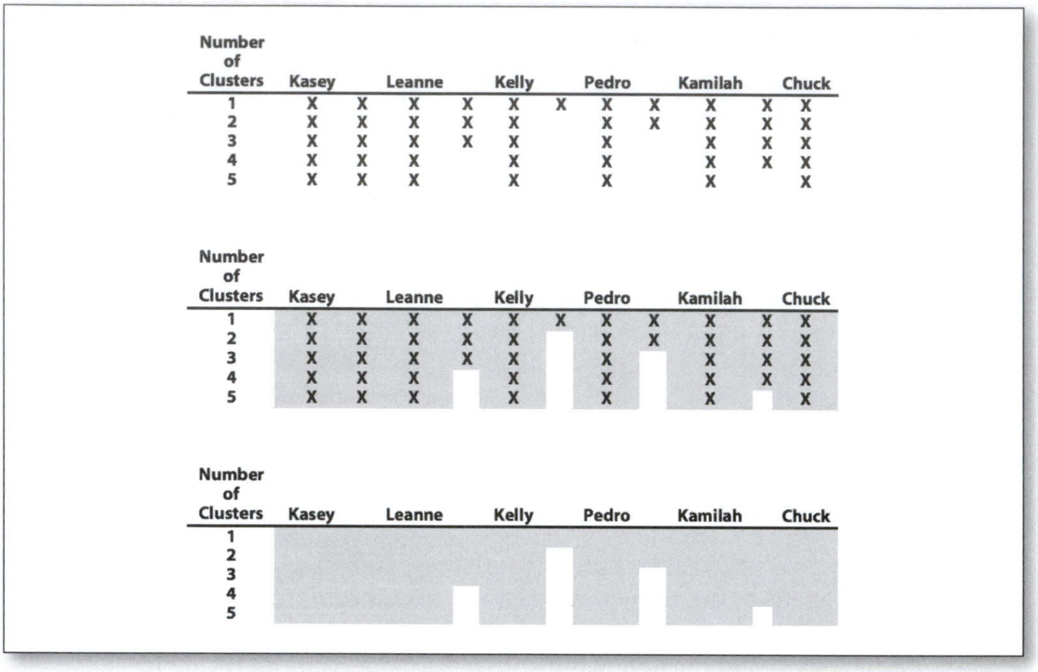

The cluster solution in the icicle plot begins at the bottom of the display and finishes at the top. In the first step of the hierarchical clustering procedure Kasey and Leanne were joined together in a cluster. To visually communicate that Kasey and Leanne have been linked, in the top and middle displays the entire column between them has been filled with *X*s to represent the fact that they have been joined or linked together to form a cluster; in the current form of the display shown below these two, we must use the tinting as our exclusive cue that Kasey and Leanne have been combined into a single cluster. At the moment following their linking, there are five clusters in the data set: Kelly, Pedro, Kamilah, and Chuck comprise four of those clusters and the cluster of Kasey–Leanne comprises the fifth. This is illustrated in the last row of the display labeled **5** under **Number of Clusters**.

In the next step of the hierarchical clustering procedure (shown in the second row from the bottom) Kamilah and Chuck were joined together in a cluster. Thus, there are now four clusters in the data set: Kelly and Pedro are each their own cluster, there is the cluster of Kasey–Leanne, and now there is also the cluster of Kamilah–Chuck. This is illustrated in the row of the display labeled **4** under **Number of Clusters**. To visually communicate that Kamilah and Chuck have been linked, the column between them from the fourth row up has been filled with *Xs* in the top two displays; again, in the current pictorial representation shown in the last display, that information is contained in the tinting.

In the next (third) step, we reduce the four clusters to three. As can be seen in the row of the display labeled **3** under **Number of Clusters**, Kelly has joined the Kasey–Leanne cluster. The next-to-last (second) step reduces the three clusters to two. In our illustration, Pedro has been linked to the Kamilah–Chuck cluster. And, at the final and least interesting step shown in the row labeled **1** under **Number of Clusters**, the Kasey–Leanne–Kelly cluster is linked to the Kamilah–Chuck–Pedro cluster to form a single set of cases.

The interpretation of a hierarchical clustering solution has a certain subjectivity associated with it. What is clear, based on the variables that were measured, is that Kasey and Leanne have more similarity than any other pair. We can also say that Kamilah and Chuck are next most similar to each other. Kelly eventually joins Kasey and Leanne, and Pedro eventually joins Kamilah and Chuck, but we know that at some point cases are forced to join together simply because the number of clusters permitted shrinks steadily as the steps progress.

So how many clusters do we have in the solution? The answer requires a subjective but educated decision by the researchers. It depends on several factors including some numerical output that we have not shown here, the knowledge of the cases that the researchers can bring to bear, and the context and purpose of the research. Our answer here is that we would be inclined to accept two clusters because all six cases would then be a part of one of the two clusters. One cluster would be the Kasey–Leanne–Kelly cluster and the other cluster would be Kamilah–Chuck–Pedro.

15A.4 k-*Means Clustering*

One of the main uses of *k*-means clustering is to cluster or group a relatively large number of cases based on a few quantitative attributes. The *k*-means clustering algorithm was named by J. MacQueen (1967), but the version of the algorithm that is generally used today was developed by Hartigan and Wong (1979). Although more modern extensions of the *k*-means algorithm have been developed, such as expectation maximization clustering (e.g., Dempster, Laird, & Rubin, 1977; Witten & Frank, 2005; Wu, 1983), *k*-means is still very commonly used and works quite well.

15A.4.1 Overview

The *k*-means clustering process is *agglomerative* in that cases are added to a cluster over the course of completing a phase in the analysis. The process is *iterative* in that the agglomerative process starts over based on the results of the last step and continues in this cyclic manner until the solution stabilizes. Unlike hierarchical clustering, researchers must specify the number of clusters at the start of the analysis. Although some statisticians have examined strategies to analytically project how many clusters should be descriptive of a given data set (see Milligan & Cooper, 1985; Steinley, 2007; Steinley & Brusco, 2011), many researchers will often perform a range of analyses and then compare the results before arriving at their judgment of the number of clusters they will accept as their solution.

15A.4.2 Phases of the Analysis

As was true for hierarchal clustering, the variables should be in z-score form at the start of the analysis. Unlike the hierarchal clustering procedure in IBM SPSS, there is no checkbox to standardize the variables on the fly—thus, this standardization step must be accomplished prior to invoking the k-means procedure.

K-means begins with a *classification* phase. It first identifies a set of k cases, where k is the number of clusters specified in setting up the analysis. These cases are selected by IBM SPSS to be quite far apart on the clustering variables and will serve as *seed points* or initial cluster centers in this phase of the analysis. Norusis (2011) reminds us to be sure that we have screened our data for outliers to prevent them from being selected as an initial seed point, as such a selection can distort the results of the analysis (e.g., the analysis can then generate clusters with very few cases far on the periphery of the data set).

Clusters are then built with a case at a time joining the cluster to which it is closest. A modified centroid method is used that involves computing the Euclidian distance between the centroid or center of the cluster (an average of the clustering variables) and the non-clustered entities. The smallest distance identifies which entity is to be absorbed by which cluster.

IBM SPSS provides a choice to users regarding the consequences of absorbing an entity into a cluster. One option, which we would not recommend to readers, is to recompute the cluster centers each time a new entity is added. The drawback to this option is that because of the way in which the analysis is structured, the order of cases in the date file can affect the outcome of the analysis.

The other option, and the one that we do recommend, is to not update the cluster centers after each new entity is added but to perform an updating once all of the cases have been assigned membership in one of the clusters; this constitutes a *reassignment* phase in which each case is reassigned to the nearest cluster. Once all of the cases have been reassigned, cluster centers based on this reconfiguration are computed. IBM SPSS then checks to see how much change in distance has occurred between the initial cluster centers and the current ones (actually, it just looks at the largest change). If that change is above a preset threshold, it starts again (iterates), using the current cluster centers as the initial centers (seed points) of another classification phase.

Iteration continues until one of two things happens: (a) the change in distance reaches its criterion threshold and (b) it reaches the number of iterations that was specified by the researcher. Thus, researchers should specify a very high number of iterations to allow the solution to reach criterion. Assuming that criterion is reached, the final cluster centers are a focal point of the results.

15A.4.3 Results of the Analysis

There are two key elements of the results that are very useful: the final cluster centers and cluster membership.

15A.4.3.1 Final Cluster Centers

The final cluster centers convey a good deal of information. These centers are the z-score means of the clustering variables for each cluster. The pattern of means for each cluster defines, in a concrete way, how to view or profile the cases in each cluster.

We can illustrate how to interpret the pattern of final cluster centers by referring to the fictional (and may we say exaggerated) results shown in Table 15a.1. In this illustration, we have used the "Big 5" personality factors as the clustering variables and have presented a three-cluster solution for convenience. Remember that these means are in z-score form, that z scores have a mean of 0 and a standard deviation of 1, that on the normal curve approximately 68% of the cases lie between ±1 *SD*, and that approximately 95% of the cases lie between ±1.96 *SD*. Hence, z scores in excess of ±1 *SD* are reasonably large, and z scores in excess of ±1.50 *SD* are quite large.

To make concrete how to interpret values in Table 15a.1, consider the mean neuroticism value of the cases classified as being members of Cluster 1. On average, these cases had a neuroticism score of 1.93. That value is almost 2 *SD* units above the mean for the entire sample and represents a very high level of neuroticism. On the other hand, these cases

Table 15a.1　Final Cluster Centers in z Score From

Variable	Cluster 1	Cluster 2	Cluster 3
Neuroticism	1.93	−1.72	0.52
Extroversion	1.56	1.68	−1.29
Openness	0.24	1.45	−1.35
Agreeableness	−1.84	0.27	1.73
Conscientiousness	−0.31	−0.87	1.41

average only 0.24 on openness. That value is about a quarter of a standard deviation above the mean of the entire sample and would certainly be considered to be very close to the full sample average. Given that context, we can profile the clusters as follows:

- Cases in Cluster 1 appear to be pretty neurotic, extroverted, and disagreeable. These are probably folks who would be quite noticeable at a social gathering and who would not get along well with others.
- Cases in Cluster 2 are psychologically stable (the other end of the neuroticism spectrum), relatively extroverted and open to new experiences, but tend toward not being that conscientious. These folks may have been the popular kids in high school.
- Cases in Cluster 3 are agreeable and conscientious and neither open to new experiences nor very social. They would probably make good students who keep to themselves.

15A.4.3.2 Cluster Membership

In the process of setting up the analysis, IBM SPSS provides users with the opportunity to save the final cluster membership of each case. It is very likely that researchers will want to do this. This cluster membership variable, coded as 1, 2, and so on corresponding to the cluster numbers in the analysis, can be used as a grouping variable in subsequent analyses. Thus, it may be useful to determine how the three cluster groups discussed above compare (e.g., in a MANOVA and discriminant analysis) with other variables that are in the data file. This allows researchers to use more subtle variables than demographic variables (e.g., sex, age) to create groups in their data analysis.

15A.5 Recommended Readings

Arabie, P., Carroll, J. D., & DeSarbo, W. S. (1987). *Three-way scaling and clustering.* Newbury Park, CA: Sage.

Breckenridge, J. N. (2000). Validating cluster analysis: Consistent replication and symmetry. *Multivariate Behavioral Research, 35,* 261–285.

Clatworthy, J., Buick, D., Hankins, M., Weinman, J., & Horne, R. (2005). The use and reporting of cluster analysis in health psychology: A review. *British Journal of Health Psychology, 10,* 329–358.

Liu, B. (2007). *Web data mining: Exploring hyperlinks, contents, and usage data.* New York, NY: Springer.

Steinley, D. (2006). *K*-means clustering: A half-century synthesis. *British Journal of Mathematical and Statistical Psychology, 59,* 1–34.

Witten, I. H., & Frank, E. (2005). *Data mining: Practical machine learning tools and techniques.* San Francisco, CA: Morgan Kaufmann.

Cluster Analysis Using IBM SPSS

15B.1 Hierarchical Cluster Analysis

The cases for our example of hierarchical cluster analysis are eight states selected haphazardly but with the intention to cover a range of general regions in the mainland United States: California (CA), Colorado (CO), Georgia (GA), Idaho (ID), Illinois (IL), Kansas (KS), Missouri (MO), and Vermont (VT). A wealth of information is available in the public domain (e.g., census data) on a state basis, and 18 widely varying quantitative variables (e.g., population, median household income, number of airports and bridges, number of Republicans sent to the 110th Congress House of Representatives, number of tornadoes per 100,000 residents) were compiled for each state. A full list of the variables is shown in the **Variable View** screenshot of the data file in Figure 15b.1. The data for this example are contained in **State Statistics**.

15B.1.1 Hierarchical Cluster Analysis Setup

Selecting the path **Analyze ➔ Classify ➔ Hierarchical Cluster Analysis** from the main menu opens the main dialog window displayed in Figure 15b.2. From the variables list panel, click over all of the variables (except **State**) to the **Variable(s)** panel. Select **State** and move it to the **Label Cases by** panel; this will place the state names (the postal abbreviations) in the output to make it possible to understand the results. Select the choice of **Cases** under **Cluster** and check both **Statistics** and **Plots** under **Display**.

Select the **Statistics** pushbutton to arrive at the screen shown in Figure 15b.3. Check both **Agglomeration schedule** and **Proximity matrix**. At the bottom of the screen,

Figure 15b.1 A Screen Shot of the Variable View Screen of the Data File Displaying the Variables Used in the Hierarchical Cluster Analysis

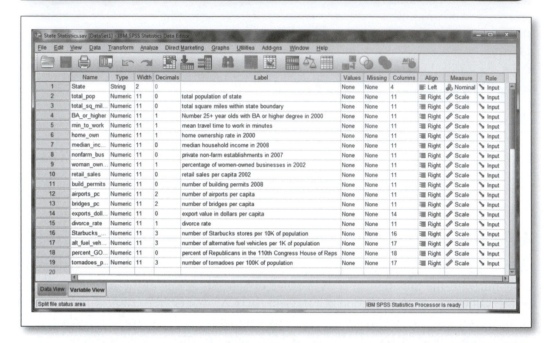

Figure 15b.2 The Main Hierarchical Cluster Screen

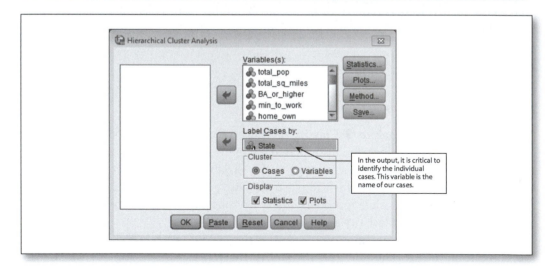

select **Range of solutions** and type in the value of **2** for **Minimum number of clusters** and **8** for **Maximum number of clusters** (this will produce a table tracking cluster membership across the cluster solutions; the vertical icicle plot does the same thing in a more visually compelling way). Click **Continue** to return to the main dialog screen.

Select the **Plots** pushbutton. As shown in Figure 15b.4, keep the defaults of **All clusters** under **Icicle** and **Vertical** under **Orientation** to obtain our vertical icicle plot. Click **Continue** to return to the main dialog screen.

Select the **Cluster Method** pushbutton. As shown in Figure 15b.5, this is the screen we use to specify our linkage method and distance measure. Many researchers will perform several analyses using various combinations of methods and distance metrics. For the sake of keeping this example relatively simple, from the drop-down menus we retain the default of **Between-groups linkage** as the method (officially known as the unweighted pair-group method with arithmetic averages method as well as the average linkage between groups method as described in Section 15A.3.6.1) and **Squared Euclidian distance** as the distance method.

This is also the screen where we specify that IBM SPSS standardize our variables. Under **Transform Values**, select from the drop-down menu **Z scores** and click **By variable**. Click **Continue** to return to the main dialog screen and click **OK** to perform the analysis.

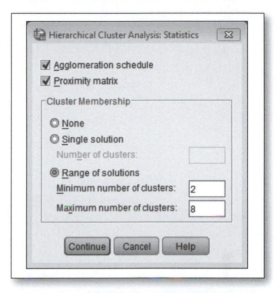

Figure 15b.3 The Statistics Screen of Hierarchical Cluster Analysis

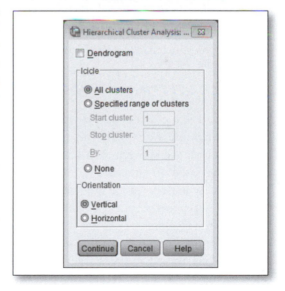

Figure 15b.4 The Plots Screen of Hierarchical Cluster Analysis

Figure 15b.5　The Method Screen of Hierarchical Cluster Analysis

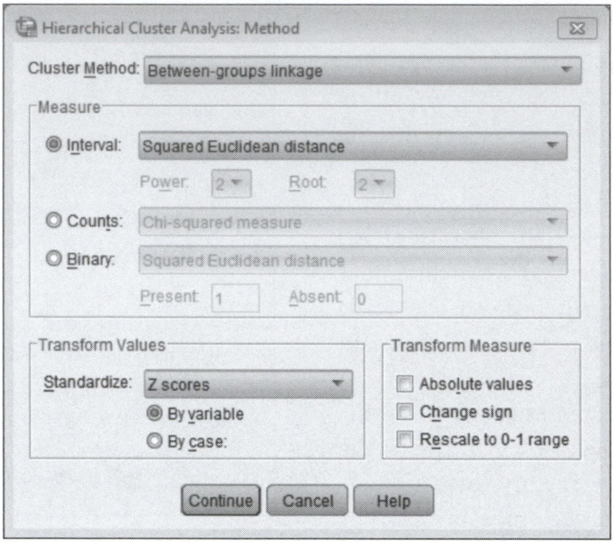

15B.1.2 Hierarchical Cluster Analysis Output

There are three main parts of the output: the proximity matrix, the agglomeration schedule, and the icicle plot. We treat each in turn.

15B.1.2.1 The Proximity Matrix

Figure 15b.6 presents the proximity matrix of squared Euclidian distances as this is the distance measure we specified in the analysis setup. Each entry is the pairwise squared Euclidian distance between the respective states. The matrix is square (redundant information is presented on either side of the diagonal) for easier reading. IBM SPSS labels this a **dissimilarity matrix** (in the note below the table) in that larger values indicate greater distances between cases. These distances are the bases on which the states will be joined together into clusters.

Notice that the smallest value in the matrix is 3.294, the distance between Georgia and Illinois. Thus, these two states are determined to be most similar based on the variables we have used in the analysis. Because they are the most similar, they will be joined together into the first cluster in the analysis.

Figure 15b.6 The Proximity Matrix

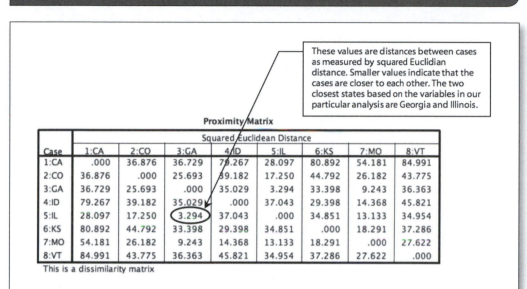

These values are distances between cases as measured by squared Euclidian distance. Smaller values indicate that the cases are closer to each other. The two closest states based on the variables in our particular analysis are Georgia and Illinois.

Proximity Matrix

Case	1:CA	2:CO	3:GA	4:ID	5:IL	6:KS	7:MO	8:VT
1:CA	.000	36.876	36.729	79.267	28.097	80.892	54.181	84.991
2:CO	36.876	.000	25.693	39.182	17.250	44.792	26.182	43.775
3:GA	36.729	25.693	.000	35.029	3.294	33.398	9.243	36.363
4:ID	79.267	39.182	35.029	.000	37.043	29.398	14.368	45.821
5:IL	28.097	17.250	3.294	37.043	.000	34.851	13.133	34.954
6:KS	80.892	44.792	33.398	29.398	34.851	.000	18.291	37.286
7:MO	54.181	26.182	9.243	14.368	13.133	18.291	.000	27.622
8:VT	84.991	43.775	36.363	45.821	34.954	37.286	27.622	.000

Squared Euclidean Distance

This is a dissimilarity matrix

15B.1.2.2 The Icicle Plot, the Agglomeration Schedule, and the Cluster Membership Table

The icicle plot is shown in Figure 15b.7. This plot is represented by the tinted bars against a white background and is most conveniently read from bottom to top. The information contained in the plot is partly summarized in the **Agglomeration Schedule** that is shown in the middle display and tabulated in the **Cluster Membership** table also shown in Figure 15b.7.

We start with the bottom of the icicle plot presenting the results for seven clusters. These seven clusters are actually the Illinois–Georgia cluster that we knew was going to be created from the proximity matrix and the remaining six states still not joined. The agglomeration schedule traces the joining together of states and/or clusters of states at each step in the analysis. Clusters are identified by IBM SPSS according to the first case number in it. Looking at **Stage 1** in the **Agglomeration Schedule** (the first row in the table), we see in the display that **Cluster 3** (Georgia) joined with **Cluster 5** (Illinois). The **Coefficients** column (these are squared Euclidian distances) shows a value of 3.294, which is the distance between Georgia and Illinois. This information is summarized in the **Cluster Membership** table; we note that in the column labeled **7 Clusters** that Georgia and Illinois are both in Cluster 3.

Figure 15b.7   The Vertical Icicle Plot, Agglomeration Schedule, and the Cluster Membership Table

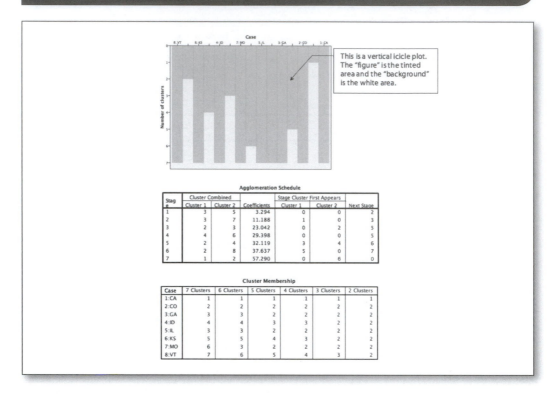

The icicle plot shows us that Missouri joined the Illinois–Georgia cluster next. This is visually depicted when we read across the plot for six clusters. In the **Agglomeration Schedule** in the row for **Stage 2** (the second row in the table), we see in the display that **Cluster 3** (Georgia, which is now linked with Illinois) joined with **Cluster 7** (Missouri). The **Cluster Membership** table in the column labeled **6 Clusters** shows that Missouri is now also in Cluster 3.

The **Coefficients** column of the **Agglomeration Schedule** (these are squared Euclidian distances) shows a value of 11.188. This value of 11.188 is the squared Euclidian distance between Missouri and the Illinois–Georgia cluster. We can obtain this value as follows from the proximity matrix. The distance between Missouri and Georgia is 9.243, and the distance between Missouri and Illinois is 13.133. Averaging the two distances yields 11.188, the value shown in the agglomeration schedule.

Tracing the clustering shown in the icicle plot informs us that Colorado joined the Illinois–Georgia–Missouri cluster next. After that, a new cluster was formed between Idaho and Kansas, followed by a joining of the Illinois–Georgia–Missouri–Colorado cluster with the Idaho–Kansas cluster. Finally, Vermont was linked to the dominant cluster, and at the end, in what might have been called an act of desperation had it been done by a human entity, the dominant cluster finally absorbed California.

That California is quite different from the other states is made evident in the agglomeration schedule. **Stage 7** is where the merge occurred, and the **Coefficient** associated with that joining is 57.290 (the average distance between California and the other seven states, which you can compute from the proximity matrix if you wish), a value quite a bit higher than the other distances shown in the agglomeration table.

One way to summarize these results is to say that of the states that we sampled and the variables on which we measured them, Illinois, Georgia, Missouri, and Colorado appear to be relatively similar to each other and that Kansas and Idaho are similar to a certain extent. However, Vermont (to a certain extent) and California (to a great extent) appear to be different from the other sampled states.

15B.1.3 Reporting Hierarchical Cluster Analysis Results

A hierarchical cluster analysis was used to describe the similarity of the following eight states: California (CA), Colorado (CO), Georgia (GA), Idaho (ID), Illinois (IL), Kansas (KS), Missouri (MO), and Vermont (VT). These states were selected haphazardly but were intended to cover a range of general locations in the mainland United States. Information in the public domain from the U.S. Census Bureau and StateMaster.com served as a source for the following variables used in the analysis: (a) total state population, (b) total square miles within the boundary of the state, (c) number of residents aged 25 years or older who hold a BA or higher degree, (d) mean number of minutes of travel time from work, (e) home ownership rate in 2000, (f) median household income in 2008, (g) private nonfarm establishments in 2007, (h) percentage of women-owned businesses in 2002, (i) retail sales per capita in 2002, (j) number of building permits issued in 2008, (k) number of airports per capita, (l) number of bridges per capita, (m) export value in dollars per capita, (n) divorce rate, (o) number of Starbucks stores per 10,000 residents, (p) number of alternative fuel vehicles per 1,000 residents, (q) percentage of Republicans elected to the 110th Congress House of Representatives, and (r) number of tornadoes per 100,000 residents. Several combinations of different distance measures and linkage methods yielded very similar findings. We report here the results for the average linkage between groups method using squared Euclidian distances.

The proximity matrix is presented in Table 15b.1 showing the pairwise squared Euclidian distance between the respective states. Distances range from a low of 3.294 between Georgia and Illinois to a high of 84.991 between California and Vermont.

The icicle plot is shown in Figure 15b.8. Georgia and Illinois were linked first. Missouri then joined the Illinois–Georgia cluster next, followed by Colorado joining

(Continued)

(Continued)

the Illinois–Georgia–Missouri cluster. After that, a new cluster was formed between Idaho and Kansas, followed by a joining of the Illinois–Georgia–Missouri–Colorado cluster with the Idaho–Kansas cluster. Finally, Vermont was linked to the dominant cluster, with California as the last state to be linked.

That California is quite different from the other states is made evident in the agglomeration schedule shown in Table 15b.2. As can be seen in the table, the average distance between California and the other seven states is 57.290, a value quite a bit higher than the other distances shown in the agglomeration table.

Table 15b.1 Proximity Matrix of Squared Euclidian Distances

	1: CA	2: CO	3: GA	4: ID	5: IL	6: KS	7: MO	8: VT
1: CA	.000	36.876	36.729	79.267	28.097	80.892	54.181	84.991
2: CO	36.876	.000	25.693	39.182	17.250	44.792	26.182	43.775
3: GA	36.729	25.693	.000	35.029	3.294	33.398	9.243	36.363
4: ID	79.267	39.182	35.029	.000	37.043	29.398	14.368	45.821
5: IL	28.097	17.250	3.294	37.043	.000	34.851	13.133	34.954
6: KS	80.892	44.792	33.398	29.398	34.851	.000	18.291	37.286
7: MO	54.181	26.182	9.243	14.368	13.133	18.291	.000	27.622
8: VT	84.991	43.775	36.363	45.821	34.954	37.286	27.622	.000

Figure 15b.8 The Vertical Icicle Plot for the Hierarchical Clustering of Eight States

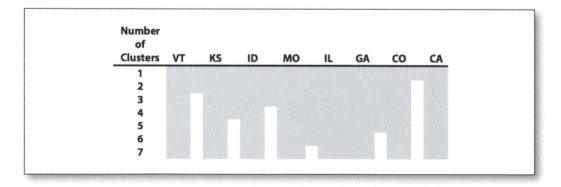

15B.2 k-Means Cluster Analysis

We will use scores on the traditional "Big 5" personality factors to cluster college students who completed a set of inventories including the NEO Five-Factor Inventory (Costa & McCrea, 1992). These scores are recorded in the data file as *T* scores (a standardized score with a mean of 50 and a standard deviation of 10), but to take you through an example analysis, we will convert them to *z* scores as the first stage of the analysis. The data are contained in the file named **Personality Cluster**.

Table 15b.2 Agglomeration Schedule

Stage	Average Distance
1	3.294
2	11.188
3	23.042
4	29.398
5	32.119
6	37.637
7	57.290

15B.2.1 z-Score Transformation

Unlike the **Hierarchical Clustering** procedure, the **K-Means Cluster Analysis** procedure in IBM SPSS does not have an option to standardize the variables. We therefore accomplish this stage of the analysis by selecting **Analyze** ➜ **Descriptive Statistics** ➜ **Descriptives** from the main menu. Move **neoneuro, neoextra, neoopen, neoagree,** and **neoconsc** to the **Variable(s)** panel and check **Save standardized values as variables** as shown in Figure 15b.9. Click **OK** to perform the analysis. We show a screen shot of the data file containing

Figure 15b.9 The Main Descriptives Screen

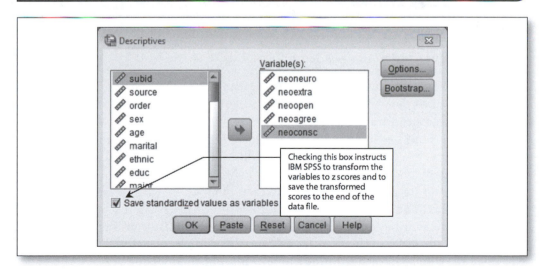

the transformed variables in Figure 15b.10. These newly created standardized variables have been named by IBM SPSS by placing an uppercase "Z" as the first character in the original variable name. For example, the variable **neoneuro** is named **Zneoneuro** in its newly created *z*-score form.

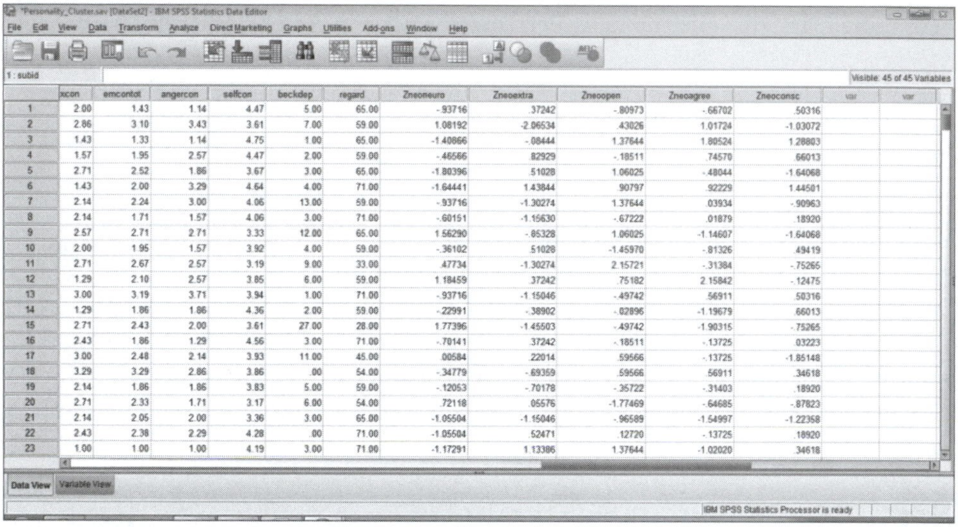

Figure 15b.10 A Screen Shot of the Variable View Screen of the Data File Displaying the Variables to Be Used in the *k*-Means Cluster Analysis

	xcon	emcontot	angercon	selfcon	beckdep	regard	Zneoneuro	Zneoextra	Zneoopen	Zneoagree	Zneoconsc	var	var
1	2.00	1.43	1.14	4.47	5.00	65.00	-.93716	.37242	-.80973	-.66702	.50316		
2	2.86	3.10	3.43	3.61	7.00	59.00	1.08192	-2.06534	.43026	1.01724	-1.03072		
3	1.43	1.33	1.14	4.75	1.00	65.00	-1.40866	-.08444	1.37644	1.80524	1.28803		
4	1.57	1.95	2.57	4.47	2.00	59.00	-.46566	.82929	-.18511	.74570	.66013		
5	2.71	2.52	1.86	3.67	3.00	65.00	-1.80396	.51028	1.06025	-.48044	-1.64068		
6	1.43	2.00	3.29	4.64	4.00	71.00	-1.64441	1.43844	.90797	.92229	1.44501		
7	2.14	2.24	3.00	4.06	13.00	59.00	-.93716	-1.30274	1.37644	.03934	-.90963		
8	2.14	1.71	1.57	4.06	3.00	71.00	-.60151	-1.15630	-.67222	.01879	.18920		
9	2.57	2.71	2.71	3.33	12.00	65.00	1.56290	-.85328	1.06025	-1.14607	-1.64068		
10	2.00	1.95	1.57	3.92	4.00	59.00	-.36102	.51028	-1.45970	-.81326	.49419		
11	2.71	2.67	2.57	3.19	9.00	33.00	.47734	-1.30274	2.15721	-.31384	-.75265		
12	1.29	2.10	2.57	3.85	6.00	59.00	1.18459	.37242	.75182	2.15842	-.12475		
13	3.00	3.19	3.71	3.94	1.00	71.00	-.93716	-1.15046	-.49742	.56911	.50316		
14	1.29	1.86	1.86	4.36	2.00	59.00	-.22991	-.38902	-.02896	-1.19679	.66013		
15	2.71	2.43	2.00	3.61	27.00	28.00	1.77396	-1.45503	-.49742	-1.90315	-.75265		
16	2.43	1.86	1.29	4.56	3.00	71.00	-.70141	.37242	-.18511	-.13725	.03223		
17	3.00	2.48	2.14	3.93	11.00	45.00	.00584	.22014	.59566	-.13725	-1.85148		
18	3.29	3.29	2.86	3.86	.00	54.00	-.34779	-.69359	.59566	.56911	.34618		
19	2.14	1.86	1.86	3.83	5.00	59.00	-.12053	-.70178	-.35722	-.31403	.18920		
20	2.71	2.33	1.71	3.17	6.00	54.00	.72118	.05576	-1.77469	-.64685	-.87823		
21	2.14	2.05	2.00	3.36	3.00	65.00	-1.05504	-1.15046	-.96589	-1.54997	-1.22358		
22	2.43	2.38	2.29	4.28	.00	71.00	-1.05504	.52471	.12720	-.13725	.18920		
23	1.00	1.00	1.00	4.19	3.00	71.00	-1.17291	1.13386	1.37644	-1.02020	.34618		

15B.2.2 k*-Means Cluster Analysis Setup*

Selecting the path **Analyze ➔ Classify ➔ K-Means Cluster** from the main menu brings us to the main dialog window displayed in Figure 15b.11. From the variables list panel, click over **Zneoneuro**, **Zneoextra**, **Zneoopen**, **Zneoagree**, and **Zneoconsc** to the **Variables** panel. Type in **4** in the panel for **Number of Clusters**. In your own research, this might be one of a range of solutions you would explore before deciding on the one you will accept, and check **Iterate and classify** under **Method**.

Click the **Iterate** pushbutton. In the **Iterate** window, shown in Figure 15b.12, we have set the **Maximum Iterations** to 50 just to ensure that we will reach the proximity criterion before running out of iterations. Make sure that **Use running means** is *not* selected, since the order of the cases in the data file will then substantially and improperly affect the solution. Click **Continue** to return to the main dialog window.

Figure 15b.11   The Main *k*-Means Cluster Screen

Select the **Options** pushbutton as shown in Figure 15b.13. In the **Statistics** panel, select **Initial cluster centers** and **ANOVA table**. For **Missing Values,** select the default of **Exclude cases listwise**. Click **Continue** to return to the main dialog window.

Select the **Save** pushbutton. In the **Save** window, as can be seen in Figure 15b.14, you should save **Cluster membership.** This will show up in the data file as a new variable. Each case will have a value of 1, 2, 3, or 4 reflecting to which cluster that case has been assigned. This cluster membership variable can then be used as an independent variable in a subsequent analysis such as a MANOVA. Click **Continue** to return to the main dialog screen and click **OK** to perform the analysis.

Figure 15b.12   The Iterate Screen of *k*-Means Cluster Analysis

Figure 15b.13   The Options Screen of *k*-Means Cluster Analysis

15B.2.3 k-Means Cluster Analysis Output

The **Save** command resulted in the **Cluster membership** results being saved to the data file. This is shown in the last column of the data file

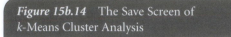

Figure 15b.14 The Save Screen of *k*-Means Cluster Analysis

in Figure 15b.15. The variable **QCL_1** can be read as follows: The **Q** stands for QUICK and the **Cl** stands for CLUSTER (**Quick Cluster** is the syntax name of the IBM SPSS procedure to perform the *k*-means analysis); the digit **1** indicates that this variable resulted from the first analysis. You can see that cases are distributed across the four clusters. For example, Cases 3, 4, and 6 are in Cluster 1, Cases 1 and 8 are in Cluster 2, and so on.

Figure 15b.15 A Screen Shot of the Data View Screen of the Data File Displaying the Cluster Membership Variable in the Last Column

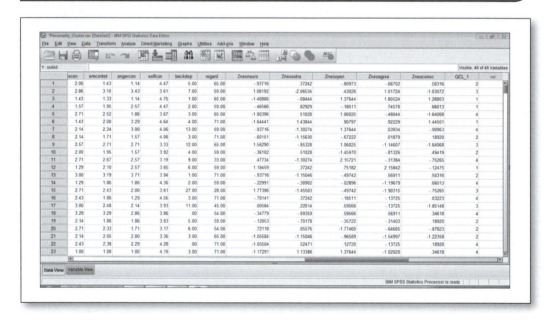

One of the first tables we examine in the output is labeled **Number of Cases in each Cluster**, shown in Figure 15b.16. What we are looking for is that the number of **Valid** and **Missing** cases is acceptable. If there are missing cases in the data file because not all the variables were complete, we want to make sure that your results are not biased (see the discussion of missing values in Chapter 3A). In the present situation, losing five cases is not problematic.

Clusters should also have, within reason, similar numbers of cases assigned to them. A solution with only a dozen or so cases here, for example, would suggest that we have an unacceptable solution probably due to the presence of outliers. In the present situation, the sizes of the clusters are, for a cluster analysis, quite similar. We can now proceed to examine the rest of the output.

Figure 15b.17 shows the **Initial Cluster Centers.** The algorithm IBM SPSS uses to select the seed points for the start of the analysis for the clusters identifies cases who are relatively far apart on the clustering variables. The values in the table are *z* scores of the selected cases. For example, the seed case for Cluster 1 has a neuroticism score of −2.23378 and an extraversion score of 2.35217.

Figure 15b.16   Number of Cases in Each Cluster

Number of Cases in each Cluster

Cluster	1	104.000
	2	113.000
	3	83.000
	4	120.000
Valid		420.000
Missing		5.000

Figure 15b.17   Initial Cluster Centers

Initial Cluster Centers

	Cluster			
	1	2	3	4
Zneoneuro Zscore: neuroticism: neo	−2.23378	.59521	3.07059	.24020
Zneoextra Zscore: extraversion: neo	2.35217	−.69359	.52471	−2.21685
Zneoopen Zscore: openness: neo	.90797	−2.52744	.59566	1.06025
Zneoagree Zscore: agreeableness: neo	.74570	−4.55200	−1.54997	.51802
Zneoconsc Zscore: conscientiousness: neo	−1.69450	.34618	−2.16543	.03671

IBM SPSS tracks how much change there is in the cluster centers from one iteration to another and provides that history in a table called **Iteration History** that we show in Figure 15b.18. We asked for 50 iterations if necessary, but IBM SPSS reached its own convergence criterion (a sufficiently small change in the cluster centers) after 25 iterations.

Figure 15b.18 Iteration History

Iteration History[a]

Iteration	Change in Cluster Centers 1	2	3	4
1	2.639	2.871	2.541	2.153
2	.461	.539	.449	.118
3	.096	.246	.166	.107
4	.021	.303	.140	.103
5	.013	.273	.215	.064
6	.040	.103	.081	.060
7	.031	.097	.070	.034
8	.018	.056	.076	.044
9	.030	.045	.061	.045
10	.075	.052	.031	.075
11	.027	.044	.023	.054
12	.033	.050	.016	.076
13	.017	.000	.024	.030
14	.025	.017	.044	.053
15	.020	.033	.024	.040
16	.021	.033	.027	.042
17	.058	.020	.030	.075
18	.067	.014	.042	.082
19	.075	.000	.099	.127
20	.042	.012	.073	.062
21	.035	.025	.042	.038
22	.000	.026	.032	.017
23	.000	.020	.027	.000
24	.000	.011	.000	.010
25	.000	.000	.000	.000

a. Convergence achieved due to no or small change in cluster centers. The maximum absolute coordinate change for any center is .000. The current iteration is 25. The minimum distance between initial centers is 4.987.

When the iteration stops, the final clusters are formed. IBM SPSS presents these cluster centers in the table labeled **Final Cluster Centers** that can be seen in Figure 15b.19. This table profiles the groups for us. Remember that the values are in *z*-score form. For example, the participants in Cluster 1 are moderately low on neuroticism ($z = -.93233$) and thus are relatively stable, are somewhat extraverted ($z = .75990$), are moderately agreeable ($z = .94476$), are moderately conscientious ($z = .81629$), and are just a little above average in openness ($z = .32671$).

We also asked for an ANOVA that tests which classifying variables are able to significantly distinguish among the groups (clusters). We show the ANOVA summary table in Figure 15b.20. The table presents a set of univariate ANOVAs, one for each classifying variable. As it turns out, the groups differ on all five of the classifying variables. The footnote to the summary table is worth attending to. As there was nothing random about the

Figure 15b.19 Final Cluster Centers

Final Cluster Centers

	Cluster 1	2	3	4
Zneoneuro Zscore: neuroticism: neo	-.93233	.32119	1.04812	-.21938
Zneoextra Zscore: extraversion: neo	.75990	-.17881	-.67690	-.02200
Zneoopen Zscore: openness: neo	.32671	-1.04458	-.06958	.74862
Zneoagree Zscore: agreeableness: neo	.94476	-.45942	-.18269	-.25981
Zneoconsc Zscore: conscientiousness: neo	.81629	.17670	-1.20131	-.04293

Figure 15b.20 An Analysis of Variance Comparing the Clusters

ANOVA

	Cluster		Error			
	Mean Square	df	Mean Square	df	F	Sig.
Zneoneuro Zscore: neuroticism: neo	66.338	3	.529	416	125.447	.000
Zneoextra Zscore: extraversion: neo	33.919	3	.763	416	44.477	.000
Zneoopen Zscore: openness: neo	67.352	3	.521	416	129.151	.000
Zneoagree Zscore: agreeableness: neo	42.516	3	.701	416	60.685	.000
Zneoconsc Zscore: conscientiousness: neo	64.276	3	.544	416	118.225	.000

The F tests should be used only for descriptive purposes because the clusters have been chosen to maximize the differences among cases in different clusters. The observed significance levels are not corrected for this and thus cannot be interpreted as tests of the hypothesis that the cluster means are equal.

selection of seed points and the subsequent efforts of the k-means procedure to maximize cluster differences, the F ratios should be taken with more than a grain of salt.

This lack of randomization in creating the groups is also in part why there is no specification provided in the IBM SPSS analysis setup for performing a multiple comparisons test—the whole point of the analysis was to create groups so that they differed quite a bit from each other on the cluster variables. The procedure therefore does not offer the option of performing multiple comparisons tests for at least two related reasons: (a) It is somewhat circular to perform such tests on groups that were designed from the outset to be quite different, and (b) the null hypothesis ordinarily in play and the distributions of the sampling statistics (see Gamst et al., 2008) underlying how we test the null hypothesis are almost certainly not appropriate to apply under these designed conditions that generated the formation of the groups.

15B.2.4 Reporting k-Means Cluster Analysis Results

There were 420 participants who had valid norm referenced NEO Five-Factor Inventory scores (Costa & McCrea, 1992) for neuroticism, extraversion, openness, agreeableness, and conscientiousness. These values were converted to z scores and were analyzed by the k-means cluster procedure of IBM SPSS. Convergence was reached in 25 iterations. Univariate ANOVAs indicated that the clustered groups differed significantly on all five variables (all ps < .001).

(Continued)

(Continued)

The final cluster centers together with the number of cases in each cluster as shown in Table 15b.3. The range of n for each cluster was 83 to 120, making for relatively equivalent sample sizes. Cases in Cluster 1 appeared to be relatively emotionally stable, agreeable, conscientious, and extraverted. Cases in Cluster 2 appeared to be relatively closed to new experiences but were otherwise relatively average on the other factors. Cases in Cluster 3 appeared to be moderately negligent, less emotionally stable, and perhaps somewhat introverted. Cases in Cluster 4 appeared to be somewhat open to new experiences but were otherwise relatively average on the other factors.

Table 15b.3   Final Cluster z Score Means on the Five Personality Variables

	Cluster 1 $n = 104$	Cluster 2 $n = 113$	Cluster 3 $n = 83$	Cluster 4 $n = 120$
Neuroticism	–.93233	.32119	1.04812	–.21938
Extraversion	.75990	–.17881	–.67690	–.02200
Openness	.32671	–1.04458	–.06958	.74862
Agreeableness	.94476	–.45942	–.18269	–.25981
Conscientiousness	.81629	.17670	–1.20131	–.04293

PART V

FITTING MODELS TO DATA

Confirmatory Factor Analysis

16A.1 Overview

The solution to many of the statistical procedures we have discussed in Parts II, III, and IV (e.g., multiple regression, discriminant function analysis, principal components analysis, and factor analysis) has involved determining the weights that variables will be assigned when we form them into one or more linear composites or variates. The variates in these analyses were not directly measured but instead were computed from the measured variables; in this sense, the variate can be conceived as a *latent* variable or construct in contrast to the variables (the so-called manifest variables) on which they are based. Thus, the prediction model in multiple regression and the components in a principal components analysis are examples of latent constructs. These latent variables are "built up" or "constructed" from the variables measured in the research.

An alternative approach when working with latent constructs in the context of factor analysis is to deduce from a sufficiently developed theory or, more commonly in behavioral and social research, hypothesize them based on a less-developed theory. This process involves specifying in advance of the statistical analysis which variables are hypothesized to be associated with which factors. We could then represent these relationships in a model and determine how well the model works in describing a given data set. In more technical words, we could propose a confirmatory model (the variables associated with the presumed factors) and assess how well the model (the hypothesized factors with their associated indicator variables) fit the data (the goodness of fit).

Confirmatory factor analysis can be a stand-alone analysis (a relatively simple structural model) where researchers wish to test the viability of a hypothesized factor structure, but it can also be embedded in a larger structural model where researchers wish to relate the factors to other variables or constructs. When a confirmatory model is included in a larger structural model, the confirmatory portion is usually referred to as a *measurement model* because it assesses the statistical quality of the factors based on the variables that are said to

represent them. A poor fit of the measurement model to the data can cause the entire structural model to perform poorly; a good fit of the measurement model does not, however,
guarantee that the larger structural model will work well.

Structural modeling is gaining widespread use in a wide range of disciplines. Our
focus in this chapter is on confirmatory models. Some resources that provide more
complete coverage of confirmatory factor analysis are Blunch (2008), Brown (2006),
Harrington (2009), Raykov and Marcoulides (2006), Schumacker and Lomax (2004),
and Thompson (2004).

16A.2 The General Form of a Confirmatory Model

Confirmatory factor analytic models are usually presented in the form of diagrams. These
models contain three kinds of elements:

- *Measured variables*, represented in the diagrams by rectangles or squares
- *Latent constructs*, represented in the diagram by ovals or circles
- *Paths*, represented in the diagram by lines with arrows pointing in a given direction
  or directions

A simplified confirmatory factor analysis model is shown in Figure 16a.1 to illustrate these
elements. We discuss each in turn.

16A.2.1 Measured Variables

Rectangles or squared-off shapes are used
to denote *measured variables*—that is, variables
that have been observed in the study, such as
items in an inventory. These variables are also
called *observed variables* (Raykov & Marcoulides,
2006) or, in the context of confirmatory factor
analysis, are often called *indicator variables*. In
Figure 16a.1, the indicator variables are represented by rectangles.

16A.2.2 Latent Variables

Rounded geometric shapes—that is,
circles and ovals—represent *latent variables*

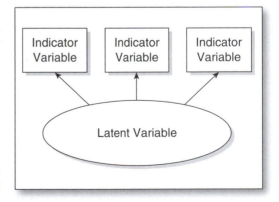

Figure 16a.1 Schematic of a Simple
Structural Diagram for a Confirmatory
Factor Analysis

or constructs. These are variables that are not directly measured in the study but are either constructed by the statistical procedure or hypothesized by the researchers (and specified in the model); they are what we mean by (how we interpret) variates. In Figure 16a.1, the single latent variable is represented by an oval.

16A.2.3 Paths

The paths show the direction of hypothesized cause or influence and are represented by lines with arrows at the end. In Figure 16a.1, the lines of influence flow from the latent variable to the indicator variables. An arrow pointing from one variable (e.g., X) to another variable (e.g., Y) can have several related interpretations, depending on the context. Among the ways to verbalize the meaning conveyed by the arrow are the following:

- X is hypothesized to cause Y.
- Y follows (in some sense or context) from X.
- One way that X can be made apparent is by measuring Y.
- X in combination with other Xs combine to form or define Y.

Each path is ordinarily associated with a coefficient known as a *path coefficient*. Path coefficients are beta weights, analogous to what we see in multiple regression analysis. These path coefficients are estimates of the predictive strength of the variable corresponding to where the path originates in predicting the variable where the path terminates, controlling for all of the other relationships specified in the model. We do not show these in Figure 16a.1 as they are produced as part of the results of the data analysis.

16A.3 The Difference Between Latent and Indicator Variables

The difference between latent and indicator variables may seem clear based on what we just discussed, but in the everyday world of research, the distinction between the two can be a little fuzzy at times. Rest assured that this fuzziness rarely gets in the way of researchers communicating about either the model or the statistical results, but it can be a little confusing at times to students who are trying to learn the topic. We therefore take a moment to offer some clarification at the very start of our Part V chapters.

16A.3.1 The Clear Differences

Relatively complex latent constructs are always recognized as such. These constructs are typically indicated by two or more variables that are often themselves (a) somewhat different and (b) indicated by or compiled on the basis of other variables. One example of a relatively complex latent construct is verbal ability, a general ability that is often assessed by testing facets such as reading comprehension, grammar, and vocabulary.

Measured variables are those on which we have directly collected information and are always recognized as such. Examples of such variables are individual items on an inventory, the time it takes to recognize a particular product on a grocery shelf, and the degree of reduction of a given symptom resulting from a particular treatment plan.

16A.3.2 The Fuzzy Differences

Between those two extremes lies a range of variables that could be identified as either latent constructs or measured variables depending on the context in which they are placed. Consider an inventory such as the Rosenberg Self-Esteem Scale (Rosenberg, 1965). It contains 10 items asking respondents to rate the extent to which they feel they are worthwhile people, their perceived general competence, the respect they have for themselves, the extent to which they possess several good qualities, and so forth. These items are clearly measured variables.

Although each item taps into an aspect of self-esteem, it is the scores of the items in combination that are taken to represent the construct; that is, after reverse scoring any negatively worded items, we sum (or average) the scores on the item to arrive at a self-esteem score. Self-esteem per se is never directly measured but is rather inferred, based on its indicators (the content represented in the items). In this sense, self-esteem is a latent construct. If placed in the confirmatory factor analysis diagram shown in Figure 16a.1 so that we might test the hypothesis that a one-factor model is a good representation of the data, self-esteem would be shown in the oval and paths would flow from it to each of the inventory items. Inventory items would each be represented by rectangles because these were measured in the data collection process.

But now consider a different context, where we might wish to focus on a broad construct such as the hypothetical latent variable of mastery of life. Such a complex construct is likely to be associated with several somewhat related but distinguishable indicators, including perhaps self-actualization, self-efficacy, and self-esteem. One way to model this is to treat mastery of life as a latent variable and to specify measures of self-actualization, self-efficacy, and self-esteem as indicators of it. In this context, if self-esteem was assessed by the Rosenberg Self-Esteem Scale, we would treat self-esteem as one of the several indicator (measured) variables in a confirmatory or measurement model.

16A.4 Contrasting Principal Components Analysis, Exploratory Factor Analysis, and Confirmatory Factor Analysis

To help establish a framework to understand confirmatory factor analysis, and to gain some perspective on principal components analysis and exploratory factor analysis, it is useful to compare these three procedures. We will do so by presenting them in structural diagrams and explicating each in turn.

16A.4.1 The Structure of Principal Components Analysis

We have presented a very simplified depiction of a principal components analysis in Figure 16a.2. To keep the figure simple enough to use for this discussion, we show only one component and only two measured variables (e.g., inventory items) associated with that component. Certain features of this model are noteworthy.

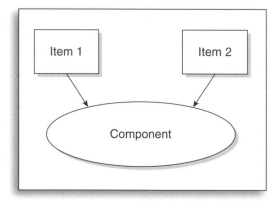

Figure 16a.2 Diagram of a Very Simple Principal Component Model

The principal component is contained in an oval, telling us that it is a latent variable. The inventory items are contained in rectangles, telling us that they are measured variables in the study. The arrows or paths point from the items toward the component, telling us that the inferential flow is inductive. This treatment is in accord with Pedhazur and Schmelkin (1991), who state that "components in PCA [principal components analysis] may be conceived of as dependent variables whose values are obtained by differentially weighting the indicators, which are treated as the independent variables" (p. 598). Within this framework, the items, taken together, cause or define the factor. Recall that variables have weights (or correlations) with the factors quantified by pattern or structure coefficients. If we were to include these coefficients, they would be placed on the connectors between the measured variables and the latent variable. This model makes clear the inductive nature of principal components analysis.

The flow of causal inference also defines the roles that these variables play in the analysis. Independent variables cause, predict, or infer dependent variables. Because the directional inference flows from the measured variables, the measured variables are the independent variables, whereas the component is the dependent variable (Hauser, 1972). The measured variables are called different names by different authors: "formative indicators" by Pedhazur and Schmelkin (1991), "producers" by Costner (1969), and "causal indicators" by Blalock (1964, 1971). We will tend to refer to them as *indicators* or *indicator variables*. Because the causal inference flows to the component, it is considered to be the dependent variable in the model.

A more complete but still simplified model of a principal components model is shown in Figure 16a.3. In this figure, we show three components, each represented by an oval to

Figure 16a.3 Diagram of a Relatively Simple Principal Components Model

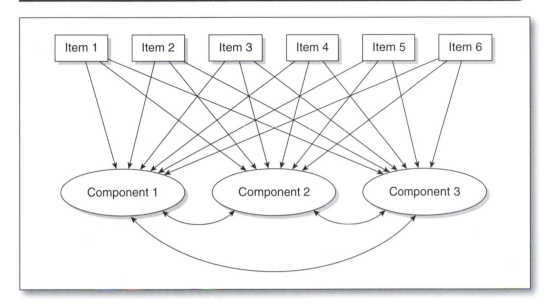

convey the idea that they are latent variables, and six indicators (measured variables or inventory items). Recall from Chapter 12A that the factor matrix shows the weights for all indicator variables on all components. Thus, we have drawn arrows from each indicator to each component.

In such an analysis depicted in Figure 16a.3, we might have certain hopes or expectations about the solution. Generally, we would anticipate that some indicators would correlate more strongly with one component and other indicators will correlate more strongly with another component. For example, we might expect Items 1 and 2 to correlate more strongly with Component 1 than with the other components, Items 3 and 4 to correlate more strongly with Component 2 than with the other components, and Items 5 and 6 to correlate more strongly with Component 3 than with the other components. The interpretation of the components would be based on what items were most strongly associated with them. For example, Component 1 would be interpreted as whatever Items 1 and 2 had in common.

In this model, we have included double-pointed arrows between pairs of components. In structural equation models, double-pointed arrows depict the notion that we are addressing the issue of correlations. In principal components analysis, our rotation strategy is going to be either varimax (which keeps factors uncorrelated) or oblique (which allows factors to be correlated). This specification applies to all the components. That is, in a varimax rotation, all the components remain uncorrelated, and in an oblique rotation, all the factors are allowed a certain amount of correlation. We have visually represented the situation in which we would obliquely rotate the factors by using the double-arrow lines between all possible pairs of components.

16A.4.2 The Structure of Principal Axis Factor Analysis

We can contrast principal components analysis with principal axis factor analysis, one of the more popular factor analytic techniques. We have presented a portion of a principal axis analysis in Figure 16a.4. Again, to keep the figure simple enough to use for this discussion, we show only one factor and only two measured variables associated with that component.

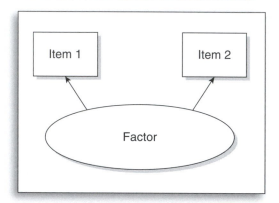

Figure 16a.4 Diagram of a Very Simple Principal Factor Model

Figure 16a.4 is analogous to our model for a principal components analysis, but there is a very important difference between that one and this one. Here, the factor, still a latent variable as shown by the oval, is conceived of as the independent variable, and the indicator variables are the dependent variables. Note that the direction of the causal flow is from the latent variable or factor to the measured variables. This is one of the major differences between principal components analysis and factor analysis. In factor analysis, the factor is seen as the focus point, and the measured variables are some of the ways that aspects of the factor can be measured. The term *indicator variable* is very descriptive (perhaps even more so than in principal components analysis) of how the measured variables are viewed in the analysis; they are the filter through which the factor is known to us.

A more complete but still simplified factor model is drawn in Figure 16a.5. Again, there are six indicators and three factors pictured in a structure similar to that in the principal components analysis. Inference flows from the latent factors to the indicators, and double-arrow lines connect each pair of factors for the same reason: Factors will all be uncorrelated (by means of a varimax rotation) or will all be allowed some correlation (by means of an oblique rotation). And again, each factor shows six paths leading from it—one to each indicator—because each indicator will receive a certain weight for each factor.

One major difference between the models for principal components analysis and principal axis factor analysis, besides the direction of the arrows and the reversal of independent and dependent variable roles, is the presence here of error elements associated with the indicators. This means that principal axis factoring explicitly recognizes

Figure 16a.5   Diagram of a Relatively Simple Principal Factors Model

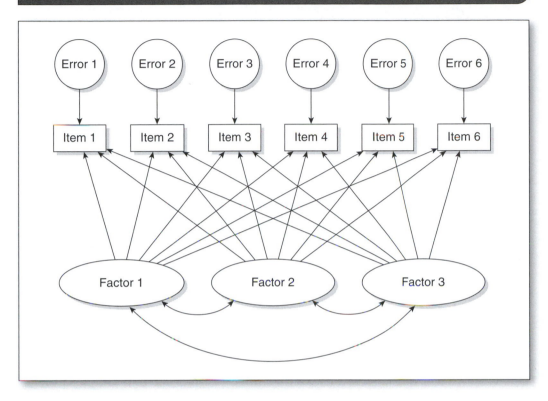

that not all the variance of the indicators will be associated with the factors. Recall from our discussion of the difference between principal components analysis and factor analysis in Chapter 12A that principal components analysis attempts to account for the total variance of the measured variables but that factor analysis attempts to account for only the variance common to the factors.

Variance that is not common or shared is said to be unique to each measured variable, and this unique variance is called *error, residual,* or *unique variance* in the structural model (Maruyama, 1998). The unique variance is usually some combination of systematic variance (e.g., another construct may actually be represented to a certain extent) and unsystematic variance (measurement error). Calling this whole term *error variance* just means that it is not part of the variance common to the set of variables in the analysis and is therefore unsystematic with respect to that common variance; it does not mean that all the variance is, in any absolute sense, completely unsystematic.

Figure 16a.6 Diagram of a Relatively Simple Confirmatory Factor Model

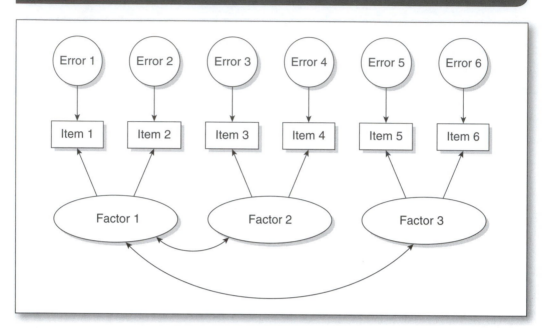

The error terms are enclosed in circles because they, too, are latent. The directional flow is from the error to the indicator, telling us what is probably obvious to most researchers: Our measurement of the indicators contains some variance not captured in the factor structure.

Note that there are no double-arrow lines connecting the error variables. That is because one of the statistical assumptions underlying the analysis is that these error terms are uncorrelated in principal axis factoring. There is some real risk, however, that such an assumption may not hold in all situations. The assumption that the errors are uncorrelated is certainly one restriction or limitation we face when using exploratory factor analysis. In addition to this restriction is the requirement that the factors must be presumed either to all be uncorrelated or to all be correlated. Add to that the atheoretical nature of exploratory analysis in general and you have the seeds of concern that have led some writers (e.g., Long, 1983) to urge great caution in using exploratory procedures lest we wind up with a "garbage in–garbage out" model.

16A.4.3 The Structure of Confirmatory Factor Analysis

We display the more complete model for confirmatory factor analysis in Figure 16a.6. Four features of this model may be noted: (a) It is more similar to principal axis factor analysis than to principal components analysis; but (b) it is also simpler than the principal axis model because instead of having each measured variable relating to every factor, the researchers now clearly specify which measured variable "belongs" to which factor; (c) not all of the factors are said to be correlated; and (d) some of the errors are hypothesized to be correlated.

The similarity between principal axis factor analysis and confirmatory factor analysis occurs because—this may seem pretty obvious—they are both addressing factor analysis. Therefore, the causal flow is from the factors to the observed variables, and one thinks of these latter variables as indicators of the factors. Furthermore, there are error terms associated with each measured variable. This is the case because factor analysis, whether in its exploratory or confirmatory form, partitions the variance of the indicators into common variance and unique variance. The analysis attempts to account for the common variance but treats the unique variance as residual or error variance.

The differences between the principal axis and confirmatory structures can be seen in the positioning of the arrows connecting (a) the factors to the indicators, (b) the factors to the factors, and (c) the errors to the errors. The first of these may be the most striking because the structure looks a lot simpler here than in principal axis factoring. In principal axis factoring, each factor is connected to all the indicators. This is the case because the factors are a weighted composite of all the measured variables. Each factor is represented by a different set of weights, but all the indicators are in the equation. For Factor 1, for instance, observed variables 1 and 2 should have, according to what the model shows, much greater weights than observed variables 3 through 6. However, for Factor 2, Indicators 3 and 4 would have the greatest weights. In a confirmatory model, we identify (hypothesize) which items are indicators of which factor.

Another difference between the principal axis and confirmatory structures is the connections between pairs of factors. Exploratory analysis decrees that what will be true for one pair of factors will be true for all pairs. If we invoke a varimax rotation, we decree that all factors will be uncorrelated; if we invoke an oblique rotation, we decree that all factors can be correlated. That restriction is lifted in confirmatory factor analysis. Researchers are able to specify the relationships they believe holds between any two pairs of factors. In Figure 16a.6, we have specified that Factor 1 is correlated with Factors 2 and 3 but that Factors 2 and 3 are uncorrelated.

In an analogous manner, researchers can also specify the associations between pairs of error terms. Because these error terms reflect unique variance, the possibility exists that this variance may be systematic and thus interpretable. It may challenge the creativity or insightfulness of the researchers, but if the theory or researchers are up to the task, it may be possible to hypothesize that some pairs of unique variance are related. In Figure 16a.6, we have specified that Errors 2 and 4, Errors 3 and 6, and Errors 5 and 6 are correlated.

16A.5 Confirmatory Factor Analysis Is Theory Based

Exploratory factor analysis represents an inductive approach in that researchers employ a bottom-up strategy by developing a conclusion from specific observations. The conclusion reached is the interpretation of the factor based on those measured variables most strongly associated with it. These measured variables thus become recognized as indicators of the factor based on the results of the statistical analysis. Although this strategy does appear to be empirically (inductively) driven, research is not conducted in a vacuum, and researchers always have some ideas about the underlying structure of the variables that they have placed together in advance. For example, researchers interested in studying a particular construct will not haphazardly develop items to write for their new inventory; rather, they will channel the content of the items to conform to what they know (or believe they know) about the construct. In this sense, no exploratory analysis is devoid of some researcher-based rationale (Gorsuch, 2003; Thompson, 2004).

Confirmatory factor analysis represents a deductive approach in that researchers employ a top-down approach by predicting an outcome from a theoretical framework. This outcome is the specification—in advance of the statistical analysis—of which measured variables are indicators of the factor. Further specification regarding the relationships between the factors and relationships between the error terms must also be put forward by the researchers.

We have talked about the theoretical framework within which one engages in confirmatory analysis and the atheoretical environment where one must of necessity engage in exploratory analysis as though the two were easily distinguishable and compartmentalized. Statistical tests that analyze exploratory research are known as "first-generation" procedures, whereas statistical tests designed to confirm a theory are known as "second-generation" procedures (Fornell, 1987). Reality, however, has a way of complicating the decisions that researchers need to make regarding which procedure is to be used in a given situation.

Theory development in the social and behavioral sciences is an ongoing process, and very little research is conducted completely outside of a theoretical context (Chin, 1998). The issue of contention is usually about the degree to which a theory has been articulated rather than whether or not there is one underlying the research. Sometimes, it is not clear if an exploratory or confirmatory approach is more appropriate, given that a particular theory may still be in the formative stage (Chin, Marcolin, & Newsted, 1996).

Furthermore, it is possible and often productive to make use of exploratory analysis as one of the theory-generating techniques open to researchers (Stevens, 2009). Thus, researchers having conducted a principal components analysis and interpreted the factors may be able to formulate some notions regarding the general construct that they were studying and begin to hypothesize what should occur under certain experimental or observational conditions. If they are able to fill in some of the details of their speculation, they may be ready to engage in confirmatory analysis the next time around.

16A.6 The Logic of Performing a Confirmatory Factor Analysis

The major objective in confirmatory factor analysis is determining if the relationships between the variables in the hypothesized model resemble the relationships between the variables in the observed data set. More formally expressed, the analysis determines the extent to which the proposed covariance matches the observed covariance.

Once a model is proposed (i.e., relationships between the variables have been hypothesized), a correlation/covariance matrix is created. The development and evaluation of a confirmatory analysis typically involves five steps (Bollen & Long, 1993): (a) model specification, (b) model identification, (c) selection of the model estimation technique (which for us is maximum likelihood), (d) model evaluation, and (e) model respecification if necessary.

16A.7 Model Specification

We will illustrate the specification of a model by using the scale assessing multicultural competence (CBMCS) developed by Gamst et al. (2004). Mental health service providers rated the 21 items on a 4-point *strongly disagree–strongly agree* scale expressing the extent to which they believed they had knowledge of multicultural issues or believed themselves to possess an ability to deliver counseling services to individuals of diverse multicultural backgrounds. In the context of this example, the four constructs corresponding to the subscales will be treated as though they are measured variables. Thus, for each subscale, the score for each respondent is the average of the items associated with the subscale, and the overall score for each subscale is the mean of those averages.

The hypothesized model is diagrammed in Figure 16a.7. In the model, the latent construct of multicultural competence of mental health providers is indicated by Sensitivity and Responsiveness to Consumers, Sociocultural Diversities, Awareness of Cultural Barriers, and Multicultural Knowledge. This model is an explanation of why these four variables relate. In the Bentler–Weeks method (Bentler & Weeks, 1980) of model specification, all variables (latent and measured) are assigned the role of either independent variables or dependent variables. Independent variables have directional paths (arrows pointing) away from the variables, whereas dependent variables have directional paths toward the variables. In Figure 16a.7, there are five independent variables as depicted by variables with originating arrows (the one factor and the four error terms) and four dependent variables as depicted by variables with arrows pointing toward them (the four measured variables).

In this proposed model, the researchers are hypothesizing that multicultural competence causes sensitivity and responsiveness to consumers, sociocultural diversities, awareness of cultural barriers, and multicultural knowledge. Also, the researchers are specifying that

Figure 16a.7   The Multicultural Competence Model

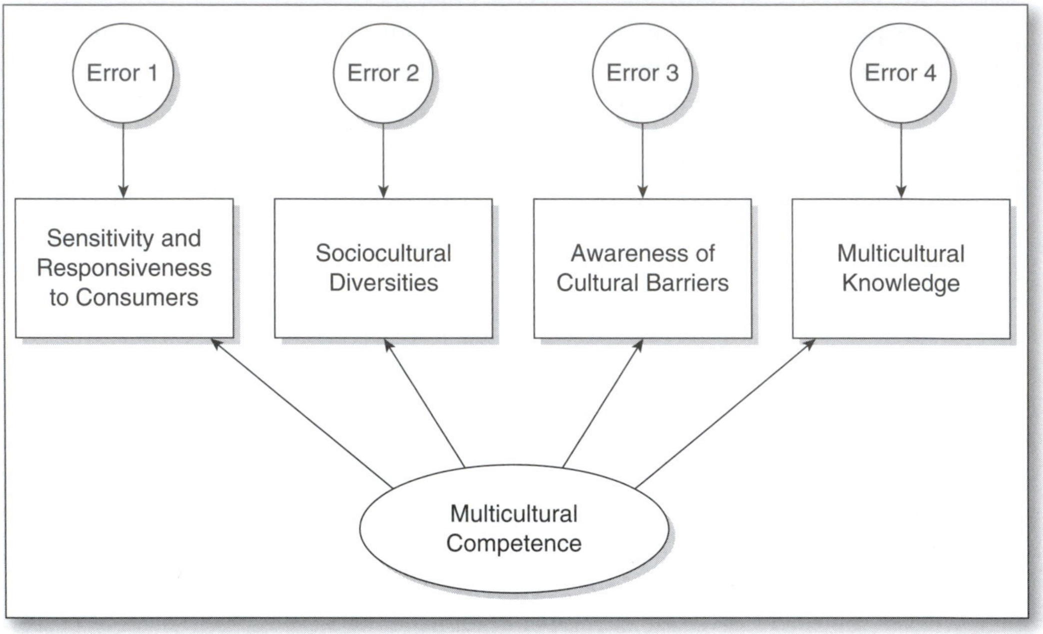

there are other influences on the indicator variables besides multicultural competence. These other influences are represented as the error or unique-variance terms.

16A.8 Model Identification

16A.8.1 Levels of Model Identification

To assess whether the proposed model fits the data, a necessary but not sufficient condition to be met is that the model must be identified (Bollen, 1989). At a very general level, model identification has to do with the difference between the number of variables in the analysis and the number of parameters that need to be estimated by the model. These parameters, or at least estimates of them, are what the structural equation model is designed to generate and are therefore unknown at the start of the analysis. The parameters in the model are as follows:

- The pattern or structure coefficients relating the independent to the dependent variables

- The correlation coefficients relating the independent variables to each other
- The variance of the independent variables

If we subtract the number of unknown parameters from the number of known or non-redundant elements, we obtain the degrees of freedom for the analysis (*df* = number of known elements – number of unknown parameters). The situation that must be met in the model identification stage is to have more known information elements than unknown parameters (Bentler & Chou, 1987).

If there are more unknown elements than known ones, the value for the degrees of freedom is negative. The model is then said to be *underidentified* and cannot be processed meaningfully in the analysis. If the numbers of known and unknown elements are equal, the model is said to be *saturated* or *just defined*. It will fit the data perfectly, but unfortunately, that fit will be artificial, and again no meaningful solution will be obtained by performing the analysis. Only when the degrees of freedom are positive (we have more known than unknown elements) can a meaningful analysis be performed. We then say that the model is *identified* (technically, positive values for degrees of freedom indicate that the model is overidentified) and that it is therefore ready to be processed.

16A.8.2 Determining the Number of Known Elements

The task in this model identification stage is to count the number of known and unknown elements and, if the initial count is insufficient, to do whatever is necessary to make sure that we wind up with more of the former than the latter. So the obvious question that can be asked at this juncture concerns what kind of elements can be counted. The answer is (a) entries in a covariance or correlation matrix for the measured (dependent) variables and (b) variances and coefficients of various sorts (correlation coefficients, pattern coefficients, structure coefficients) for the paths of the independent variables.

The number of known elements is equal to the number of unique or nonredundant entries (allowing the pairing of the variable with itself) in a matrix that represents the covariances or correlations of the indicator variables. Consider a set of three variables labeled *A*, *B*, and *C*. How many unique entries are there in the matrix? There are six: AA, BB, CC, AB, AC, and BC. If you imagine a square matrix and count the entries in its upper half plus the diagonal, you can see the six positions. Anything in the lower half is a redundancy.

Rather than physically counting this every time we start a confirmatory analysis, we can apply a simple formula to obtain the count of nonredundant elements (Raykov & Marcoulides, 2000). The formula is as follows:

$$\text{Number of nonredundant elements} = \frac{V(V+1)}{2},$$

where *V* is the number of the measured variables in the study. If $V = 3$ in our above illustration, then we have 3 multiplied by $3 + 1$ or 4 to obtain 12; divide 12 by 2 to give us 6 nonredundant elements.

We can now return to our multicultural competence example shown in Figure 16a.7. There are four indicator variables. Plugging that value into our simple formula gives us 4 multiplied by $4 + 1$ to obtain 20; divide 20 by 2 to give us 10 nonredundant elements. This value of 10 is immutable—we cannot increase this number. If there turns out to be 10 or more than 10 unknown parameters, thus yielding a zero or negative value for degrees of freedom, we must take some action to reduce that count of unknowns because we cannot raise the number of nonredundant elements.

16A.8.3 Scaling the Latent Variable

Model identification involves one other piece of business: The latent variable needs to be scaled. That is, to conduct the analysis, the latent variable must be assigned a metric of some kind. Provided that the model is viable, we would compute a multicultural competence score in a way analogous to the way in which we computed the four indicator scores—namely, by averaging the scores on all the inventory items or averaging the scores on the four indicators themselves. Either way we do it, multicultural competence would then be assessed on the same 4-point scale that we used for the items and the indicators.

In the empirical world of the researchers, if their model is workable, they would be working with the four subscales and not with the more complex larger construct (that really is the whole point of factor analysis). But the mathematical world of statistics requires that the scale of the latent variable be specified in the model or the analysis is a no-go, so we very much want to specify the construct's metric.

Note that the indicators are already measured in the course of conducting the study and so have a measurement scale already tied to them. However, in SEM where we have specified, for example, factors, each of these (unobserved) latent variables must explicitly be assigned a metric within the context of the analysis. This is normally done by constraining one of the paths from the latent variable to one of its indicator (reference) variables, such as assigning the value of 1.0 to the pattern/structure coefficient for this path. Given this constraint, the remaining paths can then be estimated. The indicator selected to be constrained to 1.0 is called the *reference item.* Typically, we select as the reference item the one that in factor analysis is most strongly correlated with the dimension represented by the latent variable, thereby allowing it to anchor the meaning of that dimension. Alternatively, we may set the factor variances to 1, thereby effectively obtaining a standardized solution, or we may select the path associated with the indicator having the best reliability (because we are tying down the measurement of the construct).

Here, we will set the coefficient to a value of 1 (actually, any positive value will suffice) on the selected path. Such an act informs IBM SPSS Amos, the statistical software that we

Figure 16a.8 The Multicultural Competence Model With Sensitivity and Responsiveness to Consumers Scaled to a Value of 1

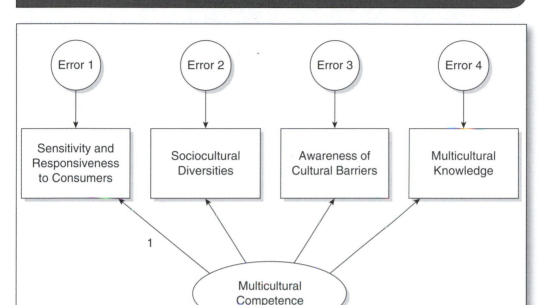

use for SEM, that the construct is to be assessed on the same metric as that indicator. In Figure 16a.8, we have identified Sensitivity and Responsiveness to Consumers as the indicator to which we will initially scale multicultural competence.

Here is why our action might seem a bit strange. One of the goals of the statistical analysis is to estimate parameters that were left unspecified by the model. The pattern or structure coefficients linking the construct and the indicators are among those parameters. But we have just filled in one of them, which sounds as though it might defeat the purpose of performing the analysis. The bad news here is that we had to make this specification in order to perform the analysis in the first place. But the good news is that SEM uses a maximum likelihood procedure that iterates its solution until it reaches a stable result. The upshot of this is that even though we have specified a value of 1 as the coefficient, the statistical procedure will use that only as a starting place and will eventually produce its own estimate. There is even more good news. Yes, we specified the coefficient leading to one of the indicators, but if we had chosen a different indicator, our solution would still be essentially the same.

16A.8.4 Determining the Number of Unknown Elements

Having done our preparation work, we now need to determine how many unknowns there are. These unknown elements will be the parameters estimated by the statistical procedure. In this model, we will need to estimate (a) the variance of the multicultural competence latent factor, (b) the variances of the four unique error terms, (c) the remaining three pattern/structure coefficients relating the latent variable to the measured variables whose coefficients are not yet specified (we have already removed from the realm of the unknown one parameter by scaling the latent factor), and (d) the four pattern/structure coefficients relating the unique variables (the error terms) to the measured variables. This gives us a total of 12 parameters (1 + 4 + 3 + 4) that we are asking the model to estimate.

16A.8.5 Resolving the Number of Known and Unknown Elements

A quick calculation to figure out if this model is identified tells us our status. Subtracting the unknowns (12) from the known elements (10) yields 2 degrees of freedom. Thus, we are (temporarily only) in a bit of trouble; the model is not yet identified and we are therefore not ready to go forward into the analysis.

The portions of the model most susceptible to specification are the paths leading from the error terms to the indicator variables. What we do here is assign them an initial value of 1 as shown in Figure 16a.9, recognizing that they will be estimated in the solution. This removes these four parameters from the list of unknowns. It also serves the added advantage of scaling these latent error terms to their respective measured variables. Because the error variables represent unique variance, the model will actually have an easy job filling in these values. Once we learn of the correlation between the indicators and the latent factor (the common variance), these values may be calculated as the residual or what remains of the total variance once the common variance is explained.

Changing the status of these parameters from unknown to known in the model now puts us in the positive range for degrees of freedom. The known elements still count to 10. The unknown parameters after all our work are (a) the variance of the latent factor, (b) the variances of the four latent error variables, and (c) the remaining three pattern/structure coefficients. That gives us a total of 8. By subtracting the number of unknown parameters from the number of known elements (10 − 8 = 2), we now have positive degrees of freedom. This model is *overidentified* (which is what we wanted to happen) and can thus be meaningfully solved.

16A.9 Model Estimation

Once we have completed the identification stage, we are ready to perform the statistical analysis. This involves mathematically building the model and estimating the relationships

Figure 16a.9 The Multicultural Competence Model With Sensitivity and Responsiveness to Consumers Scaled to a Value of 1 and the Paths From the Error Variables to the Indicator Variables Constrained to a Value of 1

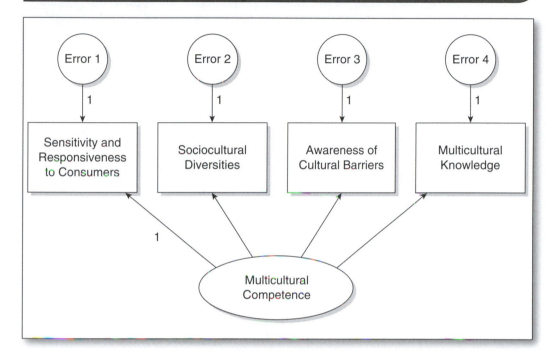

between the variables in the model. We calculate these estimates using the maximum likelihood estimation procedure, one of several methods available to researchers through the IBM SPSS Amos software. Maximum likelihood attempts to estimate the values of the parameters that would result in the highest likelihood of the data set matching the proposed model. These methods always require iterative solutions.

16A.10 Model Evaluation Overview

The proposed or hypothesized model is assessed by producing estimates of the unknown parameters. These findings are then compared with the relationships (the correlation/covariance matrices) existent in the actual or observed data. Confirmatory factor analysis assesses how well the predicted interrelationships between the variables match the interrelationships between the actual or observed interrelationships. If the two matrices (the proposed and the actual) are consistent with one another, then the model can be considered a credible explanation for the hypothesized relationships.

Stevens (2009) divides the assessment of a model into two categories: those dealing with model fit and those dealing with the individual model parameters. Assessing model fit is an omnibus or global process, analogous to eta square in ANOVA, the squared multiple correlation in multiple regression analysis, and the overall squared canonical correlation in canonical correlation analysis. If the model does not fit the data well, there is little point in examining the individual item parameters. But it is also the case that the overall fit of a model to the data may appear acceptable, yet some relationships in the model may not be supported by the data (Bollen, 1990).

16A.11 Assessing Fit of Hypothesized Models

The goal of researchers who use confirmatory factor analysis (or, more generally as we will see in later chapters, SEM techniques) is to evaluate the plausibility of their hypothesized model (i.e., the relationships between the variables). The proposed model is either guided by prior research or based on some theoretical framework. The model is then compared with the actual or observed data. If the model and observed data resemble each other, then the model is said to fit the data. Having an index that quantifies the degree of fit between the model and the data is crucial for researchers in meeting their research goals.

16A.11.1 The Multitude of Fit Indexes

Historically, chi-square was used to assess the fit of the model. The chi-square statistic is used to test the difference between the predicted and the observed relationships (correlations/covariances). Because researchers are predicting a close fit, a nonsignificant chi-square is desired. For models with relatively small cases (75–200), chi-square is an adequate measure of fit (Kenny, 2003). However, for models with more cases (which is very often the case in research designs utilizing SEM), chi-square will usually be statistically significant (the large sample size has supplied us with "too much" power to effectively rely on the chi-square test of statistical significance), suggesting a poor fit when there could be only trivial differences between the model and the data.

Most writers, such as Jöreskog and Sörbom (1996) and Bentler (1990), advise against the sole use of the chi-square value in judging the overall fit of the model because of the sensitivity of the chi-square to sample size. Larger sample sizes are associated with increased power, and with large sample sizes, the chi-square test can detect small discrepancies between the observed and predicted covariances and suggest that the model does not fit the data. A good-fitting model could be rejected because of trivial but statistically significant differences between the observed and predicted values. Chi-square is also affected by the size of the correlations in the model; larger correlations generally cause a poorer fit (Kenny, 2003). Because of these limitations, many other fit indexes were developed as alternatives or supplements to chi-square.

Efforts to identify indexes to assess the fit between the hypothesized model and the observed data continue to develop. Over the past quarter century, at least 24 fit indexes have been proposed (Klem, 2000). All of these fit indexes were developed to diminish the Type II error (i.e., concluding that the data do not support the proposed model when in fact they do). For the 24 fit measures available through statistical software programs, there is presently no general agreement on which measures are preferred (Maruyama, 1998). According to Maruyama (1998),

> The different fit indexes differ with respect to dimensions such as susceptibility to sample size differences, variability in the range of fit possible for any particular data set, and valuing simplicity of model specification needed to attain an improved fit. (p. 239)

None of the measures has a related statistical test, except for the chi-square test. The confusing consequence of these competing fit indexes is that different research studies report different fit indexes.

16A.11.2 Categorizing the Fit Indexes

Complicating this matter of competing fit indexes is the lack of consensus among SEM writers as to how we may categorize or organize this array of fit indexes, although most agree that some organizational schema is necessary (because then we might be able to report fit indexes from each category). Further complicating the decision of what fit index to report, there is disagreement about which individual fit measures might best be classified together.

Researchers have proposed various classification schemas to organize the fit indexes. For example, Arbuckle (2010) devised an eight-category scheme (parsimony, sample discrepancy, population discrepancy, information-theoretic, baseline model, parsimony adjusted, goodness of fit, and miscellaneous), whereas Tabachnick and Fidell (2007) suggest a five-category system (comparative, absolute, proportion of variance, parsimony, and residual based). Other authors (e.g., Hair et al., 2010; Jaccard & Wan, 1996) promote a three-group scheme (absolute, relative, and parsimonious). And finally, Maruyama (1998) adopts Hu and Bentler's (1999a) two-type scheme (absolute and relative but with the latter divided into four subtypes).

The most-cited organization system appears to be the three-classification scheme of absolute, relative, and parsimonious fit indexes. We add an additional category to this schema. Brief descriptions of the four categories with some of their respective target fit measures to achieve a good fit are presented below and are summarized in Table 16a.1. We also indicate what values of these indexes can represent acceptable levels of fit in our discussion below.

Table 16a.1 Absolute, Relative, and Parsimonious Fit Indexes and Target Values for Good Fit

Absolute Indexes		Relative Indexes		Parsimonious Indexes		Model Comparison Indexes	
Test	Target Value	Test	Target Value	Test	Target Value	Test	Target Value
χ^2	$p < .05$	CFI	.95	AGFI	.90	AIC	smaller
χ^2 / df	2.00	NFI	.95	PGFI	$> .50$	BCC	smaller
GFI	.90	IFI	.90	PNFI	$> .50$	BIC	smaller
RMSR	.05					ECVI	smaller
RMSEA	.08						

Note. χ^2 = Chi square test; χ^2 / df = Chi square divided by degrees of freedom test; GFI = Goodness of Fit Index; RMSR = Root Mean Square Residual; RMSEA = Root Mean Square Error of Approximation; CFI = Comparative Fit Index; NFI = Normed Fit Index; IFI = Incremental Fit Index; AGFI = Adjusted Goodness of Fit Index; PNFI = Parsimony Normed Fit Index; PCFI = Parsimony Comparative Fit Index; AIC = Akaike Information Criterion; BCC= Browne-Cudeck Criterion: BIC = Bayes or Bayesian Information Criterion; ECVI = Expected Cross Validation Index. Smaller = Smaller values indicate better fitting models.

16A.11.3 Absolute Fit Measures

Absolute fit measures indicate how well the proposed interrelationships between the variables match the interrelationships between the actual or observed interrelationships. This means how well the correlation/covariance of the hypothesized model fits the correlation/covariance of the actual or observed data. The five most common absolute fit measures assessing this general feature are the chi-square, the chi-square divided by the degrees of freedom test, the goodness-of-fit index (GFI), the root mean square residual (RMSR), and the root mean square error of approximation (RMSEA).

Because researchers are predicting a close fit, a nonsignificant chi-square is preferred. As we indicated, the chi-square test is really too powerful for most research studies. As sample size increases, power increases, and the chi-square test can return a statistically significant outcome even when the model fits the data reasonably well. An option to balance against large sample sizes driving statistical significance is to divide the chi-square value by the degrees of freedom in the analysis. Obtaining a value of less than 2 would suggest a good fit (Byrne, 1989), and obtaining a value between 2 and 5 could be considered an acceptable fit (Marsh & Hocevar, 1985).

The GFI is conceptually similar to the R^2 in multiple regression (Kline, 2011). It is the proportion of variance in the sample correlation/covariance accounted for by the predicted model, with values ranging from 0 (no fit) to 1 (a perfect fit). Although the GFI can vary from 0 to 1, theoretically it can yield meaningless negative values. By convention, GFI should be equal to or greater than .90 as indicative of an acceptable model.

The RMSR is a measure of the average size of the residuals between actual covariance and the proposed model covariance. Swanson (2005) characterizes it as the average residual correlation, and MacCallum (2009) indicates that it represents how closely the model fits the correlations among the measured variables. The smaller the RMSR, the better the fit with a target value .05 or less.

The RMSEA is the average of the residuals between the observed correlation/covariance from the sample and the expected model estimated for the population. It assesses the approximation error in the population and the precision of the fit measure, thus providing a fit index that is relatively independent of sample size (Browne & Cudeck, 1989, 1993).

Byrne (1998) states that the RMSEA "has only recently been recognized as one of the most informative criteria in covariance structure modeling" (p. 112), and this fit index has become relatively widely used (Raykov & Marcoulides, 2006). Values equal to or less than .08 are deemed acceptable, whereas values greater than .10 are generally unacceptable; values between these can be judged as borderline acceptable. The RMSEA may be somewhat inflated for sample sizes less than 200 (Paxton, Hipp, & Marquart-Pyatt, 2011), and so a reasonable model may be judged as fitting less well than is warranted under those circumstances.

16A.11.4 Relative Fit Measures

Relative fit measures are also known as comparisons with baseline measures or incremental fit measures. These are measures of fit relative to the independence model, which assumes that there are no relationships in the data (thus a poor fit) and the saturated model, which assumes a perfect fit. The incremental fit measures indicate the relative position on this continuum between worst fit to perfect fit, with values greater than .90 suggesting an acceptable fit between the model and the data.

Byrne (1998, 2010) suggests that the comparative fit index (CFI) should be the fit statistic of choice in SEM research. Knight, Virdin, Ocampo, and Roosa (1994) have suggested the following guidelines to evaluate the CFI:

- Good fit is indicated by values equal to or greater than .90. Hu and Bentler (1999a, 1999b) revised the value representing a good fit to .95.
- Adequate but marginal fit is indicated by values between .80 and .89.
- Poor fit is indicated by values between .60 and .79.
- Very poor fit is indicated by values less than .60.

Other common incremental fit measures are the normed fit index (NFI) and the incremental fit index (IFI), with values equal to or better than .95 and .90, respectively, indicating an acceptable fit.

16A.11.5 Parsimonious Fit Measures

Both the absolute and the relative measures will yield better fit measures if the models being evaluated have more parameter estimations. This is one of the by-products of the maximum likelihood method employed to estimate the parameters. Recall that the maximum likelihood method is an iterative process that compares the parameter estimates at each phase of the estimation procedure and reports the estimates that provide the best fit. With more parameters available to estimate, the greater the likelihood of developing a better fit.

To adjust for this inflated fit bias, the third classification, known as parsimonious fit measures, was developed. Parsimonious fit measures are sometimes called adjusted fit measures. These fit statistics are similar to the adjusted R^2 in multiple regression analysis in that these measures adjust for the number of estimations by penalizing models with greater parameter estimations. Kelloway (1998) warns that unlike the absolute or relative fit measures that have conventional values of .90 or .95 as acceptable models, parsimonious fit measure have no generally acceptable cutoff. Parsimonious fit measures are recommended to compare two competing models, and the model with the higher parsimonious fit measure should be judged as superior.

Common parsimonious fit measures are the adjusted GFI (AGFI) and the parsimonious GFI (PGFI). The AGFI corresponds to the GFI in replacing the total sum of squares by the mean sum of squares. A good fit is still indicated by a value of .90 or greater.

The PGFI adjusts for degrees of freedom in the baseline model. It is a variant of GFI that penalizes GFI by multiplying it by the ratio formed by the degrees of freedom in the tested model and degrees of freedom in the independence model. Similarly, the parsimonious NFI (PNFI) is a variant of the NFI. Ideally, values equal to or greater than .50 indicate an acceptable model (e.g., Mulaik et al., 1989).

16A.11.6 Model Comparison Measures

There are times when we have an interest in comparing models (an approach described in Chapters 20A and 20B on testing for model invariance), and there are additional fit indexes that can be used for this purpose. Generally, we obtain values for these indexes for each model and compare them; models associated with lower values are considered better fitting than those with larger values. Four such measures are the Akaike information criterion (AIC), the Browne–Cudeck criterion (BCC), the Bayesian information criterion (BIC), and the expected cross-validation index (ECVI). The BCC is the only measure developed for IBM SPSS Amos.

16A.11.7 Which Fit Measures to Report?

There is disagreement among SEM researchers on just which fit indexes to report. One often-cited recommendation is from Jaccard and Wan (1996), who suggest reporting at least three fit tests—one absolute, one relative, and one parsimonious—to reflect diverse criteria. Recently, with the advances of more realistic simulation studies, Kline (2011) and Thompson (2004) recommend fit measures without reference to their classification.

We suggest reporting chi-square, the GFI, the RMSEA, the CFI, and the NFI as fit measures. Although chi-square is less informative as an assessment of a single model, it is useful in comparing nested models (i.e., where one model is a subset of another model). The model with the lower chi-square value is considered to be the preferable model. The GFI should be equal to or greater than .90. Both the NFI and the CFI should achieve a value of .95 for the model to be deemed a good fit. The RMSEA is the average of the residuals between the observed correlation/covariance from the sample and the expected model estimated from the population. Loehlin (2004) proposes the following criteria for evaluating this index: (a) less than .08 indicates good fit, (b) .08 to .1 indicates a moderate fit, (c) greater than .1 indicates poor fit. In considering model comparisons, we suggest using all three of the measures shown in Table 16b.1.

16A.12 Model Estimation: Assessing Pattern/Structure Coefficients

The next step in assessing the model is to see if the factor pattern/structure coefficients are statistically significant and meaningful. Figure 16a.10 presents the pattern/structure coefficients of the four measured variables (indicators) as well as those associated with the error variables.

All the factor pattern/structure coefficients achieved statistical significance at an a priori alpha level of $p < .05$. The statistically significant pattern/structure coefficients indicate that multicultural competence is composed of the four measured variables named in the model. The pattern/structure coefficients also achieved meaningful (practical) significance with coefficients greater than .3, although the inference strength from the latent factor to awareness of cultural barriers is a bit more tenuous than the inferences to the other three indicators. Have the researchers proven their model? The answer is no. Confirmatory factor analysis is not an arena for proof, but it can be a source of support for a model and can supply enough information to researchers to cause them to reject a model if it does not fit the data very well. Even in this latter case, researchers may be motivated to modify their existing model rather than completely discarding it if they can determine what might need to be remedied so that the model may be improved.

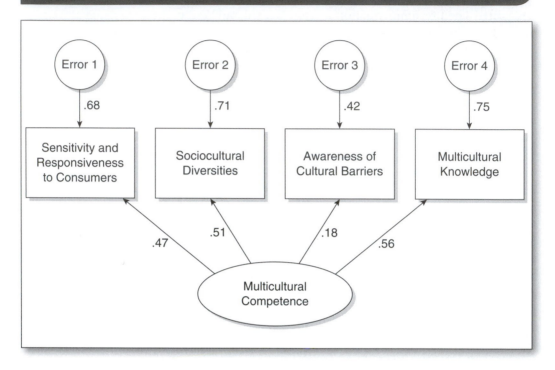

Figure 16a.10 The Multicultural Competence Model With Sensitivity and Responsiveness to Consumers Displaying the Estimated Pattern/Structure Coefficients

16A.13 Model Respecification

16A.13.1 Model Respecification: General Considerations

It is not uncommon that the initial proposed model fails to achieve an adequate fit and that the researchers consider modifying the model (i.e., respecifying). In respecifying the model, the researchers may delete the nonsignificant coefficients in an attempt to trim their models. Researchers could also add coefficients between factors and indicator variables that were previously ignored as an approach to develop their models. In either situation, the analyses are now exploratory rather than confirmatory. Byrne (2010) explains,

> In other words, once an hypothesized CFA model, for example, has been rejected, this spells the end of the confirmatory factor-analytic approach, in its truest sense. Although CFA procedures continue to be used in any respecification and reestimation of the model, these analyses are exploratory in the sense that they focus on the detection of misfitting parameters in the originally hypothesized model. (p. 89)

The researchers need to consider if the respecification is theoretically justifiable. If deleting or adding a coefficient lacks any theoretical justification, the researchers need to avoid this temptation in an attempt to improve the model fit. Steiger (1990) warns researchers of their ability to justify new parameters when he stated, "What percentage of researchers would find themselves unable to think up a 'theoretical justification' for freeing a parameter? . . . I assume that the answer . . . is near zero" (p. 175).

If a model is respecified and achieves acceptable fit with the data, this new model needs to be retested on an independent sample. This new independent sample can either be a holdout sample from the original study (provided that the sample is large enough, perhaps 400 or more) or a new sample.

16A.13.2 Model Respecification Illustration: The Original Model

To illustrate the processes of respecifying a model, the following fictional example will be used. A team of researchers assess the construct validity of a new instrument used to determine aptitude for graduate school. They have proposed two latent factors, Verbal Ability and Math Ability. Each factor has three measured (indicator) variables. The verbal factor is composed of scores from three subscales: Spelling, Grammar, and Comprehension. The math factor is composed of scores from three subscales: Word Problems, Calculations, and Conceptual Understanding. The model with a portion of its hypothetical results is presented in Figure 16a.11.

There are two latent factors in the model, and one of parameters that we specified to be estimated was the correlation between the verbal and math factors. The resulting correlation between Verbal Ability and Math Ability as shown in Figure 16a.11 was .61. There are two issues for us to consider: the pattern versus the structure coefficients and the amount of correlation between the factors.

With regard to the pattern and structure coefficients, for factors that show a moderate degree of association as ours do in our example, the pattern coefficients and the structure coefficients will differ (see our discussion of pattern and structure coefficients in Section 12A.16.3.2). We did not face this issue with only a single factor in the model, but now that we have more than one factor and because we have not specified the correlation to be taken as zero, the issue has emerged. Unlike exploratory factor analysis where we obtain both sets of coefficients, what is reported in the IBM SPSS Amos confirmatory factor analysis output are only pattern coefficients. We interpret the pattern coefficients as representing the unique relationship between the factor and the indicator variable controlling for the effects of the other factor.

With regard to the amount of correlation between the factors, our concern is with the degree of association between them. In many instances, we fully expect factors to be related. In our present example, it is very likely that a general aptitude underlies both verbal and math abilities, and so a moderate amount of correlation would be expected.

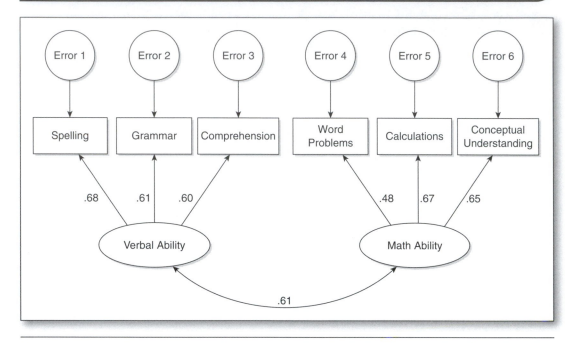

Figure 16a.11 Confirmatory Factor Analysis for Verbal Ability and Math Ability Displaying the Estimated Pattern/Structure Coefficients

Note. Goodness-of-fit index = .975; root mean square error of approximation = .085; comparative fit index = .944.

The key issue is to determine if they are so correlated as to lose their distinctiveness, and guidelines for making such a judgment are available. Bollen (1989) and Kline (2011) have suggested that a correlation between factors of .80 or greater indicates a sufficient loss of distinctiveness to be worrisome; correlations less than .80 are thus taken as indicating that the factors have sufficient discriminative validity to justify the presence of both in the model.

We also display in Figure 16a.11 the pattern coefficients as the path coefficients for each of the factors. As can be seen, the pattern coefficients are not especially high, although they are statistically significant and are therefore meaningful (i.e., they do exceed .3).

In the context of this illustration, assume that the results indicated a moderate fit between the proposed model and the observed data. The chi-square was statistically significant, indicating a lack of fit, but with a large sample size (several hundred cases) that is not surprising. Although the absolute fit measure of the GFI indicated a good fit (.975), the RMSEA indicated a marginal fit with .085. The CFI was also marginal (.944), not quite meeting the .95 criterion.

16A.13.3 Model Respecification Illustration: The Respecification

Given the tenuous degree of model fit obtained with the original model, perhaps a respecified model may better account for the observed data. As will be illustrated in Chapter 16B, the IBM SPSS Amos confirmatory factor analysis output provides modification indexes that represent suggestions to improve the fit of a model. We will adopt a couple of these proposed modifications (selecting judiciously from the list the very few that we judge make theoretical sense—selecting all or most of the proposals simply to get better fit indexes defeats the whole purpose of model fitting and, simply stated, should not be done).

Recall that the researchers need to consider if the respecification is theoretically justifiable. Because all the coefficients achieved both statistical and practical significance, deleting any of the coefficients would be counterproductive. However, it is possible to suggest additions to the model that may enhance its fit to the data. One plausible addition is adding a path (and thus a coefficient) from the latent variable of Verbal Ability to the measured variable of Word Problems (currently an indicator only of Math Ability). This path makes theoretical sense because it can be argued that verbal ability is necessary to comprehend math word problems. Another modification suggestion is that Math Ability could be indicated by the verbal indicator variable of Comprehension, and one may be able to make the case that proficient mathematical ability aids in verbal comprehension. Thus, these "cross-loadings" can make theoretical sense (certainly for our illustration purposes here).

Such a revised model with a portion of its hypothetical results is shown in Figure 16a.12. Note that the correlation between Verbal Ability and Math Ability has decreased from .61 to .44. This drop occurred because some of the variance that was "exclusive" to Verbal Ability has been "released" to the math side of the model; that is, Verbal Ability now has a path to Word Problems. At the same time, some of the variance that was exclusive to Math Ability is now reassigned to the verbal side of the model; that is, Math Ability now has a path to Comprehension.

In terms of the pattern coefficients, we see some gains here as well. The paths from the original model now show values that are a bit higher. For example, Spelling now "loads" on Verbal Ability at .71 compared with its prior value of .68, and Calculations now has a coefficient of .69 compared with its prior value of .67. The new coefficients, the ones that are "cross-loading," are not large in an absolute sense but do add explanatory power. Thus, by permitting Word Problems to be an indicator of Verbal Ability in addition to indicating Math Ability, and by permitting Comprehension to be an indicator of Math Ability in addition to indicating Verbal Ability, we have apparently reached a better understanding of the dynamics underlying these variables.

In terms of the statistical results, all the coefficients achieved statistical significance ($p < .05$). The chi-square value of .334 is nonsignificant, indicating a fit between the model and data. Improvements in the other fit indexes were also obtained. The absolute fit measure of the GFI increased to .996 and the RMSEA attenuated to .017. The CFI also increased to .998.

Figure 16a.12 A Respecified Confirmatory Model for Verbal Ability and Math Ability Displaying the Estimated Pattern/Structure Coefficients

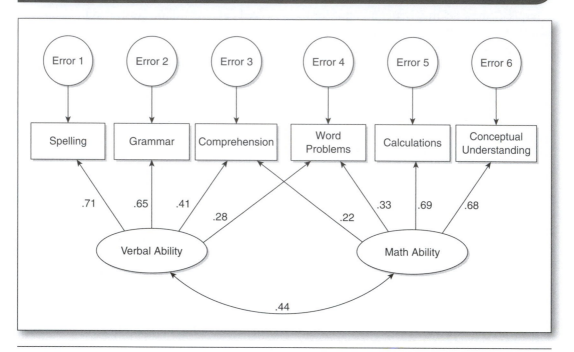

Note. Goodness-of-fit index = .996; root mean square error of approximation = .017; comparative fit index = .998.

16A.14 General Considerations

SEM is able to accommodate some departures from normality. Sample size is also something that researchers should take into consideration when performing confirmatory factor analysis or SEM in general. In the literature, sample sizes for these sorts of studies commonly run in the 200 to 400 range for models with 10 to 15 indicators. Loehlin (1992) recommends at least 100 cases and preferably 200. With more than 10 variables, sample sizes less than 200 generally cause parameter estimates to be unstable, and the tests of statistical significance tests lack a bit of power. One rule of thumb is that sample size should be at least 50 more than 8 times the number of variables in the model. Another rule of thumb, based on Stevens (2009), is to have at least 15 cases per measured variable or indicator. Bentler and Chou (1987) recommend at least 5 cases per parameter estimate (including error terms as well as path coefficients).

16A.15 Recommended Readings

Bentler, P. M. (1992). On the fit of models to covariances and methodology to the Bulletin. *Psychological Bulletin, 112,* 400–404.

Enders, C. K. (2001a). The impact of nonnormality on full information maximum-likelihood estimation for structural equation models with missing data. *Psychological Methods, 6,* 352–370.

Estrella, A. (1998). A new measure of fit for equations with dichotomous dependent variables. *Journal of Business & Economic Statistics, 16,* 198–205.

Fan, X., Thompson, B., & Wang, L. (1999). Effects of sample size, estimation method, and model specification on structural equation modeling fit indexes. *Structural Equation Modeling, 6,* 56–83.

Hu, L., & Bentler, P. M. (1999a). Cutoff criteria for fit indexes in covariance structure analysis: Conventional criteria versus new alternatives. *Structural Equation Modeling, 6,* 1–55.

Jöreskog, K. G. (1969). A general approach to confirmatory maximum likelihood factor analysis. *Psychometrika, 34,* 183–202.

Mulaik, S. (1972). *The foundations of factor analysis.* New York, NY: McGraw-Hill.

Mulaik, S. A., James, L. R., Van Alstine, J., Bennett, N., Lind, S., & Stilwell, C. D. (1989). Evaluation of goodness-of-fit indices for structural equation models. *Psychological Bulletin, 105,* 430–445.

Pearl, J. (2011). The science and ethics of causal modeling. In A. T. Panter & S. K. Sterba (Eds.), *Handbook of ethics in quantitative methodology* (pp. 338–414). New York, NY: Routledge.

Reilly, T. (1995). A necessary and sufficient condition for identification of confirmatory factor analysis models of complexity one. *Sociological Methods & Research, 23,* 421–441.

Reise, S. P., Widaman, K. F., & Pugh, R. H. (1993). Confirmatory factor analysis and item response theory: Two approaches for exploring measurement invariance. *Psychological Bulletin, 114,* 552–566.

Rigdon, E. E. (1995). A necessary and sufficient identification rule for structural models estimated in practice. *Multivariate Behavioral Research, 30,* 359–383.

Steiger, J. H. (1998). A note on multisample extensions of the RMSEA fit index. *Structural Equation Modeling, 5,* 411–419.

Thompson, B. (2000). Ten commandments of structural equation modeling. In L. G. Grimm & P. R. Yarnold (Eds.), *Reading and understanding more multivariate statistics* (pp. 261–283). Washington, DC: American Psychological Association.

Thompson, B. (2004). *Exploratory and confirmatory factor analysis: Understanding concepts and applications.* Washington, DC: American Psychological Association.

Tremblay, P. F., & Gardner, R. C. (1996). On the growth of structural equation modeling in psychological journals. *Structural Equation Modeling, 3,* 93–104.

Confirmatory Factor Analysis Using Amos

16B.1 Using Amos

In this chapter, we will demonstrate how to perform a confirmatory factor analysis using IBM SPSS Amos 19 (Arbuckle, 2010). Amos is an acronym for "Analysis of *MO*ment *Structures*" (Arbuckle, 2010). IBM SPSS Amos allows researchers to draw their hypothesized model and evaluate it. Although we will describe all of the steps involved in our analysis, we have supplied in Appendix B some of the commonly used IBM SPSS Amos commands and labels for the panels and icons used in drawing and viewing the IBM SPSS Amos diagrams; readers are encouraged to consult the material in Appendix B as we present the material in this as well as Chapters 18B, 19B, and 20B.

16B.2 Numerical Example

The data set used for this example was discussed in Chapter 16A. It concerned verbal ability and math ability factors. Our example was conceptually inspired from a data file that is supplied with IBM SPSS Amos, and the data are contained in the data file named **Verbal Math**. We will perform a two-factor confirmatory analysis. It is not unusual for researchers to compare their preferred or selected factor structure with alternative structures. We hypothesize that spelling (**spell**), grammar (**gram**), and comprehension (**comp**) are indicators of verbal ability and that solving math word problems (**prob**), performing calculations (**calc**), and conceptual understanding of mathematical concepts (**con**) are indicators of math ability.

16B.3 Model Specification

16B.3.1 Drawing the Model

To specify a model is to create a structural representation of the hypothesized relationships. We open the data file named **Verbal Math** in IBM SPSS. From the main menu, select **Analyze ➔ Amos** to bring us to the graphics window displayed in Figure 16b.1. The right portion of the window typically opens in portrait page layout (the longer axis is vertical). Because we are going to draw a two-factor structure across the screen, it would be useful to have a landscape view. Also, the default labeling schema in IBM SPSS Amos is to use the variable labels as opposed to the variable names. In our data file, the labels are rather long and will not easily fit in the rectangles for the indicator variables. Both of these matters can be quickly fixed.

Select **View ➔ Interface Properties** to reach the dialog window shown in Figure 16b.2. Make sure that the **Page Layout** tab is active (which is the default tab that is displayed). In the drop-down menu for **Paper Size**, select **Landscape Legal** and click the **Apply** pushbutton. Then, select the **Misc** tab and remove the default check mark by **Display variable labels** as shown in Figure 16b.3. Click the **Apply** pushbutton.

To draw our model, select **Diagram ➔ Draw Indicator Variable**. The cursor will change to a miniature structural diagram. We now draw the first factor. Depress the left

Figure 16b.1   Main Graphics Window for IBM SPSS Amos

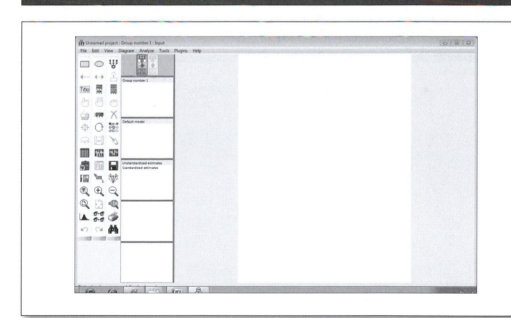

Figure 16b.2   Interface Properties Windows to Change the Page Layout

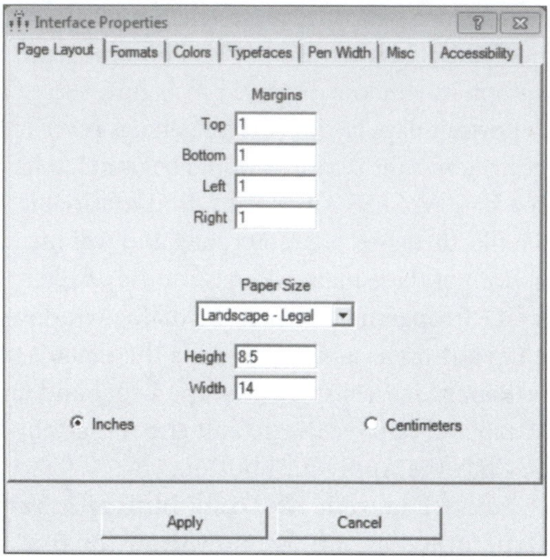

Figure 16b.3   Interface Properties Windows to Allow Variable Names for the Indicator Variables

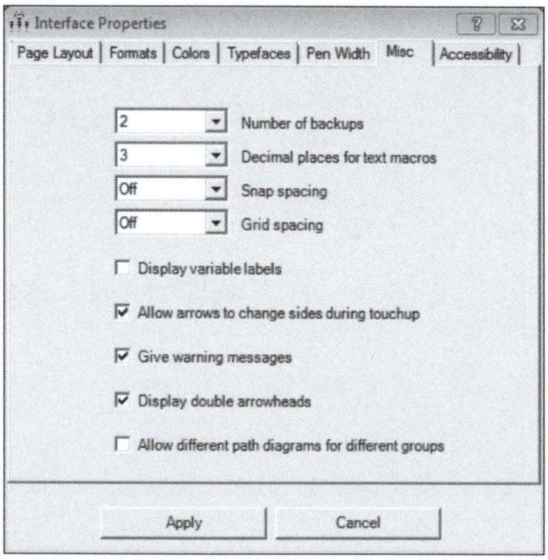

Figure 16b.4   Two Factors With Three Indicators Each

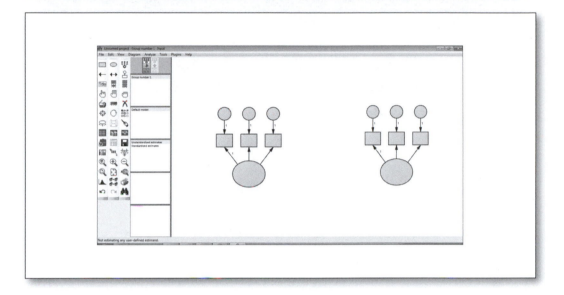

mouse button and draw a circle (or oval). With the cursor still inside the oval, click the left mouse button three times. IBM SPSS Amos automatically constructs indicator variables with associated error terms for each click of the mouse. The software selected the first indicator variable as the scaling base for the latent factor by placing an initial value of 1 (constraining the first path to unity) for the pattern/structure coefficient. Furthermore, it has also assigned a value of 1 to all the paths from the error variables to the measured variables. To generate the other factor, repeat this process. The completed diagram is shown in Figure 16b.4.

The correlation between the two latent factors needs to be represented by a curved line with a double arrow. To do this, select **Diagram** ➔ **Draw Covariance**. The cursor will change to a double arrow. Placing the cursor on the perimeter of the rightmost oval so that the perimeter is highlighted (changes color), hold down the left mouse button and draw the line over to the perimeter of the left oval. This is shown in Figure 16b.5.

16B.3.2 Naming the Measured Variables

Select **View** ➔ **Variables in Dataset**. This produces a screen containing the variables in the IBM SPSS data file as shown in Figure 16b.6. Click **spell** and drag it to the first indicator variable rectangle in the leftmost portion of the structural diagram, which we will designate as the verbal factor in a moment. Then drag **gram** and **comp** to the next two indicator

Figure 16b.5 Two Factors With Three Indicators Each and the Factors Shown to Be Correlated by a Double-Sided Arrow

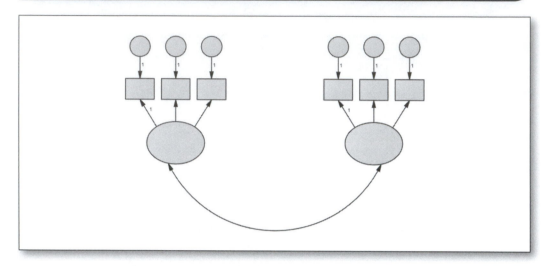

Figure 16b.6 The Variables in Dataset Window

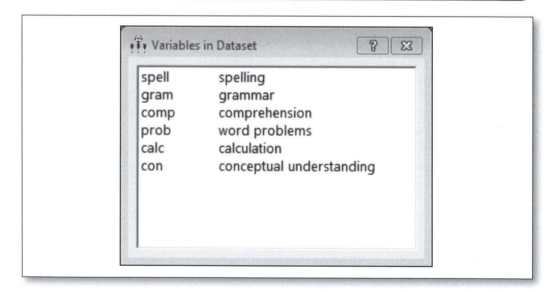

variables. The second factor is composed of **prob**, **calc**, and **con**; drag these to the next set of indicator variables, which we will designate as the math factor in a moment. The screen at this point is shown in Figure 16b.7.

Figure 16b.7 The Model With the Indicator Variable Names Included

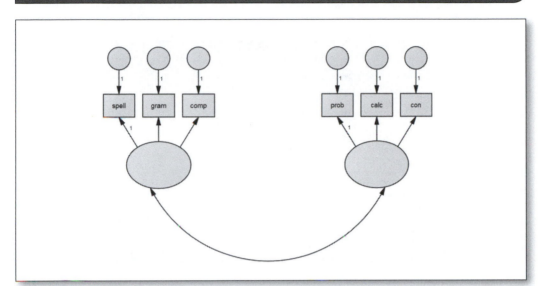

16B.3.3 Naming the Latent Factors

Next, we will name the latent variables. Selecting **View ➜ Object Properties** displays the dialog window shown in Figure 16b.8. Place the cursor in the left oval and left-click to highlight it. Then in the **VariableLabel(0) name** panel of **Object Properties** window, type **verbal**. As we type, the name appears in the oval. Then click on the other oval and type **math** in the **VariableLabel(1) name** panel. The final result is shown in Figure 16b.9.

16B.3.4 Naming the Error Variables

To name the error variables in one operation select **Plugins ➜ Name Unobserved Variables**. Selecting this option in the menu automatically names the error terms from left to right as **e1**, **e2**, and so on. This is shown in Figure 16b.10.

16B.4 Model Identification

The number of known (nonredundant) elements in the model is equal to $V(V + 1)/2$, where V is the number of the measured variables in the study. There are six measured

Figure 16b.8   The Object Properties Window

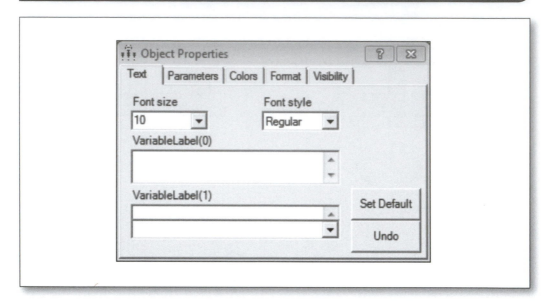

Figure 16b.9   The Model With the Latent Factors Named

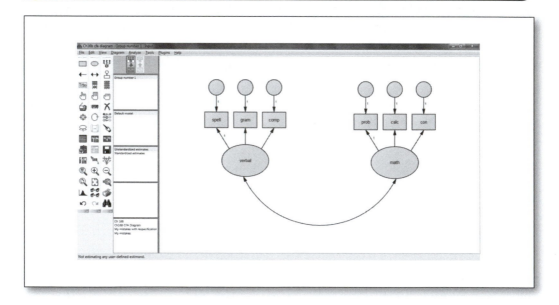

Figure 16b.10   The Model With the Error Variables Named

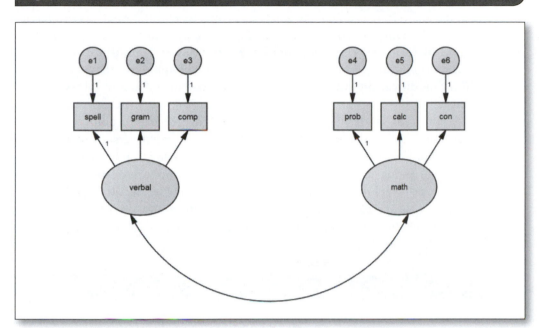

variables, and so we have (6 * 7)/2 or 21 known elements. These known elements are as follows:

- There are six variances, one for each measured variable.
- There are 15 pairwise correlations for the set of six measured variables.

The 13 unknown elements (estimated parameters) in the model are as follows:

- There is one correlation coefficient between the two latent factors.
- We are also estimating a variance for each latent factor for a total of two parameters.
- We are estimating four path coefficients (there are six, but two have already been constrained to unity).
- We are also estimating a variance for each error term for a total of six parameters.

The degrees of freedom of the model is computed as the number of known elements minus the number of estimated parameters. Here, these values are 21 − 13 for a difference of 8. The degrees of freedom are positive, and thus, the model is identified.

16B.5 Performing the Analysis

To perform the analysis, select **View** ➜ **Analysis Properties**. In the **Analysis Properties** window, select the **Output** tab as shown in Figure 16b.11. Remove the check from **Minimization history**, and check **Standardized estimates** and **Modification indices**. When **Modification indices** is checked, the value of **4** will appear in the panel labeled **Threshold for modification indices**. This value of **4** refers to chi-square values that will test the efficacy of the proposed modification. The critical value for chi-square to be statistically significant at the .05 alpha level with 1 degree of freedom is 3.84 (see Appendix A Table A2), and the value of **4** is simply a rounded version of that. One degree of freedom is invoked because it is making one assessment at a time. The problem is that it is making many assessments, and thus the alpha level becomes rather inflated. Most researchers do not take these chi-square tests (see Section 16B.7.2) literally but only as a means of spotting stronger suggestions about modifications to the model, but it is best to bear in mind that treating them as tests of significance is not strongly advised.

Figure 16b.11   The Output Tab in the Analysis Properties Dialog Window

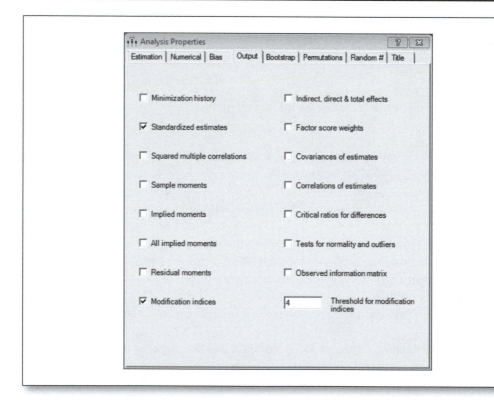

Figure 16b.12 The Estimation Tab in the Analysis Properties Dialog Window

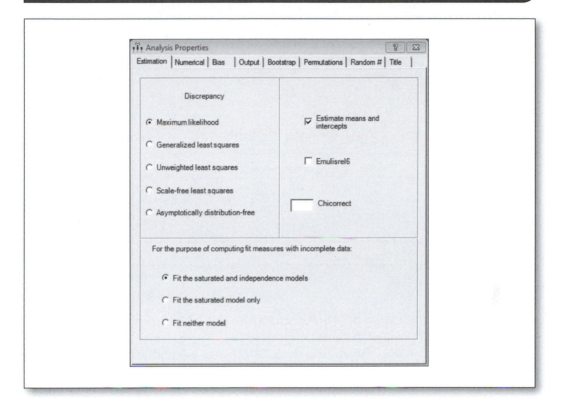

The procedure will not produce output if there are missing data (even if there is a single data value that is missing) but will instead yield an error message informing us that we have missing data. If we have missing data, IBM SPSS Amos will handle it using an FIML technique (discussed as a modern imputation method for handling missing data in Section 3a.7 of Chapter 3A), which is the recommended procedure to deal with missing data in confirmatory factor analysis and SEM in general because the estimates of the parameters tend to be less biased (Schumacker & Lomax, 2004). To invoke this procedure, we must select the **Estimation** tab in the **Analysis Properties** window. We would then check the **Estimate means and intercepts** choice; this is shown in Figure 16b.12 (for illustration purposes), but we have not checked the option because we have no missing data in our data set.

After making all of our specifications for the analysis in the **Output** window, we are ready to perform the analysis. From the main menu, select **Analyze ➜ Calculate Estimates**. At that point, IBM SPSS Amos will display the Windows **Save As** dialog screen. We must save the output file, which will contain both the graphic displays of the model and the results of the

Figure 16b.13 The Data Files Window

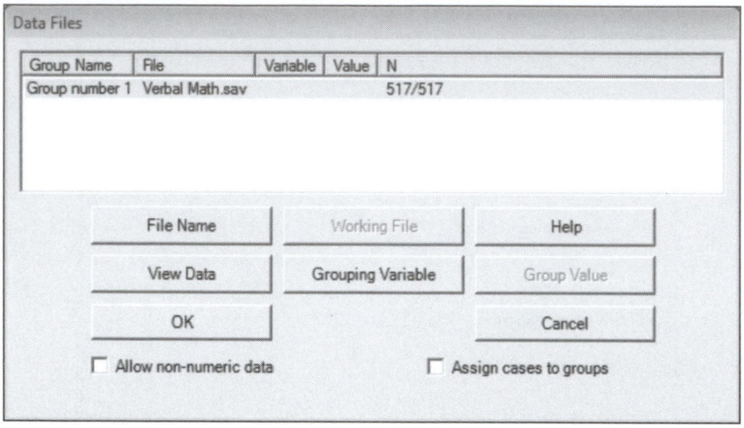

numerical calculations under a file name of our choice to a location of our choice. Once we execute the **Save As**, the output becomes available to us.

It should be noted that if we needed to make a change in the IBM SPSS data file during the same session (perhaps to correct a data entry error) and wished to once again perform the confirmatory factor analysis on the revised data set, we would need to reactivate the data file once we finished editing the data file. To reactivate the data file, select **File ➔ Data Files**. This will open the **Data Files** window (see Figure 16b.13). Despite the fact that the IBM SPSS data file name will be present in this window, it is not the updated version. To activate the updated data file, select the **File Name** pushbutton. That will bring us to the **Open** window where we would navigate to our updated data file and select it. Once a file is selected, we are returned to the **Data Files** window. Click **OK** to activate that data file.

16B.6 Working With the Analysis Output

With the variety of output ready for us, we can choose to view it in any order that makes sense or appeals to us. What follows therefore is not a mandatory fixed order of examining the output but rather our mild suggestion of what some researchers might wish to do.

Select **View ➔ Text Output**, which opens the **Amos Output** window. This **Amos Output** window contains several different screens of output. Our command places us in the

Figure 16b.14 The Initial Amos Output Window

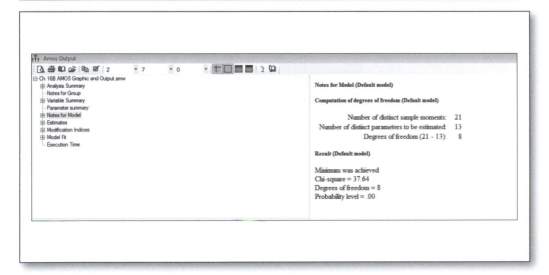

Notes for Model page shown in Figure 16b.14. The output displays the number of known elements (**Number of distinct sample moments**) as 21, the number of unknown elements (**Number of distinct parameters to be estimated**) as 13, and the **Degrees of freedom** as 8 obtained by subtracting 13 from 21.

Below this information is the chi-square result. Its value is 37.639, and with 8 degrees of freedom, it is statistically significant ($p < .001$). In isolation, we might judge from this significant chi-square that the model is not a good fit to the data. However, it is best to examine the other indexes as chi-square may have more statistical power than is useful.

16B.6.1 Model Fit

To obtain the fit indexes, select **Model Fit** in the **Text Output** menu. Some of the fit indexes shown in the output and the ones of interest to us (see Section 16A.11) are shown in Figure 16b.15. Our interest is in the rows corresponding to the **Default model**, which is the model we have specified. We ignore both the information provided for the **Saturated model**, which will artificially fit the data extremely well (see Section 16A.8.1), and the **Independence model**, which assumes that there are no relationships in the data as mentioned in Section 16A.11.4.

CMIN stands for minimum discrepancy as indexed by chi-square; this was discussed above. The target for the GFI is equal to or greater than .90 for a good fit; in the present case, its value is .975, which suggests an excellent fit. Under the heading **Baseline Comparisons**, we find both the NFI and CFI. Our target values for these indexes is .95, although .90 or above is

Figure 16b.15 Model Fit Summary

Model Fit Summary

CMIN

Model	NPAR	CMIN	DF	P	CMIN/DF
Default model	13	37.639	8	.000	4.705
Saturated model	21	.000	0		
Independence model	6	542.817	15	.000	36.188

RMR, GFI

Model	RMR	GFI	AGFI	PGFI
Default model	.139	.975	.935	.372
Saturated model	.000	1.000		
Independence model	.738	.675	.545	.482

Baseline Comparisons

Model	NFI Delta1	RFI rho1	IFI Delta2	TLI rho2	CFI
Default model	.931	.870	.945	.895	.944
Saturated model	1.000		1.000		1.000
Independence model	.000	.000	.000	.000	.000

RMSEA

Model	RMSEA	LO 90	HI 90	PCLOSE
Default model	.085	.059	.113	.016
Independence model	.261	.243	.280	.000

AIC

Model	AIC	BCC	BIC	CAIC
Default model	63.639	63.996	118.863	131.863
Saturated model	42.000	42.578	131.209	152.209
Independence model	554.817	554.982	580.305	586.305

ECVI

Model	ECVI	LO 90	HI 90	MECVI
Default model	.123	.093	.168	.124
Saturated model	.081	.081	.081	.083
Independence model	1.075	.935	1.230	1.076

acceptable; here we obtained values of .931 and .944, respectively. These values would suggest an acceptable fit. The target value for the RMSEA is .08, and the obtained value is .085 (with a 90% confidence interval of .059 to .113); this outcome would be judged to indicate a borderline acceptable fit. In summary, we would judge the model to represent an acceptable but not an excellent fit to the data.

We also show three additional fit indexes in Figure 16b.15: the AIC (63.639) and the BCC (63.996) shown in the **AIC** table and the ECVI (.123 with a 90% confidence interval of

.093 to .168) shown in the **ECVI** table. If we respecify our model, we will refer to these original values and the corresponding ones associated with the new model to determine which is a better fit.

16B.6.2 Coefficients

To obtain the coefficients that were estimated, select **Estimates** in the **Text Output** menu. A portion of the output is shown in Figure 16b.16. The **Regression Weights** table provides the raw score regression weights and the exact probability of them occurring by

Figure 16b.16 Coefficients Estimated by the Model Presented in Table Format

Estimates (Group number 1 - Default model)

Scalar Estimates (Group number 1 - Default model)

Maximum Likelihood Estimates

Regression Weights: (Group number 1 - Default model)

			Estimate	S.E.	C.R.	P	Label
spell	<---	verbal	1.000				
gram	<---	verbal	1.063	.115	9.275	***	
comp	<---	verbal	.988	.107	9.242	***	
prob	<---	math	1.000				
calc	<---	math	1.449	.185	7.847	***	
con	<---	math	1.228	.157	7.836	***	

Standardized Regression Weights: (Group number 1 - Default model)

			Estimate
spell	<---	verbal	.678
gram	<---	verbal	.611
comp	<---	verbal	.605
prob	<---	math	.482
calc	<---	math	.673
con	<---	math	.654

Covariances: (Group number 1 - Default model)

			Estimate	S.E.	C.R.	P	Label
verbal	<-->	math	.510	.082	6.219	***	

Correlations: (Group number 1 - Default model)

			Estimate
verbal	<-->	math	.613

chance if the null hypothesis is true. Coefficients that were constrained in the model speci-fication—**spell** for the **verbal** factor and **prob** for the **math** factor—cannot be estimated; thus, the value of **1** assigned to these paths to scale the latent factor appears in the table and is not tested for statistical significance.

The coefficients for the other paths are estimated and probability values (**P** values in the table) are reported. For example, the raw regression coefficient for **gram** is 1.063. The **P** value is shown as a set of three asterisks, indicating that the probability is less than .001. As may be seen, all of the estimated coefficients reached statistical significance. Thus, grammar and comprehension are statistically significant indicators of verbal abil-ity, and calculations and conceptual understanding are statistically significant indicators of math ability.

The **Standardized Regression Weights** table displays the pattern coefficients that are tra-ditionally used as the path coefficients in the structural diagram. Recall that because we have asked Amos to estimate the correlation between the factors, the standardized weights will be pattern but not structure coefficients. Pattern coefficients are correlations between the factor and the indicator variables, controlling for the correlation of all other factors with the specified factor. For example, the pattern coefficient associated with grammar is .611. Thus, the **gram** variable correlates with verbal ability .611, controlling for the correlation of verbal ability with math ability. The correlation between the two factors, as can be seen in bottom tables labeled **Covariances** and **Correlations**, was statistically significant with a value of .613. Examining the pattern coefficients generally suggests that the measured variables are excellent indictors of their respective factors.

16B.6.3 Pictorial Representation of the Output

The pattern coefficients and the correlation between the factors are shown in the **Path Diagram** (or graphics) window. Click on the name of the saved file (the name that we assigned in the **Save As** window before the analysis would be performed) that appears on the taskbar at the bottom of the screen. Choose from the drop-down menu the **Draw Indicator Variable** icon in front of the file name. The confirmatory model then appears; we show it in Figure 16b.17. To view the standardized coefficients, first click on the icon for **View the output path diagram** at the top of the panels to the left of the graphics area and then click on **Standardized estimates** in a middle panel to the left of the graphic area. All of the information that was contained in the **Estimates** output is shown in pictorial form.

16B.7 Considering the Respecification of the Model

To assess the possibility of improving model fit by effecting some respecification of the model, select **Modification Indices** in the **Text Output** menu. At this stage, our analysis

Figure 16b.17 Coefficients Estimated by the Model Placed in the Path Diagram

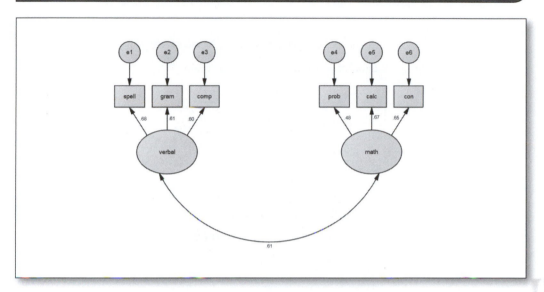

would shift from hypothesis testing to exploratory analysis, but the efforts may be useful for researchers to learn more about the topic. The two output tables presenting the **Modification Indices** are shown in Figure 16b.18.

There are two ways to improve the fit of the model: Remove or add correlations between variables and remove or add paths from the model. The top table labeled **Covariances** deals with scenarios of adding correlations between the variables, and the lower table labeled **Regression Weights** deals with scenarios of adding paths.

16B.7.1 Removing Correlations From the Model

When we specified the model originally, we may have included correlations (shown as double-arrowed curved lines in the diagram). These correlations were parameters to be estimated. It is possible that one or more of these parameters turned out to be nonsignificant or of trivial practical import. Removing such specifications from the model will tend to improve model fit, although there is no assurance that the fit would be significantly improved. Nonetheless, these correlations are candidates for removal in the respecified model. This is not a viable option in the present example as we have only one correlation between the factors and it is of reasonable magnitude.

Figure 16b.18 Modification Indices Tables

Modification Indices (Group number 1 - Default model)

Covariances: (Group number 1 - Default model)

			M.I.	Par Change
e4	<-->	verbal	9.319	.237
e3	<-->	math	13.228	.213
e3	<-->	verbal	4.356	-.108
e3	<-->	e6	5.396	.197
e2	<-->	math	5.606	-.147
e2	<-->	e6	6.229	-.225
e2	<-->	e4	4.675	.229
e1	<-->	e2	5.670	.151

Variances: (Group number 1 - Default model)

		M.I.	Par Change

Regression Weights: (Group number 1 - Default model)

			M.I.	Par Change
prob	<---	verbal	4.185	.217
prob	<---	gram	6.770	.133
comp	<---	math	5.934	.174
comp	<---	con	8.236	.091
comp	<---	calc	4.104	.056
comp	<---	prob	4.197	.059
gram	<---	con	6.361	-.085

16B.7.2 Adding Correlations to the Model

The possibility of adding one or more correlations in our model specification is addressed by the **Modification Indices** output. In the **Covariances** table under the column labeled **M.I.** (which stands for modification indices) are chi-square values. Recall from Section 16B.5 that these chi-square values are simply guides and that treating them as tests of statistical significance is not advised because of alpha inflation. Furthermore, making the changes on the basis of such "suggestions" must have some theoretical justification (we do not wish to blindly follow statistical advice that has no relationship to the content domain being studied).

For example, the second row shows the largest chi-square value of 13.228 associated with **e3** and **math**; if this change was made, we would anticipate that the overall model fit would improve. The column labeled **Par Change** (where **Par** stands for **Parameter**) shows a value of .213. This means that if we add that correlation to the model (i.e., draw a double-arrow curved line) between **e3** and **math**, we would (very approximately) obtain a correlation situation value of .213. The **e3** is the error term associated with verbal comprehension. Although such an action would increase the fit of the model, it makes no theoretical sense to correlate the verbal comprehension error term with math ability, and so we opt not to do it.

The only correlation that does make theoretical sense to add to the model is shown in the last row of the **Covariances** table. Adding a correlation between the error terms associated with spelling and grammar can be justified in that these two skills are very likely to be related.

16B.7.3 Removing Paths From the Model

As was true for correlations originally specified in the model, there may be paths that were specified in the original model that we now realize are associated with pattern coefficients that are either not statistically significant or of trivial practical import. Removing such specifications from the model will tend to improve model fit, although there is no assurance that the fit would be significantly improved.

16B.7.4 Adding Paths to the Model

The lower table (**Regression Weights**) is structured in the same way as the **Covariances** table. Paths that are not currently in the model are listed in this table together with their chi-square tests of significance and the estimated value of the new parameter. Adding a given path would improve model fit; adding several of these suggested paths might improve model fit more, but their combination is almost certainly not going to be completely additive. Again, adding a path should have some theoretical justification.

For example, the first row of the **Regression Weights** table informs us that adding a path from the **verbal** to **prob** (problem solving, one of the indicators of math ability) will improve model fit; the path coefficient is estimated to be .217. Given that problem solving involves word problems and that solving such problems might very well require a certain amount of verbal ability in addition to math ability, adding this path makes theoretical sense.

16B.7.5 The Situation With Missing Values

If we had missing values in our data set, the analysis would have been performed under the FIML imputation procedure. Once this procedure is invoked, the output does not contain the **Modification Indices** output (nor the GFI). It is still possible to engage in the model respecification process; however, researchers are on their own in determining which correlations or paths to add to the model. Thus, as long as the modifications are theoretically justifiable, model respecification can still be carried out on data sets with missing values.

16B.8 Respecifying the Model

We will make the following two changes to the model as they make theoretical sense:

- We will specify a correlation between the error terms for grammar and spelling.
- We will add a path from verbal ability to problem solving.

The newly specified model is shown in Figure 16b.19. From the main menu, select **Analyze ➔ Calculate Estimates**. This time we are not presented with a **Save As** window; instead, the analysis is performed and the new output overwrites the existing file. We need to save this newly written-over file in order to retrieve it later.

16B.9 Output From the Respecification

Select **View ➔ Text Output**, which again opens the **Amos Output** window in the **Notes for Model** page shown in Figure 16b.20. The output displays the same number of known elements (**Number of distinct sample moments**), that is, 21. What is different

Figure 16b.19   The Respecified Model With a Correlation Between the Error Terms for Grammar and Spelling and a Path From Verbal Ability to Problem Solving Added

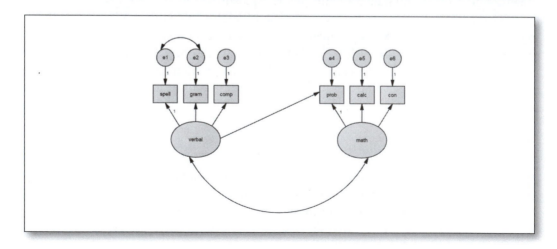

Figure 16b.20 The Amos Output Window for the Respecified Model

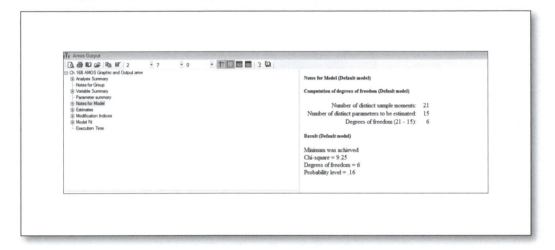

is the number of unknown elements (**Number of distinct parameters to be estimated**), which now is 15 (up from 13) because we have added two additional parameters to estimate. The **Degrees of freedom** are now 6 (down from the original 8) because we have two additional unknown elements that are subtracted from the number of known elements.

Below this information is the chi square result. Its value is 9.246, down from the value of 37.639 from the original model; with 6 degrees of freedom, it failed to achieve statistical significance and would probably bring joy to the hearts of the researchers as this represents a substantially better fit than the original model. However, it is still necessary to examine the other indexes.

To obtain the fit indexes, select **Model Fit** in the **Text Output** menu. Some of the fit indexes shown in the output and the ones of interest to us are shown in Figure 16b.21. Briefly, the GFI improved from .975 to .994, the NFI improved from .931 to .983, the CFI improved from .944 to .994, and the RMSEA improved from .085 (with a 90% confidence interval of .059 to .113) to .032 (with a 90% confidence interval of .000 to .071). Furthermore, the AIC decreased from 63.639 to 39.246, the BCC decreased from 63.996 to 39.659, and the ECVI decreased from .123 (with a 90% confidence interval of .093 to .168) to .076 (with a 90% confidence interval of .070 to .100). All of the model fit output uniformly and convincingly demonstrate that the respecified model is a superior fit to the data than the original model.

The respecified model with its estimated coefficients is shown in Figure 16b.22. The two new coefficients were both statistically significant. Thus, problem solving appears to be an indicator for both verbal and math ability.

Figure 16b.21   The Fit Indexes for the Respecified Model

Model Fit Summary

CMIN

Model	NPAR	CMIN	DF	P	CMIN/DF
Default model	15	9.246	6	.160	1.541
Saturated model	21	.000	0		
Independence model	6	542.817	15	.000	36.188

RMR, GFI

Model	RMR	GFI	AGFI	PGFI
Default model	.060	.994	.979	.284
Saturated model	.000	1.000		
Independence model	.738	.675	.545	.482

Baseline Comparisons

Model	NFI Delta1	RFI rho1	IFI Delta2	TLI rho2	CFI
Default model	.983	.957	.994	.985	.994
Saturated model	1.000		1.000		1.000
Independence model	.000	.000	.000	.000	.000

RMSEA

Model	RMSEA	LO 90	HI 90	PCLOSE
Default model	.032	.000	.071	.730
Independence model	.261	.243	.280	.000

AIC

Model	AIC	BCC	BIC	CAIC
Default model	39.246	39.659	102.967	117.967
Saturated model	42.000	42.578	131.209	152.209
Independence model	554.817	554.982	580.305	586.305

ECVI

Model	ECVI	LO 90	HI 90	MECVI
Default model	.076	.070	.100	.077
Saturated model	.081	.081	.081	.083
Independence model	1.075	.935	1.230	1.076

Figure 16b.22 The Structural Diagram for the Respecified Model

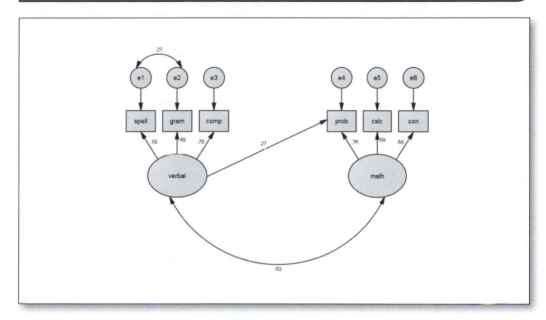

16B.10 Reporting Confirmatory Factor Analysis Results

This study tested the hypothesis that spelling, grammar, and comprehension are indicators of verbal ability and that solving math word problems, performing calculations, and conceptual understanding of mathematical concepts are indicators of math ability. A confirmatory factor analysis of the hypothesized model is shown in Figure 16b.17 and was assessed in IBM SPSS Amos 19. Figure 16b.17 also displays the path coefficients generated in the analysis.

The chi-square and fit indexes are shown in Table 16b.1. Although the chi-square test of the model was statistically significant with a value of 37.64 (8, $N = 517$), $p < .001$, the model yielded acceptable fit indexes for the GFI, NFI, and CFI; however, the RMSEA achieved a value of .09 indicating a marginal fit of the model.

Review of the modification indexes led to respecifying the model by (a) including a path from the verbal factor to the measured variable of problem solving (solving math word problems) and (b) correlating the error variances for grammar and spelling

(Continued)

(Continued)

on the grounds that these two skills are tied to each other in the instructional process. Results of the respecified model achieved a nonsignificant chi-square of 9.25 (6, $N = 517$), $p = .160$, and higher values on the GFI, NFI, and CFI. Additionally, the RMSEA was lowered to achieve a superior fit (Browne & Cudeck, 1993). The model comparison fit measures, AIC, BCC, and ECVI, were all substantially smaller in the respecified model than the original model, indicating an improved fit between the model and the data.

The results suggest that spelling, grammar, and comprehension are indicators of verbal ability but that solving math word problems, performing calculations, conceptual understanding of mathematical concepts, and problem solving are all indicators of math ability. The respecified model is shown in Figure 16b.22.

Table 16b.1   Chi-Square and Goodness of Fit Indices for Confirmatory Factor Models

Table 16b.1
Chi-square and Goodness of Fit Indices for Confirmatory Factor Models

Factor Model	χ^2	df	GFI	NFI	CFI	RMSEA	AIC	BCC	ECVI
Original	37.64*	8	.98	.93	.94	.09 (.06 to .11)	63.64	64.00	.12 (.09 to .17)
Respecified	9.25	6	.99	.98	.99	.03 (.00 to .07)	39.25	39.66	.08 (.07 to .10)

Note. χ^2 = Chi square test; *df* = degrees of freedom; GFI = Goodness of Fit Index; NFI = Normed Fit Index; CFI = Comparative Fit Index; RMSEA = Root Mean Square Error of Approximation; AIC = Akaike Information Criterion; BCC= Browne-Cudeck Criterion; ECVI = Expected Cross Validation Index.

Path Analysis: Multiple Regression

17A.1 Overview

Structural equation modeling is a statistical procedure that enables researchers to evaluate specific relationships hypothesized among a set of variables; these variables typically subsume latent variables. In SEM, we generally distinguish between two aspects of (or submodels comprising) the overall model:

- A *measurement model* that is assessed by confirmatory factor analysis. Here, we evaluate the fit between the latent constructs and their indicator variables. We have discussed this topic in Chapters 16A and 16B.
- A *structural model* in which the hypothesized interrelationships between latent constructs or between latent constructs and measured variables are assessed in terms of how well they are supported by the data. These hypothesized interrelationships are specified by (prediction) paths drawn between the variables.

Path analysis is the simplest case of SEM where we do not include latent variables. We have already broached the beginning of the topic of path models in our discussion of simple mediation in Section 8A.7. Generally, path models ordinarily contain several measured variables configured in more complex ways than simple mediation. These types of models were originally called *causal models*.

Because there are no latent variables included in a path analysis, the overall model is simpler than SEM. That is, there is no measurement model to assess, and all of the hypothesized interrelationships concern only measured variables. Path analysis also involves somewhat simpler statistical procedures than SEM. That is, the analysis may be performed in specialized SEM software; however, because there are no latent variables in the model, the analysis can also be performed using ordinary least squares multiple regression techniques (once latent constructs are included in the model, the analysis must be run in the specialized SEM software).

In this chapter and in Chapter 17B, we cover the general principles of path analysis and discuss the analysis of path structures within the context of ordinary least squares multiple regression. Chapters 18A and 18B treat path analysis using IBM SPSS Amos to perform the analysis. We will see that this latter approach allows us to perform the analysis in a more holistic manner. Chapters 19A and 19B will then transition us to SEM so that we can address the inclusion of latent variables in the model.

17A.2 Principles of Path Analysis

Path analysis was first introduced by Wright (1921) as an application of multiple regression analysis and has gained in popularity in recent years. Today, we also have the option of performing a path analysis in model-fitting programs as well as through regression. By using path analysis, researchers are able to evaluate explicitly hypothesized and often relatively complex causal (predictive) relationships between the variables represented in their data (Klem, 1995). The steps taken by researchers in conducting a path analysis are as follows:

1. Draw out the interrelationships of the variables in the form of a path diagram.

2. Indicate the hypothesized strength (e.g., relatively strong, moderate, modest, weak) and direction (direct or inverse) of each variable's presumed effect on each other in each of the paths.

3. Perform the analyses yielding the path coefficients for each path.

4. Compare the obtained path coefficients with the hypothesized path strengths and directions.

5. Evaluate how well the causal (predictive) model fits the data based on the results of the analysis.

6. Respecify (simplify) the model if it is appropriate to remove unnecessary paths.

From the standpoint of multiple regression, you would think that path analysis would be associated with the label *predictive modeling* rather than with the more commonly used term *causal modeling* because path coefficients are beta weights from the multiple regression prediction equation. Maybe invoking the term *cause* has added some extra interest in the procedure (and perhaps some controversy as well); explicating the cause of an event might suggest, to some, greater explanatory power than indicating how much we are able to predict an outcome variable.

Causal modeling in the context of path analysis really just results from synthesizing the outcome of several prediction analyses. Nonetheless, understanding the uses and limitations of path analysis is intimately related to the way in which causality is tied to the scientific method itself. Most researchers rarely make observations for their own sake. Instead, observation (data collection) serves as a means for researchers to organize or to explain the phenomena they see in the empirical world or as a way of testing their theoretical formulations. Organizing or explaining very often involves theorizing about the causal principles underlying the relationships between the variables on which they have collected data. We will therefore briefly examine the concept of causality as a foundation for our discussion of path analysis.

17A.3 Causality and Path Analysis

Most of the data to which path analysis is applied have been collected using a correlation procedure. That is, the data on most or all the variables have been collected at the same time and under the same conditions for all participants. In such a situation, the research method would not ordinarily support drawing causal inferences from the study. So how do we get from "the research method would not support drawing causal inferences" to a statistical procedure that allows researchers to evaluate a causal model? The answer is, albeit indirectly, reached via the following logic.

17A.3.1 Causality Is an Inference

We start with the principle that causality is not present in the actual observations (and is therefore not present in the data) of any piece of research. That is, we cannot directly observe or measure causality itself. When you direct your hand to the computer's mouse on the desk and move it, an observer may know that it was your effort that caused the mouse to move. But what the observer sees (i.e., what is in the province of one's actual experience) is a sequence of two events: your touching the mouse and its subsequent movement.

David Hume, the eminent British philosopher, made this case eloquently. Hume argued that all we see or can observe is co-occurrence, what we now call *correlation* or *covariation*. We see you touch the mouse (*A*) and then see it move (*B*). The former we call the cause; the latter we call the effect. Hume proposed that experiencing such sequences repeatedly throughout our lives provides us with the *sufficiency* condition for causality: Present *A* and *B* occurs (i.e., the presence of *A* is sufficient for *B* to occur). This is one of the two pieces of information we use in our attribution of causality. In addition to sufficiency, Hume suggested that we also need a condition known as *necessity*. We say that *A* is necessary for *B* if its absence is also associated with the absence of *B*. The mouse had better not move if you do not touch it.

Over a considerable history of experiencing *A* followed by *B* together with not-*A* followed by not-*B*, we build up a repertoire of the necessary and sufficient conditions associated with correlated events. Hume said that we represent this history when we assert that *A* is the cause of *B*. From Hume's analysis, we may conclude that we do not directly experience causality per se—all we have is a long series of correlations, which we have summarized within a causal linguistic structure.

17A.3.2 Causality and Research Methods

Hume's analysis in many ways captures the logic of the scientific method. Take the conceptually simplest experiment consisting of an experimental group and a control group. A treatment is presented to those in the experimental group and not presented to those in the control group, with all other conditions comparable. Any difference between the two groups can therefore be attributed with a specified degree of certainty to the treatment effect; that is, we draw the inference that the treatment has likely caused the two groups to be different.

This is a living example of Hume's analysis. The experimental group represents the sufficiency condition—present the treatment (*A*) and obtain a certain effect (*B*). The control condition represents the necessity condition—withhold the treatment (not-*A*) and do not observe the effect (not-*B*). By establishing the necessary and sufficient conditions, we are in a relatively strong position to draw the inference that the treatment causes such and such effect.

A correlation design does not permit us to observe behavior under the necessary and sufficient conditions. We are not able to systematically present and withhold a particular treatment. Cause and effect, even if they are present in the variables captured in the analysis, are inextricably woven together in such a design. At best, all we can see are some *A*s followed by *B*s and some not-*A*s followed by not-*B*s.

What we actually see in correlation data is covariation to a certain quantifiable extent. *A* and *B*, together with many other variables, can be quantitatively related to each other in terms of correlation. We can assess the degree to which each pair of variables covaries. Although we are a long way from drawing a causal inference based on an experimental manipulation, covariation presents us with a rich data source. Path analysis takes advantage of this richness.

The professional discussion concerning correlation and causality is far from over. Consider the following argument presented by Meehl and Waller (2002):

One hears the objection "Correlation does not prove causality." If *prove* means *deduce*, of course it cannot in any empirical domain—courts of law, business, common life, or sciences. However, causal inference can be strongly corroborated—*proved*, in the usual sense of the term—by correlation. (p. 284)

17A.3.3 "Causal" Analysis of Correlation Data

We are now ready to answer the question of how one can evaluate a hypothesized causal model based on correlation data. The short answer is, "Data are data," and we can do any analysis that is consistent with the underlying assumptions, provided that we can make sense of the outcome. Setting up the model in the form of a path diagram is an articulation of the hypotheses that are to be tested. The relationships between the variables are contained in the data set. All that an analysis of a structural model does is map one to the other. Perhaps the time has now come for us to talk of structural rather than causal models, given all of the excess meaning the term *causal model* carries.

17A.4 The Concept of a Path Model

Path analysis starts with researchers constructing a path diagram. Variables are connected to other variables by arrows representing hypothesized causal linkages. Multiple regression or model-fitting analyses are then computed to determine the path coefficients. These path coefficients are no more than the standardized regression coefficients (beta weights) gleaned from the appropriate analysis; we are not ordinarily focused on the raw score (unstandardized) coefficients in path analysis. We then examine the magnitudes of these coefficients to decide if the hypothesized structural model has any statistical viability (usually at .3 or greater).

We have illustrated a relatively simple structural model as the path analysis shown in Figure 17a.1. This is a somewhat different way of drawing a simple mediation model (see Section 8A.7) as an illustration of a very simple path structure. We know that this model is amenable to being evaluated by a path analysis because the variables are all measured variables (rectangles are traditionally used to denote measured or observed variables). This particular model shows the hypothesized interrelationship between the observed variables *A*, *B*, and *C*. It proposes relatively weak causal relationships (predictive paths) from *A* to *C* and a relatively strong connection between *A* and *B* and *B* and *C*. In conceptual and structural terms, this path model proposes that *A* has an effect on *C* primarily because it "causes" or acts through *B* rather than having a strong effect on *C* directly. We can say that A is hypothesized to exert a strong indirect effect on *C* through the mediation role of *B*.

17A.5 The Roles Played by Variables in a Path Structure

The variables encompassed in a path model are all measured variables. They are called by other names as well, such as *observed variables* and *manifest variables*. These measured variables can be classified in a couple of different ways. Variables can be either *endogenous* or *exogenous*, and they can also be thought of as playing the roles of *dependent variables* and

Figure 17a.1 A Simple Path Model

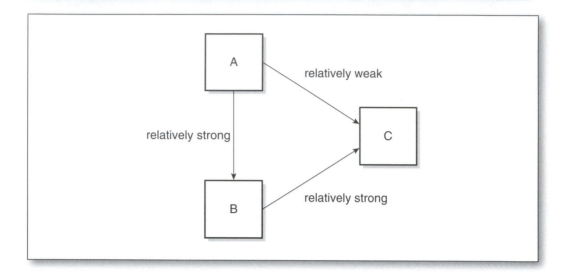

independent variables. These classification schemas often overlap with each other. Paying attention to whether or not a variable is associated with an arrow pointing to it or away from it is the key to properly identifying its roles.

17A.5.1 Endogenous and Exogenous Variables

Some variables are hypothesized in the model as being explained (having their variance accounted for) by other variables. The variables being explained are the *endogenous* variables. You can recognize such variables because they have arrows pointing toward them. In the model shown in Figure 17a.1, *B* and *C* are pointed to by arrows and are therefore classified as endogenous variables.

Some variables are not presumed to be explained by other variables in the model. Rather, they are simply taken as given in the model, presumably explained by some other factors beyond the scope of the model. These unexplained variables are the *exogenous* variables. They can be recognized because there is no arrow pointing toward them. Variable *A* in Figure 17a.1 is an exogenous variable.

17A.5.2 Dependent and Independent Variables

We talked in previous chapters about the possibility of treating a variable as either a dependent variable or an independent variable in particular statistical analyses. This possibility can be even more forcefully made here. We will use multiple regression analysis as our example statistical technique for performing a path analysis to carry this discussion. Model fitting does something similar but is a bit more complicated. If we use multiple regression to perform a path analysis, we would run enough regression analyses (one multiple regression analysis for each endogenous variable) to obtain all the path coefficients in the model. In any one of the multiple regression analyses, the criterion variable is the dependent (endogenous) variable, and the predictors are the independent variables that are hypothesized to cause it. The independent variables in the analysis are those whose arrows point to the dependent variable.

Using conceptual language, independent variables predict or cause dependent variables. This sort of a relationship is reflected in the direction of arrows in the model. A variable will be treated as a dependent variable when it has one or more arrows pointing toward it. Variables will be treated as independent variables when those variables are "doing the pointing."

In Figure 17a.1, variable *B* has an arrow pointing to it from *A*. Thus, in one regression analysis, *A* will be the predictor (independent variable) and *B* will be the criterion (dependent variable). Variable *C* also has arrows pointing to it and will therefore serve as the dependent variable in another analysis. Those arrows emerge from both *A* and *B*, and so we know that these two variables will function as the independent variables in that analysis. Because we have covered all the endogenous variables, we have covered all the regression analyses that need to be performed.

17A.5.3 Relating the Two Classification Schemas

Exogenous variables—those taken as a given in the model—do not have any arrows pointing toward them. Therefore, they always serve as independent variables and cannot serve as dependent variables. Endogenous variables—those explained by the model—will always have arrows pointing toward them. Therefore, they will always function as dependent variables in a subset of the regression analyses. It is also true, as we have seen in the example model, that some of these endogenous variables can also be the source of arrows; it is thus possible that some of these endogenous variables may be used as independent variables in other regression analyses.

17A.6 The Assumptions of Path Analysis

Pedhazur (1997) provides five assumptions underlying the application of path analysis when multiple regression is used to perform the analysis; these are in addition to all of those underlying a stand-alone multiple regression analysis. Kline (2011) discusses the assumptions for path analysis using model-fitting software such as IBM SPSS Amos. These assumptions are summarized here (with a minor variation or two):

- Relations between variables in the model are linear and causal. The relations are not curvilinear, and interaction relations are excluded. Linearity can and should be examined before the analysis is run, as described in Chapters 3A and 3B. This assumption applies to both multiple regression and model-fitting approaches.

- The errors associated with the endogenous variables are not correlated with the variables that are predicting that variable. This assumption applies to both approaches.

- There is only a one-way causal flow in the model. Such a model is called a *recursive* model. This assumption applies only to multiple regression. A double causal flow (where we see two separate straight arrows between variables *A* and *B*, one pointing from *A* to *B* and the other pointing from *B* to *A*) is only permitted in model-fitting programs.

- The variables are measured on at least an interval or near-interval (e.g., summative response) scale. This assumption applies to both approaches.

- The variables are measured without error; that is, the reliability of the measured variables is perfect. This assumption is unrealistic in behavioral science, but the analytic procedures presume that this is the case. This assumption applies to both approaches.

In addition, there is the general assumption that we have described in our multiple regression chapter that the set of variables selected for the analysis makes up the universe of all relevant variables. This is essentially the issue of specifying the model. Pedhazur (1997) states it well: "Examples of specification errors are: omitting relevant variables from the regression equation, including irrelevant variables in the regression equation, and postulating a linear model when a nonlinear model is more appropriate" (p. 288).

This admonition also applies to path analysis. If we are going to hypothesize a structural model and then evaluate how well it fits the data, it could be an exercise in futility if we had not included an important predictor in it, and it could be more work for no purpose if we included variables that were irrelevant to the predictions we were making.

17A.7 Missing Values in Path Analysis

In performing an analysis of a particular path model, it is important that the different analyses (in multiple regression) are performed on exactly the same group of cases in the data file (in model fitting, the analysis is done at one time on all the cases, so only one analysis is needed). To the extent that the sets of participants differ across regression analyses, it becomes increasingly difficult to argue that the path coefficients written into the path diagram can be compared with each other because some of them may have been based on different sets of cases. Thus, some procedure to deal with missing values is usually done just prior to running the set of multiple regression analyses. Model-fitting programs differ to a certain extent in how they arrive at this same point, but all require that all the cases have valid values on the variables used in the analysis.

In multiple regression analysis, removing those cases with missing values on any of the variables in the analysis can resolve this issue, but removing too many cases can potentially bias the sample and reduce the power and usefulness of the analysis. Another option is to use item imputation procedures as described in Chapters 3A and 3B to deal with this issue. In IBM SPSS Amos, the issue of missing data is handled by an FIML procedure (Anderson, 1957; Byrne, 2010).

17A.8 Analyzing the Path Structure

There are two ways to analyze path models: (a) multiple regression analysis and (b) estimation with a model-fitting program (Kline, 2011). The multiple regression option employs the ordinary least squares method, whereas model-fitting programs typically use maximum likelihood to calculate the path coefficients simultaneously. These two options generally produce similar but not necessarily identical results.

17A.9 The Multiple Regression Approach to Path Analysis

The multiple regression strategy to computing a path analysis employs the ordinary least squares method to calculate the path coefficients. In this approach, the path coefficients are the beta weights associated with the predictor variables in the regression equation. It is common for several multiple regression analyses to be used on different subsets of the variables before all the path coefficients are obtained.

Multiple regression was discussed in detail in Chapters 7A and 8A, but even there we held back a bit of the complexity involved. It is now time to tap into some of that complexity. Part of the language used in multiple regression refers to the "model," which we had identified as the multiple regression equation. Although that is still true, there is more to the model than just that. You can think of what is examined in multiple regression as a single-stage model (Pedhazur & Schmelkin, 1991) or as a single-stage structural model.

Single-stage structural models contain a single endogenous variable that is the dependent variable in the regression analysis. Such models also may contain any number of exogenous or predictor variables presumed to be directly related to the dependent variable. We have drawn a single-stage model using three predictors and one criterion variable in Figure 17a.2. This shows a model with three predictors (variables *J*, *K*, and *L*) and one criterion variable (variable *M*). We have included in the model the correlations

Figure 17a.2 A Single-Stage Structural Model

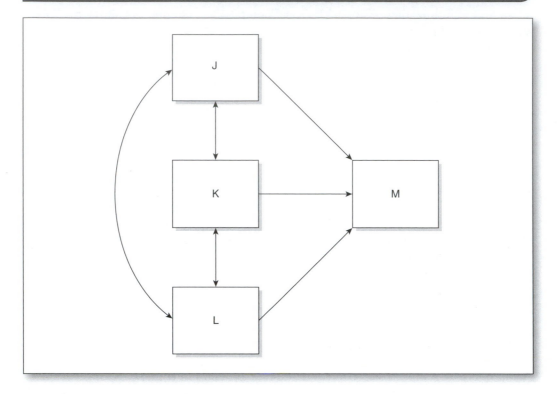

between all the pairs of predictors as represented by the bidirectional paths (the double-arrow lines).

Although the model depicted in Figure 17a.2 is too simple for most researchers to take seriously as a structural model, its underlying structure is technically subsumed under structural modeling. Because there is only one endogenous variable (a variable that can serve as a dependent variable), only one multiple regression analysis needs to be performed. The beta weights from that analysis will be placed on the paths and will be called *path coefficients*.

A single-stage model can be differentiated from a multistage model (Pedhazur & Schmelkin, 1991). The *multi* in "multistage model" indicates that more than one endogenous variable has been identified. That is, more than one variable has arrows pointing to it. Multistage structural models are what most researchers have in mind when they speak about path analysis (or structural models in general). In multistage models, we must perform more than one regression analysis. In fact, we perform as many multiple regression analyses as there are endogenous variables.

The structural model shown earlier in Figure 17a.1 is an example of a multistage model, although we did not label it as such at the time. Variables *B* and *C* are both at the receiving end of the arrows and are thus endogenous variables; they are presumed to be predicted from or caused by other variables in the model. There are thus two regression analyses needed here, one for each of these two variables to which the arrows point.

We perform one regression analysis for each endogenous variable in the structural model. Each endogenous variable becomes the dependent or criterion variable in that particular analysis. Any and all variables that are presumably causing it (i.e., any variables "pointing" to that endogenous variable) take the role of independent or predictor variables in that analysis. Remember, however, that a variable serving as a criterion (dependent) variable in one analysis could very well be one of the predictor variables in another analysis. The general rule governing the nature and number of regression analyses needed to address a path model is as follows: *Each endogenous variable involves a separate regression analysis for which it will be the dependent variable. For each analysis, all the variables pointing to that endogenous variable will serve as independent variables.*

The model in Figure 17a.1 proposes that there is a relatively strong link between *A* and *B* (that *A* is a relatively strong predictor or cause of *B*). This represents one regression analysis where the values of B are predicted from a knowledge of the corresponding values of *A*; that is, *B* will be the dependent variable and *A* will be the independent variable. The model also has two arrows pointing toward *C*, one from *A* and another from *B*. This represents the other regression analysis where *C* is predicted from both *A* and *B*; that is, *C* is the dependent variable and *A* and *B* are the independent variables.

In performing each of the regression analyses, it is mandatory that we use the standard (simultaneous) method where all the predictor variables for that particular regression analysis are placed into the equation at the same time. As you recall, the beta weights (which will be the path coefficients) are determined when statistically controlling for the influence of all the other predictors. Here, low values of some beta weights (e.g., <.2) are potentially as informative as high values (e.g., >.3) of others if we are evaluating hypotheses of weaker as well as stronger structural influences in the model.

17A.10 Indirect and Total Effects

Indirect effects involve mediator variable(s) and was a topic discussed in Section 8A.7. In our example from Figure 17a.1, *A* is hypothesized to have a direct effect on *C* and an indirect effect on *C* mediated by B. This indirect effect is calculated by multiplying the path coefficient between *A* and *B* by the path coefficient between *B* and *C*. The total effect is calculated by adding the direct effect and the indirect effect. We can do this by hand calculation in multiple regression; model-fitting programs often perform this calculation for us.

17A.11 Comparing Multiple Regression and Model-Fitting Approaches

As we have previously noted, multiple regression employs the ordinary least squares method to calculate the path coefficients; model-fitting approaches typically use maximum likelihood to calculate the path coefficients. The ordinary least squares estimation in multiple regression is known as a *partial-information* technique, whereas the maximum likelihood estimation in the model-fitting software is known as a *full-information* technique (Kelloway, 1998). The differences between the partial- and the full-information techniques (discussed in more detail in Section 18A.2) revolve around the following two interrelated features of the multiple regression and model-fitting procedures:

- *Using some or all the information in any single analysis:* In model-fitting software, all paths are estimated simultaneously. Thus, all of the information concerning the interrelationships of the variables is brought to bear in the analysis. In multiple regression, each analysis uses a different (but potentially overlapping) set of variables. Thus, any one analysis makes use of only some of the information concerning the interrelationships of the variables.
- *The iteration feature:* The maximum likelihood procedure used in model-fitting software continually reestimates the parameters until it focuses in on the values. Ordinary least squares regression is a one-shot solution based on the least squares algorithm.

17A.11.1 Current Status

Partly as a result of using all the information simultaneously and partly as a result of engaging in an iterative estimation process, the model-fitting approach seems to us to be gaining acceptance in the behavioral and life sciences. Regression analysis can certainly be used to perform path analysis, but it is our impression that more researchers are gravitating to model-fitting programs such as IBM SPSS Amos. For those who do not have access to or do not have sufficient skill to use these latter types of programs, however, it should be remembered that the path analysis results produced by the two approaches are very often similar.

17A.12 A Path Analysis Example

In this fictional example, assume that researchers are investigating the causes or predictors of academic achievement in college. They are particularly interested in the influences of three independent variables—academic self-doubt, SES, and motivation—on the dependent variable of academic achievement. The path model is presented in Figure 17a.3, where it can be

| **Figure 17a.3** | An Example of a Multistage Path Model Predicting Academic Achievement |

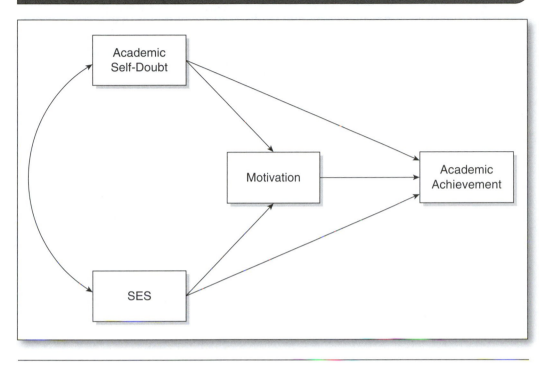

Note. SES = socioeconomic status.

seen that motivation is hypothesized to meditate the direct effects of academic Self-Doubt and SES on Academic Achievement. The correlation between the two exogenous variables (Academic Self-Doubt and SES) is represented by the double arrow connecting them. The model contains two endogenous variables (Motivation and Academic Achievement) and is considered to be a multistage structural model.

This model represents what is called a *saturated* model in the sense that every variable is hypothesized to be related to every other variable. This model not only allows researchers to examine the direct effects of Academic Self-Doubt, SES, and Motivation on Academic Achievement, but it allows us to examine some indirect effects as well. Not only are Academic Self-Doubt and SES hypothesized to directly affect Academic Achievement, they are also hypothesized to exert an effect through the Motivation variable. For example, students with less academic self-doubt may be more motivated to succeed, which in turn may yield greater academic achievement. Motivation takes on a "mediator" role in this model, and we would say that some of the causal influence of Academic Self-Doubt and SES on Academic

Achievement is mediated through Motivation (see Section 8A.7). Thus, Academic Self-Doubt and SES are said to influence Academic Achievement in two ways: (a) by exerting a direct effect on Academic Achievement and (b) by exerting an indirect effect on Academic Achievement by affecting Motivation.

17A.13 The Multiple Regression Strategy to Perform a Path Analysis

The model we are analyzing contains two exogenous variables and two endogenous variables. For every endogenous variable, a multiple regression analysis needs to be calculated. Therefore, in this example, two multiple regressions need to be conducted.

In the first regression analysis, we will focus on the Academic Achievement variable. Because the arrows are pointing to it—because causality is acting on it from the other variables—it is the dependent variable in the analysis. There are three variables identified as causes of Academic Achievement in the model: Academic Self-Doubt, SES, and Motivation. The first two are direct effects, and Motivation represents a mediated effect.

In the second regression analysis, we will focus on Motivation. It, too, is an endogenous variable and will be the dependent variable in this second analysis. Here, there are only two variables hypothesized as causally related to it—Academic Self-Doubt and SES—and these will serve as the independent or predictor variables in the regression analysis.

The beta weights (i.e., the standardized regression weights) are assigned to the appropriate paths from each analysis. Thus, we learn the values for the path coefficients in a rather piecemeal fashion. The path coefficients leading to Academic Achievement are drawn from one regression analysis, and the path coefficients leading to Motivation are drawn from the other analysis. Readers may now see why it so important to deal with missing values as we indicated earlier. Because beta weights from two separate analyses are being placed in the same model, it is necessary that the very same cases are captured in both.

We show the beta weights from these analyses as well as the correlation between the two exogenous variables in Figure 17a.4. Self-Doubt and SES are both statistically significant predictors of Motivation. Because they exceed the .3 criterion, we would also treat them as having achieved practical significance as well. We see that the beta weight leading from Academic Self-Doubt is negative, telling us that it is inversely related to Motivation (e.g., higher levels of Academic Self-Doubt are associated with lower motivational levels). The positive beta weight for SES informs us that higher status on the socioeconomic continuum predicts more motivation. Academic Self-Doubt in combination with SES predicted 36% of the variance of Motivation (this is the R^2 value) as shown in the rounded rectangle to the upper-right side of Motivation.

Only one of the three predictors of Academic Achievement yielded a significant beta weight. Motivation, with a beta weight of .49, accounted for 34% of the variance of

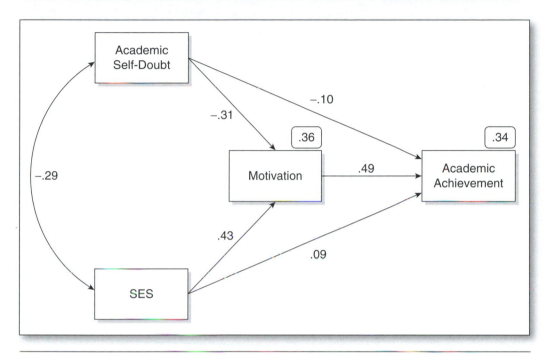

Figure 17a.4 The Path Model Displaying the Beta Coefficients, the Correlation Between the Two Exogenous Variables, and the Two R^2 Values (Shown in Rounded Rectangles to the Upper Right Side of the Endogenous Variables)

Note. SES = socioeconomic status.

Academic Achievement, controlling for the effects of Academic Self-Doubt and SES. Neither Academic Self-Doubt nor SES produced any significant direct effect on Academic Achievement. Their effect, as we can now see, was indirect; their tie to Academic Achievement was accomplished through the mediator variable of Motivation.

17A.14 Examining Mediation Effects

Having determined that Academic Self-Doubt and SES exerted indirect but not direct effects on Academic Achievement, it appears that Motivation acted as a mediator variable in the model. To act in such a manner, we might presume that, in isolation, Academic Self-Doubt and SES are each individually related to Academic Achievement. A quick analysis reveals that the correlation of Academic Self-Doubt and Academic Achievement is −.332, and the correlation of SES and Academic Achievement is .369. These Pearson correlations are also the beta coefficients in the respective simple linear regression analyses. With a sample size of 244, both of these correlations (path coefficients) are statistically significant at the .05 level. Given that neither of these paths is statistically significant in the mediated model, it would appear that complete mediation has occurred.

The indirect (mediated) effects can be evaluated for statistical significance by the Aroian test, and the difference between the unmediated and mediated paths from the exogenous variables to Academic Achievement can be evaluated by the Freedman–Schatzkin test. We performed the four analyses, two Aroian tests and two Freedman–Schatzkin tests, as described in Section 8A.7.6. In all analyses, the mediator variable was Motivation and the outcome variable was Academic Achievement; for each pair of analyses, separate tests were performed using Academic Self-Doubt and SES as the independent variables.

17A.14.1 The Aroian Tests

We performed the Aroian test by using the Preacher and Lombardelli calculator on Preacher and Leonardelli's website. The following results were obtained:

- For Academic Self-Doubt, the *z* value was -4.51662129, well in excess of our critical *z* value of 1.96 under an alpha level of .05.
- For SES, the *z* value was 5.48703317, again well in excess of our critical *z* value of 1.96 under an alpha level of .05.

We therefore conclude that Motivation significantly meditated the relationship between Academic Self-Doubt and Academic Achievement.

17A.14.2 The Freedman–Schatzkin Tests

We performed the Freedman–Schatzkin tests on a hand calculator and obtained the following results:

- For Academic Self-Doubt, the *t* value was 6.1488946 and, with 242 degrees of freedom, was well in excess of our critical *t* value of 1.98 under an alpha level of .05.
- For SES, the *t* value was 8.5400322 and, with 242 degrees of freedom, was well in excess of our critical *t* value of 1.98 under an alpha level of .05.

We therefore conclude that the direct paths from Academic Self-Doubt to Academic Achievement and from SES to Academic Achievement were each significantly reduced in the presence of Motivation as a mediating variable to the point where, in the mediated model, the mediation effect was complete.

17A.15 Respecifying the Model

We have seen that the originally proposed model, although not doing all that badly, was a bit off the mark. Two of the direct effects in the original did not statistically materialize. In model-fitting approaches, we could respecify the model and use various fit indexes to base a judgment of whether or not our respecified model was a better fit to the data. But this is multiple regression, and those tools are not part of the software. The best we can do within this approach is to respecify the model and perform the necessary multiple regression analyses again. Then we can at least place the beta weights from these new analyses on the paths.

Respecification of the model, whether executed in the context of multiple regression or model-fitting procedures, is something that is (obviously) done in hindsight. It should therefore surprise no one that the respecified model looks "slicker" than the original or, in the results from model-fitting software, fits the data at least as well as, but probably better than, the original model. Thus, the end result of a respecification process is a model that is at least as good but with fewer paths cluttering up the picture (the model is less saturated). Such an outcome is a foregone conclusion and cannot be taken as independent validation that the respecified model is a better description of the interrelationships in the data. The bottom line is this: Respecifying the model is strictly exploratory. But the exploratory-based revised model may be used as a basis for conceptualizing the phenomenon under study in future research. Used in this bottom-line fashion, there is a certain utility in the respecification process.

The respecified model together with results is shown in Figure 17a.5. The only difference here is that we have removed the two nonsignificant paths. Again, two multiple regressions were calculated. In the first model, the independent variable was Motivation, and the dependent variable was Academic Achievement. In the second model, the independent variables were Academic Self-Doubt and SES, and the dependent variable was Motivation.

The results of this model indicate that all the path coefficients achieved both practical and statistical significance (this comes as no surprise). This model appears to explain the phenomenon more efficiently, but that is true by definition when nonsignificant paths are removed. Given that truth, the respecified model does make clear that Academic Self-Doubt and SES are important variables in explaining Academic Achievement through the indirect effects they have on Motivation.

Figure 17a.5 The Respecified Path Model Displaying the New Beta Coefficients, the Correlation Between the Two Exogenous Variables, and the Two New R^2 Values (Shown in Rounded Rectangles to the Upper Right Side of the Endogenous Variables)

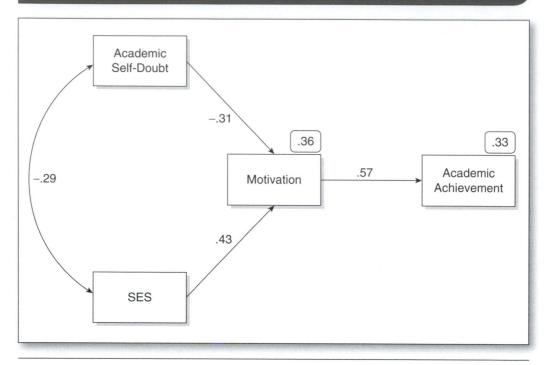

Note. SES = socioeconomic status.

17A.16 Recommended Readings

Alvarez, A. N., & Juang, L. P. (2010). Filipino Americans and racism: A multiple mediation model of coping. *Journal of Counseling Psychology, 57,* 167–178.

Pearl, J. (2011). The science and ethics of causal modeling. In A. T. Panter & S. K. Sterba (Eds.), *Handbook of ethics in quantitative methodology* (pp. 338–414). New York, NY: Routledge.

Path Analysis: Multiple Regression Using IBM SPSS

17B.1 The Data Set and Model Used in Our Example

This chapter describes how to perform a path analysis using multiple regression. The path model that represents our fictional study is shown in Figure 17b.1. The outcome variable is the amount of exercise engaged in by college students during a semester (named **exercise** in the data file). The amount of exercise in which they engage is hypothesized to be directly predictable from the degree to which students maintain a healthy diet (named **diet** in the data file), the tendency to portray themselves in a socially desirable way (named **desire** in the data file), and their levels of self-esteem (named **selfesteem** in the data file) and body-esteem (named **bodyesteem** in the data file). Social desirability and acceptance of others (named **acceptance** in the data file), self-esteem, and body-esteem are also hypothesized to exert an indirect effect on **exercise** through **diet**. In addition, self-esteem and body-esteem were hypothesized to affect social desirability and acceptance of others. Finally, it was hypothesized that acceptance of others influenced the degree of social desirability.

The data file for this example is named **Exercise**. It contains 415 cases. Because there are no missing data, all of the regression analyses will be performed on data from the same cases, and the path coefficients from separate analyses may be appropriately placed in the model as a whole.

17B.2 Specifying the Variables in Each Analysis

The multiple regression approach to path analysis requires us to perform as many analyses as there are endogenous variables in the model. In our example shown in Figure 17b.1, there

Figure 17b.1 The Path Model Predicting the Amount of Exercise in Which Students Engaged During a Semester

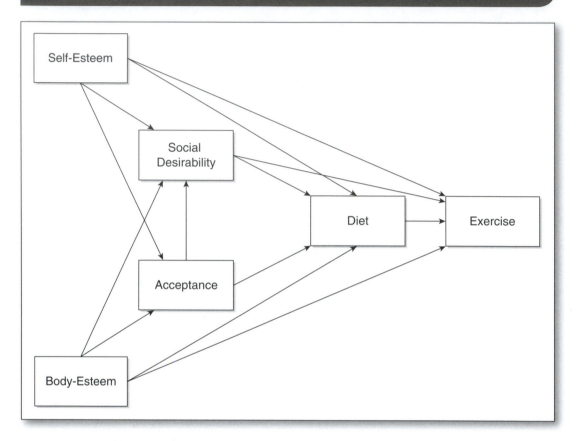

are four such variables, and so we must perform (in any order) the following four regression analyses:

- Exercise will be predicted from diet, social desirability, self-esteem, and body-esteem.
- Diet will be predicted from self-esteem, social desirability, acceptance, and body-esteem.
- Social desirability will be predicted from self-esteem, body-esteem, and acceptance.
- Acceptance will be predicted from self-esteem and body-esteem.

We have described the steps to perform and how to interpret the output of ordinary least squares regression in Section 7B.1; readers are advised to consult that material to refresh their memories as we will assume here that the basics of the procedure are already familiar.

Figure 17b.2 The Main Regression Window

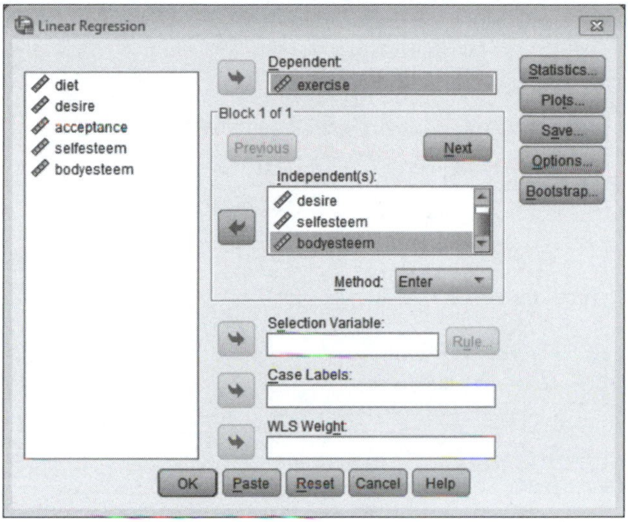

17B.3 Predicting Exercise

17B.3.1 Predicting Exercise: Analysis Setup

Open the Exercise data file and select **Analyze** ➔ **Regression** ➔ **Linear**. As shown in Figure 17b.2, we specify **exercise** as the **Dependent** variable and **diet**, **desire**, **selfesteem**, and **bodyesteem** as the **Independent** variables. Keep the **Method** as **Enter**.

In the **Statistics** window, check **Estimates** in the **Regression Coefficients** panel. Also check **Model fit**, **R squared change**, **Descriptives**, and **Part and partial correlations**. This is shown in Figure 17b.3. Click **Continue** to return to the main dialog screen and click **OK** to produce the analysis.

17B.3.2 Predicting Exercise: Output

The output of interest is shown in Figure 17b.4. As can be seen in the top table of **Model Summary**, 35% of the variance of **exercise** was explained by the prediction model. Tested with 4 and 410 degrees of freedom, the F ratio of 55.082 evaluating the value of the R^2 was statistically significant.

The standardized regression coefficients are presented in the lower table of Figure 17b.4. Both **diet** and **bodyesteem** were significant predictors of **exercise** with standardized regression

Figure 17b.3 The Statistics Window

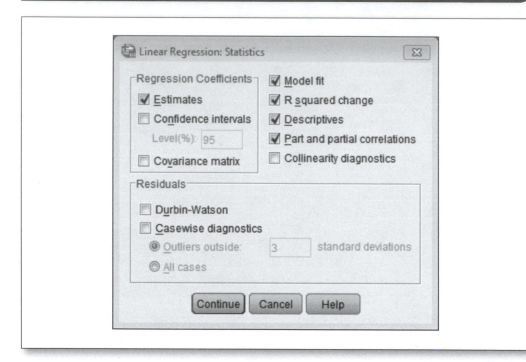

Figure 17b.4 The R^2, Test of Significance of the Model, and the Coefficients Predicting Exercise

Model Summary

Model	R	R Square	Adjusted R Square	Std. Error of the Estimate	Change Statistics				
					R Square Change	F Change	df1	df2	Sig. F Change
1	.591[a]	.350	.343	.70662	.350	55.082	4	410	.000

a. Predictors: (Constant), bodyesteem, diet, desire, selfesteem

Coefficients[a]

Model		Unstandardized Coefficients		Standardized Coefficients	t	Sig.	Correlations		
		B	Std. Error	Beta			Zero-order	Partial	Part
1	(Constant)	.034	.329		.105	.917			
	diet	.493	.047	.429	10.494	.000	.464	.460	.418
	desire	-.001	.003	-.018	-.422	.673	.177	-.021	-.017
	selfesteem	.008	.006	.058	1.194	.233	.262	.059	.048
	bodyesteem	.015	.002	.338	7.172	.000	.409	.334	.286

a. Dependent Variable: exercise

Figure 17b.5   The Path Model With Exercise and Diet Predicted

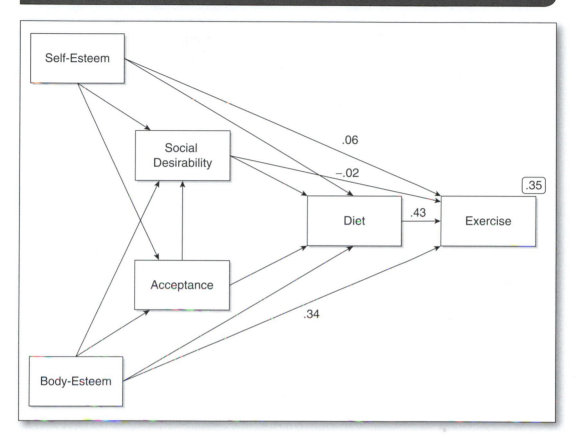

weights of .429 and .338, respectively (rounded to .43 and .34, respectively, in Figure 17b.5). The coefficients of −.018 for **desire** and .058 for **selfesteem** (rounded to −.02 and .06, respectively, in Figure 17b.5) were not statistically significant. We show the path model at this stage of the analysis in Figure 17b.5 with the values of the path coefficients and the R^2 for **exercise** included.

17B.4 Predicting Diet

17B.4.1 Predicting Diet: Analysis Setup

In this second analysis, specify **diet** as the **Dependent** variable and **selfesteem, bodyesteem, desire,** and **acceptance** as the **Independent** variables. Use the setup for the **Statistics** window as described in Section 17B.3.1.

Figure 17b.6 The R^2, Test of Significance of the Model, and the Coefficients Predicting Diet

Model Summary

Model	R	R Square	Adjusted R Square	Std. Error of the Estimate	Change Statistics R Square Change	F Change	df1	df2	Sig. F Change
1	.295ᵃ	.087	.078	.72799	.087	9.789	4	410	.000

a. Predictors: (Constant), acceptance, bodyesteem, desire, selfesteem

Coefficientsᵃ

Model		Unstandardized Coefficients B	Std. Error	Standardized Coefficients Beta	t	Sig.	Correlations Zero-order	Partial	Part
1	(Constant)	.912	.387		2.359	.019			
	selfesteem	-.011	.007	-.095	-1.600	.110	.073	-.079	-.075
	bodyesteem	.003	.002	.071	1.266	.206	.104	.062	.060
	desire	.010	.003	.165	3.205	.001	.215	.156	.151
	acceptance	.023	.005	.211	4.094	.000	.243	.198	.193

a. Dependent Variable: diet

17B.4.2 Predicting Diet: Output

The output of interest is shown in Figure 17b.6. As can be seen in the top table of **Model Summary**, approximately 9% of the variance of **diet** was explained by the prediction model. Tested with 4 and 410 degrees of freedom, the F ratio of 9.789 evaluating the value of the R^2 was statistically significant.

The standardized regression coefficients are presented in the lower table of Figure 17b.6. Both **desire** and **acceptance** were significant predictors of **diet** with standardized regression weights of .165 and .211, respectively. The coefficients of −.095 and .071 for **selfesteem** and **bodyesteem**, respectively, were not statistically significant. We show the path model at this stage of the analysis in Figure 17b.7 with the values of the path coefficients and the R^2 for **diet** added to our model.

17B.5 Predicting Social Desirability

17B.5.1 Predicting Social Desirability: Analysis Setup

In this third analysis, specify **desire** as the **Dependent** variable and **selfesteem**, **bodyesteem**, and **acceptance** as the **Independent** variables. Use the same setup for the **Statistics** window as described in Section 17B.3.1.

17B.5.2 Predicting Social Desirability: Output

The output of interest is shown in Figure 17b.8. As can be seen in the top table of **Model Summary**, approximately 16% of the variance of **desire** was explained by the prediction

Figure 17b.7 The Path Model With Exercise and Diet Predicted

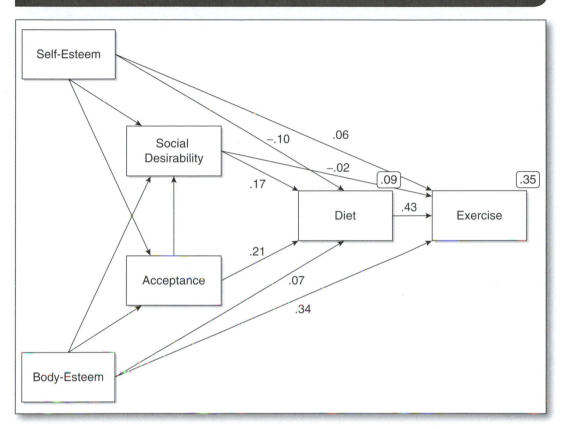

model. Tested with 3 and 411 degrees of freedom, the *F* ratio of 26.205 evaluating the value of the R^2 was statistically significant.

The standardized regression coefficients are presented in the lower table of Figure 17b.8. Both **selfesteem** and **acceptance** were significant predictors of **desire** with standardized regression weights of .221 and .211, respectively. The coefficient of .086 for **selfesteem** and **bodyesteem** was not statistically significant. We show the path model at this stage of the analysis in Figure 17b.9 with the values of the path coefficients and the R^2 for **desire** added to our model.

17B.6 Predicting Acceptance

17B.6.1 Predicting Acceptance: Analysis Setup

In this fourth analysis, specify **acceptance** as the **Dependent** variable and **selfesteem** and **bodyesteem** as the **Independent** variables. Use the same setup for the **Statistics** window as described in Section 17B.3.1.

Figure 17b.8 The R^2, Test of Significance of the Model, and the Coefficients Predicting Desire

Model Summary

Model	R	R Square	Adjusted R Square	Std. Error of the Estimate	Change Statistics				
					R Square Change	F Change	df1	df2	Sig. F Change
1	.401[a]	.161	.154	11.21665	.161	26.205	3	411	.000

a. Predictors: (Constant), acceptance, bodyesteem, selfesteem

Coefficients[a]

Model		Unstandardized Coefficients		Standardized Coefficients	t	Sig.	Correlations		
		B	Std. Error	Beta			Zero–order	Partial	Part
1	(Constant)	57.151	5.250		10.885	.000			
	selfesteem	.401	.101	.221	3.962	.000	.340	.192	.179
	bodyesteem	.052	.033	.086	1.608	.109	.245	.079	.073
	acceptance	.361	.083	.211	4.362	.000	.306	.210	.197

a. Dependent Variable: desire

Figure 17b.9 The Path Model With Exercise, Diet, and Social Desirability Predicted

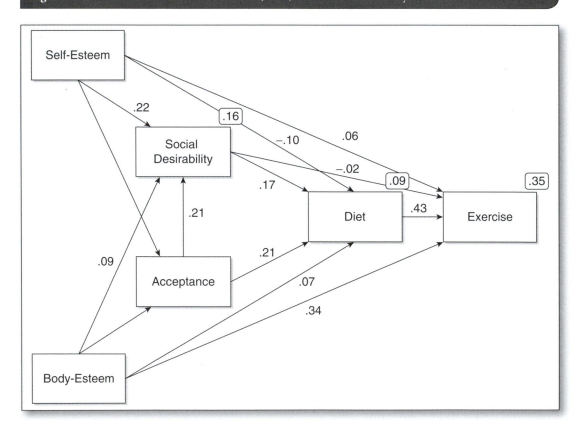

Figure 17b.10   The R^2, Test of Significance of the Model, and the Coefficients Predicting Acceptance

Model Summary

Model	R	R Square	Adjusted R Square	Std. Error of the Estimate	Change Statistics				
					R Square Change	F Change	df1	df2	Sig. F Change
1	.353ᵃ	.125	.120	6.67563	.125	29.357	2	412	.000

a. Predictors: (Constant), bodyesteem, selfesteem

Coefficientsᵃ

Model		Unstandardized Coefficients		Standardized Coefficients	t	Sig.	Correlations		
		B	Std. Error	Beta			Zero–order	Partial	Part
1	(Constant)	46.176	2.142		21.557	.000			
	selfesteem	.359	.058	.339	6.237	.000	.352	.294	.287
	bodyesteem	.009	.019	.026	.482	.630	.205	.024	.022

a. Dependent Variable: acceptance

17B.6.2 Predicting Acceptance: Output

The output of interest is shown in Figure 17b.10. As can be seen in the top table of **Model Summary**, approximately 13% of the variance of **acceptance** was explained by the prediction model. Tested with 2 and 412 degrees of freedom, the F ratio of 29.357 evaluating the value of the R^2 was statistically significant. The standardized regression coefficients are presented in the lower table of Figure 17b.10. **Selfesteem** with a standardized regression weight of .334 was statistically significant; **acceptance** with a standardized regression weight of .026 was not significant.

We show the path model at this final stage of the analysis in Figure 17b.11 with the values of the path coefficients and the R^2 for **acceptance** added to our model. As mentioned in Section 17A.13.1, it is possible to more completely explore mediation effects, principally with respect to the outcome variable (Exercise in this example) once the model is in its completed form. Here, we note that neither of the two exogenous variables (Body-Esteem and Self-Esteem) exhibit a statistically significant path to the potential mediator variable of Diet; as a consequence of this, a mediation analysis of those variables would not make sense (e.g., Body-Esteem cannot produce an indirect on Exercise through Diet if it is not related to Diet) in this context.

17B.7 Mediation Effects in the Larger Model

17B.7.1 Overview

With the overall model in place, it is possible to explore on a post hoc basis portions of the model in order to explicate simple mediation relationships if there are appropriate

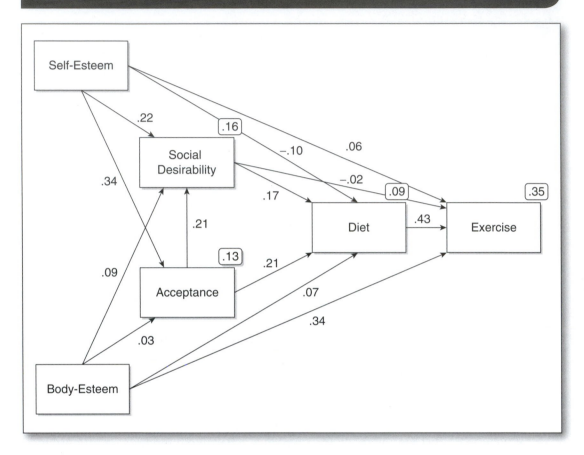

Figure 17b.11 The Path Model With Exercise, Diet, Social Desirability, and Acceptance Predicted

theoretical, research-based, or practical rationales for doing so. We will use the designations shown previously in Figure 8a.2 where X is the predictor variable, M is the mediator variable, and Y is the outcome variable. For such an analysis to make any sense, the following conditions (borrowed from Section 8A.7.2 and applied to this example) must be met:

- X must significantly predict Y in isolation. That is, it makes no sense to speak of a mediated effect of X on Y if X and Y are not correlated when considering only those two variables apart from the larger model.
- If X is going to "act through" M to influence Y, then X must significantly predict M in the larger model. If there is no significant prediction, X cannot "act through" a variable that supposedly mediates it.

- If X is going to "act through" M to influence Y, then M must significantly predict Y in the larger model. Again, the idea of "act through" implies that the effect of X is being "carried to" Y through M. If no effect is being "carried to" Y, the X cannot "act through" M to affect Y.

Such mediation analyses represent a post hoc, exploratory strategy for at least three related reasons. First, we must study the model and then select only an X, M, and Y subset of variables for which the above three conditions are true. Thus, the outcome of the entire path analysis determines which mediation relationships are meaningful to examine.

The second reason such analyses represent a post hoc strategy is that the values of the coefficients used to test the significance of mediation are driven by the particular configuration of the variables in the larger model. For example, if we had not hypothesized a direct path from Self-Acceptance to Diet, then it is quite likely that the values of the coefficients for the other predictors of Diet (Self-Esteem, Social Desirability, and Body-Esteem) would be different from what they were with the path from Self-Acceptance included. Thus, it is the obtained values of the coefficients based on the particular configuration we proposed that are placed into the mediation formulas.

The third reason such analyses represent a post hoc strategy is that the coefficients used to test the significance of mediation are *partial regression coefficients.* The term *partial* is used to remind us that their values are determined when the effects of all of the other predictors in the analysis are statistically controlled (these other predictors act as covariates). The importance of this statistical fact is that the values of the regression coefficients are very likely to be different if the set of predictor variables was different. Thus, the results of any multiple regression procedure are specific to the variables selected for the analysis—the results do not represent some absolute reality. When we select a predictor, mediator, and outcome variable from the larger model to explore, they must meet the above three conditions. But the variables we select for any one mediation analysis might not meet the above conditions or might be associated with different coefficient values in a different analysis with a somewhat different set of variables. Any mediation analysis exploring variables embedded in a larger model is thus specific to the results obtained from evaluating that model.

17B.7.2 Identifying the Variables and Their Roles

Despite its post hoc nature, it is our impression that testing for the significance of mediation effects in larger path models is relatively frequently performed in the research literature. We therefore illustrate the application of this technique here. For this analysis, we will assume that there are good reasons to explore the mediating effect of Diet on the relationship between Social Desirability and Exercise. Thus, **desire** will be the predictor (X)

Figure 17b.12 Simple Mediation Portion of the Model Shown in Figure 17b.11

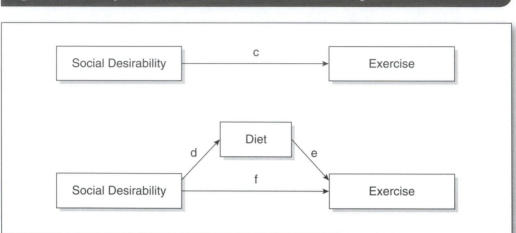

variable, **diet** will be the mediator (M) variable, and **exercise** will be the outcome (Y) variable. This extracted simple mediation relationship is drawn in Figure 17b.12.

17B.7.3 The Aroian Test

17B.7.3.1 Acquiring the Necessary Values for the Aroian Test

To perform the Aroian test (see Section 8A.7.6), here is the following information that we need (with the path letters keyed to those shown in Figure 17b.12) and the places where this information is to be found:

- The value of **d**, the raw score regression coefficient for Social Desirability predicting Diet in the mediated model. This value, obtained from Figure 17b.6 (note that the footnote to the **Coefficients** table specifies the dependent variable in the analysis), is 0.010.
- The standard error of **d**. This value, also obtained from Figure 17b.6, is 0.003.
- The value of **e**, the raw score regression coefficient for Diet predicting Exercise in the mediated model. This value, obtained from Figure 17b.4, is 0.493.
- The standard error of **e**. This value, also obtained from Figure 17b.4, is 0.047.

17B.7.3.2 Performing the Aroian Test

We placed our values in the calculator provided by Preacher and Leonardelli on their website and obtained a z value of 3.16 (rounded) with a probability level of approximately

.002. With an alpha level of .05, a *z* value of 1.96 is needed to achieve statistical significance, and we may therefore conclude, based on the Aroian test, that significant mediation occurred. Again on a post hoc basis, with the path between Social Desirability and Exercise not significant, we might characterize this mediation as being complete within the tested model.

17B.7.4 The Freedman–Schatzkin Test

17B.7.4.1 Acquiring the Necessary Values for the Freedman–Schatzkin Test

Some of the values we need are already contained in one of our output tables. The only analysis we have not performed but that supplies the rest of the information needed is the simple linear regression predicting **exercise** from **desire**. The results of this analysis are shown in Figure 17b.13.

To perform the Freedman–Schatzkin test (see Section 8A.7.6), here is the following information that we need (with the path letters keyed to those shown in Figure 17b.12) and the places where this information is to be found:

- The value of **c**, the raw score regression coefficient for Social Desirability predicting Exercise in isolation. We performed the analysis and this value, obtained from Figure 17b.13, is 0.013.
- The standard error of **c**. This value, also obtained from Figure 17b.13, is 0.003.
- The value of **f**, the raw score regression coefficient for Social Desirability predicting Exercise in the mediated model. This value, obtained from Figure 17b.4, is −0.001.

Figure 17b.13 The R^2, Test of Significance of the Model, and the Coefficients Predicting Exercise

Model Summary

Model	R	R Square	Adjusted R Square	Std. Error of the Estimate	R Square Change	F Change	df1	df2	Sig. F Change
					Change Statistics				
1	.177[a]	.031	.029	.85925	.031	13.289	1	413	.000

a. Predictors: (Constant), desire

Coefficients[a]

Model		Unstandardized Coefficients		Standardized Coefficients	t	Sig.	Correlations		
		B	Std. Error	Beta			Zero–order	Partial	Part
1	(Constant)	2.104	.351		5.997	.000			
	desire	.013	.003	.177	3.645	.000	.177	.177	.177

a. Dependent Variable: exercise

- The standard error of **f**. This value, also obtained from Figure 17b.4, is 0.003.
- The value of the Pearson correlation coefficient describing the relationship between the predictor variable of Social Desirability and the mediator variable of Diet. This value can be seen in Figure 17b.6 under the column for **Correlations** labeled as **Zero-order** (a zero-order correlation is a Pearson r with none or zero variables partialled out). The value we need is associated with the predictor variable of Social Desirability and is .215.

17B.7.4.2 Performing the Freedman–Schatzkin Test

The equation for computing the Freedman–Schatzkin test is displayed in Figure 8a.5. Substituting our values in the formula, the abbreviated computational steps using an inexpensive hand calculator are as follows:

$t = 0.013 - (-0.001)/\text{SQRT} ((0.003^2 + 0.003^2) - (2 * 0.003 * 0.003 * \text{SQRT} (1 - .215^2))$

$t = 0.014/\text{SQRT} ((0.000018) - (0.000018 * 0.976614))$

$t = 0.014/0.0007071$

$t = 19.799179$

The Student t value obtained from the Freedman–Schatzkin test is evaluated with $N - 2$ degrees of freedom. With a sample size of 415 (and thus degrees of freedom of 413), we can determine from Appendix A Table A1 displaying critical t values that we have achieved statistical significance against an alpha level of .05. Thus, within the context of the tested model, we may conclude that the direct effect of Social Desirability on Exercise was statistically negated with Diet acting as a mediator (we observed complete mediation within the context of the model).

17B.8 Reporting Path Analysis Results

This present path analysis focused on predictors of the amount of exercise in which students at University X engaged during the academic semester. The predictors, self-esteem, body-esteem, social desirability, acceptance of others, and the degree to which their diet was healthy, were configured into the hypothesized model shown in Figure 17b.1. A set of four ordinary least squares multiple regression analyses were performed to evaluate the model.

The amount of exercise was significantly predicted from attitudes toward diet, social desirability, self-esteem, and body-esteem, $F(4, 410) = 55.082$, $p < .001$, $R^2 = .350$, adjusted $R^2 = .343$; only diet and body-esteem were significant predictors in this portion of the model. The amount of diet was significantly predicted from self-esteem, body-esteem, social desirability, and acceptance, $F(4, 410) = 9.789$, $p < .001$, $R^2 = .087$, adjusted $R^2 = .078$; only social desirability and acceptance were significant predictors in this portion of the model. The amount of social desirability was significantly predicted from self-esteem, body-esteem, and acceptance, $F(3, 411) = 26.205$, $p < .001$, $R^2 = .161$, adjusted $R^2 = .154$; both self-esteem and body-esteem were significant predictors in this portion of the model. Finally, the amount of acceptance of others was significantly predicted from self-esteem and body-esteem, $F(2, 412) = 29.357$, $p < .001$, $R^2 = .125$, adjusted $R^2 = .120$; only self-esteem was a significant predictor in this portion of the model.

The path coefficients for the complete model are displayed in Figure 17b.11 and are summarized in Table 18b.1 under Direct Effects. As can be seen in Table 17b.1, the model was able to account for 35% of the variance of the amount of exercise done by the students. Almost all of this is due to the direct effects of diet and body-esteem. The model was also able to explain 16% of the variance of social desirability and 13% of the variance of acceptance of others; acceptance of others was primarily (directly) predicted by self-esteem, whereas social desirability was predicted by the direct effects of both self-esteem and acceptance of others.

One relationship that was described earlier in this paper in the process of developing the reasoning underlying the structure selected for this path model was the possible mediation of diet attitudes on the effect of social desirability on exercise behavior. In isolation, social desirability significantly predicted the amount that students exercised, $F(1, 413) = 13.29$, $p < .001$, $R^2 = .031$, adjusted $R^2 = .029$. In accord with Baron and Kenny (1986), the Aroian test (Aroian, 1944/1947), a variant of the Sobel test (Sobel, 1982, 1986), was used to evaluate the significance of the indirect path of social desirability through diet attitudes to the amount of exercise. The results of this test indicated that in the context of the larger model, a statistically significant amount of mediation was observed, $z = 3.16$, $p < .05$. In addition, the Freedman–Schatzkin test (Freedman & Schatzkin, 1992) was used to compare the magnitudes of the regression coefficients from social desirability with the amount of exercise in the unmediated and mediated models. The results of this test indicated that the unmediated coefficient was significantly greater than the mediated coefficient, $t(413) = 19.80$, $p < .05$. Given that the mediated coefficient from social desirability to exercise behavior was not significant in the mediated model, we may conclude that in the context of the larger model, complete mediation was observed.

Table 17b.1 Summary of Causal Effects of the Hypothesized Model

Outcome	Determinant	Causal Effects		
		Direct	Indirect	Total
Acceptance	Self-Esteem*	.339	---	.339
(R^2 = .13)	Body-Esteem	.026	---	.026
Social Desirability	Self-Esteem*	.221	.071	.292
(R^2 = .16)	Body-Esteem	.086	.006	.092
	Acceptance*	.211	---	.211
Diet Attitude	Self-Esteem	-.095	.109	.014
(R^2 = .09)	Body-Esteem	.071	.006	.077
	Acceptance*	.211	.036	.247
	Social Desirability*	.165	---	.165
Amount of Exercise	Self-Esteem	.058	.043	.101
(R^2 = .35)	Social Desirability	-.018	.073	.055
	Diet Attitude*	.429	---	.429
	Body-Esteem*	.338	.030	.368
	Acceptance	---	.090	.090

* $p < .05$.

Path Analysis: Structural Modeling

18A.1 The Model-Fitting Approach to Path Analysis

The present chapter is devoted to path analysis from the standpoint of a model-fitting approach, but much of what we discuss is applicable to SEM as covered in Chapters 19A and 19B. Path analysis is viewed by some researchers as less interesting than SEM because in path analysis we use only a single measure for each of the constructs in the model (Kline, 2011). However, understanding path analysis is important because (a) many studies published in the professional literature employ path analysis and (b) the principles of path analysis can be extrapolated to SEM. Sources for more complete discussions of path analysis and structural models in general include Anderson and Gerbing (1988), Bentler and Chou (1987), Bentler and Weeks (1980), Bollen (1989), Byrne (2010), Hoyle (1995), Klem (2000), Kline (2011), Loehlin (2004), Maruyama (1998), Olobatuyi (2006), Raykov and Marcoulides (2006), Schumacker and Lomax (2004), and Thompson (2000b).

Kline (2011) encourages researchers to use model-fitting software to perform a path analysis because such software provides the following: (a) how well the overall model fits the data, (b) the indirect and total effects of the predictors' variables, and (c) estimates of the path coefficients for latent variables models (as opposed to measured or observed variables) if any can be included in the model. We will discuss each in turn.

18A.1.1 Overall Fit

The overall fit of the model represents how well the model explains the data, an outcome not available in multiple regression. The best a researcher can do in regression analysis is to compare the observed correlation with the hypothesized correlations. If the two correlation matrixes are within .05 of the observed correlation matrix, then the researcher has some evidence of a proper fit (Agresti & Finlay, 2009). If multiple models are used, then the model that most closely resembles the observed model is considered "best."

Overall model fit is certainly the first thing that researchers would examine in viewing their results using model-fitting software, and it is a wonderful feeling to see, for example, the CFI hovering around .99 or the RMSEA in the neighborhood of .001. But the "quality" of the fit is driven not only by the ability of the model to represent the phenomenon under study but also by the complexity of (number of paths included in) the model. As a general rule, increases in model complexity will produce better-fitting models. When we have generated a complex model, we need to examine it with perhaps somewhat greater skepticism and ask if a simpler version of the model would not serve our research purposes just as well. This can be done either at the beginning of the research when we are designing our path structure or after data analysis when we can examine our output and determine if the model can be simplified at that time.

18A.1.2 Indirect and Total Effects

Indirect effects involve mediator variable(s), a topic discussed in Sections 8A.7 and 17A.4. In our example from Figure 17a.1, *A* is hypothesized to have a direct effect on *C* and an indirect effect on *C* mediated by *B*. This indirect effect is calculated by multiplying the path coefficient between *A* and *B* by the path coefficient between *B* and *C*. The total effect is calculated by adding the direct effect and the indirect effect. We can do this by hand calculation when we have used multiple regression to perform the path analysis; when we have used model-fitting software, these calculations are often performed for us.

18A.1.3 Working With Latent Variables

Kline's (2011) third reason to encourage researchers to use model fitting as their causal analysis method is that the statistical software enabling us to do this is also perfectly at home performing SEM—that is, including latent variables in the models that are assessed. By definition, using multiple regression precludes this option because the variables in the analysis must be represented one-for-one in the data file; that is, multiple regression must be performed on observed variables.

18A.2 Comparing Multiple Regression and Model-Fitting Approaches

As we have previously discussed in Section 17A.11, multiple regression employs the ordinary least squares method to calculate the path coefficients; model-fitting approaches typically use maximum likelihood to calculate the path coefficients. The ordinary least squares estimation in multiple regression is known as a *partial-information* technique, whereas the maximum likelihood estimation in the model-fitting program is known as a *full-information* technique (Kelloway, 1998).

The differences between the partial- and the full-information techniques revolve around two interrelated features of the multiple regression and model-fitting procedures: (a) using some or all of the information in any single analysis and (b) the iteration feature. We will discuss these features separately based on Kelloway's (1998) presentation. To keep things as simple as we can, we will focus on the path model in Figure 17a.1 as our illustration.

18A.2.1 Using Some or All of the Information

Recall that the multiple regression approach in our example in Figure 17a.1 required us to run two separate regression solutions; one involved *A* predicting *B*, and the other involved *A* and *B* predicting *C*. Thus, the information in any single regression solution we are using is based on a subset of the data set. In some sense, any information concerning *C*'s relationship to either *A* or *B* is irrelevant in the first regression solution. This can be contrasted with the model-fitting approach.

In model fitting, all the information concerning the interrelationships between all the variables is brought to bear simultaneously. The maximum likelihood procedure attempts to simultaneously generate the coefficients for all the variables with the goal of providing the best match to the data. Thus, when the model is estimating the coefficient that will work best to relate *A* and *B*, it is not doing the estimation in isolation. It is also very much involved with how *C* fits into all this because it is simultaneously working on the prediction of *C* from *A* and *B*. The coefficient it produces for the *A–B* path will therefore take into consideration how this solution relates to the one it is generating for *C*. The process is in some ways a gestalt; each part affects every other part, and it is the configuration of the parts into the whole that is paramount. In model fitting, it is the model as a whole that is fit to the data, not just a subset of the paths that the model contains. Selecting a value for one path intimately affects the values of the other paths; ultimately, the model stands or falls as a single entity rather than as a collection of separate and unrelated paths.

18A.2.2 The Iteration Process

Not only does multiple regression use only a subset of the information contained in the data set to derive the values for the coefficients, it also does so in a single evaluation of the data. For example, when the procedure is predicting *C* from *A* and *B*, it first controls for one variable and then controls for the other. These two processes—entering the variables into the equation after the other is controlled—are done independently of each other in two single assessments. The results are then summarized in the regression equation.

Model fitting typically uses an iterative maximum likelihood procedure. Not only does the procedure make use of all the information concerning the relationships between the variables simultaneously, it also does not stop with its first best guess about the value of the coefficients for all the paths. Through a process of iteration (see Section 15A.4.2), it uses its previous approximations to refine its estimates. Its target is to match the data, given the structure of the model, and we expect it to get closer and closer to that coveted match with successive attempts. At some juncture, it reaches the point of diminishing returns, and the mathematical criterion defining how much it is bettering its last attempt in effect says, "Okay, we're not making sufficient gains to keep this iterative process going. I'm going to issue the order to stop now."

18A.3 The Model-Fitting Strategy to Perform a Path Analysis With Only Measured Variables

The model-fitting approach was described in Chapter 16A in the context of confirmatory factor analysis. These procedures can also be used to perform path analysis and are probably to be preferred over multiple regression if researchers are deciding between them. In the domain of model fitting, we can distinguish between two possible sets of variables. In one set, all the variables in the model are measured or observed variables. The structural model that ties them together is evaluated through path analysis. In the other set, the variables include both latent variables and observed or manifest variables. The structural model that relates these variables together is evaluated through SEM.

18A.4 Differences Between Regression and Structural Equations

Despite the differences between regression and model-fitting analyses—ordinary least squares versus maximum likelihood with iterations, separate regression solutions for each endogenous variable independently versus simultaneous and holistic determinations of path coefficients for the entire model—there is a certain feature that these two approaches have in common. Just as separate equations are generated to predict the endogenous variables in multiple regression, so, too, are separate equations used to predict the endogenous variables in model-fitting programs. There are two differences that we note here: First, in multiple regression, these equations are computed separately, but model-fitting techniques derive the equations simultaneously. Second, the form of the equation is a bit different.

The standardized multiple regression equation is a weighted linear composite of the predictor variables. Each variable is weighted with respect to all the other predictors, and the weights are designated as beta weights. The equation is designed to predict the dependent variable; that is, the weighted composite on one side of the equation equals the predicted value of the criterion variable on the other side of the equation. How well it predicts is conveyed to us by R^2, which is the proportion of variance in the measured dependent variable that is predicted by the regression equation.

The model-fitting tradition takes a somewhat wider view, although it is not in conflict with what we have said about regression. As we have already discussed in the context of confirmatory factor analysis in Chapter 16A, the model-fitting approach explicitly notes the error variance associated with variables in the model. More specifically, model-fitting software assigns an error component to every endogenous variable.

Because these endogenous variables will serve as the dependent variables in a prediction equation, we can think of what is predicted in model-fitting methods as the combination (the sum) of the predicted value of the criterion variable and its error component (what is not able to be predicted). Conceptually, the combination of what we can and cannot predict of the dependent variable makes up all of it. Thus, *the equation is designed to yield the actual or measured variable*, which includes the part of it that is predictable and the part of it that is not. Because the error is explicitly included in the equation and we thus predict the full dependent variable, it is often referred to as a *structural equation*. The general form of the structural equation is as follows:

$$Y = b_1 X_1 + b_2 X_2 + \ldots + b_n X_n \text{ error}_Y$$

In the above equation, Y is the *measured* or *actual* dependent variable. This differs from the multiple regression equation where the target of the equation is the *predicted* value of Y, not the actual value. Here, the equation yields Y and not Y_{pred} because we have included the unaccounted for variance—the error$_Y$ term—in the equation.

The difference between the forms of the equation in multiple regression and model fitting represents the emphasis they have; they are not necessarily fundamentally different entities. Multiple regression simply focuses on generating the equation of the regression line that is the predicted value of the criterion variable. Thus, it makes sense for the multiple regression equation to yield Y_{pred}, the predicted value of the dependent variable. Model fitting is attempting to reproduce the original (observed or measured) data. Thus, it makes sense for the structural equation to yield Y, the observed value of the dependent variable. Both approaches to path analysis result in beta weights being used as the path coefficients; the difference is that these path coefficients have been derived using different analytic techniques.

18A.5 The Analysis of a Structural Model

Model-fitting software typically uses maximum likelihood to calculate the path coefficients, although other parameter estimation methods are available. Maximum likelihood attempts to estimate the values of the parameters of the model that would result in the highest likelihood of reproducing the actual data. These methods often require iterative solutions.

We have already discussed the idea of model fit and indexes to assess goodness of fit relating to confirmatory factor analysis in Sections 16A.10 and 16A.11, and all of those considerations apply to path analysis as discussed in this chapter and to SEM as discussed in Chapter 19A. Thus, we assess the overall model, but a good fit does not assure us that all of the paths are either statistically or practically significant. In path analysis and SEM, it therefore becomes important to distinguish between the overall fit of the model to the data and the accuracy of prediction in the structural equations. Accuracy of the prediction is assessed by comparing the actual values of the endogenous variables with their predicted values, usually in terms of proportion of variance that is explained (R^2).

18A.6 Configuring the Structural Model

We revisit the path model (shown in Figure 17a.3) that we used earlier to predict academic achievement. The model on which we now focus, presented in Figure 18a.1, is configured as a structural model. Note that the difference between the regression model in Figure 17a.3 and the structural model in Figure 18a.1 is the inclusion of error terms. The regression-based model does not specify any error terms; the structural model includes the error or unique influences on the two endogenous variables (motivation and academic achievement). These error or unique influences are designated by the circles labeled Error *M* and Error *A* and represent all the other influences that may affect the endogenous variables besides those specified in the model.

Their inclusion allows us to use the actual *Y* values as the criterion variables in the two structural equations; this is in contrast to path analysis using multiple regression, where the error terms are not included in the model and the regression equations therefore have the predicted *Y* values as criterion variables.

18A.7 Identifying the Structural Model

18A.7.1 Number of Known Elements

Recall from Chapter 16A that to assess whether the proposed model fits the data, a necessary but not sufficient condition is that the model must be identified. As we described in Section 16A.8, to achieve model identification we must have more known information elements than estimations of unknown parameters. The number of known elements can be determined in two ways if we wish to make the count by hand:

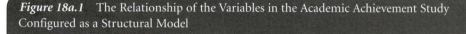

Figure 18a.1 The Relationship of the Variables in the Academic Achievement Study Configured as a Structural Model

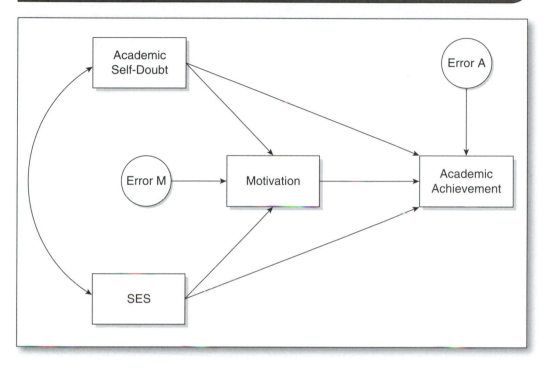

- Count the number of unique or nonredundant entries (allowing the pairing of the variable with itself) in a matrix that represents the covariances or correlations of the indicator variables.
- Count the number of variances there are in the model. This will correspond to the number of variables, but because information is the focus here and because variance is the entity that carries information, we count variances. Then add to that count the number of correlations there are in the correlation or covariance matrix (allowing the pairing of the variable with itself).

If we wish to determine the number of known elements algebraically, we can use the following formula: $V(V + 1)/2$, where V is the number of the measured variables in this study. In the present example we have $(4 * 5)/2$ or 10 nonredundant elements. These are the four variances associated with the four measured variables and the six pairs of correlations between the measured variables.

18A.7.2 Number of Unknown Elements

The following represents the number of parameters that we will be estimating in the process of performing the analysis of the model:

- The pattern/structure coefficients associated with the measured predictor variables. In this model, there are five (two predictors of motivation and three predictors of academic achievement).
- The pattern/structure coefficients relating the error terms to the endogenous variables. In this model, there are two.
- The variances of the exogenous variables. In this model, there are two.
- The variances of the error variables. In this model, there are two.
- The correlation of the two exogenous variables. In this model, there is one.

Performing the addition, we have 5 + 2 + 2 + 2 +1 for a total number of 12 unknown elements.

18A.7.3 Resolving the Count

For a model to be identified, it must have a positive number for the degrees of freedom (known elements). In this case, the number of known elements is 10 and the number of unknown parameters is 12. We therefore have a combination of known and unknown elements of −2. To achieve a positive value, we must constrain three parameters. Two of them are easy choices: the pattern/structure coefficients relating the two error terms to the endogenous variables.

For the third parameter to constrain, it is recommended that the path to be constrained is the one that our theory would predict to have the largest coefficient. If the theory does not address the magnitudes of the hypothesized causal influences, then we choose a path to constrain that makes common sense. In this instance, we select the path from academic self-doubt to motivation. From our understanding of the subject matter, we expect that greater levels of academic self-doubt produce decreased motivation. This is an inverse relationship, and if we constrain this path, we should do so using a value of −1 to reflect the presumed negative correlation of these two variables. The model that is now identified as a result of the three constraints we added is shown in Figure 18a.2. We now have 1 degree of freedom and can perform the analysis on this identified model.

18A.8 The Model Results

As recommended by Thompson (2004), we would examine selected overall fit measures of the chi-square, the NFI, the CFI, and the RMSEA. The chi-square statistic is used to test the

Figure 18a.2 The Structural Model Configured With Three Constraints so That It May Be Identified

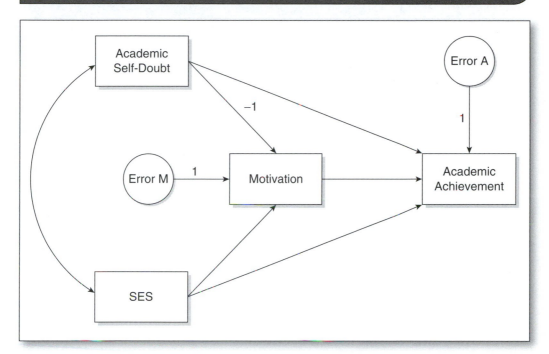

difference between the predicted and the observed relationships (correlations/covariances). Because the researchers are predicting a close fit, a nonsignificant chi-square is desired. In this example, the chi-square value was significant, indicating, at least at first glance, that there might be a poor match between the proposed model and the observed data.

We have already mentioned in Section 16A.11.1 that chi-square should be supplemented with other fit measures in judging how well the model fits the data. The CFI and the NFI are measures assessing the fit of the proposed model relative to the independence model, which assumes that there are no relationships in the data. These measures indicate the improvement of the hypothesized model compared with that baseline. Values of these indexes can range from 0 to 1, and values of .95 or greater are deemed acceptable. Because the values of the CFI and the NFI were .877 and .876, respectively, these measures do not support the model.

The RMSEA is the average of the residuals between the observed correlation/covariance from the sample and the expected model estimated from the population. A value of .08 indicates good fit. In this example, the RMSEA was .336, indicating a poor fit. Thus, all four fit indexes failed to support the proposed model.

Figure 18ab.3 The Structural Model Displaying the Beta Coefficients, the Correlation Between the Two Exogenous Variables, and the Two R^2 Values (Shown in Rounded Rectangles to the Upper Right Side of the Endogenous Variables)

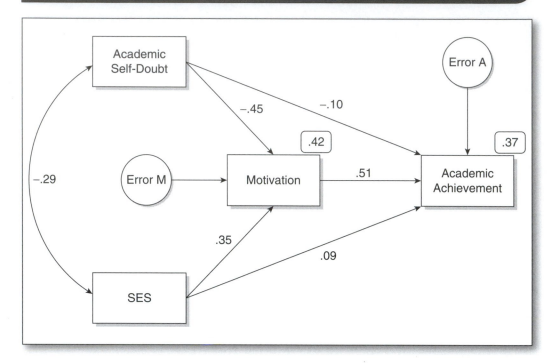

The path coefficients for the model are illustrated in Figure 18a.3. Comparing them with the results from the multiple regression analysis (Figure 17a.4) reveals them to be similar. The beta weight from academic self-doubt to motivation increased from −.31 to −.45, the beta weight from SES to motivation decreased from .43 to .35, and the beta weight from motivation to academic achievement increased from .48 to .51. The two direct paths from self-doubt and SES to achievement were virtually unchanged and still were not significant.

18A.9 Respecifying the Model

Because the model fell short of a good fit to the data, we could consider a respecification of it to see if the fit can be improved. Once again, it should be borne in mind that "retrofitting" a model is more on the exploratory side than on the confirmatory or theory-testing side of the continuum. Furthermore, we do not recommend going on a "fishing expedition," trying one modification after another until the best respecification possible is found by trial and error.

That said, IBM SPSS Amos will permit us to "go fishing" if we wish. Once the analysis is performed and we are considering which paths might be removed or *trimmed* from the model, we can identify paths for potential deletion. We can then highlight these paths to be trimmed, and IBM SPSS Amos will calculate all possible models with all combinations of those highlighted paths removed. The number of models generated by IBM SPSS Amos is equal to 2^n where n is the number of paths that are highlighted. This is the case because there are two options for each path (keep it or delete it) and that decision must be made for each of the n highlighted paths.

In the output under **Specification Search**, we can see which of those models provides the best fit. Based on model comparison indexes—we suggest examining the BCC and the BIC indexes—researchers would presumably select the one model-trimming option corresponding to the best improvement in model fit. We would strongly urge researchers to make such model selections thoughtfully and conservatively rather than just picking the model with the best improvement.

We will keep the changes simple in our working example by proposing a revised model devoid of the paths that did not reach statistical significance in the original and not trying out the options of trimming one or the other of these paths. Once again, a note of caution is appropriate here. If we presume that the model was configured based on a theoretical framework and/or prior research, then trimming the model by removing one or more paths should not be done without consideration of the theoretical (or empirical) consequences of such a reconfiguration. We will assume for illustrative purposes that removing the two nonsignificant paths does make a certain amount of sense within the theoretical context and proceed with our model trimming. The respecified model is shown in Figure 18a.4.

There are still 10 known elements in the respecified model as the number of measured variables has not changed. However, with two fewer paths in the model, the number of unknown parameters that we will be estimating in the respecified model has decreased by two. The unknown parameters are as follows:

- The pattern/structure coefficients associated with the measured predictor variables. In this model, there are three (two predictors of motivation and one predictor of academic achievement).
- The pattern/structure coefficients relating the error terms to the endogenous variables. In this model, there are two.
- The variances of the exogenous variables. In this model, there are two.
- The variances of the error variables. In this model, there are two.
- The correlation of the two exogenous variables. In this model, there is one.

Figure 18a.4 The Respecified Structural Model

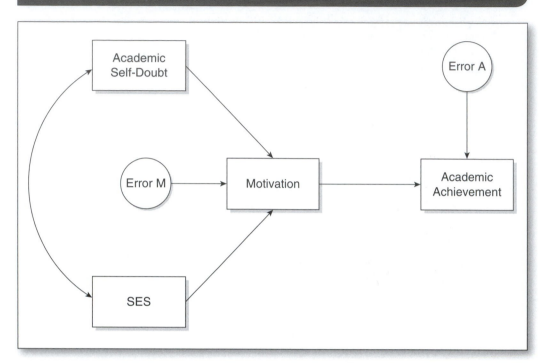

Performing the addition, we have 3 + 2 + 2 + 2 + 1 for a total number of 10 unknown elements. We will retain from the original model the constraints on the pattern/structure coefficients relating the error terms to the endogenous variables so that our respecified model can be specified; these will be iteratively estimated in the analysis in any case.

18A.10 Respecified Model Results

The chi-square was not significant this time, indicating an acceptable fit between the proposed model and the observed data. The CFI and the NFI yielded values of .985 and .977, respectively, and appear to support the model. The RMSEA was .083, just missing the .08 rule of thumb for a good fit.

The path coefficients for the respecified model are illustrated in Figure 18a.5. Examining the coefficients, we see that all the path coefficients achieved practical significance (the beta weights are above .3) and statistical significance. The beta weights shown in this revised model match the results obtained under multiple regression.

Figure 18a.5 The Respecified Structural Model Displaying the Beta Coefficients, the Correlation Between the Two Exogenous Variables, and the Two R^2 Values (Shown in Rounded Rectangles to the Upper Right Side of the Endogenous Variables)

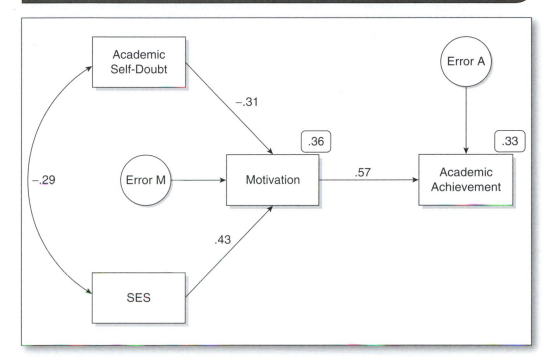

18A.11 Recommended Readings

Anderson, J. C., & Gerbing, D. W. (1988). Structural equation modeling in practice: A review and recommended two-step approach. *Psychological Bulletin, 103,* 411–423.

Chambers, W. V. (2000). Causation and corresponding correlations. *Journal of Mind and Behavior, 21,* 437–460.

Cliff, N. (1983). Some cautions concerning the application of causal modeling methods. *Multivariate Behavioral Research, 18,* 81–105.

Duncan, O. D. (1966). Path analysis: Sociological examples. *American Journal of Sociology, 72,* 219–316.

Enders, C. K. (2001b). The impact of nonnormality on full information maximum-likelihood estimation for structural equation models with missing data. *Psychological Methods, 6,* 352–370.

Everitt, B. S. (1984). *An introduction to latent variable models.* New York, NY: Chapman & Hall.

Green, S. B., Thompson, M. S., & Babyak, M. A. (1998). A Monte Carlo investigation of methods for controlling Type I errors with specification searches in structural equation modeling. *Multivariate Behavioral Research, 33,* 365–383.

Hoyle, R. H. (Ed.). (1995). *Structural equation modeling: Concepts, issues, and applications.* Thousand Oaks, CA: Sage.

Kelloway, E. K. (1995). Structural equation modeling in perspective. *Journal of Organizational Behavior, 16,* 215–224.

Kelloway, E. K. (1998). *Using LISREL for structural equation modeling: A researcher's guide.* Thousand Oaks, CA: Sage.

Leidy, N. K. (1990). A structural model of stress, psychosocial resources, and symptomatic experience in chronic physical illness. *Nursing Research, 39,* 230–236.

Maassen, G. H., & Bakker, A. B. (2001). Suppressor variables in path models: Definitions and interpretations. *Sociological Methods & Research, 30,* 241–270.

Magura, S., & Rosenblum, A. (2000). Modulating effect of alcohol use on cocaine use. *Addictive Behaviors, 25,* 117–122.

McDonald, R. P. (1996). Path analysis with composite variables. *Multivariate Behavioral Research, 31,* 239–270.

Mueller, R. O. (1997). Structural equation modeling: Back to basics. *Structural Equation Modeling, 4,* 353–369.

Rigdon, E. E. (1995). A necessary and sufficient identification rule for structural models estimated in practice. *Multivariate Behavioral Research, 30,* 359–383.

Tremblay, P. F., & Gardner, R. C. (1996). On the growth of structural equation modeling in psychological journals. *Structural Equation Modeling, 3,* 93–104.

Path Analysis: Structural Modeling Using Amos

18B.1 Overview

This chapter describes the model-fitting approach to conduct a path analysis. Model fitting is done through IBM SPSS Amos and uses maximum likelihood to calculate all the path coefficients simultaneously. This simultaneous approach is referred to as a full-information model technique and is the preferred technique if researchers have a choice between this and multiple regression, even though these two options generally produce similar results for the path coefficients.

Two points are worth noting in advance of our discussion. First, the model-fitting approach to path analysis is a special case of SEM, a topic we present in Chapters 19A and 19B. Thus, much of what we say about path analysis is applicable to SEM. Second, many of the commonly used IBM SPSS Amos commands are presented in Appendix B, and many of the fundamentals of working with IBM SPSS Amos have been discussed in Chapter 16B, and we will assume that readers are familiar with the material covered there so that we need not present the material in as much detail here.

18B.2 The Data Set and Model Used in Our Example

We will use the example from Chapter 17B but will perform a model-fitting (full-information) analysis. As will be recalled, body-esteem (**bodyesteem**) and self-esteem (**selfesteem**) are thought to be predictors of exercise in both a direct and indirect manner. Social desirability (**desire**) and acceptance (**acceptance**) of others are hypothesized to be affected by body-esteem and self-esteem and in turn predict exercise. Attitude toward diet (**diet**) is hypothesized to be a predictor of exercise (**exercise**) and in turn to be predicted by body-esteem, self-esteem, social desirability, and acceptance of others. The data file is named **Exercise**.

18B.3 Drawing the Model

In Section 16B.3.1, we showed how to change from portrait layout to landscape layout and how to use variable names rather than variable labels. This should be done here as well. There are four elements that need to be drawn in our path diagram:

- The observed variable represented by a rectangle.
- Paths are represented by lines with one-direction arrows between the observed variables.
- Error elements (also called disturbances, residuals, and unique contributions) for all endogenous variables (called Unique Variables in the Diagram drop-down menu of IBM SPSS Amos).
- A correlation between two variables.

18B.3.1 Drawing the Model

The path model that we are evaluating is shown in Figure 18b.1. Readers who are working through our example should draw a model that looks like ours. Traditionally, the flow of a path structure is from left to right, with the outcome variable at the far right of the diagram.

18B.3.2 Drawing the Observed Variables

We open the data file named **Exercise** in IBM SPSS. From the main menu select **Analyze ➔ Amos** to bring us to the graphics window. From the menu, select **Diagram ➔ Draw Observed**. A small rectangle, serving as the cursor, will appear. Left-click the mouse and drag to draw a rectangle large enough to contain the name of your variables. Move the cursor and draw a second rectangle.

18B.3.3 Drawing a Path

From the menu, select **Diagram ➔ Draw Path**. A small arrow in a rectangle, serving as the cursor, will appear. Move the blunt end of the cursor to the edge of one rectangle. When the rectangle is highlighted, click and drag to the edge of the other rectangle.

Figure 18b.1 The Hypothesized Model Predicting Amount of Exercise

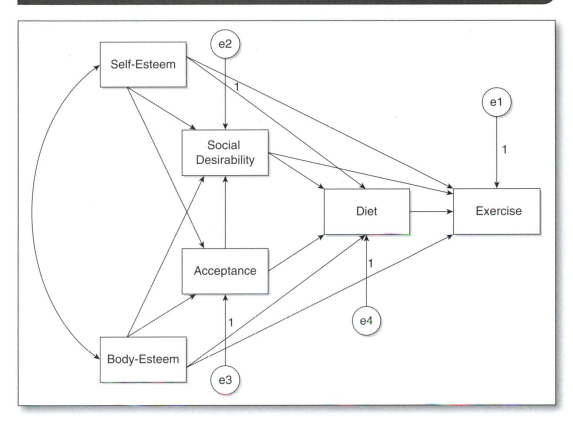

18B.3.4 Moving These Objects Around the Screen

At any point in this process, objects can be moved around the screen by dragging them. Dragging is enabled by selecting **Edit ➜ Move** from the menu. Any objects that have been "connected" will move together. To cancel the dragging capability, select **Edit ➜ Move** again.

18B.3.5 Drawing Error Elements

From the menu, select **Diagram ➜ Draw Unique Variable**. A circle/rectangle combination, serving as the cursor, will appear. Move the cursor inside an endogenous variable in the model. Once inside, the rectangle will be highlighted. Left-click the mouse; an error element will automatically be attached to the rectangle, and the path will be constrained to 1. Continuing to click will move the position of the error element around the clock so that you can select the position that best suits your needs. Repeat this for each of the four endogenous variables.

18B.3.6 Drawing a Correlation (Covariance)

From the menu, select **Diagram ➔ Draw Covariance**. A double-arrow, serving as the cursor, will appear. Move the cursor inside the rectangle for one of the variables to be correlated. Once inside, the rectangle will be highlighted. Left-click the mouse; a curved double-arrowed line will appear. Drag the line to the other variable so that this second variable becomes highlighted. To cancel this function, select **Diagram ➔ Draw Covariance** again.

18B.3.7 Naming the Measured Variables

Select **View ➔ Variables in Dataset**. This produces a screen containing the variables in the IBM SPSS data file as described in Section 16B.3.2. Drag the variables to the appropriate rectangles following the structure shown in Figure 18b.1.

18B.3.8 Naming the Error Variables

To name the error (unique) variables in one operation, select **Plugins ➔ Name Unobserved Variables**. Selecting this option in the menu automatically names the error terms.

18B.4 Model Identification

The number of known (nonredundant) elements in the model is equal to $V(V + 1)/2$, where V is the number of the measured variables in the study. There are six observed variables, and so we have $(6 * 7)/2$ or 21 known elements. These known elements are as follows:

- There are six variances, one for each measured variable.
- There are 15 pairwise correlations for the set of six measured variables.

The 20 unknown elements (estimated parameters) in the model are as follows:

- There is one correlation coefficient between self-esteem and body-esteem.
- We are estimating 13 path coefficients.
- We are estimating a variance for each error term for a total of four parameters.
- We are estimating a variance for each exogenous variable for a total of two parameters.

Figure 18b.2 The Output Tab for Analysis Properties

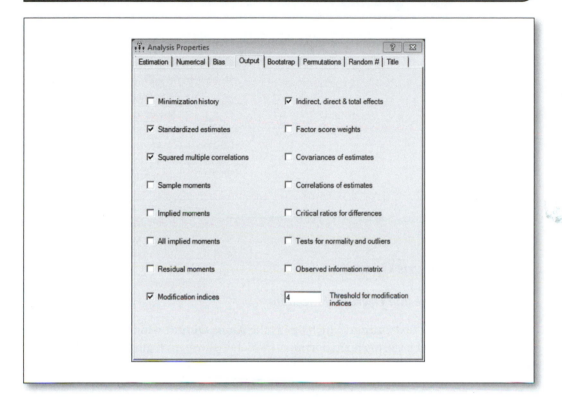

The degrees of freedom of the model is computed as the number of known elements minus the number of estimated parameters. Here, these values are 21 – 20 for a difference of 1. The degrees of freedom are positive, and thus the model is identified.

18B.5 Performing the Analysis

To perform the analysis, select **View** ➔ **Analysis Properties**. In the **Analysis Properties** window, select the **Output** tab as shown in Figure 18b.2. Remove the check from **Minimization history**, and check **Standardized estimates**, **Squared multiple correlations**, **Modification indices**, and **Indirect, direct & total effects**.

After making all of our specifications for the analysis in the Output window, we are ready to perform the analysis. From the main menu, select **Analyze** ➔ **Calculate Estimates**. At that point, IBM SPSS Amos will display the Windows **Save As** dialog screen. We must save the output file under a file name of our choice to a location of our choice. Once we execute the **Save As**, the output becomes available to us.

Figure 18b.3   The Notes for Model Output

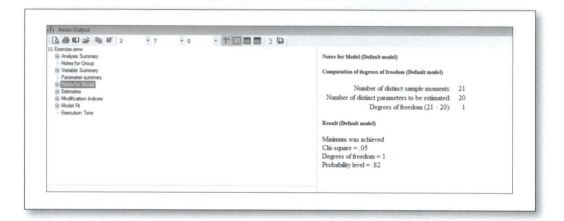

18B.6 The Analysis Output

18B.6.1 Chi-Square and Degrees of Freedom

Select **View ➔ Text Output**, which opens the **Amos Output** window, which opens in the **Notes for Model** page, the main portion of which is shown in Figure 18b.3. The output displays the number of known elements (**Number of distinct sample moments**) as 21, the number of unknown elements (**Number of distinct parameters to be estimated**) as 20, and the **Degrees of freedom** as 1 obtained by subtracting 20 from 21.

Below this information is the chi-square result. Its value is 0.052, and with 1 degree of freedom it is not statistically significant ($p = .820$). This suggests a very good fit of the model to the data.

18B.6.2 Model Fit

To obtain the fit indexes, select **Model Fit** in the **Text Output** menu. Some of the fit indexes shown in the output and the ones of interest to us are shown in Figure 18b.4. **CMIN** stands for minimum discrepancy as indexed by chi-square (see Byrne, 2010) and can be thought of simplistically as the chi-square value for the model specified by the researchers. The obtained value of chi-square is 0.052 and, with one degree of freedom, is not statistically significant (the probability **P** is .820).

The target for the GFI is equal to or greater than .90 for a good fit; in the present case its value is 1.000, which suggests an excellent fit. Under the heading **Baseline Comparisons**, we find both the NFI and CFI. Our target value for these indexes is .95, although .90 or above is acceptable; here we obtained values of 1.000 and 1.000, respectively. These values would

Figure 18b.4 Model Fit Summary

Model Fit Summary

CMIN

Model	NPAR	CMIN	DF	P	CMIN/DF
Default model	20	.052	1	.820	.052
Saturated model	21	.000	0		
Independence model	6	479.109	15	.000	31.941

RMR, GFI

Model	RMR	GFI	AGFI	PGFI
Default model	.011	1.000	.999	.048
Saturated model	.000	1.000		
Independence model	23.045	.689	.565	.492

Baseline Comparisons

Model	NFI Delta1	RFI rho1	IFI Delta2	TLI rho2	CFI
Default model	1.000	.998	1.002	1.031	1.000
Saturated model	1.000		1.000		1.000
Independence model	.000	.000	.000	.000	.000

RMSEA

Model	RMSEA	LO 90	HI 90	PCLOSE
Default model	.000	.000	.079	.892
Independence model	.273	.253	.295	.000

suggest a superb fit. The target value for the RMSEA is .08, and the obtained value is .000 (with a 90% confidence interval of .000 to .079); this outcome would be judged to indicate virtually a perfect fit. In summary, we would judge the model to represent an excellent fit to the data.

18B.6.3 Coefficients

To obtain the coefficients that were estimated, select **Estimates** in the **Text Output** menu. The unstandardized (raw) coefficients and standardized (beta) weights are shown in Figure 18b.5. A total of seven coefficients are statistically significant, and six did not reach statistical significance. Exercise amount appears to be most strongly predicted by diet (beta

Figure 18b.5   The Unstandardized (Raw) and Standardized Weights

Scalar Estimates (Group number 1 - Default model)

Maximum Likelihood Estimates

Regression Weights: (Group number 1 - Default model)

			Estimate	S.E.	C.R.	P
acceptance	<---	bodyesteem	.009	.019	.483	.629
acceptance	<---	selfesteem	.359	.057	6.252	***
desire	<---	acceptance	.361	.082	4.378	***
desire	<---	bodyesteem	.052	.033	1.613	.107
desire	<---	selfesteem	.401	.101	3.977	***
diet	<---	bodyesteem	.003	.002	1.272	.203
diet	<---	selfesteem	-.011	.007	-1.608	.108
diet	<---	desire	.010	.003	3.220	.001
diet	<---	acceptance	.023	.005	4.114	***
exercise	<---	diet	.493	.047	10.545	***
exercise	<---	desire	-.001	.003	-.424	.671
exercise	<---	selfesteem	.008	.006	1.200	.230
exercise	<---	bodyesteem	.015	.002	7.207	***

Standardized Regression Weights: (Group number 1 - Default model)

			Estimate
acceptance	<---	bodyesteem	.026
acceptance	<---	selfesteem	.339
desire	<---	acceptance	.211
desire	<---	bodyesteem	.086
desire	<---	selfesteem	.221
diet	<---	bodyesteem	.071
diet	<---	selfesteem	-.095
diet	<---	desire	.165
diet	<---	acceptance	.211
exercise	<---	diet	.429
exercise	<---	desire	-.018
exercise	<---	selfesteem	.058
exercise	<---	bodyesteem	.338

weight of .429) and body-esteem (beta weight of .338) when controlling for all of the other variables in the model.

18B.6.4 Direct, Indirect, and Total Effects

The direct, indirect, and total effects are shown in Figure 18b.6. Direct effects are those where one variable is directly predicting another. They are represented by beta weights and are the coefficients shown in path diagrams. The relationships of diet and exercise and of

Figure 18b.6 The Direct, Indirect, and Total Effects

Standardized Direct Effects (Group number 1 - Default model)

	bodyesteem	selfesteem	acceptance	desire	diet
acceptance	.026	.339	.000	.000	.000
desire	.086	.221	.211	.000	.000
diet	.071	-.095	.211	.165	.000
exercise	.338	.058	.000	-.018	.429

Standardized Indirect Effects (Group number 1 - Default model)

	bodyesteem	selfesteem	acceptance	desire	diet
acceptance	.000	.000	.000	.000	.000
desire	.006	.071	.000	.000	.000
diet	.021	.120	.035	.000	.000
exercise	.037	.005	.102	.071	.000

Standardized Total Effects (Group number 1 - Default model)

	bodyesteem	selfesteem	acceptance	desire	diet
acceptance	.026	.339	.000	.000	.000
desire	.091	.292	.211	.000	.000
diet	.091	.025	.246	.165	.000
exercise	.376	.063	.102	.052	.429

body-esteem and exercise are direct effects. These effects are shown in the top table in Figure 18b.6.

Indirect effects are those where a variable affects another through a mediating variable and are shown in the middle table of Figure 18b.6. For example, consider the indirect effect of self-esteem on diet. As the model is configured, acceptance of others mediates that effect. To determine the indirect effect, we multiply the path coefficient relating self-esteem to acceptance (.34) by the path coefficient relating acceptance to diet (.21). The product of these beta weights is .12. Note that this value appears in the cell in the middle table corresponding to the row labeled **diet** and the column labeled **self-esteem**. Generally, the variables appearing in the first column are the endogenous variables and the other variables are the predictive agents. Thus, to determine the indirect effect of **self-esteem** (the predictive agent) on **diet** (the endogenous variable), we look for **diet** in the first column and read over to the **self-esteem** column. In this analysis, none of the indirect effects are particularly strong, that is, they appear to lack practical significance.

Total effects are shown in the bottom table of Figure 18b.6. These are simply the sums of the direct and indirect effects for each endogenous variable. For example, consider the endogenous variable of **exercise**. When considering the total effect of **bodyesteem**, we add the direct effect of .338 to the indirect effect of .037 to obtain the total effect of **bodyesteem** on **exercise** of .376. One way to interpret this value is to say that for every 1 standard deviation increase in **bodyesteem** (i.e., an increase of 1 z unit), the amount of **exercise** on the average will increase by about a third of a standard deviation.

18B.6.5 The Correlation of the Two Exogenous Variables

The top tables of Figure 18b.7 present the relationship of the two exogenous variables, **bodyesteem** and **selfesteem**, and the test of significance of that correlation. The correlation was .529, which was statistically significant.

18B.6.6 The Squared Multiple Correlations

The bottom table of Figure 18b.7 presents the squared multiple correlations (R^2) of the endogenous variables. These values are the amount of variance accounted for in the model. As can be seen from the table, the model accounted for 35% of the variance of **exercise**.

Figure 18b.7 The Correlation of the Two Exogenous Variables and the R^2 for the Endogenous Variables

Covariances: (Group number 1 - Default model)

			Estimate	S.E.	C.R.	P
selfesteem	<-->	bodyesteem	70.391	7.404	9.508	***

Correlations: (Group number 1 - Default model)

			Estimate
selfesteem	<-->	bodyesteem	.529

Variances: (Group number 1 - Default model)

Squared Multiple Correlations: (Group number 1 - Default model)

	Estimate
acceptance	.125
desire	.161
diet	.087
exercise	.350

Figure 18b.8 The Structural Model With the Coefficients and R^2 Values

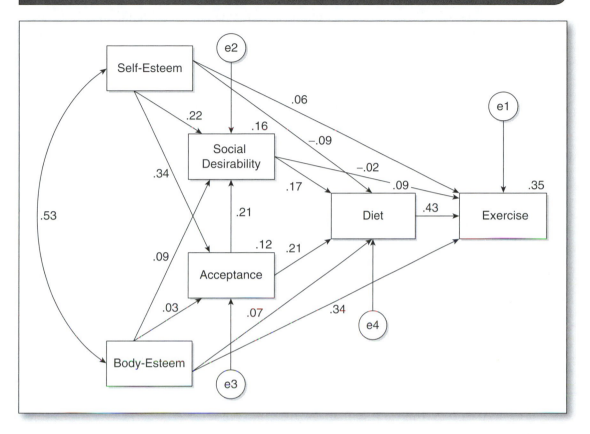

18B.7 The Structural Model

The structural model is shown in Figure 18b.8. What is displayed are as follows: the correlation between **bodyesteem** and **selfesteem**, the path coefficients, and the values of the R^2s.

18B.8 Specification Search to Delete Paths

The model shown in Figure 18b.8 is relatively busy, partly because it contains six path coefficients that are not statistically significant. Furthermore, of the seven path coefficients that are statistically significant, four do not reach a practical significance threshold of .30. Thus, the impressive values for model fit do not convey the ungainliness or unwieldiness of the model.

IBM SPSS Amos has provided a way to suggest which paths may be worthy of deletion in its **Specification Search** (see Section 18A.10). When we indicate which paths we would consider deleting, Amos will compute all possible models with all combinations of those paths removed. We could then presumably choose the best from among those alternative models. However, with many paths considered for deletion, the number of possible models can be substantial (it is equal to 2^n, where n is the number of paths under consideration).

We will adopt the following strategy to avoid a major fishing expedition:

1. First, we will delete all paths that were not statistically significant. That will trim the model down to seven paths, and we will evaluate how well that model fits the data.

2. Second, we will determine which path coefficients in that trimmed model do not reach or approach the practical significance criterion of .30. Those are the paths that we will identify in our Specification Search.

3. Third, we will consider the best model emerging from that analysis for our final version of the trimmed model.

18B.8.1 Specification Search: Removing Nonsignificant Paths

Our first job is to remove the six nonsignificant paths. These paths are as follows:

- Body-esteem to acceptance
- Body-esteem to desire
- Body-esteem to diet
- Self-esteem to diet
- Desire to exercise
- Self-esteem to exercise

To remove a path, make sure that the model is in the active window. Click on the **View the input path diagram (model specification)** icon as shown in Figure 18b.9. After clicking the icon, the path coefficients disappear (that is disturbing, but do not worry—it is the way IBM SPSS Amos has been programmed).

The **Erase objects** icon in the tool pallet to the left of the drawing area now becomes available (see Figure 18b.10). Clicking on the **Erase objects** icon turns the cursor into a version of that icon when in the graphics area. Move the cursor to a path that is targeted for deletion. Once the path is highlighted (changes to the default red color—see Figure 18b.11), select the path to delete it. The path structure resulting from removing the six paths is shown in Figure 18b.12.

Figure 18b.9 Entire Window With Input Path Diagram Icon at the Top

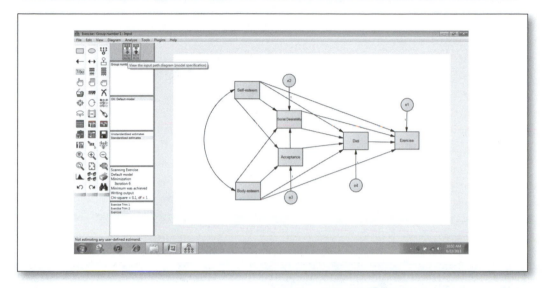

18B.8.2 Specification Search: Evaluate Results From First Trimming

Our second task is to evaluate the trimmed model. From the main menu, select **Analyze ➔ Calculate Estimates**. Selecting **View the output path diagram** icon displays the newly recalculated path coefficients. We present this in Figure 18b.13.

Select **View ➔ Text Output**, which opens the **Amos Output** window. To obtain the fit indexes, select **Model Fit** in the **Text Output** menu (see Figure 18b.14). The obtained value of chi-square is 7.25 and, with 7 degrees of freedom, is not statistically significant (the probability **P** is .40). The obtained values for the GFI, NFI, and CFI were .99, .98, and 1.00, respectively, and obtained value for the RMSEA is .01. We

Figure 18b.10 View of Window With the "Erase" Button Activated

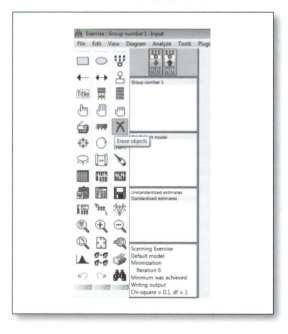

Figure 18b.11 The Highlighted Path for Deletion

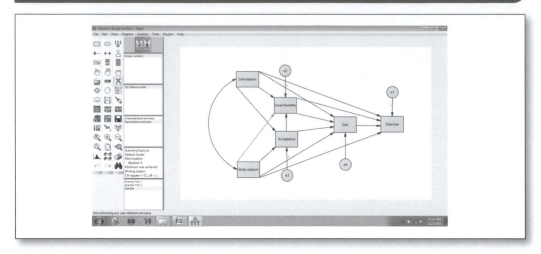

Figure 18b.12 The First Trimmed Nonsignificant Path Model

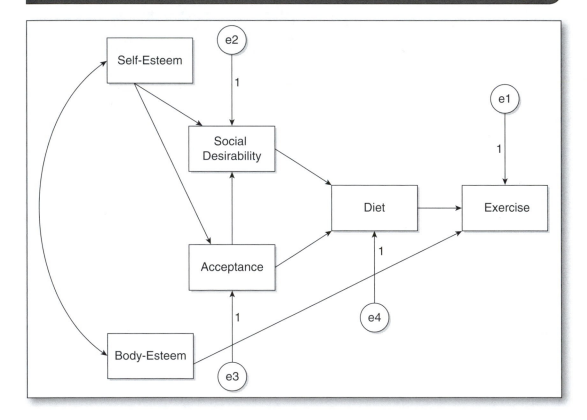

Figure 18b.13 The Diagram of the First Trimmed Model With Path Coefficients Shown

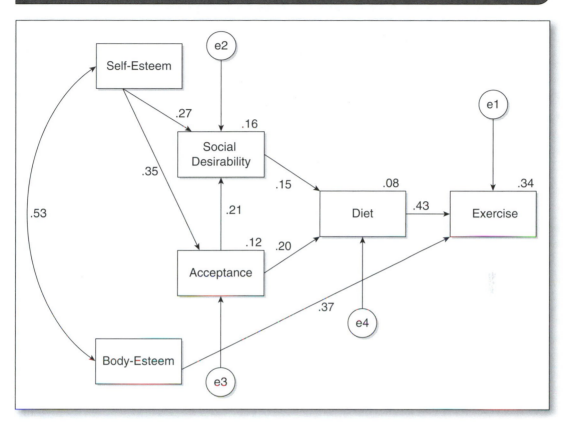

would judge the trimmed model to represent an excellent fit to the data. With fewer paths in this model than in the original one but because this trimmed model fits the data extremely well, we would consider this model to be a more parsimonious representation of the relationships among the variables.

To determine which path coefficients were statistically significant, select **Estimates** in the **Text Output** menu. The unstandardized (raw) coefficients and standardized (beta) weights are shown in Figure 18b.15. All of the seven coefficients in the trimmed model are statistically significant. Of these seven, three have achieved practical significance, that is, they exceed the threshold value of .30. One of the coefficients comes close to this value at .265, but the remaining three, although statistically significant, appear to be somewhat impractical (values ranging between .155 and .213). We will opt in this example to retain the coefficient from **selfesteem** to **desire** at .265 but place the other three into the **Specification Search**.

Figure 18b.14 First Trimmed Model Fit Summary

Model Fit Summary

CMIN

Model	NPAR	CMIN	DF	P	CMIN/DF
Default model	14	7.245	7	.404	1.035
Saturated model	21	.000	0		
Independence model	6	479.109	15	.000	31.941

RMR, GFI

Model	RMR	GFI	AGFI	PGFI
Default model	3.523	.994	.982	.331
Saturated model	.000	1.000		
Independence model	23.045	.689	.565	.492

Baseline Comparisons

Model	NFI Delta1	RFI rho1	IFI Delta2	TLI rho2	CFI
Default model	.985	.968	.999	.999	.999
Saturated model	1.000		1.000		1.000
Independence model	.000	.000	.000	.000	.000

RMSEA

Model	RMSEA	LO90	HI90	PCLOSE
Default model	.009	.000	.062	.871
Independence model	.273	.253	.295	.000

18B.8.3 Specification Search: Performing the Analysis

The **Specification Search** allows us to identify candidate paths to remove from the already trimmed model. It should be emphasized that we treat the models resulting from this procedure as statistical possibilities that we intend to evaluate with respect to our theoretical framework, the research literature, and common sense. Because we will exercise judgment in examining the results of this analysis and because we are not committed to removing any combination of them at the outset, we will put on the table all three of the following paths that failed by a substantial margin to achieve practical significance:

- Acceptance to diet
- Acceptance to desire
- Desire to diet

We suggest noting any paths that are going to be placed in the analysis as IBM SPSS Amos will remove all path coefficients from the screen once we begin our Specification Search.

Figure 18b.15 The Unstandardized (Raw) and Standardized Weights

Estimates (Group number 1 - Default model)

Scalar Estimates (Group number 1 - Default model)

Maximum Likelihood Estimates

Regression Weights: (Group number 1 - Default model)

			Estimate	S.E.	C.R.	P	Label
acceptance	<---	selfesteem	.374	.049	7.664	***	
desire	<---	selfesteem	.483	.088	5.496	***	
desire	<---	acceptance	.364	.083	4.403	***	
diet	<---	acceptance	.021	.005	3.947	***	
diet	<---	desire	.010	.003	3.131	.002	
exercise	<---	diet	.490	.046	10.715	***	
exercise	<---	bodyesteem	.016	.002	9.166	***	

Standardized Regression Weights: (Group number 1 - Default model)

			Estimate
acceptance	<---	selfesteem	.352
desire	<---	selfesteem	.265
desire	<---	acceptance	.213
diet	<---	acceptance	.195
diet	<---	desire	.155
exercise	<---	diet	.429
exercise	<---	bodyesteem	.367

To perform the **Specification Search**, return to the IBM SPSS Amos graphics window and select **Analyze ➜ Specification Search**. This opens **Specification Search** window shown in Figure 18b.16. Select the icon on the far left portion of the icon bar (see Figure 18b.16) called **Make arrows optional**. Then click on each of the paths under consideration for deletion. As shown in Figure 18b.17, the selected paths will change color.

With the three paths now selected, click the third icon from the left on the icon bar (see Figure 18b.18) called **Perform specification search**. The **Specification Search** window now displays all eight possible models. There are eight possible models in that a path can be either retained or deleted (two options) and there are three paths under consideration; thus, there are 2^3 or 8 combinations. Drag the corner of the window if necessary to enlarge it so that it displays all eight possible models as shown in Figure 18b.19.

Figure 18b.16 The Specification Search Window With the Make Arrows Optional Icon Highlighted

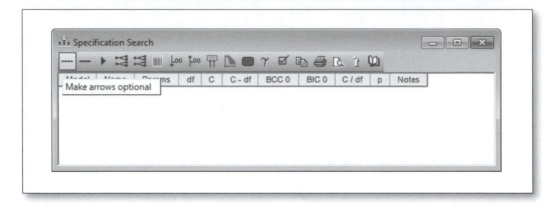

Figure 18b.17 The Specification Search Screen and the Three Paths We Have Highlighted

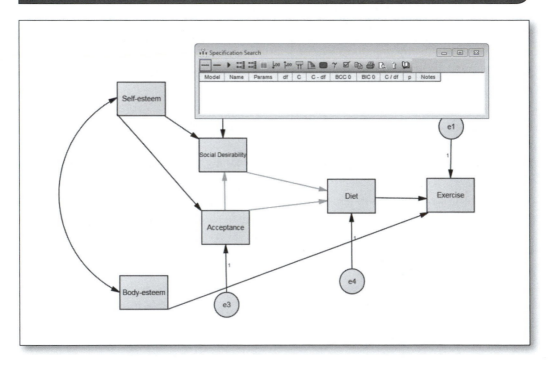

18B.8.4 Specification Search: Evaluating the Results of the Analysis

Each row in the **Specification Search** window represents one of the eight possible models. The last row contains the **Saturated** model where all variables are connected and there are no degrees of freedom; we ignore this model. For each model, the following information (reading from left to right) is displayed in columns:

- **Model**: This contains a model number that is arbitrarily assigned.
- **Name**: Every model is called the Default model.
- **Params**: This contains the number of parameters in the given model.
- **df**: This contains the number of degrees of freedom in the given model.
- **C**: This contains the chi-square value for the given model.
- **C – df**: This contains the chi-square value minus the degrees of freedom for the given model.
- **BCC**: This contains the Browne–Cudeck criterion, a model comparison index. Lower values indicate a better relative fit. Arbuckle (2010) recommends using the following interpretation guidelines for the BCC index as proposed by Burnham and Anderson (2002): Values within the range of 0 to 2 indicate that there is no evidence to rule out the model; 2 to 4 indicate that there is weak evidence to rule out the model; 4 to 7 indicate that there is definite evidence to rule out the model; 7 to 10 indicate that there is strong evidence to rule out the model; greater than 10 indicates that there is very strong evidence to rule out the model.
- **BIC**: This contains the Bayesian Information Criterion, a model comparison index; lower values indicate a better relative fit. Arbuckle (2010) recommends using the

Figure 18b.18 The Specification Search Window With the Perform Specification Search Icon Highlighted

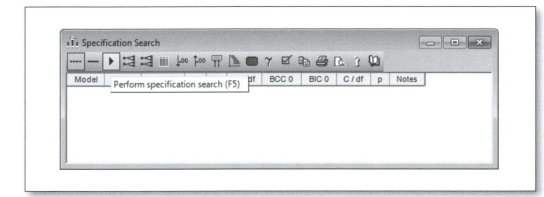

Figure 18b.19 All Possible Models Displayed in the Specification Search Window

Model	Name	Params	df	C	C - df	BCC 0	BIC 0	C / df	p	Notes
1	Default model	11	10	61.043	51.043	47.695	35.713	6.104	0.000	
2	Default model	12	9	35.885	26.885	24.571	16.583	3.987	0.000	
3	Default model	12	9	41.491	32.491	30.177	22.189	4.610	0.000	
4	Default model	12	9	42.094	33.094	30.779	22.792	4.677	0.000	
5	Default model	13	8	16.936	8.936	7.656	3.662	2.117	0.031	
6	Default model	13	8	22.541	14.541	13.261	9.267	2.818	0.004	
7	Default model	13	8	26.195	18.195	16.915	12.921	3.274	0.001	
8	Default model	14	7	7.245	0.245	*0.000*	*0.000*	*1.035*	*0.404*	
Sat	[Saturated]	21	0	0.000	0.000	6.995	34.953			

following interpretation guidelines for the BIC index as proposed by Raftery (1995): Values within the range of 0 to 2 indicate that there is weak evidence to rule out the model; 2 to 6 indicate that there is positive evidence to rule out the model; 6 to 10 indicate that there is strong evidence to rule out the model; greater than 10 indicate that there is very strong evidence to rule out the model.

- **C / df**: This contains the chi-square value divided by the degrees of freedom for the given model.
- **p**: This contains the probability level associated with the chi-square for the given model.

Selecting a row (a model) causes the model that is selected to be displayed in the graphics area. As an example, we have double-clicked the first model and presented it in Figure 18b.20. This model has the poorest fit to the data with the BCC and BIC relative fit indexes at 47.695 and 35.713, respectively. Furthermore, the model shown in Figure 18b.20 is not viable in that the only variables connected to the outcome variable are **bodyesteem** and **diet**; the other variables are just floating in space. This is a good example of what happens when all possible models are generated by a software routine without theoretical or common sense considerations.

The best of the models is the one containing the bold under the relative fit indexes. This makes it easy for users to identify the model (Model 8 in this instance) that emerged as the best of the eight possible models. We can examine this model and determine what if any further path trimming we might wish to adopt. Double-clicking Model 8 reveals the model

Figure 18b.20 The Specification Search Window With Model 1 Diagram

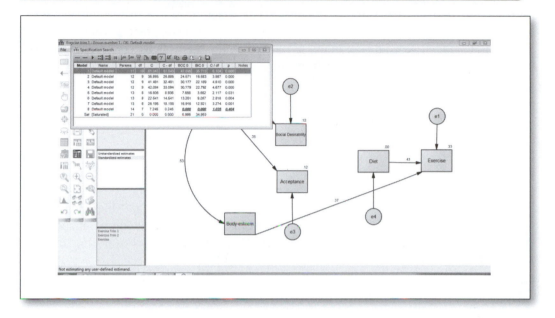

Figure 18b.21 The Specification Search Window With Model 8 Diagram

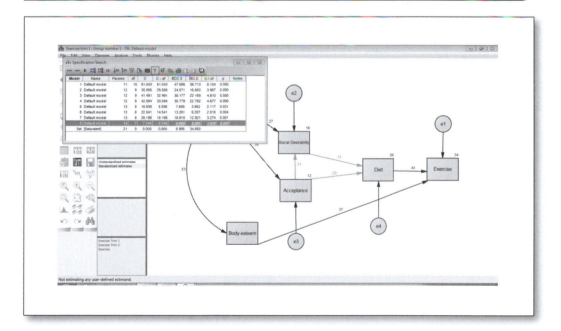

that is displayed in Figure 18b.21. The BCC and BIC relative fit indexes are at 0.000 and 0.000, respectively. Any paths that are displayed, regardless of their color, are retained by the model. Thus, despite these paths not reaching practical significance, their presence drives the model toward an excellent fit. Because these paths have reasonable theoretical grounds for being in the model, we would opt in this example to retain them. Thus, the model presented in Figure 18b.21 would be our final trimmed model.

18B.9 Reporting Path Analysis Results

The present path analysis focused on predictors of the amount of exercise in which students at University *X* engaged during the academic semester. The predictors, self-esteem, body-esteem, social desirability, acceptance of others, and the degree to which their diet was healthy, were configured into the hypothesized model shown in Figure 18b.8. The model was evaluated via IBM SPSS Amos 19 (Arbuckle, 2010). The chi-square assessing model fit, with a value of 0.052 (1, $N = 417$), $p = .820$, was not statistically significant; thus, the model appeared to be a good fit to the data. The goodness-of-fit index (GFI), the normed fit index (NFI), and the comparative fit index (CFI) all yielded values of 1.000, and the obtained RMSEA value was .001 with a 90% confidence interval of .000 to .079. All of these fit indexes indicated that the model was an excellent fit to the data.

The path coefficients are displayed in Figure 18b.8 and are summarized in Table 18b.1 under Direct Effects. Any coefficient equal to or larger than .20 is statistically significant as result of the large sample size. As can be seen in Table 18b.1, the model was able to account for 35% of the variance of the amount of exercise done by the students. Almost all of this is due to the direct effects of diet and body-esteem. The model was also able to explain 16% of the variance of social desirability and 13% of the variance of acceptance of others; acceptance of others was primarily (directly) predicted by self-esteem, whereas social desirability was predicted by the direct effects of both self-esteem and acceptance of others and to some extent indirectly by body-esteem.

Table 18b.1 Summary of Causal Effects of the Hypothesized Model

Outcome	Determinant	Causal Effects		
		Direct	**Indirect**	**Total**
Acceptance	Self-Esteem*	.338	---	.338
($R^2 = .13$)	Body-Esteem	.026	---	.026
Social Desirability	Self-Esteem*	.220	.071	.292
($R^2 = .16$)	Body-Esteem	.085	.006	.091
	Acceptance*	.210	---	.210
Diet Attitude	Self-Esteem	-.094	.120	.025
($R^2 = .09$)	Body-Esteem	.071	.021	.091
	Acceptance*	.211	.035	.246
	Social Desirability*	.165	---	.165
Amount of Exercise	Self-Esteem	.058	.005	.063
($R^2 = .35$)	Social Desirability	-.018	.071	.053
	Diet Attitude*	.429	---	.429
	Body-Esteem*	.338	.037	.376
	Acceptance	---	.102	.102

*$p < .05$.

Structural Equation Modeling

19A.1 Overview

SEM is a procedure to analyze structural models containing latent variables. It can be thought of as the union of confirmatory factor analysis and path analysis. This is because SEM is composed of two types of models: a measurement model and a structural model. Although the model as a whole is evaluated by a variety of GFIs, SEM also evaluates the measurement and the structural models separately because it is possible that they may differentially fit the data. That is, the structural equation model can be deconstructed into the structural model and the measurement model.

Once a model is proposed (i.e., relationships between the variables have been hypothesized), a correlation/covariance matrix is created. The estimates of the relationships between the variables in the model are calculated using the maximum likelihood estimation procedure just as was done in the path analysis example in Chapter 18A. The model is then compared with the relationships (the correlation/covariances matrix) present within the actual or observed data set.

19A.2 The Measurement and Structural Models

The measurement model represents the degree to which the indicator variables capture the essence of the latent factor. It is a confirmatory factor analysis for each latent variable. We call it a measurement model because the indicator variables of each factor are measured variables used to give us some access to or indication of the intangible, unmeasured latent factor. This was discussed in Chapter 16A.

The structural model is akin to path analysis (discussed in Chapter 18A) in that we are looking at the causal relationships between the variables of interest in the theory. These are typically not the indicator variables for the factors but are usually the latent variables themselves and other measured variables theoretically associated with the phenomenon addressed by the model.

SEM assesses how well the predicted interrelationships between the variables match the interrelationships between the observed variables. It has the capability to assess simultaneously both the measurement model (how well the indicator variables define their respective construct) and the structural model (how well the latent constructs relate to each other and to the other measured variables). If the two matrices (the one based on the hypothesized model and the one derived from the actual data) are consistent with one another, then the structural equation model can be considered a credible explanation for the hypothesized relationships. The degree to which matrices based on the hypothesized model and obtained data match is informed to us by the fit indexes that we have discussed in Section 16A.11.

19A.3 From Path Analysis to SEM

In our presentation of the assumptions underlying path analysis, we indicated (with very little fanfare) that the observed variables are presumed to be measured without error (Pedhazur, 1997). Maruyama (1998) assesses how well such an assumption is usually met: "Within the social sciences, assumptions about perfect reliability must be viewed as generally unrealistic. What social scientist ever has had models in which there is no measurement error?" (p. 30).

With less than perfect reliability in the measurement of our variables, some error is introduced into the analysis (Chen, Bollen, Paxton, Curran, & Kirby, 2001). If the dependent variables are less than perfectly reliable, the standard error estimate increases, which in turn weakens significance tests (Pedhazur, 1997). However, "measurement errors in the independent variable lead to underestimation of the regression coefficient" (Pedhazur, 1997, p. 34). The issue of reliability plays itself out to the advantage of the researcher in SEM. This is the case of a story with a twist. Let's look at the story briefly and then get to the twist.

The story has to do with the difference between SEM and path analysis and the impact this has on model identification. In SEM, we involve latent variables in the model. Remember from our treatment of confirmatory factor analysis that latent variables are by definition not measured—we have not collected data on them. They therefore do not have variances, and they do not appear in the correlation matrix. One consequence of this is that their attributes do not count toward the number of nonredundant (known) elements when we are identifying the model—that is, when we are determining the degrees of freedom associated with the model. Yet introduction of latent variables adds to the number of parameters (unknown elements) that we need to have the model estimate.

This increase in the number of parameters we must estimate resulting from the introduction of latent variables affects model identification. To compute degrees of freedom, we subtract the number of unknown parameters from the number of nonredundant or known elements. Model identification is achieved when the value for degrees of freedom is positive. With latent variables in the model, we have more unknown parameters to estimate than before, which therefore gives us more values to subtract, which in turn ordinarily results in us finding a negative value when we compute the degrees of freedom. As a result, the model is not identified and we cannot properly perform the analysis. The solution to this dilemma is to include additional indicator variables in the model to raise the number of known elements (the variances and correlation entries) so that when we subtract the former from the latter we arrive at a positive number.

Now for the twist in the story. Besides allowing us to identify the model and carry out the data analysis, increasing the number of indicator variables turns out to be a terrific strategy for another reason as well: It improves the reliability of our measurement. In SEM, we use at least two measured variables as indicators of the latent variable. This limiting case can be thought of as a smaller version of confirmatory factor analysis, but more measured variables may be used as indicators of the latent construct if warranted. By using at least two indicators for each latent variable, we are able to produce an estimate of the measurement error of the latent variable (the "unreliability" of the measurement operations). We do this by focusing on the variance that is common to the indicators (the common variance) and treating the variance that is not common to them (the unique variance of each measured or indicator variable) as error variance.

Consider academic self-doubt as our hypothetical example. As we have treated it in the multiple regression and in the model-fitting approaches to path analysis, it has been (it had to be) a measured variable. This variable had a certain amount of variance associated with it. Some of this variance we believed was "true score variance." But we (as the humans conducting the research) also reluctantly accept the idea that some of the variance of self-doubt was "error variance." The statistical software could not distinguish one kind of variance from another. So the statistical software simply assumed, however naively, that it was all true score variance—that the measurement was perfectly reliable or error free.

SEM relieves the analytic procedure of the need to assume that all the variance it sees in the data file is true score variance. If our interest was in academic self-doubt as a predictor, we could convert the status of that variable from that of a measured variable to that of a latent variable. To accomplish that conversion, we would need to find two or more measured variables as indicators of the construct. For example, we can propose that academic self-doubt is indicated by concerns about one's writing ability, worries about time management, anxiety about orally presenting material in class, and so on. We can then decide to measure, for the sake of simplicity in our example, two of these indicators.

This solution has at least two advantages. First, indicators of academic self-doubt are somewhat more concrete and will therefore perhaps be assessed with somewhat less measurement error. At worst, the measurement error is not likely to be greater when measuring these than when measuring self-doubt. Second, and more important, we would now have a way to estimate the measurement error for academic self-doubt if it was converted to a latent variable. Because this is the predictor of interest in the research (and not concerns about one's writing ability, worries about time management, anxiety about orally presenting material in class per se) and because we now have a way to estimate its true score variance and its error variance, we are better able to determine its effect in the model.

Assume that we have measured two indicator variables associated with academic self-doubt. Think of self-doubt as the factor and these indicators as variables correlated with or weighted on the factor. To the extent that these variables are both indicators of the factor, they will share variance. If we know their total variance (which we do know because we have data for these variables) and if we know how much of that total variance is shared or common (which the procedure calculates)—presumably representing academic self-doubt—then we are also able to determine how much variance is left over. This residual variance is variance unique to each indicator and can serve as an estimate of error variance. Thus, we (the analytic procedure) no longer have to assume that the variables of interest are perfectly measured as we did in path analysis. Because these measured variables are now converted latent variables and because we must have two or more indicators for each latent construct, we can actually estimate how far from perfection our variables have strayed.

From a research design perspective, the effort to change a path analysis design into a structural equation model means a potential gain in the precision of the research. That gain incurs a cost (is there nothing free in this world?). The researchers are going to collect more data because some of the measured variables in the path analysis are now slated to be converted latent variables, and for each latent variable that is hypothesized, we will need at least two measured indicator variables to be introduced. Furthermore, as another part of that cost, the researchers are going to have to determine how to assess the indicators. Researchers will have to decide for themselves, given the context in which they are working, whether or not they are inclined to think about designing a structural equation model when they have drawn out a path model. In many instances, we believe that the extra cost in time and resources will be judged by the researchers to be worthwhile.

19A.4 Building a Structural Model From Our Path Model

The proposed structural equation model that we will use as our example is presented in Figure 19a.1. We have used the minimum of two indicators for each for the sake of exposition.

Each endogenous variable (i.e., each indicator variable and each endogenous latent variable) has an associated error term designated **e1** through **e10**, but neither of the two exogenous variables (**Academic Self-Doubt** and **SES**) is assigned errors. Each error term is scaled to its respective endogenous variable by assigning values of 1 to those paths. These error terms represent the residual variance remaining after the prediction work has been done. For example, **e9** is the variance that is not accounted for in **Motivation** after **Academic Self-Doubt** and **SES** have done their predictive work.

Figure 19a.1 A Structural Model of Academic Achievement With Academic Self-Doubt and SES as Latent Variables

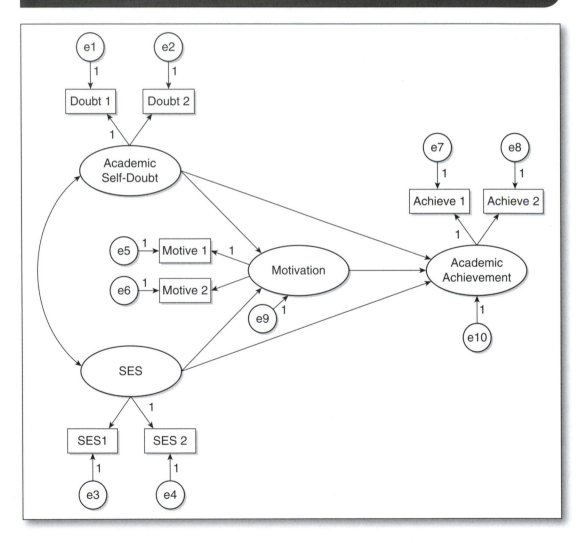

Recall from confirmatory factor analysis (see Section 16A.8.3) that researchers must scale the latent factor. This can be accomplished by selecting one of the path coefficients from each latent variable to a measured variable and fixing (constrain) that coefficient to the value to 1 (or **−1** if there is an inverse relationship between the two). This is also shown in Figure 19a.1.

19A.5 Results for Our Structural Model

In SEM, all the structural coefficients (those representing paths between latent variables) and all the measurement coefficients (those representing paths between latent variables and their indicators) are simultaneously estimated. Fit measures in an SEM analysis need to be even more cautiously interpreted. In SEM, the overall fit of a model to the data may appear acceptable, yet some relations in the model may not be supported by the data. For example, an acceptable fit index could be achieved because of the strong measurement model, even though the structural model is fairly weak. Alternatively, the structural model may be impressive but the measurement model may be quite weak, rendering the interpretation meaningless.

The results of the SEM applied to our example are as follows. The chi-square was statistically significant, presumably indicating an unacceptable fit between the proposed model and the observed data. But because the chi-square is sensitive to sample size and model complexity, we want to also use alternative fit measures to evaluate the plausibility of the proposed model. The CFI and the NFI yielded values of .983 and .962, respectively; this tends to support the model. The RMSEA was .063, indicating a good fit. Overall, we would judge the model to be a reasonably good fit to the data.

With the model appearing to represent a reasonably good fit, we can examine the path coefficients for the model. These are displayed in Figure 19a.2. All the measured variables correlated with their respective factors at a reasonably strong level. As we saw in the path analysis, neither **Academic Self-Doubt** nor **SES** were statistically significant predictors of **Academic Achievement**.

This study illustrates that even though the overall fit of a model to the data appears acceptable, some paths were not supported by the data. This acceptable fit was obtained simply because the paths in the measurement model had extremely high coefficients. To assess the accuracy of the prediction in the structural equations, we examine the proportion of variance accounted for as indexed by the R^2 values shown in rounded rectangles in the upper right area by the two endogenous variables. In this model, a weak effect size was reported for **Motivation** (.07), and a moderate effect size was found for **Academic Achievement** (.15). Is this a good model? It depends. If prior research reported greater explained variance for the endogenous variables, then this model may not contribute much to the literature. However, if the results of this model exceed what

Figure 19a.2 Results of Analyzing the Structural Model of Academic Achievement

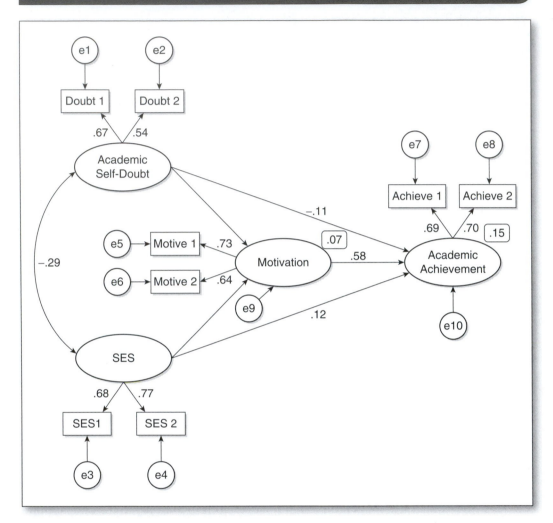

the research has thus far shown, then this model may make a positive contribution to the literature. Because results are often domain specific, it is difficult if not impossible to provide absolute standards of acceptable model fit (Jaccard & Choi, 1996) and to stipulate criterion values for size of effect.

19A.6 Recommended Readings

Anderson, J. C., & Gerbing, D. W. (1988). Structural equation modeling in practice: A review and recommended two-step approach. *Psychological Bulletin, 103,* 411–423.

Chambers, W. V. (2000). Causation and corresponding correlations. *Journal of Mind and Behavior, 21,* 437–460.

Cliff, N. (1983). Some cautions concerning the application of causal modeling methods. *Multivariate Behavioral Research, 18,* 81–105.

Duncan, O. D. (1966). Path analysis: Sociological examples. *American Journal of Sociology, 72,* 219–316.

Everitt, B. S. (1984). *An introduction to latent variable models.* New York, NY: Chapman & Hall.

Fan, X., Thompson, B., & Wang, L. (1999). Effects of sample size, estimation method, and model specification on structural equation modeling fit indexes. *Structural Equation Modeling, 6,* 56–83.

Green, S. B., Thompson, M. S., & Babyak, M. A. (1998). A Monte Carlo investigation of methods for controlling Type I errors with specification searches in structural equation modeling. *Multivariate Behavioral Research, 33,* 365–383.

Hoyle, R. H. (Ed.). (1995). *Structural equation modeling: Concepts, issues, and applications.* Thousand Oaks, CA: Sage.

Kaplan, D. (2000). *Structural equation modeling: Foundations and extensions.* Thousand Oaks, CA: Sage.

Kelloway, E. K. (1995). Structural equation modeling in perspective. *Journal of Organizational Behavior, 16,* 215–224.

Kelloway, E. K. (1998). *Using LISREL for structural equation modeling: A researcher's guide.* Thousand Oaks, CA: Sage.

Leidy, N. K. (1990). A structural model of stress, psychosocial resources, and symptomatic experience in chronic physical illness. *Nursing Research, 39,* 230–236.

Maassen, G. H., & Bakker, A. B. (2001). Suppressor variables in path models: Definitions and interpretations. *Sociological Methods & Research, 30,* 241–270.

Magura, S., & Rosenblum, A. (2000). Modulating effect of alcohol use on cocaine use. *Addictive Behaviors, 25,* 117–122.

Martens, M. P. (2005). The use of structural equation modeling in counseling psychology research. *The Counseling Psychologist, 33,* 269–298.

Martens, M. P., & Haase, R. F. (2006). Advanced applications of structural equation modeling in counseling psychology research. *The Counseling Psychologist, 34,* 878–911.

McDonald, R. P. (1996). Path analysis with composite variables. *Multivariate Behavioral Research, 31,* 239–270.

Mueller, R. O. (1997). Structural equation modeling: Back to basics. *Structural Equation Modeling, 4,* 353–369.

Rigdon, E. E. (1995). A necessary and sufficient identification rule for structural models estimated in practice. *Multivariate Behavioral Research, 30,* 359–383.

Tremblay, P. F., & Gardner, R. C. (1996). On the growth of structural equation modeling in psychological journals. *Structural Equation Modeling, 3,* 93–104.

Ullman, J. B. (2006). Structural equation modeling: Reviewing the basics and moving forward. *Journal of Personality Assessment, 87,* 35–50.

Weston, R., & Gore, P. A. (2006). A brief guide to structural equation modeling. *The Counseling Psychologist, 34,* 719–751.

Structural Equation Modeling Using Amos

19B.1 Overview

We have discussed confirmatory factor analysis models in Chapter 16A and structural path models in Chapter 18A. These two models can be combined together into more complex models known as structural equation models and analyzed through procedures known as SEM. One of the advantages of SEM is that latent variables are free of random error because, as we have seen, the error associated with the latent variables has been estimated and removed.

Using the language of SEM, structural equation models are composed of the following:

- *A measurement (confirmatory factor) model:* The measurement model assesses the relationships between the measured variables and their respective latent variables.
- *A structural (path) model:* The structural model assesses both the relationships among the hypothesized latent variables as well as the relationships between the measured variables and their respective latent variables.

Given that structural equation models are composed of both measurement and structural models, it follows that SEM is a two-stage analysis process in that we separately evaluate these two portions of the overall hypothesized model. The first portion of the model to be evaluated is the measurement model—the confirmatory factor analysis portion. It is common that two or more latent factors are included in the model, and it is also common that these two factors are not necessarily based on the same measurement operations (e.g., they may be measured on different scales from different inventories). If the measurement model has weaknesses, we would make what modifications were necessary (e.g., correlate error terms of indicator variables for a factor, remove an indicator if it was not strongly enough related to its factor, remove an entire factor if all else fails) to repair it. The strategy is to have a strong (or at least an acceptable) measurement model before evaluating the structural model because, without a strong measurement model, the latent variables would not have acceptable construct validity to use them in a path structure.

Once the measurement model is working well for us, we would proceed with the second stage of the analysis, which is to evaluate the structural model. The structural model is akin to path analysis, but instead of restricting ourselves to only measured variables, we include in the model latent variables as well or exclusively. The structural model is ultimately the primary focus of the research.

19B.2 The Example We Use

Assume that researchers are interested in understanding (predicting) academic success for students completing their first year in college. The researchers plan on using grade point average as the outcome variable as the proxy for academic success. Further assume that they wish to evaluate how various factors such as (a) encouragement from family and friends, (b) self-efficacy, (c) the characteristics of the college, and (d) the richness of college social life can affect academic success. The general roadmap (model) they put together is shown in Figure 19b.1. They hypothesize that encouragement and efficacy affect commitment and social life, which in turn affect academic performance. From

Figure 19b.1 The Hypothesized Model

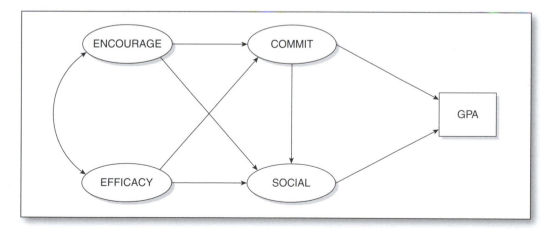

this beginning, the researchers assemble what indicator variables they need to configure the structural model.

19B.3 The Variables in Our Example Model

The data file we use for this example is named **academic performance**. The outcome variable is grade point average (named **GPA** in the data file) of students at the end of their first year of college, which is a measured variable in the data set. The latent variables in the structural model and their indicator (measured) variables are as follows:

- Encouragement from family and friends to attend a particular college. This is named **ENCOURAGE** in the model. The three indicators of **ENCOURAGE** are keyed to the people who offered the encouragement: parents of student (**parents**), role model (**role**), and relatives of student (**relatives**).
- A commitment to the college named **COMMIT**. The three indicators of **COMMIT** are keyed to different perceived attributes of the college: the reputation of the college (**reputation**), the special programs that are available in the college (**programs**), and the national ranking of the college (**ranking**).
- Academic self-efficacy, the belief that one can succeed in school; it is named **EFFICACY** in the model. The three indicators of **EFFICACY** are keyed to different kinds of abilities: belief in their writing ability (**writing**), belief in their intellect (**intellect**), and belief in their ability to succeed in college (**succeed**).
- Perceived social life that could be obtained at the college. This is named **SOCIAL**. The three indicators of **SOCIAL** are keyed to different perceived opportunities for social interaction: holding a student-elected office (**office**), joining a fraternity or sorority (**greek**), and joining school clubs (**clubs**).

19B.4 The Measurement Model

We show the measurement model in Figure 19b.2. Section 16B.3.1 discussed how to draw a diagram such as this. This is a setup for a confirmatory factor analysis. There are four factors each with three indicators. For each factor, we have constrained (initially set equal to 1) the path to its most strongly associated indicator variable: **parents** for **ENCOURAGE**, **reputation** for **COMMIT**, **writing** for **EFFICACY**, and **office** for **SOCIAL**.

We test the model as a whole, rather than deal with each factor separately, because they will all have to work together in the second stage of the analysis. This also allows us to assess collinearity, the correlation between the pairs of factors, to make sure that they are sufficiently independent of each other to function somewhat autonomously in the structural model. We have described this process in Section 16A.13 and refer readers to it if they need a refresher.

Figure 19b.2 The Measurement Model Showing the Four Factors and Their Indicators

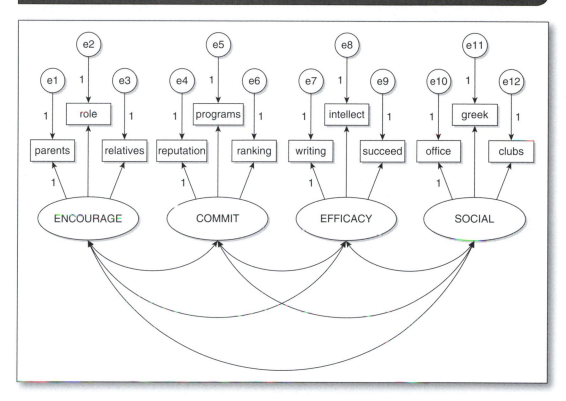

To perform the confirmatory factor analysis, select **View** ➜ **Analysis Properties**. In the **Analysis Properties** window, select the **Output** tab. Remove the check from **Minimization history** and check **Standardized estimates** and **Modification indices**. Select **Analyze** ➜ **Calculate Estimates**. Then select **File** ➜ **Save As** to save the data and output so that we can access the output.

19B.4.1 The Model Fit

Once the analysis has been performed, select **View** ➜ **Text Output**. Select **Model Fit Summary** in the **Text Output** menu as shown in Figure 19b.3. **CMIN** stands for minimum discrepancy as indexed by chi-square. The chi-square value is 75.03. With 48 degrees of freedom, it is statistically significant ($p = .008$). The GFI, NFI, and CFI were .982, .895, and .958, respectively. Based on the GFI and CFI, the model is an excellent fit; based on the NFI, the model demonstrates a less than adequate fit. The RMSEA was .028 with a 90% confidence interval of .015 to .040. Based on RMSEA, the fit would be judged as excellent. Overall, despite the results from the NFI, we would assess the model fit as excellent. Because of the quality of

Figure 19b.3 The Model Fit Summary

Model Fit Summary

CMIN

Model	NPAR	CMIN	DF	P	CMIN/DF
Default model	30	75.031	48	.008	1.563
Saturated model	78	.000	0		
Independence model	12	715.676	66	.000	10.844

RMR, GFI

Model	RMR	GFI	AGFI	PGFI
Default model	.021	.982	.971	.605
Saturated model	.000	1.000		
Independence model	.081	.833	.803	.705

Baseline Comparisons

Model	NFI Delta1	RFI rho1	IFI Delta2	TLI rho2	CFI
Default model	.895	.856	.960	.943	.958
Saturated model	1.000		1.000		1.000
Independence model	.000	.000	.000	.000	.000

RMSEA

Model	RMSEA	LO 90	HI 90	PCLOSE
Default model	.028	.015	.040	.999
Independence model	.119	.111	.127	.000

the fit, we would not examine the **Modification Indices** to see where we can improve the fit of the model. Thus, we quickly examine the coefficients and factor correlations but give the model a passing grade sufficient to be used in the full structural model in the next portion of our analysis.

19B.4.2 Coefficients

To obtain the coefficients that were estimated, select **Estimates** in the **Text Output** menu. We show the standardized regression weights in Figure 19b.4. These coefficients are all statistically significant ($p < .001$) and range from .30 (indicative of a modest strength) to .71 (indicative of substantial strength). We therefore conclude that the measured variables are all good indicators of their respective factors.

Figure 19b.4 The Standardized Regression Weights

Standardized Regression Weights: (Group number 1 - Default model)

			Estimate
parents	<---	ENCOURAGE	.702
role	<---	ENCOURAGE	.311
relatives	<---	ENCOURAGE	.501
reputation	<---	COMMIT	.568
programs	<---	COMMIT	.331
ranking	<---	COMMIT	.431
succeed	<---	EFFICACY	.685
intellect	<---	EFFICACY	.652
writing	<---	EFFICACY	.448
office	<---	SOCIAL	.712
greek	<---	SOCIAL	.302
clubs	<---	SOCIAL	.427

19B.4.3 Factor Correlations

The correlations between the pairs of factors are shown in Figure 19b.5. They range from .01 to .37, suggesting that collinearity is not an issue here. The measurement model with the parameters included is shown in Figure 19b.6.

Figure 19b.5 The Factor Correlations

Correlations: (Group number 1 - Default model)

			Estimate
ENCOURAGE	<-->	SOCIAL	-.014
ENCOURAGE	<-->	COMMIT	.282
COMMIT	<-->	SOCIAL	.269
EFFICACY	<-->	SOCIAL	.375
ENCOURAGE	<-->	EFFICACY	-.096
COMMIT	<-->	EFFICACY	.273

Figure 19b.6   The Measurement Model With Its Parameters

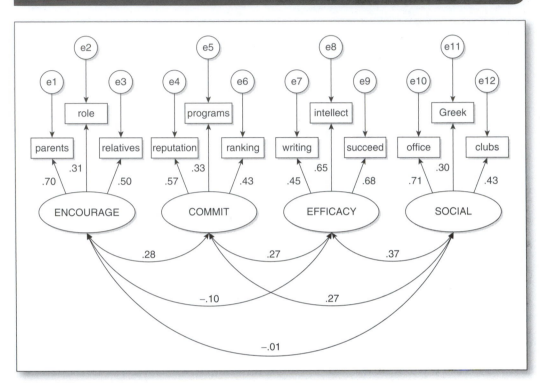

19B.5 The Variables Configured in the Full Structural Model

Figure 19b.7 shows the full structural model hypothesized by the researchers. This is the complete version of the idea presented in Figure 19b.1. We have discussed how to draw models in Chapters 16B and 17B and will not repeat that here. The full structural model includes (a) the paths relating the latent variables to each other, (b) the indicator variables associated with each latent construct (factor) with the strongest indicator for each constrained to 1 (see Section 19B.4), and (c) the correlation between the two exogenous latent constructs.

19B.6 Performing the Analysis

To perform the analysis, select **View ➔ Analysis Properties**. In the **Analysis Properties** window, select the **Output** tab as shown in Figure 19b.8. Remove the check from **Minimization history** and check **Standardized estimates**, **Squared multiple correlations**, and **Modification indices**. Select **Analyze ➔ Calculate Estimates**. Then select **File ➔ Save As** to save the data and output so that we can access the output.

Figure 19b.7 The Full Structural Model

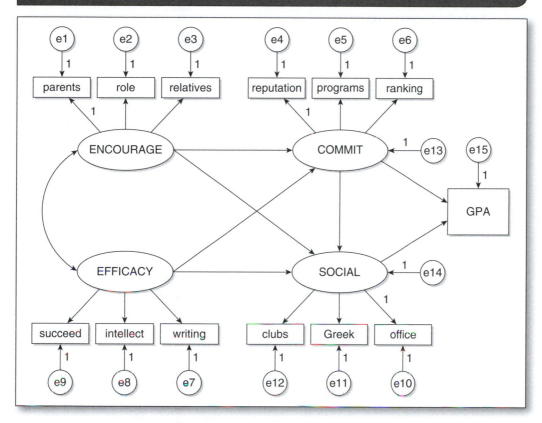

Figure 19b.8 The Analysis Properties Window

19B.7 Output for the Full Structural Model

19B.7.1 Model Identification

Once the analysis has been performed, select **View ➜ Text Output**. In the **Notes for Model** window shown in Figure 19b.9, we see that there are 91 known and 33 unknown elements. The number of known (nonredundant) elements in the model is equal to $V (V + 1)/2$, where V is the number of the measured variables in the study. There are 13 measured variables, and so we have $(13 * 14)/2$ or 91 known elements. These known elements are as follows:

- There are 13 variances, one for each measured variable.
- There are 78 [$(13 * 12)/2$] pairwise correlations for the 13 measured variables.

The 33 unknown elements (estimated parameters) in the model are as follows:

- There is one correlation coefficient between the two latent factors.
- We are also estimating a variance for each endogenous latent factor for a total of two parameters.
- We are estimating 15 path coefficients (there are 34, but 19 have already been constrained to unity).
- We are also estimating a variance for each error term for a total of 15 parameters.

The degrees of freedom of the model is computed as the number of known elements minus the number of estimated parameters. Here, these values are $91 - 33$ for a difference of 58. The degrees of freedom are positive, and thus the model is identified.

Figure 19b.9 Model Identification

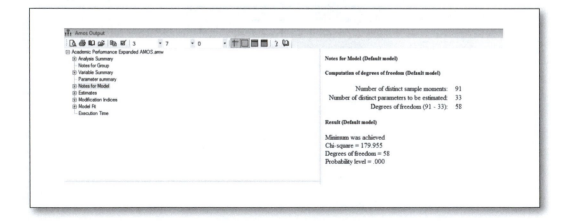

19B.7.2 Model Fit

Select **Model Fit** in the **Text Output** menu as shown in Figure 19b.10. The chi-square value is approximately 179.95. With 58 degrees of freedom, it is statistically significant ($p <$ .001). The GFI, NFI, and CFI were .961, .789, and .842, respectively. Based on these indexes, we would conclude that the model is not acceptable. The RMSEA was .055 with a 90% confidence interval of .046 to .064, suggesting an excellent fit. Generally, we are obtaining at best mixed messages and should not feel particularly comfortable with the model as formulated.

19B.7.3 Coefficients

To obtain the coefficients that were estimated, select **Estimates** in the **Text Output** menu. We show the unstandardized and standardized regression weights in Figure 19b.11. We focus on those coefficients failing to achieve statistical significance to generate ideas about what may be useful modifications to the model. There are three paths that might be dropped from the model: **COMMIT** to **SOCIAL, ENCOURAGE** to **SOCIAL**, and **COMMIT** to **GPA**.

Figure 19b.10 The Model Fit Output

Model Fit Summary

CMIN

Model	NPAR	CMIN	DF	P	CMIN/DF
Default model	33	179.955	58	.000	3.103
Saturated model	91	.000	0		
Independence model	13	852.291	78	.000	10.927

RMR, GFI

Model	RMR	GFI	AGFI	PGFI
Default model	.029	.961	.939	.613
Saturated model	.000	1.000		
Independence model	.080	.817	.787	.701

Baseline Comparisons

Model	NFI Delta1	RFI rho1	IFI Delta2	TLI rho2	CFI
Default model	.789	.716	.846	.788	.842
Saturated model	1.000		1.000		1.000
Independence model	.000	.000	.000	.000	.000

RMSEA

Model	RMSEA	LO 90	HI 90	PCLOSE
Default model	.055	.046	.064	.181
Independence model	.119	.112	.126	.000

Figure 19b.11 The Regression Coefficients

Regression Weights: (Group number 1 – Default model)

			Estimate	S.E.	C.R.	P	Label
COMMIT	<---	ENCOURAGE	.182	.053	3.463	***	
COMMIT	<---	EFFICACY	.249	.064	3.886	***	
SOCIAL	<---	EFFICACY	.576	.110	5.256	***	
SOCIAL	<---	ENCOURAGE	-.028	.067	-.416	.677	
SOCIAL	<---	COMMIT	.263	.147	1.787	.074	
parents	<---	ENCOURAGE	1.000				
role	<---	ENCOURAGE	.411	.089	4.611	***	
relatives	<---	ENCOURAGE	.644	.131	4.928	***	
reputation	<---	COMMIT	1.000				
programs	<---	COMMIT	.794	.175	4.535	***	
ranking	<---	COMMIT	.988	.204	4.850	***	
writing	<---	EFFICACY	1.000				
intellect	<---	EFFICACY	1.317	.158	8.351	***	
succeed	<---	EFFICACY	1.357	.165	8.208	***	
office	<---	SOCIAL	1.000				
greek	<---	SOCIAL	.631	.127	4.987	***	
clubs	<---	SOCIAL	1.389	.233	5.972	***	
GPA	<---	SOCIAL	.539	.115	4.689	***	
GPA	<---	COMMIT	.049	.151	.323	.747	

Standardized Regression Weights: (Group number 1 – Default model)

			Estimate
COMMIT	<---	ENCOURAGE	.311
COMMIT	<---	EFFICACY	.307
SOCIAL	<---	EFFICACY	.481
SOCIAL	<---	ENCOURAGE	-.033
SOCIAL	<---	COMMIT	.178
parents	<---	ENCOURAGE	.701
role	<---	ENCOURAGE	.311
relatives	<---	ENCOURAGE	.502
reputation	<---	COMMIT	.562
programs	<---	COMMIT	.333
ranking	<---	COMMIT	.434
writing	<---	EFFICACY	.441
intellect	<---	EFFICACY	.628
succeed	<---	EFFICACY	.714
office	<---	SOCIAL	.586
greek	<---	SOCIAL	.302
clubs	<---	SOCIAL	.417
GPA	<---	SOCIAL	.325
GPA	<---	COMMIT	.020

Before making this decision, we present the completed model in Figure 19b.12 and examine the **Modification Indices**.

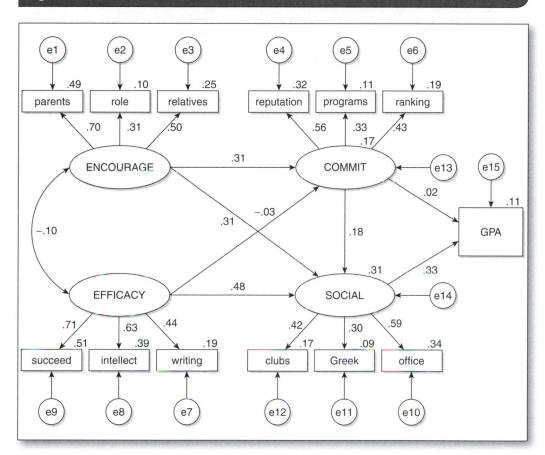

19B.7.4 Modification Indexes

The **Modification Indexes** are presented in Figure 19b.13. Based on the information in the tables, there appear to be three additions that may be added to the model making theoretical or real-world sense based on the judgment of the researchers. These are as follows:

- Correlate the error associated with **relatives** with the error associated with **reputation**. This makes sense in that relatives who encourage family members to attend a particular college may in part base their encouragement on the reputation of the school.

Figure 19b.13 The Modification Indexes

Modification Indices (Group number 1 - Default model)

Covariances: (Group number 1 - Default model)

			M.I.	Par Change
e15	<-->	EFFICACY	25.549	.061
e15	<-->	e14	15.869	-.063
e12	<-->	e15	7.416	-.103
e10	<-->	e15	7.542	-.052
e10	<-->	e12	5.445	.086
e9	<-->	e15	70.489	.137
e6	<-->	e14	4.933	.033
e6	<-->	e11	5.247	.051
e4	<-->	e14	5.369	-.027
e3	<-->	e13	5.585	.024
e3	<-->	e4	8.086	.033
e2	<-->	e14	6.457	.038
e2	<-->	e15	5.062	-.040
e2	<-->	e10	15.862	.070
e2	<-->	e5	6.437	.044
e1	<-->	e10	5.511	-.042
e1	<-->	e5	4.303	-.037

Regression Weights: (Group number 1 - Default model)

			M.I.	Par Change
GPA	<---	EFFICACY	26.727	.456
GPA	<---	clubs	5.577	-.043
GPA	<---	succeed	61.752	.301
GPA	<---	intellect	5.467	.081
GPA	<---	role	6.199	-.099
clubs	<---	GPA	6.274	-.182
office	<---	GPA	6.462	-.092
office	<---	clubs	4.202	.037
office	<---	role	13.300	.143
succeed	<---	GPA	60.696	.242
ranking	<---	greek	6.182	.067
programs	<---	role	4.349	.081
reputation	<---	relatives	6.719	.075
relatives	<---	COMMIT	5.678	.263
relatives	<---	reputation	8.992	.130
role	<---	SOCIAL	5.015	.170
role	<---	office	14.391	.125
role	<---	programs	6.360	.088
parents	<---	COMMIT	4.135	-.243
parents	<---	office	6.264	-.084
parents	<---	programs	5.627	-.084

- Correlate the error associated with **role** with the error associated with **programs**. This makes sense in that role models of students who might encourage them to attend a particular college may in part base their encouragement on the existence of special programs in the school.

- Correlate the error associated with **writing** with the error associated with **intellect**. This makes sense in that students with presumed higher intelligence should be able to produce higher quality research papers and compositions (a presumption or at least a fervent hope held by most university professors).

- Add a path from **EFFICACY** to **GPA**. This makes sense in that students who have greater self-efficacy may perform well in academics.

19B.8 Respecification of the Model

In respecifying the model, we will add the three correlations and the path from **EFFICACY** to **GPA**. We will delete the paths **ENCOURAGE** to **SOCIAL** and **COMMIT** to **GPA** but will retain the path **COMMIT** to **SOCIAL** because it might have an indirect effect on **GPA** via **SOCIAL**. The respecified model is shown in Figure 19b.14. Select **Analyze** ➔

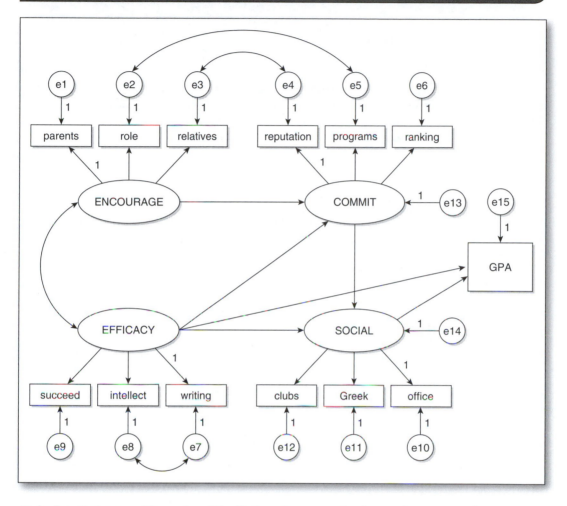

Figure 19b.14 The Respecified Model

Calculate Estimates. Then select **File ➜ Save As** to save the data and output so that we can access the output.

19B.9 Output for the Full Respecified Structural Model

19B.9.1 Model Fit

Once the analysis has been performed, select **View ➜ Text Output**. Select **Model Fit** in the **Text Output** menu as shown in Figure 19b.15. The chi-square value is 83.129. With 56 degrees of freedom, it is statistically significant ($p = .011$). The GFI, NFI, and CFI were .982,

Figure 19b.15 The Model Fit Indexes

Model Fit Summary

CMIN

Model	NPAR	CMIN	DF	P	CMIN/DF
Default model	35	83.129	56	.011	1.484
Saturated model	91	.000	0		
Independence model	13	852.291	78	.000	10.927

RMR, GFI

Model	RMR	GFI	AGFI	PGFI
Default model	.022	.982	.970	.604
Saturated model	.000	1.000		
Independence model	.080	.817	.787	.701

Baseline Comparisons

Model	NFI Delta1	RFI rho1	IFI Delta2	TLI rho2	CFI
Default model	.902	.864	.966	.951	.965
Saturated model	1.000		1.000		1.000
Independence model	.000	.000	.000	.000	.000

RMSEA

Model	RMSEA	LO 90	HI 90	PCLOSE
Default model	.026	.013	.038	1.000
Independence model	.119	.112	.126	.000

.902, and .965, respectively. Based on these indexes, we would conclude that the model is an excellent fit to the data. The RMSEA was .026 with a 90% confidence interval of .013 to .038, suggesting an excellent fit. Generally, we have a great fitting model.

19B.9.2 Coefficients

To obtain the coefficients that were estimated, select **Estimates** in the **Text Output** menu. We show the unstandardized and standardized regression weights in Figure 19b.16. All but **SOCIAL** to **GPA** achieved statistical significance.

Figure 19b.16 The Coefficients

Maximum Likelihood Estimates

Regression Weights: (Group number 1 - Default model)

			Estimate	S.E.	C.R.	P	Label
COMMIT	<---	ENCOURAGE	.119	.046	2.580	.010	
COMMIT	<---	EFFICACY	.238	.073	3.271	.001	
SOCIAL	<---	EFFICACY	.490	.124	3.943	***	
SOCIAL	<---	COMMIT	.380	.153	2.483	.013	
parents	<---	ENCOURAGE	1.000				
role	<---	ENCOURAGE	.390	.094	4.161	***	
relatives	<---	ENCOURAGE	.557	.129	4.312	***	
reputation	<---	COMMIT	1.000				
programs	<---	COMMIT	.842	.193	4.362	***	
ranking	<---	COMMIT	1.042	.231	4.503	***	
writing	<---	EFFICACY	1.000				
intellect	<---	EFFICACY	1.387	.178	7.795	***	
succeed	<---	EFFICACY	2.183	.343	6.367	***	
office	<---	SOCIAL	1.000				
greek	<---	SOCIAL	.539	.119	4.536	***	
clubs	<---	SOCIAL	1.170	.237	4.932	***	
GPA	<---	SOCIAL	.067	.071	.937	.349	
GPA	<---	EFFICACY	1.107	.169	6.552	***	

Standardized Regression Weights: (Group number 1 - Default model)

			Estimate
COMMIT	<---	ENCOURAGE	.226
COMMIT	<---	EFFICACY	.235
SOCIAL	<---	EFFICACY	.261
SOCIAL	<---	COMMIT	.205
parents	<---	ENCOURAGE	.748
role	<---	ENCOURAGE	.314
relatives	<---	ENCOURAGE	.464
reputation	<---	COMMIT	.541
programs	<---	COMMIT	.339
ranking	<---	COMMIT	.441
writing	<---	EFFICACY	.340
intellect	<---	EFFICACY	.510
succeed	<---	EFFICACY	.885
office	<---	SOCIAL	.707
greek	<---	SOCIAL	.311
clubs	<---	SOCIAL	.424
GPA	<---	SOCIAL	.049
GPA	<---	EFFICACY	.430

19B.9.3 The Respecified Model

The respecified structural model with all of the coefficients is shown in Figure 19b.17. The model is explaining 20% of the variance of **GPA**. This appears to be driven almost exclusively by **Efficacy**, with no mediating effect of **Social.**

Figure 19b.17 The Respecified Model and Its Coefficients

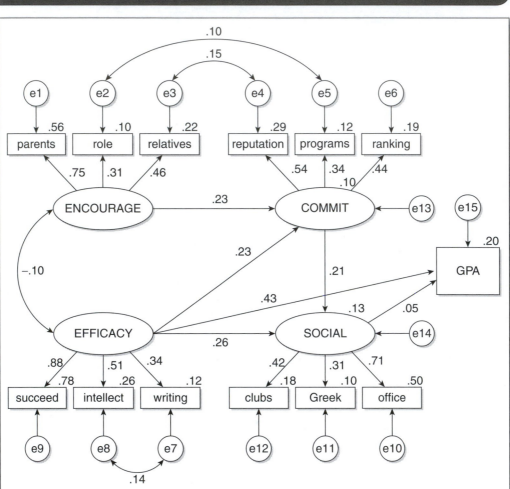

19B.10 Reporting SEM Analysis Results

The present structural model, shown schematically in Figure 19b.7, assessed the direct and indirect effects of four latent predictors on grade point average (GPA) of students after their first year of college. The model consisted of the following three structural equations (submodels). First, it was predicted that the social life of the students during the first year (Social) would affect GPA directly and that the commitment of the students to the college (Commit) would affect GPA directly as well as indirectly through Social. Second, it was predicted that both social support received by the students (Encourage) and self-efficacy (Efficacy) would have a direct effect on Social as well as both having an indirect affect via Commit. Third, it was predicted that Encourage and Efficacy would directly influence Commit. In addition, it was also hypothesized that the exogenous variables of Encourage and Efficacy would be positively correlated.

Each latent variable was measured with three indicator variables as illustrated in the measurement model in Figure 19b.2. The indicators of Encourage were represented by the people who offered the encouragement: parents of student (parents), role model (role), and relatives of student (relatives). The indicators of Efficacy were keyed to different kinds of abilities: belief in their ability to succeed in college (succeed), belief in their intellect (intellect), and belief in their writing ability (writing). The indicators of Commit were related to different perceived attributes of the college: the reputation of the college (reputation), the special programs that are available in the college (programs), and the national ranking of the college (ranking). Finally, the indicators of Social were tied to different perceived opportunities for social interaction: holding a student-elected office (office), joining a fraternity or sorority (Greek), and joining school clubs (clubs).

A two-step structural equation modeling strategy using IBM SPSS Amos 19 (Arbuckle, 2010) was used; a full-information maximum likelihood procedure was employed in estimating the parameters. This strategy involves the separate estimation of the measurement model prior to the simultaneous estimation of the measurement and three structural submodels. Although the measurement model provides an assessment of convergent validity and discriminant validity of the latent factors, the measurement model in conjunction with the structural model enables a comprehensive assessment of the full latent model.

Five criteria were employed to assess the measurement model. The chi-square test was statistically significant, $\chi^2(48, N = 700) = 75.03$, $p = .008$, suggesting that the model failed to fit the data. However, the significance of the chi-square may be caused by the large sample size in this study. Although the normed fit index (NFI) was marginal at a value of .89, the other fit measures suggested an excellent model fit to the data. The goodness-of-fit index (GFI) and the comparative fit index (CFI) were .98 and .96, respectively. The root mean square error of approximation (RMSEA) was .028 with a 90% confidence interval of .015 to .040. All coefficients achieved both statistical significance ($p < .05$) as well as practical significance (with values $\geq .30$). Thus, no modifications were conducted to improve the measurement model. Last, the correlations among the factors ranged from -.01 to .37, indicating that there is sufficient discriminant validity among the latent constructs for us to proceed (e.g., Bollen, 1989; Kline, 2011).

The second step in this two-step strategy simultaneously evaluated the coefficients of the measurement and structural submodels. All coefficients and the correlation between the exogenous variables of Encourage and Efficacy in the full structural model are presented in Figure 19b.12. The overall results suggest an unacceptable fit with a statistically significant, $\chi^2(58, N = 700) = 179.09$, $p < .001$, and GFI, NFI, and CFI of .96, .79, and .84, respectively. However, The RMSEA was .055 with a 90% confidence interval of .046 to .064, indicating an excellent fit. A total of 11% of the variance of GPA was explained by the model. Three paths failed to achieve statistical and practical significance: (a) Commit to GPA, (b) Encourage to Social, and (c) Commit to Social. The results suggest that respecifying the model may provide a better fit with the data.

In the respecified model, the paths from Commit to GPA and Encourage to Social were deleted. The path from Commit to Social was retained because both the p value (.079) and path coefficient (.18) were marginal and because of the importance of maintaining an indirect path to GPA. Based on the modification indexes, four additional parameters were imposed: (a) A correlation between the errors associated with relatives and reputation was added in that relatives who encourage family members to attend a particular college may in part base their encouragement on the reputation of the school, (b) a correlation between the errors associated with role and programs was added in that role models of students who might encourage them to attend a particular college may in part base their encouragement on the existence of special programs in the school, (c) a correlation between the error associated with writing with the error associated with intellect; and (d) a path from Efficacy to GPA was added in that students who have greater self-efficacy may very well perform well in academics. The respecified model is shown in Figure 19b.14.

Results of the respecified model reported a significant improvement over the initial model. Although significant, the $\chi^2(56, N = 700) = 83.13$, $p = .011$, was statistically significantly reduced, indicating a closer fit between the data and the model. The GFI, NFI, and CFI were .98, .90, and .96, respectively. The RMSEA was .026 with a 90% confidence interval of .013 to .038. All of these fit indexes indicate an excellent model fit with the data, with the model now explaining 20% of the variance of GPA. The respecified structural model with its parameters is shown in Figure 19b.17.

Results of the analysis indicated partial support of the model. Generally, GPA was driven by the direct effect of Efficacy; all indirect effects on GPA from Efficacy, Encourage, and Commit mediated by Social were not supported.

Model Invariance: Applying a Model to Different Groups

20A.1 Overview

In the previous chapters on confirmatory factor analysis, path analysis, and SEM, the models were analyzed with respect to a single sample or group, but it is possible to extend the reach of the analysis to situations where researchers may wish to determine if the model is equivalent for or applicable to two or more groups. The groups could represent different genders, different ethnic/racial identities, different ages, different sets of cohorts, different hospital or medical systems, and so on. When we examine such model differences across groups, we are determining if the model demonstrates the property of *invariance*—that is, if the model was as good a fit for the data of one group as it was for another. The dimensions along which we might want to evaluate such group differences include the following:

- We can assess for group invariance across the items of a factor structure. For this confirmatory factor analysis application, researchers are interested in determining if the items of an instrument bear similar relationships with their factors across different groups. If invariance is not obtained among the item pattern coefficients (that is, if the model is *noninvariant*), then the meaning of the factors is not consistent for the groups (this is known as *interpretational confounding*). For example, if a work satisfaction factor is measured by task, social, and financial indicators, then a high value of the pattern coefficient for the financial variable for one group would suggest that satisfaction might be related to their salary, but a high value of the pattern coefficient for the social variable for another group would suggest that for them, deriving satisfaction from their work primarily involves interpersonal interaction.

- We could assess for group invariance across structural models. For this application, researchers want to determine if the individual paths in a structural model are equivalent across different groups or if the path coefficients vary between groups.

20A.2 The General Strategy Used to Compare Groups

The procedure for comparing two or more groups to determine if a common model can be used to fit the data was initially developed by Jöreskog (1971). It involves, at a global level, two phases in the analysis that are somewhat analogous to what we use in ANOVA. In the first phase, we perform what amounts to an omnibus comparison to determine if there is an overall difference between the groups. This is assessed by a chi-square goodness-of-fit difference test that compares two different models. If the chi-square is statistically significant, we judge that a difference between the groups appears to exist, which permits us to engage in the second phase of the analysis. This second phase is analogous to the post hoc tests or tests of simple effects in ANOVA. Here, we determine which of the paths are associated with coefficients that differ from group to group.

20A.3 The Omnibus Model Comparison Phase

20A.3.1 The Two Models Being Compared

It is important here to understand the nature of the comparisons that IBM SPSS Amos presents to us. Let's start with what they are not. The comparisons are not a direct comparison of parameters for one group with the corresponding parameters of the other. The comparison made by IBM SPSS Amos is somewhat more indirect. The software sets up two models, and it is these two models that are compared against the data. The two models being compared are as follows:

- *The unconstrained model:* This model assumes that the groups are yielding different values of the parameters when the model is applied to the data (e.g., one or more pattern coefficients for the groups may be significantly different).
- *The constrained model:* This model assumes that the groups are yielding equivalent values of the parameters when the model is applied to the data (e.g., the pattern coefficients for the groups are not significantly different).

There are two possible outcomes resulting from this comparison that are best articulated when we consider the "objective reality" of the situation:

- *Reality Scenario A:* The two groups have significantly different values for their respective parameters. In the output, it will be found that the unconstrained and constrained models are significantly different from each other. This will be the case because the presumptions made by the unconstrained and constrained models regarding the values of the parameters are incompatible with (different from) each other. A statistically significant chi-square value reflects this incompatibility (difference).

- *Reality Scenario B:* The two groups have comparable values for their respective parameters. In the output, it will be found that the unconstrained and constrained models are not significantly different from each other. This will be the case because the presumptions of the unconstrained model (that the parameters of the groups are different) are not supported.

20A.3.2 The Unconstrained Model

We use just two groups (women and men) to keep the following discussion as simple as possible; readers should note that more than two groups may be involved in some research studies. One part of the omnibus model comparison concerns the unconstrained model. In constructing the unconstrained model, IBM SPSS Amos simultaneously estimates the parameters (e.g., the pattern coefficients in the case of confirmatory factor analysis and the path coefficients in the case of path analysis and SEM) for each group separately. At the end of this process, we have two sets of parameters, one for each group. These pairs of different parameters represent the unconstrained model. Note that there are two possible outcomes:

- The values of the corresponding parameter estimates may be extremely similar to each other.
- One or more of the values of the corresponding parameter estimates may be quite different from each other.

20A.3.3 The Constrained Model

A second part of the omnibus model comparison process creates a "null" or constrained model in which the corresponding parameters for the two groups are presumed to be equal. This presumption is the constraint that is superimposed on the model. The model then estimates all parameters simultaneously under this constraint. Under this null model, these two sets of parameters are presumed to be equal, and the statistical algorithm will make every effort to get the two values as close as it can. At the same time, however, it is estimating the parameters for the separate groups. At the end of this process, we have a null model with parameters for each group under the constraint that each pair of parameters is supposed to be the same.

20A.3.4 Chi-Square Difference Test

In a third part of the omnibus model comparison process, we obtain a chi-square difference test to determine if there is a significant difference between the fit measures for the two models. IBM SPSS Amos compares the two chi-square values—the one for the unconstrained model and the one for the constrained model—by using a chi-square difference test on these values.

If this chi-square difference test is not statistically significant, we conclude that the same model can be applied to both groups (i.e., the groups are invariant). This situation will arise when the corresponding parameter estimates are comparable. We interpret this lack of statistical significance to indicate that the same model is applicable to all of the groups—that is, we infer that the model is invariant across the groups in the analysis.

If the chi-square is statistically significant, we conclude that there are differences between the two groups (i.e., the groups are noninvariant) on at least one of the pairs of corresponding parameter estimates. To determine which corresponding parameters differ between the groups, we would next conduct the second stage of the comparison process.

20A.3.5 The Parameters That Are Compared

In the process of comparing the unconstrained and constrained models, there are several parameters that IBM SPSS Amos involves in the comparison. Our primary interest is usually in the following:

- The correlations between variables (**Structural covariances**), which in the context of confirmatory factor analysis are the factor correlations, and in the context of path analysis and SEM are the correlations of the exogenous variables
- The pattern coefficients (**Measurement weights**) in confirmatory factor analysis
- The path coefficients (**Structural weights**) in path analysis and SEM

IBM SPSS Amos also compares confirmatory factor models on the variance of the error terms (**Measurement residuals**). For path analysis and SEM, there are other parameters that are used as the basis of comparison but that are not of interest to us for the purposes of this chapter; these other parameters are as follows:

- The intercepts (structural intercepts)
- The means of the observed variables in path and the means of the latent variables in SEM (structural means)
- The variances of the error terms associated with the indicator variables of the latent factors and the endogenous observed variables (structural residuals)

20A.4 The Coefficient Comparison Phase

If the constrained and unconstrained models are different as indexed by a statistically significant chi-square value, then we hold that the model is noninvariant. Thus, one or more sets of corresponding parameters are of significantly different magnitudes, and our job is to locate where those differences lie. To reach this goal, we examine each pair of parameters that have been estimated. IBM SPSS Amos provides a pairwise comparison table in its output, showing *z* values that can be used as the basis for the comparison. At the end of this phase, we can see where the two models differ. Examination of the similarities and differences between the two models would then be related back to the theoretical framework from which the general model was drawn.

20A.5 Recommended Readings

Byrne, B. M., & Shavelson, R. J. (1987). Adolescent self-concept: Testing the assumption of equivalent structure across gender. *American Educational Research Association, 24,* 365–385.

Chen, F. F., Sousa, K. H., & West, S. G. (2005). Testing measurement invariance of second-order factor models. *Structural Equation Modeling, 12,* 471–492.

Cheung, G. W., & Rensvold, R. B. (1999). Testing factorial invariance across groups: A reconceptualization and proposed new method. *Journal of Management, 25,* 1–27.

Gregorich, S. E. (2006). Do self-report instruments allow meaningful comparisons across diverse population groups? Testing measurement invariance using the confirmatory factor analysis framework. *Medical Care, 44*(11 Suppl. 3), S78–S94.

Hofer, S. M., Horn, J. L., & Eber, H. W. (1997). A robust five-factor structure of the 16PF: Evidence from independent rotation and confirmatory factorial invariance procedures. *Personality and Individual Differences, 23,* 247–269.

Horn, J. L., & McArdle, J. J. (1992). A practical and theoretical guide to measurement invariance in aging research. *Experimental Aging Research, 18,* 117–144.

Kline, R. B. (2011). *Principles and practice of structural equation modeling* (3rd ed.). New York, NY: Guilford Press.

Lievens, F., & Anseel, F. (2004). Confirmatory factor analysis and invariance of an organizational citizenship behaviour measure across samples in a Dutch-speaking context. *Journal of Occupational and Organizational Psychology, 77,* 299–306.

MacCallum, R. C., Wegener, D. T., Uchino, B. N., & Fabrigar, L. R. (1993). The problem of equivalent models in applications of covariance structure analysis. *Psychological Bulletin, 114,* 185–199.

Meredith, W. (1993). Measurement invariance, factor analysis and factorial invariance. *Psychometrika, 58,* 525–543.

Meredith, W., & Horn, J. L. (2001). The role of factorial invariance in modeling growth and change. In L. M. Collins & A. G. Sayer (Eds.), *New methods for the analysis of change* (pp. 204–240). Washington, DC: American Psychological Association.

Reise, S. P., Widaman, K. F., & Pugh, R. H. (1993). Confirmatory factor analysis and item response theory: Two approaches for exploring measurement invariance. *Psychological Bulletin, 114,* 552–566.

Steenkamp, J.-B. E. M., & Baumgartner, H. (1998). Assessing measurement invariance in cross-national consumer research. *Journal of Consumer Research, 25,* 78–90.

Stein, J. A., Lee, J. W., & Jones, P. S. (2006). Assessing cross-cultural differences through use of multiple-group invariance analyses. *Journal of Personality Assessment, 87,* 249–258.

Vandenberg, R. J., & Lance, C. E. (2000). A review and synthesis of the measurement invariance literature: Suggestions, practices, and recommendations for organizational research. *Organizational Research Methods, 3,* 4–69.

CHAPTER **20B**

Assessing Model Invariance Using Amos

20B.1 Overview

Model invariance represents the situation in which a model can be said to apply equally well to the data obtained from two or more different groups. To the extent that this state of affairs is true, the model may be said to be invariant across the groups. We apply this invariance assessment to two types of models: confirmatory factor analysis and path analysis.

20B.2 Confirmatory Factor Analysis

20B.2.1 Numerical Example

The fictional data set used for this example is called **Cross Cultural Intelligence**. A set of researchers have hypothesized that vocabulary (**vocab**), general information (**info**), and reading comprehension (**comp**) were indicators of verbal ability and that reproducing patterns of designs of blocks (**block**), solving matrix reasoning problems (**matrix**), and identifying the missing parts of pictures (**picmiss**) were indicators of perceptual reasoning. They administered the testing battery to a sample of adults in the United States and administered a translated version of the test battery to a sample of adults in Japan. In the data file, U.S. test takers were coded as **0** and Japanese test takers were coded as **1** under the variable name **country**. This data set has a sample size of 185, which is a bit small but will serve to illustrate how to perform the confirmatory factor analysis invariance analysis.

Figure 20b.1 Hypothesized Two-Factor Model

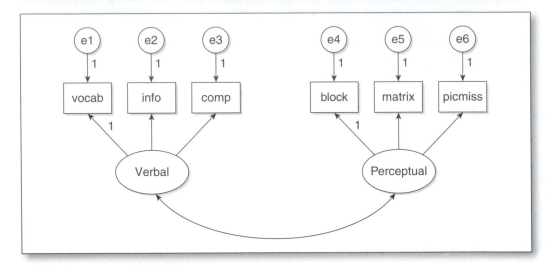

20B.2.2 Drawing the Model

To specify a model is to create a structural representation of the hypothesized relationships. Open the data file, and from the main IBM SPSS menu select **Analyze ➜ Amos** to bring us to the graphics window. Draw the model as shown in Figure 20b.1.

20B.2.3 Identifying the Two Groups

From the main IBM SPSS Amos menu, select **Analyze ➜ Manage Groups**. In the **Manage Groups** dialog window, the default expression **Group number 1** is shown (see Figure 20b.2). Highlight the expression and replace with **U.S.** (see Figure 20.3). Click the

Figure 20b.2 Initial Manage Groups Dialog Window

Figure 20b.3 Manage Groups Dialog Window With the U.S. Group Defined

Figure 20b.4 The Model With the Group Names Included

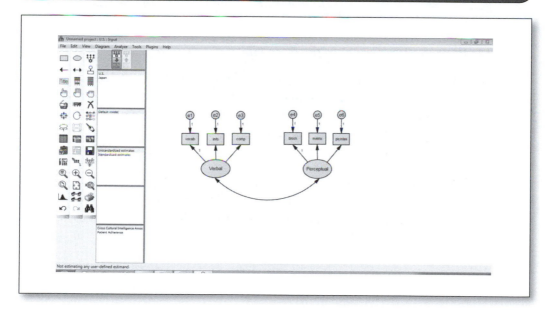

New pushbutton. We will see the expression **Group number 2**; replace that with **Japan**. Click the **Close** pushbutton. The two group names that we just defined appear in the top panel (if the cursor is moved to one of the names, the label for that panel of **Groups** will appear) to the left of the drawing area as shown in Figure 20b.4.

Figure 20b.5 The Initial Data Files Window

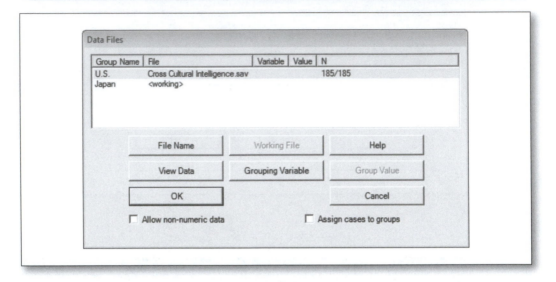

20B.2.4 Linking the Two Groups to the Data File

Having identified the names of the groups that will appear in the analysis, we now need to link these names to the **country** variable in the data file and to the values (codes) for **country**. We accomplish this by selecting **File ➜ Data Files**. Depending on your configuration (operating system, Amos embedded in IBM SPSS or installed freestanding), we achieve the next goal in one of two ways:

- If the name of the data file appears under **File** with the first group (see Figure 20b.5), then just highlight **U.S.** and select the **Grouping Variable** pushbutton (see below).
- If the label <working> is associated with both groups, then it is necessary to highlight **U.S.** and select the **File Name** pushbutton. The name of the data file (in our case **Cross Cultural Intelligence**) will appear (potentially among several others); select the appropriate data file name by double-clicking it. The **Data Files** window will now show the data file name. Then highlight **Japan** and repeat the process. The result of all this work is shown in Figure 20b.6.

This effort that we just expended was to identify the location of the data for each group. It may seem odd to some readers as both groups are "housed" in our single data file named **Cross Cultural Intelligence**. But there is good reason that we went through this process. It is very possible that in many research projects, the data for each group will be contained in

Figure 20b.6   The Data Files Window After Linking the Groups to Their Data File

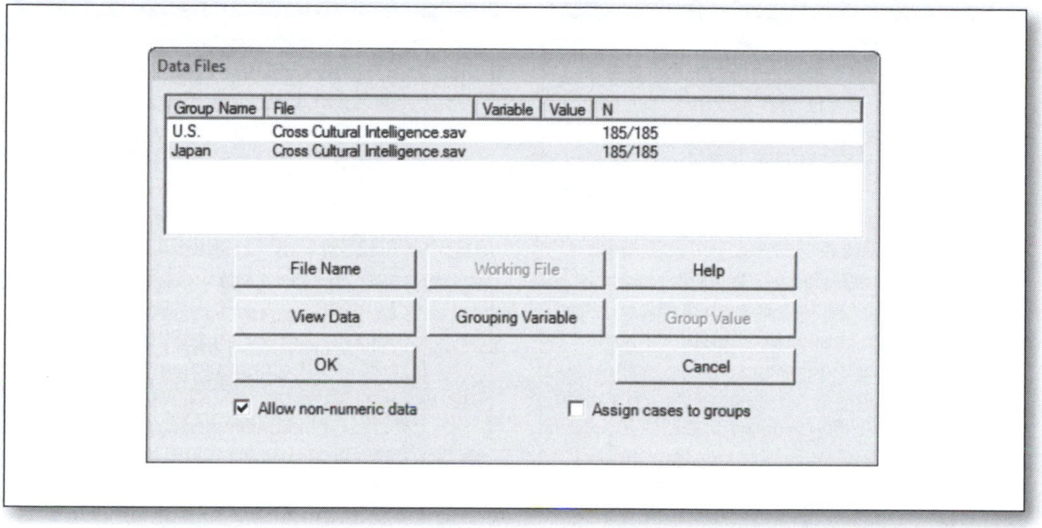

separate data files. It is a tribute to the power of IBM SPSS Amos that the software is capable of evaluating the invariance of a model based on groups located in different data sets. The only restriction is that the variables in each data file that are a part of the model must be exactly the same (e.g., if we propose that **vocab**, **info**, and **comp** are indicators of verbal ability for both Group 1 and Group 2, then the variables **vocab**, **info**, and **comp** must be contained in each data file).

Once the data files are identified, and with **Japan** still highlighted, select the **Grouping Variable** pushbutton. This opens the **Choose a Grouping Variable** window. Highlight **country** (see Figure 20b.7) and click **OK**. At this point, the **Group Value** pushbutton in the **Data Files** window is active. Selecting **Group Values** opens the **Choose Value for Group** window, which displays the value codes and the number of cases for each code. Choose the value code of **1** (because **Japan** was originally highlighted) as shown in Figure 20b.8. Click **OK**. This will return us to the **Data Files** window where we will see the code value and the sample size in the panel. Repeat this process for **U.S.**, the results of which are shown in Figure 20b.9. This completes the linkage of the groups to the data file(s).

20B.2.5 Specifying the Output

To specify what elements we wish to obtain in the output, select **View ➔ Analysis Properties**. In the **Analysis Properties** window, select the **Output** tab as shown in Figure 20b.10.

Figure 20b.7 The Choose a Grouping Variable With Country Variable Highlighted

Figure 20b.8 The Choose Value for Group Window

Figure 20b.9 The Final Configured Data Files Window

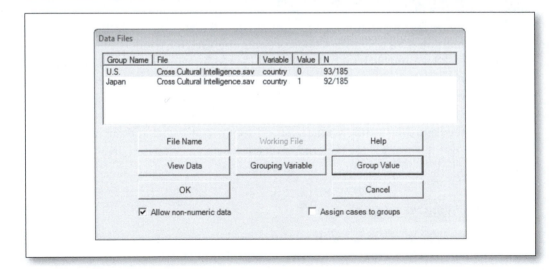

Figure 20b.10   Specifying the Output in the Analysis Properties Dialog Window

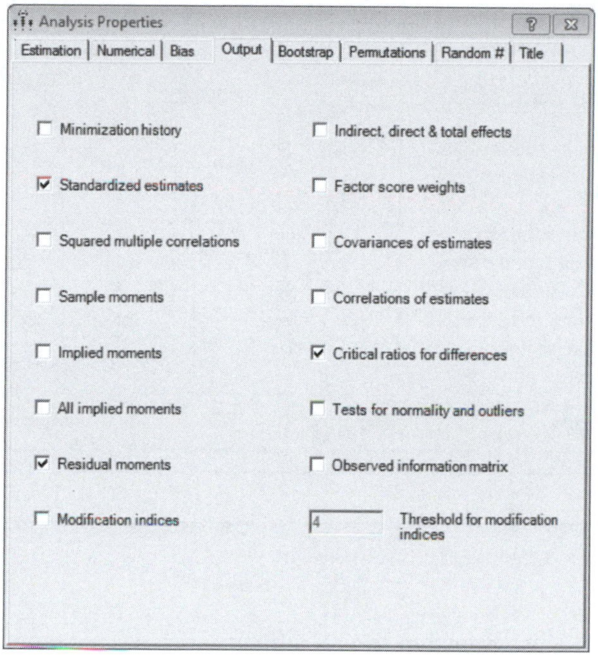

Remove the check from **Minimization history** and check **Standardized estimates**, **Residual moments**, and **Critical ratios for differences**. The **Standardized estimates** provides the pattern coefficients, the **Residual moments** addresses significant differences between the error terms (residuals) for the two groups, and the **Critical ratios for differences** addresses significant differences between the pattern coefficients associated with the respective paths. After specifying this information, just close the window.

20B.2.6 Specifying the Elements of Invariance

After making all of our specifications, select **Analyze** ➜ **Multiple-Group Analysis**. At that point, IBM SPSS Amos may display an error message that can be ignored. Click **OK** on that message, and the **Multiple-Group Analysis** window will appear as shown in Figure 20b.11. It is in this window that the main thrust of the invariance analysis—the comparison of the unconstrained and constrained models—is configured.

Figure 20b.11   The Default Choices in the Multiple-Group Analysis Window

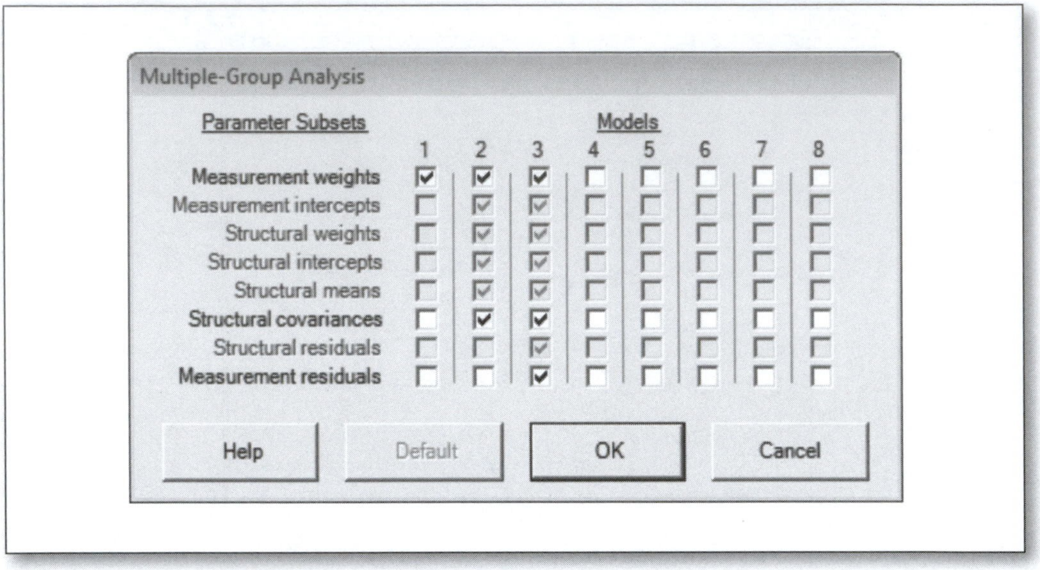

The comparison is performed in several different ways, each configured in the columns labeled by numbers. These numbers represent different bases on which the models will be contrasted, allowing researchers to successively include additional components in the comparisons.

In the default setup that we will use, IBM SPSS Amos compares the groups in three different ways. The first basis of comparison is specified in the column numbered **1**. Note that the only option that is checked is **Measurement weights**. These measurement weights refer to the pattern coefficients tying the measured or indicator variables to their respective factors and will be the only basis of comparison of the models.

The second basis of comparison is specified in the column numbered **2**. Note that both **Measurement weights** and **Structural covariances** are checked. **Structural covariances** refers to both the variances of the factors and the correlation between the two factors (the variance and covariance of the factors). In this comparison, the two models will be compared on the combination of **Measurement weights** and **Structural covariances**.

The third basis of comparison is specified in the column numbered **3**. Note that **Measurement weights**, **Structural covariances**, and **Measurement residuals** are checked. **Measurement residuals** refer to the variances of the errors. In this comparison, the two models will be compared on the combination of **Measurement weights**, **Structural covariances**, and **Measurement residuals**. Click **OK**.

Figure 20b.12 Parameter Labels Are Given

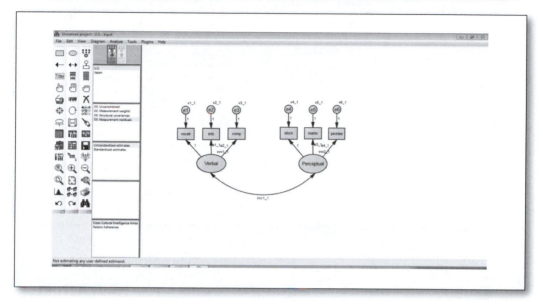

20B.2.7 Obtaining the Parameter Labels

Once we have configured our comparisons, IBM SPSS Amos will supply labels in the path diagram for the parameters. We show this in Figure 20b.12. The rubric for assigning labels is as follows:

- Paths from the observed variables to the factors are labeled as **a**. These are represented by pattern coefficients. We asked for these to be compared when we had checked **Measurement weights**.
- Variances of the factors are labeled as **vvv**. We asked for these to be compared when we had checked **Structural covariances**.
- The correlation of the factors are labeled as **ccc**. We asked for these to be compared when we had checked **Structural covariances**.
- Variances of the errors are labeled as **v**. We asked for these to be compared when we had checked **Measurement residuals**.

20B.2.8 Performing the Analysis

From the main IBM SPSS Amos menu, select **Analyze ➜ Calculate Estimates**. To address the primary interest of our analysis—whether or not the two models are equivalent—select **View ➜ Text Output**. This produces the **Amos Output** screen (see Figure 20b.13). Go directly to **Model Comparison**, shown in Figure 20b.14.

Figure 20b.13 The Initial Amos Output

Figure 20b.14 The Model Comparison Output

Nested Model Comparisons

Assuming model Unconstrained to be correct:

Model	DF	CMIN	P	NFI Delta-1	IFI Delta-2	RFI rho-1	TLI rho2
Measurement weights	4	1.184	.881	.003	.003	-.016	-.017
Structural covariances	7	4.654	.702	.010	.011	-.016	-.018
Measurement residuals	13	10.003	.694	.023	.023	-.021	-.022

The table in Figure 20b.14 presents the key results for us. It displays the comparison of the unconstrained and constrained models as we have specified our comparisons. The first row focuses only on comparing the **Measurement weights** of the groups, the second row focuses on comparing the **Measurement weights** and **Structural covariances** of the groups, and the third row focuses on comparing the **Measurement weights**, **Structural covariances**, and **Measurement residuals** of the groups

Model differences are evaluated with a chi-square test (**CMIN** in the second numerical column). For the comparison involving only the pattern coefficients, labeled as **Measurement weights** in the table, the chi-square value was 1.184. With 4 degrees of freedom (there are six indicator variables, but two—one for each factor—are constrained to 1 so that only four are free to vary), the chi-square is not statistically significant (the **P** value—the probability of the value occurring by chance if the null hypothesis is true—is .881). We therefore conclude that the unconstrained and constrained models are equally effective in describing the data.

The second comparison configuration looks at the combined factors of path coefficients and the variance/covariance of the latent variables. The chi-square value is 4.654 evaluated with 7 degrees of freedom (we gain 3 degrees of freedom from the two factor variances and the correlation between the factors) and is also not statistically significant.

The third comparison configuration looks at the combined factors of path coefficients, variance/covariance of the factors, and the variances of the error terms. The chi-square value is 10.003 evaluated with 13 degrees of freedom (we gain another 6 degrees of freedom because there are six error terms each with its own variance) and is also not statistically significant.

20B.2.9 Conclusion Drawn From the Analysis

The across-the-board nonsignificant chi-square results allow us to draw the conclusion that the two models—the unconstrained and the constrained models—are not different. We may therefore draw the inference that the two groups of test takers—those from the United States and those from Japan—can both be described by the confirmatory factor model. Thus, for both groups of individuals, vocabulary, general information, and reading comprehension can be viewed as indicators of verbal ability, and block design reproduction, solving matrix reasoning problems, and finding the missing parts of pictures can be viewed as indicators of perceptual reasoning. Note that although the factor structures are comparable, it may be that the groups might differ in their proficiency of performing on these tests (i.e., they might have different mean levels of performance on one or more of the indicator variables and/or one or both of the factors). Testing that proposition would entail performing a MANOVA and discriminant function analysis on the data.

20B.2.10 Reporting Confirmatory Factor Analysis Invariance Results

> Two dimensions of intelligence, verbal ability and perceptual reasoning, were each assessed in two different cultural environments. A sample of adult test takers from a city in the United States and another sample from a city in Japan were administered a battery of six tests to assess intellectual skill. Three of the tests, vocabulary, general information, and reading comprehension, were hypothesized to assess verbal ability; the other three tests, block design reproduction, solving matrix reasoning problems,

and finding the missing parts of pictures, were hypothesized to assess perceptual reasoning. The model is shown in Figure 20b.1, and the research issue was whether or not the confirmatory factor structure was invariant across the two different cultural samples.

The analysis was performed in IBM SPSS Amos Version 19 and evaluates the difference between an unconstrained model, which assumes that the groups are yielding different values of the parameters when the model is applied to the data, and an unconstrained model, which assumes that the groups are yielding equivalent values of the parameters when the model is applied to the data. Three types of comparisons were performed. For the comparison involving only the pattern coefficients, the chi-square value was not statistically significant, $\chi^2(4, N = 185) = 1.184$, $p = .881$. The second comparison configuration examined the combined factors of path coefficients and the variance/covariance of the latent variables. The chi-square value was not statistically significant, $\chi^2(7, N = 185) = 4.654$, $p = .702$. The third comparison configuration examined the combined factors of path coefficients, variance/covariance of the factors, and the variances of the error terms. The chi-square value was not statistically significant, $\chi^2(13, N = 185) = 10.003$, $p = .694$.

We may therefore draw the inference that the two groups of test takers—those from the United States and those from Japan—can both be described by the confirmatory factor model. Thus, for both groups of individuals, vocabulary, general information, and reading comprehension can be viewed as indicators of verbal ability, and block design reproduction, solving matrix reasoning problems, and finding the missing parts of pictures can be viewed as indicators of perceptual reasoning.

20B.3 Path Analysis

20B.3.1 Numerical Example

The fictitious data set used for this example is called **Patient Adherence**. Medical researchers were interested in predicting the degree to which patients adhered to the medication regime prescribed by their primary care physician; this was the outcome variable in the design and is labeled as **adhere** in the data file. Three variables were configured in the path structure shown in Figure 20b.15. The rapport between patient and physician was hypothesized to directly affect adherence; the data for this variable (**rapport**) were collected using a dichotomous judgment of the patient with **0** representing no rapport and **1** representing the existence of rapport. Two other quantitative variables were hypothesized as indirectly affecting adherence through their effect on patient–physician rapport. One of these was the length of time patients had been with their

Figure 20b.15 The Hypothesized Model

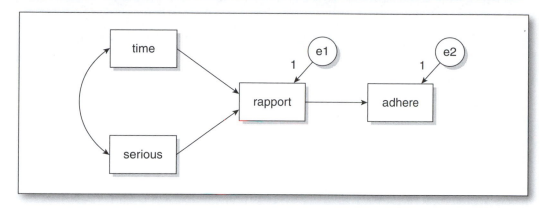

physicians (**time**); the other of these variables was the seriousness of the condition of the patients (**serious**).

The focus of this study was in differences that might be observed between patients who were members of an HMO (coded as **1**) and patients who were seen by private physicians (coded as **2**) for the variable of **facility**. At issue was whether the model was equally valid for both types of patients (i.e., whether the model was invariant).

The steps to perform the invariance analysis are very similar to what we covered in Section 20B.2, and so we will summarize those aspects of the setup and show a minimal number of screenshots; readers are referred to Section 20B.2 for more details if they need them.

20B.3.2 Drawing the Model

To specify a model is to create a structural representation of the hypothesized relationships. Open the data file and from the main IBM SPSS menu select **Analyze ➜ Amos** to bring us to the graphics window. Draw the model as shown in Figure 20b.15.

20B.3.3 Identifying the Two Groups

From the main IBM SPSS Amos menu, select **Analyze ➜ Manage Groups**. In the **Manage Groups** dialog window, the default expression **Group number 1** is shown. Highlight the expression and replace with **HMO**. Click the **New** pushbutton. Replace the expression **Group number 2** with **private**. Click the **Close** pushbutton. The two group names that we just defined appear in the top panel as shown in Figure 20b.16.

Figure 20b.16   The Model With the Group Names Included

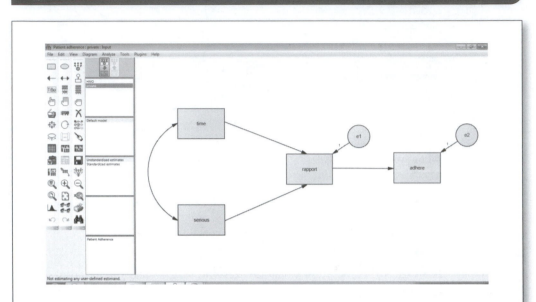

20B.3.4 Linking the Two Groups to the Data File

Having identified the names of the groups that will appear in the analysis, we now need to link these names to the medical facility variable in the data file and to the values (codes) for **facility**. We accomplish this by selecting **File ➜ Data Files**. **HMO** is highlighted. Select the **Grouping Variable** pushbutton. Then select **facility**, click **OK**, select the **Group Value** pushbutton, highlight value **1**, and click **OK**. This series of actions will link the **HMO** patients to the proper code for the proper variable in the data file. Go through the steps needed to link the value of **2** to the **private** patients under **facility**. This is shown in Figure 20b.17. Note that the sample sizes of **215/411** (i.e., 215 of the 411 cases are members of HMOs) for **HMO** patients and **196/411** for **private** patients also show in the window. Clicking **OK** brings us back to the path diagram.

20B.3.5 Specifying the Output

To specify what elements we wish to obtain in the output, select **View ➜ Analysis Properties**. In the **Analysis Properties** window, select the **Output** tab. Remove the check from **Minimization history**, and check **Standardized estimates**, **Residual moments**, and **Critical ratios for differences**.

Now select the **Estimation** tab as shown in Figure 20b.18. Check the option for **Estimate means and intercepts**. This is required because we have missing values in the data file. To

Figure 20b.17 The Data Files Window With the Group Names and Values Assigned

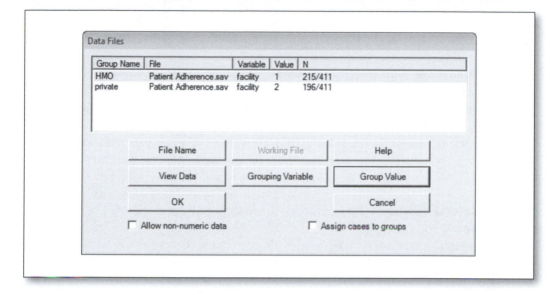

Figure 20b.18 The Estimation Tab Window Under Analysis Properties

deal with missing data, IBM SPSS Amos will perform an FIML imputation (see Section 3A.7.2). Retain the remaining defaults. After specifying this information, just close the window.

20B.3.6 Specifying the Elements of Invariance

Select **Analyze ➤ Multiple-Group Analysis**. At that point IBM SPSS Amos may display an error message that can be ignored. Click **OK** on that message and the **Multiple-Group Analysis** window will appear as shown in Figure 20b.19. It is in this window that the main thrust of the invariance analysis (the comparison of the groups) is configured.

In the default setup that we will use, IBM SPSS Amos will compare the groups in five different ways (this default setup is different from the one we saw for the confirmatory invariance analysis). Most researchers are interested in only two of the comparisons:

- **Structural weights**: These refer to the path coefficients and are specified in column 1.
- **Structural covariances**: These refer to correlation between the two exogenous variables (in our example, **time** and **serious**) and the variances and covariances of the two exogenous variables that are specified in column 4.

As there is no need to modify the contents of this window, click **OK**.

Figure 20b.19 The Multiple-Group Analysis Dialog Window

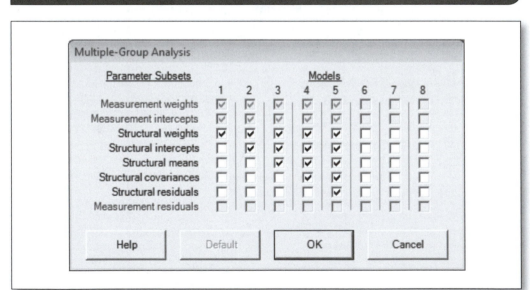

20B.3.7 Obtaining the Parameter Labels

Once we have configured our comparisons, IBM SPSS Amos will supply labels in the path diagram for the parameters. We show this in Figure 20b.20, where we show the labels for Group 1 (**HMO**) in the upper path diagram and the labels for Group 2 (**private**) in the lower path diagram. The upper path diagram shows the **HMO** parameters. The parameters for this group are displayed when we clicked **OK** in the Multiple-Group Analysis dialog window because it was identified as **Group 1**. To obtain the path diagram for the **private** group, we would click on **private** in the **Groups** panel to the left of the graphics area (see Figure 20b.20).

Figure 20b.20   The Parameter Labels Are Given for the Health Maintenance Organization and the Private Practice Groups on Two Different Screens

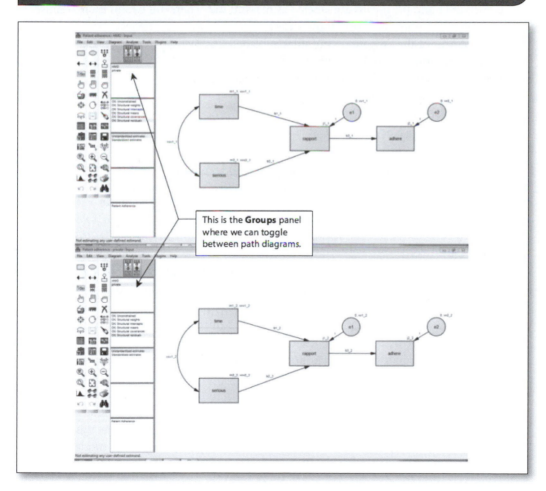

Consider the upper path diagram. Note that the top panel to the left of the graphic area contains the two groups in the analysis (**HMO** and **private**) and that the **HMO** label (recall that its code is **1** in the data file) is highlighted (we also see in the window banner the expression **Patience Adherence: HMO: Input** to reinforce that we are focused on the **HMO** group). The rubric for assigning labels is as follows:

- The correlation of the exogenous variables are labeled as **ccc**. With only two exogenous variables, we have just one correlation labeled as **ccc1_1**. This translates as correlation number 1 (the only one in this path structure) for Group 1 (HMO), that is, the group designation is provided following the underscore). If we were to highlight **private** (coded as **2** in the data file) in the top panel to the left of the graphic area, we would see the label **ccc1_2**. This general labeling strategy is used for the other parameter labels.
- Means of the exogenous variables are labeled as **m**. Note that there are two such variables and the means are labeled as **m1** and **m2**. There are two of each because we have two groups (e.g., **m1_1** and **m1_2**).
- Variances of the exogenous variables are labeled as **vvv**.
- Paths coefficients are labeled as **b**.
- Intercepts of the endogenous variables are labeled as **j**.
- Variances of the error terms are labeled as **vv**.
- Markers representing the FIML imputation procedure to estimate missing values placed by the error terms are labeled as **0**.

20B.3.8 Performing the Analysis and Obtaining the Output

From the main IBM SPSS Amos menu, select **Analyze ➜ Calculate Estimates**. To address the primary interest of whether or not the two models are equivalent, select **View ➜ Text Output**. This produces the **Amos Output** screen. Go directly to **Model Comparison**, shown in Figure 20b.21.

The table in Figure 20b.21 presents the key results. It displays the comparison of the unconstrained and constrained models. The first row focuses only on comparing the Structural weights of the groups, the second row focuses on comparing the Structural weights and Structural intercepts of the groups, the third row focuses on comparing the Structural weights, Structural intercepts, and Structural means of the groups, the fourth row adds to the above the Structural covariances, and the fifth row adds to that the Structural residuals. Our interest is limited to Structural weights and the Structural covariances.

Model differences are evaluated with a chi-square test (CMIN in the second numerical column). Only two of the comparisons are relevant for us here. For the comparison involving the path coefficients, labeled as Structural weights in first row of the table, the chi-square value was 15.227. With 3 degrees of freedom (there are three paths in the model), the chi-square is statistically significant (the *P* value—the probability of the value occurring by

Figure 20b.21 A Portion of the Amos Output

Nested Model Comparisons

Assuming model Unconstrained to be correct:

Model	DF	CMIN	P	NFI Delta-1	IFI Delta-2	RFI rho-1	TLI rho2
Structural weights	3	15.227	.002	.034	.034	-.290	-.304
Structural intercepts	5	46.582	.000	.104	.105	-.271	-.284
Structural means	7	66.858	.000	.149	.150	-.304	-.319
Structural covariances	10	74.885	.000	.167	.168	-.407	-.426
Structural residuals	12	77.494	.000	.173	.174	-.462	-.484

chance if the null hypothesis is true—is .002). We therefore conclude that some or all of the corresponding path coefficients differ between the groups. This output does not delineate which path coefficients are significantly different, and we need to consult another output table to make that determination.

The second comparison of interest lies in the comparison of the correlation and variances of the two exogenous variables (in our example, time and serious). This is shown in the fourth row labeled as Structural covariances in the table. The chi-square value was 74.885. With 10 degrees of freedom (there are three paths in the model), the chi-square is statistically significant (the P value—the probability of the value occurring by chance if the null hypothesis is true—is less than .001). We therefore conclude that either or both of the correlation or variances of the two variables differ between the groups.

20B.3.9 Pairwise Parameter Comparisons

Select from the left panel **Pairwise Parameter Comparisons**, a portion of which is shown in Figure 20b.22. As can be seen from Figure 20b.22, every possible pairwise comparison is represented. The entries in the table are z values, and landmark scores for alpha levels corresponding to .05 and .01 are 1.96 and 2.58, respectively. If we were to examine all of these comparisons, we would have an inordinate amount of alpha-level inflation. However, our interest is limited to the four path coefficients in addition to the correlations of the exogenous variables; we will therefore adopt a Bonferroni-corrected alpha level of .01 $(.05/4 = .0125)$.

Having obtained a significant chi-square for the differences between the path coefficients, most researchers would first examine these paired comparisons in the table. To

Figure 20b.22 The Pairwise Parameter Comparisons Output

Amos Output

Pairwise Parameter Comparisons (Unconstrained)

Critical Ratios for Differences between Parameters (Unconstrained)

	ccc1_1	b1_1	b2_1	b3_1	vvv1_1	vv2_1	vv1_1	vv2_1	m1_1	m2_1	j1_1	j2_1	ccc1_2	b1_2	b2_2	b3_2
ccc1_1	.000															
b1_1	3.027	.000														
b2_1	5.516	9.016	.000													
b3_1	10.184	9.781	8.507	.000												
vvv1_1	10.182	10.380	9.857	5.740	.000											
vv2_1	6.013	11.009	2.576	-7.968	-9.664	.000										
vv1_1	4.616	10.901	-3.342	-9.067	-10.079	-6.286	.000									
vv2_1	10.790	10.353	9.570	3.565	-2.805	9.231	9.907	.000								
m1_1	46.258	54.661	51.503	20.114	3.625	50.355	53.378	9.857	.000							
m2_1	20.201	50.638	33.110	-1.731	-6.961	29.006	44.656	-5.292	-38.174	.000						
j1_1	2.808	1.120	-.833	-8.008	-9.842	-1.887	-.104	-9.405	-39.830	-12.919	.000					
j2_1	19.378	20.928	18.890	3.094	-4.006	18.059	19.887	-1.077	-20.173	9.231	15.723	.000				
ccc1_2	-1.199	-3.874	-5.844	-10.434	-10.997	-6.711	-5.114	-11.057	-42.885	-17.540	-3.595	-18.767	.000			
b1_2	3.175	1.316	-8.025	-9.716	-10.352	-10.593	-9.882	-10.312	-54.554	-50.222	-1.057	-20.836	3.989	.000		
b2_2	4.904	7.532	-1.765	-8.846	-9.994	-4.432	1.440	-9.776	-52.414	-37.394	.423	-19.439	5.352	7.688	.000	
b3_2	13.564	13.420	12.184	2.974	-4.027	11.661	12.738	-1.264	-15.850	5.713	11.346	-.430	13.671	13.358	12.513	.000
vvv1_2	10.315	9.934	9.428	5.469	-.097	9.208	9.643	2.633	-3.654	6.619	9.430	3.765	9.700	9.907	9.561	3.801
vv2_2	7.661	10.377	4.693	-7.112	-9.284	2.675	7.311	-8.706	-47.248	-19.672	3.056	-16.491	6.707	10.104	6.090	-10.797
vv1_2	4.467	10.475	-3.848	-9.138	-10.108	-6.769	-.921	-9.951	-53.525	-45.487	-.019	-19.992	4.997	9.399	-2.017	-12.806
vv2_2	10.433	9.979	9.053	2.221	-4.032	8.654	9.454	-1.426	-13.333	4.027	8.806	-.730	10.708	9.931	9.297	-.333
m1_2	48.265	56.483	53.439	21.952	4.607	52.331	55.247	11.220	2.758	42.598	41.888	22.412	44.874	56.380	54.319	17.672
m2_2	20.961	43.575	31.363	-1.050	-6.664	28.043	39.195	-4.852	-38.471	2.723	13.802	-8.161	18.315	43.247	34.546	-5.037
j1_2	1.835	-.039	-2.113	-8.556	-10.109	-3.008	-1.292	-9.783	-40.304	-13.852	-.853	-16.368	2.718	-.148	-1.400	-11.863
j2_2	20.458	23.581	20.854	2.932	-4.684	19.792	22.252	-1.996	-24.488	8.846	15.966	-1.679	19.387	23.465	21.601	-.671

simplify the visual inspection of the paired comparisons tables, we have displayed in Figure 20b.23 a smaller portion of the table with ovals around the three paired comparisons for the paths. These are as follows:

- The *z* value of 1.316 represents the comparison of **b1_2** with **b1_1**, that is, the comparison of the path coefficients from **time** to **rapport** for each group. We would judge this *z* value to be nonsignificant.
- The *z* value of −1.765 represents the comparison of **b2_2** with **b2_1**, that is, the comparison of the path coefficients from **serious** to **rapport** for each group. We would judge this *z* value to be nonsignificant.
- The *z* value of 2.974 represents the comparison of **b3_2** with **b3_1**, that is, the comparison of the path coefficients from **rapport** to **adhere** for each group. We would judge this *z* value to be significant at a corrected alpha level of .01.

We are also interested in the correlation between **time** and **serious**, the two exogenous variables. This is shown in Figure 20b.24. The *z* value of −1.199 represents the comparison of **ccc1_2** with **ccc1_1**. We would judge this *z* value to be nonsignificant.

Figure 20b.23   The Paired Comparison of the Path Coefficients

Pairwise Parameter Comparisons (Unconstrained)

Critical Ratios for Differences between Parameters (Unconstrained)

	cccl_1	b1_1	b2_1	b3_1	vvvl_1
cccl_1	.000				
b1_1	3.027	.000			
b2_1	5.516	9.016	.000		
b3_1	10.184	9.781	8.507	.000	
vvvl_1	10.182	10.380	9.857	5.740	.000
vvv2_1	6.013	11.009	2.576	-7.968	-9.664
vv1_1	4.616	10.901	-3.342	-9.067	-10.079
vv2_1	10.790	10.353	9.570	3.565	-2.805
ml_1	46.258	54.661	51.503	20.114	3.625
m2_1	20.201	50.638	33.110	-1.731	-6.961
jl_1	2.808	1.120	-.833	-8.008	-9.842
j2_1	19.378	20.928	18.890	3.094	-4.006
cccl_2	-1.199	-3.874	-5.844	-10.434	-10.997
b1_2	3.175	(1.316)	-8.025	-9.716	-10.352
b2_2	4.904	7.532	(1.765)	-8.846	-9.994
b3_2	13.564	13.420	12.184	(2.974)	-4.027
vvvl_2	10.315	9.934	9.428	5.469	-.097

Figure 20b.24   The Paired Comparison of the Correlation Between the Exogenous Variables

Pairwise Parameter Comparisons (Unconstrained)

Critical Ratios for Differences between Parameters (Unconstrained)

	cccl_1	b1_1	b2_1	b3_1	vvvl_1
cccl_1	.000				
b1_1	3.027	.000			
b2_1	5.516	9.016	.000		
b3_1	10.184	9.781	8.507	.000	
vvvl_1	10.182	10.380	9.857	5.740	.000
vvv2_1	6.013	11.009	2.576	-7.968	-9.664
vv1_1	4.616	10.901	-3.342	-9.067	-10.079
vv2_1	10.790	10.353	9.570	3.565	-2.805
ml_1	46.258	54.661	51.503	20.114	3.625
m2_1	20.201	50.638	33.110	-1.731	-6.961
jl_1	2.808	1.120	-.833	-8.008	-9.842
j2_1	19.378	20.928	18.890	3.094	-4.006
cccl_2	(1.199)	-3.874	-5.844	-10.434	-10.997
b1_2	3.175	1.316	-8.025	-9.716	-10.352
b2_2	4.904	7.532	-1.765	-8.846	-9.994
b3_2	13.564	13.420	12.184	2.974	-4.027
vvvl_2	10.315	9.934	9.428	5.469	-.097

20B.3.10 Synthesis of Pairwise Comparisons

Returning to the graphics window displays the path diagram. In order to view the path coefficients, the following need to be highlighted:

- **OK: Unconstrained** in the second from the top of the left panels (the **Models** panel)
- Standardized estimates in the third from the top of the left panels (the **Parameter Formats** panel)
- The icon for **View the output path diagram** in the top left panel

We show in the upper portion of Figure 20b.25 the path coefficients for the **HMO** group. By highlighting the other group in the top panel to the left of the graphics area, the coefficients for the **private** group are displayed; we show these in the lower portion of Figure 20b.25. Toggling back and forth allows us to see the results for each group.

Figure 20b.25   Comparing the Path Coefficients of the Two Models

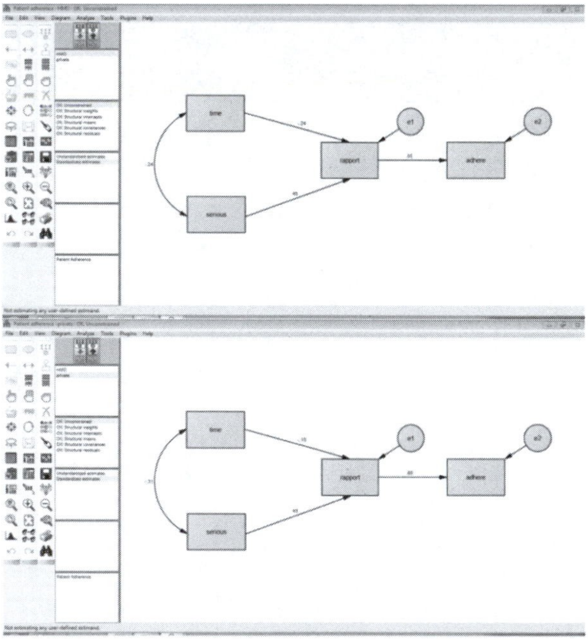

Figure 20b.26 Comparisons Between HMO and Private on Path Coefficients and Correlations

Regression Weights: (HMO - Unconstrained)

			Estimate	S.E.	C.R.	P	Label	
rapport	<---	time	-.045	.011	-4.158	***	b1	1
rapport	<---	serious	.324	.042	7.698	***	b2	1
adhere	<---	rapport	2.973	.308	9.642	***	b3	1

Standardized Regression Weights: (HMO - Unconstrained)

			Estimate
rapport	<---	time	-.244
rapport	<---	serious	.451
adhere	<---	rapport	.554

Means: (HMO - Unconstrained)

			Estimate	S.E.	C.R.	P	Label	
time			10.233	.188	54.513	***	m1	1
serious			2.433	.048	50.971	***	m2	1

Intercepts: (HMO - Unconstrained)

			Estimate	S.E.	C.R.	P	Label	
rapport			.155	.170	.913	.361	j1	1
adhere			4.469	.215	20.748	***	j2	1

Covariances: (HMO - Unconstrained)

			Estimate	S.E.	C.R.	P	Label	
time	<-->	serious	-.454	.135	-3.368	***	ccc1	1

Correlations: (HMO - Unconstrained)

			Estimate
time	<-->	serious	-.237

Variances: (HMO - Unconstrained)

			Estimate	S.E.	C.R.	P	Label	
time			7.509	.728	10.319	***	vvv1	1
serious			.487	.047	10.343	***	vvv2_1	
e1			.173	.017	10.271	***	vv1	1
e2			5.046	.492	10.265	***	vv2	1

The coefficients for the paths from the exogenous variables to rapport and the correlation between the two exogenous variables were not significantly different. These coefficients are as follows:

- The path coefficients from **time** to **rapport** were −.24 and −.15 for **HMO** and **private** patients, respectively.
- The path coefficients from **serious** to **rapport** were .45 and .43 for **HMO** and **private** patients, respectively.
- The correlations between **time** to **serious** were −.24 and −.31 for **HMO** and **private** patients, respectively.

The pairwise difference that was statistically significant was obtained for the path coefficients from rapport to adhere. These path coefficients were .55 and .69 for **HMO** and **private** patients, respectively; thus, the coefficient for private patients is significantly greater than the coefficient for HMO patients.

20B.3.11 Conclusions Drawn From the Analysis

The unstandardized and standardized partial regression coefficients and the correlation between **time** to **serious** and the probability levels are shown in Figure 20b.26 (select **View** ➡ **Text Output** and the go to **Model Comparison**). As can be seen from the output, all of the coefficients for both groups were statistically significant (i.e., all coefficients were significantly different from zero).

It appears from the results that patients who have good rapport that with the primary care physicians are more likely to adhere to their medication regime. Furthermore, the presence of rapport is more influential in affecting adherence for **private** sector patients than for **HMO** patients.

20B.3.12 Reporting Confirmatory Factor Analysis Invariance Results

Adherence to medication regimes was assessed through a path invariance design for patients who have either private sector or HMO primary care physicians. The time patients had been with their physicians, the seriousness of the condition of the patients, and whether or not patients felt rapport with their physicians (dichotomously evaluated) were placed into the path structure shown in Figure 20b.27.

The analysis was performed in IBM SPSS Amos Version 19 and evaluates the difference between a unconstrained model, which assumes that the groups are yielding different values of the parameters when the model is applied to the data, and an unconstrained model, which assumes that the groups are yielding equivalent values of the parameters when the model is applied to the data. Two sets of comparisons were of interest: the path coefficients and the correlation of the time patients had been with their physicians and the seriousness of the condition of the patients.

Both the comparisons of the respective path coefficients, $\chi^2(3, N = 411) = 15.227$, $p = .002$, and the variances/covariances of the two exogenous variables, $\chi^2(10, N = 411) = 74.885$, $p < .001$, yielded statistically significant results. In terms of the individual paths, no group difference was observed for either the path from the time patients had been with their physicians to physician rapport, $z = 1.316$, $p > .05$ or the path from the seriousness of the disorder to physician rapport, $z = -1.765$, $p > .05$. However, the path from physician rapport to the degree of adherence to the medication regime was statistically significant, $z = 2.974$, $p < .05$. The correlation between the two exogenous variables was not a contributing factor to the difference between the groups in the variance/covariance comparisons, $z = -1.199$, $p > .05$.

It appears from the results that patients who have good rapport with the primary care physicians are more likely to adhere to their medication regime. Furthermore, the presence of rapport is more influential in affecting adherence for private sector patients than for HMO patients.

Figure 20b.27 The Path Invariance Model for Adherence to a Medication Regime for Patients Seeing HMO and Private Sector Physicians

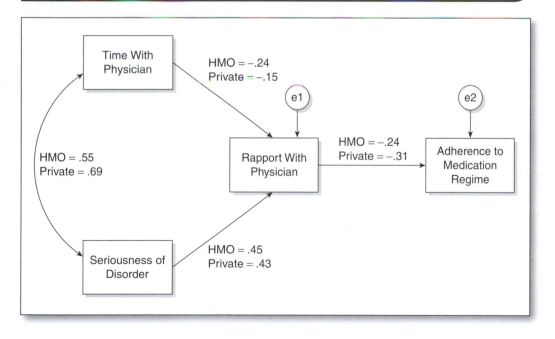

References

Agresti, A. (1996). *An introduction to categorical data analysis* (2nd ed.). New York, NY: Wiley.

Agresti, A. (2007). *Categorical data analysis* (2nd ed.). New York, NY: Wiley.

Agresti, A., & Finlay, B. (2009). *Statistical methods for the social sciences* (4th ed.). Upper Saddle River, NJ: Prentice Hall.

Aiken, L. S. (2005, April). *Interaction in multiple regression.* Paper presented at the annual meeting of the Western Psychological Association, Portland, OR.

Aiken, L. S., & West, S. G. (1991). *Multiple regression:Testing and interpreting interactions.* Newbury Park, CA: Sage.

Aiken, L. S., West, S. G., Sechrest, L., & Reno, R. R. (1990). Graduate training in statistics, methodology, and measurement in psychology: A survey of PhD programs in North America. *American Psychologist, 45,* 721–734.

Allen, M. J., & Yen, W. M. (1979). *Introduction to measurement theory.* Prospect Heights, IL: Waveland Press.

Allen, S. J., & Hubbard, R. (1986). Regression equations for the latent roots of random data correlation matrices with unities on the diagonal. *Multivariate Behavioral Research, 21,* 393–398.

Allison, P. D. (1990). Change scores as dependent variables in regression analysis. In C. C. Clogg (Ed.), *Sociological methodology* (pp. 93–114). Washington, DC: American Sociological Association.

Allison, P. D. (1999a). *Multiple regression: A primer.* Thousand Oaks, CA: Pine Forge Press.

Allison, P. D. (1999b). Comparing logit and probit coefficients across groups. *Sociological Methods and Research, 28,* 186–208.

Allison, P. D. (2002). *Missing data.* Thousand Oaks, CA: Sage.

Altman, D. G. (1991). *Practical statistics for medical research.* Boca Raton, FL: Chapman & Hall/CRC.

Alvarez, A. N., & Juang, L. P. (2010). Filipino Americans and racism: A multiple mediation model of coping. *Journal of Counseling Psychology, 57,* 167–178.

American Psychiatric Association. (2000). *Diagnostic and statistical manual of mental disorders* (4th ed., Text Revision). Washington, DC: Author.

American Psychological Association. (2009). *Publication manual* (6th ed.). Washington, DC: Author.

Anastasi, A., & Urbana, S. (1997). *Psychological testing* (7th ed.). Upper Saddle River, NJ: Prentice Hall.

Anderson, J. C., & Gerbing, D. W. (1988). Structural equation modeling in practice: A review and recommended two-step approach. *Psychological Bulletin, 103,* 411–423.

Anderson, T. W. (1957). Maximum likelihood estimates for a multivariate normal distribution when some observations are missing. *Journal of the American Statistical Association, 52,* 200–203.

Arabie, P., Carroll, J. D., & DeSarbo, W. S. (1987). *Three-way scaling and clustering.* Newbury Park, CA: Sage.

Arbuckle, J. L. (1996). Full information estimation in the presence of incomplete data. In G. A. Marcoulides & R. E. Shumaker (Eds.), *Advanced structural equation modeling* (pp. 243–277). Mahwah, NJ: Lawrence Erlbaum.

Arbuckle, J. L. (2010). *IBM SPSS Amos 19 user's guide.* Chicago, IL: SPSS.

Arce, C., & Garling, T. (1989). Multidimensional scaling. *Anuario de Psicologia, 43,* 63–80.

Aroian, L. A. (1947). The probability function of the product of two normally distributed variables. *Annals of Mathematical Statistics, 18,* 265–271. (Original work published 1944)

Attneave, F. (1950). Dimensions of similarities. *American Journal of Psychology, 63,* 516–556.

Baggaley, A. R. (1964). *Intermediate correlational methods.* New York, NY: Wiley.

Barcikowski, R. S. (1981). Statistical power with group mean as the unit of analysis. *Journal of Educational Statistics, 6,* 67–285.

Barlow, H. B. (1957). Increment thresholds at low intensities considered as signal/noise discrimination. *Journal of Physiology, 136,* 469–488.

Barnett, V., & Lewis, T. (1978). *Outliers in statistical data.* New York, NY: Wiley.

Baron, R. M., & Kenny, D. A. (1986). The moderator-mediator variable distinction in social psychological research: Conceptual, strategic, and statistical considerations. *Journal of Personality and Social Psychology, 51,* 1173–1182.

Bauer, D. J., Preacher, K. J., & Gil, K. M. (2006). Conceptualizing and testing random indirect effects and moderated mediation in multilevel models: New procedures and recommendations. *Psychological Methods, 11,* 142–163.

Beasley, W. H., & Rodgers, J. L. (2009). Resampling methods. In R. E. Millsap & A. Maydeu-Olivares (Eds.), *The Sage handbook of quantitative methods in psychology* (pp. 362–386). Thousand Oaks, CA: Sage.

Bentler, P. M. (1990). Comparative fit indexes in structural models. *Psychological Bulletin, 107,* 238–246.

Bentler, P. M. (1992). On the fit of models to covariances and methodology to the Bulletin. *Psychological Bulletin, 112,* 400–404.

Bentler, P. M., & Chou, C. P. (1987). Practical issues in structural modeling. *Sociological Methods & Research, 16,* 78–117.

Bentler, P. M., & Weeks, D. G. (1980). Linear structural equations with latent variables. *Psychometrika, 45,* 289–308.

Berk, R. A. (2003). *Regression analysis: A constructive critique.* Thousand Oaks, CA: Sage.

Berry, W. D. (1993a). *Quantitative applications in the social sciences: Vol. 92. Understanding regression assumptions.* Newbury Park, CA: Sage.

Berry, W. D. (1993b). *Understanding regression assumptions.* Newbury Park, CA: Sage.

Bickel, R. (2007). *Multilevel analysis for applied research.* New York, NY: Guilford Press.

Bird, K. D., & Hadzi-Pavlovic, D. (1983). Simultaneous test procedures and the choice of a test statistic in MANOVA. *Psychological Bulletin, 93,* 167–178.

Blalock, H. M. (Ed.). (1964). *Causal inferences in nonexperimental research.* Chapel Hill: University of North Carolina Press.

Blalock, H. M. (1971). Causal models involving unmeasured variables in stimulus-response situations. In H. M. Blalock (Ed.), *Causal models in the social sciences* (pp. 335–347). Chicago, IL: Aldine.

Blunch, N. J. (2008). *Introduction to structural equation modeling using SPSS and AMOS.* Thousand Oaks, CA: Sage.

Bochner, A. P., & Fitzpatrick, M. A. (1980). Multivariate analysis of variance: Techniques, models, and applications in communication research. In P. R. Monge & J. N. Cappella (Eds.), *Multivariate techniques in human communication research* (pp. 143–174). New York, NY: Academic Press.

Bock, H. (2008). Origins and extensions of the *k*-means algorithm in cluster analysis. *Electronic Journal for History of Probability and Statistics, 4*(2), 1–8.

Bock, R. D., & Haggard, E. A. (1968). The use of multivariate analysis of variance in behavioral research. In D. K. Whitla (Ed.), *Handbook of measurement and assessment in behavioral sciences* (pp. 100–142). Reading, MA: Addison-Wesley.

Bollen, K. A. (1989). *Structural equations with latent variables.* New York, NY: Wiley.

Bollen, K. A. (1990). Overall fit in covariance structure models: Two types of sample size effects. *Psychological Bulletin, 107,* 256–259.

Bollen, K. A., & Long, J. S. (1993). Introduction. In K. A. Bollen & J. S. Long (Eds.), *Testing structural equation models* (pp. 1–9). Newbury Park, CA: Sage.

Bollen, K. A., & Stine, R. (1990). Direct and indirect effects: Classical and bootstrap estimates of variability. *Sociological Methodology, 20,* 115–140.

Borenstein, M. (1994). The case for confidence intervals in controlled clinical trials. *Controlled Clinical Trials, 15,* 411– 428.

Borg, I., & Groenen, P. J. F. (2005). *Modern multidimensional scaling.* New York, NY: Springer.

Box, G. E. P. (1950). Problems in the analysis of growth and wear data. *Biometrics, 6,* 362–389.

Box, G. E. P., & Cox, D. R. (1964). An analysis of transformations. *Journal of the Royal Statistical Society, Series B, 26,* 211–243.

Box, G. E. P., Hunter, W. P., & Hunter, J. S. (1978). *Statistics for experimenters.* New York, NY: Wiley.

Box, J. F. (1978). *R. A. Fisher, the life of a scientist.* New York, NY: Wiley.

Box, J. F. (1987). Guinness, Gosset, Fisher, and small samples. *Statistical Science, 2,* 45–52.

Bray, J. H., & Maxwell, S. E. (1985). *Multivariate analysis of variance.* Beverly Hills, CA: Sage.

Breckenridge, J. N. (2000). Validating cluster analysis: Consistent replication and symmetry. *Multivariate Behavioral Research, 35,* 261–285.

Brown, T. A. (2006). *Confirmatory factor analysis for applied research.* New York, NY: Guilford Press.

Browne, M. W. (1975). Predictive validity of a linear regression equation. *British Journal of Mathematical and Statistical Psychology, 28,* 79–87.

Browne, M. W., & Cudeck, R. (1989). Single sample cross-validation indices for covariation structures. *Multivariate Behavioral Research, 24,* 445–455.

Browne, M. W., & Cudeck, R. (1993). Alternative ways of assessing model fit. In K. A. Bollen & J. S. Long (Eds.), *Testing structural equation models* (pp. 136–162). Newbury Park, CA: Sage.

Bryant, F. B., & Yarnold, P. R. (1995). Principal components analysis and exploratory and confirmatory factor analysis. In L. G. Grimm & P. R. Yarnold (Eds.), *Reading and understanding multivariate statistics* (pp. 99–136). Washington, DC: American Psychological Association.

Burnham, K. P., & Anderson, D. R. (2002). *Model selection and multimodel inference: A practical information-theoretic approach* (2nd ed.). New York, NY: Springer-Verlag.

Byrne, B. M. (1989). *A primer of LISREL: Basic applications and programming for confirmatory factor analytic models.* New York, NY: Springer-Verlag.

Byrne, B. M. (1998). *Structural equation modeling with LISREL, PRELIS, and SIMPLIS: Basic concepts, applications, and programming.* Hillsdale, NJ: Lawrence Erlbaum.

Byrne, B. M. (2010). *Structural equation modeling with AMOS: Basic concepts, applications and programming* (2nd ed.). New York, NY: Routledge.

Byrne, B. M., & Shavelson, R. J. (1987). Adolescent self-concept: Testing the assumption of equivalent structure across gender. *American Educational Research Association, 24,* 365–385.

Carmer, S. G., & Swanson, M. R. (1973). An evaluation of ten pairwise multiple comparison procedures by Monte Carlo methods. *Journal of the American Statistical Association, 68,* 66–74.

Carroll, J. B. (1953). An analytical solution for approximating simple structure in factor analysis. *Psychometrika, 18,* 23– 38.

Carroll, J. D., & Arabia, P. (1998). Multidimensional scaling. In M. H. Birnbaum (Ed.), *Handbook of perception and cognition: Vol. 3. Measurement, judgment and decision making* (pp. 179–250). San Diego, CA: Academic Press.

Carroll, J. D., & Chang, J. J. (1970). Analysis of individual differences in multidimensional scaling via an N-way generalization of "Eckart-Young" decomposition. *Psychometrika, 35,* 238–319.

Carroll, J. D., & Wish, M. (1974). Models and methods for three-way multidimensional scaling. In D. H. Krantz, R. C. Atkinson, R. D. Luce, & P. Suppes (Eds.), *Contemporary developments in mathematical psychology: Vol. 2. Measurement, psychophysics, and neural information processing* (pp. 57–105). San Francisco, CA: W. H. Freeman.

Cattell, R. B. (1966). The scree test for the number of factors. *Multivariate Behavioral Research, 1*, 245–276.

Chambers, W. V. (2000). Causation and corresponding correlations. *Journal of Mind and Behavior, 21*, 437–460.

Chatburn, R. L. (2011). *Handbook for health care research* (2nd ed.). Sudbury, MA: Jones & Bartlett.

Chen, F. F., Bollen, K. A., Paxton, P. M., Curran, P., & Kirby, J. (2001). Improper solutions in structural equation models. *Sociological Methods & Research, 29*, 468–508.

Chen, F. F., Sousa, K. H., & West, S. G. (2005). Testing measurement invariance of second-order factor models. *Structural Equation Modeling, 12*, 471–492.

Chen, P. Y., & Popovich, P. M. (2002). *Correlation: Parametric and nonparametric measures.* Thousand Oaks, CA: Sage.

Cheong, J., MacKinnon, D. P., & Khoo, S. T. (2003). Investigation of mediational processes using parallel process latent growth modeling. *Structural Equation Modeling, 10*, 238–262.

Chernick, M. R. (2008). *Bootstrap methods: A guide for practitioners and researchers* (2nd ed.). Hoboken, NJ: Wiley.

Cheung, G. W., & Rensvold, R. B. (1999). Testing factorial invariance across groups: A reconceptualization and proposed new method. *Journal of Management, 25*, 1–27.

Chin, W. W. (1998). Issues and opinion on structural equation modeling. *MIS Quarterly, 21*, 7–16.

Chin, W. W., Marcolin, B. L., & Newsted, P. R. (1996). A partial least squares latent variable modeling approach for measuring interaction effects: Results from a Monte Carlo simulation study and voice mail emotion/adoption study. In J. I. DeGross, S. Jarvenpaa, & A. Srinivasan (Eds.), *Proceedings of the Seventeenth International Conference on Information Systems* (pp. 21–41). Cleveland, OH.

Clatworthy, J., Buick, D., Hankins, M., Weinman, J., & Horne, R. (2005). The use and reporting of cluster analysis in health psychology: A review. *British Journal of Health Psychology, 10*, 329–358.

Cliff, N. (1983). Some cautions concerning the application of causal modeling methods. *Multivariate Behavioral Research, 18*, 81–105.

Cliff, N. (1988). The eigenvalues-greater-than-one rule and the reliability of components. *Psychological Bulletin, 103*, 276–279.

Cohen, B. H. (1996). *Explaining psychological statistics.* Pacific Grove, CA: Brooks/Cole.

Cohen, J. (1968). Multiple regression as a general data analytic system. *Psychological Bulletin, 70*, 426–443.

Cohen, J. (1969). *Statistical power analysis for the behavioral sciences.* New York, NY: Academic Press.

Cohen, J. (1977). *Statistical power analysis for the behavioral sciences* (Rev. ed.). New York, NY: Academic Press.

Cohen, J. (1982). Set correlation as a general multivariate data-analytic method. *Multivariate Behavioral Research, 17*, 301–341.

Cohen, J. (1988). *Statistical power analysis for the behavioral sciences* (2nd ed.). Hillsdale, NJ: Lawrence Erlbaum.

Cohen, J. (1990). Things I have learned (so far). *American Psychologist, 45*, 1304–1312.

Cohen, J. (1994). The earth is round ($p < .05$). *American Psychologist, 49*, 997–1003.

Cohen, J., Cohen, P., West, S. G., & Aiken, L. (2003). *Applied multiple regression/correlation analysis for the behavioral sciences* (3rd ed.). Hillsdale, NJ: Lawrence Erlbaum.

Cole, D. A., Maxwell, S. E., Avery, R., & Salas, E. (1994). How the power of MANOVA can both increase and decrease as a function of the intercorrelations among dependent variables. *Psychological Bulletin, 115*, 465–474.

Comrey, A. L., & Lee, H. B. (1992). *A first course in factor analysis* (2nd ed.). Hillsdale, NJ: Lawrence Erlbaum.

Conger, A. J., & Jackson, D. N. (1972). Suppressor variables, prediction, and the interpretation of psychological relationships. *Educational and Psychological Measurement, 32*, 579–599.

Conway, J. M., & Huffcutt, A. I. (2004). A review and evaluation of exploratory factor analysis practices in organizational research. *Organizational Research Methods, 6,* 147–168.

Cooley, W. W., & Lohnes, P. R. (1971). *Multivariate data analysis.* New York, NY: Wiley.

Cooper, H. (2010). *Reporting research in psychology: How to meet journal article reporting standards.* Washington, DC: American Psychological Association.

Coopersmith, S. (1981). *Self-esteem inventories.* Palo Alto, CA: Consulting Psychologists Press.

Cortina, J. M. (1993). What is coefficient alpha? An examination of theory and application. *Journal of Applied Psychology, 78,* 98–104.

Costa, P. T., Jr., & McCrae, R. R. (1992). *The NEO PI-R professional manual.* Odessa, FL: Psychological Assessment Resources.

Costner, H. L. (1969). Theory, deduction, and rules of correspondence. *American Journal of Sociology, 75,* 245–263.

Courville, T., & Thompson, B. (2001). Use of structure coefficients in published multiple regression articles: Beta is not enough. *Educational and Psychological Measurement, 61,* 229–248.

Cowles, M. (1989). *Statistics in psychology: An historical perspective.* Hillsdale, NJ: Lawrence Erlbaum.

Cowles, M., & Davis, C. (1982). On the origins of the .05 level of statistical significance. *American Psychologist, 37,* 553–558.

Cox, D. R. (1972). Regression models and life-tables. *Journal of the Royal Statistical Society, Series B, 34,* 187–202.

Cox, D. R., & Snell, E. J. (1989). *Analysis of binary data* (2nd ed.). London, England: Chapman & Hall.

Cox, T. F., & Cox, M. A. A. (2001). *Multidimensional scaling* (2nd ed.). Boca Raton, FL: Chapman & Hall.

Cramer, E., & Nicewander, W. A. (1979). Some symmetric, invariant measures of multivariate association. *Psychometrika, 44,* 43–54.

Crawford, C. B., & Koopman, P. (1979). Inter-rater reliability of scree test and mean square ratio test of number of factors. *Perceptual & Motor Skills, 49,* 223–226.

Cronbach, L. J. (1951). Coefficient alpha and the internal structure of tests. *Psychometrika, 16,* 297–334.

Cronbach, L. J. (1970). *Essentials of psychological testing* (3rd ed.). New York, NY: Harper & Row.

Cronbach, L. J., & Furby, L. (1970). How should we measure change? Or should we? *Psychological Bulletin, 74,* 68–80.

Cronbach, L. J., Gleser, G. C., Nanda, H., & Rajaratnam, N. (1972). *The dependability of behavioral measurements: Theory of generalizability for scores and profiles.* New York, NY: Wiley.

Cronbach, L. J., Nageswari, R., & Gleser, G. C. (1963). Theory of generalizability: A liberation of reliability theory. *British Journal of Statistical Psychology, 16,* 137–163.

Cumming, G. (2012). *Understanding the new statistics: Effect sizes, confidence intervals, and meta analysis.* New York, NY: Routledge.

D'Agostino, R. B. (1971). An omnibus test of normality for moderate and large size samples. *Biometrika, 58,* 341–348.

Darlington, R. B. (1960). *Regression and linear models.* New York: McGraw-Hill.

Darlington, R. B. (1968). Multiple regression in psychological research and practice. *Psychological Bulletin, 69,* 161–182.

Davis, C. S. (2002). *Statistical methods for the analysis of repeated measurements.* New York, NY: Springer.

Davison, M. L. (1983). *Multidimensional scaling.* New York, NY: Wiley.

de Leeuw, J., & Kreft, I. (1986). Random coefficient models for multilevel analysis. *Journal of Educational Statistics, 11,* 57–85.

DeMaris, A. (1992). *Logit modeling: Practical applications.* Newbury Park, CA: Sage.

Dempster, A. P., Laird, N. M., & Rubin, D. B. (1977). Maximum likelihood from incomplete data via the EM algorithm. *Journal of the Royal Statistical Society, Series B, 39,* 1–38.

DeStefano, C. (2012). Cluster analysis and latent class clustering techniques. In B. Laursen, T. D. Little, & N. A. Card (Eds.), *Handbook of developmental research methods* (pp. 667–686). New York, NY: Guilford Press.

Diamond, S. (1959). *Information and error: An introduction to statistical analysis.* New York, NY: Basic Books.

Diekhoff, G. (1992). *Statistics for the social and behavioral sciences: Univariate, bivariate, multivariate.* Dubuque, IA: Wm. C. Brown.

Diggle, P., Heagerty, P., Liang, K. Y., & Zeger, S. (2002). *Analysis of longitudinal data* (2nd ed.). Oxford, England: Oxford University Press.

Dobson, A. J., & Barnett, A. G. (2008). *Introduction to generalized linear models* (3rd ed.). Boca Raton, FL: Chapman & Hall/CRC.

Draper, N. R., Guttman, I., & Lapczak, L. (1979). Actual rejection levels in a certain stepwise test. *Communications in Statistics, A8,* 99–105.

Duarte Silva, A. P., & Stam, A. (1995). Discriminant analysis. In L. G. Grimm & P. R. Yarnold (Eds.), *Reading and understanding multivariate statistics* (pp. 277–318). Washington, DC: American Psychological Association.

Duncan, O. D. (1966). Path analysis: Sociological examples. *American Journal of Sociology, 72,* 219–316.

Dunlap, W. P., & Landis, R. S. (1998). Interpretations of multiple regression borrowed from factor analysis and canonical correlation. *Journal of General Psychology, 125,* 397–407.

Durbin, J., & Watson, G. S. (1971). Testing for serial correlation in least squares regression III. *Biometrika, 58,* 1–19.

Edwards, A. L. (1957). *Techniques of attitude scale construction.* New York, NY: Appleton-Century-Crofts.

Efron, B. (1975). The efficiency of logistic regression compared to normal discriminant analysis. *Journal of the American Statistical Association, 70,* 892–898.

Efron, B. (1979). Bootstrap methods: Another look at the jackknife. *Annals of Statistics, 7,* 1–26.

Ellis, M. V. (1999). Repeated measures designs. *Counseling Psychologist, 27,* 552–578.

Embretson, S. E., & Reise, S. P. (2000). *Item response theory for psychologists.* Mahwah, NJ: Lawrence Erlbaum.

Enders, C. K. (2001). A primer on maximum likelihood algorithms available for use with missing data. *Structural Equation Modeling, 8,* 128–141.

Enders, C. K. (2001). The impact of nonnormality on full information maximum-likelihood estimation for structural equation models with missing data. *Psychological Methods, 6,* 352–370.

Enders, C. K. (2010). *Applied missing data analysis.* New York, NY: Guilford Press.

Enders, C. K., & Gottschall, A. C. (2011). The impact of missing data on the ethical quality of a research study. In A. T. Panter & S. K. Sterba (Eds.), *Handbook of ethics in quantitative methodology* (pp. 357–381). New York, NY: Routledge, Taylor & Francis.

Enders, C. K., & Tofighi, D. (2007). Centering predictor variables in cross-sectional multilevel models: A new look at an old issue. *Psychological Methods, 12,* 121–138.

Estrella, A. (1998). A new measure of fit for equations with dichotomous dependent variables. *Journal of Business and Economic Statistics, 16,* 198–205.

Everitt, B. S. (1979). A Monte Carlo investigation of the robustness of Hotelling's one and two sample T_2 tests. *Journal of the American Statistical Association, 74,* 48–51.

Everitt, B. S. (1984). *An introduction to latent variable models.* New York, NY: Chapman & Hall.

Everitt, B. S., Landau, S., Leese, M., & Stahl, D. (2011). *Cluster analysis* (5th ed.). Chichester, England: Wiley.

Everitt, B. S., & Rabe-Hesketh, S. (1997). *The analysis of proximity data.* New York, NY: Wiley.

Eysenck, H. J. (1952). The uses and abuses of factor analysis. *Applied Statistics, 1,* 45–49.

Fabrigar, L. R., Wegener, D. T., MacCallum, R. C., & Strahan, E. J. (1999). Evaluating the use of exploratory factor analysis in psychological research. *Psychological Methods, 4,* 272–299.

Fairchild, A. J., MacKinnon, D. P., Taborga, M. P., & Taylor, A. B. (2009). $R2$ effect-size measures for mediation analysis. *Behavior Research Methods, 41,* 486–498.

Fan, X., Thompson, B., & Wang, L. (1999). Effects of sample size, estimation method, and model specification on structural equation modeling fit indexes. *Structural Equation Modeling, 6,* 56–83.

Fechner, G. T. (1860). *Elemente dur psychophysik* [Elements of psychophysics]. Leipzig, Germany: Breitkopf & Härtel.

Ferguson, G. A. (1954). The concept of parsimony in factor analysis. *Psychometrika, 19,* 281–290.

Ferguson, G. A., & Takane, Y. (1989). *Statistical analysis in psychology and education* (6th ed.). New York, NY: McGraw-Hill.

Férre, L. (1995). Selection of components in principal component analysis: A comparison of methods. *Computational Statistics & Data Analysis, 19,* 669–682.

Finkel, S. E. (1995). *Causal analysis with panel data.* Thousand Oaks, CA: Sage.

Fisher, R. A. (1915). Frequency distribution of the values of the correlation coefficient in samples from an indefinitely large population. *Biometrika, 10,* 507–521.

Fisher, R. A. (1921). Studies in crop variation. I. An examination of the yield of dressed grain from Broadbalk. *Journal of Agricultural Science, 11,* 107–135.

Fisher, R. A. (1925a). Applications of Student's distribution. *Metron, 5,* 90–104.

Fisher, R. A. (1925b). *Statistical methods for research workers.* London, England: Oliver & Boyd.

Fisher, R. A. (1935). *The design of experiments.* Edinburgh, Scotland: Oliver & Boyd.

Fisher, R. A. (1939). Student. *Annals of Eugenics, 9,* 1–9.

Fisher, R. A., & Eden, T. (1927). Studies in crop variation. IV. The experimental determination of the value of top dressings with cereals. *Journal of Agricultural Science, 17,* 548–562.

Fisher, R. A., & Mackenzie, W. A. (1923). Studies in crop variation. II. The manorial responses of different potato varieties. *Journal of Agricultural Science, 13,* 311–320.

Fitzmaurice, G., Laird, N. M., & Ware, J. H. (2011). *Applied longitudinal analysis* (2nd ed.). Hoboken, NJ: Wiley.

Fitzmaurice, G., & Molenberghs, G. (2009). Advances in longitudinal data analysis: An historical perspective. In G. Fitzmaurice, M. Davidian, G. Verbeke, & G. Molenberghs (Eds.), *Longitudinal data analysis* (pp. 3–30). Boca Raton, FL: Chapman & Hall/CRC.

Flicker, L., Loguidice, D., Carlin, J. B., & Ames, D. (1997). The predictive value of dementia screening instruments in clinical populations. *International Journal of Geriatric Psychiatry, 12,* 203–209.

Fornell, C. (1978). Three approaches to canonical analysis. *Journal of the Market Research Society, 20,* 166–181.

Fornell, C. (1987). A second generation of multivariate analysis: Classification of methods and implications for marketing research. In M. J. Houston (Ed.), *Review of marketing* (pp. 407–450). Chicago, IL: American Marketing Association.

Fox, J. (1991). *Regression diagnostics.* Newbury Park, CA: Sage.

Fox, J. (2000). *Multiple and generalized nonparametric regression.* Thousand Oaks, CA: Sage.

Franklin, S. B., Gibson, D. J., Robertson, P. H., Pohlmann, J. T., & Fralish, J. S. (1995). Parallel analysis: A method for determining significant principal components. *Journal of Vegetation Science, 6,* 99–106.

Frazier, P. A., Tix, A. P., & Barron, K. E. (2004). Testing moderator and mediator effects in counseling psychology research. *Journal of Counseling Psychology, 51,* 115–134.

Freedman, L. S., & Schatzkin, A. (1992). Sample size for studying intermediate endpoints within intervention trials of observational studies. *American Journal of Epidemiology, 136,* 1148–1159.

Freud, S. (1938). The interpretation of dreams. In A. A. Brill (Ed. & Trans.), *The basic writings of Sigmund Freud* (3rd ed., pp. 183–539). New York, NY: Modern Library.

Freund, R. J., & Littell, R. C. (2000). *SAS system for regression* (3rd ed.). Cary, NC: SAS Institute.

Freund, R. J., Wilson, W. J., & Ping, S. (2006). *Regression analysis: Statistical modeling of a response variable* (2nd ed.). Burlington, MA: Academic Press.

Fuller, W. A. (2009). *Sampling statistics*. Hoboken, NJ: Wiley.

Gabriel, K. R. (1969). A comparison of some methods of simultaneous inference in Manova. In P. R. Krishnaiah (Ed.), *Multivariate analysis–II* (pp. 67–86). New York, NY: Academic Press.

Galton, F. A. (1886). Regression towards mediocrity in hereditary stature. *Journal of the Anthropological Institute, 15,* 246–263.

Galton, F. A. (1888). Co-relations and their measurement, chiefly from anthropometric data. *Proceedings of the Royal Society of London, 40,* 42–73.

Gamst, G. (1985). Survival analysis: A new way to predict subscription order retention. *Newspaper Research Journal, 6,* 1–12.

Gamst, G., Dana, R. H., Der-Karabetian, A., Aragon, M., Arellano, L., Morrow, G., & Martenson, L. (2004). Cultural competency revised: The California Brief Multicultural Competence Scale. *Measurement and Evaluation in Counseling and Development, 37,* 163–183.

Gamst, G., Dana, R. H., Der-Karabetian, A., & Kramer, T. (2001). Asian American mental health clients: Effects of ethnic match and age on global assessment and visitation. *Journal of Mental Health Counseling, 23,* 57–71.

Gamst, G., Liang, C. T. H., & Der-Karabetian, A. (2011). *Handbook of multicultural measures.* Thousand Oaks, CA: Sage.

Gamst, G., Meyers, L. S., & Guarino, A. J. (2008). *Analysis of variance designs: A conceptual and computational approach with SPSS and SAS.* New York, NY: Cambridge University Press.

Garnett, J. C. M. (1919). On certain independent factors in mental measurement. *Proceedings of the Royal Society of London, Series A, 96,* 91–111.

Geisser, S., & Greenhouse, S. W. (1958). An extension of Box's results on the use of the *F* distribution in multivariate analysis. *Annals of Mathematical Statistics, 29,* 885–891.

George, D., & Mallery, P. (2003). *SPSS for Windows step by step: A simple guide and reference 11.0 update* (4th ed.). Boston, MA: Allyn & Bacon.

Gescheider, G. A. (1977). *Psychophysics: The fundamentals* (3rd ed.). Mahwah, NJ: Lawrence Erlbaum.

Ghiselli, E. E., Campbell, J. P., & Zedeck, S. (1981). *Measurement theory for the behavioral sciences.* San Francisco, CA: W. H. Freeman.

Giguère, G. (2007). Collecting and analyzing data in multidimensional scaling experiments: A guide for psychologists using SPSS. *Tutorials in Quantitative Methods for Psychology, 2,* 26–37.

Gill, J. (2001). *Generalized linear models: A unified approach.* Thousand Oaks, CA: Sage.

Glenn, N. D. (2005). *Cohort analysis* (2nd ed.). Thousand Oaks, CA: Sage.

Gliner, J. A., Leech, N. L., & Morgan, G. A. (2002). Problems with null hypothesis significance testing (NHST): What do the textbooks say? *Journal of Experimental Education, 71,* 83–92.

Glorfeld, L. W. (1995). An improvement on Horn's parallel analysis methodology for selecting the correct number of factors to retain. *Educational and Psychological Measurement, 6,* 427–439.

Goldstein, H. (2011a). Ethical aspects of multilevel modeling. In A. T. Panter & S. K. Sterba (Eds.), *Handbook of ethics in quantitative methodology* (pp. 341–355). New York, NY: Routledge.

Goldstein, H. (2011b). *Multilevel statistical models* (4th ed.). Chichester, England: Wiley.

Goodman, L. A. (1960). On the exact variance of products. *Journal of the American Statistical Association, 55,* 708–713.

Gorsuch, R. L. (1983). *Factor analysis* (2nd ed.). Hillsdale, NJ: Lawrence Erlbaum.

Gorsuch, R. L. (1990). Common factor analysis versus component analysis: Some well and little known facts. *Multivariate Behavioral Research, 25,* 33–39.

Gorsuch, R. L. (2003). Factor analysis. In J. A. Schinka & W. F. Velicer (Eds.), *Handbook of psychology: Vol. 2. Research methods in psychology* (pp. 143–164). Hoboken, NJ: Wiley.

Gorunescu, F. (2011). *Data mining: Concepts, models, and techniques.* Berlin, Germany: Springer.

Gould, W., Pitblado, J., & Sribney, W. (2006). *Maximum likelihood estimation with stata* (3rd ed.). College Station, TX: Stata Press.

Graham, J. W. (2009). Missing data analysis: Making it work in the real world. *Annual Review of Psychology, 60*, 549– 576.

Graham, J. W., Cumsille, P. E., & Elek-Fisk, E. (2003). Methods for handling missing data. In W. F. Velicer & J. A. Schinka (Eds.), *Handbook of psychology: Research methods in psychology* (Vol. 2, pp. 87–114). New York, NY: Wiley.

Graham, J. W., Olchowski, A. E., & Gilreath, T. D. (2007). How many imputations are really needed? Some practical clarifications of multiple imputation theory. *Prevention Science, 8*, 206–213.

Green, D. M., & Swets, J. M. (1966). *Signal detection theory and psychophysics.* New York, NY: Wiley.

Green, P. E., & Rao, V. R. (1972). *Applied multidimensional scaling: A comparison of approaches and algorithms.* Hinsdale, IL: Dryden Press.

Green, S. A. (1991). How many subjects does it take to do a multiple regression analysis. *Multivariate Behavioral Research, 26*, 499–510.

Green, S. B., Thompson, M. S., & Babyak, M. A. (1998). A Monte Carlo investigation of methods for controlling Type I errors with specification searches in structural equation modeling. *Multivariate Behavioral Research, 33*, 365– 383.

Greenhouse, S. W., & Geisser, S. (1959). On methods in the analysis of profile data. *Psychometrika, 32*, 95–112.

Gregorich, S. E. (2006). Do self-report instruments allow meaningful comparisons across diverse population groups? Testing measurement invariance using the confirmatory factor analysis framework. *Medical Care, 44*(11 Suppl. 3), S78–S94.

Grimm, L. G., & Yarnold, P. R. (2000). Introduction to multivariate statistics. In L. G. Grimm & P. R. Yarnold (Eds.), *Reading and understanding more multivariate statistics* (pp. 3–21). Washington, DC: American Psychological Association.

Guarino, A. J. (2004). A comparison of first and second generation multivariate analysis: Canonical correlation analysis and structural equation modeling. *Florida Journal of Educational Research, 42*, 22–40.

Guilford, J. P. (1954). *Psychometric methods.* New York, NY: McGraw-Hill.

Guilford, J. P., & Fruchter, B. (1978). *Fundamental statistics in psychology and education* (6th ed.). New York, NY: McGraw-Hill.

Guyatt, G., Jaeschke, R., Heddle, N., Cook, D., Shannon, H., & Walter, S. (1995). Interpreting study results: Confidence intervals. *Canadian Medical Association Journal, 152*, 169–173.

Hair, J. F., Jr., Black, W. C., Babin, B. J., & Anderson, R. E. (2010). *Multivariate data analysis* (7th ed.). Upper Saddle River, NJ: Prentice Hall.

Hakstian, A. R., Roed, J. C., & Lind, J. C. (1979). Two-sample T_2 procedure and the assumption of homogeneous covariance matrices. *Psychological Bulletin, 56*, 1255–1263.

Hand, D. J., & Crowder, M. (1996). *Practical longitudinal data analysis.* New York, NY: Chapman & Hall.

Hand, D. J., & Taylor, C. C. (1987). *Multivariate analysis of variance and repeated measures.* London, England: Chapman & Hall.

Hardin, J. W., & Hilbe, J. M. (2008). *Generalized linear models and extensions* (2nd ed.). College Station, TX: Stata Press.

Hardy, M. A. (1993). *Regression with dummy variables.* Newbury Park, CA: Sage.

Harlow, L. L. (2005). *The essence of multivariate thinking.* Mahwah, NJ: Lawrence Erlbaum.

Harmon, H. H. (1960). *Modern factor analysis.* Chicago, IL: University of Chicago Press.

Harmon, H. H. (1967). *Modern factor analysis* (2nd ed.). Chicago, IL: University of Chicago Press.

Harrington, D. (2009). *Confirmatory factor analysis.* New York, NY: Oxford University Press.

Harris, R. J. (1993). Multivariate analysis of variance. In L. K. Edwards (Ed.), *Applied analysis of variance in behavioral science* (pp. 255–296). New York, NY: Marcel Dekker.

Harris, R. J. (2001). *A primer of multivariate analysis* (3rd ed.). Mahwah, NJ: Lawrence Erlbaum.

Hartigan, J. A., & Wong, M. A. (1979). A K-means clustering algorithm. *Applied Statistics, 28*, 100–108.

Hartley, H. O., & Searle, S. R. (1969). On interaction variance components in mixed models. *Biometrics, 25*, 573–576.

Hauser, R. M. (1972). Disaggregating a social-psychological model of educational attainment.

Social Science Research, 1, 159–188.

Hayes, A. F. (2009). Beyond Baron and Kenny: Statistical mediation analysis in the new millennium. *Communication Monographs, 76*, 408–420.

Hayton, J. C., Allen, D. G., & Scarpello, V. (2004). Factor retention decisions in exploratory factor analysis: A tutorial on parallel analysis. *Organizational Research Methods, 7*, 191–205.

Heck, R. H., & Thomas, S. L. (2008). *An introduction to multilevel modeling techniques.* New York: Psychology Press.

Heck, R. H., Thomas, S. L., & Tabata, L. N. (2010). *Multilevel and longitudinal modeling with IBM SPSS.* New York, NY: Routledge.

Hofer, S. M., Horn, J. L., & Eber, H. W. (1997). A robust five-factor structure of the 16PF: Evidence from independent rotation and confirmatory factorial invariance procedures. *Personality and Individual Differences, 23*, 247–269.

Holloway, L. N., & Dunn, O. J. (1967). The robustness of Hotelling's T_2. *Journal of the American Statistical Association, 62*, 124–136.

Horn, J. L. (1965). A rationale and test for the number of factors in factor analysis. *Psychometrics, 30*, 179–185.

Horn, J. L., & McArdle, J. J. (1992). A practical and theoretical guide to measurement invariance in aging research. *Experimental Aging Research, 18*, 117–144.

Hosmer, D. W., Jr., & Lemeshow, S. (2000). *Applied logistic regression* (2nd ed.). New York, NY: Wiley.

Hosmer, D. W., Jr., & Lemeshow, S. (2002). *Applied survival analysis: Regression modeling of time to event data, textbook and solutions manual.* New York, NY: Wiley.

Hotelling, H. (1931). The generalization of student's ratio. *Annals of Mathematical Statistics, 2*, 360–378.

Hotelling, H. (1933). Analysis of a complex of statistical variables into principal components. *Journal of Educational Psychology, 24*, 498–520.

Hotelling, H. (1936a). Relations between two sets of variables. *Biometrika, 28*, 321–377.

Hotelling, H. (1936b). Simplified calculation of principal components. *Psychometrika, 1*, 27–35.

Howell, D. C. (1997). *Statistical methods for psychology* (4th ed.). Belmont, CA: Duxbury.

Hox, J. (2000). Multilevel analyses of grouped and longitudinal data. In T. D. Little, K. U. Schnabel, & J. Baumert (Eds.), *Modeling longitudinal and multilevel data* (pp. 15–32). Mahwah, NJ: Lawrence Erlbaum.

Hox, J. (2010). *Multilevel analysis: Techniques and applications* (2nd ed.). New York, NY: Psychology Press.

Hox, J., & Roberts, J. K. (2010). *Handbook of advanced multilevel analysis.* New York, NY: Psychology Press.

Hoyle, R. H. (Ed.). (1995). *Structural equation modeling: Concepts, issues, and applications.* Thousand Oaks, CA: Sage.

Hsiao, C. (2003). *Analysis of panel data* (2nd ed.). Cambridge, England: Cambridge University Press.

Hu, L., & Bentler, P. M. (1999a). Cutoff criteria for fit indexes in covariance structure analysis: Conventional criteria versus new alternatives. *Structural Equation Modeling, 6*, 1–55.

Hu, L., & Bentler, P. M. (1999b). Evaluating model fit. In R. H. Hoyle (Ed.), *Structural equation modeling: Concepts, issues, and applications* (pp. 76–99). Thousand Oaks, CA: Sage.

Hubert, L., Arabie, P., & Hesson-Mcinnis, M. (1992). Multidimensional scaling in the city-block metric: A combinatorial approach. *Journal of Classification, 9*, 211–236.

Huberty, C. J. (1984). Issues in the use and interpretation of discriminant analysis. *Psychological Bulletin, 95*, 156–171.

Huberty, C. J. (1989). Multivariate analysis versus multiple univariate analyses. *Psychological Bulletin, 105,* 302–308.

Huberty, C. J. (1994). *Applied discriminant analysis.* New York, NY: Wiley.

Huberty, C. J., & Barton, R. M. (1989). An introduction to discriminant analysis. *Measurement and Evaluation in Counseling and Development, 22,* 158–168.

Huberty, C. J., & Morris, J. D. (1989). Multivariate analysis versus multiple univariate analyses. *Psychological Bulletin, 105,* 302–308.

Huberty, C. J., & Olejnik, S. (2006). *Applied MANOVA and discriminant analysis* (2nd ed.). Hoboken, NJ: Wiley.

Huberty, C. J., Wisenbaker, J. M., & Smith, J. C. (1987). Assessing predictive accuracy in discriminant analysis. *Multivariate Behavioral Research, 22,* 307–329.

Huck, S. W. (2004). *Reading statistics and research* (4th ed.). New York, NY: Pearson Education.

Hummel, T. J., & Sligo, J. (1971). Empirical comparison of univariate and multivariate analysis of variance procedures. *Psychological Bulletin, 76,* 49–57.

Humphreys, L. G., & Montanelli, R. G., Jr. (1975). An investigation of the parallel analysis criterion for determining the number of common factors. *Multivariate Behavioral Research, 10,* 193–205.

Huo, Y., & Budescu, D. V. (2009). An extension of dominance analysis to canonical correlation analysis. *Multivariate Behavioral Research, 44,* 688–709.

Hutcheson, G., & Sofroniou, N. (1999). *The multivariate social scientist: Introductory statistics using generalized linear models.* Thousand Oaks, CA: Sage.

Jaccard, J., & Becker, R. A. (1990). *Statistics for the behavioral sciences* (2nd ed.). Belmont, CA: Wadsworth.

Jaccard, J., & Choi, K. W. (1996). *LISREL approaches to interaction effects in multiple regression.* Thousand Oaks, CA: Sage.

Jaccard, J., & Wan, C. K. (1995). Measurement error in the analysis of interaction effects between continuous predictors using multiple regression: Multiple indicator and structural equation approaches. *Psychological Bulletin, 117,* 348–357.

Jacoby, W. G. (1991). *Data theory and dimensional analysis.* Newbury Park, CA: Sage.

James, L. R., & Brett, J. M. (1984). Mediators, moderators, and tests for mediation. *Journal of Applied Psychology, 69,* 307–321.

James, W. L., & Hatten, K. J. (1995). Further evidence on the validity of the self typing paragraph approach: Miles and Snow strategic archetypes in banking. *Strategic Management Journal, 16,* 161–168.

Jaworska, N., & Chupetlovska-Anastasova, A. (2009). A review of multidimensional scaling (MDS) and utility in various psychological domains. *Tutorials in Quantitative Methods for Psychology, 5,* 1–10.

Jewell, D. V. (2011). *Guide to evidence-based physical therapist practice* (2nd ed.). Sudbury, MA: Jones & Bartlett.

Joachimsthaler, E. A., & Stam, A. (1990). Mathematical programming approaches for the classification problem in two- group discriminant analysis. *Multivariate Behavioral Research, 25,* 427–454.

Johnson, R. A., & Wichern, D. W. (1999). *Applied multivariate statistical analysis* (4th ed.). Upper Saddle River, NJ: Prentice Hall.

Jöreskog, K. G. (1969). A general approach to confirmatory maximum likelihood factor analysis. *Psychometrika, 34,* 183– 202.

Jöreskog, K. G. (1971). Simultaneous factor analysis in several populations. *Psychometrika, 36,* 409–426. –

Jöreskog, K. G., & Sörbom, D. (1996). *LISREL 8 user's reference guide.* Chicago, IL: Scientific Software International.

Judd, C. M., & Kenny, D. A. (1981). Process analysis: Estimating mediation in evaluation research. *Evaluation Review, 5,* 602–619.

Judd, C. M., McClelland, G. H., & Culhane, S. E. (1995). Data analysis: Continuing issues in the everyday analysis of psychological data. *Annual Review of Psychology, 46,* 433–465.

Kachigan, S. K. (1986). *Statistical analysis: An interdisciplinary introduction to univariate & multivariate methods.* New York, NY: Radius Press.

Kahane, L. H. (2001). *Regression basics.* Thousand Oaks, CA: Sage.

Kahn, J. A., Rosenthal, S. L., Succop, P. A., Ho, G. Y. F., & Burk, R. D. (2002). Mediators of the association between age of first sexual intercourse and subsequent human papillomavirus infection. *Pediatrics, 109,* 1–8.

Kaiser, H. F. (1958). The varimax criterion for analytic rotation in factor analysis. *Psychometrika, 23,* 187–200.

Kaiser, H. F. (1960). The application of electronic computers to factor analysis. *Educational and Psychological Measurement, 20,* 141–151.

Kaiser, H. F. (1970). A second-generation Little Jiffy. *Psychometrika, 35,* 401–415.

Kaiser, H. F. (1974). An index of factorial simplicity. *Psychometrika, 39,* 31–36.

Kaplan, R. M., & Saccuzzo, D. P. (2008). *Psychological testing: Principles, applications, and issues* (7th ed.). Belmont, CA: Thomson Wadsworth.

Kasser, T., & Ryan, R. M. (1993). A dark side of the American dream: Correlates of financial success as a central life aspiration. *Journal of Personality and Social Psychology, 65,* 410–422.

Kasser, T., & Ryan, R. M. (1996). Further examining the American dream: Differential correlates of intrinsic and extrinsic goals. *Personality and Social Psychology Bulletin, 22,* 280–287.

Kazelskis, R. (1978). A correction for loading bias in a principal components analysis. *Educational and Psychological Measurement, 38,* 253–257.

Kelloway, E. K. (1995). Structural equation modeling in perspective. *Journal of Organizational Behavior, 16,* 215–224.

Kelloway, E. K. (1998). *Using LISREL for structural equation modeling: A researcher's guide.* Thousand Oaks, CA: Sage.

Kenny, D. A. (2003). *Measuring model fit.* Retrieved from http://davidakenny.net/cm/fit.htm

Kenny, D. A., Bolger, N., & Kashy, D. A. (2002). Traditional methods for estimating multilevel models. In D. S. Moskowitz & S. L. Hershberger (Eds.), *Modeling intra-individual variability with repeated measures data: Methods and applications* (pp. 1–24). Mahwah, NJ: Lawrence Erlbaum.

Keppel, G. (1991). *Design and analysis: A researcher's handbook* (3rd ed.). Englewood Cliffs, NJ: Prentice Hall.

Keppel, G., Saufley, W. H., & Tokunaga, H. (1992). *Introduction to design and analysis: A student's handbook* (2nd ed.). New York, NY: W. H. Freeman.

Keppel, G., & Wickens, T. D. (2004). *Design and analysis: A researcher's handbook* (4th ed.). Upper Saddle River, NJ: Prentice Hall.

Keppel, G., & Zedeck, S. (1989). *Data analysis for research designs: Analysis of variance and multiple regression approaches.* New York, NY: W. H. Freeman.

Kessler, R. C., & Greenberg, D. F. (1981). *Linear panel analysis: Models of quantitative change.* New York, NY: Academic Press.

Keyser, V. (2010). *The predictors of self-perceived cultural competence in children's mental health providers* (Unpublished doctoral dissertation). University of La Verne, La Verne, CA.

Kim, J.-S. (2009). Multilevel analysis: An overview and some contemporary issues. In R. E. Milsap & A. Maydeu-Olivares (Eds.), *The Sage handbook of quantitative methods in psychology* (pp. 337–361). Thousand Oaks, CA: Sage.

Kim, K., & Neil, T. (2007). *Univariate and multivariate general linear models* (2nd ed.). Boca Raton, FL: Chapman & Hall/CRC.

Kirk, R. E. (1995). *Experimental design: Procedures for the behavioral sciences* (3rd ed.). Pacific Grove, CA: Brooks/Cole.

Kirk, R. E. (1996). Practical significance: A concept whose time has come. *Educational and Psychological Measurement, 56,* 746–759.

Kirk, R. E. (2008). *Statistics: An introduction* (5th ed.). Belmont, CA: Thomson/Wadsworth.

Klecka, W. R. (1980). *Discriminant analysis.* Beverly Hills, CA: Sage.

Klee, T., Pearce, K., & Carson, D. K. (2000). Improving the positive predictive value of screening for developmental language disorder. *Journal of Speech, Language, and Hearing Research, 43,* 821–833.

Klein, J. P., & Moeschberger, M. L. (2003). *Survival analysis: Techniques for censored and truncated data* (2nd ed.). New York, NY: Springer.

Kleinbaum, D. G., & Klein, M. (2005). *Survival analysis: A self-learning text* (2nd ed.). New York, NY: Springer.

Kleinbaum, D. G., Klein, M., & Pryor, E. R. (2002). *Logistic regression: A self-learning text.* New York, NY: Springer.

Klem, L. (1995). Path analysis. In L. G. Grimm & P. R. Yarnold (Eds.), *Reading and understanding multivariate statistics* (pp. 65–98). Washington, DC: American Psychological Association.

Klem, L. (2000). Structural equation modeling. In L. G. Grimm & P. R. Yarnold (Eds.), *Reading and understanding more multivariate statistics* (pp. 227–260). Washington, DC: American Psychological Association.

Kline, P. (1994). *An easy guide to factor analysis.* New York, NY: Routledge.

Kline, R. B. (2004). *Beyond significance testing.* Washington, DC: American Psychological Association.

Kline, R. B. (2011). *Principles and practice of structural equation modeling* (3rd ed.). New York, NY: Guilford Press.

Klockars, A. J., & Sax, G. (1986). *Multiple comparisons.* Beverly Hills, CA: Sage.

Knapp, T. R. (1978). Canonical correlation analysis: A general parametric significance testing system. *Psychological Bulletin, 85,* 410–416.

Knight, G. P., Virdin, L. M., Ocampo, K. A., & Roosa, M. (1994). An examination of the cross-ethnic equivalence of measures of negative life events and the mental health among Hispanic and Anglo American children. *American Journal of Community Psychology, 22,* 767–783.

Konishi, S., & Honda, M. (1990). Comparison procedures for estimation of error rates in discriminant analysis under non- normal populations. *Journal of Statistical Computing and Simulation, 36,* 105–115.

Kreft, I., & de Leeuw, J. (2007). *Introducing multilevel modeling.* London, England: Sage.

Kreft, I., de Leeuw, J., & Aiken, L. S. (1995). The effect of different forms of centering in hierarchical linear models. *Multivariate Behavioral Research, 30,* 1–21.

Kromrey, J. D., & Foster-Johnson, L. (1998). Mean centering in moderated multiple regression: Much ado about nothing. *Educational and Psychological Measurement, 58,* 42–67.

Kruskal, J. B. (1964a). Multidimensional scaling by optimizing goodness of fit to a nonmetric hypothesis. *Psychometrika, 29,* 1–28.

Kruskal, J. B. (1964b). Nonmetric multidimensional scaling: A numerical method. *Psychometrika, 29*(2): 115–129.

Kruskal, J. B., & Wish, M. (1978). *Multidimensional scaling.* Newbury Park, CA: Sage.

Kuder, G. F., & Richardson, M. W. (1937). The theory of the estimation of reliability. *Psychometrika, 2,* 151–160.

Lachenbruch, P. A. (1975). *Discriminant analysis.* New York, NY: Hafner Press.

Lane, C. J., & Zelinski, E. M. (2003). Longitudinal hierarchical linear models of the Memory Functioning Questionnaire. *Psychology and Aging, 18,* 38–53.

Lattin, J. M., Carroll, J. D., & Green, P. E. (2003). *Analyzing multivariate data.* Pacific Grove, CA: Brooks/Cole.

Lautenschlager, G. J. (1989). A comparison of alternatives to conducting Monte Carlo analyses for determining parallel analysis criteria. *Multivariate Behavioral Research, 24,* 365–395.

Lauter, J. (1978). Sample size requirements for the T_2 test of MANOVA (tables for one-way classification). *Biometrical Journal, 20,* 389–406.

Lee, E. T., & Wang, J. W. (2003). *Statistical methods for survival data analysis* (3rd ed.). New York, NY: Wiley.

Leidy, N. K. (1990). A structural model of stress, psychosocial resources, and symptomatic experience in chronic physical illness. *Nursing Research, 39,* 230–236.

Letbetter, A. (2009). Family communication patterns and relational maintenance behavior: Direct and mediated associations with friendship closeness. *Human Communication Research, 35,* 130–147.

Levine, M. S. (1977). *Canonical analysis and factor comparison.* Newbury Park, CA: Sage.

Levine, T. R., & Hullett, C. R. (2002). Eta squared, partial eta squared, and misreporting of effect size in Communication research. *Human Communication Research, 28,* 612–625.

Levy, P. S., & Lemeshow, S. (2008). *Sampling of populations: Methods and applications* (4th ed.). Hoboken, NJ: Wiley.

Lievens, F., & Anseel, F. (2004). Confirmatory factor analysis and invariance of an organizational citizenship behaviour measure across samples in a Dutch-speaking context. *Journal of Occupational and Organizational Psychology, 77,* 299–306.

Likert, R. (1932). A technique for the measurement of attitudes. *Archives of Psychology, 140,* 5–53.

Likert, R., Roslow, S., & Murphy, G. (1934). A simple and reliable method of scoring the Thurstone attitude scales. *Journal of Social Psychology, 5,* 228–238.

Link, S. W. (1994). Rediscovering the past: Gustav Fechner and signal detection theory. *Psychological Science, 5,* 335– 340.

Little, R. J. A. (1988). A test of missing completely at random for multivariate data with missing values. *Journal of the American Statistical Association, 83,* 1198–1202.

Little, R. J. A., & Rubin, D. B. (2002). *Statistical analysis with missing data* (2nd ed.). Hoboken, NJ: Wiley.

Liu, B. (2007). *Web data mining: Exploring hyperlinks, contents, and usage data.* New York, NY: Springer.

Liu, O. L., & Rijmen, F. (2008). A modified procedure for parallel analysis of ordered categorical data. *Behavior Research Methods, 40,* 556–562.

Lix, L. M., & Keselman, H. J. (2004). Multivariate tests of means in independent groups designs: Effects of covariance heterogeneity and nonnormality. *Evaluation & the Health Professions, 27,* 45–69.

Loehlin, J. C. (1992). *Latent variable models: An introduction to factor, path, and structural analysis* (2nd ed.). Hillsdale, NJ: Lawrence Erlbaum.

Loehlin, J. C. (2004). *Latent variable models: An introduction to factor, path, and structural analysis* (4th ed.). Mahwah, NJ: Lawrence Erlbaum.

Lohr, S. L. (2010). *Sampling: Design and analysis* (2nd ed.). Boston, MA: Brooks/Cole, Cengage Learning.

Long, J. S. (1983). *Confirmatory factor analysis.* Newbury Park, CA: Sage.

Lopez, R. P., & Guarino, A. J. (2011). Uncertainty and decision making for residents with dementia. *Clinical Nursing Research, 20,* 228–240.

Lord, F. M. (1953). The relation of test scores to the trait underlying the test. *Educational and Psychological Measurement, 13,* 517–548.

Lord, F. M., & Novick, M. R. (1968). *Statistical theories of mental test scores.* Reading, MA: Addison-Wesley.

Lorenz, F. O. (1987). Teaching about influence in simple regression. *Teaching Sociology, 15,* 173–177.

Luke, D. A. (2004). *Multilevel modeling.* Thousand Oaks, CA: Sage.

Lutz, J. G., & Eckert, T. L. (1994). The relationship between canonical correlation analysis and multivariate multiple regression. *Educational and Psychological Measurement, 54,* 666–675.

Maassen, G. H., & Bakker, A. B. (2001). Suppressor variables in path models: Definitions and interpretations. *Sociological Methods & Research, 30,* 241–270.

MacCallum, R. C. (2009). Factor analysis. In R. E. Millsap & A. Maydeu-Olivares (Eds.), *The Sage handbook of quantitative methods in psychology* (pp. 123–147). Thousand Oaks, CA: Sage.

MacCallum, R. C., Kim, C., Malarkey, W. B., & Kiecolt-Glaser, J. K. (1997). Studying multivariate change using multilevel models and latent curve models. *Multivariate Behavioral Research, 32,* 215–253.

MacCallum, R. C., Wegener, D. T., Uchino, B. N., & Fabrigar, L. R. (1993). The problem of equivalent models in applications of covariance structure analysis. *Psychological Bulletin, 114,* 185–199.

MacKinnon, D. P. (2008). *Introduction to statistical mediation analysis.* Mahwah, NJ: Lawrence Erlbaum.

MacKinnon, D. P., & Dwyer, J. H. (1993). Estimating mediated effects in prevention studies. *Evaluation Review, 17,* 144– 158.

MacKinnon, D. P., Fairchild, A. J., & Fritz, M. S. (2007). Mediation analysis. *Annual Review of Psychology, 58,* 593–614.

MacKinnon, D. P., Krull, J. L, & Lockwood, C. M. (2000). Equivalence of the mediation, confounding and suppression effect. *Prevention Science, 1,* 173–181.

MacKinnon, D. P., Lockwood, C. M., Hoffman, J. M., West, S. G., & Sheets, V. (2002). A comparison of methods to test mediation and other intervening variable effects. *Psychological Methods, 7,* 83–104.

Macmillan, N. A., & Creelman, C. D. (2005). *Detection theory: A user's guide* (2nd ed.). Mahwah, NJ: Lawrence Erlbaum.

MacQueen, J. (1967). Some methods for classification and analysis of multivariate observations. In L. M. LeCam & J. Neyman (Eds.), *Proceedings of the 5th Berkeley Symposium on Mathematical Statistics and Probability, 5,* 281– 297.

Magura, S., & Rosenblum, A. (2000). Modulating effect of alcohol use on cocaine use. *Addictive Behaviors, 25,* 117–122.

Mallinckrodt, B., Abraham, W. T., Wei, M., & Russell, D. W. (2006). Advances in testing the statistical significance of mediation effects. *Journal of Counseling Psychology, 53,* 372–378.

Mallows, C. L. (1973). Some comments on C_p. *Technometrics, 15,* 661–675.

Mandel, J. S., Church, T. R., Bond, J. H., Ederer, F., Geisser, M. S., Nongin, S. J., Snoever, D. C., & Schuman, L. M. (2000). The effect of fecal occult-blood screening on the incidence of colorectal cancer. *New England Journal of Medicine, 343,* 1603–1607.

Mandrekar, J. N. (2010). Receiver operating characteristic curve in diagnostic test assessment. *Journal of Thoracic Oncology, 5,* 1315–1316.

Marsh, H. W., & Hocevar, D. (1985). Application of confirmatory factor analysis to the study of self-concept: First- and higher-order factor models and their invariance across groups. *Psychological Bulletin, 97,* 562–582.

Martens, M. P. (2005). The use of structural equation modeling in counseling psychology research. *The Counseling Psychologist, 33,* 269–298.

Martens, M. P., & Haase, R. F. (2006). Advanced applications of structural equation modeling in counseling psychology research. *The Counseling Psychologist, 34,* 878–911.

Maruyama, G. M. (1998). *Basics of structural equation modeling.* Thousand Oaks, CA: Sage.

Mason, W. M., & Fineberg, S. E. (Eds.). (1985). *Cohort analysis in social research: Beyond the identification problem.* New York, NY: Springer-Verlag.

Mason, W. M., & Wolfinger, N. H. (2001). Cohort analysis. In N. J. Smelser & P. B. Baltes (Eds.), *International encyclopedia of social & behavioral sciences* (pp. 2189–2194). Amsterdam, Netherlands: Elsevier Science.

Mauchly, J. W. (1940). Significance test for sphericity of *n*-variate normal populations. *Mathematical Statistics, 11,* 37– 53.

Maxwell, S. E., & Delaney, H. D. (2000). *Designing experiments and analyzing data.* Mahwah, NJ: Lawrence Erlbaum.

Maxwell, S. E., Kelley, K., & Rausch, J. R. (2008). Sample size planning for statistical power and accuracy in parameter estimation. *Annual Review of Psychology, 59,* 537–563.

McClelland, G. H. (1993). Statistical difficulties of detecting interactions and moderator effects. *Psychological Bulletin, 114,* 376–390.

McCullagh, P., & Nelder, J. A. (1999). *Generalized linear models* (2nd ed.). Boca Raton, FL: Chapman & Hall/CRC.

McDonald, R. A., Seifert, C. F., Lorenzet, S. J., Givens, S., & Jaccard, J. (2002). The effectiveness of methods for analyzing multivariate factorial data. *Organizational Research Methods, 5,* 255–274.

McDonald, R. P. (1996). Path analysis with composite variables. *Multivariate Behavioral Research, 31,* 239–270.

McGee, V. E. (1968). Multidimensional scaling of N-sets of similarity measures. A nonmetric individual differences approach. *Multivariate Behavioral Research, 3*, 233–248.

McKnight, P. E., McKnight, K. M., Sidani, S., & Figuerdo, A. J. (2007). *Missing data: A gentle introduction.* New York, NY: Guilford Press.

McLachlan, G. J. (1992). *Discriminant analysis and statistical pattern recognition.* New York, NY: Wiley.

McLaughlin, M. L. (1980). Discriminant analysis. In P. Monge & J. Cappella (Eds.), *Multivariate techniques in human communication research* (pp. 175–204). New York, NY: Academic Press.

Meehl, P. E., & Waller, N. G. (2002). The path analysis controversy: A new statistical approach to strong appraisal of verisimilitude. *Psychological Methods, 7*, 283–300.

Menard, S. (1991). *Longitudinal research.* Newbury Park, CA: Sage.

Menard, S. (2002). *Applied logistic regression analysis* (2nd ed.). Thousand Oaks, CA: Sage.

Menard, S. (2010). *Logistic regression: From introductory to advanced concepts and applications.* Thousand Oaks, CA: Sage.

Meredith, W., & Horn, J. L. (2001). The role of factorial invariance in modeling growth and change. In L. M. Collins & A. G. Sayer (Eds.), *New methods for the analysis of change* (pp. 204–240). Washington, DC: American Psychological Association.

Mertler, C. A., & Vannatta, R. A. (2001). *Advanced and multivariate statistical methods: Practical application and interpretation.* Los Angeles, CA: Pyrczak.

Meyers, L. S., Gamst, G., & Guarino, A. J. (2009). *Data analysis using SAS enterprise guide.* New York, NY: Cambridge University Press.

Millar, R. B. (2011). *Maximum likelihood estimation and inference: With examples in R, SAS and ADMB.* Chichester, England: Wiley.

Milligan, G. W., & Cooper, M. C. (1985). An examination of procedures for determining the number of clusters in a data set. *Psychometrika, 50*, 159–179.

Milliken, G. A., & Johnson, D. E. (1984). *Analysis of messy data: Vol. 1. Designed experiments.* New York, NY: Van Nostrand Reinhold.

Mittag, K. C., & Thompson, B. (2000). A national survey of AERA members' perceptions of statistical significance tests and other statistical issues. *Educational Researcher, 29*, 14–20.

Mollenkopf, W. G. (1949). Variation of the standard error of measurement. *Psychometrika, 14*, 189–229.

Montanelli, R. G., Jr., & Humphreys, L. G. (1976). Latent roots of random data correlation matrices with squared multiple correlations on the diagonal: A Monte Carlo study. *Psychometrika, 41*, 341–348.

Morgan, G. A., Griego, O. V., & Gloeckner, G. W. (2001). *SPSS for Windows: An introduction to use and interpretation in research.* Mahwah, NJ: Lawrence Erlbaum.

Morrison, D. G. (1969). On the interpretation of discriminant analysis. *Journal of Marketing Research, 6*, 156–163.

Mosteller, F., & Tukey, J. W. (1977). *Data analysis and regression.* Reading, MA: Addison-Wesley.

Mudholkar, G. S., & Subbaiah, P. (1980). MANOVA multiple comparisons associated with finite intersection tests. In P. R. Krishnaiah (Ed.), *Multivariate analysis V* (pp. 467–482). Amsterdam, Netherlands: North-Holland.

Mueller, R. O. (1997). Structural equation modeling: Back to basics. *Structural Equation Modeling, 4*, 353–369.

Mulaik, S. (1972). *The foundations of factor analysis.* New York, NY: McGraw-Hill.

Mulaik, S. A., James, L. R., Van Alstine, J., Bennett, N., Lind, S., & Stilwell, C. D. (1989). Evaluation of goodness-of-fit indices for structural equation models. *Psychological Bulletin, 105*, 430–445.

Muller, K. E. (1982). Understanding canonical correlation through the general linear model and principal components. *American Statistician, 36*, 342–354.

Murphy, G., & Likert, R. (1937). *Public opinion and the individual.* New York, NY: Harper.

Myers, R. (1990). *Classical and modern regression with applications* (2nd ed.). Boston, MA: Duxbury Press.

Nelder, J. A., & Wedderburn, R. W. M. (1972). Generalized liner models. *Journal of the*

Royal Statistical Society, Series A (General), 135, 370–384.

Neuhaus, J. O., & Wrigley, C. (1954). The quartimax method: An analytical approach to orthogonal simple structure. *British Journal of Statistical Psychology, 7,* 81–91.

Norman, G. R., & Streiner, D. L. (2008). *Biostatistics: The bare essentials* (3rd ed.). Shelton, CT: People's Medical Publishing House.

Norusis, M. J. (2008). *SPSS statistics 17.0: Advanced statistical procedures companion.* Upper Saddle River, NJ: Prentice Hall.

Norusis, M. J. (2011). *PASW statistics 18 statistical procedures companion.* New York, NY: Pearson.

Nunnally, J. C., & Bernstein, I. H. (1994). *Psychometric theory* (3rd ed.). New York, NY: McGraw-Hill.

O'Brien, R. G., & Kaiser, M. K. (1985). MANOVA method for analyzing repeated measures designs: An extensive primer. *Psychological Bulletin, 97,* 316–333.

O'Connell, A. A., & McCoach, D. B. (2004). Applications of hierarchical linear models for evaluations of health interventions: Demystifying the methods and interpretations of multilevel models. *Evaluation & the Health Professions, 27,* 119–151.

O'Connor, B. P. (2000). SPSS and SAS programs for determining the number of components using parallel analysis and Velicer's MAP test. *Behavior Research Methods, Instruments, & Computers, 32,* 396–402.

Olejnik, S., & Algina, J. (2000). Measures of effect size for comparative studies: Applications, interpretations, and limitations. *Contemporary Educational Psychology, 25,* 241–286.

Olkin, E., & Pratt, J. W. (1958). Unbiased estimation of certain correlation coefficients. *Annals of Mathematical Statistics, 29,* 201–211.

Olobatuyi, M. E. (2006). *A user's guide to path analysis.* Lanham, MD: University Press of America.

Olson, C. L. (1974). Comparative robustness of six tests in multivariate analysis of variance. *Journal of the American Statistical Association, 69,* 894–908.

Olson, C. L. (1976). On choosing a test statistic in MANOVA. *Psychological Bulletin, 83,* 579–586.

Olson, C. L. (1979). Practical considerations in choosing a MANOVA test statistic: A rejoinder to Stevens. *Psychological Bulletin, 86,* 1350–1352.

Pagano, R. R. (1986). *Understanding statistics in the behavioral sciences* (2nd ed.). New York, NY: West.

Pampel, F. C. (2000). *Logistic regression: A primer.* Thousand Oaks, CA: Sage.

Panel on Discriminant Analysis, Classification and Clustering. (1989). Discriminant analysis and clustering. *Statistical Science, 4,* 34–69.

Park, C., & Dudycha, A. (1974). A cross-validation approach to sample size determination. *Journal of the American Statistical Association, 69,* 214–218.

Patil, V. H., Singh, S. N., Mishra, S., & Donavan, D. T. (2008). Efficient theory development and factor retention criteria: Abandon the "eigenvalue greater than one" criterion. *Journal of Business Research, 61,* 162–170.

Paxton, P. M., Hipp, J. R., & Marquart-Pyatt, S. (2011). *Nonrecursive models: Endogeneity, reciprocal relationships, and feedback loops.* Thousand Oaks, CA: Sage.

Pearl, J. (2011). The science and ethics of causal modeling. In A. T. Panter & S. K. Sterba (Eds.), *Handbook of ethics in quantitative methodology* (pp. 338–414). New York, NY: Routledge.

Pearson, K. (1901). On lines and planes of closest fit to systems of points in space. *Philosophical Magazine, 2,* 559–572.

Pedhazur, E. J. (1982). *Multiple regression in behavioral research: Explanation and prediction* (2nd ed.). New York, NY: Holt, Rinehart & Winston.

Pedhazur, E. J. (1997). *Multiple regression in behavioral research: Explanation and prediction* (3rd ed.). Orlando, FL: Harcourt Brace.

Pedhazur, E. J., & Schmelkin, L. P. (1991). *Measurement, design, and analysis: An integrated approach* (Student ed.). Hillsdale, NJ: Lawrence Erlbaum.

Peres-Neto, P. R., Jackson, D. A., & Somers, K. M. (2005). How many principal components? Stopping rules for determining the number of non-trivial axes revisited. *Computational Statistics & Data Analysis, 49,* 974–997.

Pett, M. A., Lackey, N. R., & Sullivan, J. L. (2003). *Making sense of factor analysis: The use of factor analysis for instrument development in health care research.* Thousand Oaks, CA: Sage.

Peugh, J. L., & Enders, C. K. (2005). Using the SPSS mixed procedure to fit cross-sectional and longitudinal multilevel models. *Educational and Psychological Measurement, 65,* 717–741.

Phinney, J. S., & Ong, A. D. (2007). Conceptualization and measurement of ethnic identity: Current status and future directions. *Journal of Counseling Psychology, 54,* 271–281.

Preacher, K. J., & Hayes, A. F. (2004). SPSS and SAS procedures for estimating indirect effects in simple mediation models. *Behavior Research Methods, Instruments, & Computers, 36,* 717–731.

Preacher, K. J., & Hayes, A. F. (2008). Asymptotic and resampling strategies for assessing and comparing indirect effects in multiple mediator models. *Behavior Research Methods, 40,* 879891.

Preacher, K. J., Rucker, D. D., & Hayes, A. F. (2007). Assessing moderated mediation hypotheses: Theory, method, and prescriptions. *Multivariate Behavioral Research, 42,* 185–227.

Press, S. J. (1972). *Applied multivariate analysis.* New York, NY: Holt, Rinehart & Winston.

Press, S. J., & Wilson, S. (1978). Choosing between logistic regression and discriminant analysis. *Journal of the American Statistical Association, 73,* 699–705.

Quenouille, M. H. (1949). Approximate tests of correlation in time series. *Journal of the Royal Statistical Society, Series B, 11,* 18–44.

Raftery, A. (1995). Bayesian model selection in social research. *Sociological Methodology, 25,* 111–163.

Ragsdale, C. T., & Stam, A. (1992). Introducing discriminant analysis to the business statistics curriculum. *Decision Sciences, 23,* 724–745.

Raundenbush, S. W. (2001). Comparing personal trajectories and drawing causal inferences from longitudinal data. *Annual Review of Psychology, 52,* 501–525.

Raudenbush, S. W., & Bryk, A. S. (2002). *Hierarchical linear models: Applications and data analysis methods* (2nd ed.). Thousand Oaks, CA: Sage.

Raykov, T., & Marcoulides, G. A. (2000). *A first course in structural equation modeling.* Mahwah, NJ: Wiley.

Raykov, T., & Marcoulides, G. A. (2006). *A first course in structural equation modeling* (2nd ed.). New York, NY: Routledge.

Raykov, T., & Marcoulides, G. A. (2008). *An introduction to applied multivariate analysis.* Mahwah, NJ: Lawrence Erlbaum.

Reilly, T. (1995). A necessary and sufficient condition for identification of confirmatory factor analysis models of complexity one. *Sociological Methods & Research, 23,* 421–441.

Reise, S. P., Widaman, K. F., & Pugh, R. H. (1993). Confirmatory factor analysis and item response theory: Two approaches for exploring measurement invariance. *Psychological Bulletin, 114,* 552–566.

Rice, J. C. (1994). Logistic regression: An introduction. In B. Thompson (Ed.), *Advances in social science methodology* (Vol. 3, pp. 191–245). Greenwich, CT: JAI Press.

Rigdon, E. E. (1995). A necessary and sufficient identification rule for structural models estimated in practice. *Multivariate Behavioral Research, 30,* 359–383.

Rodgers, W. L. (1982). Estimable functions of age, period, and cohort effects. *American Sociological Review, 47,* 774–787.

Romney, A. K., Shepard, R. N., & Nerlove, S. B. (1972). *Multidimensional scaling: Theory and applications in the behavioral sciences: Vol. 2. Applications.* New York, NY: Seminar Press.

Rosenbaum, M. (Ed.). (1990). *Learned resourcefulness: On coping skills, self-control, and adaptive behavior.* New York, NY: Springer.

Rosenberg, M. (1965). *Society and the adolescent self-image.* Princeton, NJ: Princeton University Press.

Rosenthal, R. (1991). *Meta-analytic procedures for social research* (Rev. ed.). Newbury Park, CA: Sage.

Rosenthal, R. (1994). Parametric measures of effect size. In H. Cooper & L. V. Hedges (Eds.), *The handbook of research synthesis* (pp. 231–244). New York, NY: Russell Sage.

Rosenthal, R., & Rosnow, R. L. (2008). *Essentials of behavioral research: Methods and data analysis* (3rd ed.). New York, NY: McGraw-Hill.

Rozeboom, W. W. (1978). Estimation of cross-validated multiple correlation: A clarification. *Psychological Bulletin, 85,* 1348–1351.

Rubin, D. B. (1976). Inference and missing data. *Biometrika, 63,* 581–592.

Rulon, P. J., & Brooks, W. D. (1968). On statistical tests of group differences. In D. K. Whitla (Ed.), *Handbook of measurement and assessment in behavioral sciences* (pp. 60–99). Reading, MA: Addison-Wesley.

Runyon, R. P., Coleman, K. A., & Pittenger, D. J. (2000). *Fundamentals of behavioral statistics* (9th ed.). Boston, MA: McGraw-Hill.

Salsburg, D. B. (2001). *The lady tasting tea.* New York, NY: W. H. Freeman.

Salthouse, T. A., Atkinson, T. M., & Berish, D. E. (2003). Executive functioning as a potential mediator of age-related cognitive decline in normal adults. *Journal of Experimental Psychology: General, 132,* 566–594.

Schafer, J. L. (1997). *The analysis of incomplete multivariate data.* New York, NY: Chapman & Hall/CRC.

Schafer, J. L., & Graham, J. W. (2002). Missing data: Our view of the state of the art. *Psychological Methods, 7,* 147–177.

Schafer, W. D. (1991). Reporting nonhierarchical regression results. *Measurement and Evaluation in Counseling and Development, 24,* 146–149.

Schiffman, S. S., Reynolds, M. L., & Young, F. W. (1981). *Introduction to multidimensional scaling theory, methods, and application.* New York, NY: Academic Press.

Schmidt, F. (1996). Statistical significance testing and cumulative knowledge in psychology: Implications for the training of researchers. *Psychological Methods, 1,* 115–129.

Schroeder, L. D., Sjoquist, D. L., & Stephan, P. E. (1986). *Understanding regression analysis: An introductory guide.* Beverly Hills, CA: Sage.

Schumacker, R. E., & Lomax, R. G. (2004). *A beginner's guide to structural equation modeling* (2nd ed.). Mahwah, NJ: Lawrence Erlbaum.

Schumacker, R. E., & Lomax, R. G. (2010). *A beginner's guide to structural equation modeling* (3rd ed.). New York, NY: Routledge.

Seaman, M. A., Levin, J. R., & Serlin, R. C. (1991). New developments in pairwise multiple comparisons: Some powerful and practicable procedures. *Psychological Bulletin, 110,* 577–586.

Senn, S. (2003). A conversation with John Nelder. *Statistical Science, 18,* 118–131.

Shadish, W. R., Cook, T. D., & Campbell, D. T. (2002). *Experimental and quasi-experimental designs for generalized causal inference.* Boston, MA: Houghton Mifflin.

Shaffer, J. P., & Gillo, M. W. (1974). A multivariate extension of the correlation ratio. *Educational and Psychological Measurement, 34,* 521–524.

Shapiro, S. S., & Wilk, M. B. (1965). An analysis of variance test for normality (complete samples). *Biometrika, 52,* 591–611.

Shapiro, S. S., Wilk, M. B., & Chen, H. J. (1968). A comparative study of various tests of normality. *Journal of the American Statistical Association, 63,* 1343–1372.

Shepard, R. N. (1962). The analysis of proximities: Multidimensional scaling with an unknown distance function. I. *Psychometrika, 27,* 125–140.

Shepard, R. N., Romney, A. K., & Nerlove, S. B. (1972). *Multidimensional scaling: Theory and application in the behavioral science: Vol. 1. Theory.* New York, NY: Seminar Press.

Sherry, A., & Henson, R. K. (2005). Conducting and interpreting canonical correlation analysis in personality research: A user-friendly primer. *Journal of Personality Assessment, 84*(1), 37–48.

Shrout, P. E., & Bolger, N. (2002). Mediation in experimental and nonexperimental studies:

New procedures and recommendations. *Psychological Methods, 7,* 422–445.

Shrout, P. E., & Fleiss, J. L. (1979). Intraclass correlations: Uses in assessing rater reliability. *Psychological Bulletin, 86,* 420–428.

Silver, N. C., & Dunlap, W. P. (1987). Averaging correlation coefficient: Should Fisher's *z* transformation be used? *Journal of Applied Psychology, 72,* 146–148.

Singer, J. D. (1998). Using SAS PROC MIXED to fit multilevel models, hierarchical models, and individual growth models. *Journal of Educational and Behavioral Statistics, 24,* 323–355.

Singer, J. D., & Willett, J. B. (1991). Modeling the days of our lives: Using survival analysis when designing and analyzing longitudinal studies of duration and the timing of events. *Psychological Bulletin, 110,* 268–290.

Singer, J. D., & Willett, J. B. (2003). *Applied longitudinal data analysis: Modeling change and event occurrence.* Oxford, England: Oxford University Press.

Snijders, T. A. B., & Bosker, R. J. (2012). *Multilevel analysis: An introduction to basic and advanced multilevel modeling* (2nd ed.). Thousand Oaks, CA: Sage.

Snyder, P., & Lawson, S. (1993). Evaluating results using corrected and uncorrected effect size estimates. *Journal of Experimental Education, 61,* 334–349.

Sobel, M. E. (1982). Aysmptotic confidence intervals for indirect effects and their standard errors in structural equation models. In N. Tuma (Ed.), *Sociological methodology* (pp. 159–186). San Francisco, CA: Jossey-Bass.

Sobel, M. E. (1986). Some new results on indirect effects in structural equation models. In S. Leinhardt (Ed.), *Sociological methodology* (pp. 290–312). Washington, DC: American Sociological Association.

Sokal, R. R., & Sneath, P. H. (1963). *Principles of numerical taxonomy.* San Francisco, CA: W. H. Freeman.

Soreide, K. (2009). Receiver-operating characteristic analysis in diagnostic, prognostic and predictive biomarker research. *Journal of Clinical Pathology, 62,* 1–5.

Soreide, K., Korner, H., & Soreide, J. A. (2011). Diagnostic accuracy and receiver-operating characteristics curve analysis in surgical research and decision making. *Annals of Surgery, 253,* 27–34.

Spatz, C. (2011). *Basic statistics: Tales of distributions* (10th ed.). Belmont, CA: Wadsworth.

Spearman, C. (1904). "General intelligence," objectively determined and measured. *American Journal of Psychology, 15,* 201–293.

Spector, P. E. (1976). Choosing response categories for summated rating scales. *Journal of Applied Psychology, 61,* 374– 375.

Spector, P. E. (1977). What to do with significant multivariate effects in multivariate analyses of variance. *Journal of Applied Psychology, 62,* 158–163.

Spicer, J. (2005). *Making sense of multivariate data analysis.* Thousand Oaks, CA: Sage.

Spink, K. S., & Nickel, D. (2010). Self-regulatory efficacy as a mediator between attributions and intention for health- related physical activity. *Journal of Health Psychology, 15,* 75–84.

SPSS, Inc. (1988). *Introduction to statistics guide SPSS-X.* Chicago, IL: Author.

SPSS, Inc. (2006). *SPSS base 15.0 user's guide.* Chicago, IL: Author.

SPSS, Inc. (2009). *PASW missing values 18.* Chicago, IL: Author.

SPSS, Inc. (2010). *IBM SPSS statistics 19 algorithms.* Chicago, IL: Author.

Stalans, L. J. (1995). Multidimensional scaling. In L. G. Grimm & P. R. Yarnold (Eds.), *Reading and understanding multivariate statistics.* Washington, DC: American Psychological Association.

Stanton, J. M. (2001). Galton, Pearson, and the peas: A brief history of linear regression for statistics instructors. *Journal of Statistics Education, 9*(3). Retrieved from http://www.amstat.org/publications/jse/v9n3/stanton.html

Steiger, J. H. (1990). Structural model evaluation and modification: An interval estimation approach. *Multivariate Behavioral Research, 25,* 173–180.

Steiger, J. H. (1998). A note on multisample extensions of the RMSEA fit index. *Structural Equation Modeling, 5,* 411– 419.

Steinley, D. (2006). *K*-means clustering: A half-century synthesis. *British Journal of Mathematical and Statistical Psychology, 59,* 1–34.

Steinley, D. (2007). Validating clusters with the lower bound for sum-of-squares error. *Psychometrika, 72,* 93–106.

Steinley, D., & Brusco, M. J. (2011). Choosing the number of clusters in *k*-means clustering. *Psychological Methods, 16,* 285–297.

Stevens, J. P. (1972). Four methods of analyzing between variation for the k group MANOVA problem. *Multivariate Behavioral Research, 7,* 499–522.

Stevens, J. P. (1980). Power of the multivariate analysis of variance tests. *Psychological Bulletin, 88,* 728–737.

Stevens, J. P. (2007). *Intermediate statistics: A modern approach* (3rd ed.). Mahwah, NJ: Lawrence Erlbaum.

Stevens, J. P. (2009). *Applied multivariate statistics for the social sciences* (5th ed.). New York, NY: Routledge.

Stevens, S. S. (1946). On the theory of scales of measurement. *Science, 103,* 677–680.

Stevens, S. S. (1951). Mathematics, measurement, and psychophysics. In S. S. Stevens (Ed.), *Handbook of experimental psychology* (pp. 1–49). New York, NY: Wiley.

Stevens, S. S. (1971). Issues in psychophysical measurement. *Psychological Review, 78,* 426–450.

Stewart, D., & Love, W. (1968). A general canonical correlation index. *Psychological Bulletin, 70,* 160–163.

Stigler, S. M. (1989). Francis Galton's account of the invention of correlation. *Statistical Science, 4,* 73–86.

Stigler, S. M. (1990). *The history of statistics: The measurement of uncertainty before 1900.* Cambridge, MA: Harvard University Press.

Stigler, S. M. (1999). *Statistics on the table: The history of statistical concepts and methods.* Cambridge, MA: Harvard University Press.

Streiner, D. L. (1998). Factors affecting reliability of interpretations of scree plots. *Psychological Reports, 83,* 687–694.

Student. (1908). The probable error of a mean. *Biometrika, 6,* 1–25.

Stuewig, J. (2010). Shrinkage. In N. J. Salkind (Ed.), *Encyclopedia of research design* (Vol. 3, pp. 1358–1360). Thousand Oaks, CA: Sage.

Swanson, H. L. (2005). Working memory, intelligence, and learning disabilities. In O. Wilhelm & R. W. Engle (Eds.), *Handbook of understanding and measuring intelligence* (pp. 409–430). Thousand Oaks, CA: Sage.

Swets, J. A. (1973). The relative operating characteristic in psychology. *Science, 182,* 990–1000.

Swets, J. A., Tanner, W. P., Jr., & Birdsall, T. G. (1961). Decision processes in perception. *Psychological Review, 68,* 302–340.

Tabachnick, B. G., & Fidell, L. S. (2007). *Using multivariate statistics* (5th ed.). Boston, MA: Pearson.

Tacq, J. (1997). *Analysis techniques in social science research.* Thousand Oaks, CA: Sage.

Takane, Y., & Hwang, H. (2002). Generalized constrained canonical correlation analysis. *Multivariate Behavioral Research, 37,* 163–195.

Takane, Y., Jung, S., & Oshima-Takane, Y. (2009). Multidimensional scaling. In R. E. Millsap & A. Maydeu-Olivares (Eds.), *The Sage handbook of quantitative methods in psychology* (pp. 219–242). Thousand Oaks, CA: Sage.

Takane, Y., Young, F. W., & de Leeuw, J. (1977). Nonmetric individual differences multidimensional scaling: An alternating least squares method with optimal scaling features. *Psychometrika, 42,* 7–67.

Tellegen, A. (1982). *Brief manual for the multidimensional personality questionnaire* (Unpublished). Department of Psychology, University of Minnesota, Minneapolis.

Tellegen, A., Ben-Porath, Y. S., McNulty, J. L., Arbisi, P. A., Graham, J. R., & Kaemmer, B. (2003). *The MMPI-2 restructured clinical (RC) scales: Development, validation, and interpretation.* Minneapolis: University of Minnesota Press (Distributed by Pearson Assessments).

Thomas, D. (1992). Interpreting discriminant functions: A data analytic approach. *Multivariate Behavioral Research, 27,* 335–362.

Thompson, B. (1984). *Canonical correlation analysis: Uses and interpretation.* Beverly Hills, CA: Sage.

Thompson, B. (1989). Why won't stepwise methods die? *Measurement and Evaluation in Counseling and Development, 21,* 146–148.

Thompson, B. (1991). A primer on the logic and use of canonical correlation analysis. *Measurement and Evaluation in Counseling and Development, 24,* 80–95.

Thompson, B. (1994). Guidelines for authors. *Educational and Psychological Measurement, 54,* 837–847.

Thompson, B. (1996). AERA editorial policies regarding statistical significance testing: Three suggested reforms. *Educational Researcher, 25*(2), 26–30.

Thompson, B. (2000a). Canonical correlation analysis. In L. G. Grimm & P. R. Yarnold (Eds.), *Reading and understanding more multivariate statistics* (pp. 285–316). Washington, DC: American Psychological Association.

Thompson, B. (2000b). Ten commandments of structural equation modeling. In L. G. Grimm & P. R. Yarnold (Eds.), *Reading and understanding more multivariate statistics* (pp. 261–283). Washington, DC: American Psychological Association.

Thompson, B. (2002). "Statistical," "practical," and "clinical": How many kinds of significance do counselors need to consider? *Journal of Counseling and Development, 80,* 64–71.

Thompson, B. (2004). *Exploratory and confirmatory factor analysis: Understanding concepts and applications.* Washington, DC: American Psychological Association.

Thompson, B., & Borrello, G. M. (1985). The importance of structure coefficients in regression research. *Educational and Psychological Measurement, 45,* 203–209.

Thompson, S. K. (2002). *Sampling* (2nd ed.). New York, NY: Wiley.

Thorndike, R. L. (1951). Reliability. In E. F. Lindquist (Ed.), *Educational measurement* (pp. 560–620). Washington, DC: American Council on Education.

Thurstone, L. L. (1927a). A law of comparative judgment. *Psychological Review, 34,* 273–286.

Thurstone, L. L. (1927b). The method of paired comparisons for social values. *Journal of Abnormal and Social Psychology, 21,* 384–400.

Thurstone, L. L. (1928). Attitudes can be measured. *American Journal of Sociology, 33,* 529–554.

Thurstone, L. L. (1929). Theory of attitude measurement. *Psychological Review, 36,* 222–241.

Thurstone, L. L. (1931). Multiple factor analysis. *Psychological Review, 38,* 406–427.

Thurstone, L. L. (1935). *Vectors of the mind.* Chicago, IL: University of Chicago Press.

Thurstone, L. L. (1947). *Multiple factor analysis.* Chicago, IL: University of Chicago Press.

Thurstone, L. L., & Chave, E. J. (1929). *The measurement of attitude.* Chicago, IL: University of Chicago Press.

Titchener, E. B. (1901). *Qualitative experiments: Vol 1. Experimental psychology: A manual of laboratory practice.* New York, NY: Macmillan.

Titchener, E. B. (1908). The tridimensional theory of feeling. *American Journal of Psychology, 19,* 213–231.

Tolman, E. C. (1932). *Purposive behavior in animals and men.* New York, NY: Appleton-Century-Crofts.

Toothaker, L. E. (1993). *Multiple comparisons for researchers.* Newbury Park, CA: Sage.

Torgerson, W. S. (1952). Multidimensional scaling: I. Theory and method. *Psychometrika, 17,* 401–419.

Torgerson, W. S. (1958). *Theory and method of scaling.* New York, NY: Wiley.

Townsend, J. T. (1971). Alphabetic confusion: A test of models for individuals. *Perception & Psychophysics, 9,* 449–454.

Tremblay, P. F., & Gardner, R. C. (1996). On the growth of structural equation modeling in psychological journals. *Structural Equation Modeling, 3,* 93–104.

Triandis, H. C., & Gelfand, M. J. (1998). Converging measurement of horizontal and vertical individualism and collectivism. *Journal of Personality and Social Psychology, 74,* 118–128.

Trusty, J., Thompson, B., & Petrocelli, J. V. (2004). Practical guide for reporting effect size in quantitative research in the *Journal of Counseling & Development. Journal of Counseling & Development, 82,* 107–110.

Tucker, L. R. (1955). The objective definition of simple structure in linear factor analysis. *Psychometrika, 20,* 209–225.

Tukey, J. W. (1977). *Exploratory data analysis.* Reading, MA: Addison-Wesley.

Tzelgov, J., & Henik, A. (1991). Suppression situations in psychological research: Definitions, implications, and applications. *Psychological Bulletin, 109,* 524–536.

Ullman, J. B. (2006). Structural equation modeling: Reviewing the basics and moving forward. *Journal of Personality Assessment, 87,* 35–50.

Vacha-Haase, T. (2001). Statistical significance should not be considered one of life's guarantees: Effect sizes are needed. *Educational and Psychological Measurement, 61,* 219–244.

Van de Vijver, J. R., van Hemert, D. A., & Poortinga, Y. H. (2008). *Multilevel analysis of individuals and cultures.* New York, NY: Psychology Press.

Velicer, W. F. (1976). Determining the number of components from the matrix of partial correlations. *Psychometrika, 41,* 321–327.

Vittinghoff, E., McCulloch, C. E., Glidden, D. V., & Shiboski, S. C. (2011). Linear and nonlinear regression methods in epidemiology and biostatistics. In C. R. Rao, J. P. Miller, & D. C. Rao (Eds.), *Essential statistical methods for medical statistics* (pp. 66–103). Burlington, MA: North-Holland.

Wagner, W. E., III. (2010). *Using SPSS for social statistics and research methods* (2nd ed.). Thousand Oaks, CA: Sage.

Walker, D. A. (2007). Estimation methods for cross-validation prediction accuracy: A comparison of proportional bias. *Multiple Linear Regression, 33,* 32–38.

Walsh, J. E. (1947). Concerning the effect of intraclass correlation on certain significance tests. *Annals of Mathematical Statistics, 18,* 88–96.

Ward, J. (1963). Hierarchical grouping to optimize an objective function. *Journal of the American Statistical Association, 58,* 236–244.

Warner, R. M. (2008). *Applied statistics.* Thousand Oaks, CA: Sage.

Watkins, M. W. (2006). Determining parallel analysis criteria. *Journal of Modern Applied Statistics, 5,* 344–346.

Weinfurt, K. P. (1995). Multivariate analysis of variance. In L. G. Grimm & P. R. Yarnold (Eds.), *Reading and understanding multivariate statistics* (pp. 245–276). Washington, DC: American Psychological Association.

Weinfurt, K. P. (2000). Repeated measures analysis: ANOVA, MANOVA, and HLM. In L. G. Grimm & P. R. Yarnold (Eds.), *Reading and understanding more multivariate statistics* (pp. 317–361). Washington, DC: American Psychological Association.

Weiss, D. J. (1972). Canonical correlation analysis in counseling psychology research. *Journal of Counseling Psychology, 19,* 241–252.

Weng, L.-J., & Cheng, C.-P. (2005). Parallel analysis with unidimensional binary data. *Educational and Psychological Measurement, 65,* 697–716.

West, S. G., Aiken, L. S., & Krull, J. L. (1996). Experimental personality designs: Analyzing categorical by continuous variable interactions. *Journal of Personality, 64,* 1–48.

Weston, R., & Gore, P. A. (2006). A brief guide to structural equation modeling. *The Counseling Psychologist, 34,* 719–751.

Wherry, R. J. (1931). A new formula for predicting the shrinkage of the coefficient of multiple correlation. *Annals of Mathematical Statistics, 2,* 440–457.

Wilkinson, L. (1975). Response variable hypotheses in the multivariate analysis of variance. *Psychological Bulletin, 82,* 408–412.

Wilkinson, L., & Task Force on Statistical Inference. (1999). Statistical methods in psychology journals: Guidelines and explanations. *American Psychologist, 54,* 594–604.

Witten, I. H., & Frank, E. (2005). *Data mining: Practical machine learning tools and techniques.* San Francisco, CA: Morgan Kaufmann.

Wood, J. M., Tataryn, D. J., & Gorsuch, R. L. (1996). Effects of under- and overextraction on principal axis factor analysis with varimax rotation. *Psychological Methods, 1,* 254–365.

Woodworth, R. S., & Schlosberg, H. (1954). *Experimental psychology* (Rev. ed.). New York, NY: Holt, Rinehart & Winston.

Wooldridge, J. M. (2009). *Introductory econometrics: A modern approach* (4th ed.). Mason, OH: South-Western/Cengage Learning.

Wright, R. E. (1995). Logistic regression. In L. G. Grimm & P. R. Yarnold (Eds.), *Reading and understanding multivariate statistics* (pp. 217–244). Washington, DC: American Psychological Association.

Wright, R. E. (2000). Survival analysis. In L. G. Grimm & P. R. Yarnold (Eds.), *Reading and understanding more multivariate statistics* (pp. 363–407). Washington, DC: American Psychological Association.

Wright, S. (1921). Correlation and causation. *Journal of Agricultural Research, 20,* 557–585.

Wu, C. F. J. (1983). On the convergence properties of the EM algorithm. *Annals of Statistics, 11,* 95–103.

Wu, C. F. J. (1986). Jackknife, bootstrap and other resampling methods in regression. *Annals of Statistics, 14,* 1261–1295.

Yin, P., & Fan, X. (2001). Estimating R_2 shrinkage in multiple regression: A comparison of different analytic methods. *Journal of Experimental Education, 69,* 203–224.

Young, F. W., & Hamer, R. M. (1987). *Multidimensional scaling: History, theory, and applications.* Hillsdale, NJ: Lawrence Erlbaum.

Young, F. W., & Hamer, R. M. (1994). *Theory and applications of multidimensional scaling.* Hillsdale, NJ: Lawrence Erlbaum.

Young, F. W., & Harris, D. F. (2008). Multidimensional scaling. In M. J. Norusis (Ed.), *SPSS statistics 17.0: Advanced statistics procedures companion* (pp. 335–404). Upper Saddle River, NJ: Prentice Hall.

Zwick, R. (1986). Rank and normal scores alternatives to Hotelling's T_2. *Multivariate Behavioral Research, 21,* 169–186.

Zwick, W. R., & Velicer, W. F. (1986). Comparison of five rules for determining the number of components to retain. *Psychological Bulletin, 99,* 432–442.

Appendix A

Statistics Tables

Appendix Table A1   Two-Tail Critical Values of Student's t Distribution For Selected Values of Degrees of Freedom

df	p = .20	p = .10	p = .05	p = .02	p = .01	p = .001
2	1.886	2.920	4.303	6.965	9.925	31.599
3	1.638	2.353	3.182	4.541	5.841	12.924
4	1.533	2.132	2.776	3.747	4.604	8.610
5	1.476	2.015	2.571	3.365	4.032	6.869
6	1.440	1.943	2.447	3.143	3.707	5.869
7	1.415	1.895	2.365	2.998	3.499	5.405
8	1.397	1.860	2.306	2.896	3.355	5.041
9	1.383	1.833	2.262	2.821	3.250	4.781
10	1.372	1.812	2.228	2.764	3.169	4.587
11	1.363	1.796	2.201	2.718	3.106	4.437
12	1.356	1.782	2.179	2.681	3.055	4.318
13	1.350	1.771	2.160	2.650	3.012	4.221
14	1.345	1.761	2.145	2.624	2.977	4.140
15	1.341	1.753	2.131	2.602	2.947	4.073
16	1.337	1.746	2.120	2.583	2.921	4.015
17	1.333	1.740	2.110	2.567	2.898	3.965
18	1.330	1.734	2.101	2.552	2.878	3.922
19	1.328	1.729	2.093	2.539	2.861	3.883
20	1.325	1.725	2.086	2.528	2.845	3.850
25	1.316	1.708	2.060	2.485	2.787	3.725
30	1.310	1.697	2.042	2.457	2.750	3.646
35	1.306	1.690	2.030	2.438	2.724	3.591
40	1.303	1.684	2.021	2.423	2.704	3.551
50	1.299	1.676	2.009	2.403	2.678	3.496
60	1.296	1.671	2.000	2.390	2.660	3.460
70	1.294	1.667	1.994	2.381	2.648	3.435
80	1.292	1.664	1.990	2.374	2.639	3.416
90	1.291	1.662	1.987	2.368	2.632	3.402
120	1.289	1.658	1.980	2.358	2.617	3.373
∞	1.282	1.645	1.960	2.326	2.576	3.291

http://itl.nist.gov/div898/handbook/eda/section3/eda3672.htm

National Institute of Standards and Technology, The NIST/SEMATECH Engineering Statistics Handbook, Web Based statistics handbook.

Developed as a joint partnership between the Statistical Engineering Division of NIST and the Statistical Methods Group of SEMATECH.

http://www.itl.nist.gov/div898/handbook/ for complete handbook.

Source: From *NIST/SEMATECH e-Handbook of Statistical Methods,* http://www.itl.nist.gov/div898/handbook/.

Appendix Table A2 Selected Critical Values of Chi-Square Distribution with Degrees of Freedom

df	p = .10	p = .05	p = .025	p = .01	p = .001		df	p = .10	p = .05	p = .025	p = .01	p = .001
1	2.706	3.841	5.024	6.635	10.828		51	64.295	68.669	72.616	77.386	87.968
2	4.605	5.991	7.378	9.210	13.816		52	65.422	69.832	73.810	78.616	89.272
3	6.251	7.815	9.348	11.345	16.266		53	66.548	70.993	75.002	79.843	90.573
4	7.779	9.488	11.143	13.277	18.467		54	67.673	72.153	76.192	81.069	91.872
5	9.236	11.070	12.833	15.086	20.515		55	68.796	73.311	77.380	82.292	93.168
6	10.645	12.592	14.449	16.812	22.458		56	69.919	74.468	78.567	83.513	94.461
7	12.017	14.067	16.013	18.475	24.322		57	71.040	75.624	79.752	84.733	95.751
8	13.362	15.507	17.535	20.090	26.125		65	79.973	84.821	89.177	94.422	105.988
9	14.684	16.919	19.023	21.666	27.877		66	81.085	85.965	90.349	95.626	107.258
10	15.987	18.307	20.483	23.209	29.588		67	82.197	87.108	91.519	96.828	108.526
11	17.275	19.675	21.920	24.725	31.264		68	83.308	88.250	92.689	98.028	109.791
12	18.549	21.026	23.337	26.217	32.910		69	84.418	89.391	93.856	99.228	111.055
13	19.812	22.362	24.736	27.688	34.528		70	85.527	90.531	95.023	100.425	112.317
14	21.064	23.685	26.119	29.141	36.123		71	86.635	91.670	96.189	101.621	113.577
15	22.307	24.996	27.488	30.578	37.697		72	87.743	92.808	97.353	102.816	114.835
16	23.542	26.296	28.845	32.000	39.252		73	88.850	93.945	98.516	104.010	116.092
17	24.769	27.587	30.191	33.409	40.790		74	89.956	95.081	99.678	105.202	117.346
18	25.989	28.869	31.526	34.805	42.312		75	91.061	96.217	100.839	106.393	118.599
19	27.204	30.144	32.852	36.191	43.820		76	92.166	97.351	101.999	107.583	119.850
20	28.412	31.410	34.170	37.566	45.315		77	93.270	98.484	103.158	108.771	121.100
21	29.615	32.671	35.479	38.932	46.797		78	94.374	99.617	104.316	109.958	122.348
22	30.813	33.924	36.781	40.289	48.268		79	95.476	100.749	105.473	111.144	123.594
23	32.007	35.172	38.076	41.638	49.728		80	96.578	101.879	106.629	112.329	124.839
24	33.196	36.415	39.364	42.980	51.179		81	97.680	103.010	107.783	113.512	126.083
25	34.382	37.652	40.646	44.314	52.620		82	98.780	104.139	108.937	114.695	127.324
26	35.563	38.885	41.923	45.642	54.052		83	99.880	105.267	110.090	115.876	128.565
27	36.741	40.113	43.195	46.963	55.476		84	100.980	106.395	111.242	117.057	129.804
28	37.916	41.337	44.461	48.278	56.892		85	102.079	107.522	112.393	118.236	131.041
29	39.087	42.557	45.722	49.588	58.301		86	103.177	108.648	113.544	119.414	132.277
30	40.256	43.773	46.979	50.892	59.703		87	104.275	109.773	114.693	120.591	133.512
31	41.422	44.985	48.232	52.191	61.098		88	105.372	110.898	115.841	121.767	134.746
32	42.585	46.194	49.480	53.486	62.487		89	106.469	112.022	116.989	122.942	135.978
33	43.745	47.400	50.725	54.776	63.870		90	107.565	113.145	118.136	124.116	137.208
34	44.903	48.602	51.966	56.061	65.247		91	108.661	114.268	119.282	125.289	138.438
35	46.059	49.802	53.203	57.342	66.619		92	109.756	115.390	120.427	126.462	139.666
36	47.212	50.998	54.437	58.619	67.985		93	110.850	116.511	121.571	127.633	140.893
37	48.363	52.192	55.668	59.893	69.347		94	111.944	117.632	122.715	128.803	142.119
38	49.513	53.384	56.896	61.162	70.703		95	113.038	118.752	123.858	129.973	143.344
39	50.660	54.572	58.120	62.428	72.055		96	114.131	119.871	125.000	131.141	144.567
40	51.805	55.758	59.342	63.691	73.402		97	115.223	120.990	126.141	132.309	145.789
41	52.949	56.942	60.561	64.950	74.745		98	116.315	122.108	127.282	133.476	147.010
42	54.090	58.124	61.777	66.206	76.084		99	117.407	123.225	128.422	134.642	148.230
43	55.230	59.304	62.990	67.459	77.419		100	118.498	124.342	129.561	135.807	149.449
44	56.369	60.481	64.201	68.710	78.750							
45	57.505	61.656	65.410	69.957	80.077							
46	58.641	62.830	66.617	71.201	81.400							
47	59.774	64.001	67.821	72.443	82.720							
48	60.907	65.171	69.023	73.683	84.037							
49	62.038	66.339	70.222	74.919	85.351							
50	63.167	67.505	71.420	76.154	86.661							
51	64.295	68.669	72.616	77.386	87.968							
52	65.422	69.832	73.810	78.616	89.272							
53	66.548	70.993	75.002	79.843	90.573							
54	67.673	72.153	76.192	81.069	91.872							
55	68.796	73.311	77.380	82.292	93.168							
56	69.919	74.468	78.567	83.513	94.461							
57	71.040	75.624	79.752	84.733	95.751							

http://www.itl.nist.gov/div898/handbook/eda/section3/eda3674.htm

National Institute of Standards and Technology, The NIST/SEMATECH Engineering Statistics Handbook, Web Based statistics handbook.

Developed as a joint partnership between the Statistical Engineering Division of NIST and the Statistical Methods Group of SEMATECH.

http://www.itl.nist.gov/div898/handbook/ for complete handbook.

Source: From *NIST/SEMATECH e-Handbook of Statistical Methods,* http://www.itl.nist.gov/div898/handbook/.

Appendix B

Selected IBM SPSS Amos Menus and Commands

Appendix Table B1   Six of the 12 IBM SPSS Amos Operations on the **File** Menu

Name on Pull-Down Menu	Icon on Pull-Down Menu	Icon on Floating Toolbar	Name on Pull-Down Menu and Floating Tool Bar	Function
New		Not Available	Start a new path diagram using the default template	To start a new project if another model is open.
Open		Not Available	Read an old path diagram from disk	Retrieves previously saved Amos files.
Save			Save the current path diagram	Saves new models as well as modifications to existing models.
Save As		Not Available	Save the current path diagram under a new name	Saves existing models with a new name.
Data Files			Select data file(s)	Locates the data file for the model analysis.
Exit		Not Available	Exit	Terminates program.

Appendix Table B2   Nine of the 20 IBM SPSS Amos Operations on the **Edit** Menu

Nine of the 20 IBM SPSS Amos Operations on the Edit Menu

Name on Pull-Down Menu	Icon on Pull-Down Menu	Icon on Floating Toolbar	Name on Pull-Down Menu and Floating Tool Bar	Function
Select			Select one object at a time	Selects single elements in the model one at a time.
Select All			Select all objects	Selects the entire model.
Deselect All			Deselect all objects	Clearing what was selected (does not erase items).
Move			Move objects	Moves object(s) within the area of the path diagram (more items can be moved simultaneously by using the select function).
Duplicate			Duplicate objects	Copies selected items from one area of the path diagram to another area of the path diagram
Erase			Erase objects	Erases selected elements from the model.
Move Parameter			Move parameter values	Moves selected output parameter for better readability.
Rotate			Rotate the indicators of a latent variable	Simultaneously moves both latent and measured variables 45 degrees to the right with each click.
Fit to Page			Resize the path diagram to fit on a page	If diagram is beyond the area of the path diagram, this function will automatically shrink entire diagram to fit the area of the path diagram.

Appendix Table B3 Four of the Nine IBM SPSS Amos Operations on the **View** Menu

Name on Pull-Down Menu	Icon on Pull-Down Menu	Icon on Floating Toolbar	Name on Pull-Down Menu and Floating Tool Bar	Function
Interface Properties		Not Available		Of the 7 tabs, the Page Layout is the most relevant. This allows the area of the path diagram to be changed from portrait to landscape (we suggest Landscape-Legal for maximum graphic area).
Analysis Properties				Of the 8 tabs, **Estimation** and **Output** are the most relevant. Under the **Estimation** tab, keep the default **Maximum Likelihood**. Check the **Estimate Means and Intercepts** only if there are missing values in your data file.
				There are 6 important options under the **Output** tab. Deselect **Minimization History** and check the following: **Standardized estimates, Squared multiple correlations, Modification indices** (only calculates if there are no missing values), **Indirect, direct & total effects** (not necessary for CFAs), and **Critical ratios for differences** (only for multiple-group analysis).
Variables in Dataset			List variables in data set	This allows dragging of the variables names and labels into the model diagram.
Text Output			View text	Provides the analysis output including model fit, parameter estimates, statistical significance for a parameter, modification indices, and model comparisons.

Appendix Table B4 Six of the 14 IBM SPSS Amos Operations on the **Diagram** Menu

Name on Pull-Down Menu	Icon on Pull-Down Menu	Icon on Floating Toolbar	Name on Pull-Down Menu and Floating Tool Bar	Function
Draw Observed			Draw observed variables	Draws a single measured (manifest) variable for the proposed model.
Draw Unobserved			Draw unobserved variables	Draws a single latent (unobserved) variable for the proposed model.
Draw Path			Draw paths (single headed arrows)	Draws the paths in SEM and path analysis.
Draw Covariance			Draw covariances (double headed arrows)	Draws the correlations among exogenous variables in SEM and path analysis as well as correlating error terms.
Draw Indicator Variable			Draw a latent variable or add an indicator to a latent variable	Simultaneously draws the latent variable, the paths, the measured variables, and the error terms for both CFA and SEM. Will also add additional measured variable(s), path(s), and error term(s) to an existing latent variable.
Draw Unique Variable			Add a unique variable to an existing variable	Draws the error terms for both latent and measured endogenous variables.

Appendix Table B5   Five of the 11 IBM SPSS Amos Operations on the **Analyse** Menu

Name on Pull-Down Menu	Icon on Pull-Down Menu	Icon on Floating Toolbar	Name on Pull-Down Menu and Floating Tool Bar	Function
Calculate Estimates			Calculate estimates	Once the model is completed, this function will analyze the model and produce all requested output.
Manage Groups		Not Available	Manage groups	Identifies multiple groups for model comparisons.
Manage Models		Not Available	Manage models	Automatically created by the **Multiple-Group Analysis** to determine invariance.
Specification Search			Specification Search	After selected paths are identified, this function assesses the alternative models for best fit.
Multiple-Group Analysis			Multiple-Group Analysis	Used to evaluate invariance among different groups or over time.

Appendix Table B6   One of the Six IBM SPSS Amos Operations on the **Plugins** Menu

Name on Pull-Down Menu	Icon on Pull-Down Menu	Icon on Floating Toolbar	Name on Pull-Down Menu and Floating Tool Bar	Function
Name Unobserved Variables	Not Available	Not Available	Not Available	Automatically names error terms and any other unnamed latent variables.

Appendix Figure B1

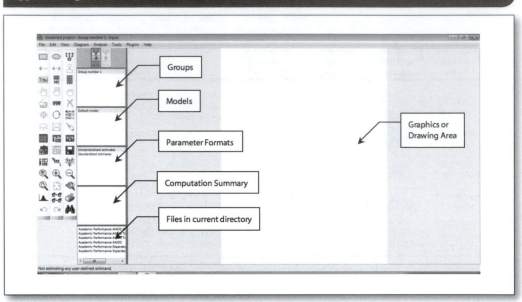

Author Index

Subject Index

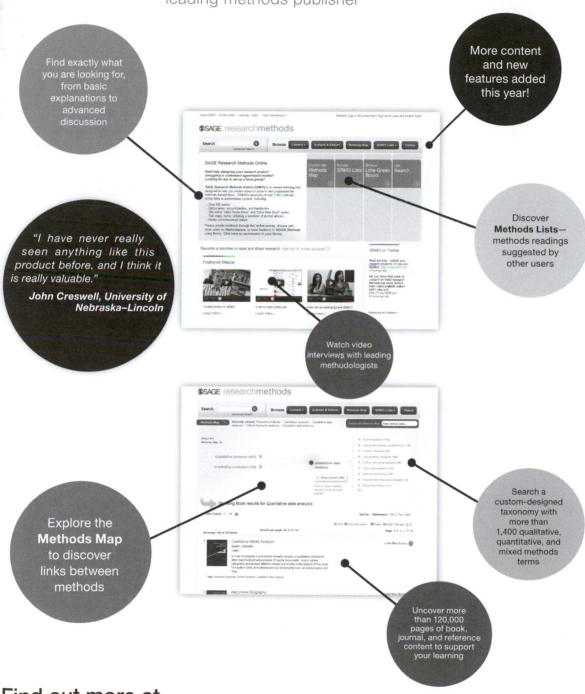

⑤SAGE research**methods**

The essential online tool for researchers from the world's leading methods publisher

Find exactly what you are looking for, from basic explanations to advanced discussion

More content and new features added this year!

"I have never really seen anything like this product before, and I think it is really valuable."

John Creswell, University of Nebraska–Lincoln

Discover **Methods Lists**— methods readings suggested by other users

Watch video interviews with leading methodologists

Explore the **Methods Map** to discover links between methods

Search a custom-designed taxonomy with more than 1,400 qualitative, quantitative, and mixed methods terms

Uncover more than 120,000 pages of book, journal, and reference content to support your learning

Find out more at
www.sageresearchmethods.com